THE OXFORD HANDBOOK

THE ARCHAEOLOGY OF RITUAL AND RELIGION

Contributors

Anders Andrén, Paul G. Bahn, Reinhard Bernbeck, Jenny Blain,
Joanna Brück, Aaron A. Burke, Roy L. Carlson, Timothy Clack,
Robin Coningham, Chantal Conneller, Zoe Crossland, Karina Croucher,
Bruno David, Michael Dietler, Chris Fowler, Paul Garwood,
Amy Gazin-Schwartz, Olivier P. Gosselain, Gunnar Haaland, Randi Haaland,
Yannis Hamilakis, Kelley Hays-Gilpin, Charles Higham, Richard Hingley,
Timothy Insoll, Tõnno Jonuks, Jody Joy, Rosemary A. Joyce, Simon Kaner,
Anders Kaliff, Julia Kindt, Vernon James Knight, Kevin Lane,
Randall McGuire, Caroline Malone, Pierre de Maret, Nicky Milner,
Kathleen Morrison, Sarah Milledge Nelson, Lukas Nickel, Terje Oestigaard,
Andrew Petersen, Paul Pettitt, Aleks Pluskowski, Daniel Potts, Neil Price,
Jeffrey Quilter, Paul Rainbird, Tom Rasmussen, Colin Renfrew,
Brian S. Robinson, Peter G. Roe, Chris Scarre, Michael Seymour,
Michael E. Smith, Anna Stevens, Simon Stoddart, James F. Strange,
Namita Sugandhi, Tim Taylor, Julian Thomas, Sam Turner, Marc Verhoeven,
Martin Welch, David S. Whitley

THE OXFORD HANDBOOK OF

THE ARCHAEOLOGY OF RITUAL AND RELIGION

Edited by
TIMOTHY INSOLL

OXFORD
UNIVERSITY PRESS

Great Clarendon Street, Oxford, OX2 6DP,
United Kingdom

Oxford University Press is a department of the University of Oxford.
It furthers the University's objective of excellence in research, scholarship,
and education by publishing worldwide. Oxford is a registered trade mark of
Oxford University Press in the UK and in certain other countries

© Oxford University Press 2011

The moral rights of the author have been asserted

First published 2011
First published in paperback 2020

All rights reserved. No part of this publication may be reproduced, stored in
a retrieval system, or transmitted, in any form or by any means, without the
prior permission in writing of Oxford University Press, or as expressly permitted
by law, by licence or under terms agreed with the appropriate reprographics
rights organization. Enquiries concerning reproduction outside the scope of the
above should be sent to the Rights Department, Oxford University Press, at the
address above

You must not circulate this work in any other form
and you must impose this same condition on any acquirer

Published in the United States of America by Oxford University Press
198 Madison Avenue, New York, NY 10016, United States of America

British Library Cataloguing in Publication Data
Data available

Library of Congress Cataloging in Publication Data
Data available

ISBN 978-0-19-923244-4 (Hbk.)
ISBN 978-0-19-885805-8 (Pbk.)

Cover photograph: Plastered skulls from the funerary
area at PPNB Tell Aswad, Syria. Laurent Dugué. Excavations
at Tell Aswad, directed by D. Stordeur, Mission El Kowm-
Mureybet Ministère Affaires Etrangères France.

Links to third party websites are provided by Oxford in good faith and
for information only. Oxford disclaims any responsibility for the materials
contained in any third party website referenced in this work.

The manufacturer's authorised representative in the EU for product safety is
Oxford University Press España S.A. of el Parque Empresarial San Fernando
de Henares, Avenida de Castilla, 2 – 28830 Madrid (www.oup.es/en).

CONTENTS

List of Figures xi
List of Tables xxi
List of Contributors xxiii

Introduction: Ritual and Religion in Archaeological Perspective 1
TIMOTHY INSOLL

PART I: ELEMENTS AND EXPRESSION

1 Monumentality 9
CHRIS SCARRE

2 Landscape 24
RANDI HAALAND AND GUNNAR HAALAND

3 Water 38
TERJE OESTIGAARD

4 Fire 51
ANDERS KALIFF

5 Myth and Folklore 63
AMY GAZIN-SCHWARTZ

6 Cosmogony 76
TERJE OESTIGAARD

7 Death 89
TIMOTHY TAYLOR

8 Taboo 105
NICKY MILNER

9 The Many Dimensions of Ritual 115
MARC VERHOEVEN

10 Personhood and the Body CHRIS FOWLER	133
11 Sacrifice TIMOTHY INSOLL	151
12 Ideology RANDALL MCGUIRE AND REINHARD BERNBECK	166
13 Feasting and Fasting MICHAEL DIETLER	179
14 Gender and Religion in Archaeology SARAH MILLEDGE NELSON	195
15 Archaeologies of the Senses YANNIS HAMILAKIS	208
16 Syncretism and Religious Fusion TIMOTHY CLACK	226
17 Technology OLIVIER P. GOSSELAIN	243
18 Rites of Passage PAUL GARWOOD	261
19 The Archaeology of Contemporary Conflict ZOE CROSSLAND	285
20 Rock Art, Religion, and Ritual DAVID S. WHITLEY	307

PART II: PREHISTORIC EUROPEAN RITUAL AND RELIGION

21 Religion and Ritual in the Lower and Middle Palaeolithic PAUL PETTITT	329
22 Religion and Ritual in the Upper Palaeolithic PAUL G. BAHN	344
23 The Mesolithic CHANTAL CONNELLER	358

24 Ritual and Religion in the Neolithic JULIAN THOMAS	371
25 Fire, Earth, Water: An Elemental Cosmography of the European Bronze Age JOANNA BRÜCK	387
26 The Iron Age JODY JOY	405

PART III: RELIGION AND RITUAL IN WORLD PREHISTORY

27 Sub-Saharan Africa TIMOTHY INSOLL	425
28 The Prehistory of Religion in China LUKAS NICKEL	442
29 The Archaeology of Religion and Ritual in the Prehistoric Japanese Archipelago SIMON KANER	457
30 Ritual and Religion in South-east Asia CHARLES HIGHAM	470
31 Historicizing Cosmologies in Australia and Papua New Guinea BRUNO DAVID	482
32 Pacific and New Zealand PAUL RAINBIRD	505
33 Walking Upside-Down and Backwards: Art and Religion in the Ancient Caribbean PETER G. ROE	519
34 Recognizing Religion in Mesoamerican Archaeology: Maya ROSEMARY A. JOYCE	541
35 Aztecs MICHAEL E. SMITH	556
36 Inca KEVIN LANE	571

37	Moche Religion Jeffrey Quilter	585
38	North America: Pueblos Kelley Hays-Gilpin	600
39	North America: Eastern Woodlands Vernon James Knight	623
40	The Religious System of the Northwest Coast of North America Roy L. Carlson	639
41	Ritual and Archaeological Visibility in the Far Northeast of North America Brian S. Robinson	656

PART IV: RELIGION AND CULT OF THE OLD WORLD

42	Prehistoric Religions in the Aegean Colin Renfrew	681
43	Ancient Greece Julia Kindt	696
44	Etruscan Ritual and Religion Tom Rasmussen	710
45	Egypt Anna Stevens	722
46	Rome: Imperial and Local Religions Richard Hingley	745
47	Maltese Prehistoric Religion Caroline Malone and Simon Stoddart	758
48	Mesopotamia Michael Seymour	775
49	Retrieving the Supernatural: Ritual and Religion in the Prehistoric Levant Marc Verhoeven	795

50	Iran Daniel Potts	811
51	Anatolia Karina Croucher	826
52	Old Norse and Germanic Religion Anders Andrén	846
53	Pre-Christian Practices in the Anglo-Saxon World Martin Welch	863
54	The Archaeology of Baltic Religions Tõnno Jonuks	877

PART V: ARCHAEOLOGY OF WORLD RELIGIONS

55	The Archaeology of Ritual and Religion in Ancient Israel and the Levant, and the Origins of Judaism Aaron A. Burke	895
56	The Archaeology of Judaism from the Persian Period to the Sixth Century AD James F. Strange	908
57	Archaeology of Hinduism Namita Sugandhi and Kathleen Morrison	921
58	Buddhism Robin Coningham	934
59	Christianity Sam Turner	948
60	Islam Andrew Petersen	967

PART VI: ARCHAEOLOGY OF INDIGENOUS AND NEW RELIGIONS

61	Shamanism Neil Price	983
62	Animism and Totemism Timothy Insoll	1004

63 Neo-Shamanism: Pagan and 'Neo-Shamanic' Interactions
   with Archaeology   1017
   JENNY BLAIN

64 Druidism and Neo-Paganism   1032
   ALEKS PLUSKOWSKI

65 Ancestor Cults   1043
   TIMOTHY INSOLL

66 Divine Kings   1059
   PIERRE DE MARET

Index   1069

List of Figures

Figure 1.1 Pentre Ifan, a megalithic monument in south-west Wales. (Photo: Chris Scarre) — 12

Figure 1.2 Stonehenge in southern Britain. (Photo: Chris Scarre) — 14

Figure 1.3 Carn Meini, Preseli Hills, south-west Wales. (Photo: Chris Scarre) — 15

Figure 1.4 The Le Ménec alignments at Carnac in southern Brittany. (Photo: Chris Scarre) — 16

Figure 2.1 The mountain associated Potala palace in Lhasa. (Photo: Gunnar Haaland) — 29

Figure 2.2 Sacred hilltops on a range as seen from Argal village, western Nepal. (Photo by kind permission of Man Badur Khattri) — 30

Figure 2.3 The iron smelter with his furnace outside the village of Oska Dencha, south-west Ethiopia. (Photo: Randi Haaland) — 31

Figure 3.1 'Baptism of the Pharaoh' where ablutions of ankh signs were poured, Karnak, Egypt. (Photo: Terje Oestigaard) — 40

Figure 3.2 Nilometer at Elephantine, Aswan, Egypt. (Photo: Terje Oestigaard) — 43

Figure 3.3 The sun above the King's Valley unites with the water in the Nile, Luxor, Egypt. (Photo: Terje Oestigaard) — 47

Figure 4.1 The rectangular platform used for Hindu cremations. From the cremation and temple site at Pashupatinath, Nepal. (Photo: Anders Kaliff) — 54

Figure 4.2 Interpretation of how a cremation may have been performed during the Bronze Age in southern Scandinavia. (Illustration: Richard Holmgren, ARCDOC) — 55

Figure 6.1 Manikarnika Ghat in Varanasi by the River Ganges, India. (Photo: Terje Oestigaard) — 79

Figure 6.2 The Aztec city Teotihuacán seen from the Moon Pyramid, Mexico. (Photo: Rune Oestigaard) — 82

Figure 6.3 Khufu's pyramid at Giza, Egypt. (Photo: Terje Oestigaard) — 84

Figure 9.1 A *Shoort* participating in the Hain initiation ritual of the Selk'nam of Patagonia. (Redrawn photo taken by Gusinde 1931, re-published by Prieto and Cárdenas 1997, fig. 144) — 119

Figure 9.2 View of the front part of one of the large T-shaped stone pillars in a ritual building at Early Neolithic Göbekli Tepe. (Redrawn from Schmidt, 2006, Abb. 92) — 125

Figure 11.1 Ancestral shrine, Goldaan House, Bonchiog, Tongo Hills, Ghana, November 2008. (Photo: T. Insoll)   157

Figure 11.2 Cow sacrifice, Yelwom shrine, Tamboog, Tongo Hills, Ghana, March 2008. (Photo: T. Insoll)   158

Figure 11.3 Blood, the residue of a cow sacrifice, Tonna'ab Yaane shrine, Tongo Hills, Ghana, August 2006. (Photo: T. Insoll)   159

Figure 14.1 Clay face with inset jade eyes from the Goddess Temple, Niuheliang, China. (Photo: Guo Dashun)   199

Figure 14.2 The outline of the Goddess Temple, Niuheliang, China. (Photo: Guo Dashan)   200

Figure 14.3 Example of Silla crown with shaman symbols, Kyongju, South Korea. (Encyclopaedia of Korean Art, used with permission)   202

Figure 15.1 Plan of the main Room A and of the adjacent rooms at the 'Mycenaean' sanctuary of Agios Konstantinos, Methana, Greece. (Photo: Y. Hamilakis)   215

Figure 15.2 Room A at the sanctuary of Agios Konstantinos, Methana, Greece. (Photo: Y. Hamilakis)   216

Figure 15.3 Animal bones from Room A at the sanctuary of Agios Konstantinos, Methana, Greece. (Photo: Kerry Harris)   217

Figure 15.4 A postal stamp issued by the Greek Postal Service in 1992, depicting Manolis Andronikos amongst some of his finds from Vergina, Greek Macedonia. (Courtesy of ELTA, the Greek Postal Service)   219

Figure 16.1 Triangle of signification through which syncretistic meanings are generated.   236

Figure 17.1 Initially soft, plastic, and moist, clay is durably transformed into a hard and resonant material through the action of fire. (© O. Gosselain)   248

Figure 17.2 The 'mystic mill' chapter, Cathedral of Vezelay (France). (Free of copyright)   250

Figure 18.1 A summary of van Gennep's tripartite *Rites de Passage* model (1960).   262

Figure 18.2 The ritual process and rites of passage in the context of Turner's model of 'social dramas'. (After Turner 1986: 293; cf. Schechner 1994, fig. 6; with additional details from Figure 18.1)   263

Figure 18.3 Thresholds, transitions, and 'journeys' (real and metaphorical) in the rites of passage process.   272

Figure 18.4 The Late Neolithic ceremonial complex at Avebury, Wiltshire, UK. (Photo: P. Garwood)   274

Figure 20.1 Barrier Canyon style rock paintings (in red), Head of Sinbad site, Utah, USA. (Photo: D. S. Whitley)   310

Figure 20.2 The Trail of Dreams, Colorado Desert region, California, USA. (Photo: D. S. Whitley)   313

Figure 20.3 Rock engravings, Willow Springs, Arizona, USA.
(Photo: D. S. Whitley) 317

Figure 21.1 Hominin cranial capacities by taxa and major increases in levels
of intentionality according to Dunbar (2003). 333

Figure 21.2 The Berekhat Ram figurine. (Collection Paul Bahn,
with permission) 334

Figure 22.1 The 'Prince' burial of Arene Candide. (Photo: P. Bahn) 345

Figure 22.2 A cast of the Cap Blanc skeleton in front of the sculpted frieze.
(Photo: P. Bahn) 347

Figure 22.3 A bear tooth and flints in a niche in the 'Lioness Chapel',
Cave of Les Trois Frères. (Photo: R. Bégouën) 353

Figure 24.1 The façade of the West Kennet long barrow, north Wiltshire.
(Photo: Julian Thomas) 372

Figure 24.2 Megalithic art at Newgrange, Ireland. (Photo: Julian Thomas) 377

Figure 24.3 Durrington Walls, Wiltshire: location of excavations 2004–7.
(Illustration: Mark Dover for Stonehenge Riverside Project) 378

Figure 24.4 Reconstruction of the Southern Circle at Durrington Walls,
constructed for a *Time Team* TV programme.
(Photo: Julian Thomas) 382

Figure 24.5 The Western Circles at Durrington Walls. (Reconstruction
image by Aaron Watson) 383

Figure 25.1 The Trundholm chariot. (©Juraj Lipták) 388

Figure 25.2 Rock art images of ships at Kasen Lövåsen, Bohuslän,
southern Sweden. (After Coles 2006, figs. 12 and 13) 392

Figure 25.3 Plan of the longhouse at Velserbroek P-63, Noord-Holland,
Netherlands. (After Therkorn 2007, fig. 12.9) 397

Figure 26.1 The Battersea Shield discovered in the River Thames
near Battersea. (© Trustees of the British Museum) 412

Figure 26.2 Nest of torques, known as Hoard L, discovered at Snettisham,
Norfolk in 1990. (© Trustees of the British Museum) 413

Figure 26.3 Bucket escutcheon, figure with headdress, from a burial at
Aylesford, Kent. (© Trustees of the British Museum) 414

Figure 27.1 Dogon masked dancers, Bandiagara Escarpment, Mali,
January 2001. (Photo: T. Insoll) 430

Figure 27.2 Iron Age burial, Ngono, Uganda. (Photo: R. MacLean) 433

Figure 27.3 *Boarbii*, Goldaana House, Bonchiog, Tongo Hills, Ghana,
November 2008. (Photo: T. Insoll) 435

Figure 28.1 Schematic drawing on a ceramic bowl from Banpo,
Shaanxi province. Fifth millennium BC. (After Goepper 1992:
168, fig. 1:1) 443

Figure 28.2 Plan of tomb 45 from Xishuipo, Puyang, Henan province, mid-fifth millenium BC. (After Goepper 1992: 19, fig. 2a) — 444

Figure 28.3 Jade *cong*, height 49.5 cm, from southern China, Liangzhu culture, around 2500 BC. (The British Museum, Asia OA 1937.4-16.188) — 446

Figure 28.4 *Zun*, late Shang period, twelfth–eleventh century BC, height 32.2 cm. (Museum Rietberg Zürich) — 452

Figure 30.1 A mortuary vessel from a Bronze Age infant's grave from Ban Non Wat, Northeast Thailand, *c.*1000 BC. — 472

Figure 30.2 Angkor Wat was the temple-mausoleum of King Suryavarman II (r. AD 1113–1150). — 479

Figure 30.3 Banteay Chmar, the spectacular ritual complex of King Jayavarman VII (r. CE 1181–1219). — 480

Figure 31.1 The sacred Djungan mountain of Ngarrabullgan, northern Australia. (Photo: Bruno David) — 489

Figure 31.2 Dugong bone mound KN17, Koey Ngurtai, Torres Strait. (Photo: Bruno David) — 494

Figure 31.3 The Himaiyu clan (Rumu) ossuary of Rupo, Papua New Guinea. (Photo: Bruno David) — 497

Figure 32.1 Standing stones and conch shell trumpets marking the burial site of Chief Roy Mata on the taboo island of Retoka (Hat Island), Vanuatu. (Photo: Paul Rainbird) — 509

Figure 32.2 The restored *Hale O Lono Heiau* at Waimea Falls Park, Oahu, Hawai'i. (Photo: Paul Rainbird) — 511

Figure 32.3 Sculpted hillside of monumental terraces topped by a 'crown' feature, Imelik State, Palau. (Photo: Paul Rainbird) — 513

Figure 33.1 The art of the earliest Antilleans: Casimiroid and Ortoiroid. ((a) Drawing: Carlos Ayes, in Ayes 1991: Illustación 2; (b) Rouse 1992: fig. 17f, drawing: Peter Roe; (c) Rouse 1992: figs. 17b, 17g, drawing: Peter Roe; (d) Drawing: Carlos Ayes, in Ayes 1990: Illustación 2) — 521

Figure 33.2 Androcentric gestation and portable wombs in Antillean art and religion. ((a)–(h) Drawing: Peter Roe; (i) Versteeg and Schinkel 1992: fig. 56; (j) Photo: Dr George P. Mentore; (k)–(l) Drawing: Peter Roe) — 522

Figure 33.3 The evolution of the three-pointer from Saladoid miniature art of personal presentation to Chican Ostionoid art of public power. (Drawings: Peter Roe) — 529

Figure 35.1 Pyramid-temple with human sacrifice, from Fray Bernardino de Sahagún. (Drawing by Rodolfo Avila, reproduced with permission from Olivier 2003: 285) — 558

Figure 35.2 Row of small platforms at Teopanzolco. (Photo: Michael E. Smith) — 559

Figure 35.3 Large cult objects. A: Smith 2008: 114; B: Seler 1990–8:
III, 100; C: Seler 1990–8: II, 169; D: Noguera 1958: pl. 26.
E: Seler 1990–8: II, 157. 560

Figure 35.4 Small cult objects. A: Seler 1990–8: II, 160; B: Kollmann 1895:
52; C: Seler 1990–8: III, 66; D: Seler 1990–8: IV, 166;
E: Seler 1990–8: II, 9.165; F: Smith in preparation. 560

Figure 37.1 Roll out drawing from a Moche vessel of the Presentation
Theme or Sacrifice Ceremony. (Illustration: Donna McClelland,
by permission of her estate) 586

Figure 37.2 A stirrup spout vessel depicting a fanged anthropomorphic
deity showing the general features of a Moche high god.
(© Dumbarton Oaks, Pre-Columbian Collection,
Washington, DC, used with permission) 590

Figure 37.3 Artistic rendering of how the Huaca de La Luna may have
appeared at the height of its development, c.AD 500–700.
(Courtesy of the Huaca de la Luna Archaeological Project) 594

Figure 37.4 The complex theme frieze as found at Huaca Cao Viejo.
(Courtesy of the El Brujo Archaeological Project,
Fundación Wiese, Lima) 596

Figure 38.1 Katsina images on pottery and rock art, fourteenth century.
(Drawing: Kelley Hays-Gilpin) 603

Figure 38.2 White Mound Black-on-white bowl fragment from NA8939,
a pithouse village site near Houck, Arizona. (Photo:
Kelley Hays-Gilpin) 605

Figure 38.3 Kiva floor plan and profile. (Drawing: Kelley Hays-Gilpin) 607

Figure 39.1 Sheet copper 'Tukabatchee plate', a ceremonial artefact in
the form of an exaggerated axe blade. (Photo: V. J. Knight) 626

Figure 39.2 Moundville, a large Mississippian ceremonial centre featuring
platform mounds arranged around a central plaza.
(Photo: V. J. Knight) 629

Figure 39.3 Paired male and female ancestor shrine figures, Etowah site,
northern Georgia. (Photo: David H. Dye) 631

Figure 40.1 Fragmentary antler spoon-handle from the Pender Canal site,
Coast Salish region, dating to 2000 BC. (Photo: Roy Carlson) 642

Figure 40.2 Bone point from a leister incised with the image of a great
blue heron, c.AD 1, Whalen Farm site, Coast Salish
region. (Photo Roy Carlson) 643

Figure 40.3 Spoon made of antler, dating to 2000 BC from the Pender
Canal site. (Photo: Roy Carlson) 644

Figure 40.4 Image of a masked dancer with a bird rattle from the Marpole
site dating c.AD 1. (Photo: Roy Carlson) 646

Figure 40.5 Small antler plaque with incised images of two bird masks back to back from southern Vancouver island dating to AD 1442. (Photo: Roy Carlson)   651

Figure 41.1 Regional map of the Far Northeast with places referred to in the text.   657

Figure 41.2 Distribution of Early and Middle period sites of the Moorehead Burial tradition.   662

Figure 41.3 Artefacts of the Early, Middle, and Late Moorehead burial tradition. (Courtesy of University or Maine [a and d]; Godfrey Collection [b and c]; Robert S. Peabody Museum, Andover [e–i]; Maine State Museum [j])   664

Figure 41.4 Petroglyph showing bird-like shaman figure and spirit helpers attributed to the Shaking Tent ceremony. (From Hedden 1983, *Maine Archaeological Society Bulletin*)   669

Figure 44.1 Drawing of upper surface of bronze liver from Piacenza, third–second century BC. (After van der Meer 1987)   713

Figure 44.2 View of present remains of Belvedere temple, Orvieto, fifth century BC. (Photo: T. Rasmussen)   716

Figure 44.3 Plan of Portonaccio sanctuary, Veii, end of sixth century BC. (After Colonna 1985)   717

Figure 45.1 (i) Temple of Hathor at Dendera. (Photo: Anna Stevens); (ii) Hypothetical reconstruction of the Early Dynastic landscape at the site of Coptos. (Reproduced courtesy of Barry Kemp)   724

Figure 45.2 A small sample of ritual objects, sourced from New Kingdom sites. (Reproduced courtesy of the Egypt Exploration Society, the National Museum of Antiquities, Leiden, Barry Kemp, and Andy Boyce)   726

Figure 45.3 Plan of the Great Aten Temple at Amarna, a scene from the Amarna tomb of the official Meryra, a stela donated at the tomb of the official Any, and small faience plaques in the shape of bovine heads. (Reproduced courtesy of the Egypt Exploration Society, Barry Kemp, and Andy Boyce)   729

Figure 45.4 The shrine for Meryka at Askut. (Reproduced courtesy of Stuart Tyson Smith)   733

Figure 46.1 The Western Roman empire, showing major sites mentioned in the text. (Drawing: Christina Unwin)   746

Figure 46.2 The centre of emperor-worship at Tarraco, Tarragona, Spain. (Drawing: Christina Unwin)   751

Figure 46.3 The Maison Carée in Nimes, France, a classical temple. (Photo: Richard Hingley)   754

Figure 47.1 Map of Malta showing main temple and burial sites, with plans of typical 'temples' (Ġgantija and Mnajdra) and reconstruction of the Brochtorff-Xagħra Circle funerary site. (Reconstruction: Steven Ashley, Libby Mulqueeney, and Caroline Malone)   759

Figure 47.2 Examples of liturgical furniture from temples and funerary sites. (Drawings: Jason Gibbon, Katherine Cooper, and Steven Ashley)   765

Figure 47.3 The cosmology of prehistoric Malta.   769

Figure 48.1 Cylinder seal, probably from Sippar, c.2300 BC. (© Trustees of the British Museum)   777

Figure 48.2 Sixty-cm-high statue of a bull, from Tell al-'Ubaid, c.2500 BC. (© Trustees of the British Museum)   782

Figure 48.3 Votive statue from Tello (ancient Girsu), c.2500 BC. (© Trustees of the British Museum)   783

Figure 49.1 Map of the Near East with prehistoric sites mentioned in Chapter 49.   796

Figure 49.2 Depiction of an animal (boar, aurochs, or lion?) in profile made from human and gazelle bones found at the PPNB burial site Kfar HaHoresh in Israel. (Photo: Nigel Goring Morris)   800

Figure 49.3 Cache of plastered skulls which founded the 'late burial ground' at PPNB Tell Aswad in Syria. (After Stordeur and Khawam 2007; photo: L. Dugué)   803

Figure 50.1 The ziggurat of Choga Zanbil. (Photo: D. T. Potts)   816

Figure 50.2 The investiture of Ardashir I (c.AD 240), left, by Ahura Mazda, right, at Naqsh-e Rustam. (Photo: D.T. Potts)   820

Figure 51.1 Map of Ancient Anatolia.   827

Figure 51.2 Plan of the Skull Building, Çayönü Tepesi. (After Schirmer 1990)   831

Figure 52.1 The picture stone from Ardre on Gotland, dated to about AD 800. (After Andrén 1993, fig. 5)   850

Figure 52.2 Plan of the ring-fort at Ismantorp on Öland, which was used temporarily between AD 200–650. (After Andrén 2006, fig. 1)   852

Figure 54.1 Map of the Baltic countries showing linguistic areas, Lithuanian Grand Duchy, Territory of Teutonic Order, Bishoprics and contemporary borders.   878

Figure 54.2 Holy hill of Tõrma in north Estonia. (Photo: Tõnno Jonuks)   886

Figure 55.1 Migdôl-style temples during the Middle and Late Bronze Ages. (Drawing: Aaron G. Burke)   899

Figure 55.2 Arad temple, Late Iron Age. (Photo by Aaron G. Burke)   901

Figure 55.3 Plan of the Royal tomb of Qatna. (After Pfälzner 2007: fig. 33, p. 57)   902

xviii LIST OF FIGURES

Figure 57.1 Sealing from Indus stamp-seal showing the so-called 'Proto Śiva' figure with horned headdress. (Photo: K. Morrison) — 924

Figure 57.2 Seventh-century Durga temple at Aihole, Karnataka. (Photo: K. Morrison) — 927

Figure 57.3 Sixteenth-century Vijayanagara temple complex dedicated to Tiruvengalanatha, a form of Vishnu. (Photo: K. Morrison) — 928

Figure 57.4 Chola king as devotee, Tiruchirapalli. Just rule was closely linked to patronage of religious institutions such as Hindu temples. (Photo: K. Morrison) — 929

Figure 57.5 Fifteenth- or sixteenth-century Naga carved on boulder outcrops in rural area near the abandoned imperial city of Vijayanagara, in southern India. (Photo: K. Morrison) — 930

Figure 58.1 The great *stupa* of the Jetavana monastery in the ancient Sri Lankan city of Anuradhapura. (Photo: R. Coningham) — 938

Figure 58.2 The monastic residence, or *vihara*, at Mohra Moradu in the Taxila Valley of Pakistan was built between the fourth and fifth centuries AD. (Photo: R. Coningham) — 939

Figure 59.1 The early medieval church of St Vincenç d'Obiols, Catalonia, Spain. (Photo: Sam Turner) — 951

Figure 59.2 The church at Çanli Kilise, Turkey (Photo: Gertrude Bell, 1907. © Newcastle University) — 953

Figure 59.3 Ruined post-medieval house in the village of Rachi, Naxos, Greece. (Photo: Sam Turner) — 956

Figure 60.1 Sixteenth-century ceramic tile in Rustem Pasha Mosque, Istanbul, Turkey depicting the Ka'ba in Mecca—the holiest shrine in Islam. (Photo: A. Petersen) — 971

Figure 60.2 Pilgrims progress around the fourteenth-century tomb of Najm al-Din Kubra at the ancient city of Kunya Urgench south of the Aral Sea in northern Turkmenistan. (Photo: A. Petersen) — 976

Figure 61.1 Prehistoric rock carvings from Siberia: (1) Oglakhty, Middle Yenisei River, (2) Middle Yenisei River, (3) Mokhsogolokh-Khaja, Middle Lena River. (After Devlet 2001: 47) — 984

Figure 61.2 Photograph of an Altai shaman, early 1920s. (After Nioradze 1925: 88) — 985

Figure 61.3 Birka chamber grave Bj.660, mid-tenth century AD. (Reconstruction: Þórhallur Þráinsson, after Price 2002: 128–31) — 996

Figure 62.1 Crocodile figurine from excavations at Yikpabongo, Koma Land, January 2007. (Courtesy of B. W. Kankpeyeng) — 1013

Figure 63.1 Stonehenge summer solstice 2001. Partying at (and on) the stones. (Photo: J. Blain) — 1023

Figure 64.1	Seahenge. (Image provided by Chris Collyer. Reproduced with permission)	1034
Figure 64.2	The St Michael ley line (cutting through Avebury and Glastonbury).	1036
Figure 64.3	Fantoft stave church, Norway. (Photo: Svein-Magne Tunli. Reproduced with permission)	1039
Figure 65.1	Tallensi ancestor shrine, Tongo Hills, Northern Ghana. (Photo: T. Insoll)	1045
Figure 65.2	Venerated Shi'a Saint's shrine, Shaikh Nasser shrine, Al-Helah, Bahrain. (Photo: T. Insoll)	1048
Figure 65.3	Ancestor-related ritual acts in the Congo. (After Hochegger 1981: 93)	1050
Figure 66.1	Leader with an anvil and ceremonial axe from a tenth-century-AD early Kisalian burial, Kamilamba, DR Congo. (Photo: P. de Maret)	1064

List of Tables

Table 9.1 The Main Anthropological Approaches to Ritual. 122
Table 20.1 Ethnography and Rock Art Origins in Far Western North America. 309
Table 45.1 Chronological List of the Ancient Egyptian Periods. 723

List of Contributors

Anders Andrén, Professor of Archaeology at the University of Stockholm, Sweden.

Paul G. Bahn, freelance writer, editor, and translator.

Reinhard Bernbeck, Professor of Anthropology at Binghamton University, USA.

Jenny Blain, Senior Lecturer in Sociology at Sheffield Hallam University, UK.

Joanna Brück, Senior Lecturer at University College, Dublin, Republic of Ireland.

Aaron A. Burke, Associate Professor of the Archaeology of Ancient Israel and the Levant in the Near Eastern Languages and Cultures department at UCLA, USA.

Roy L. Carlson, Professor Emeritus of Archaeology at Simon Fraser University in Burnaby, British Columbia, Canada.

Timothy Clack, Lecturer in Archaeology and Anthropology at the University of Oxford, UK.

Robin Coningham, Professor of Archaeology and a Pro-Vice-Chancellor at Durham University, UK.

Chantal Conneller, Lecturer in Archaeology at the University of Manchester, UK.

Zoe Crossland, Assistant Professor of Anthropology at Columbia University, USA.

Karina Croucher, British Academy Postdoctoral Fellow, based at the University of Manchester, UK.

Bruno David, QEII Research Fellow at the Programme for Australian Indigenous Archaeology, School of Geography and Environmental Science at Monash University, Australia.

Michael Dietler, Professor of Anthropology at the University of Chicago, USA.

Chris Fowler, Lecturer in Later Prehistoric Archaeology at Newcastle University, UK.

Paul Garwood, Lecturer in Prehistory at the Institute of Archaeology and Antiquity, University of Birmingham, UK.

Amy Gazin-Schwartz, Associate Professor of Archaeology at Assumption College, Worcester, MA, USA.

Olivier P. Gosselain, Professor in the Department of History, Art and Archaeology and the Department of Social Science at the Université libre de Bruxelles, Belgium, and Honorary Research Fellow in the GAES, University of the Witwatersrand, Johannesburg, South Africa.

Gunnar Haaland, Professor Emeritus at the Department of Social Anthropology, University of Bergen, Norway.

Randi Haaland, Professor of Middle Eastern and African Archaeology at the Department of Archaeology, History, Culture, and Religious Studies, University of Bergen, Norway.

Yannis Hamilakis, Professor of Archaeology at the University of Southampton, UK.

Kelley Hays-Gilpin, Professor of Anthropology at Northern Arizona University and Edward Bridge Danson Chair of Anthropology at the Museum of Northern Arizona, USA.

Charles Higham, Research Professor in the Department of Anthropology and Archaeology, University of Otago, Dunedin, New Zealand.

Richard Hingley, Professor of Roman Archaeology at Durham University, UK.

Timothy Insoll, Professor of Archaeology at the University of Manchester, UK.

Tõnno Jonuks, Senior Research Fellow at the Estonian Literary Museum in Tartu, Estonia.

Jody Joy, Curator of European Iron Age collections at the British Museum, London, UK.

Rosemary A. Joyce, Richard and Rhoda Goldman Distinguished Professor in the Social Sciences, and Professor of Anthropology at the University of California, Berkeley, USA.

Anders Kaliff, Professor in Archaeology at Uppsala University, Sweden.

Simon Kaner, Assistant Director of the Sainsbury Institute for the Study of Japanese Arts and Cultures, UK.

Julia Kindt, Senior Lecturer in Classics/Archaeology at the University of Sydney, Australia.

Vernon James Knight, Professor of Anthropology at the University of Alabama, USA.

Kevin Lane, Humboldt Fellow at the Institut für Prähistorische Archäologie of the Freie Universität Berlin, Germany.

Randall H. McGuire, Distinguished Professor of Anthropology at Binghamton University, USA.

Caroline Malone, Reader in Archaeology at Queen's University, Belfast, UK.

Pierre de Maret, Professor of Archaeology and Anthropology at the Université Libre de Bruxelles, Belgium.

Kathleen Morrison, Professor of Anthropology and Director of the Center for International Studies at the University of Chicago, USA.

Sarah Milledge Nelson, John Evans Distinguished Professor and Professor Emerita in Anthropology at the University of Denver, USA.

Nicky Milner, Senior Lecturer at the University of York, UK.

Lukas Nickel, Reader, Institute of Archaeology, University College London, and Department of the History of Art and Archaeology, School of Oriental and African Studies, UK.

Terje Oestigaard, Researcher, Nordic Africa Institute, Uppsala, Sweden.

Andrew Petersen, director of research in Islamic Archaeology at the University of Wales, UK.

Paul Pettitt, Reader in Palaeolithic Archaeology at the University of Sheffield, UK.

Aleks Pluskowski, Lecturer in Medieval Archaeology at the Department of Archaeology, University of Reading, UK.

Daniel Potts, Edwin Cuthbert Hall Professor of Middle Eastern Archaeology at the University of Sydney, Australia.

Neil Price, Professor of Archaeology at the University of Aberdeen, Scotland, and Honorary Senior Research Fellow at the Rock Art Research Institute, University of the Witwatersrand, South Africa.

Jeffrey Quilter, Deputy Director for Curatorial Affairs, Peabody Museum, Harvard University, USA.

Paul Rainbird, Honorary University Fellow, Exeter University, UK.

Tom Rasmussen, Senior Lecturer and currently Head of Art History at Manchester University, UK.

Colin Renfrew, Senior Fellow at the McDonald Institute for Archaeological Research, Cambridge, UK.

Brian S. Robinson, Associate Professor in the Anthropology Department and Climate Change Institute at the University of Maine at Orono, USA.

Peter G. Roe, Professor, University of Delaware, USA.

Chris Scarre, Professor of Archaeology at Durham University, UK.

Michael Seymour, Project Curator for Early Mesopotamia, British Museum, London, UK.

Michael E. Smith, Professor of Anthropology at Arizona State University, USA.

Anna Stevens, Assistant Director, Amarna Project, Cairo, Egypt.

Simon Stoddart, Senior Lecturer of Archaeology at Cambridge University and a fellow of Magdalene College, Cambridge, UK.

James F. Strange, Distinguished University Professor in the Department of Religious Studies at the University of South Florida, Tampa, Florida, USA.

Namita Sugandhi, Lecturer in the Department of Sociology and Anthropology, Indiana University Northwest, USA.

Timothy Taylor, Reader in Archaeology at the University of Bradford, UK.

Julian Thomas, Professor of Archaeology at Manchester University, UK.

Sam Turner, Senior Lecturer in Archaeology at Newcastle University, UK.

Marc Verhoeven, senior project manager at an archaeological consultancy in the Netherlands.

Martin Welch, Senior Lecturer in Medieval Archaeology at the Institute of Archaeology, University College London, UK.

David S. Whitley, Principal at ASM Affiliates, Inc., USA.

INTRODUCTION: RITUAL AND RELIGION IN ARCHAEOLOGICAL PERSPECTIVE

TIMOTHY INSOLL

Seven years ago this author wrote that 'religion itself is increasingly being (re)recognised as of importance within the "secular" West, a realisation which has profound implications for archaeology, considering the proportional impact of Western archaeologists on archaeological theory, interpretation and methodology' (Insoll 2004: 147). This Handbook is testimony to the accelerated pace of this interest, as are a variety of other dedicated studies that have recently appeared focusing on, for example, 'cult', 'ritual', and 'religion' (cf. Kyriakidis 2007; Barrowclough and Malone 2007; Whitley and Hays-Gilpin 2008; Morley and Renfrew 2009). It is also significant that the entries within this Handbook and the majority of the other works just referred to are not written by what might be termed 'religious' archaeologists but rather by archaeologists, perhaps with an interest in religion, or perhaps not especially so. Instead 'religion' and religious ritual has now become a routine part of the focus of archaeological attention—as it should—rather than as a specialist sub-discipline, something which it was not ten, or to a lesser extent even five years ago (Insoll 1999, 2001, 2004, 2009a).

This Handbook indicates the varied approaches that are being employed in the diverse geographical and chronological 'fields' that constitute 'archaeology'. As such it is unnecessary to provide a history of archaeological research on ritual and religion for this has been done elsewhere (Insoll 2004) and because this is a subject that most of the contributors engage with, where relevant, in their entries. Thus today a generally positive situation exists in relation to archaeological approaches to ritual and religions. A 'turn' is also increasingly evident whereby serious consideration is beginning to be given to the materiality of ritual and religions, and what this might tell us about defining religion and religions and reconstructing rituals and potentially (albeit often elusively) beliefs. This is vital for, often, archaeological consideration of ritual and religions remains underlain by assumption—that labels and definitions derived from other disciplines (religious studies or anthropology, perhaps) are 'right', and thus applicable to different contexts far removed geographically and temporally; whilst material culture might be treated as just 'there' instead of being interrogated as to how it symbolizes, represents, misleads, and informs the archaeologist attempting to explore the subtleties of ritual practice and religions (Insoll 2009a).

Meskell (2005: 1) has noted that archaeology 'has been notably remiss in producing substantive accounts of materiality for archaeological contexts'. This might be less true now (e.g. Thomas 2006–7), but in relation to thinking about the materiality of ritual and religions from an archaeological perspective was until recently correct. Anthropologists were already engaging with the materiality of religion (e.g. Keane 2008; *Material Religion* 2005–9), and archaeologists are beginning to do likewise (Insoll 2009a). This is well indicated, for instance, by Boivin's (2008, 2009) exploration of how the non-language-like qualities of material culture make it perfectly suited to emotionally and experientially directed ritual activity. In so doing she has questioned the framing of material culture 'as a passive reflection of cultural values, thoughts and cosmological beliefs that are understood to prefigure them' (2009: 266). It will be interesting to see if Boivin's emphasis upon this non-language-oriented perspective will be followed by other archaeologists seeking to explore what she describes as how ritual 'helps to grasp the elusive and unknowable at the margins' of somatic experiences (Boivin 2009: 284).

It is possible that within the framework of exploring materiality greater consideration might be given by archaeologists to the 'efficacy' and 'agency' of objects (Nooter Roberts and Roberts 2007: 10). How the interplay of the two might be teased out contextually and how as Nooter Roberts and Roberts (ibid.) discuss, 'the degree to which the efficacy of objects is due to the agency of human beings, versus how objects may possess their own powers and capacities based upon spiritual or divine intentionality and intervention'. Where the elucidation of the sacred, or the numinous—the irreducible essence of holiness which can be discussed but not defined (Otto 1950; Sharpe 1986: 164)—is perhaps in part what is sought archaeologically (Insoll 2004: 19–20) then thinking about 'things' in such a way could be vital. This differs slightly from, for instance, Keane's (2008: S124) position that 'religions may not always demand beliefs, but they will always involve material forms'. Although material culture provides the archaeologist's empirical framework we do not want to sacrifice the immaterial elements of religions on the altar of materiality. Instead the ideas expressed by Karlström (2009: 146) in relation to Buddhist archaeology and heritage in Laos are more positive as to the immaterial and its material retrieval, whereby immateriality is 'understood as the way the immaterial is conceptualised in culture, or expressed through material forms'.

This Handbook indicates the many dimensions that can be explored under the umbrella of materiality, even if this currently fashionable archaeological buzzword is not always utilized herein. For instance, framed from the perspective of ritual and religions, the senses and emotions, rites of passage, ideology, interpretations of personhood, gender and other identities, and myriad ritual actions as well as the residues of innumerable configurations of beliefs and associated religious phenomena across time and geographical space can all be linked to substance and material culture as is indicated. Foregrounding objects, efficacy, agency, and materiality as elements of archaeological research is vital in thinking about ritual and religious change over time. And here one would agree with Keane (2008: S124) that, 'material forms do not only permit new inferences, but, as objects that endure across time, they can, in principle, acquire features unrelated to the intentions of previous users or the inferences to which they have given rise in the past. This is in part because as material things they are prone to enter into new contexts.' Context is here given prominence and contexts—sites, features, layers, and profiles—are the building blocks from which the discussion in these are ultimately constructed.

It is certain that archaeological interest in religion and ritual will continue, for, as noted, it has entered the mainstream. Predicting future research trends is difficult but it is likely that the static nature of much archaeological interpretation in relation to ritual and religion will be increasingly challenged, something that is already apparent in this Handbook. The current static conceptual prevalence is potentially due to the fact that archaeologists consider static material residues, and in turn, perhaps albeit subconsciously, this static image is transferred onto the beliefs and ritual practices of both individuals and communities that generated the archaeological material. Instead it can be posited that some of this material is perhaps structured by much more fluid, dynamic, and active behaviours (Insoll 2009b: 290).

Catherine Bell (1992: 109–10) has informed us about the link between ritual and time, and via the notion of validation, the construction of memory, as well as indicating that movement can form a key component of ritual. Movement is in turn related to time and all these elements—movement, time, space, and memory—interconnect within the process of ritual action. It also needs to be recognized that ritual time is not a stable edifice of practice and custom, a simple construct. Ritual practices and the deposition events by which they are materialized archaeologically could be subject to considerable trajectories of change even over comparatively short periods of time (Insoll 2009b: 293). Yet in making this point it is not the intention necessarily to deny the existence of an underlying core of stability in practice and belief with regard to ritual. In bodily understandings in relation to the use of space, in religious beliefs, and in the metaphorical and symbolic qualities ascribed materials and objects utilized in rituals (e.g. Nooter Roberts 2000: 75–8) this can and does exist. Equally, movement can form a component of these strata of stability, for stability does not equate with 'static' (e.g. Fowler and Fowler 1986: 885, 891).

Hence challenging the static within archaeological interpretations of ritual and religions might increasingly become the focus of research. Movement can also be framed within the notion of performance, and the complementarity of 'ritual' and 'performance' has been noted (Lewis 1980: 33–5; Parkin 1992: 42–3; Schechner 2002), as have the problems inherent in a 'performance theory'-based approach to ritual (e.g. Bell 1992: 42–3). Also, as already identified, memory is a further crucial component that needs consideration in relation both to the construction and maintenance of ritual and religions. In considering interpretive options perhaps the approaches adopted with the nascent 'archaeology of memory' (e.g. Rowlands 1993; Chouin 2002; Lane 2005; Van Dyke and Alcock 2003) might be relevant (Insoll 2009b). To a degree this could be so, but it also needs to be recognized that in constructing memory with reference to places and material culture—ritual, religious, or otherwise—the importance of the body as an agent in negotiating and/or understanding these through movement perhaps again needs emphasis. This would appear to be especially so considering Vansina's (1985: 43) point that 'studies of memory emphasize that remembering is action' which perhaps returns us succinctly to ritual—as embodying practices recurrently linked to memory.

It is thus apparent that there is a shift from the cataloguing of the residues of the archaeology of ritual and religions to thinking about what they encode—actively rather than as static residues—and how this is achieved materially through engaging with materiality. These are but two emergent themes influencing recent research. The archaeology of ritual and religions is a vast subject encompassing material of myriad configurations from diverse contexts, periods, and areas. The Handbook illustrates this diversity, but is also indicative of the resonances that likewise exist across time in humanity's attempts to engage with those complex constructs we define as 'ritual and religions'.

In addressing these diverse materials the Handbook has been structured into six sections. All of these are self-explanatory as to what they contain, and break the archaeological material down singularly or in association either thematically, chronologically, geographically, or by types of ritual practices and religions.

Acknowledgements

I am especially grateful to Rachel MacLean for her assistance in the production of the volume, for formatting the entries, corresponding with, and chasing contributors where required. The Handbook could not have been completed without her help. I am also grateful to Hilary O'Shea at Oxford University Press for initiating the project and for support during its completion. Finally, I would like to thank Danielle Stordeur for permission to use the fantastic cover image from her excavations at Tell Aswad in Syria.

References

BARROWCLOUGH, D. and MALONE, C. (eds) 2007. *Cult in Context: Reconsidering ritual in archaeology* (Oxford: Oxbow Books).
BELL, C. 1992. *Ritual Perspectives and Dimensions* (Oxford: Oxford University Press).
BOIVIN, N. 2008. *Material Cultures, Material Minds: The role of things in human thought, society and evolution* (Cambridge: Cambridge University Press).
—— 2009. 'Grasping the elusive and unknowable: Material culture in ritual practice', *Material Religion*, 5: 266–87.
CHOUIN, G. 2002. 'Sacred groves in history: Pathways to the social shaping of forest landscapes in coastal Ghana', *IDS Bulletin*, 33: 39–46.
FOWLER, F. G. and FOWLER, H. W. 1986. *The Oxford Handy Dictionary* (London: Chancellor Press).
INSOLL, T. 1999. *The Archaeology of Islam* (Oxford: Blackwell).
—— (ed.) 2001. *Archaeology and World Religion* (London: Routledge).
—— 2004. *Archaeology, Ritual, Religion* (London: Routledge).
—— 2009a. 'Materiality, belief, ritual: Archaeology and material religion: An introduction', *Material Religion*, 5: 261–4.
—— 2009b. 'Materializing performance and ritual: Decoding the archaeology of movement in Tallensi shrines in northern Ghana', *Material Religion*, 5: 288–311.
KARLSTRÖM, A. 2009. *Preserving Impermanence: The creation of heritage in Vientiane, Laos* (Uppsala: Uppsala University).

KEANE, W. 2008. 'The evidence of the senses and the materiality of religion', *Journal of the Royal Anthropological Institute (NS)*: S110–S127.

KYRIAKIDIS, E. (ed.) 2007. *The Archaeology of Ritual* (Los Angeles, CA: Cotsen Institute of Archaeology).

LANE, P. 2005. 'The material culture of memory' in W. James and D. Mills (eds), *The Qualities of Time* (Oxford: Berg), pp. 19–34.

LEWIS, G. 1980. *Day of Shining Red* (Cambridge: Cambridge University Press).

Material Religion: The Journal of Objects, Art and Belief, vols. 1–5, 2005–9 (Oxford: Berg).

MESKELL, L. 2005. 'Introduction: Object orientations' in L. Meskell (ed.), *Archaeologies of Materiality* (Oxford: Blackwell), pp. 1–17.

MORLEY, I. and RENFREW, C. (eds) 2009. *Becoming Human: Innovation in prehistoric material and spiritual culture* (Cambridge: Cambridge University Press).

NOOTER ROBERTS, M. 2000. 'Proofs and promises: Setting meaning before the eyes' in J. Pemberton III (ed.), *Insight and Artistry in African Divination* (Washington: Smithsonian Institution Press), pp. 63–82.

——and ROBERTS, A. F. 2007. *Luba* (Milan: 5 Continents).

OTTO, R. 1950. *The Idea of the Holy* (Oxford: Oxford University Press).

PARKIN, D. 1992. 'Ritual as spatial direction and bodily division' in D. de Coppet (ed.), *Understanding Rituals* (London: Routledge), pp. 11–25.

ROWLANDS, M. 1993. 'The role of memory in the transmission of culture', *World Archaeology*, 25: 141–51.

SCHECHNER, R. 2002. 'Ritual and performance' in T. Ingold (ed.), *Companion Encyclopedia of Anthropology* (London: Routledge), pp. 613–47.

SHARPE, E. J. 1986. *Comparative Religion: A history* (London: Duckworth).

THOMAS, J. 2006–7. 'The trouble with material culture', *Journal of Iberian Archaeology*, 9(10): 11–23.

VAN DYKE, R. M. and ALCOCK, S. 2003. 'Archaeologies of memory: An introduction' in R. M. Van Dyke and S. Alcock (eds), *Archaeologies of Memory* (Oxford: Blackwell), pp. 1–13.

VANSINA, J. 1985. *Oral Tradition as History* (London: James Currey).

WHITLEY, D. and HAYS-GILPIN, K. (eds) 2008. *Belief in the Past: Theoretical approaches to the archaeology of religion* (Walnut Creek, CA: Left Coast Press).

PART I
ELEMENTS AND EXPRESSION

CHAPTER 1

MONUMENTALITY

CHRIS SCARRE

'Monument' today carries a double meaning, evoking size and durability on the one hand, and commemoration or memorial on the other. The term derives ultimately from the Latin *monumentum* 'something that reminds' which is related to the verb *monere* 'to remind' or 'to warn'. It was in the early seventeenth century that it was first used to indicate a structure built to commemorate an individual or event, and still later that it took on the looser meaning of something of great size, as in the word 'monumental'. The two facets—to remind and to impress—are inextricably intertwined, since a large durable structure or object evidently provides an effective means of creating a permanent memorial, and of passing on meanings and messages between generations. The messages themselves need not always be those intended by the originator of the monument, since later observers may interpret them in entirely novel and culturally specific ways. Hence monuments carry meanings far beyond the contexts of their original creation.

The construction of a monument is a consummately cultural and ideological undertaking, be it the carving of a stone or the building of a pyramid. Monuments are closely associated with social observance of death and the supernatural, and embody cosmologies in durable form. They offer unique and challenging insights into the beliefs and ritual practices of early societies. Yet they are also mutable and contingent forms, frequently reused and reinterpreted across the passage of generations. The special quality of monuments is to take ritual and cosmology beyond the realm of the domestic and quotidian, and express or embellish them in a special, dedicated setting.

Monuments are highly diverse in their form, character, and age. They include prehistoric standing stones and earthen enclosures, massive obelisks and pyramids, and memorials to the dead of recent centuries, including to those killed by conflict or natural disaster. This chapter will explore the significance of monuments in ritual and religion from the perspective of prehistoric and early historic societies, illustrated by examples from North and South America, Africa, and Europe.

1 The Powers of Place: Monuments and the Supernatural

The ritualized practices of hunter-gatherer communities commonly recognize natural features such as springs, lakes, and waterfalls as places of particular power. A number of these communities also physically altered the landscape by the construction of durable monuments. Hunter-gatherer monuments occur on every inhabited continent, from the *inuksuit* marker cairns of the Canadian Arctic to the stone rows of Australia and the Mesolithic post-holes beneath the Stonehenge car park (Hallendy 2000; Flood 1995: 275–6; Cleal et al. 1995). Many of the impressive prehistoric monuments of North America, furthermore, were constructed by societies that had not fully adopted a farming economy. In prehistoric Europe, by contrast, hunter-gatherer monuments are rare, and it was early farming communities who began to construct monuments of earth and stone.

The significance of these early monuments must be understood against the background of the widespread veneration of natural places. African ethnography throws light on the distinction through the contrast between 'places of power' and 'shrines of the land' (Colson 1997; Scarre 2008). 'Places of power' exist without human intervention and take the form of waterfalls, caves, springs or large trees. They are associated with nature spirits and are regarded as inherently sacred. The forces that they embody are considered primordial, reaching back deep into the past. 'Shrines of the land', on the other hand, are humanly built, and are associated with the spirits of those who first settled that particular location; they are essentially ancestor shrines, and focus on the continuity of human life forces rather than the powers inherent in nature. In an archaeological context, 'places of power' might be manifest as sites of offerings, without the medium of any built structure. An ethnographic example is the 'holy stone' on the Kanin Nos peninsula of northern Russia. This massive glacial erratic stands out within its landscape but has not been shaped in any way. The evidence of its special significance is provided by the offerings left around its base, which include bronze ornaments and iron rivets (Ovsyannikov and Terebikhin 1994). Archaeological deposits in caves, lakes and bogs may likewise testify to the sacred significance of these particular natural locations, in what has been termed an 'archaeology of natural places' (Bradley 2000).

Enculturated natural features such as trees or boulders might be considered 'natural monuments', becoming monuments through a process of constructive social and ritual practice rather than through their physical creation by human agents. There need be no sharp division between these and monuments that are humanly built, especially since many of the latter were created in distinct and intentional relationship to natural features of their location (rocks, trees, mountains), and may often incorporate unmodified elements or materials. Thus the megalithic tombs of Neolithic North-west Europe incorporate massive blocks of stone that are frequently unshaped. The blocks themselves were taken from outcrops and boulders, a relationship that may be especially significant if those outcrops and boulders were already regarded as sites of special ritual or mythological significance. Indeed the objective of the proceeding may have been to transfer existing 'powers of place' to newly built monuments, a suggestion that again calls to mind the distinction drawn from African ethnography between 'places of power' and 'shrines of the land', and the practice of incorporating 'powerful' stones when founding new shrines (Scarre 2004, 2008; Insoll 2006).

The veneration of natural landscape features must stretch far back into the human past, and may indeed be a fundamental characteristic of modern human cognition, along with the tendency to anthropomorphism (Mithen 1996). The anthropomorphism of animistic beliefs, through which natural features such as particular trees or stones are assumed to be imbued with intentionality and inhabited by spirits, able to enter into dialogue with humans, is especially relevant. Such understandings are classically associated with hunter-gatherer societies, and may represent a projection onto the natural world of the desire to enter into the same kind of sharing relationships as prevail within those societies themselves (Bird-David 1999). Others invoke a more cosmological explanation, referring to the 'hovering closeness of the world of myth to the actual world' among many hunter-gatherer communities (Guenther 1999: 426).

Anthropomorphism and animistic beliefs are also crucial to the understanding of many monuments, especially those that take the form of statues. Ethnographic accounts provide vivid testimony of rituals associated with such carved images that are designed to activate them. Such rituals address the figurations as if they were animate images able to see, to hear, to accept offerings, and to respond (e.g. Gell 1998). The massive statues of Easter Island may have been regarded in this way by the societies who carved and venerated them. The eyes were formed of contrastingly coloured stone inlays and may have given the statues especial potency. Most of the statues were eventually toppled forward on their faces, to cover the eyes, and in some cases the statues were also beheaded (Bahn and Flenley 1992: 165). The mode of destruction highlights the anthropomorphic power of the statues. Monuments do not need to have any resemblance to the human form, however, in order to be considered to have human qualities or to represent humans. The widespread folklore that interprets standing stones as petrified people—turned into stone for dancing on the Sabbath, for example—indicates the persistence of such beliefs down to recent times. Even burial mounds may be considered to be alive in certain traditions, as among the Mapuche of southern Chile where they may become 'ill' and require 'healing' (Dillehay 2007: 229 ff.).

Thus the creation of monuments evoked issues that go far beyond the mere commemoration of events or people. It is in this perspective that we should consider the very earliest monuments, such as the carved stone stelae from Göbekli Tepe in south-eastern Turkey. These massive limestone pillars carved with representations of wild animals in raised relief date probably to the eleventh or tenth millennium BC, and their location at a hilltop site of perhaps seasonal aggregation already associates monumentality with ritual performance and belief. Monumentalized landscapes have much earlier origins, however, if the open-air rock art of Western Europe or Australia is considered 'monumental' in character. The marking of natural surfaces, the veneration and elaboration of trees and boulders, and the use of unmodified materials in constructed settings, all exemplify the elision between 'natural' forms and 'built' forms that is fundamental to the origins of the 'monument'. It places the focus not on what (or who) is commemorated, but how that is achieved: on the specific materiality that monuments incorporate and project.

2 Connecting with the Land

Early archaeological studies of prehistoric monuments depended heavily on distributional approaches, where sites were reduced to clusters of dots on a map, or were interpreted in terms of territory and hierarchy. More recent approaches, inspired by post-processualism, have emphasized the experience of landscape and the significance of non-Western understandings of place, space, and cosmology. Thus it has been argued that early monuments may have been referencing local landforms such as rocky outcrops and mountains. The massive capstone of the Pentre Ifan chambered tomb in south-west Wales (Figure 1.1) has been claimed to mirror in some respects the prominent mountain top of Carn Ingli some 4 km to the west (Tilley 1994: 105). Ethnographic evidence from Australia indicates how the indigenous inhabitants interpreted landforms in terms of the actions and travels of creator beings during the 'dreamtime'. Uluru (Ayers Rock) in central Australia, for example, is associated in one Aboriginal tradition with a mud fight between two boys, who in death were preserved as boulders on its summit. Another tradition refers to a battle between Liru (poisonous snakes) and Kuniya (carpet snakes) that have left deep scars across the sides of

FIGURE 1.1 Pentre Ifan, a megalithic monument in south-west Wales, with the prominent mountain of Carn Ingli visible in the background.

the rock. Rubbing the rock will release some of the spiritual power generated through these associations (Layton 1986: 5–16). Among the peoples of the north-west coast of North America, features of the landscape are likewise considered the abode of supernatural beings and may be dangerous to approach. The Haida, for example, believed the coasts of the Queen Charlotte Islands were inhabited by a whole series of supernatural beings whom they referred to as the 'Ocean People' (Swanton 1905: 19–22).

Insights such as these suggest that in traditional societies landscape is conceived not as an inert three-dimensional backdrop to human action, to be exploited for its resources, but as a network of places associated with supernatural power and social or mythological meaning. It is important to recognize, however, that we see these landscapes today through modern eyes, that much of their prehistoric significance is irretrievable, and that the landscapes that we perceive today do not survive unchanged from the prehistoric past. Large and long-lived trees would have been significant elements of the prehistoric landscape, as prominent as many rock outcrops, yet in most cases tree cover has been extensively cleared and there is little to indicate their size or location. Bronze Age barrows at Buckskin in Hampshire and Deeping Saint Nicholas in Lincolnshire may have been built on the site of tree throws (Allen and Gardiner 2002; French 1994). The special significance of trees is also revealed both by ethnography and by archaeological examples such as the massive upturned tree stump within the timber circle at Holme-next-the-Sea (Shutova 2006; Brennand and Taylor 2003).

The direct relevance of ethnographic insights to specific prehistoric contexts remains problematic, but in favourable circumstances, and especially where oral or written material is available, more robust interpretations can be proposed. In southern Chile, archaeological and ethnographical approaches have been combined in a study of the monuments of the Purén and Lumaco valley area of Araucania (Dillehay 2007). Here earthen monuments of the thirteenth to nineteenth centuries AD occur in the form of *kuel* (mounds) and *rehuekuel* (levelled hilltops with groups of mounds). The mounds structure the landscape, and serve as portals for shamans, ancestors, and deities to descend from the upper world to the earth. The mounds consist of thousands of earthen loads carried by local and non-local communities. Different coloured clays and soils were dug from different places in the valley, and informants knew the source locations of the different clays and sediments which were the properties of specific lineages. Hence the materials formed direct links with different parts of the landscape and those links were themselves understood in social terms. The mounds cover the burials of deceased leaders, and form a visible network over the land. Beyond these humanly made structures were the distant sacred mountains including snow-capped volcanoes on the eastern horizon. So important were visual connections within this landscape that large tracts of forest were reportedly felled to create pathways of intervisibility between *rehuekuel* and distant sacred mountains (Dillehay 2007: 323).

Connections with the land may be affirmed in other ways. The inclusion within monuments of large stones, coloured blocks or fills, or whole uprooted trees emphasizes the symbolic resonance of the materials. Structured use of materials drawn from different places, and of different kinds, colours, and textures, may represent the incorporation of the powers and associations of the places from which those materials were taken. A number of studies have demonstrated how West European megalithic monuments sometimes (albeit rather rarely) incorporated materials of distant origin in their construction. The most famous are the so-called 'bluestones' of Stonehenge (Figure 1.2) that derive from south-west Wales.

FIGURE 1.2 Stonehenge in southern Britain, showing the prominent lintelled sarsen stone settings that form the core feature of the monument.

Measuring only 2 m in height and weighing some 1.5 tonnes, these are much smaller than the massive sarsen blocks that form the lintelled ring and trilithons, but they came from a much greater distance, some 250 kms to the west. The reason for the long-distance displacement of these 80 stones is unclear, but the fact of their removal testifies to their significance. The possibility that Preseli itself (Figure 1.3) was held by Neolithic communities to possess mystical or supernatural power, and that transporting the stones to Stonehenge was a means of appropriating that power, is persuasive (Darvill 2006; Insoll 2006).

The extraction of stone blocks and other materials will often have led to a transformation of the landscape. In the Carnac area of southern Brittany, the numerous megalithic monuments were composed of material from a series of rocky outcrops (Figure 1.4). These outcrops were dismantled and destroyed in order to feed the progressive construction of granite monuments over a period of 2,000 years. Detailed studies of the weathered surfaces of the megalithic blocks have allowed the sequence of block extraction to be reconstructed, and demonstrate that surface material—from the top or sides of an outcrop—was removed first, before attacking the core of the outcrop or quarrying into the bedrock itself. This sequence indicates that entire rock outcrops were being broken up and removed, down to ground level, for the construction of these megalithic structures. Thus a landscape of natural outcrops was steadily transformed into a landscape of built monuments (Mens 2008).

FIGURE 1.3 Carn Meini, a distinctive natural landform in the Preseli Hills of south-west Wales, probable source of some of the Stonehenge 'bluestones'.

FIGURE 1.4 The Le Ménec alignments at Carnac in southern Brittany, comprising some 1,069 standing stones arranged in eleven or twelve rows extending over more than a kilometre.

Similar transformations would have occurred with other materials: in the stripping of turf to build turf mounds, or in the felling of trees to construct massive enclosures of timber posts. Turf is a common component of prehistoric monuments in Western Europe, and its removal would have had a major visual and economic impact. As many as 30 hectares of turf grassland may have been destroyed to provide material for the Early Bronze Age barrows on King's Barrow Ridge close to Stonehenge. Converting grassland to bare chalk may have had important symbolic connotations, signifying the transition from life to death (from lush grazing land to bare inert chalk) (Parker Pearson et al. 2006: 250–2). Once again, this is not purely an economic or environmental issue, but a symbolic one. Timber-edged enclosures, for example, may have been symbolic of the forest clearings in which early ritual performances had been enacted.

Thus the act of incorporation connects monuments directly to their landscapes. Turf, timber, stones, and earth came directly from the land, and their removal created negative impacts—felling of trees, dismantling of outcrops, destruction of grassland—and converted them into the positive form of the newly built monument. Locations were chosen to draw the attention both to the monument itself and to the place where it was built. As ethnography illustrates, these may already have been places of mythological or sacred significance, or locations of assembly and ceremonial performance. The construction of monuments gave those associations novel and enduring form.

3 CONNECTING WITH PEOPLE

Monuments connect not only to the landscapes in which they were built but also to the people who built and experienced them. Many achieve their effect by virtue of size and the effort that was invested in their creation. That effort typically involved the combined labour of large numbers of people, and the act of creation was not simply the means to an end but was crucial in its own right. This is illustrated by the association of monuments with the development of a number of early states. Dramatic bursts of monument-building generate a sense of identity among those involved in the work and provide icons for the new political order. On Hawaii, episodes of temple-building coincided with periods of political tension during incipient state development during the later sixteenth century and the early nineteenth century when island-wide and then inter-island polities were created. Monumental construction is a particularly successful strategy in these circumstances since it disseminates ideology and allows leaders to promote their views, encourage social consensus, and consolidate economic resources (Kolb 2006).

The cooperative labour involved in these projects may be considered an act of social construction as much as it is one of monument-building. In southern Chile, the *kuel* of the Purén-Lumaco region were built at the time of burial in the rite of *Winkulkueltun*, and raised in successive annual ceremonies by relatives, friends, and allies of the deceased bringing additional layers of earth (Dillehay 2007: 182). The ceremonial context of construction is key to the creation and enlargement of these monuments. Similar scenarios may be posited for prehistoric monuments. Structures composed of many separate elements such as the Carnac stone rows (some of them consisting of more than 1,000 individual stones arranged in ten or more files extending over a kilometre in length (Figure 1.4)) can be envisaged as the product of additions effected over many years in a successive series of aggregations or pilgrimages that may have focused on particular ritual performances. By contrast, nearby at Locmariaquer the 300-tonne Grand Menhir Brisé, the largest standing stone of prehistoric Europe, must have been created and erected as a single project. Several thousand people would have been required for its extraction, shaping, transport, and erection, and estimates of population density suggest that those people would have needed to be drawn from extensive areas of north-west France (Scarre 2001). The renown of such an achievement would have been powerful and widespread, and the stone's subsequent fall, most likely as a result of earthquake (Boujot and Cassen 2000: 200–2), would have sent similarly powerful messages over extensive areas.

Completed monuments connect with people in a different way, commemorating individuals and the events in which they were involved. The ceremonial centres of Maya cities, for example, were furnished with monuments bearing dated inscriptions recounting the actions and genealogies of Maya rulers. These same monuments commonly depicted the rulers themselves clothed in ceremonial attire, or engaged in ceremonial acts. A well-known lintel from Yaxchilan shows the Lady Xoc drawing a thorn-lined rope through her tongue to release drops of blood to feed to gods. This depicts a specific bloodletting ceremony that took place on 28 October AD 709 (Schele and Miller 1992: 186–7). The bloodletting ritual may have been performed within the building of which the lintel forms a part. Other scenes depict rulers engaged in ritual dances, and such ceremonies may have been played out in front of large audiences. It is arguable, indeed, that the stelae commemorating these theatrical performances were erected in the public places where the performances themselves occurred. The central plazas of Maya cities were large enough to accommodate thousands of spectators, the performances themselves taking place on stages in front of the temples (Inomata 2006). Thus the monumental stelae of Maya ceremonial centres both commemorated events that had already occurred and formed the backdrop to an ongoing series of theatrical performances by the ruling elites.

In prehistoric contexts, too, material evidence indicates that monuments were active loci of ceremonial performance. The chambered tombs of Neolithic Western Europe were the setting for rituals centred upon the successive deposition of individual bodies, followed by subsequent rearrangement of the remains and the removal of selected elements. In the Orkney tombs, for example, once corpses had decayed, skulls and long bones were sometimes stacked together in particular locations within the tombs: 17 skulls in the end compartment of the tomb of Knowe of Yarso on Rousay; 23 skulls in one of side cells at Isbister on South Ronaldsay (Richards 1988; Reilly 2003). There is considerable variability in the specific practices at different times and places, but the provision of a durable entrance passage appears to have been designed to give repeated access to the chamber over a period of years or decades in order to enable practices of this kind. In some cases, the entrance passage opens at the centre of a monumental façade which may have been intended to provide an impressive backdrop to ceremonies involving veneration of the dead and the manipulation of human remains.

The scale of some of these monuments and the possible connection with concepts of pilgrimage suggests that they may have been intended (no less than Maya plazas) as places of public ceremony. British henge monuments, such as the Thornborough circles in Yorkshire or Avebury in Wessex, consist of a central space surrounded by deep ditches enclosed within massive external banks (Harding 2003). The high banks exclude the outside world—the world of everyday experience—and set these spaces apart as enclosed arenas with specific visual and acoustic properties. The avenues of standing stones that lead up to Avebury provided ceremonial pathways, to be followed perhaps by participants in the ceremonies, and the entrances into the henge itself were carefully designed for dramatic effect (Watson 2001). Other linear monuments, such as the Carnac stone rows of Brittany (Figure 1.4), which likewise led to enclosures, also strongly suggest that processions were a key part of the ceremonies which these monuments were designed to structure and frame.

4 Connecting with the Sky

The symbolism of monuments draws not only on forms and materials taken from the landscape but also on the movements of sun, moon, and stars, potent elements in the mythological and cosmological understanding of Western and non-Western societies alike. Monuments may be aligned on solar, lunar, or stellar phenomena (such as the summer or winter solstice), and in some well-documented cases incorporate celestial relationships within their very structures. Thus the Governor's Palace at the Maya city of Uxmal was oriented on the southernmost rising point of the planet Venus, a relationship supported by the numerous astronomical references in the glyphs that decorated the building (Aveni 1997: 139–42; Bricker and Bricker 1996). More widely documented are those alignments connecting monuments with the rising or setting sun, such as the well-known solstice alignments at Stonehenge, and at the megalithic tomb of Newgrange in Ireland. At Newgrange for a few days around the winter solstice the rising sun shines through the carefully constructed 'roof-box' above the passage and penetrates 20 m within the monument to illuminate the burial chamber and its human remains (O'Kelly 1982). This carefully engineered effect expresses a powerful symbolism of regeneration and rebirth.

Such relationships enhance the potency of monuments as places for the enactment of ritual. Earlier studies made claims for a proliferation of astronomical alignments. More careful assessment has subsequently urged caution. The extensive series of astronomical alignments calculated by Alexander Thom for British and Breton megalithic monuments in the 1960s and 1970s, for example, assumed a degree of precision in the construction of those monuments that is not supported by archaeology or statistical analysis (Thom 1967, 1971; Thom and Thom 1978; Ruggles 1999). The disputed methodologies that have been used to explore these relationships do not, however, detract from the importance of celestial cosmologies in the beliefs of societies whose awareness of the night sky was undimmed by modern electric lighting. Furthermore, ethnography has revealed that many traditional societies hold a belief in a three-tiered cosmos divided between underworld, this world, and an upper world. Such belief systems imbue the upper realm of the sky with particular power as the abode of supernatural beings, a belief that may find reflection in the design of the Nazca lines or the Wisconsin effigy mounds whose imagery can only be grasped from above. Prehistoric chambered tombs have also been interpreted as models of such a three-tiered cosmology, in which to enter the chamber buried within the mound is to enter the underworld of death and the spirits (Lewis-Williams and Pearce 2005).

5 FUTURE DIRECTIONS

The study of prehistoric monuments is a long-established part of archaeology with a history going back at least 300 years, but exciting directions for future research continue to be identified and explored. A century ago, diffusionist explanations were at the forefront; today, and for the coming decades, we can anticipate more precise chronologies, new insights from the analysis of human remains, and new techniques for the study of carved, painted, and weathered surfaces. Some of the greatest potential, however, lies in the domain of multi-sensory explorations that look to colour, sound, and texture to gain deeper understanding of the performative role of monumental structures. Recent approaches have drawn attention to the materiality of monuments, insisting that they are not merely ciphers or message boards, but rather that their primary impact derives from qualities of size, shape, and material. This includes notably the deployment of differently coloured materials—for example colour contrasts in alignments of standing stones (Scarre 2002), or structured soil colours in Bronze Age burial mounds that invert the normal stratigraphic order (Owoc 2002). The multi-vocality of monuments has also been recognized—that they meant different things to different people, and continue to do so into the present.

These approaches continue to privilege the visual, however, and the role of the other senses, notably touch and hearing, have only recently begun to be explored in a systematic manner. The bodily engagement of human actors—the experience of individuals entering a megalithic tomb, for example—will have made prehistoric people no less than modern visitors directly aware of the texture of surfaces, and the confined space of many burial chambers will have demanded specific postures of approach including crawling on all fours in some cases, ducking to avoid lintels in others, and squeezing through openings against roughly-textured orthostats (Cummings 2002). Direct engagement with the physicality of monuments invariably opens up new understandings and takes us away from academic studies based purely on plans, photographs, and texts.

The direct experience of monuments also has an important aural component, and the role of sound in ceremonial performance must not be overlooked. This is a difficult area which still requires a robust methodology, although exploratory studies have produced intriguing results (Watson 2006; Watson and Keating 1999, 2000; Devereux 2001; Scarre and Lawson 2006). Among the most impressive has been the study of the galleries and conduits beneath the Andean temple of Chavín de Huantar, which may have been expressly designed to produce a thunderous sound akin to applause when water rushed through them (Burger 1992: 143). Once again, the potential of the monument as a setting for theatrical performances is underlined. Monuments such as these were not merely 'mute' stone structures, but sites of ceremony and remembrance. They were key elements in human social engagement with the material world, but with a world transformed by the very monuments themselves.

Suggested Reading

The archaeology of monumentality has generated a vast and diverse literature spanning every inhabited continent and every period from the early Holocene to the recent past. For the European prehistoric material, Richard Bradley, *An Archaeology of Natural Places* (London, 2000) explores the relationship between landscape features and the construction of monuments. The connections with religion and belief are discussed in the present author's 'Shrines of the land and places of power: Religion and the transition to farming in Western Europe' in D. S. Whitley and K. Hays-Gilpin (eds), *Belief in the Past: Theoretical approaches to the study of religion* (Walnut Creek, 2008). Clive Ruggles, *Astronomy in Prehistoric Britain and Ireland* (Yale, 1999) provides an excellent examination of the complexities surrounding the interpretation of solar and lunar alignments and the relationship of monuments to celestial phenomena. The phenomenological approach is set out by Chris Tilley in the now-classic *A Phenomenology of Landscape* (Oxford, 1994). For monuments in action in an ethnohistorical context, see Tom Dillehay, *Monuments, Empires, and Resistance: The Araucanian polity and ritual narratives* (Cambridge, 2007).

REFERENCES

ALLEN, M. J. and GARDINER, J. 2002. 'A sense of time: Cultural markers in the Mesolithic of southern England?' in B. David and M. Wilson (eds.), *Inscribed Landscapes: Marking and making place* (Honolulu: University of Hawai'i Press), pp. 139–53.

AVENI, A. 1997. *Stairways to the Stars: Skywatching in three great ancient cultures* (New York: John Wiley).

BAHN, P. and FLENLEY, J. 1992. *Easter Island, Earth Island* (London: Thames and Hudson).

BIRD-DAVID, N. 1999. '"Animism" revisited: Personhood, environment, and relational epistemology', *Current Anthropology*, 40: S69–S91.

BOUJOT, C. and CASSEN, S. 2000. 'Tertres et pierres dressées', in S. Cassen, C. Boujot, and J. Vaquero (eds), *Éléments d'architecture. Exploration d'un tertre funéraire à Lannec er Godouer (Erdeven, Morbitian)*. (Chauvigny: Association des Publications Chauvinoses), pp. 181–206.

BRADLEY, R. 2000. *An Archaeology of Natural Places* (London: Routledge).

—— 2005. *Ritual and Domestic Life in Prehistoric Europe* (London: Routledge).

BRENNAND, M. and TAYLOR, M. 2003. 'The survey and excavation of a Bronze Age timber circle at Holme-next-the-Sea, Norfolk, 1998–9', *Proceedings of the Prehistoric Society*, 69: 1–84.

BRICKER, H. M. and BRICKER, V. R. 1996. 'Astronomical references in the throne inscription of the Palace of the Governor at Uxmal', *Cambridge Archaeological Journal*, 6: 191–229.

BURGER, R. L. 1992. *Chavín and the Origins of Andean Civilization* (London: Thames and Hudson).

CLEAL, R. M. J., WALKER, K. E., and MONTAGUE, R. 1995. *Stonehenge in its Landscape: Twentieth-century excavations* (London: English Heritage).

COLSON, E. 1997. 'Places of power and shrines of the land', *Paideuma*, 43: 47–57.

CUMMINGS, V. 2002. 'Experiencing texture and transformation in the British Neolithic', *Oxford Journal of Archaeology*, 21: 249–61.

DARVILL, T. 2006. *Stonehenge: The biography of a landscape* (Stroud: Tempus).

DEVEREUX, P. 2001. *Stone Age Soundtracks: The acoustic archaeology of ancient sites* (London: Vega).

DILLEHAY, T. D. 2007. *Monuments, Empires, and Resistance: The Araucanian polity and ritual narratives* (Cambridge: Cambridge University Press).

FLOOD, J. 1995. *Archaeology of the Dreamtime: The story of prehistoric Australia and its people* (Sydney: Angus and Robertson).

FRENCH, C. 1994. *Excavation of the Deeping St Nicholas Barrow Complex, South Lincolnshire* (Sleaford: Heritage Trust of Lincolnshire).

GELL, A. 1998. *Art and Agency: An anthropological theory* (Oxford: Clarendon Press).

GUENTHER, M. 1999. 'From totemism to shamanism: Hunter-gatherer contributions to world mythology and spirituality' in R. B. Lee and R. Daly (eds), *The Cambridge Encyclopedia of Hunters and Gatherers* (Cambridge: Cambridge University Press), pp. 426–33.

HALLENDY, N. 2000. *Inuksuit: Silent messengers of the Arctic* (Vancouver: Douglas and McIntyre).

HARDING, J. 2003. *Henge Monuments of the British Isles* (Stroud: Tempus).

INOMATA, T. 2006. 'Plazas, performers, and spectators: Political theaters of the Classic Maya', *Current Anthropology*, 47: 805–42.

INSOLL, T. 2006. 'Shrine franchising and the Neolithic in the British Isles: some observations based upon the Tallensi, northern Ghana', *Cambridge Archaeological Journal*, 16: 223–38.

KOLB, M. J. 2006. 'The origins of monumental architecture in ancient Hawai'i', *Current Anthropology*, 47: 657–65.

LAYTON, R. 1986. *Uluru: An Aboriginal history of Ayers Rock* (Canberra: Australian Institute of Aboriginal Studies).

LEWIS-WILLIAMS, D. and PEARCE, D. 2005. *Inside the Neolithic Mind: Consciousness, cosmos and the realm of the gods* (London: Thames and Hudson).

MENS, E. 2008. 'Refitting megaliths in western France', *Antiquity*, 82: 25–36.

MITHEN, S. 1996. *The Prehistory of the Mind: A search for the origins of art, religion and science* (London: Thames and Hudson).

O'KELLY, M. J. 1982. *Newgrange: Archaeology, art and legend* (London: Thames and Hudson).

OVSYANNIKOV, O. V. and TEREBIKHIN, N. M. 1994. 'Sacred space in the culture of the Arctic regions' in D. L. Carmichael et al. (eds), *Sacred Sites, Sacred Places* (London: Routledge), pp. 45–81.

OWOC, M. A. 2002. 'Munselling the mound: The use of soil colour as metaphor in British Bronze Age funerary colour' in A. Jones and G. McGregor (eds), *Colouring the Past: The significance of colour in archaeological research* (Oxford: Berg), pp. 127–40.

PARKER PEARSON, M., POLLARD, J., RICHARDS, C., et al. 2006. 'Materializing Stonehenge: The Stonehenge Riverside Project and new discoveries', *Journal of Material Culture*, 11: 227–61.

REILLY, S. 2003. 'Processing the dead in Neolithic Orkney', *Oxford Journal of Archaeology*, 22: 133–54.

RICHARDS, C. 1988. 'Altered images: A re-examination of Neolithic mortuary practices in Orkney' in J. C. Barrett and I. Kinnes (eds), *The Archaeology of Context in the Neolithic and Bronze Age: Recent trends* (Sheffield: Department of Archaeology and Prehistory), pp. 42–55.

RUGGLES, C. 1999. *Astronomy in Prehistoric Britain and Ireland* (New Haven and London: Yale University Press).

SCARRE, C. 2001. 'Modelling prehistoric populations: the case of Neolithic Brittany', *Journal of Anthropological Archaeology*, 20: 285–313.

——2002. 'A place of special meaning: Interpreting prehistoric monuments through landscape' in B. David and M. Wilson (eds), *Inscribed Landscapes: Marking and making place* (Honolulu: University of Hawaii Press), pp. 154–75.

——2004. 'Displaying the stones: The materiality of "megalithic" monuments' in E. DeMarrais, C. Gosden, and C. Renfrew (eds), *Rethinking Materiality: The engagement of mind with the material world* (Cambridge: McDonald Institute for Archaeological Research), pp. 141–52.

——2008. 'Shrines of the land and places of power: Religion and the transition to farming in Western Europe' in D. S. Whitley and K. Hays-Gilpin (eds.), *Belief in the Past: Theoretical approaches to the study of religion* (Walnut Creek, CA: Left Coast Press), pp. 209–26.

——and LAWSON, G. (eds) 2006. *Archaeoacoustics* (Cambridge: McDonald Institute for Archaeological Research).

SCHELE, L. and MILLER, M. E. 1992. *The Blood of Kings: Dynasty and ritual in Maya art* (London: Thames and Hudson).

SHUTOVA, N. 2006. 'Trees in Udmurt religion', *Antiquity*, 80: 318–27.

SWANTON, J. R. 1905. *Contributions to the Ethnology of the Haida: The Jessup North Pacific Expedition: Memoir of the American Museum of Natural History V, Part I* (Leiden: Brill).

THOM, A. 1967. *Megalithic Sites in Britain* (Oxford: Clarendon Press).

——1971. *Megalithic Lunar Observatories* (Oxford: Clarendon Press).

——and THOM, A. S. 1978. *Megalithic Remains in Britain and Brittany* (Oxford: Clarendon Press).
TILLEY, C. 1994. *A Phenomenology of Landscape: Places, paths and monuments* (Oxford: Berg).
WATSON, A. 2001. 'Composing Avebury', *World Archaeology*, 33: 296–313.
——2006. '(Un)intentional sound? Acoustics and Neolithic monuments' in C. Scarre and G. Lawson (eds.), *Archaeoacoustics* (Cambridge: McDonald Institute for Archaeological Research), pp. 11–22.
WATSON, A. and KEATING, D. 1999. 'Architecture and sound: an acoustic analysis of megalithic monuments in prehistoric Britain', *Antiquity*, 73: 325–36.
————2000. 'The architecture of sound in Neolithic Orkney' in A. Ritchie (ed.), *Neolithic Orkney in its European Context* (Cambridge: McDonald Institute for Archaeological Research), pp. 259–63.

Chapter 2

LANDSCAPE

Randi Haaland and Gunnar Haaland

View with a grain of sand
We call it a grain of sand,
but it calls itself neither grain nor sand.
It does just fine without a name,
whether general, particular,
permanent, passing,
incorrect, or apt.

Our glance, our touch means nothing to it.
It doesn't feel itself seen nor touched.
And that it fell on the windowsill
is only our experience, not its.
For it, it is not different from falling on anything else
with no assurance that it has finished falling
or that it is falling still.

Wislawa Szymborska: View with a grain
of Sand (p. 135)

1 Introduction

IN Chinese Mandarin there is a phrase *jing guan* (*jing* referring to something, e.g. a 'grain of sand' that is seen, and that exists whether the viewer exists or not; *guan*—the view that a viewer sees when looking at *jing*) that capture one of the many meanings of the English word *landscape*. We find this meaning fruitful for our discussion because it directs our attention to the relationship between particular viewers and the things they view. The concept covers things that exist in the viewers' natural environment as well as in man-made modifications of that environment. However, what the viewer views is not a mirror reflection of what 'exists' in a 'mind-independent' environment; what is viewed depends on the perspective of the viewer, e.g. a botanical, geological, aesthetic, emotional, etc. perspective. Han Lorzing's statement that 'I believe that "landscape" is not just an isolated, objective thing in itself. To a large extent "landscapes" are created by our perceptions... landscape is a product of the human mind' is close to our position (Lorzing 2001: 6).

The environment looked at from different perspectives can be represented in different ways. This takes us to the level of the original conceptual content of landscape in Anglo-Germanic languages, namely landscape as a painted representation of an expanse of nature as viewed by the painter and executed and judged according to aesthetic ideas current in the community of art viewers in North-western Europe at a particular time.

2 Theoretical Reflections

What we are dealing with here are the ritual perspectives of the viewer and the components in the environment that are perceived as loaded with ritual significance. We shall first try to explore some theoretical perspectives we find fruitful for interpretation of how landscapes are constituted for people dwelling in varying kinds of natural environments, as well as for different ways in which they interact with these environments. Ingold, drawing on Gibson, has argued that knowledge 'obtained through direct perception is thus practical, it is knowledge about what an environment offers for the pursuance of the action in which the perceiver is currently engaged. In other words, to perceive an object or event is to perceive what it affords... the information picked up by an agent in the context of practical activity specifies what are called the "affordances" of objects and events in the environment' (Ingold 2007: 166). Learning to attend to components in the environment is obviously of fundamental importance in peoples' acquisition of knowledge about the environment. However, they may view the environment from a different perspective from the practical one of material satisfactions. We shall here focus on viewing environment from a ritual perspective. Drawing on Barth (1975) we understand a ritual perspective on landscape as one that focuses on the way people view their environment as symbolic expressions of basic values and cosmological ideas. Following Bateson (1973) we assume that 'belief' in such values and ideas is fostered primarily in non-verbal communication and in metaphorical and mythological forms of verbal communication.

We thus see elaborations of verbal and non-verbal forms of symbolic expressions as having different qualities with regard to making the message convincing. Features of the natural environment may thus be taken as expression of ideas and values in peoples' minds; they exist as something independent of man, but given meaning as representing immaterial but meaningful dimensions of the human condition as expressed by Rappaport: 'meanings are often causal and causes are often meaningful, but because more fundamentally, the relationship between the two, in all its difficulty, tension, and ambiguity, expresses the condition of a species that lives, and can only live, in terms of meanings it itself must construct in a world devoid of intrinsic meaning but subject to natural law' (Rappaport 1979: 54). The environment people dwell in does not only offer 'affordances' for practical use; it may also offer 'food for thought', e.g. as 'affordances' for construction of meanings. Furthermore people may seek to enhance the importance of such symbolic meanings by expressing them in humanly built constructions, e.g. megaliths, temples, graves, sculptures, etc. that make them more compelling. An important difference between such representations and the original idea of landscape painting is that these representations are not intended to represent the viewed material environment at all, but rather immaterial ideas the builders are struggling to express. Paintings did not change the environment viewed, whereas modifying the material environment to represent basic ideas in material forms changes what viewers see in that environment.

We shall try to outline two theoretical perspectives we consider fruitful for interpretation of the ritual perspectives entertained in different societies. One is expressed in various publications by Lakoff and Johnson (see Lakoff and Johnson 1999 for relevant references). A central point in their cognitive theory is that understanding is based on 'imaginative structures that emerge from our experience as bodily organisms functioning in interactions with an environment' (Johnson 1987: xv and xvi).

For our purpose we find orientational metaphors interesting. Most of them have to do with spatial orientations. These spatial orientations arise from the fact that we have bodies of the sort we have and that they function as they do in our physical environment. Orientational metaphors are not arbitrary. They have a basis in our physical and cultural experience. While the polar oppositions like up–down, in–out, back–front etc. are physical in nature, the metaphors based on them vary from culture to culture. Our task is to explore how in different cultures they are taken as 'affordances' for spinning metaphoric associations into objectified forms. The up–down vertical orientation lends itself to certain types of metaphorizations, e.g. mountains are close to the sky, and the sky is often associated with 'heavenly' qualities; underground is down and below the level where humans live, and often associated with evil qualities, or bad qualities opposite to heavenly qualities. Such features of the landscape may also be taken as models for man-made constructions in the environment.

Another theoretical perspective we take from van Gennep (1960) and Turner (1969). Special types of social process that are loaded with meaning are the so-called life-cycle rituals where individuals' positions in society during a short period of time are dramatically changed both in the sense of changing rights and duties in relation to interaction partners, but also in the sense of being indoctrinated into new understandings of the nature of human and cosmological relations. According to van Gennep (1960), life-cycle rituals have a characteristic threefold structure consisting of a phase of separation; a liminal phase of transition; and a phase of reincorporation. Turner (1969) argues that the liminal phase is critical in the sense that the 'initiands' are in an ambiguous position of 'betwixt and between' where they are exposed to a range of experiences like humiliation, seclusion, and tests. The symbolism in initiation rituals is often modelled after the event of birth, the event that brings people into the world, with a person's transition to adult position in society frequently considered a second birth. In such rites of transition from birth to death, objects closely associated with the birth-giver—the woman—are frequently given ritual prominence. Likewise burials are often symbolized as transitions into another womb—the womb of mother earth (Haaland and Haaland 1995). A critical point in these rites is to communicate messages about basic values in ways that are experienced as compelling for 'initiands' as well as for other members in society. Settings for such rites very often draw on natural features that can be perceived as being 'betwixt and between' contrasting cultural categorizations of the environment, a contrast that can be perceived as analogous to the social 'betwixt and between' of transition rites. Liminal dimensions of social life may thus lead to conceptualization of specific kinds of environmental places as liminal. The ambiguity inherent in such spaces may furthermore be seen as an 'affordance' providing locations for a wider range of ritual activities of ambiguous nature like sacrifices and shamanistic performances.

3 Comparative Ethnographic and Archaeological Material

Bogs may be perceived as liminal because they are neither solid land nor lakes, and thereby be chosen as sites for performance of a range of ritual activities involving social liminality. During the Celtic and Roman Iron age in North-western Europe, bogs were used as deposition areas for human corpses that appeared to have been sacrificed. The recovered bodies were males, females, old, and young; some were strangled; some had their throats cut. Investigation of their stomach content indicates that in several cases they had been served a special gruel that may have been part of a ritual meal (Green 2002a). Human sacrifices imply that the victims are individuals set apart from the rest of the community. The ritual feeding can be interpreted as a liminal phase before the sacrificial act incorporate them in another form of imagined existence. Bogs in this region are also deposit areas for iron objects, especially weapons. Green (2002b) argues that deposited iron weapons were deliberately destroyed or 'killed' before being sacrificed. This custom of sacrifice was widely practised during the Early Iron Age from France to Denmark and especially in wetland areas that we have suggested may have been perceived as liminal landscapes.

Caves are another kind of natural formation with features that can be perceived as 'betwixt and between' in the sense that they are neither inside, nor outside the mountain; neither above, nor below the ground. Furthermore, caves lend themselves to metaphoric associations with the female body. They are, in a way, 'natural' settings for ritual activities like initiations and shamanistic performances. The rock art in European Upper Palaeolithic caves may have been connected with puberty rites. Foot and handprints of adolescents seem to have been deliberately made as part of rituals on the cave wall (Owens and Hayden 1997; see Bahn, Ch. 22, this volume). The neophytes would have been part of hunter-gatherer communities, and the painting of different animals may have been related to a totemistic world view and social organization where different social categories were associated with specific animal species. Since shamans perform in a liminal space between the world of daily practical life and the world of spirits, Lewis-Williams' argument that caves in the European Upper Palaeolithic and in Southern Africa up until recently were used for shamanistic rituals seems reasonable (see Lewis-Williams 2001 for extensive references).

The most penetrating analyses of the way cosmological ideas affect people's experience of natural environment is found in the ethnography of Australian Aborigines. According to Morphy, 'Time was created through the transformation of ancestral beings into place, the place being forever the mnemonic of the event' (Morphy 1995: 188). Features of the environment people dwell in are woven into a complex ideational world connecting events at present to the creation of the world by the ancestral beings in Dreamtime. As people move through a natural environment, a ritual perspective dominates the meanings they read from it, meanings where belief in 'the ancestral past becomes part of the subjective experience of the individual' (Morphy 1995: 189). It is a primary concern for them to acquire knowledge about components of the natural environment and the message about social order and cosmological meaning that is an integral part of these components. Moving through the landscape is a movement in relation to 'affordances' in the form of food as well as constantly reminding people of ideas also expressed in myths, rituals, songs, and dances. It is movement down a 'memory lane' where the present is blended with the past, as well as giving directions to the future.

A modern example of important messages being encoded in the environment is the fortress of Masada located on top of a 400-metre-high mountain near the Dead Sea. Masada is the location where, 1,900 years ago, after three years' resistance 960 Jews were defeated by 5,000 Roman soldiers and committed collective suicide instead of being captured by the Romans. Whatever the motives behind the suicides were, the act is so dramatic that it invites the construction of messages about its wider significance. The Jewish rabbinical tradition suppressed the memory of Masada for nearly 2,000 years because suicide was considered contrary to the beliefs of Judaism (Bruner and Gofain 1988: 63). However with the establishment of an independent Israeli state, surrounded by hostile Arab neighbours, the historic Masada events provided a source for construction of a compelling story of national solidarity and willingness to make the ultimate sacrifice of life for protection of the state of Israel. This is manifested in many ways, e.g. new recruits to the Armoured Corps of the Israel Defense Forces take their oath of allegiance at the Masada fortress and repeat the words 'Masada shall not fall again' (Bruner and Gofain 1988: 61); Israeli school children, as part of their school curriculum, visit Masada; families may hold bar mitzvahs in a synagogue at the fortress. The memory of Masada is part of an ideology emphasizing resistance and legitimating claims to land. It plays on an association with the story of David and Goliath.

Since features and activities loaded with symbolic meaning may not have left any material remains, the interpretative task is formidable. As an ethnographic example of such a situation we shall draw on Barth's (1961) argument in his Basseri monograph. The Basseri are sheep herders migrating about 500 km between the Lar lowlands in southern Iran and the Kuh-i-Bul mountains in northern Iraq. These migrations are overwhelmingly determined by natural, economic, and political considerations. However, these migratory activities that reflect technical imperatives are, according to Barth, also vested with central and crucial meanings in contexts vested with particular value, e.g. a whole range of activities such as camping, migration, and herding. The environment they move through during the great migration is experienced as a ritual landscape in which basic values are expressed.

Drawing on a study by S. Szynkiewics of a different nomadic group, the Mongols, Caroline Humphrey also expresses the idea that changing camps 'is felt to be an event outside the ordinary run of life; they put on special clothes and use festive harness for their horse... The ritualized journey is thus a spatial liminality, into and out of the otherness of "travelling that is not travelling" paradoxically an otherness which serves to reassert the nomadic way of life—thereby negating movement in the everyday world' (Humphrey 1995: 142–3). That migratory movements can be experienced as ritual is manifest in a rich inventory of verticality and body metaphors associating environmental and man-made structures (e.g. tents and sacrificial altars constructed as a heap of stones) with ideas of the energies of the world conceived as spirits. An important point made by Humphrey is that there are different rival views of landscape among the Mongols; one transmitted mainly in chiefly and lamaist rituals, and another transmitted mainly in shamanistic rituals. Shamanistic rituals are frequently performed in caves conceptualized as the mother's womb and focused on fertility cults, a metaphoric association that can be seen as a liminal phase.

In neighbouring Buddhist Tibet on the high plateau in an austere environment live the Brokpa herders. The environment exists as naturally constituted by mountains, plains, valleys, rivers, and lakes providing vegetation for an adaptation based on yak and sheep, but also exists in the herders' minds as cosmologically constituted—as a sacred realm where gods and goddesses manifest themselves in steep mountain peaks and deep lakes.

Ritual meanings (particularly for the karmic consequences of activities) are an important aspect of yak-herders' daily activities. These activities are played out in a sacred environment that 'usually comprises two matched parts, a god (mountain, rock or tree) and a goddess (lake, spring or river). The two marry. They are sometimes confused with the supernatural father and mother of the hero or king, the mountains representing both the sky and its gods (*lha*) and the lake, the underground region and its deities (*lhu*). Each community inhabiting a given site thus finds its identity in its own ancestor and holy place' (Stein 1972: 210). The verticality of the natural environment thus dominates the metaphoric constructions of the ritual landscape. It was down the mountain that the first ancestor descended from the sky to earth. Royal tombs and palaces (e.g. Potala) were analogous to mountains (Figure 2.1). Rich symbolic representations construct analogies between the human body, the tent, and the sacred mountain as pillar of the world.

A similar analogy between the body and the relation of environmental features is found in Hindu Nepal. The Magar of Nepal make an analogy between the human body and the landscape. As the human head is more pure and auspicious than other parts of the body, it has more lustre and power. Like the head of the human body, the higher hilltops are pure and more powerful than the lowland. All inferior beings and substances remain in the

FIGURE 2.1 The mountain-associated Potala palace in Lhasa.

FIGURE 2.2 To the right in the picture just beyond the rice terraces there are three almost indistinguishable sacred hilltops on a range as seen from Argal village, western Nepal.

lower places (Khattri 1999: 36). Orthodox Hindus apply the verticality metaphor to legitimize the ranking of castes according to the criterion of purity (higher caste) and pollution (lower castes).

An interesting point here is that features in the natural environment may be considered sacred because their forms lend themselves to associations with the forms of ritual objects in Hinduism, e.g. the point where three rivers merge is called Trisuli and is considered the most holy place for rituals, such as funerals, because it is associated with the holy symbol, *trisul* (trident)—one of the strong arms of lord Shiva. Likewise, three mountains, that from a specific settlement can be seen as following one behind the other, may in this settlement be associated with the *trisul* (Figure 2.2).

Verticality is also a striking dimension of the natural environment of the mountainous regions in south-western Ethiopia inhabited by Omotic-speaking people. These societies practise a caste- and gender-based division of labour with the farming caste on top and the iron-smelter and his wife at the bottom. The ranking is based on purity–pollution criteria (apparently culture historically unconnected to Hindu traditions), most clearly expressed in restrictions on commensality and sexuality, but also in a variety of other metaphors constructed as vertical, e.g. different occupational castes occupy different positions in the marketplace where the elevation of their seating correlates with their position in the caste ranking; the elevation of homestead locations also tends to correlate with caste ranking; when meeting on a hilly path the highest-ranked person will move towards the hillside and the lower caste towards the valley side (Figure 2.3). People thus move in a natural

FIGURE 2.3 The iron-smelter with his furnace located on a low slope outside the village of Oska Dencha, south-west Ethiopia. The village is located on the hilltop behind the tree.

environment that is loaded with ritual meaning expressing where people belong in the social hierarchy. The idea of the smith being polluted prevented him in the past from owning land and till the soil since his pollution would also pollute the agricultural land. The location of the site for sacrifice to ancestors is clearly based on up–down orientation with higher castes sacrificing on higher elevations and low castes in lower parts. This is related to concern about the fertility of the earth and the importance of avoiding its pollution. Iron-smelting is an activity that is believed to pollute because it involves transforming elements of the sacred earth by fire, an idea related to Omotic origin myths (Haaland, G., Haaland, R. and Data 2004).

In contrast to Tibet, a variety of myths explain how the ancestors emerged from a hole in the earth. The idea of the earth as sacred is clearly not drawing on the vertical metaphor where down is bad, but rather on the analogue between the fertility of women and the fertility of the earth. This association is manifested in traditional purification rituals. In case a high-caste man transgresses the rules of restrictions on sexual intercourse with low-caste women, he has to undergo a purification ritual whereby he creeps naked through a tunnel dug in the earth after a ram or chicken has been sacrificed at the opening and the blood sprinkled in the tunnel.

4 Earth, Land, Monuments

The idea of the earth as sacred we expect to be a dominant motive in agricultural societies where it also may be connected to ideas of descent. Among the matrilineal Khasi of Shillong and the related patrilineal Munda of Bihar megaliths (menhirs and dolmens) are material expressions of such an association.

In the archaeological record we find that the initial farming population constructed Megalithic grave monuments. These monuments were used as ossuaries, indicating ancestral cults connected with possession of agricultural land, possibly linked to the idea that people imagined themselves as descendants of land as much as the descendants of their ancestors (Joussaume 1985; Milisauskas 1978). The prominence of the megaliths in the natural environment where they stand out as landmarks indicate that they may also have served as material reminders of memories legitimating claims to land and positions. For viewers of megaliths today, Tilley has argued that they are 'the primary signifiers of the Neolithic past, of the first farming populations who transformed the natural environment on a large scale rather than simply living in it' (Tilley 1995: 50).

A very different linkage between agriculture and grave monuments are found in the Middle East. The transition to a sedentary way of life originally seems to have been brought about in locations favouring broad-spectrum resource utilization. The sedentarization process was further stimulated when people started cultivation of non-domesticated grains. Drawing on Hodder's argument that in this transition people came together at ritual centres for initiation, feasting, burials, exchange, marriage etc., we assume that this served to integrate different groups in larger systems of interaction, a process leading to increased sharing of landscape perspectives (Hodder 2007). The growth of sedentism at the time when domesticated plants appear in quantity (during the ninth millennium BP—the so-called PPNB period) is manifest in various features associated with permanent house constructions, e.g. increased 'use of skulls to build histories in houses' (Hodder

2007: 112); inventions of ovens for bread-making; change in house constructions from round to square houses with several rooms for storage (Kujit and Goring-Morris 2002); and an extensive use of lime-plastered floors, often elaborately painted. Special care seems to have been taken in making the hearths. The floors have been replastered repeatedly, indicating a remarkable continuity in house occupation. Some houses at Catal Huyuk were replastered up to 450 times in a time span of 70–100 years. Houses were rebuilt in the same place, and so were the hearths. A most important point that indicates that the house enclosed a fundamental social unit is that it is made the site for burial either below the floors, along the walls, or in its foundation. This suggests the importance of rituals taking place inside the house most probably directed towards worship of dead ancestors, typically expressing continuity with the past as well as fostering continuing solidarities for future social organization (see Akkermans and Schwartz 2003; Kuijt and Goring-Morris 2002). Hodder argues that this is related to focus on memory constructions and its social relevance (Hodder 2007).

We will suggest that the oven and its bread-based cuisine may have played a similar role in creating and maintaining memories. It was from the hearth-oven that people were fed. The food that we eat and incorporate into our body is surrounded by symbolic beliefs. Symbolic uses of food and food-related items such as ovens and hearths are embedded in material forms. In West Asia the house was the context in which food symbolism and social relations and identities were created, expressed, and maintained over time (Haaland 2007). Hence, while on the Atlantic coast the metaphoric associations between land and ancestors are manifested in physical constructions in the natural environment fostering a ritual perspective on the natural environment, the Middle Eastern material on the other hand indicates that the metaphoric associations are manifested in material constructions and activities inside the house.

In a methodologically challenging study, Julian Thomas has made a thought-provoking interpretation of the ritual landscape of Avebury as viewed by Neolithic occupants of the area. The environment is dominated by the long barrow of West Kennet, the enormous mound of Silbury Hill, three causewayed enclosures (the most famous being Windmill Hill), and Avebury Henge. Important deposits in the barrows consist of human bones indicating connections between ancestors and group land as well as being part of secret rituals communicating the importance of this connection.

Drawing on Barth's analysis of Baktaman material (Barth 1987), Thomas argues that 'the power attached to ritual knowledge derives in part from the awareness of the community at large of the existence of "secrets" which they are denied' (Thomas 1995: 36). The structure and location of the monuments are such that it is reasonable to make the assumption that people differentially positioned in society had access to view different kinds of activities surrounded by secrecy. By positioning himself in the Avebury environment and viewing what can be seen from different positions on the outside of the monuments as well as from the inside of the monuments he concludes that 'power was at least vested in access to certain forms of knowledge ... Thus while particular individuals might gain entry into the more secluded parts of these monuments, and be initiated into cardinal secrets of the community, those denied these privileges would have understandings of their own.' The ritual landscape perceived would thus differ among people who had gone through different stages in initiation to secret knowledge.

The acts and items connected with funerals are woven into complex contexts of meaning that it is not easy to interpret. As an example we can take the selection of sites for tombs in China. This is based on *feng shui*, a kind of divination that seeks to bring the graves (and other buildings as well) into the most harmonious position in relation to features (e.g. mountains, wind, and water) of the natural environment. *Feng shui* is part of a belief system that sees the world as made up of positive and negative forces. The idea of *feng shui* is to stimulate the flow of positive energies *qi* and redirect the flow of negative energies *sha*.

5 Conclusions

Looking at the natural environment from a practical perspective, a Chinese may see possibilities for resource utilization, while looking at it from a ritual perspective her concern may be how to move in relation to positive and negative energies. Since Chinese culture has a cultural continuity of at least 4,000 years, it may be possible for archaeologists to trace this belief system backwards in time from grave material. Where we cannot assume such cultural continuity the archaeologist faces a much more difficult task in connecting material objects to the belief systems that they were part of.

The natural environment people dwell in may, as the Chinese example indicates, be experienced as different landscapes depending on the perspectives from which the viewer looks at it. In contrast to the Chinese example where people's ritual perspective is anchored in ideas expressed in widely distributed cosmological beliefs, people may seek to anchor such a perspective in ideas expressing an analogy between the order in the movement of celestial bodies and the social order. Social order is precarious under any circumstance, and a fundamental problem in any society is to make belief in the principles underpinning social life convincing. Construction of monuments and performance of rituals that celebrate phases in the movement of celestial bodies may be a convenient way of fostering an idea that the social order is legitimate because it is related to undisputable observations of regularities in the movement of heavenly bodies. That Stonehenge and other prehistoric monuments are oriented in relation to sun, moon, and stars may not be so much a matter of astronomic interests, but rather a concern for order in the movement of social life. If this argument holds then the experienced ritual landscape people dwell in extends from the sky they observe to the local setting of ceremonial monuments and ritual activities.

In our view interpretation of prehistoric peoples ritual perspectives can benefit from theoretical approaches developed in cognitive sciences and in anthropology, and via comparative ethnography. The importance of comparative ethnography is that it draws attention to possible restrictions on the range of variations in ritual landscape constructions found under different circumstances, e.g. natural environments, mode of exploitation of such environments, and complexity of social organization. The possible connection between practical and symbolic 'affordances' may from this perspective be rewarding through, for example, following on from Barth's and Humphrey's work with comparative studies of ritual landscape among pastoralists in other ethnographic regions. Similarly it might be rewarding to explore ritual landscapes among communities in different adaptations under environmental circumstances that we have not touched upon here, e.g. rain forests and the arctic. Humphrey's and Morphy's documentation and analysis of landscape conceptualizations are exemplary cases that might provide models for such studies. A good starting point may be to follow Lorzing's advice and find out 'how people all over the world express themselves when they express the equivalent "for landscape" in their own language' (Lorzing 2001: 26).

Thomas's stepwise procedure is a promising approach in the use of anthropological insight in 'landscape' archaeology. By placing himself in different positions in relation to the archaeological monuments and viewing them from perspectives derived from anthropological contributions Thomas tries to imagine what the ritual landscape might have looked like for prehistoric people. This approach may be fruitful for interpretation of other enigmatic prehistoric ritual landscapes like the Nazca lines in Peru.

Suggested Reading

ABERG, A. and LEWIS, C. 2000. *The Rising Tide: Archaeology and coastal landscapes* (Oxford: Oxbow).
ALDHOUSE-GREEN, M. and ALDHOUSE-GREEN, S. 2005. *The Quest for the Shaman* (London: Thames and Hudson).
AVENI, A. F. 2000. *Between the Lines: The mystery of the giant ground drawings of ancient Nasca, Peru* (Austin: Texas University Press).
BENDER, B. 1993. *Landscape, Politics and Perspectives* (Oxford: Berg).
BRADLEY, R. 1998. *The Significance of Monuments: On the shaping of human experience in Neolithic and Bronze Age Europe* (London: Routledge).
CHAPELL, S. 2002. *Cahocia: A mirror of cosmos* (Chicago: Chicago University Press).
CHIPPINDALE, C. 1983. *Stonehenge Complete* (London: Thames and Hudson).
COSGROVE, D. E. 1984. *Social Formation and Symbolic Landscape* (London: Crook Helm Ltd).
INGOLD, T. 1993. 'The temporality of landscape', *World Archaeology*, 25(2): 52–74.
JOHNSON, M. 2007. *Ideas of Landscape* (Oxford: Blackwell).
KOPYTOFF, I. (ed.) 1987. *The African Frontier: A reproduction of traditional African societies* (Bloomington and Indianapolis: Indiana University Press).
KIRCH, P. V. and HUNT, T. L. (eds) 1997. *Historical Ecology in the Pacific Islands: Prehistoric environment and landscape change* (New Haven, CT: Yale University Press).
RAPPAPORT, R. 1990. *The Meaning of Built Environment: A nonverbal communications approach* (Tuscon: University of Arizona Press).
STEWART, P. J. and STRATHERN, A. 2003. *Landscape, Memory and History* (London: Pluto Press).
TILLEY, C. 1994. *A Phenomenology of Landscape: Places, paths and monuments* (Oxford: Berg).
TROMBOLD, C. D. 1991. *Ancient Road Networks and Settlement Hierarchies in the New World* (Cambridge: Cambridge University Press).

References

AKKERMANS, P. M. G. and SCHWARTZ, G. M. 2003. *The Archaeology of Syria: From complex hunter-gatherers to early urban societies* (Cambridge: Cambridge University Press).
BARTH, F. 1961. *Nomads of South Persia: The Basseri tribe of the Khamsen Confederacy* (Illinois: Waveland Press).

BARTH, F. 1975. *Ritual and Knowledge among the Baktamans of New Guinea* (Oslo: Universitetsforlaget).
——1987. *Cosmologies in the Making* (Cambridge: Cambridge Studies in Social Anthropology).
BATESON, G. 1973. 'Redundancy and coding' in G. Bateson (ed.), *Steps to an Ecology of Mind* (London: Fontana), pp. 411–25.
BRUNER, E. M. and GOFAIN, P. 1988. 'Dialogic narration and the paradoxes of Masada' in E. M. Bruner (ed.), *Text, Play, and Story* (Illinois: Waveland Press), pp. 56–79.
GENNEP, A. VAN 1960 [1909]. *The Rites of Passage* (Chicago: Chicago University Press).
GREEN, M. A. 2002a. *Dying for the Gods: Human sacrifices in the Iron Age and Roman Britain* (Stroud: Tempus Publishing Group).
——2002b. 'Any old iron! Symbolism and iron working in Iron Age Europe' in A. M. Green (ed.), *Artefacts and Archaeology: Aspects of the Celtic and the Roman world* (Cardiff: University of Cardiff Press), pp. 8–19.
HAALAND, G. and HAALAND, R. 1995. 'Who speaks the language of the goddess: Imagination and method in archaeological research', *Norwegian Archaeological Review*, 28: 105–73.
——— and DATA, D. 2004. 'Smelting iron: Caste and its symbolism in southwestern Ethiopia' in T. Insoll (ed.), *Belief in the Past: The proceedings of the Manchester Conference in Archaeology and Religion* (Oxford: BAR Publications in Archaeology), pp. 75–85.
HAALAND, R. 2007. 'Porridge and pot, bread and oven: Food ways and symbolism in Africa and the Near East from the Neolithic to the present', *Cambridge Archaeological Journal*, 17(2): 165–82.
HODDER, I. 2007. 'Çatalhóyük in the context of the Middle Eastern Neolithic', *Annual Review of Anthropology*, 36: 105–20.
HUMPHREY, C. 1995. 'Chiefly and shamanist landscapes in Mongolia' in H. Hirsch and M. O'Hanlon (eds), *The Anthropology of Landscape*, Studies in Social and Cultural Anthropology (Oxford: Clarendon Press), pp. 135–62.
INGOLD, T. 2007. *The Perception of the Environment: Essays in livelihood, dwelling and skill* (London: Routledge).
JOHNSON, M. 1987. *The Body in the Mind: The bodily basis of meaning, imagination, and reason* (Chicago: University of Chicago Press).
JOUSSAUME, R. 1985. *Dolmens for the Dead* (London: Batsford).
KHATTRI, M. 1999. *Sacrificial Places: An ethnoarchaeological study of the ritual landscape from Argal VDC, Western Nepal* (Masters Thesis. Bergen: University of Bergen).
KUIJT, I. N. and GORING-MORRIS, N. 2002. 'Foraging, farming, and social complexity in the pre-pottery Neolithic of the southern Levant: A review and synthesis', *Journal of World Prehistory*, 16: 361–440.
LAKOFF, G. and JOHNSON, M. 1999. *Philosophy in the Flesh* (New York: Basic Books).
LEWIS-WILLIAMS, D. 2001. *The Mind in the Cave: Consciousness and the origins of art* (London: Thames and Hudson).
LORZING, H. 2001. *The Nature of Landscape: A personal quest* (Holland: Uitgevirij).
MILISAUSKAS, S. 1978. *European Prehistory* (New York: Academic Press).
MORPHY, H. 1995. 'Landscape and the reproduction of the ancestral past' in H. Hirsch and M. O'Hanlon (eds), *The Anthropology of Landscape*, Studies in Social and Cultural Anthropology (Oxford: Clarendon Press), pp. 184–209.
——1998. *Aboriginal Art* (London: Phaidon).

Owens, D. and Hayden, B. 1997. 'A comparative study of transegalitarian hunter-gatherers', *Journal of Anthropological Archaeology*, 16(2): 121–61.
Rappaport, R. A. 1979. *Ecology, Meaning, and Religion* (Richmond, CA: North Atlantic Books).
Thomas, J. 1995. 'Politics of vision and the archaeologies of landscape' in B. Bender (ed.), *Landscape Politics and Perspectives* (Oxford: Berg), pp. 19–48.
Tilley, C. 1995. 'Art, architecture, landscape (Neolithic Sweden)' in B. Bender (ed.), *Landscape Politics and Perspectives* (Oxford: Berg), pp. 49–84.
Turner, V. 1969. *The Ritual Process: Structure and anti-structure* (Chicago: Chicago University Press).
Stein, R. A. 1972. *Tibetan Civilization* (London: Faber and Faber).

CHAPTER 3

WATER

TERJE OESTIGAARD

1 INTRODUCTION

WATER in the archaeology of ritual and religion includes water as a perspective and water as empirical data. The life-giving waters in society and religion are the fresh waters in their many facets in the hydrological cycle. Water is always in a flux. The fluid matter changes qualities and capacities wherever it is, and it always takes new forms. This transformative character of water is forcefully used in ritual practices and religious constructions. Water represents the one and the many at the same time, and the plurality of ritual institutionalizations and religious perceptions puts emphasis on water's structuring principles and processes in culture and the cosmos. Water is fundamental in many ritual practices and to conceptions of the divinities and cosmos in prehistoric religions, and consequently the study of water in ritual and religion may reveal insights into both what religion *is* and how devotees perceive themselves, the divine spheres, and their own religious practices and rituals. The pervasive role of water-worlds in society and cosmos unites micro- and macrocosmos, creates life, and legitimizes social hierarchies and religious practices and beliefs. Water is a medium which links or changes totally different aspects of humanity and divinities into a coherent unit; it bridges paradoxes, transcends the different human and divine realms, allows interactions with gods, and enables the divinities to interfere with humanity. Water is a medium for everything—it has human character because we are humans; it is a social matter but also a spiritual substance and divine manifestation with immanent powers; and, still, it belongs to the realm of nature as a fluid liquid. The hydrological cycle links all places and spheres together, and water transcends the common categories by which we conceptualize the world and cosmos (Tvedt and Oestigaard 2006). The religious water-worlds, cosmologies, beliefs, and ritual practices are evident in the archaeological record, mythology, and written sources. Hence, it is necessary to identify different types of water, the particular qualities associated with each of them, and how water materializes as religious and ritual structures, practices, and beliefs.

2 Divine Qualities of Water

Water is a medium for religious and divine interaction, it has spiritual qualities, and it might be a divinity. In order to understand the religious role of water it is analytically preferable to distinguish between 'holy' and 'sacred'. 'Holiness' may refer to the divinity and what is derived from the divinity as attributes, whereas 'sacredness' points to consecrated items where it refers to 'respected or venerated objects but not the divine itself and not to persons as individuals' (Oxtoby 1987: 434). Water is not only a mediator between humans and god(s), but the element can be a divinity itself. Hence, there is a fundamental difference between 'holy water' and 'sacred water', and the Ganges in India as the Mother Goddess in Hinduism is holy water. The water used in the Christian baptism is not a divinity, but consecrated and hence sacred water. The sacred aspects of water may also include the differentiation from other waters which may enable humans to interact with divinities or cosmological spheres and as such be an entrance to the Otherworld.

Both holy and sacred waters are within the religious realm, but the qualities and internal capacities differ, and consequently, it is important to identify these various powers and properties in order to understand why and how water is used in past and present religions.

Moreover, water can attain malevolent capacities, following Gaston Bachelard, water can be cursed; evilness can put it in active form, and thus what is evil in one aspect can become evil in the whole, and evilness is no longer a quality but a substance (Bachelard 1994: 139). Clear water, on the other hand, 'is a constant temptation for a facile symbolism of purity... it is the one that constantly breathes new life into certain old mythological forms. It gives life back to forms by transforming them, for a form cannot transform itself... Water is the most perfect liquid, it is the one from which all other solutions get their fluidity' (Bachelard 1994: 134, 93). The various types of water have different qualities, which can be separated into two overall categories with regards to religious and cultural outcome: purification and in relation to a successful harvest for the people. Purification from sins and spiritual preparations for the life hereafter is in general the most common ritual use of holy or sacred waters whereas a successful harvest can be one of the main aims of human sacrifices.

3 Ritual Use of Water and Religious Metaphors

Purification rituals may take place in almost every ritual from daily to annual ceremonies, but especially in life-cycle rites with a particular emphasis on death rituals. Funeral libations and washing of the corpse are often necessary requirements as well as beverages as gifts to the deceased. Purification rituals include not only the living and the dead, but also husbandry, statues, and temples. Common in the use of holy and sacred water for purification is the belief that different types of water have various divine capabilities to transform impurity to purity and hence annihilate sins and contamination through the rituals used. Water is also used as a medium and place for divine interaction; it represents a *liminal* zone and substance between human and gods where it is possible to transcend the earthly realm. Sacrifices have also frequently been given to holy water (the divinity itself) or to sacred water where the water is a medium enabling interaction with the cosmological spheres. Thus, the ritual uses of water may take many forms depending upon whether the water is seen as holy or sacred, and although it is difficult to trace different water rituals in the archaeological record since they do not leave any material trace as such when they are performed, there is still sufficient testimony for ritual use of water throughout history in rituals and religious metaphors.

Intensive purification rituals with water are evident from the ancient Egyptian civilization. Although it is difficult to say whether such rituals took place in the Old Kingdom, at least from the Middle and New Kingdoms the living Pharaoh was purified in numerous ceremonies (Blackman 1998: 8–10): in infancy a purification ceremony was performed which prepared the child for kingship. The ritual, which consisted of sprinkling the child with water, was not only a purification rite, but it passed on certain divine qualities and vital force to the forthcoming king. Before coronation the forthcoming king was purified in the Cool Pool and he washed his face in the waters of Nun in which the sun god washed his face. By this act he was made similar to the sun god who was asked to see him as a son. During the coronation in the 'baptism of the pharaoh', streams of vivifying ankh signs were poured over the pharaoh's head (see Figure 3.1; Gardiner 1950: 3). The purification was a renewal of the rite conducted during infancy. The gods addressed the king, 'Be pure

FIGURE 3.1 'Baptism of the Pharaoh' where ablutions of ankh signs were poured, Karnak, Egypt.

together with thy *ka*, (namely) thy great dignity of King of Upper and Lower Egypt, thou living [eternally]' (Gardiner 1950: 7). Before officiating in a temple and entering the 'House of the Morning' the Pharaoh was purified with water, which also renewed life, and, finally, at the *Sed*-festival it seems that in particular the king's hands and feet were washed (Blackman 1998: 8–10). After death, purity and purification were of utmost importance before the dead Pharaoh could enter the Solar or Osirian realm. The same lustration was also repeated in the 'Opening of the mouth' ceremony whereby water was sprinkled on the statue or the mummy (Blackman 1918: 119). The life-giving power of water was essential throughout Egyptian history restoring life to Osiris whereby he was revivified by being washed, and this water was holy rather than sacred because it represented the original waters from creation thus uniting the pharaoh with the cosmic origin, Nun, from where the Nile flowed.

Water and religion are inevitably connected to sin and defilement and in particular how to erase sin or how to prepare oneself for life after death. In this world, water has the capacity to reduce misfortunes and punishments in another world. This quality of holy water is perhaps the most important aspect of water irrespective of religion (Oestigaard 2005a: 13–14) and in Christianity, for instance, this finds its material expression in baptismal fonts throughout history. Apart from such obvious use of water which has continuity to the present, one may also trace purification processes in prehistoric death rituals. The body treatment normally includes two ritual processes: the initial preparation of the corpse by washing with water and then anointing the body with oils or other substances prior to the disposal of the corpse (Fahlander and Oestigaard 2008: 5). In contemporary societies the first ritual process most often involves purification rites with water (e.g. Oestigaard 2005b), but it is more difficult to trace similar practices in the past due to the absence of material remains. There are, however, indications that similar practices have taken place. In a cremation burial at Winterslow in Britain, together with a bronze razor, the remains of human eyebrow hairs from more than one individual were found, indicating that during the funeral there was some kind of purification ritual (Barrett 1994: 123). It is uncertain whether the eyebrow hairs were from the deceased or not, but at least one or several of the mourners had shaved parts of their body in the funeral rites. Whether water was used in this instance is difficult to say, but by highlighting the ornaments on Scandinavian razors, since they have been used in such rituals and found in burials, one may trace parts of the role of water in rituals and religion in the Bronze Age.

The common theme depicted on Bronze Age razors, but also in Bronze Age iconography in general, is a cosmology expressed by images of water and the sun in combination (Kaul 1998, 2000; Goldhahn 2005), and the sun and fire are interchangeable (Kaliff 2007). Fire and water are in most cultures and religions irrespective of time and place used as transformative mediums to express both complementary and contradictory ideas of humans, social relations, divine qualities, how interactions between humans and gods take place, and the creation and character of the cosmos itself. Because fire and water are both natural and cultural elements and constructions, they are forcefully used to express transformation and transcend, but also to define, cultural and religious categories (Bachelard 1968, 1988, 1990). The fluidity and ever-changing nature of both fire and water—and particularly when they are used in combination—make these elements unique. They might be perceived as opposites, but also as complementary to each other (Oestigaard 2003, 2008; see below). Both elements put emphasis on transformation and change, and the sun's movement—often expressed with water metaphors—represents one of the two main circles in the natural world used for spinning cultural webs of significance (Geertz 1973), the other being the hydrological circle.

4 LIFE-GIVING WATERS

The water in the hydrological circle includes rivers, rain, hail, lakes, floods, oases, swamps, bogs, wells, springs, rapids, waterfalls, snow, ice, and glaciers, etc., and also includes the transformation processes of evaporation, condensation, and freezing, and each of these forms and processes can be perceived as either holy or sacred. The attribution of religious qualities includes ecology because the absence and presence of life-giving waters are of utmost importance in order to understand and grasp the religious significance of water. The life-giving waters are for the welfare of the society, and water is seen as the divinity's grace unto humanity, giving prosperity and life to humans. This water is neither holy nor sacred as such, but the consequences of water enable life and human prosperity, which is a truly divine aim and prerequisite for humans to fulfil their homage to the gods. In other words, these waters are mandatory and prerequisites for humans to fulfil their cosmic purposes, so even though the waters in themselves do not have any spiritual qualities *apart from being a gift from the divinities*, it reveals the greatness of the gods. Hence, the seemingly neutral water is also incorporated into the religious realms since humans are dependent upon the divinities and cosmic premises for prosperity.

The absence rather than the presence of water is often more important and structuring in a given society or religion because it puts the emphasis on people's needs, but on the other hand, too much water at the wrong time of the year is as disastrous as too little water when it appears as prolonged rains or catastrophic floods washing away fields and settlements. This is particularly evident in ancient Egypt, which is commonly described as the 'Gift of the Nile'. The Egyptian civilization during the Pharaonic period (3000–332 BC) was dependent on the Nile, and the summer inundation created a civilization based on the annual floods. The life-giving water was essential not only for the economy, but also as a constitutive part of the ancient Egyptians' religious world view. All dynasties were dependent upon the Nile, but the fluctuations in the Nile flood created an interannual variability in the volume of water. The ancient Egyptians measured the maximum height of the yearly flood in the nilometers and recorded the levels in the royal annals. According to the Roman historian Pliny:

> A rise of 16 cubits is good. If less, the irrigation is incomplete. If more, the slow subsidence of the flood obstructs cultivation: the land is soaked and the proper moment for seeding is lost. If the flood is low, the parched land does not yield a crop. In either case the Province is deeply concerned. With 12 cubits famine is the result; with 13 the country goes hungry; 14 cubits bring cheers; 15 security; and 16 the joys of prosperity. [Lindsay 1968: 14]

If the flood was too high, it caused disasters; if it was too low, it led to famines.

From the early Dynastic to the Graeco-Roman period the nilometers are found in relation to sanctuaries, particularly Osiris and Isis-Sarapis temples, and Robert A. Wild has argued convincingly that the nilometers had a religious function (Wild 1981). Isis and

Sarapis possessed divine powers and caused the annual floods to come; they normally stood above the Nile as powers superior to it. Osiris, on the other hand, regularly appears as the divine power immanent within the Nile, and particularly within the waters of the flood. The low Nile was the disappearance of the god and this was mourned, and the coming of the flood was Osiris' revitalization and restoration (Wild 1981: 68–9). An inscription on the island of Siheil dates to the Ptolemaic period, but describes a seven-year famine that occurred during the reign of Djoser. The king complains that the Nile has not risen for seven years, and he confronts Imhotep, who consulted the sacred writings. He tells him 'that there is a city in the middle of the Nile called Elephantine, which is the seat from which Ra despatches life to everyone. It is the source of life, the place from which the Nile leaps forth in its flood to impregnate the lands of Egypt' (MacQuitty 1976: 127). One of the most important nilometers was located at Elephantine (Figure 3.2), thus linking the flood to the sanctuary, Ra, and the Nile; and the arrival of the flood was a religious event within the realm of rituals aiming to control the life-giving waters.

From an ecological and religious point of view water can thus be described as *benevolent* or *malevolent*, where the former is seen as a blessing or divine gift and the latter as a curse or collective penalty for moral or ritual misconduct resulting in harvest failures, famines, and death. Malevolent waters normally occur as devastating floods, too much precipitation such as prolonged rains, the *fimbulwinter* of snow, or even the lack of rain; and unsuccessful rain-making rituals or deliberately withholding the rain is generally seen as evil or as a consequence of malevolent and malignant powers. In many parts of Africa the sun has been

FIGURE 3.2 Nilometer at Elephantine, Aswan, Egypt.

seen as the enemy of mankind who was scorching up everything because it was contradicting life (Wainwright 1938: 1), and among the Bari of the White Nile in Sudan, prolonged sunshine was seen as the work of a malevolent rain-maker 'willing the sun', who could be killed if rain failed (Seligman 1932: 295).

The absence of the life-giving waters often necessitates elaborate sacrifices, which in rain-making rituals may include humans. Propitiatory sacrifices are meant to avert potential disorder or favour the realization of a project or a desired state such as to secure the fertility of the fields, to avoid famine, or to obtain rain (Valeri 1985: 41). The importance in sacrifices when humans are offered to the gods is not that the gods were 'blood-thirsty', but that the offered humans were of value to the gods (Valeri 1985: 103). Moreover, human sacrifices cannot be performed on an individual basis, but require a benefit for the collective society (Valeri 1985: 49), and it is in this light that rain-making rituals aiming to promote fertility and preventing famines and hunger have to be seen.

In the Mesoamerican civilizations, human sacrifice was seen as a form of debt payment where humans returned cosmic energy to the gods, which the gods redistributed to humans and made them fertile (Trigger 2003: 481). Thus, 'the [Mayan] gods receive from the people that which they provided in the first place—maize and water transformed into flesh and blood' (Freidel, Schele, and Parker 2001: 195), and the gods continue to provide water as rains, springs, and rivers, which enable cultivation of maize and hence, the cycle of generations was continued through time and sacrifice. Hence their living descendants in Yukatan in Mexico declare, 'Here comes the holy waters, the saint rain' when they toil in their thirsty fields looking at the black clothes covering the sun, but it is uncertain if the ancient Maya believed that the rain was like blood and that the clouds of sacrifice contained a 'holy spirit' (Freidel, Schele, and Parker 2001: 207).

Human sacrifices for procuring the life-giving waters have not been limited to Africa and Mesoamerica, and this practice was also prevalent within the pagan Nordic countries. Adam of Bremen describes sacrifices in Uppsala in Sweden of both humans and animals every ninth year. Everyone was obliged to participate or send contributions to the offering and the Christians were no exception (Adam Bremensis 1993: IV, 27). According to Adam of Bremen, if there was hunger or plague, human sacrifices were a collective act made to Thor. Snorre (1995: 25) writes that in Uppsala the king Domalde was sacrificed by his chieftains after the harvest failed for the third year. Thus, propitiatory sacrifices performed to hinder malevolent or absent waters by producing the benevolent water for society's prosperity and fertility was the king's domain, and if he failed to procure security for his people, he could be sacrificed on behalf of society therefore creating a successful harvest through the life-giving waters. Although this life-giving water is neutral but still within the divine realm, other types of waters may have been holy and revelations of the divinities themselves.

5 Sound of Water and Shamanism

Of the known Neolithic hunter-gatherer rock-engraving sites made between 4000–500 BC in Scandinavia, 25 out of about 80 sites were intentionally related to the 'sound of water'. In particular the engravings at Nämforsen and Laxforsen in Sweden are located at dangerous places with physically restricted access. The oldest rock engravings at Nämforsen are found on an island in the middle of the river, directly related to the most intensive, furious, and wildest rapids. Today the sound of the Nämforsen River is tamed by a power plant, but the Laxforsen rock engravings are, however, still situated in the furious river where the original and natural sound of the river is still possible to hear, and the roaring rapids divert the attention away from the rock art (Goldhahn 2002). Goldhahn (2002) conducted measurements of the sound levels, and the closer to the engravings, the higher was the sound of water, reaching more than 110 decibels, which equals almost the sound of a starting jumbo jet at a distance of 50 m. The height of the Laxforsen waterfalls is about 5 m whereas the falls in Nämforsen are reported to have been around 17 m. The engravings were most likely made during the summer when the rapids were at their most intense, wild, and dangerous. Thus, the sound at Nämforsen probably exceeded 110 decibels, and the physical burdens on the human mind must have been even more extreme (Goldhahn 2002: 41–3).

During the winter, the river was frozen and it was possible to travel across it. The changing character of the water-world when the ice shifted to running water puts the emphasis on the water's qualities in itself. The intentional placing of the rock engravings close to the wildest and most furious rapids suggests that the images 'gained their power' from being placed in this dangerous situation (Golhahn 2002: 44). The wild rapids in Nämforsen and Laxforsen are extreme and the sound of the water is perhaps the highest sound ever heard by the Stone Age people in this area. The cultural and religious understandings of sound levels in between 110 and 120 decibels must have been seen as a revelation of the powers of the gods and nature *par excellence* for the people who lived in an otherwise quiet environment and an animistic, religious world. The intensive sound of the river where it was at the most extreme and where the rock engravings were located are at the limit of what is possible for humans to bear physiologically and psychologically. The immanent powers of the river would have been manifested in the seasonal changes. During winters the river would have been frozen, and the silence during the winters would have been in stark contrast to the inferno during summer times. Thus, the power of water manifested itself both by sensory experiences and visualizations, and this water may have been seen as holy precisely because it revealed the most intense powers of nature.

As stated, the oldest and largest concentrations of rock engravings at Nämforsen are located next to the most vital and wild rapids, and all together there are depicted more than 1,000 images of elks with their 'life lines' (Goldhahn 2002: 43). The engravings show the skeleton with the vital, inner organs of the animals and humans depicted. The interpretations of these inner markings have been made through ethnographical analogies whereby shamans took control of the soul and spirit of the hunted prey by the use of the life line (Gjessing 1936: 140–6). The shamans used this life line to embark on journeys to other worlds and to return back to this world by the very same life line. The rock engravings may also be seen in the light of ancestral worship where the ancestors were 'attached' to the landscape and the living through sound (Nordström 1999). Goldhahn has suggested that the intensive noise of the rapids may have been a means whereby shamans achieved an altered state of consciousness or trance. Entering altered states of consciousness is not only possible by drugs, hyperventilation, or through fasting or meditation, but is also possible by sound. Hallucination can occur within a few minutes if certain senses are exposed to extremes. The loud sound of the river could have helped shamans to achieve altered states of consciousness (Goldhahn 2002: 51). Thus, this water would not have been sacred, but holy since it revealed the powers of nature and enabled shamans to become holy or part of the divine realm.

6 WATER IN THE COSMOS AND WELLS OF POWERS

Cosmologies are often perceived and depicted as transcendental water-worlds in both the lower and upper realms. These cosmic waters guarantee the life-giving waters among humans as well as facilitate interaction between the realms. The presence of water has its source in the other realms, with implications for people in this world. Floods myths are found on all continents of the world, and they are particularly important and common in the early civilizations along the great rivers such as the Nile, Tigris, Euphrates, Indus, and Yangtze (Dundes 1988). If the divinities lived in the lower realms, the water sources such as wells and bogs have been seen as entrances to the Underworld, which may explain the presence of human bog-finds. Tacitus mentions that disreputable persons were drowned, but the Gundestrup cauldron, manufactured during the second or first century BC found in Raevemose bog in Jutland, may indicate that also agricultural festivals in honour of Nerthus, where humans were sacrificed, took place in bogs (Green 2001: 114–17).

If the divinities are celestial such as the sun or the moon, the reflection of the celestial bodies in the water during day or night enables water to transfer sacrifices offered to the water to the celestial realms because the sacrifices are given to the sun or moon as they appear in the water mirror. Thus, through water, sacrifices can be given both to the lower and upper realms and as such it can be a medium and process unifying and bridging the earthly and transcendental realms. A holy river or bodies of sacred water both ends the profane and starts the divine journey, which may explain why sacrifices have been made to water throughout history; water and sun may be interchangeable (Figure 3.3), and a sacrifice to water may in fact be a sacrifice to the sun, or both, because the mirror of the sun in the water makes them the same. Wells in particular have been ascribed divine powers and seen as links between the realms, and are believed to have possessed particular qualities.

Water has been believed to have the capacity of revealing the truth. From 500 AD it seems that the Odin cult was firmly established in the Nordic regions (Hedeager 1999). In this process Odin became more powerful than the other pagan gods. In his search for knowledge and wisdom, Odin sacrificed one of his eyes in Mimir's well of wisdom. This allowed him to drink from it every day, giving him knowledge about everything, and his eye was kept in the well as a forfeit (*Edda-kvede* 1993: 12). Thus, the water was what revealed knowledge and wisdom to Odin and, even though the water was not the god in itself, it was the medium revealing the truth.

The holiness of water has also cured all kinds of sicknesses or diseases. In the Celtic religion, water had a crucial place and these perceptions were transformed and included in Christianity (Green 1986: 138). In England, water-worship was still banned into the twelfth century, but gradually the old customs and pagan aspects of water worship were hidden behind the Christian façade (Bord and Bord 1985: 19). When the Christians transformed the pagan water-beliefs, the early missionary monks included the wells in their religion (Gribben 1992: 15). The wells were believed to have various healing powers and the potential

FIGURE 3.3 The sun above the King's Valley unites with the water in the Nile, Luxor, Egypt.

to cure any kind of ailments, diseases, illnesses, or infertility (Bord and Bord 1985: 22). Thus, the outcome of the water in these wells is the same as the divine gift in the form of benevolent waters such as sufficient rains or floods, but at different levels. Whereas the latter is for the benefit of the community as a whole, the former is at a personal level enabling individual prosperity, repentance for sin, and healing.

7 Conclusions

Fresh water represents deep ontological relations, and the water-worlds in a society create opportunities for all kinds of constructions. The hydrological cycle links all places and spheres together, and the physical character of water combined with its role as a historical agent enables the medium to link the past with the present and the future (Tvedt 1997, 2002: 166–8). Water in ritual and religion is crucial for humans, gods, and everything that matters in between and beyond. Cosmologies are to a large extent dependent upon water, both physically and metaphorically, to create understandable constructions of the relations between humans, gods, and the Otherworldly spheres. Since water is both an element in nature and culture and constantly changing its character, but still being the same, it has transformative capacities which no other element has. This enables water to work and express metaphorical relations and images of contents that most often transcend consciousness; the content is beyond explicit comprehension, but nevertheless real and implicitly understandable. Water has been used for purification in rituals throughout time and in many religions. Humans have been sacrificed to ensure the life-giving waters, and water has had divine qualities or been considered as entrances to realms beyond. The cultural and religious potential of using water as a means to construct the world has thus been almost unlimited.

Suggested Reading

Assmann, J. 2005. *Death and Salvation in Ancient Egypt* (Ithaca: Cornell University Press).
Bachelard, G. 1994. *Water and Dreams: An essay on the imagination of matter* (Dallas: The Dallas Institute of Humanities and Culture).
Fagan, B. 2000. *The Little Ice Age: How climate made history 1300–1800* (New York: Basic Books).
Oestigaard, T. 2005. *Death and Life-giving Waters: Cremation, caste, and cosmogony in karmic traditions*, BAR International Series 1353 (Oxford: BAR).
Possehl, G. L. 1999. *Indus Age: The beginnings* (Philadelphia: University of Pennsylvania Press).
Tvedt, T. and Oestigaard, T. (eds) 2009. *A History of Water*, IV: *The Ideas of Water from Antiquity to Modern Times* (London: I.B.Tauris).

References

Adam Bremensis. 1993. *Beretningen om Hamburgs stift, erkebiskopenes bedrifter og øyrikene i Norden*, trans. Bjørg Tosterud Danielsen and Anne Katrine Frihagen (Oslo: Aschehougs & Co).
Bachelard, G. 1968. *The Psychoanalysis of Fire* (Boston: Beacon Press).
—— 1988. *The Flame of a Candle*, the Bachelard Translations, the Dallas Institute Publications (Dallas: The Dallas Institute of Humanities and Culture).
—— 1990. *Fragments of a Poetics of Fire*, the Bachelard Translations, the Dallas Institute Publications (Dallas: The Dallas Institute of Humanities and Culture).
—— 1994. *Water and Dreams: An essay on the imagination of matter* (Dallas: The Dallas Institute of Humanities and Culture).
Barrett, J. 1994. *Fragments from Antiquity: An archaeology of social life in Britain, 2900–1200 BC* (Oxford: Blackwell).
Blackman, A. M. 1918. 'Some notes on the ancient Egyptian practice of washing the dead', *The Journal of Egyptian Archaeology*, 5(2): 117–24.
—— 1998. 'Purification (Egyptian)' in Aylward M. Blackman (ed.), *Gods, Priests and Men: Studies in the religion of Pharaonic Egypt* (London: Kegan Paul International), pp. 3–21.

Bord, C. and Bord, J. 1985. *Sacred Waters: Holy wells and water lore in Britain and Ireland* (London: Granada).
Dundes, A. (ed.) 1988. *The Flood Myth* (Berkeley: University of California Press).
Edda-kvede (n.d.). 1993 (Oslo: Det norske samlaget).
Eliade, M. 1993. *Patterns in Comparative Religion* (London: Sheed and Ward Ltd).
Fahlander, F. and Oestigaard, T. 2005. 'The materiality of death: Bodies, burials, beliefs' in F. Fahlander and T. Oestigaard (eds), *The Materiality of Death: Bodies, burials, beliefs*, BAR International Series 1768 (Oxford: BAR), pp. 1–16.
Freidel, D., Schele, L., and Parker, J. 2001. *Maya Cosmos: Three thousand years on the shaman's path* (New York: Perennial).
Gardiner, A. 1950. 'The baptism of Pharaoh', *The Journal of Egyptian Archaeology*, 36: 3–12.
Geertz, C. 1973. *The Interpretation of Cultures* (New York: HarperCollins Publishers).
Gjessing, G. 1936. *Nordenfjelske ristninger og malninger av den arktiske gruppe*, Serie B 30 (Oslo: Instituttet for Sammenlignende Kulturforskning).
Goldhahn, J. 2002. 'Roaring rocks: An audio-visual perspective on hunter-gatherer engravings in northern Sweden and Scandinavia', *Norwegian Archaeological Review*, 35(1): 29–61.
——2005. *Från Sagaholm till Bredarör—hällbildsstudier 2000–2004*, Gotarc Serie C. Arkeologiska Skrifter No. 62 (Göteborg: Göteborgs Universitet).
——2007. *Rituelle spesialister i bronsealderen*, I: *Dödens hand—en essä om brons- och hällsmed*, Gotarc Series C 65 (Göteborg: Göteborg University).
Green, M. 1986. *The Gods of the Celts* (Gloucester: Alan Sutton).
——2001. *Dying for the Gods: Human sacrifice in Iron Age & Roman Europe* (Charleston: Tempus).
Gribben, A. 1992. *Holy Wells and Sacred Water Sources in Britain and Ireland. An Annotated Bibliography* (London: Garland Publishing).
Hedeager, L. 1999. *Skygger av en annen virkelighet. Oldnordiske myter* (Oslo: Pax Forlag A/S).
Kaliff, A. 2007. *Fire, Water, Heaven and Earth: Ritual practice and cosmology in ancient Scandinavia: An Indo-European perspective* (Stockholm: Riksantikvarieämbetet).
Kaul, F. 1998. *Ships on Bronzes: A study in Bronze Age religion and iconography* (Copenhagen: PNM Studies in Archaeology & History 3).
——2000. 'Solsymbolet', *Skalk*, (6): 28–31.
Lindsay, J. 1968. *Men and Gods on the Roman Nile* (New York: Barnes & Noble, Inc).
MacQuitty, W. 1976. *Island of Isis: Philae, temple of the Nile* (London: Macdonald and Jane's).
Nordström, P. 1999. 'Ristningarnas rytm. Om hällristningar och landskap—exemplet Boglösa Roaring Rocks 59 i Uppland' in P. Nordström and M. Svedin (eds), *Aktuell arkeologi*, VII (Stockholm: Stockholm Archaeological Report 36), pp. 127–36.
Oestigaard, T. 2003. *An Archaeology of Hell: Fire, water and sin in Christianity* (Lindome: Bricoleur Press).
——2005a. *Water and World Religions: An introduction* (Bergen: SFU & SMR).
——2005b. *Death and Life-giving Waters: Cremation, caste, and cosmogony in karmic traditions*, BAR International Series 1353 (Oxford: BAR).
——2008. 'Purification, purgation and penalty: Christian concepts of water and fire in heaven and hell' in T. Tvedt and T. Oestigaard (eds), *A History of Water*, IV: *The Ideas of Water from Antiquity to Modern Time* (London: I.B.Tauris).

Oxtoby, W. G. 1987. 'Holy, Idea of the' in M. Eliade (ed.), *The Encyclopaedia of Religion*, VI (New York: Macmillian Publishing Company), pp. 431–8.

Seligman, C. G. 1932. *Pagan Tribes of the Nilotic Sudan* (London: Routledge & Kegan Paul).

Snorre Sturluson: Norges kongesagaer, I, trans. K.-W. Hansen, J. Larsen, and Dyre Vaa, repr. 1995 (Oslo: LibriArte).

Trigger, B. 2003. *Understanding Early Civilizations: A comparative study* (Cambridge: Cambridge University Press).

Tvedt, T. 1997. *En reise i vannets historie—fra regnkysten til Muscat* (Oslo: Cappelens Forlag AS).

—— 2002. *Verdensbilder og selvbilder. En humanitær stormakts intellektuelle historie* (Oslo: Universitetsforlaget).

—— and Oestigaard, T. 2006. 'Introduction' in T. Tvedt and T. Oestigaard (eds), *A History of Water*, III: *The World of Water* (London: I.B.Tauris), pp. ix–xxii.

Valeri, V. 1985. *Kingship and Sacrifice: Ritual and society in Ancient Hawaii* (Chicago: The University Press of Chicago).

Wainwright, G. A. 1938. *The Sky-Religion in Egypt: Its antiquity and effects* (Cambridge: Cambridge University Press).

Wild, R. A. 1981. *Water in the Cultic Worship of Isis and Sarapis* (Leiden: Brill).

CHAPTER 4

FIRE

ANDERS KALIFF

1 INTRODUCTION

THE shaping of human culture is closely linked to the domestication of fire. The art of making fire has given humans the ability to survive in environments where it would not otherwise have been conceivable and has made it possible to cook food whose nutritional value could not otherwise have been fully utilized. This has formed us as people, shaping our conceptual world. Fire has been particularly significant for eschatology and the form taken by burial rituals, but also for cosmology as a whole and thus as a sacrificial medium.

Fire is nothing in itself, from the chemical point of view, just the result of a process that creates heat. At the same time, it has been obvious to people in all times, that this description does not include the whole truth. Despite the non-substance of fire, it is palpable—we see it and, above all, we feel it. The reaction between the substances can also spread to us, through the communicative essence of the fire. We are then consumed, just like the wooden sticks in the fire place. It is therefore scarcely surprising that the enigmatic nature of fire has given it a divine character, that it has even been regarded as a divinity in itself. Any child's wonder at fire, its heat and friendship, and fascination with its destructive power, demonstrates a truth about the character of fire which no other explanations can completely brush aside.

Ideas have therefore been put forward that the human fascination with fire has a shared origin at a fundamental level (e.g. Staal 2001). This does not mean that the myths and rituals connected with fire have always found the same expression in different cultural contexts. Fire as a giver of life and a destroyer can scarcely be expressed in more powerful images than in the description of the Vedic god *Agni*, a divinity who represents fire, who even is fire itself:

> Agni is brilliant, golden, has flaming hair and beard, three or seven tongues, his face is light, his eyes shine, he has sharp teeth, he makes a cracking noise, and leaves a black trail behind. He is fond of clarified butter, but he also eats wood and devours the forest. In fact, he eats everything. He is in particular a destroyer of demons and a slayer of enemies.
> [Staal 2001: 73]

The Vedic fire sacrifice, as well as its Old Iranian counterpart, is favourable as an analogy for the interpretation of fire rituals also in other Indo-European contexts. This analogy takes on an extra dimension because of the kinship between Vedic and Old Iranian fire ritual, and other Indo-European ritual traditions, in accordance with the basic similarities between languages. Just as there are linguistic similarities, there are also clear mythological parallels, which in turn reveal similar cosmological ideas (Lincoln 1986). Comparative Indo-European studies can also be valuable as analogies, regardless of whether there is any kinship between the traditions, since the use of analogies is built into every archaeological interpretation—consciously or unconsciously. My fundamental stance, however, is that the Indo-European religions also reflect a common background, with the different traditions being dialects in the same way as the Indo-European languages (Kaliff 2007), and I will apply this principle in the following discussion of the ancient Scandinavian fire ritual.

2 Ancient Scandinavian Fire Ritual

As an analogy for interpretations of ancient Scandinavian ritual, the ancient Vedic ritual tradition, along with the old Iranian and other early Indo-European ritual systems, has until recently attracted little attention in archaeology. One reason for this neglect is probably a lack of knowledge of the subject among archaeologists studying Scandinavia, combined with the view that such a comparison would be an exoticization. In addition, for several decades after the Second World War there was profound scepticism about comparative Indo-European studies, not least because of the abuse of the term Aryan (Sanskrit *Arya*) and any research that could be associated with this. In particular, the archaeology pursued in Germany under the Third Reich, when the term was used to denote an envisaged ancient people who were regarded as the ancestors of the Germanic peoples, served for a long time to cast suspicion on any research that mentioned Aryans and/or Indo-Europeans, even research with completely different foundations and aims. Archaeological research on the Indo-Europeans was thus regarded as identical with the abuse of the concept. In the last few years the attitude to comparative Indo-European research has changed somewhat. A new outlook can be discerned, as scholars show that they wish to distance themselves from the earlier abuse of research without rejecting the occurrence of an overall Indo-European cultural tradition. The archaeological perception of the spread of Indo-European culture and languages which has been in focus most in recent years has been shaped in the discussion of contacts between elite groups and centre–periphery relations in the Early Bronze Age (e.g. Kristiansen 1998, 2001, 2004; Kristiansen and Larsson 2005).

According to the Old Norse (Eddic) poem *Grímnismál* (40–1), as well as Snorri Sturluson's *Gylfaginning* (6–8), the cosmos was created from the flesh of the giant *Ymir*. In the latter variant we hear how Ymir, the first living being, is killed by the first gods. The basic features of this creation myth occur among different peoples with an Indo-European language. A similar mythological tale is *Purusasūkta* from the *Rigveda* (10.90). In this story too, the world is created when the gods cut up a cosmic giant, *Purusa* (or *Yama*). It is also this narrative that is the archetype for the Vedic fire sacrifice. The myth also occurs in, for instance, a Slavic variant, recorded in Russian folktales. The homology of the creation myths is one basic cosmological idea. This means that one entity is created using the matter in another entity. They are *alloforms*, that is alternative guises of each other. Flesh and earth, for example, are considered to be of the same material substance and can thereby be transformed into each other. In the same way, bones, the hard part inside the soft flesh, are equated with the stones in the earth and with rocks and mountains, while hair is associated with plants. The myth of a ritual death and division of a body is a narrative which can easily be transformed and rendered in sacrificial custom as well as death. The Vedic sacrifice is performed as a repetition of the creation and has cosmogonic and/or sociogonic significance, which has correspondences among other Indo-European peoples. Tacitus (*Germania* 39), for example, ascribes this meaning to the sacrifices performed by the Germanic tribe of the Semnones (Lincoln 1986: 3–7, 50–60).

An important element that derives from the original cosmological sacrifice is fire, and the god associated with it. Fire is central as a ritual tool, as is clearly and amply attested in the Vedic tradition, and for which there is also very strong archaeological evidence in ancient Scandinavia. The worship of fire as a god (*Agni*) is central to Vedic religion. There is evidence that important features of the sacrificial ritual and the design of cultic implements, for example altars, have close counterparts in other Indo-European contexts; the same applies to the crucial role of fire. In the Vedic and Iranian view, fire is a substance that is active everywhere in the cosmos. Fire is the fertile element in the cosmos; in the sky, in the storm, and in the soil, as also in man and woman (Edsman 1987: 343 f.). Fire was regarded not just as a god in itself, but simultaneously as a divine messenger, the one who conveys the sacrificial gifts to the other gods. The name Agni is clearly Indo-European in character and can be compared with Latin *ignis*, Russian *ogon*, Lithuanian *ugnis*, etc. Agni is born, according to the Vedic account, from the pieces of wood in the fire drill used to light ritual fire. He is also found in the sky, in lightning and the sun, as well as in water, whether in rain or in lakes and rivers (Staal 2001: 73, 99; cf. Parmeshwaranand 2000: 40–8).

The Vedic rituals are performed at different levels of complexity and in different contexts, from everyday rituals to more extensive ceremonies. The simplest ritual consists of a fire sacrifice to Agni (*agnihotra*), performed in a ritual enclosure in the home of the person who wishes to make the sacrifice. Three fires are needed: *gārhaptya*, the household fire; *āhavanīya*, the sacrificial fire; and *dakṣiṇāgni*, which is believed to give protection against evil. The altar for the household fire is round and is located in the west part of the enclosure, while the sacrificial altar is square and placed in the eastern part (Figure 4.1). The third altar is semicircular. There can be additional fire altars in expanded variants of the rituals, but these three always occur (Tachikawa, Bahulkar, and Kolhatkar 2001; Staal 2001: 40–1). The functions of the different altars are moreover connected to the different elements, and Agni was the link between the earth and the heavenly fire—the sun. The Iranian fire ritual is in many respects like the Vedic one, particularly when it comes to the design of the altars. In a similar way to the Vedic and Iranian tradition, in Rome there was a circular altar for Vesta (*aedes rotunda*), but also *templa quadrata*. The Greeks had a round household altar on which they offered milk and honey, and a bigger square one which was used for animal sacrifices (Staal 2001: 93, 125 ff.).

One of the most advanced Vedic sacrificial rituals is *agnicayana*. For this ceremony people built a large altar of more than a thousand fired clay bricks, which symbolizes Purusa (or Yama), the cosmological victim. The entire performance of the complex ritual

FIGURE 4.1 The rectangular platform used for Hindu cremations reflects the form of the Vedic fire-sacrifice altar. This in turn reflects the outlook on cremation as a fire sacrifice. From the cremation and temple site at Pashupatinath, Nepal.

signifies a re-creation of the cosmos, but the exact meaning of the different elements of the ritual is partly obscure. One fundamental meaning is that Agni is reborn on the sacrificial altar, and the altar is believed to be the womb from which Agni is to be born. The altar is built of clay brick in five layers, which correspond well to the body parts of the first sacrifice in the myth: marrow, bone, flesh, skin, and hair. At the same time, they are envisaged as corresponding to five zones in existence: the cosmological levels of earth, atmosphere, and heaven, together with two transitional zones. Material is taken from each part of creation in the construction of the fire altar: earth and water for the brick, grass (hair) to place on the altar, and so on. Before the building of the altar the ground is prepared through ritual ploughing and through a symbolic burial. Five heads—of human, horse, bull, ram, and goat—are buried in the ground. Together with the burial of ritual objects, including pots, and the ploughing and sowing of the ground in preparation for the altar, this symbolizes how the combination of elements contributes to the act of creation. Not only the big altar for the fire sacrifice is built for the ceremony but also other altars and ritual buildings beside it. These buildings are deliberately burned down after the lengthy ritual is completed (Staal 2001: 65 ff., 118; cf. Lincoln 1986: 60 f.).

The sacred fire and the rituals surrounding it seem to have been highly significant in different Indo-European cultural traditions. The different shapes of altar connected to these rituals, and thus to the underlying cosmology, likewise seem to have been very important and tenacious cultural implements. Proceeding from this observation, there is of course good reason to search for counterparts to the ritual of fire sacrifice and also to the altar forms in the ancient Scandinavian tradition. In view of the way the cremation ritual gained such a strong hold in South Scandinavia during the Bronze Age, we are justified here too in connecting the meaning of cremation as a sacrifice with other types of fire sacrifice

FIGURE 4.2 Interpretation of how a cremation may have been performed during the Bronze Age in Southern Scandinavia. The reconstruction is based on finds from different Swedish sites, with inspiration for the scene from Vedic rituals.

and fire rituals (see Figure 4.2). In the same way the square and the round structure is present in prehistoric stone settings, hearths, and other ritual constructions from Scandinavian pre-history, at least from the Early Bronze Age onwards. Such structures are often closely connected with ritual fire, and may in some cases be interpreted as fire altars, even if they are more often interpreted as grave markers or more generally as 'burnt mounds' or 'heaps of fire cracked stones'.

3 THE ARCHAEOLOGY OF ANCIENT FIRE SACRIFICE

Fire sacrifice has rarely been highlighted by archaeologists as a prominent ritual expression in ancient Scandinavian society. The interpretation of certain large and organized systems of hearths as ritual expressions was at first regarded as rather daring and speculative when it was put forward in the 1990s, modelled on continental find-spots and interpretations (Thörn 1996; cf. Krämer 1966). Although interpretations of certain structures as indications of rituals involving fire sacrifice had been proposed earlier (e.g. Nordén 1925; Bellander 1938), hearths, burnt mounds, and other vestiges of fires were mostly regarded a priori as being of a secular nature. It is often difficult, based solely on material remains, to determine whether a fire was used for sacred, ritual purposes or had a secular function. In particular, the hearth in the home may have been the scene of both sacred and profane activities that involved the use of fire as a medium, as the Vedic example shows. The question then is where in the archaeological record we might be able to see traces of rituals of a similar level of complexity to agnicayana, but also of rituals corresponding to the less spectacular farm and family rituals. For the former it is chiefly certain types of burnt mounds and stone settings, and features interpreted as cult houses, that are interesting. As parallels to rituals of lesser complexity, we can extend our focus to a large number of fireplaces and soot pits of different kinds. There are also structures from both the Bronze Age and the Early Iron Age that can be interpreted as buildings of a ritual nature. Some of these seem to have been enclosures without a roof, while others were probably roofed. These structures are likewise often right beside pits, bone deposits, fire-cracked stone, stone settings, and hearths, and fit well with an interpretation that they are the remains of temporary constructions used for a complex sacrificial ritual.

There are on these and other sites also extensive remains of complex structures, often designated by the non-comittal umbrella term *burnt mounds*, that occur in very different contexts. They are also often found on sites designated as cemeteries, but not infrequently on settlement sites as well, sometimes in central locations. The majority of the dated examples are from the Bronze Age. In total, however, they show a much longer chronological spread, from the Neolithic to the Late Iron Age. Some burnt mounds are indeed very good candidates for an interpretation as remains of complex altar structures. Typically, they contain a large amount of fire-cracked stone, usually together with soot and charcoal. Some burnt mounds seem to be unorganized deposits of burnt stone and other residual material, while others are complex structures. The latter often contain elements such as inner circles of stones, stone foundations under the filling, and deposits of burnt and unburnt bones and artefacts in different layers. Burials in burnt mounds have sometimes been interpreted as showing that it was practical to use the 'grave shape' of the pile. Yet why the feature had this shape from the beginning, a form that archaeologists associate with 'graves', has not usually been considered.

There are thus several reasons why burnt mounds as a type of archaeological feature deserve to be interpreted in terms of cultic instruments. In the direct written sources, the Eddic and Skaldic poems dealing with ancient Scandinavian cult, there is a special term for a holy place or sanctuary made out of stones: Old Norse *hörgr* (Swedish *harg*) seems to be referring to a rock but can also be a structure of stone or wood. It has been suggested that *hörgr* could be interpreted as a sacrificial altar of stone, located in the open air, and that it was initially a natural place in the form of a rock or an assemblage of stones, but was later developed into an altar structure (Hultgård 1996: 29 ff.; cf. Vikstrand 2001). Both burnt mounds and certain stone settings could fit the description of a *hörgr*. An interpretative problem when it comes to comparing structures from the Late Bronze Age with the instances of *hörgr* mentioned in the late pre-Christian tradition is, of course, the long distance in time. On the other hand, this need not be as problematic as it may seem at first sight. It is reasonable to assume that the pre-Christian cult in Scandinavia was a unifying phenomenon of great vitality, with the ability to remain relatively intact for a long time. Changes over time can mean that the kind of stone structure that was the *hörgr* did change, but not necessarily that these changes were so great that the origin cannot be traced. Both certain stone settings of hitherto uninterpreted function and features with burnt stone are found continuously up to the end of the pre-Christian period, even though they changed in form and to some extent in content.

One hypothesis put forward by this author claims that fire-cracked stone was produced for ritual reasons as a deliberate process, by analogy with the way the dead body was disintegrated by fire during cremation (Kaliff 1999, 2007). The intention could have been to release the life force and to free the different elements. The fire-cracked stones covering the inner structure of the burnt mounds could have been a visible sign that the fire was born from the stone. This hypothetical interpretation can be developed if we proceed from the materials that the Vedic sacrificial altar was built of, where both the design and the material reflect the elements and the cosmological creation myth. The fire-cracked stone in the burnt mounds/fire altars would thus correspond to the Vedic idea that Agni was born on the fire altar. A further parallel, which may be of great explanatory value, is that the stone was burnt to transform it in such a way that the fire became active in the material itself. This would correspond closely to the Vedic ritual as it was performed, for example, in the agnicayana, although there it is clay that is fired to make the brick used to build the altar. The brick then contains a combination of elements—earth, water, and fire—which gives it a profound symbolic meaning. If the burnt mounds are created by heating stone and then making it crack by pouring water on it, the result is a material that may have been perceived as a similar combination of elements: rock, water, fire, and perhaps also air. With this outlook the burnt stone takes on a much greater symbolic meaning than 'ordinary' stone.

Burnt mounds, besides their association with fire, are also linked to water. Evidence for this comes from their topographic location, and from the fact that many of the stones in the mounds seem to have split in water. The effect of water striking the red-hot stone may have been what was ritually intended. Both the sound and the sight of the union of the water and the red-hot stone could be regarded as living proof of the way the elements combine and change (cf. Runcis 1999). If water was poured on burnt mounds in ancient Scandinavian ritual, it could correspond to the symbolic liquid poured on the altar in the agnicayana, which was believed to bring rain and fertility. As mentioned above, the big altar for this ritual is built of clay bricks. These are fired in a kiln, like the pots in which the fire is transported during the ceremony. Through the transformation of the clay in the fire, it is believed that Agni becomes active in the material in both cases. The effect of fire on the building material for the altar and on the liturgical implements in the form of pots is therefore a crucial and meaningful part of the ritual (Staal 2001: 94, 130). From this point of view, the pots could have direct counterparts in Scandinavian tradition, whereas the altar built of fired clay has none, or at least nothing has been documented or interpreted in this way. Yet burnt stone, especially in combination with water, could have had a comparable meaning. In both cases the fire transforms one or more other elements and is combined with these.

The ritual use of burnt stone to express cosmological beliefs can be a probable interpretation for certain burnt mounds. Both the stone itself and the effect of fire and water on it can be interpreted in terms of the homologies in a creation myth of the type found in other Indo-European contexts, where different elements can be enclosed in each other and be converted into other forms. In the placing of burnt mounds in the landscape and their internal structure we find further associations with different cosmological levels. The subsequent deposition of burnt stone in pits in the ground reflects a union with the earth as another important element. Such stone is often deposited right beside or close to deposits of burnt human bone.

4 Bodies and Fire

The overall interpretation means that another idea underlying the tradition of cremation is the link to the actual destruction of the body, according to the principle that the different parts of a person then return to the basic elements of which he or she is believed to consist. What happens with the remains of the dead body itself afterwards, although it is not without significance, is of subordinate interest to the fragmentation itself. When one considers the small amount of bone and the seemingly modest burial caches in Scandinavian cremation graves from the Late Bronze Age and Early Iron Age in general, this fits well. What happened to the bones, usually the major part, that were not included in the burial cache is a question that has not yet been satisfactorily answered on the basis of the archaeological finds. The crushing and the other treatment of the bones after cremation should be viewed as a part of the ritual, to further mark the destruction of the body. Such a ritual would agree well with the outlook on death that is found in other early Indo-European traditions, particularly in Vedic practice, where death is portrayed as a dismemberment of a whole, a fragmentation and decomposition. Viewing ageing and death as a process like any other disintegration in the cosmos is fundamental for an understanding of the outlook on death in ancient Indo-European tradition.

The meaning of depositing parts of the human body in the earth and water/wetland, and the burning of the remains, agrees well with the way burnt offerings and deposits of votive gifts can be interpreted. The rituals for the dead, including cremation, mean that the body is disintegrated and reverts to its constituent parts. Deposits of just one or a few small bone fragments, a phenomenon that was very common in the Late Bronze Age and Early Iron Age, can thus be interpreted by comparison with the deposition of *astu* in Vedic tradition, the little part that is taken from the body of the deceased in the final phase of the cremation to be buried in the earth. It symbolizes the affinity of flesh with earth, alloforms of the same thing (cf. Kaliff and Oestigaard 2004: 86f.). The pattern of scattered deposits of burnt bones in cemeteries, as single fragments or in small assemblages, would thus resemble the distribution of the first cosmological sacrifice. When fragmented body parts were spread and restored to their original elements—fire, earth, stones, water—the bodies of the dead provided material for the creation of new life and the maintenance of the cosmos.

5 Fire, Rock, and Wood

Fire as one of the basic elements also has another direct connection to rock and stones. While fire is a separate element, it is also inherent in other elements. Here it is a special case, since it also represents the transformation of elements into other forms. Fire generated by a strike-a-light or a fire drill—in other words, deriving from stone or wood—can be perceived as a visible, active part released from another material. One way to interpret this is that the fire is constantly present in the stone but in 'frozen' form. It must be brought to life by people's rituals. In a similar way, it may have been imagined that something of the deceased became part of the fire at cremation, and then became concealed in the stone.

This kind of interpretation could be applied also to rock carvings. It may be noted that the carved rock faces on sites in southern Sweden show signs of fires having been lit there, as evidenced by the presence of soot and fire-cracked stone. It is also clear that fires were lit on the carved surfaces, probably as part of a ritual in which the rock was deliberately crazed (cf. Widholm 1998; Bengtsson 2004: 37–44). The carvings, of course, are also exposed towards the sky, to the light of the sun, as well as to the surrounding water. Through the water and the material on which the images are inscribed, the rock, they combine different elements: sunlight/fire, water, rock/earth. To maintain balance in the world, people must constantly perform the right acts. Perhaps the actual fertilization was conjured up by the carving on the exposed rock, with the powers combined in the images when the sun, the air, and the water penetrated the rock through the act of carving.

A special rock-carving feature, the cup mark, can act symbolically as representations of the sun, as symbolic fire-drilling holes, as symbols of fireplaces, and so on. They can moreover be viewed as passages into the stone or the earth as an element and as passages for the birth of fire from the stone. It is interesting to note that cup marks, and also in some cases petroglyphs, occur beside cremation places. Although it is scarcely likely that they could have functioned as purely functional fire-making places, they may have been symbols of this (cf. Kaliff 1997: 106–16). There is considerable ethnographic evidence that fire-drilling, with a wooden bit that is made to rotate quickly in a hole in another piece of wood, also functioned as a symbol for the human power of generation. This kind of drill has been used in different contexts to light ritual fires (cf. Heiler 1961: 43). A basic meaning of the Vedic fire rituals is that Agni is born on the fire altar and it is of the utmost importance that fire is started through friction with a rotating drill (Staal 2001: 41ff.). The Vedic ritual has parallels in the way that *nödeld*, a ritually purifying fire, was lit in Scandinavian tradition. This kind of protective fire originally had the sense of 'rubbing fire' or 'twisting fire' (Hellquist 1922: 720). Ritual annual fires in Scandinavian tradition, and fires to cure sick livestock, were lit with a fire drill—that is, through the friction of wood against wood. It was believed that *nödeld* could drive out evil when fire was born from the drilled wood (Edsman 1987: 341). The principle was similar for the Celtic fire festival on the first of May, Beltane, when the bonfire was lit with a stick rotating in a piece of wood.

A basic way to make fire, apart from the friction of wood against wood, is to strike stone against stone, or metal against stone. A spark is then visibly born from the stone. The experience of fire being born from wood and stone may have been one reason behind the belief that the different elements can be transformed into each other and that fire is inherent in other elements. If fire is concealed in other materials, it is easy to believe that life consists of a limited number of elements from which everything is compounded. New life may have been thought to emanate from the grave as a stone structure, in the same way as fire could be created from the stone. Cup marks can be viewed as symbols of fire, and they may have been cut as stylized holes for fire-drilling. Just as steel and flint conjure up a spark from the seemingly cold and dead matter, the symbolic drilling of fire in the stone may have been perceived in the same way, as a possible way to entice power out of the stone.

6 Conclusions

The most important point of departure for the interpretative perspective of this entry for *Fire* is the general cosmological beliefs in different Indo-European traditions, in which the creation of the world is associated with the gods' ritual dismemberment of the body of a primordial being. The world is then made from this being's body, each part having its counterpart in the parts of the dismembered body. Just as everything emanates from these body parts and their alloforms, everything will also return at some time to its origin, where it can then be put together and come back to life again. The meaning of human sacrificial rituals is thus to assist the divine powers to re-create and maintain the world by restoring strength to the parts of creation. A corresponding function may thus have been attached to rituals for the dead, whereby the remains of the body were similarly restored to their original elements. Seemingly contradictory features in the archaeological evidence—for example, burnt offerings compared with deposition in water or land, and in particular the cremation ritual in relation to the meaning of the deposited bones—can be given a meaningful and coherent interpretation with this approach. Both the sacrificial victim and the dead person's body are dismembered, and in this process the different parts are returned to their original states.

Suggested Reading

Kaliff, A. 2007. *Fire, Water, Heaven and Earth: Ritual practice and cosmology in ancient Scandinavia: An Indo-European perspective* (Stockholm: National Heritage Board).
Kristiansen, K. and Larsson, T. B. 2005. *The Rise of Bronze Age Society: Travels, transmissions and transformations* (Cambridge: Cambridge University Press).
Lincoln, B. 1986. *Myth, Cosmos and Society. Indo-European themes of creation and destruction* (Cambridge, MA and London, England: Harvard University Press).
Staal, F. 2001. *Agni: The Vedic ritual of the fire altar* (Delhi).

References

Bellander, E. 1938. *Bålrösen—offerrösen. Kulturhistoriska studier tillägnade Nils Åberg* (Stockholm: Generalstabens litografiska anstalt).
Bengtsson, L. 2004. *Bilder vid vatten. Kring hällristningar i Askum sn, Bohuslän,* Gotarc Serie C. Arkeologiska Skrifter 51 (Göteborg: Göteborgs Universitet).

EDSMAN, C.-M. 1987. 'Fire' in M. Eliade (ed.), *The Encyclopedia of Religion*, XIV (New York: Macmillan), pp. 340–6.
HEILER, F. 1961. *Erscheinungsformen und Wesen der Religion* (Stuttgart: W. Kohlhammer Verlag).
HELLQUIST, H. 1922. *Svensk etymologisk ordbok* (Lund: Gleerups förlag).
HULTGÅRD, A. 1996. 'Fornskandinavisk kult—finns det skriftliga källor?' in K. Engdahl and A. Kaliff (eds), *Arkeologi från stenålder till medeltid. Artiklar baserade på Religionsarkeologiska nätverksgruppens konferens på Lövstadbruk den 1–3 december 1995*, Arkeologiska undersökningar, Skrifter 19 (Linköping: Riksantikvarieämbetet), pp. 25–57.
JOHANSEN, Ø. 1979. 'New results in the investigation of the Bronze Age rock carvings', *Norwegian Archaeological Review*, 12(2): 108–14.
KALIFF, A. 1997. *Grav och kultplats. Eskatologiska föreställningar under yngre bronsålder och äldre järnålder i Östergötland*, Aun 24 (Uppsala).
——1999. 'Objekt och tanke. Speglingar av bronsålderns föreställningsvärld' in M. Olausson (ed.), *Spiralens öga. Tjugo artiklar kring aktuell bronsåldersforskning*, Avdelningen för arkeologiska undersökningar, Skrifter 25 (Stockholm: Riksantikvarieämbetet), pp. 91–114.
——2007. *Fire, Water, Heaven and Earth: Ritual practice and cosmology in ancient Scandinavia: An Indo-European perspective* (Stockholm: Riksantikvarieämbetet).
——and OESTIGAARD, T. 2004. 'Cultivating corpses: A comparative approach to disembodied mortuary remains', *Current Swedish Archaeology*, 12: 83–104.
KRÄMER, W. 1966. 'Prähistorische Brandopferplätze' in R. Degen, W. Drack, and R. Wyss (eds), *Helvetia Antiqua. Festschrift Emil Vogt* (Zürich: Schweizerische Landesmuseum), pp. 111–22.
KRISTIANSEN, K. 1998. *Europe before History* (Cambridge: Cambridge University Press).
——2001. 'Rulers and warriors: Symbolic transmission and social transformation in Bronze Age Europe' in J. Haas (ed.), *From Leaders to Rulers* (New York: Kluwer Academic/Plenum Publishers), pp. 84–104.
——2004. 'Institutioner og materiel kultur. Tvillingherskerne som religiøs og politisk institution under bronzealderen' in A. Andrén, K. Jennbert, and C. Raudvere (eds), *Ordning mot kaos. Studier av nordisk förkristen kosmologi* (Lund: Nordic Academic Press), pp. 99–122.
——and LARSSON, T. B. 2005. *The Rise of Bronze Age Society: Travels, transmissions and transformations* (Cambridge: Cambridge University Press).
LINCOLN, B. 1986. *Myth, Cosmos and Society: Indo-European themes of creation and destruction* (Cambridge, MA and London: Harvard University Press).
NORDÉN, A. 1925. *Östergötlands Bronsålder* (Norrköping: Lundbergs bokhandels förlag).
PARMESHWARANAND, S. 2000. *Encyclopaedic Dictionary of Vedic Terms*, I–II (New Delhi: Sarup and Sons).
RUNCIS, J. 1999. 'Den mytiska geografin—Reflektioner kring skärvstenshögar, mytologi och landskapsrum i Södermanland under bronsålder' in M. Olausson (ed.), *Spiralens öga. Tjugo artiklar om aktuell bronsåldersforskning*, Avdelningen för arkeologiska undersökningar, Skrifter 25 (Stockholm: Riksantikvarieämbetet), pp. 129–55.
STAAL, F. 2001. *Agni: The Vedic ritual of the fire altar* (Delhi: Motilal Banarsidass).
TACHIKAWA, M., BAHULKAR, S., and KOLHATKAR, M. 2001. *Indian Fire Ritual* (Delhi: Motilal Banarsidass).
THÖRN, R. 1996. 'Rituella eldar. Linjära, konkava och konvexa spår efter ritualer inom nord- och centraleuropeiska brons- och järnålderskulturer' in K. Engdahl and A. Kaliff (eds), *Arkeologi från stenålder till medeltid. Artiklar baserade på Religionsarkeologiska*

nätverksgruppens konferens på Lövstadbruk den 1–3 december 1995, Arkeologiska undersökningar, Skrifter 19 (Linköping: Riksantikvarieämbetet) pp. 135–48.

VIKSTRAND, P. 2001. Gudarnas platser. Förkristna sakrala ortnamn i Mälarlandskapen, Acta Academiae Regiae Gustavi Adolphi LXXVII (Uppsala).

WIDHOLM, D. 1998. *Rösen, ristningar och riter*, Acta Archaeologica Lundensia, Series Prima in 4, 23 (Lund).

CHAPTER 5

MYTH AND FOLKLORE

AMY GAZIN-SCHWARTZ

1 INTRODUCTION

FROM antiquity, people have been concerned with relics of the past. Such relics might be material, like the artefacts associated with ancient heroes collected by the Roman Emperor Augustus, or the archaic stone tools and copper artefacts preserved by the Iroquois (Bahn 1996). Myths, epics, and traditions of ritual and belief have also been preserved as relics, as 'traditional' lore and practices. The study of both folklore and archaeology has its origins in these concerns, made more formal by the pursuits of sixteenth- to nineteenth-century antiquarians in Europe and North America (Bahn 1996; Daniel 1981; Trigger 1989; Dorson 1968). Beginning in the nineteenth century, when archaeology and folkloristics began to diverge into separate disciplines, the relationships between folklore and archaeology have sometimes been quite close, and sometimes been more distant.

'Folklore' encompasses a wide range of expressive forms that people believe to be traditional (Georges and Jones 1995: 1). Since the word was first used by William Thoms in 1846 to replace what had been called 'popular antiquities' (Thoms 1965: 4–5 [1846]), folklorists have struggled to define it precisely; indeed, the American Folklore Society does not define 'folklore' (http://www.afsnet.org/aboutfolklore/aboutFL.cfm). Rather, folklore has been defined most often by a list of the traditional forms that folklorists study. These include oral traditions like stories, songs, oral histories and prayers, and also place names, traditional work practices, expressive arts, material culture, and traditions of ritual and belief. Myth, then, is the genre of folklore particularly concerned with sacred stories about cultural origins.

Folklore and myth are meaningful within specific social contexts. Social groups 'own' the folklore, subscribe to the beliefs encoded in myths, and understand the traditions and practices that folklore encompasses. The social context may be limited to small groups: families, extended families, or small villages; or it may extend to entire nations. In either case, the traditions are important elements in the ways people create and maintain cultural or social identities (Newall 1980; Giddens 1999). Folklore is often distinguished from other kinds of practices, beliefs, or texts by its mode of transmission, favouring oral over written transmission. Today, sources of folklore may include texts in archives or ethnographic collections, but the lore these texts record was usually collected from oral tradition. Oral transmission implies that items of folklore are learned through personal contact (Georges and Jones 1995).

'Folklore' and 'tradition' are often used interchangeably, and these terms sometimes suggest that the elements they refer to persist unchanged from time immemorial. It is important to recognize that, like all cultural forms, folklore and other traditions are dynamic. As Glassie writes, tradition is one of the 'many ways people convert the old into the new' (Glassie 1995: 385). A struggle to understand the dynamics of continuity and change in folklore has been particularly significant in forming archaeologists' attitudes towards folklore and myth. Understanding how folklore relates to the past requires us to understand and hold the tension between continuity and change that is expressed in the various genres of folklore.

Folklore and myth intersect with archaeology in several ways. Archaeological sites and landscape features may be the focus of traditional lore and practices. Folklore and mythology about these features reveal cultural interpretations of their meaning, and place those sites in the context of socially understood history. They may also direct our attention to landscape features that are not materially modified, but are the locus of significant cultural meaning. Folklore and myth may help archaeologists to recognize archaeological remains, and may contribute to explaining or interpreting their functions and meanings. Finally, folklore and myths continue to figure in how the public today understands the past, and thus play a role in public archaeology.

This chapter will first consider the historical relationships between folklore or myth and archaeology, primarily focusing on European and American perspectives. Because issues of authenticity affect these relationships, I will address how folklorists have dealt with those issues in this section. Next, I will examine folklore of archaeology and myth, looking at how archaeological sites are the focus of traditional stories and practices in different parts of the world. A third section will evaluate the use of folklore and myth for archaeological interpretation. Finally the role of folklore and myth in public archaeology will be discussed.

2 Folklore and Archaeology: Historical Perspectives

Historically, archaeologists have engaged with folklore and myth in a variety of ways, ranging from viewing them as documents that provide reliable information on past events and activities, to viewing them as mistaken interpretations that archaeological data can correct. Antiquarians in the early modern era rarely distinguished between observing ancient material relics and recording 'relics' of ancient practices or beliefs in the form of folk rituals and tales. They viewed both as precious remains giving insight into the origins of their own national character, or into the timeless primitive cultures they believed to be disappearing in the face of colonial and scientific advances.

Antiquarians were particularly interested in connecting European antiquities with heroes of mythology or of the Classical past. The English antiquarian Robert Plot, for example, asked his informants in Staffordshire and Oxfordshire such questions as 'Are there any ancient sepulchres hereabout of Men of Gigantic Stature, Roman Generals, and others of ancient times?' (Daniel 1981: 26; see also Dorson 1968). Analysis or interpretation of the function or meaning of monuments was less important; rather attempts were made to identify remnants of the past, and whenever possible to attach them to known personages of the past, whether mythological (such as King Arthur, Brutus), biblical, or historical (for example Roman generals, Huns). History was viewed as the works of 'great men'; and authority derived from the Bible, the Classical world, and national heroes. Such connections may have served to support developing nationalist ideologies.

By the mid-nineteenth century, archaeology and folklore began to define themselves as separate professional fields, distinct from antiquarianism. In the process of this self-definition, archaeology became the realm of physical monuments and material remains of the past, while folklore focused on verbal performances and customary activities (Bahn 1996; Daniel 1981).

Notions of history as progress, and folklore as timeless, have influenced how archaeologists view folklore in the nineteenth and first half of the twentieth centuries. Both oral traditions (folklore or myth) and material remains were viewed within a cultural evolutionary framework. Archaeology traced the material and technological progress of human cultures. Folklore was similarly viewed as the remnant of past or static cultures, as the unchanging traditions of primitive peoples. This distinction between tracing progress and recording beliefs or practices that have not progressed removes folklore from historical processes. As Whitely (2002) has pointed out, 'real' history, rooted in documents, is linear and deals with progress and change. Folklore and myth are viewed as timeless and unchanging, but simultaneously false and unreliable as historical documents. Though they are seen as timeless, folklore and myth are unreliable primarily because of a privileging of written sources over oral sources. Archaeologists, distinguishing themselves from their less scientific antiquarian ancestors, became sceptical about the value of folklore for helping them to understand the ancient past.

3 Authenticity and Continuity: Problems in Understanding Tradition

In considering the relationships between folklore and history, folklorists also have long debated questions about the historical accuracy of traditional accounts. Do traditional stories encompass 'true' histories of past events, maintaining fragments of ancient rituals or beliefs (Fleure 1948)? Or, are folk traditions unreliable as sources of history because they have been subject to influence of succeeding events and changes, or even invented in recent times (Hobsbawm and Ranger 1983; Dorson 1976; Fleure 1932; Joyner 1989)? Bendix (1997) argues that this concern with authenticity is in part a function of the search for professional legitimization for the field of folklore. Joyner argues that folklore is necessary for history not because it arose from actual historical events, but because it helps historians to understand 'the attitudes and actions of real men and women' (Joyner 1989: 11); similarly history is necessary to understand the context in which folklore arose.

This concern with the authenticity and reliability of folklore traditions underlies the frequent archaeological rejection of the value of folklore for understanding ancient monuments or other sites. In some cases, the time depth of archaeology leads to scepticism about the reliability of folklore. It is one thing to accept that stories about nineteenth-century Scottish Highland clearances, or Native American encounters with European-Americans moving west, may contain a kernel of truth, or may represent relatively accurate oral history (Mackay 1990; Spector 1993). For most archaeologists, it is another thing altogether to accept the reliability of stories about the more distant past.

There are many reasons for this scepticism. In the early days of archaeological and ethnographic interest in the Pueblo peoples of the American Southwest, for example, people attempted to match contemporary Pueblo origin myths with the locations and physical evidence of older Anasazi sites on the Colorado Plateau (Fewkes 1893). The myths did not always match the archaeology very well, and the attempts at correlation were later considered a waste of time. In Britain, the antiquarian fondness for attributing everything to the Druids led to popular and scholarly misinterpretation and romanticization that made archaeological work more difficult. How, for example, can the reality of a megalithic tomb, with its complex and problematic sequences of construction and use, confused arrangements of bodies (or lack of them), and its attribution by radiocarbon dating to a time thousands of years before any Druids, compete for attention (and ultimately for funding) with white robed priests, blood sacrifice, and mysterious ritual?

For archaeologists, 'authentic' folklore had to be verifiably historical, had to fill the role of historical documents like diaries or deeds. Long-term continuity in oral traditions was doubted, and popular (folk) traditions were viewed as inimical to scientific research (Feder 2007). To folklorists, on the other hand, 'authenticity' means that the traditions are verifiably local oral traditions—that they were transmitted in face-to-face contexts, rather than learned from books. The folklorist Henry Fleure (1932) argued that folk traditions and medieval stories might be reliable in a 'general' way, even if the specific details are incorrect. He cites as one example Geoffrey of Monmouth's story that Merlin brought the bluestone circle to Stonehenge by sea, intact from Ireland. Archaeological research demonstrates that the bluestones came from Wales, probably (he thought) by boat; so, they came by sea from elsewhere, even if not Ireland.

Seeking close agreement between verifiably oral traditions and archaeological observations betrays rather naive use of those traditions. Folklore is symbolic expression, and not necessarily meant to be taken literally. Origin myths are told in mythological language, and are symbolic and requiring interpretation. Myths reveal not facts about the past, so much as the significance of the past. We often cannot look to these stories for facts, but we can look to them for meaning. Because meaningful stories are likely to be transmitted more accurately (Connerton 1989; P. Thompson 1988; Vansina 1985), we can sometimes find within them information about very old practices, information about the uses of material culture, about the conduct of daily activities, and about the meaning of features on the landscape. As with other forms of material culture, we should expect to have to interpret the stories and to seek local interpretations of them, in order to understand their significance for constructing the past.

A second, related problem archaeologists have with the authenticity of folklore arises from the modern, Western immersion in written documents. We have come to believe that only writing can preserve accurate records; it seems impossible to accept that memories, rituals, or stories can be transmitted orally over hundreds of years. It is important to consider the context in which such stories are told. Even print-dominated modern people do remember stories, events, even smells that are associated with significant meaning or with repeated enactment. Each of us can probably come up with a list of events, people, sayings, and family stories, activities that we have remembered in quite fine detail for a long time, or that we heard from our own parents or grandparents. Even in a more oral culture, insignificant items probably are lost from memory, but significant tales remain and are carefully transmitted to successive generations. The long-term transmission of significant historical stories has been most intensively studied by oral historians working in Africa (Vansina 1985; see also Perks and Thompson 1998; P. Thompson 1988).

In addition, like other items of culture, folklore speaks with many voices, and accrues over its history aspects of each phase of that history, which must be teased out, or at the very least acknowledged. Different people may well tell different versions of the same lore. Each tradition may include both ancient references only partially understood, and more recent additions that serve to reinforce the meaning of the tradition (Hayward 1992).

Recent archaeological attitudes towards folklore still often divide along lines of reliability. For example, in two articles in *American Antiquity* in 2000, Echo-Hawk and Mason debated the archaeological value of Native American oral traditions. After a 'critical canvassing of the pros and cons attending the employment of oral traditions in archaeological reconstructions', Mason concludes that:

> archaeologists, like scientists generally, are charged with truth-seeking, however elusive it may be and however displacing or not of 'other ways of knowing.' While the purveyors of the older wisdoms are to be respected as people their recountings of ancientness are challengeable when they are thought of as data roughly on a par with, say, dendrochonology, seriation, or site distribution maps. [Mason 2000: 264]

Mason views oral tradition and archaeology or history as too distinct epistemologically to be useful to one another.

Echo-Hawk, in the same issue, takes the opposite view, arguing that oral traditions do provide 'a viable source of information about historical settings dating far back in time' (Echo-Hawk 2000: 267), and that archaeology, as a multidisciplinary field, should include oral tradition as one of the sources of data for understanding Native American sites and histories. He cites a number of cases, including Arikara and Pawnee origin stories, to support the claim that oral traditions, when properly interpreted and subject to the criteria already developed by oral historians (for example, Vansina 1985) are useful for tracing tribal histories and connections to archaeological sites and landscapes.

Following this debate, Whitely (2000) attempts to bring together the two epistemologies by arguing that archaeologists can develop criteria for evaluating the reliability of oral traditions. He uses Hopi clan-origin myths to illustrate the historical reliability and interpretive value for archaeology of oral traditions. These myths, Whitely argues, refer to specific places, many of them archaeologically known sites. They also carry information about agricultural practices, leadership, and social structure that are useful for interpreting the past, and for opening up new areas of inquiry. Rather than reverting to antiquarian methods of seeking to identify archaeology with folklore, Whitely argues for the value of folklore for archaeological interpretation.

If we recognize and accept that, like other archaeological materials and historical documents, folklore does not provide information until it is analysed and interpreted, then there are three main areas of inquiry where archaeologists in many parts of the world have found folklore and myth to be useful in understanding the past. Folklore and myth in many places are attached to archaeological sites; folklore and myth may be useful for interpreting archaeological remains; and folklore and myth form part of public understandings of the past, and therefore play a role in public archaeology.

4 Folklore of Archaeology and Archaeology of Folklore

Folklorists, ethnographers, and archaeologists have all collected material about archaeological sites in many places (for some examples see Carmichael, Hubert, Reeves, and Schanche 1994; Cruickshank 1981; Echo-Hawk 2000; Gazin-Schwartz and Holtorf 1999; Grinsell 1939, 1953, 1973, 1976; Hawkes 1954; Thompson 2004). In addition to the examples of Hopi clan-myths attached to Pueblo sites, noted above, two examples serve to illustrate the kinds of folklore that connect to archaeological monuments.

Thompson (2004) discusses the extensive connections between what archaeologists identify as Neolithic or Bronze Age megalithic tombs and folk traditions referred to as *sí*. This Irish word *sí* refers both to the monuments themselves, which take the form of circular mounds, and to the spirits believed to inhabit those mounds. In folklore, these archaeological sites are connected with the world of the dead and with inhabitants of that world, both supernatural beings and ancestral spirits. Thompson notes that applying non-native terms to both the sites ('megalithic tombs') and the spirits ('fairies') separates categories that are inextricably linked in the native Irish references. Further, these translated terms and categories denigrate the very powerful and pervasive traditions of the *sí* as quaint, backward, and picturesque. The folklore about the sites, understood in its own context, highlights the ongoing significance of the sites in Irish culture. As Holtorf (1998) and Bender (1998) argue, archaeological sites have 'life-histories' from the time they are first built, and these histories are, in part, recorded in folklore. Attention to that folklore allows archaeologists access to the significance of the sites from their original construction until today.

Thompson further uses the folklore about these sites to argue that they have been culturally significant continuously since their building. Folklore about the site of Newgrange, for example, includes information about the effects of the sun entering an opening of the tomb. This phenomenon would not have been physically visible from the time the tomb was sealed in the third millennium BC until archaeologists excavated it in 1967. Knowledge about the effects of the sun at the winter solstice seems to have been transmitted even when those effects were not visible. Folklore may thus, in this case, illustrate long-term continuity of understanding about the tomb that transcended even such cultural changes as the arrival in Ireland of Celtic-speaking peoples in the seventh century BC. Megalithic monuments throughout Europe and Asia similarly attract folklore that links their building and use to ancient peoples, mythological beings like giants, and characters in folktales (see, for example, Badone 1991; Parpola 2002). As prominent sites in the landscape, such monuments may be expected to attract attention as long as they are visible. What

Thompson argues is that their significance may also allow for transmission of ancient knowledge about the sites.

A second example illustrates how folklore can direct archaeologists' attention to culturally significant sites that may not be well marked archaeologically. Segadika (2008) has examined oral traditions about landscape features in eastern Botswana. He demonstrates that folklore, like place names and oral traditions, carries information not just about those features, but about such cultural forms as religious beliefs, gender roles, and ethnic relations. His discussion especially focuses on the cultural significance of seemingly natural places. For example, folklore attached to the hills, roads, and caves in the area explicitly links these to the activities and desires of the ancestral Batswapog spirits. One location, Dimomo cave, is associated with tales of danger, such as people experiencing unusual tiredness when they are near the cave, or people being trapped under rocks near the cave (Segadika 2008: 149–51). These tales explain that the site is powerfully associated with the spirit world, but is not likely to be marked archaeologically because the spirits do not want people to come near the cave. Segadika concludes:

> In an archaeological context, mapping the settlement patterns of the Batswapong of the Malaka area would show some places as being occupied, while others would be unoccupied or unusable, places that would be considered by the Batswapong as being fully occupied by the ancestral spirits. By the same token, the decision not to physically alter the landscape can itself be seen to be a monumental artifice based on a system and worldview that prohibits altering the earth. [Segadika 2008: 152]

Folklore, myth, and oral traditions elsewhere in the world also illustrate this principle, that it is not only the intensively marked archaeological sites that are culturally significant, but that many natural places carry powerful cultural meanings (Bradley 2000). These meanings are rarely accessible to archaeologists without reference to folklore or ethnographic materials.

Folklore and myth about archaeological sites and landscape features identify those sites as foci of activity and belief in the landscape. Sites identified in folklore, whether marked by archaeological remains or not, are distinguished from their surroundings by having particular meanings. Folklore and myth then put these sites in the context of socially and culturally understood histories. For archaeologists, these traditions may tell us where sites are located, tell us what the sites meant to local people at the time the folklore was recorded, and tell us something about what the site was used for, both at the time of its creation and in all the time since its creation.

5 Folklore, Myth, and Archaeological Interpretation

In 1951, British archaeologist J. G. D. Clark suggested that it would be profitable for (British) archaeologists to look at folklore. He was particularly concerned with the value for archaeological interpretation of understanding traditional tools and working practices, and in *Prehistoric Europe: The economic basis* (Clark 1954) he uses ethnographic records and folklore in explaining the functions of prehistoric artefacts. British and Irish folklorists have also shown a concern with material culture and traditional practices, particularly in Ireland (Evans 1957), Wales (Peate 1944, 1972) and Scotland (Fenton 1985; Grant 1961). Evans goes so far as to state that Irish rural practices and material culture represent survivals of Neolithic practices (Evans 1957: 6). Archaeologists have more recently returned to or rediscovered the use of folklore for interpretation of artefacts and material culture in general. Three more-recent examples will illustrate how folklore and myth aid in the interpretation of artefacts and of archaeological sites.

Leone and Fry (1999) and Gazin-Schwartz (2001) explore how folklore can inform interpretation of artefacts, and how archaeological and folkloristic approaches are complementary in interpretation. In the kitchen of an elite house in Annapolis, Maryland, archaeologists discovered a collection of artefacts, including blue beads, pins, buttons, bones, and glass. Thinking these artefacts might be tied somehow to African religious traditions, Leone, an archaeologist, and Fry, a folklorist, catalogued similar caches of artefacts from African-American sites in Virginia and Maryland, and used information from 'slave narratives' about healing and conjuring traditions to interpret the meanings, uses, and cultural affiliations of those caches (Leone and Fry 1999). They argued that by combining the two approaches of folkloristics and archaeology, we can turn the 'absences' of each into strengths. In the case of the caches, which they identify as bundles of artefacts used by African-American slaves in conjuring rituals, archaeology can demonstrate the time span during which such practices took place, the ritually used locations within buildings, and the geographical range over which these practices occurred. Folklore, on the other hand, provided the contexts and meanings for the practices, explained what people were doing with the bundles of artefacts and why particular artefacts were used. White buttons, for example, are related to death by their colour. The folklore allowed the archaeologists to link their finds to particular elements of West African belief systems.

Gazin-Schwartz (2001) uses Scottish folklore to identify materials used in curing rituals in historic times (the seventeenth to nineteenth century), and shows that even everyday objects like knives, string, and pins may have had ritual significance. Folklore in this case expands the definition of ritual in the context of Christian communities, and points to the significance for interpretation of attributes like the colour or form of artefacts as well as the location where they are found. In both the African-American and Scottish cases, the location of the artefacts was an important element in identifying their ritual uses.

Folklore can also be useful for interpreting archaeological sites. A number of authors have explored this in the context of interpreting San rock art in Southern Africa (Deacon 1988; Lewis-Williams 1984, 1986; Solomon 1997). Deacon (1988), for example, explores whether folklore collected in the nineteenth century can explain how San choose which rocks to mark with art, and the role of rock art in San beliefs. The animals engraved on rocks in the vicinity of springs were recorded in folklore as animals (rain-bull, lizard, elephant) associated with water and rain, and individuals who had the ritual power to bring rain were recorded as also being responsible for some of the rock art.

Similar approaches have yielded valuable insights for rock in Australia, North America and elsewhere (for examples see *World Archaeology* special edition on Rock Art, 19(2), 1987), and for artefacts at ritual sites in Kazakhstan (Lymer 2004) and elsewhere. Using folklore and archaeology to inform interpretation of votive offerings, and the locations at which they are offered, might be expected to yield fruitful results.

6 Public Archaeology and the Problem of Authenticity

Folklore and myth are elements in how the public perceives and understands the past at archaeological, historical, and religious sites today. From 'Druid' ceremonies at the summer solstice at Stonehenge to notions that extraterrestrial beings created the Nazca lines, wild tales fill public imaginations. For archaeologists, one of the problems with folklore has always been that it regularly contradicts the archaeological facts.

Archaeologists also have an obligation both to descendant communities and to the public at large who are concerned with (and perhaps paying for) archaeological research. These communities can often provide archaeologists with useful historical and contextual information about the sites and materials being excavated. Archaeologists may find that the beliefs about archaeological sites and materials held by descendant communities and the general public do not match the results they gain from archaeology, yet these beliefs remain meaningful to community members. How should archaeologists respond when we tell a landowner the chambered tomb on his property is 4,000 years old, and he replies that was the time of Adam and Eve and there were no people living where he lives back then? Examples in previous sections address some of the ways archaeologists negotiate the terrain between uncritical acceptance of all popular or folkloric interpretations, and complete rejection of the value of folklore and myth. Two additional examples from historical archaeology in the United States will illustrate this negotiation in the context of explicitly public archaeology.

Delle (2008) considers the role of public memory, social memory, and social myth in constructing histories of the Underground Railroad, and contrasts the social memories or myths with archaeological evidence. His research illustrates both the problems and the benefits archaeologists may encounter in attempting to match social myths with archaeological evidence. Delle uses the term 'social myth' (2008: 65–7) to denote those oral traditions that play a role in local identity formation and ideology. He notes that archaeological and historical research has debunked many of these oral traditions, citing, for example, archaeological interpretations of secret rooms where escaped slaves hid as 'generally mundane elements of the original architecture of buildings, features like cold cellars and cisterns long out of use and forgotten' (Delle 2008: 73). He then discusses his own excavations at the Parvin House in Pennsylvania, where the landowners claimed oral traditions about the Underground Railroad tunnels. The excavations found no evidence of tunnels in the locations the landowner identified. Despite the results of the excavation, which were reported to the landowner and published locally, the myth about the tunnels persisted.

Other work at the Thaddeus Stevens house did reveal both a tunnel and the reuse of a cistern, perhaps as a hiding place on the Underground Railroad. This research stimulated public discussion and memory about the role of local residents in the Underground Railroad. Delle ends by arguing for a greater consideration of the role of archaeology in the creation and dissolution of public and social memory and myths.

Powell and Dockall (1995) used folklore methods to integrate oral traditions and public archaeology. When they were excavating a historical African-American cemetery in Galveston, Texas, local people stopping to observe the excavations shared narratives about the history of the cemetery and the local African-American community. Powell and Dockall integrated these narratives into the research on the cemetery. Local memories aided the archaeological research in practical ways, by helping to locate graves, and by explaining evidence for disturbance in the graves. In addition, local narratives and memories helped the archaeologists to interpret puzzling features of the human remains that were excavated. For example, archaeologists recorded a high recovery rate of bones of the feet, even from graves from which the skeleton had been removed during earlier highway construction. A member of the family who operates the local funeral home explained that people are usually not buried wearing shoes, which would account for the presence of foot bones (Powell and Dockall 1995: 351). Perhaps most importantly, by using folklore methods, the archaeologists developed a collaborative approach that helped to ease tensions with the local community over the relocation of the cemetery.

7 Conclusion and Potential for Future Research

Perhaps the antiquarian perspective that viewed archaeological sites and materials, folklore, and myth as intertwined 'relics' of the past was not as misguided as later archaeologists believed. While it may not always be possible to argue that local traditions carry specific information about past rituals or beliefs about archaeological sites, it is likely that a study of folklore and myth will contribute to archaeological research and interpretation at many, or even most, sites. These contributions may be straightforward, providing details about the layout of sites or the uses of artefacts. In many cases, it will be necessary to apply the same kinds of contextual interpretation to the folklore and myths that archaeologists have to apply to material remains. Such contextual interpretation may, as Thompson (2004) argues, actually give us insights into ancient practices. Even if we cannot recognize very ancient beliefs through folklore and myth, however, we will be forced to recognize that the materials that archaeologists study have been the focus of people's interests throughout history. Perhaps folklore and myths attached to archaeological sites provide information about more recent ritual and beliefs, demonstrating continuity in cultural significance even for sites that 'go out of use'. Evidence for recent ritual activities, rather than being viewed as later intrusions into the archaeological record, can be interpreted as part of the ongoing meanings of a site. Finally, the requirements of public archaeology and collaboration often introduce folklore and mythological elements into archaeological research, and integrating these public traditions enriches archaeological interpretation.

Suggested Reading

This chapter has largely focused on British and North American examples. In this tradition, Fleure (1932) provides a good example of folklorist and antiquarian approaches to the connections between folklore and archaeology and Glassie (1977) expands that discussion to more recent historical archaeology. The links between folklore and archaeology have also been important in Scandinavia, Australia, Central Europe, and elsewhere. Gazin-Schwartz and Holtorf (1999) include case studies from other parts of the world, and useful references. Leone and Fry (1999) is a clear example of the interpretive value of collaborative research using both archaeological and folklorist methods. Recent work on indigenous archaeologies (see for example articles in Smith and Wobst 2005) expand on the issues raised in this chapter by discussing the dialogues between archaeology and indigenous traditions.

REFERENCES

BADONE, E. 1991. 'Ethnography, fiction, and the meanings of the past in Brittany', *American Ethnologist*, 18(3): 518–45.
BAHN, P. 2005. *The Cambridge Illustrated History of Archaeology* (Cambridge: Cambridge University Press).
BENDER, B. 1998. *Stonehenge: Making space* (Providence, RI: Berg).
BENDIX, R. 1997. *In Search of Authenticity: The formation of folklore studies* (Madison: University of Wisconsin Press).
BLINKENBERG, C. 1911. *The Thunderweapon in Religion and Folklore: A study in comparative archaeology* (Cambridge: Cambridge University Press).
BRADLEY, R. 2000. *An Archaeology of Natural Places* (New York: Routledge).
CARMICHAEL, D. L., HUBERT, J., REEVES, B., and SCHANCHE, A. (eds) 1994. *Sacred Sites, Sacred Places*, One World Archaeology 23 (London: Routledge).
CLARK, J. G. D. 1951. 'Folk culture and the study of European prehistory' in W. F. Grimes (ed.), *Aspects of Archaeology in Britain and Beyond* (London: Edwardo), pp. 39–48.
——1954. *Prehistoric Europe: The economic basis* (London: Methuen).
CONNERTON, P. 1989. *How Societies Remember* (Cambridge: Cambridge University Press).
CRUIKSHANK, J. 1981. 'Legend and landscape: Convergence of oral and scientific traditions in the Yukon territory', *Arctic Anthropology*, 18: 67–84.
DANIEL, G. 1981. *A Short History of Archaeology* (London: Thames and Hudson).
DEACON, J. 1988. 'The power of a place in understanding southern San rock engravings', *World Archaeology*, 20(1): 129–40.
DELLE, J. A. 2008. 'A tale of two tunnels: Memory, archaeology, and the Underground Railroad', *Journal of Social Archaeology*, 8(1): 63–93.
DORSON, R. M. 1968. *The British Folklorists: A history* (London: Routledge and Kegan Paul).
——1976. *Folklore and Fakelore: Essays toward a discipline of folk studies* (Cambridge, MA: Harvard University Press).
DUNDES, A. (ed.) 1965. *The Study of Folklore* (Englewood Cliffs, NJ: Prentice-Hall).
ECHO-HAWK, R. C. 2000. 'Ancient history in the New World: Integrating oral traditions and the archaeological record', *American Antiquity*, 65(2): 267–90.
EVANS, E. E. 1957. *Irish Folk Ways* (London: Routledge and Kegan Paul).
FEDER, K. 2007. *Frauds, Myths, and Mysteries: Science and pseudoscience in archaeology* (New York: McGraw-Hill).
FENTON, A. 1985. *The Shape of the Past: Essays in Scottish ethnology*, 2 vols. (Edinburgh: John Donald Publishers Ltd).

FEWKES, J. W. 1893. 'A-Wa'-tobi: An archaeological verification of a Tusayan legend', *American Anthropologist*, 6: 363–75.
FLEURE, H. J. 1932. *Archaeology and Folk Tradition*, The Sir John Rhys Memorial Lecture (London: The British Academy).
—— 1948. 'Archaeology and folklore', *Folklore*, 59: 69–74.
GAZIN-SCHWARTZ, A. 2001. 'Archaeology and folklore of ritual, material culture, and everyday life', *International Journal of Historical Archaeology*, 5(4): 263–80.
—— and HOLTORF, C. (eds) 1999. *Archaeology and Folklore* (London: Routledge).
GEORGES, R. A. and JONES, M. O. 1995. *Folkloristics: An introduction* (Bloomington: Indiana University Press).
GIDDENS, A. 1999. 'Runaway world', Reith Lectures (London: BBC), http://news.bbc.co.uk/hi/english/static/events/reith_99/default.htm
GLASSIE, H. 1977. 'Archaeology and folklore: Common anxieties, common hopes' in L. Ferguson (ed.), *Historical Archaeology and the Importance of Material Things*, Special Publications 2 (Columbia: Society for Historical Archaeology), pp. 23–35.
—— 1995. 'Tradition', *Journal of American Folklore*, 108(43): 395–412.
GRANT, I. F. 1961. *Highland Folkways* (London: Routledge and Kegan Paul).
GRINSELL, L. V. 1939. 'Scheme for recording the folklore of prehistoric remains', *Folk-lore*, 50: 323–32.
—— 1953. *Ancient Burial-Mounds of England*, 2nd edn (London: Methuen).
—— 1972. 'Witchcraft at barrows and other prehistoric sites', *Antiquity*, 46(181): 58–9.
—— 1973. *Folklore of Stanton Drew* (St Peter Port, Guernsey: Toucan Press).
—— 1976. *Folklore of Prehistoric Sites in Britain* (London: David and Charles).
HAWKES, J. 1954. *A Guide to the Prehistoric and Roman Monuments in England and Wales* (London: Chatto and Windus).
HAYWARD, B. 1992. *Galoshins: The Scottish folk play* (Edinburgh: Edinburgh University Press).
HOBSBAWM, E. and RANGER, T. 1983. *The Invention of Tradition* (Cambridge: Cambridge University Press).
HOLTORF, C. 1998. 'The life-histories of megaliths in Meclenburtg-Vorpommern (Germany)', *World Archaeology*, 30(1): 23–38.
JOYNER, C. 1989. 'A tale of two disciplines: Folklore and history' in D. Rohtman-Augustin and M. Povrzanovic (eds), *Folklore and Historical Process* (Zagreb: Institute of Folklore Research), pp. 9–22.
LEONE, M. and FRY, G. 1999. 'Conjuring in the big house kitchen: An interpretation of African-American belief systems based on the uses of archaeology and folklore sources', *Journal of American Folklore*, 112(445): 372–403.
LEWIS-WILLIAMS, J. D. 1984. 'Ideological continuities in prehistoric southern Africa: The evidence of rock art' in C. Shrire (ed.), *Past and Present in Hunter-Gatherer Studies* (New York: Academic Press), pp. 225–52.
—— 1986. *Believing and Seeing: Symbolic meanings in southern San rock paintings* (London: Academic Press).
LYMER, K. 2004. 'Rags and rock art: The landscapes of holy site pilgrimage in the Republic of Kazakhstan', *World Archaeology*, 36(1): 158.
MACKAY, D. 1990. 'Images in a landscape: Bonnie Prince Charlie and the Highland clearances' in F. Baker, S. Taylor, and J. Thomas (eds), *Writing the Past in the Present* (Lampeter: St Davids University College), pp. 192–203.

MASON, R. J. 2000. 'Archaeology and Native North American oral traditions', *American Antiquity*, 65(2): 239–66.

NEWALL, V. 1980. 'Introduction' in V. J. Newall (ed.), *Folklore Studies in the Twentieth Century*, Proceedings of the Centenary Conference of the Folklore Society (Totowa, NJ: Rowman and Littlefield), pp. xv–xxxii.

PARPOLA, A. 2002. 'Πανδαιη and Sītā: On the historical background of the Sanskrit Epics', *Journal of the American Oriental Society*, 122(2): 361–73.

PEATE, I. C. 1944. *The Welsh House: A study in folk culture* (Liverpool: H. Evans and Sons).

——1972. *Tradition and Folklife* (London: Faber and Faber).

PERKS, R. and THOMSON, A. (eds) 1998. *The Oral History Reader* (London and New York: Routledge).

POWELL, L. C. and DOCKALL, H. D. 1995. 'Folk narratives and archaeology: An African-American cemetery in Texas', *Journal of Field Archaeology*, 22(3): 349–53.

SEGADIKA, P. 2008. 'The domestication of landscape through naming and symbolic protection among the Batswapong peoples of eastern Botswana: Fullness and emptiness of landscapes in the eyes of the beholder' in A. P. Smith and A. Gazin-Schwartz (eds), *Landscapes of Clearance* (Walnut Creek, CA: Left Coast Press), pp. 139–53.

SMITH, C. and WOBST, H. M. 2005. *Indigenous Archaeologies: Decolonizing theory and practices*, One World Archaeology (London: Routledge).

SOLOMON, A. 1997. 'The myth of ritual origins? Ethnography, mythology and interpretation of San rock art', *The South African Archaeological Bulletin*, 52(165): 3–13.

SPECTOR, J. D. 1993. *What This Awl Means: Feminist archaeology at a Wahpeton Dakota village* (St Paul: Minnesosta Historical Society Press).

THOMPSON, P. 1988. *The Voice of the Past: Oral history*, 2nd edn (Oxford: Oxford University Press).

THOMPSON, T. 2004. 'The Irish Sí tradition: Connections between the disciplines, and what's in a word?', *Journal of Archaeological Method and Theory*, 11(4): 335–68.

THOMS, W. 1965 [1846]. 'Folklore', *The Athenaeum*, 983: 862–3; repr. A. Dundes (ed.), *The Study of Folklore* (Englewood Cliffs, NJ: Prentice-Hall), pp. 4–6.

TRIGGER, B. G. 1989. *A History of Archaeological Thought* (Cambridge: Cambridge University Press).

VANSINA, J. 1985. *Oral Tradition as History* (London: James Currey Ltd).

WHITELY, P. M. 2002. 'Archaeology and oral tradition: The scientific importance of dialogue', *American Antiquity*, 67(3): 405–15.

CHAPTER 6

COSMOGONY

TERJE OESTIGAARD

1 INTRODUCTION

COSMOGONY as a term is derived from the two Greek words *kosmos* and *genesis*. *Kosmos* refers to the order of the universe and/or the universe as the order, whereas *genesis* refers to the process of coming into being (Long 1993: 94). Thus, cosmogony has to do with founding myths and the origin and the creation of the gods and cosmos and how the world came into existence. There are schematically several different types of cosmogenic myths classified according to their symbolic structure: (1) creation from nothing, (2) creation from chaos, (3) creation from a cosmic egg, (4) creation from world parents, (5) creation through a process of emergence, and (6) creation through the agency of an earth diver. Several of these motifs and typological forms may be present in a given cosmogenic myth-system, and these types are not mutually exclusive but may rather be used in parallel in creation or origin myths (Long 1993: 94).

There are cosmogenic myths in all religions. In the Hebrew myth, there is creation from nothing: 'And God said. "Let there be light"; and there was light' (Gen. 1: 3). Importantly, in transcendental religions such as Judaism, Christianity, and Islam the omnipotent god exists totally independent of its own creation (Trigger 2003: 473), but still there are cosmogenic myths. Usually, however, cosmogony refers to a divine structuring principle where cosmos and the world are not independent of its original creation, but dependent upon the outcome of the *ritual relation* between humans and deities for its future existence, and such religions are traditionally called cosmogenic, putting the emphasis on human *rituals*. Thus, there are differences between cosmogenic and transcendental religions with regards to structures of beliefs and practices. A cosmogenic religion links humans' rituals in the present with the divine glory in the past and cosmic stability and prosperity in the future. Hence, a cosmogenic religion enables and prescribes particular types of ritual practices which are archaeologically manifest in the material culture, and all the early civilizations have been cosmogenic (Trigger 2003: 444–5) together with the majority of prehistoric religions.

Although cosmogony had been an analytical term before Mircea Eliade developed these perspectives, his writings in the 1950s (e.g. Eliade 1954, 1959a [1987]) have strongly influenced researchers' views of peoples' beliefs of the world and universe in early civilizations (Trigger 2003: 445). Cosmogony as a religious framework for understanding the world and the universe necessitates specific types of interactions and rituals with the divinities. Hence, due to the strong influence of Eliade's work on cosmogony as a principle and process, this article will focus on (1) his premises and analyses, (2) criticism and development of cosmogony as a concept, and (3) how it is possible to analyse cosmogenic rituals and religious practices as manifest in the archaeological record. This will include: (a) *rituals*, with particular emphasis on death and sacrifices in the Aztec civilization; and (b) *monuments*, with particular emphasis on the pyramids in the ancient Egyptian civilization, since these are processes and places where the dual interaction between humans and divinities took place, which recreated cosmos against the threat of chaos. Together, these case studies will illuminate the possibilities of a cosmogenic perspective in the archaeology of ritual and religion despite the difficulties with Eliade's structural universalism.

2 Cosmogony in Context

Leach argued once that 'myth implies ritual, ritual implies myth, they are one and the same' (Leach 1954: 13). Today, most researchers argue that the relationship is more complex, and that myths and rituals possess qualitatively different aspects (e.g. Bell 1992, 1997; Humphrey and Laidlaw 1994; Rappaport 2001). Following Alan Dundes, 'a myth is a sacred narrative explaining how the world and man came to be in their present form' (Dundes 1984: 1) and the creation myths give answers to the most profound human questions such as who are we, why are we here, what is the purpose of life and death, and how are humans placed in the world and cosmos in time and space? (Sproul 1979: 1). Although transcendental religions have cosmogenic myths, these do not define the ritual practice as they do in cosmogenic religions. According to Eliade, cosmogony is the dual recreation of the world and cosmos uniting micro- and macrocosmos. Thus, in cosmogenic religions the commemoration of the Creation is a re-actualization of the cosmogenic act in the rituals (Eliade 1987: 77) where 'cosmogony is the supreme divine manifestation' (Eliade 1987: 80). Cosmogony is an intimate process where humans ritually partake in the recreation of cosmos and the divinities recreate humans and the world. All creations of life, including humans, are processes in which all the forces of the universe partake, and consequently the regeneration of life and humans is also a recreation of cosmos. This approach to cosmos and the divinities has at least three consequences for an understanding of the function and importance of rituals.

First, rites are reproductions of the original creation but on a microcosmic scale. The creation of this world has the creation of the universe and the mythological beginning as its reference point. The consecration of a place is a repetition of the cosmogony and holy sites are therefore perceived as the centres of the world and temples as links between earth and heaven, but also connecting the lower realms to this world (Eliade 1987: 32–9). In the words of Eliade, 'every construction or fabrication has the cosmogony as paradigmatic model. The creation of the world becomes the archetype of every creative human gesture, whatever its plane of reference may be' (Eliade 1987: 45). Hence, every temple, holy place, or rituals which are constructed or conducted are repeating the original creation at a micro-scale and thereby humans unite and partake in the macro-cosmos. Consequently, every new town, house, temple or altar that is built stands at the 'centre of world' since these constructions involve rituals based on the original creation myth (Eliade 1993: 379), and through ritualization, these places and processes become the centre of the world—the *axis mundis* (Eliade 1987: 36–9).

Second, by 'participating ritually in the end of the world and its recreation, any . . . [man] was born anew, he began life over again with his reserve of vital forces intact, as it was at the moment of his birth' (Eliade 1987: 80). Almost all rituals include the mythological beginning and hence become cosmogenic, uniting humans with the divine spheres. Following this line of thought, life cannot be repaired, but only recreated through the symbolic repetition of the cosmogony (Eliade 1987: 82). '*The ritual makes creation over again*' (Eliade 1993: 346, original emphasis) and this is particularly seen in rites involving water ablutions. Water washes away sins and thereby purifies and gives new life to the devotee. The ritual use of water brings the devotee to 'that time' when the creation took place, but as soon as the ritual participants separate them from the water, 'every "form" loses its potentiality, falls under the law of time and of life; it is limited, enters history, shares in the universal law of change, decays, and would cease to be itself altogether were it not regenerated by being periodically immersed in the waters again' (Eliade 1993: 212). Thus, the rites are indefinite and the devotees have to conduct rituals continuously to retain their purity and spirituality as well as the proximity to the divine. With the repetition of the act of creation the sacrificer gets beyond the human state and becomes immortal by the creation ritual (Eliade 1993: 96).

Third, not only humans, but also the divinities and cosmos are dependent upon these cosmogenic myths because 'The cosmos as a whole is an organism at once real, living, and sacred' (Eliade 1987: 117). Since cosmos means, literally, ordered universe, the whole universe is interlinked and in equilibrium uniting microcosm to macrocosm through human ritual obligation. What humans do when they sin affects the cosmos since they are intimately related and indeed identical, and unless humans perform rituals there will be disequilibrium (Carrasco 1999: 184), which may even threaten the whole existence of cosmos as created by the divinities and 'by virtue of these paradigmatic models revealed to men in mythical times, the Cosmos and society are periodically regenerated' (Eliade 1954: xiv). Thus, there is a ritual reciprocity where the cosmic order created by the divinities depends upon the rituals performed: without humans' ritual engagements the divine order—cosmos—is brought into disequilibrium and deteriorates towards chaos. A cosmogenic religion prescribes certain and continuous rituals not only for the purity and the spirituality of the devotee who will be rewarded or penalized in another existence after death, but because the whole universal order depends on it, and this is an important difference between cosmogenic and transcendental religions.

3 CREMATION, CRITICISM, AND CONTRIBUTIONS

That 'every construction or fabrication has the cosmogony as paradigmatic model' (Eliade 1987: 45), uniting the regeneration of humans, the world, and cosmos through rituals, is in particular seen in Hindu cremations (Oestigaard 2005). Varanasi in India is not only a microcosm of the universe, but also a macrocosm of the body (Parry 1982: 356). Kashi (Varanasi) is the site of cosmic creation and the place where time began—it 'is both the origin-point and a microcosm of the universe; that it stands outside space and time yet all space is contained within it' (Parry 1994: 11). Death is a cosmic regeneration, and the most important cremation *ghat*—Manikarnika—is the place where the genesis of the universe occurred at the beginning of time and the place where the corpses will burn at the end of time (Parry 1994: 14). This process and place where the cosmos was created and where it will be destroyed is continuously repeated by the more than 40,000 cremations which are annually conducted (Figure 6.1). The cremation pyres burn day and night, and 'man is a replica of cosmos and is constituted by the five elements, and the life cycle and mode of thought are governed by the cosmic laws' (Prasad 1995: 99). Kashi is a microcosm of the universe and a macrocosm of the body and there is an 'equivalence between the cremation which destroys the microcosm of the physical body and the general conflagration which

FIGURE 6.1 Manikarnika Ghat in Varanasi by the River Ganges, India.

destroys the macrocosm at the end of time' (Parry 1994: 30). Cosmic dissolution and cremation are not only an end, but also a beginning and renewal of both the deceased who gain a new life and of cosmos itself, since 'the body is the cosmos the last rites become the symbolical equivalent of the destruction *and rejuvenation* of the universe' (Parry 1994: 31). Cremation is a sacrifice and on the cremation ground the creation is continuously repeated. Thus, in Varanasi time and the whole cosmos is regenerated in death by the body and the cremation rites, linking humans, gods, and cosmos through the cosmogenic event which is continuously repeated (Parry 1994: 31).

In Hindu thought, the cosmogenic model fits perfectly well, and herein lies some of the difficulties with Eliade's theories. Born in 1907, Eliade studied Sanskrit and Hindu philosophy at the University of Calcutta from 1928 to 1931 before he lived for six months in an ashram (hermitage). In 1933 he got his doctorate with the dissertation *Yoga: Essai sur les origines de la mystique indienne* (revised and published in English as *Yoga, Immortality, and Freedom* in 1958) and he was an assistant professor at the University of Bucharest from 1933 to 1939. Thus, his Hindu background has influenced the interpretations of other religions (Allen 1988: 550–1) and he emphasized non-historical universal structures rather than the historical and particular, which has been highly criticized particularly from the hermeneutical tradition (e.g. Altizer 1963; Allen 1978). Moreover, anthropologists, sociologists, and historians of religions have either ignored Eliade or simply dismissed his works, claiming that his method is uncritical, arbitrary, and subjective and hence his works cannot be taken seriously. His sweeping generalizations and universal structures are not historically falsifiable and his phenomenology is as normative as theology. Eliade's approach is, however, consistent in the way that his aim is to interpret transhistorical meaning and religious experiences making ontological claims about human nature and being as such (Allen 1988), although this is difficult within the history of religion as a human science. Eliade has, nevertheless, precisely emphasized the irreducible character of religious experience, and he has stressed that it is impossible to grasp the essence of religious experiences by means of physiology, psychology, sociology, etc. (Morris 1987: 176). Nevertheless, although one may be sympathetic to this position where one aims to understand religion on religious criteria only, 'to accept religion in its own terms is really to deny that it has any ideological function' (Morris 1987: 177) since all religious phenomena are historical and all data are conditioned and consequently religious phenomena cannot be understood outside of its 'history' (Allen 1988: 552).

A sympathetic reading of Eliade may reveal, however, new insights and knowledge of the past because, according to him, it is impossible to understand history except through imaginative recreations, and hence the method becomes 'essentially philosophical because it is concerned with essence, experience and meaning' (Berger 1986: 156). Both the reading and criticism of Eliade share some similar challenges with those surrounding interpretative archaeology. On the one hand, 'we [archaeologists] have to find our own path. The question that we need to consider is of interest outside archaeology, but the ethnographic evidence soon runs out. If they can be answered at all, it will be by archaeology alone' (Bradley 2000: 17), and archaeology has been described as science fiction because we are not simply studying the Other, but rather the *unknown*. Hence, it is possible to pursue an interpretative approach based on fictions rather than contemporary data (Fahlander 2001: 41). On the other hand, following Hodder, 'all archaeology is based on analogy and the process of analogical reasoning can be explicit or rigorous. But we cannot strictly test the analogies and hypotheses, which result from their use. Archaeologists cannot prove or falsify their hypotheses on independent data. All they can achieve is a demonstration that one hypothesis or analogy is better or worse than another, both theoretically and in relation to data' (Hodder 1982: 9). Thus, archaeology is situated in between the unknown past and known present, and this challenges our conceptions for interpretations of the past (Insoll 2007). Importantly, 'no matter how appetising some theories might appear on a meta-level, they are still useless if we cannot link them to the archaeological data' (Fahlander 2001: 11).

Hence, if a distinction is made between Eliade's theories as structural and universal explanations on the one hand, premises that have rightly been criticized, and on the other hand his theories as theoretical tools for analytical purposes, his concept of cosmogony can work as an ideal type or model for certain religious premises enabling one to gain new insights into the distant past. Therefore, the question is whether this approach to religion may contribute to other and better interpretations of the past than if one were to base one's understanding on transcendental religious or Christian prejudices. Cosmogony as a principle opens up entrances to the past since it puts the emphasis on rituals and practices which have direct material traces in the archaeological record. Death, in particular, is a dual interaction between humans and divinities where cosmos and society are recreated, and hence funerals and sacrifices as *rituals* and the construction of *monuments* unite micro- and macrocosmos through the cosmogenic myths.

4 Consuming Humans as Cosmogony

The difference between transcendental and cosmogony-centred religions is important because in transcendental religions the omnipotent god exists independent of his own creation. Consequently, sacrifice as a ritual practice has a minor ritual function in religions such as Judaism, Christianity, and Islam as opposed to cosmogenic religions where sacrifice has been one of the central features. In the early civilizations the main rationale for conducting sacrifices was to return the life-giving energy back to its divine sources and thus rejuvenate the power contrary to the rites in transcendental religions. 'In early civilizations, individual deities were not viewed as being sufficiently powerful to render them independent of human support... deities and humans were regarded as depending on each other' (Trigger 2003: 473). Sacrifice is a gift to the gods and is part of a process of exchange between gods and humans; and the logical limit of any sacrifical system, which gives it the fullest meaning, is the sacrifier's own death (Valeri 1985: 49, 62). Cosmogenically, a sacrifice is 'a religious rite in which an object is offered to a divinity in order to establish, maintain or restore a right relationship to the sacred order' (Faherty 1974: 128), and human sacrifices have been seen as the most precious offering which nourished the gods, and throughout Mesoamerica, sacrifice was seen as a form of debt repayment restoring the original harmony and balance in society and cosmos (Trigger 2003: 475–81).

Regarding the sacrifices in the Aztec cosmos (Figure 6.2), the life-giving and transformative processes necessitated that old things were destroyed and 'eaten' in order to create new things, which also included humans, as Read notes. 'Sacrifice was not just an act of destroying one thing to make another; it also was an act of eating one thing to create another, an act where living beings in this cosmos reciprocally feed each other'

FIGURE 6.2 The Aztec city Teotihuacán seen from the Moon Pyramid, Mexico. Photo: Rune Oestigaard.

(Read 1998: 134). This cosmogenic meal was a process where sacrificial bonds united death and the creation of further life. Cosmos was an ongoing and continuous production where 'transformative sacrificial acts destroy in order to create, but they also cause life-giving powers to flow' (Read 1998: 145). It was an interchange of powers between humans and non-humans (Read 1998: 147), and this had to be kept in equilibrium. 'When a child eats the substance that comes from the interior of the earth, the child ingests the weight and quality of death. All that comes from Earth Mother comes from the death that produces life. In this way, the life that is maintained at the cost of death has to be transformed into death', Carrasco argues, and 'if a human eats corn, he is required to pay his debt to the earth by giving his body when he dies. Throughout life, the human being is sinning on the earth, is building up a debt to the earth. This debt is disequilibrium, which must be paid or set back' (Carrasco 1999: 184).

Thus, it was commonly believed among the Aztecs that the gods were starved of life-giving forces, and therefore the divinities needed a continuous sacrificial cult where they were offered humans in order to sustain and maintain cosmos. Only through sacrifices could humans return the energy to the gods which the deities had given to the humans. Sacrifices of humans had therefore a rationale in the fact that flesh and blood were formed from corn and the sacrifical victims were referred to as 'tortillas for the gods' (Trigger 2003: 482–3). The human sacrifice was 'their response, and the only response that they could conceive, to the instability of a continually threatened world. Blood was necessary to save this world and the men in it' (Soustelle 2002: 99). The Aztec civilization, then, seems to have all the important characteristics of a cosmogenic religion and consequently, from an archaeology of religion point of view, cosmogony as a principle and process was not only the basis for the civilization, but one may also say that the Aztecs suffered a 'cosmic paranoia' where their striving for cosmic stability and security led to cultural and religious extremities (Carrasco 1999: 55).

5 Cosmogenic Constructions?

In ancient Egypt, as in all the other early civilizations, it was believed that the deities who had created the universe kept it functioning (Trigger 2003: 473). The mortuary cult in the Egyptian civilization has intrigued scholars and laymen from time immemorial, and the Great Pyramid in Giza is the only remainder of the ancient Seven Wonders of the World. The building of pyramids started at the beginning of the third Dynasty during the reign of Djoser (c.2650 BC). Sneferu, the first king of the fourth Dynasty (c.2625–2585 BC), was the greatest pyramid builder of all the pharaohs. He constructed four pyramids; the Bent and Red pyramids at Dashur, one in Meidum, and one in Seila. Together, these pyramids consist of 3.7 million cubic metres of stone (Verner 2003: 154), which together contained more cubic metres of stone than the Great Pyramid of his son Khufu (c.2585–2560 BC). Khufu's pyramid is the world's largest pyramid with an original height measuring 146.5 m (Figure 6.3). His successor Khafre (c.2555–2532 BC) built the second largest pyramid at Giza, and the third major pyramid in Giza was the smaller one built by Menkaure. The Old Kingdom lasted only a few centuries, but from this period 21 of the 23 major pyramids were built, standing within a 20 km stretch (Lehner 1997: 14–15). The ever-returning question of why the pyramids were built is not the focus here, but rather to highlight what a cosmogenic perspective may add to our knowledge of ancient Egyptian religion.

The Egyptian mortuary cult is exceptional in world history not only because of its size and monumentality, but also *when* the construction of the monuments took place. Contrary to most monuments of death, which are built by the descendants and the successors *after* death, the pharaohs had to build the monuments themselves while they were alive. On the one hand, one may argue that a pyramid like the one of Khufu, which is estimated to have been built by some 30,000 men (Verner 2003: 81), would have been more difficult to build by his descendents. On the other hand, the Taj Mahal in Agra in India was built over a 20-year period between c.1632–54 by the Mughal emperor Shah Jahan in memory of his deceased wife, Mumtaz Mahal, who died in 1631. It is estimated that some 20,000 workers were employed in the construction of the monument. Hence, it would have been possible for the descendants to build the pyramids, even such massive monuments as Khufu's and Khafre's pyramids, but this was not the case. Statues of pharaohs placed in temples or the ancient kings were occasionally worshipped for centuries after their death (Frankfort 1948: 55), but the overall cult put the emphasis on the pharaoh himself as an acting god. Menkaure died before he was able to complete his pyramid complex, and it was Shepseskaf who completed his father's complex in Giza, but the fact that he used mudbricks rather than stone indicates the great haste and probably reduced means he had to fulfill his duty (Verner 2003: 157–8), and there are numerous unfinished pyramids. Thus the pyramids had to be built continuously in the Old Kingdom, and this was the living pharaoh's religious obligation, not that of his successors.

FIGURE 6.3 Khufu's pyramid at Giza, Egypt.

There may be two main reasons for this in a cosmogenic perspective. First, it seems that it was the person who conducted the funeral for the late king who became the legitimate successor. This is seen in a unique scene in the burial chamber of Tutankhamun where the mummified king receives the last rites from his successor Ay, and this practice seems to have its origin in the cosmogenic myth of Osiris and Horus where Horus buried and avenged his father before he took his place as the ruler on earth (Dodson 2007: 81). Therefore, the pyramids needed to be completed when the funeral took place because otherwise the successor would not become a legitimate heir. Nevertheless, although the pharaohs' motto was 'to go beyond everything that was accomplished in the time of his predecessors' (Verner 2003: 24) and that 'ideology needs architecture for its fullest expression' (Kemp 2006: 248), there is a distinct difference if one builds the most magnificent monuments for the deceased king after his death or if the living pharaoh builds it for himself while being alive. Since the latter was the case, it may give testimony to a cosmogony where the world and cosmos had to be maintained *here and now* and not postponed for 20–30 years after a pharaoh's death.

Second, the Egyptian world order had continuously to be defended against the destructive forces of chaos, and it was only the pharaoh who could secure the divine order through rituals (Verner 2003: 22). Chaotic forces and disorder had to be controlled and tamed in order to maintain *maat* or the principle of law and order (Hornung 1982: 212–13). Building funerary monuments must therefore have had a religious and cosmogenical role in itself. The monuments were not only commemorative sepulchres, but materialized efforts to stabilize cosmos and secure welfare and prosperity through the mortuary cult. The pharaoh's power resided in him only as long as he was alive. The continuous pyramid-building in the Old Kingdom may therefore be seen as an extreme cosmogony or renewal of cosmos and rejuvenation of the pharaoh's power in his successor. Logically, since it seems that it was impossible for the successor to build the complete pyramid for the deceased king after his death, which is the usual practice in mortuary cults worldwide, it may indicate the pervasiveness of the belief and fear of cosmic threat and chaos; it was real and it was here and now. It was impossible to postpone the rituals or the funerary cult and everything had to be completed before the living pharaoh died. Thus, if Aztecs suffered a 'cosmic paranoia', one may equally label the Old Kingdom in the same way. Traditionally, the Old Kingdom has been seen as a period of stability and later changes as reflecting religious uncertainty or crises (e.g. Malek 2000: 97), but there is no correspondence between the belief in cosmic stability and actual political stability (Trigger 2003: 471). From a cosmogenic point of view, the fact that *each of the pharaohs had to build their own pyramid while they still were living*, indicates a cosmogony where literally all forces in the world and cosmos had to be employed at all times to secure the divine balance of law and order—*maat*.

6 Conclusion

Cosmogony as a religious theory and principle puts the emphasis on ritual dynamics and the dramatic importance of conducting rites when the cosmos is threatened by chaos. As a conceptual perspective, particularly in studies of early civilizations, cosmogony is an analytical tool for better understanding parts of the historic, religious processes which were at work. However, due to the heavy influence of Eliade and his works, a cosmogenic approach has its pitfalls. Although Eliade emphasized that a comparative approach is necessary in order to grasp 'the essence and the structure of religious phenomena' (Eliade 1959a: 177), the problem is that the empirical data has shown more variation than Eliade incorporated in his theories (Trigger 2003: 470–1). Moreover, when Eliade claims that the only function of myths is to create a sacred cosmos from the primordial chaos, and that all rituals are repetitions of the cosmogenic myths, he gives these structural patterns a privileged ontological status and denies that religion can be understood on other premises in terms of social, cultural, or psychological factors (Morris 1987: 181). This was in fact Eliade's project since, according to him, religious experience is always existential: 'Understanding is ecstatic and contemplative, not reductionist and analytical. Understanding is given to us, from somewhere within ourselves or from the outside, but it is not known through thinking' (Berger 1986: 151). Such a position is perhaps right from a religious point of view, but it makes religious studies difficult if not impossible.

Hence, one may say that much of the criticism of Eliade is based on his premises and not necessarily on his ideas as interpretive perspectives. The belief in universal structures was commonly held in anthropology in the 1950s, and from the 1960s in archaeology. Therefore, although 'cosmogony' is closely related to Eliade and his works, one must not dismiss it out of hand just because it was written by Eliade. Cosmogony as an analytical concept opens up new perspectives for understanding prehistoric religions. The alternative will often be to analyse religious phenomena on static, transcendental, or Christian religious terms and premises, which hinder an understanding of the function of rituals in maintaining cosmos. It is precisely because of this that a cosmogenic perspective is important in archaeological interpretation; but, as with all theory, it should be used as an entrance to gain new knowledge and not as a dogma where one religious pattern is used statically in all prehistoric societies regardless of time and space. The usefulness of cosmogony is therefore that it highlights the active and dynamic ritual processes thus stressing that it is necessary to conduct meticulous empirical analyses in order to understand how cosmogony as a process may have worked.

Suggested Reading

CARRASCO, D. 1999. *City of Sacrifice: The Aztec Empire and the role of violence in civilization* (Boston: Beacon Press).
ELIADE, M. 1954. *The Myth of the Eternal Return* (New York: Pantheon Books).
—— 1959 [1987]. *The Sacred and Profane: The nature of religion* (New York: Harcourt Brace).
OESTIGAARD, T. 2005. *Death and Life-Giving Waters: Cremation, caste, and cosmogony in karmic traditions*, BAR International Series 1353 (Oxford: BAR).
PARRY, J. 1994. *Death in Banaras*, The Lewis Henry Morgan Lectures 1988 (Cambridge: Cambridge University Press).
TRIGGER, B. 2003. *Understanding Early Civilizations: A comparative study* (Cambridge: Cambridge University Press).
VALERI, V. 1985. *Kingship and Sacrifice: Ritual and society in ancient Hawaii* (Chicago: The University Press of Chicago).

References

ALLEN, D. 1978. *Structure and Creativity in Religion* (The Hague: Mouton).
—— 1988. 'Eliade and history', *The Journal of Religion*, 68(4): 545–65.
ALTIZER, T. J. J. 1963. *Mircea Eliade and the Dialectic of the Sacred* (Philadelphia: Westminster Press).
BELL, C. 1992. *Ritual Theory, Ritual Practice* (Oxford: Oxford University Press).
—— 1997. *Ritual: Perspectives and dimensions* (Oxford: Oxford University Press).
BERGER, A. 1986. 'Cultural hermeneutics: The concept of imagination in the phenomenological approaches of Henry Corbin and Mircea Eliade', *The Journal of Religion*, 66(2): 141–56.
BRADLEY, R. 2000. *An Archaeology of Natural Places* (London and New York: Routledge).
CARRASCO, D. 1999. *City of Sacrifice: The Aztec Empire and the role of violence in civilization* (Boston: Beacon Press).
DODSON, A. M. 2007. 'The monarchy' in T. Wilkinson (ed.), *The Egyptian World* (London: Routledge), pp. 75–90.

DUNDES, A. 1984. 'Introduction' in A. Dundes (ed.), *Sacred Narrative* (Berkeley: University of California Press), pp. 1–3.
ELIADE, M. 1954. *The Myth of the Eternal return* (New York: Pantheon Books).
—— 1958. *Yoga: Immortality and freedom*, Bollingen Series LVI (New York: Pantheon Books).
—— 1959a [1987]. *The Sacred and Profane: The nature of religion* (New York: Harcourt Brace).
—— 1959b. 'Methodological remarks on the study of religious symbolism' in M. Eliade and J. M. Kitagawa (eds), *The History of Religions* (Chicago: University of Chicago Press), pp. 86–107.
—— 1993. *Patterns in Comparative Religion* (London: Sheed and Ward Ltd).
FAHERTY, R. L. 1974. 'Sacrifice' in *The New Encyclopaedia Britannica*, 15th edn, *Macropaedia*, XVI: 128–35.
FAHLANDER, F. 2001. *Archaeology as Science Fiction: A microarchaeology of the unknown*, Gotarc Serie C No. 43 (Göteborg).
FRANKFORT, H. 1948. *Kingship and the Gods: A study of ancient Near Eastern religion as the integration of society & nature* (Chicago: The University of Chicago Press).
HODDER, I. 1982. *The Present Past* (Cambridge: Cambridge University Press).
HORNUNG, E. 1982. *Conceptions of God in Ancient Egypt: The one and the many*, trans. John Baines (New York: Cornell University Press).
HUMPHREY, C. and LAIDLAW, J. 1994. *The Archetypal Actions of Ritual* (Oxford: Clarendon Press).
KEMP, B. 2006. *Ancient Egypt: Anatomy of a civilization*, 2nd edn (London: Routledge).
LEHNER, M. 1997. *The Complete Pyramids* (London: Thames and Hudson).
LONG, C. 1993. 'Cosmogony' in M. Eliade (ed.), The *Encyclopedia of Religion*, III (New York: Macmillian Publishing Company), pp. 94–100.
INSOLL, T. 2007. *Archaeology: The conceptual challenge* (London: Duckworth).
MALEK, J. 2000. 'The Old Kingdom (c.2686–2160 BC)' in I. Shaw (ed.), *The Oxford History of Ancient Egypt* (Oxford: Oxford University Press), pp. 89–117.
MORRIS, B. 1987. *Anthropological Studies of Religion: An introduction* (Cambridge: Cambridge University Press).
OESTIGAARD, T. 2005. *Death and Life-Giving Waters: Cremation, caste, and cosmogony in karmic traditions*, BAR International Series 1353 (Oxford: BAR).
PARRY, J. 1982. 'Death and cosmogony in Kashi' in T. N. Madan (ed.), *Way of Life: King, householder, renouncer: Essays in honour of Louis Dumont* (New Delhi: Vikas Publishing House Pvt Ltd), pp. 337–65.
—— 1994. *Death in Banaras*, The Lewis Henry Morgan Lectures 1988 (Cambridge: Cambridge University Press).
PRASAD, O. 1995. 'Primal elements in the Santhal musical texts' in K. Vatsyayan and B. Saraswati (eds), *Prakrti: The integral vision*, I: *Primal Elements: The oral tradition* (New Delhi: Indira Gandhi National Centre for the Arts), pp. 99–118.
RAPPAPORT, R. A. 2001. *Ritual and Religion in the Making of Humanity* (Cambridge: Cambridge University Press).
READ, K. A. 1998. *Time and Sacrifice in the Aztec Cosmos* (Bloomington: Indiana University Press).
SOUSTELLE, J. 2002. *Daily Life of the Aztecs* (New York: Dover Publications, Inc).
SPROUL, B. C. 1979. *Primal Myths: Creation myths around the world* (New York: HarperCollins Publishers).

TRIGGER, B. 2003. *Understanding Early Civilizations: A comparative study* (Cambridge: Cambridge University Press).
VALERI, V. 1985. *Kingship and Sacrifice: Ritual and society in ancient Hawaii* (Chicago: The University Press of Chicago).
VERNER, M. 2003. *The Pyramids: Their archaeology and history* (London: Atlantic Books).

CHAPTER 7

DEATH

TIMOTHY TAYLOR

1 Introduction

THERE can be no clearer a priori demonstration of ritual in past societies than the archaeological uncovery of a formal human burial. Despite considerable variation in incidence and manner, it has been found in many places and times, and appears to have emerged as a standardized routine independently on more than one occasion. Certain structured coincidences, notably the use of what are termed grave goods, and the widespread adoption of particular recurrent postures and orientations of skeletal remains and/or tombs, have led scholars to infer the existence of religious beliefs about another place. This place might be indicated by, for example, the direction of the setting sun; to reach the place, a journey must be undertaken for which the deceased will require material provisions. But burial is by no means the only intersect between death and archaeology within the framework of ritual and religion, nor (as we shall discuss later) is it a *sine qua non* for the existence of the latter.

Archaeologists' duties to the dead may be conceived of universally, and/or be subdefined by real or perceived special relationships (for example, known or projected ancestral ties). In terms of actions undertaken in the treatment of the dead, we may often be able to distinguish between coherent systems of belief by which people live and die, and ritual practice, which may be common to a wide range of communally shared or privately held beliefs (including no belief at all). The uncovery and return of the dead can thus at least appear as a material event that in its symbolism cross-cuts the avowed justifications of specific cases and individual, inner motivations.

Archaeological treatments of death in relation to belief divide sharply between those that deal with historical periods (as is the case with world religions' contexts: Insoll 2001) and those that are prehistoric. In the case of the first, it is assumed that the critical information on specific aspects of belief is known (as in the cases of Roman, Egyptian, imperial Chinese, and American colonial archaeologies of death); in the second case, there is— typically—a recourse to parallels from the anthropology of 'primitive' societies (see Parker Pearson 1999: ch. 2), that is, those non-state-level, and frequently non-agricultural societies, already reflexively categorized as 'earlier' in historically abstracted schemes of universal development (although the extent to which any such division can be maintained is debatable: Taylor 2008b).

It is clear then that relationships between the categories potentially covered by the term 'death', and the archaeology of ritual and religion are complex and potentially confusing. Shanks and Tilley (1992) described archaeology as facing a 'fourfold hermeneutic' (cf. Embree 1987), wherein archaeologists must first work interpretatively through the filters of their own sociological position (the double hermeneutic), then the sociocultural anthropological confrontation of the 'Other', which adds a further level of difficulty, to finally attempt to bridge the radical disjuncture of time involved in the study of an alien culture that no longer exists. To this complexity we must add the peculiar difficulties of the science–religion relationship. Ritual and religion raise complex definitional issues, with no final agreement in sight, except insofar as there is an emergent view that truly universal features are lacking (it can hardly be called a consensus, as many of these authors fail to consider each other's arguments; see James 1902; Kerr 1986; Harrison 1991; Clarke and Byrne 1993; Boyer 1994; Pals 1995; Whitehouse and Laidlaw 2004; Csapo 2005). This complicates the double hermeneutic and may allow projections that claim (however spuriously) to short-circuit the other levels, for example by claiming rights for the prehistoric dead beyond that of the Enlightenment duty of truth (the sole surviving duty, according to Voltaire) that is most easily assented to as consonant with the project of developing an objective discipline.

Death, obviously, is a broader subject within the archaeology of ritual and religion than recognizable funerary rites. The intersect between death and belief has resulted in many of the most significant surviving ancient finds, sites, and monuments, such as the bog bodies of North-western Europe, the Shanidar Neanderthal interments, the pyramids of Egypt, and the tombs of Queen Puabi and of the first emperor of China. We know iconographies of death, and of gods, including gods of death. Additionally, many significant ritual sites have a death-related aspect, as loci of human killing and the deposition of remains (causewayed camps, central European *Kreisgrabenanlagen*, the Aztec temples) while others were designed for ritualized activities that, though not primarily describable as religious, adumbrated a cosmology of life and death (the Roman Colosseum); in addition to discrete monuments which embody aspects of the religion–death nexus, we may also be able to identify broader landscapes. There are many difficulties in identifying ritual behaviours through discoverable surviving material and the patterning it may preserve, but it is perhaps no more problematic than any other area of archaeological inference (*pace* Whitley 2008: 552).

2 THE ANTHROPOLOGY AND SOCIOLOGY OF DEATH

As early as the fifth century BC it was possible to reflect ethnographically on differences in funerary rites as these related to deeply held beliefs about identity and propriety, as in Herodotus' description of the horror felt by two different cultures, one practising cremation and the other endo-funerary cannibalism, in the face of inducements to switch customs with one another (Hdt 3.38 and see discussion in Taylor 2002 : 83 f.). Herodotus' conclusion, essentially that human behaviour was contingent on inherited norms that could vary greatly, was to be underlined by Victorian ethnographers, such as Radcliffe Brown, W. H. R. Rivers and Sir James Frazer, who revealed an extraordinary global diversity in indigenous religious beliefs in relation to death practices. Death had a special place in the first sociological formulation of religion by Durkheim; in recent scholarship, a specific, specialized sociology of death has emerged (Clark 1993; Seale 1998) and, arguably, the broad perspective pioneered by Durkheim has been lost. As we shall see, something similar may be true in relation to 'funerary archaeology' (see below).

Durkheim frequently insisted on a structuring distinction of sacred and profane (Durkheim 2001; Fields 2001). Where these states for Durkheim are typically exclusive, defined by their set-apartness from one another, the human corpse can bring these states into a dynamic juxtaposition, being at once an object of reverence and horror, purity and corruption: for aboriginal Australian funerary rites Durkheim believed the corpse switched its sacred polarity from malevolent to beneficial during the course of the ceremony (eventually becoming profane and ordinary—a point we shall return to). Although the sacred–profane distinction 'just does not pass the test of crosscultural comparisons' (Boyer 1994: 46), the idea of sequence was to prove fertile: the idea of death as a punctuated event, with physical death (usually) preceding social death in a process choreographed in order to give meaning to status transitions more broadly, was investigated in the social anthropology of the early years of the twentieth century.

Two major attempts to synthesize and schematize the observed variance were those of Hertz (1907) and van Gennep (1960 [1908]). Hertz made important distinctions between three different sorts of human anxieties: horror of death as an event, the shock of any particular death, and fear of the dead. The first is to do with the body being rendered extraordinary and so leaving the realm of normal objects; the second relates to the rip that death makes in the social fabric, large and requiring significant repair in the case of a leader, small and possibly wholly insignificant in the case of the loss of a slave or an illegitimate child; the last is a fear of disembodied souls—entities with a potential for powerful malevolence irrespective of previous life status. Hertz argued that the nature and scale of funerary rites in all societies will vary depending on these factors, which condition the relations between the living mourners, the dead body, and the disembodied soul.

Van Gennep also argued for a universal structure in terms of the tripartite structuring of rites of passage by which individuals leave particular social statuses and are accorded new ones. His schema was to apply equally to births, deaths, and marriages and consisted of: preliminary rites of separation, when an original or old status was stripped away; liminal rites in which a transition occurred and the individual, by virtue of their statuslessness, was taboo and ritually contagious; and postliminal rites of incorporation. For the dead, van Gennep argued that primary funerary rites (corpse washing, preliminary burial, or sequestering of the corpse) led into a dangerous liminal phase where the disembodied soul would typically seek to reanimate the mortal remains, and that this danger would only lift once a secondary burial, pyre-burning, ritual ingestion, or other act was complete and so signalled the acceptance of the soul into a social world of ancestors with no possible return.

In practical terms, both Hertz and van Gennep manage to make more sense of the funerary rites accorded to socially powerful individuals than those of ordinary folk. Hertz seemed aware of this in his famous observation that 'at the death of a chief... a true panic sweeps over the group [while] the death of a stranger, a slave or a child will go almost unnoticed' (1960: 76). Obviously the death of a person in a socially pivotal position demands an orderly period of transition, in which the complexities attending a social death (issues of inheritance, succession, lineage, and so on) may be managed in a period and the authority of the deceased be maintained through elaborate and costly ritual routines. But to what extent is the apparently religious manifestation not a functional economic means for bolstering certain forms of structured inequality? Is not the hierarchization of individuals in death, under the emotional charge of some level of collective grief, not the ideal way to establish and maintain the concept of hierarchy itself? Indeed, Hocart argued that 'the first kings must have been dead kings', implying that only through the power of funerary ritual could such an absolute status be instantiated in early states (Hocart 1927; cf. the discussion in Metcalf and Huntington 1991: ch. 7, and Button 2007 for an archaeological example of this in action).

An extensive body of work exists on the death–religion nexus in sociology, philosophy, social anthropology, theology, and art history. It is too great to even fairly review here, but certain central elements should be noted. While Martin Heidegger observed that 'no one can take the Other's dying away from him' (Heidegger 1962: 284), it is also clear that the dying are ultimately deprived of their own death (as noted by Oestigaard 2004: 7), the paradoxes thereby entailed being the subject of a major philosophical study, *The Gift of Death* (Derrida 1995). Derrida nuances Heidegger's idea of authenticity as situated in acceptance of the inevitability of personal mortality, by arguing that the possibilities of moral and ethical responsibility are uniquely underpinned by such acceptance. Following Patočka, Derrida appears to distinguish fundamentally different types of religion in light of their engagement with death. For archaeologists, and especially prehistorians, this signals caution: death in world religions, and particularly in the Abrahamic tradition, at once deeply conditions modern secular metaphysics (notably, though not only, through linguistic constraint in itself) while presenting a marked, often fundamental contrast, with death concepts in non-world (a.k.a. pagan-, tribal- or primitive-) religions. These, which from a central European Christian perspective, Patočka (1990) characterizes as embodying forms of what he terms 'demonic sacralization' (notably devoid of such refined and historically derived concepts as personal responsibility, freely conceived and undertaken: see also Paul Ricoeur's introduction to Erica Abram's 1990 translation of Patočka into French), might well include the concepta, and preconceptions, of prehistoric social formations. The distinction between primitive (superstitious) modes of thinking about religion and civilized (rational) ones was also developed by Gellner (1988: although he probably underestimated the extent to which modern populations en masse had been bypassed by Enlightenment niceties).

If the existence of formally deposited human remains holds a central place in our reactions to our ancestors, it does so not only for us as members of a community of scholars but also as members of broader present societies. Death for archaeologists is a social category twice over, involving, first, the reconstruction of the conceptions of death and the dead in past communities and, second (and not necessarily), the recognition that these past communities constitute a greater category of 'the dead' to whom archaeologists undertake specific duties. These duties include a duty of truth not only in reconstructing the first category in specific cases, but in using the dead, their belongings, and detritus to uncover all possible aspects of past lifeways. They are often also perceived as extending beyond what might be dispassionately warranted by objective scientific study, and cross over explicitly into politics, ethnicity, and specific kinds of religiously underpinned reverence, as in the various contemporary 'reburial' debates. In this there are great dangers.

As noted above, W. H. R. Rivers was one of the first to note that the idea of death appears more variable than might be expected (see Metcalf and Huntington 1991: 6); indeed, as Needham was later to point out (see e.g. 1985), despite the apparent universality of the phenomenon from outside, conceptions of it and its attendant (or non-attendant) customs and symbols are far more varied, cross-culturally, than those of our shared life-processes (birth, sexual maturity, parenthood, changes in status vis-à-vis one another, and so on), which he considered relatively predictable (see also Bloch and Parry 1982). This was hardly surprising as death's contents are essentially invisible (Needham 1967; see useful discussion in Metcalf and Huntington 1991: 62 ff.). And, if this has been true of the broad present of ethnographic documentation, how much more variance must we expect in archaeological contexts and in a survey of global prehistory?

3 FUNERARY ARCHAEOLOGY

The issue of archaeological visibility in relation to death is particularly problematic. The category is often addressed obliquely, via what seems the most materially data-rich category (thus, in *The Oxford Companion to Archaeology*, death is discussed under the heading of 'Burial and tombs', and funerary archaeology considered as a subset of 'Religion': Fagan 1996: 109 f. and 590 ff.; entries by Diane Chase and Chris Scarre respectively). As with the sociology of death, funerary archaeology, since a seminal paper by Peter Ucko in 1969, has become something of a specialized subset of archaeological theory and practice (Ucko 1969; Chapman, Kinnes and Randsborg 1981; O'Shea 1984; Beck 1995; Parker Pearson 1999; Lucy 2000). Such works outline the basic processual and post-processual approaches taken to the cultural elaboration of death in past societies and investigate the visibility or otherwise of the scale of funerary rites within different contextual frameworks and touch on some unresolved issues in mortuary archaeology. Several of them reveal how an over-focus on settings (such as 'tombs' or 'cemeteries') may risk ignoring key aspects of total religious systems, at (e.g.) artefact- and landscape-level.

As we noted at the outset, the most direct archaeological evidence of ritual and religion is the context of human burial as a mortuary rite (or as part of one). Put another way, the possession of a corpse by a community becomes a pretext for ritual action, focused on death but typically ramified through symbolism to include ideas of social renewal and regeneration, the perpetuation of a cosmic order, and so on (and, as we shall see in the next section, this can be inverted, with the necessity of such symbolic ritual providing the pretext for death). The iconography, iconology, and symbolism of death can also be considered here in making some general points about cognitive development and cultural evolution over the long term as witnessed by the archaeology of death-related behaviours (in particular, issues such as the earliest evidence for ritual and the emergence of culturally elaborated, death-related behaviours and potential correspondences between art and human remains).

Two million years ago, a freshly dead australopithecine (Sterkfontein Stw 53) was butchered, the jaw cut away with a stone knife; 600,000 years ago at Bodo, Ethiopia, a cranium of early archaic Homo sapiens was intentionally defleshed; and the 800,000-year-old cannibalized remains of ten Homo antecessor individuals have been preserved at Atapuerca, Spain (Taylor 2002). Each of these acts was similarly aggressive. Although all had at least the potential to be *memento mori*, we must conclude that the normal fate of the dead in these early periods was some form of reabsorption by living systems (formally analogous with, though cognitively different from, modern Zoroastrian funerary custom, exposure, or ritual funerary cannibalism). If the dead were beautiful, the aesthetic experience would have been transitory and gustatory (Taylor 2009).

Interment, when it first appears, is thus a puzzling phenomenon among dedicated survivalists. Anatomically modern humans in the Levant were placed in caves 120,000 years ago, with pigs' jaws and burnt flint tools; 60,000 years ago at Shanidar (Iraq), a Neanderthal was perhaps buried with a garland—the 'grave of flowers'; and by 25,000 years ago elaborate burials of adults and children occur, with hundreds of drilled sea-shell beads and deer-antler tools. At Dolní Vestoniče (Czech Republic), a triple burial dating to 26,600 years ago contains two males posed to either side of a female who suffered from a congenital pelvic deformity and who could not have borne children. The hand of one of the males reaches between the female's legs, where a flint blade was placed; this zone was covered, like the heads of all three, with red ochre. Another triple burial from this time comes from Barme Grande (Italy), while double burials are known from the 'Grotte des Enfants' (France), Sungir (Russia), and Romito (Italy). The latter is the burial of a chondrodystrophic dwarf accompanied by an incredibly short woman. Perhaps the dwarf's mother, she and the disabled Dolní Vestoniče girl belong to an underrepresented group—females (75% of sexed Upper Palaeolithic remains are male: Pettitt 2011, table 6.1–2).

So only a carefully selected subset of people received 'burial', whether it was an honour or a reflex of fear. The multiple inhumations, the typical absence of obvious proximal causes of death, the elaborate poses, even the excess of decorative ornaments (literally thousands of ivory beads draping the corpses at Sungir) are consonant with ritual killing. These unusual individuals may perhaps have been excluded from reabsorption, and surrounded by magical talismans, to keep them quiet in death or to create enduring physical tableaux in the mind. Seen as a form of installation art, these bodies connect with the famous part-naked, part-adorned, large-breasted Venus figurines, carved in ivory (Taylor 2006; 2008c).

We might speculate that undying images of fertile women juxtaposed with the carefully posed, perhaps socially aberrant, skeletons lying in shallow graves, projected positive and negative ideals of beauty, the most attractive physical aspirations and the basest category transgressions. This, the first concrete aesthetic of mortality, was born of existential crisis. In the *via negativa* of these two kinds of aestheticized body, warm flesh represented by cold carved bone, and dry human bone representing the absence of moisture and softness, a conception of the soul was formed. Immortality and mortality arose together, intertwined through practice.

Not until the advent of farming, within the last 10,000 years, do we have anything like a fair reflection of a living community in what can properly be termed a necropolis. This deliberate seeding of the earth with the bones of the dead was then done for recognizably territorial reasons, using the creation of set-aside sacred space to build political entities and the resource base needed for their survival. It is no surprise that the startling image of the dead qua art object fades away at this point, to be replaced by a wealth of fancy grave goods and an often kitsch monumentality.

Where burial emerged as a ritual option it was inevitably associable with a wide range of interlaced practical and symbolic ideas, from the sequestering of corpses from scavengers and enemies (hygiene; purity) through to constructions related to territoriality and land-ownership (essentially 'caching' the dead in cemetery resources). But what also seems clear is that in the vast majority of archaeologically known cultures a range of practices arose rather than one stable template for all the deceased members of a community. In India, China, and Europe, earlier prehistoric interments may be of animals, while it is unclear that all humans were buried. In later prehistoric contexts, practices such as inhumation exist alongside cremation in many societies, with hints at less formal disposal methods for lower social strata. This has caused archaeologists many interpretive problems on the assumption that the perceived patterning must be due to overarching religious views in relation to death being expressed in a coherent way, but also subject to drift or change as religious conceptions changed for whatever internal or external reasons. But it may be that it is often a mistake to attempt to 'read' the patterns for any particular archaeological culture as reflective of a unitary religious practice.

Of the Roman Empire, where we have detailed descriptions of the forms beliefs took, Jones notes that it is not possible to argue that 'specific religions required specific funerary practices' (Jones 1987: 816). Further, from the standpoint of cognitive anthropology, Boyer (1994: 41) warns that:

> the overall consistency of people's representations about religious matters should not be taken for granted... the ancestor cult with its rituals... may well be largely independent from the ideas about witchcraft and magical capacities; although these 'systems' are likely to converge, if only because they coexist in people's minds, it would be absurd to take them a priori as an integrated worldview.

A good example might be the European 'bog body' phenomenon, which stretches from the Bronze Age through to the early medieval period with remarkable coherence when set against a variety of changing 'standard' funerary practices (Taylor 2002). This can be seen clearly in the case of Meso- and South American religious beliefs, among the Aztec, Maya, and Inca, for example, where both 'the dead' and death were used in a wide range of ways (Wilson et al. 2007; Tiesler and Cucina 2007; Arnold and Hasdorf 2008).

It is also questionable whether practices coherently 'reflect' beliefs at all; Falco Daim has drawn attention to the way in which ethnicity in early medieval Europe was constructed through funerary practices that were not necessarily taken at 'face value' (i.e. really providing for the deceased in another world: Daim 1998 and pers. comm.). This can provide one account for the relatively frequent occurrence of non-functional, proxy, or skeuo-morphic (dissembling) grave-goods, and echoes with Boyer's subsequent suggestion that scepticism concerning the basic tenets of religions, far from being insignificant 'noise', may in fact provide insights into the acquisition and fixation of beliefs (Boyer 1994: 41).

To summarize briefly here, it seems necessary that archaeologists at once try to apprehend internal (emic) understandings of death-related behaviours in connection to religion while at the same time appreciating the external, universal, or overarching effects and affordances of particular practices in terms of their ability to generate collective representations, facilitate social control, and actively create ethnic, status or gender affiliation. Because of such complexities, it is desirable that practitioners establish plausible constraints on analysis and interpretation in relation to contexts while keeping an open mind concerning what such contexts might be (*pace* Wylie 2002).

4 Identity, Exclusion, and Viscerality

This section examines physical death outside the valedictory and funerary contexts (ritual killing, human sacrifice, endo- and exo-cannibalism, etc.), indicating the importance of advancing knowledge claims antagonistic to the prevailing sociological paradigm. Child sacrifice here provides one example.

It is probably safe to say that whatever metaphysical categories for 'the dead' exist and have existed in human societies, they are only ever subsets connected to the totality of human lives and lived experiences. That is to say, the dead belong to one or more social categories, and society is as frequently defined by exclusion as incorporation—processes often primarily managed through religious practice and understood through the filters of belief. An example, contemporary but with more general (pre)historical relevance, is the 'pro-choice'/'pro-life' debate. Here, whether abortion constitutes murder of a person, and thus the production of an incorporeal soul that must be accomodated somewhere in death (as, for example, in the *limbus infantorum*), depends on when a person is deemed first to have been present. While, for the Catholic Church, the incarnation of an immortal soul is considered to occur at conception, in many societies studied by social anthropologists, a new person enters society well after parturition, often when the baby's chances of growing at least into a useful, contributory social role have been judged as good. Thus, we can see that even the apparently objective and scientific category of biological death is inevitably framed at some point ethically, morally, and spiritually. A series of initiations marks both first entry into society (typically an act of naming) and movement through its statuses, as well as physically manifesting (emically speaking) the, often gradual, establishment of what we translate as soul (though soul concepts themselves may be multiple, as in ancient Egypt).

It can be immediately perceived from the foregoing that behaviours around biological death may vary greatly within an ongoing cultural community in line with what category of being is thought to have died, and in what manner death happened. We must thus not forget the issue of the non-valorized dead, such as neonates, unrecovered war dead, and others whose typical absence from the funerary record may be sensibly inferred (sometimes from other types of material evidence, such as carvings of battle scenes). Chattel slaves, for example, being never socially alive to the enslaving community, may receive no religiously choreographed funerary rite at all (Taylor 2005). Conversely, what we may initially understand as the funerals of kings, queens, pharaohs, and so on, may be better understood as further stages in social initiation in which a secular ruler became, though a process only tangentially including what we would understand as biological death, an eternal god. According to the statuses ascribed to different beings, religious rites accorded to members of a given society may thus exclude some humans while including some apparent non-humans, such as pets, divine and totemic animals, and even inanimate objects (thus some artefact 'biographies' may have terminated in artefact death).

Archaeologists, especially prehistorians, have always to take into consideration what Margaret Masterman termed the sociological paradigm (Masterman 1970; Taylor 2007), broadly the background sociological assumptions, current among any community of academics by virtue of their belonging to a broader society, bearing on expectations of plausible behaviour. It is, for example, becoming increasingly likely, through work such as that of the Stonehenge Riverside Project, that the ceremonial landscape around Stonehenge was a ritual landscape of and for the dead (Parker Pearson and Ramilisonina 1998), and perhaps even, following the distinction made by Hertz, for rituals of death; such an explanatory possibility has been available ever since Maud Cunnington excavated an infant skeleton, its skull neatly split in two with a stone axe, at the centre of Woodhenge (Cunnington as cited in Taylor 2002: 276). That past (specifically pre-Christian and pre-Islamic) religions might include child sacrifice is made clear enough in the Old Testament, where the pattern for the Cult of Molek was of roasting first-born boys and or girls in a topeth (or roaster) outside Jerusalem; Biblical child sacrifice passages are mainly pretty literal injunctions not to do such things and it is very doubtful that coherent arguments for symbolic or euphemistic understandings can be made (Oesterley 1937, Bremmer 2007; see Leviticus 18.21; 20.2; 1 Kings 3.27; 2 Kings 16.3; 23.10; Jeremiah 3.24; 7.31; 19.5; 32.35; Deuteronomy 12.31; Ezekiel 23.39).

5 Materiality Approaches and Evolutionary Aspects

In *The Varieties of Religious Experience*, William James stressed the primacy of immediate feeling over logical exposition in religious belief; Wittgenstein, while influenced by this idea, takes a further step to argue that it is action that is foundational, echoing an earlier observation by Marrett (Kerr 1986: 158, 183; Taylor 2002: 307). Ritual, on this view, is just done; Boyer, in approving of Fortes' judgement that 'it is a short step from the notion of ritual as communication to the non-existence of ritual *per se*' (Fortes 1966; Boyer 1994: 190), is sensitive to the very same point (although in then claiming its absence from 'anthropological literature', he fails to mention the earlier thinkers). In any case, it is not hard to see how material actions—the things archaeologists may be able to track by their residues and deposits—may prompt beliefs to arise that may then provide *post factum* justification for what has been done.

Arguments for the cognitive emergence of *Homo sapiens* often rests on the interpretation of the earliest human burials on the assumption that these, if correctly identified, imply minds complex enough for the idea of a religiously conceived 'beyond'; these often conflate four things, viz. (i) the emergence by whatever means of religion; (ii) the increasing emotional impact of death with increased intelligence (as pining becomes concrete bereavement and is then formalized by mourning); (iii) specific treatment patterns for corpses, some of which may be, more or less accidentally, more archaeologically visible; (iv) some belief in souls.

Death marks the point where active human subjects become objects whose volition is *de facto* absent, but whose wishes may remain potent projections in the minds of those left alive, in whatever relation to the deceased. In a way, death produces in the human body a reduced object, that is thereby analogous to a human being but is not it. This insight was made by Levi-Strauss (1985) in relation to all art objects, and in special connection to masks. The mask-building transformation of prehistoric treatments of the dead, not just the ochre crusts of the Middle Upper Palaeolithic in Europe, but the clay-covered cowrie-eyed Jericho skulls, and the Chalcolithic 'cenotaph' graves of Varna, all suggest an impulse to aestheticize death, not in a trivial 'prettying-up' fashion, but in a profound religious sense of making a physical commentary on mortality, memory, and identity.

If we have this knowledge now, when did we not have it? Did it simply occur when a certain modern human cognitive threshold was passed? Perhaps we avoided the reality even as it first revealed itself, adopting it in performance and countering it in figurative art. The common assumption that knowledge of mortality inevitably arose past a certain stage in encephalization rests on questionable foundations (Parker Pearson 1999: 164; Taylor 2002). Personal mortality is an idea that requires inculcation (for instance, children often believe that death may be a reversible process). The fact that some living things, including some members of an on-going community, are known to have died, does not lead to any straightforward conclusion concerning mortality as a universal condition. In band-level societies, such as those presumed to have uniformly characterized the period from the emergence of our genus a little before 2 million years ago to some 10,000 years ago, when farming first began, the observation that people of different ages, from infancy to mature years, died from time to time would obviously have framed death as a possibility but not, in the absence of genealogical history, an inevitability. That is why Tambiah (1990: 113 f.) is correct to list consciousness of the possibility of death as a finality as a fundamental anxiety, rather than consciousness of inevitable mortality.

Personal mortality could, of course, have been deduced on the basis of not even the most elderly person being able to recall back more than three or four generations, but such an idea of sequential generations may not have been obvious to communities lacking a system of memorialization through cumulative, shared funerary structures. That those certainly began to exist from around the time farming first emerged has often been taken, with a fair degree of plausibility, as evidence that genealogy had begun, with its attendant concomitants for inheritance, group membership, projected social worlds of ancestors, and so on. Prior to this point, it must be said, any systematic funerary archaeological records are scanty and infrequent, and may thus not be most safely interpreted as a reverential and religious reflex in the face of inevitable mortality.

One of the most energetic areas of current debate centres on the relationships (however understood) of scientific study and on-going religious belief (e.g. Dawkins 2006; McGrath 2004; 2007; Bentley 2008). It is clear that wherever individual scholars stand on this, the activities of archaeologists in relation to death as a category and 'the dead', however materially defined but usually in the form of residual human skeletal elements or other biological material, may themselves be interpreted in ritual terms, and not always sympathetically (*vide* the claims of modern pagan groups to 'know', through an act of self-identification, the religious outlooks of some of those represented by the archaeological dead and, through that, to understand the ongoing ritual requirements—often antithetical to scientific study—that the dead demand). The death–religion nexus has also been addressed from evolutionary, psychological, behavioural and cognitive perspectives, but this in many ways represents a separate body of transdisciplinary work, often avowedly atheistic and scientific where the previously described body was at least agnostic, historical, and humanistic (Boyer 1994; Whitehouse and Laidlaw 2004).

6 Conclusions

Given what else might or might not be done with corpses, the uncovery of the kind of formal burial, so archetypal in our own practitioner ideas of uncovering past belief systems (as noted at the outset) at least reveals the existence of a grammar of a type Wittgenstein (among others) associated a priori with ritual behaviour, while noting that such behaviours might not connect in any consistent way with any particular religious beliefs (Wittgenstein 1953; 1979; cf. Kerr 1986). That is to say, it is possible that the observed ritual behaviours prompt the development of a specific kind of religious belief, as I have argued in relation to the extensive use of inhumation, especially in later prehistoric communities, and the emergence of a set of broadly uniform ideas concerning the soul. Ironically (perhaps) the archaeological creation of a material category of 'prehistoric ancestors' can be seen as, arguably, a major factor in the restructuring of indigenous belief systems around the dead, where archaeologically uncovered ancestors become a significant factor in political struggles (such as aboriginal land claims) where the dice are heavily loaded in favour of large-scale interests, such as property and mining companies.

The situation is even more problematic because, given strong claims for the domains of religion and science to be partly separate yet partly overlapping (Gould 2002; McGrath and McGrath 2007), and given the inadvisability (essentially, futility) of scientists asserting religion to be disprovable (McGrath 2004; cf. Dawkins 2006; Dennett 2003 and see contributions to Bentley 2008), it must be admitted that entities such as 'the immortal soul' (or, indeed, ghosts) are possible metaphysical realities. It follows that we cannot dismiss out of hand the possibility that death rituals have had or promise actual efficacy in relation to some transcendent reality. Neither, however, should we presume that, simply by being 'prehistoric' or otherwise ancient, past communities might not have been capable of scepticism (or some species of agnosticism) while yet participating in activities around death that might appear to us now as profoundly steeped in sincere beliefs.

Suggested Reading

Further readings on death with special relevance to archaeology are as follows: for the anthropological background the single essential source is Metcalf and Huntington's 1991 volume, *Celebrations of Death: the anthropology of mortuary ritual* (2nd edn) while for a good sociological overview see Davies' *Ritual and Remembrance: Responses to death in human societies* (1994). From the perspective of archaeological method, Carr's 1995 article, 'Mortuary practices: Their social, philosophical-religious, circumstantial and physical determinant' is recommended, while a broad range of studies is represented by Chapman, Kinnes, and Randsborg's *The Archaeology of Death* (1981). Synthetic accounts that deal with the issues archaeologically but from an anthropologically informed perspective are the standard text,

Parker-Pearson's *The Archaeology of Death and Burial* (1999), and the more controversial reassessment of a range of data in Taylor's *The Buried Soul: How humans invented death* (2002).

REFERENCES

ANDRÉN, A., JENNBERT, K., and RAUDVERE, C. (eds) 2006. *Old Norse Religion in Long-term Perspective* (Lund: Nordic Academic Press).

ARIÈS, P. 1981. *The Hour of our Death*, trans. Helen Weaver (New York: Vintage Books).

ARNOLD, B. 1995. '"Honorary males" or women of substance? Gender, status and power in Iron Age Europe', *Journal of European Archaeology*, 3(2): 153–68.

ARNOLD, D. and HASTORF, C. (eds) 2008. *Heads of State: Icons, power, and politics in the ancient and modern Andes* (Walnut Creek, CA: Left Coast).

BAR-YOSEF, O., VANDERMEERSCH, B., ARENSBURG, B., et al. 1992. 'The excavations in Kebara Cave, Mt Carmel', *Current Anthropology*, 33(5): 496–550.

BARLEY, N. 1995. *Dancing on the Grave: Encounters with death* (London: John Murray).

BARRETT, J. 1990. 'The monumentality of death: The character of Early Bronze Age mortuary mounds in southern Britain', *World Archaeology*, 22(2): 179–89.

BECK, B. 1995. 'The anthropology of the body', *Current Anthropology*, 16: 486–7.

BENTLEY, A. (ed.) 2008. *The Edge of Reason: Science and religion in modern society* (London: Continuum).

BINFORD, L. R. 1972. 'Mortuary practices: Their study and potential' in L. R. Binford (ed.), *An Archaeological Perspective* (New York: Seminar Press), pp. 108–243.

BINFORD, S. R. 1968. 'A structural comparison of disposal of the dead in the Mousterian and the Upper Palaeolithic', *Southwestern Journal of Anthropology*, 24: 139–54.

BLOCH, M. 1981. 'Tombs and states' in S. C. Humphreys and H. King (eds), *Mortality and Immortality: The anthropology and archaeology of death* (London: Academic Press), pp. 137–47.

BLOCH, M. and PARRY, J. (eds) 1982. *Death and the Regeneration of Life* (Cambridge: Cambridge University Press), pp. 187–210.

BOYD, B. 1992. 'The transformation of knowledge: Natufian mortuary practices at Hoyonim, Western Galilee', *Archaeological Review from Cambridge*, 11(2): 19–38.

BOYER, P. 1994. *The Naturalness of Religious Ideas: A cognitive theory of religion* (Berkeley: University of California Press).

BREMMER, J. N. (ed.) 2007. *The Strange World of Human Sacrifice*, Studies in the History and Anthropology of Religion 1 (Leuven: Peeters).

BROWN, J. A. 1981. 'The search for rank in prehistoric burials' in R. Chapman, I. Kinnes, and K. Randsborg (eds), *The Archaeology of Death* (London: Carlisle Press), pp. 25–37.

——1995. 'On mortuary analysis: With special reference to the Saxe-Binford research program' in L. A. Beck (ed.), *Regional Approaches to Mortuary Analysis* (New York: Plenum Press), pp. 3–26.

BUTTON, S. 2007. 'Mortuary studies, memory, and the Mycenaean polity' in N. Yoffee (ed.), *Negotiating the Past in the Past: Identity, memory and landscape in archaeological research* (Tucson: University of Arizona Press), pp. 76–103.

BYRD, B. F. and MONAHAN, C. M. 1995. 'Death, ritual and Natufian social structure', *Journal of Anthropological Archaeology*, 14: 251–87.
CARR, C. 1995. 'Mortuary practices: Their social, philosophical-religious, circumstantial and physical determinant', *Journal of Archaeological Method and Theory*, 2(2): 105–200.
CHAPMAN, J. 1994. 'The living, the dead and the ancestors: Time, life cycles and the mortuary domain in later European prehistory' in J. Davies (ed.), *Ritual and Remembrance: Responses to death in human societies* (Sheffield: Sheffield Academic Press), pp. 40–85.
CHAPMAN, R. 1987. 'Mortuary practices: Society, theory building and archaeology' in A. Boddington, N. Garland, and R. C. Janaway (eds), *Death, Decay and Reconstruction* (Manchester: Manchester University Press), pp. 198–213.
——1995. 'Landscapes and mortuary rites' in A. Beck (ed.), *Regional Approaches to Mortuary Analysis* (New York: Plenum Press), pp. 29–51.
——KINNES, I., and RANDSBORG, K. (eds) 1981. *The Archaeology of Death* (London: Carlisle Press).
CHASE, D. 1996. 'Burial and tombs' in B. Fagan (ed.), *The Oxford Companion to Archaeology* (Oxford: Oxford University Press), pp. 109–10.
CLARK, D. (ed.) 1993. *The Sociology of Death* (Oxford: Blackwell).
CLARK, G. A. and NEELEY, M. 1987. 'Social differentiation in European Mesolithic burial data' in P. Rowley-Conwy, M. Zvelebil, and H. P. Blankholm (eds), *Mesolithic Northwest Europe, Recent trends* (Sheffield: Department of Archaeology and Prehistory, University of Sheffield), pp. 121–30.
CLARKE, P. B. and BYRNE, P. 1993. *Religion Defined and Explained* (New York: St Martin's Press).
CRAIG, C. R., KNÜSEL, C. J., and CARR, G. C. 2005. 'Fragmentation, mutilation and dismemberment: An interpretation of human remains on Iron Age sites' in M. Parker-Pearson and I. J. N. Thorpe (eds), *Violence, Warfare and Slavery*, British Archaeological Reports International Series 1374 (Oxford: Archaeopress), pp. 165–80.
CRAWFORD, S. 1991. 'When do Anglo-Saxon children count?', *Journal of Theoretical Archaeology*, 2: 17–24.
——1993. 'Children, death and the afterlife in Anglo-Saxon England', *Anglo-Saxon Studies in Archaeology and History*, 6: 83–91.
CSAPO, E. 2005. *Theories of Mythology* (Oxford: Blackwell).
DAIM, F. 1998. 'Archaeology, ethnicity and the structures of identification: The example of the Avars, Carantanians and Moravians in the eighth century' in W. Pohl and H. Reimitz (eds), *Strategies of Distinction: The construction of ethnic communities, 300-800* (Leyden: Brill), pp. 71–94.
DANIELL, C. 1997. *Death and Burial in Medieval England* (London: Routledge).
DAVIES, J. (ed.) 1994. *Ritual and Remembrance: Responses to death in human societies* (Sheffield: Sheffield Academic Press).
DAWKINS, R. 2006. *The God Delusion* (New York: Bantam).
DE EUR, A. 1993. *Les sépultures moustériennes* (Paris: Éditions du CNRS).
DENNETT, D. 2003. *Freedom Evolves* (London: Allen Lane).
DERRIDA, J. 1995. *The Gift of Death*, trans. D. Wills (Chicago and London: Chicago University Press).
DURKHEIM, E. 2001. *The Elementary Forms of Religious Life*, trans. Karen Fields (Oxford: Oxford University Press).
EMBREE, L. 1987. 'Archaeology: The most basic science of all?', *Antiquity*, 61: 75–8.

FAGAN, B. F. (ed.) 1996. *The Oxford Companion to Archaeology* (New York: Oxford University Press).

FIELDS, K. 2001. 'Introduction' in Durkheim, *The Elementary Forms for Religious Life* (Oxford: Oxford University Press).

FLEMING, A. 1973. 'Tombs for the living', *Man*, 8(2): 177–93.

FORTES, M. 1966. 'Religious premises and logical technique in divinatory ritual', *Philosophical Transactions of the Royal Society of London*, 251: 409–22.

FRANKENSTEIN, S. and ROWLANDS, M. J. 1978. 'The internal structure and regional context of Early Iron Age society in south-western Germany', *London Institute of Archaeology Bulletin*, 15: 73–112.

GARGETT, R. H. 1989. 'Grave shortcomings: The evidence for Neanderthal burial', *Current Anthropology*, 22(1): 1–23.

—— 1999. 'Middle Palaeolithic burial is not a dead issue: The view from Qazfeh, Saint-Césaire, Kebara, Amud and Dederiyeh', *Journal of Human Evolution*, 37(1): 27–90.

GELLNER, E. 1988. *Plough, Sword and Book: The structure of human history* (London: Collins and Harvill).

GENNEP, A. VAN 1960 [1908]. *The Rites of Passage* (Chicago: University of Chicago Press).

GOULD, S. J. 2002. *The Structure of Evolutionary Theory* (Cambridge, Mass.: Harvard University Press).

HÄRKE, H. 1997. 'Material culture as myth: Weapons in Anglo-Saxon graves' in C. K. Jensen and K. H. Høilund Nielson (eds), *Burial and Society: The chronological and social analysis of burial data* (Aarhus: Aarhus University Press), pp. 119–25.

HARRISON, J. E. 1991 [1903]. *Prolegomena to the Study of Greek Religion*, Mythos Series (Princeton: Princeton University Press).

HAYDEN, B. 1993. 'The cultural capacities of Neanderthals: A review and re-evaluation', *Journal of Human Evolution*, 24: 113–46.

HEIDEGGER, M. 1962. *Being and Time* (New York: Harper and Row).

HERTZ, R. 1907. 'Contribution à une étude sur la représentation collective de la mort', *Année sociologique*, 10: 48–137.

—— 1960. 'A contribution to the study of the collective representation of death' in R. Hertz, *Death and the Right Hand*, trans. R. Needham and C. Needham (New York: Free Press).

HOCART, A. M. 1927. *Kingship* (Oxford: Oxford University Press).

INSOLL, T. (ed.) 2001. *Archaeology and World Religion* (London: Routledge).

JAMES, W. 1902 [2002]. *The Varieties of Religious Experience: A study in human nature* (Mineola, NY: Dover).

JENNBERT, K. 2006. 'The heroized dead: People, animals, and materiality in Scandinavian death rituals, AD 200–1000' in A. Andrén, K. Jennbert, and C. Raudvere (eds), *Old Norse Religion in Long-term Perspective* (Lund: Nordic Academic Press), pp. 135–40.

JONES, R. F. J. 1987. 'Burial customs of Rome and the Provinces' in J. Wacher (ed.), *The Roman World* (London: Routledge and Kegan Paul), pp. 812–31.

KERR, F. 1986. *Theology after Wittgenstein* (Oxford: Blackwell).

KINNES, I. 1975. 'Monumental function in British Neolithic burial practices', *World Archaeology*, 7(1): 16–29.

KNÜSEL, C. J. and CAR, G. C. 1995. 'On the significance of the crania from the River Thames', *Antiquity*, 69: 162–9.

LÉVI-STRAUSS, C. 1985. *The Way of the Masks*, trans. S. Modelski (London: Jonathan Cape).

LUCY, S. 2000. *The Anglo-Saxon Way of Death* (Stroud: Sutton).

McGrath, A. 2004. *Dawkins' God: Genes, memes and the meaning of life* (Oxford: Blackwell).
—— and Collicutt McGrath, J. 2007. *The Dawkins Delusion* (London: SPCK).
Masterman, M. 1970. 'The nature of a paradigm' in I. Lakatos and A. Musgrave (eds), *Criticism and the Growth of Knowledge* (Cambridge: Cambridge University Press).
Metcalf, P. and Huntington, R. 1991. *Celebrations of Death: The anthropology of mortuary ritual* (Cambridge: Cambridge University Press).
Morris, I. 1992. *Death-ritual and Social Structure in Classical Antiquity* (Cambridge: Cambridge University Press).
Needham, R. 1967. 'Percussion and transition', *Man*, n.s. 2: 606–14.
—— 1985. *Exemplars* (Berkeley: University of California Press).
Oesterley, W. O. E. 1937. *Sacrifices in Ancient Israel: Their origin, purposes, and development* (New York: Macmillan).
Oestigaard, T. 2004. *Death in World Religions* (Bergen: BRIC Press).
O'Shea, J. M. 1984. *Mortuary Variability: An archaeological investigation* (Orlando: Academic Press).
Pals, D. L. 1995. *Eight Theories of Religion*, 2nd edn (Oxford: Oxford University Press).
Parker Pearson, M. 1982. 'Mortuary practices, society and ideology: An ethnoarchaeological case study' in I. Hodder (ed.), *Symbolic and Structural Archaeology* (Cambridge: Cambridge University Press), pp. 99–113.
—— 1999. *The Archaeology of Death and Burial* (Gloucester: Sutton).
—— and Ramilisonina. 1998. 'Stonehenge for the ancestors: The stones pass on the message', *Antiquity*, 74: 308–26.
Patocka, J. 1990. *Essais hérétiques sur la philosophie de l'histoire* (Paris: Verdier).
Quinn, J. 2006. 'The gendering of death in eddic cosmology' in A. Andrén, K. Jennbert, and C. Raudvere (eds), *Old Norse Religion in Long-term Perspective* (Lund: Nordic Academic Press), pp. 54–7.
Randsborg, K. 1981. 'Burial, succession and early state formation in Denmark' in R. Chapman, I. Kinnes, and K. Randsborg (eds), *The Archaeology of Death* (London: Carlisle Press), pp. 105–21.
Saxe, A. A. 1971. 'Social dimensions of mortuary practices in a Mesolithic population from Wadi Halfa, Sudan', *American Antiquity*, 36(3): 39–57.
Scarre, C. 1994. 'The meaning of death: Funerary beliefs and the prehistorian' in C. Renfrew and E. B. W. Zubrow (eds), *The Ancient Mind: Elements of cognitive archaeology* (Cambridge: Cambridge University Press), pp. 75–83.
—— 1996. 'Religion' in B. Fagan (ed.), *The Oxford Companion to Archaeology* (Oxford: Oxford University Press), pp. 590–3.
Seale, C. 1998. *Constructing Death: The sociology of dying and bereavement* (Cambridge: Cambridge University Press).
Seters, J. van 2003. 'From child sacrifice to paschal lamb: A remarkable transformation in Israelite religion', *Old Testament Essays*, 16(2): 453–63.
Shanks, M. and Tilley, C. 1992. *Re-Constructing Archaeology: Theory and practice*, 2nd edn (London: Routledge).
Shennan, S. 1975. 'The social organisation at Brančֹ', *Antiquity*, 49: 279–88.
Tambiah, S. J. 1990. *Magic, Science, Religion, and the Scope of Rationality* (Cambridge: Cambridge University Press).
Taylor, T. 2002. *The Buried Soul: How humans invented death* (London: 4th Estate).

TAYLOR, T. 2005. 'Ambushed by a grotesque: Archaeology, slavery and the third paradigm' in M. Parker Pearson and I. J. N. Thorpe (eds), *Warfare, Violence and Slavery in Prehistory*, BAR International Series 1374 (Oxford: BAR), pp. 225–33.
—— 2006. 'Why the Venus of Willendorf has no face', *Archäologie Österreichs*, 17(1): 26–9.
—— 2008a. 'Materiality' in R. A. Bentley, H. D. G. Maschner, and C. Chippindale (eds), *Handbook of Archaeological Theories* (Lanham: AltaMira), pp. 297–320.
—— 2008b. 'Prehistory vs. archaeology: Terms of engagement', *Journal of World Prehistory*, 21: 1–18.
—— 2008c. 'The Willendorf Venuses: Notation, iconology and materiality', *Mitteilungen der Anthropologischen Gesellschaft Wien* (MAGW), 138 (Vienna).
—— 2009. 'The first aesthetic of death' in P. Picq (ed.), *100 000 ans de beauté* (Paris: Gallimard/Babylone), pp. 102–5.
—— forthcoming. 'Concentric ambiguities: A theoretical approach to Neolithic Kreisgrabenanlagen' in F. Bertemes et al. (eds), *Neolithic Circular Enclosures in Europe* (Halle: Martin-Luther-Universität).
TIESLER, V. and CUCINA, A. 2007. *New Perspectives on Human Sacrifice and Ritual Body Treatments in Ancient Maya Society* (New York: Springer).
TRINKAUS, K. M. 1995. 'Mortuary behavior, labor organization, and social rank' in L. A. Beck (ed.), *Regional Approaches to Mortuary Analysis* (New York: Plenum Press), pp. 53–75.
WAIT, G. A. 1985. *Ritual and Religion in Iron Age Britain*, BAR British Series 149 (Oxford: BAR).
WHITEHOUSE, H. and LAIDLAW, J. (eds) 2004. *Ritual and Memory: Toward a comparative anthropology of religion* (Walnut Creek, CA: AltaMira).
WHITLEY, D. S. 2008. 'Religion' in R. Bentley, H. Maschner, and C. Chippindale (eds.), *Handbook of Archaeological Theories* (Lanham: AltaMira), pp. 547–66.
WILLIAMS, H. 1997. 'Ancient landscapes and the dead: The reuse of prehistoric and Roman monuments as early Anglo-Saxon burial sites', *Medieval Archaeology*, XLI: 1–32.
WILSON, A. S., TAYLOR, T., and CERUTI, M. C. 2007. 'Stable isotope and DNA evidence for ritual sequences in Inca child sacrifice', *Proceedings of the National Academy of Science (PNAS)*, 104(42): 16456–61.
WITTGENSTEIN, L. 1953. *Philosophische Untersuchungen—Philosophical Investigations*, trans. G. E. M. Anscombe (Oxford: Basil Blackwell).
—— 1979. *Wittgenstein's Lectures, Cambridge, 1932–1935: From the notes of Alice Ambrose and Margaret Macdonald* (Totowa, N.J.: Rowman and Littlefield).
WYLIE, A. 2002. *Thinking from Things: Essays in the philosophy of archaeology* (Berkeley, CA: University of California Press).

CHAPTER 8

TABOO

NICKY MILNER

1 INTRODUCTION: THE CONCEPT OF TABOO

THE word *taboo* was first introduced into European languages by Captain Cook in his description of his third voyage around the world, when he visited Polynesia. Here, he witnessed the ways in which the word taboo was used for certain avoidance customs ranging across widely different things such as rights over an object, a supreme chief's relation to petty dignitaries, food restrictions of women, and the sacredness of places of sacrifice. Cook died during his last voyage but his successor, King, continued his journal which included further examples of taboo:

> Mention hath already been made, that women are always *tabooed*, or forbidden to eat certain kinds of meats. We also frequently saw several at their meals, who had the meat put into their mouths by others; and on our asking the reason of this singularity were told that there were *tabooed*, or forbidden, to feed themselves. This prohibition, we understood, was always laid on them after they had assisted at any funeral, or touched a dead body, and also on other occasions. It is necessary to observe that, on these occasions, they apply the word *taboo* indifferently both to persons and things. Thus they say the natives were *tabooed*, or the bay was *tabooed*, and so of the rest. This word is also used to express anything sacred, or eminent, or devoted. Thus the king of Owhyhee was called *Eree-taboo*; a human victim *tangata taboo*; and in the same manner, among the Friendly Islanders, Tonga, the island where the king resides, is named *Tonga-taboo*. [Cook 1784, cited in Steiner 1967: 27]

Cook was read widely, particularly in Britain. The customs described seemed extraordinary to people in Europe and the word *taboo* rapidly came into use, as well as becoming a major descriptive category of ethnography (Steiner 1967). Robertson Smith was one of the first scholars to study the concept and drew a line between religious behaviour, concerned with ethics and gods, and non-religious magical behaviour, using the term taboo to describe non-religious rules of conduct, particularly concerned with pollution. Rules of holiness he held to be intelligible, whereas non-religious taboos he held to be primitive and savage (see Douglas 1999). Sir James Frazer (1875) wrote the first essay on taboo in the ninth edition of the *Encyclopaedia Britannica*, where he tried to classify and understand the nature of magical thinking. He took an evolutionary approach which has been heavily criticized by Steiner (1967). His work suggested that a confusion between uncleanness and holiness marks primitive thinking. Studies of taboo and ritual abstention were advanced by a number of scholars in the nineteenth and twentieth centuries including van Gennep (1909), Mead et al. (1937), Radcliffe-Brown (1948), Freud (1950) and a thorough critique of them all is provided by Steiner (1967) in his collection of lectures entitled *Taboo*.

In Steiner's work it becomes clear that the definition of the word *taboo* is problematic and varies between cultures, but essentially it is concerned with:

1. all the social mechanisms of obedience which have ritual significance
2. with specific and restrictive behaviour in dangerous situations
3. with the protection of individuals who are in danger
4. with the protection of society from those endangered—and therefore dangerous—persons (Steiner 1967: 20–1).

Steiner (1967: 33) analyses the ways in which taboo has been translated into European languages, usually as *prohibited* and/or *sacred* but he sees problems with these translations because these words cannot be expressed in Polynesian terms and modern European languages lack a word with the Polynesian range of meaning. The distinction between prohibition and sacredness is artificially introduced by the Western world. This is an important concept because of the link between impurity and prohibition and sacredness. For the Polynesians there are few words which indicate sacredness without implying prohibition, but there are many words which mean dirty or defiled. So, a notion of something being unfit for consumption could be made without reference to sacredness and prohibition. Only some notions of impurity were connected with taboo. As Steiner (1967: 35) stresses, this does not fit for other cultures such as Indian caste society where the concept of pollution is paramount.

The word seems to be used widely nowadays largely to mean something which is prohibited, and very often in connection with things which are not talked about, 'a taboo subject'. It is, however, given a broad definition in the Oxford English Dictionary:

> As originally used in Polynesia, Melanesia, New Zealand, etc.: Set apart for or consecrated to a special use or purpose; restricted to the use of a god, a king, priests, or chiefs, while forbidden to general use; prohibited to a particular class (esp. to women), or to a particular person or persons; inviolable, sacred; forbidden, unlawful; also said of persons under a perpetual or temporary prohibition from certain actions, from food, or from contact with others. [Oxford English Dictionary, OED online]

In terms of archaeological studies, *taboo* appears to get little attention, perhaps because it is so very difficult to study. Many of the kinds of taboos presented in the Polynesian accounts do not leave material traces. For example, the taboo of touching dead bodies, the taboo of men and women eating together, the taboo of women entering sacred places, and tabooing the bay are all actions which would be impossible to identify in the archaeological record. However, one area of taboo connected with religion and ritual which does have some potential for archaeological study, is that of food. Many cultures and religions have strict rules which prohibit the consumption of, usually, certain types of animal. This chapter will first present an important example, that of the prohibition of the pig, providing theories on its origins as well as interpretations as to why pig consumption taboos developed. Second, the following section will use a number of archaeological case studies to explore the ways in which such religious and ritual prohibitions may be identified in the archaeological record, and will consider the problems involved in interpreting them.

2 Pig Prohibition

And the swine, though he divide the hoof, and be clovenfooted, yet he cheweth not the cud; he is unclean to you.
 Of their flesh shall ye not eat, and their carcass shall ye not touch...

Leviticus 11: 7–8

The main centre of pork avoidance is the Near East, but the prohibition of the pig is in fact widespread across the world and occurs among Jews, Muslims, Hindus, Ethiopian Christians, Yezidi, Mandaeans, and Lamaists amongst others (Diener and Robkin 1978: 495). The religious taboo of swine consumption is one of the more significant markers of some of these religions and poor adherence to the prohibition can be considered as grave religious insults or cultural transgressions (Lobban 1994: 57).

The history of pork avoidance is extremely complex and culturally specific and a detailed picture of early practices through the Near East and the Mediterranean can be found in Simoons (1994: ch. 2). Pork avoidance in this area, however, is generally accepted to have originated from ancient Egypt. One of the key explanations is that pig taboos became more common when Seth, a god with whom the pig was associated, lost favour and the god Horus, his rival, became more important. The legend suggests that Seth, disguised as a pig, attempted to destroy the eye of Horus (probably the moon) and that Horus avenged himself by establishing pig sacrifice to the moon (ibid: 99). It is only in the writings of Herodotus, the Greek Historian (c.484–425 BC) that a taboo is made explicit, in his Book II on the history of the Middle East region:

> The pig is regarded among them as an unclean animal, so much so that if a man passing accidentally touches a pig, he instantly hurries to the river, and plunges in with all his clothes on. Hence, too, the swineherds, notwithstanding that they are of pure Egyptian blood, are forbidden to enter into any of the temples which are open to all other Egyptians... They do not offer swine in sacrifice to any of their gods, excepting Bacchus and the Moon, whom they honor in this way at the same time, sacrificing pigs to both of them at the same full moon, and afterward eating of the flesh. [Lobban 1994: 69]

It is considered likely that by the time of the Egyptian New Kingdom (sixteenth century BC) there was probably a formal taboo, perhaps for the nobility, although pork was still widely eaten by the poor (Lobban 1994). It is important to note that Moses was a high-ranking civil servant in Egypt during the reign of Pharoah Rameses II, in which he may have been exposed to food preferences and prohibitions, for instance the pig. However, Moses fled from Egypt into the wilderness but it is thought he did not abandon this already-established taboo (Lobban 1994: 59).

Pork avoidance is found in the first five books of the Old Testament, known as the Pentateuch to Christians and the Torah to the Jews, and Soler (1979) demonstrates how prohibitions on food develop through these chapters. These books tell the story from the creation of the World to the death of Moses, to whom the laws of prohibition are attributed. Food is first mentioned in the first book, Genesis, where God gives Man plants as food. As well as meat being tabooed, the fruit of two trees is also proscribed, but this prohibition is broken by Adam and Eve. Later on, the Flood is a point when God decides to do away with his Creation, but spared Noah and his family, and a pair of each species of animal. A new era began and at this point God allows every moving thing that lives to be food (ibid.), however, blood remains sacred, and only when meat becomes desacralized through bleeding does it become permissible. It is only when Moses appears in the text that prohibition of certain animals is introduced, and the taboo concerning blood remains. Within Jerusalem, the setting apart of the blood becomes the occasion of a ritual: before the meat can be eaten, the animal is presented to the priest who performs a peace offering and pours the blood on the altar.

The two most significant books concerning prohibition are Leviticus and Deuteronomy. The texts are largely similar but neither of them provide a clear explanation about why certain foods were tabooed; they simply set out the distinctions between clean and unclean species (ibid: 59). An animal is clean if it has a hoofed foot, a cloven hoof, and if they chew the cud. The hoofed foot is a distinctive trait between herbivores and carnivorous animals which have claws. Birds are also unclean. Other criteria are added however. The second criterion is chewing the cud. Ruminants eat grass by regurgitating it and chewing it again. Cloven hoofed animals such as cows and sheep are also clean. This latter criterion eliminates animals even though they are herbivorous, such as the horse, ass, hare and rock badger.

In early Christianity, there was considerable controversy about the food bans in Leviticus. Christians did not adopt the Jewish view that the pig was an unclean animal because in the New Testament Acts 10: 9–16 this food restriction was abandoned (Lobban 1994: 59); consequently pork consumption became more general (Simoons 1994: 32). With the establishment of Islam, the negative attitudes toward pig and pork were also adopted with the Prophet Mohammed singling out the pig as the only animal to be prohibited, which also served to distinguish Muslims from Christians (ibid: 33). Reference is made to Sura 5:3 'Forbidden unto you (for food) are carrion and blood and swine flesh...' (Lobban 1994: 59).

The search for an explanation of the origin of pig taboo is apparently at least as old as the ancient Greeks (Lobban 1994). It is interesting, however, that despite many years of scholarship, there is little agreement as to why this important taboo exists. Speculation that pork avoidance stems from practical reasons such as the pig's dirty habits or disease at least dates back to the medieval rabbi and Jewish scholar, Moses Maimonides (AD 1135–1204) who explains that if Hebrew law had permitted the eating of pork, markets and even homes would have been dirtier than any latrine (Simoons 1994: 66). But more recently veterinary sciences have disputed these claims and many scholars have sought cultural and social routes for this widespread taboo (e.g. Bennett 1970; Douglas 1966, 1972; Simoons 1994; Lobban 1994).

Others, however, have provided ecological explanations. The idea that the pig was banned because it was ecologically maladaptive and would have been difficult to keep in certain environmental conditions (Coon 1951; Harris 1972, 1973, 1974), has been dismissed on a number of grounds by Simoons (1994). For instance, there is little evidence to support pigs being affected by environmental deterioration at the time of Moses. Pigs are very versatile in their eating habits, which means that they can live in a number of habitats. In addition, evidence for them in the form of bones from archaeological sites does exist, suggesting that it was possible for them to live in some ecological niches at this time.

The symbolic explanations, put forward by Douglas in her book *Purity and Danger* (1966) are perhaps most well known. Douglas saw some important taxonomic patterns in the laws which are presented. The animals that the Hebrews herded (sheep, goat, and cattle) were clean and served as a model for what was acceptable for eating. They are ungulates who chew the cud and have cloven hoofs. Douglas argues that the pig was banned because it does not chew the cud. She suggested that there was an emphasis on holiness as an essential goal of the ancient Hebrews. In Leviticus, only one reason is given for the laws and that is the need for 'holiness', meaning both sanctification and separation, which related to food consumption. However, Douglas's work was subsequently criticized for only concentrating on animal taxonomy and not on the broader social thinking and activities of the Hebrews. Consequently, in later publications she develops her theories and suggests that it was important to the Hebrews to be set apart from other ethnic groups. In addition, the pig bore a burden of multiple pollution because not only was it taxonomically abhorrent, it was also raised by non-Hebrews and ate carrion (Douglas 1972, 1973, 1975).

Soler's (1979) views are very similar to those of Douglas, but he sees the separation of the Hebrews from other peoples as being the most important aspect of the laws, rather than the taxonomy. The explanation of the rules that is given is that the elimination of non-hoofed animals was seen as eliminating carnivores from the diet. Carnivores are meat eaters, but animals should be vegetarian and must not be blemished, as set out in Genesis (see above). That animals should chew the cud is seen as a further effort to include the herbivores but exclude the carnivores.

3 Archaeology and Taboo

In order to identify patterns in the archaeological record, such restrictions or taboos can only be identified through careful analyses of the faunal remains. But, as in any archaeozoological study, it is important to consider the taphonomic constraints as well as the cultural patterning of the material. The faunal remains have to be interpreted in the light of patterns of disposal, recovery, and preservation. Faunal remains can be discarded in a number of places depending on the situation: household waste may be disposed of differently to waste produced in sanctified places, and a range of locations may be used such as pits or general refuse layers. How waste is disposed of will depend on whether it remains representative of that activity or not. For instance, waste placed into secure locations such as covered pits or in water may not be affected so much as waste placed into open refuse layers where dogs and other animals may scavenge and radically change the composition of the assemblage. In addition, sometimes waste is carted away and put on fields or gardens. The conditions of the burial environment also need to be considered. If soils are acid most bones are likely to be destroyed; in neutral or alkaline soils larger bones tend to survive better than the smaller ones. Finally, the archaeological methods used in the recovery of bones are an important consideration. Sites are excavated in different ways with different priorities, resources, and questions. Not every bone is always kept and therefore there may be some distinct biases in collections. In addition, if sediments are not sieved the smaller bones such as fish and bird bone may go unnoticed (Woolgar et al. 2006). With these caveats in mind, it is possible to examine archaeological food waste and consider whether there is evidence of certain foods being tabooed.

There are a number of archaeozoological studies which have looked at whether it is possible to identify religious dietary laws in the archaeological record. For instance, in terms of the Muslim diet there are a number of patterns which may be observable in the archaeological record (Insoll 1999: 95–100). There are some differences between Islamic schools and issues of non-observance must be acknowledged but, overall, there are three categories of food: *halal* (lawful), *haram* (prohibited), and *makruh* (reprehensible). For instance, alcohol, spilt blood, pork, dogs, excrement, carrion, and milk of animals whose flesh is not eaten are prohibited. In addition, there are laws regarding slaughter and animals must be killed facing the *qiblah* (the point toward which Muslims turn to pray), the name of God invoked, and the throat of the animal cut.

In a study of a number of sites in Jordan, Insoll (1999: 96–9) considers whether such dietary laws can be identified. In Muslim period deposits, few pig bones were found, most of which were considered as residual. However, at Pella, there was a context where pig bones strongly suggested the continued use of this animal into the Muslim period, and this has been interpreted as perhaps the toleration of a small Christian or recently converted Muslim population. *Halal* slaughter will be harder to find because a skilled person will cleanly cut the throat and is unlikely to cut down to the bone. In the Jordanian examples, little differentiation could be made between pre-Muslim and Muslim butchery methods.

Another important example is provided by the work of Ijzereef (1989) where the analysis of over 100,000 animal bones in Amsterdam was carried out in order to investigate whether animal bones can tell us about the social differences between individual households. The material studied was from about 100 cesspits and refuse layers from two excavations of seventeenth- and eighteenth-century sites. From about 1600 the area was inhabited by Portuguese Jews. The data was sorted according to period, location, and different percentages of the various species. The main criterion used to separate cesspits of the Jewish and non-Jewish households was the percentage of pig bones. On that basis, four groups could be distinguished: those with no pig remains (Jewish households); those with 0–1% of pig remains (Jewish households, perhaps with contamination from later layers); 1–5% of pig remains (non-kosher households, or Jews with non-Jewish residents living in the same house); more than 5% pig remains, usually about 15% (non-Jewish households).

In addition, there were other very specific differences between these households, in that there was also a lack of hind-limb bones of cattle and sheep; this is considered non-kosher because of the presence of the sciatic nerve which is difficult to remove. There was also a lack of calf bones; Jewish butchers only bought adult oxen. In addition, the chicken bone quantities are very high, as opposed to non-Jewish contexts where duck was more common. The chicken sesamoid bones (in the leg) tended to have a lead seal attached to them, showing that they were slaughtered on a Thursday, probably for consumption on the Friday night. Finally, eel, an animal which is considered to be impure, was also absent, and fish and shellfish were very low in numbers. This analysis of animal bones allowed a study to be made of the distribution of Jewish and non-Jewish households.

However, such studies do not always provide such clear-cut evidence. Investigations by Coningham and Young (1999) focused on caste in South Asia and questioned whether this was visible archaeologically. One area of study was that of diet and the faunal remains from the site of Anuradhapura, Sri Lanka, were examined; an early historic urban site (first millennium BC–fifth century AD). The remains were compared from a trench excavated within the centre of the city and one located within the north-east of the city, with the hope of identifying spatial variation within diet between the two, which might conform to patterns of modern South Asian communities where selected diets are restricted to caste and are distributed differentially in urban locations. The *Laws of Manu* records the regulations of diet, compiled between the second century BC and second century AD. For instance, they forbid all carnivorous and one-hoofed animals, all solitary and unknown beasts, all five-toed animals, animals which eat fish, and village pigs. In addition, any man who kills a horse, deer, elephant, fish or snake will be degraded to a mixed caste.

In the trench excavated within the city centre, cattle, horse, pig, and deer (forbidden) and buffalo, porcupine, hare, and terrapin (permitted) were found. In the trench to the north-east of the city, cattle, horse, pig, and deer (forbidden) and terrapin (permitted) were found. There is a similarity between forbidden species in both trenches, and many from the latter trench had cut marks. It is noted that the presence of cattle bone is particularly surprising in both areas given that there was a major beef-eating taboo on the island after AD 100. It appears in this instance, that the formal caste-based models which have been put forward have not been found in the archaeological record, and that the spatial differentiation observed today is a relatively recent phenomenon. However, Coningham and Young do caution that taboo and other symbolic pressures often distort the archaeological record.

Religious food avoidances can be even more complicated when they do not constitute a total ban but instead may be related to certain times of the year. For example, in Britain in the medieval period the Church began to place greater emphasis on the avoidance of meat and fasting (Woolgar 2006). The commonly held belief was that when the outer man fasted, the inner man prayed. Fasting was seen as a preparation for spiritual acts, like communion. By about 1300 abstinence of meat was often practised on Wednesdays, Fridays, and Saturdays, through Lent, the eves of the great Marian feasts, the eves of the feasts of the Apostles and three days before the Ascension. Personal devotion may have added further days. In some contexts, it appears that fish was eaten instead of flesh (Serjeantson 2006). However, identifying these sorts of avoidances is very difficult in the archaeological record because meat was not totally prohibited and will be found alongside fish remains on archaeological sites.

In examining whether taboo foods can be found in the archaeological record, it would appear that there certainly are instances where this can be identified, but the key here is that they belong to periods where there are historical accounts and the religious practices are known. The question remains, however, whether it is possible to identify taboo in the archaeological record from sites where the religion or ritual practices are not fully understood.

In the study of prehistory, taboo foods are rarely mentioned. One recent exception concerns discussions surrounding isotopic studies of human bones dated to the Mesolithic Neolithic transition. Here it has been suggested that there is a sharp shift in diet from marine-based foods like fish, shellfish, and seal, to a diet dominated by terrestrial foods (Schulting and Richards 2002; Richards and Schulting 2003). This has been described as a taboo, a cultural prohibition on marine foods, by Thomas (2003) who compares it to ethnographic examples, including the Rangi of Tanzania who forbade the eating of fish because they were scaled and conceptually similar to snakes. Clearly some significant changes did occur in diet at this time but it is important to be cautious in assigning a lack of a certain category of food to taboo, particularly from one line of evidence, i.e. stable isotopes. This approach has been criticized partly on the grounds that archaeozoological data at some coastal sites demonstrate that marine foods were still being consumed and suggests that not everyone 'turned their backs on the sea' (Milner et al. 2004, 2006).

Ethnographic research can be used to demonstrate how complex taboos can be and to highlight the difficulties for archaeologists in interpreting the material remains, particularly for hunter-gatherers. Politis and Saunders (2002) provide a useful case study to demonstrate this. Their work involved the exploration of a range of evidence concerning species avoidance in Amazonia, and specifically on the Nukak. The white-lipped peccary is an interesting example. These animals in Nukak mythology were originally people who ate *seje* fruits from the ancestral palms and became peccaries. They are hunted by adult and adolescent males usually at some distance from the residential camp. Although women and children may play a supporting role they do not participate in the killing, processing, and consumption of the meat which can last about four days. The processing of the peccary produces some interesting patterns of bone disposal. First, the head and some viscera are discarded in a temporary butchery spot. Then, the ribs, vertebrae, pelvis and scapulae are discarded in the area around a grill on the outskirts of the base camp. Sometimes the humerus and femur bones are also left there and broken for marrow. The tibia, fibula, ulna, metacarpals and metatarsals, carpals, tarsals, and phalanges are then discarded within the base camp. Most of the activity takes place outside the base camp. An archaeological analysis of the landscape would show a wide distribution of bone discard (depending on taphonomic conditions outlined above) which would be very different to other animals which are not tabooed. However, very rarely is such a large area considered archaeologically and a small-scale excavation of the base camp would create a very different pattern, perhaps missing the consumption of the peccary altogether.

4 Conclusions

Taboo has been examined extensively in anthropology and sociology yet it has received little attention in archaeology due to the difficulties of finding material evidence. For the world religions, even if there is controversy surrounding interpretations as to *why* certain foods have been prohibited, there is detailed information in religious texts about *what* is tabooed. This information is useful to archaeologists when they are excavating sites that were populated by people who held religious beliefs, in order to look for change and spatial differentiation. It is much harder to identify food taboos associated with ritual and religion when studying prehistory. It may be possible to identify changes in diet, or animals which are absent from the archaeological record and taboo may be one of the reasons for this, although others such as complex disposal rituals should also be taken into account. With detailed examination of food waste disposal across a site it may also be possible to identify patterns which clearly stand out and may be related to the more complex taboos concerned with gender and age. Without historical records, however, these interpretations can only ever be conjecture.

Suggested Reading

Simoons (1994), *Eat Not This Flesh*, provides a number of chapters covering the history of prohibition and cultural variations for a number of foods: pork, beef, chicken and eggs, horseflesh, camelflesh, dogflesh, and fish. In order to understand more fully the history of anthropological research into taboo, Steiner's (1967) book on *Taboo*, provides a critical analysis of key papers written in the nineteenth and early part of the twentieth century. Mary Douglas (1966) was influenced by Steiner, and examines in detail prohibition in the Old Testament in her book *Purity and Danger: An analysis of concepts of pollution and taboo*. Politis and Saunders (2002) provide a detailed picture of the complexities of taboo which often do not focus on single animals, but which concern prohibition for certain members of societies in certain situations, and this should serve as a reminder to archaeologists not to be simplistic in their archaeological interpretations.

References

BENNETT, M. K 1970. 'Aspects of the pig', *Agricultural History*, 44: 223–35.
CONINGHAM, R. and YOUNG, R. 1999. 'The Archaeological visibility of caste: An introduction' in T. INSOLL (ed.), *Case Studies in Archaeology and World Religion. The proceedings of the Cambridge Conference*, BAR International Series S755 (Oxford: Archaeopress), pp. 84–93.
COOK, J. 1784. *A Voyage to the Pacific Ocean in the Years 1776, 1777, 1778, 1779 and 1780* (London: G. Nicol and T. Cadell).
COON, C. S. 1951. *Caravan* (New York: Henry Holt).
DIENER, P. and ROBKIN, E. E. 1978. 'Ecology, evolution, and the search for cultural origins: the question of Islamic pig prohibition', *Current Anthropology*, 19(3): 493–540.
DOUGLAS, M. 1966. *Purity and Danger: An analysis of concepts of pollution and taboo* (New York: Praeger).
——1972. 'Deciphering a meal', *Daedalus*, 101(1): 61–82.
——1973. *Natural Symbols: Explorations in cosmology*, 2nd edn (London: Barrie and Jenkins).
——1975. *Implicit Meanings: Essays in anthropology* (London and Boston: Routledge and Kegan Paul).
——1999. *Implicit Meanings: Selected essays in anthropology*, 2nd edn (London and New York: Routledge).
FREUD, S. 1950. *Totem and Taboo* (London: Routledge and Kegan Paul).
GENNEP, A. VAN 1904. *Tabou et Totémise à Madagascar* (Paris: E. Leroux).
HARRIS, M. 1972. 'The riddle of the pig', *Natural History*, 81(8): 32–8.
——1973. 'The riddle of the pig II', *Natural History*, 82(2): 20–5.
——1974. *Cows, Pigs, Wars and Witches: The riddles of culture* (New York: Random House).
IJZEREEF, F. G. 1989. 'Social differentiation from animal bone studies' in D. Serjeantson and T. Waldron (eds), *Diet and Crafts in Towns: The evidence of animal remains from the Roman to the post-medieval periods*, BAR British Series 199 (Oxford: BAR), pp. 41–54.
INSOLL, T. 1999. *The Archaeology of Islam* (Oxford: Blackwell).
LOBBAN, R. A., JR 1994. 'Pigs and their prohibition', *International Journal of Middle East Studies*, 26(1): 57–75.

MEAD, M., CRAIG, O. E., and BAILEY, G. N. 1937. 'Tabu' in E. R. A. Seligman (ed.), *Encyclopaedia of the Social Sciences*, VII (New York: Macmillan), pp. 502–5.

MILNER, N. et al. 2004. 'Something fishy in the Neolithic? A re-evaluation of stable isotope analysis of Mesolithic and Neolithic coastal populations', *Antiquity*, 78: 9–22.

—— 2006. 'A response to Richards and Schulting', *Antiquity*, 80: 456–8.

POLITIS, G. G. and SAUNDERS, N. J. 2002. 'Archaeological correlates of ideological activity: Food taboos and spirit-animals in an Amazonian Hunter-gatherer society', in P. Miracle and N. Milner (eds), *Consuming Passions and Patterns of Consumption* (Cambridge: McDonald Institute Monographs), pp. 113–30.

RADCLIFFE-BROWN, A. R. 1948. *The Andaman Islanders* (Cambridge: Cambridge University Press).

RICHARDS, M. and SCHULTING, R. J. 2003. 'Sharp shift in diet at onset of Neolithic', *Nature*, 425: 366.

SCHULTING, R. J. and RICHARDS, M. P. 2002. 'The wet, the wild and the domesticated: The Mesolithic-Neolithic transition on the west coast of Scotland', *European Journal of Archaeology*, 5(2): 147–89.

SERJEANTSON, D. 2006. 'Fish consumption in medieval England' in C. M. Woolgar, D. Serjeantson, and T. Waldron (eds), *Food in Medieval England: Diet and nutrition* (Oxford: Oxford University Press), pp. 102–30.

SIMOONS, F. J. 1994. *Eat Not This Flesh: Food avoidances in the Old World*, 2nd edn (Madison: University of Wisconsin Press).

SOLER, J. 1979. 'The semiotics of food in the Bible' in R. Forster and O. Ranum (eds), *Food and Drink in History* (Baltimore: Johns Hopkins University Press), pp. 126–38.

STEINER, F. 1967. *Taboo* (Harmondsworth: Penguin Books).

THOMAS, J. 2003. 'Thoughts on the "repacked" Neolithic revolution', *Antiquity*, 77(295): 67–74.

WOOLGAR, C. M. 2006. 'Group diets in late medieval England' in C. M. Woolgar, D. Serjeantson, and T. Waldron (eds), *Food in Medieval England: Diet and nutrition* (Oxford: Oxford University Press), pp. 191–200.

WOOLGAR, C. M., SERJEANTSON, D. and WALDRON, T. 2006. 'Introduction' in C. M. Woolgar, D. Serjeantson, and T. Waldron (eds), *Food in Medieval England: Diet and nutrition* (Oxford: Oxford University Press), pp. 1–10.

CHAPTER 9

THE MANY DIMENSIONS OF RITUAL

MARC VERHOEVEN

1 INTRODUCTION

FROM the beginnings of the discipline, archaeologists have excavated, catalogued, and interpreted objects that almost certainly had important ritual and religious significance, such as burials, temples, henge monuments, decorated human skulls, and figurines. However, explicit methodologies for reconstructing ancient ritual and religion have been largely absent. Moreover, their role in both the past and in archaeological practice has been under-theorized (Garwood et al. 1991; Fogelin 2007; Kyriakidis 2007a; Trigger 1999: 141). The main reason for this neglect probably is that as ritual and religion are related to the supernatural, they are generally considered to be beyond the archaeologists' grasp. Furthermore, it is known from other social sciences, such as ethnography, that ritual practice and religious thought can be very complex. How, many archaeologists ask themselves, can the fragmented archaeological record ever cover this complexity?

In recent years, however, ritual and religion have come to the fore as important areas of investigation in archaeology. There now even appears to be a sub-discipline called the archaeology of religion (Insoll 2004; Whitley and Hays-Gilpin 2008; Steadman 2009). As we shall see, this is probably due to the realization that ritual and religion were important and integral parts of life in ancient communities, and not dealing explicitly with these subjects will impoverish our understanding of them. Moreover, modern understanding of the practice and materiality of ritual and religion has resulted in a positive attitude towards the 'eloquence' of the archaeological record. Indeed, the number of convincing archaeological studies about ritual and religion seems to be steadily increasing.

In this chapter, I wish to make a further contribution to this field by focusing on theoretical and methodological aspects of the study of ritual. The objective is to present the reader with a general background with regard to two main questions: what is ritual and how can it be approached and reconstructed in archaeology? Given its long and rich research history on ritual, social anthropology shall play a major role as a 'frame of reference'.

2 Defining Ritual

In a recent debate about the archaeology of ritual (Kyriakidis 2007b), the necessity of defining ritual was contested. Bell (2007), for instance, argues that there is never going to be agreement on such a definition because ritual has too many functions and meanings and, according to her, no scientific field moves forward because of a good definition. Bell suggests that we should rather look at what ritual does (by means of the concept of ritualization, see below). Bowie (2000: 22), in her handbook on the anthropology of religion, further adds that 'we need to remember that we are constructing a category... based upon European languages and cultures, and that the term has no necessary equivalent in other parts of the world. At best we are therefore looking at a clumsy process of translation...'. Moreover, definitions have the problem of having to be broad enough to include a wide variety of activities, but at the same time they have to preserve some explanatory value.

Notwithstanding these sensible arguments, I believe that by considering definitions of ritual we can learn something about it. As Kyriakidis (2007a) notes, a definition need not to be universally accepted in order to be useful.

3 Definitions

Firth's definition of ritual, formulated as long ago as 1951, is still useful for introductory purposes. Firth (1951: 222) considered ritual to be: 'a kind of patterned activity oriented towards the control of human affairs, primarily symbolic in character with a non-empirical referent, and as a rule socially sanctioned'. By this general definition we are immediately made aware that ritual seems to be a multifaceted phenomenon, as a number of different aspects are mentioned: formalism, explicit symbolism, reference to the supernatural, and social sanctioning.

In fact, most other definitions of rituals mention the different aspects of it. I shall give a few other famous examples. In his important book on ritual and religion in the 'making of humanity', Rappaport (1999: 24) defines ritual as 'the performance of more or less invariant sequences of formal acts and utterances not entirely encoded by the performers'; whilst according to Tambiah (1979: 119), 'Ritual is a culturally constructed system of symbolic communication. It is constituted of patterned and ordered sequences of words and acts, often expressed in multiple media, whose content and arrangement are characterized in varying degree by formality (conventionality), stereotypy (rigidity), condensation (fusion), and redundancy (repetition).'

My final two examples are from archaeologists. Renfrew and Kyriakidis have recently defined ritual as 'practices that are time-structured and involve performance, with the repetition of words and actions in formalized ways' (Renfrew 2007a: 109–10); 'an etic category that refers to set activities with a special (not-normal) intention-in-action, and which are specific to a group of people' (Kyriakidis 2007a: 294). It is instructive to look somewhat closer at the various properties mentioned in these definitions, which can be grouped into a number of basic attributes.

3.1 Basic Attributes

Bell (1997: 138–69) has distinguished six basic attributes of ritual, which are neither exclusive nor definitive. The categories are: (1) formalism, (2) traditionalism, (3) disciplined invariance, (4) rule-governance, (5) sacral symbolism, and (6) performance.

3.1.1 Formalism

This refers to a limited and rigidly organized set of expressions and gestures, a restricted code of communication or behaviour, in contrast to a more open and elaborated code. Formality should be understood in terms of contrast and degree. Thus, formal activities are explicitly contrasted with informal contexts. Moreover, activities can be formalized to different degrees.

3.1.2 Traditionalism

This is the attempt to make activities appear to be identical to, or consistent with, preceding cultural practices. It serves as a powerful tool of legitimation and may be expressed as repetitions of past activities, adaptations of these in new settings, or the invention of practices to evoke links with the past.

3.1.3 Disciplined invariance

This can be defined as a disciplined set of actions characterized by precise repetition and physical control: 'The emphasis may be on the careful choreography of actions, the self-control required by the actor, or the rhythm of repetition in which the orchestrated activity is the most recent in an exact series that unites past and future' (Bell 1997: 150).

3.1.4 Rule-governance

This refers to explicitly formulated norms (rules), which are imposed upon, and are meant to restrict, human action and interaction.

3.1.5 Sacral symbolism

This denotes the use of sacred, non-profane, symbols. For Bell (1997: 159) sacredness is not related to the supernatural only, but also to special activities that 'evoke experiences of a greater, higher, or more universalized reality—the group, the nation, humankind, the power of God, or the balance of the cosmos'.

3.1.6 Performance

Mentioned in many definitions, this is the deliberate self-conscious practice of often highly symbolic actions in public. Performances are often dramatic actions which provide multisensory experiences that can be memorable and even shocking. Moreover, performance creates a special context, one in which a clear difference is made with the surrounding world. A quite dramatic example of a ritual performance is the Hain initiation ritual of the sub-recent Selk'nam hunter-gatherers of Patagonia, in which so-called Shoorts (Figure 9.1) actively terrorized the initiates (Chapman 1982; 1997; Verhoeven 2010).

Based on these key principles, I define ritual as performances which are distinguished in both space and time, marked by explicit material and immaterial symbolism, often (but not always) related to the supernatural, in which behaviour is guided and restricted by tradition, rules and repetition. Note that this definition is only about the *form* of rituals. With regard to *function* and *meaning* I propose that rituals are practices in which symbolic communication serves to establish relationships between humans and/or supernatural beings.

3.2 Types of Rituals

There are many different rituals in which the above-listed attributes play various roles: marriages, circumcision, baptism, funerals, prayer, Christmas, harvest rituals, coronations, etc. It is helpful to classify such rituals. First of all, a basic distinction can be made between rituals of world religions (Christianity, Islam, etc.), in which ritual actions are often prescribed in written scriptures, and rituals in 'traditional' religions (e.g. in small-scale societies in New Guinea), which lack written creeds (Bowie 2000: 26).

Another fundamental distinction is often made between religious and non-religious rituals. Obviously, religious rituals refer to ceremonies that involve a belief in supernatural beings (which is the most basic definition of religion), while non-religious rituals do not. Examples of the former would be prayer, baptism, shamanistic rites, pilgrimages, etc., while illustrations of profane rituals are coronations, birthdays, greetings, etc. However, the distinction between the sacred and the profane, or the supernatural and the social, is often difficult to make and in many contexts even not present at all. For instance, since the fundamental work of Durkheim (1995), it is acknowledged that religious rituals have important social functions, with regard to, for example, social cohesion, uniting people by their belief, and the establishment and maintenance of power structures, making social differences appear as supernatural. A second problem with the distinction is that it appears to be meaningless in many societies. This so-called holism will be discussed later, but first let us further deal with ritual typology.

Six basic categories of ritual action, which seem to comprise most (but of course not all) rituals, are: (1) rites of passage; (2) calendrical and commemorative rites; (3) rites of exchange and communion; (4) rites of affliction; (5) rites of feasting, fasting and festivals; and (6) political rituals (Bell 1997).

3.2.1 Rites of passage

As is well-known, these are so-called life-cycle rituals, which mark a person's transition from one social stage to another. Examples are birth, puberty rituals, marriage, and death. According to van Gennep (1960), all rites of passage are marked by a tripartite structure, consisting of separation, transition, and incorporation. Victor Turner (1969) is perhaps best known for his work on the transitional—or so-called liminal—stage, marked by ambiguity and anti-structural traits (for a more recent example see Guenther 1999). The work of Hertz

FIGURE 9.1 Dramatic ritual performance: a *Shoort* participating in the Hain initiation ritual of the Selk'nam of Patagonia. Typically, the man representing the spirit (probably a manifestation of the sun) is naked and decorated by painted abstract symbols. The mask seems to be made of Guanco hide stuffed with leaves or dry grass. (Redrawn photo taken by Gusinde 1931; republished by Prieto and Cárdenas 1997, fig. 144).

(1960) on the different elements of funerals—i.e. the three so-called *dramatis personae*: the corpse, the soul, and the mourners—is useful to better understand this transformation and the anxieties it involves (Metcalf and Huntington 1991; Parker Pearson 1999).

3.2.2 Calendrical and commemorative rites

These are rituals that are basically structured by time. Calendrical rites predictably occur at fixed times and are related to, for example, changes in seasons, agricultural work, and other activities. Examples are harvest rituals and rituals accompanying winter and summer solstices. Commemorative rites are rituals in which important historical events are recalled or celebrated.

3.2.3 Rites of exchange and communion

These denote human–divine interactions, with the human expectation of getting something back for their gifts to supernatural beings. Such ritual acts of exchange often establish intricate mutual dependencies between the natural and supernatural worlds, with the purpose of ensuring the prosperity of both. Offerings (of incense, flowers, and so on) to the gods are the most straightforward examples. Sacrifices are special forms of offerings. As Hubert and Mauss (1964) have set out, in sacrifices the offerings are sanctified, i.e. made holy. In this process of sanctification the sacrificed objects are most often destroyed: burned to transfer them to the gods or eaten to share it with them. Many of the special, or 'structured' deposits (Hill 1995) encountered by archaeologists, such as depositions of either unused or deliberately broken and damaged bronze objects in wet contexts in the Netherlands (Fontijn 2002), are interpreted as rites of exchange and communion (see e.g. Bradley 1990).

3.2.4 Rites of affliction

These have the purpose of abating the negative influence of supernatural beings. Purification and healing (e.g. exorcism) are the most central elements of this type of rituals.

3.2.5 Rites of feasting, fasting, and festivals

These are all social dramas marked by the overt public display of adherence to social and often religious norms and values. Perhaps the potlatches of the Northwest Coast Indians of North America are the most famous instances of feasting. It is not only, as it is well-known, a competitive feast focused on display and exchange to enhance status and prestige; it is also a negotiation between humans, other natural beings and objects, and supernatural beings, which all depend on each other (Goldman 1975). Feasting, especially competitive feasting, has been popular among archaeologists to explain various aspects of the past, such as the domestication of plants in the Near East (Hayden 1990), the politics of food (Dietler and Hayden 2001), and Neolithic pottery decoration (Nieuwenhuyse 2007).

3.2.6 Political rituals

These, finally, are practices that 'specifically construct, display and promote the power of political institutions (such as king, state, the village elders) or the political interests of distinct constituencies and subgroups' (Bell 1997: 128). Such political power is often established by using symbolism to inflict a notion of social cohesion based on shared norms and values, which are then argued to be 'natural'.

3.3 Approaches

Perhaps to complicate matters even further, there are not only many different definitions, attributes, and types of rituals, but, in fact following from this multidimensionality, there are also numerous approaches to the study of it. In each of these approaches ritual is defined and interpreted by focusing on particular aspects of it. Table 9.1 presents a general overview of the most common anthropological approaches, their emphasis ('dimension') and their main proponents.

These different theories have been extensively dealt with elsewhere (see, for example, Cunningham 1999; Morris 2006; Verhoeven 2002a); here I shall just briefly deal with so-called cognitive approaches and practice approaches.

3.3.1 Cognitive approaches

In cognitive approaches, obviously, the relations between the human mind and ritual and religion are analysed. For instance, concerning himself with the question of why, in general, religion is so widespread and why religions often have so many features in common, Boyer (2001) has argued that this is because of human cognition. He maintains that intuitively people differentiate between the natural and the supernatural. Religious representations, then, are 'good to think with' and are persistent components of human minds. Due to the constraints of our mental activities, such representations have many features in common, such as the structure of rituals (e.g. the tripartite structure of rites of passage) and the belief in supernatural beings. Perhaps unfortunately for archaeologists, material culture (religious objects) hardly figures in Boyer's theory, which is almost wholly concerned with 'internal' mechanisms (the mind). Other cognitive researchers, including Donald (1991) and McCauley and Lawson (2007) and the archaeologists Renfrew (2007b) and Mithen (1996), however, have stressed that 'external' elements, the environment and objects (including literacy), were and are of crucial importance in our cognitive development. There is a dialectic, then, between our brains and our surroundings. The neurophysiologist Diamond (1988), for instance, investigated the impact of the environment on the anatomy of the brain, based on experimental studies with rats. She distinguished so-called enriched and impoverished environments. Enriched environments consisted of sufficiently large and diversified surroundings with a number of species; in impoverished environments a single animal was enclosed in a monotonous surrounding. Diamond found that enriched or impoverished environments respectively had positive and negative effects on brain growth throughout the life of rats. Very probably this holds for humans as well.

McCauley and Lawson have put forward a unified theory about religious ritual that not only acknowledges the important role of external objects, but also the contextual nature of

Table 9.1 The Main Anthropological Approaches to Ritual.

Approach	Dimension	Main proponents
Intellectualism	explaining the world	Frazer (1990), Goody (1961), Horton (1973), Spencer (1885), Tylor (1929)
Emotionalism	dealing with emotions	Freud (1985), Malinowski (1982), Tarlow (1999)
Functionalism	regulating society: function	Durkheim (1995), Evans-Pritchard (1937), Radcliffe-Brown (1956), Rappaport (1999)
Symbolism	symbolic communication: meaning	Douglas (1973), Geertz (1973), Tambiah (1979), Turner (1969), van Gennep (1960)
Structuralism	underlying structural system	Leach (1976), Lévi-Strauss (1968)
Cognitive approaches	cognitive elements of ritual form	Boyer (2001), Humphrey and Laidlaw (1994), Lewis-Williams (2008), McCauley and Lawson (2002), Whitehouse (2004), Renfrew (2007b)
Marxist approaches	ideology	Bloch (1989), Godelier (1977)
Relational approaches	holism	de Coppet (1992), Descola (1994), Dumont (1980), Houseman and Severi (1998)
Performance approaches	drama, *communitas*	Schechner (1994), Schieffelin (1985), Staal (1989), Turner (1982)
Practice approaches	action, ritualization	Bell (1993), Bourdieu (1977)

religious practice. Their theory has been recently summarized for archaeologists (McCauley and Lawson 2007), including a glossary of the rather idiosyncratic terms used, and need not be further elaborated upon here. However, one of the useful observations they make is that, however strange they may be, religious rituals are actions too, guided by the same cognitive system that guides everyday practice. This brings us to the second set of approaches to be discussed.

3.3.2 *Practice approaches*

In what, for want for a better term, has been called practice approaches here, it is explicitly acknowledged that ritual is social action, i.e. that it is only through the performance of activities that ritual has meaning. These approaches are largely based on Bourdieu's *Theory of Practice*, which stresses the active and recursive relationships between social practice and rules and norms (as particularly materialized in architecture). Bourdieu himself (1977) has regarded rituals as specific activities which create certain situations by correctly performing according to rules. The power of rituals lies in the act of acceptance of these rules, which seemingly are immanent. Moreover, rituals transform differences of a biological or social nature in culturally meaningful distinctions. Ritual, according to Bourdieu, is a type of social strategy that simultaneously integrates and differentiates the social world; it is not a separate domain, but a practical (and special) activity among others. An important term that has surfaced within practice approaches is that of *ritualization*, which due to its archaeological potential will be discussed separately in somewhat more detail.

3.4 Ritualization

In general terms, ritualization can be described as the process in which different forms of behaviour are modified and combined to form a ritual. Humphrey and Laidlaw (1994, 2007) have in this respect argued that ritual is a quality that actions can come to have, instead of being a separate category of special events. Thus, many different activities may be ritualized and, vice versa, ritual activities always have non-ritual connotations. Notwithstanding the ties with everyday activities, it is clear that rituals are special in some way. According to Humphrey and Laidlaw what sets ritual apart from other activities is that in ritual intentionality is displaced; ritual participants at the same time are and are not the source of their actions. Both non-religious and religious activities can have different degrees (from low to high) of ritualization.

Bell (1993) is perhaps best known for her work on ritualization, which also for her is meant to indicate that ritual is deeply embedded in social systems and that ritual actions derive their significance from the interplay and contrasts with other practices. According to her, ritualization is accomplished by, first, the generation of a privileged position among other activities. Thus, a structured symbolic environment is created, characterized by the use of a space to which access is restricted, a special time, restricted codes of communication, special persons and objects, special verbal and gestural combinations, particular physical or mental states, and especially formalization. Second, through generation of the structured environment, ritualized agents are produced. Following Bourdieu (1977), it is argued that the active and dialectical relationship between the cognitive frameworks ('habitus') of participants and ritual practice is a continuous process of interpretation, reinterpretation, and change. Ritual, then, does not reflect or reproduce existing norms and values, but rather negotiates these. Therefore, rituals are often strategic actions, which are not necessarily representative of a commonly accepted religion. Likewise, rituals may be less structured or rule-bound than theoretically expected, for ritualization involves complex interactions between different participants with perhaps conflicting agendas (see also Knottnerus 1997).

One of the archaeologists who has explicitly used the concept of ritualization is Bradley (2005) in his study of ritual and domestic life in prehistoric Europe. Bradley questions the—on the basis of state-religions—often-assumed division between non-ritual and ritual (or sacred and quotidian) activities, contexts, and objects in the small-scale prehistoric communities of Europe. By taking ritual to be practice/performance that can occur in many contexts, he has looked for evidence of ritual activities in different places. It appears that, indeed, rituals were performed in many different contexts, which would traditionally be called sacred or profane. For instance, it seems that mortality and the agricultural cycle were related in various ways in different parts of Neolithic Europe. For instance, artefact assemblages of megalithic tombs often referred to the domestic domain, while causewayed enclosures showed combinations of human bones and farm animals. Likewise, votive deposits of this period were dominated by artefacts related to food consumption.

3.5 Ethnocentrism, the Sacred–Profane Dichotomy, and Holism

Now that the structure and nature of ritual has been summarized, one of the main problems with it can be dealt with, i.e. ethnocentrism, including the sacred–profane distinction.

The work of Bradley, among others (e.g. Insoll 2007), has made us aware that our preconceptions about what ritual is (or should be) may limit a true understanding of the past. Recently Price (2008), among others, has in this respect argued that our modern, post-Enlightenment, ritual and religious practices, which are often taken as models, are very probably not applicable to small-scale, pre-state, prehistoric societies. As he points out, the concept of religion as something orthodox, marked by strict rules of obedience and behaviour and worship would probably not have been understood by pre-Christian communities in Europe. For these people ritual and religion would have been embedded in many, if not all, aspects of life. Boundaries between the natural and supernatural probably were loose and permeable. For example, the Viking gods (such as Odin, Thor, and Freya), did not have to be worshipped in the modern Western sense of the concept. They only demanded a recognition that they were part of both the natural and supernatural world. Denial of this would disturb the balance in the 'socio-cosmic universe' (de Coppet and Iteanu 1995), and therefore life itself. As Price (2008: 147) indicates, asking a Viking whether (s)he believed in the gods would be to ask if (s)he believed in the sea.

In a comparable critique of what we may conveniently label ethnocentrism, Brück (1999) has argued that due to our modern Western rationality, rituals—with no intrinsic means–ends relationship—are often regarded as distinctly sacred, non-functional, and irrational actions. This kind of rationality, however, is not found in all societies. In fact, it is by now well-known that strict separations (between for example, nature and culture, the sacred and profane, the living and the dead, objects and people, etc.) are utterly meaningless to many 'traditional' small-scale communities all over the world (e.g. Descola and Pálsson 1996). These communities, then, may be regarded as holistic, since they live by relations, rather than by separations. They are probably closer to the prehistoric communities that many archaeologists study than the state-societies that implicitly serve as models for reconstructing the past. In fact, prehistorians are increasingly finding evidence of this holism in the archaeological record (see e.g. Verhoeven 2004).

It seems to be the case, then, that the sacred–profane dichotomy (Eliade 1954), which is still explicitly, but more often implicitly, used, is far too simple. Certainly, there are, and undoubtedly were, sacred and profane contexts, but it is probably more productive to view the holy and quotidian as the two extreme ends of a continuum. Many contexts and activities are situated somewhere between these extremes, having different degrees or qualities of both the holy and the domestic.

3.6 Ritual and Religion

Finally, with regard to defining rituals, a few words on the relationships between ritual and religion are in order. First, we have seen that there are both religious and non-religious rituals, but it may now be added that there is a continuum between religiousness and non-religiousness. Second, I think we have to agree with the premise of practice theory that

THE MANY DIMENSIONS OF RITUAL 125

FIGURE 9.2 View of the front part of one of the large T-shaped stone pillars in a ritual building at Early Neolithic Göbekli Tepe (pillar 33 in building D): indicating symbolic connections between different animals. (Redrawn from Schmidt 2006, Abb. 92).

ritual activity is not a secondary aspect of religion (subordinate to beliefs, which would be primary), but that it is central. It is through ritual action that religious beliefs are communicated, negotiated, and transmitted. For archaeologists this central position of ritual is exciting, as the remains of these activities present major opportunities for studying ancient religions. But how can ritual be detected and studied?

4 Recognizing and Reconstructing Ritual

4.1 Framing

As already indicated at the beginning of this chapter, there seems to be ample evidence in the archaeological record for ritual and religious objects and contexts. An example of this are a series of circular stone buildings with megalithic decorated T-shaped pillars and large stone sculptures with various human and animal depictions at the Early Neolithic (c.9100–8500 cal BC) site of Göbekli Tepe in south-eastern Turkey (Figure 9.2). Virtually all researchers agree that this site must have had major ritual and religious significance (Schmidt 2006, 2007).

I shall return to the problem of interpreting such material, but first we must ask why and how archaeologists recognize such ritual objects and contexts. We have seen that rituals are usually marked by special symbolic behaviour and the use of special contexts and objects. These latter may be recovered in the archaeological record, and with regard to this I have introduced the notion of *framing* (Verhoeven 2002a, 2002b). Framing can be defined as the way, or performance, in which people and/or activities and/or objects are set off from others, spatially and/or chronologically, for ritual purposes. It is mainly achieved by creating a special place, a special time, and by the use of uncommon objects, whether on a micro (e.g. individual) or macro (e.g. public) scale. To quote Douglas (1966, 64) 'a ritual provides a frame. The marked off time or place alerts a special expectancy, just as the oft-repeated "Once upon a time" creates a mood receptive to fantastic tales.' In archaeology, framing may be recognized by trying to detect deviations from the 'norm' at the site or area investigated. Note that this is different from approaches based on checklists of universal—often ethnocentric—indications for ritual (see e.g. Insoll 2004: 59). With regard to buildings, for instance, peculiarities in location, shape, texture, colour, size, orientation, and construction material in buildings, as well as the presence of special features, inventories, and symbols might be the starting point for detecting framing and ritual.

While the concept of framing acknowledges the special nature of rituals, it does not resurrect the sacred–profane distinction; rather it is a way of getting access to ritual and religion in ancient communities. As we have seen, ritual can pervade all aspects of life: many 'profane' or 'domestic' objects may have religious meaning. However, as a starting point, for archaeologists it is virtually impossible to detect this. Therefore, I argue that an analysis of prehistoric ritual should *start* with distinguishing the most 'obvious' framed objects and deposits. Once detected, these should be contextualized, for example by looking for spatial associations, with the potential of gaining access to the less obvious ritual significance of other elements and contexts, such as the temporal distinction of spaces for ritual purposes.

An example of this is provided by the analysis of a mortuary ritual in a burnt Neolithic tell settlement in northern Syria. The initially framed elements of this ritual consisted of two human skeletons surrounded by large loaf-shaped clay objects, which may have represented mythical creatures, given that some of them were marked by the horns of wild sheep. In relating this ritual to architecture, artefacts, and formation processes, it seems that the settlement was most likely not burnt accidentally, as was previously assumed, but purposely set on fire as part of an abandonment/mortuary ritual (Verhoeven 2000).

4.2 Contextualization

In order to investigate whether framing has been reliably reconstructed and to make the archaeological study of ritual productive, a few basic research directions can be proposed, all of which have to do with *contextualization*. First of all, one has to make sure that the excavated evidence allows reconstructions of the functions and meanings of supposedly ritual and religious objects. When the objects are too fragmented, or when there is too little context, the information may simply be not good enough for beneficial reconstructions (Malone et al. 2007). Second, as ritual often seems to be deeply embedded in social life, and as it potentially leaves traces in different contexts, it should be attempted to relate it to other aspects of the archaeological record. Cooperation between specialists (e.g. the palaeobotanist, the archaeozoologist, the lithic expert, etc.) can be particularly helpful in this respect. Third, not only good archaeological context needs to be generated, but also profitable interpretative context ('thick description'). Ethnography can be particularly helpful here, not so much to provide direct analogies but to make one aware of types, structures, functions, and meanings of ritual practices in non-Western contexts, if only to counter ethnocentric presuppositions. More in general, the rich body of literature on ritual in the social sciences is an extremely valuable resource (hence the attention paid to it in this chapter). The different approaches as listed in Table 9.1 each highlight different aspects of ritual, which can be relevant for the specific contexts studied (e.g. rites of passage for burials) or preferred interpretations (e.g. relational approaches for dealing with links between the natural and the supernatural).

5 Conclusion

Given the many different definitions, attributes, typologies, and approaches used by researchers, as well as the fact that in many societies ritual and religion are inextricably bound up with every other aspect of life, it has been argued that ritual is not only a multidimensional, but also a holistic phenomenon. Thus, in many contexts rituals are basic mechanisms for the proper operation of the 'socio-cosmic universe', relating social and supernatural domains. Ethnocentric assumptions regarding the sacred and profane, or other taken-for-granted distinctions should therefore be treated with suspicion, especially when dealing with small-scale prehistoric societies. The many dimensions of ritual make it not only a very interesting but also a rather difficult subject, especially for archaeologists who have to work with material culture only. However, there are many clues in the past as well as in the present, which promise to make the archaeology of ritual and religion not only a challenging, but also a very promising field of research.

SUGGESTED READING

There is a plethora of literature about ritual in both anthropology and archaeology. In Table 9.1 some of the major publications of the various anthropological approaches to ritual have been referred to; they can be found in the bibliography. Two more general useful publications on the anthropology of ritual and religion are Bowie (2000) and Morris (2006). Probably still the best book on ritual only is Bell's *Ritual: Perspectives and dimensions* of 1997. There is also the *Journal of Ritual Studies*, which deals with all aspects of ritual and it is aimed at an interdisciplinary audience. For the study of ritual in archaeology the recent books of Barrowclough and Malone (2007), Insoll (2004), Kyriakidis (2007b), Steadman (2009), and Whitley and Hays-Gilpin (2008) provide excellent backgrounds with regard to theory, methods, and data.

ACKNOWLEDGEMENTS

First of all, I would like to thank Tim Insoll for giving me the opportunity to write a chapter in this volume. Moreover, his editorial comments improved the paper. Rachel MacLean is also thanked for her work in this regard. Jenny Wagstaffe of Oxford University Press made all the necessary arrangements for publishing this contribution. Ans Bulles corrected the English text and Mikko Kriek made the drawings.

REFERENCES

BARROWCLOUGH, D. A. and MALONE, C. (eds) 2007. *Cult in context: Reconsidering ritual in archaeology* (Oxford: Oxbow Books).
BELL, C. 1993. *Ritual Theory, Ritual Practice* (New York/Oxford: Oxford University Press).
—— 1997. *Ritual: Perspectives and dimensions* (New York/Oxford: Oxford University Press).
—— 2007. 'Response: Defining the need for a definition' in E. Kyriakidis (ed.), *The Archaeology of Ritual* (Los Angeles: Cotsen Institute of Archaeology at UCLA), pp. 277–88.
BLOCH, M. 1989. *Ritual, History and Power: Selected papers in anthropology* (London: Athlone Press).
BOURDIEU, P. 1977. *Outline of a Theory of Practice* (Cambridge: Cambridge University Press).
BOWIE, F. 2000. *The Anthropology of Religion* (Oxford: Blackwell).
BOYER, P. 2001. *Religion Explained: The human instincts that fashion gods, spirits and ancestors* (London: William Heinemann).
BRADLEY, R. 1990. *The Passage of Arms: An archaeological analysis of prehistoric hoards and votive deposits* (Cambridge: Cambridge University Press).

—— 2005. *Ritual and Domestic Life in Prehistoric Europe* (New York: Routledge).
BRÜCK, J. 1999. 'Ritual and rationality: Some problems of interpretation in European archaeology', *European Journal of Archaeology*, 2(3): 313–44.
CHAPMAN, A. 1982. *Drama and Power in a Hunting Society: The Selk'nam of Tierra del Fuego* (Cambridge: Cambridge University Press).
—— 1997. 'The great ceremonies of the Selk'nam and the Yámana: A comparative analysis' in C. McEwan, L. A. Borrero, and A. Prieto (eds), *Patagonia: Natural history, prehistory and ethnography at the uttermost end of the earth* (Princeton: Princeton University Press), pp. 82–109.
CUNNINGHAM, G. 1999. *Religion and Magic: Approaches & theories* (Edinburgh: Edinburgh University Press).
COPPET, D. DE (ed.) 1992. *Understanding Rituals* (London/New York: Routledge).
—— and ITEANU, A. (eds) 1995. *Cosmos and Society in Oceania* (Oxford: Berg).
DESCOLA, P. 1994. *In the Society of Nature: A native ecology in Amazonia* (Cambridge: Cambridge University Press).
—— and PÁLSSON, G. (eds) 1996. *Nature and Society: Anthropological perspectives* (London: Routledge).
DIAMOND, M. C. 1988. *Enriching Heredity: The impact of the environment on the anatomy of the brain* (New York: The Free Press).
DIETLER, M. and HAYDEN, B. (eds.) 2001. *Feasts: Archaeological and ethnographic perspectives on food, politics and power* (Washington: Smithsonian Institution Press).
DONALD, M. 1991. *Origins of the Modern Mind: Three stages in the evolution of culture and cognition* (Cambridge: Harvard University Press).
DOUGLAS, M. 1966. *Purity and Danger: An analysis of the concepts of pollution and taboo* (London/New York: Routledge).
—— 1973. *Natural Symbols: Explorations in cosmology* (New York: Vintage Books).
DUMONT, L. 1980. *Homo hierarchicus: The caste system and its implications* (London/Chicago: University of Chicago Press).
DURKHEIM, E. 1995 [1912]. *The Elementary Forms of Religious Life* (New York, etc.: Free Press).
ELIADE, M. 1954. *The Sacred and the Profane: The nature of religion* (New York: Harcourt Brace Jovanovich).
EVANS-PRITCHARD, E. E. 1937. *Witchcraft, Oracles and Magic among the Azande* (Oxford: Oxford University Press).
FIRTH, R. 1951. *Elements of Social Organization* (London: Watts).
FOGELIN, L. 2007. 'The archaeology of religious ritual', *Annual Review of Anthropology*, 36: 55–71.
FONTIJN, D. 2002. *Sacrificial Landscapes: Cultural biographies of persons, objects and 'natural places' in the Bronze Age of the Southern Netherlands, c. 2300-600 BC* (Leiden: Analecta Praehistoria Leidensia 33/34).
FRAZER, J. G. 1990 [1911]. *The Golden Bough: A study in magic and religion* (London: Macmillan).
FREUD, S. 1985 [1913]. 'Totem and taboo' in: *The Pelican Freud Library* 13 (Harmondsworth: Pelican Books).
GARWOOD, P., JENNINGS, D., SKEATES, R. and TOMS, J. (eds) 1991. *Sacred and Profane: Proceedings of a conference on archaeology, ritual and religion, Oxford, 1989* (Oxford: Oxford University Committee for Archaeology).
GEERTZ, C. 1973. *The Interpretation of Cultures* (New York: Basic Books).

Gennep, A. van 1960 [1909]. *The Rites of Passage* (Chicago: the University of Chicago Press).
Godelier, M. 1977. *Perspectives in Marxist Anthropology* (Cambridge: Cambridge University Press).
Goldman, I. 1975. *The Mouth of Heaven: An introduction to Kwakiutl religious thought* (New York: John Wiley).
Goody, J. 1961. 'Religion and Ritual: The definitional problem', *British Journal of Sociology*, 12: 142–64.
Guenther, M. 1999. *Tricksters & Trancers: Busman religion and society* (Bloomington/Indianapolis: Indiana University Press).
Gusinde, M. 1931. *Die Feuerland-Indianer, Band I: Die Selk'nam* (Mödling bei Wien: Verlag der Internationalen Zeitschrift *Anthropos*).
Hayden, B. 1990. 'Nimrods, piscators, pluckers, and planters: The emergence of food production', *Journal of Anthropological Archaeology*, 9: 31–69.
Hertz, R. 1960 [1907]. 'A contribution to the study of the collective representation of death' in R. Needham and C. Needham (trans.), *Death and the Right Hand* (New York: Free Press).
Hill, J. D. 1995. *Ritual and Rubbish in the Iron Age of Wessex: A study on the formation of a specific archaeological record*, BAR British Series 242 (Oxford: BAR).
Horton, R. 1973. 'Lévy-Bruhl, Durkheim and the scientific revolution' in M. Horton and R. Finnegan (eds), *Modes of Thought* (London: Faber and Faber), pp. 249–305.
Houseman, M. and Severi, C. 1998. *Naven or the Other Self: A relational approach to ritual action* (Leiden: Brill).
Hubert, H. and Mauss, M. 1964 [1898]. *Sacrifice: Its nature and functions* (Chicago: University of Chicago Press).
Humphrey, C. and Laidlaw, J. 1994. *The Archetypal Actions of Ritual: A theory of ritual illustrated by the Jain rite of worship* (Oxford: Clarendon Press).
Insoll, T. 2004. *Archaeology, Ritual, Religion* (London/New York: Routledge).
—— 2007. *Archaeology: The conceptual challenge* (London: Duckworth).
Knottnerus, D. 1997. 'The theory of structural ritualization' in B. Markovsky, M. J. Lovaglia, and L. Troyer (eds), *Advances in Group Processes*, XIV (Greenwich: JAI Press), pp. 257–79.
Kyriakidis, E. 2007a. 'Archaeologies of ritual' in E. Kyriakidis (ed.), *The Archaeology of Ritual* (Los Angeles: Cotsen Institute of Archaeology at UCLA), pp. 289–308.
—— ed., 2007b. *The Archaeology of Ritual* (Los Angeles: Cotsen Institute of Archaeology at UCLA).
Leach, E. R. 1976. *Culture and Communication: The logic by which symbols are connected* (Cambridge: Cambridge University Press).
Lévi-Strauss, C. 1968. *Structural Anthropology* (London: Allen Lane, The Penguin Press).
Lewis-Williams, J. D. 2008. 'Religion and archaeology: An analytical materialist account' in D. S. Whitley and K. Hays-Gilpin (eds), *Belief in the Past: Theoretical approaches to the archaeology of religion* (Walnut Creek: Left Coast Press), pp. 23–42.
McCauley, R. N. and Lawson, E. T. 2002. *Bringing Ritual to Mind: Psychological foundations of cultural forms* (Cambridge: Cambridge University Press).
—— 2007. 'Cognition, religious ritual and archaeology' in E. Kyriakidis (ed.), *The Archaeology of Ritual* (Los Angeles: Cotsen Institute of Archaeology at UCLA), pp. 209–54.
Malinowski, B. 1982 [1925]. *Magic, Science and Religion and Other Essays* (London: Souvenir Press).

MALONE, C., BARROWCLOUGH, D. A. and STODDART, S. 2007. 'Introduction' in D. A. Barrowclough and C. Malone (eds), *Cult in Context: Reconsidering ritual in archaeology* (Oxford: Oxbow Books), pp. 1–7.

METCALF, P. and HUNTINGTON, R. 1991. *Celebrations of death: The anthropology of mortuary ritual* (Cambridge: Cambridge University Press).

MITHEN, S. 1996. *The Prehistory of the Mind* (London: Thames and Hudson).

MORRIS, B. 2006. *Religion and Anthropology: A critical introduction* (Cambridge: Cambridge University Press).

NIEUWENHUYSE, O. 2007. *Plain and Painted Pottery: The rise of Late Neolithic ceramic styles on the Syrian and northern Mesopotamian plains* (Turnhout: Brepols).

PARKER PEARSON, M. 1999. *The Archaeology of Death and Burial* (Stroud: Sutton).

PRICE, N. S. 2008. 'Bodylore and the archaeology of embedded religion: Dramatic license in the funerals of the Vikings' in D. S. Whitley and K. Hays-Gilpin (eds), *Belief in the Past: Theoretical approaches to the archaeology of religion* (Walnut Creek: Left Coast Press), pp. 143–65.

PRIETO, A. and CÁRDENAS, R. 1997. *Introduction to Ethnographic Photography in Patagonia* (Punta Arenas: Hernán Pisano Skarmeta).

RADCLIFFE-BROWN, A. R. 1956. *Structure and Function in Primitive Society* (London: Cohen and West).

RAPPAPORT, R.A. 1999. *Ritual and Religion in the Making of Humanity* (Cambridge: Cambridge University Press).

RENFREW, C. 1985. *The Archaeology of Cult: The sanctuary at Phylakopi* (London: Thames and Hudson).

——2007a. 'The archaeology of ritual, of cult, and of religion' in E. Kyriakidis (ed.), *The Archaeology of Ritual* (Los Angeles: Cotsen Institute of Archaeology at UCLA), pp. 109–22.

——2007b. *Prehistory: Making of the human mind* (London: Weidenfeld and Nicolson).

SCHECHNER, R. 1994. 'Ritual and performance' in T. Ingold (ed.), *Companion Encyclopedia of Anthropology: Humanity, culture and social life* (London/New York: Routledge), pp. 613–47.

SCHIEFFELIN, E. L. 1985. 'Performance and the cultural construction of reality', *American Ethnologist*, 12: 707–24.

SCHMIDT, K. 2006. *Sie bauten die ersten Tempel: das rätselhafte Heiligtum der Steinzeitjäger* (München: C. H. Beck).

——2007. 'Die Steinkreise und die Reliefs des Göbekli Tepe' in C. Lichter (ed.), *Vor 12.000 Jahren in Anatolien: die ältesten Monumente der Menschheit* (Stuttgart: Theiss), pp. 83–96.

SPENCER, H. 1885. *A System of Synthetic Philosophy 6: Principles of sociology 1* (London: Williams and Norgate).

STAAL, F. 1989. *Rules without Meaning: Ritual, mantras and the human sciences* (New York, etc.: Peter Lang).

STEADMAN, S. R. 2009. *Archaeology of Religion: Cultures and their beliefs in worldwide context* (Walnut Creek: Left Coast Press).

TAMBIAH, S. J. 1979. *A Performative Approach to Ritual* (Oxford: Oxford University Press).

TARLOW, S. 1999. *Bereavement and Commemoration: An archaeology of mortality* (Oxford: Blackwell).

TRIGGER, B. 1999. 'Reconnoitring religion', *Cambridge Archaeological Journal*, 9(1): 139–41.

TURNER, V. 1969. *The Ritual Process: Structure and anti-structure* (Chicago: Aldine).

——1982. *From Ritual to Theater and Back: The human seriousness of play* (New York: PAJ Publications).

TYLOR, E. B. 1929. *Primitive Culture*, 2 vols. (London: John Murray).
VERHOEVEN, M. 2000. 'Death, fire and abandonment: Ritual practice at Late Neolithic Tell Sabi Abyad, Syria', *Archaeological Dialogues*, 7(1): 46–83.
VERHOEVEN, M. 2002a. 'Ritual and its investigation in prehistory' in H. G. K. Gebel, B. D. Hermansen, and C.H. Jensen (eds), *Magic Practices and Ritual in the Near Eastern Neolithic*, Studies in Early Near Eastern Production, Subsistence, and Environment 8 (Berlin: Ex Oriente), 5–40.
—— 2002b. 'Ritual and ideology in the pre-pottery Neolithic B of the Levant and South-East Anatolia', *Cambridge Archaeological Journal*, 12(2): 233–58.
—— 2004. 'Beyond boundaries: Nature, culture and a holistic approach to domestication in the Levant', *Journal of World Prehistory*, 18(3): 179–282.
—— 2010. 'Social complexity and archaeology: A contextual approach' in D. Bolger and L. Maguire (eds), *The Development of Pre-state Communities in the Ancient Near East* (Oxford: Oxbow), pp. 11–21.
WHITEHOUSE, H. 2004. *Modes of Religiosity: A cognitive theory of religious transmission* (Walnut Creek: Left Coast Press).
WHITLEY, D. S. and HAYS-GILPIN, K. 2008. 'Religion beyond icon, burial and monument: An introduction' in D. S. Whitley and K. Hays-Gilpin (eds), *Belief in the Past: Theoretical approaches to the archaeology of religion* (Walnut Creek: Left Coast Press), pp. 11–22.
—— —— (eds) 2008. *Belief in the Past: Theoretical approaches to the archaeology of religion* (Walnut Creek: Left Coast Press).

CHAPTER 10

PERSONHOOD AND THE BODY

CHRIS FOWLER

1 INTRODUCTION

THIS chapter will explore religious beliefs about personhood and religious practices relating to those beliefs. The first part will focus on concepts of the person, particularly the constitution of the person. The second part will examine the role of embodied ritual action in generating and transforming persons according to cosmological principles and within a religious framework. Examples are selected from ethnographic, historical, and archaeological sources. Until recently there has been relatively little research on personhood in archaeology and little of that explicitly addresses religious beliefs and practices (for notable exceptions see Graves 2008; Meskell and Joyce 2003; Oliver 2009). Although it discusses some important archaeological work, this chapter highlights areas of enquiry which could be pursued in future archaeological studies much more than it summarizes a tradition of archaeological research, and is more for archaeologists interested in personhood, ritual, and religion than it is about the work of previous archaeologists.

2 CONCEPTUALIZING PERSONHOOD

2.1 Religious Beliefs about the Constitution of Personhood

A person is a composite being, with distinct yet interwoven aspects. For communities with religious beliefs, personhood is a divinely sanctioned condition. Aspects of the person have spiritual qualities and one or more elements of the person may be immortal in origin and destiny: for instance, the soul that comes from God. Other elements may be mortal and ephemeral. Relationships between aspects of the person are complex. A person is first constituted during conception, though some aspects may precede birth and survive death and there are many different beliefs about when full personhood is achieved or how the relationship between personal aspects changes over time, especially following death. For Fortes (1987) Tallensi personhood could only be fully achieved once the male life-cycle was completed: i.e. after a man had successfully matured, married, procreated, died, and divination had confirmed the person as an ancestor to a lineage. Personhood was therefore a state of ancestry, a religiously sanctioned social condition dependent on practices and relationships during life. Indeed, the dead may be treated differently depending on the state of personhood achieved in life: unbaptized children were buried away from sacred ground in medieval Ireland (Finlay 2000), while among the Islamic Rajput caste of the rural Punjab children who 'die before they are made Muslims by having the call to prayer (*azan*) recited in their ear' are similarly buried outside the graveyard and full funeral rites are only accorded to adults who have married and borne children (Alvi 2001: 60–1). Often, personhood is not considered a static and uniform condition, but changes throughout the lifecourse. Religious beliefs concern not only ordinary states of personhood, but also *idealized* states of personhood which largely cannot be attained in this life, but must be aspired to in order to achieve that state following death.

Aspects of the person, and relationships between them, are specific to each religion, yet there are also broad points of commonality, particularly between traditions with shared heritage. For instance, the 'soul' is defined, and related to the 'body', in varied yet related ways in Zoroastrian, Jewish, Christian, and Islamic traditions. In Zoroastrianism the person consists of *ēwēnag* (form), *frawahr* (spirit), *tan* (body), *gyān* (vital soul) and *ruwān* (soul) (Williams 1997: 163). Form and spirit exist only in the spiritual world; the other aspects dwell in the material world during life. The material world is the work of the Creator (sky, earth, water, fire, plants, certain animals, and human beings are the seven 'creations' which must be respected), but the world is also permeated by the evil influences of the Hostile Spirit. These threaten the human person through the body. Body and soul are intertwined, and the body is to be kept in a pure state where it is fertile. Following the death of the body and the extinguishing of the vital soul (*gyan*), the soul (*ruwan*) passes through judgement and on to the afterlife. Bodily rewards and punishments described in heaven and hell are parables for spiritual rewards and punishments. Surrendering the body to evil forces leads towards damnation, but the body is not itself sinful (Williams 1997).

The unity or separability of the soul and body have been debated in Jewish traditions along with the nature of God and the nature of the soul itself (see Jacobs 1997 for a historical perspective on changing Jewish concepts of the soul and afterlife). The Kabbalistic view is that the soul has three parts: the *nefesh*, the lowest part, which remains with the corpse after death; the *ruah* which is punished for sins committed during life for one year then ascends to heaven; and the *neshamah* which ascends immediately following death (Jacobs 1997: 83). Greek Orthodox Christians draw from Old Testament concepts of complete integration of body and soul and Resurrection, fused with a Platonic view of the soul (Ware 1997). Here the soul also consists of three aspects: conscious intellect associated with the head; desire or appetite associated with the lower body; and will or spirit associated with the chest (Morris 1994: 36–7). But perhaps more important to Christian thought than the relationship between body and soul is that between flesh and spirit. While the sinful, fallen, mortal, and earthly flesh (the opposite of the ethereal spirit) is to be chastised, the body provides an image to be aspired to. The 'body' most commonly refers to the single human body, but here also the Eucharist taken in Communion, and the body of the congregation (see below). The human body is a divine form, since humanity was made in the image of God. The heart is where relationships between aspects of personhood and other forces are resolved, within each person. The heart therefore symbolizes complete personhood with God. In Islamic beliefs the matter of the body gives rise to the soul on conception. The soul can be 'selfish' providing ongoing temptations to be struggled with, and is a constant version of the self unlike the continually changing, growing, ageing body. After death the soul remains with the body, and will reanimate the body during Resurrection and both will be physically rewarded or punished in the afterlife (Winter 1995: 42–3).

In each of these traditions the soul is equated with consciousness and understanding (including will and thought) and an enduring sense of self, while the spirit is often perceived as life-force or fertile energy—but both aspects of the person have divine origins. The body itself is also divine in origin and not evil, although it is susceptible to evil through its matter (e.g. flesh) or the infiltration of the body by polluting forces. After death the person lives a second time (often following a period of limbo or purgatory before the Resurrection), and good ways of relating to others followed in life ensure good treatment in death when an idealized version of personhood is, all being well, attained. While heaven and hell are divided (though Zoroastrians believe that all will eventually be united with God following the end of time), personal identity in the world of the living and the afterlife otherwise mirror one another so those who attain goodness in life are made good after death. In some faiths virtuous conduct is not sufficient alone for salvation—the person must also have true faith in God and salvation.

There are also similarities between the concept of personhood in Central and Eastern Asian religious traditions. The key aspects of the person in Sikhism are body (*tan*) and soul (*atma*). Sikhs believe in reincarnation, and desire release from it; that release provides oneness with God. There is no hell to torment the soul or body, and asceticism is eschewed. In Hindu traditions matter in the womb receives a soul (*atman*) only when a body is fully formed (Parry 1994: 167–8). Souls pass through hell prior to reincarnation: they are tormented with memories of their previous lives while an embryo in the womb following reincarnation, but this consciousness is removed from them by Vishnu during birth (Doniger 1997: 174). The body is composed of worldly elements and each of these is charged in a certain way, like humours. But the person is not simply a fusion of body and soul: there are other key concepts used to understand personhood, including mind and spirit, while caste membership is another vital aspect of personhood, related to the reincarnation of the soul. In Buddhism the body is mortal, and the soul (which is again conscious) transcends death to be reborn. *Nirvana*, a release from the constant cycle of death and rebirth, is sought by following Buddha's 'middle way' between asceticism and indulgence. Collins (1997) argues that while this release promotes immateriality as the aspiration of Buddhist persons, such aspirations are nonetheless expressed materially in Buddhist objects, buildings, and bodies. These often present people experiencing blissful realizations in balanced, aesthetically pleasing and tranquil surroundings. At the same time, the body in Buddhism is essentially base, needing food (which is often seen as repulsive), producing waste, and continually decaying; as with all religions good bodily conduct is necessary in order to attain a desirable state of personhood or, more accurately in this case, dissolution from personhood. Various techniques, such as meditations, assist in achieving the necessary understanding of person and world to achieve *nirvana*, a fine illustration of the extent to which states of personhood have to be understood, achieved, and eventually surrendered, in many religious contexts.

In Taoist traditions spiritual aspects are identified with body parts, so that *ch'i* (energy or breath) associated with the mind is located in the head, *shen* (soul, spirit, or will) in the heart, and *ching* (intuitive essence) is located in the belly. These qualities are also present in the cosmos, as spirits in heaven consist of *ch'i*, earth spirits exhibit *shen*, and water spirits of the underworld *ching* (Saso 1997). A person dies when *ch'i* and *ching* are exhausted, and their soul leaves the body and is purified in the fires or waters of the underworld before ascending to heaven. The Taoist tradition of balancing body and world forms part of various Asian religions, and its principles are both shared by and inverted in Asian shamanic practices—shamans summon spirits, while Taoists seek to empty the body and cosmos of impurities (Saso 1997: 246).

These Asian religions share a complex understanding of the body in which its parts and elements are charged in specific ways. The fate of the person after death differs significantly from the monotheistic religions originating in the Near East: in most cases there is no heaven or afterlife for a soul following the death of its singular body, but rather cycles of reincarnation providing the soul with many bodies, many different perspectives from which relationships are built. In Hinduism there are many lives and many gods; many relationships must be negotiated, and repeated cultivation of good relationships lead to the attainment of no relationships at all. In Buddhism there is a desire for complete dissolution requiring no god. In Sikhism, God may only be found when the cycle of reincarnation is broken: good relationships lead to oneness with God.

I would present a number of important caveats here. The composition of the person and relationship with divinity are central theological concerns and as such are highly contentious, making it impossible to accurately synopsize traditions of belief. Sacred texts may be read in conflicting ways, and be taken to support contrasting understandings of social relations and personhood in accordance with local social and political trends in any period as well as over time. Religious traditions encapsulate many sub-traditions, with differing perspectives on fundamental issues. For instance, there have been varied Judeo-Christian perspectives on whether the material body and world were made by God or by demonic forces (e.g. the Archons of the Gnostics), and whether there was one event of creation or two (the first producing Adam as a spiritual being in the image of God, the second producing the material world and the human body, into which this spiritual being was cast [Perkins 1995]). As with the Gnostic reworking of Genesis, the role of scripture in such religious traditions needs to be set against other cultural and socio-political factors. Religious beliefs and practices change, as do the institutions operating them—for instance, some movements within Christianity and Islam have hierarchies of religious practitioners, while others reject such intermediaries with God. Communities may draw on a combination of religious traditions: for instance, Kerala Christian communities studied by Busby (1997) illustrated a similar concept of bodily constitution and personhood to Hindu Indians studied by Marriott (1976). Specific traditions, religious and secular, can therefore combine different features of belief systems, including combinations of animistic, totemic, and other practices (cf. Fowler 2004a: 122–6; Insoll 2004: 114).

Each variation, each combination, involves subtle differences in understandings of personhood and the configuration and fate of the mortal person. Even concepts that archaeologists may see as fundamental to personhood, such as the human body, may be understood in very different ways and seen as less fundamental than other aspects which scholars translate through terms such as 'spirit'. Nonetheless, perspectives on personhood are inextricable from understandings of divine power, cosmogony, the appropriateness of having special intermediaries with the divine, and concepts of mortality and what follows death. Understandings of personhood cut to the core of religious practices. And because soul, spirit, and similar concepts are invisible (though often inseparable from physical practices and believed to have visible manifestations), archaeologists interested in evidence for how personhood is shaped in religious practices must concentrate on how the human body is situated alongside substances and forms (including other 'bodies' and body parts) which may convey spiritual qualities important to personhood. The body and its representation are therefore key issues for archaeological investigations of personhood.

2.2 Relational Personhood and the Body Transcending Scale

Relational personhood—understanding each person as defined in relation to others—is a key feature of religious morality and, as such, many religious observances concern the appropriate ways to relate to others: mortals, divine and demonic beings, and the wider environment. In his treatise on Christian personhood, Alistair McFadyen (1990: ch. 1) argues that the Holy Trinity provides the model for Christian persons: God is neither a singular individual being nor three separate persons. God exemplifies a relationship between (divine) persons which also constitutes a (divine) person—the Father, Son, and Spirit are defined by their relationships. McFadyen (1990: 63) defines the Holy Spirit as 'the organisational energy of communication': the Spirit does not share the substance of the Father and Son, but provides the energy through which the Father creates the Son. The mortal Christian person is equally composite, uniting the soul, mind, and body, and defined by potential relationships with God, with saints, with the Devil, and with other mortals. Here, the personification of God in human form (or the creation of Man in the image of God) means that the mortal person mirrors the divine person.

However, it is not only the single person that assumes the divine form of the body. Dahlberg (1991: 47) observes that 'human generation follows the pattern of the Incarnation, for both express a harmonious unity of divinity and flesh. The Catholic mass replicates this pattern again, on a higher plane: the host itself regenerates the communicant'. Christian Communion is, put simply, the act of uniting the body of the single worshipper with that of the congregation by sharing the body and blood of Christ (cf. Ware 1997: 94), in which the substance of the body is transformed and personhood transcends the scale of the individual person: 'Whereas in ordinary eating food is changed into the person who consumes it—fish, bread and milk become human flesh and blood—here the reverse happens: we become what we eat, and through Holy Communion our bodies are changed into the members of Christ's body' (Ware 1997: 102–3). This pattern, of the replication of personhood in the same form at different scales, is a fractal one, meaning that the same pattern is evident at whatever scale is chosen, and that one (e.g. a single person) is also a part of a larger collectivity or whole (e.g. the congregation, God). Such fractal patterns are common in many cultural contexts (cf. Fowler 2008a). Religious communities are often described as one family of brothers and sisters and in some cases the sins or misdemeanours of one person may be visited spiritually on another member of the social body, rather than that specific individual. Restrictions from Communion during menstruation or following sexual emission in the Greek Orthodox Church, for instance, may aim to prevent polluting the wider body, illustrating these fractal relations where the sacred body appears at a number of scales.

Plato, whose thought is so influential in European religious traditions, exemplifies the presence of fractal thinking in his view that the person is a minor copy of the cosmos—both are bodies, both have souls (Ware 1997: 111–13). Effectively, the person, visualized through the body, is variously compared with God or gods, with the world or cosmos, and with the community. There are many ways that such fractal patterns, such expressions of the same principles in microcosm and macrocosm are made evident in archaeologically visible ways, such as through the design and treatment of architecture, landscapes, and material culture (Fowler 2008a and 2008b). One example would be religious architecture. It could be suggested that the physical structure of the Christian church often emulates the concept of the shared body, with the congregation forming the body and the chancel forming the head (including the choir, the voice) where the priest and altar (often covering sacred relics) are located. The head, the holiest part of the person often equated with the soul in Christian thought, faces east, the holiest direction, where the sun rises and the Garden of Eden lies within the cosmos. Gilchrist (1999: 83–7) argues that late medieval Church plans emulated the crucified body of Christ, and also presented an image of the Christian life course: the font for baptism near the door (entering the living community), the congregation gathered in the nave (the community of the living), and the chancel and altar hidden behind the rood screen as emblematic of Heaven (entered following death and Resurrection). She has also suggested that this vision of the Church as Christ's body may explain why many English medieval nunnery cloisters were located to the north of the transcept: the Virgin Mary was at the right hand of Christ during the Crucifixion (Gilchrist 1994: 133–43). Many early churches were small, making the body and congregration seem large, while, for instance, Gothic churches are vast, illustrating the smallness of the individual in relation to the vast congregation and host. In these cases the architecture plays a mediating role in relations of scale and senses of proximity to the divine alongside changing socio-political relations.

Where religious space is not separated from dwelling space domestic architecture may provide similar opportunities for analysis. Batammaliba houses are built from earth, water, and pebbles as the body is made from flesh, blood, and bones. House construction mirrors the growth of a human being and the creation of the world. The Batammaliba pantheon is ruled by an androgynous sun god and the house, which has bodily features including organs like eyes, and has both male and female genitals. Houses are equated not with an individualized and singularly sexed body, but the divine social body, combining male and female characteristics in a form of greater unity. Each house is the dwelling place of the family while 'foundation' houses are an embodiment of the entire clan. These houses also connect the living with the ancestral dead, transcending scales of time in drawing together the community (Preston Blier 1987; Tilley 1999: 41–9).

Another avenue to explore is the treatment of the human body following death. Many religious discourses concern the fragmentation of the person following death, and mortuary practices variously preserve the integrity of the body or accentuate its fragmentation. For instance, medieval Christian discourses presented the possibility of physical reconstitution at the Resurrection, with beasts regurgitating limbs they had consumed so these could rejoin the resurrected bodies (Bynum 1991: 12–13). The part will rejoin the whole—the promise of redemption is one of an infinite fractal integration (limbs rejoin bodies, individuals rejoin communities, communities are joined with God). Among many religious communities with a belief in the Resurrection any part of the body will support regeneration of the whole: in Islamic teachings, body parts removed in life, like hair, will rejoin the body (hence ritual purification prior to cutting hair—Winter 1995: 40). Medieval burial practices attempted to address concerns over the fate of the person following death (Gilchrist and Sloane 2005), and Christians were buried prepared for the Resurrection. Some were equipped with prosthetics needed to help them travel to the final judgement or amulets to protect or heal them at the Resurrection (Gilchrist 2008). Medieval images of hell often include the fragmented bodies of the damned divided from God—these fragments are not assembled in fractal relations but remain isolated. Images of decay and corruption also throw the sanctity of the redeemed fractal, connected body into relief. Such imagery is not uncommon: broken body parts are a motif evident in ancient Egyptian religious iconography of hell (Meskell and Joyce 2003: 145–53). The fragmentation of the person in hell need not mean that indivisible persons were celebrated in life in these instances: some aspect(s) of individual character may be preserved for the next life, but in both cases the person was a composite of different aspects and relationships. The fear associated with the loss of parts of the self in medieval Europe was related to a feared loss of an idealized 'wholeness' associated with the next life, but that 'wholeness' was reliant on relationships with others (including God) and relationships between affiliated parts; it was not a monadic condition.

Persons are often understood as composite beings which can be 'decomposed' and 'recomposed' through their relations with others, including spiritual entities. While in some communities decomposition and recomposition occur mainly following death, in others such processes may be common. Personhood among the Classic Maya was clearly composite, and some aspects of personhood such as *way* (spirit companion or co-essence) and *bah* (image or visage) could be made evident through such material media as masks or animal skins. Other aspects like *ik* (breath), names, *k'ik* (a vital energy conveyed through the blood), and *b'ak* (bone) were depicted emanating from, accompanying, or produced out of the body in Mayan artwork (Meskell and Joyce 2003: 24–9, 89, *inter alia*). The decay of the flesh did not seem to mark the disintegration of the person as many of the personal aspects were materialized in other media, and personhood persisted through the fragmented parts that remained. Meskell and Joyce (2003: 142) argue that '[b]odily integrity was less important for the Classic Maya than the extension of bodily connections into the future, achieved through the use of bones by living people, including as body ornaments'. In some cases persons risk the loss of some parts in their encounter with spiritual beings. Rituals may focus on this anxiety, so that, for instance, shamans in Northern Eurasia may conduct rituals to retrieve pieces of the 'body-soul' (a soul divisible into parts corresponding to body parts) which may be lost to spirits during hunting and other dangerous interactions (Ingold 1986: 246–7).

Personhood may also be understood as embedded in the wider world beyond the human body, and distributed among things, plants, animals, and places. For Iteanu, the Orokaivan person consists of *hamo* (biography), *ahihi* (image), *jo* (inside), and *onderi* (wild spirit) (Barraud et al. 1994; Iteanu 1995). Following death, the *ahihi* is invested in shell goods, feathers, and similar display items, the *onderi* emerges to take the form of wild animals in the forest, while the *jo* is extinguished. During this process the *hamo*, the person's lived biography is forgotten as they are transformed—the person will be remembered through the presence of their image. The qualities associated with aspects of personhood in Melanesia (and elsewhere) may be distributed throughout the world of the living as well as relocated to other planes of existence. Sequences of mortuary rites celebrate the person, but also then deconstitute them: where aspects of personhood are invested in pigs, crops, shell goods, and so on, these are gathered together in the mortuary act and then redistributed following death (e.g. among the 'Are'Are—Barraud et al. 1994: 53–5). The living person is dissolved so that some aspects of the person are assured ongoing existence in the social world, and items like shell goods come to be associated with the 'fame' or 'image' of the ancestors. Death is necessary for social regeneration as well as cosmic regeneration.

Within Hinduism and Buddhism personal dissolution is the most desirable goal. Here (and wider afield) the body is described as a vessel which is made, contains energies conveyed through substances, and is broken through mortuary rites which refine the substances constituting it (Collins 1997: 191). Hindu bodies are cremated, and the remains ideally washed away in the sacred river: the power of fire and water are such that they can refine bodily substance. By contrast, in Zoroastrian practice the elements of fire and earth are too respected to be polluted with death, and the body was historically exposed to the air and left for vultures at 'Towers of Silence'. Unlike for Zoroastrians, the Hindu soul must be released to be recycled and this requires the purification of the body into a more ethereal state, not just its destruction. Fractal relations in time are evident in the Hindu mortuary rites which reprise the sequence of cosmogony: a scaling principle links the cycle of death and rebirth with the cosmic cycles of world destruction and world renewal. At Varanasi, the most sacred site where cremations can occur, Vishnu sat in a phallic column of flame and created the world from the waters of a flood—the world is repeatedly destroyed and created in a cosmic cycle like the cycles of death and reincarnation. In other religions spiritual energies must be released from the body, and these are sometimes invested in tombs or in the landscapes where people dwell, through mortuary rites which gradually deconstitute the body (e.g. Bloch 1982).

There have already been archaeological attempts to consider past mortuary practices as transformations in personhood which can inform us about past concepts of the person (e.g. Brück 2001, 2004, 2005, 2006; Fowler 2003, 2004b; Jones 2002, 2004; Thomas 2002) and religious beliefs (e.g. Gilchrist and Sloane 2005; Williams 2001), and this may continue to be a fruitful avenue of research. A further avenue ripe for enquiry is the treatment of the living human body. The person is not an isolated entity that becomes completely bounded at conception in most views of the world, but is physically vulnerable to a range of outside forces, some of which may injure and some of which may enhance the person. The body (singular and collective) is a vital locus of personhood (both singular and collective), which is at risk from hostile forces (sin, evil, witchcraft, sorcery, demons, etc.). The body is carefully monitored through ritual and religious practices to preserve it from such hostile forces, which may be seen or unseen. In some religions these evil forces originate externally to the body (e.g. Zoroastrian bodies and persons are not evil but rather can come to house evil forces—Williams 1997: 159), but in others, as in the Catholic notion of Original Sin, they also inhere in the flesh of which the mortal body consists, and in yet others there may be an active will within the person over which they have no control and which may practise witchcraft following ill thoughts about others. Evil has no place in the idealized religious order, and must be not only prevented from entering bodies, but ultimately purged from the cosmos—which at its smallest scale is the person. The person is vulnerable to divine and supernatural forces, including influences hostile to the person, body, and soul. Specific practices, such as prayers, purifications, dressing, body modification, pilgrimages, and sacrifices direct the person through complex interactions with such forces, and I will discuss examples of these later.

2.3 Special Religious Persons and Divine Persons

Not all bodies are treated in the same way, and not all persons are ordinary. I outlined above how the constitution of the human person is understood, but this covers significant variation within any community as to how states of personhood are achieved and experienced. For instance, the Hindu caste system plays a major role in shaping personhood, where persons are defined according to their cosmologically sanctioned place in the social body, as do life stages and membership of different cults (Marriott 1976). Special religious identities come in various forms. As well as lay persons, there are priests, shamans, ascetics, monks and nuns, holy persons, deified emperors, avatars, and those temporarily possessed by divine powers. Members of religious orders are often required to pass through special rites of passage: these may be lengthy and involve the 'death' of one personal identity and the assumption of another along with ritual acts of purification (Gilchrist 1994: 18–19). There are also unholy persons, such as witches, and those possessed by demonic powers.

Not all persons are human, and not all beings can be easily reconciled with the categories of mortal and divine. There are categories of beings whose personhood is uncertain—they are given life in religious thought but are not human—for instance, religious icons (e.g. Faure 1995; Gell 1998: ch. 7). Personal relations may be formed with images of saints, petitioned by the living (Graves 2008). Jose Oliver (2009) has studied the role of *cemi* idols in Taino society, sacred animate objects with many of the qualities of persons and with whom human persons form special partnerships. The intersection between the human and the divine is a difficult matter which may be hard to discern, and much religious art consists of quasi-human monsters and hybrids. Such beings are not ordinary persons, but are divine or demonic—they transcend the boundaries of normal personhood. Among Mayan communities, Joyce (2001: 191) describes a Mayan anxiety over uncertainties as to the inability to know whether beings are mortal or divine, object or subject.

Saints and other divine persons often have atypical relations with the normal course of personhood following death. Catholic saints are special, sacred persons, whose bodies demonstrate their sacred nature in life and after death through the production of miracles. The making of relics from the bodies of Catholic saints might seem to contradict the emphasis on redemption as wholeness, but parts of saint's bodies were often seen as incorruptible and each part effectively made the whole present (Bynum 1991: 265–97). The bodies and body parts of saints exhibit such overwhelming divinity that their pure bodies are supernaturally 'fertile' in special ways. Contact with their bodies, it is hoped, may transfer the supernatural quality of the Holy Spirit and inspire miraculous regeneration of the ailing body of the supplicant. Some Chinese Buddhist monks have been mummified while the cremated remains of others have been kept as relics, as have their monastic attributes like bowls and particularly the robes which convey the *dharma* (true knowledge) realized by that monk (Faure 1995). In both cases relics attracted pilgrims and their presence at specific shrines was contested (e.g. Faure 1995: 217–9). Catholic relics were taken on progresses and, when relics were removed from one place to another, this was often seen as the will of the saint and added to the sanctity of the new locale.

In Christianity Christ is a divine person who has also been a mortal person—as an aspect of God (the Son) incarnate in a mortal body and its flesh, Christ also had a mortal soul (Ware 1997: 92). It is significant that there are no relics of the body of Christ (see Bynum 1991: 11–12). Instead, Christ is present on earth as the body in the Eucharist and in Heaven through his Ascension following his death and resurrection. Equally, there are no bodily relics of the Virgin Mary, who was spared death and ascended directly to Heaven (Gilchrist pers. comm.) The 'three bodies' of Buddha are worth consideration in comparison with the bodies of Christ. The 'body of truth' of Buddha's teachings are the first body, the human body of Siddhatta Gautama is the second, and 'Buddha bodies' or relics of the Buddha's body, form a third (Faure 1995). Indeed, Buddha's cremated remains were separated into eight portions, each given to representatives of a specific community who built a *stupa* over them (the cremation urn and pyre debris were also treated as relics and commemorated by other *stupas*) (Coningham 2001: 65). Collins (1997) points out that the Buddhist monastic community also embodies the key concepts in Buddhist thought and practice. While the teachings of Buddha form a 'body', in Sikhism the sacred text is named after and treated as the body of the Guru Granth Sahib; it is fanned when hot, and covered when cold (Nesbitt 1997: 300–2). Thus, the sacred knowledge of special persons like Buddha and Guru Granth Sahib transcends the death of their mortal human bodies to become incorporated in other bodies.

3 RITUAL, PERSONHOOD, AND BODILY ACTION

3.1 Traditions of Bodily Practice

Religious concepts of the person feed into regulatory ideals for social interaction and for embodied action. They are part of a moral code and narrative structure for the relation between each person and other persons, divine beings, and natural and supernatural forces. Such ideals exist in the plural in most communities, and there are orthodox and unorthodox persons (e.g. ascetics) as well as ordinary and special persons. In this section I will outline some of the ways that personhood is shaped with reference to these religious ideals. It should be borne in mind that these are also expected, desirable, or ideal actions and practices and are not always followed literally—they nonetheless form principles structuring ritualized action against which further agency is made sensible. The reasons given for the same practice may vary over time and within a faith (e.g. Jacobs 1997: 83; Starrett 1995: endnote 3); practice and belief are mutually constitutive but either may be revised while the other remains the same. One key purpose that seems to underlie much religious practice is the attainment of a particular way of being in order to honour a divine being and/or the desired cosmic order. One goal or desired result of much religiously sanctioned personal conduct is the attainment of a perfect state of being or the cessation of being through a particular way of life.

Studying depictions of bodily engagement in religious practices may provide clues to understanding states of personhood in past communities. Persons, and their bodies, are constituted and 'trained' through their participation in traditions of practice—traditions which are sanctioned by religious beliefs—and interpretations of those practices. Following orthodox practices may be important in attaining idealized states of personhood. Some traditions require the body to be still and calm, stressing mental reflection, while others direct the body towards ecstatic activity. Buddhist prayers are designed to align the body and cosmos and promote flows of forces between them while keeping the body still. Virtuous Muslims may repeat ritualized bodily practices following the examples set by the Prophet Muhammed's and consciously 'embody' Islam in their daily lives (e.g. Starrett

1995). Not all bodily practices stem from scriptures but may relate to the influence of particular social and political institutions and may also be translated in syncretism so that, for instance, Christian pilgrimage routes may overlay landscapes with existing religious monuments and continue some of the embodied practices involved in those pilgrimages.

3.2 Rituals of Atonement: Purity and Bodily Boundaries

Just as the relationship between the material body (as a whole, or as a congregation of parts or substances) and spiritual qualities or forces (e.g. soul, spirit, breath, image) varies, so there are accordingly a wide variety of ways that the body can be treated in attaining a desired state of personhood. Nonetheless, as Mary Douglas (1966) illustrated, rules about pollution and purity are extremely widespread and underlie explicitly verbalized codes of moral action. Pollution occurs where substances, things, and people are where they should not be, causing ambiguity. It is a risk associated with crossing boundaries. Ambiguous states need to be resolved, and transgressions atoned for, through cleansing ritual action. Purity can be associated with sterility and virginity as a material (or a person) is kept separated from other materials or persons. Especially pure bodies may in some cases be potent, however. For Zoroastrians, bodily purity involves heightened fertility, and bodies must be purified prior to religious ceremonies (Williams 1997: 159–65). Among medieval Catholic ascetics, pure bodies could be sustained without food and become conduits to sacred power, including after death. The immaculate conception of the Virgin Mary arguably illustrates a victory of purity over the sinful flesh, while Purgatory provides an image of a liminal state in which the soul is purified before it can enter Heaven. But not all material is polluting and fertility, sacred energy, or potency do not only come from pure, that is separated, substance; they can also come from materials which are so decomposed and intermixed as to be no longer identifiable into separate elements. Thus mixed midden material may be fertile and potent rather than polluting: one substance rather than many.

Ascetics may demonstrate their sanctity by their ability to defy and overcome pollution (e.g. the Aghori ascetics in India: Parry 1994: ch. 8), but most people avoid polluting contact because it is through such contact that evil forces may be transmitted. Proper personhood demands repeated atonement for necessary movement through boundaries, and the boundaries of the body have to be carefully policed for transgression. It is through the body, after all, that forces harmful to the soul, spirit, or other unseen aspects of the person infiltrate. This infiltration can come, for instance, via food or via bodily fluids from another person. One's own bodily fluids and *exuviae* may be harmful as once they have left the body they should not return to it—cut hair or nails, shed skin, faeces, etc, are all forms of 'dirt' or 'matter out of place' which are neither of the body nor not of the body (Douglas 1966: 24–7, *inter alia*). In many cases 'wasted' bodily substance is especially polluting, particularly menstrual blood and semen which could potentially have given life. Therefore, bodily boundaries are carefully monitored through ritual action according to religious beliefs. As the Islamic body is resurrected with all its parts reassembled, ritual washing is necessary before shaving (Winter 1995: 40). Acts of physical purification are necessary in order to achieve spiritual purification, and such physical purification is achieved through the use of water and/or fire. For instance, immersion in water of all or part of the body is a fundamental religious practice in Christianity (baptism), Islam (daily ablutions, washing feet in particular before entry to sacred space), Zoroastrianism (daily ablutions and baths associated with rites of passage), and Hinduism (cremation and immersion in sacred river). Williams (1997: 165) describes Zoroastrian ritual washing and prayers as 'performed in order to reseal symbolically the boundary which has been ruptured by matter leaving the system (i.e. body)'.

Bodies can be protected as well as purified. Witchcraft is believed to provide contact with the person through use of their *exuviae*. In seventeenth-century Europe 'witch bottles' filled with urine and nails were buried under floorboards to ward off witchcraft and harm witches (Merrifield 1955). The bodies of the living may also be possessed by the dead (e.g. Vitebsky 1993) or by unseen spirits (e.g. Rasmussen 1995). Bodily pollution or overly potent or evil influences or spirits may be protected against through a variety of body modification and body dressing practices including tattooing and the wearing of veils (e.g. Rasmussen 1995, Gell 1993). As well as being used in tattoos, apotropaic symbols are sometimes located at the entrances and boundaries to buildings and enclosures, including knot-work and mazes designed to confuse evil spirits (Gell 1998: 83–90). It has been suggested in some societies pots are decorated like human bodies due to the conception of the human body as a vessel (David et al. 1988). Pots contain substances that pass into the body, potentially requiring the same protection as human bodies.

The role of orthodox ritual specialists, and proscriptions on those specialists, varies alongside the relationship between the person and the divine. Not all religions have such specialist persons (e.g. Sikhism where there is no priestly community), but all have ritual observances in which someone plays a specialized role. Where they form a special category of person, ritual specialists stand in a unique position with regard to normal observances. For instance, Catholics perceive sexual relations in heterosexual marriage as a manifestation of divinely sanctioned bodily fertility. Priests mediate in the relationship between the congregation and God. Catholic priests may only be male (male priesthood is often justified by pointing out, among other things, that it is the male aspect of God which was embodied in Christ [Graham 1995: 38]). Priests do not engage in marriage and sexual relations (Dahlberg 1991: 48). The role of a priest is therefore 'pure' and clearly demarcated. Protestants each individually form a direct relationship with God and do not place the same emphasis on the divinity of bodily substance and fertility: their ministers may marry and practice sexual relations, while Communion is an allegorical act (Dahlberg 1991: 48). In Protestant thought the perfection of the soul is not related to the form and substance of the body, and there are no daily rites to maintain the purity of the body—though there may be daily prayers and gatherings in which the mind, heart, and voice are directed towards the divine. Protestant ministers are subject only to the same rules of probity as other members of the congregation.

3.3 Rituals of Devotion: Beneficial Bodily Contact and Personal Transformation

I have already argued that the body is often understood as permeable to outside forces, and that the limits of the person extend beyond the skin. Pilgrims to sites of healing frequently leave intimate personal items, things associated with the ailing body (e.g. cloths used to wash afflicted body parts in holy springs), emblems of consumption (e.g. bottles, cigarettes) or signs of their journey (e.g. holy water from distant sites, shells, and pebbles) at holy wells, springs, and shrines. Miniature body parts have been worn as badges by pilgrims and deposited as votive offerings at Catholic shrines—and Gallo-Roman wooden body parts have also been found at a spring in France (Vatin 1972). Such practices form a bodily and personal connection between the person, the sacred place, and the divine. Indeed, sacred places are often so because of the bodily presence of some divine being whether formed by ancestral beings, the footprints of saints, or formed on the resting places of holy bodies. Some sacred places focus on living holy persons. In Stirrat's (1991) study of Sinhalese shrines, living unorthodox holy men are the focus of these shrines and their bodily presence mark the connection between the human and the divine. Lay persons form special relations with particular holy men who intercede with God, as often also happens with Catholic saints. Visiting sacred places builds a personal relationship intended to transform the supplicant, therefore, and this is often manifested as an indirect or direct contact between mortal and divine bodies. As Dahlberg (1991: 45) notes, observing a pilgrim at Lourdes, 'she ran her hands over various parts of the statue of Our Lady of St Pé and then touched the corresponding parts of her own body, as though she were attempting to "put on" the perfect body of the statue'. Dahlberg's study also indicated that 'sick' pilgrims were placed physically and spiritually closer to sacred forces at Lourdes by 'well' pilgrims, and seen as mediating with the divine. It is as if the bodies of the afflicted had a closer relation with divine forces, and that a kind of beneficial transfer of spiritual energy was being sought through their afflicted bodies.

Pilgrimages and similar acts of religious devotion at sacred places are emphatically bodily acts, considered to transform the person, often physically but always spiritually. In this sense they may in some cases perform a similar role to rites of passage (Turner and Turner 1978: 12): they may or may not relate to life stages, but they may bring about a significant change in identity. This can be seen in the Muslim *hajj*: those who have undertaken this act of pilgrimage take the honoric '*hajji*'. Pilgrimages are not the only acts of religious devotion which make demands of bodily sacrifice (of labour, time, effort, even of bodily substance from sweat to blood) or are intended to heal the afflicted. Indeed, a useful technique for studying concepts of the body and person in anthropology has been to attend to healing, magic, and ritual practices which attempt to cure, restore, and keep well the body and person. There are Neolithic sites in the British Isles which seem to present restricted access to relic remains (e.g. Fowler 2004b), and the use of complexes of monuments from the Neolithic and Early Bronze Age may attest to long journeys and large gatherings akin to pilgrimages. Archaeological studies of relics and pilgrimages alongside techniques that shape, maintain, and undo bodily boundaries may be fruitful avenues for understanding past religious attitudes to the body and concepts of the person.

4 CONCLUSION

The role of social and political trends or institutions in the maintenance or mutation of religious practice is undeniable. Religious beliefs about the body and person can change significantly over time, and there is great diversity in religious conceptions of personhood as well as the strategies pursued in attempting to achieve ideal personhood. Nonetheless, personal conduct is often directed towards achieving an idealized version of personhood following death: ancestorhood, holiness, a place in heaven, an end to the cycle of life and death, etc. The ritual observances that shape personhood also renew the world, ensuring continuities such as the custodianship of sacred places and the reproduction of other beings, for instance. Religious ideals about personhood stress the integration of the person in a wider community and cosmos. Persons are therefore presented as relational, and the kinds of relationships persons are expected to pursue are cosmologically sanctioned. This close relationship between cosmology and personhood is significant for archaeologists since studies of past cosmologies are already well established, including in prehistoric archaeology where discussion of religion is more limited.

Only a small number of archaeological studies foreground the body and personhood in their studies of past religious communities, though this number is growing. Beliefs about personhood are fundamental features of religions. While these issues are challenging for archaeologists to investigate using the fragmentary remains of past activity, archaeological studies of past sacred architecture, mortuary practices, and other phenomena can shed light on concepts of personhood. Ritual and ritualized habitual acts serve as key mechanisms by which religious concepts become installed in the person; these acts play a key role in the shaping of a desired personhood. The body, and the direction of embodied experience, is something which archaeologists are well positioned to study, while archaeologists have also begun to interpret diverse forms of relational personhood (e.g. Jones 2005; Harris 2006; Whittle 2003: ch. 3; and see Fowler 2004a; 2010). Cross-pollination between archaeology, history, sociology, anthropology, and religious studies may prove extremely productive for each discipline in understanding the relationships between cultural practices, material culture, and concepts of the body and person.

Acknowledgements

While writing this chapter I was fortunate to attend the World Archaeological Congress in Dublin, and there benefited from conversations with several people on this topic, including Chris Knüsel and Rachel Scott. I would like to thank Roberta Gilchrist, Mark and Liz Jackson, Elizabeth Kramer Fowler, Sam Turner, and Jane Webster for similar discussions and/or comments on a draft text.

Suggested Reading

There is no source that deals comprehensively or comparatively with archaeological evidence for concepts of the person across many different religious traditions. Roberta Gilchrist has produced archaeological studies of European Christian religious persons (e.g. Gilchrist 1994; and co-authored with Barney Sloane, Gilchrist and Sloane 2005), while Lynn Meskell and Rosemary Joyce (2003) have co-authored a comparative discussion of Classic Mayan and ancient Egyptian communities which addresses personhood and the body in these two contexts with their differing religious traditions. Historians have also studied religious bodies and persons, including monks, nuns and bodily relics (e.g. Bynum 1991). Both *Religion and the Body* (Coakley 1997) and *Religious Reflections on the Human Body* (Law 1995) provide valuable edited collections of studies in comparative contemporary and historical world contexts, though are not concerned with archaeological evidence. Important anthropological discussions on rites of passage and personhood can be found in the work of Maurice Bloch (e.g. 1989), Victor Turner (1969), and Arnold van Gennep (1960). The anthropology of Mircea Eliade (1957) and Mary Douglas (1966, 1970) provide insightful comparative considerations of the relationship between cultural practices, religion and cosmology. Marcel Mauss (1985), Nancy Munn (1986), and Marilyn Strathern (1988) have made particularly important contributions to the study of personhood in anthropology, and I have discussed archaeological and anthropological studies of personhood more elsewhere (Fowler 2004a; 2010).

References

Alvi, A. 2001. 'The category of the person in rural Punjab', *Social Anthropology* 9(1): 45–63.
Barraud, C. et al. 1994. *Of Relations and the Dead: Four societies viewed from the angle of their exchanges* (Oxford: Berg).
Bloch, M. and Parry, J. 1982. 'Introduction: Death and the regeneration of life' in M. Bloch and J. Parry (eds), *Death and the Regeneration of Life* (Cambridge: Cambridge University Press), pp. 1–44.
—— 1989. 'Death and the concept of the person' in S. Cederroth, C. Corlin, and J. Lindstrom (eds), *On the Meaning of Death* (Cambridge: Cambridge University Press), pp. 11–29.
Brück, J. 2001. 'Body metaphors and technologies of transformation in the English Middle and Late Bronze Age' in J. Brück (ed.), *Bronze Age Landscapes: Tradition and transformation* (Oxford: Oxbow), pp. 149–60.
—— 2004. 'Material metaphors: The relational construction of identity in Early Bronze Age burials in Ireland and Britain', *Journal of Social Archaeology*, 4: 307–33.
—— 2005. 'Fragmentation, personhood and the social construction of technology in Middle and Late Bronze Age Britain', *Cambridge Archaeological Journal*, 16(3): 297–315.
—— 2006. 'Death, exchange and reproduction in the British Bronze Age', *European Journal of Archaeology*, 9(1): 73–101.
Busby, C. 1997. 'Permeable and partible persons: A comparative analysis of gender and the body in South India and Melanesia', *Journal of the Royal Anthropological Institute*, 3: 261–78.
Bynum, C. W. 1991. *Fragmentation and Redemption: Essays on gender and the human body in medieval religion* (New York: Zone Books).
Coakley, S. (ed.) 1997. *Religion and the Body* (Cambridge: Cambridge University Press).
Collins, S. 1997. 'The body in Theravāda Buddhist monasticism' in S. Coakley (ed.), *Religion and the Body* (Cambridge: Cambridge University Press), pp. 185–204.
Coningham, R. 2001. 'The archaeology of Buddhism' in T. Insoll (ed.), *Archaeology and World Religion* (London: Routledge), pp. 61–95.
Dahlberg, A. 1991. 'The body as a principle of holism: Three pilgrimages to Lourdes' in J. Eade and M. J. Sallnow (eds), *Contesting the Sacred: The anthropology of Christian pilgrimage* (London: Routledge), pp. 30–50.

DAVID, N., STERNER, J., and GAVUA, K. 1988. 'Why pots are decorated', *Current Anthropology*, 29(1): 365–89.
DONIGER, W. 1997. 'Medical and mythical constructions of the body in Hindu texts' in S. Coakley (ed.), *Religion and the Body* (Cambridge: Cambridge University Press), pp. 167–84.
DOUGLAS, M. 1966. *Purity and Danger: An analysis of the concepts of pollution and taboo*, 1994 edn (London: Routledge).
—— 1970. *Natural Symbols: Explorations in cosmology* (London).
ELIADE, M. 1957. *The Sacred and the Profane: The nature of religion* (London: Harcourt Brace Jovanovich).
FAURE, B. 1995. 'Substitute bodies in Chan/Zen Buddhism' in J. Law (ed.), *Religious Reflections on the Human Body* (Bloomington: Indiana University Press).
FINLAY, N. 2000. 'Outside of Life: infant burials from cillin to cist', *World Archaeology* 31(3): 407–22.
FORTES, M. 1987. 'The concept of the person' in M. Fortes (ed.), *Religion, Morality and the Person: Essays in Tallensi religion* (Cambridge: Cambridge University Press).
FOWLER, C. 2003. 'Rates of (ex)change: Decay and growth, memory and the transformation of the dead in Early Neolithic Southern Britain' in H. Williams (ed.), *Archaeologies of Remembrance: Death and memory in past societies* (New York: Kluwer Academic/Plenum Press), pp. 45–63.
—— 2004a. *The Archaeology of Personhood: An anthropological approach* (London: Routledge).
—— 2004b. 'In touch with the past? Bodies, monuments and the sacred in the Manx Neolithic' in V. Cummings and C. Fowler (eds), *The Neolithic of the Irish Sea: Materiality and traditions of practice* (Oxford: Oxbow), pp. 91–102.
—— 2008a. 'Fractal bodies in the past and present' in D. Borić and J. Robb (eds), *Past Bodies* (Oxford: Oxbow Press), pp. 47–57.
—— 2008b. 'Landscape and personhood' in B. David and J. Thomas (eds), *Handbook of Landscape Archaeology* (Walnut Creek, CA: Left Coast Press), pp. 291–9.
—— 2010. 'From identity and material culture to personhood and materiality' in M. Beaudry and D. Hicks (eds), *The Oxford Handbook of Material Culture Studies* (Oxford: Oxford University Press).
GELL, A. 1993. *Wrapping in Images: Tattooing in Polynesia* (Oxford: Clarendon).
—— 1998. *Art and Agency: An anthropological theory* (Oxford: Clarendon).
GENNEP, A. VAN 1960. *The Rites of Passage* (London: Routledge and Keegan Paul).
GILCHRIST, R. 1994. *Gender and Material Culture: The archaeology of religious women* (London: Routledge).
—— 1999. *Gender and Archaeology: Contesting the past* (London: Routledge).
—— 2008. 'Magic for the dead? The archaeology of magic in later medieval burials', *Medieval Archaeology*, 52: 119–59.
—— and SLOANE, B. 2005. *Requiem: The medieval monastic cemetery in Britain* (Museum of London Archaeology Service).
GRAHAM, E. 1995. *Making the Difference: Gender, personhood and theology* (London: Mowbray).
GRAVES, P. 2008. 'From an Archaeology of iconoclasm to an anthropology of the body: Images, punishment and personhood in England, 1500–1660', *Current Anthropology*, 49(1): 35–57.
HARRIS, O. 'Identity, emotion and memory in Neolithic Dorset', PhD thesis, Cardiff University.
INGOLD, T. 1986. *The Appropriation of Nature: Essays on human ecology and social relations* (Manchester: Manchester University Press).
INSOLL, T. 2004. *The Archaeology of Ritual and Religion* (London: Routledge).

ITEANU, A. 1995. 'Rituals and ancestors' in D. de Coppet and A. Iteanu (eds), *Cosmos and Society in Oceania* (Oxford: Berg), pp. 135–63.
JACOBS, L. 1997. 'The body in Jewish worship: Three rituals examined' in S. Coakley (ed.), *Religion and the Body* (Cambridge: Cambridge University Press), pp. 71–89.
JONES, A. 2002. 'A biography of colour: Colour, material histories and personhood in the early Bronze Age of Britain and Ireland' in A. Jones and G. MacGregor (eds), *Colouring the Past* (Oxford: Berg), pp. 159–74.
——2004. 'Matter and memory: Colour, remembrance and the Neolithic/Bronze Age transition' in E. DeMarrais, C. Gosden, and C. Renfrew (eds), *Rethinking Materiality: The engagement of mind with the material world* (Cambridge: MacDonald Institute for Archaeological Research), pp. 167–78.
——2005. 'Lives in fragments? Personhood and the European Neolithic', *Journal of Social Archaeology*, 5: 193–224.
JOYCE, R. 2001. *Gender and Power in Prehispanic Mesoamerica* (Austin: University of Texas Press).
LAW, J. (ed.) 1995. *Religious Reflections on the Human Body* (Bloomington: Indiana University Press).
MCFADYEN, A. 1990. *The Call to Personhood: A Christian theory of the individual in social relationships* (Cambridge: Cambridge University Press).
MARRIOTT, M. 1976. 'Hindu transactions: Diversity without dualism' in B. Kapferer (ed.), *Transaction and Meaning: Directions in the anthropology of exchange and symbolic behaviour* (Philadelphia: Institute for the study of Human Issues), pp. 109–37.
MAUSS, M. 1985. [Trans.] 'A category of the human mind: The notion of person; the notion of self' in M. Carrithers, S. Collins, and S. Lukes (eds) (1985), *The Category of the Person: Anthropology, philosophy, history* (Cambridge: Cambridge University Press), pp. 1–25.
MERRIFIELD, R. 1955. 'Witch bottles and magical jugs', *Folklore*, 66(1): 195–207.
MESKELL, L. and JOYCE, R. 2003. *Embodied Lives: Figuring ancient Mayan and Egyptian experience* (London: Routledge).
MORRIS, B. 1994. *Anthropology of the Self: The individual in cultural perspective* (Pluto Press: London).
MUNN, N. 1986. *The Fame of Gawa: A symbolic study of value transformation in a Massim (Papua New Guinea) society* (Durham: Duke University Press).
NESBITT, E. 1997. 'The body in Sikh tradition' in S. Coakley (ed.), *Religion and the Body* (Cambridge: Cambridge University Press), pp. 289–305.
OLIVER, J. 2009. *Caciques and Çemi idols: The web spun by Taino rulers between Hispanola and Boriquén* (Tuscaloosa: University of Alabama Press).
PARRY, J. 1994. *Death in Banaras* (Cambridge: Cambridge University Press).
PERKINS, P. 1995. 'Creation of the body in Gnosticism' in J. Law (ed.), *Religious Reflections on the Human Body* (Bloomington: Indiana University Press), pp. 21–35.
PRESTON BLIER, S. 1987. *The Anatomy of Architecture: Ontology and metaphor in Batammaliba architectural expression* (Chicago: University of Chicago Press).
RASMUSSEN, S. 1995. *Spirit Possession and Personhood among the Kel Ewey Tuareg* (Cambridge: Cambridge University Press).
SASO, M. 1997. 'The Taoist body and cosmic prayer' in S. Coakley (ed.), *Religion and the Body* (Cambridge: Cambridge University Press), pp. 231–47.
STARRETT, G. 1995. 'The hexis of interpretation: Islam and the body in the Egyptian popular school', *American Ethnologist*, 22(4): 953–69.

STIRRAT, R. 1991. 'Place and person in Sinhala Catholic pilgrimage' in J. Eade and M. J. Sallnow (eds), *Contesting the Sacred: The anthropology of Christian pilgrimage* (Routledge: London), pp. 122–36.

STRATHERN, M. 1988. *The Gender of the Gift: Problems with women and problems with society in Melanesia* (Berkeley: University of California Press).

THOMAS, J. 2002. 'Archaeology's humanism and the materiality of the body' in Y. Hamilakis, M. Pluciennik, and S. Tarlow (eds), *Thinking Through the Body: Archaeologies of Corporeality* (London: Kluwer Academic/Plenum), pp. 29–46.

TILLEY, C. 1999. *Metaphor and Material Culture* (Oxford: Blackwell).

TURNER, V. 1969. *The Ritual Process: Structure and anti-structure* (New York: Aldine De Gruyter).

——and TURNER, E. 1978. *Image and Pilgrimage in Christian Culture: Anthropological perspectives* (Columbia University Press: New York).

VATIN, C. 1972. 'Wooden sculpture from Gallo-Roman Auvergne', *Antiquity*, 44: 39–42.

VITEBSKY, P. 1993. *Dialogues with the Dead: The Discussion of Mortality among the Sora of Eastern India* (Cambridge: Cambridge University Press).

WARE, K. 1997. '"My helper and my enemy": The body in Greek Christianity' in S. Coakley (ed.), *Religion and the Body* (Cambridge: Cambridge University Press), pp. 90–110.

WHITTLE, A. 2003. *The Archaeology of People: Dimensions of Neolithic Life* (London: Routledge).

WILLIAMS, A. 1997. 'Zoroastrianism and the body' in S. Coakley (ed.), *Religion and the Body* (Cambridge: Cambridge University Press), pp. 155–66.

WILLIAMS, H. 2001. 'An ideology of transformation: Cremation rites and animal sacrifice in early Anglo-Saxon England' in N. Price (ed.), *The Archaeology of Shamanism* (London: Routledge), pp. 193–212.

WINTER, M. 1995. 'Islamic attitudes towards the human body' in J. Law (ed.), *Religious Reflections on the Human Body* (Bloomington: Indiana University Press), pp. 36–45.

CHAPTER 11

SACRIFICE

TIMOTHY INSOLL

1 CONCEPT AND DEFINITIONS

'SACRIFICE' is defined by the *Oxford Handy Dictionary* as 'slaughter of animal or person, surrender of a possession, as offering to a deity; what is thus slaughtered or surrendered; giving up something (usu. valuable) for sake of something else, thing so given up, loss so entailed' (Fowler and Fowler 1986: 795). This definition neatly encompasses all the elements with which the archaeology of sacrifice should be concerned. Or does it? In reality it extends beyond what this entry focuses upon in including in its latter component the notion of secular 'sacrifice', of giving something up. Instead religious sacrifice is the concern here and thus returns to the etymological origins of 'sacrifice' as derived from the Latin *sacrificium* (*sacer*, 'holy' and *facere* 'to make') and described by Henninger (2005: 7997) as carrying 'the connotation of the religious act in the highest, or fullest sense'.

Henninger (ibid.), in his admirable discussion of sacrifice, proceeds also to note that 'offering', i.e. 'the presentation of a gift' is used as a synonym for 'sacrifice'. Again, this is not the concern in this chapter, for though 'offering' can constitute sacred ritual action, it differs from sacrifice in lacking the destructive element that is perhaps its defining criteria and which offers the potential to recognize the sacrificial act as opposed to the making of an offering in the archaeological record. Destruction might thus be considered the sacrificial mechanism and this can be focused upon humans and animals, as well as inanimate objects such as weapons, pots, plants, and crops, textiles, etc. The latter are also included within the definition of sacrifice proposed here, for sacrifice is not solely concerned with the 'immolation by death (at least symbolically)' of living beings as many of the contributors in Bourdillon and Fortes (1980: 16) suggest. Such a perspective wrongly denies the indisputable role of objects within sacrifice.

However, the religious element has to be given pre-eminence in considering sacrifice as defined here for the destruction of objects can also occur within the framework of what Bourdillon (1980: 13) refers to as 'prestigious killings' as in the North American Kwakiutl potlatch which is concerned 'with status, a material benefit' (ibid.) rather than religious belief. Thus religion provides the intellectual rationale, but the intentions underpinning sacrifice can also be as broad as the material sacrificed and could include expiation, praise or homage, supplication, thanksgiving (Carter 2003: 5; Henninger 2005: 8001), and communion or communication. But a further commonality to sacrifice exists, as Fortes (1980: xiii) notes, in that it 'is a special ritual procedure for establishing or mobilising a relationship of mutuality between the donor (individual or collective) and the recipient'.

2 SACRIFICE AS A FOCUS OF STUDY

The attention paid to sacrifice by scholars is vast. However, this is primarily by theologians, historians of religion (e.g. Carter 2003), and anthropologists (e.g. Bourdillon and Fortes 1980) rather than archaeologists. It is both impossible and unnecessary to attempt to summarize this, though it is useful to note a couple of points of potential relevance to archaeologists here. First, that sacrifice was formerly placed 'at or near the beginning of a chronological sequence' of evolutionary studies of religion (Carter 2003: 8) as exemplified by the works of, for example, Tylor (1929) or Robertson Smith (1894). Second, and somewhat similarly in terms of the associated evolutionary temporal connotations, Carter (2003: 8) describes how sacrifice was often identified as the 'essence of religion' as evident in, for instance, the writings of Frazer (1911–15) or Freud (1938). Hence sacrifice has been presumed to be a 'primordial' ritual action, and epistemologically, sacrifice has assumed a prominent place in discussions of the origins of religion as well as in the seminal 'proto' anthropological studies on religion (e.g. Carter 2003).

3 THE ARCHAEOLOGY OF SACRIFICE

Archaeological evidence for sacrifice has also been found in myriad contexts, both geographically and temporally. Primary attention has often been given to blood sacrifice, especially of humans, for it is frequently the focus of morbid popular curiosity (Law 1985: 53), matched only, perhaps, by interest in archaeological evidence for cannibalism even where convincing proof is lacking (Hughes 1991: 24). Instances of human sacrifice in the archaeological record are varied and include, for example, the burial of five or more persons, perhaps slaves, on the roof of an *eze Nri* title-holder's burial chamber dated to the ninth to eleventh centuries AD at Igbo-Richard, part of the Igbo-Ukwu site complex in Eastern Nigeria (Shaw 1970: 565; Ray 1987: 68). Another example is provided by the extensive evidence for human sacrifice at Kerma in the Sudan. Here, Bonnet (2004: 76) describes how 'the last rulers of Kerma pushed this custom to the limits of demographic possibility, since the human sacrifices associated with the great royal tumuli were in their hundreds'. This is seemingly not an exaggeration for in the *Kerma Classique* period (*c.*1750–1550 BC) large numbers of people linked to the royal court were sacrificed and placed to accompany royal burials in a sacrificial corridor leading towards the funerary chamber in the grave tumuli (Bonnet 2004: 72, 76–7).

Similar evidence for the practice of large-scale human sacrifice has also, famously, been recorded at Aztec sites. As Brumfiel (2007: 266–7) describes, Aztec state religion combined warfare with the natural cycles that sustained life. Diurnal and seasonal cycles were embedded in longer cycles of destructive chaos and orderly creation. The Aztecs believed that the four previous creations had been destroyed, with the present one destined to meet the same fate via earthquakes, and its continued existence would only be 'so long as it was strengthened by human sacrifice' (ibid.: 267). Hence both cosmic cycles and the need for human sacrifice were represented in the material culture of the Aztec state, as in, for example, the Aztec calendar stone with at its centre a sacrificial knife protruding from the mouth of the deity (Brumfiel 2007: 267–8).

The sacrifice of animals is also frequently attested archaeologically either in association with humans, or individually, or in association with objects. Again the sacrificial evidence from the sites at Kerma is relevant, and where sheep and goats, occasionally dogs, and cattle were sacrificed and placed in or around tombs. One spectacular tomb from the *Kerma Moyen* period (2050–1750 BC), interpreted as of a prince, was found accompanied by 4,351 cattle bucrania from animals sacrificed to accompany the deceased which had been deposited in the southern part of the tumuli (Bonnet 2004: 75, 89). A spectacular animal sacrificial deposit was also recorded at the Maussolleion of Halikarnassos (modern Bodrum) in Turkey dated to *c*.353/52 BC (Jeppesen et al. 1981). Five cattle, 25 sheep/goats, 8 lambs and kids, 3 cocks, 8 pigeons, 10 hens, and 26 hen's eggs were recovered deposited as either near-complete carcasses or butchered segments. These had been laid on a smooth clay floor and were covered with a pile of stone. This seemingly single depositional event was interpreted as possibly 'ritualized presentation of a meal for the dead' (Hojlund 1981: 84).

Animal sacrifices can also be cremated, as Williams (2001) describes for Anglo-Saxon England. For example, at the site of Spong Hill animal remains were recovered from nearly half the cremation burials suggesting that animal sacrifice formed a widespread element of funerary ritual (ibid.: 197). The species represented were varied but the most common were horse and sheep/goat. The species selected for sacrifice do not appear to precisely reflect the economy of Anglo-Saxon England and instead functioned to, as Williams (2001: 199) notes, 'set up symbolic associations between animal species and the physical remains of the dead through the ritual process'.

Evidence for the sacrifice of objects is similarly varied. For example, Bradley (1998) discusses many examples of material—metal weapons, shields, ornaments, tools—that were recovered from bogs and watery deposits in the Bronze and Iron Ages in Western and Northern Europe. Bradley (1998) describes these predominantly as 'votive offerings' (ibid.: 200) for he defines sacrifice as 'of living matter, whether plants or animals, whilst artefacts can only be offerings' (Bradley 1998: 1990). This can be questioned for whilst it is possible that some of these artefact deposits were hoards or votive offerings, it is equally plausible that some might be 'sacrificial'. A suggestion that can be made as Bradley's definition of sacrifice is limited in excluding artefacts, as these could also have been considered as imbued with 'life' that even in relation to animals and plants (both alive and processed) can vary significantly (Insoll 2007a). Moreover destruction, identified as significant in defining sacrifice here, seems to have been sometimes employed in relation to dealing with these artefacts (e.g. Bradley 1998: 176), potentially strengthening an alternative 'sacrificial' interpretation.

This chapter could be entirely filled with a list of archaeological finds of sacrificial material, but this is irrelevant. Of greater significance is considering the questions that might be asked in investigating sacrifice archaeologically. For example:

1. Are there differences in the species and materials sacrificed by cultivators, herders, and hunter-gatherers?
2. In blood sacrifice what species are sacrificed and how might these interrelate with other possible elements of systems of belief such as totemism?
3. What faunal remains, body parts, or parts of objects are represented? Do the deposition patterns differ and are especial parts given prominence?
4. Can the sacrificial ritual and any accompanying beliefs be reconstructed?
5. What is the context of sacrifice and does it allow inferences about seasonality or time of sacrifice?

It is useful to consider these questions and the archaeological possibilities they raise in a little more detail, and at the outset to recognize that they are in fact interconnected.

3.1 Are there Differences in the Species and Materials Sacrificed by Cultivators, Pastoralists/Herders, and Hunter-gatherers?

This question raises interesting ideas in relation to the evolution of religions and their connection with concepts of settlement permanence versus mobility, ties to the land, and interrelation with phenomena such as ancestor cults. For instance, Henninger (2005: 7998) proposes that 'the most extensive development of ritual slaying is found among cultivators' with emphasis placed upon blood as 'a power-laden substance that brings fertility'. In contrast, he argues that blood sacrifice is usually not found among hunter-gatherers where instead a small symbolic part of the animal slain during hunting might be offered but the actual kill is not equivalent to a sacrificial act.

Attitudes to animals differ (Ingold 2000: 72, 74), but whether such a general interpretation is universally supported by archaeological evidence is of course debatable, though it merits further investigation. Certainly, in hunter-gatherer contexts archaeological evidence for blood sacrifice has been found, as in the cemeteries at the Mesolithic site of Skateholm in southern Sweden where dogs had been sacrificed and included in some burials (Zvelebil 1996: 48, 2000: 40). However at these sites, evidence indicating increasing sedentism was found rather than a fully mobile hunter-gatherer economy (Zvelebil 1996, 2008).

3.2 In Blood Sacrifice what Species are Sacrificed and how Might these Interrelate with Other Possible Elements of Systems of Belief such as 'Totemism'?

Certain repetitive general patterns would also seem to exist with regard to the species that are the focus of sacrifice and these hold potential archaeological implications. Blood sacrifice, besides humans which seems to have been largely uncommon outside certain contexts, is primarily of domesticated animals: reindeer, horses, camels perhaps amongst herders; cattle, sheep, goats, pigs, fowls, and dogs amongst cultivators (Henninger 2005: 7998). The rarity of sacrificing wild animals and fish and birds other than fowls or doves has also been remarked upon (ibid.). Beattie (1980: 31) suggests that this emphasis placed upon domestic animals is because they 'are identified with the home, and with the human group that lives there; with *man* [*sic*], as against "nature"'. The interpretation proposed by Zvelebil (1996: 56) to explain the dog sacrifice at Skateholm would seem to concur with this. For he suggests that dogs were sacrificed at Skateholm as they were considered domesticated, thus following Ingold's (1986) assertion that sacrifice is only applicable to domesticated species, as animals subordinate to humans.

This is broadly what is represented by the species acceptable for sacrifice amongst the Tallensi of Northern Ghana, where wild animals are almost wholly precluded and domesticates are the focus of sacrifice. However, a uniform assumption that all domesticates are acceptable is simplistic. Shrines will accept the cow, sheep, goat, donkey, cat, dog, fowl, guinea fowl, and dove, but not the horse, camel, pig, or duck—though the duck will be accepted if a turtle, that is obviously not a domesticate, cannot be found for sacrifice if this is what the shrine or soothsayer has said is required, reasoning behind this being that both the turtle and duck are defined as aquatic. Unacceptable animals for sacrifice, although domesticates, include the horse, camel, pig, and generally, the duck. The pig is defined as unacceptable, not because of religious sanctions, it is kept and its meat consumed, but because it is considered as being like a bush (wild) animal (Insoll in preparation a). There is also an emphasis placed upon familiarity with the animals sacrificed by the ancestors, with the pig described as not known at a very early stage by the ancestors, as it was too recently acquired. This point could probably be extrapolated to the horse, but here its association with Muslim slavers (see Allman and Parker 2005) might also be a factor of consequence in precluding its use in sacrifice (Insoll in preparation).

Although the prevalence of domestic animals in sacrifice would seem to be almost universal, archaeological examples to the contrary can be found. An example of this is seemingly provided by Moszynska (1978) in discussing material from the site of Ust-Polui in the Lower Ob region of Siberia where large quantities of animal bones were recorded that had been placed in heaps on the ground. These were interpreted as the residue of sacrifice conducted within Shamanic frameworks of belief. The species present included reindeer, recorded elsewhere as sacrificed within shamanic contexts (Jordan 2001: 96), but also beaver, hare, sable, squirrel, elk, and, nearby, dog and human. Hence besides the reindeer, dogs, and humans, wild species are represented and Moszynska (1978: 472) also refers to an account that observed that 'reindeer, red game, and waterfowl' were sacrificed. Such evidence is unusual and it is possible that the report on Ust-Polui is unreliable for both the contextual and dating evidence can be challenged, but alternatively if it is correct it might provide evidence for the sacrifice of wild animals.

Further research possibilities exist in exploring which species are sacrificed. Beattie (1980), for instance, in considering sacrifice in general, does not proceed to explore the possibilities of metaphor or metonym linked with the dominant role of domesticated animals in sacrifice, but potentially these could be considered. However it should be noted that in making this point no attempt is being made to try and go back to, for example, Robertson Smith's (1894) or Durkheim's (2001) positions linking on certain occasions the totem and sacrifice, and the eating of the totem (Carter 2003: 54, 128). But this stated, equally, it is possible that in some instances concepts of totem, even if read only as 'symbol', and prohibition perhaps linked with what is or is not sacrificed.

3.3 What Faunal Remains, Body Parts, or Parts of Objects are Represented? Do the Deposition Patterns Differ and are Especial Parts Given Prominence?

The presence or absence of certain faunal remains or body parts and a possible emphasis placed upon parts of objects or certain categories of material culture or materiality in sacrificial deposits might be of significance. The predominance of skulls as possible objects of power is an example of this. This might be what is represented archaeologically at the Classic period (twelfth–sixteenth centuries AD) site of Obalara's Land at Ife, Nigeria, where one of the emphases seems to have been placed upon skulls and heads. Thus gagged and decapitated human heads are represented on a pot found whilst piles of sorted human remains including a compact group of both fragmentary and complete human skulls were also recorded (Garlake 1974). This was perhaps representative of human sacrifice but also post-mortem human decapitation (Ogundiran 2002: 50–1; Insoll 2004: 108–9).

Amongst the Tallensi, skulls of sacrificial animals are given to 'leaders'—Earth priests, chiefs, elders—rather than ordinary people. The skull indicates superiority and leadership and thus placing the skull in a shrine is an indication of the shrine's superiority and also indicates that the sacrifice has been completed as from the skull it is easy to identify what has been sacrificed (Insoll in preparation) (Figure 11.1). Similarly, the division of a sacrifice can be of the utmost significance and this might relate to consumption for, as Carter (2003: 6) notes, 'consumption is frequently an important part of sacrifice-like activities'. This can also have profound archaeological implications, for because of social and ritual reasons, the sacrificed animal might be widely dispersed according to known criteria, post-butchery.

Lienhardt (1961: 24), for instance, clearly indicates how a sacrificed cow is divided among different kin by the Dinka of the Sudan. A similar process of division is evident with the Tallensi where different kin groups and religious title-holders take their share of the sacrificial beast but the details vary according to the shrine where the sacrifice was completed (Insoll in preparation). Hence, for example, from a cow sacrifice at the Yelwom shrine in Tamboog in the Tongo Hills of Northern Ghana, the Tengdaana will get the head, horns, the tail, part of the skin, and the rear hind leg, whilst the Tibil Gaadan (Gadan Yire) who is an elder and part of the Tengdaana's family will get the left fore leg, and the 'nephews' (the sons of women from the Tengdaana's family who have married out) get the neck (Insoll in preparation) (Figure 11.2).

In archaeological terms the existence of such sacrifice patterns amongst the Tallensi means that faunal remains rarely enter the archaeological record (Insoll 2007b: 331). Instead they are distributed throughout the landscape where the meat and marrow is consumed and certain elements might be incorporated in ancestral shrines as described, or in diviners' or soothsayers' bags. The faunal remains that are included in the latter are selectively chosen for symbolic purposes so that, for example, a sheep's horn will represent a shrine, a chicken's foot the obligation to present a fowl for sacrifice, and a sheep's jaw that a witch might be seeking to destroy you (Fortes 1987: 19; Insoll in preparation).

The examples just discussed, excluding that from Ife, are derived from ethnographic observation, but indicate the potential in thinking about the patterning represented by faunal and other remains in possible sacrificially related archaeological contexts. Moreover, considering the interconnection between different substances and materials

FIGURE 11.1 Ancestral shrine formed of skulls, jaw bones etc. about to be sacrificed to, Goldaan House, Bonchiog, Tongo Hills, Ghana, November 2008.

beyond a cruder consideration of body parts might also be useful. This might be of significance for Werbner (1989: 135) emphasizes how in his anthropological examples of sacrifice from Southern Africa, the sacrificial rite is underpinned by 'transformation'—'opposed by counter transformation, sequences of animal substances by counter-sequences of non-animal substances, rites in phases of ritual by anti rites in counterphases of play'. The latter might be irrelevant or difficult to infer from archaeological evidence, but the former might be something to explore in relation to considering sacrifice via archaeological deposits, i.e. potential relationships between bones and pots or stones and bones or metals, wood etc.

FIGURE 11.2 Cow sacrifice, Yelwom shrine, Tamboog, Tongo Hills, Ghana, March 2008.

3.4 Can the Sacrificial Ritual and any Accompanying Beliefs be Reconstructed?

As noted in the introduction to this volume and throughout the entries, ritual has been the obsession of archaeologists often to the detriment of recognizing its probable function within a framework of religion (Insoll 2004). Sacrifice is often tightly structured according to precise ritual frameworks dictating what, when, where, and how the sacrifice must be completed. Besides ethnography, an insight into this is provided by, in some instances, iconographic data.

A good example is provided by ancient Greek sacrifice that is depicted pictorially, as well as recorded historically, and evident archaeologically. Ekroth (2005), for example, discusses in precise detail the treatment of blood at Greek sacrifices based on iconographical

FIGURE 11.3 Blood, the residue of a cow sacrifice, Tonna'ab Yaane shrine, Tongo Hills, Ghana, August 2006.

evidence. Representations of sacrificial ritual in vase paintings allow the suggestion to be made (supported by written sources [Ekroth 2002: 242–76]) that the blood from regular animal sacrifices was kept, prepared, and consumed after a small amount had been sprinkled upon the altar (Ekroth 2005: 9) (Figure 11.3). Complex sacrificial ritual actions can be reconstructed because of the supporting iconographic data which, though it cannot be read 'as exact depictions of reality or as snapshots of antiquity', indicates 'some degree of correspondence between what is shown and what went on at ancient sacrifices' (ibid: 20).

Also of interest is the sceptical view in relation to human sacrifice in ancient Greek religion taken by Hughes (1991), who reinterprets various archaeological case studies and in so doing reconstructs and suggests quite different ritual practices to those proposed by the original excavators. An instance of this is provided by his reinterpretation of the supposed evidence for cannibalism recovered from the basement rooms of a Late Minoan house (c.1450 BC) at Knossos. Rather than being 'indicative of human sacrifice and ritual consumption', Hughes (1991: 23) tentatively suggests on the basis of the cut-mark evidence on the children's bones found that this is possibly indicative of 'defleshing before reburial', i.e. secondary burial practices and not sacrifice. Hence this is still the residue of the archaeology of ritual action, but of a quite different type to sacrifice.

The repetitive actions in relation to material things inherent in ritual (Insoll 2004: 78; Bell 1992), including that of sacrifice are, theoretically at least, amenable to archaeological investigation. Context can be critical in assessing the longevity of sacrificial practice and the established nature of the sacrificial ritual, the latter possibly accompanied by actions of burning, libations, blood-letting and butchery, and the deposition of objects and materials, as well as the archaeologically invisible elements such as invocations and prayers.

Although a checklist approach to investigating ritual and its potentially associated beliefs is generally inadvisable for the exceptions tend to outnumber the supposed universalities (Insoll 2004; 2007c), Henninger (2005: 7999) makes some interesting points about the location of sacrifice that might be useful in archaeological interpretation. For instance, he suggests that if the recipient of the sacrifice is thought to dwell in heaven then smoke and burning might be the agent of sacrifice and the open air will be preferred as the place of sacrifice, involving a natural high place such as a mountain or hill or human-constructed roof or temple tower, or the sacrificial material will be hung on a tree or stake. Alternatively, sacrificial materials will be buried or blood poured into the earth if the focus is chthonic; whilst if water-associated beliefs are the focus, then sacrifices will be left in bodies of water and water courses etc., and if it is the dead, then the grave will be the focus of sacrifice.

This is of course a general and simplistic framework, exceptions and complications can be added based even on the one ethnographic Tallensi example drawn upon earlier. These could include the integration of burning, via the roasting of a fowl or the liver of a cow in a 'non-sky'-related context such as an Earth shrine where the sacrifice was completed; or communication with the ancestors (deceased) through the agency of sacrifice at household shrines which have no physical connection with graves or human remains (Insoll 2008). But leaving aside these, and the numerous other exceptions that could probably be found, certain recurring elements could exist which might allow the reconstruction of aspects of sacrificial ritual at a level of detail beyond that of recognizing the potential sacrificial intent underpinning the archaeological deposits alone.

Such a degree of interpretation is facilitated where supporting sources of evidence are available such as historical sources or ethnographic accounts. Simpson (1967: 190), for example, comments on the comparatively rich records that exist on Scandinavian pre-Christian beliefs and rituals as opposed to those of contemporary Anglo-Saxon England. Her focus is upon sacrifice and these sources provide rich descriptions of sacrificial rituals, beliefs, and contexts, as in Adam of Bremen's famous second-hand account of the great temple at Uppsala, Sweden in the eleventh century AD. To quote (ibid.: 193):

> The sacrifice is performed thus: nine head of every living male creature are offered, and it is the custom to placate the gods with the blood of these. The bodies are hung in a grove which stands beside the temple. This grove is so holy for the heathens that each of the separate trees is believed to be divine because of the death and gore of the objects sacrificed; there dogs and horses hang together with men.

However, it also has to be admitted, as was conceded in relation to the Greek iconographic evidence previously, that literal truth is of course not necessarily represented in historical sources or myths. Mallory (1989: 132–3) provides a useful example of this in discussing how the ideals of Indo-European religious belief—i.e. the tripartite conceptual system of Indo-European mythology—should, ideally, be translated into the archaeological record in relation to, for example, ritual animal sacrifice. Hence the horse as the focal point of Indo-European sacrifice, perhaps via the agency of the *asvamadha* ceremony where various rituals were completed and the horse was ultimately smothered and dismembered into three portions, could theoretically be archaeologically manifest. Nonetheless, archaeological reality is in general not so kind, for as Mallory (1989: 142) notes, 'ideal worlds of myths, one may argue, are just that, and although they may be an expression of social realities, these need never take the corporeal forms required by the archaeologist'. This is echoed by Hughes (1991: 3), who warns us about the relationship between myth and ritual in ancient Greek religion when he suggests myth in regard to human sacrifice 'is more a testament to the capacity and breadth of the imagination of the Greeks than a documentary record of their practices' (ibid.: 193). Hence comparative historical, mythological, or iconographic evidence is not a panacea for reconstructing sacrificial ritual.

Yet the optimistic reliance upon these sources for the reconstruction of sacrificial ritual is unnecessary. For where written sources are lacking, as in northern Ghana until the late nineteenth century (Allman and Parker 2005), it is possible to get an insight into the sacrificial ritual and, potentially, the beliefs that underpin it from archaeological evidence. The deposition of pots in the great Tallensi earth shrine of Nyoo would seem to be indicative of sacrificial ritual combining the deposit of the pots, some seemingly broken *in situ*, around a series of stone arrangements possibly arranged according to known criteria as seating places for elders, Earth priests, and chiefs (Insoll 2009). Furthermore, the sacrificial action in Nyoo was perhaps underpinned by beliefs involved in returning the pots, made of clay, to the medium, the earth, from which they came before altering by human hand and fire (Insoll 2010). The whole, based on ethnographic analogy, potentially also accompanied by other ritual performative actions such as movement, perhaps dance (Insoll 2009). In this instance ethnographic analogy has assisted archaeological interpretation of sacrificial ritual but only partially. For the deposits in Nyoo were dated by OSL to between the mid-third and mid-eleventh centuries AD and are thus from substantially before Tallensi oral historical memory and before they existed as a 'defined' ethnolinguistic group (Insoll, Kankpeyeng, and MacLean 2007).

In considering this example, the issue of belief is also encountered. As ritual is embedded within religion, at least in reference to the rituals that are the focus of this volume, then belief in the efficacy of sacrifice must presumably exist as well or it becomes wanton destruction. Hence beliefs, unattainable as they might be archaeologically, are locked into the contexts and deposits. As noted, the reasons for completing a sacrifice can be varied and theories on the role and function of sacrifice have proliferated (see Carter 2003). One of specific potential interest archaeologically is the degree of pragmatism underpinning sacrifice, i.e. in it functioning as a way of obtaining and possibly controlling sources of food and especially protein. Although it is undesirable to descend to a level of ecological determinism in relation to interpreting sacrifice (see Schlee 1992: 120 for cogent criticism), acknowledging a degree of pragmatism has implications for how we might view our faunal remains outside of sacrificial contexts. This is because meat, blood, skins (and objects) obtained sacrificially can be moved outside the 'sacred' and desacralized in more profane uses, though sacrifice was their original ritual role and purpose. This is not a return to Hubert and Mauss's (1964) interpretation that the sacrificial 'victim' (Carter 2003: 89) serves as an 'intermediary' between the sacred and profane but merely an observation that in material archaeological terms sacrifice can extend beyond the context of the immediate sacrifice, deposits, and ritual itself.

3.5 What is the Context of Sacrifice and Does it Allow Inferences about Seasonality or Time of Sacrifice?

This is intertwined with the previous question and its separation is somewhat arbitrary for, again, belief and ritual cannot be divorced from its consideration. Henninger (2005: 8000) outlines two main times of sacrifice, regular sacrifices and extraordinary sacrifices. The types of material present might indicate the time of sacrifice where this is tied into the agricultural or vegetative year or the seasonal cycle, as with the Tallensi Boardam festival, a harvest festival allied with the completion of initiation rites (Fortes 1987: 47), and within which sacrifice plays a significant part.

Alternatively, where perhaps a range of comparative sacrificial deposits exist, an unusual or anomalous focus of sacrifice may indicate an 'extraordinary' sacrificial occurrence. Could this be perhaps what was represented in Benin, southern Nigeria, where the remains of at least 41 young women aged between 15–35 years were recorded who had been dropped, clothed, down a cistern in deposits dated to the mid-thirteenth century AD (Connah 1975: 66)? Of interest is that there were some 10 m of deposits above these human sacrifices within which were pieces of iroko timber, described by Connah (ibid.) as 'today often regarded as the Oba's (Ruler's) timber', whilst pieces of valuable elephant tusk had been placed towards the top of the deposits in the cistern. Connah (2001: 160) would seem to be right in stating that this must represent 'ritual sacrifice of a sort indicative of strongly centralized authority', but was this an extraordinary event or a regular sacrificial occurrence? Documentation for the use of cisterns to dispose of bodies exists (Connah 1975: 66), but the scale of the sacrifice and the links with authority seemingly attested by the iroko wood and the ivory suggest that should comparative archaeological examples become available in the future more might perhaps be inferred about the significance and timing of this sacrifice.

4 FUTURE DIRECTIONS IN INVESTIGATING THE ARCHAEOLOGY OF SACRIFICE

It is evident in the preceding discussion that although a broad definition of sacrifice was provided at the outset encompassing objects, plants, animals, and humans, the discussion has predominantly focused on issues surrounding blood sacrifice. This might seem to undermine the definition itself and lend credence to the view that sacrifice can only operate in relation to living things. However, this is not so. Conversely, it reflects where the predominant archaeological focus has been placed thus far and in so doing serves to illustrate that perhaps a primary future direction lies in thinking about and investigating materiality, context, and deposition patterns of sacrifice more broadly construed. To achieve this we perhaps need to revisit existing archaeological material, as well as ethnography, literary sources, oral history, myth, and iconography (the prior cautions noted) to think about how objects, materials, animals, people, and places are potentially conceptualized as living, dead, personified, animated, created, and destroyed. For these all interrelate with and invest meaning in the archaeology of sacrifice.

Suggested Reading

There is no one key text for the archaeology of sacrifice. The examples chosen and discussed in this chapter obviously reflect the author's interests. Suggestions for further reading are thus limited and comprise, first and foremost, Henninger's (2005) encyclopaedia entry and Carter's (2003) selection of readings on sacrifice. Neither of these is 'archaeological', so researching sacrifice in the archaeological record is again down to personal preference and material of sacrificial relevance can be found in literature concerned with most periods and regions.

References

ALLMAN, J. and PARKER, J. 2005. *Tongnaab* (Bloomington: Indiana University Press).
BEATTIE, J. H. M. 1980. 'On understanding sacrifice' in M. F. C. Bourdillon and M. Fortes (eds), *Sacrifice* (London: Academic Press), pp. 29–44.
BELL, C. 1992. *Ritual Theory, Ritual Practice* (Oxford: Oxford University Press).
BONNET, C. 2004. 'The Kerma culture' in D. A. Welsby and J. R. Anderson (eds), *Sudan. Ancient treasures* (London: British Museum Press), pp. 70–89.
BOURDILLON, M. F. C. 1980. 'Introduction' in M. F. C. Bourdillon and M. Fortes (eds), *Sacrifice* (London: Academic Press), pp. 1–27.
——and FORTES, M. (eds) 1980. *Sacrifice* (London: Academic Press).
BRADLEY, R. 1998. *The Passage of Arms* (Oxford: Oxbow Books).
BRUMFIEL, E. M. 2007. 'Huitzilopochtli's conquest: Aztec ideology in the archaeological record' in T. Insoll (ed.), *The Archaeology of Identities. A reader* (Abingdon: Routledge), pp. 265–80.
CARTER, J. (ed.) 2003. *Understanding Religious Sacrifice: A reader* (London: Continuum).
CONNAH, G. 1975. *The Archaeology of Benin* (Oxford: Clarendon Press).
——2001. *African Civilisations* (Cambridge: Cambridge University Press).
DURKHEIM, E. 2001. *The Elementary Forms of Religious Life* (Oxford: Oxford University Press).
EKROTH, G. 2002. *The Sacrificial Rituals of Greek Hero-Cults in the Archaic to the Early Hellenistic Periods* (Liege: Centre International d'Etude de la Religion Grecque Antique).
——2005. 'Blood on the altars? On the treatment of blood at Greek sacrifices and the iconographical evidence', *Antike Kunst*, 48: 9–29.
FORTES, M. 1980. 'Preface: Anthropologists and theologians: Common interests and divergent approaches' in M. F. C. Bourdillon and M. Fortes (eds), *Sacrifice* (London: Academic Press), pp. v–xix.
——1987. *Religion, Morality and the Person* (Cambridge: Cambridge University Press).

Fowler, F. and Fowler, H. 1986. *The Oxford Handy Dictionary* (Oxford: Oxford University Press).

Frazer, J. G. 1911–1915. *The Golden Bough: A study in magic and religion* (London: Macmillan).

Freud, S. 1939. *Totem and Taboo* (Harmondsworth: Penguin).

Garlake, P. 1974. 'Excavations at Obalara's Land, Ife: An interim report', *West African Journal of Archaeology*, 4: 111–48.

Henninger, J. 2005. 'Sacrifice' in L. Jones (ed.), *Encyclopedia of Religion*, XII, 2nd edn (Detroit: Thomson Gale), pp. 7997–8008.

Hojlund, F. 1981. 'The deposit of sacrificed animals at the entrance to the tomb chamber' in K. Jeppesen, F. Hojlund, and K. Aaris-Sorensen (eds), *The Maussolleion at Halikarnassos*, I: *The Sacrificial Deposit* (Moesgard: Jutland Archaeological Society Publications), pp. 21–90.

Hubert, H. and Mauss, M. 1964. *Sacrifice: Its nature and function* (Chicago: Chicago University Press).

Hughes, D. D. 1991. *Human Sacrifice in Ancient Greece* (London: Routledge).

Ingold, T. 1986. *The Appropriation of Nature* (Manchester: Manchester University Press).

—— 2000. *The Perception of the Environment* (London: Routledge).

Insoll, T. 2004. *Archaeology, Ritual, Religion* (London: Routledge).

—— 2007a. *Archaeology: The conceptual challenge* (London: Duckworth).

—— 2007b. '"Totems", "Ancestors", and "Animism": The archaeology of ritual, shrines, and sacrifice amongst the Tallensi of northern Ghana' in D. Barrowclough and C. Malone (eds), *Cult in Context* (Oxford: Oxbow Books), pp. 326–33.

—— 2007c. 'Natural or human spaces? Tallensi sacred groves and shrines and their potential implications for aspects of Northern European prehistory and phenomenological interpretation', *Norwegian Archaeological Review*, 40: 138–58.

—— 2008. 'Negotiating the archaeology of destiny: An exploration of interpretive possibilities through Tallensi shrines', *Journal of Social Archaeology*, 8: 380–403.

—— 2009. 'Materialising performance and ritual: Decoding the archaeology of shrines in northern Ghana', *Material Religion*, 5: 288–311.

—— 2010. 'Pots and earth cults: The context and materiality of archaeological ceramics amongst the Tallensi of northern Ghana and their interpretive implications' in N. Naguib and B. De Vries (eds), *Heureux qui comme Ulysses a fait un Beau Voyage: the movements of people in time and space.* (Bergen: Bric Press), pp. 189–212.

—— in preparation. *Theoretical Explorations in African Archaeology. Contexts, materials, persons, and animals* (Oxford: Oxford University Press).

——, Kankpeyeng, B., and MacLean, R. 2007. 'Shrines, rituals, and archaeology in northern Ghana', *Current World Archaeology*, 26: 29–36.

Jeppesen, K., Hojlund, F., and Aaris-Sorensen, K. 1981. *The Maussolleion at Halikarnassos*, I: *The Sacrificial Deposit* (Moesgard: Jutland Archaeological Society Publications).

Jordan, P. 2001. 'The materiality of shamanism as a "world-view": Praxis, artefacts and landscape' in N. Price (ed.), *The Archaeology of Shamanism* (London: Routledge), pp. 87–104.

Law, R. 1985. 'Human sacrifice in pre-colonial West Africa', *African Affairs*, 84: 53–87.

Lienhardt, G. 1961 [1987]. *Divinity and Experience: The religion of the Dinka* (Oxford: Oxford University Press).

Mallory, J. P. 1989. *In Search of the Indo-Europeans* (London: Thames and Hudson).

Moszynska, W. 1978. 'An ancient sacrificial site in the Lower Ob region' in V. Dioszegi and M. Hoppal (eds), *Shamanism in Siberia* (Budapest: Akademiai Kiado), pp. 469–79.

OGUNDIRAN, A. O. 2002. 'Filling a gap in the Ife-Benin interaction field (13th–16th centuries AD): Excavations in Iloyi Settlement, Ijesaland', *African Archaeological Review*, 19: 27–60.

RAY, K. 1987. 'Material metaphor, social interaction and historical reconstructions: Exploring patterns of association and symbolism in the Igbo-Ukwu corpus' in I. Hodder (ed.), *The Archaeology of Contextual Meanings* (Cambridge: Cambridge University Press), pp. 66–77.

ROBERTSON SMITH, W. 1894. *The Religion of the Semites: The fundamental institutions* (London: A. and C. Black).

SCHLEE, G. 1992. 'Ritual topography and ecological use: The Gabbra of the Kenyan/Ethiopian borderlands' in E. Croll and D. Parkin (eds), *Bush Base: Forest farm* (London: Routledge), pp. 110–128.

SHAW, T. 1970. *Igbo-Ukwu* (Evanston: Northwestern University Press).

SIMPSON, J. 1967. 'Some Scandinavian sacrifices', *Folklore*, 78: 190–202.

TYLOR, E. B. 1929. *Primitive Culture*, 2 vols. (London: John Murray).

WERBNER, R. 1989. *Ritual Passage. Sacred Journey* (Washington: Smithsonian Institution Press).

WILLIAMS, H. 2001. 'An ideology of transformation: Cremation rites and animal sacrifice in early Anglo-Saxon England' in N. Price (ed.), *The Archaeology of Shamanism* (London: Routledge), pp. 193–212.

ZVELEBIL, M. 1996. 'Ideology, society and economy of the Mesolithic communities in temperate and Northern Europe', *Origini*, 20: 39–69.

——2008. 'Innovating hunter-gatherers: The Mesolithic in the Baltic' in G. Bailey and P. Spikins (eds), *Mesolithic Europe* (Cambridge: Cambridge University Press), pp. 19–59.

CHAPTER 12

IDEOLOGY

RANDALL MCGUIRE AND REINHARD BERNBECK

1 INTRODUCTION

IDEOLOGIES thrive in the imagination and in the desires of different social groups. Ideologies move in the space between thought and knowledge that every society generates. Ideologies reflect in oblique ways the standpoint of social groups and spring from the interests of those social groups. They create opinions and dictate both mundane and ritual behaviours in order to validate these interests. They make these interests look real by turning assumptions into beliefs, transferring them into the taken for granted notions of everyday opinions, and reiterating them to reinforce them as an indispensable entity for social life and for its analysis. Ideologies, based on supposedly shared ethical or moral premises, tend to generate opposition and confrontation by nourishing and excluding identities in a social group which, due to their support of opposing interests, fractures into factions; on the other hand, they provide closure to open-ended questions and deepen conflicts. Ritual, religion, political discourse, and visual representations are loaded with ideologies.

Archaeologists have rarely taken up the complex concept of ideology. When discussing past ideologies, archaeologists mainly use the term as a substitute for 'world view', 'religion', or 'political doctrine'. However, 'ideology' is not a coherent sphere of collective thought that can be investigated like a landscape or group of material objects. Instead, it refers to a complex set of relations between people and their surroundings that is centred on power differentials. Another aspect is the ideological nature of archaeological thought itself. When we speak of archaeological theories, we treat ideologies of interpretation in a fashion similar to that of past worldviews. The realm of theoretical discourse and the power relations established by it are—wrongly—treated as if this was a level playing field of equal interactions among (interested) archaeologists.

2 A BRIEF HISTORY OF THE CONCEPT OF IDEOLOGY

The term ideology originated in the aftermath of the French Revolution (Polowetzky 1993). The French scientist Destutt de Tracy applied the positivist paradigm from the natural sciences onto ideas. 'Ideologists' claimed to have a privileged access to reality, one that enabled them to represent the world as it really is.

Marx and Engels (1970) wrote *The German Ideology* as a challenge to the German Romanticism and Idealism of Hegel's students. They saw this work—not published until 1932—as a work of self-clarification. Marx and Engels argued that ideology is not simply 'consciousness', or 'ideas' but instead a false representation of the relationship between consciousness and being. Marx and Engels 'turned Hegel on his feet' by arguing that real social conditions and not the mind or ideas produce the contradictions that move history forward. In their formulation, ideologies primarily served to advance the interests of the ruling class by representing the particular interests of dominant groups as the general interests of society.

Marx did not use the term ideology in any of his further works. Most notably *Capital* makes no mention of ideology. Instead, Marx confronts misrepresentations of reality as 'commodity fetishism', where social relationships between people appear as if they were relations between things. Capitalist production breaks down into many steps the process of making objects, so that workers no longer recognize the input of their own labour. Instead, the finished thing turns into a mystical entity with monetary value that falsely appears to be unrelated to the workers' labour. By the same processes, the very human ability to perform work becomes a commodity that capitalists buy in a 'labour market'. Through this process capitalism alienates the worker from his labour.

The German Ideology tackles misrepresentation mainly as an effect of political relations, whereas Marx's later focus on commodity fetishism is the 'economic side' of ideology. Both of these concepts are important to understand how human beings live in an imagined relationship to reality. Commodity fetishism and ideology also set up two intertwined genealogical lines leading to modern concepts of ideology.

2.1 Western Marxism

Western Marxism developed the first line in the early twentieth century by integrating notions of ideology and commodity fetishism to understanding social life. Georg Lukács (1971) argued that commodity fetishism seeps into the social life beyond the economic sphere. Relations between human beings themselves become reified. Lukács maintains that in the process, objects take on an abstract appearance of existing in and by themselves, uncontrollable in an opaque world. Scholars of the Frankfurt School emphasized Marx's concept of ideology to elaborate on Lukacs's ideas (Arato and Gebhardt 1982; Rush 2004). They separated 'traditional' and 'critical' theory. Traditional theories take a 'realist' perspective of a presumed neutral and independent mind. The naivety of traditional theory leads to the acceptance of a capitalist logic of instrumental reasoning that seeks to optimize gains and by that reifies social relations, alienating people from themselves and nature. In contrast, critical theory recognizes that historically and socially created ideologies mediate our perceptions of the world. Thus, to gain knowledge, scholars must first investigate how their own ideological position mediates their understanding of the world. Critical theory reveals the ideological content and reification of instrumental reasoning. In the second half of the twentieth century, Jürgen Habermas's (1984) theory of communicative action adds to this critique of a dominant reason by dividing the social universe into one sphere ruled by instrumental reason, science and reification, which he calls the system. The other is the 'lifeworld', a realm of communicative reason. Built of unquestioned and unquestionable elements, Habermas conceptualizes actions in the lifeworld as largely discursive events where the optimizing relation between means and ends so typical of instrumentality, becomes inseparably merged, as in chatting or communication during a collective meal.

The second genealogical line continued to use the term ideology and led to the equation of ideology with false consciousness, first mentioned by F. Engels. Many Marxists compounded the facile understanding of 'false consciousness' with a simplified reading of Engels' comment that the economic base determines superstructures 'in the last instance'. Proponents of Social Democracy and the Second International promoted the notion that economic relations determine ideas. The communist bloc propagated this vulgar materialism in their doctrine of 'historical materialism'.

Western Marxist theorists, including Lukács, opposed the idea of ideology as false consciousness by emphasizing that thought and knowledge about the world could change practices and thus the world itself. Lukács also defined ideology as the collective consciousness of specific classes, rather than a 'false consciousness'. The Italian communist Antonio Gramsci (1992) refuted the concept of ideology as a product of economic relations and instead argued that ideology caused economic relations. He concluded that ideology and culture are of central importance for all political relations, foreshadowing the cultural studies paradigm. He contended that people have two 'consciousnesses', one non-discursive, and the other 'explicit or verbal'. The non-discursive results in a naive reproduction of the hegemonic ideas of social elites and institutions such as church, state, and schools.

Gramsci's concept of hegemony refers to ideas that are both cultural and political. Institutions of the state, including law, police, or military, use hegemony to enforce submission. Scott (1990: 70–85) discusses two readings of Gramsci's notion of hegemony. The 'thick version' claims that people actively subscribe to ideas that enhance their own subordination. The 'thin version' posits that a dominant class defines 'for subordinate groups what is realistic and what is not realistic and to drive certain aspirations and grievances into the realm of the impossible' (Scott 1990: 74). Gramsci claimed that a social group could only become politically dominant after having gained a hegemonic, culturally compelling position in civil society by integrating to some extent subordinate groups' interests.

We can summarize the relation between hegemony and ideology as follows:

- ideology is deeply embedded in civil society and serves to subdue subaltern classes to political power
- ideology as a 'cement' of society is both practical and grounded in thought
- ideological hegemony means co-optation of the ruled by their rulers in a cultural network that is not specifically political but serves political ends anyway
- subordinate groups employ counter-hegemonies to try and transform dominant hegemonic leadership.

2.2 French Structural Marxism and Althusser

Louis Althusser's main work on ideology (1972) departs radically from much earlier thought. Building on Gramsci, Althusser differentiates historically specific, practised ideologies located in what he calls 'ideological state apparatuses' (ISA) from 'ideology in general'.

He differentiates ISA such as schools, church, or family from 'repressive state apparatus' (RSA) that include the police and the army. The two kinds of apparatuses make up a state but do not seamlessly merge into a whole: while the RSA is coherent, ISAs do not form a totality. Instead, they are themselves de-centred and contradictory.

However, Althusser's main contributions to theories of ideology are his reflections on 'ideology in general'. He contends that ideology is universal in how humans relate to the world and not just a product of the consciousness of some dominant class intent on ruling others, nor a warped reflection of reality. Ideology produces subjects, people who perceive themselves as 'free subjects' but who are, as the notion implies, 'subjected' (Althusser 1972: 182). Subjection means that individuals are 'always already subjects' (Althusser 1972: 176): they have a name, religion, nationality, language, and culture at birth. Existence as a human being implies being placed inside pre-existing ideology. Second, ideology constitutes subjects through relentless symbolical 'hailing'. Althusser refers to Blaise Pascal's example of the person who kneels in a church and by that practical act believes. One does not kneel because one believes; it is enough to kneel in order to believe. Practice induces dispositions of the mind. Althusser turns ideology into something material and performative. This reversal of conventional concepts of ideology fits Althusser's general stance on history as the effect of structures from which spring human practices that create subjects.

Abercrombie et al. (1980) have critiqued Althusser's and Gramsci's position as a 'dominant ideology thesis' where ideologies dupe lower classes into willing submission despite stark economic inequalities—an abbreviation of 'thick versions' of hegemony. In contrast Abercrombie et. al (1980) argue that dominant ideologies merely integrate ruling classes, whereas subordinate groups form their own, opposing ideas. This critique fails to address the complexity of Althusser's and Gramsci's thought. Their dismissal of categorical divides makes it clear that neither of them envisioned a ruling class cunningly creating an ideological scheme of domination. Rather ideology produces collective, de-centred subjects who paradoxically imagine themselves as centred 'egos'. Contrary to Marx, ideologies do not exist in the collective imaginary of some ruling class but rather are made up by the collective imaginary of the lower social strata. According to Balibar (1993: 13), upper classes appropriate this imaginary, rework it and return it in altered form to subordinate groups. The degree to which subordinates accept the returned imaginary measures the success of a ruling ideology. Ideologies conceal this relationship between the subaltern imaginary and dominant ideology.

2.3 Ideology, Discourse, and Hegemony

According to Althusser, ideology produces collective and individual subjects. Michel Foucault instead claims that subjects are shaped by discourses. Foucault objects to the notion of ideology because peoples' attempts to unveil what ideology silences and hides presume some truth beyond what is criticized. Foucault opposes this claim to truth arguing that truth is not to be had, not even relationally—as in 'closer' or 'further from it'. Instead Foucault explores the establishment of 'truth regimes' (1984: 60), the conditions that turn specific discourses into apparent truths and others into falsehoods.

Laclau and Mouffe's (1985) discourse theory diverges from Foucault in several ways. They claim that there is literally nothing outside of discourse and merge the concept of a discourse with the notion of hegemony. Laclau and Mouffe see hegemony as a particular emergence of meaning in discourse that is driven not by interests of a collective or individual subject but by discourse itself. Laclau and Mouffe (1985: 136–7) call the practice of chaining discursive notions to a major concept 'hegemonic articulation', an activity that is political because different hegemonic formations may end up in relationships of antagonism and struggle. They agree with Foucault on the impossibility of a subject that is at the origin of a discourse; there is no other possibility than constantly shifting 'subject positions' that are provided by discourse itself.

Slavoj Zizek (1994, 2008) analyses how ideology appears in the contemporary world in culture, politics, religion, and daily life. He begins with the Lacanian triad of the Imaginary, the Symbolic, and the Real. The Imaginary is closely related to the emergence of an 'image' of self in early childhood. The desire to render all and everything meaningful is, according to Zizek, an anthropological universal that requires a symbolic sphere which is mainly the realm of language. Zizek claims that language constitutes a universe in itself that does not denote reality. It is an entire world apart. Finally, the 'Real' is not reality as we experience it, but reality as we would experience if we were not wrapped in the symbolic realm. Zizek reads contentions that we are at an 'end of ideology' or that we need to create a 'post-ideological' (2008: 295–6) world as 'ideology par excellence' (1994: 17), since such contentions are typically ideological positions unrecognized by those who hold them. This means that the unexamined, taken-for-granted aspects of theory, methods, or practices, in archaeology or elsewhere, are more likely to be ideological in character than those that individuals contest. Zizek's observations on cultural production, and his insistence on identifying the many instances and types of misrepresentation in the symbolic realm, provide a good example for a critical archaeology that recognizes both past beliefs and its own products as misrecognitions.

3 IDEOLOGY AND ARCHAEOLOGY

The archaeological discourse on ideology begins with the work of Karl Marx. Archaeologists initiated this discourse in the middle of the twentieth century but with the exception of V. Gordon Childe, mid-century archaeologists denied, ignored, or were simply ignorant of the Marxist origin of the concept. Partly as a result of their failure to engage Marxist scholarship they misread the idea of ideology as a reified 'world view'. Towards the end of the twentieth century many archaeologists initiated a serious, explicit engagement with Marxism and the concept of ideology (Patterson 2003). At the same time, other archaeologists picked up strands of feminist and post-modernist thought that also use a Marxist-derived notion of ideology.

3.1 V. Gordon Childe

In the 1930s, V. Gordon Childe (1936) explicitly adopted a Marxist concept of ideology as a false consciousness that served elite interests. He stressed 'the obvious truth that men cannot live without eating', such that 'the way people get their living should be expected in the long run to "determine" their beliefs and institutions' (Childe 1979: 94). Childe sought to show that in any given environment, with a given set of tools and knowledge, one form of organization secures the smoothest and most efficient exploitation of that environment—people included—while any other is likely to impede production or may even paralyse it. And in general just one *kind* of ideology—institutions, beliefs, and ideals—will keep that organization functioning most smoothly. He placed ideology firmly in the realm of myth, ritual, and religion, and seems to have regarded magic, religion, and ideology as aberrations, forms of social pathology that blocked progress in social evolution. Because class struggle pervades *all* aspects of the life of class societies, magic, religion, and ideology as systems of mystification and control are essential features of elite power.

In his later years, Childe (1956) considered the relationship of knowledge and history and retained a notion of ideology as false consciousness. Childe argued that a society's knowledge is not always progressive, and critique is necessary to reveal this. For Childe, the convergence between knowledge as a model of the 'real world' and that society's means of production provides the measure of a society's fitness to survive. Ideology as individual delusion or social illusion could hamper a society's knowledge, and the ability to act and progress. Childe saw the development of knowledge as a dialectic in which people achieved understanding through the negation of error and argued that ideology interferes with the progress of knowledge. Thus, ideology as an integral part of human history is for Childe distinct from knowledge. He had no problem in claiming the latter for the discipline of archaeology.

3.2 Neo-Evolutionists and Cultural Ecologists

In the 1960s, the term 'ideology' came into common use among Anglophone archaeologists. Most of them did not refer to Marx or Childe but rather drew their ideas from the Neo-evolutionary theory of Leslie White and/or the cultural ecology of Julian Steward. Neo-evolutionists tended to equate ideology with the 'ideational' or realm of ideas as opposed to material relations and processes of life. Cultural ecologists on the other hand, usually spoke of ideology as information that regulated adaptive systems.

White (1949: 366) defined culture as people's extra-somatic means of adaptation and divided it into three subsystems: technology, society, and ideology. The process of cultural change begins in the technological subsystem and changes in this subsystem lead to changes in the social subsystem that then result in changes in ideology. White's students equated ideology with the totality of mental culture including world view, beliefs, and value systems (Demarest 1992: 1). As solely the outcome of a process of culture change, ideology becomes trivial and epiphenomenal.

The new archaeologists of the 1960s picked up this broad view. Many also accepted that ideology was a consequence rather than a dynamic, active element of cultural change. White's three subsystems guided Binford (1962: 24–5) in his division of material culture into technomic, sociotechnic, and ideotechnic artefacts. He embraced White's definition of ideology as an operational subsystem of culture that rationalized social structures and enabled individuals to function in society. In historical archaeology, James Deetz (1977) drew on structuralism rather than White but he too equated ideology simply with the realm of ideas, namely as a colonial world view he called the Georgian Order.

Julian Steward's (1955) ideas of cultural ecology and multilinear evolution differed from White's but both approaches viewed culture as an adaptive system and ideology as ideas.

Steward, however, did not categorize ideas, beliefs, and values as epiphenomena. He instead argued that each society had a cultural core of traits closely related to subsistence activities. The core includes economic arrangements and related political, religious, and social patterns. As part of the cultural core, world views could play an active role in adaptation. Roy A. Rappaport (1967) showed how ritual pig feasts, myths, and folk taxonomies of highland New Guinea articulated with and regulated ecological relations. In archaeology, cultural ecologists rejected the view of ideology as trivial and examined how religion functioned in adaptation and in cultural evolution as a source of information, as a regulating mechanism for decision-making, and as propaganda (Demarest and Conrad 1992).

Making ideology synonymous with ideas deprives the concept of any real analytical power (Burke 2006: 130). Such reified, essentialist concepts of ideology oversimplify how ideas articulate with other aspects of social relations and imply that society as a whole shared a world view, values, and beliefs. Yet in reality we never find such uniformity within cultures. Rather, ideas exist in a pluralistic, strife-ridden social world made up of social groups or individuals who share some elements of a world view but diverge and clash on others. To understand how ideas come to be, affect cultural change, and enable and transform social relations, many Marxist, post-processual, and feminist archaeologists have adopted an explicitly Marxist notion of ideology.

3.3 Marxist Archaeology and Ideology

In the mid-1970s, several Western archaeologists began an explicit and sustained use of Marxist theory in their research that continues to the present (Patterson 2003: 91). They drew on a wide range of Marxist theory including classical Marxism, French structural Marxism, critical theory, and Hegelian Marxism. These approaches defined ideology in various ways and gave it different weight in analyses. Almost all of these authors rejected the notion that the economic base determined ideology and instead argued that ideology exists in a reflexive relationship to the economy and material culture. They directly challenged the processual archaeology equation of ideology with ideas. In their studies they demonstrated how people used ideology to legitimize and manipulate social relations of inequality and exploitation.

During the 1970s many British scholars embraced Jonathan Friedman's (1979) structural Marxist theory. Friedman challenged the structural causality of Althusser and argued for a more historical approach whereby scholars explained a given social form by exposing the structural transformation that created it. In their epigenetic model of early civilizations, Friedman and Rowlands (1978) emphasized the generative role of ideology in class formation and interpreted ideology in emergent class societies as religious expressions that legitimate the sanctity of chiefs by positioning them as intermediaries between natural and supernatural worlds.

In the United States, Mark Leone and his students (Leone 1995, 2005; Palus et al. 2006) proposed a critical archaeology derived from structural Marxism and critical theory. Leone defined ideology as the taken-for-granted beliefs and assumptions that serve to mystify the true nature of social relations and thus maintain relations of exploitation by outwardly resolving contradictions that still exist within society. Leone urged scholars to expose how such ideologies were created. He hoped that people would transform relations of exploitation once scholars pulled away the veil of ideology. Others have employed the Althusserian idea of interpellation to elaborate the many practical ways in which material aspects of ideologies contribute to the shaping of subjectivities of various dominant and subordinate groups (Bernbeck 2003–4, 2008).

Leone's Annapolis project investigated how the plan, architecture, landscape, and material culture of the city established and reinforced a Georgian (Enlightenment) Order (read ideology) of individualism, rationalism, equality, and social contract. The project also sought to reveal to modern tourists how the historic district of the city had been manipulated to reinforce an ideology of modern capitalism and the contradictions and social inequalities that the hegemonic history of Annapolis obscured. This challenge to the ideological narrative about Annapolis failed to overcome the official. The public responded to the alternative vision of the project by reinterpreting it in terms of assumptions directly derived from a capitalist ideology.

Marxist archaeologists have mostly rejected the dominant ideology thesis that underlies the early critical archaeology (McGuire 1988; Burke 1999). They point out that it is unlikely that elite constructions such as formal gardens duped waged and enslaved workers into a false consciousness that hid from them the reality of their oppression. Instead, they emphasize the negotiation of ideology in class conflict. Specifically they examine how dominant classes use dominant ideologies to create class-consciousness for themselves and how subordinate classes manipulate these ideologies in struggles against domination (Shackel and Palus 2006). In this light, the failure of the Annapolis Project's public programmes to emancipate tourists in Annapolis is clear. Annapolis attracts tourists primarily from privileged classes and these tourists interpreted the message of the programme using their class ideology.

After some self-critique, Leone adopted a post-Marxist approach that uses Habermas's notion of communicative action and Foucault's idea of governmentality (Palus, Leone, and Cochran 2006). He recognized that people who have been directly and negatively affected by the contradictions of interests, inequalities, and exploitation of capitalism would be the most receptive to ideological critiques. Since 1990, Annapolis archaeologists have worked in collaboration with African-American communities (Palus, Leone, and Cochran 2006).

In the 1980s some US archaeologists took inspiration from a Marxist anthropological political economy and used dialectics as a way to understand the lived experience of people (McGuire 1992; Marquardt 1992; Delle 1998; Wurst 2006). Following the critical archaeology they also adopted a self-reflexive awareness of archaeology's place in the modern world. A reflexive, Marxist archaeology recognizes that class exploitation always intersects with other forms of exploitation such as sexism and racism. This approach places the motor for social change in the conflicts that result from the ambiguities, tensions, and contradictions that exist within social relations. Social relations can only exist in historical contexts and structures, and between living human beings; they do not exist in the abstract. Therefore, human action in the form of collective agency makes history as it both transforms and reproduces social structures. They also argue that the economy and ideology do not exist as separate levels of society but rather form a social totality. Thus it is nonsensical to speak of base determining superstructure because the existence of the base necessarily requires and entails the existence of the superstructure. It is the relationship between modes of production and superstructure that shapes society so that ideology becomes an active force in social change. From this perspective, a single class does not possess ideology and ideology does not hide reality but rather ideology exists in processes that negotiate, and transform social relations (Burke 2006: 141).

These archaeologists tend to view ideology as a relational component of lived experience (Burke 2006: 137). Ideology has observable material and behavioural manifestations. Ideology may have multiple functions in the negotiation of social relations. No unified ideology exists because the same sets of beliefs and symbols may evoke different meanings in different social sectors and at different times. Ideologies are the product of, and a prerequisite for, a group attaining a political consciousness and serve to integrate social groups (classes, genders, professions, lineages, etc.) in power struggles. Specifically, a ruling class needs to remain coherent to dominate others by relying on a unified ideology that at the same time mystifies such domination by representing its particular interests as those of all. This ideology may be accepted by subordinate classes or they may rework it into subordinate ideologies. Conflict may result from inconsistencies between the ideology of elites and the ideology of subordinates. Change in consciousness moves people to actions that transform the reality again challenging the ideal. Subordinate ideologies therefore may reveal power relations but, because they are cultural, they also mystify reality and serve to reproduce and legitimate inequalities in society if subordinate groups come to dominate. As Burke (2006: 141) notes, 'ideology is continually emergent. It is not an entity, but a highly dynamic process that always changes in response to its engagement in the world and the patterning of relationships between social groups.'

3.4 Post-processualist Archaeology

Post-processual archaeology borrowed heavily from Marxism, including a definition of ideology as a mystifying force in social relations that generate and reproduce conflicts of interest (Miller and Tilley 1984). Post-processualists drew on French structuralist Marxism and the Frankfurt School. Marxist and post-processual archaeologies have similarities but their differences are not trivial. Both view archaeology as a politically engaged practice that is more than a search for knowledge and study ideological uses of the past in the present.

Post-processual approaches to ideology differ from Marxist concepts of ideology because the post-processualists emphasize the relationship between ideology and individual agents. Miller and Tilley (1984: 14) asserted that 'ideology and power are inextricably bound up with social practices; they are a component of human *praxis*, by which is to be understood the actions of agents on and in the world, serving as an integral element in the production, reproduction, and transformation to the social'. The post-processualists find ideology in the consciousness of individuals, specifically in the meanings that social actors use to make sense of the world (Shanks 1992). In contrast, Marxists tend to spotlight ideology as it is manifest in relations between social groups, with a focus on how ideology forms class consciousness.

3.5 Feminist Archaeology

If ideology is an active component of social relations that masks or builds group consciousness and reproduces or instigates transformations of social inequalities, then ideology must be in the service of particular group interests (Burke 2006: 134). These can be class-specific, but ideology can also serve racial, ethnic, and gender interests. Feminists and feminist archaeologists use Marxist-derived concepts of ideology (Weedon 1987: 29–32). The most obvious distinction between the two approaches is that Marxists focus more on class and feminists on gender.

Second-wave feminists in the early 1960s read French structuralist Marxism and critical theory (Weedon 1987: 29–32) and rejected the idea that the economic base determines ideology, as well as the juxtaposition of ideology as false consciousness and purportedly true knowledge. They viewed gender ideologies as being interrelated but not reducible to ideologies of class and class relations. Third-wave feminists in the 1990s incorporated postmodern ideas into feminism. Some of them dropped the concept of ideology to discuss the negotiation of gender relations in terms of discourse. Like post-processual archaeologists they stress the potential of individual agency (Gilchrist 1999: 26).

Margaret Conkey and Joan Gero (1991: 5) identified three goals to a feminist archaeology: (1) to expose gender bias in archaeological inquiry, (2) to find women in the archaeological context and identify their participation in gender relations, gender ideologies, and gender roles, and (3) to problematize underlying assumptions in Western culture about gender and difference. Ideology figures prominently in these goals and in feminist scholars' efforts to realize them (Nelson 2007; Joyce 2008). Feminist archaeologists confront ideologies of gender in the past and in the present.

4 Ideology and Archaeology at the Turn of the Twenty-First Century

In the 1990s, many archaeologists invoked ideology. This was particularly the case in studies of chiefdoms or mid-range societies. Archaeologists argued that the lack of institutionalized instruments of power in such societies give ideologies a crucial position in legitimating and reproducing chiefly power. However, Marx's theories have found their strongest proponents in Anglo-American archaeology among those scholars who study the modern world (McGuire 2008). Historical archaeologists have maintained a very active engagement with questions of ideology throughout the turn of the twenty-first century (Burke 2006; Palus et al. 2006).

By the first decade of the twenty-first century, ideology has lost much of its appeal in prehistoric archaeology. In part, this results from the critique of the dominant ideology thesis (Abercrombie et al. 1980). The realization that ideology does not in some simple way dupe people led some archaeologists to overemphasize agency. Post-processual archaeologists now argue that archaeologists should understand change in terms of the action of individuals. The archaeological literature is littered with statements about why the individual is the only force capable of creating cultural change (Hodder 2000). Post-processual theorists would have us believe that their positions are radical and transformative of capitalism (Shanks and Tilley 1987). Other authors have argued that the post-modernist focus on the individual is not really radical at all, but rather fits nicely as a component of the dominant ideology globalization and modern consumer capitalism (Thomas 2004; McGuire and Wurst 2002).

What happens when we ignore ideology or assign it to the scrap heap? Or to put it another way, after the pendulum of theoretical discourse has swung to the extreme of a history driven by human agents, why does ideology matter? At a most basic level, the explicit abandonment of ideology as a facet of all human life puts those who do so at the centre of a deeply ideological position—that of 'absolute knowing'. In its present use, such a denial prevents us from recognizing the individual agent of post-modern theory as an ideology. Ideologies of individual agency—at the extreme, methodological individualism—shatter notions of the social whole so that social relations seem only to exist as a network of interpersonal relations. The idea that a society, a class, genders, or other totalities might be more than the sum of their individual parts is thus lost as today's individuals consume identities and perform personalized subjectivities, destroying notions of solidarity and commonality in the process. Any projection of such late capitalist conditions into a closer or farther-away past serve only to reconfirm the very ideological conditions of their making. Forgetting about ideology makes it impossible to form a coherent praxis based on shared consciousness.

Suggested Reading

The primary literature on ideology can be pretty daunting to the novice reader. Terry Eagleton's (1991) *Ideology: An introduction* and David Hawkes' (2003) *Ideology* provide good summaries to start with. Chris Weedon's (1987) *Feminist Practice and Poststructuralist Theory* contains a brief discussion of ideology in feminism. An excellent reader of basic texts is Zizek's edited volume *Mapping Ideology* (1994). A student interested in understanding more about ideology should read the primary literature beginning with Marx and Engel's (1970) *The German Ideology* and following the historical development of the concept from Lukács through Zizek as cited in the article. Within archaeology Miller and Tilley (1984), McGuire (1992), Burke (1999, 2006), Leone (2005), and Palus, Leone, and Cochran (2006) provide good discussions of ideology.

References

ABERCROMBIE, N., HILL, S., and TURNER, B. S. 1980. *The Dominant Ideology Thesis* (London: Allen and Unwin).

ALTHUSSER, L. 1972. 'Ideology and ideological state apparatuses. (Notes towards an investigation)' in L. Althusser (ed.), *Lenin and Philosophy* (New York: Monthly Review Press), pp. 127–88.

ARATO, A. and GEBHARDT, E. 1982. *The Essential Frankfurt School Reader* (London: Continuum).

BALIBAR, E. 1993. 'The non-contemporaneity of Althusser' in E. A. Kaplan and M. Sprinker (eds), *The Althusserian Legacy* (London: Verso), pp. 1–16.

BERNBECK, R. 2003–4. 'Politische Struktur und Ideologie in Urartu', *Archäologische Mitteilungen aus Iran und Turan*, 35: 267–312.

——2008. 'Royal deification: An ambiguation mechanism for the creation of courtier subjectivities' in N. Brisch (ed.), *Religion and Power: Divine kingship in the ancient world and beyond* (Chicago: University of Chicago Oriental Institute Press), pp. 157–70.
BINFORD, L. R. 1962. 'Archaeology as anthropology', *American Antiquity*, 28(2): 217–25.
BURKE, H. 1999. *Meaning and Ideology in Historical Archaeology* (New York: Plenum Press).
——2006. 'Ideology and the material culture of life and death' in M. Hall and S. W. Silliman (eds), *Historical Archaeology* (Oxford: Blackwell Publishing), pp. 128–46.
CHILDE, V. G. 1936. *Man Makes Himself* (New York: The New American Library).
——1956. *Society and Knowledge* (New York: Harper and Brothers).
——1979. 'Prehistory and Marxism', *Antiquity*, LIII: 93–5.
CONKEY, M., and GERO, J. 1991. 'Tensions, pluralities, and engendering archaeology: An introduction to women and prehistory' in J. Gero and M. Conkey (eds), *Engendering Archaeology* (Oxford: Basil Blackwell), pp. 3–30.
DEETZ, J. 1977. *In Small Things Forgotten* (New York: Anchor Books).
DELLE, J. A. 1998. *An Anthropology of Social Space* (New York: Kluwer/Plenum).
DEMAREST, A. A. 1992. 'Archaeology, ideology and pre-Columbian cultural evolution: The search for an approach' in A. A. Demarest and G. W. Conrad (eds), *Ideology and Pre-Columbian Civilizations* (Santa Fe: School of American Research Press), pp. 1–13.
——and CONRAD, G. W. (eds) 1992. *Ideology and Pre-Columbian Civilizations* (Santa Fe: School of American Research Press).
EAGLETON, T. 1991. *Ideology: An introduction* (London: Verso).
FOUCAULT, M. 1984. *The Foucault Reader*, ed. Paul Rabinow (New York: Pantheon Books).
FRIEDMAN, J. 1979. *System, Structure and Contradiction* (Copenhagen: The National Museum of Denmark).
——and ROWLANDS, M. (eds) 1978. *The Evolution of Social Systems* (London: Duckworth).
GILCHRIST, R. 1999. *Gender and Archaeology: Contesting the past* (London: Routledge).
GRAMSCI, A. 1992. *Prison Notebooks* (New York: Columbia University Press).
HABERMAS, J. 1984. *The Theory of Communicative Action* (Boston: Beacon Press).
HAWKES, D. 2003. *Ideology*, 2nd edn (London: Routledge).
HODDER, I. 2000. 'Agency and individuals in long-term processes' in M. Dobres and J. Robb (eds), *Agency in Archaeology* (London: Routledge), pp. 21–33.
JOYCE, R. A. 2008. *Ancient Bodies, Ancient Lives: Sex, gender, and archaeology* (London: Thames and Hudson).
LACLAU, E. and MOUFFE, C. 1985. *Hegemony & Socialist Strategy: Towards a radical democratic politics* (London: Verso).
LEONE, M. P. 1995. 'A historical archaeology of capitalism', *American Anthropologist*, 97(2): 251–68.
——2005. *The Archaeology of Liberty in an American Capital: Excavations in Annapolis* (Berkeley: University of California Press).
LUKÁCS, G. 1971. *History and Class Consciousness: Studies in Marxist dialectics* (Boston: MIT Press).
MCGUIRE, R. 1988. 'Dialogues with the dead, ideology and the cemetery' in M. P. Leone and P. B. Potter Jr (eds), *The Recovery of Meaning, Historical archaeology in the Eastern United States* (Washington: Smithsonian Institution Press), pp. 435–80.
——1992. *A Marxist Archaeology* (Orlando: Academic Press).
——2008. *Archaeology as Political Action* (Berkeley: University of California Press).

McGuire, R. H. and Wurst, L. 2002. 'Struggling with the past', *International Journal of Historical Archaeology*, 6: 85–94.
Marquardt, W. H. 1992. 'Dialectical archaeology', *Archaeological Method and Theory*, 4: 101–40.
Marx, K. and Engels, F. 1970. *The German Ideology* (New York: International Publishers).
Miller, D. and Tilley, C. (eds) 1984. *Ideology, Power and Archaeology* (Cambridge: University of Cambridge Press).
Nelson, S. M. 2007. *Women in Antiquity: Theoretical approaches to gender and archaeology* (Walnut Creek, CA: AltaMira).
Palus, M. M., Leone, M. P., and Cochran, M. D. 2006. 'Critical archaeology: Politics past and present' in M. Hall and S. W. Silliman (eds), *Historical Archaeology* (Oxford: Blackwell Publishing), pp. 84–106.
Patterson, T. C. 2003. *Marx's Ghost: Conversations with archaeologists* (Oxford: Berg).
Polowetzky, M. 1993. *A Bond Never Broken: The relations between Napoleon and the authors of France* (London: Associated University Presses).
Rappaport, R. A. 1967. *Pigs for the Ancestors: Ritual in the ecology of a New Guinea people* (New Haven: Yale University Press).
Rush, F. (ed.) 2004. *The Cambridge Companion to Critical Theory* (Cambridge: Cambridge University Press).
Scott, J. 1990. *Domination and the Arts of Resistance: Hidden transcripts* (New Haven: Yale University Press).
Shackel, P. and Palus, M. 2006. 'Remembering an industrial landscape', *International Journal of Historical Archaeology*, 10(1): 49–72.
Shanks, M. 1992. *Experiencing the Past: On the character of archaeology* (London: Routledge).
—— and Tilley, C. 1987. *Social Theory and Archaeology* (Cambridge: Polity Press).
Steward, J. 1955. *Theory of Cultural Change* (Urbana-Champagne: University of Illinois Press).
Thomas, J. 2004. *Archaeology and Modernity* (London: Routledge).
Weedon, C. 1987. *Feminist Practice and Poststructuralist Theory* (Oxford: Basil Blackwell).
White, L. 1949. *The Science of Culture* (New York: Farrar and Straus).
Wurst, L. 2006. 'A class all its own: Explorations of class formation and conflict' in M. Hall and S.W. Silliman (eds), *Historical Archaeology* (Oxford: Blackwell Publishers), pp. 190–208.
Zizek, S. 1994. 'Introduction: The spectre of ideology' in Slavoj Zizek (ed.), *Mapping Ideology* (London: Verso), pp. 1–33.
—— 2008. *In Defense of Lost Causes* (London: Verso).

CHAPTER 13

FEASTING AND FASTING

MICHAEL DIETLER

1 INTRODUCTION

FOOD and drink have an especially prominent place in ritual and religion because they are 'embodied material culture' (see Dietler 2001, 2005). That is, they are material objects produced specifically to be destroyed by a form of consumption that involves ingestion into the human body. This fact lends them a heightened symbolic and affective resonance in the social construction of the self (Falk 1994). Moreover, given that eating and drinking are social acts that must be repeated virtually every day for biological survival, they occupy a salient place among the various routinized practices that, as Bourdieu (1990) explained, serve to inculcate habitus—that is, the set of embodied dispositions that structure action in the world and that unconsciously instantiate social roles and cultural categories and perceptions of identity and difference. Furthermore, because sustaining this process of consumption requires continual replenishing production through both agricultural and culinary labour, this domain of material culture is one where the intimate linkages between the domestic and political economy are especially evident (Goody 1982; Sahlins 1972). In addition, alcohol, as a special form of food with psychoactive effects, has a particularly salient role in ritual because of its transformative properties (Dietler 1990, 2006a; Heath 1987, 2000).

Feasting and fasting are two alternative ways to mobilize the symbolic power of food and drink, through either ritualized commensal consumption or refusal of consumption. Although ethnographic and historical research has shown that both practices are common in societies around the world and throughout history, the archaeological visibility of fasting is far more limited than that of feasting. This undoubtedly explains why the surge of recent interest by archaeologists in feasting (e.g. Benz and Gramsch 2006; Bray 2003a; Dietler 1990, 1996, 2001, 2006b; Dietler and Hayden 2001; Hayden 1990, 1996, 2001; Mills 2004; Wright 2004) has not been accompanied by a similar pursuit of fasting. This article examines the symbolic logic and material basis of both practices through a theoretical discussion based upon comparative ethnographic and historical data.

2 Feasting

Feasting may be defined as a form of ritual activity centred on the communal consumption of food and drink. Rituals of this kind have played many important social, economic, and political roles in the lives of peoples around the world. As with other types of ritual, feasts provide an arena for both the highly condensed symbolic representation and the active manipulation of social relations, and they have an inherent political dimension (see Dietler 1996, 2001, 2006b; Hayden 1996, 2001).

Some scholars (e.g. Hayden 2001; Wills and Crown 2004) suggest that feasts need not be rituals, but this stems from an eccentric understanding of the nature of ritual. Identifying feasts as rituals does not mean that they are necessarily highly elaborate ceremonies. Nor need rituals necessarily be 'sacred' in character (see Moore and Myerhoff 1985). The defining criterion of rituals is that they are in some way symbolically differentiated from everyday activities in terms of forms of action or purpose: in Kertzer's (1988: 9) phrase, they are 'action wrapped in a web of symbolism'. In fact, feast is the term that is used precisely to designate those food-consumption events that are in some way symbolically differentiated from daily meals. The ritual symbolism of feasting is constituted through a complex semiotic relationship to daily consumption patterns, and both form part of a common semiotic field (see Douglas 1984; Elias 1978). In order to understand the symbolic logic of feasts and the social roles they play, it is clearly necessary to examine feasts and daily meals together and to explore the various ways in which both symbolic differentiation and commonality are invoked in different contexts within the overall system of foodways (see below).

Perhaps the most famous examples of feasting are the Potlatch of Native Americans of the Northwest coast and the competitive feasts of New Guinea bigmen (Codere 1950; Feil 1984; Lemonnier 1990; Perodie 2001; Powdermaker 1932; Suttles 1991). These became well known in the anthropological literature because of the overtly agonistic escalating nature of the feasts, where lavish hospitality was used to crush guests under an obligation to respond with ever more generous hospitality in events that could take over a decade to prepare. Although such escalating feasts are known from other contexts as well (e.g. Rehfisch 1987), these are, in fact, not representative of feasting in general. Usually there are culturally specific behavioural sanctions and moral philosophies of legitimate power that restrict the escalation of such commensal practices and assure that cases of this extreme type are fairly unusual. But, as shown later, some degree of social competition is involved in all feasting. That is, those who do not keep up in their fulfilment of expected hospitality fall behind. Such practices always affect the *relative* status and influence of participants and the quality of relationships. In this sense, feasting is always competitive in its effects, even though the political implications may be subtle, limited, and thoroughly euphemized.

Ethnographic and historical studies have documented the prevalence, importance, and diversity of feasting in most regions of the world. Cases from Africa (e.g. Anigbo 1996; Dietler 2001; Goody 1982; Halperin and Olmstead 1976; Rehfisch 1987; Richards 1939; Saul 1983), the Pacific (Feil 1984; Hogbin 1970; Kirch 2001; Lemonnier 1990; Powdermaker 1932; Volkman 1985; Wiessner 2001), Latin America (Bartlett 1980; Cancian 1965; Kennedy 1978), and East and South-east Asia (Adams 2004; Clarke 2001; Friedman 1984; Hayden 2003) are particularly abundant in this literature, but other regions are also well represented. However, with a few notable exceptions (e.g. Bell 1997: 120–8; Friedman 1979, 1984; Lemonnier 1990), treatment of feasting was often somewhat anecdotal, and explicit systematic attempts to develop a detailed cross-cultural theoretical framework for understanding feasting as a distinctive ritual practice did not appear until the theme was taken up by archaeologists in the 1990s (Dietler 1990, 1996, 2001; Gero 1992; Hayden 1990, 1996, 2001). Moreover, ethnographic accounts usually had not focused sufficiently upon the material dimension that is crucial for archaeologists to be able to detect and interpret feasting in the record of material remains of the past revealed through excavation. This problem stimulated several archaeologists to undertake primary ethnographic (or 'ethnoarchaeological') research on feasting that has further improved understanding of the practice in various ways (e.g. Adams 2004; Arthur 2003; Clarke 2001; Dietler and Herbich 2001, 2006; Hayden 2003; Wiessner and Tumu 1998). Recently, a growing body of archaeological studies has begun to demonstrate the deep antiquity of feasting and its historical significance, in cases ranging from the ancient Near East and Egypt (Benz and Wächtler 2006; Pollock 2003; Schmandt-Besserat 2001; Smith 2003) to South, Central, and North America (Blitz 1993; Bray 2003b; Brown 2001; Clark and Blake 1994; Goldstein 2003; Jennings 2005; Kelly 2001; Knight 2001; Lau 2002; LeCount 2001; Mills 2004, 2007; Morris 1979; Phillips and Sebastian 2004; Potter 2000; Potter and Ortman 2004; Rosenswig 2007; Smith et al. 2003), prehistoric Europe (Benz and Gramsch 2006; Dietler 1990, 1996, 1999, 2006b; Müller 2006; Ralph 2005; Wright 2004), South-east and East Asia (Junker 1999; Nelson 2003) and beyond.

What all of this research has shown is that, among the various forms of ritual activity, feasts have some distinctive properties. The symbolic power of feasts derives from the fact that food and drink serve as the media of expression, and commensal hospitality constitutes the syntax in the context of a ritual of consumption. Food and drink are highly charged symbolic media because, as noted above, they are 'embodied material culture' produced specifically for ingestion into the body. They are a basic and continual human physiological need that are also a form of highly condensed social fact embodying relations of production and exchange and linking the domestic and political economies in a highly personalized way. Moreover, although eating and drinking are among the few biologically essential acts, they are never simply biological acts. Rather, they are learned *'techniques du corps'* (Mauss 1935)—culturally patterned techniques of bodily comportment that are expressive in a fundamental way of identity and difference. Moreover, people consume not abstract calories or protein, but food and drink: a form of material culture subject to almost unlimited possibilities for variation in terms of ingredients, techniques of preparation, patterns of association and exclusion, modes of serving and consumption, aesthetic evaluations, and so forth. This presents the potential for a vast array of highly charged symbolic elaborations of foodways. However, it must be remembered that food is not only a sign system, and its consumption is not only the consumption of signs. It is also a material construction of the self in much more than a figurative sense, and the study of feasting should also be grounded in analysis of the material conditions and social relations of production and distribution.

Both food and drink are a highly perishable form of material good, the full politico-symbolic potential of which is realized in the performative drama of public consumption events that constitute a prime arena for the reciprocal conversion of what Bourdieu (1990) metaphorically called 'symbolic capital' and economic capital. Public distribution and consumption of a basic need derives added symbolic salience from its demonstration of confidence and managerial skill in the realm of production. More importantly, however, consumption is played out in the extremely potent idiom of commensal hospitality. Commensality is a powerfully expressive trope of intimacy that creates and reproduces relationships capable of encompassing even sustained aggressive competition by effectively euphemizing it in a symbolic practice that encourages collective misrecognition of the self-interested nature of the process. This feature is crucial to understanding the political dimensions of feasting rituals.

3 Feasting and the Political Economy

Feasts serve a wide variety of important structural roles in the broader political economy. They create and maintain social relations that bind people together in various intersecting groups and networks on a wide range of scales, from the local household cluster to the regional political community. For example, they are extremely important in establishing sentiments of friendship, kinship, and group solidarity, as well as in cementing bonds between affine groups and political links between leaders of various kinds. In this sense, they perform, at a variety of scales, the classic integrative function of creating community that was identified by earlier functionalist analysts of ritual (Bell 1997; Turner 1969). Feasting rituals, in effect, act as a form of symbolic metaproduction, constituting and euphemizing broader social relations in terms of the basic commensal unit.

Among other things, this enables feasts to act frequently as the nodal contexts that articulate regional exchange systems: commensal hospitality establishes relationships between exchange partners, affines, or political leaders, and provides the social ambiance for the exchange of valuables, bridewealth, and other goods which circulate through a region. Feasts may also provide the main context for the arbitration of disputes, the passing of legal judgments, and the public acting out of sanctions (ridicule, mimicry, ostracism, etc.) that maintain social control within a community. In the religious sphere, these 'social dramas' of consumption also serve to reinforce commitment to basic religious values and to provide links to the gods or ancestors that can also be used to define the structure of relations between social groups or categories within a region or community (see Bell 1997: 120–8). In the form of 'work feasts', they also provide a crucial mechanism for the process of labour mobilization that underlies the political economy and they serve to articulate indirect conversions between spheres of exchange (see Dietler and Herbich 2001).

It is important to emphasize that feasting is not simply a feature of state politics or elite classes or status groups: this practice permeates all levels of society and operates in a wide range of social formations. Recent studies have demonstrated well the significance of feasting to the construction of power and status in various state structures ranging from Mesopotamia to Mycenae, the Maya, and many others (e.g. Bray 2003a; Dietler 1999, 2001; Dietler and Hayden 2001; Jennings 2005; Lau 2002; LeCount 2001; Rosenswig 2007; Wright 2004). Given the scale and frequent ostentation of state- or elite-sponsored feasting, this is likely to be the form most immediately visible to archaeologists. But feasting is also a feature of social practice at other levels of these same state societies, often in different forms, and it is equally crucial to political action in societies without social classes, centralized political structures, or formal political roles (see Blitz 1993; Clark and Blake 1994; Dietler 1990, 1996, 2001; Dietler and Hayden 2001; Hayden 1990, 1996, 2001, 2003; Potter 2000; Mills 2004; Sadr 2004). Understanding the ways feasting operates in these diverse contexts requires moving beyond examination of general structural roles to explore the dynamic nature of feasts as privileged ritual sites of micro-political and economic practice and the implications this has for social change.

4 Feasts and Commensal Politics

Feasting is a form of 'commensal politics' (Dietler 1996). That is, like other ritual, it has an inherently political dimension (Bell 1997; Kelly and Kaplan 1990; Kertzer 1988), but with some distinctively specific aspects. Commensal hospitality may be viewed as a specialized form of gift exchange that establishes the same relations of reciprocal obligation between host and guest as between donor and receiver in the exchange of other more durable types of objects (Mauss 1966; Sahlins 1972). The major difference is that food is destroyed in the act of commensal consumption at a feast, and destroyed by ingesting it into the body. This is a very literal embodiment of the gift and the social debt that it engenders. Aside from the powerful symbolic dimension of this practice, it also results in the pragmatic fact that, unlike durable valuables, the food consumed cannot be recirculated (or 'reinvested') in other gift-exchange relationships: food must be produced anew through agricultural and culinary labour in order to fulfil reciprocal obligations.

Commensal hospitality is a practice that serves to establish, reproduce, and transform social relations. This is why feasts are often viewed as mechanisms of social solidarity that serve to create a sense of community. However, as Mauss (1966) long ago pointed out these are relations of reciprocal obligation that, while establishing social bonds, simultaneously serve to create and define differences in status. The relationship of giver to receiver, or host to guest, translates into a relationship of social superiority and inferiority unless and until the equivalent can be returned. In this feature, the potential of hospitality to be manipulated as a tool in defining social relations, lies the crux of commensal politics. The hospitality of feasting is, of course, only one of many potential fields of political action that may be variably articulated. Feasting may be strategically used by individuals or groups either to complement or to compete against forms of prestige and power derived from other domains of competition for symbolic capital, such as warfare, magic, gift-giving, public oratory, etc. (cf. Bourdieu 1990; Lemonnier 1990; Modjeska 1982; Strathern 1971). However, the special attribute of feasting is that, because of the intimate nature of the practice of sharing food and the symbolic power of the trope of commensality, of all forms of gift prestation it is perhaps the most effective at subtly euphemizing the self-interested nature of the process and creating a shared 'sincere fiction' (in Bourdieu's phrase, 1990: 112) of disinterested generosity.

Furthermore, like all ritual, feasts provide a site and a medium for the highly condensed symbolic representation of social relations. However, again as with other ritual, they express idealized concepts: the way people *believe* relations exist, or should exist, rather than how they are necessarily manifested in daily activity. Such representations may either camouflage, naturalize, or contest asymmetries of power; and struggles over the control of representations and their interpretation by differentially situated actors are an important site of historical change. However, in addition to this idealized representation of the social order, rituals also offer the potential for manipulation by individuals or groups attempting to alter or make statements about their relative position within that social order as it is perceived, presented and contested. As such, feasts are subject to simultaneous manipulation for both ideological and more immediately personal goals. In other words, individuals and groups can use feasting to compete against each other without questioning a shared vision of the social order that the feast reproduces and naturalizes, or they can use feasting to simultaneously struggle for personal position *and* promote contrasting visions of the proper structure of the social world.

5 Types of Feasts

A variety of more or less useful classifications of feasts and feasting have been proposed based upon a range of criteria. These include such things as the scale of inclusion of participants (household feasts, neighborhood feasts, community feasts, etc.), the specific cultural contexts (funerary feasts, marriage feasts, initiation feasts, war feasts, curing feasts, harvest feasts, etc.), social and economic functions (religious feasts, labour feasts, community celebrations, solidarity feasts, economic feasts, etc.), or differences in the symbolic logic of modes of commensal politics (empowering feasts, patron-role feasts, and diacritical feasts) (e.g. see Adams 2004; Benz and Gramsch 2006; Dietler 1996, 2001; Hayden 2001; Kirch 2001; LeCount 2001; Turkon 2004). The heuristic value of such classifications is, of course, entirely relative to the problems they are intended to solve, the subtlety of the analysis they permit, and their logical consistency. None can provide a straightforward correspondence to consistently characteristic types of material signatures (e.g. rare foods, large quantities of food, exceptional serving vessels, special locations or architectonic distinction, etc.) because of the multitude of ways that feasts can be symbolically distinguished from daily meals and the fact that these can overlap with the ways that food is used to create status and category distinctions among consumers. This renders Hayden's (2001) desire for a single archaeological typology of feasting based on types of material remains a quixotic goal, as the interpretation of feasting evidence in the archaeological record must always rely upon richly textured and culturally specific contextual arguments grounded in a cross-cultural theoretical understanding of the complexities of feasting in order to determine what roles the practice was serving and how it worked in a particular case. This is not to say, however, that greater attention to the material attributes of feasting is not warranted. Quite the contrary: it is essential (see Adams 2004; Clarke 2001; Hayden 2003; Turkon 2004).

It is also important to be aware that, like other ritual, feasting is a polysemic activity: several different social roles may be served by the same event. Hence, what one analyst might classify as an 'alliance and cooperation feast' may be simultaneously serving economic and status distinction functions: these need not be separate *kinds* of feasts. For example, a 'work feast' used to mobilize labour may be at the same time creating prestige and social capital, sentiments of community, and social category distinctions. Indeed, nearly all feasts actually serve in some ways to define social boundaries while simultaneously creating a sense of community. That is, nearly all feasts serve to mark, reify, and inculcate diacritical distinctions between social groups, categories, and statuses while at the same time establishing relationships across the boundaries that they define. Gender categories and age distinctions, for example, are very commonly signalled through feasting even among peoples with a strongly egalitarian political ethos. Such categorical differentiation between men and women, between elders and younger men, and between kinship groups are commonly signalled at feasts by permutations of such things as (1) spatial distinctions (i.e. segregation or other structured differential positioning of individuals or groups while eating), (2) temporal distinctions (such as the order of serving or consumption), (3) qualitative distinctions (in the kinds of food, drink, or service vessels that different people are given or are allowed to consume), (4) quantitative distinctions (in the relative amounts of food or drink served to different categories of people), or (5) behavioural distinctions (i.e. differences in expected bodily comportment between different categories of people during and after feasting, including such things as permissible signs of intoxication, talking while eating, reaching for food, serving or being served, withdrawing from the meal first, etc.). Similarly, social groups or networks of various kinds (affines, age grades, etc.) are frequently marked by the same kinds of practices that are used to make other insider vs. stranger distinctions. Concepts of ethnicity, for example, very frequently involve beliefs (of variable accuracy) about distinctive food tastes and culinary practices. Feasts can be a theatre for the symbolic manipulation of such culinary distinctions in the expression of sentiments of inclusion and exclusion at various levels.

As noted earlier, the meaning of a feast event both derives from and plays upon the meaning of consumption in the context of daily meals, but is, at the same time, dramatically transformed by the symbolic framing devices that distinguish it as a theatre of ritual action. The ways in which feasts are symbolically marked as distinct from daily practice are variable, and extremely important to understand. This fact poses certain dangers for archaeological interpretation because similar symbolic devices can be used to mark categories of events as well as categories of people. Particular care must be taken not to mistake the kinds of practices that may be used to differentiate feasts in general (as ritual events) from everyday informal consumption (or those used to mark different kinds of feasts) for those used to differentiate, for example, social classes in societies having 'diacritical' feasts. In many cases, this former distinction (i.e. marking feasts as ritual events) is accomplished simply by differences in the sheer quantity of food and drink proffered and consumed, or by a change in the location and/or timing of consumption. However, the same types of devices used as symbolic diacritica in marking social distinctions may be employed to distinguish ritual from quotidian practice. For example, either feasts or categories of people may be marked by special foods (e.g. ones which are expensive, rare, exotic, especially rich, particularly sweet, intoxicating, etc.). Alternatively, special service vessels or other paraphernalia (including special forms of clothing or other bodily adornment), or special architectural staging, may be employed for this marking purpose. Finally, atypical complexity in recipes or in the structured order of service and consumption may also be used to invoke such distinctions (see Douglas 1984).

There is no simple, universal rule of thumb that will enable the archaeologist to distinguish readily between practices marking boundaries between categories of events or persons. But disentangling the symbolic logic is possible for archaeologists through careful and critical evaluation of the contextual and associational patterns of the evidence and a multi-stranded, thickly textured interpretive argument. To use a highly simplified hypothetical example: special types of ceramic tableware that are found only in funerary contexts, but in *all* funerary contexts are more likely representative of event-marking practices; whereas those found exclusively in male graves, but in *all* male graves, probably imply both a ritual and categorical distinction; while huge, ostentatious bronze drinking vessels found only in a limited number of very wealthy burials most likely indicate the operation of 'diacritical feasts' in marking social class. But the plausibility of such an interpretation will depend upon other evidence from settlement data as well.

6 Feasting and Gender

As noted earlier, gender is one cultural category of social identity that is nearly everywhere marked, reified, and naturalized to some extent through feasting practices. In fact, gender is one of the most common categorical distinctions made through food/drink-related practices in general, albeit in a wide variety of culturally specific ways (Bacon 1976; Child et al. 1965; Counihan and Kaplan 1998; Dietler 1990, 2001; Gefou-Madianou 1992; McDonald 1994). Such categorical boundary-marking at feasts may be based upon various permutations of the kinds of symbolic diacritica noted above. These patterns of gender differentiation may also vary greatly between social classes, such that behaviour considered appropriate for women may be quite different in upper and lower class contexts within the same society.

It is also important to emphasize that feasting practices, while marking boundaries of gender identities in the ways noted above, simultaneously express relationships of mutual dependence across those boundaries, which, in turn, represent and naturalize ideologies structuring larger societal relations of production and authority. In addition to the various aspects of symbolic representation noted above, feasting frequently is sustained by a gendered asymmetry in terms of labour and benefits. Specifically, women, by providing the agricultural and, especially, culinary labour that are essential for feasts, very often largely support a system of feasting in which men are the primary beneficiaries in the political arena. This is one of the main reasons why there is such a strong linkage between polygyny and male political power in Africa and elsewhere (cf. Boserup 1970: 37; Clark 1980; Dietler and Herbich 2001; Friedman 1984; Geschire 1982; Lemonnier 1990; Vincent 1971).

Whether one interprets this as labour exploitation frequently hinges upon a subtle contextual consideration of the question posed by Clark for the Kikuyu: are women 'controllers of resources or themselves resources controlled by men?' (Clark 1980: 367). While exploitation is frequently a justifiable analytical conclusion, this is by no means a pattern that is universal or even generalizable in a simple way. For example, in some societies there is typically a more balanced, or even male-dominated, pattern of labour in the production of feasts (although this generally does not extend to the preparation of daily meals). Moreover, women may share in the status and political benefits from their labour by being members of an influential household or lineage (in matrilineal contexts). Their labour (and male dependence upon it) may also be overtly recognized and valued, and women may even derive considerable categorical and individual status from their central role in the furnishing of hospitality or in maintaining commensal relations with the gods (e.g. Gero 1992; March 1998). And, in many societies, women do host their own work feasts and other feast events, although usually on a smaller scale than men.

The relationship between feasts and gender is clearly a complex but analytically rich and important one. Feasts are intimately implicated in the representation, reproduction, and transformation of gender identity, as well as in the gendered structuring of relations of production and power in society. This means both that feasting is an important and potentially productive avenue for understanding gender relations and roles, and that gender must be an essential consideration in any analysis of feasting (Bray 2003c; Dietler 2001; Gero 1992).

7 Fasting

Fasting may be defined as *voluntary* complete or partial abstention from consuming food and/or drink for a period of time. The voluntary aspect distinguishes fasting from periods of hunger or famine imposed by economic or ecological conditions. Like feasting, fasting is a symbolic act that is wrapped in ritual and frequently accompanies rites of passage. Practices such as dieting for weight loss and anorexia nervosa (defined as pathological food avoidance) that are distinctive to certain Western societies in recent periods (and especially to women in those societies) have an ambiguous relationship to ritual fasting, although they also have a strongly symbolic component (Bell 1997; Counihan 1998; Habermas and Beveridge 1992; Reischer and Koo 2004).

Obviously, when fasting is total, it can be practised for only a limited time before death ensues. But fasting is usually highly selective in terms of both the categories of food and drink to be avoided and the timing of such avoidance: for example, the Roman Catholic practice of not eating meat on Fridays is a targeted form of fasting with categorical and temporal limits. Fasting can also be practised either over an extended period of time (e.g. a hunger strike), or intermittently (e.g. Mormon Fast Sundays), or both (e.g. Islamic Ramadan, in which fasting extends over a month, but for only part of each day).

Fasting in some form has been a significant part of the ritual practices of most of the major world religions for centuries, as well as many other religious traditions studied by anthropologists (e.g. Buitelaar 1993; Bynum 1987; Grimm 1996; Lambert 2003; Rader 1987). It is used to show piety, devotion, penitence, and self-control, to effect purification in preparation for certain tasks or ritual transformations, and to provoke altered states of consciousness. But fasting has also been deployed as a non-religious ritual, including especially the political hunger strike as a form of non-violent protest (Ellmann 1993).

Like feasting, fasting relies upon a semiotic connection to daily food consumption for its symbolic force: daily consumption patterns will determine such things as what foods are to be avoided, when consumption can occur, and who participates together. Fasts sometimes also involve the substitution of certain unusual or less desirable foods for more common ones rather than complete abstention, and these choices also depend upon a relationship to the structure of daily consumption. Fasting is also frequently linked in an intimate way to feasting. For example, feasting frequently marks the beginning or end of a fast (as with Mardi Gras, Eid, and feasts ending various initiation fasts), and alternate rituals of fasting and feasting may structure temporality over the course of the year. However, fasting plays upon the trope of refusal or negation of consumption rather than elaboration. When done individually, for example by anorexic individuals in Western societies, this can constitute a symbolic rejection of sociality (Bell 1985; Brumberg 1988; Bynum 1987). But fasting generally has a collective aspect and, every bit as much as feasting, it serves as an instrument for the construction of community, social identity, and prestige (Knutsson and Selinus 1970).

Over the past century, a significant literature on fasting has emerged from the fields of social anthropology, history, theology, medicine, and psychology (e.g. Buitelaar 1993; Bynum 1987;

Lambert 2003; Rader 1987), along with many ethnographic and historical studies that document the practice without a primary focus on it (e.g. Malinowski 1922; Powdermaker 1960; Richards 1939; Shack 1971; Young 1971). But the topic has received relatively little attention in archaeology. Unlike feasting, fasting is virtually impossible to detect archaeologically in the absence of texts. The practice of fasting requires no material equipment, and episodes of collective fasting are not usually long enough to cause major bodily trauma that might be detected through, for example, osteological or bone chemistry analysis. And even if such traces of trauma were to be found, it would be extremely difficult, if not impossible, to differentiate them from trauma caused by non-voluntary forms of nutritional deprivation, such as famines or the lean times of periodic hunger that often precede the harvest in many agrarian societies (Shipton 1990). Some scholars have attempted to use such things as stable isotope analysis of human bone to complement textual records in evaluating the impact of fasting in historical periods (e.g. see Müldner and Richards 2005). But the search for evidence of fasting in prehistoric periods remains far more problematic than that for traces of feasting, and we know correspondingly less about its potential existence and significance.

Suggested Reading

Feasting and fasting are two alternative ways to mobilize the symbolic power of food and drink, through either ritualized commensal consumption or refusal of consumption. Feasting has become a popular theme in recent archaeological work, with several edited volumes offering a good perspective on the range of theoretical and methodological approaches and epistemological issues. See especially Dietler and Hayden (2001), Bray (2003a), Mills (2004), and Wright (2004). A number of individual articles and books have also served as key contributions to the development of the theoretical analysis of feasting in archaeology and cultural anthropology, including Powdermaker (1932), Codere (1950), Friedman (1979), Dietler (1990, 1996), Hayden (1990, 1996), Lemonnier (1990), Gero (1992), Clark and Blake (1994). Because of its archaeological invisibility, fasting has failed to attract the same attention among archaeologists, although it has been a subject of anthropological and historical research. See especially Knutsson and Selinus (1970), Bynum (1987), Habermas and Beveridge (1992), Buitelaar (1993), Ellman (1993), Grimm (1996), Counihan (1998), Lambert (2003), Reischer and Koo (2004).

References

ADAMS, R. L. 2004. 'An ethnoarchaeological study of feasting in Sulawesi, Indonesia', *Journal of Anthropological Archaeology*, 23: 56–78.

ANIGBO, O. A. C. 1996. 'Commensality as cultural performance: The struggle for leadership in an Igbo village' in D. Parkin, L. Calplan, and H. Fisher (eds), *The Politics of Cultural Performance* (Oxford: Berghahn Books), pp. 101–14.

ARTHUR, J. W. 2003. 'Brewing beer: status, wealth and ceramic use alteration among the Gamo of south-western Ethiopia', *World Archaeology*, 34(3): 516–28.

BACON, M. K. 1976. 'Cross-cultural studies of drinking: integrated drinking and sex differences in the use of alcoholic beverages' in M. Everett, J. Waddell, and D. Heath (eds), *Cross-cultural Approaches to the Study of Alcohol: An interdisciplinary perspective* (The Hague: Mouton), pp. 23–33.

BARLETT, P. F. 1980. 'Reciprocity and the San Juan fiesta', *Journal of Anthropological Research*, 36: 116–30.

BELL, C. 1997. *Ritual: Perspectives and dimensions* (Oxford: Oxford University Press).

BELL, R. M. 1985. *Holy Anorexia* (Chicago: University of Chicago Press).

BENZ, M. and GRAMSCH, A. 2006. 'Zur sozio-politischen Bedeutung von Festen. Eine Einführung anhand von Beispielen aus dem Alten Orient und Europa', *Ethnographisch-Archaeologische Zeitschrift*, 47(4): 417–37.

—— and WÄCHTLER, N. 2006. 'Von der Integration zur Distinktion. Die feiernde Elite der Frühdynastischen Zeit', *Ethnographisch-Archaeologische Zeitschrift*, 47(4): 463–83.

BLITZ, JOHN. 1993. 'Big pots for big shots: Feasting and storage in a Mississippian community', *American Antiquity*, 58: 80–96.

BOSERUP, E. 1970. *Women's Role in Economic Development* (London: Allen and Unwin).

BOURDIEU, P. 1990. *The Logic of Practice* (Stanford: Stanford University Press).

BRAY, T. L. (ed.) 2003a. *The Archaeology and Politics of Food and Feasting in Early States and Empires* (New York: Kluwer Academic/Plenum Publishers).

—— 2003b. 'Inka pottery as culinary equipment: Food, feasting, and gender in imperial state design', *Latin American Antiquity*, 14(1): 3–28.

—— 2003c. 'To dine splendidly: Imperial pottery, commensal politics, and the Inca state' in T. L. Bray (ed.), *The Archaeology and Politics of Food and Feasting in Early States and Empires* (New York: Kluwer Academic/Plenum Publishers), pp. 93–142.

BROWN, L. A. 2001. 'Feasting on the periphery: The production of ritual feasting and village festivals at the Cerén site, El Salvador' in M. Dietler and B. Hayden (eds), *Feasts: Archaeological and ethnographic perspectives on food, politics, and power* (Washington DC: Smithsonian Institution Press), pp. 368–90.

BRUMBERG, J. J. 1988. *Fasting Girls: The emergence of anorexia nervosa as a modern disease* (Cambridge, MA: Harvard University Press).

BUITELAAR, M. 1993. *Fasting and Feasting in Morocco: Women's participation in Ramadan* (Oxford: Berg).

BYNUM, C. W. 1987. *Holy Feast and Holy Fast: The religious significance of food to medieval women* (Berkeley: University of California Press).

CANCIAN, F. 1965. *Economics and Prestige in a Maya Community* (Stanford: Stanford University Press).

CHILD, I. L., BARRY, H., and BACON, M. K. 1965. 'A cross-cultural study of drinking. 3. Sex differences', *Quarterly Journal of Studies in Alcohol (Supplement)*, 3: 49–61.

CLARK, C. M. 1980. 'Land and food, women and power, in nineteenth century Kikuyu', *Africa*, 50: 357–70.

CLARK, J. E. and BLAKE, M. 1994. 'The power of prestige: Competitive generosity and the emergence of ranked societies in Lowland Mesoamerica' in E. Brumfield and J. Fox (eds), *Factional Competition and Political Development in the New World* (Cambridge: Cambridge University Press), pp. 17–30.

CLARKE, M. J. 2001. 'Akha feasting: an ethnoarchaeological perspective' in M. Dietler and B. Hayden (eds), *Feasts: Archaeological and ethnographic perspectives on food, politics, and power* (Washington DC: Smithsonian Institution Press), pp. 144–67.

CODERE, H. 1950. *Fighting with Property: A study of Kwakiutl potlatching and warfare, 1792–1930* (Seattle: University of Washington Press).

COUNIHAN, C. M. 1998. 'An anthropological view of Western women's prodigious fasting' in C. M. Counihan and S. L. Kaplan (eds), *Food and Gender: Identity and power* (Newark, NJ: Gordon and Breach), pp. 99–124.

—— and KAPLAN, S. L. (eds) 1998. *Food and Gender: Identity and power* (Newark, NJ: Gordon and Breach).

DIETLER, M. 1990. 'Driven by drink: The role of drinking in the political economy and the case of Early Iron Age France', *Journal of Anthropological Archaeology*, 9: 352–406.

—— 1996. 'Feasts and commensal politics in the political economy: food, power, and status in prehistoric Europe' in P. W. Wiessner and W. Schiefenhövel (eds), *Food and the Status Quest : An interdisciplinary perspective* (Providence, RI: Berghahn Books), pp. 87–125.

—— 1999. 'Rituals of commensality and the politics of state formation in the "princely" societies of Early Iron Age Europe' in P. Ruby (ed.), *Les princes de la Protohistoire et l'émergence de l'état* (Naples: Cahiers du Centre Jean Bérard, Institut Français de Naples 17—Collection de l'École Française de Rome 252), pp. 135–52.

—— 2001. 'Theorizing the feast: Rituals of consumption, commensal politics, and power in African contexts' in M. Dietler and B. Hayden (eds), *Feasts: Archaeological and ethnographic perspectives on food, politics, and power* (Washington DC: Smithsonian Institution Press), pp. 65–114.

—— 2005. 'Introduction: Embodied material culture', *Archaeological Review from Cambridge*, 20(2): 3–5.

—— 2006a. 'Alcohol: Anthropological/archaeological perspectives', *Annual Review of Anthropology*, 35: 229–49.

—— 2006b. 'Feasting und kommensale Politik in der Eisenzeit Europas. Theoretische Reflexionen und empirische Fallstudien', *Ethnographisch-Archaeologische Zeitschrift*, 47(4): 541–68.

—— and HAYDEN, B. (eds) 2001. *Feasts: Archaeological and ethnographic perspectives on food, politics, and power* (Washington DC: Smithsonian Institution Press).

—— and HERBICH, I. 2001. 'Feasts and labor mobilization: Dissecting a fundamental economic practice' in M. Dietler and B. Hayden (eds), *Feasts: Archaeological and ethnographic perspectives on food, politics, and power* (Washington DC: Smithsonian Institution Press), pp. 240–64.

—— —— 2006. 'Liquid material culture: Following the flow of beer among the Luo of Kenya' in H.-P. Wotzka (ed.), *Grundlegungen. Beiträge zur europäischen und afrikanischen Archäologie für Manfred K. H. Eggert* (Tübingen: Francke Verlag), pp. 395–408.

DOUGLAS, M. 1984. 'Standard social uses of food: Introduction' in *Food in the Social Order*, ed. M. Douglas (New York: Russell Sage Foundation).

ELIAS, N. 1978. *The History of Manners* (New York: Pantheon Books).

ELLMANN, M. 1993. *The Hunger Artists: Starving, writing, and imprisonment* (Cambridge, MA: Harvard University Press).

FALK, P. 1994. *The Consuming Body* (London: Sage).

FEIL, D. K. 1984. *Ways of Exchange: The Enga Tee of Papua New Guinea* (St. Lucia: University of Queensland Press).

FRIEDMAN, J. 1979. *System, Structure and Contradiction in the Evolution of 'Asiatic' Social Formations* (Copenhagen: National Museum of Denmark).
——1984. 'Tribes, states, and transformations' in M. Bloch (ed.), *Marxist Analyses and Social Anthropology* (London: Tavistock), pp. 161–202.
GEFOU-MADIANOU, D. (ed.) 1992. *Alcohol, Gender and Culture* (London: Routledge).
GERO, JOAN M. 1992. 'Feasts and females: Gender ideology and political meals in the Andes', *Norwegian Archaeological Review*, 25: 15–30.
GESCHIRE, P. 1982. *Village Communities and the State: Changing relations among the Maka of south-eastern Cameroon since the colonial conquest*, trans. J. Ravell (London: Kegan Paul).
GOLDSTEIN, P. S. 2003. 'From stew-eaters to maize drinkers: The chicha economy and the Tiwanaku expansion' in T. L. Bray (ed.), *The Archaeology and Politics of Food and Feasting in Early States and Empires* (New York: Kluwer Academic/Plenum Publishers), pp. 143–72.
GOODY, J. 1982. *Cooking, Cuisine and Class: A study in comparative sociology* (Cambridge: Cambridge University Press).
GRIMM, V. 1996. *From Feasting to Fasting, the Evolution of a Sin: Attitudes to food in Late Antiquity* (London: Routledge).
HABERMAS, T. and BEVERIDGE, A. 1992. 'Historical continuities and discontinuities between religious and medical interpretations of extreme fasting', *History of Psychiatry*, 3(12): 431–55.
HALPERIN, R., and OLMSTEAD, J. 1976. 'To catch a feastgiver: Redistribution among the Dorze of Ethiopia', *Africa*, 46: 146–65.
HAYDEN, B. 1990. 'Nimrods, piscators, pluckers and planters: The emergence of food production', *Journal of Anthropological Archaeology*, 9: 31–69.
——1996. 'Feasting in prehistoric and traditional societies' in P. W. Wiessner and W. Schiefenhövel (eds), *Food and the Status Quest: An interdisciplinary perspective* (Providence, RI: Berghahn Books), pp. 127–48.
——2001. 'Fabulous feasts: Prolegomenon to the importance of feasting' in M. Dietler and B. Hayden (eds), *Feasts: Archaeological and ethnographic perspectives on food, politics, and power* (Washington DC: Smithsonian Institution Press), pp. 23–64.
——2003. 'Were luxury foods the first domesticates? Ethnoarchaeological perspectives from Southeast Asia', *World Archaeology*, 34: 458–69.
HEATH, D. B. 1987. 'Anthropology and alcohol studies: Current issues', *Annual Review of Anthropology*, 16: 99–120.
——2000. *Drinking Occasions: Comparative perspectives on alcohol and culture* (Philadelphia: Brunner/Mazel).
HOGBIN, I. 1970. 'Food festivals and politics in Wogeo', *Oceania*, 40: 304–28.
JENNINGS, J. 2005. 'La chichera y el patrón: chicha and the energetics of feasting in the prehistoric Andes', *Archaeological Papers of the American Anthropological Association*, 14: 241–59.
JUNKER, L. 1999. *Raiding, Trading, and Feasting: The Political Economy of Philippine Chiefdoms* (Honolulu: University of Hawaii Press).
KELLY, J. D. and KAPLAN, M. 1990. 'History, structure, and ritual', *Annual Review of Anthropology*, 19: 119–50.
KELLY, L. S. 2001. 'A case of ritual feasting at the Cahokia site' in M. Dietler and B. Hayden (eds), *Feasts: Archaeological and ethnographic perspectives on food, politics, and power* (Washington DC: Smithsonian Institution Press), pp. 334–67.

KENNEDY, J. G. 1978. *The Tarahumara of the Sierra Madre: Beer, ecology, and social organization* (Arlington Heights, IL: AHM).

KERTZER, D. I. 1988. *Ritual, Politics, and Power* (New Haven, CT: Yale University Press).

KIRCH, P. V. 2001. 'Polynesian feasting in ethnohistoric, ethnographic, and archaeological contexts: A comparison of three societies' in M. Dietler and B. Hayden (eds), *Feasts: Archaeological and ethnographic perspectives on food, politics, and power* (Washington DC: Smithsonian Institution Press), pp. 168–84.

KNIGHT, V. J. 2001. 'Feasting and the emergence of platform mound ceremonialism in eastern North America' in M. Dietler and B. Hayden (eds), *Feasts: Archaeological and ethnographic perspectives on food, politics, and power* (Washington DC: Smithsonian Institution Press), pp. 311–33.

KNUTSSON, K. E. and SELINUS, R. 1970. 'Fasting in Ethiopia: An anthropological and nutritional study', *The American Journal of Clinical Nutrition*, 23: 956–69.

LAMBERT, D. 2003. 'Fasting as a penitential rite: A biblical phenomenon?', *Harvard Theological Review*, 96(4): 477–512.

LAU, G. 2002. 'Feasting and ancestor veneration at Chinchawas, North Highlands of Ancash, Peru', *Latin American Antiquity*, 13: 279–304.

LECOUNT, L. J. 2001. 'Like water for chocolate: Feasting and political ritual among the Late Classic Maya at Xunantunich, Belize', *American Anthropologist*, 103(4): 935–53.

LEMONNIER, P. 1990. *Guerres et festins: paix, échanges et compétition dans les Highlands de Nouvelle-Guinée* (Paris: CID-Maison des Sciences de l'Homme).

MCDONALD, M. (ed.) 1994. *Gender, Drink and Drugs* (Oxford: Berg).

MALINOWSKI, B. 1922. *Argonauts of the Western Pacific* (New York: Dutton).

MARCH, K. S. 1998. 'Hospitality, women, and the efficacy of beer' in C. M. Counihan and S. L. Kaplan (eds), *Food and Gender: Identity and power* (Newark, NJ: Gordon and Breach), pp. 45–80.

MAUSS, M. 1935. 'Les techniques du corps', *Journal de Psychologie*, 32: 271–93.

——1966. *The Gift: Forms and functions of exchange in archaic societies*, trans. I. Cunnison (London: Routledge and Kegan Paul).

MILLS, B. J. (ed.) 2004. *Identity, Feasting, and the Archaeology of the Greater Southwest* (Boulder, CO: University of Colorado Press).

——2007. 'Performing the feast: Visual display and suprehousehold commensalism in the Puebloan Southwest', *American Antiquity*, 72(2): 210–39.

MODJESKA, N. 1982. 'Production and inequality: Perspectives from central New Guinea' in A. Strathern (ed.), *Inequality in New Guinea Societies* (Cambridge: Cambridge University Press), pp. 50–108.

MOORE, S. F. and MYERHOFF, B. G. 1985. 'Introduction: secular ritual: forms and meanings' in S. F. Moore and B. G. Myerhoff (eds), *Secular Ritual* (Assen/Amsterdam: Van Gorcum), pp. 3–24.

MORRIS, C. 1979. 'Maize beer in the economics, politics, and religion of the Inca empire' in C. Gastineau, W. Darby, and T. Turner (eds), *Fermented Foods in Nutrition* (New York: Academic Press).

MÜLDNER, G. and RICHARDS, M. P. 2005. 'Fast or feast: Reconstructing diet in later medieval England by stable isotope analysis', *Journal of Archaeological Science*, 32(1): 39–48.

MÜLLER, J.-M. 2006. 'Die feiernde Elite. Mykenische Feste in archäologischen Befund', *Ethnographisch-Archaeologische Zeitschrift*, 47(4): 485–520.

NELSON, S. M. 2003. 'Feasting the ancestors in early China' in T. L. Bray (ed.), *The Archaeology and Politics of Food and Feasting in Early States and Empires* (New York: Kluwer Academic/Plenum Publishers), pp. 65–89.

PERODIE, J. R. 2001. 'Feasting for prosperity: A study of southern Northwest coast feasting' in M. Dietler and B. Hayden (eds), *Feasts: Archaeological and ethnographic perspectives on food, politics, and power* (Washington DC: Smithsonian Institution Press), pp. 185–214.

PHILLIPS, D. A., and SEBASTIAN, L. 2004. 'Large-scale feasting and politics: An essay on power in precontact Southwestern societies' in B. J. Mills (eds), *Identity, Feasting, and the Archaeology of the Greater Southwest* (Boulder, CO: University of Colorado Press), pp. 233–58.

POLLOCK, S. 2003. 'Feasts, funerals, and fast food in early Mesopotamian states' in T. L. Bray (ed.), *The Archaeology and Politics of Food and Feasting in Early States and Empires* (New York: Kluwer Academic/Plenum Publishers), pp. 17–38.

POTTER, J. M. 2000. 'Pots, parties, and politics: Communal feasting in the American Southwest', *American Antiquity*, 65: 471–92.

—— and ORTMAN, S. G. 2004. 'Community and cuisine in the prehispanic Southwest' in B. J. Mills (ed.), *Identity, Feasting, and the Archaeology of the Greater Southwest* (Boulder, CO: University of Colorado Press), pp. 173–91.

POWDERMAKER, H. 1932. 'Feasts in New Ireland: The social function of eating', *American Anthropologist*, 34: 236–47.

RADER, R. 1987. 'Fasting' in M. Eliade (ed.), *The Encyclopedia of Religion* (New York: Macmillan), pp. 289–90.

RALPH, S. 2005. 'Eat, drink and be Roman? Feasting in later Iron Age and early Roman Britain', *Archaeological Review from Cambridge*, 20(2): 32–52.

REHFISCH, F. 1987. 'Competitive beer drinking among the Mambila' in M. Douglas (ed.), *Construstive Drinking: Perspectives on drink from anthropology* (Cambridge: Cambridge University Press), pp. 135–45.

REISCHER, E. and KOO, K. S. 2004. 'The body beautiful: Symbolism and agency in the social world', *Annual Review of Anthropology*, 33: 297–317.

RICHARDS, A. L. 1939. *Land, Labour and Diet in Northern Rhodesia* (London: Oxford University Press).

ROSENSWIG, R. M. 2007. 'Beyond identifying elites: Feasting as a means to understand early middle formative society on the Pacific coast of Mexico', *Journal of Anthropological Archaeology*, 26: 1–27.

SADR, K. 2004. 'Feasting at Kasteelberg? Early herders on the west coast of South Africa', *Before Farming (Online Journal)*, 2004(3): 1–17.

SAHLINS, M. 1972. *Stone Age Economics* (London: Tavistock).

SAUL, M. 1983. 'Work parties, wages, and accumulation in a Voltaic village', *American Ethnologist*, 10: 77–96.

SCHMANDT-BESSERAT, D. 2001. 'Feasting in the ancient Near East' in M. Dietler and B. Hayden (eds), *Feasts: Archaeological and ethnographic perspectives on food, politics, and power* (Washington DC: Smithsonian Institution Presso, pp. 391–403.

SHACK, W. A. 1971. 'Hunger, anxiety and ritual: Deprivation and spirit possession among the Gurage of Ethiopia', *Man*, 6(1): 30–45.

SHIPTON, P. M. 1990. 'African famines and food security: Anthropological perspectives', *Annual Review of Anthropology*, 19: 353–94.

SMITH, M. E., WHARTON, J. B., and OLSON, J. M. 2003. 'Aztec feasts, rituals, and markets: Political uses of ceramic vessels in a commercial economy' in T. L. Bray (ed.), *The*

Archaeology and Politics of Food and Feasting in Early States and Empires (New York: Kluwer Academic/Plenum Publishers), pp. 235–68.

SMITH, S. T. 2003. 'Pharaohs, feasts, and foreigners: Cooking, foodways, and agency on ancient Egypt's southern frontier' in T. L. Bray (ed.), *The Archaeology and Politics of Food and Feasting in Early States and Empires* (New York: Kluwer Academic/Plenum Publishers), pp. 39–64.

STRATHERN, A. 1971. *The Rope of Moka: Big-men and the ceremonial exchange in Mount Hagen, New Guinea* (Cambridge: Cambridge University Press).

SUTTLES, W. 1991. 'Streams of property, armor of wealth: The traditional Kwakiutl potlatch' in A. Jonaitis (ed.), *Chiefly Feasts: The enduring Kwakiutl potlatch* (Seattle: University of Washington Press), pp. 71–133.

TURKON, P. 2004. 'Food and status in the prehispanic Malpaso valley, Zacatecas, Mexico', *Journal of Anthropological Archaeology*, 23: 225–51.

TURNER, V. 1969. *The Ritual Process: Structure and anti-structure* (Ithaca, NY: Cornell University Press).

VINCENT, J. 1971. *African Elite: The big men of a small town* (New York: Columbia University Press).

VOLKMAN, T. A. 1985. *Feasts of Honor: Ritual and change in the Toraja Highlands* (Urbana, IL: University of Illinois Press).

WIESSNER, P., and TUMU, A. 1998. *Historical Vines: Enga networks of exchange, ritual, and warfare in Papua New Guinea* (Washington DC: Smithsonian Institution Press).

WIESSNER, P. W. 2001. 'Of feasting and value: Enga feasts in a historical perspective (Papua New Guinea)' in M. Dietler and B. Hayden (eds), *Feasts: Archaeological and ethnographic perspectives on food, politics, and power* (Washington DC: Smithsonian Institution Press), pp. 115–43.

WILLS, W. H., and CROWN, P. L. 2004. 'Commensal politics in the prehispanic Southwest' in B. J. Mills (ed.), *Identity, Feasting, and the Archaeology of the Greater Southwest* (Boulder, CO: University of Colorado Press), pp. 153–72.

WRIGHT, J. C. (ed.), 2004. *The Mycenaean Feast* (Athens: American School of Classical Studies).

YOUNG, M. 1971. *Fighting with Food: Leadership, values and social control in a Massim society* (Cambridge: Cambridge University Press).

CHAPTER 14

GENDER AND RELIGION IN ARCHAEOLOGY

SARAH MILLEDGE NELSON

1 INTRODUCTION

SEEKING evidence of religion and looking for gender are both relatively new pursuits in archaeology. The breakthrough paper for gender in archaeology was a strongly processual analysis of why gender needed attention in archaeology, and did not touch on religion (Conkey and Spector 1984). Because gender itself was considered a marginal pursuit, those who sought to make it mainstream tended to shy away from other marginal topics, which at the time included approaching religion in archaeology. And yet there is a natural affinity between the topics of gender and religion. Rituals may differ by gender, or may be separated by gender in many cultures, and the ability to reach the spirits is often perceived as essentially female (Nelson 2008; Tedlock 2005). Gender may be attributed to supernatural entities.

While the topic of gender and religion in archaeology implies goddesses to many readers, gender is relevant to several other aspects of religion and ritual. The officiants of rituals may be gendered, those taking part in rituals may be gendered, and those omitted from certain rituals may be gendered. In fact, instead of being an obvious starting point, goddesses have been a problem for gender archaeology. This explains, at least in part, why the topic of religion was not embraced earlier by the majority of archaeologists interested in gender. But this is not to say that goddesses were ignored. The enthusiastic embrace of ancient goddesses by third-wave feminists was not always based on a critical approach to the past (e.g. Conkey and Tringham 1995). Thus mainstream Anglo-American archaeologists interested in questions of gender shied away from topics that combined gender and religion.

The era when processualism was becoming established as the proper and scientific way to do archaeology coincided with a revitalized feminist movement. Those few women who had carved a niche for themselves in the then male-dominated world of archaeology tended to pursue topics which were amenable to processual methods and intent. It was much safer to 'engender' (Gero and Conkey 1991) subsistence and settlement, lithics and pottery than to approach religion especially when the topic, such as gender, was already suspect.

Looking back at the first attempts to add gender to the archaeological agenda, the rarity of attention to religion is striking, In the groundbreaking book, *Engendering Archaeology*

(Gero and Conkey 1991), 'religion' does not appear in the index, although there are four entries under 'rituals' and three more under 'ceremonial', which are the same chapters using 'ritual' and 'ceremony' as synonyms. It is useful to inquire what was meant by these expressions at the time. Joan Gero (1991: 185) suggests that, although males at the Huaricoto site in Peru were hunters as well as makers of ceremonial blades, the stone tools used for preparing ceremonial meat might have been associated with women, and even made by them. Thus the concept of ceremony is assumed rather than explicated. Patty Jo Watson and Mary Kennedy (1991: 263) refute the notion of shamans as the impetus behind the beginnings of plant cultivation (growing gourds for rattles) in their brief brush with gender and religion. They point out that 'we are leary [sic] of explanations that remove women from the one realm [plants] that is traditionally granted them, as soon as innovation or invention enters the picture'. Watson and Kennedy are not specifically denying the possible ritual use of cucurbits, but the attribution of plant domestication to a presumed male shaman. It is not clear whether they are suggesting that the shaman was not necessarily male, or that the male shaman was stealing the show.

Cheryl Claassen (1991: 294) writes of ritual in the context of burials in shell mounds. She proposes that 'shellfish were gathered seasonally and ceremoniously. It was the shell itself that was valued, to erect monuments and create a burial context for a specific subset of community members including many women who themselves may have been shellfishers, provisioners of storable protein, and shamans by virtue of an ideological system that associated shell with value, procreation, and death'. Classen asserts that collecting shellfish had religious as well as economic connotations, but she does not elaborate.

Susan Pollock (1991: 380–2), writing about images of Sumerian women, notes that banqueting scenes include both women and men, but that contest scenes portray only men. She envisions both these types of scenes as depictions of rituals, but notes that women, although present, are shown as passive in the rituals while men are active. These attempts at engendering rituals do not come to grips with either gender or rituals, but they represent a tentative beginning. None of these papers make gender and religion their focus.

In the volume of volunteered papers that emerged from the first widely attended meeting on feminist archaeology, the only paper that approaches questions of ideology is Nelson's (1991), which discusses the archaeology of Niuheliang, a site in China with a structure called a 'Goddess Temple', although 'ideology' (considered a safer term than 'religion') was mentioned in three other papers but was not a central focus. The first conference volume on gender to appear in Australia avoids the topic of gender and religion altogether.

Another perspective on religion and gender in archaeology can be gained by examining the book of critiques of gendered archaeology published by students at the University of Michigan (Bacus et al. 1993). This volume does not include ideology, ritual, or ceremony in its index, but, unlike the previously described volumes, examines 13 papers with references to religion and gender. The papers under this heading include several on figurines, fertility cults, goddesses, and iconography as popular topics, but most of these were by authors outside mainstream archaeology, for example art historians or cultural anthropologists using archaeological data. The students tend to critique these papers severely for lacking in rigour.

Thus, religion and gender did not play a big part in early discussions of ancient gender in archaeology. This lack of interest is in strong contrast to other circles, in which ancient goddesses were at the centre of the discussion. Marija Gimbutas' 1974 book, *The Gods and Goddesses of Old Europe, 7000–3500 BC: Myths, legends and cult images*, was eagerly devoured by some groups of feminists of the 1970s, and became the centre of something of a cult on its own. Later books by Gimbutas about 'Old Europe' gave the goddesses precedence (*Goddesses and Gods* . . . 1982), and her final book omitted gods from the title altogether (*The Language of the Goddess*, 1989). Many other goddess books followed, based on archaeological data but for the most part not written by archaeologists. Although Gimbutas was well established as a mainstream archaeologist, her work on goddesses was critiqued by other women archaeologists. Most archaeologists were leery of the topic of religion.

Thus in the very early stages of feminist archaeology, religion itself was almost taboo, and ritual and ceremony were rarely central to any argument. The study of gender had not gone beyond the constraints of processual archaeology, and had barely thought about challenging gender stereotypes of religion in the past.

Since gender itself is often difficult to approach with archaeological data, and religion is likewise difficult, the combination of gender and religion has seemed like skating on very thin ice. Archaeological manifestations of material culture which could be interpreted as indicating both gender and religion are uncommon. Solid evidence of gender mostly comes from depictions of gendered persons and sexable burials. These contexts may or may not have material culture which can be definitively related to religion. It is useful to examine the types of evidence that have been used to discuss gender and religion, before turning to religious episodes that can be discussed in terms of gender.

2 TYPES OF EVIDENCE

Burials are often examined in terms of ritual and ideology. In this section, three Chinese Neolithic examples demonstrate various types of evidence that have been discussed in terms of religion: Xishuipo with dragon and tiger mosaics surrounding a burial, Yuanjunmiao with special burials of girls, and Niuheliang with jade emblems.

The burial in central China at Xishuipo, Puyang, Henan is best known in terms of its interpretation as evidence of Neolithic sky lore. The burial complex surrounds a burial described as male. The skeleton is extended, head to the south, between two shell mosaics depicting animals. On the east is a saurian creature described as a dragon, and on the west is a mammal with a long tail, designated a tiger. Chinese sky lore includes the Blue Dragon of the East and the White Tiger of the West, and these are therefore seen as proof of the Neolithic origins of this belief. In much later burials, the guardian animals of the four directions were often painted on the four walls of elite burials. Near the head of the central burial three human skeletons are arranged as if they were guarding the feet of the central burial. This complex is enthusiastically described as a male shaman and his entourage (Zhang 2005), and as proof that the belief in animals of the four directions goes back to the Neolithic. The connection between shamanism and the astronomical symbolism is not explored.

Another Chinese burial ground, at Yuanjunmiao, is said to be for adults only, with the exception of three subadults, who are identified as girls by the hairpins they wear, also found in adult female burials. These are interpreted as shamans, on the basis of the elaborateness of their burials, and the assumption that spiritual paths were the only ones available to females.

The sex of burials is often questioned, especially when the buried person appears to be of ritual importance. For example, the 'Princess of Vix', an Iron Age burial in France, was once described as a transvestite male priest, although 'the simpler interpretation of women in positions of power and authority is more likely' (Arnold 1991: 373). Arnold comes to this conclusion on the basis of other similar graves of high status women of the period. The central burial in Monte Alban's Tomb Seven has likewise been the focus of gender discussions in the context of both religion and rulership. The principal burial in this richest of all Mesoamerican burials (McCafferty and McCafferty 2003) was declared to be male by the excavators. However, the skeletal material allows some doubt as to its sex, and the accompanying artefacts suggest that it represents objects associated with supernatural females. These examples show that sex and gender have had various interpretations in contexts that include ritual.

2.1 Rock Art

Rock art is frequently discussed in terms of both gender and religion. Ritual sites have been identified on the basis of depictions painted or engraved on walls. A thorough discussion of rock art and gender can be found in Kelley Hays-Gilpin's (2004) excellent book which is devoted to this topic. In this section only a few examples of the ways rock art has been interpreted as gendered can be mentioned, since it is found all over the world, and is very often given gendered interpretations. In rock art research, depictions of humans are often ambiguous as to their sex or gender, but the ambiguity has not always deterred gendered interpretations.

Rock art may define sacred areas, which may also be gendered. Ruth Whitehouse (2002) describes sites in southern Italy, including a cult cave, the Grotta di Porta Badisca, with Neolithic paintings. Whitehouse suggests that this cave, accessed through tunnels that required crawling on all fours, was the site of male initiation ceremonies. In studying the differences between the more accessible paintings near the mouth of the cave and those deep within the cave, she found that those in the inner recesses tended to be less interpretable. She concludes that women made the paintings and held their rituals closer to the mouth of the cave. She thus explains differences in men's and women's religious experiences based on the placement and presumed gender of these depictions in caves.

2.2 Buildings

Buildings which are associated with ritual may have gender components. In the Neolithic Hongshan culture of north-east China, a building was partly unearthed which was dubbed the 'Goddess Temple' because it contained fragments of human statues with breasts. A smiling face with inset green jade eyes is thought to represent the goddess (Figure 14.1). Although this building is 22 m long, it is only 2 m wide for most of its length (Figure 14.2). It seems more likely to have been a shrine than a temple. The site of Niuheliang, which includes the Goddess Temple, is mostly mortuary in nature, with both inhumations and bundle burials. The site of Dongshanzui, on the main Daling River, some 45 km distant

FIGURE 14.1 Clay face with inset jade eyes from the Goddess Temple, Niuheliang, China.

by road, consists of low 'altars' with walls connecting them, and female statues that suggest an interest in maternal and child health.

Other temples with obvious female imagery include those of Neolithic Malta. The shapes of these temples imply female curves, and the 'goddesses' whose statues which have been found are curvy and well fed. One figure portrays a well-fed woman reclining on a couch. These sculptures and the rounded architecture have led researchers to call the buildings goddesses. Since a portly woman is portrayed, she is often seen as the Great Mother. Such pronouncements need to be treated as hypotheses.

2.3 Figurines

Figurines from the European Upper Palaeolithic are mostly female (Delporte 1979), although a few are known which are ungendered or (fewer still) definitely male. When the first examples were found, they were interpreted as representations of goddesses, and later were more specifically called 'Venus' figurines, implying sexuality. Although one archaeologist proclaimed, 'The first God was a Goddess!!!' (Renaud 1929) for the most part the religion, if any, indicated by the figurines was presumed to serve male purposes, and be related to sexuality and fertility. The likelihood that Palaeolithic hunters might have needed to keep down their birth rate is never considered in these discussions.

The figurines from the Jomon period in Japan are shaped in general like humans, but they are probably intended to imply the realm of the spirits. They were once used as evidence of visitors from outer space. Nevertheless, most of them do have gender indicated,

FIGURE 14.2 The outline of the Goddess Temple, Niuheliang, China.

and they are mostly female (Ikawa-Smith 2002). The nature of the religion that may be associated with them is not at all clear from the material remains, however.

Something must be said about the religion of 'Old Europe' about which Marija Gimbutas wrote prolifically. She portrayed the Neolithic as a period of peace, in which women were in charge of both the religious and secular spheres. The humanoid figurines are often covered with painted symbols, which were interpreted by Gimbutas as religious symbolism. This peaceful and profoundly religious society was destroyed eventually by warrior peoples speaking Indo-European languages, according to Gimbutas' reconstruction.

The occurrence of gendered pairs of figurines in tombs in Western Mexico made it possible for Melissa Logan (2007) to study the varieties of poses and combinations—usually clearly depicted as a male and a female, but not always. The fact that they were buried in tombs seems to connect the figurine pairs with religion, but its nature is impossible to specify. Still, it seems that both men and women were involved in the religious system, and that the couples were significant.

Joyce Marcus used figurines from Formative Oaxaca to describe women's rituals, largely based on the figurines that are found in various contexts, including residences and burials. 'As in many village cultures all over the world, it was the task of women to communicate with recent ancestors' (1998: 1). Most of the rituals were held within the household, and the figurines were both made and used by women. Most commonly the figurines depicted females, which Marcus suggests indicates that the ancestors mostly consulted were females. When they were arranged in ritual scenes they 'constituted a venue to which the spirits of recent ancestors could return' (1998: 3). Based on ethnographic material, and similar features in ancient houses Marcus argues that women practised divination and healing. Burials of women may contain multiple figurines. One burial from Tlatilco in the Basin of Mexico was buried with 20 figurines in two clusters, suggesting religious ritual.

Diane Bolger (2003) shows that religion is just one type of information that can be teased out of figurines and their context. In ancient Cyprus, figurines have been used to describe many aspects of daily life. Bolger shows that, among other things, gender and ritual change through time, and the figurines can be an index of that change.

2.4 Paintings

Paintings that include ritual scenes were studied by Joan Connelly (2007) to understand the roles of priestesses in ancient Greece. Connelly's examination of various kinds of art—paintings on pottery and walls, sculptures, and friezes—finds many priestesses in the ancient Greek world, as well as literary references to goddesses. Objects that are known to indicate religious officiants are made use of to identify women priests, when inscriptions are absent or unclear.

2.5 Objects

Objects may be called upon in other contexts to discuss religious ceremonies. It is likely that bells and flutes found in Neolithic China indicate religious ceremonies. Pure gold crowns in the Silla kingdom of southern Korea (Figure 14.3) have been said to indicate not only royalty, but also shamanism (Kim 1997). The sacred objects of the family of the Japanese emperor—mirror, sword, and curved jewel—are related to shrine activities, where the officiating priest may be male or female. The ancient objects themselves are kept in dedicated shrines. Spindle whorls are associated with goddesses in Mesoamerica, as well as with royal women (McCafferty and McCafferty 2003). Burned hemp seeds in Siberian tombs seem to represent a final ceremony within the tomb, probably related to reaching spirits.

Gender and religion are thus most often established when either male and female bodies or depictions of men and women are found in clear association with ceremonial objects, buildings, or ritual areas. But occasionally it is possible to consider religious activities and gender, to which we now turn.

FIGURE 14.3 Example of Silla crown with shaman symbols, Kyongju, South Korea.

3 Religious Activities

Religious activities, such as sacrifices, divination, curing, and communicating with spirits or powers are often, but not always, gendered. This is one of the areas in which gender mistakes are often made, because of a propensity to read present gender relationships into the past. For example, shamans, who may often perform these activities, are often presumed to be male when traces of those activities are found in the past. Recent research on shamans in ancient East Asia (Nelson 2008) indicates that this was not the case in that region and time, possibly because women have been seen as naturally more able to reach the spirits. In fact, it has been claimed that women are shamans as often as men in many cultures (Tedlock 2005). Some of the activities which may be discernable with archaeological data include travelling to reaching the spirits, making sacrifices, divination, and curing.

3.1 Sacrifices

The gender of the person who made sacrifices that may be evident or inferred in archaeological contexts is impossible to ascertain directly. Sometimes it is inferred, as when weapons that were deposited in wells are presumed to represent males, and jewellery females (Levy 2007). Other kinds of presumed sacrifices include humans embedded in the understructure of buildings in Shang China and earlier contexts, and the bog bodies of Northern Europe. In these cases the gender of the sacrificial victim can be determined, but not that of the sacrificer. It seems that males were often the preferred human sacrifice in burials of the Shang dynasty, generally in both men's and women's royal graves (Keightley 1999).

3.2 Divination

Divining the future is often a religious ritual. It has been performed by many cultures, with different objects of material culture treated in various ways to interpret the future (Nelson 2003). The nature of the divination usually reveals nothing of the gender of the diviner, although it can be presumed that the diviner is perceived as either able to read messages about the future, in touch with powers who control the future, or both. In East Asia, two quite different ways to tell the future were through the use of oracle bones and yarrow sticks. Oracle bones made of mammal scapuli with holes bored in them to make them crack in the fire are found as early as 6000 BC in East Asia, although the best known are those of the Shang dynasty which contain writing and reveal a great deal about the religious system of the time. The writing tells the topic of the divination and sometimes the name of the diviner. From this we learn that some of the royal ladies were among the diviners. Furthermore, the basic meaning of the Chinese character for those who contact the spirits, *wu*, is 'female diviner'. Although the distinction between male *xi* and female *wu* was not always made, it seems clear that the original designation applied to women. Thus it cannot be known, but can be inferred, that the makers and users of the most ancient oracle bones, those who told the future, were women. Such bones with bored holes but without writing have been found in the Korean peninsula and the Japanese islands through the early centuries AD. Since women shamans are known from both archaeology (e.g. *haniwa* figurines from the Kofun period in Japan) and historical records (the Chinese *Weizhi* [Seyock 2004], the *Samguk Sagi* of Korea [Ilyon 1972]).

Less is known about the archaeology of throwing the yarrow sticks, since, being perishable, they are rarely found in archeological contexts. Chinese histories credit ancient sages with their invention. It seems that a question was asked and the sticks thrown, giving an answer to a question about the future depending on the configuration of flat and round sides. It may be that the *Yi Qing* is a codified reading of the answers given by the sticks. Thus later history genders the yarrow stick throwers as male, but we know nothing about the gender of early prognosticators.

3.3 Healing

Healing the sick is part of religious practice in many cultures. Sites of early temples in Greece are said to be places where people came to be cured (Connelly 2007), but this cannot be inferred from the buildings themselves unless there are depictions that can be interpreted in this way. Tholos (round) buildings with underground mazes have been interpreted as snake pits, known from literary sources to have been a treatment for nervous disorders.

4 CONCLUSION

There is a rich field of data waiting to be tapped with which to explore a variety of questions about ritual, religion, and gender. Possible future research directions include the question of gender and leadership, especially religious leadership, although the religious and the secular are often intertwined, even in complex societies. Several questions are implicit in the way that gender and religion have been discussed using archaeological materials. Sometimes the question involves the identification of gender—does the religion involve men only, women only, third genders? Sometimes it is a matter of restoring gendered officiants where they have been overlooked. Sometimes it is a matter of distinguishing between what counts as religion and what is a reflection of daily life, such as the division of labour by gender.

Some of the early questions posed by feminists included the notion of women's status being lower than men, more or less worldwide. This premise was not challenged, but the question was how did it come about? The standard saying in anthropology was that the first social divisions were by sex and age. In the context of ritual and religion, this precept turns out not to be universal, and perhaps the result of the domination of male scholarship in the present, rather than the domination of males in the past.

Goddesses are usually inferred from depictions of females, whether sculpted or painted. But whether it is appropriate to see all goddesses as the same, branding them as Earth Mothers, Fertility Goddesses, and so forth, does not do justice to the data. Stephanie Buden (2002) has made a giant stride in this direction in terms of interpreting the goddess figures of ancient Cyprus. She suggests that sexuality without fertility was another trait of some goddesses.

When the powers are anthropomorphized, their gender may reflect the ways that people in the culture are expected to live their gendered lives. Peggy Sanday (1981) calls origin myths involving female and male gods 'scripts' for proper gendered behaviour. Looked at in this light, the structure of the religion itself becomes important for understanding gender relations and roles. It raises the question of why the powers have any gender at all? Sometimes they do not. For example, the spirits appealed to on the Shang oracle bones are both personal and impersonal. Powers of the four directions, natural phenomena such as winds and rain, and places such as rivers and mountains, have no gender. On the other hand, spirits of the ancestors, who were once living people, are specified, not just according to their gender, but by their temple name. Particular ancestors were called upon and queried about the future, not generic deceased members of the family. Cult was performed for both female and male ancestors, because they could both influence the fortunes of living people.

While it is true that in China there are origin myths, in the form they have been handed down they are not very developed. Only one of the founders is female—her name is Nuwa, Changing Woman. But while she is the only woman, she is also the only one assigned cosmological significance, for she is said to have propped up the corner of the sky with stones of five colors (Wu 1982). The other culture heroes are named for a specific addition to human life—Have Nest, Divine Farmer, etc. (Chang 1986).

Like everything else in archaeological explanations, understanding a religion is important for understanding gender. A culture that emphasizes warriors is likely to have more important male than female gods. But even the fierce and warlike Aztecs had female powers—as we have seen, they are identifiable as female by their association with weaving implements. While feminist archaeologists have tended to examine questions that are specific to a given culture, and to scrutinize details that might indicate gender more closely than previous work has done, the time is ripe to address the Big Questions that can be approached with comparative data.

Suggested Reading

For many, Marija Gimbutas (1989) is the authority on gender and religion in archaeology. Her work discusses the figurines of Old Europe, cult buildings, and symbolic markings on various objects. A critique of this work is valuable (Conkey and Tringham 1995). For a regional example of taking both gender and religion seriously, see Nelson (2008).

References

Arnold, B. 1991. 'The deposed princess of Vix: The need for an engendered European prehistory' in D. Walde and N. Willows (eds), *The Archaeology of Gender* (Calgary: Archeological Association, University of Calgary), pp. 366–74.

Bacus, E. A., Barker, A., and Bonevich, J. D. 1993. *A Gendered Past: A critical bibliography of gender in archaeology* (Ann Arbor: University of Michigan Museum of Anthropology).

Bolger, D. 2003. *Gender in Ancient Cyprus: Narratives of social change on a Mediterranean island* (Walnut Creek, CA: AltaMira).

BUDEN, S. L. 2002. 'Creating a goddess of sex' in D. Bolger and N. Serwint (eds), *Engendering Aphrodite: Women and Society in ancient Cyprus* (Boston: American Schools of Oriental Research), pp. 315–24.
CHANG, K. C. 1986. *The Archaeology of Ancient China* (New Haven: Yale University Press).
CLAASSEN, C. 1991. 'Gender, shellfishing, and the Shellmound Archaic' in J. Gero and M. Conkey (eds), *Engendering Archaeology: Women in prehistory* (Oxford: Blackwell), pp. 2276–300.
CONKEY, M. W. and SPECTOR, J. D. 1984. 'Archaeology and the study of gender', *Advances in Archaeological Method and Theory*, 7: 1–38.
—— and TRINGHAM, R. E. 1995. 'Archaeology and the goddess: Exploring the contours of feminist archaeology' in D. C. Stanton and A. J. Stewart (eds), *Feminisms in the Academy* (Ann Arbor: University of Michigan Press), pp. 102–39.
CONNELLY, J. B. 2007. *Portrait of a Priestess* (Princeton: Princeton University Press).
DELPORTE, H. 1979. *L'Image de la Femme dans l'Art Préhistorique* (Paris: Picard).
GERO, J. 1991. 'Genderlithics: Women's roles in stone tool production' in J. Gero and M. Conkey (eds), *Engendering Archaeology: Women in prehistory* (Oxford: Blackwell), pp. 163–93.
—— and CONKEY, M. (eds) 1991. *Engendering Archaeology: Women in prehistory* (Oxford: Blackwell).
GIMBUTAS, M. 1974. *The Gods and Goddesses of Old Europe* (Berkeley: University of California Press).
—— 1982. *The Goddesses and Gods of Old Europe* (Berkeley: University of California Press).
—— 1989. *The Language of the Goddess* (San Francisco: Harper & Row).
HAYS-GILPIN, K. A. 2004. *Ambiguous Images: Gender and rock art* (Walnut Creek, CA: AltaMira).
IKAWA-SMITH, F. 2002. 'Gender in Japanese prehistory' in S. M. Nelson and M. Rosen Ayalon (eds), *In Pursuit of Gender: Worldwide archaeological approaches* (Walnut Creek, CA: AltaMira), pp. 323–54.
ILYON 1972. *Samguk Yusa*, trans. Tae-Hung Ha and Grafton K. Mintz (Seoul: Yonsei University Press).
KEIGHTLEY, D. 1999. 'At the beginning: The status of women in Neolithic and Shang China', *Nannu*, 1: 1–63.
KIM, Y.-C. (ed.) 1977. *Women of Korea: A History from Ancient Times to the Present*. Seoul: Ehwa University Press.
LEVY, J. 1995. 'Heterarchy in Bronze Age Denmark: Settlement pattern, ritual, and gender' in R. M. Ehrenreich, C. L. Crumley, and J. E. Levy (eds), *Heterarchy and the Analysis of Complex Societies*, Archeological Papers of the American Anthropological Association No. 6(1) (Washington, DC), pp. 41–53.
—— 2007. 'Gender, Hierarchy and Heterarchy' in S. M. Nelson (ed.), *Women in Antiquity: Theoretical approaches to gender and archaeology* (Walnut Creek: AltaMira Press), pp. 189–216.
LOGAN, M. 2007. 'Gender Archaeology in Late Formative Western Mexico', MA Thesis, University of Colorado at Denver.
MCCAFFERTY, GEOFFREY G., and MCCAFFERTY, S. D. 2003. 'Questioning a queen? A gender-informed evaluation of Monte Alban Tomb 7' in S. M. Nelson (ed.), *Ancient Queens: Archaeological explorations* (Walnut Creek, CA: AltaMira), pp. 41–58.
MARCUS, J. 1998. *Women's Ritual in Formative Oaxaca, Figurine-making, Divination, Death and the Ancestors*, Memoirs of the Museum of Anthropology, University of Michigan No. 33 (Ann Arbor).

NELSON, S. M. 1991. 'The "Goddess Temple" and the status of women at Niuheliang, China' in D. Walde and N. Willows (eds), *The Archaeology of Gender* (Calgary: Archeological Association, University of Calgary), pp. 302–8.
—— 2003. 'The Queens of Silla: Power and connections to the spirit world' in S. M. Nelson (ed.), *Ancient Queens: Archaeological explorations* (Walnut Creek, CA: AltaMira), pp. 77–92.
—— 2004. *Gender in Archaeology: Analyzing power and prestige* (Walnut Creek, CA: AltaMira).
—— 2008. *Shamanism and the Origin of States* (Walnut Creek, CA: Left Coast Press).
POLLOCK, S. 1991. 'Women in a men's world: Images of Sumerian women' in J. Gero and M. Conkey (eds), *Engendering Archaeology: Women in prehistory* (Oxford: Blackwell), pp. 366–406.
RENAUD, E. B. 1929. 'Prehistoric female figures from America and the Old World', *Scientific Monthly*, 28: 507–12.
SANDAY, P. R. 1981. *Female Power and Male Dominance: On the origins of sexual inequality* (Cambridge: Cambridge University Press).
SEYOCK, B. 2004. *Auf dem Spuren der Ostbarbaren*. Tübingen: Bunka, Vol. 8.
TEDLOCK, B. 2005. *The Woman in the Shaman's Body* (New York: Bantam Books).
WATSON, P. J. and KENNEDY, M. 1991. 'The development of horticulture in the eastern woodlands of North America: Women's role' in J. Gero and M. Conkey (eds), *Engendering Archaeology: Women in prehistory* (Oxford: Blackwell), pp. 255–75.
WHITEHOUSE, R. 2002. 'Gender in the south Italian Neolithic: A combinatory approach' in S. M. Nelson and M. Rosen Ayalon (eds), *In Pursuit of Gender: Worldwide archaeological approaches* (Walnut Creek, CA: AltaMira), pp. 15–42.
WU, K. C. 1982. *The Chinese Heritage* (New York: Crown Publishers).
ZHANG, Z. 2005. 'The Yangshao period: Prosperity and transformation of prehistoric society' in K. C. Chang and X. P. Pingfang (eds), *The Formation of Chinese Civilization* (New Haven: Yale University Press), pp. 43–84.

CHAPTER 15

ARCHAEOLOGIES OF THE SENSES

YANNIS HAMILAKIS

1 What is the Archaeology of the Senses?

It will be easier to start by describing what the archaeology of the senses is not. It is not an attempt to produce a long-term developmental history of the sensory modalities of humanity, from early prehistory to the present. Such an effort would be akin to writing 'the history of everything' as a single narrative, or as one volume. It is not an effort to reconstruct past sensory and sensuous experience, in other words to understand, to feel, to sense, how past people sensed and felt in their interaction with the material world and with other humans. Sensory and sensuous experience is socially and historically specific, and our bodies and sensory modalities too are the products of our own historical moment, thus rendering attempts at sensory empathy with past people problematic. It is not a sub-discipline of archaeology either, in the same way that we have an archaeology of food, of death, of pottery, of ethnicity, or colonialism. Such a compartmentalization is not only unfeasible (for the senses do not occupy the same ontological ground as, say, pottery, or a historical phenomenon such as colonialism), but it would have also deprived this approach of its potential to cross-fertilize all aspects of the archaeological endeavour.

So, what is it? I hope that a more complete answer to this question will emerge at the end of this chapter, but for the sake of convenience, let me offer a working definition here: the archaeologies of the senses are attempts to come to terms with the fully embodied, experiential matter-reality of the past; to understand how people produce their subjectivities, their collectively and experientially founded identities, how they live their daily routines and construct their own histories, through the sensuous and sensory experience of matter, of other animate and inanimate beings, human, animal, plant, or other. In other words, they are attempts to come to terms with the skin and the flesh of the world. The archaeologies of the senses do not ask the questions: did this roast pig taste for the people in the Neolithic the same as it does to us today? Or did this Early Bronze Age Aegean pot with this plastic external decoration and its rough surface, produce the same tactile feelings of roughness to the Early Bronze Age people in the Aegean as it does to the pottery analyst today? Not only are these questions impossible to answer, but they are also wrongly phrased—we only need to be reminded of the context-specific nature of sensory experiences even within our own era. But the archaeologies of the senses do pose the following questions: what is the *range* and *form* of taste or tactile experiences in any given context, and how and why do they change across space and time? Why is it that these specific pots with their distinctive surfaces with plastic decoration, appear and disappear suddenly, what is the context of their use, and how does their distinctive tactile experience relate to the tactile experience of other pots, spatially and chronologically? How do the tactile experiences they afford relate to the olfactory and taste experiences of their content, and, of course, the visual experience in the context of their use (a dark cave or a tomb, perhaps, where tactility then becomes crucial in recognizing the shape of the pot and its content)? And how does the olfactory and taste experience of roast pig, and of burning fat relate to the range of other culinary sensory experiences in that context? What kind of occasion does this experience produce, and what kind of temporality does it relate to? How do the sensory experiences of hunting an animal, of killing it, sometimes as part of a sacrificial ceremony, of listening to the screams of the animal as it senses its death, of seeing the bright red colour of blood and of meat, of partaking of the skinning, the chopping, and cooking of the carcass, of being infused with smoke and smells, and of course with the sensory and embodied presence of others, produce feelings and emotions, time, identities, and personal and collective histories? How does the relatively infrequent bodily consumption of meat in a context, say Mediterranean prehistory, where daily routines are structured around a diet based on cereals and legumes (mostly of pale colours, with tastes and odours less strong than that of meat and fat), produce time, history, memory, and identity? And what kind of prospective memories would these events and experiences have sedimented onto the bodies of the participants, and how were these memories materially reactivated during a subsequent occasion? Finally, how do these sensory experiences and associated memories operate within the field of political economy, how do they structure the bio-political reality of a given context?

It is often assumed that sensory experience is too ephemeral and immaterial to be of use to archaeology, yet the examples I have cited in the passage above, and a growing body of work in a number of disciplines (cf. Seremetakis 1994; Sutton 2001, 2010, for anthropology; Rodaway 1994 for geography) should convince us that, in fact, the opposite is the case: sensory experience is material, it requires materiality in order to be activated, and its past and present material traces are all around us, whether it is the burnt bones of a pig that was sacrificed and then consumed, or the traces left on a rock which was repeatedly hit deliberately to produce sound. Why is it then that sensory and sensuous archaeologies is a project that is still at its infancy? To answer this question will require a close and detailed examination which should explore, side by side, the social and philosophical western conceptions of the body and of the bodily senses since classical times, but also the development of official, professional archaeology, as a specific device of Western modernity. It is well known that archaeology, as an organized discipline and as we know and practise it today in the West, is the outcome and at the same time an essential device of Western capitalist modernity, with close affinities with the colonial and national projects and with the post-Enlightenment philosophical traditions (cf. Hamilakis and Duke 2007; Thomas 2004). What is less well known or even systematically overlooked is that, in the same way that modernity is not a monolithic concept, modernist archaeology is diverse and multifaceted: diverse modernities have often resulted in alternative archaeologies, often incorporating features that we associate with pre-modern attitudes and practices (cf. Hamilakis 2007; Hamilakis and Momigliano 2006).

It is fair to say, however, that dominant and influential versions in Western modernist archaeology relied on a philosophical and social framework which consistently denigrated sensory experience, set out the framework of the five senses commonly known today, constructed a distinctive hierarchy within the Western sensorium (lower senses: touch, smell, taste; higher senses: vision, hearing), and elevated the autonomous vision to the highest position. Of course this framework is part and parcel of a Cartesian view of the world, with its well known binarisms of mind/body, mental/material, culture/nature, and male/female, to name but a few. Contemporary Western archaeology is still primarily visual, one only needs to reflect (another visual word) on its vocabulary, but it harbours at the same time a tension: a tension between this occularcentric tradition on the one hand, and the inherently multisensory nature of both material culture, and of the archaeological processes on the other. As Ingold has already noted (2000), the solution is not to demonize vision but to *re-materialize* it, to fully integrate it again within the multisensory human and archaeological experience. Besides, vision and sight as modalities have been hardly homogeneous throughout history; suffice only to mention the sense of vision as extramission, encountered amongst philosophers and authors in classical antiquity, in Byzantium, and in other contexts (cf. Bartsch 2000: 79, and below): the idea that the eyes emit as well as receive rays of light, a notion that makes vision akin to the sense of touch.

There have been several attempts in recent years to produce archaeologies of the senses, with varied degrees of success (cf. Insoll 2007). Some researchers have tried to isolate a single sensory modality (as defined by the Western sensorium), say, the auditory sense, and have attempted to reconstruct on that basis acoustic or other properties and effects of past material culture, the megalithic monuments of southern England for example (e.g. Devereux and Jahn 1996; Watson 2001; Watson and Keating 1999). Others have focused on concrete pictorial and other material representations of sensuous social actions, contexts rich in such evidence such as Mesoamerica (e.g. Hauston and Taube 2000); and others still have concentrated mostly on megalithic monuments, primarily in Northern Europe and within a theoretical context which they define as landscape phenomenology, they have explored primarily the visual (but more recently, other sensory) effects of these monuments (e.g. Tilley 1994, 2004, 2008).

A detailed critique of these approaches is beyond the scope of this chapter, but suffice to say here that, notwithstanding the immense value of these attempts as the first exploratory endeavours in a new field, the problems with them are considerable. Despite the analytical convenience, the focus on one single sense ignores two fundamental facts: that the dominant Western sensorium with its five autonomous senses may not be the most appropriate framework for understanding past sensory experience; ethnographic work (e.g. Geurts 2002) has shown than non-Western societies may valorize other modalities, balance for example, beyond our own definitions. More importantly, however, sensuous experience is always *synaesthetic*—it involves multiple sensory modalities working in unison (Porath 2008; cf. Hamilakis 2002; in preparation). Representational studies on the senses are important; yet, sensuous interactions are primarily experiential, and in many cases do not involve representations. Whenever these are available, they should be studied not only as depictions of sensuous experience, but also, and perhaps primarily, as material that elicits sensuous experience in itself, through vision, touch, or perhaps other senses.

Finally, work on landscape phenomenology is still heavily biased towards vision as a separate entity, despite recent efforts to include other senses, and often resorts to structuralist binarisms. Moreover, it often relies on a limited set of data, primarily landscape and architecture; very little use is made of detailed on-site, artefactual, or bioarchaeological data, even when these are available (cf. Brück 2005). More seriously, it mostly assumes a solitary observer, more often than not the archaeologist herself, who experiences a site or a monument as if *for the first time*. Yet, as Bergson has taught us (1991), there is no experience which is not full of memories (cf. Jones 2007). It is this neglect of the *mnemonic sensuous field*, of the fact the sensuous experience of past people would have been filtered though countless past multisensory memories, produced through *collective interaction* rather than though a solitary encounter, which renders many of these approaches problematic.

Still, the archaeologies of the senses constitute a growing and dynamic field of enquiry, in tandem with the growth of the field in other disciplines, and perhaps the only approach which challenges both the cognitivist discourses of much recent theoretical work as well as the residual functionalism of much of scientific archaeology. In fact, the archaeologies of the senses have the ability to bridge these divides, and with their emphasis on the thingness of things, on the materials (Ingold 2007) as well as on materiality, to bring together in a fruitful collaboration hitherto disparate efforts, from zooarchaeology and soil micromorphology to explorations on temporality and the philosophy of archaeology. Recent studies along these lines (e.g. Boivin 2004; Boivin et al. 2007; Cummings 2002; Goldhahn 2002; Hamilakis 1998, 1999, 2002; Morris and Peatfield 2002; Rainbird 2002; Skeates 2008, 2010) have already demonstrated the enormous potential that lies ahead (cf. Insoll 2007).

2 RELIGION AND RITUAL: REDUNDANT CONCEPTS?

Several contributors to this book have problematized the notions of religion and of ritual more generally and in archaeology (see Introduction and Chapter 11). I tend to side with the scholars who insist that these two concepts should be kept apart, not only because of the difficulty of talking about religion for much of human history, but also because the term ritual or rather the more useful concept of ritualization as a process (cf. Bell 1992, 2007) has the potential to inform our understanding of situations and phenomena which are definitely not religious in any sense. The fundamental problem with both religion and ritual is that as categories they are the result of the modernist Western mentality I referred to, and the one which has been responsible for the dichotomous thinking which the archaeologies of the senses have attempted to overcome. It is this thinking that has produced the additional dichotomies between secular and religious, and ritual versus practical. It is often repeated that archaeologists in particular have used the concept of ritual whenever they have faced a difficulty in finding a practical or economic explanation for an observed pattern (Insoll 2004: 1–2), perpetuating thus the dichotomous Cartesian logic. There are, however, some interesting recent developments in this debate. Some anthropologists of religion, for example, emphasize the need to view religions not as systems of beliefs but as material and sensory practices. 'Religions may not always demand beliefs, but they always involve material forms', states Webb Keane (2008a: S124; cf. also 2008b), whereas the recent launch of the journal *Material Religion* points to the same direction (see also the special issue of this journal on *Archaeology and Material Religion* 5(3), 2009). Archaeologists have critiqued the use of the concept of ritual in their own discipline, and have attempted to bridge the divide between special, 'ritual' occasions and contexts, and the routines and practices of domestic and daily life (e.g. Bradley 2005; Brück 1999).

The approach I am advocating here, however, proposes a more radical break. Its starting point is that religions and ritual—if seen as overarching, and in many ways abstract, concepts—are of limited value in understanding past human experiences. A sensory and sensuous archaeology instead begins with the human body, or rather the *trans-corporeal, somatic landscape* and its culturally defined but universally important sensory modalities; the multisensory interactions with the material world; the interweaving of the senses in experiential interactions (intersensoriality and cultural synaesthesia); and social and collective bodily memory, seen as a meta-sense linked both to remembering *and* forgetting which are activated and re-enacted through the senses. Some of these social sensory interactions may be formalized, performative and repetitive (i.e. 'ritual'), some not; some taking place within the context of organized religions, some not; but all are important in social production and reproduction, in the construction of human histories and identities. In other words, an archaeology of the senses goes beyond the religious and the secular, the ritual and the ordinary/mundane, showing the futility of such dichotomous thinking. I will try to illustrate these thoughts with the case studies below.

3 The Sensory World of a Byzantine Church

Reading Byzantine theological texts one gets the impression that Eastern Orthodox Christianity is an austere, spiritual world, where the bodily senses are seen as the portals to sin and to depravity, and they are thus banished. Yet, partaking of a religious ceremony inside a Byzantine church would testify otherwise. The experience here is clearly multisensory, almost carnal, as all sensory modalities are activated in unison and play a fundamental role in the ceremonies (Caseau 1999: 103). Churches are not simply the places where the believer communicates with God, but rather the materialization of heaven on earth (Ware 1963: 269–80). The different material entities, from architecture and the organization of space, to the iconography on the walls and the ceilings as well as on portable panels, the candles and the oil lamps, the incense, the singing and the Eucharist, the decorative flowers, and of course, the multisensory bodies of the priests and of the congregation, are all participants in a theatrical drama where sensorial stimuli and interactions are the key ingredients. In many cases, it is the interaction across the various material media that produces mnemonic and highly evocative effects in this performance.

Conventional art historical traditions have treated much of the material culture of Byzantine churches as works of art, to be appreciated and perceived through the sense of autonomous vision, and in galleries lit with steady, harsh and cold light (cf. James 2004; Pentcheva 2006). Yet, in Byzantine churches, the figures of saints on the walls and on portable media were lit by oil lamps and candles, and the flickering of their light produces the effect of movement, of human forms becoming animated, and fully participating in the ceremony. In some cases, the selection of certain materials seems to have been governed by the desire to create the sense of movement and animation, to facilitate this theatre of reflections and shadows. The use of mosaics is a case in point. As Liz James has noted:

> [mosaics] made of thousands of glass tesserae, all acting as little mirrors, formed one vast reflective surface which glinted and sparkled as light played across it. Offsetting the tesserae of a mosaic changed the spatial relations around the mosaic and encouraged a sense of movement. It would also change the appearance of an image. In the apse of Hagia Sophia [in Istanbul], the Virgin's robe alters in colour as the light moves around it. [2004: 527–8]

The same goes for the use of enamel to decorate silver icons (Pentcheva 2006: 640–1). These techniques render these artefacts dynamic and constantly changing, resistant to attempts by scholars who may wish to photograph them, that is to render them two-dimensional and static: the multiple reflections of lights would result in constant changes of the expression of the image (2006: 644). Byzantine icons are often equated with the later, better-known, flat wood panels, yet an earlier (ninth–eleventh centuries AD) middle Byzantine tradition of silver-relief icons, often decorated with enamel, invites a tactile experience, and enacts the dominant, in Byzantine theological mentality, view of vision as extramission: in Byzantine churches, vision was a tactile sense, as rays of light were thought to reach out of the eye to touch and feel surfaces (James 2004: 528; Nelson 2000: 150; Pentcheva 2006: 631). But these objects were meant to be experienced with the whole body, not just through tactile vision: images and icons were touched and kissed; they came alive in ceremonies where sermons and singing were prominent, not as theological rhetoric and content (which most people could not understand) but primarily as spoken words and songs, in other words as sound and hearing (James 2004: 527); and they were decorated with aromatic flowers and were infused with incense.

The use of incense and of fragrant smell within the Byzantine churches deserves special mention. Smell is a peculiar sense; it invades human bodies at will, being the most difficult to shut out and control, and occupying at the same time that liminal space between the material and immaterial. As Alfred Gell has noted, '[t]o manifest itself as a smell is the nearest an objective reality can go towards becoming a concept without leaving the realm of the sensible altogether' (1977: 29). It is perhaps these properties that have led to the association of fragrant smells and perfumes not only with magic and dreaming, but also with transcendence and with rituals aimed at communicating with the divine. Incense in particular, with its smoke as well as smell, provides a visual and olfactory bridge between the human and the divine worlds (Pentcheva 2006: 650). Within the church, incense produces a spatial realm that is no longer of this world, but rather paradise itself. The fragrant smell envelops the bodies of the participants, as well as the bodies of saints on the wall, and it neutralizes individual bodily odour, creating thus the collectivity of the worshippers (Kenna 2005: 58). It also marks specific locales within the church, as the priest would often stop and infuse with incense special spots, the icon of the patron saint for example. But it also marks distinctive moments within the service, focusing the congregation's attention to transitions within the liturgy (Kenna 2005: 65), marking thus time, and inviting the congregation to cross themselves or to engage in other ritualized actions. Incense, of course, is also used in religious rituals outside the church, often with similar effects, in producing a locale as sacred (the corner with the Christian icons within the house, for example), or marking time within the day (e.g. the time of the evening Mass) and within the annual religious calendar.

4 AT A 'MYCENAEAN' SANCTUARY

Very little is known about 'Mycenaean' (meant here as chronological rather than ethnic signifier) 'religious' practice. The societies of the Aegean in the fourteenth and thirteenth centuries BC, with which this problematic label is normally associated, after the site-type of Mycenae in the Peloponnese, have been constructed in the late nineteenth and the twentieth centuries AD as the beginnings of Greek civilization, as the mythical heritage of the Homeric epics, and very often as a warlike society, in opposition to the 'peaceful' and serene 'Minoans' of Crete (cf. Darcque et al. 2006; Hamilakis and Momigliano 2006). As in my previous example, the documentary evidence for this period—if used on its own—offers, if not a misleading picture, certainly a partial and fragmentary one: the documents of Linear B are of administrative nature, concerned with the interests of 'palatial' institutions. They do however, mention deities, and more importantly, provisions of food commodities and offerings for sanctuaries and religious festivals (cf. Bendall 2007; Palaima 2004). Archaeological work has offered some concrete examples of such sanctuaries, with Phylakopi on the Aegean island of Melos being the most prominent, thanks to its detailed study and publication (Renfrew 1985). Yet, much of the discussion has focused on the criteria for identifying sacred, cultic localities; the nature of the divinities; and on potential links with the later, Classical Greek religion, often leading to unfounded extrapolations and desperate searches for continuities. It is only very recently that social practice and ritualized embodied interactions have attracted attention. A key factor in this recent shift is the realization that eating and drinking ceremonies formed a central part in the religious rituals (Hamilakis 2008).

The sanctuary of Agios Konstantinos, located on the east coast of the Methana peninsula (in the north-east Peloponnese) was excavated in the 1990s by Eleni Konsolaki. It forms part of a large architectural complex, with many rooms, including a megaron (the formal, elite reception building of Mycenaean centres) (Konsolaki 2004). The room that seems to have been the focus of cultic activity, room A (Figures 15.1 and 15.2) is only 4.30 m x 2.60 m, and yet is full of material traces of intense ritualized ceremonies: more than 150 clay figurines, mostly of bovines, but also humans (riders, charioteers, bull-leapers, one single female), and clay models of thrones, tripod tables, a bird, and a fragmentary boat, scattered over a stone bench and its three, low stone steps. Other features in the room included a low stone platform along one of its walls, a partly paved floor, a hearth full of ash and burnt animal bones, drinking vessels, cooking pots, a triton shell with its apex deliberately broken, and ceramic vessels associated with libations, including an animal-head rhyton (libation vessel) resembling the head of a fantastic beast, something between a pig and fox. The finds seem to constitute a single, destruction layer (cf. Hamilakis and Konsolaki 2004; Konsolaki 2002).

It is tempting to impose a literary/documentary and mythological/genealogical grid upon this site, and attempt to relate it to a deity mentioned in the Linear B or even in later, classical sources, and even attach a set of beliefs to this material, positioning it thus along the long line of perceived continuity of Greek religion. Alternatively, and the approach advocated here, is to engage with the embodied, sensory, material practices, and connect them to their historical social context at large. My starting point is the bare bones found in and around the hearth. These humble, fragmentary, mostly burnt, bones—some brown-black, more greyish white—come mostly from juvenile and neonatal pigs

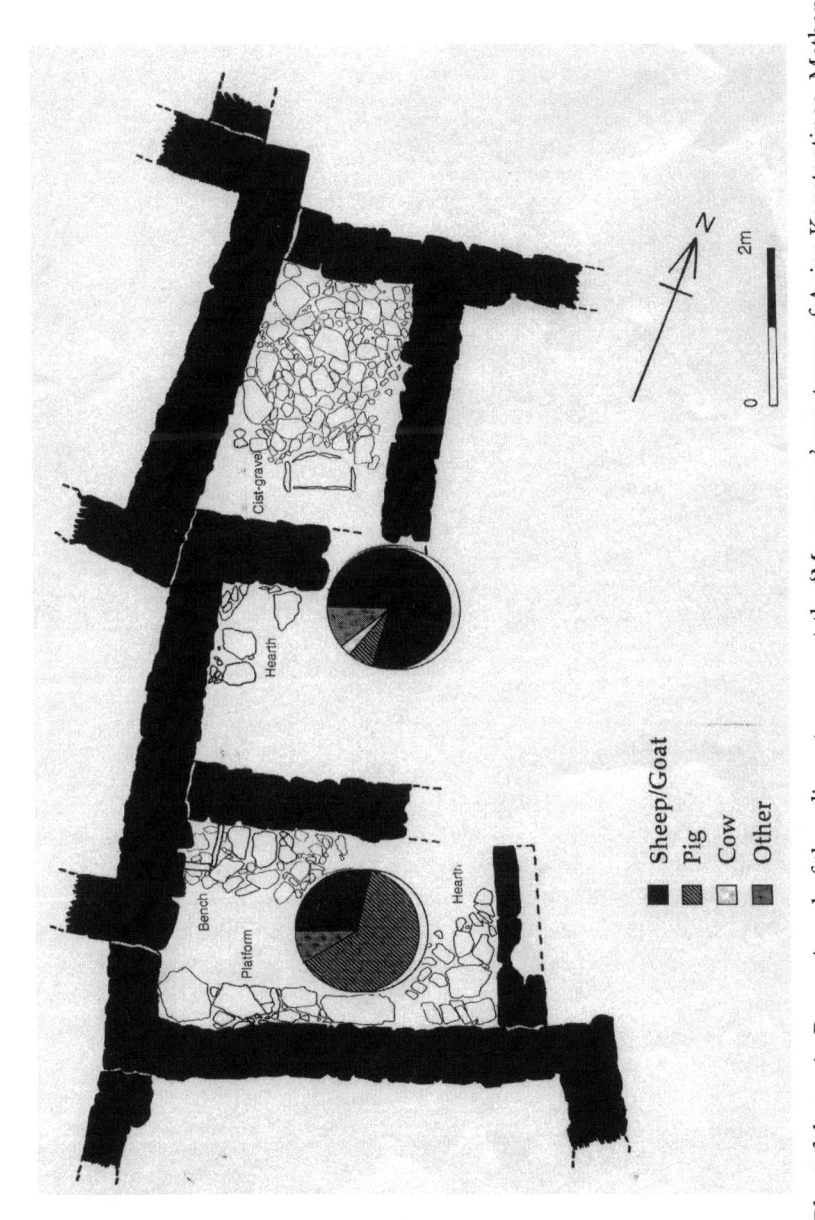

FIGURE 15.1 Plan of the main Room A and of the adjacent rooms at the 'Mycenaean' sanctuary of Agios Konstantinos, Methana, Greece.

FIGURE 15.2 Room A at the sanctuary of Agios Konstantinos, Methana, Greece.

(Figure 15.3). Whole carcasses seemed to have been brought into the room, and they must have been either boiled in cooking pots or roasted in the hearth, possibly on spits (a stone spit stand was also found next to the hearth); some of them were eaten (witness the filleting cut marks), and then the bones were thrown into the hearth and burned; some, perhaps the youngest animals, could have been thrown in the hearth with the meat attached: food for people but also burnt offerings for deities, the earth, the elements, or non-human entities. Inside the room other bones of sheep and goat were found but, unlike pigs which were whole, they were represented mostly by their meat bearing elements; while some of them were burnt, most of them were not; their bones did not seem to have constituted burnt offerings to non-human beings. Many limpet shells were also found in the room, as were eight drinking vessels (*kylikes*). What we have here, therefore, is strong zooarchaeological evidence for the practice of animal burnt sacrifices in the Late Bronze Age, a practice hitherto undocumented, and one which is also encountered in later classical periods (and in Homeric epic) but in different form.

We are dealing here with a small space, possibly with restricted access, but one which was the focus not only of exhibition and depositional practices (of figurines, of bones, of artefacts), but also of intense embodied ceremonies with strong sensory effects: the smells of cooking meat, of fat burning, the smoke produced by the hearth, the tasting of food and drink, the sensorial experiencing of marine as well as terrestrial foods, the intoxicating

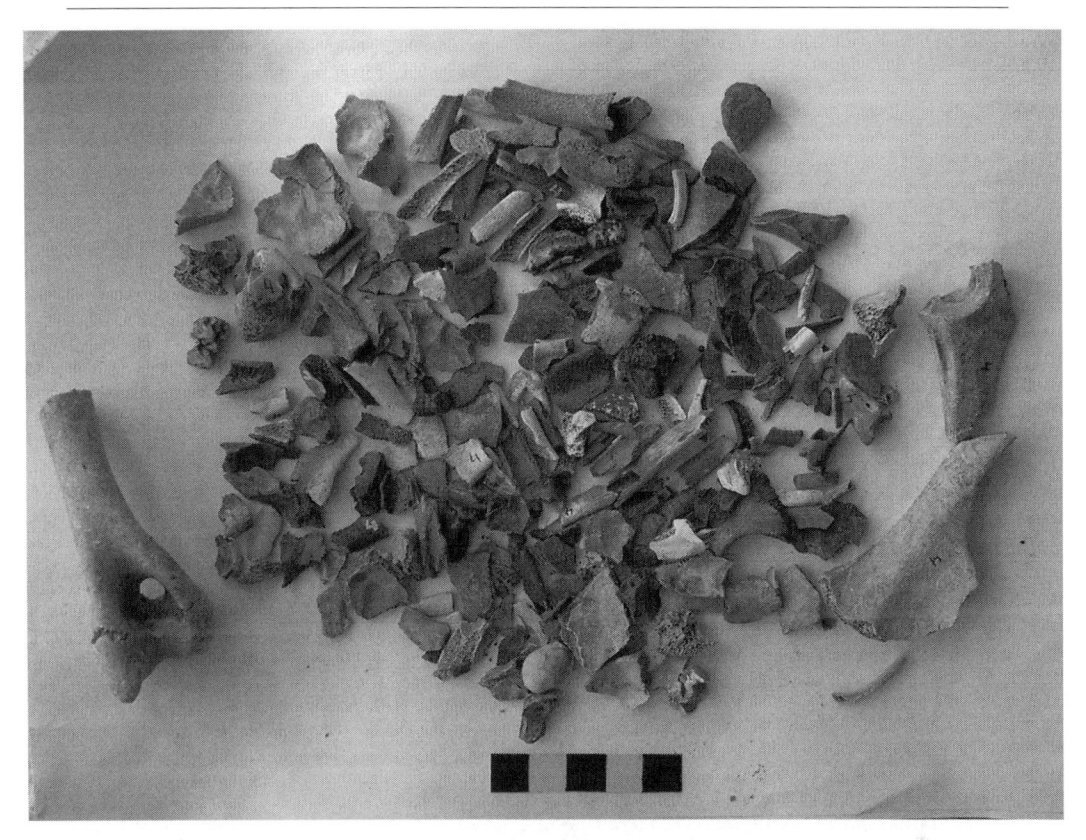

FIGURE 15.3 Animal bones from Room A at the sanctuary of Agios Konstantinos, Methana, Greece. The assemblage is dominated by the burnt bones found in and around the hearth, the remnants of burnt sacrifices.

effects of alcohol, and possibly the sound and music generated by the modified triton shell which would have produced a fully embodied tactile experience, not just an aural one. The physical proximity and restriction would have amplified these effects, and the smoke and smells would have infused and enveloped the bodies of the participants, producing a transcendental locale, as well as unified sensory and corporeal landscape. And all this in front of the large accumulation of figurines, and perhaps a large wooden statue, standing on the partly paved floor (Konsolaki 2002: 32). The ingredients for these sensory events were not unusual: the animals are the ones we encounter in all contexts of the same period, the materials used in the production of artefacts are neither exotic not rare. Yet, these sensory events would have disrupted the temporality of the everyday, by virtue of their special features such as the burnt offerings, the consumption of alcohol, the consumption of meat in a society with cereals as the staple diet, but mostly by virtue of the special locale within which they were taking place. They would have produced strong mnemonic effects on the bodies of the few participants, which could have been then narrated and recalled in future occasions and other locales. These sensory memories would have also bonded these people together, conferring upon them a sense of entitlement and special status as the few participants in sensorially strong, and emotionally special, transcendental events.

5 The Sensory Archaeology of a Contemporary Shaman

The hero at the centre of the third case study is not a shaman in the sense of the neo-pagan traditions and practices, explored by other entries in this volume (e.g. see Chapters 61, 63, and 64). This is in fact the story of a celebrated archaeologist, Manolis Andronikos (1919–92), the excavator of the site of Vergina in northern Greece, where in 1977 he unearthed the so-called tomb of Philip II of Macedonia, and subsequently other tombs (Figure 15.4). I have explored Andronikos's archaeological life and his national biography in some detail elsewhere (Hamilakis 2007), but here I want to summarize and comment on some specific features of this story, more pertinent to the theme of this chapter.

Why have I used the metaphor of shamanism to describe Andronikos? To answer the question, I will need to say a word or two on the national and social context. As part of a broader study, I have claimed that within the modern Hellenic national imagination, archaeological monuments and sites (especially the Classical ones) have become sacralized. This sacralization was the outcome of a series of processes and factors: the affinities of national ideologies with religious systems of thinking (e.g. Anderson 1991: 10–12; Llobera 1994; cf. Hamilakis 2007: 85 for further references); the veneration of Greek Classical antiquities by the Western elites since the Renaissance, especially in more recent centuries; the fact that several iconic national monuments are places of ancient worship; and last but not least, the fundamental role of Greek Orthodox Christianity in modern Hellenic national imagination, which has led to a fusion I have termed *Indigenous Hellenism*. Within this framework of sacralization, Andronikos became a key figure, in fact the most venerated figure in Greek archaeology. He was a public intellectual of considerable standing well before his moment of destiny, the discovery of the undisturbed tomb at Vergina in 1977. But it was that discovery which elevated him to the supreme position, especially since the find was seen by him, by the Greek authorities, and by the majority of Greek citizens, as proving beyond any dispute the Hellenicity of Macedonia, an issue that has been the apple of discord between Greece and its northern neighbours, most recently with the Former Yugoslav Republic of Macedonia.

Andronikos had the conventional training of the classical archaeologist in Greece including a spell in Oxford, was participating in the international fora of his discipline, was a brilliant and inspiring teacher, and enjoyed the respect of his peers. But his main audience was always the general Greek public, and it was with them that he was in constant communication, through his popular books, his newspaper column, and his public speeches. In addition, although he had no apparent intellectual contact with recent phenomenological writings, he often claimed both in his scholarly and his popular writings that the archaeologist engages in an experiential, sensuous and bodily contact with the material past: 'the archaeologist sees and touches the content of history; this means that he perceives in a sensory manner the metaphysical truth of historical time' (Andronikos 1972). His writings and his speeches evoked the sensory reception of materiality, leading a commentator to write, after Andronikos's death, a piece dedicated to his hands, with the synaesthetic title: 'The touch that could see' (Georgousopoullos 1995).

FIGURE 15.4 A postal stamp issued by the Greek Postal Service in 1992, depicting Manolis Andronikos amongst some of his finds from Vergina, Greek Macedonia.

The most important materialization of his sensory, existential philosophy was his discovery of the fourth-century BC underground tomb (tumulus) at Vergina. He choreographed and performed that moment in a ceremonial manner. He planned the opening of the tomb for 8 November, a day that in the Orthodox calendar is dedicated to the archangels Michael and Gabriel, the guards of the underworld, and he makes much in his writings of that 'coincidence' (Hamilakis 2007: 142 with references). The theatrical moment of the opening of the tomb was his descent to the underworld, where he uncovered, amongst many other things, a golden chest with cremated bones. At that moment, he was overcome with emotion and religious piety, as he was standing 'like a Christian, in front of the holy relics of a saint' (Andronikos 1997: 142). Andronikos, unlike many other shamans, did not have to reach altered states of consciousness through various bodily techniques (cf. Price 2001), but he did share with them the fundamental ability of all shamans, the mediation between different worlds (cf. Eliade 1972: 51). He communicated with the ancestors through this touch, and upon his return from the underworld he told a story of familial connections and national continuity: the celebrated dead, despite the on-going academic debates on his identity, was named as Philip II, was reunited with his national family; and a new grave, the new museum-crypt of Vergina, was created for his secondary burial, now a locale for perpetual, national veneration of both the ancient dead and the shaman-archaeologist.

6 CONCLUSIONS

The archaeologies of the senses do not simply offer some colourful detail of past life; they do not fill the gaps in a picture already drawn by other archaeological approaches, a picture of social organization, states, organized religions, technology, trade, subsistence, and ritual symbolism. The archaeologies of the senses in fact can succeed where abstract, top-down, functionalist, symbolist, textualist, and cognitivist approaches have failed. For example, we cannot fully understand the great iconoclastic dispute in eighth- to ninth-century AD Byzantium, if we fail to see it as a sensory debate, over whether sight or hearing hold primacy in communicating with the divine (James 2004: 529), a debate which concluded with the reinstatement of icons, as multisensory performative objects, rather than mere visual representations. We cannot comprehend what made a small and humble room in a remote location the special focus of a 'Mycenaean' cult if we fail to see it as a portal to other, transcendental worlds (cf. Hume 2007), reached through strong and special sensory experiences. We cannot easily explain why archaeologists like Andronikos become iconic, shamanistic figures (complicating thus our idea of modernist archaeology) and why the antiquities they 'touch', reanimate, and 'resurrect', acquire such immense force in national imagination, as has happened in contemporary Greece, if we fail to comprehend the potency of their sensory archaeology. The archaeologies of the senses do not constitute an added, optional ingredient to our mix of theories and methodologies; rather, they demand nothing less than a paradigmatic shift.

SUGGESTED READING

A pioneering collection on the senses is Howes (1991); the same author and the Concordia University inter-disciplinary group on the senses of which he has been a leading figure, continue to produce some important works (e.g. Classen et al. 1994; Howes 2003). A recent series of readers, focusing, however, rather unfortunately on single (Western) senses is the one produced by Berg Publishers (Bull 2003; Classen 2005; Drobnick 2006; Korsmeyer 2005; for a more integrated attempt see Howes 2005). Jütte (2005) provides a long-term analysis of attitudes towards the senses in the West, from antiquity to the present. The journals *Body and Society* and especially the recently launched *The Senses and Society* publish interesting interdisciplinary material. In anthropology, the pioneering works are by Stoller (e.g. 1989; 1997), Feld (1982), and Seremetakis (1994), a volume particularly relevant to archaeology due to its linking the senses with material culture and memory. Sutton's ethnography (2001) tackles the neglected dimension of the sensory importance of eating (on which see also, from a philosophical point of view, Curtin and Heldke 1992). For other interesting anthropological work see Desjarlais (2003), and Hirschkind (2007). Amongst recent historical works, see Hoffer (2003), whilst the monograph by Woolgar (2006) has particular resonance to archaeology. Film studies (e.g. MacDougall 2006), architecture (e.g. Barbara and Perliss 2006) and contemporary art (e.g. Drobnick 2004; Jones 2006) have long been fertile grounds for the exploration of sensuous and sensory experience, while interesting insights can be found in the interdisciplinary collection on sound and listening edited by Erlmann (2004).

In archaeology there is still little writing on the topic. Most attempts have been already mentioned in the main body of the chapter. Hamilakis et al. (2002) provides a critique of archaeology's attitudes towards the body, and includes several studies on sensory experience. Edwards et al. (2006) includes studies by archaeologists and anthropologists with a special focus on museums and colonialism. Other attempts that do not directly address the topic but are linked in some way to the archaeology of the senses are works on embodiment (e.g. Meskell and Joyce 2003), the collection by Jones and MacGregor (2002), and the literature on visual culture and archaeology (e.g. Skeates 2005; Smiles and Moser 2005), although this body of work does not always situate visuality within a critical sensory history and theory of archaeology. The recent discussion between contemporary artists and archaeologists (e.g. Renfrew 2003; Renfrew et al. 2004) sometimes touches upon issues of sensory experience, although not as frequently and as thoroughly as it should.

REFERENCES

ANDERSON, B. 1991. *Imagined Communities: Reflections on the origins and spread of nationalism* (London: Verso).
ANDRONIKOS, M. 1972. 'Arhaiologia kai hronos' ['Archaeology and time'], *To Vima*, 12 October 1972.
——1997. *To Hroniko tis Verginas* [*The Chronicle of Vergina*] (Athens: MIET).
BARBARA, A. and PERLIS, A. 2006. *Invisible Architecture: Experiencing places through the sense of smell* (Milan: Skira).
BARTSCH, S. 2000. 'The philosopher as Narcissus: Vision, sexuality, and self-knowledge in classical antiquity' in Robert S. Nelson (ed.), *Visuality Before and Beyond the Renaissance* (Cambridge: Cambridge University Press), pp. 70–97.
BELL, C. 1992. *Ritual Theory, Ritual Practice* (New York: Oxford University Press).
——2007. 'Response: Defining the need for a definition' in E. Kyriakidis (ed.), *The Archaeology of Ritual*, Cotsen Institute of Archaeology, Advance Seminar 3 (Los Angeles), pp. 277–8.
BENDALL, L. M. 2007. *The Economics of Religion in the Mycenaean World*, School of Archaeology, Monograph No. 67 (Oxford: Oxford University School of Archaeology).
BERGSON, H. 1991. *Matter and Memory* (New York: Zone Books).
BOIVIN, N. 2004. 'Mind over matter? Collapsing the mind–matter dichotomy in material culture studies' in E. DeMarrais, C. Gosden, and C. Renfrew (eds), *Rethinking Materiality: The engagement of mind with the material world* (Cambridge: MacDonald Institute), pp. 63–71.
——BRUMM, A., LEWIS, H., et al. 2007. 'Sensual, material and technological understanding: Exploring soundscapes in South India', *Journal of the Royal Anthropological Institute*, 13(2): 267–94.

BRADLEY, R. 2005. *Ritual and Domestic life in Prehistoric Europe* (London: Routledge).
BRÜCK, J. 1999. 'Ritual and rationality: Some problems of interpretation in European archaeology', *European Journal of Archaeology*, 2(3): 313–44.
—— 2005. 'Experiencing the past? The development of a phenomenological archaeology in British prehistory', *Archaeological Dialogues*, 12(1): 45–72.
BULL, M. (ed.) 2003. *The Auditory Culture Reader* (Oxford: Berg).
CASEAU, B. 1999. 'Christian bodies: The senses and early Byzantine Christianity' in E. James (ed.), *Desire and Denial in Byzantium* (Aldershot: Ashgate), pp. 101–9.
CLASSEN, C. (ed.) 2005. *The Book of Touch* (Oxford: Berg).
—— HOWES, D., and SYNNOT, A. 1994. *Aroma: The cultural history of smell* (New York and London: Routledge).
CUMMINGS, V. 2002. 'Experiencing texture and transformation in the British Neolithic', *Oxford Journal of Archaeology*, 21(3): 249–61.
CURTIN, D. W. and HELDKE, L. M. (eds) 1992. *Cooking, Eating, Thinking: Transformative philosophies of food* (Bloomington and Indianapolis: Indiana University Press).
DARCQUE, P., FOTIADIS, M., and POLYCHRONOPOULOU, O. (eds) 2006. *Mythos: La préhistoire égéenne du XIXe au XXIe siècle après J.-C.*, Bulletin de Correspondence Hellénique, Suppl. 46 (Paris and Athens: ÉFA)
DESJARLAIS, R. 2003. *Sensory Biographies: Lives and deaths among Nepal's Yolmo Buddhists* (Berkeley: University of California Press).
DEVEREUX, P. and JAHN, R. G. 1996. 'Preliminary investigations and cognitive considerations of the acoustic resonances of selected archaeological sites', *Antiquity*, 70: 665–6.
DROBNICK, J. (ed.) 2004. *Aural Cultures* (Toronto: YYZ Books).
—— (ed.) 2006. *The Smell Culture Reader* (Oxford: Berg).
EDWARDS, E., GOSDEN, C., and PHILIPS, R. B. (eds) 2006. *Sensible Objects: Colonialism, museums and material culture* (Oxford: Berg).
ELIADE, M. 1972. *Shamanism: Archaic techniques of ecstasy* (Princeton: Princeton University Press).
ERLMANN, V. (ed.) 2004. *Hearing Cultures: Essays on sound, listening and modernity* (Oxford: Berg).
FELD, S. 1982. *Sound and Sentiment: Birds, weeping, poetics and song in Kaluli expression* (Philadelphia: University of Pennsylvania Press).
GELL, A. 1977. 'Magic, perfume, dream' in I. Lewis (ed.), *Symbols and Sentiments: Cross-cultural studies in symbolism* (London and New York: Academic Press), pp. 25–38.
GEORGOUSOPOULOS, K. 1995. 'The touch that could see', *I Lexi*, 125: 6–9 (in Greek).
GEURTS, K. L. 2002. *Culture and the Senses: Bodily ways of knowing in an African community* (Berkeley: University of California Press).
GOLDHAHN, J. 2002. 'Roaring rocks: An audio-visual perspective on hunter-gatherer engravings in Northern Sweden and Scandinavia', *Norwegian Archaeological Review*, 35(1): 29–61.
HAMILAKIS, Y. 1998. 'Eating the Dead: Mortuary feasting and the political economy of memory in Bronze Age Crete' in K. Branigan (ed.), *Cemetery and Society in the Bronze Age Aegean* (Sheffield: Sheffield Academic Press), pp. 115–32.
—— 1999. 'Food technologies/technologies of the body: The social context of wine and oil production and consumption in Bronze Age Crete', *World Archaeology*, 31(1): 38–54.
—— 2002. 'The past as oral history: Towards an archaeology of the senses' in Y. Hamilakis, M. Pluciennik, and S. Tarlow (eds), *Thinking Through the Body: Archaeologies of corporeality* (New York: Kluwer/Plenum), pp. 121–36.

—— 2007. *The Nation and its Ruins: Antiquity, archaeology and national imagination in Greece* (Oxford: Oxford University Press).
—— 2008. 'Time, performance and the production of a mnemonic record: From feasting to an archaeology of eating and drinking' in L. Hitchcock, R. Laffineur, and J. Crowley (eds), *DAIS: Feasting in the Aegean Bronze Age* (Liege and Austin: University of Liege and University of Texas at Austin), pp. 3–17.
—— in preparation. *Archaeologies of the Senses* (Cambridge: Cambridge University Press).
—— and DUKE, P. (eds) 2007. *Archaeology and Capitalism: From ethics to politics* (Walnut Creek, CA: Left Coast Press).
—— and KONSOLAKI, E. 2004. 'Pigs for the gods: Burnt animal sacrifices as embodied rituals at a Mycenaean sanctuary', *Oxford Journal of Archaeology*, 23(2): 135–51.
—— and MOMIGLIANO, N. (eds) 2006. *Archaeology and European Modernity: Producing and consuming the 'Minoans'*, Bottega D'Erasmo, Creta Antica 7 (Padua: Aldo Ausilio).
——, PLUCIENNIK, M. and TARLOW, S. (eds) 2002. *Thinking Through the Body: Archaeologies of corporeality* (New York: Kluwer/Plenum).
HAUSTON, S. and TAUBE, K. 2000. 'An archaeology of the senses: Perception and cultural expression in ancient Mesoamerica', *Cambridge Archaeological Journal*, 10(2): 261–94.
HIRSCHKIND, C. 2007. *The Ethical Soundscape: Cassette sermons and Islamic counterpublics* (New York: Columbia University Press).
HOFFER, P. C. 2003. *Sensory Worlds in Early America* (Baltimore: Johns Hopkins University Press).
HOWES, D. (ed.) 1991. *The Varieties of Sensory Experience: A sourcebook in the anthropology of the senses* (Toronto: University of Toronto Press).
—— 2003. *Sensual Relations: Engaging the senses in culture and social theory* (Ann Arbor: Michigan University Press).
—— (ed.) 2005. *Empire of the Senses: The sensual culture reader* (Oxford: Berg).
HUME, L. 2007. *Portals: Opening doorways to other realities through the senses* (Oxford: Berg).
INGOLD, T. 2000. 'Stop, look and listen! Vision, hearing and human movement' in T. Ingold, *The Perception of the Environment: Essays in livelihood, dwelling and skill* (London: Routledge), pp. 243–87.
—— 2007. 'Materials against materiality', *Archaeological Dialogues*, 14(1): 1–16.
INSOLL, T. 2004. *Archaeology, Ritual, Religion* (London: Routledge).
—— 2007. *Archaeology: The conceptual challenge* (London: Duckworth).
JAMES, L. 2004. 'Senses and sensibility in Byzantium', *Art History*, 27(4): 522–37.
JONES, A. 2007. *Memory and Material Culture* (Cambridge: Cambridge University Press).
—— and MACGREGOR, G. (eds) 2002. *Colouring the Past: The significance of colour in archaeological research* (Oxford: Berg).
JONES, C. A. (ed.) 2006. *Sensorium: Embodied experience, technology, and contemporary art* (Cambridge, MA: MIT Press).
JÜTTE, R. 2005. *A History of the Senses: From antiquity to cyberspace* (Cambridge: Polity).
KEANE, W. 2008a. 'The evidence of the senses and the materiality of religion' in M. Engelke (ed.), *The Objects of Evidence: Anthropological Approaches to the Production of Knowledge*, Journal of the Royal Anthropological Institute, Special Issue, pp. S110–S127.
—— 2008b. 'On the materiality of religion', *Material Religion*, 4(2): 230–1.
KENNA, M. 2005. 'Why does incense smell religious? Greek Orthodoxy and the anthropology of smell', *Journal of Mediterranean Studies*, 15(1): 51–70.

Konsolaki, E. 2002. 'A Mycenaean sanctuary at Methana' in R. Hägg (ed.), *Peloponnesian Sanctuaries and Cult* (Stockholm: Swedish Institute at Athens), pp. 25–36.

—— 2004. 'Mycenaean religious architecture: The archaeological evidence from Ayios Konstantinos, Methana' in M. Wedde (ed.), *Celebrations: Sanctuaries and vestiges of cult activity* (Bergen: The Norwegian Institute at Athens), pp. 61–94.

Korsmeyer, C. (ed.) 2005. *The Taste Culture Reader* (Oxford: Berg).

Llobera, J. 1994. *The God of Modernity: The development of nationalism in Western Europe* (Oxford: Berg).

MacDougall, D. 2006. *The Corporeal Image: Film, ethnography, and the senses* (Princeton: Princeton University Press).

Meskell, L. and Joyce, R. 2003. *Embodied Lives: Figuring ancient Maya and Egyptian experience* (London: Routledge).

Morris, C., and Peatfield, A. 2002. 'Feeling through the body: Gesture in Cretan Bronze Age religion' in Yannis Hamilakis, M. Pluciennik, and S. Tarlow (eds), *Thinking through the Body: Archaeologies of corporeality* (New York: Kluwer/Plenum), pp. 105–20.

Nelson, R. S. 2000. 'To say and to see: Ekphrasis and vision in Byzantium' in R. S. Nelson (ed.), *Visuality Before and Beyond the Renaissance* (Cambridge: Cambridge University Press), pp. 143–68.

Palaima, T. 2004. 'Sacrificial feasting in the Linear B documents' in J. Wright (ed.), *The Mycenaean Feast*, Hesperia Special Volume 73(2) (Princeton: The American School of Classical Studies) pp. 97–126.

Pentcheva, B. V. 2006. 'The performative icon', *Art Bulletin*, 88(4): 631–55.

Porath, N. 2008. 'Seeing sound: Consciousness and therapeutic acoustics in the inter-sensory shamanic epistemology of the Orang Sakai of Riau (Sumatra)', *Journal of the Royal Anthropological Institute*, 14(3): 647–63.

Price, N. (ed.) 2001. *The Archaeology of Shamanism* (London: Routledge).

Rainbird, P. 2002. 'Making sense of petrogryphs: The sound of rock art' in B. David and M. Wilson (eds), *Inscribed Landscapes: Marking and making place* (Honolulu: University of Hawaii Press), pp. 93–103.

Renfrew, C. 1985. *The Archaeology of Cult: The sanctuary at Phylakopi* (London: The British School at Athens).

—— 2003. *Figuring It Out: The parallel vision of artists and archaeologists* (London: Thames and Hudson).

——, Gosden, C., and DeMarrais, E. (eds) 2004. *Substance, Memory, Display: Archaeology and art* (Cambridge: The MacDonald Institute for Archaeological Research).

Rodaway, P. 1994. *Sensuous Geographies: Body, sense, and place* (London: Routledge).

Seremetakis, N. C. (ed.) 1994. *The Senses Still: Perception and memory as material culture in modernity* (Chicago: Chicago University Press).

Skeates, R. 2005. *Visual Culture and Archaeology: Art and social life in prehistoric south east Italy* (London: Duckworth).

—— 2008. 'Making sense of the Maltese temple period: An archaeology of sensory experience and perception', *Time and Mind*, 1(2): 207–38.

—— 2010. *An Archaeology of the Senses: Prehistoric Malta* (Oxford: Oxford University Press).

Smiles, S. and Moser, S. (eds) 2005. *Envisioning the Past: Archaeology and the image* (Oxford: Blackwell).

Stoller, P. 1989. *The Taste of Ethnographic Things: The senses in anthropology* (Philadelphia: The University of Pennsylvania Press).

—— 1997. *Sensuous Scholarship* (Philadelphia: The University of Pennsylvania Press).

SUTTON, D. 2001. *Remembrance of Repasts: An anthropology of food and memory* (Oxford: Berg).
——2010. 'Food and the senses', *Annual Review of Anthropology*, 39: 209–23.
THOMAS, J. 2004. *Archaeology and Modernity* (London: Routledge).
TILLEY, C. 1994. *A Phenomenology of Landscape* (Oxford: Berg).
——2004. *The Materiality of Stone* (Oxford: Berg).
——2008. *Body and Image* (Walnut Creek: Left Coast Press).
WARE, T. 1963. *The Orthodox Church* (Harmondsworth: Penguin).
WATSON, A. 2001. 'The sounds of transformation: Acoustics, monuments and ritual in the British Neolithic' in Neil Price (ed.), *The Archaeology of Shamanism* (London: Routledge), pp. 178–92.
——and KEATING, D. 1999. 'Architecture and sound: An acoustic analysis of megalithic monuments in prehistoric Britain', *Antiquity*, 73: 325–36.
WOOLGAR, C. M. 2006. *The Senses in Late Medieval England* (New Haven: Yale University Press).

CHAPTER 16

SYNCRETISM AND RELIGIOUS FUSION

TIMOTHY CLACK

1 Introduction

GLOBALIZATION, development, international migration, and the creation and mobilization of innovative expressions of identity have impacted the world in far reaching ways. In consequence of the cultural change, which underpins these processes, conceptualizations such as 'religion', 'ideology', and 'fundamentalism' have come under considerable scrutiny in popular, policy, and intellectual circles. This has precipitated the erosion of scholarly assumptions and implicit understandings concerning terminology, taxonomy, and definition. Nonetheless recomprehension and readjustment within certain disciplinary traditions has been slow and contested (Barzilai 2003; de Vos 2006; Gilman 2006). In archaeology and anthropology, with more nuanced appreciations of cultural articulation and context, this has been less of an issue (see Insoll 2006; Geertz 1977). What is surprising, however, is that the notion of syncretism or religious fusion has received comparatively little attention in either discipline. This despite the fact religion must have been a hugely important element of the human past (Insoll 1999a, 2001), as it is in the present, and most likely will be in the future. At a time when the archaeological discipline has become theoretically and philosophically mindful such a lacuna is cause for concern. It is vital this oversight is both recognized and addressed.

It is envisaged archaeology can positively supplement wider understandings of syncretism and thus corresponding research is of both local interest and global significance. For example, archaeology can augment interpretations by giving temporal depth to anthropological appreciations of experience and identity, in recognizing how the past is recapitulated in the present, and in identifying the materiality of assimilation and contestation. This paper sketches out definitional and conceptual issues relating to syncretism and provides a limited overview of anthropological and archaeological approaches to the theme. The following sections outline two broad theoretical bases for archaeological research into religious fusion, make some comment as to the potential and future for related archaeological investigations, and highlight archaeological and anthropological research currently subsumed within such foundations. The final section covers a theme that cuts through all theoretical approaches to syncretism and that is the correspondence between power and religious fusion. It is suggested that future investigations into this area will augment wider scholarly investigations into identity, structure and agency, colonialism, and ritual and religion.

2 Definition and Background

At this point it would make sense to offer a definition for syncretism but this is difficult. Attempts have been made to distinguish syncretism from other cultural process and the following example from the Oxford English Dictionary is considered an inclusive characterization, as good as any other, but one that still seems somewhat clumsy in its conceptualization of opposition and mixing:

> The attempted union or reconciliation of diverse or opposite tenets or practices, especially in religion. Religious syncretism exhibits blending of two or more religious belief systems into a new system, or the incorporation into a religious tradition of beliefs from unrelated traditions. This can occur for many reasons, and the latter scenario happens quite commonly in areas where multiple religious traditions exist in proximity.

Another problem is the history of the term itself. Syncretism has meant lots of different things at different times. As two anthropologists note in their introduction to the influential work *Syncretism/Anti-Syncretism*, '"syncretism" is a contentious term' (Shaw and Stewart 1994: 1). Nonetheless the academy has been enduringly enchanted with it (Magowan and Gordon 2001: 253). The term is derived from the ancient Greek words *syn* 'with' and *krasis* 'mixture' (Shaw and Stewart 1994: 3) and has been used in Christian theology since the early seventeenth century (van der Veer 1994: 196). Most frequently the syncretistic notion is utilized to describe the mixture of traditional and world religions, especially those brought into contact during the histories of colonialism. On the whole it is not evident that the concept of syncretism denotes anything different from the apparently synonymous terms 'creolization' and 'hybridity' and because of this some have suggested disposing of the category completely (Leopold and Jensen 2004a: 8). What is more, standard attempts to articulate the meanings of these synonymous terms are reliant on a host of other imprecise verbs suggesting a 'coming-together' e.g. assimilate, amalgamate, blend, borrow, combine, fuse, influence, integrate, join, mix, unify, and unite. Perhaps the English lexicon has a surfeit of labels for this process exactly because it is so difficult to conceptualize. The sheer volume of alternatives of course adds to the opaqueness and imprecision.

The use of the term syncretism to denote religious mixing, separate from wider cultural bricolage, has proved advantageous in ethnographic studies (Shaw and Stewart 1994) although one might take issue with the category deployed in this way for being too vague and indefinite. Similar reasoning has precipitated claims that 'bewildered scholars tend to redefine the category each time there is a new subject under study' (Leopold and Jensen 2004a: 7). History of religion confirms that 'every religion is in essence syncretistic—there are no pristine origins or essences' (Leopold and Jenson 2004a: 5). This sentiment links the theme of syncretism with the past and the archaeological enterprise. If the simple fact of syncretism is that it 'is for many reasons a persistent and universal phenomenon in human history' and that 'it cannot but happen, unless people live in entire isolation' (Kraemer 1956: 389), then any appreciation of the past requires comprehension of syncretistic process. Moreover archaeology might be able to provide, through cultural and material comparison, analysis as to why syncretism is a universal constant of the human condition. However, simply to note all religions are mixtures is not that helpful and akin to 'explaining the phenomenon of syncretism with syncretism' (Pakkanen 1996: 86). Thus greater precision is needed concerning the many intricacies of cultural process. Concepts need to be disentangled if attempts to comprehend them are to be successful, otherwise convolution and confusion is inevitable.

The anthropologist Thomas Eriksen has provided some useful distinctions between various categories of cultural mixing (2007: 172). The basis of these definitions should be adopted in the promotion of analytic conformity:

- *Cultural pluralism* describes the relative boundedness of the constituent groups or categories that make up a society.
- *Hybridity* describes individuals or cultural forms that are reflexively mixed, that is syntheses of cultural forms or fragments of diverse origins.
- *Diasporic identity* describes an essentially social category consisting of people whose primary subjective belonging is to another country, region, or group.
- *Transnationalism* describes a social existence attaching individuals and groups not primarily to one particular place but to several or none.
- *Diffusion* describes the flow of substances and meanings between societies, whether it is accompanied by actual social encounters or not.
- *Creolization* describes cultural phenomena that result from the displacement and the ensuing social encounter and mutual influence between/among groups, creating an ongoing dynamic interchange of symbols and practices, eventually leading to new forms with varying degrees of stability.
- *Syncretism* describes the amalgamation of formerly discrete worldviews, cultural meanings, and in particular religion.

Eriksen's scheme provides useful demarcations between distinct forms of cultural mixing. Leopold and Jensen (2004a: 5) ask 'do we locate syncretism in mind, culture or in politics?' This relates to whether syncretism can optimally be understood in terms of psychology and cognition, through linguistics, symbolism and discourse, or through political power and social orchestration. Therefore it is also worthwhile to emphasize the various broad-brush types of syncretism which have been identified. The sheer number and variance demonstrate why an all-encompassing definition is problematic:

- *Unconscious mode of syncretism* describes the overlooked and unrecognized results of natural interaction. This is most apparent between similar religious elements and such change would normally be considered adaptation or assimilation rather than innovation (Droogers 1995).
- *Interpenetrating mode of syncretism* describes the consequences of dominant religious cultures forced upon minority ones (Bastide 1978).
- *Discursive mode of syncretism* describes how innovations do not necessarily result from intercultural contact but they may originate as part of discursive differences in competing factions of mutual religious backgrounds (Pachis 2004).

- *Contextual mode of syncretism* describes the hidden antecedents of religious adaptation—the traces of historical developments (Pakkanen 1996).
- *Performative mode of syncretism* describes the processes of categorization, reclamation, subversion and reiteration linked to religious meaning (Vroom 1989).
- *Cognitive mode of syncretism* describes the 'blending' of symbolic domains based on inference systems. The mind being so composed that it makes particular selections out of the various impressions it is given and is predisposed to make sense of these (Boyer 2001).

Syncretistic orchestrations are diverse in character. Similar to the transformative notions of habitus (Bourdieu 1977) and structuration (Giddens 1986) syncretism should be identified as an essential 'organic' character of culture. Moreover in line with these sociological theories of cultural transformation it is also evident that syncretism denotes both process and the result of process.

3 ANTHROPOLOGY OF SYNCRETISM

Early anthropologists observed syncretism through theological spectacles. In the works of Evans-Pritchard (1940, 1956), for example, it has been suggested that value-laden concepts such as syncretism were allowed to enter the anthropological vocabulary—although he was consciously aware of the distinction between missionary and anthropologist (Stewart 1995: 16). This is hardly surprising for the discipline itself originated as one of many intellectual tools involved in the consolidation and rationalization of imperialistic agendas (Feuchtwang 1973; Thomas 1994; van Bremen and Shimizu 1999). Early anthropologists dealt in the collection, collation, and dissemination of information significant in the successful administration of colonial territories. Thus missionaries were colleagues held in high esteem, particularly respected for their linguistic skills, but pursuing recognizably different agendas. In appreciation of these problems, syncretism has been a term treated with considerable caution. For many anthropologists the term cannot be salvaged and thus alternatives are used, e.g. 'religious adaptation' (Fardon 1990: 48), 'bricolage' (Camaroff 1985: 12) and 'conservatism' (Wilson 1961: 548). A notable exception to this is South American anthropology which has consistently applied the term in a positive manner. In the work of Melville Herskovits, for instance, syncretism was not a form of religious relapse rather a stage for cultural integration that was involved in the creation of nationalistic identities (Apter 1991). This regional distinction concerning anthropological approaches to syncretism (i.e. Africa = negative/South America = positive) could be linked to the political ideologies of New World countries in the post-colonial period that espoused 'melting-pot' strategies of nation-building (see Stewart 1995: 17–20).

Contemporary research has seen syncretism return to the mainstream anthropological lexicon. In this perspective syncretism should not be utilized as a categorization but rather to denote processes and systems of religious synthesis with particular powers, structures, and agencies. Thus one should focus upon the discourses of syncretistic workings (Shaw and Stewart 1994: 7). This focus recognizes that syncretism is distinguished from other forms of cultural change in its sole application to observable religious phenomena

(Magowan and Gordon 2001: 255). As noted, every religion is syncretistic—synthetically incorporating exogenous cultural, material, and ritual elements over time. The only authentic dimension to religions concerns the synchronicity of the syncretistic mix (Mosko 2001: 260). Thus syncretistic agendas seek to inform about modification, assimilation, interpretation, and origination (Mosko 2001: 271; Shaw and Stewart 1994: 128). Moreover the agenda embodies the processes of moral, spiritual, and emotional synchronicity (Magowan 2001: 278; Robbins 2004: 314). In anthropological employment the term is almost exclusively applied within a relativist framework (van der Veer 1994: 197). Within such a cosmopolitan and pluralist scaffold equal theological and ritual perspectives can be modelled. In this sense—rather ironically—instead of countering the effects of syncretistic progress multiculturalism simply redirects further syncretization (Stewart 1995: 20).

Local variations or versions of world religions have often been mechanically labelled as syncretistic (Peel 1968: 140). This is actually an example of anti-syncretism. It is crucial that the category anti-syncretism is accepted for this relates to the processes that precipitate notions of authenticity, purity, and primordiality. These political overtones performatively devalue the syncretistic religion as an inferior caricature of the original. Thus anti-syncretistic discourses imply impurity, weakness (Kiernan 1994: 70), confusion, and disorder (Mosko 2001: 260). Indeed one commentator stresses the socio-political power of the category by commenting that the syncretistic religion 'becomes the bridge over which Africans are brought back to heathenism' (Sundkler 1961: 397). In the anti-syncretistic sense religions are value-laden and variable but always against the notional backdrop of authenticity and purity. The instrumentalist critique of stable primordial traditions (see Droogers and Greenfield 2001; Hobsbawm and Ranger 1983) has shown such entities to be fallacies. Despite this of course all religions are convinced of their own orthodoxy and orthopraxy (Shaw and Stewart 1994: 133). The acceptance of the category anti-syncretism is significant in that it allows syncretism to successfully throw off its pejorative associations with missionary theology.

Although syncretism has regained currency in anthropology there is opposition from certain quarters. Most notable perhaps is the challenge to the association of syncretism with the 'emerging consensus' amongst anthropologists that secularization is not a real force. David Gellner (1997, 2001), for example, has taken this supposed relationship to task by showing secularization has both happened and is happening. Therefore it should be noted that syncretism can be bound up with secularization but it does not have to be. In the past secularization was less pervasive a force so such discussion has less impact on archaeological theory. Nonetheless when it comes to theoretical developments archaeology has long had a profitable, albeit somewhat parasitic, relationship with anthropology and the case of syncretism is no exception.

4 ARCHAEOLOGY OF SYNCRETISM

The archaeology of syncretism is in its infancy and in the main would be considered a sub-theme of research into colonialism, migration, or economic 'trade and exchange' networks. In archaeology, from the diffusionist roots of the discipline (e.g. Childe 1931, 1949) to the multivocality of the present (e.g. Grossman 2005; Habu et al. 2007; Hodder 1992), the meaning of the term has been treated as largely self-evident. This suggests that dominant cultural ideas permeate through porous ethnic and linguistic boundaries and replace obsolete indigenous ones. This 'colonial approach' to syncretism can be easily observed in the classic and still dominant model of Romanization—the imperialist process by which the Roman provinces were 'civilized' (Collingwood 1932; Haverfield 1923). In this view syncretism is erroneously seen in terms of a period of adjustment resulting from the diffusion of religions prior to complete colonization (e.g. Millett 1990; Woolf 1998).

This view has been subject to severe critique on multiple grounds which are significant for all archaeological research into syncretism. First, there is ignorance of the capacity of agents to find their own way of 'becoming Roman' (see Hingley 1995, 1996; see also Dobres and Robb 2000 for wider discussion of agency theory in archaeology). Second, Roman culture was never static; rather it comprised a 'fluid repertoire of styles and practices altered ... by absorbing and adapting influence from the provinces' (Webster 2001: 105; see also Barrett 1988, 1989). Third, knowledge concerning the executors and consequences of the imperial agenda has given primacy to the Roman elite and has ignored how processes would have operated at the lower social levels (Beard et al. 1998). Fourth, Romanization was not, as the name suggests, a one-side process presupposing a linear dissemination of ideas throughout the empire from centre to provincial periphery. Webster (2001) brings these critiques together and demonstrates in an exceptionally well-argued paper, concerning the Romano-Celtic interface, that both the classic account of religious colonialism coordinated by imperial elites (Collingwood 1932) and the account of the nativist school proposing Roman religion was largely ignored (Forcey 1997; Reece 1988) are flawed. What is actually evidenced in this context is a syncretistic fusion of religious world views taking place on all social levels. Thus the significance of bottom-up cultural and religious development is acknowledged (Webster 1997, 2001).

In reaction to the absence of explicated meanings in traditional approaches to religion, there have been significant theoretical and methodological enhancements to recent archaeological appreciations of syncretistic process. These have noted that syncretism has not been studied in appropriate detail previously together with its significance to conceptualizing past identities (Insoll 2004b; Webster 2001). These accounts recognize that syncretistic fusion usually involves the creation of new religious expressions and narratives. There is most definitely a future for the archaeology of syncretism but how might such a project be structured? Historical archaeology—in its widest sense—appears an obvious framework for exploration. This necessitates a concern with the local as well as the global. Further syncretism can be used to model and explain 'intermediate' forms of conversion and indigenization. Clearly the project is entwined within the wider concerns of archaeology of religion and the methodologies utilized therein should be of use. For example, the materiality of innovative syncretistic expressions could be archaeologically visible in certain contexts. In investigating this material the appreciation of 'structuring principles' would be most useful, e.g. architecture, personal possessions, diet, calendrical, and temporal systems (see Insoll 1999b, 2004b).

Prehistory is also a fertile area for investigation. As Larsson (2006: 99) points out in reference to the Scandinavian Early Bronze Age, 'here we are faced with archaeological data that strongly support the idea of religious syncretism, certainly among the warrior and chiefly strata of society'. Moreover indigenous developments and borrowing may well have been rife within other elements of society (see Larsson 1999; Kristiansen and Larsson 2005). It is now well documented that simply assuming religion in prehistoric societies related wholly to economics or social organization, because such evidence is more archaeologically visible, is reckless (Insoll 2004a; cf. Hawkes 1954). Unfortunately one cannot offer a framework or toolkit for the analysis of prehistoric or historic syncretism because, as will be demonstrated in the theoretical discussions below, context is vital. In the main, though, approaches to syncretism can be conveniently divided into cognitive and experiential. It is interesting therefore that such theory has not already penetrated archaeological discourses for we are well aware of the same 'schizophrenic split' characterizing theoretical approaches to the Neolithic and Palaeolithic (see Insoll 2004a).

5 Experiential–Performative Approaches to Syncretism

One must consider the dynamics of syncretism in order to offer both descriptive and explanative analysis. In theology Kamstra (1967) has suggested the comparison of different ongoing hermeneutic activities to comprehend syncretistic processes. This is because '[t]o be human is to be a syncretist' (Kamstra 1970: 23). Comparison is of course no easy task because '[t]he term does not always communicate anything definite, and the meaning that is intended could often be more clearly expressed if another term was used' (Baird 1991: 59). Indeed to some, any characterization of religion or belief system as being syncretistic does little more than admit 'each has a history and can be studied historically' (1991: 63). Both archaeology and history indicate that the interrelationship between ideas and movements was a vital component of the human past despite the many manipulative forces engineered and deployed at various times to disrupt such contact. These disruptive forces incorporate the various social facets of nation-building, communicative media, the human propensity to categorize, and other mechanisms of conformity that engineer 'in-groups' and 'out-groups' e.g. in reference to religion these could include liturgies, codified beliefs, and ritual performance. Syncretism is a significant dimension of human experience.

Articulation of religion through syncretistic performance has been linked to the notion of transposition. Transposition is the variation of significance of any phenomenon, occurring in the dynamic of religions, while its form remains quite unaltered (van der Leeuw 1938). Such understandings influenced the activities of missionaries.

Although the ideology of missions and their complicity with wider colonial projects have been criticized, the insights that religions 'live by being active' or that 'ceaseless agitation is the life movement' (van der Leeuw 1938) are profound. This is because without syncretism religions would quickly become outdated, stagnant, and ultimately obsolete. Religions retain relevancy through fusion with processes and expressions of modernity. This is not to doubt the importance of tradition and heritage to ritual and experience, rather noting that without relevancy to the present the 'potency' of the past would diminish. This notion of experiential adaptation and cyclical relevancy has been linked to hermeneutics. Hendrik Vroom (1989) proposes that the syncretistic incorporation of external elements into a religious tradition is enacted through a hermeneutic process involving a 'reinterpretation of old beliefs and a re-configuration (particularly) of basic insights' (Vroom 1989: 26). Such reinterpretation accommodates profound changes and explains how certain religions potentially lose their original meaning and identity. Integration occurs with other religions but also with components of a secular world. Interestingly this also explains how secular views can gain religious significance and secular objects become sacred through involvement in ritual activity.

In various attempts to enhance earlier phenomenological accounts Michael Pye (1971, 1994) highlights 'ambiguity' as the essence of syncretism. This is because the many descriptions of syncretism give the term its breadth of meaning. He also notes, through the concept of 'transportations', that the notion of syncretistic ambiguity also reveals something about the very nature of religion and humankind. The ambiguity of religion and religious experience has been, quite rightly, stressed in archaeology where sophisticated attempts to understand religion recognize that it includes irrational, intangible, and indefinable elements (Insoll 2004a: 7; 2004c: 1). It is vital to realize that we will never be able to fully comprehend religious fusion. This relates not only to our obvious inability to conceptualize religion itself but also to the difficulties in appreciating the character of fusion. Accordingly, attempts to conceptualize fusion lead to a collision of meanings.

Pye (1971) uses his phenomenological framework to restrict the uses of syncretism to refer to short term religious processes, i.e assimilation, standardization, and dissolution. Further he develops the useful distinction between syncretism 'from within' and 'from without'. In this sense from within is an introverted form of syncretism that highlights elements of religions that continue to exist within a religious system even though they have lost their original meanings. The meaningfulness of these elements continues but the meaning has been rearticulated (1971: 85–90). This in part relates to performativity— religions being performed through categories, identities, and rituals (see Butler 1993). Syncretistic alienation between elements and structures results in parody and subversion. In recognizing syncretism 'from within', recognition of syncretism 'from without' is facilitated. One is able to acknowledge 'parallel hermeneutic activity in quite diverse traditions' because 'in any religion considered dynamically, syncretisms may be seen to be in the process of being unmasked and broken off while at the same time new ones are being built up again' (Pye 1971: 87).

Syncretism 'from without' is extrovert and aspires to penetrate existing belief systems— missionary activity being an obvious example. The study of the dynamics of religious fusion involves reference to the hermeneutical activities of agents operating with varying degrees of self-reflexivity. The advantage of this approach is that syncretism is seen as a mode of religious production rather than deviation from religious authenticity. As Leopold and Jensen (2004b: 25) point out, in such a scheme emphasis is placed on 'the dynamic processes between religious systems, regarding them as fluid, negotiable traditions rather than fixed entities'. This conceptualization is not without problems. Although offering a more rigid structure for categorizing syncretism it excludes other religious manifestations—especially longer-term ones—which do not fit within the categorical matrix. Perhaps in recognition of this Rudolf (1992) concerns himself with the description of what he considers to be three universal conditions for syncretism: *encounter, contact,* and *confrontation*. In this scheme syncretism is grounded in history and attempts to understand the present involve analysis of the past. This is interesting from an archaeological standpoint because it could pave the way for inter/disciplinary involvement in attempts to comprehend the present and future as well as the past. It has long been recognized that the present can assist in the comprehension of the past. As Ricoeur (1985: 17; in Insoll 2004a: 129) notes, myth and ritual provide the means to 'recapitulate the past in the present'.

Baird (1991) prefers a phenomenological definition of syncretism that stresses the intentionality of experience. He proposes that a distinction should be made between a syncretism that is reflective and conscious as opposed to one that is simply spontaneous. In this scheme syncretistic description is reserved for cases where 'two conflicting ideas or practices are brought together and are retained without the benefit of consistency' (ibid.: 63). This configuration demonstrates various elements can be brought together without any being offered primacy. In contrast 'reconception' or 'synthesis' occurs when various elements are harmonized, even if they previously appeared to be in conflict, through modification. Logic is used to demonstrate that truly conflicting concepts cannot be united and that it is contradictory to characterize such modification as harmonization (1991: 64; see also Hocking 1956; Mackintosh 1956). The problem here is not the logic of classifications which are sound, but that the spontaneity of syncretistic expression and the consequential unconscious experiential changes arguably offer more insight into the phenomenon of syncretism. One gets the sense that in teasing apart intentional syncretism from unconscious reconception, the ethereal elements of syncretistic experience have been cut away. While obviously acknowledging the utility of logic in the analyses of philosophy, and indeed the whole academic enterprise, certain elements of the human condition can be illogical or irrational and thus philosophically absurd. Indeed there is an entire branch within philosophy of religion dedicated to this area (see Kenny 1983; Mawson 2005; Plantinga and Wolterstorff 1983).

Applications of phenomenological methods in archaeology have been in vogue for over a decade (e.g. Tilley 1994; Thomas 1996). The success of these is not to be debated here having been covered at length elsewhere (see Brück 2005; Insoll 2004a for review). It does need to be mentioned, however, that all experiential–performative approaches to syncretism are likely to be plagued by similar limitations. These include the apparent colonization of past worlds with the experiences of the present, the fact that justice can never be done to the diversity of human experience, the primacy afforded to visual perception, and the exclusion of routine practice in phenomenological accounts.

6 POWER AND SYNCRETISM

The theme of power has received much archaeological attention particularly concerning its relation to structure and agency (see Milledge Nelson 1997; Miller and Tilley 1984; Steele and Shennan 1995). Power is a vital dynamic of syncretism. Foucault (1972a, 1972b) influentially demonstrated how power and knowledge are inextricably related. At the same time syncretism is inextricably linked to social or hegemonic paradigms. Andrew Apter (1991), using cultural hermeneutics, demonstrated that syncretism is discursive, that it can be a force of both hegemonic and counter-hegemonic strategy, and that it is always elemental in cultural processes of revision and resistance. Thus rituals are optimally considered as rallying points rather than permanent distinctive features. Rituals, despite regulations and portrayals of conformity, are performed in a range of constantly evolving forms. These are embodied, interpreted, and understood in diverse ways. According to Benavides (1995) syncretism relates to power through the psychological compulsion of indigenous groups to acquire prestigious elements from colonial enterprises. This adoption results in the formation of pidgin religious expressions but unlike their linguistic counterparts these are not necessarily short-lived, temporary cultural formations. Such formations also relate to power through an individual's self-conscious identification with a religious community and through the mastery of a symbolic code. There is a hierarchy to the navigation of ritual and symbolic order:

> The equivalent of Creoles can be found in those situations in which an accommodation of sorts has been reached and a new system of meanings has been born, related but not identical to the mother group. It is ... not justified to assume that the grammatical structure of Creoles (or the symbolism of new religious formations) is intrinsically less complex than the source language, or less able to make communication possible: the only criteria that can be used to place Creoles and source languages in a hierarchy depend upon the social and ultimately political prestige and power of the source language. [Benavides 2002: 492]

Syncretism is different from but related to creolization. The notions of creolization as deployed in linguistics (e.g. Blevins 1995; Lambropoulos 2001) might offer enhancement to archaeologies of religious fusion. Language, it can be argued, is a microcosm for wider cultural structures. On the one hand, of course, it can be suggested that such theorization 'overplays' the significance of language in understanding culture. On the other hand linguistic concepts and categories are interpretive tools with which we make the worlds we inhabit. Culture can be understood as a technology deployed in interpreting 'the-world' within which one is a 'being-in'.

The use of linguistic insights has been common in studies of creolization (Stewart 2007) and these have shown creolization is fundamentally about power. For example, the model of the creole continuum, used in linguistics to describe intermediate languages in various countries, has been used to make sense of the apparent continua of cultural repertoires in world societies and also to explain the effects of colonialism. In the linguistic model intermediate language forms (mesolects) originate from a 'standard' form (acrolect) and evolve into a fully creole form (basilect). Anthropologists (e.g. Eriksen 2007; Hannerz 1987) have suggested that urban elites and other migratory sections of societies tend to travel and absorb globally circulating cultural forms. '[T]his world of movement and mixture', suggests Hannerz (1987: 551), 'is a world in creolization'. This has led to assertions that the processes of globalization and urbanization have resulted in the entities once called 'cultures' becoming 'creolized subcultures' (Hannerz 1992: 218). Perhaps such creolization should not only be considered a phenomenon of the present but also of the past. However, there are problems with such an approach and these will be outlined. The main issue concerns the notion of true standard forms or acrolects and whether such things actually exist. Creolization is also highly political. In Mauritian society, for example, there is considerable tension between the forces of cultural fusion and multiculturalism (Eriksen 1997). 'Let the colours of the rainbow remain distinctive', said the Archbishop of Mascareignes in the early 1990s, 'so that it can be beautiful'. Indeed politicians and citizens alike believe that concord is maintained on the crowded, culturally heterogeneous island only because there is a 'precarious numerical equilibrium and functioning politics of compromise between the ethnic groups' (Eriksen 2007: 173).

It has been suggested that the colonial enterprise, and even the Caribbean experience in particular, exercises copyright over the meaning of creolization (Vale de Almeida 2004). This is not the dominant view as the term, like syncretism, has escaped its original context and moved beyond its original meaning (see Stewart 2007). Semiotic approaches to both creolization and syncretism have also emphasized power in the production of meaning. There are layers of power structures within societies that impose different modes of religious constructions. Boundaries around religions, and for that matter cultures and languages, do not simply relate to the exercise of power but mutual intelligibility (Benavides 2002). Further, in the essay 'Syncretism, Power, Play', Droogers (1995) highlights dynamics of meaning generation based on the dialectics between actors and symbols. According to this approach meanings are produced through metaphors. A triangle of signification exists through which syncretistic meaning is found (Figure 16.1). Hence in satisfying the human predilection for clarification and classification syncretism operates through an inventory of meanings. These are selectively adopted on the basis of intuitive intelligibility usually grounded in the orchestration of power structures.

Essentially interaction between multiple religions always involves the articulation of dominance, legitimacy, and sanction (Benavides 1995). Selection acknowledges the repertoire of religious elements that were not adopted and thus allows power to be fully implicated in patterns of adoption. Acknowledging this precipitates the realization that syncretistic religious formations do not have 'surfaces' or 'cores' but rather 'elements' that are the outcome of selection. Syncretistic approaches must overcome these inside–outside, giving–receiving dualisms by emphasizing mutual relations. Webster (1997: 330) points out that archaeology has a penchant for reiterating similar dichotomies, e.g. Christian–pagan and civilized–barbarian. These long-lived 'Othering' strategies, evident throughout

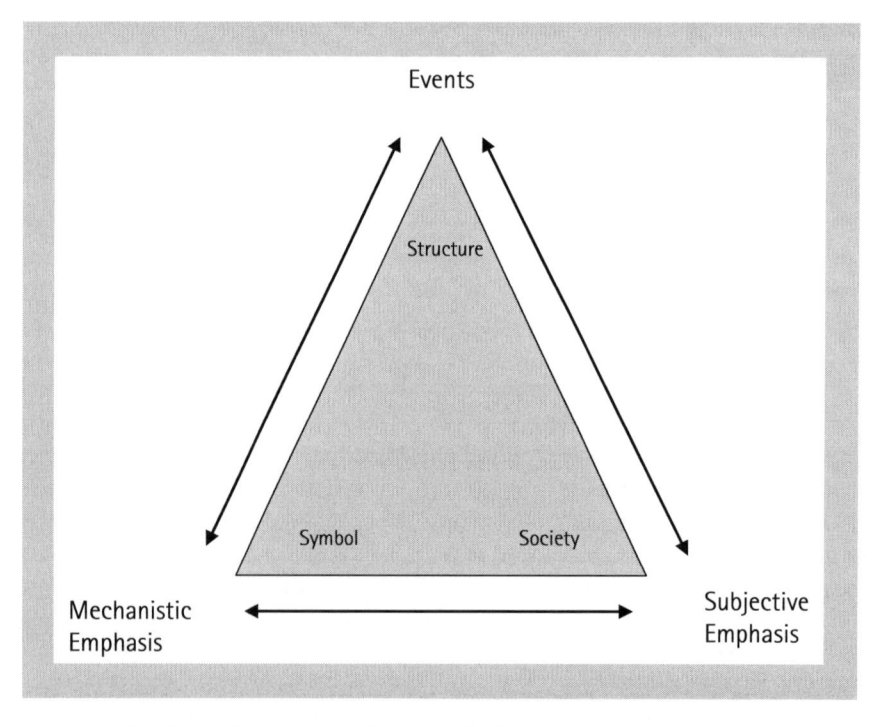

FIGURE 16.1 Triangle of signification through which syncretistic meanings are generated.

nineteenth-century colonialism, need to be excised. As well as manipulating syncretistic process, however, power is both challenged and negotiated by syncretism. An obvious example to cite here are societies dominated by world religions such as Christianity and Islam. Despite power structures deployed in processes of conversion, for example regulatory texts and the codification of belief, there are always apparent parallel processes involving the indigenization of ideology. These processes make things relevant according to local order and cultural attunements.

7 Conclusion

In theorizing syncretism only one thing can be claimed for certain—that the concept is at once fascinating, confusing, and intellectually fertile. The term has a complex history but this should not detract from its future application. Syncretism offers the means to interpret coalescing religious ideologies, practices, and beliefs. As an interpretive aid it offers significant scope to better understand a range of time periods and geographical locations, for religions have always been dynamic and permeable. A final point to note is that religious syncretism is seldom followed by social syncretism (Bastide 1978) so it could not be utilized as an instrument of cosmopolitan development. This probably relates to the fact the mind organizes information according to inferences and other interpretive mechanisms (see Boyer 2001). This mental predisposition makes certain religious elements more intuitive, thus they permeate through cultural boundaries and survive syncretistic assimilations.

Acknowledgements

I would like to thank Chris Gosden, Renee Hirschon, Timothy Mawson, and the editor for discussion of several of the themes in this paper.

Suggested Reading

Antes, P., Geertz, A. W. and Warne, R. (eds) 2005. *New Approaches to the Study of Religion* (New York: de Gruyter).
Apter, A. 2002. 'On African origins: Creolization and connaissance in Haitian vodou', *American Ethnologist*, 29(2): 233–61.
Benavides, G. 2002. 'Power, intelligibility and the boundaries of religions', *Historical Reflections/Réflexions Historiques*, 27(3): 481–98.
Black, L. T. 1994. 'Religious syncretism as cultural dynamic' in T. Irimoto and T. Yamada (eds), *Circumpolar Religion and Anthropology: An anthropology of the north* (Tokyo: University of Tokyo Press), pp. 221–36.

Böhlig, A. 1975. 'Der Synkretismus des Mani' in A. Dietrich (ed.), *Synkretismus im persisch-syrischen Kulturgebiet* (Göttingen: Vanderhoeck and Ruprecht), pp. 144–69.

Brook, T. 1993. 'Rethinking syncretism: The unity of the three teachings and their joint worship in late-imperial China', *Journal of Chinese Religions*, 21: 13–44.

Carlson, J. 1992. 'Syncretistic religiosity: The significance of this tautology', *Journal of Ecumenical Studies*, 29(1): 24–34.

Colpe, C. 1977. 'Syncretism and secularisation: Complementary and antithetical trends in new religious movements', *History of Religions*, 17: 158–76.

Droge, A. J. 2001. 'Retrofitting/Retiring "Syncretism"', *Historical Reflections/Réflexions Historiques*, 27(3): 375–88.

Droogers, A. and Greenfield, S. M. (eds) 2001. *Reinventing Religions: Syncretism and transformation in Africa and the Americas* (Lanham, MD: Rowman and Littlefield).

Geertz, A. W. 1997. 'From stone tools to flying saucers: Tradition and invention in Hopi prophecy' in M. Mauzé (ed.), *Past Is Present: Some uses of tradition in native societies* (Lanham, NY: University Press of America), pp. 175–94.

Gort, J. D., Vroom, H. M., Fernhout, R., and Wessels, A. (eds) 1989. *Dialogue and Syncretism: An interdisciplinary approach* (Amsterdam: Rodopi).

Hsü, E. 1995. 'The manikin in man: Culture crossing and creativity' in G. Aijmer (ed.), *Syncretism and the Commerce of Symbols* (Göteborg: Institute for Advanced Studies in Social Anthropology), pp. 156–204.

Morrison, K. 1990. 'Baptism and alliance: The symbolic mediations of religious syncretism', *Ethnohistory*, 37: 416–37

Parkin, D. 1970. 'Politics of ritual syncretism: Islam among the non-Muslim Giriama of Kenya', *Africa*, 45: 217–33.

Seiwert, H. 1996. 'What is new with religious contact today?' in I. Doležalová, B. Horyna, and D. Papousek (eds), *Religions in Contact* (Brno: CSSR).

References

Apter, A. 1991. 'Herskovits's heritage: Rethinking syncretism in the African diaspora', *Diaspora: Journal of Transnational Studies*, 1(3): 235–60.

Baird, R. 1991. 'Syncretism and the history of religions' in R. Baird (ed.), *Essays in the History of Religion* (New York: Peter Lang), pp. 59–71.

Barrett, J. 1988. 'Fields of discourse: Reconstituting a social archaeology', *Critique of Anthropology*, 7(3): 5–16.

—— 1989. 'Render Unto Caesar' in J. Barrett, A. P. Fitzpatrick, and L. Macinnes (eds), *Barbarians and Romans in North-West Europe* (Oxford: BAR), pp. 231–41.

Barzilai, G. 2003. *Communities and Law: Politics and cultures of legal identities* (Ann Arbor, MI: University of Michigan Press).

Bastide, R. 1978. 'Problems of religious syncretism' in H. Sebba (ed.), *The African Religions of Brazil: Towards a sociology of the interpenetration of civilizations* (Baltimore, MD: Johns Hopkins University Press).

Beard, M., North, J. and Price, S. 1998. *Religions of Rome*, I: *A History* (Cambridge: Cambridge University Press).

BENAVIDES, G. 1995. 'Syncretism and legitimacy in Latin American religion' in A. M. Stevens-Arroyo and A. I. Perez y Mena (eds), *Enigmatic Powers: Syncretism with African and indigenous peoples' religions among Latinos* (New York: Bildner Center for Western Hemisphere Studies), pp. 19-46.

——2002. 'Power, intelligibility and the boundaries of religions', *Historical Reflections/ Réflexions Historiques*, 27(3): 481-98.

BLEVINS, J. P. 1995. 'Syncretism and paradigmatic opposition', *Linguistics and Philosophy*, 18: 113-52.

BOURDIEU, P. 1977. *Outline of a Theory of Practice* (Cambridge: Cambridge University Press).

BOYER, P. 1990. *Tradition as Truth and Communication* (Cambridge: Cambridge University Press).

——2001. *Religion Explained: The evolutionary origins of religious thought* (New York: Basic Books).

BREMEN, J. VAN and SHIMIZU, A. (eds) 1999. *Anthropology and Colonialism in Asia and Oceania* (London: Curzon Press).

BRÜCK, J. 2005. 'Experiencing the past? The development of a phenomenological archaeology in British prehistory', *Archaeological Dialogues*, 12(1): 45-72.

BUTLER, J. 1993. *Bodies That Matter: On the discursive limits of 'sex'* (London: Routledge).

CAMAROFF, J. 1985. *Body of Power, Spirit of Resistance: The culture and history of a South African People* (Chicago: University of Chicago Press).

CHILDE, V. G. 1931. *The Forest Cultures of Northern Europe: A study in evolution and diffusion* (Bradford: Moonraker).

——1949. *Social Worlds of Knowledge* (London: Oxford University Press).

COLLINGWOOD, R. G. 1932. *Roman Britain* (Oxford: Clarendon).

DOBRES, M. and ROBB, J. (eds) 2000. *Agency in Archaeology* (London: Routledge).

DROOGERS, A. 1995. 'Syncretism, power, play' in G. Aijmer (ed.), *Syncretism and the Commerce of Symbols* (Göteborg: Institute for Advanced Studies in Social Anthropology), pp. 38-59.

——and GREENFIELD, S. M. 2001. 'Recovering and reconstructing syncretism' in S. M. Greenfield and A. Droogers (eds), *Reinventing Religions: Syncretism and transformation in Africa and the Americas* (Lanham: Rowman and Littlefield), pp. 21-42.

ERIKSEN, T. H. 1997. 'Multiculturalism, individualism and human rights: Romanticism, the Enlightenment and lessons from Mauritius' in R. Wilson (ed.), *Human Rights: Culture and context* (London: Pluto).

——2007. 'Creolization in anthropological theory in Mauritius' in C. Stewart (ed.), *Creolization: History, ethnography, theory* (Walnut Creek, CA: Left Coast Press), pp. 153-76.

EVANS-PRITCHARD, E. E. 1940. *The Nuer: A description of the modes of livelihood and the political institutions of a Nilotic people* (Oxford: Clarendon Press).

——1956. *Nuer Religion* (Oxford: Clarendon Press).

FARDON, R. 1990. *Localizing Strategies: Regional traditions of ethnographic writing* (Edinburgh: Scottish Academic Press).

FEUCHTWANG, S. 1973. 'The discipline and its sponsors' in T. Asad (ed.), *Anthropology and the Colonial Encounter* (London: Ithaca Press), pp. 35-46.

FORCEY, C. 1997. 'Technologies of power in Roman Britain' in K. Meadows, C. Lemke, and J. Heron (eds), *TRAC 1996: Proceedings of the Sixth Annual Theoretical Roman Archaeology Conference*. Oxford: Oxbow, pp. 15-21.

FOUCAULT, M. 1972a. *The Archaeology of Knowledge* (New York: Harper).

FOUCAULT, M. 1972b. *Discipline and Punishment: The birth of the prison* (New York: Pantheon).
GEERTZ, C. 1977. *The Interpretation of Cultures* (New York: Basic Books).
GELLNER, D. 1997. 'For syncretism: The position of Buddhism in Nepal and Japan compared', *Social Anthropology* 5(3): 277–91.
—— 2001. 'Studying secularisation, practicing secularisation: Anthropological imperatives', *Social Anthropology*, 9(3): 337–40.
GIDDENS, A. 1986. *The Constitution of Society: Outline of a theory of structuration* (Cambridge: Polity).
GILMAN, N. 2006. 'The prophet of post-Fordism' in N. Lichtenstein (ed.), *American Capitalism: Social thought and political economy in the twentieth century* (New York: University of Pennsylvania Press), pp. 109–32.
GREENFIELD. S. M. and DROOGERS, A. (eds) 2001. *Reinventing Religious: Syncretism and transformation in Africa and the Americas* (Lanhan: Rowman & Littlefield).
GROSSMAN, H. E. 2005. 'Syncretism made concrete' in D. Deliyannis and J. Emerick (eds), *Archaeology in Architecture: Essays in honor of Cecil Striker* (Mainz: Ph. von Zabern), pp. 82–104.
HABU, J., FAWCETT, C., and MATSUNGA, J. M. (eds) 2007. *Evaluating Multiple Narratives: Beyond nationalist, colonialist, imperialist archaeologies* (New York: Springer).
HANNERZ, U. 1987. 'The world in creolisation', *Africa*, 57: 546–59.
—— 1992. *Cultural Complexity: Studies in the social organization of meaning* (Ithaca, NY: Columbia University Press).
HAVERFIELD, F. 1923. *The Romanization of Roman Britain* (Oxford: Clarendon Press).
HAWKES, C. 1954. 'Archaeological theory and method: Some suggestions from the Old World', *American Anthropologist*, 56: 155–68.
HINGLEY, R. 1995. 'Britannia, Origin Myths and the British Empire' in S. Cottam, D. Dungworth, S. Scott, and J. Taylor (eds), *TRAC 1994: Proceedings of the Fourth Annual Theoretical Roman Archaeology Conference* (Oxford: Oxbow), pp. 11–23.
—— 1996. 'The legacy of Rome: The rise, decline and fall of the theory of Romanization' in J. Webster and N. Cooper (eds), *Roman Imperialism: Post-colonial perspectives* (Leicester: Leicester University Press), pp. 35–48.
HOBSBAWM, E. and RANGER, T. 1983. *The Invention of Tradition* (Cambridge: Cambridge University Press).
HOCKING, W. E. 1956. *The Coming of World Civilization* (London: Harper).
HODDER, I. 1992. *Theory and Practice in Archaeology* (London: Routledge).
INSOLL, T. 1999a. *Case Studies in Archaeology and World Religion* (Oxford: BAR).
—— 1999b. *Archaeology of Islam* (Oxford: Blackwell).
—— 2001. *The Archaeology of World Religion* (London: Routledge).
—— 2004a. *Archaeology, Ritual, Religion* (London: Routledge).
—— 2004b. 'Syncretism, time and identity: Islamic archaeology in West Africa' in D. Whitcomb (ed.), *Changing Social Identity with the Spread of Islam: Archaeological perspectives* (Chicago: Oriental Institute), pp. 89–101.
—— 2004c. 'Are archaeologists afraid of gods? Some thoughts on archaeology and religion' in T. Insoll (ed.), *Belief in the Past: The proceedings of the 2002 Manchester Conference on Archaeology and Religion* (Oxford: Archaeopress), pp. 1–6.
—— (ed.) 2007. *The Archaeology of Identities: A reader* (London: Routledge).
KAMSTRA, J. H. 1967. *Encounter or Syncretism: The initial growth of Japanese Buddhism* (Leiden: Brill).

—— 1970. *Synkretisme op de Grens tussen Theologie en Godsdienstfenomenologie* (Leiden: Brill).

KENNY, A. 1983. *Faith and Reason* (Irvington, NY: Columbia University Press).

KIERNAN, J. 1994. 'Variations on a Christian theme: the healing synthesis of Zulu Zionism', in C. Stewart and R. Shaw (eds), *Syncretism/Anti-Syncretism: the politics of religious synthesis* (London: Routledge), pp. 69–84.

KRAEMER, H. 1956. *Religion and the Christian Faith* (Philadelphia: Westminster Press).

KRISTIANSEN, K. and LARSSON, T. B. 2005. *The Rise of Bronze Age Society: travels, transmissions and transformations* (Cambridge: Cambridge University Press).

LAMBROPOULOS, V. 2001. 'Syncretism as mixture and method', *Journal of Modern Greek Studies*, 19: 221–35.

LARSSON, T. B. 1999. 'The transmission of elite ideology: Europe and the Near East in the second millennium BC' in J. Goldhahn (ed.), *Rock Art as Social Representations* (Oxford: BAR), pp. 49–64.

—— 2006. 'Review of Timothy Insoll: Archaeology, ritual, religion', *Norwegian Archaeological Review*, 39(1): 98–9.

LEEUW, G. VAN DER 1938. 'The dynamics of religion, syncretism, mission' in J. E. Turner (ed.), *Religion in Essence and Manifestation: A study in phenomenology* (Princeton, NJ: Princeton University Press), pp. 609–12.

LEOPOLD, A. M. and JENSEN, J. S. 2004a. 'General introduction' in A. M. Leopold and J. S. Jensen (eds), *Syncretism in Religion: A reader* (London: Equinox), pp. 1–8.

—— —— 2004b. 'Introduction to Part II' in A. M. Leopold and J. S. Jensen (eds), *Syncretism in Religion: A reader* (London: Equinox), pp. 14–28.

MACKINTOSH, H. R. 1956. *Types of Modern Theology* (London: Nisbet and Co).

MAGOWAN, E. 2001. 'Syncretism or synchronicity? Remapping the Yolngu feel of place', *Australian Journal of Anthropology*, 12(3): 275–90.

—— and GORDON, J. 2001. 'Introduction', *Australian Journal of Anthropology*, 12(3): 253–8.

MAWSON, T. 2005. *Belief in God* (Oxford: Oxford University Press).

MILLEDGE NELSON, S. 1997. *Gender in Archaeology: Analyzing power and prestige* (Westport, CA: AltaMira Press).

MILLER, D. and TILLEY, C. (eds) 1984. *Ideology, Power and Prehistory* (Cambridge: Cambridge University Press).

MILLETT, M. 1990. *The Romanization of Britain: An Essay in Archaeological Interpretation* (Cambridge: Cambridge University Press).

MOSKO, M. 2001. 'Syncretistic persons: Sociality, agency and personhood in recent charismatic ritual practices among the North Mekeo (PNG)', *Australian Journal of Anthropology*, 12(3): 259–74.

PACHIS, P. 2004. 'Religious tendencies in Greece at the dawn of the 21st century: An approach to contemporary Greek reality' in A. M. Leopold and J. S. Jensen (eds), *Syncretism in Religion: A reader* (London: Equinox), pp. 348–61.

PAKKANEN, P. 1996. 'Definitions: Re-evaluation of concepts' in P. Pakkanen (ed.), *Interpreting Early Hellenistic Religion: A study based on the mystery cult of Demeter and the cult of Isis* (Athens: Layias and Souvatzidakis), pp. 85–100.

PEEL, J. D. 1968. 'Syncretism and religious change', *Comparative Studies in Society and History*, 10: 121–41.

PLANTINGA, A. and WOLTERSTORFF, N. (eds) 1983. *Faith and Rationality* (Notre Dame, IN: University of Notre Dame Press).

PYE, M. 1971. 'Syncretism and ambiguity', *NUMEN*, 18: 83–93.
——1994. 'Syncretism versus synthesis', *Method & Theory in the Study of Religion*, 6: 217–29.
REECE, R. 1988. *My Roman Britain* (Cirencester: Cotswold Studies).
RICOEUR, P. 1985. 'The History of Religions and the Phenomenology of Time Consciousness' in J. Kitagawa (ed.), *The History of Religions: Retrospect and prospect* (London: Collier Macmillan), pp. 13–30.
ROBBINS, J. 2004. *Becoming Sinners: Christianity and moral torment in a Papua New Guinea society* (Berkeley, CA: University of California Press).
RUDOLF, K. 1992. 'Syncretism: From theological invective to a concept in the study of religion' in D. Warburton (ed.), *Geschichte und Probleme der Religionswissenschaft* (Lieden: Brill), pp. 193–213.
SHAW, R. and STEWART, C. 1994. 'Introduction: Problematizing syncretism' in C. Stewart and R. Shaw (eds), *Syncretism/Anti-Syncretism: The politics of religious synthesis* (London: Routledge), pp. 1–26.
STEELE, J. and SHENNAN, S. (eds) 1995. *Archaeology of Human Ancestry: Power, Sex and Tradition* (London: Routledge).
STEWART, C. 1995. 'Relocating Syncretism in Social Science Discourse' in G. Aijmer (ed.), *Syncretism and the Commerce of Symbols* (Göteborg: Institute for Advanced Studies in Anthropology), pp. 13–37.
——1999. 'Syncretism and its synonyms: Reflections on cultural mixture', *Diacritics*, 29(3): 40–62.
——2007. 'Creolization: History, ethnography, theory' in C. Stewart (ed.), *Creolization: History, ethnography, theory* (Walnut Creek, CA: Left Coast Press), pp. 1–25.
SUNDKLER, B. G. M. 1961. *Bantu Prophets in South Africa* (London: Oxford University Press for the International African Institute).
THOMAS, J. 1996. *Time, Culture and Identity: An interpretive archaeology* (London: Routledge).
THOMAS, N. 1994. *Colonialism's Culture: Anthropology, travel and government* (London: Polity).
TILLEY, C. 1994. *A Phenomenology of Landscape: Places, paths and monuments* (Oxford: Berg).
VALE DE ALMEIDA, M. 2004. *An Earth Colored Sea: 'Race', culture and the politics of identity in the post-colonial Portuguese-speaking world* (Oxford: Berghahn).
VEER, P. VAN DER. 1994. 'Syncretism, multiculturalism and the discourse of tolerance', in C. Stewart and R. Shaw (eds), *Syncretism/Anti-syncretism: the politics of religious synthesis* (London: Routledge), pp. 196–211.
VOS, G. A., DE 2006. 'Ethnic pluralism: Conflict and accommodation' in L. Romanucci-Ross, G. A. de Vos, and T. Tsunda (eds), *Ethnic Identity* (Westport, CA: AltaMira), pp. 1–32.
VROOM, H. M. 1989. 'Syncretism and dialogue: A philosophical analysis' in J. D. Gort, H. M. Vroom, R. Fernhout, and B. Eerdmans (eds), *Dialogue and Syncretism: An interdisciplinary approach* (Grand Rapids, MI: Eerdmans), pp. 26–35.
WEBSTER, J. 1997. 'Necessary comparisons: A post-colonial approach to religious syncretism in the Roman provinces', *World Archaeology*, 28(3): 324–38.
——2001. 'Creolizing the Roman provinces', *American Journal of Archaeology*, 105: 209–25.
WILSON, M. 1961. *Reaction to Conquest* (London: Oxford University Press).
WOOLF, G. 1998. *Becoming Roman: the origins of provincial Roman civilization in Gaul* (Cambridge: Cambridge University Press).

CHAPTER 17

TECHNOLOGY

OLIVIER P. GOSSELAIN

1 INTRODUCTION

POPULAR conceptions of 'technology' tend to associate that term with activities governed by science and involving important 'hardware' content; i.e., tools, devices, machines. Conversely, 'technique' would pertain to more mundane activities; built upon non-reflexive routines and implying more direct forms of engagements with materials. This view has been severely challenged for the last three decades. As stressed by Haudricourt (1964) and Sigaut (1987), the 'technology' label should more appropriately designate the 'science of techniques', which is above all 'a science of human activities' (Haudricourt 1964: 28). In this chapter, I will accordingly use the term 'technique' and 'technical practice' in reference to any action upon matter, hereby conceived as a dynamic combination of both tangible (actors, actions, instruments, materials, energy...) and intangible (knowledge, representations) components.

That being said, associating techniques with concepts such as 'religion' and 'rituals' may sound a bit unsettling, especially for a Western audience. Granted, we may all think of one or several examples of such association. The Christian cross, for instance, is the main component of a Roman killing technique used together to materialize a religious affiliation and what believers deem to be the core of the Christ's message. Similarly, the design of the tyre-less tractor used in modern Amish communities has clearly been influenced by religious considerations (Morel 2002: 64–6). Apart from these obvious examples, however, a more general consensus is that techniques are essentially utilitarian in nature: they aim at fulfilling basic needs, in the most efficient and rational way possible. Such a 'standard view' (Pfaffenberger 1992) relegates social and symbolic preoccupations to the back of a 'technical core' supposedly governed by physical and functional constraints. Religious aspects, if any, would simply be adjunct to a set of practices and implements that develop essentially outside the cultural field.

This view is not only at odds with the way in which non-Western societies conceive and engage in technical practice (see below), but also the way in which, from antiquity to modern times, techniques and technical actors used to be considered in Western societies. As notably illustrated by Eliade (1962; but see also Gille 1980; Sigaut 1987), inventors and civilizing heroes—purveyors of techniques—have often been associated with magicians or portrayed as tricksters, who relied on ruse and artifices in the conduct of technical activities. In fact, up to the early seventeenth century, science, technique, and magic developed in close association (Hansen 1986, cited in Sigaut 1987: 17). Things started to change dramatically with the scientific revolution of the seventeenth and eighteenth centuries. On the one hand, techniques were considered from a purely utilitarian and positivist point of view; on the other hand, scholars began to associate them with brainless routine, a segment of human practices less likely than others to give access to cultural values, knowledge, and identities (Sigaut 1987). Having started in Classical Greece, but clashed for centuries with the realities of technical practice (Svenbro 2006), the laicization of techniques was now complete, albeit in a way that subordinated them to a new scientific ideology and mainly provided an impoverished grid of interpretation.

Starting with Mauss (1979 [1934]), social scientists have since then attempted sporadically to break the ideological covering under which techniques were buried. It is only by the late 1970s, however, that a new conception has started to be imposed as a viable alternative, thanks to a multiplication of anthropological, archaeological, and sociological case studies. What follows is a short overview of the way in which social sciences reinvested the technical domain and renewed it with a more culturally oriented conception of techniques that included its religious and ritual dimensions.

2 Technological Style and *Chaîne Opératoire*

For archaeologists on both sides of the Atlantic, 1977 was the year two seminal papers on style came out, that would respectively mark the end and the beginning of an era. The first was by Martin Wobst. It envisioned style as residing in the parts of an artefact relating to its participation in processes of information exchange. In other words, only visible, non-functional, and non-technical parts of an artefact were deemed 'stylistic' and said to inform us about the deliberate marking of social boundaries. Although Wobst did not address the issue of technology, his definition of style may be seen as the epitome of a dualist conception of human practices that clearly separates technique from culture. Widely discussed and criticized during the following decade, it has since been largely abandoned (see David and Kramer 2001: 177–83; Martinelli 2005). The second publication was by Heather Lechtman, a scientist with experience in physics and anthropology, and training in metallography. She viewed style as liable to reside in any part of an artefact, since it corresponded to the material expression of cultural patterning, to which members of a cultural community remained largely oblivious. Style thus reflected pre-existing cultural values rather than the active signalling of identities. Lechtman's decisive contribution came with the concept of 'technological style', defined as a package of 'the many elements that make up technological activities—for example, by technical modes of operation, attitudes toward materials, some specific organization of labor, ritual observances—elements which are unified non randomly in a complex of formal relationships' (1977: 6; see also Lechtman 1984). In Lechtman's view, technology was thus not only intrinsically stylistic; it was also 'culture' in the full sense of the term—an idea quite at odds with the prevailing processualist conceptions of the time (see discussions in Dobres 2000; Childs 1991; Childs and Killick 1993).

Here, I will briefly evoke the historical and anthropological background of her study, for it illustrates how religious beliefs may combine with technical practices, and how we may grasp this interrelation from material analysis. As with many other archaeologists interested in the development of Andean metallurgy, Lechtman was struck by the very late inception of the bronze technique in the area. During two millennia, Andean metallurgists produced artefacts made from metal alloys—copper with a small proportion of gold and silver—that all had a gilded or silvered appearance. Such colours could be obtained with pure gold or pure silver, but not copper. In that case, the most convenient technique would have been to plate golden or silver leaf on a copper core, a technique used in most parts of the world. Yet, Andean metallurgists relied on a more complex procedure, consisting of a surface depletion of metal alloys aiming at 'developing' gold or silver surfaces. According to Lechtman, such a technique only made sense if the importance of these two metals in Andean cosmologies is considered—gold being assimilated to the sweat of the sun and silver to the tears of the moon—and the fact that Andean people assimilated the outer appearance of things to their inner essence. Thus, using gold or silver plating would have been cheating with nature and the gods: to do things appropriately, gold and silver had to be *embodied* in the copper core, even if this led to their temporary disappearance. In later publications, Lechtman (1984, 1996) showed how such correlation between cosmological representations and technical practice did not only concern metallurgy but also weaving: clearly, Andean technologies shared a common 'technological style' insofar as their constituting elements were unified non-randomly, according to a similar cultural logic.

If not an instant hit, the concept of 'technological style' was definitely growing: by the early 1990s a whole generation of archaeologists were exploiting it outside the Andean and metallurgical domains. Such success may be explained by at last three reasons. First, the concept came at the right moment to rejuvenate a debate on style that was mainly concerned with artefact typologies and the marking of identities. Second, Lechtman demonstrated that there could be more in laboratory analyses than the seemingly useless—and definitely boring— columns of number that had plagued much of the archaeometrical literature so far. In that regard, her case study illustrated how careful laboratory analyses were actually the best way to explore such crucial aspects as the technical embodiment of cosmological representations. Third, and more importantly, Lechtman's work was in step with a growing body of studies developing nearly independently among English-speaking (Pfaffenberger 1992; Dobres 2000) and French anthropologists and emphasizing the cultural dimension of techniques.

The latter gravitated around the Musée de l'Homme and the team 'Techniques & Culture' at the CNRS, and included people such as Hélène Balfet, Bob Creswell, François Sigaut, Marie-Claude Mahias, Pierre Lemonnier, and Marie-Noël Chamoux—some of whom had been the students of André Leroi-Gourhan and André-Georges Haudricourt (themselves former students of Marcel Mauss). All these scholars did not approach techniques from the same angle: some focused on economy; others on history and cultural geography, or social and symbolic dimensions. Yet they all shared the belief that ethnography would benefit as much from an analysis of technical systems as it already did from that of social or matrimonial systems. They also shared a common analytical tool—the *chaîne opératoire* or operational sequence—initially developed by Leroi-Gourhan (1964), and corresponding to the analysis of the series of operations involved in any transformation of matter (Balfet 1991; Lemonnier 1992: 26; see also Creswell 1983).

English-speaking scholars tend sometimes to confuse this concept of *chaîne opératoire* with a theoretical or philosophical point of view; a way of stressing the cultural dimension of technical actions. Actually, the *chaîne opératoire* is an *analytical tool* aiming at documenting activities in the field or in the archaeological record and, as importantly, for ordering the data in view of subsequent comparisons. What is actually compared, as well as how things are interpreted, depends largely on theoretical perspective (e.g., Marxism, structuralism) of scholars. *Chaîne opératoire* remains nevertheless a powerful analytical tool because it imposes systematization in data collection, as well as the acknowledgement of a variety of elements—location, actors, gestures, tools, raw materials, duration, organization, vocabulary, rituals, and taboos, etc.—that are invariably brought together in the conduct of technical activities. Such a collection of elements reminds us of the 'package' evoked by Lechtman (1977: 6) in her definition of 'technological style'. As an analytical framework, however, the *chaîne opératoire* allows for a more systematic and comprehensive exploration of the nature of, and relationships between, the constitutive elements of techniques.

Given the topic of this handbook, I will focus on studies that aim at exploring the social and symbolic dimensions of techniques. Pioneered by people such as Pierre Lemonnier (1986, 1992, 1993), they currently constitute an impressive body of work. Their basic assumption, rooted in structuralism, is that all techniques of a given society form a 'system', within which various categories of tools, devices, actions, materials, and knowledge are interrelated, both socially and historically (Gille 1978; Lemonnier 1992; for a similar conception among English-speaking historians, see especially Hughes 1983). These elements, as well as their combinations, are 'arbitrary', in the sense that they do not stem from technical or functional constraints, but are chosen, deliberately or not, among equally viable options. They are also 'conventional', in the sense that they are generally congruent with, and constitutive of a wider system of social conventions. (Petroski [1993: 220–5] provides a good example of the combined effect of arbitrariness and conventionality in retracing the changing packaging of McDonald hamburgers.) In order to approach the social logic that lies behind technical choices, data collected through *chaîne opératoire* analyses must be compared at three levels: (1) elements constituting a given technique; (2) set of techniques developed by a given society, whose interrelation constitute a 'technical system'; (3) relationships between a technical system and other elements of social organization (Lemonnier 1983). As stressed by Mahias (2002: 43–44), anthropologists have focused in particular on the first and third levels of comparison, perhaps because such analyses do not require exhaustive inventories of techniques. Her detailed comparison of several production techniques in India demonstrates, however, that one does not require exhaustiveness for reconstructing a technical system, especially if paying attention to elements such as vocabulary or body grammars.

The following section summarizes some of the post-1970 anthropological contributions to the study of techniques.

3 GREAT EXPECTATIONS

Iron-smelting and blacksmithing have been especially explored in Africa, where these activities are not only surrounded by rituals and taboos, but also associated with human gestation, fertility, and rituals of power in a variety of ways. Such an association materializes, notably, in furnaces being conceived as a female belly/uterus and decorated accordingly with breasts, genitals, scarification, and necklaces; in bellows being conceived as male genitals and bellowing noise as the sound of sexual intercourse; in songs praising the fertility of the furnace/bride; or in blacksmithing hammers being used both as symbols and makers of political power (see, among many others, Barndon 1996; Childs 1991; Childs and Killick 1993; David and Kramer 2001: 328–47; Haaland et al. 2002; Herbert 1993; Maret 1985; Schmidt 1997). According to Rowlands and Warnier, the analogy between smelting and the reproduction process may be less indicative of a representation of fertility as a metaphor of iron-working, than of a context in which 'smelters and smiths appear to have regarded themselves as facilitators in what we would call a *natural process* by which certain materials in nature transformed themselves into a substance which could be adapted to culturally useful ends' (1993: 541). Hence their possible intervention outside the field of iron-making (e.g., for curing presumably frigid or barren women), and the ambiguous social position of blacksmiths (Hoberg 2001; Maret 1980), that culminates throughout the African Sahel in blacksmithing being often practised by members of endogamous socio-professional sub-groups or 'castes', who act as main ritualists. Comparing data collected in Nepal and East Africa in view of assessing the technical grounding of the symbols people 'spin' around iron-working, Haaland et al. (2002) also point out that smelting and forging do not offer the same potential in that regard. The first centres on an invisible process of transformation in which objects and actions are strongly reminiscent of sexual intercourse and gender imagery. The second is a visible process through which the blacksmith gives shape to the bloom, an activity that 'can be made relevant to understanding domains related to the theme of giving shape and creating order' (2002: 53). In Africa, this would explain the frequent occurrence of blacksmiths' tools and mentions in kingship rituals (Maret 1985, Ch. 66, this volume; Reid and MacLean 1995).

Pottery-making is also an activity 'good to think' for those who practise it (Lévi-Strauss 1988). Following Lechtman, Sillar (1996) provides a fascinating illustration of a south-central Andean 'technical system' in which pottery techniques, food production, food processing, and mortuary practices are connected, both metaphorically and practically, through a series of transformation processes—digging, drying, soaking—that seem to structure both the technical and the social world (Figure 17.1). This symbolic emphasis on transformation in pottery making is a common phenomenon that has been commonly discussed in relation to African material (Berns 1993; Barley 1994; Gosselain 1999; McLeod 1984). Throughout the continent there exists what Barley calls a 'potting model' (Barley 1994: 138), associating pots and pottery techniques to transitory states, fertility, death, and bodily cavities, and placing them as efficient tools for explaining natural processes or shaping cultural ones. For example, pottery-making is metaphorically associated with human gestation—in much the same way as iron-smelting—with a pot/foetus thought to result from the mixing of female (clay) and male (water or temper) elements, hardened in a fire/uterus, and born with the help of a potter/midwife, who may subsequently strengthen it through similar treatments as those used for newborns (see examples in Gosselain 1999). Similarly, potters, pots, and pottery tools and techniques may appear in puberty rites, marriage ceremonies, or funerals. The breaking of a vessel, for instance, may materialize death; yet pots may also serve as receptacles for ancestors and media for communicating with them (Berns 2000; Sterner 1989).

As in the Andean example evoked above, David (1992: 193) observes that some north Cameroonian populations liken the grave to a pottery vessel, a granary and a uterus, 'all appropriate abodes for the process of ancestralization through germination, gestation, and

FIGURE 17.1 Initially soft, plastic, and moist, clay is durably transformed into a hard and resonant material through the action of fire. Such properties provide a series of technical metaphors that have been heavily exploited throughout the world.

possibly fermentation'. Pots are also frequently likened to human beings, in Africa as in other parts of the world, which translates into parallels between body and vessel ornamentation, with numerous occurrences of clay, clay firing, and fired products in creation myths and proverbs, or pottery parts being designated after body parts (David et al. 1988; Erikson 2002; Gosselain 1999, 2008; Mahias 1993; Ritz 1989). Combined with the fact that pottery-making is usually practised within domestic contexts, this anthropomorphization of pots and potting processes is often viewed as the main reason why the craft is preponderantly in the hands of female potters across the world (e.g. Vincentelli 2003): as women give birth to human beings, so should they also 'give birth' to human-like objects. But controlling natural elements such as clay and fire also places them in an ambiguous position, both dangerous and powerful. As blacksmiths, they may consequently occupy a singular social position and act as prominent ritualists and/or providers of ritual tools and metaphors (Barley 1994; see Mahias [1993] and Saraswati [1978] for examples in India). The context in which potters enter the craft, as well as the way they practise it may also be surrounded by a series of taboos and rituals aiming at protecting individuals from the dangers of manipulating clays and fired products.

Of course, the symbolic prominence of fire and heat are not confined to pottery- or iron-making (see de Heusch 1972, 1982; Jacobson-Widding 1989). In the Irian Jaya region of New Guinea, for example, large circular fires are used for cooking meat and tubers (with the help of heated stones), for heating blocks of stone in order to obtain plates from which axes will be roughed out, and for making salt. The connection transcends technical actions and devices, since both stones and salt are considered as the body parts of mythical heroes, classed among 'hot things' (with pork grease), and cooked in highly socialized contexts. According to Pétrequin et al. (2000: 562–3), the underlying logic pertains to hot, dead organisms that must be cooked and distributed in a ritual anthropophagous context in order to reproduce the ideal functioning of society. And as for metal or pottery objects, the fact that production techniques are embedded in mythology and social practice transforms certain axes, salt-making tools or objects made with pork tusks into sacred objects, that are subsequently used for ensuring the fertility and power of lineages. Note that such a combination of technical, symbolic, and social concerns has also been splendidly illustrated by Lemonnier (1993) in his study of the Anga eel-trap or, more recently, drums used by Ankave people in ritual ceremonies (Lemonnier 2004).

In the Irian Jaya example, fire and heating were the nodes linking food preparation, salt-making, the shaping of stone axes, and social order. In India, Mahias (2002) documents a different linking process, centred on milk and especially the production of butter—one of the 'ramparts' of ritual purity—through churning. Besides the uses of lacteous products and the references made to the processes of milk transformation in ritual contexts, 'churning' stands as a prominent metaphor in mythological accounts and daily life. For example, the components and structuring principles of the universe are said to proceed from a churning of the 'sea of milk', accomplished by gods and demons with the help of a mountain serving as a rotating whipping tool and set in motion with a snake/rope. This rotating device, used throughout India for churning milk, is similar to that formerly used for producing fire, a technique strongly associated with the act of procreation. Interestingly, after the introduction and generalization of matchsticks, the technique has survived in ritual contexts, such as the lighting of sacrificial fires or funeral pyres. (Frazer [1984: 74–88] cites a similar example: on Easter day, Greek Orthodox priests lit a fire in front of the church with a flint and steel. The faithful took brands from this fire and re-lit their own kitchen fires.) As concluded by Mahias (2002: 58–9), similar gestures and modes of action 'reveal' the fire hidden in the wood or the butter hidden in the milk. In both cases, the aim is to overturn a primary state, chaotic or inert, in order to transform it into something both fertile and having the ability to create, be it the cosmological or the social order. The symbolic

FIGURE 17.2 The 'mystic mill' chapter, Cathedral of Vezelay (France). After its inception in the twelfth century, the mill became the main metaphor for explaining the incarnation of Christ and the Church. Here, Moise pours the grains (words of God) into a mill (the Christ) activated by Paul, who collected the flour.

representation is thus an integral part of the techniques, but it requires a material (technical) support to be *activated*. In other words, rituals are not simply 'nurtured' by technical metaphors, or technical mimicking: their ability to transform people and the world may be drawn from technical actions themselves.

Europe and the Mediterranean world provide another fascinating example of the symbolic dimension and ritual exploitation of food processing. As the main staple food for millennia, bread has become a metaphor for life. Since antiquity, it was associated with gestation and the human body, since yeast makes the dough bulge as the 'breath of life' makes the foetus grow in a woman's womb (Gélis 1984). Every tool and device used in the bread-making process is thus embedded in a similar web of significance (Macherel and Zeebroek 1994). For example, the oven is likened to a uterus and the wooden stick used for cleaning the oven to a penis. Also, the word 'placenta' is a scientific translation of the popular word 'cake' (Gélis 1984). Through centuries, the Christian Church manipulated these powerful symbols, adapting them to its own agenda and developing new metaphors, in close connection with technical innovations. After its inception in the twelfth century, for instance, the mill became the main metaphor used for explaining the incarnation of

Christ and the Church: the mill transformed the grains of the Christ's words into hosts (the body of Christ) that would subsequently be shared by the faithful, through a process that reified the role and position of the Virgin, the Apostles, the pope, the bishops, and the priests (Figure 17.2; Pierce 1966; for a further illustration, see the Host Mill altar piece [around 1470], Ulm, Ulmer Museum, Germany). As in the case of iron- or pottery-making, and with striking symbolic correspondences, bread-making techniques served thus as a convenient referent for explaining and teaching religion, for reifying a social (and religious) order, and for making sense of biological experiences.

4 Problems and Prospects

Cultural approaches to technology have of late clearly influenced anthropological and archaeological reasoning. Even if former techno-functional conceptions are currently being recycled into neo-Darwinian research programs (e.g. O'Brien and Lyman 2003), those remain fortunately marginal. As put by Küchler (2006: 325), '"technological determinism" gave way . . . to a large number of theoretical frameworks that have in common to largely accept as a premise that there are social influences in technology, having replaced the earlier impact-driven theory with a notion of a "seamless web" of social and technological dynamics'. We cannot ignore, however, that these theoretical frameworks have also brought their share of conceptual and methodological problems. What follows is a brief evocation of some questions generated by studies that seek to explore the symbolic dimensions of technical practices.

To start with the trivial, the quest for 'world views' and 'symbolic logics' should not make us forget that there is always more at play in technical processes than religious or ritual concerns. Doing things is not just enacting world views; it is also responding to economic, social, political, ecological, *and* functional concerns. The nature and characteristics of the action itself, the materials involved and the surrounding environment also play a crucial role, in channelling behaviour—or, more appropriately, creating the conditions of its actualization (Ingold 2000, 2007; Lemonnier 1992; van der Leeuw 1992). In their eagerness to denounce the fallacies of the materialistic approach to technology, some, for example, have gone as far as stating that 'pottery- and iron-making are social rather that material necessities' (Pinçon 1999: 4), a conception as misleading as the ones it seeks to oppose. Indeed, thinking about the relationship between procedures, goals, and meaning is not a question of calculating their respective weight, but, more simply, of acknowledging their simultaneous occurrence and complete tangling (Lemonnier 1991: 17).

This said, an ongoing question concerns the actual meaning of those symbolic representations embedded in, and generated by, technical practice. Here, I am considering the actors' point of view as well as that of those scientists interested in a better understanding of cultural practices. When considering the anthropological and ethnoarchaeological literature of the last decades, one gets the impression that the 'social representations' attached to technical procedures pertain largely to the religious and magical domains. To paraphrase Bourdieu (1980: 88), they also appear as big 'structured' and 'structuring' principles—or logics—that not only loom over individuals and societies, but also overflow the boundaries of individual techniques. What is, then, their capability to affect technical choices, beyond rationalizing, at a representational level, a set of practices already acquired through socialization processes? And could it be that such systems exist *outside* history?

A related question is that most—if not all—the symbolic systems evoked above develop within a web of metaphors linked to transformation processes: natural/biological transformation, technical transformations, social transformations, ritual transformations. Of course, there are notable differences in the nature and association of these metaphorical referents, which allows for singling out sub-Saharan systems of thought from New Guinean ones, for instance, or Indian and European ones. But there are also similarities, as notably highlighted by Haaland et al. (2002). And even when considering discrete areas, the tendency is for symbolic systems to overlap social boundaries. What is therefore their cultural and historical significance?

In a cross-cultural comparison of taboos, rituals, and representations linked to pottery making in sub-Saharan Africa, for example, I identified a similar logic spreading throughout the continent and materializing in associations between pots and people, pots and uterus, potters and pregnant women, pottery-firing and birthing, or the breaking of a pot and death (Gosselain 1999). Those associations are shared by people living in distinct cultural contexts, with few—if any—historical ties. Hence they do not provide any clue in regard to social boundaries or culture dynamics. We have seen, moreover, that these metaphors are also widely attested outside the African continent. So, when the archaeologist Goce Naumov (2006) observes parallels between pots, ovens, houses, women, wombs, and burials, in Neolithic cultures of the Balkans, he rightly concludes that the symbolic system is built upon notions of transformation, regeneration, and female fertility. Does it follow, however, that since similar conceptions have been documented among modern Slavic populations, archaeological evidence 'reveal[s] the deep roots of several Slavic rites and practices from the [nineteenth] and [twentieth] centuries' (Naumov 2006: 84)? I would say no.

More prosaically, if people living in different contexts draw similar symbols from pottery-making, it is because these symbols are 'afforded' (in the sense developed by Gibson [1979]) by the physical characteristics of the activity; because the very materiality of the craft offers a set of representational possibilities and opportunities. To be sure, such 'affordances' are always numerous. Their recognition and exploitation may also vary according to the cultural background of individuals. But some affordances are so salient as to literally 'impose' themselves on us. Pottery-making, for example, necessarily involves the shaping of a moist, plastic material, and its transformation by fire into a different material. When related to other salient qualities, such as the biological functioning of the human body, it seems nearly unavoidable that similar symbolic representations will be generated. This is not new. In his *Psychoanalysis of Fire*, first published in 1938, Bachelard (1987) already documented these 'natural analogies', to which humans gain access by virtue of their own nature (see also Eliade 1962). As concluded by Lemonnier (2006) in his comparison of witchcraft in Papua-New Guinea and fifteenth- and sixteenth-century Europe, such categories of symbols may be likened to a sort of 'background noise', that hampers the exploration of cultural specificities and dynamics, in diverting our attention toward universal cognitive processes.

If, on the contrary, we consider these natural analogies as a baseline, a first level of potentialities offered to people by simply being and acting in the world, the next logical step is to explore how such potentialities are actually exploited in the course of history. This direction has notably been followed by Webb Keane (2005). Drawing on the 'logical-causal' model of semiotics developed by Charles Sanders Peirce, he emphasizes the ongoing potential of objects to bring new realizations into new historical contexts, due to their material qualities. Such qualities form 'bundles', which are only partially exploited by semiotic ideologies, opening the way for new significations. As put by Keane (2005: 12), 'the work of selecting and stabilising the relevant bundles of iconicity and indexicality, the semiotic ideology this involves, is a project that can in principle never be completed, or fully consolidated. As such, semiotic ideology is necessarily historical.'

To come back to pottery-making, one sees that the potentialities offered by the craft do not necessarily relate to its pyrotechnological aspects. Socrates, for instance, compared a life conducted without thinking to the attempt of shaping a pot without following, or even knowing technical procedures (De Botton 2001: 21). The focus was thus put on the complexity of the craft (used here as a metaphor for existence) and on the subsequent impossibility of carrying it out by mere intuition. A similar metaphor is developed by Mintzberg, who urges modern corporate managers to 'craft' strategies with 'an intimate knowledge of the materials at hand' (1987: 67). But even if considering the metaphorical use of potting techniques in relationships with natural and cultural transformations, as I have done so far, one does not need to dig much to see the diversity of ways in which it may be stated from one population to the next (e.g. Barley 1994; Gosselain 1999). Rather than seeking to reconstruct coherent and widely shared structures of thought through comparison, we should thus focus on internal variations within such systems and, above all, look for the development of systems of opposition within sets of adjacent (or more remote) populations. This certainly requires a shift in the spatial scale of analysis, as well as the level of detail taken into consideration, but not necessarily a rejection of structuralism. On the contrary, exploring the processes that underlie regional systems of opposition is a way of concretizing its potentials as a historical method (de Heusch 1993).

Another question, related to the preceding, is what people actually know about, think about, and do with the symbolic and ritual aspects of technical processes (see especially Dobres and Hoffman 1994). Those 'underlying logics' reconstructed from observations and interviews often appear to exist beyond the grasp of the people we work with. As put by a Cameroonian informant, 'when ancestors leave you prescriptions they never take the trouble to explain the meaning' (Gosselain 1999: 206). Symbolic systems would thus loom over people and have a deep impact on practice, without people being necessarily aware of their existence or having the capacity to alter or adapt them to changing circumstances. This later conception has been strongly criticized by the historian Marcia Wright (2002). Reconstructing the life trajectory of a Tanzanian master smelter, she shows that the stability and importance of rituals in iron-smelting may have been overemphasized by ethnoarchaeologists. Indeed, post-1950 reconstructions were decontextualized performances achieved mainly by individuals whose role in the activity had formerly been peripheral. They consequently placed processes and rituals at the 'heart' of the event, for such components of the technique were those that they could more easily single out and analyse 'scientifically'. The biography of Mzee Stephano—the master smelter—reveals, on the contrary, that symbolic prescriptions were easily downplayed in the normal course of activities, for instance when faced with an economic challenge such as an increase in the regional demand for iron tools (e.g., the smelting took place within the village, it involved male and female individuals unrelated to the craft). Neither sticking to the 'tradition' nor fully embracing colonial practice, Mzee Stephano was simply adapting to a changing context, without compromising his craft, identity, or social position.

Wright's observations are reminiscent of those made by Michael Rowlands and Jean-Pierre Warnier in regard to iron-smelting in the Cameroonian grassfields. First, they identify what they call a 'secularization' or 'disenchantment' of the symbolism of iron production in certain communities; second, and more importantly, the symbolic code is seen to allow 'the producers to have a fairly clear representation of what is going on, and how to cope with technical breakdowns' (Rowlands and Warnier 1997: 538). Such a representation, they add, constitutes 'an intellectual *bricolage*', 'functionally equivalent to the scientific and empirical knowledge of the metallurgical engineer'. Instead of viewing symbols and rituals as the passive (and mainly involuntary) testimonies of a wider system of thought—that mainly exists *outside* the field of technical activities—we should thus consider them as tools in their own right; that is, as components of any artisan's toolkit, liable to be used and adapted strategically in the course of activity.

This opens a series of possibilities that do not necessarily exclude one another, contrary to what Rowlands and Warnier seem to imply in their critic of van der Merwe and Avery's (1987) functional interpretation of magic in African iron-smelting. At a first, basic level, controlling or coaxing natural forces, ancestors, and deities would be a way of coping with the uncertainties surrounding most technical processes, even in overtly laicized contexts of production (Svenbro 2006: 33–5)—a required skill, thus, but not necessarily one that supersedes others. For example, I have often been struck by those artisans who, having vehemently stressed the importance of respecting taboos while carrying out an activity, would, if faced with unexpected failures, explain them in purely technical terms (e.g. 'the clay was not sufficiently dry', 'there has been a gust of wind during firing'). Clearly, resorting to symbols and rituals did not exonerate them from developing an accurate knowledge and mastery of technical actions. Should such symbols and rituals be conceived therefore as a sort of supplementary safeguard? Or is it, as suggested by Gell (1988: 7–8), that 'magical thought formalizes and codifies the structural features of technical activity, imposing on it a framework of organization which regulates each successive stage in a complex process'? This conception of magic as adjunct to technical practices and serving cognitive ends (just as the 'intellectual *bricolage*' highlighted by Rowlands and Warnier [1997]), seems to be corroborated by historical documents such as the written formula of Western medieval dyers or painters (Pastoureau 2006: 64–7). Two categories of texts are indeed uncovered by historians: short, practical ones, that may have been used in workshops on a daily basis, and long, philosophically oriented ones, whose actual purpose remains unclear.

Other kinds of relationships between techniques and magic should also be envisioned, as suggested by van der Merwe and Avery (1987). For instance, esoteric knowledge is a way of maintaining a monopoly on craft activities, but also of negotiating social status. Here again, practices and representations depend heavily on historical and cultural contexts. For instance, many Kanuri blacksmiths of eastern Niger, who had formerly occupied a low social position when practising the craft, have reinvented themselves as Muslim scholars. They explained to me that they owned their power and knowledge—widely recognized locally—from carrying a 'blacksmith's hammer' in one hand and the Koran in the other. In other words, it is the combined use of Muslim and non-Muslim esoteric knowledge that empowers them and provides an efficient way to redefine their social position. Yet, knowledge and skills do not necessarily need to be conceptualized as 'esoteric' for being attributed magic-like qualities and exploited in social negotiations. Jeanjean (1999) provides a fascinating example of the way in which town sewer workers of Montpellier (France) tend to mask technical skills and knowledge when operating in public, presenting successful interventions as strokes of luck. Success is not associated to the rational linking of particular actions, but to an undetermined 'something else', from which sewer workers draw their power in the eyes of watchers. There is something akin to magic, concludes Jeanjean (1999: 81), when soiled waters spring again; an effect deliberately sought by workers for, as in the case of Kanuri *mallam*, it allows them to redefine their professional image.

Finally, the symbolic aspects of craft activities may also be exploited outside the technical domain, by a wider range of actors. This is the case in southern Togo, where blacksmithing has become one of the main expressions of social order for Ewe people (Mace 1998). Said to be the abode of Nyiglà, a powerful voodoo that protects the whole community, the smithy is regarded not only as the production place of necessary tools, but also as a shelter, a safeguard against the troubles and dangers having plagued the country since the re-election of G. Eyadéma in 1993 and the devaluation of money in 1994. Technical and symbolic values are thus used by a community to define and reinforce itself vis-à-vis others, through a process that, even if relying on ancient—so-called 'traditional'—world views, is plainly inscribed in modernity.

5 CONCLUSIONS

If anything, I hope to have made clear that techniques are not only cultural productions in their own right, but cultural productions that should be taken most seriously by social scientists. They correspond to 'ongoing and unfinished process[es]...through which people, society, and materials together weave and reweave the meaningful conditions of everyday life', as put by Dobres (2000: 4). They are thus 'ways' of acting upon the world, not only to fulfil economic or biological needs, but also to fulfil social, political, religious and symbolic ones. Besides illustrating the rich symbolic web that surrounds technical practices, recent anthropological and sociological studies have also documented their ability to create crucial aspects of the world inhabited by humans. And this goes far beyond the daily production of material culture or the modification of the physical environment. As we have seen, techniques are also used to transform people through the ages of life; to create, maintain, or abolish meaningful boundaries such as gender, age groups, and social entities; to generate social order and political power; to carry on ritual actions; and to cope with the uncertainties of daily life. In other words, techniques play a role in transformations that largely exceed action upon matter. Exploring these crucial issues requires first that we get rid of the positivist and utilitarian ideology that shaped our relations to techniques since the eighteenth century; second, we should develop more appropriate methods for exploring both the historical dimension of technical systems and processes of individual appropriation and transformation of practices. Some steps have already been made in that direction, as I showed above.

In closing this chapter, I would like to stress that the salutary turn taken by social scientists in regard to techniques and material culture could also benefit those interested in rituals and religion. Mitchell (2006) reminds us that performances taking place during feasts and rituals have transformative potentialities that develop from an interaction between things, places, time, and the body. In this regard, rituals should be taken as seriously as techniques; that is, not simply considered as categories of actions that lack technical motivation (e.g. Whitehouse 2002). Indeed, if rites, myths, and actions upon matter are completely intricate in technical practice, why should ritual actions be analysed as a distinct category of cultural production, disconnected from other realms of human experience? As with Lemonnier (2006: 38–9), I suspect that *chaîne opératoire* analyses of rituals will open new avenues in the study of religion.

Suggested Reading

From the mid-1970s onward, hundreds of ethnographic studies aiming at documenting the cultural dimension of technical practices have emerged throughout the world, forming a field of investigation that, while incredibly heterogeneous in regard to the nature and purpose of individual contributions, has had a deep and lasting impact on anthropological and archaeological practice. Here are some references that may prove useful for archaeologists. Readers interested should look at issues of *Techniques & Culture, Technology and Culture, History of Technology*, or *Journal of Material Culture*, among others. They should also consult the recent compilation of ethnoarchaeological studies made by David and Kramer (2001) and publications such as Cohen and Pestre (1998), Dobres (2000), Dobres and Hoffman (1999), Küchler (2006), Lemonnier (1993, 2004), Mahias (2002), and Pfaffenberger (1992). Part 3 ('Skill') of Ingold (2000) is also of great interest, for it covers topics not addressed in other works. And, of course, readers would be well advised to check the works of Leroi-Gourhan, Haudricourt or Balfet, some of which are referenced in this chapter.

References

BACHELARD, G. 1987 [1938]. *Psychoanalysis of Fire* (London: Beacon Press).
BALFET, H. (ed.) 1991. *Observer l'action technique. Des chaînes opératoires, pour quoi faire?* (Paris: Editions du CNRS).
BARLEY, N. 1994. *Smashing Pots: Feats of clay from Africa* (London: The British Museum Press).
BARNDON, R. 1996. 'Fipa ironworking and its technological style' in Peter Schmidt (ed.), *The Culture and Technology of African Iron Production* (Gainesville: University of Florida Press), pp. 58–74.
BERNS, M. 1993. 'Art, history, and gender: Women and clay in West Africa', *The African Archaeological Review*,11: 129–48.
—— 2000. 'Containing power: Ceramic and ritual practice in Northeastern Nigeria' in Christopher Roy (ed.), *Clay and Fire: Pottery in Africa*, Iowa Studies in African Art 4 (Iowa City: The University of Iowa), pp. 53–76.
BOTTON, A. DE 2001. *The Consolations of Philosophy* (London: Gardners Books).
BOURDIEU, P. 1980. *Le sens practique* (Paris: Editions de Minuit).

CHILDS, T. 1991. 'Style, technology, and iron-smelting furnaces in Bantu-speaking Africa', *Journal of Anthropological Archaeology*, 10: 332–59.
——and KILLICK, D. 1993. 'Indigenous African metallurgy: Nature and culture', *Annual Reviews of Anthropology*, 22: 317–37.
COHEN, Y. and PESTRE, D. 1998. 'Présentation', *Annales Histoire Sciences Sociales*, 53(4–5): 721–44.
CRESWELL, R. 1983. 'Transferts de techniques et chaînes opératoires', *Techniques & Culture*, 2: 143–63.
DAVID, N. 1992. 'The Archaeology of ideology: Mortuary practices in the Central Mandara Highlands, Northern Cameroon' in Judy Sterner and Nicholas David (eds), *An African commitment: Papers in honour of Peter Lewis Shinnie* (Calgary: University of Calgary Press), pp. 181–210.
——and KRAMER, C. 2001. *Ethnoarchaeology in Action* (Cambridge: Cambridge University Press).
——STERNER, J. and GAVUA, K. 1988. 'Why pots are decorated', *Current Anthropology*, 29(3): 365–89.
DOBRES, M.-A. 2000. *Technology and Social Agency* (Oxford: Blackwell).
——and HOFFMAN, C. 1994. 'Social agency and the dynamics of prehistoric technology', *Journal of Archaeological Method and Theory*, 1(3): 211–58.
——(eds.) 1999. *The Social Dynamics of Technology: Practice, politics, and world views* (Washington, DC: Smithsonian Institution Press).
ELIADE, M. 1962. *The Forge and the Crucible: The origin and structure of alchemy* (Chicago: The University of Chicago Press).
ERIKSON, P. 2002. 'Le masque matis. Matière à réflexion, réflexion sur la matière', *L'Homme*, 161: 149–64.
FRAZER, J. 1984 [1915]. *Le rameau d'or. 4. Balder le magnifique* (Paris: Robert Laffont).
GÉLIS, J. 1984. *L'arbre et le fruit. La naissance dans l'Occident moderne, XVIe–XIXe siècles* (Paris: Fayard).
GELL, A. 1988. 'Technology and magic', *Anthropology Today*, 4(2): 6–9.
GIBSON, J. 1979. *The Ecological Approach to Visual Perception* (Boston: Houghton Mifflin).
GILLE, B. (ed.) 1978. *Histoire des techniques* (Paris: Gallimard).
——1980. *Les mécaniciens grec. La naissance de la technologie* (Paris: Editions du Seuil).
GOSSELAIN, O. 1999. 'In pots we trust: The processing of clay and symbols in sub-Saharan Africa', *Journal of Material Culture*, 4(2): 205–30.
——2008. 'Ceramics in Africa' in Helain Selin (ed.), *Encyclopaedia of the History of Science, Technology, and Medicine in Non-Western Cultures* (New York: Springer), pp. 464–77.
HAALAND, R., HAALAND, G., and RIJAL, S. 2002. 'The social life of iron: A cross-cultural study of technological, symbolic, and social aspects of iron making', *Anthropos*, 97(1): 35–54.
HANSEN, B. 1986. 'The complementarity of science and magic before the scientific revolution', *American Scientist*, 74(2): 128–36.
HAUDRICOURT, A.-G. 1964. 'La technologie, science humaine', *La Pensée*, 115: 28–35.
HERBERT, E. 1993. *Iron, Gender, and Power: Rituals of transformation in African societies* (Bloomington: Indiana University Press).
HEUSCH, L. DE 1972. *Le roi ivre ou l'origine de l'état* (Paris: Gallimard).
——1982. *Rois nés d'un coeur de vache* (Paris: Gallimard).
——1993. 'Maintenir l'anthropologie', *Social Anthropology*, 1(3): 247–84.
HOBERG, I. 2001. 'Etre artisan en Afrique orientale', *Journal des Africanistes*, 71(2): 139–63.

HUGHES, T. 1983. *Networks of Power. Electrification in Western society, 1880-1930* (Baltimore: Johns Hopkins University Press).

INGOLD, T. 2000. *Perception of the Environment: Essays in livelihood, dwelling and skill* (London: Routledge).

—— 2007. 'Materials against materiality', *Archaeological Dialogue*, 14(1): 1–16.

JACOBSON-WIDDING, A. 1989. 'Notion of heat and fever among the Manyika of Zimbabwe' in A. Jacobson-Widding and D. Westerlund (eds), *Culture, Experience and Pluralism: Essays on African ideas of illness and healing* (Uppsala: Centraltryckeriet), pp. 27–44.

JEANJEAN, A. 1999. 'Travailler et penser une matière impensable' in Marie-Pierre Julien and Jean-Pierre Warnier (eds), *Approches de la culture matérielle. Corps à corps avec l'objet* (Paris: L'Harmattan), pp. 73–85.

KEANE, W. 2005. 'The hazards of new clothes: What signs make possible' in S. Küchler and G. Were (eds), *The Art of Clothing. A pacific experience* (London: UCL Press), pp. 1–16.

KÜCHLER, S. 2006. 'Process and transformation: Introduction' in C. Tilley, W. Keane, S. Kuchler, M. Rowlands, and P. Spyer (eds), *Handbook of Material Culture* (London: Sage Publications), pp. 325–8.

LECHTMANN, H. 1977. 'Style in technology: Some early thoughts' in H. Lechtman and R. Merrill (eds), *Material Culture: Style, organization, and the dynamics of technology* (St Paul: American Ethnological Society), pp. 3–20.

—— 1984. 'Andean value systems and the development of prehistoric metallurgy', *Technology and culture*, 25: 1–36.

—— 1996. 'Cloth and metal: The culture of technology' in E. H. Boone (ed.), *Andean Art at Dumbarton Oaks*, I (Washington, DC: Dumbarton Oaks Research Library and Collections), pp. 33–44.

LEEUW, S. VAN DER 1993. 'Giving the potter a choice. Conceptual aspects of pottery techniques' in Pierre Lemonnier (ed.), *Technological Choices: Transformation in material cultures since the Neolithic* (Routledge, London), pp. 238–88.

LEMONNIER, P. 1983. 'L'étude des systèmes technique, une urgence en technologie culturelle', *Techniques & Culture*, 1: 11–34.

—— 1986. 'The study of material culture today: Toward an anthropology of technical systems', *Journal of Anthropological Archaeology*, 5: 147–86.

—— 1991. 'De la culture matérielle à la culture? Ethnologie des techniques et préhistoire', *25 ans d'études technologiques en préhistoire* (Antibes: Editions APDCA), pp. 15–20.

—— 1992. *Elements for an Anthropology of Technology*, Anthropological Paper No. 88 (Ann Arbor: Museum of Anthropology, University of Michigan).

—— 1993. 'The eel and the Ankave-Anga of Papua New Guinea: Material and symbolic aspects of trapping' in C. Hladik et al. (eds), *Tropical Forests, People and Foods: Biocultural interactions and applications to development* (Paris: UNESCO, MAB), pp. 673–82.

—— (ed.) 1993. *Technological choices: Transformations in material culture since the Neolithic* (London: Routledge).

—— 2004. 'Mythiques chaînes opératoires', *Techniques & Culture*, 43–4: 25–43.

—— 2006. *Le sabbat des lucioles. Sorcellerie, chamanisme et imaginaire cannibale en Nouvelle-Guinée* (Paris: Stock).

LEROI-GOURHAN, A. 1964. *Le Geste et la Parole*, I: *Technique et Langage* (Paris: Albin Michel).

LÉVI-STRAUSS, C. 1988. *The Jealous Potter* (Chicago: The University of Chicago Press).

MACE, A. 1998. 'Tradition, technique et modernité: approche des Ewé de Tsévié (Sud-Togo)', *Socio-Anthropologie*, 3: 1–7.

MACHEREL, C. and ZEEBROEK, R. 1994. 'Le pain était leur corps' in C. Macherel and R. Zeebroek (eds), *Une vie de pain. Faire, penser et dire le pain en Europe* (Bruxelles: Crédit Communal), pp. 11–39.

MCLEOD, M. 1984. 'Akan Terracota' in John Picton (ed.), *Earthenware in Asia and Africa* (London: Percival David Foundation), pp. 365–81.

MAHIAS, M.-C. 1993. 'Pottery techniques in India: Technical variants and social choice' in P. Lemonnier (ed.), *Technological Choices. Transformation in material cultures since the Neolithic* (London: Routledge), pp. 157–80.

——2002. *Le barattage du monde. Essai d'anthropologie des techniques en Inde* (Paris: Editions de la Maison des Sciences de l'Homme).

MARET, P. (de) 1980. 'Ceux qui jouent avec le feu: la place du forgeron en Afrique Centrale', *Africa*, 50(3): 263–79.

——1985. 'The smith's myth and the origin of leadership in Central Africa' in R. Haaland and P. Shinnie (eds), *African Iron Working* (Oslo : Norwegian University Press), pp. 73–87.

MARTINELLI, B. 2005. 'Style, technique et esthétique en anthropologie' in B. Martinelli (ed.), *L'interrogation du style* (Aix en Provence: Presses de L'Université de Provence), pp. 19–48.

MAUSS, M. 1979 [1934]. 'Body techniques' in *Sociology and Psychology* (London: Routledge), pp. 95–123.

MERWE, N. J. VAN DER and AVERY, D. H. 1987. 'Science and magic in African technology: Traditional iron-smelting in Malawi', *Africa*, 57(2): 143–72.

MINTZBERG, H. 1987. 'Crafting strategy', *Harvard Business Review* (July–August): 66–74.

MITCHELL, J. 2006. 'Performance' in C. Tilley et al. (eds), *Handbook of Material Culture* (London: Sage Publications), pp. 384–401.

MOREL, C. 2002. *Les décisions absurdes. Sociologie des erreurs radicales et persistantes* (Paris: Gallimard).

NAUMOV, G. 2006. 'The vessel, oven and house in symbolical relation with the womb and women: Neolithic bases and ethnographic implications' [text in Russian], *Studia Mythologica Slavica*, 9: 59–95.

O'BRIEN, M. and LYMAN, L. (eds) 2003. *Style, Function, Transmission: Evolutionary archaeological perspectives* (Salt Lake City: University of Utah Press).

PASTOUREAU, M. 2006. *Bleu. Histoire d'une couleur* (Paris: Seuil, Points Histoire).

PÉTREQUIN, P., PÉTREQUIN, A.-M., and WELLER, O. 2000. 'Cuire la pierre et cuire le sel en Nouvelle Guinée: des techniques actuelles de régulation sociale' in P. Pétrequin, P. Fluzin, J. Thiriot, and P. Benoit (eds), *Arts du feu et productions artisanales* (Antibes: Editions APDCA), pp. 545–64.

PETROSKI, H. 1993. *The Evolution of Useful Things* (New York: Alfred A. Knopf).

PFAFFENBERGER, B. 1992. 'Social anthropology of technology', *Annual Review of Anthropology*, 21: 491–516.

PIERCE, J. 1966. 'Memling's mills', *Studies in Medieval Cultures*, 2: 111–19.

PINÇON, B. 1993. 'Propos sur la technique' in *Journées de réflexion sur les finalités et l'avenir du modèle de société occidental* (Neuchâtel: Université de Neuchâtel), pp. 1–9.

REID, A. and MACLEAN, R. 1995. 'Symbolism and the social contexts of iron production in Karagwe', *World Archaeology*, 27(1): 144–61.

RITZ, U. 1989. '"Niemand zerbricht einen Wassertopf beim ersten tolpern": zur Analogie von Topf und Mensch bei den Asante (Ghana)', *Paideuma*, 35: 207–19.

Rowlands, M. and Warnier J.-P. 1993. 'The magical production of iron in the Cameroon Grassfields' in T. Shaw et al. (eds), *The Archaeology of Africa: Food, metals and towns*, One World Archaeology 20 (London: Routledge), pp. 512–50.

Saraswati, B. 1978. *Pottery-making Cultures and Indian Civilization* (Abhinav Publications).

Schmidt, P. 1997. *Iron Technology in East Africa: Symbolism, science, and archaeology* (Bloomington: Indiana University Press).

Sigaut, F. 1987. 'Préface: Haudricourt et la technologie' in A.-G. Haudricourt (ed.), *La technologie, science humaine* (Paris: Editions de la Maison des Sciences de l'Homme), pp. 9–34.

Sillar, B. 1996. 'The dead and the drying. Techniques for transforming people and things in the Andes', *Journal of Material Culture*, 1(3): 259–89.

Sterner, J. 1989. 'Who is signalling whom? Ceramic style, ethnicity and taphonomy among the Sirak Bulahay', *Antiquity*, 63: 451–9.

Svenbro, J. 2006. 'Les démons de l'atelier. Savoir-faire et pensée religieuse dans un poème d' "Homère"', *Cahiers d'Anthropologie Sociale*, 1: 25–36.

Vincentelli, M. 2003. *Women Potters: Transforming traditions* (New Brunswick: Rutgers University Press).

Wobst, M. 1977. 'Stylistic behavior and information exchange' in C. E. Cleland (ed.), *Papers for the Director: Research essays in honor of James B. Griffin* (Ann Arbor: Museum of Anthropology, University of Michigan), pp. 317–42.

Wright, M. 2002. 'Life and technology in everyday life: Reflections on the career of Mzee Stefano, master smelter in Ufipa, Tanzania', *Journal of African Cultural Studies*, 15(1): 17–34.

CHAPTER 18

RITES OF PASSAGE

PAUL GARWOOD

1 Introduction: van Gennep's Ritual Process—An Anthropological Classic and its Archaeological Legacy

In William Golding's *Rites of Passage* trilogy of novels (1980, 1987, 1989), set in the nineteenth century, a disparate group of passengers embark on a sea voyage to a colonial destination. They submit themselves to a journey that divorces them from the world they knew, entering a liminal domain of 'otherness', unsettling social inversions and dangerous ordeals, where each person is transformed in some way, before arriving in their new world—a place of social order renewed, akin but different to the one left behind. These allegorical novels, which explore life-course transitions, journeys of self-discovery and passages to new realms, give some indication of how widely and how diffusely the idea of 'rites of passage' has pervaded Western consciousness. Indeed it seems possible to extend the theme of personal change through real or metaphorical journeys with tripartite structures (departure–other-world/out-of-time experiences–arrival/return), into any context or genre of representation (as Hollywood 'road movies' demonstrate *ad nauseam*).

Our present conceptualization of 'rites of passage' stems from the work of the Belgian anthropologist Arnold van Gennep, whose book *Les Rites de Passage*, published in French in 1911 and belatedly in English in 1960, remains extraordinarily influential as the point of departure for discussions of transition rituals. Only Victor Turner's elaboration of some of van Gennep's themes, especially in relation to liminality (1967, 1969), the idea of *communitas* (1969, 1974), and performance (1982), have had similar far-reaching impact on how rites of passage are understood. According to van Gennep, the purpose of rites of passage is 'to ensure a change in condition or a passage from one magico-religious or secular group to another' (1960: 11). He argued that such rituals must be understood in their entirety and that all share a tripartite structure—comprising beginnings (rites of separation), middles (rites of liminality), and ends (rites of reaggregation) (1960: 191–2; see Figure 18.1). The apparent universality of this ritual process (cf. Metcalf and Huntington 1991: 30) suggests a single cultural logic for managing human encounters with the supernatural. Rites of

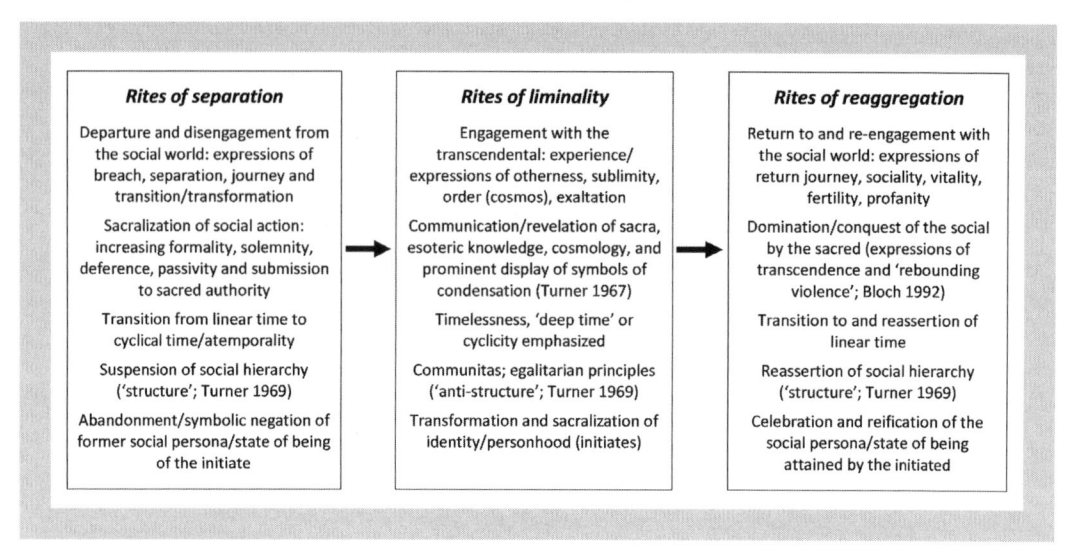

Rites of separation	Rites of liminality	Rites of reaggregation
Departure and disengagement from the social world: expressions of breach, separation, journey and transition/transformation	Engagement with the transcendental: experience/ expressions of otherness, sublimity, order (cosmos), exaltation	Return to and re-engagement with the social world: expressions of return journey, sociality, vitality, fertility, profanity
Sacralization of social action: increasing formality, solemnity, deference, passivity and submission to sacred authority	Communication/revelation of sacra, esoteric knowledge, cosmology, and prominent display of symbols of condensation (Turner 1967)	Domination/conquest of the social by the sacred (expressions of transcendence and 'rebounding violence'; Bloch 1992)
Transition from linear time to cyclical time/atemporality	Timelessness, 'deep time' or cyclicity emphasized	Transition to and reassertion of linear time
Suspension of social hierarchy ('structure'; Turner 1969)	Communitas; egalitarian principles ('anti-structure'; Turner 1969)	Reassertion of social hierarchy ('structure'; Turner 1969)
Abandonment/symbolic negation of former social persona/state of being of the initiate	Transformation and sacralization of identity/personhood (initiates)	Celebration and reification of the social persona/state of being attained by the initiated

FIGURE 18.1 A summary of van Gennep's tripartite *Rites de Passage* model (1960), showing some of the key characteristics and qualities of different parts of the ritual process as identified by Van Gennep (1960), Turner (1967, 1969, 1974), and Bloch (1992).

separation dissolve society and guide participants into a domain where ordinary social affairs are excluded; in the liminal stage people find themselves betwixt and between heaven and earth, in the presence of supernatural powers, where social norms are suspended; finally, rites of re-aggregation provide a way to reconstitute social order. This is not a process without risks; as Mary Douglas observed, van Gennep 'saw society as a house with rooms and corridors in which passage from one to another is dangerous' (1966: 96).

Although there have been critiques of van Gennep's approach (e.g. Gluckman 1962), as well as occasional attempts to question the validity of the tripartite rites of passage structure (e.g. Werbner 1989), his model remains central to anthropological conceptions of ritual, repeatedly drawn upon for general interpretative purposes and widely applied in every imaginable cultural context. Some anthropologists have even proposed that *all* rituals are in some way rites of passage (e.g. Parkin 1992). In contrast, despite mention of rites of passage in archaeology, especially in reviews of anthropological approaches to ritual or as allusions to practices supposedly represented in the material evidence, especially in 'liminal' contexts, there is no concerted discussion of van Gennep's ideas to be found anywhere. Remarkably, most recent general discussions of ritual in archaeology barely mention rites of passage at all (e.g. Brück 1999b; Insoll 2004a, 2004b; Bradley 2005; Diaz-Andreu et al. 2005).

2 ALL THINGS LIMINAL

The emphasis on liminality in the archaeology of ritual can be explained in part by the influence of Victor Turner, who extended van Gennep's model to encompass many kinds of 'social dramas' (legal, political, or religious), which all require similarly structured redressive processes to re-establish order and validate new social and moral conditions (summarized succinctly in diagrammatic form: 1986: 293; cf. Schechner 1994: fig. 6; see Figure 18.2). Turner focused especially on liminal stages and their shared symbolic and performative properties: 'milieus detached from mundane life... characterized by the presence of ambiguous ideas, monstrous images, sacred symbols, humiliations, esoteric and paradoxical instructions, the emergence of "symbolic types" represented by maskers and clowns, gender reversals, anonymity and many other phenomena' (Turner 1990: 11). Combinations of symbols drawn from both nature and culture are especially common in such liminal contexts: a good example is the association of uprooted tree, winged angel, fairy lights, sweets, tinsel, and colourfully wrapped gifts found in many Western houses at

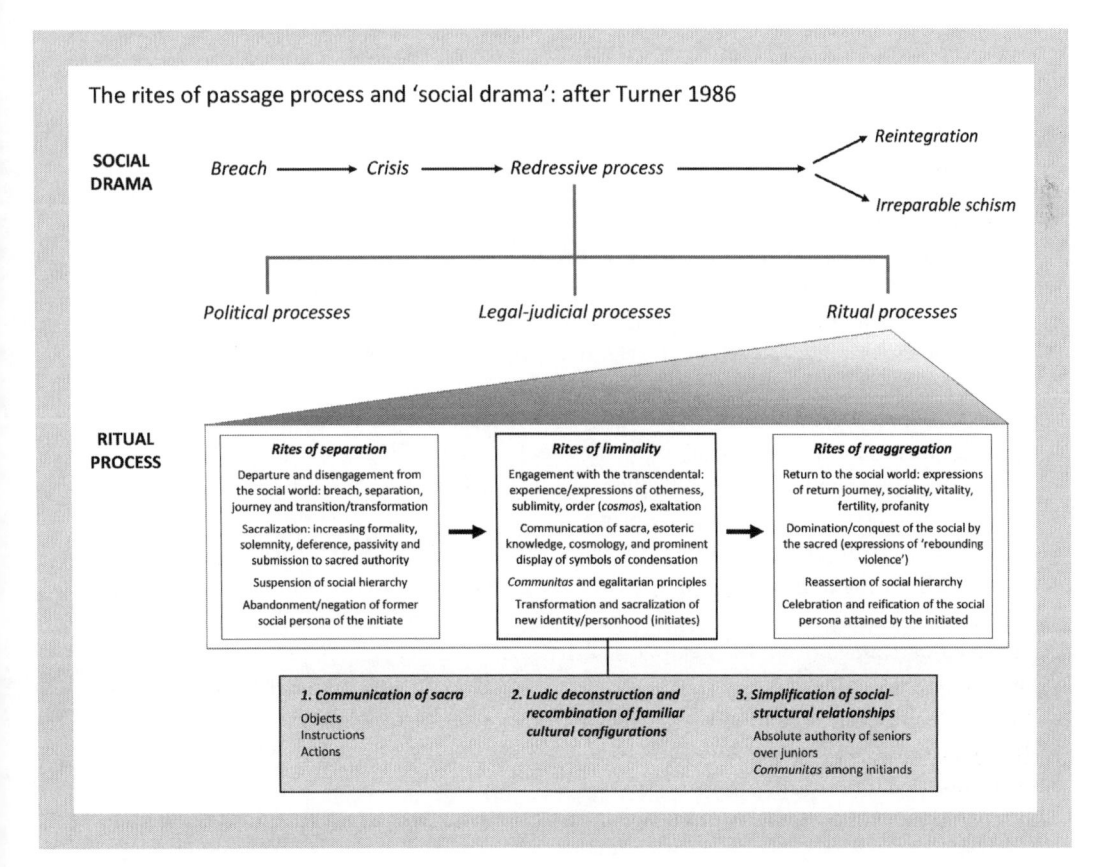

FIGURE 18.2 The ritual process and rites of passage in the context of Turner's model of 'social dramas'.

Christmas time—when the moral economy of the 'family' is affirmed as transcendent over secular values and market principles (Kuper 1993). Reversals of fundamental assumptions during liminal states can also cause intense stress, forcing participants to reconstruct their understanding of the world: for example, the revelation for male Orokaiva initiates that wild pigs are not simply 'public enemies' and sources of food but also the equivalents of men—virile, cunning, and dangerous (H. Whitehouse 2000: 30). Central to these themes is the idea that liminality represents anti-structure as opposed to the structure of the social world—a structure which is first dissolved in rites of separation and later reconstituted in rites of reaggregation. In liminal conditions, according to Turner, a form of sociality entirely different to that of the everyday world is brought to the fore—*communitas*—where social hierarchy is overturned in favour of egalitarian religiosity and shared identity (1974).

In this context it is notable that ritual in archaeology is usually explored as an undifferentiated kind of esoteric or 'irrational' action, opposed to utilitarian or 'rational' behaviour (cf. Brück 1999b)—a characterization that clearly approximates most closely to the *liminal* stage defined by van Gennep and Turner. It is therefore unsurprising that archaeological studies of ritual tend to emphasize 'otherness', heightened or extreme modes of expression and symbolic communication. Although archaeologists have become quite comfortable discussing 'ritual' in these narrow terms, they usually ignore the different characteristics and purposes of the rites at other stages of the ritual process.

3 RITES OF PASSAGE AS JOURNEYS

The act of going somewhere else to gain access to the liminal, and to return, requires movement, real or imagined: journeys can therefore be seen as an intrinsic feature of the ritual procress (cf. Helms 1988). As Humphrey and Laidlaw observe: 'Rites of passage have three stages... not because they are *rites* of passage but because they are rites of *passage*' (1994: 125, their emphases). It is especially important, however, to distinguish the specific purpose of each ritualized journey in relation to the *overall* ritual process in which such a journey is set, and the different expressive qualities and symbolic references of rites of separation and reaggregation. For example, in Western mortuary traditions, processional movement as part of the rite of separation (i.e. to church and churchyard) tends to emphasize increasing formality and collectivity as the domain of the sacred is approached; whereas movement for the living during the aggregational stage (i.e. in leaving the churchyard and progressing to the everyday world) tends to be informal and sectional. Movements during liminal stages of rites of passage, when the participants are 'neither here nor there', are different again. These 'journeys' are effectively *outside* time and may be perceived as real, re-lived, or metaphorical passages in other places/times—of deities or heroes, celestial bodies, ancestral wanderings, travels on the paths of the dead, and so forth—which initiates temporarily participate in. Social norms are suspended, notions of shared identity, origins and solidarity (*communitas*) confirmed, and religious and moral truths revealed. Pilgrimages, in this context, are perhaps better understood as extended rites of separation, with progressive disengagement from the secular world and gradual religious inculcation of the initiate, whose encounter with the sacred is realized fully only in the liminal context of the cult centre or shrine (Morinis 1992).

Other kinds of journeys, such as holidays, of course involve similar processes of separation–liminality–return, while mythic narratives are often constructed with the same basic structure as rites of passage. It has even been suggested that 'ritual is only another mythology, another language, the outward dramatization of a basic and recurrent framework or "myth"' (Dowden 1999: 239). This view has few adherents amongst anthropologists as it privileges the semiotic and textual properties of mythic tales (typical of Western literary criticism) over the performative and practical properties of ritual emphasized recently in anthropology (cf. Bell 1992; Grimes 2003; Schechner 1994; Turner 1974: 1982). It is one thing to listen to or read a story in order to be entertained or instructed, quite another to 'live through it' by engaging in a series of ritual acts—involving intense physical and emotional experiences—in order to achieve a fundamental transformation of personhood that seems sublimely 'real' to the participant (cf. Bourdieu 1977: 135, on the *embodiment* of dispositions and beliefs).

4 Technologies of Transformation

The particular purpose of rites of passage is described succinctly by Ronald Grimes: 'To enact any kind of rite is to *per*form, but to enact a rite of passage is also to *trans*form' (2003: 7, his emphases). The stress laid on efficacy by Schechner (1994) similarly points to the practicality and intentionality of rites of passage, which serve (as van Gennep specified originally) to make things—and especially people—different (cf. Grimes 2003: 7; Turnbull 1990: 77–9). It is unsurprising, in this context, that death and rebirth are widely used metaphorically to signal the profound, irreversible nature of the process of transformation, as well as the particular qualities of the changes involved (Bloch and Parry 1982; cf. Hayden 2003: 58, on shamanic initiation rites). It is tempting, in this light, to conceive of rites of passage as *technologies* of person transformation (Bourdieu 1977: 135).

Indeed, technical acts are often subject to ritualization themselves. This theme has been explored with respect to metal smelting, both by anthropologists and archaeologists, who draw attention to the widespread symbolic significance of metalworking practices and furnaces (e.g. Budd and Taylor 1995; Haaland et al. 2004; Herbert 1993). As Rowlands and Warnier note, 'The idea that a technical process recapitulates more general ideas about natural reproduction in a mythological and cosmological context re-establishes the link between magic, fertility and technology' (1993: 513). Even so, the relationships between rites of passage and technology (e.g. in terms of productivity, transformation, performance, practicality, deference to authority, and revelation) have received little attention. This is especially surprising in relation to the social construction of skill-reproducing groups (Sigaut 1994: 448), the organization of which is often managed by rites of passage (e.g. the induction of craftsmen into guilds, or clerks into the clergy, during the Middle Ages; cf. Cullum 2004). The metaphorical and practical 'making' of people, in ways that combine technical, biological, and religious processes, can also be seen in political contexts, for example in the investiture of chiefs by iron smiths in West African societies (Herbert 1993: 136–7).

It is notable, in this context, that the material culture of rites of passage is almost always interpreted in symbolic terms. Rather than *reflections of* categories, however, artefacts in rituals may serve as *tools for* changing or making things sacred. The material constituents of rituals are not just means of symbolic communication or irrational expressions of belief but 'substances and processes that are generative: they create change' (La Fontaine 1985: 189). From an archaeological perspective, the objects sometimes described as having 'meaning' in rituals (e.g. in funerary assemblages) could equally be seen as resources in ritual acts that—just like manufacturing processes—require specific raw materials and technical procedures to achieve replicable outcomes. Whilst Brück is right to reject the dichotomization of secular/practical/technological and sacred/esoteric/aesthetic as a product of Western Enlightenment rationalism (1999b), the separation between ritual and technology dissolves still further once rites of passage are recognized as practices that are creative of new things through combinations of learnt skills, requisite materials, and practical *chaînes opératoires* (cf. Pfaffenberger 1988: 244).

5 Rites of Passage, Cosmic Order, and Classificatory Schemes

Although van Gennep highlighted the strong resemblances among different rites of passage, there has been a tendency to subdivide them into contrasting categories: for example, rites concerned with social transitions can be contrasted with those focused on natural cycles, while rites that achieve individual status transitions can be contrasted with those that achieve group transitions (La Fontaine 1985: 27). Inevitably, perhaps, the idea of rites of passage has become identified most closely with stages in the life course, while other kinds of rites of passage have attracted less attention (cf. Gilchrist 1999: 94–5). Different kinds and scales of social complexity, with potential variation in rites of passage according to status group and cultural identity, have also received scant attention in anthropology and archaeology, except in terms of relationships between elite and commoner rituals (cf. Bloch 1987).

It is also evident that rites of passage are fundamentally gendered, with pronounced contrasts between male and female rites in terms of their scale, biological symbolism, and social and religious significance (e.g. see Gilchrist 1999: 94–100; Muir 2005: 33). In many respects, of course, rites of passage act as a primary means of *creating* gender differences (Lutkehaus 1995) and of vindicating these with reference to an ideal model of cosmic order. In this context, the prominence given to gender distinctions in funerary ritual may have little to do with asserting the gender of the dead person, which in most cases is not in dispute, but instead relate to religious or moral discourses on gender relations, reproduction, and ideal life courses through the construction of powerful images of what gendered persons 'should be like', or 'will be', at least among the society of the dead.

Initiation rites, more widely, involve not just a change of status but disclosure of secret knowledge and deeper understanding of the sacred (Whitehouse 2000: 19). Such rites of passage are intimately bound up with the reproduction of both social and cosmic order (ibid.: 19–21). Indeed, in some cultural contexts, the recognition and reproduction of classificatory order through rites of passage may in themselves be seen as one means by which the cosmos itself is reproduced: in ancient Egypt, for example, the maintenance of moral and classificatory order in the life course was perceived as an important way of protecting a cosmos that was constantly under threat (David 2002: 271).

6 Power, Sacred Conquest, and Rites of Reaggregation

The act of processing from one status category to a 'higher' one in rites of passage is usually mediated by people thought to possess special sacred knowledge and expertise. Participation in rites of passage thus involves conscious commitment to a model of social and moral hierarchy in which certain people are superior to others. This produces 'an apparition of the world where everything is in its place and where the power-holders are at the source of everything' (Bloch 1989: 128). Indeed, Bloch has argued that the fundamental characteristic of ritual is 'deference' to greater authorities (2005). Rites of passage, from this perspective, are a practical and ideological means of creating social differentiation and hierarchy that is represented as all-encompassing and beyond contention (cf. Bloch 1985, 1986, 1987). This helps to explain the extraordinary scale of social effort invested in coronation and other rites of political succession, especially by elite groups in complex societies (Cannadine and Price 1987), as well as competitive staging of transition rituals where relationships between political power, social structure, and cosmic order need to be reconstituted and confirmed anew (e.g. in Balinese and Madagascan kingdoms: cf. Geertz 1980; Bloch 1986).

There may, however, be another dimension to the expression of power in rites of passage, indeed one that is intrinsic to ritual generally. Violence has long been recognized as a feature of rites of passage (cf. Schechner 1994), but most explanations have focused not on the nature of the ritual process but either on psychological drives (such as collective catharsis; Girard 1977, 1987), or on primordial mythic narratives (such as the 'hunt'; Burkert 1987). More recently, Bloch has proposed an alternative explanation in terms of 'rebounding violence' (Bloch 1992). He has argued that in ritual creativity is seen to derive from 'a transcendental force that is mediated by authority... this fact legitimates, even demands, the violent conquest of inferiors by superiors who are closer to the transcendental' (Bloch 1986, 189). These ideas have interesting implications for archaeological interpretations of deliberate artefact breakage, fragmentation processes, and human and animal sacrifice (cf. Carrasco 1999; Chapman 2000; Green 2001).

7 Themes in the Archaeology of Rites of Passage

The virtual absence of discussions of rites of passage in archaeology is puzzling given the attention paid recently to questions of social and cultural identity, personhood, and social being and becoming (e.g. Thomas 1996; Dobres and Robb 2000; Meskell and Joyce 2003; Fowler 2004). It is notable, in particular, that attempts to theorize the relationship between agency and structure rarely recognize the episodic temporality and uneven intensity of different social practices and their modes of signification. In particular, generative principles and dispositions may be created in the course of short-term social events, like rituals, rather than day-to-day practices. In this context, rites of passage are fundamental to the creation of social order, and plainly represent some of the most intense, emotionally charged and socially transformative episodes in people's lives, yet archaeologically they are usually treated abstractly—as invisible *prior* events that once determined the social identities of the individuals whose bodies or actions are encountered in the material evidence.

Nevertheless, it is still possible to recognize several interpretative themes in recent archaeological study that draw heavily on the idea of rites of passage. These are discussed below under the following headings: states of being and personhood; passages to other worlds; boundaries, portals, thresholds, and transformations; and liminality and sacred domains.

7.1 States of Being and Personhood

The identification in archaeology of distinct person-kinds produced through rites of passage, primarily in terms of age and gender categories but also sacred and political categories such as shamans and chiefs, is dominated by the evidence from mortuary contexts (Lucy 2005). Indeed, it is difficult to identify rites of passage events in the archaeological record *except* where funerary rituals involved burial acts as part of the process of transformation. The dominance of mortuary studies in this area, however, has not only severely biased the conceptualization of rites of passage, marginalizing all other kinds of transition such as initiation and marriage, but has also often led to misunderstandings about the significance of the person-kinds and status-sets reified through mortuary practices.

All too often, archaeologists have 'read-off' funerary categories as reflections of living social 'types', with the assumption that these represent identities constituted in the course of rites of passage enacted while the dead person was living. This approach is profoundly misleading: it denies the particular processes and intentions of ritual acts involving mortuary deposition and especially the highly creative nature of mortuary ritual (Parker Pearson 1999). Above all, funerals are in themselves rites of passage involving *transformations* of identity and states of being, whether this takes the dead *beyond* social categorization entirely (e.g. Nilsson Stutz 2003: 67), creates a new kind of 'social' identity, or even reintegrates the dead *into* society (e.g. Fowler 2004: 81). In each case, funerary rituals may act as 'a kind of initiation where the deceased is the person who is initiated' (Oestigaard 2004: 120). Burials, therefore, are not fossilizations of status-identities which 'once were', but instead constitute sacralized identities that 'will be', or perhaps, where special emphasis is placed on lost potentiality, 'could have been' (cf. Bloch and Parry 1992; Mizoguchi 2000; Garwood 2007).

Interpretations of burials as propositional acts are now commonplace in studies of ancient societies, both material and text-based (e.g. see Harlow and Laurence 2008: 23), with shared themes such as the ideological constitution of communities of the dead (e.g. Shanks and Tilley 1982; Morris 1987: 39–43), the representation of stereotypical identities in social and political discourses (e.g. Thomas 1991; Sørensen 1997; Gowland 2008), and the creation of new kinds of identity appropriate to the domains which the dead inhabit (e.g. Williams 2001). These are all widely represented in archaeological studies, some of which pay a modicum of attention to the *ritual* constitution of the dead. It has been suggested, for example, that Anglo-Saxon cremation rites which incorporated animal sacrifices were part of a wider ideology (and technology) of transformation managed by shamans or drawing upon shamanic ideas (ibid.). Animals, in this context, may have been perceived as vessels for ancestral spirits or qualities, acting either as agents for transformation or as new elements of a person's identity—animal and human combined in the fire to forge ancestral beings. In this interpretation, 'cremation served to destroy and rebuild the identity of the deceased into a new ancestral form' (ibid.: 207).

An especially interesting theme emerging in this wider context relates to the idea of *potentiality* in rites of passage. It is usually assumed that such rites celebrate new identities and statuses as given and complete things: in other words, that the individuals concerned, in passing through the ritual process, become full realizations of the person-kinds intended. This seems far too simplistic: rites of passage just as often create *unfinished* identities—prototypical forms that individuals make real through appropriate kinds of conduct, decisions, and social relationships before their personhood is fully realized (cf. La Fontaine 1985: 188–9; Strathern 1993: 46). In Classical Athens, for example, three-year old boys took part in ritualized drinking banquets on the *Choes* day of the *Anthestria* festival, as a celebration of now-recognizable sociality, survival of infancy, and '*prospective* role as adult members of the community' (Ham 1999: 6, my emphasis). In Anglo-Saxon England, while a transition in female identity is visible in the funerary record at the age of 10–12, a threshold probably related to puberty and child-bearing potential, the accumulation of female items in grave assemblages peaks in late teenage years, suggesting cumulative growth and enhancement (and also further potentiality) of this kind of personhood over several years (Stoodley 2000). In Aztec Mesoamerica, rites surrounding the recognition of infants as social beings involved the display of miniature versions of gendered adult artefacts and clothing, including dressing the children in small versions of adult apparel: from a very early stage an Aztec child was thus a male or female adult-to-be (Joyce 2000).

Great care is needed, therefore, in interpreting systems of social classification exhibited in funerary events. Death rituals serve as technologies for the construction of 'persons' that never were: potentiality is emphasized over actuality; 'initiations' in death transform individuals into person-kinds not yet attained in life; and people are recreated as sacred stereotypes that can properly inhabit the domain of the dead. Funerary rites of passage thus provide us with a means of exploring imagined classificatory order, ideal types, and of constructions and transformations of personhood *after* death. Only very rarely is it possible to recognize material representations of 'biographies' or life courses, either artefactually (e.g. as cumulative ornament sets on funerary dress; Sørensen 1997) or recorded directly on human bodies (e.g. using tattoos, scarification, piercings and tooth-filing [Joyce 2000: 477–8; cf. Fowler 2004: 79–81; Sofaer 2006]).

Moving beyond the mortuary sphere there have been a few attempts to identify material evidence for rites of passage such as birthing and female initiation. It has been suggested, for example, that Upper Palaeolithic painted caves were used for the initiation of children into secret societies (Owens and Hayden 1997), while some hut structures in the Mesolithic of North-west Europe may have been used for the seclusion of initiates or giving birth (Finlay 2006: 54–5). More widely, it may be possible to identify a range of shamanic artefacts and representations, including use of therianthropic imagery (e.g. antler headdresses), in both non-mortuary (e.g. spirit possession: Conneller 2006: 106–7; Hayden 2003: 59–60; Jordan 2001) and mortuary contexts (e.g. funerary costumes; Piggott

1962). Figurative representations may also provide a means of exploring non-funerary rites of passage, especially in combination with written sources, as in the case of ancient Egyptian male circumcision rituals (Janssen and Jannsen 1990: 90–5), and notably in recent studies of the constitution of person kinds in the classical world (e.g. Laurence 2000, 2007; Revell 2005; Serwint 1993) and Mesoamerica (e.g. Joyce 2000). Ray Laurence's interpretation of Emperor Augustus' *Ara Pacis* monument in Rome (2000: 447–53) also highlights how the life course—and by implication rites of passage—can be used for symbolic purposes in political discourse, especially as a metaphor for processes of change and transformation.

An intriguing dimension of the material culture of rites of passage is the treatment of objects as 'living' things. Artefacts may be seen to have distinct life courses, with their own 'biographies' (sometimes paralleling, sometimes transcending those of their human hosts) and they may be used in ritual acts (e.g. 'sacrifice') as substitutes for living kinds. Several interpretations of prehistoric long houses, for example, use ethnographic comparisons to define symbolic schemes centred on the house as a kind of body with its own cycle of birth–ageing–death–decay... and perhaps rebirth (Bradley 1998b: 42–8; Hugh-Jones 1996; Whittle 2003: 139–42). It is surprising, however, that the idea of rites of passage is very rarely used to try to understand how such processes were structured and marked, even though house 'foundation deposits' could easily be seen to relate to a birth rite of passage, while burning events could mark part of the death ritual of the house and proper treatment of its 'body' (i.e. as an act of cremation) (see: Brück 1999a; Nowakowski 2001). The same observations apply to other structures such as shrines, which are usually regarded simply as stages for ritual acts or as repositories of sacred objects, rather than as built forms and deposits that may be assembled/configured 'organically' in a creative process that embodies individual and/or collective life courses (as Insoll describes in the case of Tallensi personal shrines and concepts of destiny; 2008: 386–8). Similarly, the staged production processes involved in the making of objects sometimes bear close similarities with the structuring of rites of passage (e.g. in metal smelting and casting, which takes ores from a raw state, through a 'liminal' process of molten dissolution and fluidity, through to 'rebirth' in a new hardened form; cf. Herbert 1993).

7.2 Passages to Other Worlds (and Back Again)

Movement is fundamental to rites of passage, both in a practical sense of traversing boundaries and entering/leaving liminal domains, and in a symbolic sense where change is expressed through spatial shifts in bodily positions and dispositions (Parkin 1992). The archaeology of ritualized movement is an expanding field of enquiry across a wide range of cultural/period-specific contexts, with diverse attention paid to the geography, staging, semiotics, and phenomenology of sacred journeys.

The most sustained analytical and interpretative approaches to the study of ritualized movement in archaeology can be found in European prehistory (e.g. Tilley 1994; 1999), especially in relation to the complex linear and circular architectural forms of the British Neolithic. These include fully enclosed pathways like cursuses (e.g. Harding 1999; Loveday 1999), demarcated routes ('avenues') to ceremonial enclosures (e.g. Barrett 1994: 1–69; Thomas 1993) and internal passageways within or through complex circular structures such as timber circles and henges (e.g. Pollard 1995; Owoc 2001; Thomas 1999: 62–88). In some cases these studies relate ritualized movement directly to reconstructions of prehistoric cosmology (e.g. in the proposed articulation of movement, rites of transition, natural cycles and orientations, and conceptions of time: e.g. Harding et al. 2006; Owoc 2001; Pollard and Ruggles 2001). In other cases there is greater emphasis on the experiential qualities of controlled movement through sacred landscapes, including bodily alignment on fundamental symbolic significata, mystification and revelatory transitions across boundaries (e.g. Thomas's description of the West Kennet Avenue approach to Avebury Henge; 1993).

It is rare, however, to find explicit reference in these studies to rites of passage and there is usually little or no discussion of the specific stages of the ritual process in which such journeys fall. One exception is Tilley's discussion of the Bronze Age rock-carving complex at Hogsbyn in southern Sweden, which is interpreted as 'a symbolic resource forming an important focus for the ordering of calendrical and initiation rites' (1999: 154). Tilley draws particular attention to the spatial organization of the carved surfaces along a path, forming a *sequence* of stages/scenes for ritual acts that perhaps embodied a mythic narrative of travel and transformation (reflected by abundant boat, foot, and shoe carvings). Also striking is the way that groups of carved surfaces are spatially separated, suggesting a discontinuous process of engagement with the sacred that parallels the organization of many systems of initiation: it is possible that initiates returned to Hogsbyn on several occasions, each time travelling one step further on their journey of revelation (ibid.).

7.3 Boundaries, Portals, Thresholds, and Transformations

Another powerful analytical approach to the archaeology of rites of passage focuses on the architectural structuring of ritualized action. This theme is explored by Parker Pearson and Richards who observe that, 'Walls, gateways and entrances serve to mark transitions between domains such as inside/outside, sacred/profane, male/female, public/private, enemy/friend, elite/commoner or initiate/uninitiated' (1994: 24). Architectural forms thus reify conceptual divisions, define bounded contexts for the spatial articulation of cultural meanings, and guide the enactment of specific practices. Portals—especially—provide means of traversing classificatory boundaries and thus act as (liminal) thresholds between different conceptual domains and states of being (ibid.: 25). The principal interpretative difficulty relates to the very nature of rites of passage. As total processes of transformation, such rites require people to traverse at least two critical thresholds and often many more lesser barriers (Figure 18.3), in each case marked by alerting performative acts, the presence of key players in the ritual drama, architectural features (such as gates and screens), visual media (such as powerful symbols or images), and the deposition of objects and substances. It is often difficult, however, to discern at which stage in the ritual process the various social, architectural, visual, and material 'markers' of transition rites fall, and thus their particular social and religious significance.

Material deposits at entrances to sacred spaces, for example, are often read simply as the outcomes of ritual acts at liminal points (e.g. sacrifices or votive payments for crossing sacred thresholds), yet their meanings will have been quite different depending on whether the actors were entering (in the final transition from the social to the sacred) or leaving (to embark on rites of aggregation to return to the social world). The material outcomes of

The ritual process: rites of passage, thresholds, transitions, and 'journeys'

Social world	Rites of separation	Rites of liminality	Rites of reaggregation	Social world
	'Journey' Abandonment/negation of former social persona (may be a staged process through series of ritual acts)	Sacred 'space' Otherness Transcendence Sublimity Order Revelation Transformation	**'Journey'** Celebration/reification of the social persona/state of being attained (may be staged through series of ritual acts)	
	Departure Breach Separation Transition	Arrival/entry Accession Integration Transition	Departure Progression Separation Transition	Arrival/return Conquest? Integration Transition

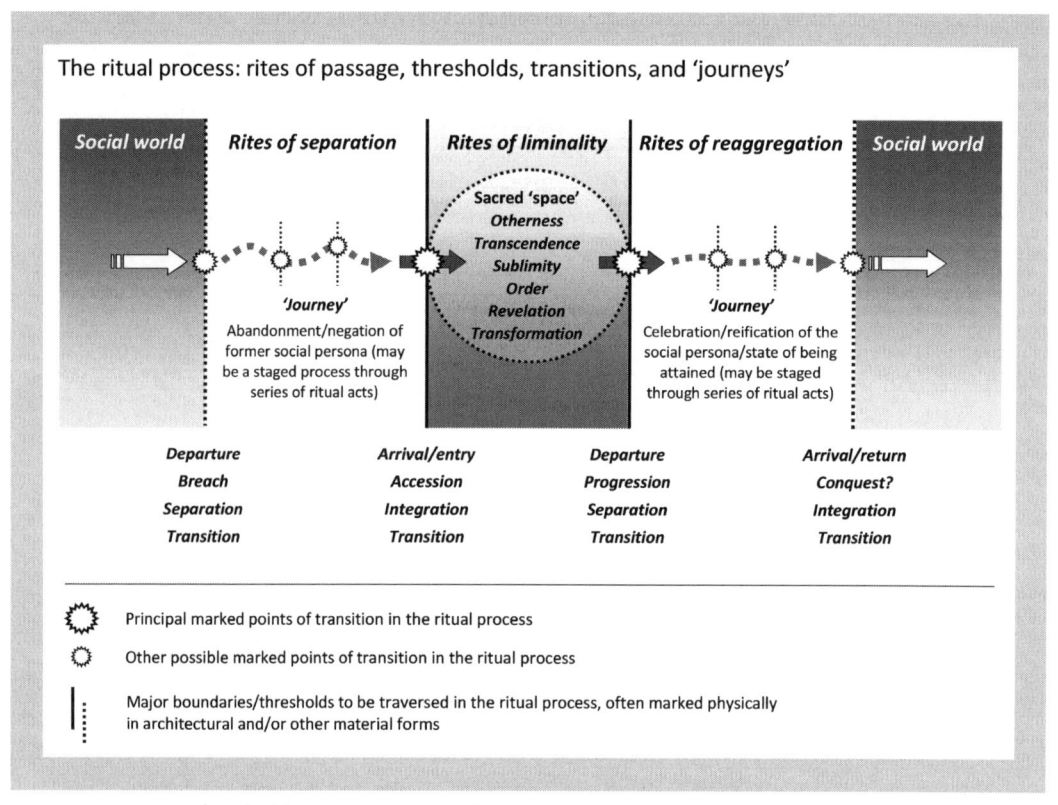

- ✸ Principal marked points of transition in the ritual process
- ○ Other possible marked points of transition in the ritual process
- ┆ Major boundaries/thresholds to be traversed in the ritual process, often marked physically in architectural and/or other material forms

FIGURE 18.3 Thresholds, transitions, and 'journeys' (real and metaphorical) in the rites of passage process. These may be marked physically—and ritualized performances guided—by architectural structures, pathways, and places of material deposition.

some of these acts might appear similar but in fact have profoundly different meanings at different stages in the ritual process. The breaking of ceramic vessels, for example, might signify—on entry to the sacred domain—the destruction of symbols of everyday sociality such as eating and drinking. Alternatively, it could just as easily represent—on leaving the sacred domain—the fragmentation of sacralized objects that could not pass into the everyday world where their sanctity might be subverted, or perhaps the conquest of the everyday through acts of violence and destruction. It is evident that we should aim to comprehend the *full* ritual process, and how it is structured spatially, in order to make sense of specific stages of ritualized action encountered in the archaeological record.

This problem is evident in interpretations of Early Neolithic causewayed enclosures in North-west Europe (Edmonds 1993; Thomas 1999: 34–53) which often draw on the idea of rites of passage to explain artefact deposition. Although the particular classificatory principles and meanings proposed for these enclosures (such as outside–inside, nature–culture dichotomies) are diverse, the placed deposits of artefacts, human and animal bones, and burnt organic materials in ditch terminals are thought to mark depositional acts at liminal points between outside and inside, and—in the case of multi-circuit enclosures—through concentrically ordered hierarchical nesting of spaces (e.g. Whittle et al. 1999: 347–90). This is convincing at a general level but there is little attempt in these studies to distinguish directionality in the ritual process nor the particular transitional stages being marked out, even though this is critical to an understanding of the specific meanings being evoked by depositional events during rites of passage.

The grand architectural designs, structural features, and qualities of Late Neolithic monumental architecture in Europe are also routinely interpreted in terms of the spatial organization of ceremonial performances (e.g. Barrett 1994; Pollard 1995), although references to rites of passage again tend to be more allusory than analytical. Whether the interpretative methodology is essentially symbolist or phenomenological in inspiration, the idea of rites of passage is used mainly as a means of descriptive characterization of *possible* practices, rather than as a means of interrogating the evidence. Even so, the particular emphasis given to movement towards, within, and through monuments, the distinctive kinds of agency within them, and especially the points of transition at thresholds between significant spaces, all provide a basis for studies of rites of transition. The impressive well-preserved monumental architecture of the Avebury (Figure 18.4) and Stonehenge monument complexes in southern England, in particular, have attracted repeated attempts to make sense of their forms and meanings in terms of both design symbolism and as stages for practices with particular performative constraints and qualities (e.g. Barrett 1994; Parker Pearson and Ramilisonina 1998; Thomas 1993).

Similar theoretical and interpretative approaches have been applied to smaller-scale Neolithic buildings. The performative qualities of the passage into the 'shrine' building within the late Neolithic settlement at Barnhouse, Orkney, which had a hearth placed within the entrance, invite specific interpretations of transformations (and perhaps purifications or ordeals) by fire when crossing the boundary between everyday life and the domain of the sacred (Hill and Richards 2005; cf. Parker Pearson and Richards 1994: 25–6). The setting of this building within a long-lived settlement and its architectural parallels with both contemporary 'house' designs and the entrance passages of earlier tombs suggest it was conceived as an 'abode of the ancestors'. As cremation was one aspect of contemporary mortuary ritual, the fiery journey across the entrance threshold may in this context have been a means to transform initiates into the 'temporary dead' to gain admission into the company of ancestral beings.

In many of these studies, however, it is evident that insufficient attention is paid to the directionality of movement (and thus orientation of perception), the particular meanings of ritualized actions, and the wider purposes of the ritual process reified in monumental architecture. In European prehistory, just as in other areas and periods of study, it is remarkable just how selectively archaeologists have chosen the aspects of monuments they wish to study, and yet how generalizing they are in making sweeping interpretations based on such studies. It is possible, for example, to proceed along the Stonehenge Avenue in both directions, yet in the archaeological literature prehistoric ceremonies appear only to have involved progress towards Stonehenge, not away; similarly, Avebury has four entrances/exits, yet again we are invited to follow (or emulate) the progress of the faithful along only one approach route (and never to leave). Plainly, whether we want to study these practices in terms of rites of passage, or some other mode of ritual performance, this requires an interpretative framework that recognizes fully the significance of the complete sequence of

FIGURE 18.4 The Late Neolithic ceremonial complex at Avebury, Wiltshire, UK. Top: the West Kennet Avenue. Bottom: the south entrance to Avebury henge enclosure, showing the massive portal stones forming part of the main stone circle, and parts of the South Circle in the background. This architecture has often been interpreted as a stage for ceremonial processions and the traversing of monumentalized boundaries/thresholds to gain access to a series of nested 'sacred' spaces (e.g. Barrett 1994, Thomas 1993), although usually only in one direction (as implied here; from the Sanctuary, via the West Kennet Avenue, to Avebury henge enclosure).

actions necessary to achieve the intentions of the ritual, and to contextualize this process in socio-spatial terms within the wider cultural landscape.

7.4 Liminality and Sacred Domains

Interpretations of sacred buildings and landscapes as liminal places/spaces inhabited during ritual performances also have widespread currency in archaeology. These emphasize the representation and experience of otherness, sacrality, purity, and order, as well as some of the social and performative qualities recognized in rites of liminality (such as *communitas*, solidarity, and ecstasy). The particular qualities of spaces and how these are interpreted will, however, vary cross-culturally (e.g. the idea of 'cleanliness' as an expression of moral good or purity is appropriate in some cultural contexts but not others), so that no universal spatial syntax or symbolic scheme exists for recognizing or giving meaning to 'liminality' (Parker Pearson and Richards 1994: 26). The fundamental properties of liminal places and spaces, therefore, are dictated by what is seen to be 'otherworldly' in contradistinction to what is perceived to be 'normal', the nature of both being socially constructed and culture-relative.

The experiential qualities that make places 'other', and how these are woven into ritual performance, have attracted considerable recent attention. This is greatly complicated, however, by the diversity of formal, material, and aesthetic attributes that may be regarded as expressions of the sacred, and by the very different kinds of places that may be seen as stages for rites of liminality. These range from caves (Owens and Hayden 1997) and huts for shamanic rituals or initiations (Gulløv and Appelt 2001; Finlay 2006: 54–5), through every kind of mortuary architecture, to grandiose temple precincts (Oestigaard 2004). At one level, of course, *all* sacred places serve to create worlds of difference, entered by the faithful to encounter, engage with, and perceive the reality of transcendant order and power (LeFebvre 1991; Parker Pearson and Richards 1994; Bradley 1998b, 68–72; Rowlands and Tilley 2006). Sensations of transcendance, in this context, may be stimulated especially through material forms and properties that surpass ordinary human frames of reference in space and time, and the use of materials or images that symbolize or appear to derive from sacred domains. Built structures may thus be made exceptionally durable, using materials such as stone that convey a sense of timelessness, transcending the human life course and even natural processes (see Parker Pearson and Ramilisonina 1998), and so massive that they overwhelm whatever is considered to be a 'human' bodily scale. They may incorporate special substances 'of' or 'for' the sacred, and representations that personify the presence of deities or spirits, such as decorative schemes, icons, or statuary. Sacred architecture may also be designed to embody especially powerful 'condensation' symbols (Turner 1967: 28–9); evident, for example, in the architectural designs of medieval Christian churches (cf. Gilchrist 1999: 83–7).

Sensations of otherness are also achieved through dramatic use of objects, images and substances that cause anxiety, suppress semantic logic, disorientate, and induce hallucinations, including drugs and alcohol (e.g. Sherratt 1991) and playing of musical instruments such as drums (e.g. Moore 2006). The monumental architecture of Neolithic Europe again provides an especially rich range of studies of this kind, focusing on the symbolic and experiential properties of entoptic phenomena (e.g. Dronfield 1995: 1996), colour (see Jones and MacGregor 2002), and strange and other-worldly acoustic effects (e.g. Watson 2001: 188–9). Very similar discussions of the qualities of liminality and otherness can be found in interpretations of cave sites, with particular emphasis on altered states of consciousness induced by sensory deprivation in dark cold places, sound and lighting effects, and striking visual imagery (e.g. Owens and Hayden 1997; Lewis-Williams 2002; R. Whitehouse 2001).

The builders of sacred architecture also routinely co-relate places in the constructed landscape with *natural* features and phenomena, that appear—from the perspective of the human observer—to exist outside history. In other words, the 'foreground' of dynamic social action is construed with reference to the 'background' of unchanging order exemplified by 'eternal' physical forms and cycles in the natural world (Hirsch 1995; Tilley 1994). This is the main focus for archaeological discussions of cyclical, collective rites of passage, such as annual rites of renewal and regeneration (e.g. fertility rites). For example, it is common in many cultural contexts to find liminal places in locations such as mountain tops, springs, or caves, which—from the perspective of daily life—seem to be situated in the background margins of the cultural landscape, occupying points of contact with other planes of existence (e.g. the sky, water, underworld) and the abodes of deities, spirits, or ancestors (Bradley 2000: 28–32, 97–103). These relationships can be further articulated through a range of devices embodied in building locations and designs, such as the framing of vistas or creation of lines of sight that reference unchanging natural features (e.g. mountain peaks: Tilley 1994: fig. 2.8) or astronomical phenomena (e.g. solar and lunar cycles: Owoc 2001; Pollard and Ruggles 2001). Non-monumentalized settings for periodic rituals of reproduction and creation can also be recognized both in 'domestic' contexts (Bradley 2005; Hill 1995; cf. Bourdieu 1977: 127–32) and large-scale communal sacrificial acts including distinctive forms of material deposition that evoked ideas of gift-giving (e.g. metalwork deposition in rivers as 'gifts to the gods' during the European Bronze Age and Iron Age: Barrett 1989b; Bradley 1998a).

It is important to recognize, however, that the inhabitation of sacred places in the course of ritual performances, and the meanings given to particular practices within these places, can be understood only as one part of a process that entailed a *series* of transformations in the course of rites of passage. In order to explore and make sense of liminal rites it is therefore necessary to arrive at an understanding of the wider spatial articulation of ritual actions, their purpose, and the course that the passage through liminal places took. The common tendency in archaeology to focus on just the liminal stage of the ritual process ignores how 'liminality' is a conditional construct that only makes sense with reference to what went before and what comes after. This problem is illustrated by the idea of 'ancestor rites' which is used widely in European prehistory for explaining the great attention paid to human remains and monument building (e.g. Bradley 1998b: 36–67; Barrett 1989a; Parker Pearson and Ramilsonina 1998; Pollard and Ruggles 2001: 80). Whilst the interpretative models proposed are often thought-provoking, the term 'ancestor' is used mainly as a vague metaphor for practices that gave prominence to the dead, the past, origins, and community identity (in various combinations), especially in monumentalized 'liminal' settings. The specific *purposes* of the ancestral rites alluded to, their spatial organization, and the whole process of engagement with the 'ancestors', including their wider cosmological significance, are not explained in detail (cf. Whitley 2002; Whittle 2003: 124–32).

8 CONCLUSION: AN ARCHAEOLOGY OF RITUAL

The argument that ritual is incapable of differentiation from other kinds of practice, at least from a material perspective (Brück 1999b), may be more a reflection of methodological inadequacies in archaeological study than a real condition of social action. Rituals in all cultural contexts draw upon a wide range of formal and stylistic features that are intended deliberately to set them apart from everyday routines, as means of *ritualization* of certain kinds of action (Bell 1992: 90). These include various kinds of 'alerting' phenomena, the display of exceptionally prominent and/or formalized symbolic media, and self-conscious referencing of otherness and timelessness (Lewis 1980, 20–36; Barrett 1991; Bell 1992). As this differentiation of practices commonly has distinctive material features, it is within the capabilities of archaeologists to distinguish 'ritual' from non-ritual, not in universalizing terms but in terms sensitive to the particular cultural contexts they are exploring. As Owoc suggests, 'what must be comprehended are the ways in which *indigenous actors* in the past and present make distinctions between different forms of practice' (2001: 28, her emphasis). This is easier to recognize than often imagined: it is usual, for example, for categorically differentiated kinds of practice to be separated *spatially* and given distinctive architectural settings and material culture repertoires for their proper performance.

Even so, rites of passage, like all ritual actions 'exist in the moments of their enactment and then disappear' (Grimes 2003: 7). At first sight, such a transient phenomenon as ritual performance appears to evade archaeological recognition, yet passages through the ritual process clearly have an intrinsic materiality, potentially comprising many different kinds of physical acts, built stages, representations, and objects. Rites of passage may thus be manifested in specific kinds of material culture, spatially patterned placement of artefacts, and distinctive architectural forms designed to guide and facilitate repeat performances. The main difficulty for archaeology, it would seem, is that rites of passage are best understood as whole processes—each stage being articulated with and made sensible by their relation to the others—but not every stage may be equally discernible materially. Yet it is perfectly possible to *imagine* the full rites of passage structure and thus contextualize and give meaning to the particular stage(s) encountered in the evidence, both in terms of the specific purposes of rites and the wider cultural schemes and principles these reproduced in practice. Unfortunately, most discussions of rites of passage in archaeology are selective and partial, focusing on specific features of ritualized passages such as thresholds, or on particular stages of the ritual process such as liminality, and thus fail entirely to address the fundamental transformative qualities of rites of passage as total social processes.

It is perhaps unsurprising, as a consequence, that even the most compelling interpretations of built structures and depositional practices in terms of ritual action can seem insubstantial, while others are routinely given to evasions and abstractions in their treatment of the subject. This may in fact be a symptom of a more general malaise: it is apparent that discussions of ritual in archaeology have been so mesmerized by questions of theoretical construction and empirical identification that the essential qualities, purposes and structures of ritual have been forgotten. By repositioning rites of passage at the heart of an archaeology of ritual it may be possible to refocus attention on what makes ritualization such a necessary part of human cultural life, what the specific purposes of ritual acts were, and how—practically and materially—rituals were performed by social actors in the past.

Suggested Reading

There is an extensive and dynamic anthropological literature on rites of passage, exemplified by van Gennep's classic work (1960), Victor Turner's influential explorations of liminality, *communitas*, the ritual process and performance (1967, 1969, 1974, 1982), and Maurice Bloch's account of ritual transformation and violence in *Prey into Hunter* (1992). Other important studies include La Fontaine's survey of initiation rites (1985), revealing discussions of mortuary rites of passage by Bloch and Parry (1982) and Metcalf and Huntingdon (1991), considerations of ritualized journeys and pilgrimages by Helms (1988) and Morinis (1992), and recent reflections on the rites of passage idea such as Grimes' *Deeply into the Bone* (2003). There is, of course, a wealth of ethnographic literature bearing on this subject, including thematic surveys of topics such as gender and female initiation (e.g. Lutkehaus and Roscoe 1995). In contrast, there is little previous archaeological writing concerned explicitly with rites of passage: rare exceptions include discussions by Brück (1999a), Carrasco (1999), Garwood (2007), Joyce (1999), Owens and Hayden (1997), and Stoodley (2000). More generally, rites of passage are discussed only briefly or by implication (e.g. Bradley 1998a, 2000, 2005; Díaz-Andreu et al. 2005; Fowler 2004; Gilchrist 1999; and Whittle 2003).

References

BARRETT, J. 1989a. 'The living, the dead and the ancestors: Neolithic and Early Bronze Age mortuary practices' in J. Barrett and I. Kinnes (eds), *The Archaeology of Context in the Neolithic and Bronze Age* (Sheffield: Department of Archaeology and Prehistory, University of Sheffield), pp. 2–8.
—— 1989b. 'Food, gender and metal: Questions of social reproduction' in M.-L. Sørensen and R. Thomas (eds), *The Bronze Age-Iron Age Transition in Britain*, BAR International Series 484 (Oxford: BAR), pp. 304–20.
—— 1991. 'Towards an archaeology of ritual' in P. Garwood, D. Jennings, R. Skeates, et al. (eds), *Sacred and Profane: Archaeology, ritual and religion* (Oxford: Oxford University Committee for Archaeology Monograph), pp. 1–9.
—— 1994. *Fragments from Antiquity* (Oxford: Blackwell).
BELL, C. 1992. *Ritual Theory, Ritual Practice* (Oxford: Oxford University Press).
BLOCH, M. 1985. 'From cognition to ideology' in R. Fardon (ed.), *Power and Knowledge: Anthropological and sociological approaches* (Edinburgh: Scottish Academic Press), pp. 21–48; repr. in M. Bloch, 1989. *Ritual, History and Power: Selected papers in anthropology* (London: Athlone Press), pp. 106–36.
—— 1986. *From Blessing to Violence: History and ideology in the circumcision ritual of the Merina of Madagascar* (Cambridge: University of Cambridge Press).

—— 1987. 'The ritual of the royal bath in Madagascar: the dissolution of death, birth and fertility into authority' in D. Cannadine and C. Price (eds), *Rituals of Royalty: Power and ceremonial in traditional societies* (Cambridge: Cambridge University Press), pp. 271–97; repr. in M. Bloch, 1989. *Ritual, History and Power: Selected papers in anthropology* (London: Athlone Press), 187–211.

—— 1992. *Prey into Hunter: The politics of religious experience* (Cambridge: Cambridge University Press).

—— 2005. 'Ritual and deference' in M. Bloch (ed.), *Essays on Cultural Transmission* (Oxford: Berg), pp. 123–37.

—— and PARRY, J. 1982. 'Introduction: Death and the regeneration of life' in M. Bloch and J. Parry (eds), *Death and the Regeneration of Life* (Cambridge: Cambridge University Press), pp. 1–44.

BOURDIEU, P. 1977. *Outline of a Theory of Practice* (Cambridge: Cambridge University Press).

BRADLEY, R. 1998a. *The Passage of Arms: An archaeological analysis of prehistoric hoards and votive deposits*, 2nd edn (Oxford: Oxbow Books).

—— 1998b. *The Significance of Monuments* (London: Routledge).

—— 2000. *An Archaeology of Natural Places* (London: Routledge).

—— 2005. *Ritual and Domestic Life in Prehistoric Europe* (London: Routledge).

BRÜCK, J. 1999a. 'Houses, lifecycles and deposition on Middle Bronze Age settlements in southern England', *Proceedings of the Prehistoric Society*, 65: 1–22.

—— 1999b. 'Ritual and rationality: Some problems in interpretation in European archaeology', *European Journal of Archaeology*, 2(3): 313–44.

BUDD, P. and TAYLOR, T. 1995. 'The faerie smith meets the bronze industry: Magic versus science in the interpretation of prehistoric metal-making', *World Archaeology*, 27(1): 133–43.

BURKERT, W. 1987. 'The problem of ritual killing' in R. Hamerton-Kelly (ed.), *Violent Origins: Ritual killing and cultural formation* (Stanford: Stanford University Press), pp. 149–76.

CANNADINE, D. and PRICE, C. (eds) 1987. *Rituals of Royalty: Power and ceremonial in traditional societies* (Cambridge: Cambridge University Press).

CARRASCO, D. 1999. *City of Sacrifice: The Aztec empire and the role of violence in civilization* (Boston: Beacon Press).

CHAPMAN, J. 2000. *Fragmentation in Archaeology* (London: Routledge).

CHATTERTON, R. 2006. 'Ritual' in C. Conneller and G. Warren (eds), *Mesolithic Britain and Ireland: New approaches* (Stroud: Tempus), pp. 101–20.

CONNELLER, C. 2006. 'Death' in C. Conneller and C. Warren (eds), *Mesolithic Britain and Ireland: New approaches* (Stroud: Tempus), pp. 139–64.

CULLUM, P. 2004. 'Boy/man into clerk/priest: The making of the late medieval clergy' in N. McDonald and W. Ormrod (eds), *Rites of Passage: Cultures of transition in the fourteenth century* (York: York Medieval Press), pp. 51–65.

DAVID, R. 2002. *Religion and Magic in Ancient Egypt* (London: Penguin).

DÍAZ-ANDREU, M., LUCY, S., BABIĆ, S., et al. 2005. *The Archaeology of Identity: Approaches to gender, age status, ethnicity and religion* (London: Routledge).

DOBRES, M-A. and ROBB, J. E. (eds) 2000. *Agency in Archaeology* (London: Routledge).

DOUGLAS, M. 1966. *Purity and Danger* (London: Routledge and Kegan Paul).

DOWDEN, K. 1999. 'Fluctuating meanings: "Passage rites" in ritual, myth, odyssey, and the Greek romance', *Bucknell Review*, 43(1): 221–43.

DRONFIELD, J. 1995. 'Migraine, light and hallucinogens: the neurocognitive basis of Irish megalithic art', *Oxford Journal of Archaeology*, 14(3): 261–75.

Dronfield, J. 1996. 'Entering alternative realities: Cognition, art and architecture in Irish passage-tombs', *Cambridge Archaeological Journal*, 6(1): 37–72.

Edmonds, M. 1993. 'Interpreting causewayed enclosures in the past and the present' in C. Tilley (ed.), *Interpretative Archaeology* (Oxford: Berg), pp. 99–142.

Finlay, N. 2006. 'Gender and personhood' in C. Conneller and G. Warren (eds), *Mesolithic Britain and Ireland: New approaches* (Stroud: Tempus), pp. 35–60.

Fowler, C. 2004. *The Archaeology of Personhood* (London: Routledge).

Garwood, P. 2007. 'Vital resources, ideal images and virtual lives: Children in Early Bronze Age funerary ritual' in S. Crawford and G. Shepherd (eds), *Children, Childhood and Society*, British Archaeological Reports, International Series 1696 (Oxford: Archaeopress), pp. 63–82.

Geertz, C. 1980. *Negara: The theatre state in nineteenth century Bali* (Princeton: Princeton University Press).

Gennep, A. van 1960 [1908]. *The Rites of Passage*, trans. M. B. Vizedom and G. L. Caffee (Chicago: University of Chicago Press).

Gilchrist, R. 1999. *Gender and Archaeology: contesting the past* (London: Routledge).

Girard, R. 1977. *Violence and the Sacred* (Baltimore: Johns Hopkins University Press).

—— 1987. 'Generative scapegoating' in R. Hamerton-Kelly (ed.), *Violent Origins: Ritual killing and cultural formation* (Stanford: Stanford University Press), pp. 73–105.

Gluckman, M. 1962. *Les Rites de Passage* in M. Gluckman (ed.), *Essays on the Ritual of Social Relations* (Manchester: Manchester University Press), pp. 1–52.

Golding, W. 1980. *Rites of Passage* (London: Faber).

—— 1987. *Close Quarters* (London: Faber).

—— 1989. *Fire Down Below* (London: Faber).

Gowland, R. 2008. 'Age, ageism and osteological bias: The evidence from Late Roman Britain' in M. Harlow and R. Laurence (eds), *Age and Ageing in the Roman Empire*, Supplementary Series 65 (Portsmouth, RI: Journal of Roman Archaeology), pp. 153–69.

Green, M. A. 2001. *Dying for the Gods: Human sacrifice in Iron Age and Roman Europe* (Stroud: Tempus).

Grimes, R. L. 2003. *Deeply into the Bone: Re-inventing rites of passage* (Berkeley: University of California Press).

Gulløv, H. C. and Appelt, M. 2001. 'Social bonding and shamanism among late Dorset groups in high arctic Greenland' in N. Price (ed.), *The Archaeology of Shamanism* (London: Routledge), pp. 146–63.

Haaland, G., Haaland, R., and Dea, D. 2004. 'Smelting iron: Caste and its symbolism in south-western Ethiopia' in T. Insoll (ed.), *Belief in the Past*, BAR International Series 1212 (Oxford: BAR), pp. 75–86.

Ham, G. L. 1999. '*Choes* and *Anthestria* reconsidered: Male maturation rites and the Peloponnesian wars', *Bucknell Review*, 43(1): 203–18.

Harding, J. 1999. 'Pathways to new realms: Cursus monuments and symbolic territories' in A. Barclay and J. Harding (eds), *Pathways and Ceremonies: The cursus monuments of Neolithic Britain*, Neolithic Studies Group Seminar Papers 4 (Oxford: Oxbow Books), pp. 30–8.

——, Johnson, B., and Goodrick, G. 2006. 'Neolithic cosmology and the monument complex of Thornborough, North Yorkshire', *Archaeoastronomy*, 20: 28–53.

Harlow, M. and Laurence, R. 2008. 'Introduction: Age and ageing in the Roman Empire' in M. Harlow and R. Laurence (eds), *Age and Ageing in the Roman Empire*, Supplementary Series 65 (Portsmouth, RI: Journal of Roman Archaeology), pp. 9–24.

HAYDEN, B. 2003. *Shamans, Sorcerers and Saints: A prehistory of religion* (Washington: Smithsonian Books).
HELMS, M. 1988. *Ulysses' Sail: An ethnographic odyssey of power, knowledge and geographical distance* (Guildford: Princeton University Press).
HERBERT, E. W. 1993. *Iron, Gender and Power: Rituals of transformation in African society* (Bloomington and Indianapolis: Indiana University Press).
HILL, J. D. 1995. *Ritual and Rubbish in the Iron Age of Wessex*, BAR British Series 242 (Oxford: BAR).
HILL, J. and RICHARDS, C. 2005. 'Structure 8: Monumentality at Barnhouse' in C. Richards (ed.), *Dwelling among the Monuments: The Neolithic village of Barnhouse, Maehowe passage grave and surrounding monuments at Stenness* (Cambridge: McDonald Institute for Archaeological Research), pp. 157–94.
HIRSCH, E. 1995. 'Introduction. Landscape: Between place and space' in E. Hirsch and M. O'Hanlon (eds), *The Anthropology of Landscape: Perspectives on place and space* (Oxford: Clarendon Press), pp. 1–30.
HUGH-JONES, C. 1996. 'Houses in the Neolithic imagination: An Amazonian example' in T. Darvill and J. Thomas (eds), *Neolithic Houses in Northwest Europe and Beyond* (Oxford: Oxbow Books), pp. 185–93.
HUMPHREY, C. and LAIDLAW, J. 1994. *The Archetypal Actions of Ritual: A theory of ritual illustrated by the Jain rite of worship* (Oxford: Oxford University Press).
INSOLL, T. 2004a. *Archaeology, Ritual, Religion* (London: Routledge).
——2004b. 'Are archaeologists afraid of gods? Some thoughts on archaeology and religion' in T. Insoll (ed.), *Belief in the Past*, BAR International Series 1212 (Oxford: BAR), pp. 1–6.
——2008. 'Negotiating the archaeology of destiny: An exploration of interpretative possibilities through Tallensi shrines', *Journal of Social Archaeology*, 8(3): 380–403.
JANSSEN, R. and JANSSEN, J. 1990. *Growing Up in Ancient Egypt* (London: Rubicon).
JONES, A. and MACGREGOR, G. (eds) 2002. *Colouring the Past: The significance of colour in archaeological research* (Oxford: Berg).
JORDAN, P. 2001. 'The materiality of shamanism as "world view": praxis, artefacts and landscape' in N. Price (ed.), *The Archaeology of Shamanism* (London: Routledge), pp. 87–104.
JOYCE, R. 2000. 'Girling the girl and boying the boy: The production of adulthood in ancient Mesoamerica', *World Archaeology*, 31(3): 473–83.
KUPER, A. 1993. 'The English Christmas and the family: Time out and alternative realities' in D. Miller (ed.), *Unwrapping Christmas* (Oxford: Clarendon Press), pp. 157–75.
LA FONTAINE, J. S. 1985. *Initiation: Ritual drama and secret knowledge across the world* (Harmondsworth: Penguin).
LAURENCE, R. 2000. 'Metaphors, monuments and texts: The life course in Roman culture, *World Archaeology*, 31(3): 442–55.
——2007. 'Gender, age and identity: The female life course at Pompeii' in M. Harlow and R. Laurence (eds), *Age and Ageing in the Roman Empire*, Supplementary Series 65 (Portsmouth, RI: Journal of Roman Archaeology), pp. 94–110.
LEFEBVRE, H. 1991. *The Production of Space* (Oxford: Blackwell).
LEWIS, G. 1980. *Day of Shining Red: An essay on understanding ritual* (Cambridge: Cambridge University Press).
LEWIS-WILLIAMS, D. 2002. *The Mind in the Cave* (London: Thames and Hudson).
LOVEDAY, R. 1999. 'Dorchester-on-Thames: Ritual complex or ritual landscape?' in A. Barclay and J. Harding (eds), *Pathways and Ceremonies: The cursus monuments of Neolithic Britain*, Neolithic Studies Group Seminar Papers 4 (Oxford: Oxbow Books), pp. 49–63.

Lucy, S. 2005. 'The archaeology of age' in M. Díaz-Andreu, S. Lucy, S. Babić, et al.(eds), *The Archaeology of Identity: Approaches to gender, age status, ethnicity and religion* (London: Routledge), pp. 43–66.

Lutkehaus, N. C. 1995. 'Feminist anthropology and female initiation in Melanesia' in N. C. Lutkehaus and P. B. Roscoe (eds), *Gender Rituals: Female initiation in Melanesia* (London: Routledge), pp. 3–29.

—— and Roscoe, P. B. (eds) 1995. *Gender Rituals: Female initiation in Melanesia* (London: Routledge).

Meskell, L. and Joyce, R. 2003. *Embodied Lives: Figuring ancient Maya and Egyptian experience* (London: Routledge).

Metcalf, P. and Huntingdon, R. 1991. *Celebrations of Death: Anthropology of mortuary ritual*, 2nd edn (Cambridge: Cambridge University Press).

Mizoguchi, K. 2000. 'The child as a node of past, present and future' in J. Sofaer Derevenski (ed.), *Children and Material Culture* (London: Routledge), pp. 141–50.

Moore, J. D. 2006. '"The Indians were much given to their taquis": Drumming and generative categories in ancient Andean funerary processions' in T. Inomata and L. S. Coban (eds), *Archaeology of Performance: Theaters of power, community and politics* (Lanham: AltaMira), pp. 47–79.

Morinis, A. 1992. 'Introduction' in A. Morinis (ed.), *Sacred Journeys: The anthropology of pilgrimage* (London: Greenwood Press), pp. 1–28.

Morris, I. 1987. *Burial and Ancient Society: The rise of the Greek city state* (Cambridge: Cambridge University Press).

Muir, E. 2005. *Ritual in Early Modern Europe*, 2nd edn (Cambridge: Cambridge University Press).

Nilsson Stutz, L. 2003. *Embodied Rituals and Ritualized Bodies: Tracing ritual practies in late Mesolithic burials* (Lund: Wallin and Dahlholm Boktryckeri AB).

Nowakowski, J. 2001. 'Leaving home in the Cornish Bronze Age: Insights into planned abandonment processes' in J. Brück (ed.), *Bronze Age Landscapes: Tradition and transformation* (Oxford: Oxbow Books), pp. 139–48.

Oestigaard, T. 2004. 'Kings and cremations: Royal funerals and sacrifices in Nepal' in T. Insoll (ed.), *Belief in the Past*, BAR International Series 1212 (Oxford: BAR), pp. 115–24.

Owens, D. and Hayden, B. 1997. 'Prehistoric rites of passage: A comparative study of transegalitarian hunter-gatherers', *Journal of Anthropological Archaeology*, 16: 121–61.

Owoc, M.A. 2001. 'Bronze Age cosmologies: The construction of time and space in southwestern funerary/ritual monuments' in A. T. Smith and A. Brookes (eds), *Holy Ground: Theoretical issues relating to the landscape and material culture of ritual space objects*, BAR International Series 956 (Oxford: BAR), pp. 27–38.

Parker Pearson, M. 1999. *The Archaeology of Death and Burial* (Stroud: Tempus).

—— and Ramilisonina. 1998. 'Stonehenge for the ancestors: The stones pass on the message', *Antiquity*, 72: 308–26.

—— and Richards, C. 1994. 'Ordering the world: Perceptions of architecture, space and time' in M. Parker Pearson and C. Richards (eds), *Architecture and Order: Approaches to social space* (London: Routledge), pp. 1–37.

Parkin, D. 1992. 'Ritual as spatial direction and bodily division' in D. de Coppet (ed.), *Understanding Rituals* (London: Routledge), pp. 11–25.

Pfaffenberger, B. 1988. 'Fetishised objects and human nature: Towards an anthropology of technology', *Man*, 23: 236–52.

Piggott, S. 1962. 'From Salisbury Plain to South Siberia', *Wiltshire Archaeological and Natural History Magazine*, 58: 93–7.
Pollard, J. 1995. 'Structured deposition at Woodhenge', *Proceedings of the Prehistoric Society*, 61: 137–56.
—— and Ruggles, C. 2001. 'Shifting perceptions: Spatial order, cosmology and patterns of deposition at Stonehenge', *Cambridge Archaeological Journal*, 11: 69–90.
Revell, L. 2005. 'The Roman life course: A view from the inscriptions', *European Journal of Archaeology*, 8(1): 43–63.
Rowlands, M. and Tilley, C. 2006. 'Monuments and memorials' in C. Tilley, W. Keane, S. Kuechler, et al. (eds), *Handbook of Material Culture* (London: Sage Publications), pp. 500–15.
—— and Warnier, J-P. 1993. 'The magical production of iron in the Cameroon Grassfields' in T. Shaw, P. Sinclair, B. Andah, et al. (eds), *The Archaeology of Africa: Food, metals and towns* (London: Routledge), pp. 512–50.
Schechner, R. 1994. 'Ritual and performance' in T. Ingold (ed.), *Companion Encyclopaedia of Anthropology* (London: Routledge), pp. 613–47.
Serwint, N. 1993. 'Female athletic costume at the Heraia and prenuptial initiation rites', *American Journal of Archaeology*, 97(3): 403–22.
Shanks, M. and Tilley, C. 1982. 'Ideology, symbolic power and ritual communication: a reinterpretation of Neolithic mortuary practices' in I. Hodder (ed.), *Symbolic and Structural Archaeology* (Cambridge: Cambridge University Press), pp. 129–54.
Sherratt, A. 1991. 'Sacred and profane substances: The ritual use of narcotics in later Neolithic Europe' in P. Garwood, D. Jennings, R. Skeates, et al. (eds), *Sacred and Profane: Archaeology, ritual and religion*, Oxford University Committee for Archaeology Monograph 32 (Oxford), pp. 50–64.
Sigaut, F. 1994. 'Technology' in T. Ingold (ed.), *Companion Encyclopaedia of Anthropology* (London: Routledge), pp. 420–59.
Sofaer, J. R. 2006. *The Body as Material Culture* (Cambridge: Cambridge University Press).
Sørensen, M.-L. S. 1997. 'Reading dress: The construction of social categories and identities in Bronze Age Europe', *Journal of European Archaeology*, 5(1): 93–114.
Stoodley, N. 2000. 'From the cradle to the grave: Age organization and the early Anglo-Saxon burial rite', *World Archaeology*, 31(3): 456–72.
Strathern, M. 1993. 'Making incomplete' in V. Broch-Due, I. Rudie, and T. Bleie (eds), *Carved Flesh/Cast Selves: Gendered symbols and social practices* (Oxford: Berg), pp. 41–52.
Thomas, J. 1991. 'Reading the body: Beaker funerary practice in Britain' in P. Garwood, D. Jennings, R. Skeates, et al. (eds), *Sacred and Profane: Archaeology, ritual and religion*, Oxford University Committee for Archaeology Monograph 32 (Oxford), pp. 33–42.
—— 1993. 'The politics of vision and the archaeologies of landscape' in B. Bender, J. Gledhill, and B. Kapferer (eds), *Landscape: Politics and perspectives* (Oxford: Berg), pp. 19–48.
—— 1996. *Time, Culture and Identity: An interpretive archaeology* (London: Routledge).
—— 1999. *Understanding the Neolithic* (London: Routledge).
Tilley, C. 1994. *A Phenomenology of Landscape: Places, paths and monuments* (Oxford: Berg).
—— 1999. *Metaphor and Material Culture* (Oxford: Blackwell).
Turnbull, C. 1990. 'Liminality: A synthesis of subjective and objective experience' in R. Schechner and W. Appel (eds), *By Means of Performance: Intercultural studies of theatre and ritual* (Cambridge: Cambridge University Press), pp. 50–81.

TURNER, V. 1967. *The Forest of Symbols: Aspects of Ndembu ritual* (Ithaca: Cornell University Press).
——1969. *The Ritual Process: Structure and anti-structure* (Chicago: Aldine).
——1974. *Dramas, Fields and Metaphors: Symbolic action in human society* (Ithaca: Cornell University Press).
——1982. *From Ritual to Theatre* (New York: Performing Arts Journal Publications).
——1986. *On the Edge of the Bush* (Tucson: University of Arizona Press).
——1990. 'Are there universals of performance in myth, ritual and drama?' in R. Schechner and W. Appel (eds), *By Means of Performance: Intercultural studies of theatre and ritual* (Cambridge: Cambridge University Press), pp. 8–18.
WATSON, A. 2001. 'Round barrows in a circular world: monumentalizing landscapes in Early Bronze Age Wessex' in J. Brück (ed.), *Bronze Age Landscape. Tradition and Transformation* (Oxford: Oxbow Books), pp. 207–16.
WERBNER, R. 1989. *Ritual Passage, Sacred Journey: The process and organization of religious movement* (Washington: Smithsonian Institution Press).
WHITEHOUSE, H. 2000. *Arguments and Icons: Divergent modes of religiosity* (Oxford: Oxford University Press).
WHITEHOUSE, R. 2001. 'A tale of two caves: The archaeology of religious experience in Mediterranean Europe' in P. F. Biehl, F. Bertemes, and H. Meller (eds), *The Archaeology of Cult and Religion* (Budapest: Archaeolingua Alapítvány), pp. 161–7.
WHITLEY, J. 2002. 'Too many ancestors', *Antiquity*, 76: 119–26.
WHITTLE, A. 2003. *The Archaeology of People: Dimensions of Neolithic life* (London: Routledge).
——POLLARD, J., and GRIGSON, C. 1999. *The Harmony of Symbols: The Windmill Hill causewayed enclosure* (Oxford: Oxbow Books).
WILLIAMS, H. 2001. 'An ideology of transformation: Cremation rites and animal sacrifice in early Anglo-Saxon England' in N. Price (ed.), *The Archaeology of Shamanism* (London: Routledge), pp. 193–212.

CHAPTER 19

THE ARCHAEOLOGY OF CONTEMPORARY CONFLICT

ZOE CROSSLAND

1 INTRODUCTION

THE last decade of the twentieth century witnessed the forensic exhumation of human remains on an unprecedented scale. Drawn into what had previously been the terrain of forensic anthropology, archaeologists have been called on to deal with the large numbers of mass graves uncovered at multiple sites across the world (Haglund et al. 2001; Haglund 2001; Hunter and Simpson 2007). The extraordinary numbers of people killed by the violent conflicts and abuses of the twentieth century have demanded that an account be made, and the nature of the deaths means that often archaeological exhumation is an important first step in this accounting. Early exhumations of mass graves took place during and after the Second World War (Mant 1987); the most well-known is perhaps the German-sponsored investigation into the massacre of Polish soldiers by Soviet troops at the site of Katyn (Paul 1991; Sanford 2005). The number and frequency of mass-grave exhumations has grown enormously in recent years, and the forensic archaeological field has become more professionalized, with a major landmark being the formation of the Argentine Forensic Anthropology Team in the mid-1980s (Snow et al. 1984; Doretti and Snow 2003). Since then forensic techniques for the detection and excavation of mass graves have developed rapidly (e.g. Haglund 2002, Schmitt 2002; Wright et al. 2005). These excavations reside within the medico-legal world of forensic science, and have been little studied in mainstream archaeological texts, although the recent turn towards the archaeology of the contemporary past has encouraged an interest in the abject horrors of modernity (Buchli and Lucas 2001; Gonzalez-Ruibel 2006).

This relative lack of engagement may derive in part from the dominant focus of archaeological approaches to warfare and conflict, which have traditionally been theorized within a social evolutionary frame, in terms of tribal and chiefly violence (e.g. Ferguson and Whitehead 1992; Redmond 1994; papers in Martin and Frayer 1997) and particularly in relation to state-making practices (Carneiro 1992; Cohen 1984; Haas 1982; LeBlanc 1999; Webster 1975; Wilson 1987). Recent scholarship by archaeologists and others has broadened the range of approaches, particularly through the study of recent and historical warfare (e.g. Carman 1997, 1999a, 1999b, 2002; Carman and Harding 2004; Pollard and Banks 2006, 2007; Saunders 2004b, 2007; Schofield et al. 2002). The major themes that emerge from this literature include the increasingly pressing question of the memory and commemoration of recent conflict (e. g. Boorman 1988; Gilchrist 2003a; King 1998; Moriarty 1995; Rowlands 1999; Saunders, N. J. 2002, 2004b); critique of the dominant narratives of military history, which have viewed warfare primarily in terms of tactics and technology, men's identities, and practices of power and domination (Gilchrist 2003b; Tarlow 1997; Vandkilde 2003); and the materiality of conflict and of human life (Saunders 2003a, 2003b; also papers in Saunders 2004a; Schofield 2005). In contrast, forensic archaeological or anthropological accounts have tended to remain outside of the frame of theoretical debate in archaeology. Here it should be noted that while forensic archaeology as a field is distinguished from forensic anthropology in the UK (the one focusing more on the context of excavation and depositional analysis, the other more on the osteological analysis of human remains), in the US the term 'forensic anthropology' encompasses both specialisms. Additionally, as this chapter explores, the term 'forensic' is often used to cover a broad spectrum of archaeological interventions, many of which are not concerned with providing legal evidence. In many cases the impulse to excavate is humanitarian rather than forensic in orientation.

The lack of engagement between mainstream archaeological theory and forensic archaeology is all the more striking because of the association of violent conflict with present-day state making and the definition of nation (Skurski and Coronil 2006; Tilly 2002). Much attention has been paid to the ways in which archaeological practice is caught up in conflict over boundaries, territory, and the definition of ethnicity and faith (Abu El-Haj 2001; Arnold 1990, 2002, 2006; Díaz-Andreu 2001; Meskell 1997; Pollock 2008); attempts to control historical narratives associated with the self-definition of state and of nation are often fraught with allusions to past conditions (see papers in Gillis 1994). The classificatory policies of colonial empire-building—the map and census, and the delimitation of territory were also often underwritten by appeals to the past as Benedict Anderson has explored (1991; also Kuklick 2001; Silverberg 1968) and these continue to resonate (e.g. Labadi 2007; van Eeden 2004). Archaeological narratives have been shown to have underwritten state projects of population control and definition both in the metropole (e.g. papers in Kohl and Fawcett 1995; McCann 1990; Champion 2001; Leoussi 2001) and on the colonial frontier (e.g. Silberman 2001; Robertshaw 1990). In the case of Rwanda for example, colonial scholarship constructed Tutsi and Hutu as phenotypically distinct, projecting these perceived racial differences back into the past in a search for the 'original' occupants of the land (Twagiramutara 1989). This acted to fix social and political identities that had previously been somewhat fluid, and contributed to creating the conditions within which the genocide of 1994 took place (Mamdani 2001: 41–75; also Longman 2001). An archaeology of contemporary conflict therefore involves consideration of the role and ethics of archaeological knowledge practices, excavating the disciplinary histories of archaeology and anthropology, and tracing their role in defining populations and groups with reference to the material evidence of the past (see for example papers in Hamilakis and Duke 2007; Meskell and Pels 2005; Starzmann, Pollock, and Bernbeck 2008). This is as much the case for forensic archaeological practice as it is for other aspects of the recent past.

It is striking how archaeological engagement with conflict shifts into a different register when the subject is interpersonal violence in the contemporary past. In this case archaeological evidence of violence against people is composed within a forensic framework, usually for use as part of the prosecution of human rights abuses. Although the techniques and activities of forensic archaeologists originally developed, as the name suggests, in the context of criminal prosecutions (Haglund 1998), the work also has a humanitarian aspect which can be in tension with the legal need for excavated evidence (Fondebrider 2002). The location of archaeological exhumation within a medico-legal framework acts to make sense of past violence through the deployment of secular, medically tinged analysis tied to a humanitarian narrative of aid and a legal narrative of justice. Thomas Laqueur, in his exploration of the origins of nineteenth-century humanitarianism has shown how medical writings of the eighteenth and nineteenth centuries amassed and ordered facts in order to testify to and make visible the suffering of others, in the process demonstrating possibilities for action and intervention. In the search for medical truth located in the trustworthy corpse, the pain-filled body created a point of connection between those who suffered and those who would come to their aid, while also remaining the site of scientific enquiry. The dead, unlike the living, offered truths through autopsy, and could be represented through narratives that offered a model for social action (Laqueur 1989: 176–8). In the same way, the humanitarian procedures of forensic archaeological practice attempt to understand the death of the deceased through measurement and analysis (cf. Laqueur 2002). It is part of its representational force and evocative power that such a seemingly scientific and rational mode of operation should be enacted in situations of apparent irrationality, fear, and social breakdown, whether this be widespread societal destruction as in Rwanda or the former Yugoslavia, or more narrowly situated in the untimely and violent death of those victims of individual murderers.

If the work of forensic and humanitarian archaeological practice acts to make sense of violent contexts retrospectively, then at least three dimensions can be recognized in these sense-making acts. First, through its participation in efforts to prosecute those held to be responsible for political violence and other acts of aggression, archaeology works to remake the world by ensuring the appropriate punishment of crime. In the process of bringing illegitimate or delegitimized violence within the structured realm of legislation and the balance of the law the preceding violence is often figured as senseless or chaotic (cf. Donham 2006: 20). Second, the identification of remains and their return to families where possible, brings the dead back into regularized funerary practice and the world of grief and mourning usually associated with the dead. In so doing archaeological practice acts to alleviate the violence enacted upon the dead and their friends and relatives. Finally, the very act of cordoning off and securing an area of violence and horror (e.g. Skinner 1987: 277–8), of bringing scientific techniques and practices to bear on a locus of disorder and destruction has a powerful symbolic force. The treatment of mass graves as crime scenes acts to demarcate the boundaries in time and space of these violent acts, containing them and managing them. The concern with crime-scene contamination expresses this need to clarify and delineate the violent conditions without outside influence. In the rest of this review I start by looking at the complex relationship between archaeology's forensic role in assembling evidence for judicial scrutiny, and its humanitarian focus in relation to funerary ritual and the return of human remains to families. I then move on to discuss archaeology's scientific operations as sense-making acts in the context of its location within mortuary practices more broadly.

2 Human Rights, Humanitarianism, and Mortuary Ritual

Talal Asad notes that despite the long history of anthropological interest in religion and ritual, the complementary category of the secular has evaded the critical gaze (Asad 2003: 21; although see Taylor 2007). Although the secular and rationalist orientation of forensic archaeological practice sets it aside from religious beliefs and practices, its operations demonstrate how it is involved with definitions of the sacred and profane (themselves contingent historical categories as Asad observes), and in maintaining boundaries between the dead and the living. This becomes visible not only in forensic archaeologists' acknowledgement of diverse beliefs about, and treatment of, the dead body (e.g. Williams and Crews 2008; Skinner 2007; Vanezis 1999; Rainio et al. 2001), but also in the ways in which forensic practice itself is differently inflected according to the context within which it operates. Forensic archaeological practice can, therefore, tell us something about the constitution of the secular and its relationship to concerns that would normally be understood to occupy the ground of religious belief, or more generally, would be defined in opposition to secular reason.

Huge efforts can be expended in searching for the dead, and not simply for the purposes of criminal prosecution. One of the most striking illustrations of this is the work coordinated by the International Commission on Missing Persons (ICMP) in the former Yugoslavia, where tens of thousands of individuals were killed and buried in mass graves. Much of the work there now focuses primarily on identifying human remains for relatives (e.g. Wagner 2008). The excavations allow comparison of DNA profiles from blood samples donated by living family members to DNA obtained from the exhumed dead (Weaver 2003). These efforts speak to the perceived need for the dead body in order to carry out proper funerary ritual, illustrating how archaeological work responds to the exigencies of the absent body, whether in contexts of accidental death, or in cases of murder or political violence (Stover and Shigekane 2002; Fondebrider 2002: 889–90). As the work of forensic anthropologists extends into human rights work more broadly written, it expands to include the identification of bodies, not for the purposes of legal proceedings, but to enable them to be returned to families for proper burial (Burns 2007: 204–7; Ferllini 1999). This movement illustrates how archaeological exhumation is located firmly within funerary ritual, a stage, as Istvan Rév has emphasized, on the body's journey from the liminality of the temporary grave to the reincorporation of final burial (1995, 2005). In the practice of exhumation the dead body is brought back into the realm of the living, often as part of a ritualized process of transition and incorporation, to use van Gennep's terms (van Gennep 1969). István Rév's discussion of the search for the bodies of Imre Nagy and other politicians executed after the Hungarian Revolution in 1958, conceptualizes their exhumation and reburial as part of funerary practice, arguing that the disinterment of the dead may be understood within the framework of temporary burial outlined by Hertz (1960), despite their somewhat different location within the ritual cycle of separation and incorporation. Sant Cassia has explored the personal responses to exhumed bodies of the missing among relatives in Cyprus, looking at the ways in which relationships to the bodies of the dead are negotiated and maintained through the process of mourning (2005, 2006). He notes that the archaeological exhumations act to invert the normal process of funerary ritual in Greek Cyprus, allowing the dead to begin to enter in to the ritual process of the funeral and reburial (2006: 210–11). His work in Cyprus encourages a view of the forensic exhumation as a point where grieving starts, and this seems to be borne out by comments from family members in other parts of the world when confronted with the excavated traces of their relatives (e.g. Crossland 2000: 154). In its extension of humanitarian care for those who have suffered violent and untimely deaths, forensic practice establishes a bond of commonality with the efforts of mourners to understand and make sense of the death of their friends and relatives (Laqueur 1989; Panourgiá 1995: 206–7). At the same time it brings a particular history and set of attitudes that developed in the context of Western European medical, legal, and scientific practice. The attitudes have informed the routine dissociation of some corpses from social concerns and funerary requirements (Blakely and Harrington 1997; Crossland 2009a; Richardson 1987).

Reflecting this tension, the knowledge produced through archaeological exhumation focuses on two aspects of the dead's bodily histories. In the context of mass graves, the personal identification and naming of the dead is essential in order to allow funerary ritual to take place. However, the search for knowledge of the circumstances of death and deposition for the purposes of mounting legal cases tends to focus on the cause and manner of death (Fondebrider 2002: 888). Identification is often difficult, or costly if DNA analysis is the only possible route, and is in any case often unnecessary for the prosecution of crimes within the context of human rights law as developed since the Second World War (Burns 1998; Cerone 2007). The deployment of archaeological and anthropological evidence in the prosecution of war crimes, crimes against humanity, and the crime of genocidal targeting of ethnic, racial, religious, or national communities often revolves primarily around identifying group affiliation, cause, and manner of death (Mufti and Stover 2004: 29). The forensic requirements for demonstrating this kind of crime do not necessarily entail the personal identification of individual human remains. A salient example is the forensic archaeological work carried out at Ovčara near Vukovar in the former Yugoslavia under the auspices of the United Nations. Archaeological excavation was undertaken in order to independently assess witness testimony recording the abduction and execution of patients and staff from Vukovar hospital in November 1991. Work at the site established that a mass grave existed and the number of bodies buried within it. It was also possible to clarify the conditions under which the massacre took place and to demonstrate that a graveside mass execution took place consistent with oral testimonies (Fenrick 1994; Stover and Peress 1998). The evidence produced through exhumation substantiates and makes material the written and oral testimony of witnesses, as well as documentary evidence of crimes (Weiss 2009). In the prosecution of crimes, the power of archaeological exhumation is often in its public documentation of an open secret that was already known, as Winifred Tate has outlined (2007; also Taussig 1999). The focus of archaeological and anthropological analysis in the prosecution of human rights abuses is usually on establishing whether those killed were civilians, ascertaining the manner of death, and whether the murders were systematic and widespread (Mufti and Stover 2004: 29–30). The last is of particular importance in establishing genocidal intentions on the part of those charged. Consequently, establishing the cause and manner of death often becomes the most pertinent issue. In this case the legal desiderata can overshadow the needs and desires of families and survivors, leading to potential conflict when the families are treated as marginal to the proceedings of exhumation and prosecution, as Fondebrider has noted in relation to UN investigations (2002: 887).

In the drama of exhumation the claims and views of relatives are often understood to be endowed with a moral force that asserts their rights to the bodies against those of other participants. The practice of exhumation therefore acts as a focal point for the personal and psychological grief of mourning, sometimes coming into conflict with societal concerns and legal and scientific claims on the body. Like funerary practices exhumation is work carried out for both the living and the dead, existing often uncomfortably at the point where competing needs and desires intersect. As in the funerary setting claims are often made that the living are facilitating the wishes of the dead; in the context of forensic practice this is understood as a desire on the part of the dead to act as witness in the pursuit of justice (e.g. Whitaker 2000). This justification emerges out of the tension between the competing needs, all focused on the dead body, of legal and/or medical evidence, political narratives, and the desires of relatives and survivors for remembrance and mourning (Crossland 2009b).

The numbers and actions involved in mass murder often seem ungraspable, and one perspective that allows a glimpse of the scale and extent of violence while also remembering those who were killed is that of the case study. This narrows down the focus to individual cases, which act metonymically to represent the full horror of the violence (Laqueur 2002: 178). This is an approach that has been called upon in the work of the Argentine Forensic Anthropology Team, who, in their efforts to identify the remains of people disappeared by the state, worked to create histories and memories of those buried anonymously (Salama 1992). The focus on the case study and the deployment of archaeological practice as part of a societal duty of care is consistent with exhumation's location within both medical and forensic contexts (Crossland 2009a). Within this framework a humanitarian desire to help can be expressed as the tracing of an individual case history, or as the search for knowledge, broadly written. While the individual case history acts to reunite the biography of the dead person with the medico-legal facts that are produced upon and through their body, the broader search for knowledge without this grounding in the dead person's history and biography risks becoming detached from the desires and needs of living relatives and families. In this sense, forensic anthropology can run into similar ethical issues to those around human remains more broadly (Thompson 2001; Steele 2008). Increasingly, the results of exhumations are used to assess and refine methodologies, aiming ultimately at the better prosecution of crimes (e.g. Kimmerle et al. 2008; Komar 2003; Schaefer 2008; Šlaus et al. 2003). Recently forensic anthropologists and archaeologists have been drawn into ethical debates over research carried out to this end on human remains from mass graves in the former Yugoslavia. The controversy over claims that samples of bone were kept for study without the consent of relatives (Banning and DeKoning 2004) has obvious parallels with the storm over retention of human tissue at Alder Hey Hospital in Liverpool, as has been noted by John Hunter and Margaret Cox (2005: 215). Both cases illustrate how their positioning as simultaneously humanitarian intervention and scientific practice can encourage a view of the dead as evidence in the service of a greater societal good in which the needs and desires of relatives are overlooked (see also Marks 2005).

In the context of exhumation the reappearance of the dead can create new possibilities for action, as Katherine Verdery has explored (1999). Narratives that are located in the humanitarian traditions of the individual case-history may be rejected, whether because of opposition to the knowledge practices within which the bodies are embedded or because of a need to claim and re-make the collective death of those excavated, as Layla Renshaw has observed (2007: 249). Equally, the powerful political resonances that are evoked in these contexts can overwhelm the personal histories of the dead (Ferrándiz 2006: 10). The corpse can act as a powerful metaphorical extension of the body politic and this is often in some tension with its desired incorporation into funerary ritual and personal frameworks of grief and memorialization (Sassòli and Tougas 2002). During excavations of people murdered by Argentina's military regime of 1976-83, opposition to the exhumations was expressed by some human rights groups. In this case the memory of the missing dead was recognized as a more powerful force for social justice without a body to tie it to individual memory and funerary ritual (Crossland 2002). Consequently, the state-sponsored commemoration of the dead and disappeared through the dedication of sculptures, parks, and other monumental spaces can be viewed as problematic by relatives and survivors (e.g. Huyssen 2003), not least because of the manner in which these memorials are constructed to channel and control remembrance and incorporate memory into collective narratives, often politicized and partial (Rowlands 1999).

Archaeological exhumation itself creates another axis for the creation and maintenance of memory (Basu 2007; Renshaw 2007; Sanford 2003), although this can come into conflict both with survivors and relatives who resist the framing of the body as evidence (Crossland 2000) or are reluctant to accept the new memories created through exhumation (Ferrándiz 2006). Rév observes that 'an unknown grave is a historical fact... it has a definitive historical place... as a consequence of... the fact that its exact location is not known' (1995: 36). Grave sites are therefore often as potent as the bodies themselves in the creation of political narratives. The location of grave sites in imaginary places, or their deliberate forgetting in some cases, can be undermined through the delving of archaeologists and human rights investigators into the earth and into the past (Ferrandíz 2006: 9). Enabling the dead to undergo the appropriate funerary ritual, exhumation can also facilitate social reincorporation, banishing the ghosts who haunt survivors. This banishment may not always be welcomed, however (Crossland 2002). Bloch and Parry note that within mortuary traditions that extend funerary rites past the first burial, the first disposal of the body tends to be associated with the polluting aspects of death, often tied to the time-bound individual and his or her history and individual biography, whereas in the subsequent second burial regenerative aspects are often brought to the fore, drawn upon in the remaking of the social order and the re-establishment of authority (1982: 11). Certainly the debates over forensic excavation, subsequent funerary ritual and associated commemorative practices are strongly associated with conflict over how the world should be remade and the normal order of things re-established, suggesting that it can be conceptualized within this frame. Bringing forensic excavation within the realm of mortuary practices more broadly written, both in its connection with funerary ritual, and in terms of its medico-legal history of post-mortem interventions opens up questions about the attitudes and beliefs about the body that are worked through in the practice of exhumation.

3 FORENSIC ARCHAEOLOGY AS SENSE-MAKING PRACTICE

In response to the mounting body of experience in mass-grave excavation, forensic archaeologists are developing guidelines and protocols for dealing with the exhumation of the dead in a variety of international contexts (Steele 2008). As well as building on established archaeological methodologies, these draw upon Western European criminal, legal, and medical traditions to promote a cross-culturally applicable model of practice. John Hunter and Barry Simpson observe that this universal orientation is an idealized model that has to adapt to local needs and demands (2007: 268). One of the first actions at a crime scene is to define and map its limits, often including cordoning off the site to avoid unnecessary interference by the press and members of the public, while also regulating access among members of the investigating team (Geberth 1983; Hunter and Cox 2005: 1–27; Skinner and Lazenby 1983). This concern with the delineation of space is sometimes linked to anxieties about the shielding of the work of excavation from the gaze of onlookers, sympathetic or otherwise (e.g. Skinner 1987; Wright et al. 2005: 156–7; cf. Brkic 2003). Forensic archaeologists come under scrutiny from a range of gazes: the media, state bureaucrats, international observers, military and police representatives, as well as relatives and representatives of human rights organizations. This can make the space of excavation a charged and uncomfortable place (Crossland 2002: 124–7; Klonowski 2007: 161; Skinner 2007: 268). As well as controlling access to the gravesite, the marking out of the scene of death and its environs both protects those working within it and delineates the grave as outside of social space. Instead, a new, carefully regulated place is defined (Skinner et al. 2003: 83), within which secular scientific practice is deployed to order and measure the violence that it delimits.

In a forensic context the careful control of evidence is imperative in order to ensure that the crime scene is not contaminated and the archaeological evidence will be viable in court (Dilley 2005; Galloway et al. 1990; Geberth 1983; Hunter and Knupfer 1996). In archaeology this may be translated into a distinction between exhumation and excavation (e.g. Connor and Scott 2001: 4), where exhumation is characterized as unstructured, sometimes chaotic, and destructive. An exhumed body is removed from the grave with little attention paid to scientific methodology, to recording context, or to the wider setting within which the body is located. Concern is often expressed in the forensic archaeological literature about situations where uncontrolled and unscientific exhumation has taken place, not least because this can often preclude identification and return of individuals to relatives, as well as foreclosing the possibility that the remains can be used as evidence in court (e.g. Klonowski 2007: 158–68; Joyce and Stover 1991: 241; Stover et al. 2003: 663). An excavated body in contrast, is one that is carefully removed from the grave, where thought is paid to the traces of human actions that led to its deposition in the ground, and close attention paid to the clues and signs left behind by those responsible for its burial. Excavations are carefully controlled; attempts are made not to introduce new elements into the grave, to keep the site as clean and uncontaminated as possible, free from the traces of archaeologists who mediate the body's extrication.

However, the discussion of contamination also works to reveal the death pollution associated with exhumation, particularly when dealing with the decomposing and 'abject' dead (Buchli and Lucas 2001: 10–11; Mitrović 2008; Skinner 1987: 278). Forensic archaeology, particularly in contexts of recent mass graves is an emotionally and physically difficult task and it is understandable that practitioners would want to leave the dirt and decay behind at the site. Mark Skinner, for example, recommends that a field decontamination area be established where possible, aside from where people normally wash (Skinner 1987: 275–6). Although this is not always possible in difficult field conditions, this ideal acts to separate the everyday washing areas from those especially dedicated to cleaning oneself of the pollution from the grave. These practices operate within the realm of rationality as defined by forensic practice, yet are also important boundary markers between the dead and the living. A concern with pollution, while framed in terms of rational and common-sense logic, has resonances with mortuary practices more broadly, and in this respect it is also significant that archaeological exhumation is often brought in to scenes and places of disorder and chaos, a rationalist project to bring order and sense to worlds where chaos and destruction seem to have reigned. In this context, death pollution can be managed and shouldered in the service of reordering and remaking the world through exhumation and subsequent funerary ritual. This is sometimes expressed explicitly in popular accounts, which tie the dirt and degradation of the grave to a transcendent narrative of redemption through archaeological and anthropological practice (e.g. Koff 2004: 51–5). The symmetry between the concern with the bounded and carefully controlled scene of exhumation, and the emphasized need to keep clean and to keep work items away from living quarters (Wright et al. 2005: 141) also suggests ways in which the concern with death pollution makes itself felt. The boundaries between the grave site and the world of the living are carefully managed, as far as is practicable, through maintaining the chain of custody, and through thorough labelling and storage of excavated human remains and associated artefacts (Burns 2007; Hunter and Simpson 2007: 285–6; Skinner 1987: 276; Skinner and Lazenby 1983).

Hunter and Cox's (2005) recent edited volume on forensic archaeology pays thoughtful attention to the ethical and affective dimensions of forensic archaeological practice. These are dimensions that are often omitted from forensic texts. In dealing with these broader issues the authors' account raises questions of pollution in relation to forensic practice. Most notable is how the concern with controlling and delimiting the space of excavation and maintaining the integrity of the chain of custody merges into issues of health and safety. The authors outline the need for spotlessly clean equipment and appropriate clothing that will avoid the transfer of fibres from archaeologist to grave site. This speaks to a concern with evidence and the potential for undermining the legal case if close attention is not paid to its collection (ibid.: 98–9). They then move on to warn of the risks of contamination to archaeologists from the grave, whether from disease or trauma (ibid.: 99). This, in contrast, speaks to questions of illness and personal risk rather than the work of forensic evidence collection, and suggests that there is an anxiety about contamination that works both ways. The concern with the proper use of latex gloves demonstrates the movement between the different conceptions of contamination:

> Rubber gloves are essential for all scene of crime work and are best worn doubled up when dealing with human remains. This... allows the outer glove to be replaced without risk of contamination or risk to the individual... Unlike more traditional archaeological scenarios, there are *no* occasions at a scene of crime where it is permissible to use bare hands. [Hunter and Cox 2005: 100]

Here close attention is paid to the boundary between the forensic archaeologist and the context of excavation, as the discussion moves from maintaining the integrity of the scene of crime, to the risk to the archaeologist, and then back again. The doubled gloves act as a barrier that protects the person excavating ('without... risk to the individual') but also prevents the archaeologist from contaminating the evidence ('there are *no* occasions at a scene of crime where it is permissible to use bare hands'). Not only does the archaeologist's presence need to be minimized in order to avoid contaminating the evidence, but the boundaries between living and the dead need to be carefully delineated. Although framed within a secular discourse of rationality the easy movement between best-practice recommendations for the correct collection of evidence and the application of the appropriate health and safety measures hints at an underlying anxiety about pollution, one that escapes the rationalist and secular framework that forensic archaeology occupies.

The careful extrication of the forensic practitioner from the crime scene is reinscribed through the common emphasis in both the popular and academic literature on the need for objectivity, neutrality, and expert independence (see Aronson 2007). An objective stance removes the archaeologist from the crime scene emotionally and politically, working to maintain the representational boundaries between expert and evidence that are delineated materially through forensic practice. Hunter and Cox note that there is some tension between the demand for objectivity within the context of forensic work and the social relationships within which forensic archaeologists are located (2005: 210–11). The objective forensic attitude has been associated with a purging of emotion and a traditionally dispassionate and neutral voice in textbooks, with little acknowledgement or discussion of the emotional issues involved with excavating and analysing the dead (e.g. Krogman and Işcan 1986). However, increasingly archaeologists and biological anthropologists are acknowledging a range of issues that had not previously been raised, including questions of ethics, personal involvement, and professionalization (although see Peter Pels (2005) for a critical discussion of ethics in anthropology). This shift can be seen for example in the change in orientation over the two volumes edited by William Hagland and Marcella Sorg on forensic taphonomy (Haglund and Sorg 1997, 2002).

The idiom of objectivity most often drawn upon in forensic texts derives from a nineteenth-century tradition of 'mechanical objectivity', an orientation that works to record its facts exactly as found, and with minimal interference from the observer (Daston and Galison 1992, 2007). Lorraine Daston and Peter Galison have shown that this ideal was established relatively late in the nineteenth century, demonstrating that 'objectivity' itself encompasses a range of historically contingent positions. What is significant about this form of objective account is the way in which it acts to circumscribe the character and expression of affective response. This move is both productive and problematic in the context of forensic archaeological practice, in that it provides an avenue to disengage from the horror of the abuses inflicted upon the people excavated, while neither acknowledging any room for affective response on the part of the excavator, nor providing space for engagement with relatives and survivors outside of the narrow confines of data collection and presentation. Popular accounts of forensic practice frequently delineate the moments of emotional eruption when the analyst loses his or her ability to suppress an affective response (e.g Koff 2004: 46–7, 152–5). This is portrayed as a threat to the necessary professional distance that should be maintained. This 'necessary inhumanity' is also deeply embedded in the medical histories of post-mortem intervention that Ruth Richardson has delineated (1987, 2000), itself the subject of debate within the medical field (e.g. Bertman and Marks 1989; Smith and Kleinman 1989; Miles 1991). While distancing strategies are clearly helpful in negotiating the difficult terrain of human exhumation, it is useful to unpack the historically and culturally specific baggage that comes with this concept of objectivity. In fact, the different orientations of forensic practice that already exist demonstrate a range of possibilities. This can be illustrated through comparison of the differing approaches to forensic practice in the context of mass graves and human rights violations.

In the case of the UK and US, forensic archaeology emerged in the context of domestic crime scene analysis, usually dealing with the excavation and analysis of the individual burials and skeletal remains (Hunter 1994, 1999; Cox 2001; Morse et al. 1976; 1983; Stewart 1979). This expertise has since been called upon in international contexts (for example by the United Nations to investigate war crimes and genocide in the former Yugoslavia and Rwanda [Saunders, R. 2002; Stover and Peress 1998; Haglund et al. 2001]). In Argentina and Guatemala, in contrast, forensic archaeology/anthropology teams were established using local team members, trained in place to investigate widespread political violence and disappearances (Joyce and Stover 1991; Stover 1985). This greater involvement with the community and better understanding of the local context of disappearance and exhumation have led to a greater focus on working with families of the dead and developing close links with local human rights organizations among the Argentine Forensic Anthropology Team (EAAF) and the Guatemalan Forensic Anthropology Foundation (FAFG) (Bernardi and Fondebrider 2007: 209–10; Doretti and Fondebrider 2001: 142; Suasnávar and Moscoso Moller 1999). Building upon its experiences in Argentina and abroad, the EAAF advocates a broadly interdisciplinary approach that is sensitive to particular local circumstances and encourages the training of autonomous teams of forensic specialists in place. Although ante-mortem interviews and community outreach are increasingly being recognized as a key component of forensic archaeological practice throughout the field (Burns 1998; Hunter and Cox 2005: 214; Hunter and Simpson 2007: 276–8; Simmons and Haglund 2005: 171; Steadman and Haglund 2005: 4) a more complete integration of local communities into the forensic investigation along the model established in South and Central America is still viewed as problematic by some practitioners in that it compromises the independence of the forensic team (Rainio et al. 2007: 59).

Whereas most forensic practice in Europe and North America tends to make efforts to control and regulate access to the crime scene, in the context of Central and South America the approach has been to integrate relatives and survivors in the investigation in so far as this is possible. This is a model that has also been found to work in other parts of the world (Stover and Shigekane 2002). The EAAF start their work with interviews and the collection of oral testimony with local communities, not focusing solely on the collection of ante-mortem data, but working more broadly with local human rights organizations and community groups both to explain their work and acknowledge the histories that people want to tell (Fondebrider pers. comm. 2008). Clearly, funding and field constraints can make this approach difficult in many cases, such as in the former Yugoslavia (Klonowski 2007). In Guatemala, Victoria Sanford has documented the excavations of mass graves in Plan de Sánchez by the FAFG. In this case the grave site was treated as a location for grieving and commemoration, with flowers and candles being placed within the grave and adjacent to putatively identified human remains (Sanford 2003). In other cases such as Iraqi Kurdistan, the Balkans, and Ethiopia, relatives have worked alongside forensic archaeologists (Fondebrider 2002; Hunter and Simpson 2007: 277–8; Stover 1992; although also see Tumini et al. 2007). In Spain, recent excavations of mass graves from the civil war have been organized by relatives. These exhumations fall outside of the strictly forensic sphere, instead constituting part of a project of collective memory. In this case Layla Renshaw has shown how the demand for rigorous control of the chain of evidence recedes, while the idiom of scientific neutrality is maintained as part of the performance of exhumation (2007; also Gassiot and Steadman 2008).

Clearly the different contexts and requirements of varying excavations create different parameters and possibilities for forensic archaeological practice and these are continually being explored and reinvented on the ground. Yet in the theoretical literature the habitual emphasis on the detached 'mechanical objectivity' of Western scientific practice tends to act to foreclose the possibility of full recognition of the affective, religious, and sacred dimensions of forensic archaeological work, and not simply in contexts where archaeologists work primarily to retrieve and identify human remains rather than to prosecute crimes. In so doing, this framing of forensic archaeological work acts to describe and circumscribe the field of secular humanitarianism, delineating it as part of the realm of universal rationality, and disavowing the contribution of culturally embedded, religious, ritualized, and affective forms of belief (see also Wylie 2005). These aspects exist both within the traditions of practice of forensic archeology, and in the contexts of death and bodily disposal that it encounters. As John Hunter and Barry Simpson observe:

> [w]e are accustomed to believe that western (ie., UK and US) standards are the appropriate standards to apply worldwide, but that fails to take into account local values, traditional justice systems, and ethnic and religious beliefs within societies for whom UK and US attitudes of justice may be neither appropriate nor relevant. [Hunter and Simpson 2007: 268]

4 CONCLUSION

Increasingly there are calls for forensic archaeologists and anthropologists to engage more widely with the issues raised in their practice (Cox 2001; Hunter and Cox 2005: 204–25). The context of forensic excavation reveals the brutality and trauma of violence in all its tangibility and corporeality, and encourages a focus on the articulation of individuals and their everyday lives with the social and political structures that lead to the wrenching of people from networks of home and family, and their violent death and deposition in the earth. Steadman and Haglund note the potential for cross-cultural synthesis of forensic anthropological results to create a 'new, objective perspective on some of the most notorious, as well as forgotten, events of the 20th century' (2005: 2). In starting to place mass graves within wider social and political contexts (Hunter and Simpson 2007: 270), traditions and histories of forensic practice itself are also opened up to analysis and question. The present theoretical framework within which much of forensic practice is situated provides little room for exploration of these issues, instead leaving this to popular forensic archaeology texts or to ethnographic or sociological study (examples of the latter include Basu 2007; Ferrándiz 2008; Ferrándiz and Baer 2008; Sant Cassia 2005, 2006; Sanford 2003) In her influential book on the political lives of dead bodies, Katherine Verdery asks after the power of dead bodies to attract attention and to become the focal point for political claims. She begins with their materiality, noting how the tangibility of the corpse locates it firmly in place, while also allowing the past to be materialized in the present. Yet, the significance of corpses, she concludes, comes less from their tangible presence, and more from the particular properties that make them powerful political symbols. These include the dead body's connection to the sacred, through the association of death with religious rites and its connection to the everyday, through its lived biography (1999: 31–3). Forensic and humanitarian archaeology's location as a necessary stage in the completion of funerary rites positions it as part of the production of the sacred. This entails a recognition that while the sacred nature of exhumed bodies need not be understood in religious terms as Ronald Dworkin has argued, neither is it particularly helpful to follow Dworkin in understanding the body's sanctity as a transhistorical and universal entity (Dworkin 1993).

Corpses share some of their power to fascinate and enchant with those objects chosen for museological display (Elliot 1994) and they raise similar questions of epistemic practice and politics (Curtis 2003). Archaeological practice acknowledges the significance of the corpse and its sacral dimensions precisely through the great efforts made to search for, recover, and identify the dead, complete and whole, ready to be placed in holy ground. This recognition opens up rather than closes down possibilities for future engagement, not least in its acknowledgement of the historical specificicity of archaeological assumptions about the appropriate post-mortem treatment of the dead body. While the space of exhumation is the key locus for the production of forensic archaeological knowledge, it also acts as an important site of encounter and commemoration for relatives of the dead and missing (Stover and Shigekane 2002: 860–1), and as such always holds the potential for the creation of new and sometimes unexpected contexts for interaction and mourning (Ferrándiz and Baer 2008). Wendy Brown has argued that the loss of confidence in modernity's key underpinnings has led to a suspicion of the meta-narratives of progress and universal rights without offering any political substitute (Brown 2001). Arguably, in forensic archaeology's practical engagement with these issues in day-to-day practice new formulations are being worked out on the ground in response to the dead and the living in a bricolage of techniques and discursive frameworks (Stover and Ryan 2001). In placing the humanitarian intervention of forensic archaeological practice within a broader historical perspective, its role in the production of the field of the secular is clarified, and the meaning of secular practice itself expanded.

Acknowledgements

Many thanks to Luis Fondebrider, John Hunter, Adam Rosenblatt, Tim Thompson, and Lindsay Weiss for helpful comments. Thanks too to Susan Pollock, Caroline Steele, and Jamie Johns for help in tracking down references.

Suggested Reading

John Hunter and Margaret Cox's *Forensic Archaeology: Advances in theory and practice* provides a useful introduction and overview to the subject. For discussion of the humanitarian issues around finding and returning human remains see the 2002 issue of the *International Review of the*

Red Cross 84(848). Insightful ethnographic accounts of archaeological exhumations have been written by Victoria Sanford and Paul Sant Cassia. For discussion of the meaning of present-day secularism, see Talal Asad and Charles Taylor; Wendy Brown's work is helpful and relevant in considering the position of forensic excavation in relation to such transnational forces as humanitarianism, secularism, and international law.

References

ABU EL-HAJ, N. 2001. *Facts on the Ground: Archaeological practice and territorial self-fashioning in Israeli society* (Chicago: University of Chicago Press).
ANDERSON, B. 1999. *Imagined Communities*, rev. edn (London: Verso).
ARNOLD, B. 1990. 'The past as propaganda: Totalitarian archaeology in Nazi Germany', *Antiquity*, 64(244): 464–78.
—— 2002. 'Justifying genocide: The supporting role of archaeology in "ethnic cleansing"' in A. L. Hinton (ed.), *Annihilating Difference: The anthropology of genocide* (Berkeley: University of California Press), pp. 95–116.
—— 2006. 'Pseudoarchaeology and nationalism' in G. G. Fagan (ed.), *Archaeological Fantasies: How pseudoarchaeology misrepresents the past and misleads the public* (London: Routledge), pp. 154–79.
ARONSON, J. D. 2007. *Genetic Witness: Science, law, and controversy in the making of DNA profiling* (New Brunswick: Rutgers University Press).
ASAD, T. 2003. *Formations of the Secular: Christianity, Islam, modernity* (Stanford, Calif.: Stanford University Press).
BANNING, C. and DE KONING, P. 2004. 'Without the consent of next-of-kin in Bosnia and Kosovo—Tribunal collected bones', Kosova Action Network Website, posted 16 September, accessed 11 Jan. 2009, <http://www.kan-ks.org>
BASU, P. 2007. 'Palimpsest memoryscapes: Materializing and mediating war and peace in Sierra Leone' in F. de Jong and M. Rowlands (eds), *Reclaiming Heritage: Alternative imaginations in West Africa* (Walnut Creek, CA: Left Coast Press), pp. 231–59.
BERNARDI, P. and FONDEBRIDER, L. 2007. 'Forensic archaeology and the scientific documentation of human rights violations: An Argentinean example from the early 1980s' in R. Ferllini (ed.), *Forensic Archaeology and Human Rights Violations* (Springfield, IL: Charles C. Thomas), pp. 205–32.
BERTMAN, S. L. and MARKS, S. C. 1989. 'The dissection experience as a laboratory for self discovery about death and dying', *Clinical Anatomy*, 2(2): 103–13.
BLAKELY, R. L. and HARRINGTON, J. M. (eds) 1997. *Bones in the Basement: Postmortem racism in nineteenth century medical training* (Washington, DC: Smithsonian Institution Press).
BLOCH, M. and PARRY, J. (eds) 1982. *Death and the Regeneration of Life* (Cambridge: Cambridge University Press).
BOORMAN, D. 1988. *At the Going Down of the Sun: British First Word War memorials* (York: Ebor Press).
BRKIC, C. A. 2003. 'Adiyo, Kerido', *Public Archaeology*, 3: 95–9.
BROWN, W. 2001. *Politics Out of History* (Princeton: Princeton University Press).
BUCHLI, V. and LUCAS, G. (eds) 2001. *Archaeologies of the Contemporary Past* (London: Routledge).

BURNS, K. R. 1998. 'Forensic anthropology and human rights issues' in K. J. Reichs (ed.), *Forensic Osteology: Advances in the identification of human remains* (Springfield, IL: Charles C. Thomas), pp. 63–85.

—— 2007. *Forensic anthropology training manual* (Upper Saddle River, NJ: Prentice Hall International) (2nd edition).

CARMAN, J. (ed.) 1997. *Material Harm: Archaeological studies of war and violence* (Glasgow: Cruithne Press).

—— 1999a. 'Beyond the Western way of war: Ancient battlefields in comparative perspective' in J. Carman and A. F. Harding (eds), *Ancient Warfare: Ancient perspectives* (Stroud: Sutton), pp. 39–55.

—— 1999b. 'Bloody meadows: The place of battle' in S. Tarlow and S. West (eds), *The Familiar Past? Archaeologies of later historical Britain* (London: Routledge), pp. 233–45.

—— 2002. 'Paradox in places: Twentieth century battlefield sites in long-term perspective' in J. Schofield, W. G. Johnson, and C. M. Beck (eds), *Matériel Culture: The archaeology of twentieth-century conflict* (London: Routledge), pp. 9–21.

—— and HARDING, A. (eds) 2004. *Ancient Warfare: Archaeological perspectives* (Stroud: Sutton).

CARNEIRO, R. L. 1992. 'The role of warfare in political evolution: past results and future projections' in G. Ausenda (ed.), *Effects of War on Society* (San Marino: Center for Interdisciplinary Research on Social Stress), pp. 87–102.

CERONE, JOHN P. 2007. 'The nature of international criminal law and implications for investigations' in R. Ferllini (ed.), *Forensic Archaeology and Human Rights Violations* (Springfield, IL: Charles C. Thomas), pp. 24–54.

CHAMPION, T. 2001. 'The appropriation of the Phoenicians in British imperial ideology' in M. Díaz-Andreu (ed.), 'Archaeology and Nationalism', special issue of *Nations and Nationalism: Journal of the Association for the Study of Ethnicity and Nationalism*, 7(4): 451–65.

COHEN, R. 1984. 'Warfare and state formation: Wars make states and states make war' in R. B. Ferguson (ed.), *Warfare, Culture, and Environment* (New York: Academic Press), pp. 329–58.

CONNOR, M. and SCOTT, D. D. 2001. 'Paradigms and perspectives', *Journal of Historical Archaeology*, 35(1): 1–6.

COX, M. 2001. 'Forensic archaeology in the UK. Questions of socio-intellectual context and socio-political responsibility' in V. Buchli and G. Lucas (eds), *Archaeologies of the Contemporary Past* (London: Routledge), pp. 145–57.

CROSSLAND, Z. 2000. 'Buried lives: Forensic archaeology and the disappeared in Argentina', *Archaeological Dialogues*, 7(2): 146–59.

—— 2002. 'Violent spaces: Conflict over the reappearance of Argentina's disappeared' in J. Schofield, C. Beck, and W. G. Johnson (eds), *Matériel Culture: The archaeology of twentieth-century conflict* (London: Routledge), pp. 115–31.

—— 2009a. 'Acts of estrangement: The making of self and other through exhumation', *Archaeological Dialogues*, 16(1): 101–25.

—— 2009b. 'Of signs and traces: Dead bodies and their evidential traces', *American Anthropologist*, 111(1): 69–80.

CURTIS, N. G. W. 2003. 'Human remains: The sacred, museums and archaeology', *Public Archaeology*, 3: 21–32.

DASTON, L. and GALISON, P. 1992. 'The image of objectivity', *Representations*, 40: 81–128.

—— 2007. *Objectivity* (New York: Zone Books).

Díaz-Andreu, M. 2001. 'Introduction: Nationalism and archaeology' in M. Díaz-Andreu (ed.), *Archaeology and Nationalism*, special issue of *Nations and Nationalism: Journal of the Association for the Study of Ethnicity and Nationalism*, 7(4): 429–40.

Dilley, R. 2005. 'Legal matters' in J. R. Hunter and M. Cox (eds) 2005. *Forensic Archaeology: Advances in theory and practice* (London: Routledge), pp. 177–203.

Donham, D. L. 2006. 'Staring at suffering. Violence as a subject' in E. G. Bay and D. L. Donham (eds), *States of Violence: Politics, youth, and memory in contemporary Africa* (Charlottesville: University of Virginia Press), pp. 16–33.

Doretti, M. and Fondebrider, L. 2001. 'Science and human rights: Truth, justice, reparation and reconciliation, a long way in Third World countries' in V. Buchli and G. Lucas (eds), *Archaeologies of the Contemporary Past* (London: Routledge), pp. 138–44.

—— and Snow, C. 2003. 'Forensic anthropology and human rights: The Argentine experience' in D. W. Steadman (ed.), *Hard Evidence: Case studies in forensic anthropology* (New Jersey: Prentice Hall), pp. 290–310.

Dworkin, R. 1993. *Life's Dominion: An argument about abortion, euthanasia, and individual freedom* (New York: Knopf).

Eeden, J. van 2004. 'The colonial gaze: Imperialism, myths, and South African popular culture', *Design Issues*, 20(2): 18–33.

Elliot, J. D. 1994. 'Drinking from the well of the past: Historical preservation and the sacred', *Historic Preservation Forum*, 8(3): 26–35.

Fenrick, W. J. 1994. *Mass Graves: Ovcara*, Annexes X. A Final Report of the United Nations Commission of Experts established pursuant to Security Council Resolution 780 (1992).

Ferguson, R. B. and Whitehead, N. L. (eds) 1992. *War in the Tribal Zone* (Santa Fe: School of American Research Press).

Ferllini, R. 1999. 'The role of forensic anthropology in human rights issues' in S. I. Fairgrive (ed.), *Forensic Osteological Analysis: A book of case studies* (Illinois: Charles C. Thomas), pp. 287–302.

Ferrándiz, F. 2006. The return of Civil War ghosts. *Anthropology Today*, 22(3): 7–12.

—— 2008. 'Cries and whispers: exhuming and narrating defeat in Spain today', *Journal of Spanish Cultural Studies* 9(2): 177–92.

—— and Baer, A. 2008. 'Digital memory: The visual recording of mass grave exhumations in contemporary Spain', *Forum: Qualitative Social Research*, 9(3): article 35, Online Journal: <http://www.qualitative-research.net>

Fondebrider, L. 2002. 'Reflections on the scientific documentation of human rights violations', *International Review of the Red Cross*, 84(848): 885–91.

Galloway, A., Birkby, W. H., Kahana, T., et al. 1990. 'Physical anthropology and the law: Legal responsibilities of forensic anthropologists', *Yearbook of Physical Anthropology*, 33: 39–58.

Gassiot, E. and Steadman, D. W. 2008. 'The political, social and scientific contexts of archaeological investigations of mass graves in Spain', *Archaeologies: Journal of the World Archaeological Congress*, 4(3): 429–44.

Geberth, V. J. 1983. *Practical Homicide Investigation: Tactics, procedures, forensic techniques* (New York: Elsevier).

Gennep, A. van. 1969. *The Rites of Passage* (Chicago: University of Chicago Press).

Gilchrist, R. (ed.) 2003a. 'The social commemoration of warfare', *World Archaeology*, 35(1).

—— 2003b. 'Towards a social archaeology of warfare', *World Archaeology*, 35(1): 1–6.

Gillis, J. 1994. *Commemorations: The politics of national identity* (Princeton NJ: Princeton University Press).

GONZALEZ-RUIBAL, A. 2006. 'The dream of reason: An archaeology of the failures of modernity in Ethiopia', *Journal of Social Archaeology*, 6(2): 175–201.
HAAS, J. 1982. *The Evolution of the Prehistoric State* (New York: Columbia University Press).
HAGLUND, W. D. 1998. 'The scene and context: Contributions of the forensic anthropologist' in K. J. Reichs (ed.), *Forensic Osteology: Advances in the identification of human remains*, 2nd edn (Springfield, IL: Charles C. Thomas), pp. 41–61.
—— 2001. 'Archaeology and forensic death investigations', *Historical Archaeology*, 35(1): 26–34.
—— 2002. 'Recent mass graves: An introduction' in W. D. Haglund and M. H. Sorg (eds), *Advances in Forensic Taphonomy: Method, theory, and archaeological perspectives* (Boca Raton: FL: CRC Press), pp. 243–61.
——, CONNOR, M. and SCOTT, D. D. 2001. 'The archaeology of contemporary mass graves', *Historical Archaeology*, 35(1): 57–69.
—— and SORG, M. H. 1997. *Forensic Taphonomy: The postmortem fate of human remains* (Boca Raton, FL: CRC Press).
—— —— 2002. *Advances in Forensic Taphonomy: Method, theory and archaeological perspectives* (Boca Raton, FL: CRC Press).
HAMILAKIS, Y. and DUKE, P. (eds) 2007. *Archaeology and Capitalism: From ethics to politics* (Walnut Creek, CA: Left Coast Press).
HERTZ, R. 1960. *Death and the Right Hand* (Glencoe, IL: Free Press).
HUNTER, J. R. 1994. 'Forensic archaeology in Britain', *Antiquity*, 68: 758–69.
—— 1999. 'The excavation of modern murder' in J. Downes and T. Pollard (eds), *The Loved Body's Corruption: Archaeological contributions to the study of human mortality* (Glasgow: Cruithne Press), pp. 209–23.
—— and KNUPFER, G. C. 1996. 'The police and judicial structure in Britain' in J. R. Hunter, C. A. Roberts, and A. Martin (eds), *Studies in Crime: An introduction to forensic archaeology* (London: Routledge), pp. 24–39.
—— and Cox, M. (eds) 2005. *Forensic Archaeology: Advances in theory and practice* (London: Routledge).
—— and SIMPSON, B. 2007. 'Preparing the ground: Archaeology in a war zone' in R. Ferllini (ed.), *Forensic Archaeology and Human Rights Violations* (Springfield, IL: Charles C. Thomas), pp. 266–92.
HUYSSEN, A. 2003. 'Memory sites in an expanded field: the memory park in Buenos Aires' in *Present Pasts: Urban palimpsests and the politics of memory* (Stanford, CA: Stanford University Press), pp. 94–109.
JOYCE, C. and STOVER, E. 1991. *Witnesses from the Grave: The stories bones tell* (Boston: Little, Brown and Company).
KIMMERLE, E. H., JANTZ, R. L., KONIGSBERG, L. W., et al. 2008. 'Skeletal estimation and identification in American and East European populations', *Journal of Forensic Sciences*, 53(3): 524–32.
KING, A. 1998. *Memorials of the Great War in Britain: The symbolism and politics of remembrance* (Oxford: Berg).
KLONOWSKI, E. 2007. 'Forensic anthropology in Bosnia and Herzegovina: Theory and practice amidst politics and egos' in R. Ferllini (ed.), *Forensic Archaeology and Human Rights Violations* (Springfield, IL: Charles C. Thomas), pp. 148–69.
KOFF, C. 2004. *The Bone Woman: A forensic anthropologist's search for truth in the mass graves of Rwanda, Bosnia, Croatia, and Kosovo* (New York: Random House).
KOHL, P. and FAWCETT, C. (eds) 1995. *Nationalism, Politics and the Practice of Archaeology* (Cambridge: Cambridge University Press).

KOMAR, D. 2003. 'Lessons from Srebrenica: The contribution and limitations of physical anthropology in identifying victims of war crimes', *Journal of Forensic Sciences*, 48(4): 713–16.

KROGMAN, W. M. and IŞCAN, M. Y. 1986. *The Human Skeleton in Forensic Medicine* (Springfield, IL: Charles C. Thomas).

KUKLICK, H. 2001. 'Contested monuments: The politics of archaeology in Southern Africa' in G. W. Stocking (ed.), *Colonial Situations: Essays on the contextualisation of ethnographic knowledge* (Madison, WI: University of Wisconsin Press), pp. 135–69.

LABADI, S. 2007. 'Representations of the nation and cultural diversity in discourses on World Heritage', *Journal of Social Archaeology*, 7(2): 147–70.

LAQUEUR, T. W. 1989. 'Bodies, details and the humanitarian narrative' in L. Hunt (ed.), *The New Cultural History* (Berkeley and Los Angeles: University of California Press), pp. 176–204.

—— 2002. 'The dead body and human rights' in S. T. Sweeney and I. Hodder (eds), *The Body* (Cambridge: Cambridge University Press), pp. 75–93.

LEBLANC, S. A. 1999. *Prehistoric Warfare in the American Southwest* (Salt Lake City, UT: University of Utah Press).

LEOUSSI, A. S. 2001. 'Myths of ancestry' in M. Díaz-Andreu (ed.), Archaeology and Nationalism, special issue of *Nations and Nationalism: Journal of the Association for the Study of Ethnicity and Nationalism*, 7(4): 467–86.

LONGMAN, T. 2001. 'Christian churches and the genocide in Rwanda' in O. Bartov and P. Mack (eds), *In God's Name: Genocide and religion in the twentieth century* (Oxford: Berghahn Books).

MCCANN, W. J. 1990. '"Volk und Germanentum": The presentation of the past in Nazi Germany' in P. Gathercole and D. Lowenthal (eds), *The Politics of the Past* (London: Routledge), pp. 74–88.

MAMDANI, M. 2001. *When Victims Become Killers: Colonialism, nativism, and the genocide in Rwanda* (New Jersey: Princeton University Press).

MANT, A. K. 1987. 'Knowledge acquired from post-war exhumations' in A. Boddington, A. N. Garland, and R. C. Janaway (eds), *Death, Decay and Reconstruction: Approaches to archaeology and forensic science* (Manchester: Manchester University Press), pp. 65–78.

MARKS, J. 2005. 'Your body, my property: The problem of colonial genetics in a postcolonial world' in L. Meskell and P. Pels (eds), *Embedding Ethics* (Oxford: Berg), pp. 29–45.

MARTIN, D. L. and FRAYER, D. W. 1997. *Troubled Times: Violence and warfare in the past* (Australia: Gordon and Breach).

MESKELL, L. 1997 (ed.). *Archaeology under Fire: Nationalism, politics and heritage in the Eastern Mediterranean and Middle East* (London: Routledge).

—— and PELS, P. (eds) 2005. *Embedding Ethics* (Oxford: Berg).

MILES, S. H. 1991. 'The anatomy lesson', *Clinical Anatomy*, 4(6): 456–9.

MITROVIĆ, S. 2008. 'Fresh scars on the body of archaeology' in *Past Bodies: Body centered research in archaeology* (Oxford: Oxbow Books), pp. 79–89.

MORIARTY, C. 1995. 'The absent dead and figurative First World War memorials', *Transactions of the Ancient Monuments Society*, 39: 7–40.

MORSE, D., CRUSOE, D., and SMITH, H. G. 1976. 'Forensic archaeology', *Journal of Forensic Sciences*, 21(2): 323–32.

—— DUNCAN, J., and STOUTAMIRE, J. 1983. *Handbook of Forensic Archaeology and Anthropology* (Tallahassee, FL: Florida State University Foundation).

MUFTI, H. and STOVER, E. 2004. 'Iraq: State of the evidence', *Human Rights Watch*, 16(7E): 1–41.

PANOURGIÁ, N. 1995: *Fragments of Death, Fables of Identity: An Athenian anthropography* (Madison: University of Wisconsin Press).

PAUL, A. 1991. *Katyn: Stalin's massacre and the seeds of Polish resurrection* (Annapolis: Charles Scribner Book Company).

PELS, P. 2005. '"Where there aren't no ten commandments": Redefining ethics during the *Darkness in El Dorado* scandal' in L. Meskell and P. Pels (eds), *Embedding Ethics* (Oxford: Berg), pp. 69–99.

POLLARD, T. and BANKS, I. 2006. *Past Tense: Studies in the archaeology of conflict* (Leiden: Brill Academic Publishers).

—— 2007. *War and Sacrifice: Studies in the archaeology of conflict* (Leiden: Brill Academic Publishers).

POLLOCK, S. 2008. 'Archaeology as a means for peace or a source of violence? An introduction', *Archaeologies: Journal of the World Archaeological Congress*, 4(3): 356–67.

RAINIO, J., LALU, K., RANTA, H., et al. 2001. 'Practical and legal aspects of forensic autopsy expert team operations', *Legal Medicine*, 4: 220–32.

—— —— and ANTTI, S. 2007. 'International forensic investigations: Legal framework, organisation, and performance' in R. Ferllini (ed.), *Forensic Archaeology and Human Rights Violations* (Springfield, IL: Charles C. Thomas), pp. 55–75.

REDMOND, E. M. 1994. *Tribal and Chiefly Warfare in South America* (Ann Arbor: University of Michigan Museum of Anthropology).

RENSHAW, L. 2007. 'The Iconography of exhumation: Representations of mass graves from the Spanish Civil War' in T. Clack and M. Brittain (eds), *Archaeology and the Media* (Walnut Creek, CA: Left Coast Press), pp. 237–51.

RÉV, I. 1995. 'Parallel autopsies', *Representations*, 49: 15–39.

—— 2005. *Retroactive Justice: Prehistory of post-communism* (Stanford, CA: Stanford University Press).

RICHARDSON, R. 1987. *Death, Dissection, and the Destitute* (London: Routledge and Kegan Paul).

—— 2000. 'A necessary inhumanity?', *Medical Humanities*, 26(2): 104–6.

ROBERTSHAW, P. (ed.) 1990. *A History of African Archaeology* (London: James Currey).

ROWLANDS, M. 1999. 'Remembering to forget: Sublimation as sacrifice in war memorials' in A. Forty and S. Küchler (eds), *The Art of Forgetting* (Oxford: Berg), pp. 129–45.

SALAMA, M. C. 1992. *Tumbas Anonimas. Informe Sobre la Identificacion de Restos de Víctimas de la Represión Ilegal* (Buenos Aires: Equipo Argentino de Antropología Forense).

SANFORD, G. 2005. *Katyn and the Soviet Massacre of 1940: Truth, justice and memory* (London: Routledge).

SANFORD, V. 2003. *Buried Secrets: Truth and human rights in Guatemala* (New York: Palgrave Macmillan).

SANT CASSIA, P. 2005. *Bodies of Evidence: Burial, memory and the recovery of missing persons in Cyprus* (New York, Oxford).

—— 2006. 'Recognition and emotion: Exhumations of missing persons in Cyprus' in Y. Papadakis, N. Peristianis, and G. Welz (eds), *Divided Cyprus: Modernity, history and an island in conflict* (Bloomington: Indiana University Press), pp. 194–213.

SASSÒLI, M. and TOUGAS, M.-L. 2002. 'The ICRC and the missing', *International Review of the Red Cross*, 84(848): 727–50.

SAUNDERS, N. J. 2002. 'Excavating memories: Archaeology and the Great War 1914–2001', *Antiquity*, 76(291): 101–8.

SAUNDERS, N. J. 2003a. 'Crucifix, calvary, and cross: Materiality and spirituality in Great War landscapes', *World Archaeology*, 35(1): 7–21.

SAUNDERS, N. J. 2003b. *Trench Art: Materialities and memories of war* (Oxford: Berg).

—— 2004a. 'Material culture and conflict. The Great War, 1914–2033' in N. J. Saunders (ed.), *Matters of Conflict: Material culture, memory and the First World War* (London: Routledge), pp. 5–25.

—— (ed.) 2004b: *Matters of Conflict: Material culture, memory and the First World War* (London: Routledge).

—— 2007. *Killing Time: Archaeology and the First World War* (Sutton: Stroud).

SAUNDERS, R. 2002. 'Tell the truth: The archaeology of human rights abuses in Guatemala and the former Yugoslavia' in J. Schofield, W. G. Johnson, and C. M. Beck (eds), *Matériel Culture: The archaeology of twentieth-century conflict* (London: Routledge), pp. 103–14.

SCHAEFER, M. C. 2008. 'A summary of epiphyseal union timings in Bosnia males', *International Journal of Osteoarchaeology*, 18(5): 536–45.

SCHMITT, S. 2002. 'Mass graves and the collection of forensic evidence: Genocide, war crimes, and crimes against humanity' in W. D. Haglund and M. H. Sorg (eds), *Advances in Forensic Taphonomy: Method, theory, and archaeological perspectives* (Boca Raton, FL: CRC Press), pp. 277–92.

SCHOFIELD, J. 2005. *Combat Archaeology: Material culture and modern conflict* (London: Duckworth).

——, JOHNSON, W. G., and BECK, C. M. 2002. *Matériel Culture: The archaeology of twentieth-century conflict* (London: Routledge).

SILBERMAN, N. A. 2001. 'If I forget thee, O Jerusalem: Archaeology, religious commemoration and nationalism in a disputed city, 1801–2001' in M. Díaz-Andreu (ed.), Archaeology and Nationalism, special issue of *Nations and Nationalism: Journal of the Association for the Study of Ethnicity and Nationalism*, 7(4): 487–504.

SILVERBERG, R. 1968. *Mound Builders of Ancient America: The archaeology of a myth* (Greenwich, CT: New York Graphic Society Ltd).

SIMMONS, T. and HAGLUND, W. D. 2005. 'Anthropology in a forensic context' in J. R. Hunter and M. Cox (eds), *Forensic Archaeology: Advances in theory and practice* (London: Routledge), pp. 159–76.

SKINNER, M. F. 1987. 'Planning the archaeological recovery of evidence from recent mass graves', *Forensic Sciences International*, 34: 267–87.

—— 2007. 'Hapless in Afghanistan: Forensic archaeology in a political maelstrom' in R. Ferllini (ed.), *Forensic Archaeology and Human Rights Violations* (Springfield, IL: Charles C. Thomas), pp. 233–65.

—— and LAZENBY, R. A. 1983. *Found! Human Remains: A field manual for the recovery of the recent human skeleton* (Burnaby, BC: Archaeology Press).

—— ALEMPIJEVIC, D., and DJURIC-SREJIC, M. 2003. 'Guidelines for international forensic bio-archaeology monitors of mass grave exhumations', *Forensic Science International*, 134: 81–92.

SKURSKI, J. and CORONIL, F. 2006. 'States of violence and the violence of states' in F. Coronil and J. Skurski (eds), *States of Violence* (Ann Arbor: University of Michigan Press), pp. 1–31.

ŠLAUS, M., STRINOVIC, D., ŠKAVIC, J. and PETROVECKI, V. 2003. 'Discriminant function sexing of fragmentary and complete femora: Standards for contemporary Croatia', *Journal of Forensic Sciences*, 48: 509–12.

SMITH, A. C. and KLEINMAN, S. 1989. 'Managing emotions in medical school: students' contacts with the living and the dead', special issue: Sentiments, Affect and Emotion (March), *Social Psychology Quarterly*, 52(1): 56–69.

SNOW, C. C., LEVINE, L., LUKASH, L., et al. 1984. 'The investigation of the human remains of the disappeared in Argentina', *American Journal of Forensic Medicine and Pathology*, 5: 297–9.

STARZMANN, M. T., POLLOCK, S., and BERNBECK, R. (eds). 2008. *Archaeologies: Journal of the World Archaeological Congress* (Special Issue, Imperial Inspections: Archaeology, War and Violence), 4(3).

STEADMAN, D. W. and HAGLUND, W. D. 2005. 'The scope of anthropological contributions to human rights investigations', *Journal of Forensic Sciences*, 50(1): 1–8.

STEELE, C. 2008. 'Archaeology and the forensic investigation of recent mass graves: Ethical issues for a new practice of archaeology', *Archaeologies: Journal of the World Archaeological Congress*, 4(3): 414–28.

STEWART, T. D. 1979. *Essentials of Forensic* Anthropology (Springfield, IL: Charles C. Thomas).

STOVER, E. 1985. 'Scientists aid search for Argentina's "Desaparecidos"', *Science*, 230(4680): 56–7.

——1992. *Unquiet Graves: The search for the disappeared in Iraqi Kurdistan* (New York: Middle East Watch and Physicans for Human Rights).

——and PERESS, G. 1998. *The Graves: Srebrenica and Vukovar* (Zurich: Scalo Publishers).

——and RYAN, M. 2001. 'Breaking bread with the dead', *Historical Archaeology*, 35(1): 7–25.

——, HAGLUND, W. D., and SAMUELS, M. 2003. 'Exhumation of mass graves in Iraq: Considerations for forensic investigations, humanitarian needs, and the demands of justice', *Journal of the American Medical Association*, 290(5): 663–6.

——and SHIGEKANE, R. 2002. 'The missing in the aftermath: When do the needs of victims' families and international war crimes tribunals clash?', *International Review of the Red Cross*, 84(848): 845–66.

SUASNÁVAR, J. S. and MOSCOSO MOLLER, F. 1999. 'La arqueología en el esclarecimiento histórico' in J. P. Laporte and H. L. Escobedo (eds), *Simposio de Investigaciones Arqueologicas en Guatemala, 1998* (Guatemala: Museo Nacional de Arqueología y Etnología), 858–75.

TARLOW, S. 1997. 'An archaeology of remembering: Death, bereavement and the First World War', *Cambridge Archaeological Journal*, 7: 105–21.

TATE, W. 2007. *Counting the Dead: The culture and politics of human rights activism in Colombia* (Berkeley and Los Angeles: University of California Press).

TAUSSIG, M. 1999. *Defacement: Public secrecy and the labor of the negative* (Stanford, CA: Stanford University Press).

TAYLOR, C. 2007. *A Secular Age* (Cambridge, MA and London: Belknap Press of Harvard University Press).

THOMPSON, T. J. U. 2001. 'Legal and ethical considerations of forensic anthropological research', *Science and Justice*, 41(4): 261–70.

TILLY, C. 2002. 'War making and state making as organized crime', repr. in C. L. Besteman (ed.), *Violence: A reader* (Basingstoke: Palgrave), pp. 35–60.

TUMINI, M. C., GARAY, L. S., and BANCHIERI, C. M. 2007. 'Argentina: Procesos de exhumaciones: un espacio possible' in P. Pérez-Sales and S. Navarro García (eds), *Resistencias contra el Olvido. Trabajo Psicosocial en Procesos de Exhumaciones* (Barcelona: Gedisa Editoria), pp. 157–85.

TWAGIRAMUTARA, P. 1989. 'Archaeological and anthropological hypotheses concerning the origin of ethnic divisions in sub-Saharan Africa' in R. Layton (ed.), *Conflict in the Archaeology of Living Traditions* (London: Routledge), pp. 88–96.

VANDKILDE, H. 2003. 'Commemorative tales: Archaeological responses to modern myth, politics, and war', *World Archaeology*, 35: 126–44.
VANEZIS, P. 1999. 'Investigation of clandestine graves resulting from human rights abuses', *Journal of Clinical Forensic Medicine*, 6: 238–42.
VERDERY, K. 1999. *The Political Lives of Dead Bodies: Reburial and postsocialist change* (New York: Columbia University Press).
WAGNER, S. E. 2008. *To Know Where He Lies: DNA technology and the search for Srebrenica's missing* (Berkeley: University of California Press).
WEAVER, K. 2003. 'Identifying the fallen', *British Medical Journal*, 326: 1110.
WEBSTER, D. 1975. 'Warfare and the evolution of the state: A reconsideration', *American Antiquity*, 40: 464–70.
WEISS, L. 2009. 'Terra incognita: The material world in international criminal courts' in D. Boric (ed.), *Excavating Memories* (Oxford: Oxbow Press), pp. 185–95.
WHITAKER, R. 2000. 'When bones speak', *The Independent on Sunday*, 19 November: 13–20.
WILLIAMS, E. D. and CREWS, J. D. 2008. 'From dust to dust: Ethical and practical issues involved in the location, exhumation, and identification of bodies from mass graves', *Croatian Medical Journal*, 44(3): 251–8.
WILSON, D. J. 1987. 'Reconstructing patterns of early warfare in the lower Santa Valley: New data on the role of conflict in the origins of complex north-coast society' in J. Haas (ed.), *The Origins and Development of the Andean State* (Cambridge: Cambridge University Press), pp. 59–69.
WRIGHT, R., HANSON, I., and STERENBERG, J. 2005. 'The archaeology of mass graves' in J. R. Hunter and M. Cox (eds), *Forensic archaeology: Advances in theory and practice* (London), pp. 137–58.
WYLIE, A. 2005. 'The promise and perils of an ethic of stewardship' in L. Meskell and P. Pels (eds), *Embedding Ethics* (Oxford: Berg), pp. 47–68.

CHAPTER 20

ROCK ART, RELIGION, AND RITUAL

DAVID S. WHITLEY

1 INTRODUCTION

ROCK art is landscape art: paintings and engravings placed on cave and rock-shelter walls and ceilings, and open boulders and cliff faces. It also includes earth figures or geoglyphs—rock alignments and intaglios—and cupules or ground cups. Although there are accounts of rock art made as graffiti or for other secular purposes (e.g., Layton 1992: 72–7), probably the majority was made for religious reasons. We know this archaeologically based on the restricted nature of the iconography of many corpora of art, sometimes by its location in unusual places (such as the dark zones of caves, where it was both difficult to create and hard to see), and occasionally by associations with other ceremonial objects. Equally importantly, ethnographic accounts worldwide commonly emphasize its religious origin. Though it is likely that the meaning and origin of some prehistoric rock art differed from known ethnographic examples, the anthropological accounts, carefully applied, are our best guides to understanding the potential range of variability in prehistoric cases, if only to avoid the imposition of our contemporary Western biases on the archaeological past. Indeed, the most commonly suggested popular rock art explanations—boundary and trail markers, or directional signs—exactly reflect these kinds of biases. Speaking to these interpretations, California ethnographer Alfred L. Kroeber wrote almost a hundred years ago that:

> It has sometimes been conjectured the symbols served as boundary markers, direction signs, or for some analogous practical purpose. Yet this interpretation fits neither their character, their location, nor the habits of native life. The Indian knew the limits of his territory and his way around it; and as for strangers, his impulse would have been to obscure their path rather than blazon it. [1925: 939]

This overview begins, accordingly, with a summary of global rock art ethnography (cf. Morwood and Hobbs 1992; Clottes 2002; Whitley 2005). Significant methodological approaches for archaeological analyses are considered next, before concluding with a review of studies addressing a key rock art research issue: the origin and nature of the earliest known religions, seen globally and regionally.

2 Global Rock Art from an Ethnographic Perspective

Rock art is often conceptualized primarily as a hunter-gatherer phenomenon—hence the occasional use of the generic term 'cave art', implying just this association. Although hunter-gatherers commonly made this art, it was also produced by agriculturalists, occasionally even in state-level societies (e.g. Stone 1995; Betts 2001). Given the diversity in religions that this implies, a similar wide range of variation is known for the described origins of this art, what it symbolizes, which social and gender groups made it, and how it was used ritually—with distinctions sometimes existing even between why the art was made and how it was subsequently employed. Further complicating this circumstance, the origin, meaning, and use of rock art does not perfectly correlate with specific kinds of religious systems (such as shamanism versus totemic cults versus formal priestly religions).

The easiest way to conceptualize the variability in rock art globally is then to consider the origins and functions of the art in terms of two very broad categories: art intended to portray visionary or altered states of consciousness (ASC) imagery; and motifs made to illustrate other subjects and/or created for other reasons. This distinction roughly, but imperfectly, parallels the difference between shamanic and non-shamanic religions. Although visionary art is a product of shamanic religions, as we will see, non-visionary rock art was created by both shamanistic and non-shamanistic cultures.

3 Visionary Rock Art

Visionary or ecstatic states are important in many religions, but they are central components of shamanism, which maintains that an individual may have direct interaction with the supernatural world through an ASC. Shamanistic rock art for this reason commonly portrays visionary imagery, symbolizing in a general sense a supernatural experience or event. Despite this commonality, shamanistic rock art was made for a variety of purposes, by a full range of social and gender groups beyond the shaman alone, depending upon cultural context (Table 20.1). Further, although the particular purposes for making the art varied, at a certain level these can all be understood as demonstrating either the acquisition or the manipulation of supernatural power. The reasons for making this art include shamanic power acquisition, puberty and cult initiations, life crises, curing, sorcery, rain-making, game charming and hunting magic, and world renewal.

Table 20.1 Ethnography and Rock Art Origins in Far Western North America.

Tribe/ Group	Shamanic Art			Shamanistic Art				Non-Visionary Art
	Owned Sites	Communal Sites	Unknown ownership	Puberty		Life Crises	
				Boys	Girls		
Yokuts	X			-	-	-	X
W. Mono	X			-	-	-	X
Chumash	X			-	-	-	X
Gabrielino	X			?	X	-	X
Luiseño	X			X	X	-	X
Cahuilla	X			?	X	-	X
Kumeyaay	X			X	X	-	X
Cupeño			X	?	X	-	?
Serrano			X	?	X	-	?
Mojave		X		X	-	-	X
Quechan		X		X	-	-	X
Cocopa			X	X	-	-	?
So. Paiute		X		-	-	-	X
No. Paiute		X		-	-	-	X
Shoshone		X		-	-	-	X
Seri			X	?	?	?	?
Interior Salish		X	X	X	X	?	
Thompson River		X	X	X	X	?	
Nez Percé			?	X	X	X	?
Shushwap			?	X	X	X	?
Kutenai			?	X	?	X	?
Okanagan			X	X	X	X	?
Modoc			?	X	X	X	X
Klamath			X	X	X	X	X
Sinkaietk			X	X	X	X	?
Yakama			X	X	X	X	?
Wasco			?	X	X	?	?
Warm Springs		?	X	X	?	?	
Coeur d'Alene		?	X	?	?	?	
Flathead			?	X	X	?	?
Lilloet			?	X	X	?	?
Spokan			?	X	X	?	?

Key: Present x
Suspected ?
Absent -

3.1 Shamanic Power Acquisition

A common form of rock art was created by shamans following their initial success at contacting the supernatural world and obtaining its potency, usually through the receipt of an animal spirit helper or familiar (Figure 20.1). In much of Native America, shamanic vision quests were often lengthy and private, although the art that was created after the ASC

FIGURE 20.1 Barrier Canyon style rock paintings (in red), Head of Sinbad site, Utah, USA. Although Archaic (c.3500–5000 BP) in age, these are interpreted as shamanistic in origin, partly because of the human–bison conflation on the left—possibly a spirit helper for the central shaman figure. The snake above the central anthropomorph likewise may symbolize a rattlesnake helper, one of the more common shamanic animal familiars in Native America.

was in some cultures placed in the middle of villages (Whitley 2000)—hence there is no necessary correlation between rock art made as a result of private versus public ceremonies, and viewshed or accessibility. Among the San or Bushmen of southern Africa, in contrast, shamans received their power in a public Trance Dance (Lewis-Williams 1981, 2002a). In both cases the shamans painted or engraved motifs, usually subsequent to the ASC, portraying their spirit helpers, themselves in their transformed supernatural state, and/or the events they experienced while in an ASC. This is illustrated by an ethnographic comment concerning the making of Native California rock paintings:

> Specifically [made by] doctors, *po'hage* [i.e., shamans]. They painted their 'spirits' (*anit*) on rocks 'to show themselves, to let people see what they had done. The spirit must come first in a dream [vision]'. [Driver 1937: 126]

Because the actions of shamans and their spirit helpers were considered fully equivalent, ethnographic accounts often state that spirit helpers themselves made the art, rather than the shamans. For example:

> One night a medicine man [i.e., shaman] of the Wishram [tribe] mixed some paint made from roots. Then an unseen power guided his hand and his brush across the stone... The man could not see what he was painting. He worked hard, so that his work would be done before morning came... Later he was found, in a trance, at the foot of a rock. A ghostly eye was looking down at him and on the people who came to him. All knew that *Tahmahnawis* [powers, spirits] had painted it. [Ranck 1926: 1]

Because trance experiences include optical and bodily hallucinations, ASC-influenced imagery has a series of formal visual characteristics (discussed below). Due to the fact that the hallucinations are intrinsically difficult to describe, a series of common bodily reactions to ASCs were also used as verbal and graphic metaphors for a supernatural experience. Although these reactions varied from individual to individual, and even from specific experience to experience, they are the result of hard-wiring in the human neurophysiological system, and are restricted to a limited range of possible outcomes. These served as a set of typical cross-cultural ASC metaphors. The most common of these are death, flight, bodily transformation, aggression/fighting, going underwater, and sexual arousal (Whitley 1994, 1998a, 2000). These constitute the subject matter or symbolic themes that characterize much shamanic rock art.

In some cases—notably, among the Numic speaking (Shoshone and Paiute) tribes of the North American Great Basin and the Yokuts of California—shamans alone made visionary rock art, though some important ritual distinctions existed even between these two large groups. Yokuts shamans owned their individual rock art sites, for example, whereas no such ownership pertained among the Numic. In other cultures, such as the Columbia Plateau tribes, shamans made rock art, but so did non-shaman adults during life crises, and male and female adolescents at puberty (below). A distinction can then be seen between *shamanic* art that was specifically made by a shaman, and *shamanistic* art that was created by non-shamans but within the context of shamanic beliefs and practices (cf. Taçon 1983). Further, the relationship between rock art rituals and mythology also varied tribally. Among some groups (such as the Yokuts and the Numic) there was no correlation whatsoever. Among others, such as the Yuman-speaking tribes (Mojave, Quechan, and Cocopa) in the Colorado River area, the association was complete: shamanic and shamanistic rock art were both created at the locations of specific relevant mythic events (Whitley 2000).

3.2 Shamanistic Puberty and Cult Initiations

The creation of rock art as part of puberty initiations is especially common—but not universal—in Native America, though the specific circumstances varied substantially from tribe to tribe (Whitley 2006; cf. Driver 1941; Minor 1973). On the Columbia Plateau, as noted above, boys and girls were sent to remote spots by their parents on individual puberty initiations where they were expected to receive supernatural power in the form of a spirit helper, and then draw or incise an image of the spirit, and also document aspects of the initiatory rite (Hays-Gilpin 2004). The youths apparently achieved an ASC as a result of fasting, isolation, sleep deprivation and physical exertion. Creating rock cairns and alignments (discussed below), usually at higher elevations distant from the rock art itself, was part of the ritual process, with ritual behaviour then involving movement across the landscape (Whitley 2006; Whitley et al. 2004).

Boys' group initiations were conducted among the Yuman-speaking tribes where the young males were sent on a lengthy desert run along the 'Trail of Dreams' (Figure 20.2), the purpose of which was to have a dream or vision (induced by fasting, sleeplessness, and exertion). This imparted supernatural power, depicted in the visionary imagery they inscribed at a specific spot along the trail. Subsequently their nasal septums were pierced, which allowed them to attain warrior status and (eventually) enter the land of the dead (Whitley 2006). Shamanistic cults, with formal group puberty initiations, also existed among some tribes (Whitley in press), with membership required to attain leadership or elite social roles. The *Chingichngish* religion, practised by the Luiseño and Kumeyaay in south-western California, had both boys' and girls' group initiations. These culminated in the painting of the spirit helpers they received during jimsonweed (*Datura wrightii*) or tobacco-induced ASCs (Whitley 2006).

3.3 Life Crises

Rock art was created by adults as part of individual vision quests by the Columbia Plateau tribes during so-called 'life crises'—the birth of a child, for example, or the death of a spouse, or even a bad string of gambling luck. The purpose in this case was to restore or enhance the supernatural potency that they had first obtained during their original puberty initiation.

3.4 Power Manipulation

Shamans also created rock art during rituals involving the manipulation of their supernatural power. These included a wide range of activities, such as healing, sorcery, rain-making, finding lost objects and game, hunting magic, and prognostication (Keyser and Whitley 2006). Concerning sorcery, for example:

> [T]he bewitcher generally goes off to a quiet place to make his spell. He draws an image of his victim and with a sharpened stick pierces the image where the heart is. [Trippel 1889: 582]

FIGURE 20.2 The Trail of Dreams, Colorado Desert region, California, USA. This was (and continues to be) used by Quechan-speaking boys for their puberty initiation—a lengthy run through the desert, during which they are expected to receive visions signalling their acquisition of supernatural power, following by a nasal septum piercing ceremony. Imagery of their visions, typically geometric patterns corresponding to the mental light images generated during ASCs, are inscribed at a site along this trail, corresponding to the location of an important mythic event—the first (mythic) puberty initiation. Boys were required to maintain this ritual trail, by tamping it down with logs and by sprinkling the edges with broken quartz, so it could be better seen at night during their run.

This statement illustrates an important fact: shamanistic rock art motifs were conceptualized not as symbols, but as material 'spirit objects' more akin to 'pagan idols' than texts or abstract signs (Whitley 2009).

3.5 Shamanic World Renewal

The shamanic world view was based on belief in the existence of a fundamental dialectical opposition (Meyerhoff 1976): a precarious and unresolvable balance between opposing forces, such as good and bad, or light and dark. Many shamanic rituals, as a result, were concerned with maintaining the cosmic equilibrium, to ensure the safety and security of the world. In at least some cases, shamanic rock art was created as a result of these kinds of rituals. Among horticulturalist groups in lowland South America, for example, Reichel-Dolmatoff (1967) documented shamans creating visionary imagery in a ritual associated with supernatural negotiations with the Master of the Game spirit, intended to ensure the supply of hunted meat for the coming year.

As these examples illustrate, visionary rock art was made in shamanistic societies by a very wide range of individuals, for a variety of purposes. Identifying the content of a rock art corpus as shamanistic (below) is not then the conclusion of interpretive analysis, but just a mid-way point towards determining the ritual nature and significance of the art.

4 Non-Visionary Rock Art

Although the ethnography of non-visionary rock art is less studied than the visionary art, a substantial amount has been compiled about non-shamanistic rock art rituals and imagery, especially in Australia (e.g., Layton 1992; Morwood and Hobbs 1992). This demonstrates that it was made by both shamanistic and totemic or priestly religions, again for many different reasons. These are best summarized partly by reference to kinds of art, and in part with respect to the nature of the differing ritual practices.

4.1 Cupules and Vulva-Forms

Engraved or incised cups or pits are common in many parts of the world, with three ritual origins and purposes known within the limits of Native California alone (Heizer 1953; Minor 1973; Parkman 1986, 1993; Smith and Lerch 1984; Whitley 2000, 2006). In northern California cupules were called 'rain-rocks', and they were made, by shamans, to bring either rain or the wind. The purpose behind rain-making in this region was to ensure the yearly riverine salmon runs (requiring seasonal stream flooding). These rituals can best then be understood as a kind of world renewal ceremony conducted by shamans making non-visionary rock art.

So-called 'pit-and-groove' rocks were pecked in central California (in the San Francisco Bay region) by wives and sometimes husbands who were having difficulty conceiving. Known as 'baby rocks', they were created during a private fertility rite. The intent of the ritual was to produce and collect rock powder or dust, which was placed in the woman's vagina (and, sometimes, on other parts of the woman's and/or man's body) prior to intercourse. The underlying concept behind this action was the fundamental shamanistic belief that supernatural power existed within sacred rocks and that, by gathering some of the rock powder and anointing the body with it, the individual's own potency would be enhanced and fertility improved (Whitley 2000).

Cupules were also made by girls during puberty initiations in south-central California and the Great Basin (Whitley 2006). By grinding briefly in all of the many cups on a given rock, the girls were said to reconnect with all of the earlier and older women of the tribe. This represents an example of non-visionary art created by non-shamans, within the context of shamanistic cultures and religions.

Cups and rings, in contrast, were created by Hawai'ian women following childbirth, in a ritual intended to ensure the health of the newborn (cf. McBride 1969: 35; Beckwith 1970: 89–90). This involved hiding and thereby preserving the infant's umbilical cord, and creating a cup and ring or cupule, symbolic of the umbilicus—and thus the child's connection to its mother. Given the common occurrence of cupules and similar kinds of rock art worldwide, it is likely that many other ritual origins and functions were also involved in their creation.

Vulva-form motifs are also common worldwide, and they are almost invariably interpreted as evidence of fertility rituals of some kind. In some ethnographic cases this is clearly justified. Polynesian girls' puberty ceremonies involved a 'clitoris stretching' ceremony, for example, after which an engraved 'portrait' of the girl's genitalia was created (Lee 1992). In the Great Basin region of North America, in contrast, vulva-forms may have been made by male shamans, in acts of sorcery (Whitley 1998b). Although this interpretation is inferential, it is based on the androcentric tribal belief in this region that female genitalia were inherently dangerous, and that looking at them would cause spiritual harm.

4.2 Earth Figures and Rock Alignments

Earth figures (geoglyphs, intaglios, and rock alignments), and standing or stacked stones/cairns are found in a number of world regions, and are widely considered a kind of rock art. The ethnographic record demonstrates that this class of feature is often the result of ritual, though again the origin and meaning of specific examples vary widely.

Rock alignments and walls, talus pits, and stacked stones are common components of many archaeological records, especially in far western North America (e.g. von Werlhof 1987). Traditionally these were interpreted as hunting-related: 'dummy hunters' and hunting blinds (e.g. Heizer and Baumhoff 1962). Although there are accounts of hunting structures, much more commonly described in the ethnography is the construction of these features as part of shamanistic vision quest rituals: rock walls, stone rings, rock 'seats', and talus pits as locations where an individual conducted a vision quest; and rock alignments and cairns resulting from the physical exertion undertaken during the quest (Whitley 2006; Whitley et al. 2004). Although efforts have been made to identify an iconography in the rock alignments, the Native American ethnography demonstrates that the alignments resulted from *instrumental actions* that had no specific referential meaning (cf. Whitley 2005): they were ritual constructions, not iconographic imagery.

The lack of referential meaning in western North American rock alignments is, however, not universal. In Australia, Aboriginal 'Rock alignments and artificial rockpiles are consistently interpreted as the bodies or paraphernalia of totemic beings changed by themselves into lithic form' (Gould 1969: 144; cf. Layton 1992: 35). Typical of much Australian rock art (see below), they are identified with specific mythic actors ('totemic beings') and their actions at particular locations, and were used in rituals associated with those actors and events (such as circumcision). In these cases the exact meaning of the rock features is encoded in mythology, which is to say oral tradition, reflecting the controlled nature of knowledge in many traditional societies.

The large intaglios made and used by Yuman-speakers along the Colorado River in North America provide a useful contrast with the Aboriginal rock alignments. The Native American sites consist of iconic imagery, ritual pathways, and dance circles cleared in the desert pavement at the locations of mythic events. They chart the movement of the cultural hero Mastamho as he created the region and its people, and established their customs, with the imagery portraying the mythic actors and events pertinent to each location (Whitley 2000; von Werlhof 2004). These sites were used in ritual pilgrimages led by shamans, during which supplicants were purified and re-experienced the mythic creation of the world.

4.3 Pilgrimage Commemoration

The Yuman-speakers' creation and use of rock art in pilgrimages is not unique. Rock engravings of an individual's clan symbol were made by male members of the Hopi tribe in Arizona, during their salt expedition (Titiev 1937; Michaelis 1981; Schaafsma 1981). Although the resulting images outwardly appear secular in meaning, they were created during this ritual pilgrimage at a specific spot and hence, in this circumstance, are religious in intent. Religious symbolism here is based on context and setting—a specific ritual act and location—rather than iconographic form alone (Figure 20.3).

4.4 Cult Ceremonies

Rock art was also created in non-shamanic cult ceremonies, especially in Australia where the connections between kinship, mythology, landscape, and religious practice were fundamental and very intricate (cf. Elkin 1964). In the Australian case it is useful to bear in mind the distinction between *identification* and *meaning* (Panofsky 1983). Identification concerns an outward depiction or illustration: 'this is a painting of a horse'. Meaning, in contrast, concerns symbolic intent or interpretive significance. Most imagery has multiple levels of meaning. A horse motif might signal the wealth or status of the painter; membership in a clan or a secret cult society; or an animal spirit helper. (To an archaeologist, a horse painting in a specific context might also indicate that the rock art was created during the historical period after horses were introduced into the given region—further demonstrating the different levels of meaning that symbols may encode.) All of these are distinct kinds of meaning; not all of them are mutually exclusive, but each is distinguishable from identification alone.

Because many Aboriginal rock-art-making cults were secret societies, specific identifications and certain levels of meaning were restricted to initiated members; many of these

FIGURE 20.3 Rock engravings, Willow Springs, Arizona, USA. This site is an important ritual location on the Hopi Salt Pilgrimage, where participants pecked their clan signs into the rocks. Visible here are the Corn and Bear clan symbols. Although these images outwardly concern social organization (clan membership), they are religious in intent at this location and in this context. This site is unfortunately located adjacent to a modern road and vandalism is evident to the lower right.

identifications and meanings are either lost or will never be shared with outsiders. But this does not mean that all of the meaning of this art is beyond our knowledge, nor that the specific artist's commentary is required to understand each motif. Although there are variations from the general pattern (see, e.g. Layton 1992: 31–32; Chippindale et al. 2000), this art commonly portrays mythic ancestors and actors (especially totemic beings and animals), their paths across the landscape (including trails and springs), and other animal and plant species, and perhaps implements, associated with these beings (cf. Layton 1992). The sites themselves are typically locations of mythic events (e.g. a waterhole used by a specific mythic being, or the origin point for an animal species). And the art was often made (and maintained, through re-painting) during cult initiations and ceremonies, including so-called 'increase rites', by specific secret societies—including both men's and women's groups. The increase rites were more properly world renewal ceremonies inasmuch as they were intended to ensure the continued existence of specific animal or plant species, rather than any increase in their numbers (cf. Elkin 1964: 205).

4.5 War Events and Honors

'Biographic style' rock art is common on the northern Plains of North America (Klassen 1998; Keyser 2004; Keyser and Klassen 2001). This is characterized by realism in depiction and a thematic emphasis on military feats, such as the warriors themselves, their battle scenes, and raiding and capture. Associated with the 'horse cultures' that developed among Native American tribes after the reintroduction of this animal into the Americas by the Spanish, this art is protohistorical/historical in age. Partly because of this fact, the specific iconographic details of biographic art are well documented (cf. Keyser 2004). Although these outwardly concern warfare—seemingly a secular topic—the art is placed at sacred locations on the landscape: sites where warriors went to conduct vision quests, often locations with earlier rock art. Understanding this art requires recognizing that, in Native American terms, all success results from supernatural power (including military achievements), and is a product of interaction with the spirits. Biographic art in this sense is best understood as a commemoration not simply of warfare, but instead of the inseparability of religious belief and practice from other aspects of social life. Warriors made biographic art not to document their heroism in any mundane sense, but to acknowledge the importance of the supernatural in their success: they were heralded warriors not simply because they were skilful and fierce, but also because they properly maintained their relationships with supernatural power.

As the above summary illustrates, the ethnographic reasons for making rock art varied substantially, even among hunter-gatherers and, more to the point, even among shamanistic hunter-gatherer cultures alone. There are also anecdotal ethnographic accounts suggesting additional origins and meanings to rock art (e.g., Odak 1992), beyond those outlined here. These circumstances point to the fundamental difficulty of archaeological—that is, truly prehistoric—rock art interpretation, the next topic for discussion.

5 Methodological Approaches for Archaeological Cases

Taçon and Chippindale (1998) have usefully grouped archaeological approaches to rock art interpretation as *informed*, based on informants or insider's information of some kind; or *formal*, with analyses emphasizing the qualities of the art, its associations, and contexts. Although the distinction is imperfect (see below), informed studies commonly attempt to identify symbolism and meaning, contributing to an understanding of the religious implications of the art. Formal approaches, in contrast, more frequently consider the social and adaptive ramifications of the art and are thereby less often directly concerned with religion.

Informed approaches include ethnographic interpretation, the Direct-Historical Approach, and different kinds of ethnographic analogy (Whitley 2005). As Conkey (1997) has noted, ethnographic interpretation—the use of directly relevant anthropological accounts of the making and meaning of the art—is responsible for many of the recent advances in rock art research. It needs to be emphasized however that, contrary to common perceptions, ethnographic approaches are *interpretive* in that they require the compilation, synthesis and analysis of 'raw' ethnographic data, not simply a search for full symbolic exegesis in published accounts. Methodological guides to ethnographic interpretation have been provided by Taçon (1992), Layton (2001), Whitley (2005, 2007), and Sundstrom (2000, 2006). Direct ethnographic interpretations have been particularly common in Southern African (e.g. Lewis-Williams 1981, 2002a; Lewis-Williams and Pearce 2004) and North American (e.g. Conway and Conway 1990; Whitley 2000; Keyser and Klassen 2001; Keyser 2004; Francis and Loendorf 2002) rock art studies, both of which are regions with detailed ethnographic records, and relatively recent contacts between traditional and Western cultures.

The Direct-Historical Approach (cf. Wedel 1938) is appropriate in regions with good ethnographic records and, typically (but not invariably), a prehistoric record that extends into the relatively recent past. The concept behind the approach is straightforward: archaeologists can trace ethnographic practices back in time by examining continuity in iconography, production techniques, site location and structure, and various kinds of archaeological associations (e.g., Whitley et al. 1999; see below). But the goal of the Direct-Historical Approach is not simply to extend ethnographic interpretations into the prehistoric past. Equally important is the identification of change over time (Huffman 1986), in order to determine when an ethnographic model is no longer applicable. Generally speaking, the Direct-Historical Approach is particularly valuable for studies of prehistoric religion because different aspects of cultural and social traditions change at different rates. Religious beliefs and practices typically are conservative (Steward 1955; Lévi-Strauss and Eribon 1991 etc.), and alter much more slowly than technology and subsistence (Sahlins 1985). Moreover, traditional religious beliefs often continue among indigenous groups into contemporary times, despite their outward adoption of Western religions (White 1963; Elkin 1964; Bean and Vane 1978).

Ethnographic analogy involves the application of an interpretation developed (e.g., from directly relevant anthropological accounts) for one group or region to another. Perhaps the best-known ethnographic analogy in rock art interpretation was the early twentieth-century theory that Western European Upper Palaeolithic rock art was an expression of hunting magic (Reinach 1903), due to putative equivalences between Palaeolithic cultures and Australian Aborigines and their rock art. This analogical interpretation was rejected once it was demonstrated both that the Palaeolithic art emphasizes animal species that were not commonly major components of the prehistoric diet, and when the symbolism and meaning of ethnographic Australian Aboriginal art proved to be much more complex than 'hunting magic' alone (above). Despite this specific failure, ethnographic analogies are potentially useful, especially when there are strong links between the source and target groups (e.g. if both groups are members of the same linguistic family, and/or share the same general symbolic and ritual systems). They are also valuable as initial interpretive hypotheses, which then can be evaluated with additional kinds of evidence (Whitley 2005).

As noted above, most formal analytical approaches emphasize the social and adaptive implications of rock art rather than its ritual significance. But two formal models have been developed that specifically concern rock art's religious implications: the Neuropsychological (N-P) model for trance imagery, and the Ritual Form model. The N-P model was developed by Lewis-Williams (Lewis-Williams and Dowson 1988; Lewis-Williams 1991, 2001, 2002b) in order to determine whether corpora of prehistoric rock art portray the mental imagery of trance, and hence whether they likely originated from shamanistic practices. Strictly, the model examines the content and form of the iconography, and is not concerned with its symbolic meaning. Using clinical and ethnographic accounts, Lewis-Williams initially developed a series of expectations for the nature of the mental images generated during ASCs. Although these experiences vary from person to person, and even from specific incident to incident, the model is based on the fact that hard-wiring in the human brain results in a limited range of potential reactions. These include the nature of the initial mental images that are commonly experienced (geometric light patterns called entoptic designs, such as zigzags); the way that mental imagery typically advances through progressive stages (starting with entoptics and eventually including fully iconic imagery); and the fashion in which images of all types are variably perceived (often superimposed, repeated, fragmented, inverted, and so on, rather than visualized in a 'normal' manner; e.g. with a horizontal ground-line and real-world orientation). Lewis-Williams inferred that rock art intended to portray trance imagery would include all or many of these characteristics. He tested the model using two ethnographically known cases of shamanistic rock art. Based on the model's fit with these two control cases, he used it to examine European Upper Palaeolithic art (below), concluding that at least some of it portrays trance imagery and thus likely depicts shamanistic visions.

The Ritual Form model was developed by Ross and Davidson (2006), based on an earlier synthesis of ethnographic ceremonies provided by Rappaport (1999). The goal of the model is to determine, using systematic criteria, if a corpus of rock art was created in ritual rather than due to secular activities, and to identify the structural form of the ritual rather than its symbolism or content. The emphasis in analysis, accordingly, is repeated and stylized behaviour, as expressed in seven features (e.g. use of specialized places, invariant action, etc.). Ross and Davidson (2006) used the model to analyse central Australian rock art, determining that this art includes both ritual and secular corpora, that possible contemporaneous but different ritual forms coexisted, and that ritual forms may have changed over time.

6 ROCK ART AND THE ORIGIN OF RELIGIONS

An important rock art research topic is the origin of religions, a problem that has been considered at both global (i.e. the first appearance of religion worldwide) and regional (the earliest religion in a specific area) scales, with studies conducted in Western Europe, Southern Africa, Siberia and North-east Asia, Australia, and North America.

European Upper Palaeolithic rock art, dating between 36,000 and 10,000 YBP, is currently considered the earliest rock art and, perhaps, the earliest evidence of systematic ritual. Future discoveries in other regions may change this understanding, but it seems clear that this art, and the religion that it expresses, only appeared with the arrival of anatomically and behaviourally modern humans in Western Europe, *Homo sapiens sapiens*, but not Neanderthal. The origin and meaning of this art have been debated since the sites were first discovered by science in the late nineteenth century, with interpretations ranging from hunting-magic, to totemic signs, mythological markers, art for art's sake, and shamanism, among others. Although there is no consensus among all researchers, the strongest empirical case has been presented for the shamanistic interpretation (Lewis-Williams and Dowson 1988; Lewis-Williams 1991, 2002b; Dowson and Porr 2001; Clottes and Lewis-Williams 1998; Whitley 2009). This includes the facts that the corpus of art replicates the features identified by the N-P model for the mental imagery of trance; much of the art occurs in cave dark zones, where sensory deprivation easily can result in ASCs; and it also includes subjects correlating with common shamanistic themes (such as the conflation of human and bison into a single compound being).

Early art is also present, though barely studied, in Southern Africa. Paintings dating from about 27,000 BP are present at Apollo 11 Cave, Namibia (Wendt 1976). Like the European Upper Palaeolithic art, these include an example of a human–animal conflation; in this case a lion with human legs and feet. Partly based on this discovery, the earliest African art and religion likewise have been interpreted as shamanistic in origin (Lewis-Williams 1984; Lewis-Williams and Pearce 2004).

Australian Aboriginal rock art, at least ethnographically, is primarily totemic, not shamanistic, and two studies have been completed examining the time-depth of the so-called Aboriginal 'Dreamtime' religion (Taçon et al. 1996; David 2002). Although the conclusions of these two analyses differ, both concur that, relative to the great length of human occupation of the continent, this religion appeared recently in the prehistoric past (at most around 6,000 years ago). This leaves uncertain the form and nature of the original Australian Aboriginal religion(s), though another analysis suggests that shamanism may have been responsible for some of the early rock art on the continent (Chippindale et al. 2000).

Siberian and North-east Asian shamanism, in contrast, has been presumed both the source for New World religions and, for that reason, necessarily quite ancient (e.g. Kroeber 1923; Furst 1977; LaBarre 1980). Archaeological research in the region has proven this inference wrong, at least with respect to time-depth. The consensus is that shamanism only developed in this area at the end of the Neolithic or beginning of the Bronze Age—approximately 4,000 years ago (Devlet 2001; Jacobson 2001; Rozwadowski 2001, 2004; Rozwadowski and Kosko 2002). The nature and substance of earlier religion(s) in this region are, so far, undetermined.

The implications of this circumstance are uncertain with respect to the frequently noted similarities between Siberian and North American shamanism (e.g., Schlesier 1987). Rock art studies demonstrate about 12,000 years of continuity in site use, the tools used to create rock engravings, the general composition of the iconographic corpus, and a series of specific iconographic attributes for rock art in eastern California, suggesting that shamanism was the initial New World religion (Whitley et al. 1999)—as researchers had long assumed. Generally supporting this evidence are independent data indicating at least 7,000 years of hallucinogen use in the Americas (e.g., Boyd 2003), illustrating that interest in ASC also has great time-depth. Shamanism was clearly the earliest religion in the Americas but it appears to pre-date Siberian shamanism by roughly 8,000 years, and therefore is not clearly a direct off-shoot of Palaeolithic Siberian religion. Whether the striking ethnographic similarities between North American and Siberian shamanism are instead the result of recent cultural diffusion, east to west, or the reverse, is still uncertain (Whitley 2004, 2009).

These studies demonstrate that, at least in some regions, shamanism was the earliest religion. The existing evidence suggests that this may also be true globally in the sense that the first appearance of shamanism was an expression of the evolution of behavioural and cognitive modernity. But no research has yet been conducted on the earliest religion(s) in most regions of the world, and it may be some time before we have a complete understanding of the appearance and evolution of early human ritual and belief.

7 ROCK ART AND THE ARCHAEOLOGY OF RELIGION

Rock art research still confronts a number of methodological and technical challenges, but this is true of the archaeology of religion generally, not just of rock art specifically. And despite these challenges, rock art studies have already demonstrated their value to the understanding of prehistoric ritual and belief. This is especially true with respect to small-scale hunter-gatherer societies, where rock art is often the most visible, and richest, evidence for prehistoric ritual and belief. Indeed, although hunter-gatherers traditionally were derided as entirely gastrically or practically oriented (e.g., Steward 1938: 46, 1941: 216, 1955: 114), the rock art record shows something else: their artistic sensibilities and iconographic systems were complex, implying an equivalent sophistication for their religious beliefs and practices. We will only understand these prehistoric cultures when we understand their religions, and rock art provides an accessible line of evidence for this goal.

Suggested Reading

A useful overview of world rock art is provided by Clottes (2002). Research, methodological and site management summaries may be found in Whitley (2000b, 2005). Good syntheses of European Upper Palaeolithic, South African, and Australian rock art have been published by Lewis-Williams (2002b), Lewis-Williams and Pearce (2004), and Morwood (2002), respectively.

References

BEAN, L. J. and VANE, S. B. 1978. 'Cults and Their Transformations' in R. F Heizer (ed.), *Handbook of North American Indians*, VIII: *California* (Washington: Smithsonian Institution), pp. 662–72.
BECKWITH, M. 1970. *Hawaiian Mythology* (Honolulu: University of Hawaii Press).
BETTS, A. V. G. 2001. 'The Middle East' in D. S. Whitley (ed.), *Handbook of Rock Art Research* (Walnut Creek, CA: AltaMira), pp. 786–824.
BOYD, C. E. 2003. *Rock Art of the Lower Pecos* (College Station: Texas A&M University Press).
CHIPPINDALE, C., SMITH, B., and TAÇON, P. 2000. 'Visions of dynamic power: Archaic rock paintings, altered states of consciousness and "Clever Men" in Western Arnhem Land (NT), Australia', *Cambridge Archaeological Journal*, 10(1): 63–101.
CLOTTES, J. 2002. *World Rock Art* (Los Angeles: Getty Conservation Institute).
——and LEWIS-WILLIAMS, J. D. 1998. *The Shamans of Prehistory: Trance and magic in the painted caves* (New York, Harry N. Abrams).
CONKEY, M. 1997. 'Making a Mark: Rock Art Research', *American Anthropologist*, 99: 168–72.

CONWAY, T. and CONWAY, J. 1990. *Spirits on Stone: The Agawa pictographs* (San Luis Obispo: Heritage Discoveries Publication #1).

DAVID, B. 2002. *Landscapes, Rock Art and the Dreaming: An archaeology of preunderstanding* (London: Leicester University Press).

DEVLET, E. 2001. 'Rock art and the material culture of Siberian and Central Asian shamanism' in N. Price (ed.), *The Archaeology of Shamanism* (London: Routledge), pp. 43–55.

DOWSON, T. A. and PORR, M. 2001. 'Special objects—special creatures: Shamanistic imagery and the Aurignacian art of south-west Germany' in N. Price (ed.), *The Archaeology of Shamanism* (London: Routledge), pp. 165–77.

DRIVER, H. E. 1937. 'Cultural element distributions: VI, Southern Sierra Nevada', *University of California Anthropological Records*, 1(2): 53–154.

——1941. 'Cultural element distributions: XVI, Girls' puberty ceremonies in North America', *University of California Anthropological Records*, 6(2).

ELKIN, A. P. 1964. *The Australian Aborigines* (New York: Doubleday).

FRANCIS, J. E. and LOENDORF, L. L. 2002. *Ancient Visions: Petroglyphs and pictographs from the Wind River and Bighorn country, Wyoming and Montana* (Salt Lake City: University of Utah Press).

FURST, P. T. 1977. 'The roots and continuities of shamanism' in A. T. Brodzy, R. Daneswich, and N. Johnson (eds), *Stones, Bones and Skin: Ritual and shamanic art* (Toronto: Society for Art Publications), pp. 1–28.

GOULD, R. A. 1969. *Yiwara: Foragers of the Australian desert* (New York: Charles Scribner's Sons).

HAYS-GILPIN, K. 2004. *Ambiguous Images: Gender and rock art* (Walnut Creek, CA: AltaMira).

HEIZER, R. F. 1953. 'Sacred rain rocks of California', *University of California Archaeological Survey Report 20*.

——and BAUMHOFF, M. A. 1962. *Prehistoric Rock Art of Nevada and Eastern California* (Berkeley: University of California Press).

HUFFMAN, T. N. 1986. 'Cognitive studies of the Iron Age in Africa', *World Archaeology*, 18: 84–95.

JACOBSON, E. 2001. 'Shamans, shamanism, and anthropomorphizing imagery in prehistoric rock art of the Mongolian Altay' in H. P. Francfort and R. N. Hamayon (eds), *The Concept of Shamanism: Uses and abuses*, X (Budapest, Czech Republic: Akadémiai Kiadó, Bibliotheca Shamanistica), pp. 277–96.

KEYSER, J. D. 2004. *Art of the Warrior: Rock art of the American Plains* (Salt Lake City: University of Utah Press).

——and KLASSEN, M. A. 2001. *Plains Indian Rock Art* (Seattle: University of Washington Press).

——and WHITLEY, D. S. 2006. 'Sympathetic magic in western North American rock art', *American Antiquity*, 71(1): 3–26.

KLASSEN, M. A. 1998. 'Icon and narrative in contact transition rock art at writing-on-stone, Southern Alberta, Canada' in C. Chippindale and P. S. C. Taçon (eds), *The Archaeology of Rock Art* (Cambridge: Cambridge University Press), pp. 42–72.

KROEBER, A. L. 1923. 'American culture and the Northwest coast', *American Anthropologist*, 25: 1–20.

——1925. 'Handbook of the Indians of California', *Bureau of American Ethnology, Bulletin 78* (Washington, DC: Smithsonian Institution).

LaBarre, W. 1980. *Culture in Context* (Durham, NC: Duke University).
Layton, R. 1992. *Australian Rock Art: A new synthesis* (Cambridge: Cambridge University Press).
—— 2001. 'Ethnographic study and symbolic analysis' in D. S. Whitley (eds), *Handbook of Rock Art Research* (Walnut Creek, CA: AltaMira), pp. 311–32.
Lee, G. 1992. *The Rock Art of Easter Island: Symbols of power, prayers to the gods*, Monumenta Archaeologica 17 (Institute of Archaeology, UCLA).
Lévi-Strauss, C. and Eribon, D. 1991. *Conversations with Claude Lévi-Strauss*, trans. P. Wissing (Chicago: University of Chicago Press).
Lewis-Williams, J. D. 1981. *Believing and Seeing: Symbolic meaning in southern San rock paintings* (London: Academic Press).
—— 1984. 'Ideological continuities in prehistoric Southern Africa' in C. Schrire (ed.), *Past and Present in Hunter-gatherer Studies* (New York: Academic Press), pp. 225–52.
—— 1991. 'Wrestling with analogy: A methodological dilemma in Upper Paleolithic art research', *Proceedings of the Prehistoric Society*, 57(I): 149–62.
—— 2001. 'Brain-storming images: Neuropsychology and rock art research' in D. S. Whitley (ed.), *Handbook of Rock Art Research* (Walnut Creek, CA: AltaMira), pp. 332–57.
—— 2002a. *A Cosmos in Stone: Intepreting religion and society through rock art* (Walnut Creek, CA: AltaMira).
—— 2002b. *The Mind in the Cave: Conscousness and the origins of art* (London: Thames and Hudson).
—— and Dowson, T. A. 1988. 'The signs of all times: Entoptic phenomena in Upper Palaeolithic art', *Current Anthropology*, 29: 201–45.
—— and Pearce, D. 2004. *San Spirituality: Roots, expression, and social consequence* (Walnut Creek, CA: AltaMira).
McBride, L. R. 1969. *Petroglyphs of Hawaii* (Hilo: The Petroglyph Press).
Meyerhoff, B. 1976. 'Shamanic equilibrium: Balance and mediation in known and unknown worlds' in W. D. Hand (ed.), *American Folk Medicine* (Berkeley: University of California Press), pp. 99–108.
Michaelis, H. 1981. 'Willowsprings: A Hopi petroglyph site', *Journal of New World Archaeology*, 4(2): 3–32.
Minor, R. 1973. 'Known origins of rock paintings of southwestern California', *Pacific Coast Archaeological Society Quarterly*, 9(4): 29–36.
Morwood, M. J. 2002. *Visions from the Past: The Archaeology of Australian Aboriginal Art* (Crows Nests, NSW, Australia: Allen & Unwin).
—— and Hobbs, D. R. (eds) 1992. *Rock Art and Ethnography*, Occasional AURA Publication No. 5 (Melbourne: Australian Rock Art Assoc.)
Odak, O. 1992. 'Ethnographic context of rock art sites in East Africa' in M. J. Morwood and D. R. Hobbs (eds), *Rock Art and Ethnography*, Occasional AURA Publication No. 5 (Melbourne: Rock Art Assc.), pp. 67–70.
Panofsky, E. 1983. *Meaning in the Visual Arts* (Chicago: University of Chicago Press).
Parkman, B. 1986. 'Cupule petroglyphs in the Diablo Range, California', *Journal of California and Great Basin Anthropology*, 8: 246–59.
—— 1993. 'Creating thunder: The western rain making process', *Journal of California and Great Basin Anthropology*, 15: 90–110.
Ranck, G. 1926. 'Tribal lore of Wishram Indians rich in traditions of Columbia', *The Sunday Oregonian*, 7 February, Portland.

Rappaport, R. A. 1999. *Ritual and Religion in the Making of Humanity* (Cambridge: Cambridge University Press).
Reichel-Dolmatoff, G. 1967. 'Rock paintings of the Vaupes: An essay of interpretation', *Folklore Americas*, 27(2): 107–13.
Reinach, S. 1903. 'L'art et la magie: a propos des peintures et des gravures de l'age du Renne', *L'Anthropologie*, 14: 257–66.
Ross, J. and Davidson, I. 2006. 'Rock art and ritual: An archaeological analysis of rock art in arid Central Australia', *Journal of Archaeological Method and Theory*, 13(4): 305–41.
Rozwadowski, A. 2001. 'Sun Gods or shamans? Interpreting the "solar-headed" petroglyphs of Central Asia' in N. Price (ed.), *The Archaeology of Shamanism* (London: Routledge), pp. 65–86.
—— 2004. *Symbols through Time: Interpreting the rock art of Central Asia* (Poznan: Institute of Eastern Studies, Adam Mickiewicz University).
—— and Kosko, M. M. (eds) 2002. *Spirits and Stones: Shamanism and rock art in Central Asia and Siberia* (Poznan: Instytut Wschodoznawcze, Poznanskie Studia Wschodoznawcze 4).
Sahlins, M. 1985. *Islands of History* (Chicago: University of Chicago Press).
Schaafsma, P. 1981. 'Kachinas in rock art', *Journal of New World Archaeology*, 4(2): 25–32.
Schlesier, K. H. 1987. *The Wolves of Heaven: Cheyenne shamanism, ceremonies, and prehistoric origins* (Norman: University of Oklahoma).
Smith, G. and Lerch, M. 1984. 'Cupule petroglyphs in Southern California', *San Bernardino Museum Quarterly*, 32.
Steward, J. H. 1938. 'Basin-Plateau Aboriginal Sociopolitical Groups', *Bureau of American Ethnology* Bulletin 120 (Washington, DC).
—— 1941. 'Element Distributions: XIII, Nevada Shoshoni', *University of California Anthropological Records*, 4(2): 209–359.
—— 1955. *Theory of Culture Change: The methodology of multilinear evolution* (Chicago: University of Chicago).
Stone, A. 1995. *Images from the Underworld: Naj Tunich and the tradition of Maya cave painting* (Austin: University of Texas Press).
Sundstrom, L. 2000. 'Rock art studies and the direct ethnographic approach: Case studies from the Black Hills country', *1999 International Rock Art Congress Proceedings*, I: 105–110.
—— 2006. 'Reading between the lines: Ethnographic sources and rock art interpretation approaches to ethnography and rock art' in J. D. Keyser, G. Poetschat, and M. W. Taylor (eds), *Talking with the Past: The ethnography of rock art* (Portland: Oregon Archaeological Society), pp. 49–68.
Taçon, P. S. C. 1983. 'An analysis of Dorset Art in relation to prehistoric culture stress', *Etudes/Inuit/Studies*, 7(1): 41–65.
—— 1992. '"If you miss all this story, well bad luck": Rock art and the validity of ethnographic interpretation in western Arnhem Land, Australia' in M. J. Morwood and D. R. Hobbs (eds), *Rock Art and Ethnography*, Occasional AURA Publication No. 5 (Melbourne: Australian Rock Art Assoc.), pp. 11–18.
—— and Chippindale, C. 1998. 'An archaeology of rock art through informed methods and formal methods' in C. Chippindale and P. S. C. Taçon (eds), *The Archaeology of Rock Art* (Cambridge: Cambridge University Press), pp. 1–10.
—— Wilson, M., and Chippindale, C. 1996. 'Birth of the rainbow serpent in Arnhem Land rock art and oral history', *Archaeology in Oceania*, 31(3): 103–24.
Titiev, M. 1937. 'A Hopi salt expedition', *American Anthropologist*, 37: 244–58.

TRIPPEL, E. J. 1889. 'The Yuma Indians', *Overland Monthly*, second series, 13(78): 561–84 and 14(79): 1–11.

WEDEL, W. R. 1938. 'The direct-historical approach in Pawnee archaeology', *Smithsonian Miscellaneous Collections*, 97(7) (Washington, DC).

WENDT, W. E. 1976. '"Art mobilier" from the Apollo 11 Cave, South West Africa: Africa's oldest dated works of art', *South African Archaeological Bulletin*, 31: 5–11.

WERLHOF, J. VON 1987. *Spirits of the Earth: A study of earthen art in the North American deserts*, I: *The North Desert* (El Centro, CA: Imperial Valley College Desert Museum Society).

—— 2004. *That They May Know and Remember*, II: *Spirits of the earth* (Ocotillo: Imperial Valley College Desert Museum Society).

WHITE, R. C. 1963. 'Luiseño Social Organization', *University of California Publications in American Archaeology and Ethnology*, 48: 91–194.

WHITLEY, D. S. 1994. 'Shamanism, natural modeling and the rock art of far western North America' in S. Turpin (ed.), *Shamanism and Rock Art in North America*, Special Publication 1 (San Antonio: Rock Art Foundation, Inc.), pp. 1–43.

—— 1998a. 'Cognitive Neuroscience, Shamanism and the rock art of Native California', *Anthropology of Consciousness*, 9: 22–36.

—— 1998b. 'Finding rain in the desert: Landscape, gender, and far western North American rock art' in C. Chippindale and P. S. C. Taçon (eds), *The Archaeology of Rock Art* (Cambridge: Cambridge University Press), pp. 11–29.

—— 2000. *The Art of the Shaman: The rock art of California* (Salt Lake City: University of Utah Press).

—— 2004. 'The Archaeology of Shamanism' in *The Encyclopedia of Shamanism* (Santa Barbara, CA: ABC-Clio), pp. 15–21.

—— 2005. *Introduction to Rock Art Research* (Walnut Creek, CA: Left Coast Press).

—— 2006. 'Rock art and rites of passage in far western North America' in J. D. Keyser, G. Poetschat, and M. W. Taylor (eds), *Talking with the Past: The ethnography of rock art* (Portland: Oregon Archaeological Society), pp. 295–326.

—— 2007. 'Indigenous knowledge and 21st century archaeological practice: An introduction', *SAA Archaeological Record*, 7(2): 6–8.

—— 2009. *Cave Paintings and the Human Spirit: The origin of creativity and belief* (Amherst: Prometheus Books).

—— in press. 'Hunter-gatherer religion and ritual' in V. Peters, P. Jordan, and M. Zevelebil (eds), *The Oxford Handbook of the Archaeology and Anthropology of Hunter-Gatherers* (Oxford: Oxford University Press).

——, DORN, R. I., SIMON, J. M., et al. 1999. 'Sally's Rockshelter and the archaeology of the vision quest', *Cambridge Archaeological Journal*, 9: 221–47.

——, LOUBSER, J. H. N., and HANN, D. 2004. 'Friends in low places: Rock art and landscape on the Modoc Plateau' in C. Chippindale and G. Nash (eds), *The Figured Landscapes of Rock Art: Looking at pictures in place* (Cambridge University Press, Cambridge), pp. 217–38.

PART II

PREHISTORIC EUROPEAN RITUAL AND RELIGION

CHAPTER 21

RELIGION AND RITUAL IN THE LOWER AND MIDDLE PALAEOLITHIC

PAUL PETTITT

1 INTRODUCTION

To many Palaeolithic archaeologists religious belief would join language and symbolism as possessions unique to *Homo sapiens* that arose with, or later than, our biological origins after 200,000 years ago. To this list one might add indirect reciprocity, large degrees of interindividual and intergroup altruism, and morality (Schloss 2006: 195). The search for what constitutes 'cognitive modernity', at least for archaeologists, has been a major palaeoanthropological concern for two decades. A key issue is whether or not the shift towards more planned behaviour in the landscape, effective and broad spectrum resource acquisition, and use of symbols occurred suddenly and relatively late in our evolutionary development (Mellars 1998; Klein 2000) or more gradually over the late Middle Pleistocene and Upper Pleistocene, paralleling the evolution of anatomically modern humans from our presumed ancestor species *Homo heidelbergensis* (McBrearty and Brooks 2000). Although a few specialists have invoked the connectedness of religious thought with cognitive evolution, religion has been curiously neglected in palaeoanthropological discussions as to what makes us modern humans and how this arose. This may in large part be due to the perceived lack of clear data pertinent to the issue, although this limit could equally apply to the search for the evolutionary origins of modern cognition and language.

Factors stimulating the unfolding of religious belief and practice over the course of premodern hominin evolution could be social, economic, intellectual, and emotional. It is clear how these may have manifested themselves: social competition between individuals as well as the need for group solidarity in a hostile environment; stimuli for the advantageous sharing of resources; provision of an intellectual explanation for natural phenomena in order to render the world credible; allaying of confusion, anxiety, and fear; and providing the acceptance of the inevitability of death. I distinguish here between 'religion', a working definition of which might be shared belief in supernatural agencies potentially active within the world, and 'ritual', which might be defined from an archaeological perspective at least as habitual manifestations of religious beliefs which may leave material remains in the archaeological record.

To a certain extent, searching for religion over the remote time of the Lower and Middle Palaeolithic involves an uneasy mix of baseline projections derived from evolutionary psychology and cognitive science, and the search for material evidence that might plausibly be seen to be indicative of ritual (or ritualized) activities. With such an endeavour it is difficult to avoid the 'checklist' approach to the archaeological record, whereby the appearance of certain 'innovative' phenomena are seen to be indicative of new behaviours and even new cognitive thresholds, most notably, for example, with the appearance of 'modern' human behaviour noted above. Our own species, *Homo sapiens*, is beyond the scope of this chapter; I restrict my discussion to pre-modern hominins of the genera *Australopithecus*, *Paranthropus*, and *Homo*. Thus while my coverage formally relates to archaeological periods, I must inevitably include hominins for whom an archaeological record has yet to be found or may not exist. As the emergence of the archaeological record (currently recognized in East Africa ~2.6 Myr BP) relates to changes in carcass butchery for which systematic creation of simple tools of stone was employed, the distinction between 'Palaeolithic' and 'Pre-Palaeolithic' hominins has no meaning in the context of religion, and given the increasing recognition of simple stone tools among primates (e.g. Whiten et al. 1999; Mercader et al.2002; Mitani et al. 2002; van Schaik et al. 2003) it is in any case likely that the archaeological record will eventually extend back much further, perhaps even to the emergence of the *Homininae* in the Late Miocene/Early Pliocene.

2 NATURAL THINGS, SUPERNATURAL AGENCY, AND THE PSYCHOLOGICAL ORIGINS OF RELIGION

At first sight, religion and its associated habitual and often elaborate rituals, might be seen as maladapted to the evolutionary world; it is costly and does not have an immediate material return. Cognitive scientists, however, stress that an awareness of the supernatural and the emergence of religion, occurred as converging by-products of cognitive and emotional mechanisms that evolved under natural selection for mundane adaptive tasks (Atran 2002, 2006; Atran and Norenzayan 2004). In this sense, 'brains have been disposed by evolution to believe' (Atkins 2006: 133) and even evolutionary materialists concede that religion plays a role in human well-being (Schloss 2006: 191). It is easy to see how these converging mechanisms rapidly came to be used to rationalize or solve existential problems that otherwise have no worldly solution, such as the inevitability of death or the threat of deception by others. Research in this area based on cognitive psychology, neuroscience, cultural anthropology, and archaeology is beginning to reach maturity, and a number of generalizations can now be seen to be shared between all modern religious systems. In a phylogenetic sense these shared beliefs are best explained as deriving from our evolutionary origins (Power Bratton 2006: 217–8; Boyer 2008). These 'universals' include:

- The cosmos and its living creatures have inherent worth.
- Religious and ecological preservation are integrally linked: individuals and communities have responsibility towards the environment.

- The world is infused with supernatural agency: humanity is spiritually linked to (and affected by) the cosmos.
- Individuals maintain social relationships with supernatural agents.
- Individuals generally entertain highly anthropomorphic expectations about these supernatural agents.
- The minds of supernatural agents are *implicity* expected to function like our own, even though this is at odds with our *explicit* beliefs about them.
- Individuals are usually willing to subscribe to the religious norms of their own social groups, at the expense of being viewed as wrong by other groups.
- Individuals are only aware of some of their beliefs; a large amount of implicit, unconscious tenets underlies them.
- Religious beliefs are often concerned with issues of purification and danger, invoking ritual behaviour designed to deal with these.

The most obvious use of religion is to encode and preserve ecological information:

> The World's religions have historically served as important cultural reservoirs of ecological understanding. Religious myths and rituals order and convey information about the geography and availability of natural resources, the behaviour of important food species or predators, and the habits and properties of plants. Although religious traditions often emphasise species or environmental features with consumptive value, such as salmon, bison, or dependable springs, the World's diversity of religious art and myth contains myriad accounts of species not directly utilised by humans. Religion appreciates the ecological roles of organisms of little caloric importance, such as ravens and eagles, and utilises these creatures to symbolise natural processes. The buffalo dances of the native American peoples depict bison behaviour and movements... myths about salmon... describe not just the migratory patterns, but also the relationship of salmon to other species... [Power Bratton 2006: 208]

The origin of deities and other supernatural agents may, therefore, be seen as personifications of ecological processes.

3 VOICES IN THE WIND: INDIVIDUAL AGENCY AND THE ORIGINS OF RELIGION

Unless one believes in the currently undemonstrated notion that religions were *revealed* to hominins through real supernatural agency, the appropriate place to start a search for their intellectual origins is with the individual. Bodily experience of the sensual world must inevitably be the root of any kind of supernatural belief, and knowledge among indigenous peoples has been described as 'anthropocosmic' in the sense that humans are usually seen to play active roles in the cosmic process (Grim 2006: 91). Thus, the issue of religious origins must be intimately connected to individual agency. As Atran (2006: 411) has noted:

> a reasonable speculation is that agency evolved as hair-triggered response in humans, who needed to react 'automatically' under conditions of uncertainty to potential threats (and opportunities) by intelligent predators (and protectors). From this evolutionary perspective,

agency is a sort of 'innate reasoning mechanism'...whose original evolutionary domain encompasses animate objects but which inadvertently extends to moving dots on computer screens, voices in the wind, faces in the clouds, and virtually any complex design or uncertain situation of unknown origin.

Religion therefore involves a costly commitment to a counter-intuitive world of supernatural agents who are believed to master existential anxieties (Atran and Norenzayan 2004); the greater an individual's faith in these agents the greater society's trust in their abilities to help others.

In this way the very symbols of the ecological world become active agents linked with human individuals in meaningful and potent ways. It is not difficult to see how these relationships arise from the strong desire for survival and a great need for meaning. From a modern sociobiological perspective the need for an individual to decipher his or her reality stems from the stark awareness that the randomness of evolution and contingency, the importance of competition as a driving force in evolution, and the reductive argument that genes are the basis of evolution are all that are required to understand why we are here—'what's in it for me is the ancient refrain of all life' (Barash, quoted in Schloss 2006: 190). In this sense the construction of religious belief is a process of observation and replication. A cultural filter will determine what species and phenomena are worthy of record and the appropriate way to codify this. One might expect such codes to have been constantly under selection over human evolution. In this way, not only is important information about the resource environment preserved, but often, regulation is put in place and contributes towards keeping resource extraction below the environmental carrying capacity (ibid.: 209). Rituals, or at least the physical aspects of them, probably began as reproductions of actual phenomena (many still are, such as the shaking of Himalayan faith healers simulating the flapping of wings as a metaphor for travelling between worlds [Miller 1997]).

Dunbar (2003) has interpreted brain evolution in terms of intentional states—reflexive sequences of belief states—which range from one (I believe that...) to the normal human limit of four. Theory of mind, which in modern humans emerges at four to five years, requires level two (I believe that you believe...). Of import here is that, to Dunbar, while requiring individuals to conform to social norms requires only three levels of intention (I *want* you to *believe* that you must behave how we *want*), religion, at least as we know it, requires level four intention (I have to *believe* that *you suppose* that there are supernatural beings *who understand* that *you and I desire* that things happen in a certain way). To Dunbar, religion can therefore be seen in social rather than individual perspective (ibid.: 177). Dunbar has suggested that levels of intentionality have increased over the course of hominin evolution; equating these with increasing brain size, group size, and grooming time (Figure 21.1). This would grant australopithecines approaching two levels of intentionality (thus a theory of mind), archaic *Homo* such as *Homo erectus* and *Homo heidelbergensis* three levels (thus enough for social norms to develop and one might argue simple religious beliefs) and four levels to Neanderthals and anatomically modern humans. In light of the latter it is perhaps not surprising that it is with both Neanderthals and modern humans that burial of the dead was from time to time practised (see below).

Thus while the origins of religious imperatives derive from the individual, belief and practice inevitably become social phenomena, and it follows that religion may be used by individuals to negotiate positions in society. Gamble (1999: 80) has profitably used *attachment* (greeting) and

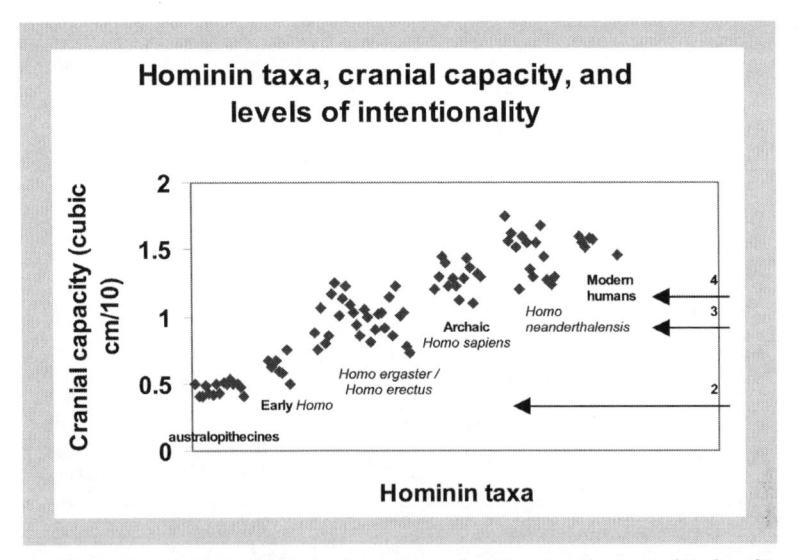

Hominin taxa, cranial capacity, and levels of intentionality

FIGURE 21.1 Hominin cranial capacities by taxa and major increases in levels of intentionality according to Dunbar (2003). Plotted using data from Aiello and Dunbar (1993). Cranial capacity plotted at cm^3/10, arrows refer to boundaries between levels of intentionality (2 levels = between apes and australopithecines; 3 levels = between *Homo erectus*/*Homo ergaster* and archaic *Homo sapiens*, 4 levels between archaic *Homo sapiens* and Neanderthals/modern humans).

detachment (mortuary) *rituals* as an interpretative heuristic for Palaeolithic social life. Of relevance here are Leroi-Gourhan's (1993) observation that the rhythms of everyday actions link the social with the technical and Gosden's (1994) point that such rhythms may become instinctive and habitual. By such mechanisms individual agency may be given social, and in some cases religious, meaning. One might reasonably expect places of aggregation—where hominins came together to share resources and socialize—to have formed foci for habitual activities, out of which ritual might emerge.

Before considering further the emergence of a spatial element to ritual, it is necessary to consider what could be the earliest known archaeological manifestations of any kind of belief system; these are natural objects resembling the human body (or parts of it) which have received minor amounts of intentional modification in order to bring out the similarity further. Three of these *pierres figures* are known, two from the Lower Palaeolithic and one from the Middle. A Lower Palaeolithic assemblage at Berekhat Ram in the Golan Heights, Israel, dominated by Levallois flakes and containing a handful of bifaces dated imprecisely to between 230,000 and 780,000 BP (most probably 350–500,000 BP), yielded a small (3.5 cm in maximum dimensions) pebble of basaltic tuff containing scoria clasts resembling a human torso and head (Goren-Inbar and Peltz 1995; see Figure 21.2). This has been the subject of optical and scanning electron microscope study by D'Errico and Nowell (2000), who concluded that, unlike other pieces of scoriae found at the locale, grooves found on the neck and sides of the piece were consistent with those produced by flint points used experimentally and thus that the figurine was intentionally modified. Similarly, the

FIGURE 21.2 The Berekhat Ram figurine.

Middle Acheulian (~400,000 BP) deposits at Tan-Tan, on the banks of the River Draa in Morocco, yielded a quartzite cobble (5.8 cm in maximum dimension) again reminiscent of a human body and modified with eight grooves and with red pigment (Bednarik 2003). Finally, the Middle Palaeolithic cave site of La Roche Cotard (Indre-et-Loire, ~32,000 BP) yielded a block of flint around the periphery of which several flakes have been removed and through which a natural perforation runs, into which a bone splinter has been wedged. It has been suggested that the overall effect is to resemble a face (Marquet and Lorblanchet 2003), with the protruding ends of the bone splinter effecting the eyes.

Although one cannot at present rule out a purely fortuitous association of the removals and bone wedge with the cobble, and also the observation that the piece can hardly be described as artistically achieved (Pettitt 2003) the possibility remains that it, too, can be placed in the *pierres figures* category. While a sample of three, widely spaced in Pleistocene time, is hardly grounds for robust interpretation of *pierres figures* as unambiguous indicators of early symbolism, let alone ritual, we should not write them off as casual 'lithic doodles' as Dennell (2008: 285) has noted. Instead, he argues that like the appearance of precocious lithic technologies in the Lower Palaeolithic such as end-scrapers and burins at Berekhet Ram, symbolism (and by extension perhaps, ritual) drifted in and out of use over evolutionary time. In this case 'rather than dismissing objects as nonsymbolic that would be regarded as symbolic if found in later contexts, it might be advisable to consider instead why they are so rare, and under what circumstances they might occur' (ibid.: 285). Perhaps one might also view in this light six large mammal bones recovered from the Lower Palaeolithic site of Bilzinsleben (discussed below) that bear fine engraved lines which have been interpreted by the excavators as geometric symbols (Mania and Mania 2005: 110–14). These all bear numerous parallel, radiating or diverging lines of a regularity that it is difficult to see arising simply from butchery or from using them as small 'work surfaces' on which perhaps hides were cut. One tarsal of straight-tusked elephant from Bilzingsleben bears on its concave surface a number of superimposed rectangles. Although these need of course bear no relation to religion or ritual, it is their context that makes them interesting in this light, as discussed below.

4 Ritual Space

The aggregation of hominins at certain locales probably has a very long antiquity (Gamble 1999, 2007) and the sharing of resources—particularly meat—is likely to have played an important role in social negotiation at these places (Roebroeks 2001). Sharing of resources—and one should include stone in this—is essentially a process of fragmentation, whereby resources are divided into smaller units which are then dispersed according to social rules. By the Mid-Upper Palaeolithic at least, certain human bodies were being fragmented and circulated as relics, presumably for use in rituals, the nature of which would have been determined by religious doctrine. These processes, however, begin at spatial locales, where individual agency is focused and magnified by the group context. Originally these locales would have been entirely natural—familiar places, strange places, places where resources were abundant, places of danger, places of safety—but at some evolutionary point humans began artificially creating such places. Such spaces for ritual create microcosmic places for engaging with the macrocosm (Grim 2006: 96) and a legitimate goal for archaeological enquiry is how and in what contexts the creation of ritual space evolved. By the Upper Palaeolithic there is abundant evidence for the deliberate sequestering of space for ritual, both among camp sites and in deep caves, but unambiguous evidence for the non-utilitarian use of space in the Lower and Middle Palaeolithic is difficult to find. It is easy to see how certain places may inherit specific meanings to which religious notions might on occasion be attached. Here, I discuss two sites—one predating the archaeological record and the other Lower Palaeolithic—separated by some 3 million years and thus each effectively unique. Thus while one should obviously be cautious about over-interpretation or, especially, generalization, they at least provide indications about the types of behaviour one might reasonably expect for these remote periods.

The 3–3.5 Myr-old locality AL-333/333w at Hadar (Ethiopia) lies on a steep hill slope, and yielded >200 hominid fossils representing nine adults, two juveniles, and two infants (MNI = 13) assigned to *Australopithecus afarensis* within a small area (Aronson and Taieb 1981: 189, Johanson et al. 1982). These stand out against a poor background of mammalian fauna at the site, and seem to have been covered by sediments fairly rapidly. The lack of palaeontology suggests that there was little activity in this point of the landscape. The site stands out from other Hadar localities as it is, as Johanson and Shreeve (1989: 87) note, 'just hominids littering a hillside'.

How the hominins came to be deposited at the site has attracted considerable debate. A dynamic event such as a flood can be ruled out on sedimentological grounds, and lack of carnivore modifications of the bones rules out predation; furthermore it is difficult to see how an entire group could become bogged down on a wet plain to die together on a hill. One cannot rule out the hypothesis that at least 13 dead individuals came to lie on the hill within a short space of time, because they had been deliberately placed there by their conspecifics. The locale seems to have been a relatively quiet area on an otherwise dynamic and dangerous landscape. Perhaps it was given meaning as bodies could be placed in the long grass, minimizing the possibility that carnivores would scavenge from them. One needs invoke no specific meaning to this further than the desire to protect corpses from scavenging, but it is easy to see how, at some cognitive stage in hominin evolution, such places might begin to acquire further meaning. Similarly, one might expect dangerous areas of intense carnivore activities, such as Swartkrans, South Africa, where carcasses of *Paranthropus* and early *Homo* accumulated (Brain 1993) also to attract meaning as places of fear and avoidance. Thus might the landscape begin to be imbued with meaning—places of life, places of opportunity, places of danger, places of death. Recognizing at which point/s such places are enculturated with supernatural meaning remains, of course, archaeologically intractable at present, although given the human brain's propensity to hear voices in the wind as noted above, it is not inconceivable that simple emotional and non-prosaic meanings were given to locales very early on in the evolution of the homininae, perhaps from the point that a theory of mind emerged.

At Bilzingsleben, in the Wipper Valley, Germany, archaeological preservation was exceptional due to the activities of a travertine spring. Around 600 m^2 of the site has been excavated, around half of which contained rich evidence of Lower Palaeolithic settlement during interglacial conditions in either Marine Isotope Stage 9 or 11, broadly between ~300–400,000 BP (Mania 1991; Mania and Mania 2005). Activities at a lake edge occurred in a mixed forest rich in shrub trees, juniper, and oak. Remains of a camp site, including six activity areas and three oval/circular ring-distributions of travertine blocks and bones which may represent windbreaks have been recovered. Cranial fragments and isolated teeth of at least three hominins (two adults and one juvenile) were recovered from the site, classified either as late *Homo erectus* or *Homo heidelbergensis*, two of which (Adult 2 and the juvenile) derived from the *in situ* archaeology of the camp site. Although the integrity of the spatial features remains to be demonstrated, Gamble (1999: 159–61, 165–71) used ring and sector analysis of the spatial patterning of the most circular of these, suggesting instead that the patterning pertains to activities (specifically drop and toss zones) around natural foci such as trees.

This is of no concern here, but the use of space at the site may be. Whatever their specific nature, each ring-like structure at Bilzingsleben appears to have been associated with an area of burning, and an activity area usually consisting of elephant bones and a large travertine block interpreted as an 'anvil'. Of particular interest is Zone V (Mania and Mania 2005: 102), which consists of a sub-circular 'pavement' formed from a single layer of flat stones trodden into the soft sediments of the lake edge. An area of burning was located towards its centre, a large travertine block severely affected by heat at its eastern periphery, and a quartzite 'anvil' in its western periphery next to a large bovid skull retaining its horn cores. The lack of splintered bone, hammerstones, or other tools on the pavement contrasts markedly with the rest of the settlement area, and Mania and Mania (ibid.: 102) have suggested that the area around the anvil and bovid skull was intentionally cleaned. The two refitting cranial fragments of Hominin 2 were recovered over 3 m apart on this 'pavement', in close proximity to the anvil/skull, and in 'smashed and macerated condition' (ibid.: 113), in addition to the juvenile mandible. Small fragments of bone preserved in the natural crevices of the quartzite 'anvil' show that bones were smashed upon it, but rather than forward a prosaic interpretation (marrow acquisition, for example) the excavators suggest that this was an area of 'special cultural activities' (ibid.: 102) which 'probably played a role in some kind of ritual behaviour' (ibid.: 113), further evidenced by a 'linear structure of large pebbles, which seem to run towards the circular area and which ends appear to have been marked by... elephant tusks'. Recovery of engraved marks on four large mammal bones from the site might also indicate further forms of symbolic activity, as noted above.

Gamble (1999: 171–2) offers an intriguing interpretation of Bilzingsleben. A frequently visited locale in an ecologically rich setting wherein carnivore activity seems to have been absent, he sees the relative security provided by the area as fostering relatively large gatherings of individuals. It is easy to see how Gamble's 'attaching rituals' could become embroiled with the use of the locale as a place imbued with meaning (perhaps as a place of safety and opportunity), with religious belief in this case literally unfolding out of the habitual rituals practised at the locale. To Gamble, the attaching rituals involved setting up the anvils, a 'structured activity, the start of rhythmic gesture', with each individual contributing materials. Although, however, his interpretation is convincing, from the perspective of this chapter we arrive at the inevitable interpretative limits; we can observe specific use of space and perhaps fairly confidently assume that meaning was given to it by the temporary performance of an attachment ritual, but we can go no further.

5 Treatment of the Dead

The development of mortuary activity is intimately connected with the use of space to contain the dead, although the interpretative limit in Palaeolithic archaeology is that we cannot, at least before the Upper Palaeolithic, confidently demonstrate that treatment of the dead is ritual in nature, i.e. that it stems from religious imperatives. A handful of examples of cut marks on hominin remains exist, notably:

- on the ~2 Myr-old Stw 53 maxilla from Sterkfontein, South Africa, assigned to early *Homo* or late *Australopithecus* (Pickering et al. 2000)
- on several Lower Palaeolithic hominins from the Gran Dolina at Atapuerca, Spain (*Homo antecessor* ~900,000 BP, Arsuaga et al. 2003: 77–8; Fernández-Jalvo et al. 1999)
- on the cranium from the Lower Palaeolithic (Acheulian) site of Bodo, Ethiopia classified as *Homo heidelbergensis* (White 1986)
- on several cranial fragments of the archaic hominin remains from the Acheulian site of Castel di Guido near Rome, Italy around 300–340,000 BP (Mariani-Costantini et al. 2001)
- in the Middle Palaeolithic (*Homo neanderthalensis*) at Moula Guercy cave, France (MNI = 6, Defleur et al. 1993), Combe-Grenal shelter, France (Le Mort 1989), Krapina, Croatia (Russell 1987, but cf. Orschiedt 2008) and on the Engis 2 child calvarium, Belgium (Russell and le Mort 1986).

These examples demonstrate that pre-modern hominins were at times removing soft tissues from the dead although it is unresolved as to whether this was 'nutritional cannibalism' or something more ritualized. In a number of cases it would appear that cut and scrape marks represent defleshing rather than the removal of major muscles. Elsewhere (Pettitt 2002, 2011) I have suggested an outline evolutionary development of mortuary activity, in which Lower Palaeolithic *Homo heidelbergensis* populations would on occasion deposit the dead in natural features ('Funerary Caching'), which was developed in some Neanderthal societies whereby sites were deliberately modified in order to contain the dead by excavating simple graves. A final development among Neanderthals was the use of specific places to contain multiple corpses, such as at the La Ferrassie rockshelter (Dordogne), Shanidar Cave (Iraq), and Amud Cave (Israel). I noted that Neanderthal mortuary activity (simple inhumation, secondary processing and burial, infants buried in pits, use of sites for multiple burials) was more variable than that observed for the earliest *Homo sapiens* populations, from which I inferred that the hypothesis that Neanderthals obtained the idea of burial (and whatever beliefs might accompany it) from *Homo sapiens* was unlikely.

The accumulation of the bodies of at least 32 individuals assigned to *Homo heidelbergensis* in the Sima de los Huesos ('Pit of the Bones') at Atapuerca, Spain, constitutes the earliest example of the use of a particular place for mortuary disposal. Between 400–500,000 BP thousands of bones accumulated in the 13-metre-deep pit mainly comprising bears (*Ursus deningeri* MNI = 166), several felids and canids, and the hominins, the latter heavily skewed towards prime adults (Arsuaga et al. 1997; Bischoff et al. 2003). Lack of decent degrees of carnivore gnawing show that they were not responsible for the deposition of the hominin bodies, and degrees of articulation, and lack of damage and considerable mixing of the hominin bones, suggest that they are either *in situ* or have not moved far. Consensus seems to be that they were deliberately placed here, perhaps at the top of the shaft which may have been open to the air at the time (Arsuaga et al. 1997: 124; Arsuaga et al. 2003: 88). The lack of any archaeology in the pit save for one Acheulian biface (ibid.: 88) suggests further a non-prosaic nature of the accumulation, although a specifically 'ritual' function has been questioned on taphonomic grounds (Fernández-Jalvo and Andrews 2001). Different weathering states on the hominin bones suggest that they were deposited on separate occasions over a very long period of time, perhaps as the individuals of concern were pathological (Y. Fernández-Jalvo pers. comm.). For now, it is perhaps best to assume no more than the repeated selection of a certain place for the disposal of the dead.

A parsimonious reading of the Eurasian Middle Palaeolithic record shows that between 30–40 simple inhumations of *Homo neanderthalensis* are known, with more inclusive estimates approaching 60 (see Pettitt 2002 and 2011 and references therein). These burials, all without the inclusion of grave goods, span the period from 80,000–34,000 BP, perhaps a little earlier, and overlap with the dates for the earliest burials of *Homo sapiens* (e.g. at Skhūl and Qafzeh caves, Israel ~120,000–90,000 BP). Both young and old Neanderthals were buried, and examples fall into distinct regional groups, notably south-west France, Germany, and the Levant. Given the relatively low number of burials known despite a rich Middle Palaeolithic record, one cannot conclude from this that 'Neanderthals buried their dead'; it may be more apposite to conclude that some Neanderthals buried some of their dead, some of the time. While it is unclear whether these simple inhumations were undertaken for prosaic reasons, the use of sites for multiple burials and the possible use of grave markers might suggest that some underlying belief accounts for the burials. The representation of multiple Neanderthals among fragmentary remains at several sites is intriguing: at least 25 individuals at Krapina (Trinkaus 1995); 20 at L'Hortus, France, among which young adults dominate (de Lumley 1972); at least 22 at la Quina, France (Defleur 1993); 7 at La Ferrassie of which 2 are juveniles and 3 foeti/neonates (Defleur 1993); at least 7 at Shanidar cave, Iraq (Trinkaus 1982); and 2 in the Feldhoffer cave in the Neander Valley (Schmitz et al. 2002), and in Amud and Tabun caves, Israel (Hovers et al. 1995). At La Ferrassie, several of the grave pits—those of children—seem to have been covered with large boulders, one of which bore 'cup marks' (Peyrony 1934). It is tempting to view the latter as specific grave markers. Thus, while there are no unambiguous indications of a religious imperative for the burials that do exist in the Middle Palaeolithic, some suggestions that it was more than prosaic corpse disposal do exist. Whether or not religious beliefs underpinned Neanderthal burials it seems reasonable to conclude that the deliberate sequestering of space for non-prosaic activity was certainly practised. Furthermore, Dunbar's inclusion of Neanderthals into the 'fourth level intentionality' strengthens the notion that by the Late Middle Palaeolithic at least nascent (mortuary) rituals and presumably some kind of underlying beliefs had emerged.

6 Conclusion: The Evolutionary Emergence of Religion and Ritual: Do Evolutionary Schema have Any Import?

The history of current world religions carries, in my opinion, two major observations for the emergence of extant religions over the course of human evolution. First, these 'truths' were 'revealed' only to *Homo sapiens*, and secondly, from the perspective of the longevity of humans on the planet they were revealed suddenly, and very late. Leaving aside the question as to whether there is any reality to these beliefs or whether they are colourful examples of the interaction of individual agency, place and society as discussed above—intellectually I favour the latter—the lesson is that religions will, over deep time, come and go, contextualized in specific societal constructs. All of the direct information that we have pertaining to religion relates solely to one human species, and it may therefore not be justifiable to draw any specific conclusions from this that has relevance to cognitively pre-modern hominins. But, I suggest, it would be surprising if a gradual, cumulative model for the emergence of religion and ritual applies to the Lower and Middle Palaeolithic. It seems to me far more likely that issues of rapid emergence and contingency would have pertained over deep time; creative interactions of individual agency, social conditions, and environmental contexts evolved, grew, and eventually became extinct in no different a way than the waxing and waning of hominin species and dispersals over the course of the Pliocene and Pleistocene. In this case, the search for evolutionary 'patterns' of increasing complexity of religion and ritual over the course of hominin evolution might, like the search for a 'centre' for the emergence of 'modern' human behaviour, be futile.

Beliefs and rituals will come and go, and if a gradual increase in the cognitive complexity of belief did occur it has to be said that the archaeological record is particularly mute about its character and is likely to remain so. It is, of course, tempting to 'read' the record for signs of gradualism; individual agency and the derivation of shared beliefs from the observation of natural phenomena among hominins of the australopithecine grade; the contextualization and wider interindividual promulgation of these among the *Homo erectus* grade, incorporation of beliefs about death and place with the *Homo heidelbergensis* grade culminating in cultural variation in mortuary rituals in the *Homo neanderthalensis* and early *Homo sapiens* grade, for instance. But this may be illusory; our 'evidence' for these is minimal, and generalizations may mask the cultural variation between individuals and groups that could have very deep evolutionary history.

Dunbar's (2003) work discussed above carries significant implications for the evolutionary history of human religion. If a certain cognitive threshold must be crossed before religious systems as we know them can be conceived and maintained, the very real possibility exists that religion *sensu stricto* is a unique characteristic of symbolically and linguistically empowered *Homo sapiens*. In this case the 'religions' of the Lower and Middle Palaeolithic were probably very different to those of the last few tens of thousands of years and might justifiably be termed 'less complex' than those of the Upper Palaeolithic and thereafter.

Acknowledgments

I am grateful to F. LeRon Schults and Mark White for their comments on a draft of this paper; to Yolanda Fernández-Jalvo for discussing the nature of the Sima de los Huesos accumulation; Paul Bahn for the Berekhat Ram illustration, and to Tim Insoll and Rachel Maclean for their kind invitation to contribute to this volume.

Suggested Reading

An excellent overview of the cognitive, evolutionary and psychological evolution of religion is S. Atran (2002), *In Gods We Trust: the evolutionary landscape of religion* (Oxford: Oxford

University Press). A useful, concise, summary of the argument that religion is an inevitable by-product can be found in P. Boyer (2008), 'Religion: Bound to believe?', *Nature*, 455, 1038–9. A number of papers in P. Clayton and Z. Simpson (eds), *The Oxford Handbook of Religion and Science* (Oxford: Oxford University Press) are pertinent to the evolution of religion, particularly those by Grim (indigenous lifeways and religion), Schloss (evolutionary theory), Bratton (ecology), and Atran (cognition). No specific consideration of the archaeological contribution to the origins of ritual and religion exists, but consideration of specific phenomena pertinent to the argument can be found in C. Gamble (1999), *The Palaeolithic Societies of Europe* (Cambridge: Cambridge University Press) (gesture, performance and social negotiation; space) and C. Gamble (2007), *Origins and Revolutions* (Cambridge: Cambridge University Press); and P. Pettitt (2002), 'The Neanderthal dead: Exploring mortuary variability in Middle Palaeolithic Eurasia', *Before Farming*, 2002/1, <http://www.waspress.co.uk/journals/beforefarming/journal_20021> (burial).

References

Aiello, L. C. and Dunbar, R. I. M. 1993. 'Neocortext size, group size, and the evolution of language', *Current Anthropology*, 34(2): 184–93.

Aronson, J. L. and Taieb, M. 1981. 'Geology and palaeography of the Hadar hominid site, Ethiopia' in G. Rapp and C.F. Vondra (eds), *Hominid Sites: Their geologic settings* (Boulder: Westview), pp. 165–95.

Arsuaga, J. L., Martínez, I., Gracia, A., et al. 1997. 'Sima de los Huesos (Sierra de Atapuerca, Spain), the site', *Journal of Human Evolution*, 3: 109–27.

——Carbonell, E., and Bermúdez de Castro, J. M. 2003. *The First Europeans: Treasures from the hills of Atapuerca* (New York: American Museum of Natural History/Junta de Castilla y León).

Atkins, P. 2006. 'Atheism and science' in P. Clayton and Z. Simpson (eds), *The Oxford Handbook of Religion and Science* (Oxford: Oxford University Press), pp. 124–36.

Atran, S. 2002. *In Gods We Trust: The evolutionary landscape of religion* (Oxford: Oxford University Press).

——2006. 'The scientific landscape of religion: Evolution, culture, and cognition' in P. Clayton and Z. Simpson (eds), *The Oxford Handbook of Religion and Science* (Oxford: Oxford University Press), pp. 407–29.

——and Norenzayan, A. 2004. 'Religion's evolutionary landscape: Counterintuition, commitment, compassion, communion', *Behavioural and Brain Sciences*, 27: 713–70.

Bednarik, R. 2003. 'A figurine from the African Acheulian', *Current Anthropology*, 44(3): 405–12.

Bischoff, J. L., Shamp, D. D., Aramburu, A., et al. 2003. 'The Sima de los Huesos hominids date to beyond U/Th equilibrium (>350Kyr) and perhaps to 400–500 kyr: New radiometric dates', *Journal of Archaeological Science*, 30: 275–80.

Boyer, P. 2008. 'Religion: Bound to believe?', *Nature*, 455: 1038–9.

Brain, C. K. 1993. *Swartkrans: A cave's chronicle of early man* (Pretoria: Transvaal Museum).

Defleur, A. 1993. *Les Sépultures Moustériennes* (Paris : Editions CNRS).

——Dutour, O., Valladas, H., et al. 1993. 'Cannibals among the Neanderthals', *Nature*, 362: 214.

DEFLEUR, A., WHITE, T., VALENSI, P., et al. 1999. 'Neanderthal cannibalism at Moula-Guercy, Ardèche, France', *Science*, 286: 128–31.

DENNELL, R. 2008. *The Palaeolithic Settlement of Asia* (Cambridge: Cambridge University Press).

D'ERRICO, F. and NOWELL, A. 2000. 'A new look at the Berekhat Ram figurine: implications for the origins of symbolism', *Cambridge Archaeological Journal*, 10(1): 123–67.

DUNBAR, R. I. M. 2003. 'The social brain: Mind, language, and society in evolutionary perspective', *Annual Review of Anthropology*, 32: 163–81.

FERNÁNDEZ-JALVO, Y., CARLOS DIEZ, J., CÁCERES, I., et al. 1999. 'Human cannibalism in the Early Pleistocene of Europe (Gran Dolina, Sierra de Atapuerca, Burgos, Spain)', *Journal of Human Evolution*, 37: 591–622.

——and ANDREWS, P. 2001. 'Atapuerca, le conte des deux sites', *L'Anthropologie*, 105: 223–6.

GAMBLE, C. 1999. *The Palaeolithic Societies of Europe* (Cambridge: Cambridge University Press).

——2007. *Origins and Revolutions* (Cambridge: Cambridge University Press).

GOREN-INBAR, N. and PELTZ, S. 1995. 'Additional comments on the Berekhat Ram figurine', *Rock Art Research*, 12(2): 131–2.

GOSDEN, C. 1994. *Social Being and Time* (Oxford: Blackwell).

GRIM, J. 2006. 'Indigenous lifeways and knowing the world' in P. Clayton and Z. Simpson (eds), *The Oxford Handbook of Religion and Science* (Oxford: Oxford University Press), pp. 87–107.

HOVERS, E., RAK, Y., LAVI, R., et al. 1995. 'Hominid remains from Amud Cave in the context of the Levantine Middle Palaeolithic', *Paléorient*, 21(2): 47–61.

JOHANSON, D. C., TAIEB, M., and COPPENS, Y. 1982. 'Pliocene hominids from the Hadar formation, Ehtiopia (1973–1977): Stratigraphic, chonological, and paleoenvironmental contexts, with notes on hominid morphology and systematics', *American Journal of Physical Anthropology*, 57: 373–402.

——and SHREEVE, J. 1989. *Lucy's Child: The Discovery of a Human Ancestor* (London: Penguin).

KLEIN, R. G. 2000. 'Archaeology and the evolution of human behavior', *Evolutionary Anthropology*, 9: 17–36.

LE MORT, F. 1989. 'Traces de décharnement sur les ossements néanderthaliens de Combe-Grenal (Dordogne)', *Bulletin de la Société Préhistorique Française*, 83(3): 79–87.

LEROI-GOURHAN, A. 1993. *Gesture and Speech* (Cambridge, MA: MIT Press).

LUMLEY, H. DE 1972. 'Les Neanderthaliens' in H. de Lumley (ed.), *La Grotte del Hortus (Valflaunès, Hérault)* (Marseilles: Université de Provence), pp. 375–86.

MCBREARTY, S. and BROOKS, A. S. 2000. 'The revolution that wasn't: A new interpretation of the origin of modern human behaviour', *Journal of Human Evolution*, 39: 453–63.

MANIA, D. 1991. 'The zonal division of the Lower Palaeolithic open air site Bilzingsleben', *Anthropologie*, 29: 17–24.

——and MANIA, U. 2005. 'The natural and socio-cultural environment of *Homo erectus* at Bilzingsleben, Germany' in C. Gamble and M. Porr (eds), *The Hominid Individual in Context* (London: Routledge), pp. 98–114.

MARIANI-COSTANTINI, R., OTTINI, L., CARAMIELLO, S., et al. 2001. 'Taphonomy of the fossil hominid bones from the Acheulian site of Castel di Guido near Rome, Italy', *Journal of Human Evolution*, 41: 211–25.

MARQUET, J.-C. and LORBLANCHET, M. 2003. 'A Neanderthal face? The proto-figurine from La Roche-Cotard, Langeais (Indre-et-Loire, France)', *Antiquity*, 77: 661–70.

MELLARS, P. A. 1998. 'Neanderthals, modern humans and the archaeological evidence for language' in N. G. Jablonski and L. C. Aiello (eds), *The Origin and Diversification of Language*, Memoirs of the Californian Academy of Sciences 24 (San Francisco: University of California Press), pp. 89–115.

MERCADER, J., PASANGER, M., and BOESCH, C. 2002. 'Excavation of a chimpanzee stone tool site in the African rainforest', *Science*, 296: 1452–5.

MILLER, C. J. 1997. *Faith Healers in the Himalayas* (Delhi: Book Faith India).

MITANI, J. C., WATTS, D. P., and MULLER, M. N. 2002. 'Recent developments in the study of wild chimpanzee behaviour', *Evolutionary Anthropology*, 11: 9–25.

ORSCHIEDT, J. 2008. 'The Krapina case: New results on the question of cannibalism of Neanderthals', *Quartär*, 55: 63–81.

PETTITT, P. 2002. 'The Neanderthal dead: Exploring mortuary variability in Middle Palaeolithic Eurasia', *Before Farming*, 2002/1, <http://www.waspress.co.uk/journals/beforefarming/journal_20021>.

——2003. 'Is this the infancy of art? Or the art of an infant? A possible Neanderthal face from La Roche-Cotard, France', *Before Farming*, 2003/4, <http://www.waspress.co.uk/journals/beforefarming/journal_20034/news/index.php>.

——2011. *The Palaeolithic Origins of Human Burial* (London: Routledge).

PEYRONY, D. 1934. 'La Ferrassie : Moustérien—Périgordien—Aurignacien', *Préhistore*, 3: 1–92.

PICKERING, T. R., WHITE, T. D., and TOTH, N. 2000. 'Brief communication: Cutmarks on a Plio-Pleistocene hominid from Sterkfontein, South Africa', *American Journal of Physical Anthropology*, 111: 579–84.

POWER BRATTON, S. 2006. 'Ecology and religion' in P. Clayton and Z. Simpson (eds), *The Oxford Handbook of Religion and Science* (Oxford: Oxford University Press), pp. 207–25.

ROEBROEKS, W. 2001. 'Hominid behaviour and the earliest occupation of Europe: An exploration', *Journal of Human Evolution*, 41(5): 437–61.

RUSSELL, M. D. 1987. 'Mortuary practice at the Krapina Neanderthal site', *American Journal of Physical Anthropology*, 72: 381–97.

SCHAIK, C. P. VAN, and LE MORT, F. 1986. 'Cutmarks on the Engis 2 calvaria?', *American Journal of Physical Anthropology*, 69: 317–23.

SCHAIK, C. P. VAN, ANCRENAZ, M., BORGEN, G., et al. 2003. 'Orangutan cultures and the evolution of material culture', *Science*, 299: 102–5.

SCHLOSS, J. P. 2006. 'Evolutionary theory and religious belief' in P. Clayton and Z. Simpson (eds), *The Oxford Handbook of Religion and Science* (Oxford: Oxford University Press), pp. 187–206.

SCHMITZ, R., SERRE, D., BONANI, G., et al. 2002. 'The Neanderthal type site revisited: Interdisciplinary investigations of skeletal remains from the Neander Valley, Germany', *Proceedings of the National Academy of Sciences (USA)*, 99: 13342–7.

TRINKAUS, E. 1982. 'Trauma among the Shanidar Neanderthals', *American Journal of Physical Anthropology*, 57: 61–76.

——1995. 'Neanderthal mortality patterns', *Journal of Archaeological Science*, 22: 121–42.

WHITE, T. D. 1986. 'Cut marks on the Bodo cranium: A case of prehistoric defleshing', *American Journal of Physical Anthropology*, 69: 503–9.

WHITE, T. D. and JOHANSON, D. C. 1989. 'The hominid composition of Afar Locality 333: Some preliminary observations' in G. Giacobini (ed.), *Hominidae: Proceedings of the 2nd International Congress of Human Paleontology, Turin, September 28–October 3 1987* (Milan: Jaca), pp. 97–102.

WHITEN, A., GOODALL, J., MCGREW, W. C., et al. 1999. 'Cultures in chimpanzees', *Nature*, 399: 682–5.

CHAPTER 22

RELIGION AND RITUAL IN THE UPPER PALAEOLITHIC

PAUL G. BAHN

1 INTRODUCTION

WHEN assessing potential evidence of ritual and religion in the Upper Palaeolithic—the period from roughly 40,000 to 10,000 years ago—it is often difficult to decide whether one is seeing something of deep significance or instead something mundane: was all cave art necessarily profoundly meaningful and mystical? Do footprints in deep caves represent ritual visits, or simply the bravado of youngsters? Was the breakage of an object a ritual, or an accident? Were bone fragments stuck into cave walls and floors as part of a ritual or for practical reasons? Is the positioning of a bear skull part of a mystical rite, or the result of a child playing with it? It is all too easy to project our own preconceptions and wishful thinking onto the mute archaeological evidence, and one could cite countless examples of unwarranted and purely speculative hypotheses involving ritual in this period. The evidence requires a more objective and sober assessment.

2 BURIALS

In any account of Upper Palaeolithic ritual, two major categories of evidence are usually called upon—i.e. burials and Ice Age art. Many burials have been found (Harrold 1980; Binant 1991); formal interment seems to have begun in the Gravettian period (c.28–22,000 years ago) (Formicola 2007); most elaborate examples date to that period, as well as the Magdalenian (c.16–12,000 years ago). Some contain grave goods, such as the 'Prince' burial of Arene Candide (Liguria, Italy), found in 1942 and dating to 23,440 BP; he was accompanied by four perforated antler batons and held a 23 cm flint blade in his right hand (Pettitt et al. 2003) (Figure 22.1). The two children of Sungir, Russia, buried head to head about 24,000 years ago, were accompanied by numerous remarkable objects including

FIGURE 22.1 The 'Prince' burial of Arene Candide.

ivory animal carvings; bracelets and rings; disc-shaped pendants; and 16 spears, points, and daggers of ivory (Bader and Lavrishin 1998). Like the adult buried at Sungir, they also had about 3,500 mammoth-ivory beads each, which had presumably been attached in rows to garments. These, like other beads and items of jewellery found in many burials, may simply represent funerary clothing, rather than everyday wear, but the presence of prestigious objects placed with the dead certainly suggests a belief in some kind of afterlife.

Quantities of red ochre are frequently found in Upper Palaeolithic burials, and are generally thought to be symbolic of life or blood. However, red pigment may also have been applied to corpses not so much out of pious beliefs about life blood, or in order to restore an illusion of health and life to dead cheeks, but rather to neutralize odours and to help preserve the body (Audouin and Plisson 1982). It is often difficult to tell whether a body had its flesh painted, or merely its bones. If the whole body was painted at death, or just before, the lumps of pigment placed with the corpse may represent supplies of body-paint for the afterworld. In some cases, one can at least be certain that the pigment was of great importance: for example in Australia, the Lake Mungo 3 burial, dating to perhaps 40,000 years BP, is an adult covered in red ochre which must have been transported some distance—the nearest known sources may be 100–200 km to the north-west (Bowler 1998).

A few burials appear to have received special treatment: for example, at the Abri Pataud (Dordogne, France), excavation in 1958 unearthed a 16-year old girl of $c.$20,500 BP, who seems to have been buried with her newborn (presumably stillborn) child in her arms; some time later, her skull was removed from the body, and placed 4 m away, protected by stone blocks (Movius 1975). At Le Mas d'Azil (Ariège, France), the skull of a female adolescent, without jaws or teeth, was found near the entrance of the decorated gallery; each eye socket was filled with a disc carved from a deer vertebra (Sacchi and Vaquer 1996: 42, 49); unfortunately these unique discs were subsequently lost.

In addition, it is possible to argue that those who were buried—or at least those with elaborate burials—were special people in some way. Much speculation is certainly possible about the social standing of those selected for complex burial, especially children—some have even contemplated human sacrifice (Formicola 2007). Occasionally they have some physical anomaly: at Sungir, for example, one of the children is a girl with short, bowed femurs. However, the most intriguing example is in the triple burial of Dolní Vestonice (Czech Republic), found in 1986 and dating to 26,640 BP. The three skeletons, all of young people between 17 and 20, comprise a probable female flanked by two definite males. The right male lay on his stomach, his left arm covering the female's hand, and his skull smashed; the left male lay on his side, with both arms covering her pelvis, a piece of wood skewering his sacrum. All three skulls were in soil impregnated with red ochre, and there was also a considerable concentration of ochre under the female's pelvis and between her thighs. Of particular interest is the fact that the female's bones show several pathological deformations, suggesting that she had rickets or encephalitis. In her mouth was a fragment of burnt reindeer pelvis, perhaps a clamp to bite on during times of great pain, as it shows traces of scratches and pressure. A variety of scenarios have been proposed for this unique group, ranging from a failed birth (with the two men providing help and comfort) to the sacrifice of two males to accompany the dead female (Oliva 2001; Bahn 2002b). The enigma remains complete, but it is certainly possible that some kind of ritual was involved here.

At the Italian site of Romito, excavations in front of the shelter revealed six Upper Palaeolithic skeletons: notably a grave found in 1963 containing a small middle-aged female with her arms round an adolescent male dwarf—the earliest dwarf known anywhere in the world, since this layer of the site has been dated to 11,150 years ago (Frayer et al. 1988). This kind of age would also be perfectly acceptable for the site's engravings. This individual, just over a metre tall, was clearly very special within his society, since he survived to an age of about 17 despite his physical impediments—and it may be no coincidence that he was buried in this very special place, in a decorated shelter.

The only other burial known in an Ice Age decorated shelter, at Cap Blanc in France (Bahn 2002a) (Figure 22.2), was also that of a very special person, who may have been the artist. This young lady, 25–35 years old, had an ivory point in her abdominal area, which may perhaps have been her cause of death. But in any case, her burial in such a special place, in front of the very centre of a sculpted frieze, may indicate a noteworthy social or religious status.

The decorated cave of Cussac (Dordogne, France), discovered in 2000, contains at least half a dozen human skeletons, some of them in cave bear hollows and associated with red ochre. One of them has been dated to c.25,000 years ago, which fits the stylistic age of the cave's engravings (Aujoulat et al. 2002). These are thought to be the work of one artist, and so it is quite possible that the artist is one of the bodies found here: moreover, since one skeleton is still fairly complete and unscattered, there is a possibility that the cave's mouth

FIGURE 22.2 A cast of the Cap Blanc skeleton in front of the sculpted frieze.

was deliberately sealed after the bodies were placed inside—the first such case ever found for the Upper Palaeolithic.

3 Portable Art

Thousands of portable art objects are known from the Upper Palaeolithic, particularly of Eurasia, but most of them have no readily apparent symbolic or ritual role. Occasionally, however, their context can suggest such a function: for example, at the Magdalenian rock shelter of Duruthy (Landes, France), a 'sanctuary' was unearthed in 1961, comprising four horse carvings in a limited area, together with the remains of two horse skulls, and fragments of six horse jaws, two of which formed a kind of box (Arambourou 1978: 50, 116–24). Indeed the horse seems to have played a prominent role in Magdalenian beliefs, not only in cave art in general, but also—at least in the Pyrenees—in other ways, since horse skulls or teeth have been found placed in the fireplaces of several major decorated caves such as Erberua and Labastide (Bahn 1982: 21). Recently, further evidence of the central role of the horse has been found in the Cantabrian cave of La Garma where remains of this species dominate in some parts of the site, including an equid skull inside a structure, with its dome of bone removed (Arias 2009).

Some categories of portable art—most notably engraved plaquettes of stone, but also some stone carvings and bone cutouts in Pyrenean caves (Bahn and Vertut 1997: 98)—have been found broken, with fragments of the same specimen being metres apart (for example, at the German open-air site of Gönnersdorf, fragments of the same plaquette have been found up to 30 m apart). While taphonomic factors (i.e. accidental breakage) may sometimes be responsible, there are definitely cases where the dispersal of fragments was purposeful, and indeed some pieces have proved impossible to find and are therefore absent. A few (e.g. in the Pyrenean caves of Labastide and Enlène) bear marks of blows, suggesting deliberate breakage; however, while traces of burning are frequent, this may simply mean that the slabs were used as lamps or heating devices. Only a percentage of plaquettes in any site bear engravings—e.g. at Gönnersdorf, only 5–10 per cent of the tons of schist plaquettes brought into the site were engraved, and seem to be distributed at random among the rest (Bosinski 1984: 318)—which suggests that the engravings lost all value once the ritual had been performed, and they had been broken or dispersed; or merely that they never had any ritual significance, and were done simply to pass the time, for practice, for storytelling, or perhaps even to personalize one's private bed-warmer!

A different kind of breakage has been found in Moravia and neighbouring areas, where, around 22,000 years ago, hundreds of terracotta figurines were made at sites such as Dolní Vestonice and Pavlov. The thousands of fragments comprise small figurines of animals and a few humans; a hearth or 'oven' for their manufacture has also been found. Tests have shown that they were fired at temperatures from 500° to 800° centigrade, and the shape of their fractures implies that they were broken by thermal shock—in other words, they were placed, when still wet, in the hottest part of the fire, and thus deliberately caused to explode. Rather than carefully made art objects, therefore, their lack of finish and the manner of their breakage suggest that they have been used in some special ritual (Soffer et al. 1993).

Finally, one prominent category of portable art object is that of the female figurines, or 'Venuses', most of which date to the Gravettian period (Delporte 1993). Most specimens from Western Europe (many of stone) have been found in caves or rock shelters, while almost all those from Central and Eastern Europe (usually of mammoth ivory) have come from open-air settlements, and sometimes seem to have had a special role in the home. For example, one from the Russian site of Kostenki I, found in 1983, and dating to about 23,000 years ago, was upright in a small pit, leaning against the wall and facing the centre of the living area and the hearths; the pit was filled with soil mixed with red ochre, and was capped by a mammoth shoulder-blade (Praslov 1985: 182–3). Pits in other Russian sites have sometimes contained one, two, or three such figurines, but we do not know if these pits were ritual or for storage. The statuettes have often been interpreted by Russian scholars as a mother- or ancestor-figure, a mistress of the house.

4 Cave Art

Where Ice Age cave art is concerned, the earliest interpretation was to see it, along with portable art, as merely 'art for art's sake'—i.e. that the art was essentially meaningless, and merely decorative, made by hunters with time on their hands; and indeed a certain amount of it could certainly be seen as decoration, or a means of telling and recording stories or myths. However, in the early twentieth century 'art for art's sake' was rapidly replaced by notions of 'sympathetic magic' imported from ethnographic studies of Australian Aborigines and South African San, the so-called Bushmen. These notions were eagerly adopted by Henri Breuil, the dominant figure in cave art studies; and so for the next 50 years most cave art was thus attributed to 'hunting magic', even though there was not a single recognizable hunting scene among the thousands of images, and despite the fact that very few caves contained any animal figures marked by possible 'missiles'. Nevertheless, the few images which seemed to be marked in that way were presented as characteristic of the art (Bahn 1991; Bahn and Vertut 1997).

Similar notions of fertility magic were also highly popular, despite the complete absence of copulation scenes in the art; the importance and ubiquity of the human vulva in Ice Age art were routinely exaggerated (Bahn and Vertut, ibid.). However, a few caves do contain fissures, ranging from small (e.g. Ekain) to huge (e.g. Gargas, Tito Bustillo), whose entrance and sides are thickly coated with red ochre; and the obvious interpretation is that these were meant to represent vulvas, and presumably had some kind of symbolic or religious significance.

The second half of the twentieth century was marked by the new approach of Annette Laming-Emperaire (1962) and André Leroi-Gourhan (1965) who, taking their lead from pioneering work by Max Raphael (1945), decided to abandon ethnographic parallels and to study cave art itself, in terms of quantities of different animals, and their distribution in each cave. This work led to many important new insights; and, while much of it is now outdated, some of its basic findings of regularities and rules still appear valid.

One of the most important advances produced by this new approach was the emphasis on planning. Whereas before, decorated caves had been seen as a more-or-less random accumulation of individual figures, the new rules and regularities discovered by Laming-

Emperaire and Leroi-Gourhan revealed that the art had often been carefully thought out in terms both of where it was placed in the caves, and of which species were placed in which areas. Leroi-Gourhan took this idea to extremes, believing that there was a cave 'blueprint', and that most decorated caves should be seen as single compositions, laid out as closely to the template as possible. Today each cave is seen as unique in terms of its layout and decoration; but nevertheless some of Leroi-Gourhan's regularities and rules have stood the test of time and of new discoveries. There is a definite syntax and a great deal of planning in cave art, often involving the use or enhancement of natural shapes in rocks and concretions. Leroi-Gourhan certainly believed that much cave art was an expression of some kind of religious belief, and that the caves could be considered 'sanctuaries' (1964, 1965).

The early part of the twentieth century had also seen various ideas based on shamanism and totemism applied to selected aspects of cave art, with little or no success. Later, in a new theory loosely based on Siberian shamanism, André Glory (1968) suggested that many of the figures in Palaeolithic art were 'ongones', spirits which took the form of 'zoomorphs', 'anthropomorphs', and 'polymorphs', and which were asked to help in hunting, matters of health, and so on. However, Leroi-Gourhan—who was an expert on Siberian ethnography as well as on cave art—was adamant (1977) that the phenomenon of historical shamanism could not validly be applied to the European Ice Age.

Sadly, in a great leap backwards, the end of the twentieth century—despite Leroi-Gourhan's warning—saw the re-emergence of long-abandoned notions of 'shamanism' in cave art studies. This time around they were linked to neuropsychological data concerning 'altered states of consciousness' and 'trance'—whose three stages were supposedly linked to different motifs in the art, since the artists had reproduced their visions on the walls—as well as to a few ethnographic parallels from Southern Africa (Clottes and Lewis-Williams 1996; Lewis-Williams 2002). Unfortunately, this entire approach proved bogus, being founded on a distortion, misuse, or misunderstanding of the term 'shaman' and the phenomenon of 'shamanism'; on outdated, distorted, or utterly erroneous neuropsychological data; and on highly selective and distorted data from Southern African rock art motifs and ethnographic testimony (see Helvenston and Bahn 2005, 2006). The supposed 'three stages of trance', one of the cornerstones of this approach, and copied endlessly from author to author without the slightest effort to check their validity, only occur when one has ingested a very small range of hallucinogens, most notably LSD, and certainly have no applicability whatsoever to Ice Age art.

The resulting obsession with 'trance' interpretations led to some amazing claims—for example, that the supposedly mutilated hand stencils in France's Gargas Cave (see below) were the result of people cutting their fingers off so that the pain might help induce altered states of consciousness (Clottes and Lewis-Williams 1996: 96). Besides, the above-mentioned careful planning of much cave art and the tremendous artistry involved in its production cry out against it being simply an accumulated record of images seen in trance. Moreover, 'trance' (which is never clearly defined—there are over 70 kinds!) is in no way a reliable indicator of true shamanism—most often in Siberia, the shaman simply pretends to enter an altered state of consciousness (Hamayon 1995).

One of the favourite pieces of evidence used by the proponents of the 'shamanic' hypothesis was the therianthropes, half-man/half-animal figures, which they naturally saw as depicting shamans. Unfortunately, such figures are extraordinarily rare in cave art—about six are known—so they cannot possibly be seen as representative of Ice Age art, let alone a key to its understanding. In any case, why should one see them as shamans rather than mythical beings, or gods, or sorcerers, or men dressed as animals, or simply creatures of the imagination? Another constant theme was that the cave wall represented a 'veil' between this world and that of the spirits, and that the artists constantly sought to reach through the veil, or to depict animals emerging through it. However, such a notion has nothing to do with shamanism, and is simply wishful thinking, with no supporting evidence at all.

Hand stencils are quite common in caves and may have had both secular and ritual functions. What has caused much ink to flow for the past century is whether some of them are mutilated, and, if so, whether the cause was pathological or due to a ritual. This particularly applies to the cave of Gargas, which contains over 200 hands, most of which are incomplete, ranging from some with a single phalange missing to hands with almost no fingers at all (Barrière 1976). It would, however, be a foolish idea for hunter-gatherers to sacrifice so many of their fingers to a ritual, and most specialists today believe that the fingers were actually bent over for some reason when the stencils were made. Similarly, at the Spanish cave of Maltravieso it used to be thought that the hand stencils all had the little finger missing, which must therefore have been a ritual mutilation, since no medical condition could produce this phenomenon. However, ultraviolet light has now shown that all the Maltravieso hands were intact when stencilled, and that the little fingers were later painted over (Ripoll et al. 1999).

A different kind of retouching is also presumably of ritual significance—some drawings in caves were touched up, while a few (e.g. hand stencils in Cosquer) were scratched out. In several caves, it seems to have been of importance to mark walls and concretions with fingers dipped in paint—Cougnac has hundreds of such marks, while in other sites such as La Garma or Tito Bustillo they are grouped in particular chambers or walls.

One aspect of cave art remains of unquestionable value in examining its role, namely its location. Some of the art is 'public' or 'open', and was clearly meant to be seen by other people: at Candamo (Asturias) figures placed in a niche 12 m up were made more visible from below by concretions being broken; while stalagmites and stalactites in front of the main decorated panel at Cougnac were broken to make it readily visible. However, much cave art is very 'private' or 'hidden' and was made after a journey involving some physical effort or hardship—e.g. in extremely narrow passages (Fronsac, La Pasiega), up chimneys (Bernifal), or in remote inaccessible chambers (Le Combel). In other words, some images were never intended to be viewed by people, but instead were made to be seen by (or offered to) something non-human, either gods, or spirits, ancestors, or natural forces (Bahn 2003). The ultimate example of this phenomenon has been found in the cave of Pergouset (Lot) where the engraved art begins only after a long crawl down a narrow, low, and unpleasant passage; and one of the engraved figures, a horse head, was made at arm's length inside a fissure into which the artist could not possibly have inserted his or her head (Lorblanchet 2001: 63–4). In other words, even the artist never saw this figure, which was 'drawn blind'; it was not meant to be seen by human eyes but can plausibly be argued to be some kind of votive offering. This view of some cave art as 'offerings' is echoed by possible ex-votos (see below).

5 Cave Activities

In addition to parietal art, many caves contain a wide variety of other vestiges of the Upper Palaeolithic which have often been interpreted in terms of religion or ritual. For example, 'lithophones'—i.e. 'draperies' of folded calcite formations—often resound when struck with a hard object (wooden sticks seem to produce the clearest and most resonant notes), and this was clearly noticed by Palaeolithic people, since some of the lithophones are somewhat battered, and are decorated with painted lines and dots (Dams 1985). Many of the known examples are in the Lot region of France (e.g. at Pech Merle, Les Fieux, Roucadour); moreover, most of them are in or near large chambers which could have held a large audience.

Studies have also been made of the acoustics of a few decorated caves (e.g. Dauvois 1994), and it has sometimes been found that the best acoustics coincide with the richest decoration, and the poorest with little or no decoration. Naturally one cannot assume that all making of sounds or music in caves was ritual or religious in nature, but it seems a reasonable assumption that, if ceremonies of some kind were performed in such a setting, full advantage would have been taken of its acoustic properties, including echoes which must have been both baffling and impressive.

One of the most popular theories about the Upper Palaeolithic use of caves is that they would have been a perfect setting for the initiation of youngsters, indelibly imprinting crucial tribal information onto impressionable minds (Pfeiffer 1982); not only would the darkness, strange formations and acoustics have played a major role, but engravings could have been made to appear and disappear by moving the light source, while painted animals would have seemed to move in the flickering light. Obviously, there is not a shred of actual evidence for this theory, but it is certain that youngsters were no strangers to deep dark caves in this period: indeed almost all the footprints found so far are from children or adolescents. However, this may be due to bravado, curiosity, and exploration rather than to rituals. For example, in the Pyrenean cave of Fontanet, a little child seems to have been chasing a puppy, while in Niaux youngsters were clearly playing, making the most perfect footprints that they could. In Le Tuc d'Audoubert, the chamber next to the famous clay bison figures contains numerous heel prints, as well as holes and lines made in the floor (Bégouën and Breuil 1958), and a circle of small stalactites stuck into the floor (Clottes 2007: 45). Much has been speculated about ritual dances, but it seems equally probable that these were bored children, passing the time while the adults made the figures.

Similarly, some clay 'sausages' on the ground near the bison have traditionally been interpreted as phalluses, or occasionally as horns, by adherents of fertility- or hunting-magic theories, but a study by a sculptor (Beasley 1986) suggested, far more plausibly, that they are simply the result of testing the clay's plasticity, and the position of palm- and fingerprints on them supports this.

Other traces of strange activities abound. For example, in Italy's Toirano Cave, pellets of clay seem to have been thrown forcefully against the back wall of the innermost chamber, 400 m from the entrance, probably at least 12,000 years ago (Blanc 1957)—perhaps a meaningful ritual, but equally possibly an example of play. In France's Chauvet cave, much excitement was caused by the discovery of a cave-bear skull placed on a rock in a decorated chamber (Chauvet et al. 1995); but rather than evidence for some kind of cave-bear cult (a once-popular notion, especially for the Middle Palaeolithic, but long discredited thanks to taphonomic studies) this could again be an example of a child playing inside the cave. There is no way of deciding between the two possibilities on present evidence.

In certain cases, it is very difficult to see anything other than some kind of ritual or religious behaviour in action: for example, in both Montespan and Le Tuc d'Audoubert (deep Pyrenean caves containing clay sculptures), a headless snake skeleton was found, which seems a remarkable coincidence. And in Les Trois Frères, the 'Chapelle de la Lionne' is a small chamber containing one prominent depiction of a lioness on a stalagmite flow; not only has this image been repeatedly pounded on the head and shoulder, but objects have been found carefully placed in niches below the depiction and in the chamber's walls—flint tools, a bear tooth, and a burnt seashell (Bégouën and Clottes 1980) (Figure 22.3). Special objects associated with a special depiction in a very special place—everything clearly suggests that these were 'ex-votos' of some kind, offered to something non-human, just as some cave art, as mentioned above, was also probably a kind of offering.

Finally, much has been made in recent years of fragments of bone found stuck into wall-fissures or into the ground in many caves, mostly in the Pyrenees but also in Chauvet and elsewhere. For some reason, these have all been ascribed to some kind of ritual, inevitably

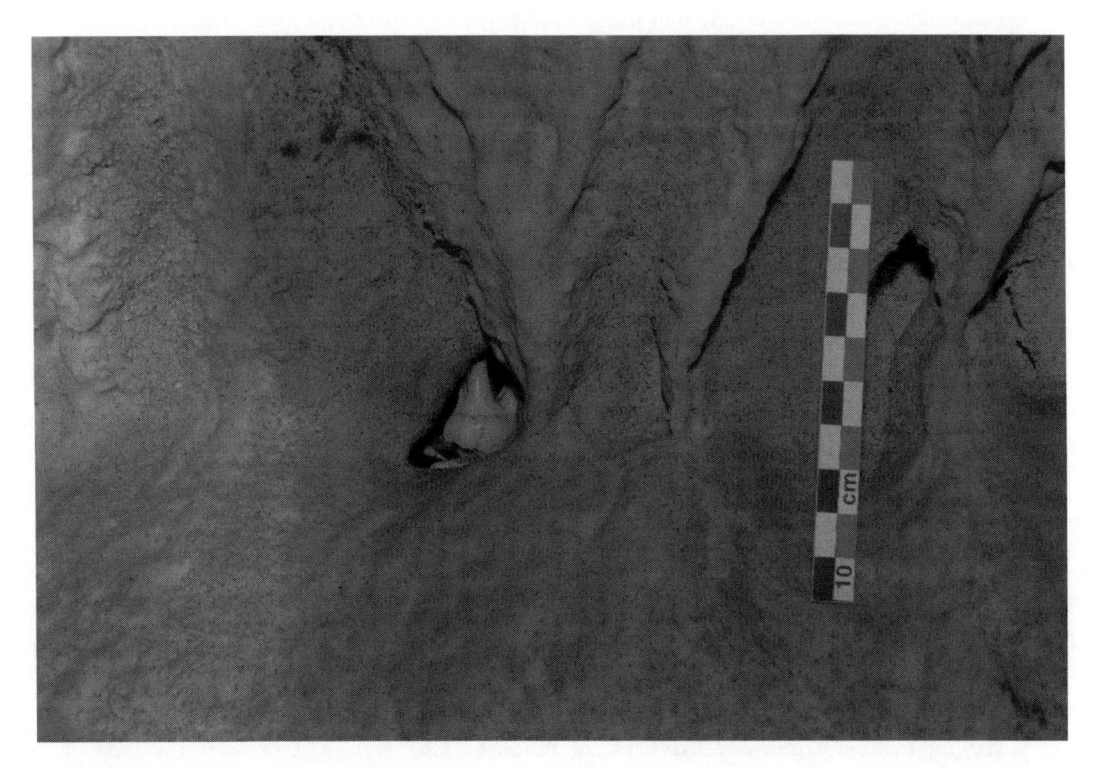

FIGURE 22.3 A bear tooth and flints in a niche in the 'Lioness Chapel', Cave of Les Trois Frères.

involved with penetrating the entirely fictitious 'veil' (see above) to reach the spirit world (Clottes 2007: 51). In most cases, however, a far more mundane explanation seems preferable—i.e. these were nails and pegs, used to store materials and containers above the humid floor, and out of the reach of children or animals. Bone lasts far longer than wood, which rots quickly in damp caves, and indeed this use of bone pegs can be found throughout the world in many different cultures, including at the present-day. Strangely, the advocates of 'veil piercing' do not mention the existence of rings carved into limestone walls and ceilings not only in the Upper Palaeolithic (Pair-non-Pair, Abri Pataud, Cap Blanc, Angles-sur-l'Anglin) but also in the medieval period (e.g. Cave Pataud), which presumably served the same purpose. Further evidence to support the functional interpretation is the existence in some rock art—notably in South Africa's Cederberg region—of actual depictions of bags hanging from pegs driven into cracks in rock-shelter walls (Parkington 2003: 20, 60)! Many wooden pegs are still to be found lodged in cracks in Cederberg rock shelters (ibid.: 20). The same can be seen in Saharan rock art, while similar pegs are still to be found wedged into the walls of countless Saharan rock shelters (J.-L. Le Quellec pers. comm.).

In addition, flint tools, blades, and animal teeth are also sometimes found concealed in niches in caves, or sticking out of holes in the wall (e.g. at Bernifal). Except in special locations (as in Les Trois Frères, mentioned above), it is hard to decide whether this is necessarily ritual, or simply a means of storing or caching a valuable object.

It has been argued that some of the bone fragments in cave walls are in positions that cannot have been functional (Clottes 2007: 43), but how can we be sure? Of course the bones occasionally found stuck deeply into the ground (e.g. in Chauvet and Enlène) cannot have been used for suspending objects. However, even if one assumes that these vertical bones were not involved in some kind of game—and one cannot safely make that assumption (cf. the stalactite ring, above)—this does not necessarily link them to any kind of ritual or religious activity. They remain one of the countless enigmas of the Upper Palaeolithic period.

6 Conclusion

All of the blanket explanations put forward so far for cave art are deeply flawed, usually bending the facts to fit the theory, grossly exaggerating the frequency of certain pet themes, or employing erroneous data on neuropsychology and ethnography. Clottes (2007: 51) has even claimed that all decorated caves are the result of magico-religious practices; but it is hard to see what can justify such a statement. Those who make such claims tend to ignore the open-air rock art of the Upper Palaeolithic, perhaps because it looks more secular; but we know from studies of rock art in places such as Australia that open-air rock art can be just as mystical, powerful, or dangerous as anything in deep caves. Future discoveries and studies will doubtless bring new questions as well as new theories, but it is vital that the evidence be assessed soberly and objectively, without preconceptions or fantasy.

One can rarely be sure that any aspect of the material culture of the Upper Palaeolithic is linked to religion or ritual—most evidence can also have a more mundane explanation—but it is very difficult to imagine a secular explanation for the 'Chapel of the Lioness' in Les Trois Frères, and for the most hidden of the cave art, which thus provide our best insights into the symbolism, spirituality, and beliefs of these hunter-gatherers. It is inaccessibility of different kinds which seems to be the crucial factor in most of the 'private' art. Indeed, one often has the impression that it was the overcoming of obstacles, the suffering of discomforts and dangers, which was more important than the actual images produced—or that it was the process of journeying to a location and leaving an image there which counted, rather than the image itself, or its appearance, degree of completeness, or durability. There was clearly a tremendously strong motivation behind this phenomenon, which must have been 'religious' in some way.

Acknowledgements

I am most grateful to Robert Bégouën for specially supplying Figure 22.3, and giving permission to reproduce it here.

Suggested Reading

Bahn, P. G. and Vertut, J. 1997. *Journey through the Ice Age* (London: Weidenfeld and Nicolson/Berkeley: University of California Press).
Binant, P. 1991. *La Préhistoire de la Mort: Les premières sépultures en Europe* (Paris: Editions Errance).
Laming-Emperaire, A. 1962. *La Signification de l'Art Rupestre Paléolithique* (Paris: Picard).
Leroi-Gourhan, A. 1964. *Les Religions de la Préhistoire* (Paris: Presses Universitaires de France).
——1965. *Préhistoire de l'Art Occidental* (Paris: Mazenod).
Lorblanchet, M. 1995. *Les Grottes Ornées de la Préhistoire. Nouveaux regards* (Paris: Editions Errance).
Luquet, G. H. 1926. *L'Art et la Religion des Hommes Fossiles* (Paris: Masson).
Patte, E. 1960. *Les Hommes Préhistoriques et la Religion* (Paris: Picard).
Pfeiffer, J. E. 1982. *The Creative Explosion: An enquiry into the origins of art and religion* (New York: Harper and Row).

References

Arambourou, R. 1978. *Le Gisement Préhistorique de Duruthy à Sorde-l'Abbaye (Landes). Bilan des Recherches de 1958 à 1975*, Mémoire 13 de la Société Préhistorique Française.
Arias, P. 2009. 'Rites in the dark? An evaluation of the current evidence for ritual areas at Magdalenian cave sites', *World Archaeology*, 41(2): 262–94.
Audouin, F. and Plisson, H. 1982. 'Les ocres et leurs témoins au Paléolithique en France: enquête et expériences sur leur validité archéologique', *Cahiers du Centre de Recherches Préhistoriques*, 8: 33–80.
Aujoulat, N., Geneste, J.-M., Archambeau, C., et al. 2002. 'La grotte ornée de Cussac—Le Buisson-de-Cadouin (Dordogne): premières observations', *Bulletin de la Société Préhistorique Française*, 99(1): 129–37.

Bader, N. O. and Lavrishin, Y. A. (eds) 1998. *Upper Palaeolithic Site Sungir (graves and environment)* (Moscow: Scientific World) (in Russian).

Bahn, P. G. 1982. 'Homme et cheval dans le Quaternaire des Pays de l'Adour' in J. Robert (ed.), *Les Pays de l'Adour, Royaume du Cheval* (Lourdes: Musée Pyrénéen), pp. 21–6.

—— 1991. 'Where's the beef? The myth of hunting magic in palaeolithic art' in P. Bahn and A. Rosenfeld (eds), *Rock Art and Prehistory (Papers from the 1st AURA Congress, Darwin, 1988)* (Oxford: Oxbow Books), pp. 1–13.

—— 2002a. 'The Cap Blanc lady' in P. Bahn (ed.), *Written in Bones: How human remains unlock the secrets of the dead* (Newton Abbot: David and Charles), pp. 108–13.

—— 2002b. 'The triple burial of Dolní Vestonice' in P. Bahn (ed.), *Written in Bones. How human remains unlock the secrets of the dead* (Newton Abbot: David and Charles), pp. 56–8.

—— 2003. 'Location, location: What can the positioning of cave and rock art reveal about Ice Age motivations?' in A. Pastoors and G.-C. Weniger (eds), *Cave Art and Space: Archaeological and architectural perspectives* (Wissenschaftliche Schriften des Neanderthal Museums), pp. 11–20.

Barrière, C. 1976. *Palaeolithic Art in the Grotte de Gargas*, BAR International Series No. 14, 2 vols. (Oxford: BAR).

Beasley, B. 1986. 'Les bisons d'argile de la grotte du Tuc d'Audoubert', *Bulletin de la Société Préhistorique Ariège-Pyrénées*, 41: 23–30.

Bégouën, H. and Breuil, H. 1958. *Les Cavernes du Volp: Trois-Frères—Tuc d'Audoubert* (Paris: Arts et Métiers Graphiques).

Bégouën, R. and Clottes, J. 1980. 'Apports mobiliers dans les cavernes du Volp (Enlène, Les Trois Frères, le Tuc d'Audoubert)' in M. Almagro (ed.), *Altamira Symposium* (Madrid: Ministerio de la Cultura), pp. 157–88.

——, Fritz, C., Tosello, G., et al. 2009. *Le Sanctuaire Secret des Bisons* (Paris: Somogy Editions d'Art).

Binant, P. 1991. *La Préhistoire de la Mort: Les premières sépultures en Europe* (Paris: Editions Errance).

Blanc, A. C. 1957. 'A new paleolithic cultural element, probably of ideological significance: The clay pellets of the Cave of the Basua (Savona)', *Quaternaria*, 4: 1–9.

Bosinski, G. 1984. 'The mammoth engravings of the magdalenian site Gönnersdorf (Rhineland, Germany)' in H.-G. Bandi, W. Huber, M.-R. Sauter and B. Sitter (eds), *La Contribution de la Zoologie et de l'Ethologie à l'interprétation de l'art des peuples chasseurs préhistoriques*, 3e colloque de la Société suisse des Sciences Humaines, Sigriswil 1979 (Fribourg: Editions Universitaires), pp. 295–322.

Bowler, J. M. 1998. 'Willandra Lakes revisited: Environmental framework for human occupation', *Archaeology in Oceania*, 33: 120–55.

Chauvet, J.-M., Brunel Deschamps, E., and Hillaire, C. 1995. *Chauvet Cave: The discovery of the world's oldest paintings* (London: Thames and Hudson); US edition: *Dawn of Art, The Chauvet Cave: The oldest known paintings in the world* (New York: Abrams).

Clottes, J. 2007. 'Un geste paléolithique dans les grottes ornées: os et silex plantésin' in R. Desbrosse and A. Thévenin (eds), *Arts et Cultures de la Préhistoire. Hommages à Henri Delporte*, Documents Préhistoriques 24 (Paris: Editions du Comité des Travaux Historiques et Scientifiques), pp. 41–54.

—— and Lewis-Williams, D. 1996. *Les chamanes de la Préhistoire. Transe et Magie dans les Grottes Ornees* (Paris: Le Seuil).

Dams, L. 1985. 'Palaeolithic lithophones: Descriptions and comparisons', *Oxford Journal of Archaeology*, 4: 31–46.

DAUVOIS, M. 1994. 'Les témoins sonores paléolithiques extérieur et souterrain' in M. Otte (ed.), *'Sons Originels', Préhistoire de la Musique Actes du Colloque de Musicologie, Dec. 1992* (Liège: ERAUL 61), pp. 11–31.

DELPORTE, H. 1993. *L'Image de la Femme dans l'Art Préhistorique*, 2nd edn (Paris: Picard).

FORMICOLA, V. 2007. 'From the Sunghir children to the Romito dwarf: Aspects of the Upper Paleolithic funerary landscape', *Current Anthropology*, 48(3): 446–53.

FRAYER, D. W., MACCHIARELLI, R. and MUSSI, M. 1988. 'A case of dwarfism in the Italian late Upper Paleolithic', *American Journal of Physical Anthropology*, 75: 549–65.

GLORY, A. 1968. 'L'énigme de l'art quaternaire peut-elle être résolue par la théorie du culte des ongones?' in E. Ripoll (ed.), *Simposio de Arte Rupestre, Barcelona 1966*, Diputación Provincial de Barcelona, pp. 25–60.

HAMAYON, R. N. 1995. 'Pour en finir avec la "transe" et l' "extase" dans l'étude du chamanisme', *Etudes mongoles et sibériennes*, 26: 155–90.

HARROLD, F. B. 1980. 'A comparative analysis of Eurasian Palaeolithic burials', *World Archaeology*, 12: 195–211.

HELVENSTON, P. A. and BAHN, P. G. 2005. *Waking the Trance Fixed* (Kentucky, USA: Wasteland Press).

—— 2006. 'Archaeology or Mythology? The "three stages of trance" model and South African rock art' in Y. Gauthier, J.-L. le Quellec and R. Simonis (eds), *Hic sunt leones. Mélanges Sahariens en l'honeur d'Alfred Muzzolini*, Cahier 10 de l'Association des Amis de l'Art Rupestre Saharien, pp. 111–26.

LEROI-GOURHAN, A. 1977. 'Le préhistorien et le chamane. Voyages chamaniques', *L'Ethnographe*, 74–5(2): 19–25.

LEWIS-WILLIAMS, D. 2002. *The Mind in the Cave* (London: Thames and Hudson).

LORBLANCHET, M. 2001. *La grotte ornée de Pergouset (Saint-Géry, Lot): un sanctuaire secret paléolithique*, Documents d'Archéologie française 85 (Paris: Maison des Sciences de l'Homme).

MOVIUS, H. L. JR (ed.) 1975. *Excavation of the Abri Pataud, Les Eyzies (Dordogne)* (Harvard, Cambridge, MA: Peabody Museum of Archaeology and Ethnology).

OLIVA, M. 2001. 'Les pratiques funéraires dans le Pavlovien morave: Révision critique', *Préhistoire Européenne*, 16–17: 191–214.

PARKINGTON, J. 2003. *Cederberg Rock Paintings* (Cape Town: Creda Communications).

PETTITT, P., RICHARDS, M., MAGGI, R., et al. 2003. 'The Gravettian burial known as the Prince ('Il Principe'): New evidence for his age and diet', *Antiquity*, 77: 15–19.

PRASLOV, N. D. 1985. 'L'art du Paléolithique Supérieur à l'est de l'Europe', *L'Anthropologie*, 89: 181–92.

RAPHAEL, M. 1945. *Prehistoric Cave Paintings* (Washington, DC: Pantheon Books, Bollingen Series).

RIPOLL, S., RIPOLL, E., and COLLADO, H. 1999. *Maltravieso, El Santuario Extremeño de las Manos* (Cáceres: Memorias, Museo de Cáceres).

SACCHI, D. and VAQUER, J. 1996. *Connaître la Préhistoire des Pyrénées* (Bordeaux: Sud-Ouest).

SOFFER, O., VANDIVER, P., KLÍMA, B., et al. 1993. 'The pyrotechnology of performance art: Moravian venuses and wolverines' in H. Knecht, A. Pike-Tay, and R. White (eds), *Before Lascaux: The complex record of the Early Upper Paleolithic* (Boca Raton: CRC Press), pp. 259–75.

CHAPTER 23

THE MESOLITHIC

CHANTAL CONNELLER

1 INTRODUCTION

UNTIL recently there has been little attempt to reconstruct Mesolithic ritual or religious practices. The Mesolithic has traditionally been viewed as a period of 'impoverishment', lacking the cave art and funerary monuments of adjacent periods; a time when life was too difficult to devote time to practices not necessary for physical survival. Since art and monuments are the main media through which archaeologists have also inferred ritual and religious practices, the Mesolithic even seemed to lack the methodological basis whereby archaeologists could go beyond functional considerations of Mesolithic lifeways. Since the pioneering work of Clark (1952), reinforced by the palaeoeconomic and processual schools of archaeology, economic and ecological considerations have dominated understandings of Mesolithic lifeways.

Before the mid-1970s there had been little consideration of Mesolithic religion and beliefs beyond a few cursory mentions in syntheses of the period and site reports. Uncertainty about the age of some of the earlier finds of Mesolithic burials confined discussion to a few key burial sites and finds of material culture. So Srejović speculated on the mythology behind the Lepenski Vir statuettes, naming them accordingly: Danubius was seen as the creator, while the Ancestress and Ancestor were the representative founders of the Lepenski Vir people (Srejović 1972). Clark briefly considered the significance of the red deer frontlets discovered at Star Carr, suggesting they may have functioned as 'head-dresses for some kind of ritual dance designed perhaps to improve the hunter's luck, to increase the fertility of the deer on which he so largely depended, or merely to promote natural increase in general' (Clark 1954: 170). Syntheses of the period briefly discuss the burials of Téviec and Hoëdic, Brittany and the nest of skulls at Grosse Ofnet, Germany (Clark 1967, 1980), but these are secondary to concerns with economy and the process of neolithicization.

In recent years there has been more interest in reconstructing Mesolithic ritual practices. This work has two separate foci: first the discovery of Mesolithic cemeteries in Scandinavia and the radiometric dating of earlier cemetery excavations elsewhere has stimulated an interest in Mesolithic ritual and beliefs. Much of the focus of early work on the cemeteries was concerned with ranking, status, and the identification of complex hunter-gatherers. However Larsson's initial work on the Skateholm cemeteries explicitly focused on funerary practices and wider beliefs (Larsson 1988, 1989a, 1989b, 1990, 2004). The most extensive analysis of Mesolithic mortuary ritual is that undertaken by Nilsson Stutz (2003a and b) on the cemeteries of Vedbæk Bøgebakken, Denmark, and Skateholm I and II, Sweden. Nilsson Stutz has used the French technique *anthropologie de terrain* (Duday et al. 1990) where burials are viewed as the preserved material part of a series of gestures related to the funerary process, these gestures being reconstructed through a form of forensic archaeology. This technique is combined with practice theory, whereby the embodied action of funerary practices are considered to be both structured by, but able to affect broader systems of values and beliefs. Hence the archaeological remains are conceived as traces of dynamic ritual practices rather than static indicators of social standing.

A second important influence has been the use of direct historic analogy to elucidate Mesolithic religious practices. Building on much earlier work and regional traditions of research (e.g. Gurina 1956) in recent years explicit parallels have been drawn between Mesolithic practices and a set of beliefs found across a variety of northern Eurasian hunter-gatherer groups (Zvelebil 1993, 1996, 2003a and b, 2004, 2008; Schmidt 2000). These include the concept of a three-tiered world and the role of the shaman as religious specialist who interceded with various animal spirits, or the 'master of animals'. In a similar vein, anthropological accounts (e.g. Ingold 2000; Tanner 1979; Descola 1997) that stress the very different understandings that hunter-gatherers have of the relationship between humans and animals (with animals seen as friends or relatives or spiritual beings) have stimulated interest in the treatment of animals in archaeological contexts.

2 Rites of Passage

With the exception of mortuary practices, little work has been undertaken on rituals associated with the life cycle. Only a few tentative hypotheses have been put forward regarding the ritual associated with major stages in human life.

2.1 Birth

Birth represents a rite of passage both for the mother and the child, an event that can change identities and produce new social persona. Invariably a dangerous time for both individuals, birth can be seen as dangerous or polluting or associated with apotropaic rituals. Strassburg (2000) argues that an elliptical structure unearthed at the site of Gongehusvej 7, Vedbæk, Denmark represents a birthing hut. The remains of several infants, possibly including twins, surrounded the house. This, he suggests, seems reminiscent of anthropological examples, where pregnant individuals are secluded as they approach childbirth because they are seen as either polluting or powerful. From this liminal space the adult would be reincorporated into society with a new social position, that of mother. However, more recent publications on Gongehusvej 7 (Brinch Petersen and Meikeljohn 2003) suggest rather more complexity to the site than Strassburg's theory can encompass, with a variety of individuals buried and cremated at the site, from infants, through older children and adolescents to adult individuals, probably of both genders. One cremation of a young woman was covered with the articulated body of a three-month-old roe deer faun; this may lend weight to Strassburg's idea of a concern with young individuals at the site.

More broadly a concern with the dangers associated with childbirth can be seen in the cemeteries, particularly in Scandinavia. The individuals buried at Skateholm I and II and Vedbæk Bøgebakken represent a carefully selected portion of the population with a significant component of young women, often with rich grave goods. Both Orme (1981) and Strassburg (2000) have argued that these are individuals who died in childbirth, and that it may be this very concern around lives cut short in traumatic fashion, or in a dangerous liminal state, that gained these individuals admittance to these cemeteries.

2.2 Initiation

Differing treatment of infants and children across Europe may hint at the presence of additional rites of passage—initiation ceremonies that conferred full social status on an individual. Infants and young children are represented in the Scandinavian cemeteries, whereas older children are not. This may suggest that infants were seen as part of their parents, lacking full social status. Older children, though separate from their parents, appear to have lacked the full social persona that permitted them to be buried in these cemeteries. This suggests the presence of further rites of passage, initiation rituals that may have served to transform children into full members of the social group. In contrast, at Zvenieki, Latvia, children buried alone have grave goods, which Janik (2000) suggests means that they were seen as individuals in their own right.

Further evidence of initiation rituals come from an unlikely source: a flint nodule with engraved cortex from the Danish Maglemosian (early Mesolithic) site of Holmegård V (Fischer 1975). Refitting knapping debris revealed a 21-cm-long elongated flint nodule, on the outer surface of which had been scratched a variety of geometric designs. The scratches form a series of motifs of the kind known from decorated Mesolithic bone and antler tools and include heavily stylized male figures. Most of the flint waste belonging to the nodule was recovered in a small compact heap. However some pieces were found to be missing: four of the most regular and blade-like flakes seem to have been deliberately removed. Fischer suggests that the ornamentation of the flint core was a symbolic act intimately connected with the use of the missing flakes. Fischer strongly connects this to maleness—both through the gender of the human figures, but also through the phallic shape of the flint nodule. This could suggest a male rite of passage—possibly circumcision—in which the flint blades were used.

2.3 Death

In contrast to these more obscure examples that hint at rites of passage concerned with earlier life stages, there is ample evidence for ritual practices concerned with death and burial. Archaeologists have in certain cases been able to reconstruct some of the rituals accompanying burial. Larsson (1989b, 1990, 2004) has elucidated ritual activity at the Skateholm cemeteries, noting the presence of wooden structures built over graves at Skateholm I that appear to have been burned down as part of the burial ritual and a mortuary house at Skateholm II containing layers of red ochre and soot. Further evidence that fire could be an important part of the mortuary rite is provided by the presence of cremations and hearths located near several of the graves. Food refuse was also present in the fill of some of the graves at Skateholm, suggesting feasting accompanying the burial of the dead. Food also appears to have been interred with the dead, occasionally fish stews in organic containers, which Larsson (2004) suggests may indicate belief in an afterlife.

At the Breton shell-midden cemetery of Téviec we also find evidence of ritual practice associated with fire and feasting. Pequart and colleagues (Pequart et al. 1937; Schulting 1996) identified both 'feasting' and 'ritual' hearths. These appear to have been associated with the burial rite, with feasting hearths generally being associated with the larger graves. These hearths are generally large and contain considerable quantities of bone and charcoal. Ritual hearths seem to have been lit directly on the covering slabs of the graves. These tend to contain one or two mandibles of red deer or pig, which were considered to have represented funerary offerings.

A central part of the funerary rite is the treatment of the body. Particularly arresting is the sheer variability in the way cadavers were treated in Mesolithic Europe: burials of complete bodies; scattered, disarticulated material; and cremations are all present. Bodies can be found in large cemeteries, in single graves, or in small groups. Individual burials can be extended, crouched, sitting up, or multiple. Bodies can be absent from grave pits and can be human, canine, or feline. The body can be adorned with grave goods or bare, lying on a structure in the grave, or in a container or wrapping. It is worth noting that this variation does not simply reflect regional practices, but can be present within a single cemetery (Larsson 1989b). Skateholm II for example contains single, double, and multiple graves; individuals that were buried extended, crouched, or sitting up, intact or disarticulated, and can be human, canine, or absent. Some graves contain very rich grave goods. If ritual suggests some form of routinized sacred action what are we to make of the sheer variation of Mesolithic practices?

In dealing with this variation, Nilsson Stutz (2003a: 322) suggests that we need to attempt to elucidate the concept of the ideal or 'proper' burial that societies at Skateholm I and II and Vedbæk held in order to understand whether the variation observed occurs within or outside social norms. Her work indicates the dominant burial practice at the three sites was primary burial, meaning the dead were buried intact, probably a few days after death had occurred, before the body started to decay. Single burials dominate and the cadaver was laid out, on its back with the limbs in extension. The individual was often given grave goods and covered with ochre. At Skateholm individuals are buried on their side or sitting up in sufficient numbers for this to be considered part of the norm at the site. The individual was sometimes placed on a structure (antlers, wooden padding, soft padding) within the burial pit. The smaller, or more repeated changes from the norm can be attributed to change over time in the guiding principles that motivated treatment of the dead. Radical variations from these broad norms include grave 13 at Skateholm I, for example, where the disarticulated remains of a man were found: only the left hand and right foot bones were articulated; the right hand and the left foot were missing. A transverse arrowhead was found embedded in a section of the pelvis. Such radical differences in treatment of particular bodies may reflect the identity of the individual or the manner of their death (Nilsson Stutz 2003a: 338).

Nilsson Stutz's work represents an essential first step towards an understanding of Mesolithic ritual practice. Others have argued however that cemeteries do not represent the idealized mortuary treatment, in fact quite the reverse. Both Orme (1981) and Strassburg (2000) have argued that the cemeteries represent unusual or 'deviant' burials. Orme (1981: 244) points out that the Vedbæk cemetery consists only of the very young (0–1 year old), young women (18–20 years) and old individuals (40–60 years). Infants and the very old, she suggests, based on ethnographic analogy, are often singled out for special treatment because of their tenuous hold on life, while death in childbirth was considered particularly dangerous. Strassburg (2000) argues that Vedbæk and the Skateholm cemeteries represent the interment of dangerous individuals, who had died in traumatic circumstances. As well as young women often accompanied by infants who he suggests had died in childbirth, he draws attention to the number of individuals with traumatic injuries (old men with violent blows to their skulls, individuals pierced with arrowheads). These people he suggests were seen as a danger to the living, thus their burial represents an attempt to remove them from circulation, so that either these dangerous dead could not haunt the living or that their souls would not be reborn into new bodies.

The continued focus on the cemeteries as the 'norm' of Mesolithic funerary practice means the status of the disarticulated human remains frequently found on Mesolithic settlement sites remains uncertain. The manipulation of human body parts is a common feature of Mesolithic approaches to death, one which has however been frequently overlooked (Cauwe 2001). This manipulation occurs within cemeteries (e.g. Skateholm I, Téviec), but it is more frequently seen through the presence of isolated human elements both on living sites and places set apart from domestic activity such as rivers and certain caves across Europe (Strassburg 2000; Conneller 2006) and through the presence of more spectacular or formal arrangements of disarticulated material (e.g. Cauwe 2001). There is a tendency for the patterning in this material to be dismissed, particularly by archaeologists working in Scandinavia (though see Andersson et al. 2004), as the product of taphonomy or unintentional processes (such as human elements falling from excarnation platforms) (Larsson et al. 1981). Nilsson Stutz (2003a) is correct when she states we need to consider carefully whether such material can be described as the remnants of ritual practice; however, it could have important implications for interpreting Mesolithic beliefs and understandings of death. The presence of isolated human material suggests that some bones circulated with the living for some time. This could indicate reverence for the bones of ancestors, which may have circulated as relics.

3 Sacred Places

Though the Mesolithic has traditionally been seen as a period lacking in built monuments, a number of recent finds suggests this is not entirely the case. From the series of large posts from the Stonehenge area (Allen and Gardiner 2002), to single posts or totem poles at the Scanian Mesolithic sites of Årup and Tågerup (Andersson et al. 2004), a pattern of wooden landscape markers is emerging. Furthermore a number of archaeologists have argued that shell middens, as gleaming white mounds visible from a distance, in some cases hundreds of metres in length, often containing human remains and arguably representing evidence for feasting, were comparable to Neolithic long mounds and chambered tombs (e.g. Pollard 1990).

Archaeologists have also posited that particular 'natural' places had particular potency (Bradley 2000). Certain landscape features appear to have been marked through burial of the dead, or through deposition of animal or human body parts or significant artefacts. Many cemeteries, for example, have a strong association with water. Vedbæk Bøgebakken was situated on the shores of a lagoon (Albrethsen and Brinch Petersen 1976); the Skateholm cemeteries on islands in a lagoon, with Skateholm II submerged during the later Mesolithic (Larsson 2004); Oleniostrovski on an island in Lake Onega (O'Shea and Zvelebil 1984). At Møllegabet II, a submerged site off the coast of Denmark, an individual was even buried in a canoe which had been submerged just off the shoreline (Grøn and Skarup 1993: 47). Both the canoe and the body were wrapped in birch bark. Isolated human bones are also commonly found at lake-edge sites in Southern Scandinavia (Strassburg 2000), particularly in the early part of the Mesolithic. The same occurs in Britain, with human bone recovered from aquatic contexts at Thatcham, Berkshire and Staythorpe, Nottinghamshire (Conneller 2006).

A number of finds of complete animals may also suggest aquatic offerings. A series of complete or near complete elk and aurochs skeletons have been found across Southern Scandinavia (Strassburg 2000). Such finds tend to be interpreted as animals that have escaped the hunter, only to die later from their wounds. However some of the associations of these animals are unusual and hint at something more. The five elks from Lundby, Denmark, were deposited in piles one of which was associated with an elk antler staff (Møller Hansen 2005). At Prejlerup, Denmark, an aurochs had been shot with 15 arrows. A similar case of potential overkill is in evidence in Wales at Lydstep Haven, where a pig was found in a waterlogged context, pinned down by a tree and with two microliths embedded in its neck (Chatterton 2006). Particular body parts also appear to have been preferentially deposited in wetland areas. At Star Carr, Yorkshire, there is a big emphasis on antlers. At the Scanian site of Bökkeberg red deer left scapulae and left-sided antlers are concentrated in a 70 m² area of the site alongside human bone and decorated objects (Andersson et al. 2004). Artefacts were also deposited into wetlands in large numbers: 23 slotted bone points were recovered from Åamossen in southern Scania, Sweden and 108 large blades were deposited parallel to each other at Rönneholm, Scania (Andersson et al. 2004).

Aquatic locations were not the only category of place marked as sacred. Caves were significant places, marked out by the deposition of Mesolithic skeletal material across Europe (e.g. Cullen 1995; Orschiedt 2002; Cauwe 2001). In Britain, the majority of Mesolithic human bone recovered derives from caves. This mainly consists of isolated elements, but also includes burials, such as Gough's Cave and the cemetery site of Avelines' Hole (Schulting 2005; Conneller 2006). The majority of these caves do not contain contemporary lithic or faunal material, so appear to have been set apart from everyday life, unlike most of the continental cemeteries. The caves also tend to contain Upper Palaeolithic material and late glacial fauna, consisting of both extinct animals (horse, reindeer, etc.) and animals much larger than their Mesolithic counterparts (red deer). These strange implements and alarming animals may have added to the 'otherness' of the cave. In North-west Europe several caves have yielded patterned arrangements of human bone or other evidence of ritual. In Germany is the famous Ofnet site, one of three where nests of skulls have been recovered (Orschiedt 2002). At Grotte de Perrats, France, the remains of eight disarticulated individuals were found with numerous cut marks (Boulestin 1999). In Belgium at the site of Abri des Autours, a series of human finger bones were found inserted in a crevice in the cave wall (Cauwe 2001). This practice strongly recalls the fragments of animal bone inserted into crevices at Upper Palaeolithic cave art sites in southwest France, interpreted by Clottes and Lewis-Williams (1998) as an attempt to push offerings through the cave wall membrane into the underworld.

The site of Lepenski Vir shows the complexity of people's relationships with sacred elements of the landscape. Both the Danube and the trapezoidal mountain opposite the site were highly significant as symbolic resources and a guiding principle in people's lives. Houses were orientated to face the river, while their trapezoidal shape echoes that of the mountain, as does the trapezoidal stone arrangements of hearth surrounds (Borić 2002). The houses contain the famous sculptures, several of which appear to represent human/fish therianthropes. Burials were not orientated north–south or east–west, but rather in relation to the river—usually parallel or perpendicular to it. Again these patterns highlight the importance of the river. A number of burials were placed in extended position, parallel to the river, with the head facing downstream. Radovanović (1997) has suggested that this could have symbolized an idea about the souls of the deceased going down the river. Borić has pointed out that large anadromous fish—up to 5 m in length—swam upstream every spring to spawn. He suggests that in the context of the fish/human sculptures, these large fish may have been seen as the ancestors returning every year. Borić also points out the presence of two old men at Padina, buried in the sitting up position, with their backs leaning against spurs of bedrock facing the Danube. Similar burials were found at Lepenski Vir and Vlasac; in the context of the importance of the river it seems appropriate that the dead should also watch over it.

4 SHAMANISM

Shamanism has recently become a major research topic in the Mesolithic. This is part of a broader trend in early prehistory stemming from cave art studies, particularly Lewis-Williams and Dowson's influential work on cave art (Lewis-Williams and Dowson 1988). Strassburg (2000: 86), for example, relates abstract and figurative designs on Mesolithic artefacts to Lewis-Williams and Dowson's three stages of trance. However archaeological concepts of shamanism have a longer history through the use of direct historic analogy in parts of Northern Europe with extant hunter-gatherer groups (e.g. Gurina 1956). Much of the stimulus for the Mesolithic work derives from Zvelebil's revival of direct historical analogy in determining Mesolithic worldviews. In a series of papers Zvelebil (1993, 1996, 2003a, 2003b, 2008) argues for continuity in cosmology and belief between Mesolithic people and contemporary and historic Northern Eurasian hunter-gatherers. Zvelebil summarizes the common aspects of a boreal belief system as follows:

1. the concept of the three-tiered world with an upper world (world of spirits), middle world (world of living), and underworld (world of the dead) linked by a pillar, tree, or river
2. the world perceived as inhabited by supernatural beings
3. nature perceived as a 'giving environment', lacking the dichotomization of nature and culture of modern worldviews

4. ideas of reciprocal relations with animals, with animals needing to be treated with respect in order that they continue to give themselves up to the hunter
5. the concept of the soul as possessed by both humans and animals
6. the shaman as religious specialist and mediator between the worlds
7. the importance of elk, bear, and waterbirds.

Zvelebil's northern hunter-gatherer cosmology fits broadly within current definitions of animism as outlined by Descola (1997) and Ingold (2000), in which ideas of the giving environment and reciprocity with animals and animal souls are key features of a world view depending on the continuing circulation of essences. Recognition of shared elements in Eurasian and American hunter-gatherer world views appears increasingly accepted by anthropologists (Viveiros de Castro 1998; Fausto 2007). Zvelebil's scheme however differs from this anthropological work in the detail of the features he sees as shared between temporally distinct groups. It is this level of detail that means—if Zvelebil's framework is accepted—that features of Mesolithic archaeology can be interpreted in great depths; so the reason many Mesolithic cemeteries were located adjacent to water becomes because water was seen as an entrance to the underworld, the world of the dead; the amber elk, bear, and waterbirds found across the Baltic become representations of the shaman's animal helpers. Waterbirds amongst several Eurasian groups act as messengers to the dead, thus the infant from Vedbæk Bøgebakken buried on a swan's wing has been interpreted as referencing this symbolism (Zvelebil 2003b).

Other archaeologists have argued that shamanic equipment can be identified in the Mesolithic record. Larsson (1988: 48) suggests that the elk-headed staffs found in Southern Scandinavia (most notably with the 'big dog' burial at Skateholm II) functioned as drumsticks for shamanic trance drums. Strassburg (2000: 90) identifies shamanic masks, one made from the skull of an old aurochs from Fulemile on Funen, the other a depiction of a horned figure on an antler staff from Bodal Mose, Åmose, Zealand. Several archaeologists have also identified shamanic burials: Gurina (1956), the original excavator of Oleni'ostrov Mogilnik, Karelia suggested the shaft burials at the site as shamanic, again based on direct historical analogy with local hunter-gatherer groups, an interpretation echoed by O'Shea and Zvelebil (1984) and Schmidt (2000). Schmidt also suggests that the androgenous body form of the individual from grave XV at Skateholm II led to this person being marked out for shamanhood, a fact reflected in the grave goods which have both male and female associations. More recently Porr and Alt (2006) have identified the rich burial of Bad Dürrenberg, Germany as a shaman's grave. Osteoarchaeological studies indicate a cranial pathology that might have caused altered states of consciousness. Porr and Alt suggest that elements of the woman's condition may have been interpreted as possession by spirits and resulted in a high social (shamanic) status, as reflected in the grave goods.

5 ANIMALS

In animist ontologies, animals have varied roles. Certain species, or particular animals, are viewed as possessing a soul; animals can be seen as friends, spiritual beings (such as the 'master of the animals') and as spiritual helpers or messengers (Tanner 1979; Ingold

2000; Jordan 2003). Common amongst such groups are ideas of 'perspectivism' (Viveiros de Castro 1998), whereby animals, whilst amongst themselves, are perceived to indulge in human-like social relations. Certainly, the idea of animals as purely resources is a misleading one; however to what extent can the material traces of these posited animist ontologies be perceived in the Mesolithic record?

Jordan has undertaken ethnoarchaeological work in order to find material correlates of the northern hunter-gatherer cosmology (2003). Amongst the Evenki—as amongst many hunter-gatherer groups—animal remains have to be treated with respect; bear bones are deposited in deep pools, elk bones are returned to the forest. Jordan suggests archaeologists should seek patterns of structured deposition in similar contexts. As outlined earlier in this chapter, both Strassburg (2000) and Chatterton (2006) have argued that animal body parts, and even whole animals, were deposited in waterlogged areas. Work at the site of Star Carr suggests the potency of animal bodies extended, on occasions, even to objects made from their remains. Wetland depositionary practices involved 193 barbed points and 21 antler frontlets. The fact that both these object categories were made from red-deer antler suggests that this species was most important to the inhabitants of the site and that the antlers may have been the body part that best represented the animal's animus (Conneller 2004).

In investigating Mesolithic attitudes to animals, the animal masks from Star Carr and Fulemile, mentioned above, also deserved further consideration. To these can be added three German examples of perforated red-deer antler frontlets from the sites of Bedburg Königshoven, Berlin Biesdorf and Hohen Viecheln (Street 1991; Chatterton 2003). In many societies, masks are not a means of concealment, but rather have fundamental effects on the body of the wearer, producing a transformed or human/animal composite body (Strassburg 2000; Conneller 2004). These masks should perhaps be viewed as the material media for the transformations between human and animal bodies that a perspectivist ontology permits.

Borić (2005) suggests similar bodily transformations are in evidence at Lepenski Vir, represented in the composite human/fish boulder artwork. However Borić also suggests that the close proximity of the boulders to burials of the dead indicates the art is objectifying the change of bodies through the life cycle by making reference to bodily changes between human and animal. Metamorphosis in Borić's view is the final stage of the life cycle, with the ancestors transformed into migratory fish moving up and down the Danube in an annual cycle.

These examples suggest that particular species only were perceived as spiritually important to particular Mesolithic societies. On occasions even particular animals within a single species were marked as important. Eleven dogs were buried at the Skateholm cemeteries. As amongst the human population of the cemeteries, canine bodies were dealt with in a variety of ways. One dog is amongst the richest in the cemetery, buried with an antler, three flint blades, and a unique, ornamented antler hammer; another was buried with a flint flake and strewn with red ochre. However, two additional dogs were killed and thrown into human graves. Larsson suggests that dogs served as substitutes for their masters, when their bodies could not be recovered (Larsson 1990: 157). However, as ambiguous animals, existing between human and animal cultures, we can perhaps see particular dogs only as having the particular qualities that allowed them to be full participants in human ritual practices. This is echoed in the beliefs of the Evenk, who distinguish two types of dogs. Dogs with particular talents only are considered to possess a soul and thus accorded human-like burials (Grøn pers. comm.).

6 Conclusions: The Future for Mesolithic Ritual and Religion

There have been huge advances in understandings of Mesolithic ritual and religion in recent years, not least because these have finally been accepted as legitimate topics for debate. However, this is still a young field and much remains to be interrogated. The cemeteries still tend to dominate discussions of ritual and religion within these new approaches, just as they dominated approaches to understanding Mesolithic society in the 1970s and 1980s. Other sources need to be explored; the disarticulated remains that are frequent finds on Mesolithic sites potentially suggest very different ritual practices and understandings of the body from those the cemeteries provide. A further challenge is to move towards a fuller understanding of ritual than that simply based on the treatment of the dead. To do this we need to investigate other categories of evidence: artefacts, faunal remains, landscapes, using new methodologies, and theoretical approaches. Direct historic analogy, the major current model employed, though attractive, is highly problematic and can undermine a rigorous approach to the evidence. As for any model, differences between source and subject need to be made evident and perhaps these approaches are too young to have yet undergone a thorough exploration of the evidence. However, overall we can remain extremely optimistic for the future; it is heartening that Mesolithic archaeologists have finally stepped onto the last rung of the 'ladder of inference' (Hawkes 1954).

Suggested Reading

Liv Nilsson Stutz's book *Embodied Rituals and Ritualised Bodies* (2003a) is the most thoughtful and thorough approach to Mesolithic mortuary ritual. A good recent summary of the Scandinavian evidence for mortuary ritual is that by Larsson (2004), 'The Mesolithic period in Southern Scandinavia, with special reference to burials and cemeteries' in A. Saville (ed.) *Mesolithic Scotland and its neighbours* (Edinburgh: Society of Antiquaries for Scotland). Zvelebil's ideas of northern hunter-gatherer ideology are outlined in a number of publications, most recently in a volume edited by Geoff Bailey and Penny Spikins (2008), *Mesolithic Europe* (Cambridge: Cambridge University Press). An original approach to shamanism and ritual in Mesolithic Scandinavia more generally has been outlined by Jimmy Strassburg (2000) in *Shamanic Shadows: One hundred generations of undead subversions in Southern Scandinavia*. Finally a synthesis of evidence for ritual practices in Mesolithic Britain has been complied by Richard Chatterton in Chantal Conneller and Graeme Warren (eds), *Mesolithic Britain and Ireland*.

References

ALBRETHSEN, S., and BRINCH PETERSEN, E. 1976. 'Excavation of a Mesolithic cemetery at Vedbaek, Denmark', *Acta Archaeologica*, 47: 1–28.

ALLEN, M. J., and GARDINER, J. 2002. 'A sense of time: Cultural markers in the Mesolithic of Southern England' in D. Bruno and M. Wilson (eds), *Inscribed Landscapes: Marking and making place* (Honolulu: University of Hawaii Press), pp. 139–53.

ANDERSSON, M., KARSTEN, P., KNARRSTRÖM, B., et al. 2004. *Stone Age Scania* (Malmö: Riksantivarieämbetets Förlag Skrifter 52).

BORIĆ, D. 2002. 'The Lepenski Vir conundrum: Reinterpretation of the Mesolithic and Neolithic sequences in the Danube Gorges', *Antiquity*, 76: 1026–39.

——2005. 'Body metamorphosis and animality: Volatile bodies and boulder artworks from Lepenski Vir', *Cambridge Archaeological Journal*, 15(1): 35–69.

——and STEFANOVIĆ, S. 2004. 'Birth and death: Infant burials from Vlasac and Lepenski Vir', *Antiquity*, 78: 526–46.

BOULESTIN, B. 1999. *Approche taphonomique des restes humains. Le cas des Mésolithiques de la grotte des Perrats et le problème du cannibalisme en préhistoire récente européenne* (Oxford: BAR).

BRADLEY, R. 2000. *An Archaeology of Natural Places* (New York: Routledge).

BRINCH PETERSEN, E., and MEIKELJOHN, C. 2003. 'Three cremations and a funeral: Apects of burial practice in Mesolithic Vedbaek' in L. Larsson, H. Kindgren, K. Knutsson, et al. (eds), *Mesolithic on the Move: Papers presented at the Sixth International Conference on the Mesolithic in Europe, Stockholm 2000* (Oxford: Oxbow Books), pp. 485–93.

CAUWE, N. 2001. 'Skeletons in motion, ancestors in action: Early Mesolithic collective tombs in southern Belgium', *Cambridge Archaeological Journal*, 11(2): 147–63.

CHATTERTON, R. 2003. 'Star Carr reanalysed' in J. Moore and L. Bevan (eds), *Peopling the Mesolithic in a northern environment* (Oxford: BAR), pp. 69–80.

——2006. 'Ritual', in C. Conneller and G. Warren (eds), *Mesolithic Britain and Ireland: New perspectives* (Stroud: Tempus), pp. 101–20.

CLARK, J. G. D. 1952. *Prehistoric Europe: The economic basis* (London: Methuen).

——1954. *Excavations at Star Carr* (Cambridge: Cambridge University Press).

——1967. *The Stone Age Hunters* (London: Thames and Hudson).

——1980. *Mesolithic Prelude* (Edinburgh: Edinburgh University Press).

CLOTTES, J. and LEWIS-WILLIAMS, J. D. 1998. *The Shamans of Prehistory: Trance and magic in the painted caves* (New York: Harry N. Abrams).

CONNELLER, C. J. 2004. 'Becoming deer: Corporeal transformations at Star Carr', *Archaeological Dialogues*, 11(1): 37–56.

——2006. 'Death' in C. Conneller and G. Warren (eds), *Mesolithic Britain and Ireland: New perspectives* (Stroud: Tempus), pp. 139–64.

CULLEN, T. 1995. 'Mesolithic mortuary ritual at Franchthi Cave, Greece', *Antiquity*, 69: 270–89.

DESCOLA, P. 1997. 'Constructing natures' in P. Descola and G. Palsson (eds), *Nature and Society: Anthropological perspectives* (London: Routledge), pp. 82–102.

DUDAY, H., COURTRAUD, P., CRUBÉZY, E., et al. 1990. 'L'anthropologie "de terrain": reconnaissance et interprétation des gestes funéraires' in E. Crubézy et al. (eds), Anthropologie et Archéologie: Dialogue sur les essembles funéraires. *Bulletin et Mémoires de la Société d'Anthropologie de Paris* 2(3–4): 29–50.

FAUSTO, C. 2007. 'Feasting on people: Eating animals and humans in Amazonia', *Current Anthropology*, 48: 497–530.

FISCHER, A. 1975. 'An ornamented flint core from Holmegård V, Zealand, Denmark', *Acta Archaeologica*, 45: 155–68.

GRØN, O. and SKAARUP, J 1993. 'Møllegabet II: A submerged Mesolithic site and a "boat burial" from Ærø', *Journal of Danish Archaeology*, 10: 38–50.
GURINA, N. 1956. *Oleneostrovski mogilnik. Materialy I issledovaniya po areologgi SSSR* 47.
HAWKES, C. 1954. 'Archaeological theory and method: Some suggestions from the Old World', *American Anthropologist*, 56: 153–68.
INGOLD, T. 2000. *The Perception of the Environment* (London: Routledge).
JANIK, L. D. 2000. 'Construction of the individual and transmission of knowledge among early and Mid-Holocene communities of Northern Europe' in J. Sofaer Derevenski (ed.), *Children and Material Culture* (London: Routledge), pp. 117–30.
JORDAN, P. 2003. 'Investigating post-glacial hunter-gatherer landscape enculturation: Ethnographic analogy and interpretative methodologies' in L. Larsson, H. Kindgren, K. Knutsson, et al. (eds), *Mesolithic on the Move: Papers presented at the Sixth International Conference on the Mesolithic in Europe, Stockholm 2000* (Oxford: Oxbow Books), pp. 128–38.
LARSSON, L. 1988. *The Skateholm Project 1: A Late Mesolithic settlement and cemetery complex at a southern Swedish lagoon* (Stockholm: Almquist and Wicksell International).
——1989a. 'Ethnicity and traditions in Mesolithic mortuary practices of Southern Scandinavia' in S. J. Shennan (ed.), *Archaeological Approaches to Cultural Identity* (London: Unwin Hyman), pp. 210–18.
——1989b. 'Late Mesolithic settlements and cemeteries at Skateholm, S. Sweden' in C. Bonsall (ed.), *The Mesolithic in Europe* (Edinburgh: John Donald), pp. 367–78.
——1990. 'Dogs in fraction, symbols in action' in B. Vermeersch and van Peer (eds), *Contributions to the Mesolithic in Europe* (Leuven: Leuven University Press).
——2004. 'The Mesolithic period in Southern Scandinavia, with special reference to burials and cemeteries' in A. Saville (ed.), *Mesolithic Scotland and its Neighbours* (Edinburgh: Society of Antiquaries for Scotland), 371–92.
——, MEIKELJOHN, C., and NEWELL, R. R. 1981. 'Human skeletal material from the Mesolithic site of Agerod I: HC, Scania, southern Sweden', *Fornvänen*, 76: 161–8.
LEWIS-WILLIAMS, J. D. and DOWSON, T. A. 1988. 'The signs of all times: Entoptic phenomena in Upper Palaeolithic Art', *Current Anthropology*, 29: 201–45.
MØLLER HANSEN, K. 2005. 'Preboreal elk bones from Lundby Mose', in L. Larsson, H. Kindgren, K. Knutsson, D. Loeffler, and A. Åkerkind (eds), *Mesolithic on the Move: Papers presented at the Sixth International Conference on the Mesolithic in Europe, Stockholm 2000* (Oxford: Oxbow Books), pp. 521–6.
NILSSON STUTZ, L. 2003a. *Embodied rituals and ritualised bodies*, Acta Archaeologica Lundensia, Series 8, No. 46 (Stockholm: Almqvist and Wiksell International).
——2003b. 'A taphonomy of ritual practice, a "field"-anthropological study of late Mesolithic burials' in L. Larsson, H. Kindgren, K. Knutsson, et al. (eds), *Mesolithic on the Move: Papers presented at the Sixth International Conference on the Mesolithic in Europe, Stockholm 2000* (Oxford: Oxbow Books), pp. 527–35.
ORME, B. 1981. *Anthropology for Archaeologists* (London: Duckworth).
ORSCHIEDT, J. 2002. 'Die Kopfbestattungen der Ofnet-Höhle: Ein Beleg für Kriegerische Auseinderstezungen im Mesolithikium', *Archäologische Informationen*, 24: 199–207.
O'SHEA, J., and ZVELEBIL, M. 1984. 'Oleneostrovski Mogilnik: Reconstructing the social and economic organisation of prehistoric foragers in northern Russia', *Journal of Anthropological Archaeology*, 3: 1–40.
PEQUART, M., and PEQUART, S.-J. 1934. 'La necropole mesolithique de l'ile d'Hoedic (Morbihan)', *L'Anthropologie*, 44: 1–20.

——, Pequart, S. J., Boule, M., et al. 1937. *Teviec: Station-Necropole Mesolithique du Morbihan* (Paris: Institut de Paleontologie Humaine).
Pollard, A. 1990. 'Down through the ages: A reconsideration of the Oban cave sites', *Scottish Archaeological Review*, 7: 57–84.
Porr, M. and Alt, K. W. 2006. 'The burial of Bad Dürrenberg, Central Germany: Osteopathology and osteoarchaeology of a Late Mesolithic shaman's grave', *International Journal of Osteoarchaeology*, 16: 395–406.
Radovanović, I. 1997. 'The Lepenski Vir Culture: a contribution to interpretation of its ideological aspects', in *Antidoron Dragoslavo Srejović completis LXV annis ab amicis collegis discipulis oblatum* (Belgrade: Centre for Archaeological Reasearch, University of Belgrade), pp. 85–93.
Schmidt, R. 2000. 'Shamans and northern cosmology: The direct historic approach to Mesolithic sexuality' in R. Schmidt and B. Voss (eds), *Archaeologies of Sexuality* (London: Routledge), pp. 220–35.
Schulting, R. J. 1996. 'Antlers, bone pins and flint blades: The Mesolithic cemeteries of Téviec and Hoëdic, Brittany', *Antiquity*, 70: 335–50.
——2005. '"Pursuing a rabbit in Burrington Coombe": New research on the Early Mesolithic burial cave of Aveline's Hole', *Proceedings of the University of Bristol Speleological Society*, 23(3): 171–265.
Srejović, D. 1972. *Europe's First Monumental Sculpture: New discoveries at Lepenski Vir* (London: Thames and Hudson).
Strassburg, J. 2000. *Shamanic Shadows: One hundred generations of undead subversions in southern Scandinavia*, Stockholm Studies in Archaeology 20 (Stockholm: Stockholm Universitet).
Street, M. 1991. 'Bedburg Königshoven: A pre-boreal Mesolithic site in the Lower Rhineland, Germany' in N. Barton, A. Roberts, and D. Roe (eds), *The Late Glacial in Europe: Human adaptation and environmental change at the end of the Pleistocene* (London: Council for British Archaeology), pp. 256–70.
Tanner, A. 1979. *Bringing Home Animals* (London: C. Hurst).
Viveiros de Castro, E. 1998. 'Cosmological deixis and Amerindian perspectivism', *Journal of the Royal Anthropological Institute*, 4: 469–88.
Zvelebil, M. 1993. 'Concepts of time and "presencing" in the Mesolithic', *Archaeological Review from Cambridge*, 12(2): 51–70.
——1996. 'Hunter-gatherer ritual landscapes: Spatial organisation, social structure and ideology amongst hunter-gatherers of Northern Europe and Western Siberia', *Analecta Praehistorica Leidensia*, 29: 33–50.
——2003a. 'Enculturation of Mesolithic landscapes' in L. Larsson, H. Kindgren, K. Knutsson, et al. (eds), *Mesolithic on the Move: Papers presented at the Sixth International Conference on the Mesolithic in Europe, Stockholm 2000* (Oxford: Oxbow Books), pp. 65–73.
——2003b. 'People behind the lithics: Social life and social conditions of Mesolithic communities in temperate Europe' in J. Moore and L. Bevan (eds), *Peopling the Mesolithic in a northern environment* (Oxford: BAR), pp. 1–26.
——2004. 'Social structure and ideology of the late Mesolithic communities of north Temperate Europe', in G. A. Clark and M. Gonzales-Morales (eds), *The Mesolithic of the Atlantic Facade* (Tempe: Arizona State University Anthropological Research Papers 35), pp. 23–37.
——2008. 'Innovating hunter-gatherers: The Mesolithic in the Baltic' in G. Bailey and P. Spikins (eds), *Mesolithic Europe* (Cambridge: Cambridge University Press), pp. 18–53.

CHAPTER 24

RITUAL AND RELIGION IN THE NEOLITHIC

JULIAN THOMAS

1 INTRODUCTION: A FEAR OF GODS?

THE archaeological record of the Neolithic period in Europe potentially provides rich raw material for the student of prehistoric ritual and religion. This includes megalithic tombs associated with protracted funerary practices, complex artefacts which imply symbolic significance, ceremonial monuments which could enclose groups of participants, and ambiguous, highly formalized types of visual expression such as figurines and megalithic art. Accordingly, the Neolithic has provided a focus for debates on the archaeology of ritual in recent years (e.g. Barrett 1991; Bradley 2005; Shanks and Tilley 1982; Thomas 2004, *inter alia*). Yet as Timothy Insoll has pointed out, the same period has seen a surprising reluctance on the part of archaeologists to explicitly address questions of *religion* (Insoll 2004a: 1; 2004b: 77). Insoll suggests a number of reasons why this might be the case: the embedding of archaeologists within a secular contemporary culture; concerns over the generality of the term 'religion'; the evanescence of religious meanings. In this contribution, I will attempt to explain the decline of debate on Neolithic religion, and suggest ways in which the field might be revitalized, before turning to the question of ritual through a specific example.

Insoll (2004a: 2) expresses some reservations over any rigid distinction between world religions and 'traditional' or 'primal' religion, noting that it is possible for the categories to overlap or coincide. Yet it is clear that this division lies behind some of the concerns that have been raised over the investigation of prehistoric religion. Consider, for instance, John Barrett's criticism of the notion that megalithic tombs were the temples of a unified, pan-European cult (1994: 50). Barrett specifically calls into question Stuart Piggott's comparison between the architecture of the West Kennet long barrow (Figure 24.1) and that of medieval parish churches (Piggott 1962: 61). Piggott's analogy, says Barrett, relates to a 'religion of the book' and its liturgy, so that the spatial organization of the church is to some extent prescribed by a pre-existing text. 'There never was a single body of beliefs which characterised "Neolithic religion"', he contends (Barrett 1994: 50). Megalithic tombs reveal a

FIGURE 24.1 The façade of the West Kennet long barrow, north Wiltshire.

wide range of different practices, which cannot be reduced to a single cultural scheme. Rather, there are broad elements of shared symbolism, deployed in entirely different ways within separate local traditions.

World religions, such as Christianity, Islam, and Buddhism, are distinguished by an imperative to proselytize, and consequentially have creeds, scriptures, and liturgies that are of potentially universal applicability, and which can be transferred between contexts (Keane 2008: 112). These texts (written or verbal) represent an objectification or distillation of a religious tradition, and are a kind of 'blueprint' for religious conduct. Where these texts exist, it may be that an archaeology of scriptural religion is a relatively straightforward task, evaluating the relationship between the text and the archaeological evidence. But in the case of traditional religions, the challenge that presents itself *appears* to be one of reconstructing religious ideas or beliefs on the basis of material residues. It is arguable that the present generation of archaeologists have intuitively recoiled from such an enterprise, because it implies that abstract ideas precede and underlie acts in the physical world. This perception is manifested in Durkheim's claim that religious performances 'are merely the external envelope concealing mental operations' (quoted by Insoll 2004a: 3). Such a view relies on a Cartesian model of the human being as a corporeal shell concealing an inner world of thought, from within which our actions emanate. Accordingly, archaeologists have drawn a distinction between ritual (which is concerned with practices with tangible outcomes) and religion (which is metaphysical), and elected to concern themselves exclusively with the former.

However, it may be possible to circumvent this problem, and provide a different foundation for an archaeology of Neolithic religious activity. Arguing against the notion of a universal definition of religion, Talal Asad (1993: 29) rejects Clifford Geertz's view that religion can be understood as a symbolic system that is virtually autonomous from power and practices (see Geertz 1973: 91). For Asad, religion is never a state of mind, but a practical knowledge of institutions and conventions, which amounts to a mode of conduct in the world. As he points out, it is perfectly possible for people to live a religious life without being able to explicitly articulate their religious knowledge (Asad 1993: 36). It is conceivable that some of our difficulties arise from the centrality of *belief* in Christianity, the religion with which many archaeologists working on the European Neolithic are most familiar. This focus on belief cannot necessarily be extended to all religions, and in any case 'belief' can refer to shared, public understandings. In the Christian tradition since St Augustine the notion that belief is an inner state has formed part of a more general preoccupation with inwardness, in which the route to the deity is found through the contemplation of the inner self (Ruel 1997: 56–9; Taylor 1989: 127).

As Webb Keane has recently argued, it is more helpful to emphasize the primacy of religious acts and phenomena over inner states, and he identifies the former as semiotic forms (Keane 2008: 114). Such forms have a worldly character that renders them open to experience and interpretation, through which understandings are generated. In this sense, beliefs may be 'parasitic' upon practices, rather than underlying or generating them. Religious actions and paraphernalia can persist over time and space, and thus be reinterpreted and incorporated into new human projects. Yet, says Keane, although religious phenomena have a tangible quality that allows beliefs to cluster around them, they generally also have the capacity to evoke an 'ontological divide'. That is, their performance alerts one to the proximity of abnormal or even sacred agencies (ibid.: 120). In these terms, the investigation of Neolithic religious activity would cease to be the search for specific deities and spirits, beliefs about the order of the cosmos, or systems of symbols, hidden beneath the surface of the archaeological evidence. Rather, the focus might fall on practices, performances, and materials, and the ways in which they functioned to generate and transform understandings of the seen and unseen worlds. In this sense, the rigid separation of religion and ritual begins to narrow somewhat. Yet as we shall see, the study of Neolithic religion to date has been dominated by the conviction that the material evidence is the outward manifestation of beliefs that were widespread and enduring.

2 THE VARIETIES OF NEOLITHIC RELIGIOUS EXPERIENCE

As we have already noted, one of the perennial themes in Neolithic archaeology over the past century has been the notion that megalithic tombs were the creation of some form of widely distributed cult. In much the way that we have just noted, similar ways of treating the dead have been inferred to derive from a shared set of beliefs concerning death and rebirth (Fleming 1969: 297). But beyond this, the idea of 'megalithic missionaries' dispersed from the eastern Mediterranean can be attributed to the particular predisposition of culture-historic archaeology to identify sets of artefacts and monuments as the material signatures of distinct groups of people. The gradual development of Gordon Childe's ideas concerning megalith-builders in Britain are instructive in this context. In *The Dawn of European Civilization* Childe emphasized the continuity between the British Mesolithic and Neolithic, but argued that megalithic tombs represented an exogenous element, introduced from Mediterranean Europe through coastal trade (1925: 287, 291). However, having collaborated with Stuart Piggott on a study of British Neolithic pottery and its continental affinities, Childe became convinced that the country had been colonized by representatives of the 'Western Neolithic' family of cultures, the Windmill Hill people (1931: 41). Childe reasoned that the Western Neolithic cultures were peasant folk who had originated in Africa, perhaps the Nile Delta, and had slowly migrated across Europe (1935: 74). However, megalithic architecture was not a primary feature of Western Neolithic groups. Because Childe saw human beings as fundamentally conservative, he was reluctant to recognize new cultural elements being spontaneously created within prehistoric cultures. As a result, he argued that the megaliths must have had a separate origin, perhaps with the early Minoan tombs of the Aegean. The introduction of an exotic form of mortuary activity from the eastern Mediterranean was most easily explained in terms of religious fanatics who braved the long journey to Britain in order to impose themselves on the Windmill Hill folk as 'chiefs and wizards', a 'spiritual aristocracy' (Childe 1940: 78; 1957: 326). The architectural variability of Neolithic tombs was consequently attributed to schisms between different elements of the megalithic cult.

What is important to recognize is that Childe's explanation was a *deus ex machina* (if the term is not inappropriate in this context). Unable to find a place for megaliths within the cultural repertoire of the Windmill Hill people, he was obliged to identify an alternative origin for them. As culture-history views all human products as the materialization of the cognitive cultural norms of specific communities, a means had to be devised to account for this extraneous architectural form. Since funerary rites were attributed to religious belief, the incursion of a Mediterranean cult provided an adequate rationalization. However, Childe resisted the temptation to speculate over the content of the megalithic religion. Yet as Ronald Hutton has elegantly demonstrated, this silence would soon be filled by ideas of a 'Great Goddess' that had been developing within Romantic thought during the previous century (Hutton 1997: 92). As Hutton points out, the association of the earth with the female sublime is a thoroughly modern conception, dressed up as a rediscovered primal truth. The various elements of the Goddess theory (a central female deity presiding over a golden age of matriarchy that was eventually destroyed by patriarchal warrior bands from the north) were eventually pulled together by the classicist Jane Ellen Harrison at the start of the twentieth century (ibid.: 93).

In Britain, the vision of the Great Goddess was championed by Jacquetta Hawkes during her later career, by when she had elected to write to a more popular audience. In *A Land*, Hawkes described the worship of the Goddess or Earth Mother as having been brought to Britain from the Mediterranean, and characterizes the female deity and her son/lover as the archetypal gods of the ancient world, from which all others were derived (1951: 158). She went on to argue that the scarce chalk figurines from some causewayed enclosures, and the disputed figure from Grimes Graves flint mine, were representations of the 'White Goddess'. Here, Hawkes was explicitly leaning on Robert Graves's work of poetic mythology (1948), which draws together themes from Welsh, Irish, Greek, and Middle Eastern texts.

As with her reliance on Jungian psychology (Hutton 1997: 96) this reveals a willingness to see Neolithic religious practices as having been underpinned by symbols and themes that remained unchanged for millennia, and which relate to fundamental human dispositions. This kind of essentialism was characteristic of its time.

For Hawkes, it was the Great Goddess who presided over the rituals that took place in megalithic tombs, whose swollen mound containing a hidden chamber within which bodies might be crouched in a foetal position betrayed a symbolism of birth and regeneration rather than death and ancestry (Hawkes 1951: 159). She went on to propose that Neolithic society had been matriarchal, and that the lack of representations of warfare and killing attributable to the period demonstrated that the good sense and 'earthiness' of the women had restrained the aggressive urges of the men (ibid.: 160). Sadly, the growing evidence for village massacres and skeletal trauma indicates that the European Neolithic was no idyllic age of peaceful coexistence (Price, Wahl, and Bentley 2006; Schulting and Wysocki 2005; Wahl and König 1987; Wild et al. 2004). Yet Hawkes proposed that it was the Beaker folk who brought warlike ways to Britain, identifying them as Indo-European 'high pastoralists, a restless patriarchal society in which the masculine principle had raised the Sky God to pre-eminence' (Hawkes 1951: 161).

The idea that shared material patterns betrayed shared spiritual beliefs was further developed by O. G. S. Crawford in his *The Eye Goddess* (1957), in which he proposed that a fertility cult with a female deity had spread from Western Asia to North-west Europe during the Neolithic. The cult's defining material trait was the motif of the female face or the eye, which degenerated into the spirals and concentric circles of megalithic art. However, the concept of the Neolithic mother goddess reached its apogee in the work of Marija Gimbutas (1982). Gimbutas presented an Old European world view, which she argued to have been codified in a plethora of symbols, most notably female figurines (1982: xv). This religious symbolism had originated in the Palaeolithic, and had not been immediately transformed by the introduction of agriculture to the continent. It related to a mythology of birth, death, and the renewal of life, which was central to a society in which women had been clan-heads and queen-priestesses. A single Great Goddess had been venerated throughout the continent, and as in Hawkes' account had been supplanted by the warrior gods of the Indo-European Kurgan folk (Gimbutas 1982: 321). Like Hawkes and Crawford, Gimbutas tended to conflate material from over a wide geographical area, in the service of a rather grand vision. The cost of this was a degree of insensitivity to the contexts from which figurines were recovered, and the practices in which they may have been engaged (Bailey 2005: 149; Meskell 1995: 75). Despite these failings, Gimbutas continues to have a massive following in the eco-feminist movement, for, however flawed her methodology, the image of a peaceful matriarchal past is a deeply attractive one (Meskell 1995: 75). Equally, the notion of a primordial female deity remains a potent one within mainstream Neolithic archaeology, emerging periodically as a default explanation (see Cassen 2000: 242 for comments on the place of the Great Goddess in French archaeology).

The development of processual archaeology in the 1960s and 1970s coincided with a decline in the investigation of Neolithic religion. This is slightly surprising, for while some culture-historic archaeologists had declared matters of belief to be beyond the competence of the discipline (Hawkes 1954), the New Archaeologists had sought to demonstrate that all aspects of culture had an adaptive significance. Thus Binford (1971) had presented mortuary rites as a means by which the loss of a social actor might be communicated to the group as a whole, enabling their roles and statuses to be passed on to others. So it might have been expected that the systemic role of ritual and religion in prehistoric European societies would have been explored by processual archaeologists. Such had been the perceived excesses of the Goddess cultists, however, that the period was largely given over to the debunking of arguments connecting putative prehistoric migrations with Earth Mother beliefs (e.g. Renfrew 1967: 276). Thus Fleming (1969: 248) offered a detailed evaluation of the evidence for the worship of female deities in the Neolithic of Western Europe, and concluded that the forms of expression represented by statue-menhirs, gallery-graves, and other megalithic art were localized and chronologically dispersed. Rather than a universal Great Goddess, they probably amounted to localized traditions of limited duration. It was only later that the idea of a 'cognitive processualism' developed, bringing with it the implication that religious ideas might play a part in the collective adaptation of human communities (Renfrew 1994: 48). Once again, though, this form of archaeology identifies religion with belief, and locates belief inside the human mind.

If much of Neolithic archaeology has sought the root of diverse forms of symbolic behaviour in a uniform and enduring body of religious beliefs, a rather different form of essentialism has emerged in recent years. With various collaborators, David Lewis-Williams has explored the proposition that all religions are attempts to codify and interpret ecstatic experiences, which are the outcome of mental states produced by the brain under unusual conditions (Lewis-Williams and Pearce 2005: 25). Broadly speaking, religions involving the experience and exegesis of such altered states are referred to as 'shamanism'. The Neolithic involved new ways of understanding these mental states, which were increasingly cast as an esoteric knowledge that was revealed only to a restricted elite. Thus the complicated imagery of megalithic art inside chambered tombs in Brittany and Ireland demonstrates the efforts of emerging elites to control and restrict hallucinatory religious experience (Figure 24.2), and to monopolize the revelations that flowed from it (Lewis-Williams and Dowson 1993: 60). Attempting to refine this neuro-psychological model, Jeremy Dronfield produced a classification of the types of imagery associated with a variety of forms of mind-altering practice. He argued that migraine, flickering lights, and the use of hallucinogenic substances might all have been responsible for generating the images that were translated into Irish passage tomb art (Dronfield 1994: 545; 1995: 272). However, Dronfield (1996) went on to emphasize the particular importance of 'subjective tunnel experiences' (such as tunnel vision), which were monumentalized in the increasingly lengthy passages of the Irish tombs. These he reasoned to have represented the entrance to an alternative reality experienced within the architecture.

While the neuro-psychologists break radically with some aspects of previous interpretations of Neolithic religious practice, they nonetheless sustain the view that acts in the physical world are the outcomes of mental states, although in this case chemically induced rather than transmitted as collective norms. Rather than imagining universal bio-psychological states being passed through some form of cultural filter and contextually rationalized, it might be profitable to consider shamanic practices as both corporeal and social. Drug-taking and the induction of trance states are embodied experiences, often conducted collectively: they are never raw cognitive stimuli over which cultural understanding is draped. While altered states may have formed an element of Neolithic ceremonial activities, they would always have been understood from within established expectations, and sanctioned by social convention. As with the preoccupation with belief as the focal element of prehistoric religion, we would do well

FIGURE 24.2 Megalithic art at Newgrange, Ireland.

to shift our concern toward practice, and its place within the social lives of embodied subjects embedded in cultural traditions.

3 THE ARCHAEOLOGY OF RITUAL REVISITED

We can turn now from religion to ritual, a topic that has been more thoroughly investigated within Neolithic archaeology. We can begin with a paradox: much of the recent archaeological literature expresses a desire to break down the opposition between ritual and the everyday, and yet there are certain kinds of performances, such as funerals and initiations, that we are happy enough to label as 'rituals' (Brück 1999: 316). The recent work conducted under the aegis of the Stonehenge Riverside Project at the Late Neolithic henge monument of Durrington Walls in Wiltshire has brought this problem into focus, by revealing evidence for a range of different practices, some of which we might wish to identify as 'ritual' or 'ritualized' (Parker Pearson et al. forthcoming) (Figure 24.3). Durrington Walls has a significant place in the history of archaeological attempts to grapple with the issue of ritual, and back in 1984 Colin Richards and the author used the material from Geoffrey Wainwright's excavations of 1966–7 in order to try and establish a method for identifying ritual using the structural qualities of the archaeological evidence (Richards and Thomas 1984; Wainwright and Longworth 1971). Following Maurice Bloch (1974: 58), we argued that ritual represents a formalized and restricted form of communication, sanctioned by

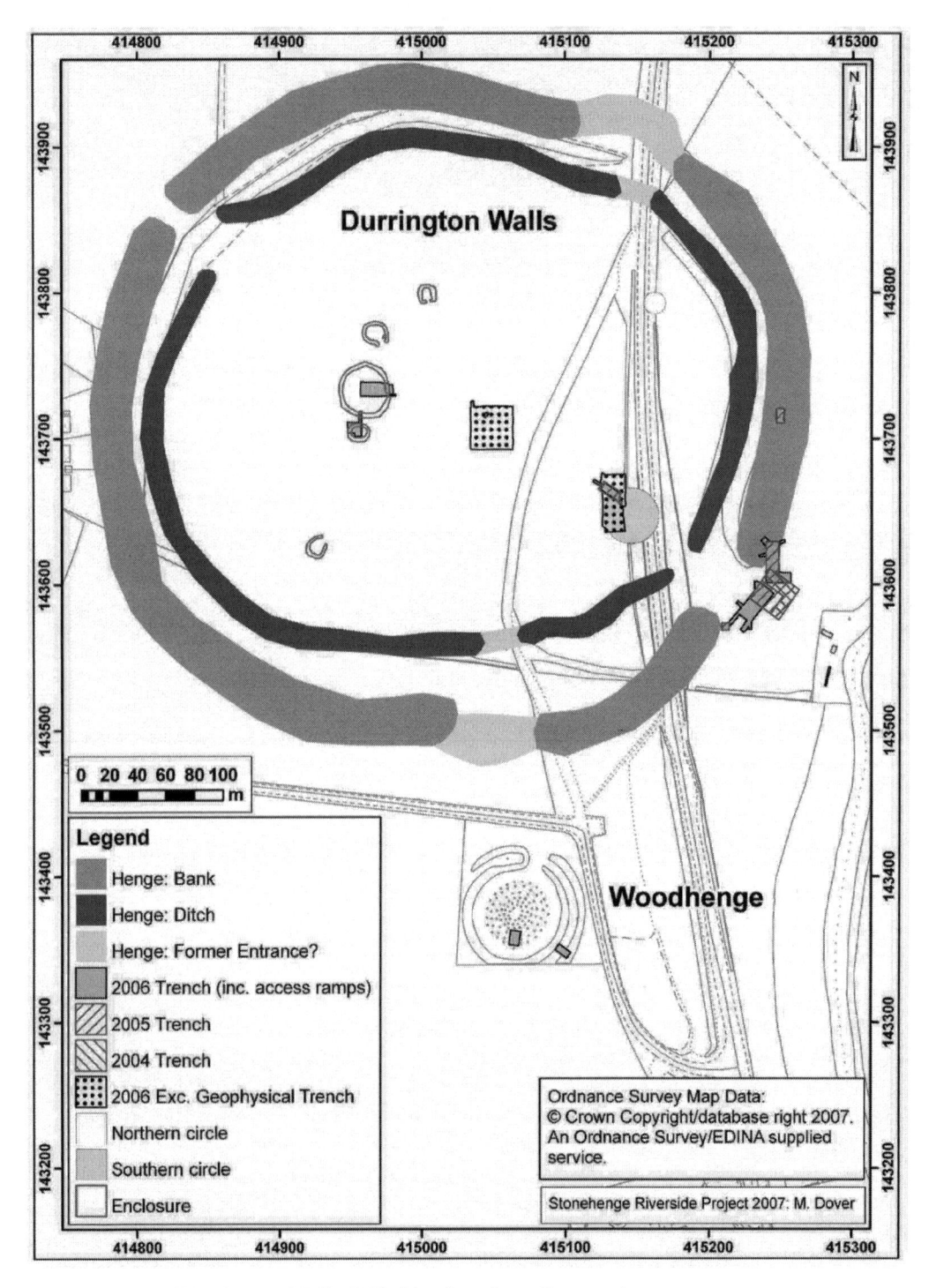

FIGURE 24.3 Durrington Walls, Wiltshire: location of excavations 2004–7.

tradition, which enables dominant messages to be expressed in ways that are not susceptible to evaluation. Ritual employs archaic forms of speech, rhyme, and song, and prescribed bodily postures and patterns of movement in order to convey cardinal truths, which are not to be argued with.

We suggested that the same formality and restriction should be manifested in the use and deposition of material culture, and set out to demonstrate that the spatial variation in pottery decoration, and the representation of stone tools and faunal remains within the Durrington henge was highly patterned, reflecting control, segregation, and ordering in the use of material symbols. Different patterns of deposition and association were suggested for the northern and southern timber circles, the midden and platform, and the henge ditch. Over the past 20 years, the debate has moved on, and new excavations have clarified the structural sequence at Durrington Walls. It is now appropriate to reflect on how our views of the practices documented by the internal features within the henge might be affected by these developments.

Recently, a number of authors have drawn attention to the presumed separation of ritual from everyday life in archaeological thought. Richard Bradley (2005: 28), for instance, has noted that domestic activity is often imagined to have been spatially separate from, and to have followed a different logic to, ritual. Similarly, Joanna Brück (1999: 317) identifies the distinction between irrational, non-productive, highly symbolic ritual and practical, functional, technical action with modern Western rationality. Ritual, she argues, is perceived as not doing anything, so that it comes to be understood as signifying something else, or at best as functioning ideologically, to mask and misrepresent social reality. Yet in premodern contexts, ritual is not separated from the secular. In what Brück refers to as animist or monist systems of thought, there is no distinction between functional and symbolic action. A single practical logic governs all forms of action, and ritual is understood as having tangible outcomes, in terms of curing, divination, or intercession with spirits.

Brück's argument is that if we persist in distinguishing between ritual and the everyday, we are likely to neglect apparently mundane contexts in which deposition was nonetheless governed by cultural logics quite distinct from our own. She therefore recommends dispensing with the category of ritual altogether. But on the other hand, she recognizes in passing the existence of rites of transformation, such as burial and marriage, but she is not clear about how these should be dealt with archaeologically (Brück 1999: 329). Now, we can agree with virtually all of Brück's argument, especially when she advocates above all the investigation of past rationalities, without having to accept her conclusion that we should not talk about ritual at all. Instead, it may be that we should identify ritual not as a separate sphere of practice, but as a distinct *mode of conduct*, which people move into and out of in the course of their day. An obvious example would be the way in which an industrial worker might break off from their labours, unroll a mat, and pray for a few minutes. The worker's comportment signals that something has changed, even if he has not entered a consecrated space or made use of sanctified artefacts.

In the contemporary West, ritual may have been set apart from the everyday, but this should perhaps alert us to the very different role and significance that ritual can have in different societies. In modern nation states, ritual still serves to bring the past to mind, to reinforce social ties, or to sustain minority identities (James 2003: 107). But it is less often understood as having a tangible efficacy, as Brück maintains. The distinction between ritual and mundane action lies not between different logics, but in an intensification or heightening of the experience of one's immediate situation, including cosmological relations. This is brought about through submitting oneself to a discipline, which draws on tradition and precedent, and establishes distinctive social conditions (Barrett 1991: 4). Revealingly, the Ndembu word for 'ritual' also means 'obligation' (Turner 1969: 11). Ritual is based on memory, reiterating or quoting past events and utterances, but as a heightening of experience it is itself often highly memorable (Connerton 1989: 44). As Victor Turner pointed out, symbols are the basic elements of ritual, but these symbols may be less concerned with communication than with expression, which is to some degree open to interpretation (Turner 1967: 19). People often know what acts and utterances are required to make ritual efficacious, without actually knowing what they mean (Lewis 1980: 6).

Moreover, although everything in ritual is a symbol, these should not be thought of as arbitrary signifiers, so that ritual becomes an empty code that merely refers to other things. On the contrary, ritual symbols bring powers, connotations, virtues, and allusions to bear on a specific location, and render them manipulable. Ritual symbols provide a microcosm that is networked to the macrocosm, offering influence in the world at large through performative engagement. Brück is correct in saying that in pre-modern worlds there may be no distinction between sacred and secular, meaning and function, so that powers and spiritual qualities may be immanent in the world as a whole. Nonetheless, there may be places, occasions, and persons that allow privileged access to these powers and qualities, and this is often what ritual provides, in non-Western contexts.

Some rituals constitute ceremonial events, distinct from everyday life, or punctuating the seasonal cycle (van Gennep 1960). But there are also everyday observances, like daily prayer or formalized ways of serving and consuming food. In these circumstances, elements of ritual are not only embedded in mundane activity, but they take on a habitual character which make them unconsidered aspects of personal and group identity. It follows from this that from an archaeological point of view there will be a very fuzzy line around the edge of what we consider to be ritual activity. At one end of the continuum there will be distinctive rites and ceremonies, but we should expect these to shade out into varying degrees of ritualization, including the unconsidered and the unconscious.

4 Reconsidering Ritual at Durrington Walls

This picture perhaps better expresses the situation now revealed at Durington Walls, where new fieldwork has identified a complex and protracted structural sequence. The different elements of the site that were effectively treated as equivalents in the 1984 analysis are not necessarily contemporary, their character has often been reassessed, and the nature of deposition varies between the repetitive and the episodic. The platform outside the southern timber circle has been identified as a fragment of a metalled avenue that connects the circle with the river Avon; the 'midden' may represent one or more terraced buildings; and much of the feasting activity on the site (see Albarella and Serjeantson 2002) appears to pre-date the construction of the henge bank and ditch, which themselves seem to represent a final statement terminating the complex (Parker Pearson 2007: 129; Parker Pearson et al. 2007: 631).

At the Southern Circle, what had formerly been designated 'Circle 1B' (that is, part of the first-phase structure) is likely to have been integral to the second phase, where the smaller post-holes may have supported shuttering or fencing, creating a secluded inner space within the timber circle (Thomas 2007). Such a space would have been similar in size and character to the space within the sarsen trilithon horseshoe at Stonehenge, now demonstrated to have been roughly contemporary with the Southern Circle (Parker Pearson et al. 2007: 626). Indeed, the stone settings at Stonehenge and the Southern Circle can now be seen as complementary structures, similar in architectural organization and forming the two ends of a unified pattern of movement down the river Avon and the two avenues. The first phase of the Southern Circle was thus a simpler structure, very comparable with the Northern Circle. It probably consisted of four central posts, surrounded by a single ring of lesser posts, approached by an avenue and crossed by a façade. The implication of this is that the second phase stands alongside Woodhenge and Stonehenge as examples of an extremely elaborate architecture which built on simpler precedents (Pollard and Robinson 2007: 167).

Following the 1967 excavation at Durrington Walls, Wainwright argued that the Southern Circle had been a massive roofed timber building, and that within this structure offerings of pottery, stone, and animal bones had been placed at the feet of the posts supporting the roof (Wainwright with Longworth 1971: 23–38). However, the recognition that the circle was incomplete supports the view that the structure was composed of free-standing posts (Figure 24.4). Hence it is unlikely that objects would have survived un-weathered on the surface to be incorporated into the 'weathering cones' left behind by the rotting out of the posts. These Wainwright argued to have been created by the eroding-back of the post-packing, creating features that trapped most of the artefacts recovered from the circle. Excavations in 2005–6 demonstrated that these were actually re-cut pits, dug into the tops of the post-holes after the timbers had rotted out (Thomas 2007: 151). Within these re-cuts, finds formed dense clusters, obviously placed or tipped rather than having fallen haphazardly into the cut. There was often a distinct sequence to the deposition, with spreads of animal bone succeeded by layers of knapping waste, followed by the placing of individual grooved-ware sherds.

Importantly, all of this material must have been deposited after the timber circle had fallen into ruin, a point that was barely addressed in the 1984 paper. The placing of these deposits therefore appears to have been *commemorative* in character, creating an 'architecture of memory' which referred to the vanished monument, very probably at the same time as the natural amphitheatre of Durrington Walls was being enclosed by the henge ditch. So, although the re-cutting was a singular event rather than a repetitive practice, it was very explicitly one that drew on and cited the past. Moreover, it is highly significant that the spatial distribution of artefacts in the re-cuts echoed that of the antler picks which had been deposited in the original packing of the post-holes. In both cases, the post-holes around the entrance to the circle were emphasized. The deliberate deposition of the antler picks used to excavate ditches, pits and shafts during the Neolithic is a fine example of a ritualized act that punctuates the cycle of labour and construction. More than a generation later, antlers and posts were cited and brought back to notice through the act of re-cutting. All of these acts are ritual, not just because they were highly structured, but because they betray a mode of conduct in which people were highly attentive to substances and materials, their histories, powers, and connotations.

FIGURE 24.4 Reconstruction of the Southern Circle at Durrington Walls, constructed for a *Time Team* TV programme.

Two hundred metres west from the Southern Circle, a group of at least six penannular structures have been revealed by geophysical survey, arranged around a terrace overlooking the timber circle and the eastern entrance (Thomas 2007: 152). Two of these were investigated in the summer of 2006, and rather than burials or timber circles, they proved to contain buildings similar to those that had been investigated in a Late Neolithic settlement at the eastern entrance of Durrington Walls (Parker Pearson 2007: 133). However, both were contained within timber palisades as well as hengiform ring-ditches. The larger one, in Trench 14, also had a façade of massive posts immediately in front of the building, in close-set pairs which may indicate that they were the wooden equivalent of the Stonehenge trilithons. In other words, these structures combined the characteristic grooved-ware house form with architectural elements that were associated with timber circles. While the surface had been subject to erosion before a thick layer of colluvium had been laid down, there were no finds at all on the house floors or in the post-holes. A large pit outside Building 14 contained quantities of animal bone and grooved ware, giving the impression of the clearing-up operations required to keep the structure clean. This contrasts very markedly with the general filthiness of the eastern-entrance houses. Beside the façade posts, another shallow pit contained the butchered remains of two pigs, with numerous articulated bones indicating a rather more prompt burial than the clean-up pit.

While the eastern-entrance houses demonstrate ritual acts of various kinds conducted in what was broadly a domestic setting (see Parker Pearson 2007: 138), the western enclosures suggest the same kind of building being subject to a very different kind of conduct, as well as

FIGURE 24.5 The Western Circles at Durrington Walls.

being structurally elaborated in order to provide deeply secluded spaces. They may simply have represented elite residences, but the evidence could also be read to indicate that they were shrines, cult-houses, or spirit-lodges (Figure 24.5). Overall, the evidence from the internal structures at Durrington Walls does not show that this was a 'ritual site', for there is no such thing. There are simply sites at which ritual has taken place, and at Durrington a variety of acts of various degrees of ritualization, from formal rites to habitual practices, were woven into a complicated history, marking moments of crisis, transformation, and daily routine.

5 Conclusion

Despite a long history of research, the archaeology of ritual and religion in Neolithic Europe has yet to realize its potential. This chapter has suggested some ways in which the rich evidence available to us can be used to address these issues. The way forward lies with abandoning the attempt to reconstruct past mental states, and recognizing that both ritual and religion involved practices enacted in the material world.

Acknowledgements

Thanks to Tim Insoll for the invitation to contribute to this volume. Part of the text was delivered at a meeting of the Neolithic Studies Group, and I should like to thank Stuart Needham for organizing that event.

SUGGESTED READING

Hutton's (1997) discussion of invocations of the mother goddess gives a good sense of the way that archaeologists addressed Neolithic religion in the interwar years. Bradley (2005) addresses aspects of ritualization in European prehistory, while Brück (1999) provides a more focused discussion of the pitfalls of identifying ritual archaeologically. Richards and Thomas (1984) includes an early attempt to define criteria for the archaeological recognition of ritual, while Barrett (1994) provides a cogent argument for doubting the existence of a coherent 'Neolithic religion'.

REFERENCES

ALBARELLA, U. and SERJEANTSON, D. 2002. 'A passion for pork: Meat consumption at the British Late Neolithic site of Durrington Walls' in P. Miracle and N. Milner (eds), *Consuming Passions and Patterns of Consumption* (Cambridge: McDonald Institute), pp. 33–49.
ASAD T. 1993. *Genealogies of Religion* (Baltimore: Johns Hopkins University Press).
BAILEY, D. W. 2005. *Prehistoric Figurines: Representation and corporeality in the Neolithic* (London: Routledge).
BARRETT, J. C. 1991. 'Towards an archaeology of ritual' in P. Garwood, D. Jennings, R. Skeates, et al. (eds), *Sacred and Profane* (Oxford: Oxford University Committee for Archaeology), pp. 1–9.
——1994. *Fragments from Antiquity: An archaeology of social life in Britain, 2900–1200 BC* (Oxford: Blackwell).
BINFORD, L. R. 1971. 'Mortuary practices: their study and their potential', in J. Brown (ed.), *Approaches to the Social Dimension of Mortuary Practice* (Arlington: Society for American Archaelogy), pp. 6–29.
BLOCH, M. 1974. 'Symbols, song, dance and features of articulation', *Archives of European Sociology*, 15: 55–81.
BRADLEY, R. J. 2005. *Ritual and Domestic Life in Prehistoric Europe* (London: Routledge).
BRÜCK, J. 1999. 'Ritual and rationality: Some problems of interpretation in European Archaeology', *Journal of European Archaeology*, 2: 313–44.
CASSEN, S. 2000. 'Stelae reused in the passage graves of Western France: History of research and sexualisation of the carvings' in A. Ritchie (ed.), *Neolithic Orkney in its European Context* (Cambridge: McDonald Institute), pp. 233–46.
CHILDE, V. G. 1925. *The Dawn of European Civilisation* (London: Kegan Paul).
——1931. 'The continental affinities of British Neolithic pottery', *Archaeological Journal*, 88: 37–66.
——1935. *The Prehistory of Scotland* (London: Kegan Paul).
——1940. *Prehistoric Communities of the British Isles* (London: Chambers).
——1957. *The Dawn of European Civilisation*, 6th edn (London: Routledge and Kegan Paul).
CONNERTON, P. 1989. *How Societies Remember* (Cambridge: Cambridge University Press).
CRAWFORD, O. G. S. 1957. *The Eye Goddess* (London: Phoenix House).
DRONFIELD, J. 1994. 'Subjective vision and the source of Irish megalithic art', *Antiquity*, 69: 539–49.

—— 1995. 'Migraine, light and hallucinogens: The neurocognitive basis of Irish megalithic art', *Oxford Journal of Archaeology*, 14: 261–75.

—— 1996. 'Entering alternative realities: Cognition, art and architecture in Irish passage tombs', *Cambridge Journal of Archaeology*, 6: 7–72.

FLEMING, A. 1969. 'The myth of the mother-goddess', *World Archaeology*, 1: 247–61.

GEERTZ, C. 1973. 'Religion as a cultural system' in C. Geertz (ed.), *The Interpretation of Cultures* (New York: Basic Books), pp. 87–125.

GENNEP, A. VAN 1960. *The Rites of Passage* (London: Routledge and Kegan Paul).

GIMBUTAS, M. 1982. *Goddesses and Gods of Old Europe* (London: Thames and Hudson).

GRAVES, R. 1948. *The White Goddess: A historical grammar of poetic myth* (London: Faber and Faber).

HAWKES, C. F. C. 1954. 'Archaeological theory and method: Some suggestions from the Old World', *American Anthropologist*, 56: 155–68.

HAWKES, J. 1951. *A Land* (London: Cresset Press).

HUTTON, R. 1997. 'The Neolithic great goddess: A study in modern tradition', *Antiquity*, 71: 91–9.

INSOLL, T. 2004a. 'Are archaeologists afraid of gods? Some thoughts on archaeology and religion' in T. Insoll (ed.), *Belief in the Past* (Oxford: Archaeopress), pp. 1–6.

—— 2004b. *Archaeology, Ritual, Religion* (London: Routledge).

JAMES, W. 2003. *The Ceremonial Animal: A new portrait of anthropology* (Oxford: Oxford University Press).

KEANE, W. 2008. 'The evidence of the senses and the materiality of religion', *Journal of the Royal Anthropological Institute*, Special Issue 2008: S110–27.

LEWIS, G. 1980. *Day of Shining Red: An essay on understanding ritual* (Cambridge: Cambridge University Press).

LEWIS-WILLIAMS, J. D. and DOWSON, T. A. 1993. 'On vision and power in the Neolithic: Evidence from the decorated monuments', *Current Anthropology*, 34: 55–65.

—— and PEARCE, D. 2005. *Inside the Neolithic Mind* (London: Thames and Hudson).

MESKELL, L. 1995. 'Goddesses, Gimbutas and "New Age" archaeology', *Antiquity*, 69: 74–86.

PARKER PEARSON, M. 2007. 'The Stonehenge Riverside Project: Excavations at the east entrance of Durrington Walls' in M. Larsson and M. Parker Pearson (eds), *From Stonehenge to the Baltic*, BAR International series 1692 (Oxford: BAR), pp. 125–44.

——, CLEAL, R., MARSHALL, P., et al. 2007. 'The age of Stonehenge', *Antiquity*, 81: 617–39.

—— POLLARD, J. RICHARDS, C., et al. forthcoming. 'The Stonehenge Riverside Project: Exploring the Neolithic landscape of Stonehenge', *Documenta Praehistorica*, 35.

—— and RAMILSONINA 1998. 'Stonehenge for the ancestors: The stones pass on the message', *Antiquity*, 72: 308–26.

PIGGOTT, S. 1962. *The West Kennet Long Barrow: Excavations 1955–56* (London: Her Majesty's Stationery Office).

POLLARD, J. and ROBINSON, D. 2007. 'A return to Woodhenge: The results and implications of the 2006 excavations' in M. Larsson and M. Parker Pearson (eds), *From Stonehenge to the Baltic*, BAR International series 1692 (Oxford: BAR), pp. 159–68.

PRICE, T. D., WAHL, J., and BENTLEY, R. A. 2006. 'Isotopic evidence for mobility and group organisation amongst Neolithic farmers at Talheim, Germany, 5000 BC', *European Journal of Archaeology*, 9: 259–84.

RENFREW, C. 1967. 'Colonialism and megalithismus', *Antiquity*, 41: 276–88.

—— 1994. 'The archaeology of religion' in C. Renfrew and E. Zubrow (eds), *The Ancient Mind: Elements of cognitive archaeology* (Cambridge: Cambridge University Press), pp. 47–54.

RICHARDS, C. C. and THOMAS, J. S. 1984. 'Ritual activity and structured deposition in later Neolithic Wessex' in R. Bradley and J. Gardiner (eds), *Neolithic Studies* (Oxford: BAR), pp. 189–218.

RUEL, M. 1997. *Belief, Ritual and the Securing of Life: Reflexive essays on Bantu Religion* (Leiden: Brill).

SCHULTING, R. and WYSOCKI, M. 2005. '"In this chambered tumulus were found cleft skulls . . .": An assessment of the evidence for cranial trauma in the British Neolithic', *Proceedings of the Prehistoric Society*, 71: 107–38.

SHANKS, M. and TILLEY, C. Y. 1982. 'Ideology, symbolic power and ritual communication: A reinterpretation of Neolithic mortuary practices' in I. Hodder (ed.), *Symbolic and Structural Archaeology* (Cambridge: Cambridge University Press), pp. 129–54.

TAYLOR, C. 1989. *Sources of the Self: The making of the modern identity* (Cambridge: Cambridge University Press).

THOMAS, J. S. 2004. 'The ritual universe' in I. Shepherd and G. Barclay (eds), *Scotland in Ancient Europe* (Edinburgh: Society of Antiquaries of Scotland), pp. 171–8.

——2007. 'The internal features at Durrington Walls: Investigations in the Southern Circle and western enclosures, 2005–6' in M. Larsson and M. Parker Pearson (eds), *From Stonehenge to the Baltic*, BAR International series 1692 (Oxford: BAR), pp. 145–58.

TURNER, V. 1967. *The Forest of Symbols: Aspects of Ndembu ritual* (Ithaca: Cornell University Press).

——1969. *The Ritual Process: Structure and anti-structure* (New York: Aldine De Gruyter).

WAHL, J. and KÖNIG, H. G. 1987. 'Anthropologisch-traumatologisch untersuchung der menschlichen skelettreste aus dem Bandkeramischen massgrab bei Talheim, Kreis Heilbronn', *Fundberichte Baden-Württemberg*, 12: 65–193.

WAINWRIGHT, G. J. and LONGWORTH, I. H. 1971. *Durrington Walls: Excavations 1966–1968* (London: Society of Antiquaries).

WILD, E. M., STADLER, P., HÄUSSER, A., et al. 2004. 'Neolithic massacres: Local skirmishes or general war in Europe?', *Radiocarbon*, 46: 377–85.

CHAPTER 25

FIRE, EARTH, WATER
An Elemental Cosmography of the European Bronze Age

JOANNA BRÜCK

1 Introduction: Ritual and Religion in the European Bronze Age

IN 1902, a farmer ploughing land reclaimed from a bog at Trundholm on the island of Zealand, Denmark, found fragments of an extraordinary bronze object (Glob 1973: 99–103; Kaul 2004b). The Trundholm chariot, as it has come to be known, is a model of a chariot or wagon, some 59 cm long (Figure 25.1). It is drawn by a horse, and is carrying what is usually interpreted as a representation of the sun. It was deliberately broken before being deposited in the bog. In this single find are combined several of the most significant aspects of Bronze Age cosmology: a concern with elements of the natural world, in this case the sun and its nemesis, the watery underworld; an interest in travel, transformation, and fertility, signified by the deliberate destruction of the chariot of bronze drawing the sun on its diurnal and seasonal cycle; and a belief in the importance of animals in mediating between the world of the living and that of the supernatural.

The European Bronze Age (c.2300–800 BC) was a period of dramatic social and economic change. The occurrence of rich single graves is thought to indicate the development of social stratification, with some authors arguing for the emergence of chiefly hierarchies (e.g. Renfrew 1974; Kristiansen 1998). The appearance of hill forts, particularly in the later part of the period, and the first specialized weaponry, notably rapiers and swords, suggests that the Bronze Age was characterized—at least at times—by intense interpersonal and intercommunity competition (e.g. Osgood and Monks 2000). There was a dramatic rise in the intensity of interaction between different geographical regions, as the exchange of raw materials and finished artefacts increased (e.g. Kristiansen 1998). Doubtless, the

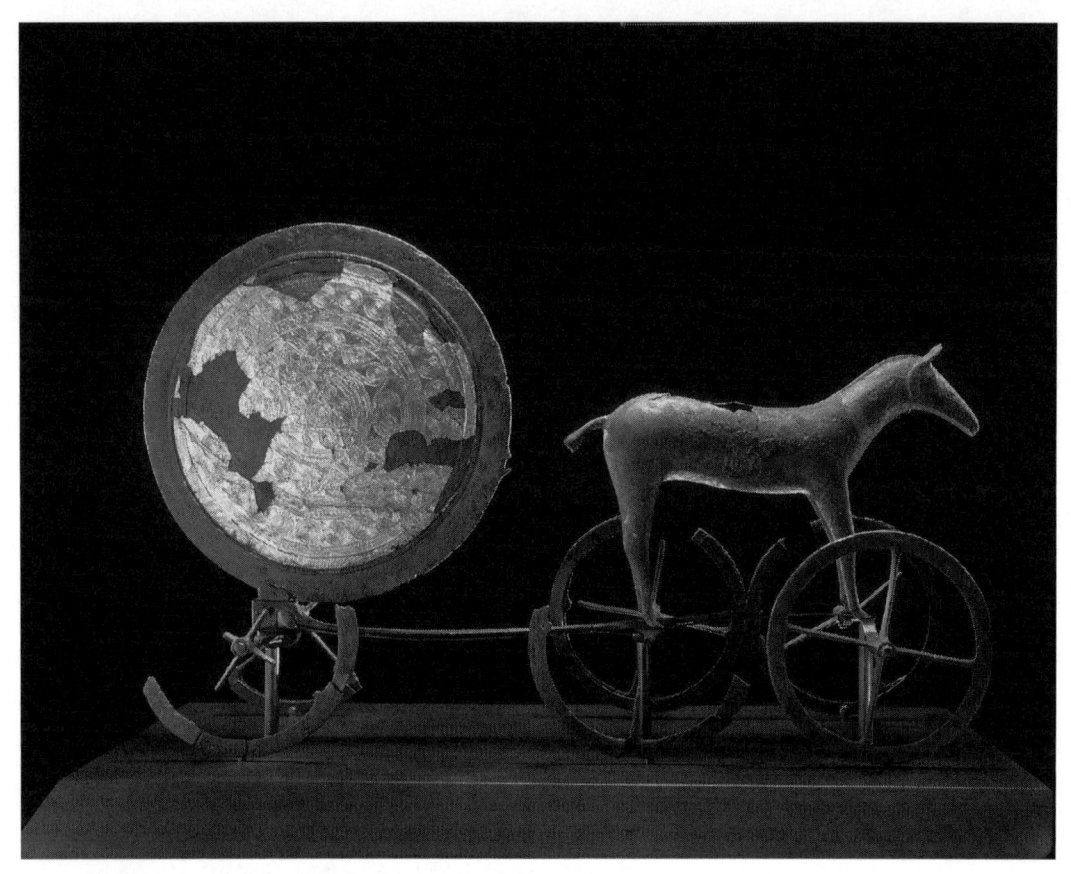

FIGURE 25.1 The Trundholm chariot.

introduction of metalworking played a significant role in these changes: it provided a new medium for both the accumulation and display of wealth and associated social status and, as such, its introduction may have resulted in an increase in social differentiation and competition. Against this backdrop, Bronze Age ritual and religion can be seen to have played a significant role in the construction, definition, and maintenance of social relationships.

This chapter will consider the character and role of ritual and religion in the European Bronze Age, and will address a series of interlinked themes and issues. The sites discussed range geographically from Scandinavia to the Mediterranean, and from Ireland to Hungary. There is considerable diversity in the available evidence for ritual practice across Europe, but there are also striking similarities that speak of the intensity of inter-regional interaction. Religious iconography, although relatively rare, provides insights into elements of Bronze Age belief systems, but the names and characteristics of particular deities are lost to us. In addition, there is a wealth of information on a range of ritual practices that can cast light on the role of religion in Bronze Age society.

2 SPECIAL PLACES

The deposition of metalwork and other finds in special places is one of the key ritual practices of the European Bronze Age. Wet places, in particular, were singled out for attention. Bronze objects, often comprising high-status items such as swords, bronze shields, and objects of probable ritual significance such as the *lures*, or bronze horns, of the Nordic Bronze Age, were thrown into rivers, lakes, and bogs (e.g. Hundt 1955; Torbrügge 1971; Bradley 1990; Hansen 1994; Fontijn 2002). For example, the large number of objects deposited at the confluence of the rivers Havel and Spree at Berlin-Spandau, northern Germany, included swords, axes, spearheads, daggers, and rapiers, mostly of northern German and southern Scandinavian types, but including also a small number of exotic imports (Schwenzer 1997). These were deposited over a lengthy period of time, probably a century or more, and some of the weapons were unused. A special platform had been built projecting into the Spree, so that those who made these offerings were set apart from their audience, enhancing the visual potency of the act of deposition. Rivers are of course natural geographical boundaries, and as such provide a perfect example of the interplay between political power and religious beliefs. It seems likely that they were considered liminal places in Bronze Age cosmographies, providing a point of access to the underworld and its powers. Those who deposited metalwork into the water enhanced their own status in the eyes of their community by propitiating the gods; at the same time, we might interpret such acts as political posturing at what may have been boundaries between neighbouring groups. The choice of the confluence of two rivers is particularly significant in this instance: as a place of convergence and separation, this location highlighted in both practical and metaphorical terms the travels and intercommunity connections that facilitated the acquisition of those very objects that were deposited into the water.

Locations such as rivers and bogs may have marked out the edges of the familiar, but deposits in water took place too at the heart of the settled landscape. Wells and waterholes were foci for the deposition of special objects (e.g. Wyss 1996). For example, a collection of items including an iron dagger handle, birch-bark vessels, bone and antler artefacts, and human remains were found at the base of a wood-lined well at Gánovce, Poprad, Slovakia (Furmánek and Vladár 1996: 498). At Yarnton, Oxfordshire, England, part of the right humerus of an adult human was recovered from a waterhole that formed one element of an extensive area of Bronze Age settlement (Hey 2006: 123); this item was worn smooth and had a notch cut at one end. Similar finds are known from springs: for instance a flanged axe was recovered from a sulphur spring at Schams near Pignia, south-east Switzerland (Wyss 1996: 421). Doubtless, the life-giving properties of water, and the magical qualities of places where it emerged from beneath the ground, meant that such locations may have been associated with particular spirits or deities to whom offerings needed to be made.

Other features of the natural landscape, for example caves, were also a focus of interest (e.g. Schauer 1981; Almagro-Gorbea 1996: 46; Warmembol 1996). The Sculptor's Cave at Covesea, Moray, Scotland, produced a range of objects of Late Bronze Age date including bronze armrings, a number of pieces of ring money (composite bronze and gold objects) and a large quantity of human remains, predominantly those of children (Benton 1931; Shepherd 2007). The relatively high percentage of skull and mandible fragments in the entrance passages suggests the display of heads at the entrance to the cave (similar evidence has been noted at caves in other regions, for example the Trou del Leuve in Belgium: Warmembol 1996: 216). Fragments of mandibles and atlas vertebrae were more numerous than the skulls themselves, however, suggesting that many of the latter were removed from the site once the heads had started to decay and the jaws dropped off. It seems likely that sites such as this were viewed as entrances to the underworld, places of danger and liminality at which the domains of the living and the dead collided, and where gods, spirits and ancestors could be addressed and propitiated. As perilous meeting-points between the worlds of darkness and light, caves may have been considered suitable places to conduct rites of passage. Interestingly, the Sculptor's Cave is in an inaccessible location on the shore of Moray Firth, a large coastal inlet, and is best approached from the sea; this quality may have enhanced its liminality, making it an especially suitable location for ritual activities.

Mountain tops, passes, and rocky outcrops also attracted particular attention. For example, a large number of artefacts including spindle whorls, bronze pins, rings, and socketed arrowheads were deposited in crevices in the Totenstein, a dramatic granite outcrop near Königshain, east Germany (Buck 1996: 280), while a hoard of two axes and a spearhead were found on the Hannig Pass between the Saas and Matter valleys in the Swiss Alps (Wyss 1996: 424–5). The Minoan peak sanctuary at Atsipadhes Korakias in west-central Crete produced a large number of terracotta animal and human figurines, along with anatomical models, particularly of human limbs (Peatfield 1992). The raised arms of some of the human figures have been interpreted as gestures of worship, while the anatomical models suggest that those who came to the site may have sought the healing of particular bodily ills. Many of these finds had been deliberately broken, and their fragments placed in rock clefts on and near two natural terraces at the top of the mountain. The presence of jars and rhytons suggests that libations were offered to the gods at this site, while cups and dishes may indicate feasting activities.

Together, these and similar finds suggest that Bronze Age people viewed prominent features of the natural landscape as sacred places (Schauer 1996; Wyss 1996; Bradley 2000). Caves, bogs, mountains, and other features were viewed with awe and reverence and were seen as locations which provided a conduit between heaven, earth, and the underworld. As such, they were considered to possess liminal or other-worldly characteristics that facilitated various types of transformation, including the handling of the dead and the healing of the sick. In some cases, these special places may have marked out political or cultural boundaries because of their 'otherness'. As part of the sacred geographies of Bronze Age societies, such locations provided a context in which ideas of danger, difference, and distance could be addressed and mediated, in some cases through physically arduous acts of pilgrimage such as entering the earth or scaling mountain heights. Distinctions between self and other and between the familiar and the foreign were central to the activities that were carried out at these sites.

Yet, there is evidence to suggest that the dichotomy that is drawn between culture and nature in the modern Western world may not have been articulated so sharply in the Bronze Age. Rather, the deposition of offerings at natural features suggests that these were imbued with special powers and may have been considered animate entities in their own right so that the contemporary objectification of the landscape as something qualitatively different to and outside of the human social world may not have applied (for detailed discussion see Insoll 2007). Although we tend to classify such locations as 'natural' places, they were of course often altered—in both subtle and dramatic ways—through human intervention. As such, they must be considered significant elements of a thoroughly socialized and meaningful landscape whose very shape was maintained through social practice and which in turn helped to define and sustain particular forms of social relationship.

3 COSMOLOGY AND RELIGIOUS BELIEFS

In the absence of written texts, it is of course difficult to reconstruct the content of Bronze Age belief systems. The large number of votive deposits in wet contexts has led certain authors to propose the existence of a water cult (e.g. Burgess 1980: 350–1). Certainly, water was a significant component of Bronze Age cosmographies, but research on the religious symbols and iconography of the period suggest it was just one part of a particular categorization of the world and its elements.

Studies of Bronze Age iconography have identified a number of possible religious symbols including ships, waterbirds, chariots, horses, the sun, and the wheel (e.g. Kossack 1954; Sprockhoff 1955; Gelling and Davidson 1969; Larsson 1998; Kaul 1998; Kaul 2004a). These symbols became particularly prevalent in the Late Bronze Age, although their origins lie in earlier periods. They were produced in a variety of media, including stone, bronze, and ceramics. For example, the rock art of Scandinavia has been a focus of study for many years (Figure 25.2; e.g. Malmer 1981; Coles 2005; Bertilsson 1987). Although everyday activities such as hunting are frequently portrayed, it is widely accepted that much of the imagery was of ritual significance (e.g. Norbladh 1989; Bradley 1997; Goldhahn 1999; Tilley 1999: ch. 5; Kaul 2004c). Images of boats are frequent, and the prows and sterns of certain examples are shaped like horse heads. In some of these vessels stand figures with raised arms, perhaps performing acts of worship, while on other ships acrobats are depicted performing leaps and somersaults. Some boats are shown with the sun (depicted as a cup-mark or a wheel) directly above them, while others appear to carry the sun on a stand or altar. A concern with fertility is indicated by scenes showing sexual intercourse between two people or between men and animals. Ceremonial processions showing men holding aloft elaborate axes and *lures* (bronze horns) are known (Maier 1997: fig. 2; Coles 2003). Such objects are themselves usually found as part of votive deposits in bogs in the same regions (indeed, a number of the *lures* found in bronze hoards were ritually decommissioned by having their mouthpieces torn off: Broholm et al. 1949: 15–16). Some of the human figures depicted on rock art wear special costumes, such as horned helmets, while others take on animal characteristics, such as the heads or wings of birds. This suggests that there may have been a shamanistic element to some of the rites depicted, with shape-shifting humans acquiring some of the abilities of animal spirits (Kristiansen and Larsson 2005: 320–2).

The famous Trundholm chariot has already been mentioned above, but other model chariots or wagons are also known (Pare 1989). These include two bronze wagon models from a Late Bronze Age cemetery at Gross Perschnitz, Silesia, northern Germany, which were deposited in a pit along with a pair of arm-rings (Maraszek 1997). These, like other examples from the same region, were each drawn by a trio of waterbirds. The more complete of the two

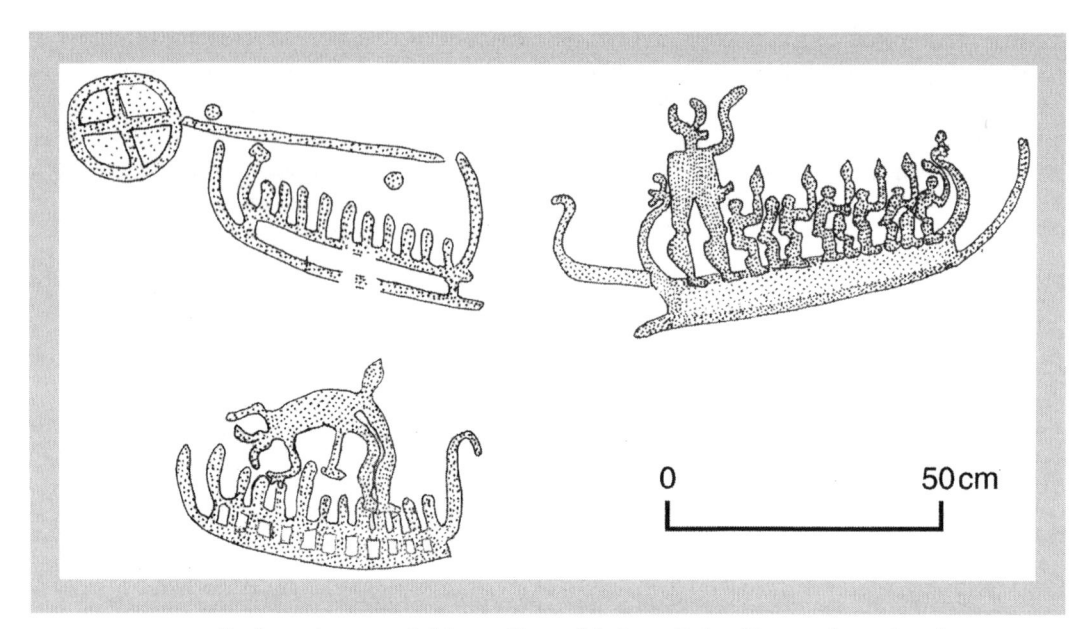

FIGURE 25.2 Rock art images of ships at Kasen Lövåsen, Bohuslän, southern Sweden.

ceramic wagon models from Dupljaja, Banat, Serbia, was also drawn by waterbirds and carried a standing anthropomorphic figurine with a bird-shaped head (Bošković 1959; Pare 1989: 84). A number of rich Late Bronze Age burials have produced model wagons carrying bronze vessels which acted as containers for the cremated remains of the deceased (ibid.: 82). The example from Acholshausen in Bavaria, southern Germany, was adorned by a pair of waterbirds attached to each of the two axles (Peschenck 1972: figs. 3–5).

A range of similar symbolic references can be identified on other classes of metalwork. The large bronze bucket from Unterglauheim, Bavaria, southern Germany, was decorated with embossed 'Vogelbarke' motifs, comprising ships with bird-headed prows and sterns carrying the sun (Jacob 1995: 103–4, figs. 50, 312); inside the bucket were deposited two further bronze vessels, two small gold bowls, and a cremation. A ship was engraved on one of two bronze scimitars deposited in a bog at Rørby, Denmark (Rønne 2004), while an axe from Hermannshagen in the Mecklenburg-Vorpommern region, northern Germany, bears a sunburst or star motif on one of its faces (Schwartz 2004a). The razors that accompanied Late Bronze Age cremations in Denmark were sometimes decorated with incised depictions of boats, while in other cases their handles were rendered as horse heads (Kaul 1998), and it is likely that these artefacts were used to prepare the bodies of the dead for the funerary rite. In the mortuary context, the use of boat symbolism was not confined to grave-goods, but was employed in other ways too. For example, ship-shaped stone settings surround a number of Late Bronze Age burials on the island of Gotland in the Baltic Sea (Capelle 1986), while the similarity between the oak coffin from the barrow at Loose Howe, Yorkshire, northern England, and contemporary log boats is striking (Elgee and Elgee 1949: 91–2).

One of the most extraordinary finds of recent years is the Nebra disc (Meller 2004a; 2004b). This large bronze disc, measuring some 32 cm in diameter, was found in a hoard along with two swords, two axes, two spiral arm-rings and a chisel on the Mittelberg, a hill in Saxony-Anhalt, eastern Germany. Pieces of gold foil attached to the disc represent the sun, moon, and stars, and it has been argued that this object facilitated observation of the movement of celestial bodies and calculation of calendrical dates (Schlosser 2004; but see Pásztor and Roslund 2007). Two gold strips (one of which is now lost) formed opposing arcs each spanning some 80 degrees around the edge of the disc. These divide the circumference of the disc into four, representing perhaps the four seasons, each marked out by the rising and setting of the sun at different points on the horizon. A third, shorter arc on the lower edge of the disc may represent a ship on its celestial travels.

Overall, this body of iconography has been interpreted to indicate the concern of a predominantly agricultural society with the passing of the seasons and the cyclical regeneration of life. It has often been suggested that Bronze Age societies regarded the sun as a deity that travelled by day in a chariot through the heavens and by night in a ship across the watery underworld (Gelling and Davidson 1969; Kaul 1998; Kaul 2004a; Kristiansen and Larsson 2005: 294–308; Bradley 2006). Both boats and chariots came to be linked with cycles of death and rebirth and it is hardly surprising that they were considered a suitable means of transporting the dead to the afterlife (Bradley 1997). Similar motifs recur throughout Indo-European mythology (Kristiansen and Larsson 2005: ch. 6): later Greek myths recount how the sun god Apollo left Delphi each winter in a chariot drawn by swans, while ships were considered appropriate vessels for the souls of the dead by, amongst others, the ancient Egyptians and the Vikings. In addition, the choice of natural places such as caves, bogs, and mountains as foci for deposition and other ritual activities suggests that Bronze Age belief systems divided the cosmos into three distinct parts: the sky (a world of light and life symbolized by the sun, wheels, and horses), the earth (the land of the living), and the underworld (a watery place of darkness and death, symbolized by the moon, ships, and waterbirds) (Randsborg 1993: 119–20; Goldhahn 1999; Kristiansen and Larsson 2005: 355, fig. 167; Bradley 2006). The location of barrows on hilltops in Norway, Britain, and elsewhere may suggest that those who had successfully made the passage to ancestorhood were considered to reside in the uppermost level of this tripartite scheme.

4 RITUAL, POWER, AND EXCLUSION

Who, then, were the practitioners of Bronze Age rituals? Burials of a number of possible ritual specialists have been identified. One of the most famous is that from Hvidegård, just north of Copenhagen, Denmark (Glob 1973: 116). Here, the cremation burial of a man was accompanied by a sword, fibula, and a small leather bag which contained, amongst other things, the tail of a grass snake, a falcon's claw, the jaw of a squirrel, a fragment of amber bead, a piece of bark, a number of different dried roots, a small cube of wood, a pair of bronze tweezers, and a bronze razor with a handle shaped like a horse's head. A cremation burial from the Late Bronze Age cemetery at Budapest, Hungary, contained 23 small clay objects including wheel-, disc-, star-, and crescent-moon-shaped artefacts (Kalicz-Schreiber 1991). These have been interpreted as part of the toolkit of a priest or shaman. Bird-shaped ceramic rattles have been found in graves at sites such as Korbovo and Male Vrbica, north-east Serbia (Vasic and Vasic 2000: figs. 12 and 15), their shape suggesting that these may have played a role in ritual activities and were not simply musical instruments or toys.

Similarly, sets of animal astragali (usually sheep/goat or cattle) from burials at sites such as Volders in the Austrian Tyrol may have been used in divination (Schauer 1996: 396).

Depictions of the participants in Bronze Age rituals (both mortal and immortal) are known in a range of media. Phallic figures, sometimes wearing horned helmets or carrying swords, are shown engaged in a variety of activities on the rock art of Bronze Age Scandinavia: they are depicted standing on boats, carrying *lures* and other high status metalwork in processions, ploughing, fighting, and hunting (see examples in *corpora* such as Burenhult 1973; Bertilsson 1987; Coles 2005). The references to human fertility, as well as the character of the activities involved, suggests that at least some of these scenes depict particular rituals or mythological narratives. The small bronze figurines found in hoards at Fårdal in northern Jutland and Grevensvænge in south Zealand, Denmark, have been interpreted either as deities or priests and priestesses (Glob 1973: 163, 165, figs. 64, 67, 70; Kaul 2004d). The female figures wear short corded skirts and neck-rings and some perform acrobatic feats like those depicted elsewhere on rock art panels; the men wear horned helmets and carry axes. At Ralaghan, County Cavan, Ireland, a wooden 'idol', just over 1 m tall, was found in a bog (Coles 1990: 320–2), while Minoan iconography indicates that goddesses and their female officiants played a particularly important role in the religious rituals of Bronze Age Crete (Gesell 1983). In most of these examples, of course, it is difficult to distinguish deities from ritual specialists and other participants; indeed, it is likely that this ambivalence was deliberate.

There are particularly strong links between the religious symbols discussed above and activities that appear to have defined and underpinned the status of Bronze Age elites, notably exchange, feasting and warfare (Kristiansen 1998). It would hardly be surprising if at least some of those who officiated in religious ceremonies held positions of special social and political power within their communities. Religious symbols often occur on high-status metalwork associated with fighting and feasting. For example, the bronze greave from a hoard at Rinyaszentkirály, south-west Hungary, is ornamented with depictions of wheels and waterbirds (Kemenczei 2003: 171, fig. 38); bronze armour of this quality is likely to have been worn only by those of high status. Similarly, an axe from a rich burial at Osternienburg, Saxony-Anhalt, Germany, is decorated with the so-called 'Vogelbarke' motif showing a ship with a bird-headed prow and stern (Schwartz 2004b). The flesh-hook from the bog at Dunaverney, County Antrim, Northern Ireland, is embellished with small bronze models of two ravens and a family of swans, and it has been suggested that this imagery calls to mind a broader cosmological distinction between air and water, black and white, death and life (Bowman and Needham 2007: 94). The bronze amphora from Gevelinghausen in Westphalia, western Germany, contained a cremation and was decorated with a series of 'Vogelbarken', each carrying one or two sun motifs represented by embossed concentric circles (Jockenhövel 1974). In other cases, the paraphernalia worn by religious specialists were made of precious materials. For instance, the gold 'hat' from Ezelsdorf-Buch, Germany, is decorated with rows of repoussé discs and wheel-motifs, and surmounted by a star or sunburst (Schauer 1986; Springer 1999).

The relationship between high-status artefacts and religious imagery suggests that the elites of the Bronze Age drew part of their power from their role in ritual and religious life. In particular, the use of symbols associated with deities and with concepts of fertility and rebirth would have legitimated the position of particular individuals, so that they were seen to hold the power of life and death over the people around them and to be responsible for the cyclical regeneration of the natural world. Like the sun itself, ships, horses, and chariots were used by the elites in warfare and on trading expeditions, so that the role and activities of deities and elites became elided (Kristiansen 1998; Kristiansen and Larsson 2005: 45).

5 THE SPECIAL AND THE EVERYDAY: TRANSFORMING PEOPLE, OBJECTS, AND PLACES IN THE EUROPEAN BRONZE AGE

Our previous discussion of special places hints that for much of Europe, built shrines or other special-purpose structures for ritual activities are largely unknown. One of the few examples in Northern Europe is the putative shrine found in a bog at Bargeroosterveld in the province of Drenthe, Netherlands (Waterbolk and van Zeist 1961). This consisted of a setting of wooden posts forming a small, square building some 1.8 x 1.8 m in size, probably with open sides and an open roof. Five pieces of timber that had been dressed to resemble horns were also found, and the excavators suggested that these originally formed the ends of the cross-pieces that tied the uprights together at roof-level; these 'horns' had been broken off, suggesting deliberate destruction of the building. Three bronze hoards were found nearby. There are rather more examples of buildings that can be interpreted as shrines in the Mediterranean region. For example, the *taula* monuments of Menorca consist of a substantial stone upright surmounted by a horizontal slab of stone (Waldren 1982: 335-6). Some of these monuments are several metres high, and they are often enclosed by a stone wall. Excavations at a number of sites have produced large quantities of animal bone, suggestive of feasting activities, and studies of the astronomical alignments of some of the *taulas* indicate an interest in marking out significant points in the solar calendar, for example the midsummer sunrise (Hochsieder and Knösel 1995). Further east, some of the rooms in Minoan palaces have been interpreted as shrines, with the presence of libation tables, so-called 'horns of consecration', lustral basins (sunken areas that may have been used for ritual cleansing), and frescos depicting acts of offering and sacrifice indicating their probable religious significance (Gesell 1985; Rutkowski 1986). Elsewhere, however, ritual activities often took place in the open air. In other words, special-purpose buildings accessible only to high-status individuals were—outside of the Mediterranean world—rarely constructed, suggesting that architecture was not used as a means of exclusion from ritual activities. Of course, this need not mean that there was open access to sites where ritual activities were carried out, and a variety of taboos and proscriptions may have protected such places from the eyes of many members of the community. Indeed, the inaccessible nature of locations such as caves and mountains may have facilitated this process.

Ritual activities were not solely carried out at 'natural places', however. In addition, Bronze Age houses and settlements were important foci for ritual practice (e.g. Furmánek and Jakab 1997; Brück 1999a). Items of probable cultic significance are known from some sites, while at many others, votive deposits attest to the intertwining of ritual and domestic life. For example, at Itford Hill in Sussex, England, a chalk phallus was deposited in a post-hole that formed part of the porched entrance to roundhouse D (Burstow and Holleyman 1957: 176). At

Jędrychowice, Opole, Poland, the flexed body of an adult female was found on the base of pit 261a, while disarticulated human remains (mostly skull fragments) were recovered from 13 other pits in this defended settlement (Gedl and Szybowicz 1997: 27, fig. 7). A spearhead was found lying almost horizontally in the top of one of the post-holes of house 4 at Rhenen-Remmerden, Utrecht, Netherlands (van Hoof and Meurkens 2007: 92), suggesting that it was deposited in this feature after the post had been removed. At Velserbroek P-63, Noord-Holland, Netherlands, a pit containing two cattle skulls and a calf burial marked out the threshold between what may have been the main occupation area and the byre in the earliest longhouse (Figure 25.3; Therkorn 2007: fig. 12.9).

It has been suggested that such deposits marked out either liminal points in space (especially boundaries and entrances) or moments of temporal disjunction (for example, foundation or abandonment) (Brück 1999a; 2006; Gerritsen 1999). They may have acted as offerings to ensure the well-being of the household and the activities that supported it, particularly agricultural production, so that the annual agricultural cycle may have become metaphorically linked with both places of spatial transformation and the life cycle of the settlement and its inhabitants. Alternatively, such offerings may be interpreted as attempts to shape personal destiny through intercession with the ancestors (Insoll 2008), so that the diversity of the deposits reflect the specificities of individual life histories. Doubtless, such ritual activities were not restricted to an elite but were likely to have involved all members of the household, albeit perhaps on different occasions. Perhaps most importantly, it suggests that there was no strict demarcation between the ritual and domestic spheres, and that the ritual–secular divide that characterizes the modern Western world cannot be imposed onto the past (Brück 1999b; Bradley 2005).

The items that form part of votive deposits in settlement contexts were, in many cases, deliberately broken or burnt prior to deposition. For instance, roundhouse 648 at Trethellen Farm in Cornwall, England, was demolished and sealed with layers of earth, stone, and occupation debris, among which were found the smashed and burnt fragments of a quernstone (Nowakowski 1991). It seems likely that this item was deliberately destroyed as part of a ritual to mark out the 'death' of this house. Such practices are interesting, as they reflect similar activities in other contexts, including hoards and burials. For example, a bronze shield was found placed face down in a ditch at the foot of South Cadbury hill fort, Somerset, England (Coles et al. 1999); a blunt-ended tool (possibly a wooden stake) had been driven through it in three places as it lay on the ground. The artefacts in the hoard from Crévic, Meurthre-et-Moselle, north-east France, were all broken; they included an axe and a spearhead that had been deliberately bent and battered in an act that would have required considerable force, and three bracelets whose terminals had been torn off (Nebelsick 2000: 160, fig. 11.1). Certainly, it is difficult to explain the bending of these items in practical terms and it seems likely that this was a means of ritually decommissioning artefacts of particular social potency. Fire and fragmentation were, of course, also frequently employed in Bronze Age funerary rites, both in the Late Bronze Age when cremation became the dominant form of funerary treatment for the dead across most of Europe (e.g. Coles and Harding 1979: 359, 500), and during earlier periods. For example, at Grünhof-Tesperhude, Lower Saxony, north Germany, a rectangular wooden mortuary house was built over an oak coffin containing the bodies of a woman and child; this structure was fired prior to the erection of a substantial mound (Kersten 1936). Grave-goods, too, were often broken: for example, smashed drinking vessels are frequently found in Mycenean burials on both Crete and mainland Greece and can be interpreted either as

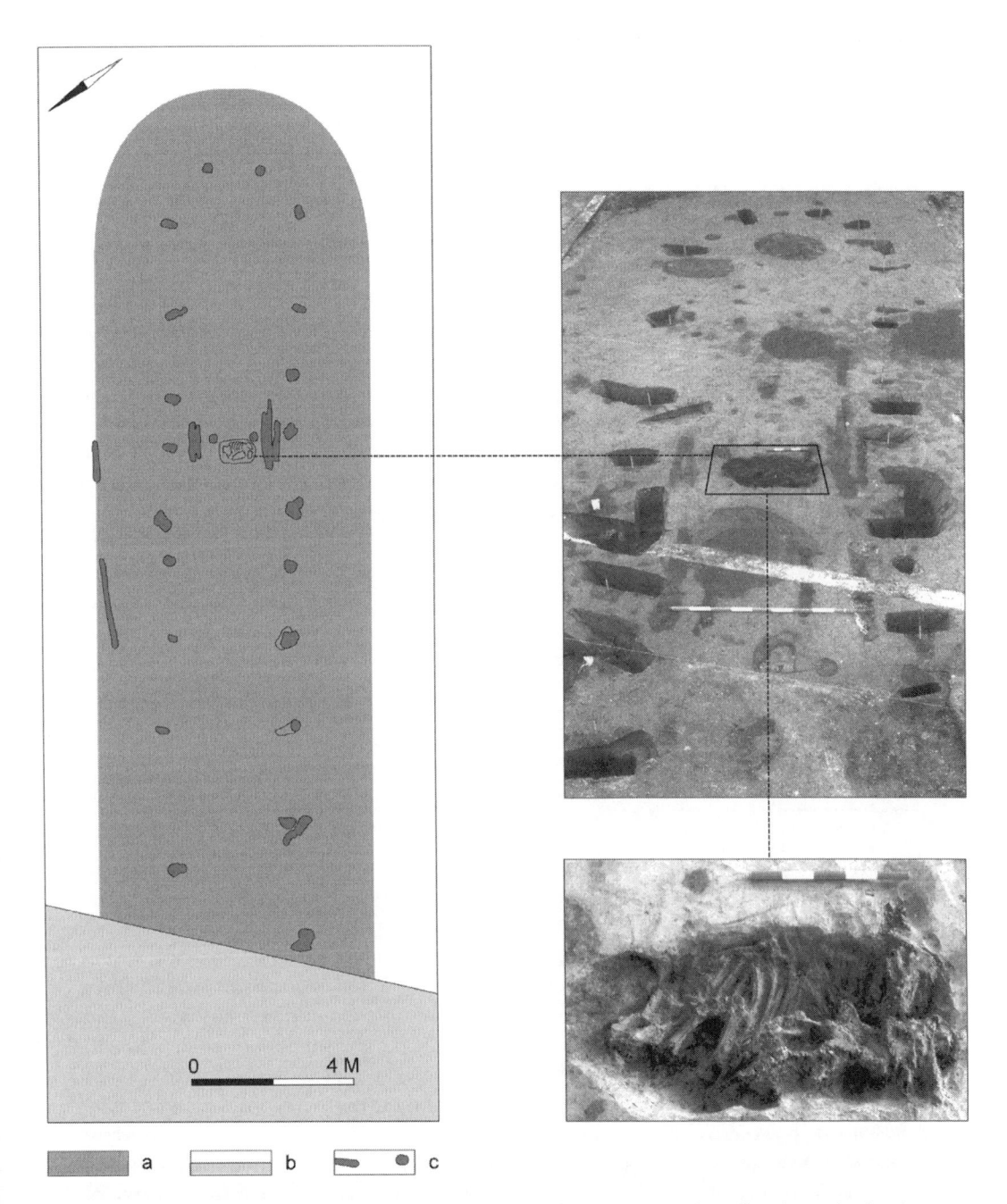

FIGURE 25.3 Plan of the longhouse at Velserbroek P-63, Noord-Holland, Netherlands, showing location of the pit containing the burial of a calf and two cattle skulls.

offerings to the dead or as the remains of mortuary feasts (Åström 1987: 215). Similarly, deliberately bent swords and daggers are known from Mycenean tombs at Pylos on the Peloponnese peninsula and Ialysos, Rhodes (ibid.).

Acts of deliberate burning and breaking did not merely symbolically signify death, however. Contemporary technologies such as metalworking and potting subjected artefacts to fire and fragmentation both in the early stages of the productive process (for example, the smelting and casting of copper alloys) and in later recycling (the use of grog temper in pottery, for instance). As such, we can suggest that the deliberate destruction of both people and artefacts acted not only as a means of transformation but was considered essential to the regeneration of life in the face of death (Fendin 2000; Brück 2006). This means that the sorts of concerns indicated in Bronze Age iconography (diurnal and seasonal cycles of death and rebirth) were reflected in the depositional activities that were carried out in the home as well as elsewhere in the landscape. It is therefore likely that transformative technologies of various sorts (including metalworking and cooking) were surrounded by ritual (e.g. Budd and Taylor 1995; cf. Hingley 1997). Certainly, the artefacts and refuse associated with such activities were often disposed of with particular care. For example, at King's Stables, County Armagh, Northern Ireland, an artificial pool which was constructed in the Late Bronze Age lay just 200 m north-east of the contemporary Haughey's Fort. This pool produced 18 clay mould fragments for the production of bronze swords, along with animal bones and part of a human skull (Lynn 1977). Similarly, a cave at Kallmünz, near Regensburg in Bavaria, produced a hoard of broken bronze objects (Schauer 1981: 411); it seems likely that the magical, dangerous, and transformative character of metalworking made these items a particularly apt form of votive deposit for such a liminal place (cf. Hingley 1997).

6 Conclusion

It is evident from our discussion that ritual and religious practice was a central component of everyday life in the European Bronze Age. No strict distinction can be drawn between ritual, on the one hand, and domestic or technological activities on the other. At the same time, access to certain rites, symbols and significant places may have been restricted, so that political power and religious beliefs were intertwined. The cosmography of the European Bronze Age divided the world and its inhabitants into different elements and classes, and although comparisons can be drawn between the activities carried out on settlements and those that took place on the margins of the settled landscape, the differences were perhaps equally important (Fontijn 2002). The significance of these distinctions has yet to be fully understood, however, and the conceptual categorization of the Bronze Age universe requires further investigation, particularly outside of the Nordic region. Although it is widely believed that many of the ritual activities discussed above were the preserve of Bronze Age elites, this assumption requires detailed re-evaluation in the light of evidence for votive deposition on settlement sites; indeed, the identity of those elites and their relationships with other members of their communities remains unclear. As the discovery of the Nebra disc demonstrates so well, new finds continue both to challenge and enhance our understanding of Bronze Age ritual and religion. The passage of the seasons and the movement of heavenly bodies are a focus of concern in many societies both past and present; what is required is a detailed appreciation of the specific ways in which the religious beliefs and practices of the period addressed such concerns as well as their role in shaping Bronze Age social and political relationships.

Acknowledgements

Thanks to Katharina Becker, Harry Fokkens, Anthony Harding, Brendan O'Connor, and Jo Sofaer for advice and information. I am grateful also to Regine Maraszek for arranging permission for the reproduction of Figure 25.1 and to Harry Fokkens for providing the original version of Figure 25.3. All errors are, of course, my own.

Suggested Reading

Hänsel, A. and Hänsel, B. (eds) 1997. *Gaben an die Götter. Schätze der Bronzezeit Europas* (Berlin: Freien Universität Berlin/Staatliche Museen zu Berlin).
Harding, A. 2000. *European society in the Bronze Age* (Cambridge: Cambridge University Press), ch. 9.
Huth, C. (ed.) 1996. *Archäologische Forschungen zum Kultgeschehen in der jüngeren Bronzezeit und frühen Eisenzeit Alteuropas* (Regensburg: Universitätsverlag Regensburg GmbH).
Kaul, F. 2004. *Bronzealderens religion* (Copenhagen: Det Kongelige Nordiske Oldskriftselskrab).
Meller, H. (ed.) 2004. *Der geschmiedete Himmel. Die weite Welt im Herzen Europas* (Stuttgart: Theiss).
Orrling, C. (ed.) 1998. *Communication in Bronze Age Europe: Transactions of the Bronze Age symposium in Tanumstrand, Bohuslän, Sweden, September 7–15, 1995* (Stockholm: Museum of National Antiquities Studies 9).

References

Almagro-Gorbea, M. 1996. 'Sacred places and cults of Late Bronze Age tradition in Celtic Hispania' in C. Huth (ed.), *Archäologische Forschungen zum Kultgeschehen in der jüngeren Bronzezeit und frühen Eisenzeit Alteuropas* (Regensburg: Universitätsverlag Regensburg GmbH), pp. 43–79.
Åström, P. 1987. 'Intentional destruction of gravegoods' in R. Laffineur (ed.), *Thanatos: les coutumes funéraires en Egée à l'Âge du Bronze* (Liège: Université de Liège), pp. 213–17.
Benton, S. 1931. 'The excavations of the Sculptor's Cave, Covesea, Morayshire', *Proceedings of the Society of Antiquaries of Scotland*, 65: 177–216.
Bertilsson, U. 1987. *The Rock Carvings of Northern Bohuslän: Spatial structures and social symbols* (Stockholm: Stockholm Studies in Archaeology 7).
Bošković, D. 1959. 'Quelques observations sur le char cultuel de Dupljaja', *Archaeologia Jugoslavica*, 3: 41–5.

Bowman, S. and Needham, S. 2007. 'The Dunaverney and Little Thetford flesh-hooks: History, technology and their position within the Later Bronze Age Atlantic zone feasting complex', *Antiquaries Journal*, 87: 53–108.

Bradley, R. 1990. *The Passage of Arms: An archaeological analysis of prehistoric hoards and votive deposits* (Cambridge: Cambridge University Press).

—— 1997. 'Death by water: Boats and footprints in the rock art of western Sweden', *Oxford Journal of Archaeology*, 16(3): 315–24.

—— 2000. *An Archaeology of Natural Places* (London: Routledge).

—— 2005. *Ritual and Domestic Life in Prehistoric Europe* (London: Routledge).

—— 2006. 'Danish razors and Swedish rocks: Cosmology and the Bronze Age landscape', *Antiquity*, 80: 372–89.

Broholm, H. C., Larsen, W. P. and Skjerne, G. 1949. *The Lures of the Bronze Age: An archæological, technical and musicological investigation* (Copenhagen: Gyldendal).

Brück, J. 1999a. 'Houses, lifecycles and deposition on Middle Bronze Age settlements in southern England', *Proceedings of the Prehistoric Society*, 65: 245–77.

—— 1999b. 'Ritual and rationality: Some problems of interpretation in European archaeology', *Journal of European Archaeology*, 2(3): 313–44.

—— 2006. 'Fragmentation, personhood and the social construction of technology in Middle and Late Bronze Age Britain', *Cambridge Archaeological Journal*, 16(2): 297–315.

Buck, D.-W. 1996. 'Symbolgut, Opferplätze und Deponierungsfunde der Lausitzer Gruppe' in C. Huth (ed.), *Archäologische Forschungen zum Kultgeschehen in der jüngeren Bronzezeit und frühen Eisenzeit Alteuropas* (Regensburg: Universitätsverlag Regensburg GmbH), pp. 271–300.

Budd, P. and Taylor, T. 1995. 'The faerie smith meets the bronze industry: Magic versus science in the interpretation of prehistoric metal-making', *World Archaeology*, 27(1): 133–43.

Burenhult, G. 1973. *The Rock Carvings of Götaland* (Lund: Gleerup).

Burgess, C. 1980. *The Age of Stonehenge* (London: J. M. Dent).

Burstow, G. P. and Holleyman, G. A. 1957. 'Late Bronze Age settlement on Itford Hill, Sussex', *Proceedings of the Prehistoric Society*, 23: 167–212.

Capelle, T. 1986. 'Schiffsetzungen', *Prähistorische Zeitschrift*, 61: 1–63.

Coles, B. 1990. 'Anthropomorphic wooden figures from Britain and Ireland', *Proceedings of the Prehistoric Society*, 56: 315–33.

Coles, J. 2003. 'And on they went... processions in Scandinavian Bronze Age rock carvings', *Acta Archaeologica*, 74: 221–50.

—— 2005. *Shadows of a Northern Past: Rock carvings of Bohuslän and Ostfold* (Oxford: Oxbow Books).

—— 2006. 'Beacon on the ridge: Rock carvings at Kasen Lövåsen, Bohuslän, Sweden', *Proceedings of the Prehistoric Society*, 72: 319–39.

—— and Harding, A. 1979. *The Bronze Age in Europe: An introduction to the prehistory of Europe, c.2000–700 BC* (London: Methuen).

——, Leach, P., Minnitt, S. C. et al. 1999. 'A later Bronze Age shield from South Cadbury, Somerset, England', *Antiquity*, 73: 33–48.

Elgee, H. W. and Elgee, F. 1949. 'An Early Bronze Age burial in a boat-shaped wooden coffin from north-east Yorkshire', *Proceedings of the Prehistoric Society*, 15: 87–106.

Fendin, T. 2000. 'Fertility and the repetitive partition: Grinding as a social construction', *Lund Archaeological Review*, 6: 85–97.

FONTIJN, D. 2002. *Sacrificial Landscapes: Cultural biographies of persons, objects and 'natural' places in the Bronze Age of the Netherlands, c.2300–600 BC* (Leiden: Faculty of Archaeology, University of Leiden).

FURMÁNEK, V. and JAKAB, J. 1997. 'Menschliche Skelettreste aus bronzezeitlichen Siedlungen in der Slowakei' in K.-F. Rittershofer (ed.), *Sonderbestattungen in der Bronzezeit im östlichen Mitteleuropa. Kolloquium der Arbeitsgemeinschaft Bronzezeit in Pottenstein 1990* (Espelkamp: Verlag Marie Leidorf), pp. 14–23.

—— and VLADÁR, J. 1996. 'Kultstätten und Votivdeponierungen in der Bronzezeit Slowakei' in C. Huth (ed.), *Archäologische Forschungen zum Kultgeschehen in der jüngeren Bronzezeit und frühen Eisenzeit Alteuropas* (Regensburg: Universitätsverlag Regensburg GmbH), pp. 497–516.

GEDL, M. and SZYBOWICZ, B. 1997. 'Bestattungen in bronzezeitlichen Siedlungen Polens' in K.-F. Rittershofer (ed.), *Sonderbestattungen in der Bronzezeit im östlichen Mitteleuropa. Kolloquium der Arbeitsgemeinschaft Bronzezeit in Pottenstein 1990* (Espelkamp: Verlag Marie Leidorf), pp. 24–41.

GELLING, P. and DAVIDSON, P. 1969. *The Chariot of the Sun and other Rites and Symbols of the Northern Bronze Age* (London: J. M. Dent and Sons, Ltd).

GERRITSEN, F.A. 1999. 'To build and to abandon: The cultural biography of late prehistoric farmhouses in the southern Netherlands', *Archaeological Dialogues*, 6: 78–114.

GESELL, G. C. 1983. 'The place of the goddess in Minoan Society' in O. Krzyszkowska and L. Nixon (eds), *Minoan Society: Proceedings of the Cambridge Colloquium 1981* (Bristol: Bristol Classical Press), pp. 93–9.

—— 1985. *Town, Palace and House Cult in Minoan Crete* (Göteborg: Paul Åströms Förlag).

GLOB, P. V. 1973. *The Mound People: Danish Bronze-Age man preserved* (London: Book Club Associates).

GOLDHAHN, J. 1999. 'Rock art and the materialisation of a cosmology: The case of the Sagaholm barrow' in J. Goldhahn (ed.), *Rock Art as Social Representation*, BAR International Series 794 (Oxford: BAR), pp. 77–100.

HANSEN, S. 1994. *Studien zu den Metalldeponierungen während der älteren Urnenfelderzeit zwischen Rhônetal und Karpatenbecken* (Bonn: Universitätsforschungen zur prähistorischen Archäologie 21).

HEY, G. 2006. 'Scale and archaeological evaluations: What are we looking for?' in G. Lock and B. L. Molyneaux (eds), *Confronting Scale in Archaeology: Issues of theory and practice* (New York: Springer), pp. 113–27.

HINGLEY, R. 1997. 'Iron, ironworking and regeneration: A study of the symbolic meaning of metalworking in Iron Age Britain' in A. Gwilt and C. Haselgrove (eds), *Reconstructing Iron Age societies: New approaches to the British Iron Age* (Oxford: Oxbow), pp. 9–18.

HOCHSIEDER, P. and KNÖSEL, D. 1995. *Les Taules a Menorca: un estudi arqueo-astronòmica* (Mahón: Institut Menorquí d'Estudis).

HOOF, L. VAN and MEURKENS, L. 2007. 'Rhenen-Remmerden revisited: Some comments regarding site structure and the visibility of Bronze Age house plans' in S. Arnoldussen and H. Fokkens (eds), *Bronze Age Settlements in the Low Countries* (Oxford: Oxbow), pp. 81–93.

HUNDT, H.-J. 1955. 'Versuch zur Deutung der Depotfunde der nordischen jüngeren Bronzezeit, unter besonderer Berücksichtigung Mecklenburgs', *Jahrbuch des Römisch-Germanischen Zentralmuseums*, 2: 95–140.

INSOLL, T. 2007. '"Natural" or "human" spaces? Tallensi sacred groves and shrines and their potential implications for aspects of Northern European prehistory and phenomenological interpretation', *Norwegian Archaeological Review*, 40(2): 138–58.

——2008. 'Negotiating the archaeology of destiny: An exploration of interpretative possibilities through Tallensi shrines', *Journal of Social Archaeology*, 8(3): 380–403.

JACOB, C. 1995. *Metallgefässe der Bronze- und Hallstattzeit in Nordwest-, West- und Süddeutschland*, Prähistorische Bronzefunde Band 9 (Stuttgart: Steiner).

JOCKENHÖVEL, A. 1974. 'Eine Bronzeamphore des 8. Jahrhunderts v. Chr. von Gevelinghausen, Kr. Meschede, (Sauerland)', *Germania*, 52: 16–54.

KALICZ-SCHREIBER, R. 1991. 'Die spätbronzezitliche Gräberfeld in Budapest', *Praehistorische Zeitschrift*, 66: 161–96.

KAUL, F. 1998. *Ships on Bronzes. A study in Bronze Age religion and iconography* (Copenhagen: National Museum).

——2004a. *Bronzealderens Religion* (Copenhagen: Det Kongelige Nordiske Oldskriftselskrab).

——2004b. 'Der Sonnenwagen von Trundholm' in H. Meller (ed.), *Der geschmiedete Himmel. Die weite Welt im Herzen Europas* (Stuttgart: Theiss), pp. 54–7.

——2004c. 'Die Sonnenschiffe des Nordens' in H. Meller (ed.), *Der geschmiedete Himmel. Die weite Welt im Herzen Europas* (Stuttgart: Theiss), pp. 58–63.

——2004d. 'Schiffe als "Tempel" der Bronzezeit—die Figurenensembles von Fårdal und Grevensvaenge' in H. Meller (ed.), *Der geschmiedete Himmel. Die weite Welt im Herzen Europas* (Stuttgart: Theiss), pp. 71–3.

KEMENCZEI, T. 2003. 'Bronze Age metallurgy' in Z. Visy (ed.), *Hungarian Archaeology at the Turn of the Millennium* (Budapest: Ministry of National Cultural Heritage), pp. 167–74.

KERSTEN, K. 1936. 'Das Totenhaus von Grünhof-Tesperhude, Kreis Herzogtum Lauenburg', *Offa*, 1: 56–87.

KOSSACK, G. 1954. *Studien zur Symbolgut der Urnenfelder- und Hallstattzeit Mitteleuropas*, Römisch-Germanisch Forschungen 20 (Berlin: de Gruyter).

KRISTIANSEN, K. 1998. *Europe before History* (Cambridge: Cambridge University Press).

——and LARSSON, T. B. 2005. *The Rise of Bronze Age Society: Travels, transmissions and transformations* (Cambridge: Cambridge University Press).

LARSSON, T. B. 1998. 'Symbols in a European Bronze Age cosmology' in C. Orrling (ed.), *Communication in Bronze Age Europe: Transactions of the Bronze Age symposium in Tanumstrand, Bohuslän, Sweden, September 7–15, 1995* (Stockholm: Museum of National Antiquities Studies 9), pp. 9–16.

LYNN, C. J. 1977. 'Trial excavations at the King's Stables, Tray Townland, County Armagh', *Ulster Journal of Archaeology*, 40: 42–62.

MAIER, S. 1997. 'Klingende Zeugen der Bronzezeit. Die ältesten spielbaren Blechinstrumente aus den Opfermooren Nordeuropas' in A. Hänsel and B. Hänsel (eds), *Gaben an die Götter. Schätze der Bronzezeit Europas* (Berlin: Freien Universität Berlin/Staatliche Museen zu Berlin), pp. 77–81.

MALMER, M. 1981. *A Chronological Study of North European Rock Art* (Stockholm: Almqvist and Wiksell).

MARASZEK, R. 1997. 'Kultgerät im mittleren Oderraum: die Deichselwagen' in A. Hänsel and B. Hänsel (eds), *Gaben an die Götter. Schätze der Bronzezeit Europas* (Berlin: Freien Universität Berlin/Staatliche Museen zu Berlin), pp. 71–5.

MELLER, H. 2004a. 'Der Körper des Königs' in H. Meller (ed.), *Der geschmiedete Himmel. Die weite Welt im Herzen Europas* (Stuttgart: Theiss), pp. 94–7.

——2004b. 'Die Himmelsscheibe von Nebra' in H. Meller (ed.), *Der geschmiedete Himmel. Die weite Welt im Herzen Europas* (Stuttgart: Theiss), pp. 22–31.

NEBELSICK, L. 2000. 'Rent asunder: Ritual violence in late Bronze Age hoards' in C. Pare (ed.), *Metals Make the World Go Round: The supply and circulation of metals in Bronze Age Europe* (Oxford: Oxbow Books), pp. 160–75.

NORDBLADH, J. 1989. 'Armour and fighting in the South Scandinavian Bronze Age, especially in view of rock art representations' in T. Larsson and H. Lundmark (eds), *Approaches to Swedish Prehistory: A spectrum of problems and perspectives in contemporary research*, British Archaeological Reports International Series 500 (Oxford: BAR), pp. 323–33.

NOWAKOWSKI, J. 1991. 'Trethellan Farm, Newquay: The excavation of a lowland Bronze Age settlement and Iron Age cemetery', *Cornish Archaeology*, 30: 5–242.

OSGOOD, R. and MONKS, S. 2000. *Bronze Age Warfare* (Stroud: Sutton).

PARE, C. 1989. 'From Dupljaja to Delphi: The ceremonial use of the wagon in later prehistory', *Antiquity*, 63: 80–100.

PÁSZTOR, E. and ROSLUND, C. 2007. 'An interpretation of the Nebra disc', *Antiquity*, 81: 267–78.

PEATFIELD, A. 1992. 'Rural ritual in Bronze Age Crete: The peak sanctuary at Atsipadhes', *Cambridge Archaeological Journal*, 2(1): 59–87.

PESCHENK, C. 1972. 'Ein reicher Grabfund mit Kesselwagen aus Unterfranken', *Germania*, 50: 29–56.

RANDSBORG, K. 1993. 'Kivik. Archaeology and iconography', *Acta Archaeologica*, 64(1): 1–147.

RENFREW, A. C. 1974. 'Beyond a subsistence economy: The evolution of prehistoric Europe' in C. B. Moore (ed.), *Reconstructing Complex Societies*, Supplement to the Bulletin of the American Schools of Oriental Research 20 (Cambridge, MA), pp. 69–95.

RØNNE, P. 2004. 'Guss und Verzierung der Nordischen Krummschwerter' in H. Meller (ed.), *Der geschmiedete Himmel. Die weite Welt im Herzen Europas* (Stuttgart: Theiss), pp. 64–5.

RUTKOWSKI, B. 1986. *The Cult Places of the Aegean* (New Haven: Yale University Press).

SCHAUER, P. 1981. 'Urnenfelderzeitlicher Opferplätze in Höhlen und Felsspalten' in H. Lorenz (ed.), *Studien zur Bronzezeit. Festschrift für Wilhelm Albert von Brunn* (Mainz: Philipp von Zabern), pp. 403–18.

——1986. *Die Goldblechkegel der Bronzezeit—Ein Beitrag zur Kulturverbindung zwischen Orient und Mitteleuropa* (Bonn: Habelt).

——1996. 'Naturheilige Plätze, Opferstätten, Deponierungsfunde und Sybolgut der jüngeren Bronzezeit Süddeutschlands' in C. Huth (ed.), *Archäologische Forschungen zum Kultgeschehen in der jüngeren Bronzezeit und frühen Eisenzeit Alteuropas* (Regensburg: Universitätsverlag Regensburg GmbH), pp. 381–416.

SCHLOSSER, W. 2004. 'Die Himmelsscheibe von Nebra—astronomische Untersuchungen' in H. Meller (ed.), *Der geschmiedete Himmel. Die weite Welt im Herzen Europas* (Stuttgart: Theiss), pp. 44–7.

SCHWARTZ, R. 2004a. 'Äxte aus dem Hohen Norden—zur geschichte der Bronzeaxt aus Hermannshagen' in H. Meller (ed.), *Der geschmiedete Himmel. Die weite Welt im Herzen Europas* (Stuttgart: Theiss), pp. 178–9.

——2004b. 'Mit der Vogelbarke ins Totenreich—das Beil aus Osternienburg' in H. Meller (ed.), *Der geschmiedete Himmel. Die weite Welt im Herzen Europas* (Stuttgart: Theiss), pp. 78–9.

SCHWENZER, S. 1997. '"Wanderer kommst Du nach Spa...". Der Opferplatz von Berlin-Spandau. Ein Heiligtum für Krieger, Händler und Reisende' in A. Hänsel and B. Hänsel (eds.), *Gaben an die Götter. Schätze der Bronzezeit Europas* (Berlin: Freien Universität Berlin/Staatliche Museen zu Berlin), pp. 61–6.

SHEPHERD, I. A. G. 2007. '"An awesome place": The Late Bronze Age use of the Sculptor's Cave, Covesea, Moray' in C. Burgess, P. Topping, and F. Lynch (eds), *Beyond Stonehenge: Essays on the Bronze Age in honour of Colin Burgess* (Oxford: Oxbow Books), pp. 194–203.

SPRINGER, T. 1999. 'The golden cone of Ezelsdorf-Buch: A masterpiece of the goldsmith's art from the Bronze Age' in K Demakopoulou, C. Eluère, J. Jensen et al. (eds), *Gods and Heroes of the European Bronze Age* (London: Thames and Hudson), pp. 176–81.

SPROCKHOFF, E. 1955. 'Das bronzene Zierband von Kronshagen bei Kiel. Eine Ornamentstudie zur Vorgeschichte der Vogelsonnenbarke', *Offa*, 14: 5–120.

THERKORN, L. 2007. 'Marking while taking land into use: Some indications for long-term traditions within the Oer-IJ estuarine region' in S. Arnoldussen and H. Fokkens (eds), *Bronze Age Settlements in the Low Countries* (Oxford: Oxbow), pp. 149–64.

TILLEY, C. 1999. *Metaphor and Material Culture* (Oxford: Blackwell).

TORBRÜGGE, W. 1971. 'Vor- und Frühgeschichtliche Flussfunde. Zur Ordnung und Bestimmung einer Denkmälergruppe', *Bericht der Römisch-Germanisch Kommission*, 51–2: 1–146.

VASIC, V. and VASIC, R. 2000. 'Funcion depuradora de los humedales 1: una revision bibliografica sobre el papel de los macrofitos', *Sehumed*, 16: 131–9.

WALDREN, W. 1982. *Balearic Prehistoric Ecology and Culture: The excavation and study of certain caves, rock shelters and settlements*, British Archaeological Reports, International Series 149 (Oxford: BAR).

WARMENBOL, E. 1996. 'L'or, la mort et les Hyperboréens. La bouche des enfers ou le Trou de Han à Han-sur-Lesse' in C. Huth (ed.), *Archäologische Forschungen zum Kultgeschehen in der jüngeren Bronzezeit und frühen Eisenzeit Alteuropas* (Regensburg: Universitätsverlag Regensburg GmbH), pp. 203–34.

WATERBOLK, H. and VAN ZEIST, W. 1961. 'A Bronze Age sanctuary in the raised bog at Bargeroosterveld (Dr.)', *Helinium*, 1: 5–19.

WYSS, R. 1996. 'Funde von Pässen, Höhen, aus Quellen und Gewässern der Zentral- und Westalpen' in C. Huth (ed.), *Archäologische Forschungen zum Kultgeschehen in der jüngeren Bronzezeit und frühen Eisenzeit Alteuropas* (Regensburg: Universitätsverlag Regensburg GmbH), pp. 417–28.

CHAPTER 26

THE IRON AGE

JODY JOY

1 INTRODUCTION

THE popular image of Iron Age religion is of religious ceremonies, officiated by druids in sacred groves. Scholarly accounts utilize two main sources of evidence: literary and archaeological. Many are based on evidence gathered largely from classical texts and early medieval Irish and Welsh literature (e.g. Ross 1967; Green 1986). The archaeological evidence which is put forward is often comprised of data which cannot easily be explained by functional interpretations, or common sense. Few studies integrate both literary and archaeological evidence well. A dichotomy can also be observed between accounts based on literary evidence which examine religion and archaeological evidence which is often interpreted as evidence for symbolic, ritual activity.

The chronological and geographical scope of this chapter stretches from 800 BC–first century AD and focuses on Western Europe, particularly Britain and France. This in part reflects biases in the literary evidence and previous work. There are parallels between debates over religion and the notion of the Celts (see Collis 2003). Some studies specifically refer to 'Celtic' rather than Iron Age religion and its distribution is often seen to match the distribution of Celts. Like interpretations of Celts, universal accounts are also popular and similarity in religious beliefs is often implied across large geographical areas and over long time spans.

In this chapter the existence of a single universal European Iron Age religion is refuted. Although regional and temporal similarities can be observed, the specific details of practice are different. Instead it is argued that for the most part Iron Age religion was practised on a local scale. Relationships with the supernatural were negotiated within systems of belief that were intimately bound up and connected with every other aspect of life.

2 LITERARY EVIDENCE

Like Celtic Art, studies of Iron Age religion occupy their own niche, separate from mainstream archaeology. Studies largely reliant on the literary evidence are perceived by many Iron Age specialists to lack credibility (Fitzpatrick 2007: 289) as an idealized, universal picture of religion is presented (Fitzpatrick 1991) following a straightforward, uncritical application of the literature (Webster 1994: 1). The way in which textual sources are applied also displays an element of 'pick and choose archaeology': something is mentioned in a text and evidence is then sought from the archaeological record to back it up. Evidence to the contrary is often ignored. Recent trends in archaeological theory also mean that site-specific or regional explanations are often favoured over universal accounts (see Collis 2008: 35). As a consequence many Iron Age specialists now avoid references to religion, or evidence derived from classical and medieval texts, preferring instead to examine ritual practice.

Use of writing was limited among Iron Age peoples (although see Williams 2007) but accounts of them are documented in contemporary Greco-Roman texts. These date to as early as the sixth century BC, but the majority were written after 120 BC when the Romans came into direct contact with Iron Age peoples in southern France (Webster 1995a: 445). It is possible to highlight general themes in this evidence. There are descriptions of different gods (Cunliffe 2005: 573) and there is also broad agreement that people believed in an afterlife (Wait 1995: 491; Cunliffe 2005: 572). A group of religious specialists, the Druids, are referred to by 20 classical authors (see Kendrick 1927; Piggott 1968; Green 1997; Webster 1999: table 1). A broadly consistent account of the Druids as philosophers is portrayed by writers during the second and first centuries BC (Webster 1999: 4; Fitzpatrick 2007: 289). Caesar describes the Druids as a group of religious specialists who acted as intermediaries with the gods. In addition to officiating at religious ceremonies, the Druids also acted as judges arbitrating disputes and as teachers of religious knowledge (Webster 1999: 6; Fitzpatrick 2007: 290). First century AD writers place a different emphasis, describing Druids as magicians or seers (Webster 1999: 4), or portraying them as healers, detailing the importance of natural foci to Iron Age religion, such as sacred groves (Fitzpatrick 2007: 289). Some authors also state that human sacrifice was undertaken (see Webster 1999: table 1; Cunliffe 2005: 573).

There are a number of problems associated with the classical literary evidence. Contemporary classical texts were produced by an external, conquering society (Webster 1995a: 445). Specific passages may have been included to make a moral argument rather than to document historical fact and we cannot be certain of their veracity (see discussion of Tacitus in Hutton 2007: 3–6). As we have seen, the majority of accounts of Iron Age religion were written by Romans describing practices in Gaul in the second–first century BC. These cannot easily be projected backwards in time, or to other regions. Many descriptions relate Iron Age practices to Roman counterparts. For example, the roles of various gods are often equated with, or converted to, their closest Roman equivalent (Webster 1995b; Cunliffe 2005: 573). Other significant practices may have been missed or ignored. For example, the emphasis on the natural elements of Iron Age religion reflect a concern for nature in classical religion (Webster 1995a) and the change in emphasis noted in the literature of the first century AD (see Wait 1985: 204) could be an entirely literary construct (Webster 1995a: 448).

Data gathered from medieval Irish and Welsh literature, written in the vernacular, have also been used as sources of evidence. The literature describes popular myths, first written down by Christian monks. Many of these myths are thought to have ancient origins (Green 1995a: 482) and evidence from these texts has been backtracked onto the Iron Age. Since the mid-1980s the veracity of the Irish and Welsh vernacular literature has been questioned by historians (see Hutton 1991: 144–50). For example, we do not know what influence the Christian beliefs of the monks played in determining the information recorded (Wait 1985: 12). Monks were also influenced by Greco-Roman literature and it is possible old deities were fitted into a structure inspired by classical religion (Hutton 1991: 296). The age of the texts has also been questioned and few now believe many are older than the eighth century AD, meaning that the pre-Christian past was already semi-mythical before these texts were written (ibid.: 148).

It is important to note that many of the older studies of religion are heavily reliant on Irish and Welsh texts. In addition to the problems with these sources highlighted by historians, the methodology often applied in these accounts of religion was also problematic. Many sought to find similarities between medieval Irish and Welsh and classical texts as a means of validation. However, as Fitzpatrick pointed out, using this approach religion is presented as 'timeless'; 'a tradition flowing uninterrupted from the pre-Roman Iron Age to the medieval' (1991: 127), and temporal changes and spatial differences are lost, despite the fact that the classical literary evidence indicates changes in practices and beliefs over time as different authors describe different time spans and encounter different groups of people (Nash 1976: 120; Webster 1999: 8). As Webster (1997) has noted for deposition in wells and shafts, there is also a danger of 'text expectations': because something is mentioned in texts it must therefore have happened.

Despite problems with the nature of the evidence and its interpretation in the past, classical texts *are* contemporary accounts of Iron Age religion and used critically potentially contain much information (Webster 1995a: 445).

3 ARCHAEOLOGICAL EVIDENCE

Although recent work has examined everyday ritual practices (see below) for the most part archaeological evidence for Iron Age ritual activity has been attributed to data which cannot be explained easily by functional or practical means (see Brück 1999; Insoll 2004). This section of the chapter is divided into depositional types and contexts, which have been interpreted as evidence for religious beliefs and ritual practice. As with other archaeological accounts of Iron Age ritual and religion this could also be described as a list of the 'unexplainable'.

3.1 Shrines and 'Sacred' Spaces

Occasionally formalized structures, which have been interpreted as shrines or sacred spaces, can be recognized, although it must be emphasized that evidence for prescribed ritual space elsewhere is rare. The term *Viereckshanzen*, or quadrangular enclosure, describes a series of rectilinear enclosures defined by an earth bank and ditch, enclosing an area of about 1 ha. Originally used to describe sites from Bavaria, the term has been extended to sites across Europe (see Büchsenschütz and Olivier 1989). It was widely assumed that these sites served a common cult function, although Webster (1995a: 453) has questioned this interpretation suggesting that the category may cross-cut a variety of site types, and some may have been settlements (see Büchsenschütz and Olivier 1989).

Following extensive excavations in northern France another type of site has been uncovered defined by large deposits of artefacts, and human and animal remains, and often structures, within an enclosure (see Brunaux 1988: 12). Similar sites dating to the late Iron Age have also been discovered in Britain, for example at Hayling Island and Harlow (Drury 1980; King and Soffe 2001; Haselgrove 2005). They have been interpreted as sanctuaries with offerings and ritual activities taking place within the enclosure. The most famous French site is Gournay-sur-Aronde (Brunaux 1988: 13–16). Dating from the fourth–first centuries BC, it is located on the slope of a valley near a stream, on the borders of four tribal territories. A huge number of artefacts were deposited including more than 2,000 broken weapons and 3,000 animal bones in a single ditch dated to the second century BC.

These temple sites are quite common in France and they provide evidence for complex rituals and ceremonies which have been formalized through human division of space. They show similarities in form and construction but detailed excavation has revealed that often very complicated but significantly different practices occurred at each of them.

3.2 Iconography

There are very few representations of gods. The majority that survive are made of stone. There are a small number of wooden figures, often from watery contexts, but as wood rarely survives we do not know how widespread they were. In Britain and Ireland (Coles 1990: table 1) anthropomorphic wooden figurines have been discovered dating from the Bronze Age–fourth century BC. These include figures standing in a small boat from Roos Carr, Holderness. A large assemblage of wooden carvings of humans and bits of humans were also recovered from Sources de la Seine, France in 1963 (Deyts 1983). These date from the first century BC–first century AD and are very different in character to the British and Irish figures (Coles 1990: 329). Deyts (1983: 167–72) interpreted them as votive offerings.

Stone carvings are also rare. Up to fifty miniature chalk carvings have been discovered in East Yorkshire on Iron Age and Roman sites. Many of these represent a warrior with a sword positioned on the back. Stead (1988) interpreted these as representing a god, mythical figure, or ancestor and suggested they had a ritual or magical function. A series of early Iron Age statues have been discovered in Baden-Württemberg, Germany. One of the most famous is the statue from Hirshlenden, Germany, of a warrior wearing a neck-ring which originally stood on top of a burial mound dating to 500 BC, or later (Megaw and Megaw 2001: 45). The deceased could have had the status of a warrior, or perhaps some religious authority (see Fitzpatrick 2007: 304). Another is the ragstone head from Mšecké Žehrovice, near Prague, Czech Republic. It depicts a stylized image of a moustachioed male wearing a neck-ring or torque, which has been interpreted as depicting a deity (Green 1997: 59), or hero (Venclová 1998).

3.3 Time

Inscribed bronze plaques from Coligny and Villards d'Héra in France have been interpreted as calendars. Although these date to the late second or early third centuries AD, they are different from Roman calendars and the language used is Gaulish or Gallo-Latin (Fitzpatrick 1996: 385–6). Ross (1995: 433) suggested that the Coligny calendar represents a system of dividing time derived from the knowledge of the Druids. Whether or not the information is derived from Druids, there is consensus that these calendars represent knowledge from pre-Roman times (Fitzpatrick 1996: 386), indicating astronomical knowledge and the ordering of time.

3.4 Burials

Burials provide the most abundant evidence for Iron Age beliefs; the dead are buried by the living and burials are primary evidence for the motivations and beliefs of past peoples (Parker Pearson 1999). Burial practices vary significantly. For example, in Britain from the fifth–first centuries BC two regional inhumation burial rites in East Yorkshire and Devon and Cornwall can be observed (Whimster 1977; Ashbee 1979; Dent 1985; Cunliffe 1988; Nowakowski 1991; Stead 1991a). Middle Iron Age burials elsewhere are uncommon, although some inhumation cemeteries, sited just outside settlements have been recently discovered (e.g. King et al. 1996; Hey et al. 1999; Cunliffe and Poole 2000: 152–70). Cremation burials occur in south-east England (see Birchall 1965; Stead 1976) after 100 BC. Later, local burial traditions can also be identified, for example in south Dorset (Wheeler 1943; Woodward 1993) and Gloucestershire (Staelens 1982).

Rituals associated with the disposal of the dead were often complex. In many cases, interrogation of what may first appear to be a simple deposit reveals a complicated series of preceding events. In southern England throughout the Iron Age, complete bodies and bits of bodies were deposited at settlement sites in pits, ditches and enclosure boundaries (Whimster 1981; Hill 1995; Carr and Knüsel 1997). Several stages, or separate rituals can explain the presence of these bits of bodies. The dead were exposed (perhaps in open pits and ditches, or on platforms) and allowed to decompose for a period before some bits were selected and incorporated into pit or enclosure deposits (Carr and Knüsel 1997: 171). We do not know what happened to the rest of the body, or why some body parts were selected for deposition and not others but there is evidence that some body parts were favoured above others. For example, at some sites skull fragments are more common than other parts of the skeleton (Cunliffe 2005: 552–3).

British burials have been interpreted in many different ways. It is often assumed that people were buried with grave-goods for use in another life. This is seen as proof of belief in the existence of 'other-worlds'. However, not all people were buried with grave-goods and practices varied widely over time and space, suggesting that this belief was not universal, or that to some access to the afterlife was achieved by different means. Indeed, for large parts of the Iron Age in Britain we do not know how people disposed of their dead as no archaeologically visible remains survive. In other societies practising exposure it is believed that the newly dead occupy a liminal state and the soul can only be freed from the body through decomposition. Carr and Knüsel (1997: 168–9) suggest it was important for people to see and smell the decay of bodies and witness the transition from the human to spirit world. The adoption of cremation in south-east England has been used to support evidence from classical authors indicating belief in a human soul and reincarnation as the spirit is released from the body by fire. However, as Fitzpatrick (1997: 239) argues, the association between cremation and the existence of a soul is not universal and the adoption of a new burial rite does not necessarily indicate new religious beliefs.

Fitzpatrick (1997) illustrated the different rituals associated with cremation and burial at Westhampnett, West Sussex, a large cemetery containing over 160 cremation burials. To one side of the cemetery four enclosures were uncovered, which have been interpreted as shrines or a religious site. The remains of cremation pyres were also found on the perimeter of the cemetery. Fitzpatrick (ibid.: 241) suggested a possible sequence of rites undertaken at the site. After death the deceased was adorned in the costume appropriate to age, sex, and status. The body was then carried to the religious site and laid out. Pyre material was gathered and the pyre constructed. Animals were sacrificed and the deceased was placed on the pyre, which was then lit and the body cremated. The pyre was left to cool; afterwards human bone was collected and a selection representative of all parts of the body, costume fittings, and animal remains removed. The pyre site was dug over and the burnt pots smashed. The selected human, costume, and animal remains were taken to the cemetery, wrapped in a cloth or placed in a bag. A grave was dug, in it was placed the wrapped cremated remains, pots and wooden vessels. The burial was then covered with straw and filled in. The final act was to erect a marker for the grave. Each of these stages was suggested to have been marked by ceremonies and rituals and the whole process could have occurred over an extended period of time.

Across much of Britain from the fourth century BC–first century AD there is a tradition of burials with offensive weapons, like swords or spears (Collis 1973; Hunter 2005: 50–6). These graves are relatively rare but are found in all of the 'formal' burial traditions identified above. They are often interpreted as the graves of warriors or seen as evidence for a warrior cult. Although there is a broad tradition of 'warrior burial', the exact details of each burial are different, meaning that the ceremonies, rituals and local context of beliefs leading to each was different (see Price 2008 who makes this point in his interpretation of Viking ship burials). The same argument could also be put forward for burials with mirrors (Joy 2010), or cremation burials containing feasting equipment.

3.5 Bog Bodies

Well-preserved human remains have also been discovered in bogs in Britain, Ireland, Denmark, the Netherlands, and north-west Germany. They date from 500 BC–AD 100 and many show signs of violent death or 'overkill' (see Asingh 2007; Joy 2009). Describing this evidence and drawing on information from classical texts, Glob (1969) believed these people were victims of ritual sacrifice. They were deposited in bogs as offerings to the gods and may have gone willingly to their deaths, or were perhaps prisoners of war or criminals. However, bog bodies are found over an extended period of time and across a wide geographical area and although practices may be related there can be no single explanation as to why people were placed in bogs. Kelly (2006), for example, noted that many Irish bog bodies were found close to ancient land boundaries, suggesting that the bodies served a protective function.

3.6 Watery Deposition

Deposition of well-made artefacts, particularly weaponry, in watery deposits such as rivers, lakes, and bogs has long drawn attention (e.g. Fitzpatrick 1984; Bradley 1990). Significant quantities of metalwork have been recovered from some rivers in Britain and Ireland, particularly the Thames, Witham, and Bann (Garrow 2008: 27; MacDonald 2007: 178). Of the material discovered in the Thames there is a definite bias towards weaponry, particularly spears, swords, and daggers, although it should be emphasized that coins, currency bars, cauldrons, and brooches have also been discovered (Fitzpatrick 1984: 179, table 12.1). Unlike many Bronze Age artefacts, deliberate breakage was not an important consideration as the majority of artefacts were deposited undamaged (MacDonald 2007: 178).

In continental Europe deposits of artefacts have also been discovered in ancient riverbeds around Lake Neuchâtel, Switzerland, at La Tène, Cornaux, and Port Nidau (Bradley 1990: 157). At La Tène, over a period of 40 years, excavators discovered hundreds of objects, particularly weapons such as swords (see de Navarro 1972), but also items of jewellery, tools, pots, quern-stones, and cauldrons, as well as human and animal remains (Vouga 1923; Dunning 1991; Egloff 1991). Although poorly excavated, many of these objects were found in a former channel of the River Thielle, between the remains of two bridges or jetties constructed in the mid-third century BC (Bradley 1990: 157; Parker Pearson in Field and Parker Pearson 1993: 179; MacDonald 2007: 175). De Navarro (1972: 17) noted that some artefacts were damaged before they were deposited. A submerged bridge was also discovered a few kilometres from La Tène, at Cornaux-Les Sauges (Egloff 1987: 30; Dunning 1991: 368). It is dated to around 300 BC and was repaired in 120–116 BC (Parker Pearson in Field and Parker Pearson 2003: 181). Like La Tène, artefacts uncovered include weapons and tools as well as animal and human remains (ibid.). At Port Nidau, 60 swords and an equal number of spearheads as well as a helmet were discovered from an ancient course of the River Zihl (Müller 1991: 528).

As objects in water could not easily be retrieved, it has long been suggested that artefacts were placed in water as an offering to a deity or god and that water was numinous in Iron Age religion (e.g. de Navarro 1972: 17; Fitzpatrick 1984: 183). Deposits were made from natural locations as well as man-made structures such as causeways and jetties. Deposition in a lake at Llyn Cerrig Bach, Anglesey is thought to have been from a natural rock platform (Fox 1947: 69–70), or possibly a causeway (MacDonald 2007: 174). Objects, including swords and spears, were also found in the River Witham at Fiskerton, Lincolnshire, next to a wooden causeway (Field and Parker Pearson 2003). The quantity of objects deposited varied, ranging from single deposits to hundreds, even thousands of objects. Weapons were frequently selected for deposition and many artefacts were deliberately broken. Deliberate breakage has been interpreted as 'ritual killing' of the artefact (see discussion in MacDonald 2007: 172). Human remains discovered at La Tène, in the Thames (although many of these date to the Bronze Age) and at Llyn Cerrig Bach, have prompted speculation that some artefacts were deposited as a part of burials, or even that human sacrifices took place (for discussions of sacrifice see Webster 1994: 6–8; Aldhouse Green 2001; Hutton 2007: 130–3). Animal bone could represent the remains of feasts accompanying depositional acts. There were no butchery marks on the animal bone from Llyn Cerrig Bach indicating that animals could have been sacrificed (MacDonald 2007: 185).

This data hints at the varied and complicated rituals associated with watery deposition. Many artefacts deposited in rivers in Britain, such as the Battersea Shield (Figure 26.1) and Waterloo Helmet, are well made and ornamented with art. Because of this they are usually considered to have been made for and used by the elite. This raises the question of what were the social and religious contexts and motivations for their deposition and should these necessarily be viewed separately (Fitzpatrick 1984: 185). Despite similarities in the data,

FIGURE 26.1 The Battersea Shield discovered in the River Thames near Battersea.

practices varied markedly over time and space. Clearly water was important to Iron Age beliefs and objects may have been deposited as propriety offerings but practices and rituals differed, implying that different kinds of offerings were being made to different gods for different reasons.

3.7 Hoards

Deposition of metalwork such as coins, torques, and weapons also occurred in non-watery contexts. For example, up to 25 hoards of gold neck-rings, or torques, and coins have been discovered across Central and Western Europe (Fitzpatrick 2005: 159), the majority date from the third–first centuries BC (ibid.: 174–82). At Snettisham, Norfolk at least 12 hoards of objects, including torques, coins, and ingots dating from the second–first centuries BC have been discovered (Stead 1991b) (Figure 26.2).

Unlike watery deposits, hoards can easily be retrieved and many have been interpreted as being deposited for safe-keeping in troubled times. For example, Stead (ibid.: 455–63) suggested that the remains from Snettisham were hidden as a 'treasury' with the intention of retrieval. More recently this type of common-sense interpretation has been contested as patterns in the positioning and composition of artefacts in hoards have been uncovered. Often hoards are placed in significant positions in the landscape, on hills or in the boundary ditches of settlements (see Hingley 1990, 2005). Deposition at Snettisham was on Ken Hill, an area of higher ground. Excavation of the site in the early 1990s also revealed a large enclosure but it is not certain if it is contemporary. Many of the artefacts were deliberately damaged, some were even melted. These factors caused Fitzpatrick (1992) to argue that it is not possible to rule out the interpretation that the Snettisham deposits were votive. Many other hoards contain artefacts that were deliberately broken or artefacts that could have easily been recycled. The hoards of torques and coins were buried close to springs or lakes, or within man-made enclosures; specific types of coin were also selected and torques were often broken before they were deposited (Fitzpatrick 2005: 172). As a result

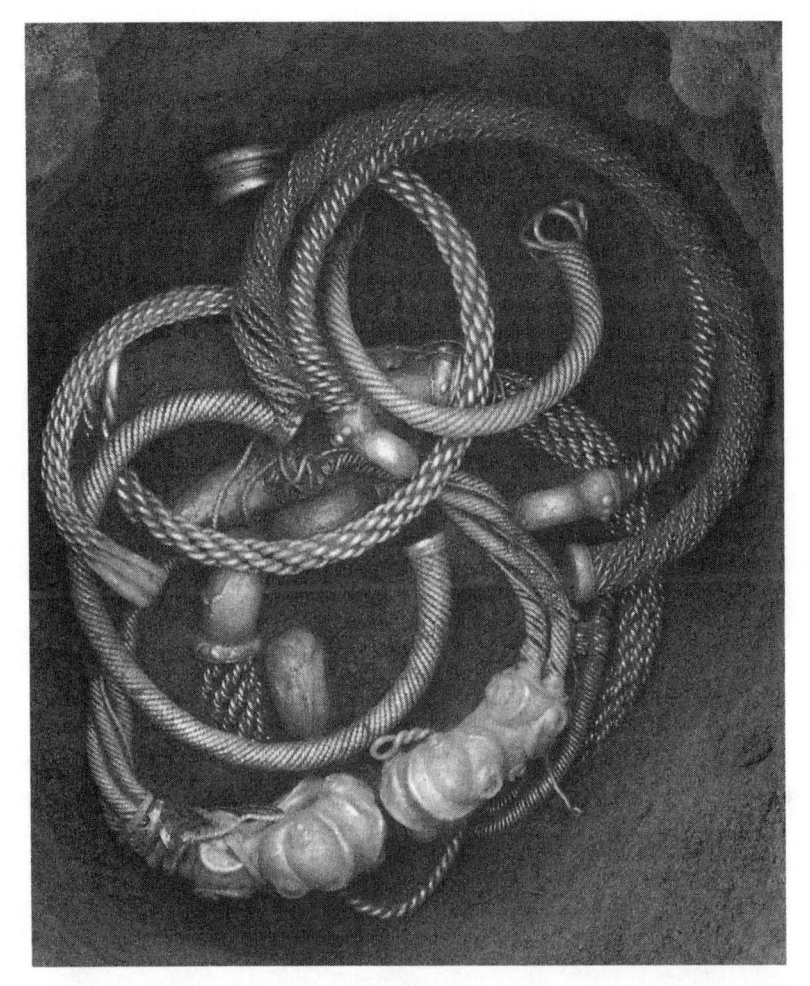

FIGURE 26.2 Nest of torques, known as Hoard L, discovered at Snettisham, Norfolk in 1990.

of these unexplainable factors, hoards are now most often interpreted as votive offerings and potential sources of information on systems of belief (Hunter 1997: 108).

Like offerings in water, practices varied and valuable objects were selected for deposition indicating the central role of religion and ritual activities in social negotiations of power. For example, many hoards from England and Wales dating to the middle decades of the first century AD, like Severn Sisters, Glamorgan, contain artefacts that mix Roman and Iron Age technologies and styles (Davis and Gwilt 2008: 146). These most commonly appear at the 'frontier regions', which saw most resistance to Roman occupation.

3.8 'Religious Equipment'

Some objects whose function cannot easily be explained have been interpreted as specifically religious or ritual objects (see discussion in Fitzpatrick 2007). For example, Fitzpatrick

(1996: 389) suggested that anthropomorphic-handled short swords, found in small numbers across Europe, were used in practices or ceremonies associated with marking and keeping time. Headdresses, such as the 'crown' from a grave at Deal, Kent have been interpreted as symbols of status worn by religious leaders (Stead 1995: 86). Depictions of human heads wearing horned helmets or headdresses are also found on the bronze handle escutcheons of wooden buckets from first century BC cremation burials at Alkham, Aylesford (Figure 26.3) and Baldock (see Fitzpatrick 2007: 303).

3.9 'Archaeology of the Everyday'

In his classic study *Ritual and Rubbish in the Iron Age of Wessex*, Hill (1995) demonstrated that finds from prehistoric settlements may well have been just as meaningful to those depositing them as objects from graves or hoards. He found that often pits and ditches were filled in ordered ways with clear patterns or rules dictating associations between artefacts and the particular fill layer they were placed in. For Hill, 'these patterns demonstrate that excavated settlement evidence, and the associated artefacts and ecofacts, were structured according to symbolic schemes, rationalities and common senses very different from our own' (1995: 126). Deposition in pits and other settlement contexts is part of everyday practice but this practice was grounded in belief and these actions, although they may not make sense to us, are entirely logical given a particular awareness of the world (see Brück 1999: 321).

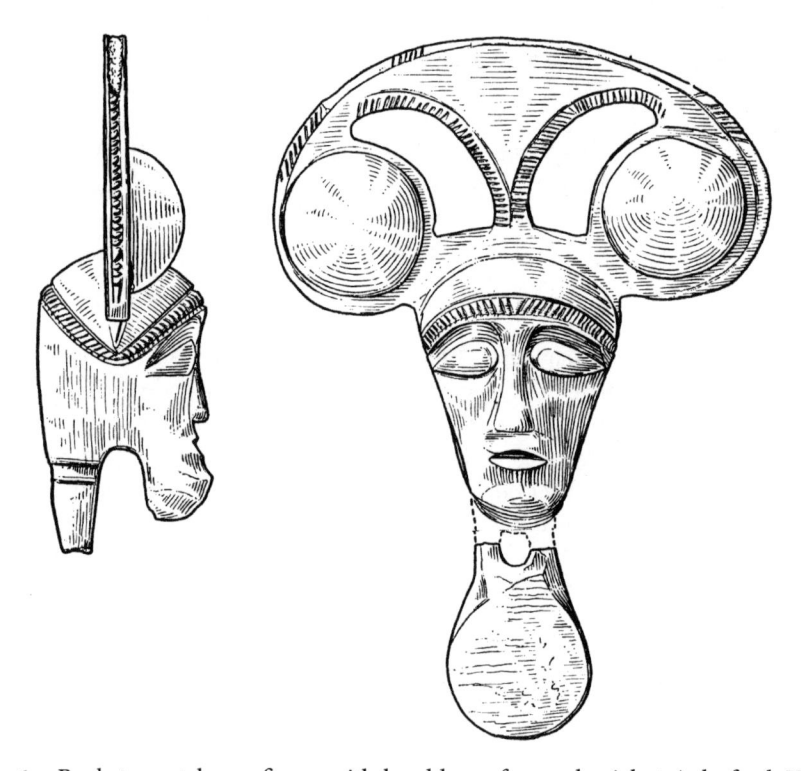

FIGURE 26.3 Bucket escutcheon, figure with headdress, from a burial at Aylesford, Kent.

In Britain and Ireland the entrances to roundhouses, dating from the late Bronze Age and throughout the Iron Age, are often orientated to the east or south-east. Practical explanations include the suggestion that it was to allow in more light, for privacy, or to avoid prevailing winds (see Hingley and Miles 1984: 63). Others have indicated this layout had cosmological significance (Parker Pearson 1996: 119), linking the position of doorways to the orientation of shrines (Wait 1985: 177), the rising sun (Oswald 1997: 94), and the 'correct' direction to enter a roundhouse (Hill 1994: 6). Pope (2007) has recently challenged this cosmological model on the basis that it implies a universal explanation and that we cannot so easily set common-sense ideas against cosmological ones. There is no reason why these explanations should be contradictory given a particular understanding of the world. It was propitious to orient doorways towards the rising sun. At the same time doorways were orientated towards the morning light and through standardization doorways in settlements did not face one another, ensuring privacy.

4 FUTURE DIRECTIONS

Interpretations of religion based on literary accounts and ritual based on archaeological evidence should be reintegrated. The way in which both strands of evidence have been studied is problematic. Literary accounts are too often taken at face value and changes over time neglected, meaning that a universal Iron Age religion is presented. Fitzpatrick (2007) has attempted to look for evidence of religious practitioners, such as the Druids. Although he argues that there is little evidence for an organized priesthood throughout much of the Iron Age, importantly he uses the full range of evidence to reach his conclusions.

Until recently the archaeology of ritual and religion has been an account of the unexplainable. However, as accounts of the 'everyday' demonstrate, religion is manifest in everyday life (Hill 1995; Brück 1999; Insoll 2004; Bradley 2005; Whitley and Hays-Gilpin 2008: 17) and all actions take place within the context of a particular belief system. Following Brück (1999), Iron Age people applied a specific view of the world to all actions and future research should focus on understanding systems of belief. The motivations behind structured deposition in pits may not make practical sense from our perspective. However, for Iron Age people deposition was clearly important and may have served practical functions to mark boundaries and/or served as offerings to deities. Depositional events may also have marked events in the life cycle, such as marriage, or the transition from juvenile to adult, or significant times of year, linked to agricultural, solar, and lunar cycles (Jones 2007).

With the notable exception of Green (1995b), associations between religion and gender have been relatively neglected. Many objects discussed above are martial in character and were most probably associated with men. Ritual artefacts and deposition associated with women are less obvious (see discussion in Fitzpatrick 1984: 186–7). In Britain mirror burials (Giles and Joy 2007) have been viewed as the female equivalent of male warrior burials but discoveries such as the burial from Bryher, Isles of Scilly (Johns 2006), which contained weapons and a mirror, should caution us over putting forward simplistic gender associations. Accounts based on literary evidence highlight the role of male Druids acting as mediators with the gods. However, as MacDonald (2007: 187) points out, classical texts also detail the role of religious women (see also Green 1995b: ch. 7), for example Tacitus describes 'witch-like' women in his description of the Roman attack on Anglesey. Religious roles were likely not as clearly defined as they are today. For example, the man from Deal, Kent, buried with a priestly crown or headdress as well as weapons may have performed different roles throughout his lifetime as 'warrior', 'leader', or 'religious specialist'.

5 Conclusions

It is easier to summarize what Iron Age religion is not rather than to detail what it is. On the whole, it lacks images of deities and formalized, humanly made religious structures like shrines or temples. Intentional deposition dominates the archaeological record but this was rarely recorded in contemporary Greek and Roman accounts. The location of deposits was important. They were most often made in water or located in relation to water in the landscape, high places, or boundaries. These locations may have been numinous. Many objects were broken or 'ritually killed' before they were deposited. The structured nature of more everyday deposits in pits, enclosure ditches, and post-holes, and the complex ceremonies associated with disposal of the dead, also show beliefs were not divorced from everyday life. Different social dimensions of religion can also be viewed. Evidence for religious practice of the elites is most evident in the archaeological record, for example rich graves, or the deposition of well-made martial equipment in rivers. Social status can be enhanced through religious practice. By officiating at religious ceremonies and conducting them in a particular way it is possible to emphasize a certain viewpoint.

Practices varied across time and space and there is no evidence for a single Iron Age religion. Instead the evidence points to local patterns of belief and behaviour, but with some common conceptions such as the importance of water. Despite the problems of interpreting the archaeological data and reconciling this with the literary evidence, understanding belief systems is essential to understanding Iron Age society.

Acknowledgements

I would like to thank Andrew Fitzpatrick, Duncan Garrow, J. D. Hill and Ben Roberts for reading previous drafts of this chapter, and Stephen Crummy for his help with illustrations. All errors remain my own.

Suggested Reading

Ross (1967) and Green (1986) give excellent accounts of Iron Age religion primarily using literary evidence. Webster (1994; 1995a; 1995b; 1997; 1999) examines the literary evidence critically. Wait's (1985) study of religion in Britain is extensive, but now dated. Cunliffe (2005: 543–78) provides a concise summary. Kendrick (1927) and Piggott (1968) are the classic accounts of the Druids. Cunliffe (2010) provides a recent, succinct introduction to the Druids. MacDonald (2007: 171–89) gives an up-to-date summary of watery deposition, but see also Fitzpatrick (1984) and Bradley (1990). Glob (1969) produced the classic study of bog bodies. Brunaux's (1988) account of sanctuaries in Gaul is engaging. For accounts of hoards see Hingley (1990, 2005), Hunter (1997), and Fitzpatrick (2005). See also Hill (1995) for explanation of structured deposition in pits and Brück (1999) for her discussion of ritual.

References

Aldhouse Green, M. 2001. *Dying for the Gods: Human sacrifice in Iron Age and Roman Europe* (Stroud: Tempus).
Ashbee, P. 1979. 'The Porth Cressa cist-graves, St Mary's, Isles of Scilly: A postscript', *Cornish Archaeology*, 19: 61–80.
Asingh, P. 2007. 'The bog people' in P. Asingh and N. Lynnerup (eds), *Grauballe Man: An Iron Age bog body revisited* (Moesgaard: Jutland Archaeological Society), pp. 290–323.
Birchall, A. 1965. 'The Aylesford-Swarling Culture', *Proceedings of the Prehistoric Society*, 31: 241–367.
Bradley, R. 1990. *The Passage of Arms: An archaeological analysis of prehistoric hoards and votive deposits* (Cambridge: Cambridge University Press).
—— 2005. *Ritual and Domestic Life in Prehistoric Europe* (London and New York: Routledge).
Brück, J. 1999. 'Ritual and rationality: Some problems of interpretation in European archaeology', *European Journal of Archaeology*, 2(3): 313–44.
Brunaux, J. L. 1988. *The Celtic Gauls: Gods, rites and sanctuaries*, trans. D. Nash (London: B. A. Seaby Ltd).
Büchsenschütz, O. and Olivier, L. (eds) 1989. *Les Viereckschanzen et les enceintes quadrilaterals en Europe Celtique* (Paris: Proceedings of the 9th Colloquium of the AFEAF).
Carr, G. and Knüsel, C. 1997. 'The ritual framework of the early and middle Iron Ages of central southern Britain' in A. Gwilt and C. Haselgrove (eds), *Re-constructing Iron Age Societies* (Oxford: Oxbow Monographs 71), pp. 167–73.
Coles, B. 1990. 'Anthropomorphic wooden figures from Britain and Ireland', *Proceedings of the Prehistoric Society*, 56: 315–33.
Collis, J. 1973. 'Burials with weapons in Iron Age Britain', *Germania*, 51: 121–33.
—— 2003. *The Celts: Origins, myths and inventions* (Stroud: Tempus).
—— 2008. 'The Celts as "grand narrative"' in A. Jones (ed.), *Prehistoric Europe: Theory and practice* (Oxford: Blackwell Publishing), pp. 35–53.
Cunliffe, B. 1988. *Mount Batten Plymouth: A prehistoric and Roman fort* (Oxford: Oxford University Committee for Archaeology, Monograph 26).
—— 2005. *Iron Age Communities in Britain: An account of England, Scotland and Wales from the seventh century BC until the Roman Conquest*, 4th edn (London: Routledge).
—— and Poole, C. 2000. *The Danebury Environs Programme: The prehistory of a Wessex landscape, II/iii: Sudden Farm, Middle Wallop, Hants, 1991 and 1996* (Oxford: English Heritage and Oxford University Committee for Archaeology, Monograph 49).
—— 2010. *Druids: a very short introduction* (Oxford: Oxford University Press).
Davis, M. and Gwilt, A. 2008. 'Material, style and identity in the first century AD metalwork, with particular reference to the Severn Sisters Hoard' in D. Garrow, C. Gosden, and J. D. Hill (eds), *Rethinking Celtic Art* (Oxford: Oxbow Books), pp. 146–84.
Dent, J. 1985. 'Three cart burials from Wetwang, Yorkshire', *Antiquity*, 59: 85–92.

DEYTS, S. 1983. *Les bois sculptés des sources de la Seine (XLII supplément à Gallia)* (Paris: Editions du CNRS).

DRURY, P. J. 1980. 'Non-classical religious buildings in Iron Age and Roman Britain: A review' in W. Rodwell (ed.), *Temples, Churches and Religion: Recent research in Roman Britain*, BAR British Series 77 (Oxford: BAR), pp. 45–78.

DUNNING, C. 1991. 'La Tène' in S. Moscatiabó (eds), *The Celts* (Milano: Bompiani), pp. 366–8.

EGLOFF, M. 1987. '130 years of archaeological research in Lake Neuchâtel, Switzerland' in J. M. Coles and A. J. Lawson (eds), *European Wetlands in Prehistory* (Oxford: Clarendon Press), pp. 23–32.

——1991. 'Celtic craftwork at La Tène' in S. Moscati, O. H. Frey, V. Kruta, et al. (eds.), *The Celts* (Milano: Bompiani), pp. 369–71.

FIELD, N. and PARKER PEARSON, M. 2003. *Fiskerton an Iron Age Timber Causeway with Iron Age and Roman Votive Offerings: The 1981 excavations* (Oxford: Oxbow Books).

FITZPATRICK, A. P. 1984. 'The deposition of La Tène Iron Age metalwork in watery contexts in southern England' in B. Cunliffe and D. Miles (eds), *Aspects of the Iron Age in Central Southern Britain* (Oxford: University of Oxford Committee for Archaeology), pp. 178–90.

——1991. 'Celtic (Iron Age) religion: Traditional and timeless?', *Scottish Archaeological Review*, 8: 123–8.

——1992. 'The Snettisham, Norfolk, hoards of Iron Age torques: Sacred or profane?', *Antiquity*, 66: 395–8.

——1996. 'Night and day: The symbolism of astral signs on later Iron Age anthropomorphic short swords', *Proceedings of the Prehistoric Society*, 62: 373–98.

——1997. *Archaeological Excavations on the Route of the A27 Westhampnett Bypass, West Sussex, 1992*, II: *The Cemeteries* (Salisbury: Wessex Archaeology Report 12).

——2005. 'Gifts for the golden gods: Iron Age hoards of torques and coins' in C. Haselgrove and D. Wigg-Wolf (eds), *Iron Age Coinage and Ritual Practice*, Studien zu Fundmunzen der Antike (Mainz am Rhein: Phillipp von Zaberg), pp. 157–82.

——2007. 'Druids: Towards an archaeology' in C. Gosden, H. Harrerow, P. de Jersey, and G. Lock (eds), *Communities and Connections: Essays in honour of Barry Cunliffe* (Oxford: Oxford University Press), pp. 287–315.

FOX, C. 1947. *A Find of the Early Iron Age from Llyn Cerig Bach, Anglesey* (Cardiff: The National Museum of Wales).

GARROW, D. 2008. 'The time and space of Celtic Art: Interrogating the "Technologies of Enchantment" database' in D. Garrow, C. Gosden, and J. D. Hill (eds), *Rethinking Celtic Art* (Oxford: Oxbow Books), pp. 15–39.

GILES, M. and JOY, J. 2007. 'Mirrors in the British Iron Age: Performance, revelation, and power' in M. Anderson (ed.), *The Book of the Mirror* (Cambridge: Cambridge Scholars Press), pp. 18–34.

GLOB, P. V. 1969. *The Bog People: Iron-Age man preserved* (London: Faber and Faber).

GREEN, M. 1986. *The Gods of the Celts* (Gloucester: Alan Sutton).

GREEN, M. J. 1995a. 'The gods and the supernatural' in M. J. Green (ed.), *The Celtic World* (London: Routledge), pp. 465–88.

——1995b. *Celtic Goddesses: Warriors, virgins and mothers* (London: British Museum Press).

——1997. *Exploring the World of the Druids* (London: Thames and Hudson Ltd).

HASELGROVE, C. 2005. 'A trio of temples: A reassessment of Iron Age coin deposition at Hayling Island, Harlow and Wanborough' in C. Haselgrove and D. Wigg-Wolf (eds), *Iron*

Age Coinage and Ritual Practice, Studien zu Fundmunzen der Antike (Mainz am Rhein: Phillipp von Zaberg), pp. 381–418.

HEY, G., BAYLISS, A., and BOYLE, A. 1999. 'Iron Age inhumation burials at Yarnton, Oxfordshire', *Antiquity*, 73: 551–62.

HILL, J. D. 1994. 'Why we should not take the data from Iron Age settlements for granted: Recent studies in intra-settlement patterning' in A. Fitzpatrick and E. Morris (eds), *The Iron Age in Wessex: Recent work* (Salisbury: Trust for Wessex Archaeology), pp. 4–8.

—— 1995. *Ritual and Rubbish in the Iron Age of Wessex: A study of the formation of a specific archaeological record*, BAR British Series 242 (Oxford: BAR).

HINGLEY, R. 1990. 'Iron Age "currency bars": The archaeological and social context', *Archaeological Journal*, 147: 91–117.

—— 2005. 'Iron Age "currency bars" in Britain: Items of exchange in liminal contexts?' in C. Haselgrove and D. Wigg-Wolf (eds), *Iron Age Coinage and Ritual Practice*, Studien zu Fundmunzen der Antike (Mainz am Rhein: Phillipp von Zaberg), pp. 183–205.

—— and MILES, D. 1984. 'Aspects of Iron Age settlements in the Upper Thames valley' in B. Cunliffe and D. Miles (eds), *Aspects of the Iron Age in Central Southern Britain* (Oxford: Oxford University Committee for Archaeology, Monograph 16), pp. 52–71.

HUNTER, F. 1997. 'Iron Age hoarding in Scotland and northern England' in A. Gwilt and C. Haselgrove (eds), *Re-constructing Iron Age Societies* (Oxford: Oxbow Monograph 71), pp. 108–34.

—— 2005. 'The image of the warrior in the British Iron Age: Coin iconography in context' in C. Haselgrove and D. Wigg-Wolf (eds), *Iron Age Coinage and Ritual Practice*, Studien zu Fundmunzen der Antike (Mainz am Rhein: Phillipp von Zaberg), pp. 43–68.

HUTTON, R. 1991. *The Pagan Religions of the ancient British Isles: Their nature and legacy* (Oxford: Blackwell).

—— 2007. *The Druids* (London: Hambledon Continuum).

INSOLL, T. 2004. *Archaeology, Ritual, Religion* (London: Routledge).

JOHNS, C. 2006. 'Iron Age sword and mirror cist burial from Bryher, Isles of Scilly', *Cornish Archaeology*, 41–2: 1–80.

JONES, M. 2007. 'A feast of Beltain? Reflections on the rich Danebury harvests' in C. Gosden, H. Hamerow, and P. De Jersey (eds), *Communities and Connections: Essays in honour of Barry Cunliffe* (Oxford: Oxford University Press), pp. 142–53.

JOY, J. 2009. *Lindow Man* (London: British Museum Press).

—— 2010. *Iron Age mirrors: a biographical approach*, BAR British Series 518 (Oxford: BAR).

KELLY, E. P. 2006. *Kingship and Sacrifice: Iron Age bog bodies and boundaries*, Guide No. 35 (Dublin: Archaeology Ireland Heritage).

KENDRICK, T. D. 1927. *The Druids* (London: Methuen and Co. Ltd).

KING, A. and SOFFE, G. 2001. 'Internal organisation and deposition at the Iron Age temple on Hayling Island, Hampshire' in J. Collis (ed.), *Society and Settlement in Iron Age Europe: Actes du XVIIIe Colloque de l'AFEAF, Winchester (April 1994)* (Sheffield: J. R. Collis Publications), pp. 111–24.

KING, R., BARBER, A., and TIMBY, J. 1996. 'Excavations at West Lane, Kemble: An Iron Age, Roman, and Saxon burial site and a medieval building', *Transactions of the Bristol and Gloucestershire Archaeological Society*, 114: 15–54.

MACDONALD, P. 2007. *Llyn Cerrig Bach: A study of the copper-alloy artefacts from the insular La Tène assemblage* (Cardiff: University of Wales Press).

Megaw, R. and Megaw, V. 2001. *Celtic Art: From its beginnings to the Book of Kells*, rev. and expanded edn (London: Thames and Hudson).

Müller, F. 1991. 'The river site of Port Nidau' in S. Moscati, O. H. Frey, V. Kruta, et al. (eds), *The Celts* (Milano: Bompiani), pp. 528–9.

Nash, D. 1976. '"Reconstructing Poseidonios" Celtic ethnography: Some considerations', *Britannia*, 7: 111–26.

Navarro, J. M. de 1972. *The Finds from the Site of La Tène* (Oxford: Oxford University Press).

Nowakowski, J. A. 1991. 'Trethallan Farm, Newquay: The excavation of a lowland Bronze Age settlement and Iron Age cemetery', *Cornish Archaeology*, 30: 5–242.

Oswald, A. 1997. 'A doorway on the past: Practical and mystic concerns in the orientation of roundhouse doorways' in A. Gwilt and C. Haselgrove (eds), *Re-constructing Iron Age Societies* (Oxford: Oxbow Monograph 71), pp. 87–95.

Parker Pearson, M. 1996. 'Food, fertility and front doors in the first millennium BC' in T. C. Champion and J. R. Collis (eds), *The Iron Age in Britain and Ireland: Recent trends* (Sheffield: Sheffield Academic Press), pp. 117–32.

——1999. *The Archaeology of Death and Burial* (Stroud: Sutton Publishing).

Piggott, S. 1968. *The Druids* (London: Thames and Hudson).

Pope, R. 2007. 'Ritual and the roundhouse: A critique of recent ideas on the use of domestic space in later British prehistory' in C. Haselgrove and R. Pope (eds), *The Earlier Iron Age in Britain and the Near Continent* (Oxford: Oxbow Books), pp. 204–28.

Price, N. S. 2008. 'Bodylore and the archaeology of embedded religion: Dramatic license in the funerals of the Vikings' in D. S. Whitley and K. Hays-Gilpin (eds), *Belief in the Past: Theoretical approaches to the archaeology of religion* (Walnut Creek: Left Coast Press), pp. 143–66.

Ross, A. 1967. *Pagan Celtic Britain: Studies in iconography and tradition* (London: Routledge and Kegan Paul Ltd).

——1995. 'Ritual and the Druids' in M. J. Green (ed.), *The Celtic World* (London: Routledge), pp. 423–44.

Staelens, Y. J. E. 1982. 'The Birdlip Cemetery', *Transactions of the Bristol and Gloucestershire Archaeological Society*, 100: 19–31.

Stead, I. M. 1976. 'The earliest burials of the Aylesford culture' in G. de G. Sieveking, I. M. Longworth, and K. E. Wilson (eds), *Problems in Economic and Social Archaeology* (London: Duckworth), pp. 401–16.

——1988. 'Chalk figurines of the Parisi', *Antiquaries Journal*, 68: 9–29.

——1991a. *Iron Age Cemeteries in East Yorkshire: Excavations at Burton Fleming, Rudston, Garton-on-the-Wolds, and Kirkburn*, English Heritage Archaeological Report 22 (London: English Heritage).

——1991b. 'The Snettisham treasure: Excavations in 1990', *Antiquity*, 65: 447–65.

——1995. 'The metalwork' in K. Parfitt (ed.), *Iron Age Burials from Mill Hill, Deal* (London: British Museum Press), pp. 58–111.

Venclová, N. 1998. *Mšecké Žehrovice in Bohemia: Archaeological background to a Celtic hero 3rd–2nd centuries BC* (Sceaux: Chronothèque 2).

Vouga, P. 1923. *La Tène: monographie de la station publiée au nom de la commission des fouilles de La Tène* (Leipzig: Karl W. Hiersemann).

Wait, G. A. 1985. *Ritual and Religion in Iron Age Britain*, BAR British Series 149 (Oxford: BAR).

——1995. 'Burial and the otherworld' in M. J. Green (ed.), *The Celtic World* (London: Routledge), pp. 489–511.
WEBSTER, J. 1994. 'The just war: Graeco-Roman texts as colonial discourse' in S. Cottam, D. Dungworth, S. Scott, et al. (eds), *Proceedings of the 4th Annual Theoretical Roman Archaeology Conference, Durham 1994* (Oxford: Oxbow Books), pp. 1–10.
——1995a. 'Sanctuaries and sacred places' in M. J. Green (ed.), *The Celtic World* (London: Routledge), pp. 445–64.
——1995b. 'Translation and subjection: Interpretation and the Celtic gods' in J. D. Hill and C. G. Cumberpatch (eds), *Different Iron Ages: Studies on the Iron Age in temperate Europe*, BAR International Series 602 (Oxford: BAR), pp. 175–84.
——1997. 'Text expectations: The archaeology of "Celtic" ritual wells and shafts' in A. Gwilt and C. Haselgrove (eds), *Re-constructing Iron Age Societies* (Oxford: Oxbow Monograph 71), pp. 134–44.
——1999. 'At the end of the world: Druidic and other revitalisation movements in post-conquest Gaul and Britain', *Britannia*, 30: 1–20.
WHEELER, R. E. M. 1943. *Maiden Castle, Dorset* (Oxford: Oxford University Press).
WHIMSTER, R. P. 1977. 'Harlyn Bay reconsidered: The excavations of 1900–1905 in the light of recent work', *Cornish Archaeology*, 16: 61–88.
——1981. *Burial Practices in Iron Age Britain: A discussion and gazetteer of the evidence c.700 BC–AD 43*, BAR British Series 90 (Oxford: BAR).
WHITLEY, D. S. and HAYS-GILPIN, K. 2008. 'Religion beyond icon, burial and monument: An introduction' in D. S. Whitley and K. Hays-Gilpin (eds), *Belief in the Past: Theoretical approaches to the archaeology of religion* (Walnut Creek: Left Coast Press), pp. 11–22.
WILLIAMS, J. 2007. 'New light on Latin in pre-conquest Britain', *Britannia*, 38: 1–11.
WOODWARD, A. 1993. 'Discussion' in D. E. Farwell and T. I. Molleson (eds), *Poundbury*, II: *The Cemeteries* (Dorchester: Dorset Natural History and Archaeological Society Monograph Series 11), pp. 215–39.

PART III

RELIGION AND RITUAL IN WORLD PREHISTORY

CHAPTER 27

....

SUB-SAHARAN AFRICA

....

TIMOTHY INSOLL

1 INTRODUCTION
....

THE contribution made by African anthropology to global understandings of religions and their associated ritual practices has been immense as attested by the impact of the work of, for example, Evans-Pritchard (1956), Fortes (1987), Goody (1962), and Turner (1969). In comparison that of archaeology has been relatively insignificant. This is not because of a lack of material, but rather because of a lack of interest, until recently, by archaeologists in looking at religion in Africa (de Maret 1994; Insoll 2004). Exceptions exist, but these primarily relate to ancient Egypt (e.g. Kemp 1995; Richards 2005), or world religions such as Christianity in Ethiopia and the Sudanese Nile Valley (e.g. Phillipson 1998; Edwards 1999; Finneran 2002) or Islam in its regional or continental aspects (Insoll 1996, 2003).

This is unfortunate as the archaeology of sub-Saharan Africa has much to contribute to our understanding of religions, empirically within the continent itself, but also hermeneutically in providing analogies and new perspectives potentially relevant elsewhere, for as de Maret (1994: 184) notes, 'Africa, with its extraordinary diversity and continuity, offers exceptional opportunities for this type of study.' Moreover, it would appear almost certain that the early modern forerunners of ourselves, *Homo sapiens sapiens*, originated in Africa c.150,000–100,000 years ago and spread out from there via the so-called 'Out of Africa II' migration that took place from c.100,000–80,000 years ago (Stringer and Gamble 1993: 38). Hence the earliest evidence for 'symbolic' or non-utilitarian behaviour associated with early modern humans has been recovered from this continent indicating its pre-eminent role in what might later form part of the behaviours that could be termed 'ritual' or 'religious'. This includes an engraved fragment of mammal bone and two pieces of ochre 'deliberately engraved with abstract patterns interpreted as symbolic, meaningful representations' (D'Errico et al. 2001: 309), as well as 39 beads produced from the shell of the mollusc *Nassarius kraussianus*, recovered from contexts dated to c.70,000 years ago at Blombos Cave in South Africa (D'Errico et al. 2005).

Also from South Africa, the material from Klasies River Mouth is very significant in considering the evidence for the origins of behavioural modernity and anatomy in sub-Saharan Africa (Deacon and Deacon 1999; McBrearty and Brooks 2000; Wadley 2001; Barham and Mitchell 2008). This site yielded early modern human skeletal remains mostly from a horizon dated to 90,000 years ago, but also from contexts dated to between 110,000–120,000 years ago (Singer and Wymer 1982). Deacon and Deacon (1999: 104–5) suggest that some of these remains show evidence of charring, 'impact fractures and cut marks', possibly consistent with cannibalism, 'inspired by ritual rather than hunger' (ibid.: 105); though Barham and Mitchell (2008: 250) note that alternative interpretations can be proposed.

Equally, though this is more controversial, some of the earliest putative evidence anywhere for what can be very loosely described as 'symbolic' behaviour has been recorded in sub-Saharan Africa. This is provided by the so-called 'Australopithecine cobble' from Makapansgat in the northern region of South Africa which is a reddish-brown jasperite cobble of $c.83$ mm in length by 69 mm in width and 38 mm in thickness. Bednarik (1998: 6) microscopically analysed this artefact and notes that although it bears no trace of intentional modification, it can be recognized as representing something 'resembling the reconstruction of an australopithecine face, wearing a friendly if somewhat mischievous grin'. Hence he suggests that it was collected by australopithecines for its visual qualities and is therefore justifiably described as the earliest 'palaeoart' (2.5 to 3 million years ago) found to date (ibid.: 7). Obviously, even if the interpretation is accepted in the first instance, this is not being included as suggestive of australopithecine 'ritual' or 'religion'. This is an absurd concept and proposition.

Instead these examples serve to indicate, in totality, the immense importance of sub-Saharan Africa within a consideration of the archaeology of ritual and religion and also how it is impossible, nor necessarily desirable, to provide a chronological overview within the remits of this chapter. Hence emphasis will be placed upon considering examples of categories of archaeological evidence and potential associated research questions that might facilitate the archaeological investigation of ritual and religion in sub-Saharan Africa. In so doing, the approach adopted by de Maret (1994) in one of the first, if not the first, consideration of the same subject is broadly adopted, but at the same time, altered, updated, and amplified. However, it should be noted that world religions are excluded from this consideration because of the comparatively substantial archaeological effort that has been expended in their investigation (see above). Thus 'prehistoric' and indigenous African religions are the primary focus.

2 Defining African Indigenous Religions

Whether the concept of African 'indigenous' or 'traditional' religions is at all applicable (Shaw 1990), and whether if so defined these should be seen as a singular religion (Idowu 1973) or multiple religions (Mbiti 1989: 1) has been the subject of extensive debate (e.g. Shaw 1990: 345; Morris 2006: 149). Common sense would dictate that these should be considered in the plural, as African indigenous religions, but that they contain certain key recurring elements that also have material correlates, as will be explored. These could include a belief in a high or sky god, beliefs in a lesser tier of spirits or divinities, ancestral veneration and propitiation, belief in the power of certain material substances, and, according to Morris (2006: 151), the recognition of witchcraft as 'a constituent part of African religious culture'—the latter more broadly framed by Mbiti (1989: 189) as 'mystical power, magic, witchcraft and sorcery'.

Similarly, the degree to which religiosity can be presumed to imbue both African thought and life has also been considered by scholars (Mbiti 1989: Morris 2006: 149). This has direct implications for how the archaeological record is conceptualized as to what constitutes the residue of the 'sacred' and what the 'profane' (Insoll 2004). Here it is perhaps best to agree with Mbiti (1989: 15) who suggests that religion in African life is an 'ontological phenomenon', meaning in turn that for archaeological purposes all aspects of material culture can be (but need not be) considered under the remit of 'religion'. Such a theoretical approach is facilitated by an emphasis placed upon context in identifying in specific archaeological situations how broad the notion of 'religion' or religiosity extends into the domain of material culture.

It is recognized that this is something of an ideal construct and that great diversity is evident in the archaeological record of a continent approximately 6,000 km east to west by 7,000 km north to south at its widest points (Meadows 1999: 163) in how religions are made materially manifest. Nonetheless, categories of evidence that can be considered include, for example, rock art, portable art, materiality and technology, death and burial, and shrines and monuments.

3 ROCK ART

Rock art comparable in date to that recorded in Palaeolithic European contexts is known from sub-Saharan Africa (Bahn and Vertut 1988: 27). Portable art, seven stone slabs bearing traces of animal figures rendered in charcoal, ochre, and white were recorded at Apollo II cave in Namibia in contexts dating to probably sometime between 19,000–27,500 years ago (Kinahan 1995: 187). Besides providing early evidence for rock art, sub-Saharan Africa has contributed significantly to worldwide debates on the archaeological interpretation of religion based on this category of evidence. Key here has been the three-stage trance or altered state of consciousness model derived from San ethnography of Southern Africa that has in turn been used to interpret rock art in, for example, Upper Palaeolithic contents in Europe (e.g. Lewis-Williams and Dowson 1988; Lewis-Williams 2002). The Apollo II evidence has been suggested as perhaps indicating shamanic trance (Kinahan 1995: 187). These shamanic interpretations have been much criticized both in their Southern African context and analogical application elsewhere (e.g. Solomon 1997, 2000; Kehoe 2001), and unfortunately, the debate over what constitutes 'shamanism' and how generally applicable it is has become somewhat polarized (Insoll 2004: 141–2).

One of the most useful discussions of the relevance of 'shamanism' in the African context is provided by Lewis (1997), who argues that using the term 'shaman' faces the same sort of transference difficulties as other emic/vernacular terms such as 'totem'. This is a valid point (see Chapter 62, 'Animism and Totemism', for more discussion of 'shaman' and 'totem') and Lewis (1997: 123) suggests that the recognition of shamanism is valid in the African context but not as mis-conceptualized by Eliade (1964) in his influential study, *Shamanism: Archaic techniques of ecstasy*. The archaeological recognition of 'shamanism' is currently fashionable (Insoll 2004: 141), but in sub-Saharan Africa its relevance outside of a few specific contexts such as parts of Southern Africa perhaps needs further consideration. This point is made in relation to interpreting rock art or other categories of archaeological evidence for as with 'totem' (see Chapter 62), African-derived vernacular alternatives need evaluating, as well as the applicability of less geographically binding terms such as 'healer', 'ritual expert', 'specialist' (Mbiti 1989: 162), 'priest', or 'possession' to describe relevant roles and associated phenomena. It is likely that the 'shaman' debate both in general archaeological terms and in the African context will continue (see e.g. Layton 2000).

Besides the shamanism debate, the ongoing project, less well remarked, of recording the massive inventory of rock art in many regions of sub-Saharan Africa is continuing, as in, for instance, the Sudan (Kleinitz and Olsson 2005; Kleinitz and Koenitz 2006), Burkina Faso (Barbaza and Jarry 2004), or Angola (Gutierrez 2008).

4 PORTABLE RITUAL OBJECTS

In comparison to rock art, research by archaeologists on what could be termed 'portable ritual objects' is less prolific. For example, our understanding of the clay figurines assumed to have ritual purposes from Jenne-jeno in Mali, or various sites associated with the so-called Sao in Chad is still meagre. At Jenne-jeno over seventy human or animal representations have been found dating from between the eleventh and fifteenth centuries AD (S. K. McIntosh 1995). Some may have functioned as toys, but others appear to have served ritual purposes. The latter include a single kneeling figure with arms crossed over its torso, perhaps associated with 'ancestor worship' (R. J. and S. K. McIntosh 1979: 53). Other terracotta figurines were found associated with funerary urns and what are termed 'rain-making altars' (R. J. and S. K. McIntosh 1988: 156). But, unfortunately, the great majority of figurines known are from looted sites and thus without context (Schmidt and McIntosh 1996).

The origins and etymology of the So or Sao also remain obscure (Lebeuf et al. 1980; Insoll 2003: 278), and the function of figurines produced between *c.* the tenth to sixteenth centuries AD largely unknown. These include human heads, torsos, full figures, masks, and animals such as hippopotami, lizards, sheep, and porcupines modelled in clay. Lebeuf and Masson Detourbet (1950: 68–9) refer to a '*sanctuaire*' excavated at Tago in which figurines were recorded *in situ*. In one level (II), three human figurines were recorded looking to the east with one placed upon part of a funerary jar accompanied by four balls of fired clay put at the cardinal points. Arranged around these figures were groups of other figurines, some interpreted as wearing zoomorphic masks, as well as, nearby, cylindrical stone pounders, ochre, animal bones, and a 'ritual' hearth. Overall, Sao beliefs are described by Lebeuf and Masson Detourbet (1950), briefly summarized, as encompassing an ancestor cult, a form of totemism, and beliefs in various spirits. Certainly, many more possibilities for research exist in relation to this material should archaeological work ever be possible in Chad again.

In contrast, renewed investigation of the Nok area in Central Nigeria has begun to place the terracotta figurines in context (Rupp, Ameje, and Breunig 2005). For instance, it was observed that most Nok settlements were located on mountain tops and were of considerable size, as with the site of Kochio that was defended with a wall partially cut from the underlying granite with a further area walled with granite slabs of 'megalithic dimension' at the centre of the site (ibid.: 287). This research is of particular significance as the Nok terracottas are dated to *c.*500 BC to AD 200 and are therefore presumed to be the earliest figurative sculptures known from sub-Saharan Africa. However, other than being treated as 'art', very little was known about their possible social or religious meanings, or ritual usage. Similarly, our understanding of the terracotta figurines from Koma Land in Northern Ghana has been advanced recently by renewed archaeological research (Kankpeyeng and Nkumbaan 2008), as described in Chapter 62, 'Animism and Totemism'.

Sculptures, figurines, 'fetishes', shrines, and ritual objects made in wood and other plant materials, cloth, leather and skins, and animal parts (bones, blood, feathers), by their perishable nature rarely survive in the archaeological record. These, however, may have constituted the majority of portable ritual objects. An exception to their general non-survival is provided by a zoomorphic wooden head radiocarbon dated to the eighth–ninth centuries AD from Angola. De Maret (1995: 240) suggests, not unfeasibly, that the shape of the head perhaps indicates that an aardvark was represented. This is of interest because the aardvark is known from ethnography to be thought of as an anomalous creature, 'good to think' (de Maret ibid.).

This is a direct reference to Lévi Strauss (1964: 89), and Roberts (1995), in his inspiring book, *Animals in African Art*, expands upon why some animals and not others are frequently the focus of sub-Saharan African artistic expression. Common amongst these are creatures considered 'preposterous' (ibid.: 18), which is conceptually similar to Douglas's (1999: 51) notion of the 'anomalous' creature. These could include, for example, pangolins, the spotted hyena, mudfish, crocodiles, and the aardvark (Roberts 1995). The latter is considered to be 'an odd assortment of other animal's parts', with a peniform snout, and human-like characteristics in usually bearing one offspring at a time and sleeping on its back (Roberts 1995: 80).

Thinking about wooden sculpture, figurines, and portable ritual objects as a whole in such a way raises various interesting research possibilities. These pertain to what both ethnographic and art historical studies might tell us about human–animal relations, concepts, and their interface with, for example, medicine and ritual practice, for as was defined at the outset of this entry a belief in the efficacy of powerful substances is a recurring characteristic of African indigenous religions. Hence to exclude considerations of materials and substances in thinking about portable ritual objects would be flawed. The composite objects illustrated by Roberts (1995), as with the Sapo mask from Liberia conjoining multiple animal parts from 'ferocious' species with fur, iron tacks, other materials, and human hair, to create a 'fearsome' symbol of 'civilizing, moral forces and agents of social control' (ibid.: 155) provides just such an example. This is indisputably a material masterpiece but is also an ontological statement and a reflection of metaphoric and metonymic thinking. These may rarely survive in the archaeological record but still make us consider the fusion of ontology, substance, material, ritual, and medicine that can be inherent in, or act in relation to, portable ritual objects (Insoll in preparation b).

In thinking about portable ritual objects in such ways, interdisciplinary perspectives can be gained from art history, ethnography, and anthropology. Dieterlen (1989: 34), for instance, in considering Dogon masks from Mali emphasizes how these as well as costumes, ornaments, and the associated performative and ritual actions such as songs, mimes, rhythms, and dances are integrated into the mythology, cosmogony, and history of the Dogon (Figure 27.1). They bring to life 'ancestors' (ibid.; see also van Beek 1988: 60 for the role of ancestors in Dogon religion) from the whole ontological spectrum, vegetal, animal, and human. But strip away the masks, fibre costumes, and performers, as

FIGURE 27.1 Dogon masked dancers, Bandiagara Escarpment, Mali, January 2001.

preservation conditions in the archaeological record inevitably will; what remains? Other tangible elements of Dogon masquerade and performance survive, relating to the sensory, auditory dimension. These are what Dieterlen (1989: 43) refers to as the 'lithophones', described as, 'sonorous uncarved rocks...found in almost all the caves, rock shelters or faults in the plateau in which the stages of cosmogony are represented by various furnishings and wall-paintings. They are beaten with round stones on a precise spot on their surface or corner, visibly worn by the blows.' Hence context is reinforced by this ethnographic example, physically in relation to ritual setting and its durable manifestation and also via the senses, the latter often ignored by archaeologists but whose role can be vital in ritual and religion (e.g. Scarre and Lawson 2006), and whose cultural prominence can vary with attendant archaeological implications (Insoll 2007a: 49–56).

5 MATERIALITY AND TECHNOLOGY

Similar themes are continued in thinking about materiality and technology within the frameworks of the archaeology of ritual and religion in sub-Saharan Africa. Substances, materials, and technologies are obviously not necessarily conceptually inert (Insoll 2007a). Instead they can function within religious systems of belief and be subject to ritual sanction, and it is now well established that technology should not be divorced from its social and symbolic contexts (Hodder 1982). This has perhaps been most fully explored in relation to iron production and technology in sub-Saharan Africa (e.g. Herbert 1993; Reid and MacLean 1995; Schmidt 1997). Herbert (1993) has, famously, considered how gender prohibition and ritual sanction structured iron production across the continent south of the Sahara. Moreover, sub-Saharan African iron-working analogies have also had a major impact upon how people working elsewhere have interpreted archaeological evidence for metallurgy (e.g. Giles 2007; Haaland 2007).

Less well known, but potentially equally significant in considering the possible ritual and religious roles played in conceptualizing materiality and technology are ceramics, for a belief in the inherent power of clay has been noted by various observers of African potters (e.g. Herbert 1993: 207–9; Gosselain and Livingstone Smith 2005: 40). Hence prohibitions and taboos could exist in regard to how clay should be extracted and handled as Frank (1998: 79) relates for the Mande of Mali who believe that raw clay has *nyama*, 'a kind of vital energy or "heat" that pervades all things'. Clay can be seen as a powerful substance and this, besides technical considerations, might also help explain why old pots are often ground down as grog in new pots (Barley 1984). Gosselain and Livingstone Smith (2005: 41) refer to how Fulani/Gurma (Burkina Faso) and Songhai/Zarma (Niger) potters' recycle archaeological sherds into grog, 'to tie new vessels with those of the ancestors'. Perhaps the act of renewal achieved through adding ground pot to new vessels serves to enhance or 'temper' the powerful qualities of clay, besides its more practical purpose of stopping the clay sticking to the tools used (Insoll 2010).

Such beliefs are less universal than those surrounding iron working but do offer possibilities for archaeological interpretation. And these ideas have been explored recently in relation to considering what factors might underlie the deposition of a large spread of pottery recorded during excavations in a Tallensi earth shrine, the Nyoo shrine, in Northern Ghana that was dated by OSL to between the mid-third and mid-eleventh centuries AD (Insoll, Kankpeyeng, and MacLean 2007; Insoll 2009; see also Chapter 11, 'Sacrifice').

Both technologies also explicitly relate to gender. In iron working, Herbert (1993: 25) states that 'the smith and smelter are always male', and describes how the furnace can be modelled upon the female form with the provision of clay breasts, incised scarification marks, navels, and a gynecomorphic parallel often evident in how the bloom in the furnace is thought of as analogous to the foetus in the womb, with the furnace opening sometimes considered similar to the vulva, in giving birth (access) to the iron. In contrast to male-dominated iron production, women produce pots in the vast majority of societies that have been documented in sub-Saharan Africa (e.g. Berns 1993; Frank 1998; Gosselain 1999). In general, the link between women and pots would seem to be due to the connection with the Earth and the metaphor of fertility, with its recurrence being almost what Jacobson-Widding and van Beek (1990: 24) refer to as 'a leitmotif in agricultural and semi-agricultural societies all over sub-Saharan Africa'.

6 Death and Burial

All aspects of evidence should be considered, where possible, alongside each other, and so conceptualized, death and burial forms part of life (Insoll 2004: 66). The archaeological evidence for death related material in sub-Saharan Africa is both immense and varied (Figure 27.2). The extent to which this has been interpreted, as opposed to described or reported, also varies. Although stated as 'an understanding of the past based on data recovered from burials' (Child and De Maret 1996: 51), the research completed in the Upemba Depression in the Luba heartland of south-eastern Congo provides a good example of where interpretation, pertinent both to the archaeology of ritual and religion, but also ethnicity, and the concept of 'history' has been maximized.

Burial evidence indicates that the area was continuously occupied from *c.* the seventh century AD through to the present. A long sequence is thus represented but the term 'Luba', a reference to the dominant contemporary ethno-linguistic group, is not used to describe the archaeological material, for prior to this point in time the sequence is defined by the chronological markers of Kamilambian (seventh century AD), ancient Kisalian (eighth to tenth centuries AD), Classic Kisalian (tenth to thirteenth centuries AD), and Kabambian (thirteenth to seventeenth centuries AD). But even though interpretive subtlety is evident in the sequence proposed, Childs and De Maret (1996: 56) emphasize that continuity is apparent in the burial rituals, pottery, and objects such as ceremonial axes present in the graves in indicating that the people of the Kisalian and Kabambian periods should be regarded as the ancestors of the modern Luba.

Although great selectivity has necessarily had to be employed within the confines of this entry, the spectacular funerary evidence indicating very interesting human–animal relationships at Kerma in the Sudan has to be mentioned. The close relationship between the population of Kerma and its animals has been remarked upon based on evidence from burials and cemeteries (Bonnet 2004: 74). This includes the 'omnipresence of leather' (ibid.) in the form of clothes, chests, bags, hides etc. and animal remains from sacrifices accompanying the dead (see also Chapter 11, 'Sacrifice'). The latter are of particular interest because some of the sheep placed next to corpses in tombs dated to *c.*2500 BC wore leather caps crowned with a disc of ostrich feathers. Bonnet (2004: 82) notes that these are generally young animals and that 'the headdress most likely had a religious character'. Quite what this signifies is unclear but the making of a statement perhaps about concepts of personhood in relation to humanizing or altering animals would not seem an unfeasible inference, albeit a purely hypothetical one.

FIGURE 27.2 Iron Age burial, Ngono, Uganda.

Considering issues of how prominence is accorded the dead and their physical remains and how this might contrast with the processes of refocusing attention away from the corporeal remains and onto the construction of less tangible ancestors also merits research. These are themes considered in Chapter 65, 'Ancestor Cults', and are of relevance in the sub-Saharan African archaeological context. But gaining inferences upon these processes based on archaeology alone would be difficult, though hypotheses might be developed through ethnography. David's (1992) ethnoarchaeological study of the funerary practices of various unhierarchized agricultural societies in the central Mandara Mountains of Cameroon is useful in this respect for all these groups have ancestor cults. The evidence presented indicates, for example, how the form of the grave or tomb can have relevant symbolic connotations. Thus the bell or flagon-shaped tomb of the Mofa or Kapsiki signifies, according to David (1992: 193), 'hut, granary, pot and uterus, all appropriate abodes for the process of ancestralization through germination, gestation and conceivably also fermentation'.

The concept of secondary burial can also be significant in constructing and attaining ancestral status. Ethnography has again contributed to our understanding of these processes, with perhaps the most influential work being that of Metcalf and Huntington (1991), building upon the seminal study of Hertz (1960) looking at rites of separation, transition, and incorporation. This both draws upon sub-Saharan African material, notably from Madagascar (Metcalf and Huntington 1991: 113–30), and has influenced work completed on sub-Saharan African material by others (e.g. David 1992: 182–3). Moreover, material relating to secondary burial and treatment of skeletal remains might also be of importance in providing an insight into people's symbolic relationship with body parts as represented by their sorting and deposition. For something is achieved through these activities and via analogy, potentially, insight could be gained into the operation of similar processes in the past, beyond the fact that they might attest to the possible previous existence of some form of liminality concept. An example of this is provided by Mangut's (1998: 223–4) discussion of skull treatment and deposition in Ron abandoned settlements on the fringes of the Jos Plateau in central Nigeria, work that merits further expansion and reinterpretation.

7 SHRINES AND MONUMENTS

Significant research has also been completed upon both the archaeology and ethnoarchaeology of shrines and sacred groves in sub-Saharan African recently (e.g. Sheridan and Nyamweru 2008; Dawson 2009). Mathers (2003) has explored the relationship between shrines, 'land gods' (ibid.: 32) as places of power, and their links with the founding of settlements and the domestication of the landscape amongst the Kusasi of Northern Ghana, whilst of particular importance is the work that has been undertaken by Chouin (2002, 2008) on the sacred groves of Southern Ghana. The recurring relationship between sacred groves and former settlements has been explored within the framework of perceiving groves as anthropogenic 'creations' and *'lieux de memoire'* (Chouin 2002: 42, 45). In many ways, though Chouin (ibid.: 42) does not exactly state this himself, his point that 'the landscape should be interpreted both as a diachronic accumulation of memorial sediments extending deep into the past, and as a synchronic construction that reshapes a heritage into a present reality' could be extended to the concept of African indigenous religions themselves in their constant interplay between past and present.

Hence sacred groves function much more than as places of sacrifice or as shrines. At sites such as Eguafo sacred groves were found to be associated with abandoned settlements that were politically significant in the past. Even at Asantemanso 30 km south of Kumasi, the most sacred forest of the Ashanti state coincided with a site 'which is the presumed cradle of the Ashanti nation' (Chouin 2002: 43), and where occupation has been dated to c.AD 800. Ethnobotanical research in Tallensi sacred groves indicates similar processes in operation, at groves where human agency potentially contributed to the predominance of species represented (Insoll 2007b). The transformative aspects of sacred groves and shrines is also clearly indicated by Chouin's (2008: 187) ethnoarchaeological research showing how in the face of development pressures groves can be cleared and instead the focal point of the sacred protected by a walled enclosure of cement blocks. Such radical transformations, have, as yet unexplored potential for considering the evolution of religious structures and ritual spaces in sub-Saharan Africa with perhaps interpretive implications beyond the African context.

Shrines and the substances from which they are made can also offer possibilities for exploring via archaeology ritual relationships and obligations, and religious links and influences. This is because shrines can be 'franchised' (Insoll 2006) creating extensive ritual networks actualized through the movement of ideas and tangible materials such as stone, clay, other medicinal substances, or animal remains from the 'parent' shrine (Insoll 2006). Kuba and Lentz (2002: 393) refer to how the stone that forms the centre of a Dagara earth shrine in south-west Burkina Faso and north-west Ghana 'is a surprisingly mobile object', and how power is transferred to other stones surrounding the earth shrine thus producing 'children' of the mother shrine that can in turn form shrines elsewhere. Similarly, among the Tallensi powerful shrines such as Tonna'ab Yaane are franchised (Allman and Parker 2005), via the *Boarbii*, 'the shrine's child' and the *Boarchii*, 'the shrine gourd' (Figure 27.3). These are constructed from various elements including medicinal substances, cow horns, skin, gourds, feathers, and blood (Insoll in preparation). The implications of these processes for interpreting archaeological materials elsewhere are profound in thinking about, for example, why 'exotic' rock is found in Neolithic ritual contexts in the British Isles at sites such as Stonehenge and West Kennet Long Barrow (Insoll 2006).

Where the category of 'shrines' ends and 'monuments' begins is arbitrary. Natural 'monumentality' can exist with regard to both the form and sheer survival of, for instance, sacred groves in areas otherwise largely denuded of tree cover as in northern Ghana (Insoll 2007b). Great Zimbabwe, a massive site in Zimbabwe covering some 700 ha that dates from its main period of use to *c*.AD 1270 to 1450, might be better defined as a 'monument', though equally contains shrines, as well as various other elements. Huffman (1996) has developed interesting, if debatable hypotheses that draw upon ethnographic analogy to contextualize the site, its components, setting, architecture, and small finds in relation to each other in seeking to interpret the symbolic, ritual, and ultimately religious purpose of the site. Hence, for example, he suggests (Huffman 1996: 134–5) that the most famous objects recovered from the site, the carved soapstone birds that seem to represent raptors, were symbols of the mediating role of royal ancestors. An interpretation derived from ethnography, as in the Shona tradition that eagles can be mediators between God and man.

Finally, megaliths are an important but little understood category of relevant monuments in sub-Saharan Africa. These can interrelate with many of the categories already described such as death and burial, materiality, and technology. Four main distributions of megalithic monuments are found in sub-Saharan Africa, in Central Africa, West Africa,

FIGURE 27.3 *Boarbii*, Goldaana House, Bonchiog, Tongo Hills, Ghana, November 2008.

Ethiopia, and Madagascar (Joussaume 1988). As well as between regions, within these regions, diversity in megalithic monument form, size, and interpretations of purpose obviously varies significantly. It is impossible to describe all these monuments here and again a selective approach has had to be employed.

In Central Africa megalithic monuments are found both in the Central African Republic and Cameroon. David (1982), for example, investigated the *tazunu*, 'standing stones', of the western Central African Republic and eastern highland Cameroon. At least 200 *tazunu* exist and are usually formed of oval mounds or tumuli of earth and granite rubble ranging in size from 25 m^2 to 2000 m^2, some containing interior cists, sometimes later exterior ones, and topped with standing stones up to 4 m in height and up to 100 in number. David (1982: 75) suggests a mean date in the early to middle first millennium BC for these monuments and proposes that they are probably funerary monuments though not necessarily tombs. Zangato (1999: 46) has more recently revisited these monuments and based upon 62 dates obtained presents a reconstructed sequence characterized by three periods: Balimbe, Gbabiri, and recent. The main period of *tazunu* is reconstructed as being associated with the Gbabiri of 950 cal BC to 1600 cal AD.

Asombang's (2004) research looking at the standing stones of north-west Cameroon is also of interest in the context of considering the archaeology of ritual and religion in sub-Saharan Africa. This is because he indicates the complexity of the monuments and stresses that this must be accordingly reflected in interpretation. Moreover, Asombang (2004: 300) indicates, based on ethnohistorical testimony and ethnoarchaeological observation, that the survival of standing stone settings need not necessarily imply a ritual function. One example provided is in the parallels found for 3 x 3 m rectangular stone alignments or platforms recorded within megalithic monuments with granary bases used to protect bamboo granary structures and their contents from insect damage. Crucial here are the 'de-ritualized' interpretive pointers Asombang presents, though it should be noted that 'ritually' associated granaries could also exist!

Beyond function and date attention could be focused upon the stone from which the megaliths are made, how they are finished, and what in some instances they might depict. A key site in this respect is Tondidarou in Mali where *c*.150 standing stones were recorded dating from, possibly, the seventh to ninth centuries AD. These stones range in height between 50 cm and 2 m and some are phallic in form and often decorated with incisions and patterns (Dembele and Person 1993: 446–7). This is unlikely to be a direct representation of such drastic alteration of the penis but could be an allusion to scarification of other aspects of the body. Moreover, some of the stones also represented navels, everted umbilical hernias, features that can also be represented on the phallic stones themselves (see Dembele and Person 1993: 447). Hence, again, interesting statements about bodies and persons seem to be made that could be further explored in relation to the context of the stones and their parallels with similar figurative megaliths elsewhere such as the less stylized phallic stones, the *Akwanshi* of the Cross River region of eastern Nigeria that can include arms on the side of the phallus as well as facial features, navels, and scarification marks (see Allison 1968: 29–30; Ray 2004: 193–4).

8 Future Directions in Investigating the Archaeology of Ritual and Religion in Sub-Saharan Africa

The future focus of archaeological research on ritual and religion in sub-Saharan Africa is potentially various. Greater attention could be paid to charting trajectories of religious change, fusion, and syncretism in relation to material culture. Sub-Saharan African indigenous religions have never been static phenomena but have been adaptable and as their continued existence today indicates, resilient. Similarly, conceptually 'decompartmentalizing' religion itself might be useful so that, for instance, the interface between 'religion' and 'medicine' is recognized. This is of great pertinence in conceptualizing religion in sub-Saharan Africa (Morris 2006: 151), but 'medicine' is a term rarely used in archaeological contexts, certainly with reference to religion. In so doing, a return to the more fluid types of definitions discussed by W. H. R. Rivers (1924: 4) is made, where 'medicine' is not distinguished from 'magic', a term that is less useful here, but also 'religion', and in so doing this perhaps permits an exploration of a more encompassing archaeology of ritual and religion in sub-Saharan Africa.

Suggested Reading

The references provided in the text should obviously be followed according to areas or subjects of interest. In more general terms de Maret's (1994) article on what he terms 'Traditional African Religious Expression' should be looked at. Whilst for a summary of the anthropological background the relevant chapter in Morris (2006), *Religion and Anthropology*, is useful.

References

Allison, P. 1968. *African Stone Sculpture* (London: Lund Humphries).
Allman, J. and Parker, J. 2005. *Tongnaab* (Bloomington: Indiana University Press).
Asombang, R. N. 2004. 'Interpreting standing stones in Africa: A case study in north-west Cameroon', *Antiquity*, 78: 294–305.
Bahn, P. and Vertut, G. 1988. *Images of the Ice Age* (New York: Facts on File).
Barbaza, M., and Jarry, M. 2004. 'Le Site de Tondiedo a Markoye (Burkina Faso). Elaboration d'un Modele Théorique pour l'Étude de l'Art Rupestre Protohistorique du Sahel Burkinabe', *Sahara*, 15: 83–96.
Barham, L. and Mitchell, P. 2008. *The First Africans* (Cambridge: Cambridge University Press).
Barley, N. 1984. 'Placing the West African Potter' in J. Picton (ed.) *Earthenware in Asia and Africa* (London: Percival David Foundation of Chinese Art), pp. 93–105.

BEDNARIK, R. G. 1998. 'The "Australopithecine" cobble from Makapansgat, South Africa', *South African Archaeological Bulletin*, 53: 4–8.

BEEK, W. VAN 1988. 'Functions of sculpture in Dogon religion', *African Arts*, 21(4): 58–65, 91.

BERNS, M. 1993. 'Art, history, and gender: Women and clay in West Africa', *African Archaeological Review*, 11: 129–48.

BONNET, C. 2004. 'The Kerma culture', in D. A. Welsby and J. R. Anderson (eds), *Sudan: Ancient treasures* (London: British Museum Press), pp. 70–89.

CHILDS, S. T. and DE MARET, P. 1996. 'Re/Constructing Luba Pasts', in M. Nooter Roberts and A. F. Roberts (eds), *Luba Art and the Making of History* (New York: Museum for African Art), pp. 49–59.

CHOUIN, G. 2002. 'Sacred groves in history: Pathways to the social shaping of forest landscapes in coastal Ghana', *IDS Bulletin*, 33: 39–46.

——2008. 'Archaeological perspectives on sacred groves in Ghana' in M. J. Sheridan and C. Nyamweru (eds), *African Sacred Groves: Ecological dynamics and social change* (Oxford: James Currey), pp. 178–94.

DAVID, N. 1982. *Tazunu*: Megalithic monuments of Central Africa', *Azania*, 17: 43–77.

——1992. 'The archaeology of ideology: Mortuary practices in the Central Mandara Highlands, northern Cameroon' in J. Sterner and N. David (eds), *An African Commitment* (Calgary: University of Calgary Press), pp. 181–210.

DAWSON, A. (ed.) 2009. *Shrines in African Societies* (Calgary: University of Calgary Press).

DEACON, H. J. and DEACON, J. 1999. *Human Beginnings in South Africa* (Walnut Creek, CA: Altamira).

DEMBELE, M. and PERSON, A. 1993. 'Tondidarou, un foyer original du megalithisme africain dans la vallée du fleuve Niger au Mali' in J. Devisse (ed.), *Vallées du Niger* (Paris: Reunion des Musees Nationaux), pp. 441–55.

D'ERRICO, F., HENSHILWOOD, C., and NILSSEN, P. 2001. 'An engraved bone fragment from c.70,000-year-old MSA levels at Blombos Cave, South Africa: Implications for the origin of symbolism and language', *Antiquity*, 75: 309–18.

—— ——, VANHAEREN, M., and VAN NIEKERK, K. 2005. '*Nassarius kraussianus* Shell Beads from Blombos Cave: Evidence for symbolic behaviour in the Middle Stone Age', *Journal of Human Evolution*, 48: 3–24.

DIETERLEN, G. 1989. 'Masks and mythology among the Dogon', *African Arts*, 22(3): 34–43, 87–8.

DOUGLAS, M. 1999. *Implicit Meanings: Selected essays in anthropology* (London: Routledge).

EDWARDS, D. 1999. 'Christianity and Islam in the Middle Nile: Towards a study of religion and social change in the long term' in T. Insoll (ed.), *Case Studies in Archaeology and World Religion*, BAR S755 (Oxford: Archaeopress), pp. 94–104.

ELIADE, M. 1964 (1989). *Shamanism: Archaic techniques of ecstasy* (London: Penguin).

EVANS-PRITCHARD, E. E. 1956. *Nuer Religion* (Oxford: Oxford University Press).

FINNERAN, N. 2002. *The Archaeology of Christianity in Africa* (Stroud: Tempus).

FORTES, M. 1987. *Religion, Morality and the Person* (Cambridge: Cambridge University Press).

FRANK, B. 1998. *Mande Potters and Leather-Workers* (Washington: Smithsonian Institution Press).

GILES, M. 2007. 'Making metal and forging relations: Ironworking in the British Iron Age', *Oxford Journal of Archaeology*, 26: 395–413.

GOODY, J. 1962. *Death, Property, and the Ancestors* (London: Tavistock).

GOSSELAIN, O. 1999. 'In pots we trust: The processing of clay and symbols in sub-Saharan Africa', *Journal of Material Culture*, 4: 205–30.

—— and LIVINGSTONE SMITH, A. 2005. 'The source. Clay selection and processing practices in sub-Saharan Africa' in A. Livingstone Smith, D. Bosquet, and R. Martineau (eds), *Pottery Manufacturing Processes: Reconstitution and interpretation*, BAR S1349 (Oxford: Archaeopress), pp. 33–47.

GUTIERREZ, M. 2008. 'L'Art rupestre de la province de Namibe, Angola: Étude des sites par rapport a leur position topographique', *Journal of African Archaeology*, 6: 21–32.

HAALAND, R. 2007. 'Say it in iron: Symbols of transformation and reproduction in the European Iron Age', *Current Swedish Archaeology*, 15: 1–20.

HERBERT, E. 1993. *Iron, Gender and Power* (Bloomington: Indiana University Press).

HERTZ, R. 1960. *Death and the Right Hand*, trans. R. Needham and C. Needham (London: Cohen and West).

HODDER, I. 1982. *Symbols in Action* (Cambridge: Cambridge University Press).

HUFFMAN, T. 1996. *Snakes and Crocodiles: Power and symbolism in ancient Zimbabwe* (Johannesburg: Witwatersrand University Press).

IDOWU, E. B. 1973. *African Traditional Religion: A definition* (London: SCM Press).

INSOLL, T. 1996. *Islam, Archaeology and History: Gao region (Mali) ca.AD 900–1250*, BAR S647 (Oxford: Tempus Reparatum).

—— 2003. *The Archaeology of Islam in Sub-Saharan Africa* (Cambridge: Cambridge University Press).

—— 2004. *Archaeology, Ritual, Religion* (London: Routledge).

—— 2006. 'Shrine franchising and the Neolithic in the British Isles: Some observations based upon the Tallensi, northern Ghana', *Cambridge Archaeological Journal*, 16: 223–38.

—— 2007a. *Archaeology: The conceptual challenge* (London: Duckworth).

—— 2007b. 'Natural or human spaces? Tallensi sacred groves and shrines and their potential implications for aspects of Northern European prehistory and phenomenological interpretation', *Norwegian Archaeological Review*, 40: 138–58.

—— 2009. 'Materialising performance and ritual: Decoding the archaeology of shrines in northern Ghana', *Material Religion*, 5: 288–311.

—— 2010. 'Pots and earth cults: The context and materiality of archaeological ceramics amongst the Tallensi of northern Ghana and their interpretive implications', in N. Naguib and B. De Vries (eds), *Heureux qui comme Ulysses a fait un Beau Voyage: the movements of people in Time and Space* (Bergen: Bric Press), pp. 189–212.

—— in preparation. *Theoretical Explorations in African Archaeology: Contexts, materials, persons, and animals* (Oxford: Oxford University Press).

——, KANKPEYENG, B., and MACLEAN, R. 2007. 'Shrines, rituals, and archaeology in northern Ghana', *Current World Archaeology*, 26: 29–36.

JACOBSON-WIDDING, A. and VAN BEEK, W. 1990. 'Chaos, order, and communion in African models of fertility' in A. Jacobson-Widding and W. van Beek (eds), *The Creative Communion: African folk models of fertility and the regeneration of life* (Uppsala: Uppsala University Press), pp. 15–43.

JOUSSAUME, R. 1988. *Dolmens for the Dead* (London: Guild Publishing).

KANKPEYENG, B. and NKUMBAAN, S. N. 2008. 'Rethinking the stone circles of Komaland: A preliminary report on the 2007/2008 fieldwork at Yikpabongo, Northern Region, Ghana' in T. Insoll (ed.), *Current Archaeological Research in Ghana*, BAR S1847 (Oxford: Archaeopress), pp. 95–102.

KEHOE, A. 2001. *Shamans and Religion* (Prospect Heights: Waveland Press).

KEMP, B. J. 1995. 'How religious were the ancient Egyptians?', *Cambridge Archaeological Journal*, 5: 25–54.
KINAHAN, J. 1995. 'Charcoal drawing of an antelope and charcoal drawing of animal–human figure' in T. Phillips (ed.), *Africa: The art of a continent* (London: Royal Academy of Arts), pp. 187–8.
KLEINITZ, C. and OLSSON, C. 2005. 'Christian period rock art landscapes in the Fourth Cataract Region: The Dar el-Arab and et-Tereif rock art surveys', *Sudan and Nubia*, 9: 32–9.
—— and KOENITZ, R. 2006. 'Fourth Nile Cataract petroglyphs in context: The ed-Doma and Dirbi rock art survey', *Sudan and Nubia*, 10: 34–42.
KUBA, R. and LENTZ, C. 2002. 'Arrows and earth shrines: Towards a history of Dagara expansion in southern Burkina Faso', *Journal of African History*, 43: 377–406.
LAYTON, R. 2000. 'Review feature. Shamanism, totemism and rock art: *Les Chamanes de la Préhistoire* in the context of rock art research', *Cambridge Archaeological Journal*, 10: 169–86.
LEBEUF, J.-P. and MASSON DETOURBET, A. 1950. *La Civilisation du Tchad* (Paris: Payot).
——, TREINEN-CLAUSTRE, F., and COURTIN, J. 1980. *Le Gisement Sao de Mdaga* (Paris: Societe d'Ethnographie).
LÉVI-STRAUSS, C. 1964 (1991). *Totemism* (London: Merlin Press).
LEWIS, I. M. 1997. 'The shaman's quest in Africa', *Cahier d'Études Africaines*, 145: 119–35.
LEWIS-WILLIAMS, D. 2002. *The Mind in the Cave* (London: Thames and Hudson).
LEWIS-WILLIAMS, J. D. and DOWSON, T. A. 1988. 'The signs of all times: Entoptic phenomena in Upper Palaeolithic art', *Current Anthropology*, 29: 201–45.
MCBREARTY, S. and BROOKS, A. S. 2000. 'The revolution that wasn't: A new interpretation of the origin of modern human behaviour', *Journal of Human Evolution*, 39: 453–563.
MCINTOSH, R. J. and MCINTOSH, S. K. 1979. 'Terracotta statuettes from Mali', *African Arts*, 12(2): 51–3.
—— —— 1988. 'From siécles obscurs to revolutionary centuries in the Middle Niger', *World Archaeology*, 20: 141–65.
MCINTOSH, S. K. (ed.) 1995. *Excavations at Jenne-jeno, Hambarketolo, and Kaniana (Inland Niger Delta, Mali), the 1981 Season* (Los Angeles: University of California Press).
MANGUT, J. 1998. 'An archaeological investigation of Ron abandoned settlements on the Jos Plateau: A case of historical archaeology' in K. W. Wesler (ed.), *Historical Archaeology in Nigeria* (Trenton: Africa World Press), pp. 199–241.
MARET, P. DE 1994. 'Archaeological and other prehistoric evidence of traditional African religious expression' in T. D. Blakely, W. E. A. van Beek, and D. L. Thomson (eds), *Religion in Africa* (London: James Currey), pp. 182–95.
—— 1995. 'Zoomorphic head' in T. Phillips (ed.), *Africa: The art of a continent* (London: Royal Academy of Arts), p. 240.
MATHERS, C. 2003. 'Shrines and the domestication of landscape', *Journal of Anthropological Research*, 59: 23–45.
MBITI, J. S. 1989. *African Religions and Philosophy* (Oxford: Heinemann).
MEADOWS, M. E. 1999. 'Biogeography' in W. M. Adams, A. S. Goudie, and A. R. Orme (eds), *The Physical Geography of Africa* (Oxford: Oxford University Press), pp. 161–72.
METCALF, P. and HUNTINGTON, R. 1991. *Celebrations of Death: The anthropology of mortuary ritual* (Cambridge: Cambridge University Press).
MORRIS, B. 2006. *Religion and Anthropology: A critical introduction* (Cambridge: Cambridge University Press).
PHILLIPSON, D. 1998. *Ancient Ethiopia* (London: British Museum Press).

Ray, K. 2004. 'Boka Botuom and the decorated stones of the Cross River region, eastern Nigeria' in A. Reid and P. Lane (eds), *African Historical Archaeologies* (New York: Kluwer Plenum), pp. 189–217.

Reid, A., and MacLean, R. 1995. 'Symbolism and the social contexts of iron production in Karagwe', *World Archaeology*, 27: 144–61.

Richards, J. E. 2005. *Society and Death in Ancient Egypt: Mortuary landscapes of the Middle Kingdom* (Cambridge: Cambridge University Press).

Rivers, W. H. R. 1924 (2002). *Medicine, Magic and Religion* (London: Routledge).

Roberts, A. F. 1995. *Animals in African Art* (New York: Museum for African Art).

Rupp, N., Ameje, J., and Breunig, P. 2005. 'New studies on the Nok culture of central Nigeria', *Journal of African Archaeology*, 3: 283–290.

Scarre, C. and Lawson, G. (eds) 2006. *Archaeoacoustics* (Cambridge: McDonald Institute for Archaeological Research).

Schmidt, P. 1997. *Iron Technology in East Africa* (Oxford: James Currey).

——and McIntosh, R. J. 1996. *Plundering Africa's Past* (Oxford: James Currey).

Shaw, R. 1990. 'The invention of "African Traditional Religion"', *Religion*, 20: 339–53.

Sheridan, M. J. and Nyamweru, C. (eds) 2008. *African Sacred Groves: Ecological dynamics and social change* (Oxford: James Currey).

Singer, R. and Wymer, J. 1982. *The Middle Stone Age at Klasies River Mouth in South Africa* (Chicago: University of Chicago Press).

Solomon, A. 1997. 'The myth of ritual origins? Ethnography, mythology and interpretation of San rock art', *South African Archaeological Bulletin*, 52: 3–13.

—— 2000. 'On different approaches to San rock art', *South African Archaeological Bulletin*, 55: 77–8.

Stringer, C. and Gamble, C. 1993. *In Search of the Neanderthals* (London: Thames and Hudson).

Turner, V. 1969. *The Ritual Process* (Harmondsworth: Penguin).

Wadley, L. 2001. 'What is cultural modernity? A general view and South African perspective from Rose Cottage Cave', *Cambridge Archaeological Journal*, 11: 201–21.

Zangato, E. 1999. *Societes Prehistoriques et Megalithes dans le Nord-Ouest de la Republique Centrafricaine*, BAR S768 (Oxford: Archaeopress).

CHAPTER 28

THE PREHISTORY OF RELIGION IN CHINA

LUKAS NICKEL

1 INTRODUCTION

RESEARCH into prehistory, a term describing a stage in the development of societies before the advent of writing, mainly relies on information provided by archaeology. In China, written sources begin to fill in the gaps of the archaeological record during the second half of the second millennium BC, when ritual practitioners began to meticulously document on turtle shells and cattle scapula their communications with the supernatural powers they believed in. In Anyang, the last capital of the Shang dynasty (c.1600–1046 BC) hundreds of thousands of so-called oracle bones have been found (Thorp 2006: 122; Bagley 1999: 130). The inscriptions which use an early form of Chinese script which is largely still legible, are records of divination carried out at the Shang court, inquiring about harvest and natural phenomena, matters of warfare and personal welfare of the king. It thus was the royal diviners, persons in charge of the communication with the supernatural beings of Shang religion, who put an end to 'prehistory' in China.

Over the following millennium, scribes and educated noblemen produced an ever-growing corpus of literature: philosophical texts, chronicles, dedicatory inscriptions, legal contracts, poems, and diaries. They wrote, however, only rarely explicitly about the principles of their beliefs, leaving information about their religious environment in scattered remarks in texts mainly dealing with other questions. The first thoroughly documented religion was Buddhism, a foreign faith which became known in China at the end of the Han dynasty (206 BC–AD 220). While for the first millennium BC a multitude of data about wars, diplomatic encounters between states, events at the courts and observations of natural disasters are recorded with precision, and 'history' is well established, 'prehistory'—in its literal sense—of religion in China, one may propose, lasted even beyond the point when writing was developed. This chapter will introduce evidence for religion in both late Neolithic and early historic China, mainly relying on archaeological sources.

Religion is used here as a general term for human beliefs in the supernatural which may have had its visual expression in acts of veneration, sacrifices, and rituals.

2 Early Evidence for Religious Activity

From the sixth millennium BC wide parts of what is now northern and central China were inhabited by advanced Neolithic societies. They left archaeological traces which point towards religious activity. The following paragraphs will introduce a small selection of finds from cultures of northern, eastern, and south-western China which may have had a religious significance to the early inhabitants of this area.

Several cultures of the fifth and fourth millennium BC in northern China which are traditionally summarized under the name Yangshao, do display features that suggest religious activity. Designs on the red pottery typical for central and western-central China, featuring abstract motifs or schematic drawings of fish, frogs, and other animals, have been interpreted as having a religious meaning (Chang 1999: 49–52 and fig. 1.4). In Banpo, the so far best-researched Neolithic settlement near modern Xian, Shaanxi province, dating to about 4500 BC, black designs on red pottery show stylized animals seen frontally (Figure 28.1). Foundations of a large hall were discovered which may have served as a gathering place and a religious focus point. Human skulls lay under the floor and walls of the building, suggesting a sacrificial activity during the erection of the structure (Zhang Zhongpei 2005: 78).

In Xishuipo in Puyang county, modern Henan province, one tomb (no. 45), dating to the middle of the fifth millennium BC, contained four skeletons: three male and one female. It is possible that the three skeletons accompanying the main burial were sacrificial victims. Clam-shell mosaics laid out on the ground to both sides of the main skeleton depicted animals. Below the feet of the main skeleton more shells and two human bones formed another mosaic which is not clearly recognizable (Figure 28.2). The animal depictions may have had a religious meaning for the people who made them.

FIGURE 28.1 Schematic drawing on a ceramic bowl from Banpo, Shaanxi province, fifth millennium BC.

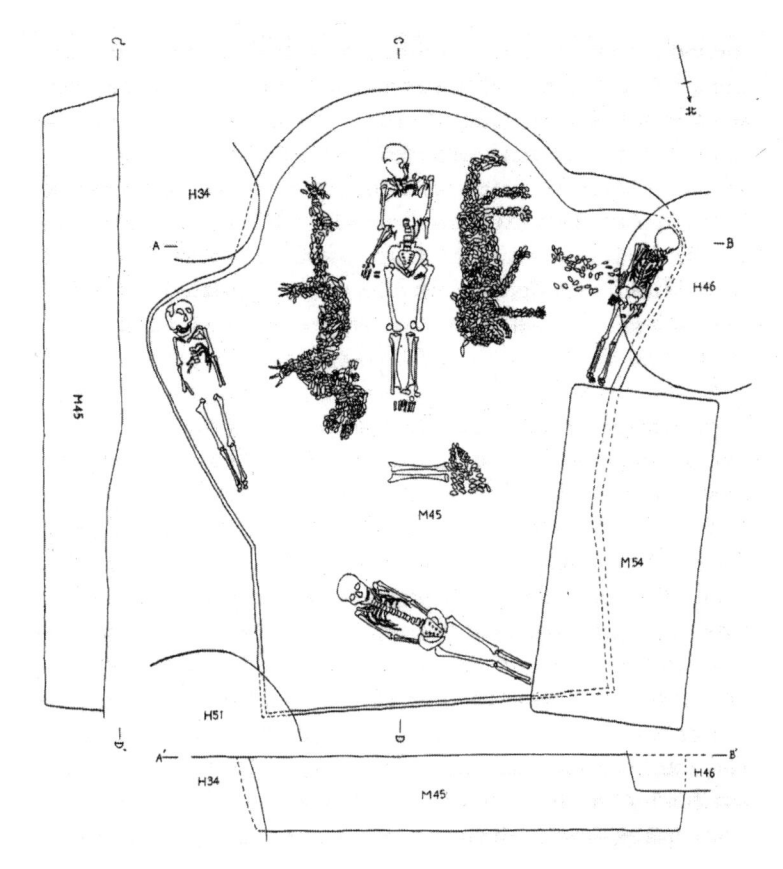

FIGURE 28.2 Plan of tomb 45 from Xishuipo, Puyang, Henan province, mid-fifth millenium BC.

Many early religions employed anthropomorphic images for the depiction of supreme beings. In Christian thinking, humans were even thought to have been shaped as images of God, which gave them a special position among other parts of the creation (Erickson 1994: 498–510). An obvious rarity of human-shaped motifs in painting, sculpture or relief decoration may suggest that the visualization of supreme beings did play only a minor role in the imagination of northern Chinese peoples, a characteristic which appears to have persisted in that area until the unification of the country by the First Emperor in 221 BC (Nickel 2006). Only cultures on the periphery of the modern Chinese territory like the Majiayao culture (3300–2050) in Qinghai in the west, the Hongshan culture (4700–2900 BC) in Liaoning in the northeast, and several Neolithic cultures in the south showed more interest in human and animal-shaped objects. Many of the finds with anthropomorphic decoration have been summarized by Helmut Brinker (Brinker 1995). Vases from Majiayao sites displayed, next to abstract painted motifs, masks or whole human bodies in relief, sometimes with explicit sexual connotations (Rawson 1996: 36–9; Zhang Zhongpei 2005: 76 and fig. 3.49).

Human figures made of clay and remains of non-residential buildings have been found in the Hongshan culture sites Dongshanzui and Niuheliang in modern Liaoning province. Dongshanzui was active in the middle of the fourth millennium BC. The site was enclosed by a wall and contained several architectural structures with stone-laid foundations as well as burials and earth mounds. Painted clay cylinders often interpreted as columns, small animal-shaped jade carvings, and 20 female figurines, the tallest of which is nearly 80 cm in height, support the identification as a religious site (Chang 1986: 186; Barnes 1999: 109–10). Remains of much taller clay figures were found in Niuheliang, active about the same time. A human figure with eyes inlaid in jade was about life-size, while others were more than twice as tall. The site also contained a pyramid-shaped structure made of stone, several large tombs, more clay cylinders and fragments of wall paintings (*Hongshan* 1994). Both sites may have served as political and religious centres of the Hongshan culture, though the beliefs which led to their construction are not known anymore.

In the east-coast region, during the middle and late phases of the Dawenkou culture (4100–2600 BC), centred in modern Shandong province, tombs of differing sizes were built which suggests growing social differentiation (Barnes 1999: 110). Large burials had ledges running around the tomb chamber providing room for the placement of burial goods. The special care for the dead again points towards the religiosity of the Dawenkou society.

Dawenkou was superseded by several late Neolithic societies traditionally summarized under the name Longshan culture which occupied the Shandong peninsula, the middle and lower reaches of the Yellow River and parts of the eastern coast during the third millennium BC. Longshan sites are characterized by the prevalence of black ceramics and the use of jade, ivory, and turtle shells. Some ceramic vessels, especially high-stemmed cups made of an extremely thin, polished ware—so-called eggshell ceramics—were too fragile to be of everyday use. The objects quite certainly had a religious significance to their owners. One can hypothesize that they served in cults involving libation ceremonies.

Clear evidence for buildings with religious purpose is still missing for many Neolithic cultures of the northern plains. More to the south, in the Yangzi River delta, one such site has been reported. In Yaoshan, a large settlement of the Liangzhu culture (3400–2250 BC) of modern Zhejiang and Jiangsu province, a square structure of pounded earth was found. The platform was located in close proximity to a group of well-equipped tombs. It was described by the excavators as an altar serving the tombs of shamans (*Wenwu* 1988: 32–3). In other sites even larger rectangular elevated platforms were found which contained tombs of high-ranking persons (Chang 1999: 61–3).

Liangzhu culture is famous for the abundance of jade objects found in its tombs. The manufacture of jades required an advanced technology and points towards division of labour. The most significant shapes of jades were *bi*, *cong*, and *yue*. While *bi* were flat discs with a hole drilled through its centre, *cong* were hollow cylinders, the outer cross-section of which were fashioned as squares with rounded sides (Figure 28.3). *Yue* were flat axes originally attached to a wooden haft. The sheer amount of these objects found in elite tombs—tomb 20 in Fanshan, for instance, contained 547 jade items—as well as their weight—the largest *cong* known was discovered in tomb 12 in Fanshan and weighs 3.5 kg (Shao Wangping 2005: 112)—suggest that they were not just personal ornaments but had a special significance.

Engraved in some of the jades were frontal depictions of a hybrid creature with a feather headdress. Sometimes the motif was reduced to a pair of eyes (for an illustration see Shao Wangping 2005: fig. 4.44). The headdress may signify some sort of religious figure, while the discs, cylinders, and axes were probably used in rituals by the elite of the highly stratified Liangzhu society.

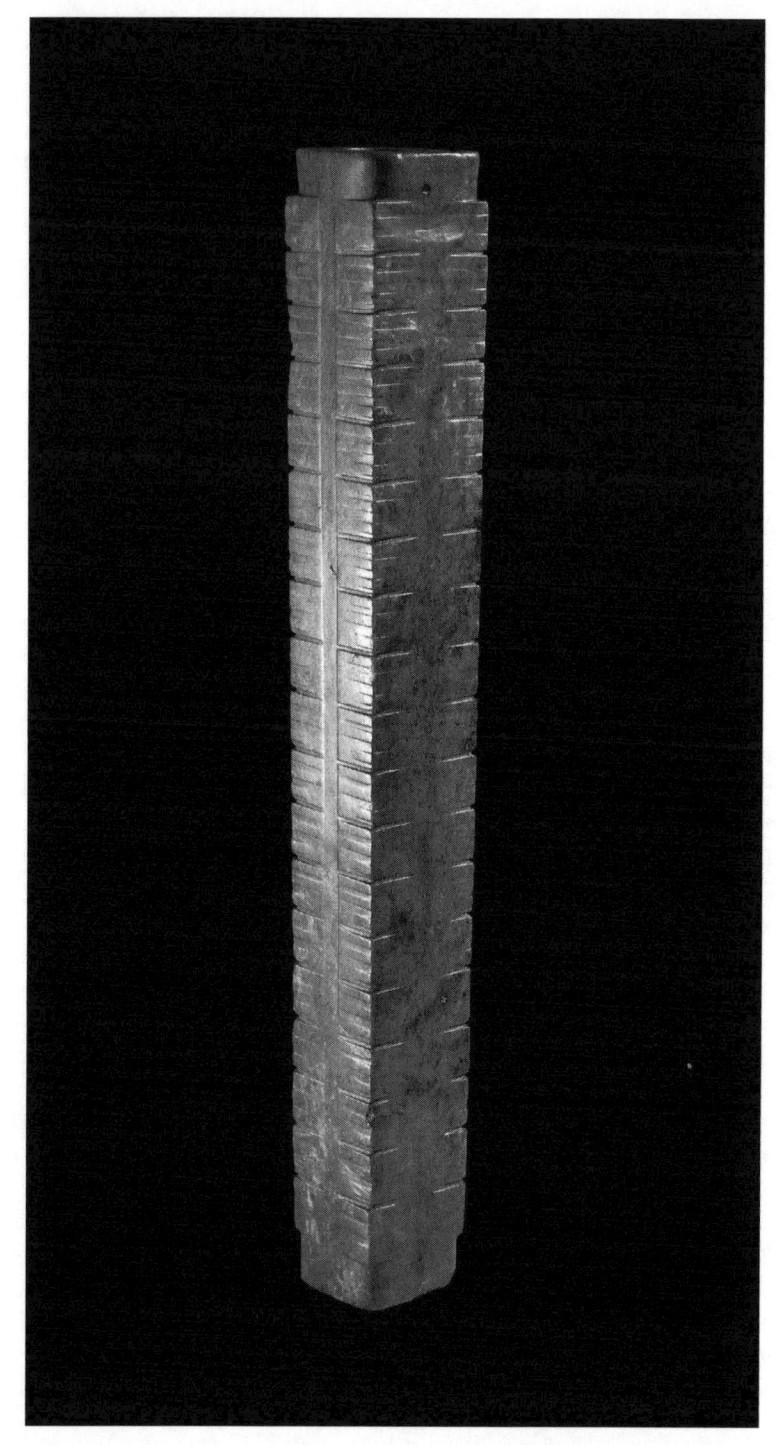

FIGURE 28.3 Jade *cong*, height 49.5 cm, from southern China, Liangzhu culture, around 2500 BC.

In the area to the south and south-west along the middle reaches of the Yangzi river, excavated tombs document an accumulation of wealth and a hierarchical division of society. Numerous non-utilitarian objects again point towards religious activity. From the Qujialing culture (3000–2600 BC) several conical ceramic objects more than 1 m tall with projecting spikes are known. It has been suggested that these impressive objects represented phalli and were used in fertility cults (Zhang Xuqiu 1992; Wiedehage 1995a). In Dengjiawan, a settlement of the Shijiahe culture (2400–2000 BC), thousands of small clay figurines of human and animal shape, most of them between 5 and 10 cm tall, were found. Since all of them were located in pits and none was excavated in a tomb, they certainly served ritual functions outside the funeral context (Wiedehage 1995b; Zhang and Okamura 1999: 89; for more information on the Shijiahe site see Shao Wangping 2005: 106–12).

Neolithic cultures discovered in the northern plains, the Shandong peninsula, the eastern coastline and the valley of the Yangzi River left remains which were linked to the religious ideas of their owners. While beliefs and rituals undoubtedly existed, it is difficult to clearly identify the ideas that initiated the creation of non-utilitarian buildings, tomb furnishings, and objects. It is generally assumed, however, that by the early second millennium BC several Neolithic cultures developed a ritual system, which helped to establish ideas of kingship and visualize the social structure of their societies (Gao Wei 1989).

3 Interpretation of Archaeological Finds

While the non-utilitarian character of some of the objects recovered from Neolithic sites suggests ritual uses, the identification of underlying ideas proved to be difficult. Next to the general problem of reconstructing beliefs of non-literate societies from the scattered archaeological evidence, in the Chinese case research often has been influenced by assumptions drawn from a vast corpus of literature from early historic times. Perhaps even more than in Biblical archaeology (for this see Insoll 2001: 10–15; Lane 2001), excavated material has been used as an illustration of religious ideas and ritual practices as described in texts—many of which were compiled in the late first millennium BC or later—rather than as independent sources of information.

One prime example for the impact of late texts upon the interpretation of archaeological material is the discussion about the clam-shell mosaics in tomb 45 in Xishuipo, Henan province (middle of fifth millennium BC), mentioned above. The mosaics to the sides of the main burial depict two animals which are often interpreted as the earliest depictions of two animals of the cardinal directions, the 'Blue Dragon of the East' and the 'White Tiger of the West', the pair being one of the most widespread cosmological motifs in Han period art and popular religion from the second century BC onwards. May we really assume that these two depictions in Xishuipo are the earliest evidence of a cosmological idea popular in early medieval China? The animal depiction in itself does not readily support this interpretation. One has an elongated head, a lean, S-shaped body, a long tail and two extremities with claws. It bears resemblance to a crocodile, but may as well fit later conventions in representing dragons. The other animal has a thick body, a rounded head, four extremities, and a pronounced tail. The people who made the mosaic may have meant any feline animal, such as a leopard, a female lion, a panther, or even a dog. Only a viewer accustomed to Han and post-Han representational practices will recognize the animals as 'tiger' and 'dragon' without hesitation.

Dragon and tiger as an iconographic pair were often depicted in Chinese art from the second century BC onwards. They first appear in the decoration of censers with mountain-shaped lids (*boshanlu*) and wine warmers made of bronze (the earliest example is possibly found on a high-stemmed mountain censer dating to the middle second century BC; see Fong 1980: pl. 20). In the following centuries the pair became one of the most frequently used motifs in the imagery of folk religion. Before the Han dynasty, however, the motif was hardly employed. The only earlier depiction which may be interpreted as dragon and tiger was found framing a celestial chart on the lid of a lacquered box from the tomb of Zeng Hou Yi (died 433 BC; see Harper 1999: 833–40; Falkenhausen 2006: 313), but the identification of the crude line drawings of two animals is far from certain. In literature, dragon and tiger as a pair are mentioned in works from the late third century onwards. A clear cosmological connotation was first applied to them in the *Chuci* and the *Huainanzi*, mainly dated to the third and second century BC (Nickel 1997).

Both the archaeological record and the received texts suggest that dragon and tiger as a pair, and the cosmological ideas connected to them, only became widespread from around 200 BC. It is possible, of course, that the Han-period texts referred to an ancient belief system that was, until then, only communicated orally. But between the Xishuipo tomb and the next assumed depiction of the topic there is a wide gap of 4,000 years. If dragon and tiger as a cosmological pair and as symbols of East and West were really an ancient idea that was transmitted over several thousand years to Han-period astrologers, one would expect it to have been depicted at least occasionally, especially since ritual bronzes of the Shang and Zhou periods were extensively decorated with zoomorphic motives. Without such a link, however, it is difficult to assume an intellectual continuity from the fifth millennium BC to the Han period. What animals the Niuheliang people wanted to depict and which ideas they connected to them we may find out at some point, but for the moment the application of later ideas might limit rather than facilitate our search.

4 SHAMANISM

The interpretation of the two animals in tomb no. 45 in Xishuipo as dragon and tiger, the celestial animals of the cardinal directions (as well as the subsequent reading of more clamshells and two human bones placed to the feet of the main tomb occupant as the constellation Big Dipper, *beidou*), resulted in the assumption that the tomb was built for a shaman (Chang 1999: 50–2), a person capable of communication and interaction with supreme beings and the non-human world (Eliade 1951; Price, Ch. 61, this volume). Without the equation of the animal depictions in tomb no. 45 with the animals of the cardinal directions the shamanistic interpretation would become far less obvious.

Many scholars believe that shamanistic practices have been an important aspect of religiosity in Neolithic East Asia. K. C. Chang proposed that shamanism was a substratial feature that differentiated Neolithic and Bronze Age societies on Chinese soil from that of other areas (ibid.: 52; Chang 1986: 418). David Keightley challenged the argument of shamanistic prevalence in Shang and pre-Shang China (Keightley 1998: 821–4). While oracle bone inscriptions indicate that exorcism and other rites usually connected to shamanism were practised in Anyang, clear reference to shamanism we find only in transmitted texts from the second half of the first millennium BC onwards.

The earliest written source explicitly mentioning shamanism is the Guo Yu ('Sayings of the States', fifth and fourth centuries BC). The text puts shamanistic practices into the distant past:

> At that time there were certain persons who were so perspicacious, single-minded, and reverential that their understanding enabled them to make meaningful collation of what lies above and below, and their insight to illumine what is distant and profound. Therefore the spirits would descend into them. The possessors of such powers were, if men, called *hsi* (shamans), and, if women, *wu* (shamanesses). It is they who supervised the positions of the spirits at the ceremonies, sacrificed to them, and otherwise handled religious matters. [Bodde 1961: 390]

Later texts, like the Chuci ('Elegies of Chu', third to second century BC), also include descriptions of shamanistic procedures. During the late Warring States and Han periods, such practices were apparently not uncommon (Chang 1983: 44–55; for a recent study of late Zhou understanding of shamanism see Fu-shih Lin 2009). If these were, at the time, indigenous or foreign cults is still unclear. Intensive contacts with nomadic tribes from the Ordos region, southern Siberia and Mongolia during the second half of the first millennium BC would allow the authors to report on foreign, in their eyes 'primitive' practices, which they may then have been placed into the story line of their own early history. While the archaeological evidence may be insufficient to prove the prevalence of shamanism in Neolithic China, the cult was certainly well established in the early historic period (Puett 2004: 194).

5 ANCESTOR WORSHIP

Ancestor worship and beliefs in the potency of the dead is one religious framework that continued to strongly influence the Chinese mind throughout the historic period. Judging from the sheer wealth of funerary objects placed in elite tombs of Longshan sites in Shandong or Liangzhu graveyards in eastern China, it seems safe to assume that elements of ancestor cults already developed during the late Neolithic. Keightley saw the 'remarkable care with which the inhabitants of Neolithic China treated their dead' as an indication that ancestor worship had its roots even in the fifth and fourth millennia BC (Keightley 2004: 5).

Even if many richly equipped elite tombs of the Neolithic have been discovered during excavations, the finds only allow very few uncontroversial explanations. We may state that the bereaved felt it necessary to provide the dead with food and drink vessels, which possibly contained food and beverages during the time of the burial. This should mean that the dead would exist and remain active in some form after the funeral. Other objects, like the jade *cong* and *bi* in Liangzhu-culture tombs, appear to be indicators of status and wealth and a growing division of society, as only a minority of tombs were equipped with such items. The social hierarchy obviously extended beyond death.

6 Shang Religious Practice

How complex early beliefs connected to ancestors may actually have been can only be understood when looking at the Shang dynasty situation from about 1250 BC, the moment when diviners began to document their communications with gods and ancestors on oracle bones. It emerges that the Shang kings did not just venerate their immediate predecessors, but had established a long line of ancestors reaching back to times before the founding of the dynasty. Next to the main line of their ancestors, they were also aware of secondary lineages and, for instance, spouses of kings. By worshipping their ancestors the Shang kings defined their own position in a historic timeline as well as in a social framework. Ancestors were impersonalized to give them a broader functionality. They were not addressed by using their personal name, but by temple names—posthumous ritual titles given to them according to their position in the lineage extending back to a founding ancestor. The types and amount of sacrifices were determined by the ancestors' rank rather than by any personal virtue. Offerings were provided following a ritual cycle which grew more systematic in time. It constituted the first steps towards the development of a calendrical system (Keightley 2004: 8).

Both male and—to a lesser extent—female ancestors were offered sacrifices and rituals. Sacrifices were often provided in connection with inquiries about present and future events. Others were made to inform the ancestors about current affairs. Some inscriptions show that the diviners tried to gain the assistance of ancestors or to influence and instrumentalize their powers. It was even possible to pledge with ancestors, offering additional human or other sacrificial victims in case of success. For the Shang kings, sacrifices and rites directed towards ancestors were much more than simply a sign of respect for their predecessors. 'The worship of the ancestors not only validated status; it gave access to power' (Keightley 2004: 11).

Access to power certainly extended to the divinatory practitioners who made the inscriptions and read the answers indicated by cracks in the surface of the bone or shell when heated in fire. Even if the questions, comments, and reports inscribed in the surfaces of bones and shells can be read by modern scholars, it so far has been impossible to define a systematic way in which the cracks may have been interpreted and the responses of the gods and ancestors understood. At the end of the Anyang period it appears that the king himself became the only diviner, excluding other members of the elite and divination practitioners from the process and strengthening the influence of the ruler (Keightley 1999: 243; for a detailed explanation of the divination process see also Thorp 2006: 172–85).

Next to their ancestors, the Shang worshipped several other powers. The highest institution in the pantheon was Di, the High God, who was able to command most aspects of the natural environment and social relations. Di presided over natural powers embodied in the earth, mountains, rivers and the sun, a group of 'Former Lords' which stood outside the royal ancestral lineage, as well as the predynastic and dynastic ancestors of the Shang house (Keightley 2004: 6–11). Each of the powers influenced a wide range of natural phenomena and matters of the Shang state, although functions were not exclusively assigned. The majority of the offerings and inquiries documented in the inscriptions addressed, however, the direct ancestors of the kings, indicating that these were the most appropriate access point for communication with the beings beyond the human world.

To our knowledge, no attempt has been made to visualize the world the ancestors and other powers were residing in, nor the gods and ancestors themselves. As already noted for most Neolithic societies of central China, in Anyang the beings worshipped were not represented in art. The utensils used in rituals, however, were produced and decorated with utmost care. The finely decorated vessels, food and beverage containers, drinking cups, offering plates, spoons and ladles, many of which were made of cast bronze, represent the highest achievements of Shang craftsmanship (Figure 28.4). The intricate ornamentation on most bronzes displays, next to birds, dragons and other motifs, stylized two-eyed masks, which were perhaps reminiscent of the mask designs often engraved into Neolithic jades. The possible significance of the complex mask designs has been widely discussed (Kesner 1991; Allen 1992; Bagley 1992) without achieving a consensus.

Next to one of the best-preserved Shang elite tombs, the tomb of Lady Hao, consort of the Shang king Wu Ding (reigned until 1189 BC), remains of a building were found. It was a large, rectangular structure on a platform measuring 5 x 6.5 m, covered by a roof resting on wooden columns. The find supports the idea that special altars or offering halls were dedicated to the cults of certain ancestors and other powers (Thorp 2006: 186; for the tomb see Bagley 1999: 194–202). Large numbers of animals—cattle, sheep and dogs—as well as human victims were killed during the sacrifices. Grain and warm alcoholic drinks were among the offerings as well (Keightley 1999: 258). Other activities during the rituals may have included dance performances (Eno 2009: 94–5).

Anyang was not the only religious centre in the late second millennium BC. Judging from the archaeological finds of bronze vessels, other less-literate regional courts in northern China and the Yangzi valley adopted aspects of the Shang ritual system and possibly shared Shang beliefs (Bagley 1999: 171–80, 208–29). One culture located in the area of Sanxingdui, Sichuan province, developed a visibly diverging religious practice. In Sanxingdui, a site that can roughly be dated to around 1200 BC (Bagley 1999: 212–19; 1988), huge, often more than life-size bronze sculptures and masks with human features and protruding eyes were cast, in this case possibly visualizing the supreme beings the people of the region believed in. The casting technology used for making the figures as well as the types and styles of bronze vessels indicate that this southern court stood in contact with Anyang and other bronze-producing centres. The sculptures found in the pits undoubtedly served in a religious environment quite different from that of the Shang court. Sanxingdui religion ceased to exist before its underlying ideas had been documented in writing.

The Zhou dynasty which succeeded the Shang in 1046 BC, apparently followed many of the Shang ritual practices. Sacrificial bronze vessels of comparable types and functions continued to be used. Only from the late tenth century BC onwards the archaeological as well as literary evidence suggest wide-ranging shifts in society and religion (Shaughnessy 1999: 332). Jessica Rawson observed a standardization in vessel shapes and ornaments, changing burial patterns, and the inclusion of new grave goods into the tomb inventory such as chariot parts instead of complete carriages and bells used in ritual music, all of which points towards an alteration in ritual procedure (Rawson 1999: 414–23; Falkenhausen 2006: 43–52).

From around 550 a shift towards more personalized tombs can be observed. The strict ritual regulations previously meticulously followed now were less strictly observed. Tombs tended to excel in size, while the amount of ritual vessels decreased or was replaced by low-quality objects or ceramic substitutes. In Qin, the westernmost state of Zhou China, tombs contained growing numbers of objects for personal use and tended to take the shape of

FIGURE 28.4 *Zun*, late Shang period, twelfth–eleventh century BC, height 32.2 cm.

underground households. The idea of the tomb as a living place for the dead which may have developed, at the time, as a regional characteristic (Falkenhausen 2006: 312–21), became of growing importance in the following centuries and turned into a standard feature of tombs during the Han period (Nickel 2000).

In the course of the second half of the first millennium BC the amount of tombs documented by archaeological excavations keeps increasing, suggesting that wider strata of society were willing to build (and were able to afford) well-equipped and durable tombs (compare the survey of Eastern Zhou finds in Wu Hung 1999: 717–18). Received contemporary texts, growing numbers of documents found in tombs as well as the more detailed archaeological record point towards a diversification of beliefs among which the Shang ritual system and the traditional sacrifices to the ancestors became of decreasing importance (Thote 2009; Falkenhausen 1999). Ghosts, souls, immortals, natural powers, a complete underground bureaucracy governing the dead, as well as complex cosmologies, begin to fill our picture of human imagination in ancient China (Brashier 1996; Harper 1999; Loewe and Shaughnessy 1999: 978–82; Poo 1998, 2004). Many ideas which become now apparent, however, may have existed before but were not recognizable by archaeological evidence alone, which indicates that our understanding of the prehistory of religion in China will have to remain a tentative and incomplete one.

7 CONCLUSIONS

Over the last 20 years China developed with tremendous pace. Highways, railway lines, and canals are now criss-crossing the country, while high-rising residential and industrial buildings extend into the outskirts of cities and into previously agriculturally used areas. The dramatic reshaping of the modern landscape has a significant impact on our knowledge of ancient China: large-scale surveys and excavations undertaken at the construction sites provide a wealth of archaeological information. The enormous corpus of newly-found 'raw' data, however, is only slowly getting reviewed and assessed. Moreover, scholars in related fields such as history or the study of religions are only beginning to incorporate the finds into their discussion. While the rich literary heritage will remain an invaluable basis for exploring beliefs of peoples in ancient China, we may expect that archaeology will become of growing importance in this inquiry. Even if settlements, tombs, and artefacts may only provide indirect and limited insight into the thoughts and imagination of the people who made them, the sheer number of archaeological remains that came to light during the recent economic boom will soon allow an increasingly differentiated interpretation of early societies and their religious concepts.

SUGGESTED READING

ALLEN, S. (ed.) 2005. *The Formation of Chinese Civilisation: An archaeological perspective* (New Haven and London: Yale University Press; Beijing: New World Press).
LAGERWEY, J. (ed.) 2004. *Religion and Chinese Society* (Hong Kong: The Chinese University Press).

LAGERWEY, J. and KRALINOWSKI, M. (eds) 2009. *Early Chinese Religion* (Leiden/Boston: Brill).
LOEWE, M. and SHAUGHNESSY, E. L. (eds) 1999. *The Cambridge History of Ancient China* (Cambridge: Cambridge University Press).
OVERMYER, D. L. et al. 1995. 'Chinese religions: The state of the field. Part 1: Early religious traditions: The Neolithic period through the Han dynasty', *Journal of Asian Studies*, 54(1): 124–59.
THORP, R. L. 2006. *China in the Early Bronze Age: Shang civilization* (Philadelphia: University of Pennsylvania Press).

REFERENCES

ALLEN, S. 1992. 'Art and meaning' in Roderick Whitfield (ed.), *The Problem of Meaning in Early Chinese Ritual Bronzes*, Colloquies on Art and Archeology in Asia No. 15 (London: SOAS), pp. 9–33.
——(ed.) 2005. *The Formation of Chinese Civilisation: An archaeological perspective* (New Haven and London: Yale University Press; Beijing: New World Press).
BAGLEY, R. W. 1988. 'Sacrificial pits of the Shang period at Sanxingdui in Guanghan County, Sichuan Province', *Ars Asiatiques*, 43: 78–86.
——1992. 'Meaning and explanation' in Roderick Whitfield (ed.), *The Problem of Meaning in Early Chinese Ritual Bronzes*, Colloquies on Art and Archeology in Asia No. 15 (London: SOAS), pp. 34–55.
——1999. 'Shang archaeology' in M. Loewe and E. L. Shaughnessy (eds), *The Cambridge History of Ancient China* (Cambridge: Cambridge University Press), pp. 124–231.
——(ed.) 2001. *Ancient Sichuan: Treasures from a lost civilization* (Princeton: Princeton University Press).
BARNES, G. 1999. *The Rise of Civilisation in East Asia: The archaeology of China, Korea and Japan* (London: Thames and Hudson).
BODDE, D. 1961. 'Myths of ancient China' in Samuel N. Kramer (ed.), *Mythologies of the Ancient World* (New York: Doubleday).
BRASHIER, K. E. 1996. 'Han Tantalogy and the division of souls', *Early China*, 21: 125–58.
BRINKER, H. 1995. 'Vom Ursprung des Menschenbildes' in Roger Goepper (ed.), *Das Alte China: Menschen und Götter im Reich der Mitte* (Essen: Hirmer), pp. 13–35.
CHANG, K. C. 1983. *Art, Myth and Ritual: The path to political authority in ancient China* (Cambridge, MA: Harvard University Press).
——1986. *The Archaeology of Ancient China*, 4th edn (New Haven: Yale University Press).
——1999. 'China on the eve of the historical period' in M. Loewe and E. L. Shaughnessy (eds), *The Cambridge History of Ancient China* (Cambridge: Cambridge University Press), pp. 37–73.
ELIADE, M. 1951. *Le Chamanisme et les techniques archaïques de l'extase* (Paris: Payot).
ENO, R. 2009. 'Shang state religion and the pantheon of oracle texts' in John Lagerwey and Marc Kralinowski (eds), *Early Chinese Religion* (Leiden, Boston: Brill), pp. 41–102.
ERICKSON, M. 1994. *Christian Theology* (Grand Rapids, MI: Baker Book House).
FALKENHAUSEN, L. VON 1999. 'The waning of the Bronze Age: Material culture and social developments, 770–481 BC' in M. Loewe and E. L. Shaughnessy (eds), *The Cambridge History of Ancient China* (Cambridge: Cambridge University Press), pp. 450–544.

—— 2004. 'Mortuary behaviour in pre-imperial Qin: A religious interpretation' in J. Lagerwey (ed.), *Religion and Chinese Society* (Hong Kong: The Chinese University Press), pp. 109–72.

—— 2006. *Chinese Society in the Age of Confucius (1000–250 BC): The archaeological evidence* (Los Angeles: Cotsen Institute of Archaeology, University of California).

FONG, W. (ed.) 1980. *The Great Bronze Age of China* (New York: The Metropolitan Museum of Art).

GAO W. 1989. 'Longshan shidai de lishi [History of the Longshan period]' in *Qingzhu Su Bingqi kaogu wushiwu nian lunwen ji* (Beijing: Wenwu Press), pp. 235–44.

GOEPPER, R. (ed.) 1995. *Das Alte China—Menschen und Götter im Reich der Mitte* (Essen: Hirmer).

HARPER, D. 1999. 'Warring states natural philosophy and occult thought' in M. Loewe and E. L. Shaughnessy (eds), *The Cambridge History of Ancient China* (Cambridge: Cambridge University Press), pp. 813–84.

Hongshan 1994. *Liaoning Hongshan wenhua tan miao zhong* [Temples, altars and mounded tombs of the Hongshan culture in Liaoning] (Beijing: Wenwu Press).

INSOLL, T. (ed.) 2001. *Archaeology and World Religion* (London and New York: Routledge).

KEIGHTLEY, D. N. 1998. 'Shamanism, death, and the ancestors: Religious mediation in Neolithic and Shang China (*ca.*5000–1000 BC)', *Asiatische Studien*, 52(3): 763–831.

—— 1999. 'The Shang: China's first historical dynasty' in M. Loewe and E. L. Shaughnessy (eds), *The Cambridge History of Ancient China* (Cambridge: Cambridge University Press), pp. 232–91.

—— 2004. 'The making of the ancestors: Late Shang religion and its legacy' in John Lagerwey (ed.), *Religion and Chinese Society* (Hong Kong: The Chinese University Press), pp. 3–64.

KESNER, L. 1991. 'The Taotie Reconsidered: Meaning and Functions of the Shang Theriomorphic Imagery', *Artibus Asiae* 51(1–2): 29–53.

LAGERWEY, J. (ed.) 2004. *Religion and Chinese Society* (Hong Kong: The Chinese University Press).

LANE, P. 2001. 'The archaeology of Christianity in global perspective' in T. Insoll (ed.), *Archaeology and World Religion* (London and New York: Routledge), pp. 148–81.

LIN F. 2009. 'The image and status of shamans in ancient China' in J. Lagerwey and M. Kralinowski (eds), *Early Chinese Religion* (Leiden, Boston: Brill), pp. 397–458.

LOEWE, M. and SHAUGHNESSY, E. L. (eds) 1999. *The Cambridge History of Ancient China* (Cambridge: Cambridge University Press).

NICKEL, L. 1997. 'Review essay of Roger Goepper (ed.), *Das Alte China*', *Mitteilungen der Deutschen Gesellschaft für Ostasiatische Kunst*, July 1997: 30–3.

—— 2000. 'Some Han-dynasty paintings in the British Museum', *Artibus Asiae*, 60(1): 59–78.

—— 2006. 'Tonkrieger auf der Seidenstrasse? Die Plastiken des Ersten Kaisers von China und die hellenistische Skulptur Zentralasiens', *Zurich Studies in the History of Art/Georges Bloch Annual*, 13–14: 124–49.

OVERMYER, D. L. et al. 1995. 'Chinese religions: The state of the field. Part 1: Early religious traditions: The Neolithic period through the Han dynasty', *Journal of Asian Studies*, 54(1): 124–59.

POO M. 1998. *In Search of Personal Welfare: A view of ancient Chinese religion* (Albany: State University of New York Press).

—— 'The concept of ghost in ancient Chinese religion' in J. Lagerwey (ed.), *Religion and Chinese Society* (Hong Kong: The Chinese University Press), pp. 173–93.

PUETT, M. 2004. 'The ascension of the spirit: Toward a cultural history of self-divinization movements in early China' in J. Lagerwey (ed.), *Religion and Chinese Society* (Hong Kong: The Chinese University Press), pp. 193–222.
RAWSON, J. 1996. *Mysteries of Ancient China—New Discoveries from the Early Dynasties* (London: The British Museum).
—— 1999. 'Western Zhou archaeology' in M. Loewe and E. L. Shaughnessy (eds), *The Cambridge History of Ancient China* (Cambridge: Cambridge University Press), pp. 352–449.
SHAO W. 2005. 'The formation of civilization: The interaction sphere of the Longshan period' in S. Allen (ed.), *The Formation of Chinese Civilisation: An archaeological perspective* (New Haven and London: Yale University Press; Beijing: New World Press), 85–124.
SHAUGHNESSY, E. L. 1999. 'Western Zhou history' in M. Loewe and E. L. Shaughnessy (eds), *The Cambridge History of Ancient China* (Cambridge: Cambridge University Press), pp. 292–351.
THORP, R. L. 2006. *China in the Early Bronze Age: Shang civilization* (Philadelphia: University of Pennsylvania Press).
THOTE, A. 2009. 'Shang and Zhou funeral practices: Interpretation of material vestiges' in J. Lagerwey and M. Kralinowski (eds), *Early Chinese Religion* (Leiden, Boston: Brill), pp. 103–42.
Wenwu 1988/1. 'Yuhang Yaoshan Liangzhu wenhua jitan yizhi fajue jianbao' ['Preliminary report on the excavation of a sacrificial altar of the Liangzhu culture in Yaoshan, Yuhang'], *Wenwu*, 1988/1: 32–51.
WHITFIELD, R. (ed.) 1992. *The Problem of Meaning in Early Chinese Ritual Bronzes*, Colloquies on Art and Archeology in Asia No. 15 (London: SOAS).
WIEDEHAGE, P. 1995a. 'Phallus' in R. Goepper (ed.), *Das Alte China—Menschen und Götter im Reich der Mitte* (Essen: Hirmer), pp. 183–5.
—— 1995b. 'Figurengruppe aus Menschen und Tieren' in R. Goepper (ed.), *Das Alte China—Menschen und Götter im Reich der Mitte* (Essen: Hirmer), pp. 185–7.
WU H. 1999. 'The art and architecture of the Warring States period' in M. Loewe and E. L. Shaughnessy (eds), *The Cambridge History of Ancient China* (Cambridge: Cambridge University Press), pp. 651–744.
—— 2005. 'On tomb figurines: The beginning of a visual tradition' in Wu Hung and K. R. Tsiang (eds), *Body and Face in Chinese Visual Culture* (Harvard: Harvard University Press), pp. 13–47.
XU J. 2001. 'Sichuan before the Warring States period' in R. W. Bagley (ed.), *Ancient Sichuan: Treasures from a lost civilization* (Princeton: Princeton University Press), pp. 21–58.
Zeng Hou Yi. 1992. *Zeng Hou Yi mu wenwu yishu* [Art and artefacts from the tomb of Zeng Hou Yi] (Wuhan: Hubei Meishu chubanshe).
ZHANG, C. and OKAMURA, H. 1999. 'Excavation of Cities: Shijiahe and Yinxiangcheng' in R. Whitfield and Wang Tao (eds), *Exploring China's Past: New discoveries and studies in archaeology and art* (London: Saffron), pp. 87–94.
ZHANG X. 1992. *Changjiang zhongyou xinshiqi shidai wenhua gailun* [Discussion of the middle reaches of the Changjiang during the Neolithic period] (Wuhan), pp. 224–30.
ZHANG Z. 2005. 'The Yangshao period: Prosperity and the transformation of prehistoric society' in S. Allen (ed.), *The Formation of Chinese Civilisation: An archaeological perspective* (New Haven and London: Yale University Press; Beijing: New World Press), pp. 44–83.

CHAPTER 29

THE ARCHAEOLOGY OF RELIGION AND RITUAL IN THE PREHISTORIC JAPANESE ARCHIPELAGO

SIMON KANER

1 INTRODUCTION

THIS chapter will review the evidence and interpretation of the development of ritual traditions in the prehistoric Japanese archipelago prior to the appearance of Buddhism in the mid-sixth century AD. Key sites and materials will be selected from the Jomon period (c.14,000 BC–c.500 BC), the Yayoi period (c.500 BC–AD 300 AD), and the Kofun period (AD 300–710). A number of good general surveys of Japanese archaeology are available in English (Aikens and Higuchi 1982; Pearson 1992; Imamura 1996; Mizoguchi 2002).

The early occupants of the archipelago left behind a rich material culture, large parts of which are interpreted as being ritual in nature. Interpretations draw on traditional Japanese ethnology, which is in turn heavily influenced by studies of the 'native' religious traditions, and are often considered to have coalesced under the broad rubric of Shintoism (Harris 2001). This chapter, rather than adopting this usual, rather essentialist, discourse used for the development of 'early Japanese religion', presents case studies from each period. These case studies, while reflecting the distinctive nature of specific contextual materials from the archipelago, illustrate more general processes whereby local ritual traditions develop, interact, influence one another, and are transformed over time through the playing-out of generative schema, rich in symbolism and embedded in the social reproduction and transformation of communities at the local and regional scales.

While introducing a series of key sites, this chapter will adopt a thematic approach to evidence for religious activity in the Japanese archipelago including: cosmology; the transformative qualities of 'ritual' material culture; evidence for 'ritual specialists'; the existence of generative schema behind the diversity of ritual traditions; monumentality; the ritualization of the expression of human–animal relationships; and the ritual expression of transitions during the life cycles of individuals and communities.

2 THE ARCHAEOLOGY OF RELIGION AND RITUAL IN JAPAN

The word for religion, 'an overarching term encompassing a variety of spiritual traditions' was only introduced into Japan in the 1850s, translated as *shukyo* (Thal 2005: 8). This term (a Buddhist term for 'sectarian teachings'), however, 'emphasized religion as a doctrine rather than as ritual' (ibid.: 8). In an intriguing twist, in the compromise between Western imposed freedoms of religious belief, and the constraints of an emerging state doctrine (i.e. State Shinto), a number of state-supported shrines were treated as 'not religion'.

For many in Japan, the origins of Shinto lie in the prehistoric period, in particular the Yayoi (Harris 2001). Mori Mizue, writing on the 'dawn of Shinto' notes the contrast between the hunting and gathering Jomon period and the rice-agriculture-based Yayoi period, noting that 'the least we can say is that the excavations of ritual sites from the Yayoi period leave little doubt that during this period, people believed in, and worshipped, spiritual powers that controlled the weather and the crops. These sites bespeak the existence at this early date of what we may call *kami* workship' (Mori 2003: 12). However, the same authority acknowledges that recent archaeological discoveries have blurred the boundaries between Yayoi and Jomon so that 'the animism of the Jomon period will also have to be taken into account as a possible ancestor of Shinto' (ibid.: 14).

Perhaps the most influential study of archaeological traces of early ritual practices in Japan is the monumental survey of Shinto archaeology edited by Oba Iwao, professor at Kokugakuin University in Tokyo, for long the centre for the study of Shinto and the training of Shinto priests (Oba 1983). Oba was responsible for some very significant archaeological investigations at sites including the Oyu stone circles in Akita Prefecture in the 1950s. Histories of Japanese religion often begin with a consideration of the earliest periods (e.g. Earhart 2004: 22–8; Kasahara 2001: 27–46).

3 RITUAL PRACTICES AMONG LATE PALAEOLITHIC AND JOMON FORAGERS (14,000–500 BC)

The period from the late glacial to the first millennium BC is known by the term Jomon, which refers to the cord-marking on many of the pottery vessels which characterize the period (Habu 2004; Kobayashi 2004). This single name, however, represents a great diversity of material expressions, although there are shared characteristics. It would, nevertheless, be misleading to assume that there was any unity of religious system or ritual structures. People during this long period did dedicate considerable energies to what archaeologists recognize as ritual facilities, and the performative aspects of the rituals thought to have been carried out are expressed both in the spatial layout of these facilities, and by many of the aspects of the material culture with which they are associated.

The most recent extensive survey of ritual activity during the Jomon period identified a series of themes: beliefs connected with hunting and fishing; burials and the cult of the dead; upright stones, stone pillars, and phallic stones; anthropomorphic and zoomorphic ceramic figurines; and clay masks (Naumann 2000). Kobayashi Tatsuo and his colleagues have proposed that many Jomon sites were constructed so as to be aligned on the movements of celestial bodies, notably the sun and the moon, and key landscape features such as distinctive mountain peaks, and have postulated a Jomon cosmology based around the relatively permanent settlements of pit houses, many of which developed a circular structure (Kobayashi 2004). During the long Jomon period, divided into six sub-divisions, a multitude of regional and local cultures developed, giving rise to a great range of material culture forms (in particular pottery styles) thought to reflect considerable cultural diversity, within a broader cultural co-tradition (Kobayashi 2004).

In his 1908 synthesis of Japanese archaeology, the Scottish doctor and amateur archaeologist Neil Gordon Munro described the stone circles at Oshoro, near the port of Otaru in Hokkaido (Munro 1908). He suggested that the stones, although not megalithic, were laid out oriented to movements of the celestial bodies, indicating an early interest in cosmology. There are several hundred such sites around the Japanese archipelago (Suzuki 2007), with a distribution from Hokkaido to Kagoshima, though the majority are in eastern Japan. These sites are widely regarded as burial sites or regional ritual centres (Kodama 2003). Among the most famous are the double rings of Manza and Nonakado at Oyu in Akita (Aikens and Higuchi 1982) and Komakino in Aomori (Kodama 2003).

While there is evidence for intensification of human–animal relationships in the Jomon, including signs of hunting pressure on deer populations from the Late Jomon, and suggestions of the management of wild boar, including transporting them to parts of the archipelago where they were not native, notably Hokkaido and some smaller offshore islands, there is no proof of domestication of any species other than the dog. On occasion, as at the Incipient Jomon rock shelter at Kamikuroiwa on Shikoku, dogs were treated to careful burial (Aikens and Higuchi 1982). However, at a number of sites animal bones are found suggesting that their deposition served some religious or cultic purpose from the Early Jomon. These include Mawaki in Ishikawa Prefecture, where the bones of dolphins appear to have been treated in a very specific fashion:

> In a small place, together with bones of other animals and fish, the bones of about 300 dolphins were found. Their skulls had been deposited in a special way: some in a fan-like circle, the muzzles facing inwards, or with two skulls lying parallel or muzzle to muzzle. In the same place a carved pole was found, 2.5 m long, diameter 45 cms. Three zones are carved out, but only a part of the middle zone is well-enough preserved to recognise a round center as big as the palm of a hand, and two crescents each to the left and right of it' [Naumann 2002: 12]

and Higashi Kushiro in Hokkaido 'where dolphin bones were laid out radially, the muzzles pointing outwards, covered with red iron oxide' (Naumann 2002: 12).

One of the most beguiling elements of Jomon ritual material culture are the ceramic figurines and the suggestively phallic stone bars of various shape (Kaner 2009; Mizoguchi 2007; Naumann 2000). Parts of more than 15,000 individuals are now recorded on the Jomon figurine database. In 2006, at Meotoshi in Yamanashi Prefecture, a large quantity of figurine fragments were recovered from the evocatively named 'woman man stone' site (Bunkacho 2007). The site is located on a level terrace against the spectacular backdrop of the three peaks of the Kofu Komagadake mountain range, and was a centre for ritual activities for over 1,000 years, between 5500–4500 BP in the Middle Jomon period. These rituals appear to have focused on the huge 'woman-man stone', some 2.5 m long and 1.7 m high, a natural boulder, which is located at the middle of the site. Other remains included a cluster of 18 pit buildings, a single arranged stone feature and a short distance away, an associated dump area. Centred on this large boulder were discovered some 70 figurine fragments, along with stone bars, miniature pottery vessels, and other objects of ritual nature. The deposits contained a large proportion of ash, suggesting that fire played a significant role in these ritual practices. As is typical of many figurine assemblages, there was considerable variation within the group from Meotoishi. Yamanashi Prefecture is famous for its figurines: in the 1970s the Shakado site produced over 1,000 figurine fragments, all broken (Yamagata 1992) and over 1,800 figurine fragments have been recovered from the largest Jomon site yet discovered, from Sannai Maruyama in Aomori Prefecture (Habu 2008).

Jomon burial traditions are every bit as complex as those of complex hunter-gatherers the world over. They have been analysed mainly from the perspective of attempting to understand what they can tell us about the nature of Jomon social organization, although this discourse has, somewhat inevitably, given the parameters of the debate, become bogged down in a sterile argument over where there was, or was not, any institutionalized social hierarchy present during the Jomon, with evidence for ascribed (rather than simply achieved) social status (Kaneko 2005).

The presence of a large number of cemeteries throughout the archipelago, lend themselves to a historical analysis, in which changes in the material aspects of burial rites can be observed. Several of the best-known cemeteries from sites such as Tsukomo were excavated many years ago (Harunari 1986). Recent examples include Mukaisamada A and D in Akita Prefecture (Bunkacho 2002). These burial grounds often had long histories of use—as did many of the settlements themselves. Sannai Maruyama, for example, one of the largest Jomon settlements yet discovered, was occupied for around 1,900 years (Habu 2008). Differences in body orientation and the clustering of graves have suggested to some archaeologists that family or lineage groupings are represented spatially (for example Harunari Hideji 2002 and Hayashi Kensaku 2001). The elaborate burials also suggest a belief in the afterlife, and a concern with managing ancestral spirits.

Mukaisamada is part of a large ritual complex dating to the early part of the Final Jomon, located on a terrace overlooking the Komata River in northern Akita Prefecture. The complex comprised two circular arrangements of stones. To the east was a circle some 13 m in diameter, centred on a stone-surrounded hearth, some 1.4 m in length, around which were located a large number of grave pits and a dump area. The ritual areas appeared to have been separated off from the valley beyond by an earthen bank or mound. From the dump area and the earthen mound were recovered large quantities of artefacts which may have featured in ritual practices, including ceramic and stone figurines, engraved stone plaques, stone bars, along with stone beads and other accessories. Many of these objects are thought to have been used as part of the funerary rites associated with the many graves at the site. The assemblage suggested to the excavators that this was a site where objects were 'sent off', along with the spirits of the departed.

Two approaches dominate the interpretation of the archaeology of the Jomon period. The first, largely inspired by Marxist writings, considers that Jomon societies were unable to progress beyond the hunting and gathering mode of production, as they did not adopt agriculture. This meant that they became 'trapped' in a cycle of stagnation, expressed through increasingly useless rituals. The cultural dynamic here is one of stadial cultural evolution and progress, and Jomon societies were unable to do this. Such an approach overlooks the creativity and agency inherent in Jomon societies. Jomon peoples developed their own very sophisticated ways of expressing their relationship with the other world through local cults and ritualized practices. Central to these practices was a recognition of the ability for human beings to be transformed into other entities, which we would regard as either animate or inanimate. The power to transform is an essential attribute of the religious systems which developed, a power which is embodied in the transformative qualities of the clay used to create the great range of ceramic forms in the Jomon, which underpinned the success of the subsistence strategies adopted over ten millennia: cooking the rich resources available to the foragers and transforming them into edible foodstuffs.

The second theme is that various ritual practices, from burial with grave goods to the construction of stone-built monuments, were expressions of social power rather than ritual power or religious authority. This theme is at the forefront of discussions by scholars such as Junko Habu and Oki Nakamura who have argued that there was a degree of inherited, or ascribed, social status in the Jomon period, and that the primary function of ritual practice was to express and legitimate this ascribed status. There remains considerable disagreement about this (Habu 2004).

An alternative approach to these issues in Jomon religion is to accept, as does much recent anthropological theory, that there is nothing 'natural' or 'primitive' about an egalitarian ideology, but that it has to be proactively and discursively maintained. Add to this the way in which religious traditions are reproduced and transformed in small-scale societies (Barth 1988; Kaner 2007), and we have the foundations for a new approach to Jomon religion which not only accepts the distinctiveness of Jomon spiritual experience (avoiding the teleology of looking for the origins of Shinto), but also accepts that this distinctively religious aspect of Jomon life was not epiphenomenal to subsistence or social organization, but was deeply implicated in and causal to Jomon ways of life.

The foraging communities who occupied the Japanese archipelago during the Jomon period developed an elaborate cosmology which related fixed locations in the landscape to movements of the celestial bodies. Stone circles and other features were aligned on distinctive landscape elements notably rivers. Ritual specialists, if they existed, are thought to have been part-time, although some scholars, notably Watanabe Hitoshi (1998) consider that they may have represented a class of person in whom a certain stratification of authority and power may have been embodied. Certain burials, for example one from Yamaga in Kyushu, with shell armlets and jadeite axes, are cited as evidence for this (Kobayashi 2004). The ceramic figures and pottery masks, and the intriguing emerging representative designs embedded in many of the Jomon cooking vessels, suggest a concern with transformation and the awareness of the potential to take on different personalities.

4 THE ELABORATION OF RITUAL AUTHORITY: RELIGION AND RICE-GROWING IN THE YAYOI (500 BC–AD 300)

As is the case in much of the rest of the world, the adoption of agriculture is considered to be one of the great disjunctures in the history of the occupation of the Japanese archipelago. The appearance of wet rice agriculture in north-west Kyushu around 900 cal BC, associated with the construction of paddy fields and other new technologies, notably metalworking and silk weaving, all introduced from the continent, marked the beginning of an inevitable demise in Jomon cultural manifestation, and its replacement with a set of ritual and religious practices, greatly influenced by the agricultural way of life. Rice itself, given such prominence in subsequent constructions of Japanese identity (Ohnuki-Tierney 1994), and its preparation and consumption may well have been circumscribed by ritual and belief (Hosoya 2009). Religion and ritual continued to play a major structural role in the reproduction and transformation of communities and societies in the archipelago, albeit in a different form to that of the preceding Jomon period. Kobayashi Tatsuo (2004) and others have argued that the native Jomon populations attempted to use ritual in order to 'resist' the spread of the agricultural lifestyle as suggested by the large number of ceramic figurines manufactured in western Japan in the final stages of the Jomon period.

Any such putative Jomon 'resistance' was, however, ultimately overcome and many of the distinctive Jomon ritual objects and presumably practices gave way to Yayoi successors. Yayoi archaeologists have typically recognized the following as the material traces of ritual activity: bronze bells and mirrors, elaborate bronze weapons and talc imitations/skeumorphs, oracle bones suggesting divination, and a rich, if very heterogeneous, mortuary record (Hudson 1992: 156–68), which tracks the 'development of formal cemeteries... linked to an increasing concern with ancestral rights to land'. Koji Mizoguchi has expanded on this theme in recent publications (2005), in which he argues for greater awareness of expressions of lineage and differentiations between lineage groupings.

Did the ways in which ritual and religious practices were implicated in Yayoi life differ greatly from Jomon ritual traditions? We have less evidence for the spatial ordering of ritual activities from most Yayoi settlements. And yet the continuing importance of initiation rites involving bodily mutilation including tooth filing suggests that life-history rituals continued to be important. In addition, it appears that Yayoi people developed new ways of communicating with the spirit world, including the use of divination involving the interpretation of burnt animal bones. Yayoi people also innovated with ways of portraying what are interpreted as winged shamans and other activities, through etchings on pottery vessels, particularly from sites such as Karako-Kagi in Nara, and representational scenes of a probable mythological nature on some 10 per cent of the 400 or so bronze bells which they deposited in western Honshu at field margins and away from everyday settlement.

Mark Hudson has suggested a structured set of relationships between some of the key aspects of Yayoi society, emphasizing the role of warfare and increasing social cohesion: 'the need for warfare and social cohesion was negotiated through the ritualisation of war and its association with hunting' (1992: 149). In this relationship, the ritualization of warfare is represented by the development of 'wide-bladed, impractical ritual objects' derived from 'actual weapons' and seeing 'weapons... become objects of worship' (ibid.). Hudson continues:

> Ritual weapons were also made of wood and were probably used in performances, such as those described in the Wei Zhi and depicted on bronze mirrors. This mirror provides a clear link between (mock) warfare and the hunting of deer. If we agree that the deer represented land spirits in agricultural ritual, then I believe we can understand why hunting and warfare scenes are so common in Yayoi art. Hunting and warfare were a metaphor for the control of the wild or, in other words, the domestication of both rice and society. [Ibid.: 149]

Indeed, Edward Kidder has argued that human action during the Yayoi was greatly constrained by 'an overarching fear of malignant spirits' which represents 'the bonding feature of Wa society' (2007: 228):

> we find a psychologically insecure mentality that acts only after divination, depends on the interpretation of dreams, looks for signs and omens to guide future action, explains ordinary occurrences (such as diseases) as the work of hostile spirits, sees life in inanimate objects with nefarious potential, and believes in physical transformation. [Ibid.: 228]

These new religious configurations gave rise to some new forms of sacred place. As part of a move towards enclosure, seen clearly in the moated settlements of the Yayoi, such as Ikegami-Sone and Yoshinogari (Mizoguchi 2002: 3), sacred precincts around central 'shrine-like' buildings began to appear. The monumentalization of Yayoi ritual architecture represents the expression of a new exclusivity in Japanese religious tradition. Some commentators, such as Kidder (2007: 77) consider these structures to be 'special, raised floor dwellings for their spiritual-political leaders', based on the ground plans of arrangements of large post-holes and engravings on pottery sherds. Kidder continues: 'The type persisted as an elite dwelling and was for structural form adopted for the first of the religious shrines—Izumo Taisha and Ise Jingu both have elevated floors—presumably because it was the shaman's house' (ibid.). The largest example known is from the Yoshitake-Takagi location of the Iimori site in Fukuoka, dating to the Middle Yayoi, a structure with six posts along one side and five posts along the other estimated to have been some 12 m high and with over 120 m^2 of floor space (Kidder 2007: 78). An example at Ikegami Sone was associated with a 'ritual well' (Inui 1999).

Several archaeologists have argued for a religious 'revolution' between the Middle and the Late Yayoi periods, which gave rise to the ideological underpinnings for the state-level polities which came about during the later third century in the Kansai region of central Honshu. Gina Barnes (2007: 114–15) describes this process partly in terms of 'ritual replacement': 'The emergence of paramount chiefs following the demise of bronze bell ritual... indicates greater hierarchisation of society and is interpreted as ritual replacement: a shift from worshipping the "spirit of the rice" to the worshipping the "spirit of the ruler"' (ibid.: 114). Barnes further notes that: 'In the Japanese case, archaeologists put the onus of action on the populace, who transfer their focus of attention from fertility rituals to individuals whom they recognise as their leaders, revering them as gods in and of themselves' (ibid.: 115).

Koji Mizoguchi developed a related theme. He identifies the person interred in grave three at Yoshitake-Takagi in Fukuoka as a 'shaman' or a 'shamanistic leader', 'mediating the relationship between the community and the supernatural as an Other' (2002: 154). This person, whose physical remains have long since vanished in the acid-rich soil, was buried with 'a bronze mirror with sophisticated geometric patterns, two bronze daggers, a bronze spearhead, a bronze halberd, and a C-shaped stone bead... as well as numerous stone cylindrical beads, probably making up a necklace' (Mizoguchi 2002: 153–4). Mizoguchi argues that this person had both religious authority (expressed through the mirror) and social authority (expressed through the weapons), and represented a form of 'community leadership' (ibid.).

By the second century AD we have forms of evidence not available to us for the earlier period. These are the accounts of life in the archipelago left to us by the historians who compiled the Wei Zhih, a sixth-century Chinese account, which includes details of embassies sent from the land of Wa, equated with one of the polities in the archipelago. These accounts, the first eye-witness descriptions of the Japanese archipelago and its inhabitants, describe the presence of special diviners in missions sent from Japan to the Chinese court:

> there is always one man who does not comb his hair, does not remove the lice, lets his clothes become dirty, does not eat meat, and does not get near women. He is like a mourner and works like a diviner or an ascetic/abstainer. If there is good luck, in view of this they will all give him slaves and valuable things, but if disease or injuries occur, they dispatch him because as the diviner he had not been respectful [of his vows]. [Kidder 2007: 15]

The chronicles also describe divination using oracle bones, and the magic nature of rulership, as embodied in the figure of Queen Himiko and her brother (Barnes 2007; Hudson 1992: 173; Kidder 2007).

A number of spheres of activity, including some completely new ones, became heavily ritualized during the Yayoi period. Changes in attitudes towards animals and plants expressed new relationships involving domestication and shifts in perceptions of the wild and the tame. Transformation continued to be an important feature of ritual material culture; but instead of, as in the Jomon, elaborate ceramic forms fulfilling this role, now it was the transformative qualities of metal, in particular bronze, that characterize this. Violent feuding, perhaps fuelled by competition over land and water, fed the development of the ritualized display of arms and armour. The nature of ritual authority underwent considerable changes, in particular around the middle of the third century AD, as leaders consolidated their positions by gathering in control of access to the gods and spirits. Whereas Jomon rituals appear to have been focused on the settlements which were at the centre of their cosmology, Yayoi rituals moved out across the landscape, reflecting the increased human involvement in constructing and cultivating paddy fields and associated irrigation systems.

5 The Appropriation of Religious Power by the Tomb-Builders of the Kofun Period (c. AD 250–710)

In the early third century AD, large mounded tombs, many with a distinctive keyhole shaped plan, began to be constructed in the archipelago. These tombs give the name Kofun, literally 'old tombs', to the period in which the first state-level society appeared in the Kinai region, around modern-day Nara and Osaka. This construction of monumental tombs grew out of earlier Yayoi burial traditions, represented by the large mound at Tatetsuki in Okayama (Kondo 1977), or the huge tomb associated with the large settlement of Yoshinogari in Kyushu (Barnes and Hudson 1991). But the construction of tombs in the Kofun period was implicated in the formulation of a new religious tradition involving new cult practices adopted from the East Asian continent and the influence of Daoist beliefs. Within the domestic context, ritual spaces became increasingly formalized within distinct elite residential compounds. Liminal areas, including offshore islands, perhaps most notably Okinoshima (Matsumae 1993), and mountains, such as Mount Miwa in Nara Prefecture, became the foci of cult activities involving the deposition of a range of ritual material culture. These developments reflect new cosmological beliefs expressing how the newly emergent paramount rulers saw their place in the world and beyond. The final resting places of the deceased elite were protected by terracotta tomb guardians, set up around the flanks of the great tombs (Maison 2001). Although the earliest Japanese quasi-historical chronicles, the *Kojiki* (Philippi 1977) and the *Nihongi*, also known as the *Nihon Shoki* (Aston 1972), were only written down in the eighth century and were undoubtedly coloured by the viewpoint of the ruling lineage whose rule they sought to legitimate, they provide important evidence for the nature of belief and cult activity during the period of the tombs and during this time, ritual authority accrued to the rulers themselves.

Recent scholarship on the Early Kofun period has emphasized its ritual nature. Gina Barnes reflects a contemporary Japanese view that this period saw the emergence of a central authority in the archipelago which brought together the various regional groupings through 'a new religious framework which adopted Chinese conceptions' (2007: 179). These Chinese conceptions were, according to Barnes, likely to have included the cult of the Queen Mother of the West, while elements such as the worship of females with divine powers, marriage with gods, and associations with mountains, materialized through ritual paraphernalia including staffs made of jade and bronze mirrors with 'beast-deity' patterns, all creating strong links to political authority. The location of Makimuku in Nara Prefecture was closely involved with this process of the emergence of centralized political authority, and focused upon one of the most distinctive landscape features in the vicinity, Mount Miwa. Gina Barnes and Edward Kidder have both made recent compelling arguments for the significance of the Miwa Court. Barnes has proposed that this court was based on the concept of 'godly authority' (*shinken*) which expresses the 'charisma' and religious 'attractiveness' of the Miwa cult figures. Barnes argues that 'the authority of Miwa was established on the basis of deity-beast mirror procurement and on the creation of a new religious cult to respect Himiko (= Princess Yamato) as the supplier of the mirrors and to worship her husband Oho-mono-nushi-no-kami as the god who oversaw these wonderful "things"' (2007: 183). And this authority in turn was 'constantly exercised' by recreating a set of values—'respect, moral standing, affection, wealth and enlightenment'—'in the performance of rituals and the use of material objects [such as beast-deity mirrors and jade staffs] to mystify central power. This materialisation of the ideology served to both reinforce and extend Miwa authority and become a form of "governance"' (ibid.: 185).

There is still debate about the nature of the social formations of the Kofun period, which witnessed the construction of some of the largest monuments of the ancient world, the great mounded tombs, including that designated as the final resting place of the fifth-century ruler Nintoku. Supplementing the archaeological record are the accounts of this period written down in the early eighth century, the Kojiki and Nihon Shoki, full of evocative detail about the events and rulers of the centuries around the arrival of a new foreign religion, Buddhism, introduced from the Korean peninsula in the middle of the sixth century. At about the same time as the King of Paekche on the south-western peninsula was despatching sutras and Buddha statues to his counterpart in central Honshu, a massive volcanic eruption of Mount Haruna in eastern Honshu buried an entire Kofun-period landscape, preserving for archaeology the layout of an elite residential compound at Mitsudera in modern-day Gunma Prefecture, the investigation of which in the 1980s provided a hitherto unparalleled glimpse into domestic ritual practices of the higher echelons of regional society at the time (Ishino 1992).

By the end of the period of tomb-building, a Chinese-style cosmology had been adopted by Japanese elites at least, represented by the explicit Chinese iconography of the Takamatsuzuka tomb, whose discovery caused a sensation in 1973, and problems of conservation continue to be of national interest today (Kidder 1972; Bunkacho 2008). Takamatsuzuka is located in the Asuka region in the south of the Nara Prefecture, where traces of many of the earliest Buddhist temples are also to be found. The tomb mound, some 16 m in diameter and 5 m high, contained a stone burial chamber decorated with frescos derived from Korean and ultimately Chinese models: brightly adorned courtiers and the four principal cosmological beasts, the Azure Dragon, the Black Tortoise, the White Tiger and the Vermilion Bird, all beneath a map of the stars depicted on the ceiling. This was the tomb of a high-ranking nobleman or perhaps a member of the royal family, and encapsulates the arrival of a new religious sensibility in the centre of power in the archipelago, just prior to the abandonment of monumental tomb-building in favour of the Buddhist cremation rites.

The spread of Buddhism accompanied the increasing hegemony of the Yamato court across large swathes of the Japanese archipelago. Regional administrative centres were established, each with a standard-format Buddhist temple. Over the coming centuries, Buddhism and the traditional Japanese ritual practices coexisted through a kind of ecumenical syncretism, which was only seriously challenged in the nineteenth century with the promulgation of the new modern nation state of Japan under the banner of a freshly reinvigorated nationalist ideology which rejected the 'foreign' tenets of Buddhism, and fostered a new, and ultimately pathological, ideology, that of State Shinto (Breen and Teeuwen 2000).

6 Conclusions

The archaeology of religion is undergoing a renaissance (Insoll 2004; Renfrew and Morley 2007; Barrowclough and Malone 2007). Many of the elements of the archaeology of religion and ritual in early Japan appear to have been identified at the dawn of anthropological interest, notably Edward Tylor's influential *Primitive Culture* of 1871, which presented examples of animism, shamanism, fertility cults, and the nature of religious authority. But just as anthropology has moved on from regarding such religious manifestations as resulting from 'primitive' epistemologies, so are studies of religion and ritual in the early Japanese archipelago moving on from looking for the origins of 'Shinto'. Tim Ingold (2006) has recently written of animism (the imputation of life to inert objects) as a relational ontology, just as Bird-David (1999) has described it as a 'relational epistemology' (2002: 72): it is 'a condition of being alive to the world, characterized by a heightened sensitivity and responsiveness, in perception and actions, to an environment that is always in flux, never the same from one moment to the next' (Ingold 2006: 10). Life in an animistic universe, with relationships with the spirit world being mediated by shamans, is a theme which runs throughout interpretations of ritual and religion in the Japanese archipelago prior to the appearance of Buddhism. The case studies presented above, however, indicate that the nature of the spirit worlds depended on differing sets of relational ontologies, each of which had their own internal cohesion, worked out and expressed through place-specific rituals and rituals marking various stages of personhood—from birth to death.

Suggested Reading

A good starting point is a special issue of the *Japanese Journal of Religious Studies* (Vol. 19 Nos. 2–3) on archaeological approaches to ritual and religion in Japan (1992), edited by Mark Hudson and Simon Kaner. Edward Kidder's volume on Himiko (Kidder 2007) provides an excellent account of Yayoi- and Kofun-period archaeology, relating many of the key archaeological discoveries and themes, to the earliest Japanese and Chinese written sources that relate back to Japanese pre- and protohistory, in particular regarding cult and belief. Koji Mizoguchi's (2002) volume presents the archaeology of the Japanese archipelago from the Palaeolithic to Kofun periods with a very interesting theoretical perspective.

References

Aikens, C. M. and Higuchi, T. 1982. *The Prehistory of Japan* (New York and London: Academic Press).
Aston, W. G. 1972. *Nihongi: chronicles of Japan from the Earliest times to AD 697 (translation of the Nihongi otherwise called the Nihon Shoki)*. London, Transactions of the Japan Society 1896, reprinted Charles E. Tuttle Co. Inc.
Barnes, G. L. 2007. *State Formation in Japan: Emergence of a 4th-century elite* (London: Routledge).
—— and Hudson, M. 1991. 'Yoshiongari: a Yayoi settlement in northern Kyusu', *Monumenta Nipponica*, 46: 211–35.
Barrowclough, D. and Malone, C. 2007. *Cult in Context* (Oxford: Oxbow Books).
Barth, F. 1988. *Cosmologies in the Making* (Cambridge: Cambridge University Press).
Bird-David, B. 1999. 'Animism revisited: Personhood, environment and relational epistemology', *Current Anthropology*, 40: 67–91; repr. in Graham Harvey (ed.) 2002. *Readings in Indigenous Religions* (London and New York, Continuum), pp. 72–105.
Breen, J. and Teeuwen, M. (eds) 2000. *Shinto in History* (Honolulu: Hawaii University Press).
Bunkacho. 2002. 'Mukaisamada A and D' in Bunkacho (ed.), *Hakkutsu sareta Nihon retto [The Japanese Archipelago Excavated]* (Tokyo: Asahi Shimbun), pp. 22–3.
—— 2007. 'Meotoishi' in Bunkacho (ed.), *Hakkutsu sareta Nihon retto [The Japanese Archipelago Excavated]* (Tokyo: Asahi Shimbun), pp. 26–7.
—— 2008. 'Takamatsuzuka kofun' ['The Takamatsuzuka kofun'] in Bunkacho (ed.), *Hakkutsu sareta Nihon retto [The Japanese Archipelago Excavated]* (Tokyo: Asahi Shimbun), pp. 18–24.
Earhart, H. B. 2004. *Japanese Religion: Unity and diversity* (Belmont: Wadsworth/Thomson).
Habu, J. 2004. *Ancient Jomon of Japan* (Cambridge: Cambridge University Press).
—— 2008. 'Growth and decline in complex hunter-gatherer societies: A case study from the Jomon period Sannai Maruyama site, Japan', *Antiquity*, 317: 571–84.
Harris, V. 2001. *Shinto: The sacred art of ancient Japan* (London: British Museum Press).
Harunari, H. 1986. 'Rules of residence in the Jomon period based on the analysis of tooth extraction' in R. Pearson (ed.), *Windows on the Japanese Past: Studiesn in Archaeology and Prehistory* (Michigan: Center for Japanese Studies), pp. 293–310.
—— 2002. *Jomon shakai ronkyu [A Study of Jomon Society]* (Tokyo: Hanawa Syobo Co. Ltd).

HAYASHI, K. 2001. *Jomon shakai no kokogaku* [*The Archaeology of Jomon Society*] (Tokyo: Doseisha).
HOSOYA, L. A. 2009. 'Sacred commonness: archaeobotanical approach to Yayoi social stratification—the Central Building Model and Osaka Okegami Sone site' in K. Ikeya, H. Ogawa, and P. Mitchell (eds), *Interaction between hunter-gatherers and farmers: from prehistory to the present*. Senri Ethnological Studies, 73: 99–177.
HUDSON, M. 1992. 'Rice, bronze and chieftains: An archaeology of Yayoi ritual', *Japanese Journal of Religious Studies*, 19(2–3): 139–90.
IMAMURA, K. 1996. *Prehistoric Japan* (London: UCL Press).
INGOLD, T. 2006. 'Rethinking the animate, re-animating thought', *Ethnos*, 71(1): 9–20.
INOUE, N. (ed.) 2003. 'Shinto: A short history' (London and New York: Routledge Curzon).
INSOLL, T. 2004. *Archaeology, Ritual, Religion* (London: Routledge).
INUI, T. 1999. *Yomigaeru Yayoi no toshi to shinden: Ikegami-Sone iseki—saidai Kenbutsu no kozo to bunseki* [*An introduction to the Yayoi shrine and city: Structure and analysis of the giant architecture at Ikegami Sone*] (Tokyo: Hihyosha).
ISHINO, HIRONOBU 1992. 'Rites and rituals of the Kofun period', *Japanese Journal of Religious Studies*, 19(2–3): 191–216.
KANEKO, A. 2005. 'Transegalitarian society and the mortuary system of the Kamegaoka culture: The mortuary system in the northern part of the Tohoku region in the Final Jomon period', *Nihon Kokogaku*, 19: 1–28.
KANER, S. 2007. 'Cult in context in prehistoric Japan' in D. Barrowclough and C. Malone (eds), *Cult in Context* (Oxford: Oxbow Books).
—— (ed.) 2009. *The Power of Dogu: Ceramic figures from ancient Japan* (London: British Museum Press).
KASAHARA, K. (ed.) 2001. *A History of Japanese Religion* (Tokyo: Kosei Publishing Co).
KIDDER, J. E. 1972. 'The newly discovered Takamatsuzuka tomb', *Monumenta Nipponica* 27: 245–51.
—— 2007. *Himiko and Japan's Elusive Kingdom of Yamatai* (Honolulu: Hawaii University Press).
KOBAYASHI, T. 2004. *Jomon Reflections* (Oxford: Oxbow Books).
KODAMA, D. 2003. 'Komakino stone circle and its significance for the study of Jomon social structure: Hunter-Gatherers of the North Pacific Rim', in J. Habu, J. M. Savelle, S. Koyama et al. (eds), *Hunter-Gatherers of the North Pacific Rim*, Senri Ethnological Studies, 63: 235–62.
KONDO, Y. 1977. 'Kofun izen no funkyubo—Tatetsuki iseki o megutte' ['Burial mounds before Kofun: the tatetsuki site'], *Okayama Daigaku Bungakubu Gakujitsu Kiyo*, 37: 1–15.
KOSUGI, Y. 2003. *Jomon no matsuri to kurashi* [*Jomon Festivals and Lifestyles*] (Tokyo: Iwanami Shoten).
MCCALLUM, D. F. 2003. 'Review article: *The emergence of Japanese kingship*, by Joan R. Piggott', *Journal of East Asian Archaeology*, 5(1–4): 73–100.
MAISON DE LA CULTURE DE JAPON À PARIS (eds) 2001. *Haniwa* (Paris: Fondation du Japon).
MATSUMAE, T. 1993. 'Early kami worship', in D. Brown (ed.), *The Cambridge History of Japan*. Volume 1. *Ancient Japan* (Cambridge: Cambridge University Press), pp. 317–58.
MIZOGUCHI, K. 2002. *An Archaeological History of Japan 30,000 BC to AD 700* (Philadelphia: University of Pennsylvania Press).
—— 2005. 'Genealogy in the ground: Observations of jar burials of the Yayoi period, northern Kyushu, Japan', *Antiquity*, 304: 316–26.

—— 2007. 'The emergence of anthropomorphic representation in the Japanese archipelago: a social systemic perspective' in C. Renfrew and I. Morley (eds), *Image and Imagination* (Cambridge: McDonald Institute for Archaeological Research), pp. 185-98.

MORI, M. 2003. 'Ancient and classical Japan: The dawn of Shinto' in N. Inoue, S. Ito, and M. Mori (eds), *Shinto: A short history*, trans. and adapted M. Teeuwen and J. Breen (London: Routledge Curzon), pp. 12-62.

MUNRO, N. G. 1908. *Prehistoric Japan* (Yokohama).

NAUMANN, N. 2000. *Japanese Prehistory: The material and spiritual culture of the Jomon period* (Berlin: Harrassowitz Verlag).

OBA, I. (ed.) 1983. *Shinto kokogaku koza* [*Survey of Shinto Archaeology*] (Tokyo: Yuzankaku).

OHNUKI-TIERNEY, E. 1994. *Rice as Self: Japanese identities through time*. Princeton: Princeton University Press.

PEARSON, R. 1992. *Ancient Japan* (Washington, DC: Sackler Galleries).

PHILIPPI, D. L. 1977. *Kojiki* (Tokyo: University of Tokyo Press).

RENFREW, C. and MORLEY I. (eds) 2007. *Image and Imagination* (Cambridge: McDonald Institute).

RYANG, S. 2004. *Japan and National Anthropology: A critique* (London and New York: Routledge Curzon).

SUZUKI, K. (ed.) 2007. 'Nihon no suton sakuru' ['Stone circles in Japan'], *Kikan Kokogaku* 101.

THAL, S. 2005. *Rearranging the Landscape of the Gods: The politics of a pilgrimage site in Japan, 1573-1912* (Chicago: University of Chicago Press).

TYLOR, E. B. 1871. *Primitive Culture: Researches into the development of mythology, philosophy, religion, art and custom* (London).

WATANABE, H. 1998. 'Jomon dogu to joshin shinko. Minzokushiteki joho no kokogaku e no taikeiteki enyo ni kansuru kenkyu' ['Jomon clay figurines and the goddess cult: An ethnoarchaeological study'], *Kokuritsu Minzokugaku Hakubutsukan Kenkyu Hokoku*, 22(4): 829-973 and 23(1): 129-251.

YAMAGATA, M. 1992. 'The Shakado figurines and Middle Jomon ritual in the Kofu basin', *Japanese Journal of Religious Studies*, 19(2-3): 129-38.

CHAPTER 30

RITUAL AND RELIGION IN SOUTH-EAST ASIA

CHARLES HIGHAM

1 INTRODUCTION: THE FIRST FARMERS

DURING the second millennium BC, Neolithic rice farmers began to explore and settle the broad plains that flank the major rivers of South-east Asia. Here they interacted with the scattered groups of hunter-gatherers whose ancestors had adapted to the inland forests and the rich coasts over the previous 50,000 years. These farmers originated in the Yangtze valley to the north, and brought with them not only their cultivated rice and domestic stock, but also their rituals (Rispoli 2008). Documenting their ritual behaviour relies entirely on their treatment of the dead. We know that for millennia in their Chinese homeland, the dead were interred in lineage cemeteries, accompanied by offerings appropriate to individual status. This practice continued in South-east Asia, as seen in the extensive exposure of a Neolithic cemetery at the site of Ban Non Wat in North-east Thailand (Higham and Higham 2009; Higham and Kijngam 2009). Here, the first phase of the cemetery dates to about 1460 BC and lasted for at least two generations.

Adult corpses were buried in two different ways. Most lay on their backs in a grave, but two were found in a seated position within a large lidded ceramic vessel. Infants were invariably placed in a lidded pot appropriate to their smaller size. The two adult jar burials present intriguing evidence for rituals of death. In the first place the vessels are remarkable for their size, large enough to contain a man in one case, and woman in the other. The necks of each are too small for the insertion of a body, and both were broken at the side to create access. One of these vessels was elaborately decorated with incised and painted designs along the shoulder, while the body was embellished with red painted designs in a complex curvilinear pattern. Both graves contained a small pot as a mortuary offering, as well as a freshwater bivalve shell. These shells recur in burials of the Bronze and Iron Ages in later burials at Ban Non Wat. Their careful placement relative to the skeletons are suggestive of a ritual and symbolic value that might well be connected with the idea of rebirth.

Men and women interred supine in a grave were always accompanied by a range of offerings. These include the complete or partial skeletons of domestic pigs. The inclusion of animal bones in this manner also continued throughout the prehistoric occupation of this and other South-east Asian sites. Food for the afterlife is a ready interpretation of this practice, but it is also likely that they reflect communal feasting at the time of burial, by members of the community. The living also considered it important to place complete ceramic vessels with the dead. At Ban Non Wat, these reflect a highly sophisticated tradition of pottery-making, for not only are the vessels large and shapely, but they were also decorated with incised and painted designs of considerable complexity (Higham and Kijngam 2011). Some of the motifs have been matched from north-east Thailand into northern Vietnam and southern China. Highly stylized, they represent human figures and animals.

2 Khok Phanom Di and Coastal Hunter-Gatherers

Identical human figures were found on a pot of the same date from the site of Khok Phanom Di (Higham and Thosarat 2004). This large mound, formerly located at the mouth of the Bang Pakong River that debouches into the Gulf of Siam, was occupied from about 2000 to 1500 BC. It is thought that the initial settlers there were coastal hunter-gatherers, who interacted, possibly intermarried, with intrusive Neolithic farmers (Bentley et al. 2007). Certain aspects of their death rites are remarkable. The dead were wrapped in naturally occurring asbestos sheeting, covered in red ochre and placed on wooden biers. Some women were accompanied by the ceramic anvils used to this day to shape clay into pots. Men by contrast were buried with large, turtle carapace ornaments that were probably worn on the chest. None, however, has survived intact for they were ritually smashed before being placed in the grave. In about 1500 BC, a woman was buried in a particularly deep grave. Her body, covered in blood-red ochre, was covered in over 120,000 shell beads that would have radiated sunlight when worn. Two horned shell discs lay on her chest. A stack of clay cylinders, preforms for shaping ceramic vessels, covered her body. She must have been a potter, for her tools of trade lay in a shell container beside her right ankle. A smaller version of this grave lay alongside: there, lay an infant little over a year old at death accompanied by a miniature anvil. It seems that children began to fashion clay at a very young age. The succeeding phase at this site saw a rich woman interred in a rectangular mortuary building with clay wall foundations and a clay floor (Higham and Bannanurag 1990).

3 The Bronze Age

The Bronze Age of South-east Asia has for long seemed anomalous: elsewhere, early metallurgy is usually accompanied by a sharp rise in social differentiation as some individuals or groups within a community attain prominence. This situation results from the few sites that have been excavated, and the small scale of the areas opened. At Ban Non Wat, however, many of the 637 burials so far revealed date to six phases in the Bronze Age, and have revealed a very complex set of rituals again associated with death. The first Bronze

FIGURE 30.1 A mortuary vessel from a Bronze Age infant's grave from Ban Non Wat, Northeast Thailand, portraying a stylized human face, c.1000 BC.

Age phase saw seven burials of far greater complexity than had been the practice during the preceding Neolithic. One young woman in a deeply cut grave lay in a wooden boat-shaped coffin. A generation or two later, in about 1000 BC, three rows of burials in the second Bronze Age phase contained the remains of men, women, infants, and children buried with such wealth that they can realistically be described as princely. The body was first wrapped in a fabric shroud, and then placed in a wooden or a clay coffin. Further aspects of ritual behaviour may be identified in the presence of ash and flecks of charcoal on or under the skeleton as if burning was part of the mortuary procedure.

The dead wore many items of personal jewellery, fashioned from exotic marine shell, marble, and bronze. On occasion, the shell and marble bangles literally covered the arms from shoulder to wrist. Necklaces and belts were made up of thousands of disc-shaped shell beads. Similar shell beads often covered the skulls, suggesting that the body was covered in a sequined mask or hat. Bivalve shells were strategically placed relative to the corpse, and up to 40 or 50 ceramic vessels lay beyond the head and feet in a grave up to 5 m long. Some vessels had been placed upside-down over the face, some elaborately painted with curvilinear patterns clearly derived from Neolithic prototypes of the human figure. The finest such vessel, however, accompanied an infant. It was painted with a highly stylized human face, with eyes and a mouth (Figure 30.1). Could it be a revered ancestor, indicating ancestor worship?

There is some evidence in this early Bronze Age cemetery to support the notion of ancestor worship, which was such a prominent part of the rituals in China during this same period. The two richest graves were large enough to contain two people, one having two men, the other two women. Both men had been partially exhumed after burial. Cuts from a sharp implement, perhaps a bronze axe, had severed the lower femora and the neck of one man, and the bones had been removed, and then replaced in a neat stack between the skull and the feet. Most of the other man's bones had similarly been replaced, with the skull balanced on top of them. One of the women remained untouched, but her companion had been disturbed after interment and once again the bones replaced. The same treatment, with particular attention being paid to the positioning of the disturbed skull, was identified in two other burials. Why should this be? One answer is that these were revered ancestors for ensuing generations, and their bones were exhumed as ritual acts, perhaps in an ancestral ceremonial cult.

4 THE IRON AGE

This initial stellar display of Bronze Age wealth did not last. Later burials of this period were markedly poorer, although in one instance, a man was buried with 28 clay moulds for casting bronze axes and bangles. He was interred just before the beginning of the Iron Age, during the fifth century BC, and it was with this period, that we encounter further compelling evidence in South-east Asia generally for ritual and religion. It was then that South-east Asian communities intensified their contacts with the civilizations of China and India. Chinese influence was most keenly felt in the Red River valley of Vietnam, and across the region of southern China known as Lingnan. Both were firmly in the sights of Chinese imperial ambition, and through both archaeological research and surviving texts, we can pinpoint important aspects of religion and ritual. In Cambodia and Thailand, the strongest external contacts were now through maritime trade that incorporated both India and China, and beyond to the Red Sea and Mediterranean lands.

There are few, if any, clearer reflections of ritual in a prehistoric context than those found in the Dian chiefdom of Yunnan Province, China (Huang Ti and Wang Dadao 1983). At the royal necropolis of Shizhaishan, and its contemporary site at Lijiashan, the elite in society were interred in magnificent wooden tombs, embellished with lacquer decoration, and containing remarkable bronzes in the form of drums and situlae. These were filled with cowrie shells, symbols of wealth and fertility. On the top of the drums, religious and ritual scenes are represented in the form of the actors themselves, cast in bronze. The most detailed scene comes from burial 12. We see a raised dais, with a steeply pitched roof. It shelters the Dian paramount chief, depicted larger than life, presiding over a meeting that involves two rows of seated men, each with a drinking cup beside him, Sixteen drums are lined along the edge of the platform, beyond which a crowd is busily engaged in cooking food. Two tigers are involved in the melee of people, one feeding on a dog, another tied to a post. One man carries a large fish, a slaughterman brandishes a knife over a sheep and a pig. Human sacrifice is involved: a man is tied to a post, another is partially consumed by a snake. The scene has been interpreted as the enactment of a ceremony in which sub-chiefs are swearing their allegiance to the paramount, to a background of feasting and human sacrifice.

Women also played a prominent role in seasonal rituals. A tableau from burial 12 shows an elite woman borne aloft on a palanquin by four sturdy men. She is presiding over a ceremony involving three sacrificial victims. A woman is tied to a post, and two are restrained in the stocks or bound and kneeling. Women are seen bringing baskets of fish and meat. Huge drums are set on the ground, and in the centre of the ceremony, a large snake slithers up a pillar. In the Chinese Book of Rituals, the *Li Ji*, snakes are symbols of regeneration, since they emerge afresh after sloughing their skins. This scene, then, is interpreted as a sacrificial ceremony to celebrate a successful harvest.

Dian houses are depicted in minute detail. An example from burial 13 shows a festive occasion in a large house, raised on piles. A musical ensemble plays, people are feasting, animals are tethered to the house posts and in an attic room, a couple is engaged in a romantic interlude.

As one proceeds from the Dian area down the valley of the Red River to the delta, one reaches the domain of the Dong Son chiefs. Here, great ceremonial drums cast in bronze played a prominent role in the rituals of the leaders: Chinese sources describe how they were beaten to summon people to war. These drums were richly decorated with scenes that reveal a wide range of activities. We see drums being beaten, for example, on board warships. The Ngoc Lu drum is famous for its size, and the depiction of four drums being played during a ceremonial occasion (Pham Huy Thong et al. 1990). They were placed on the ground, while drummers sat on a raised platform and beat the drum from above. This was linked with a procession of feathered warriors, and a group of musicians wearing feathered headdresses that incorporated a bird's head. Ethnographic films shot in the highlands of Vietnam almost a century ago reveal almost identical scenes. The drums usually incorporate a frieze of crane egrets, a bird of the marshlands that is thought to have been totemic to the Dong Son paramounts.

Dong Son drums were traded south into the valleys of the Mekong and Chao Phraya rivers, on into the islands of South-east Asia and as far east as New Guinea. This clear evidence for widespread exchange may be linked with the burgeoning maritime trade routes linking South-east Asia with India and beyond. Such seafaring brought more than desirable glass or hardstone beads to the coastal communities. Asoka, the third king of the Mauryan dynasty in India, was an enthusiastic convert to Buddhism (Glover 1998). In the third century BC, he sent Buddhist missionaries to South-east Asia to spread the word, we even know their names: Gavampti, Sona, and Uttara. This might well explain how it is that at the Iron Age cemetery of Ban Don Tha Phet in central Thailand archaeologists have recovered a carnelian lion ornament, dating to this same period. A lion was used then to symbolize the Buddha. Several more lion carnelians have been found in Myanmar (Moore 2007). Buddhism was not the only new religion to attract the attention of South-east Asian leaders. Trade links also brought the Hindu religion to South-east Asia 2,000 years ago.

5 EARLY STATES

We have a detailed description of an early South-east Asian trading state, following a visit to the Mekong Delta by Kang Tai, an emissary of the Chinese emperor. Sent to explore a maritime trade route in the third century AD, he encountered a state controlled by a ruling dynasty, with its own legal and taxation systems, which kept written records, and defended cities. When these very sites were identified by archaeologists, they uncovered brick foundations for temples and cremation cemeteries containing golden plaques bearing Buddhist religious texts. On occasion, wooden statues of the Buddha have been dredged from the delta mud. A burial mound at Go Thap, which was occupied during the sixth century AD, contained brick-lined pits containing human cremations. Three hundred and twenty-two gold leaves were found, decorated with images of Hindu gods. A turtle represents Visnu; an eagle, his mount, Garuda. A second such cemetery at Nen Chua incorporated a large brick and stone building that housed a stone *linga* or phallus, symbolizing potency and regeneration as well as a trinity of Hindu gods (Le Xuan Diem et al. 1995).

This period from about 250 to 550 AD is usually referred to as Funan, a name given it by the Chinese (Pelliot 1903). There is no doubting that Indian gods were adopted with enthusiasm by the leaders, who also assumed resounding Sanskrit names, such as Jayavarman, protégé of victory, or Rudravarman, protégé of Siva. From 550 AD, a network of powerful chiefdoms emerged in the interior of Cambodia, under the generic name Chenla. By this period, paramounts were setting up inscriptions to record their august genealogies and achievements. These were carved in Sanskrit, but some texts were also written in Old Khmer. These provide us with a vital glimpse of the religious beliefs under the veneer of Hindu worship. The Chenla cities, such as Isanapura, were dominated by impressive brick temples set within walled precincts. The exterior walls were decorated in stucco with painted scenes of courtly life while in the gloomy interior there stood the stone *linga* which would once have been gilded and covered with a jewelled cap. Although Hindu gods are often named in the associated inscriptions, we also find reference to the local deities, which surely have a deep ancestry stretching back into the prehistoric period. We find, for example, references to the god of the clouds, or of a tree, and an old and a young god. The name given to many deities is *kpon*, and these are localized in their distribution, and might well represent ancestral family gods (Vickery 1998). Continuing into the present, there are few Cambodian or Thai homes or businesses that do not have a spirit house in the grounds, where ancestors are worshipped and provided with food and drink.

As Chenla rulers increased their power over the people, so they themselves assumed divine status. The *vrah kamraten an* was accorded this divine title posthumously. But Jayavarman I in 664 AD was given the title during his own lifetime.

If Hinduism linked with local traditional gods dominated in the Chenla chiefdoms of Cambodia, Buddhism was more popular in the early state of Dvaravati in Chao Phraya valley to the west. Dvaravati, meaning 'that which has gates', was probably a series of independent statelets, each having its own centre enclosed by a moat and defensive bank. Excavations in these sites invariably encounter the foundations of religious buildings, usually of laterite foundations with a brick superstructure. The latter was decorated in painted stucco. The buildings include *stupas* and *caityas*. The former is a circular structure constructed to house sacred relics. The latter would normally contain images of the Buddha. Pong Tuk is one such site, where excavations have also uncovered the foundations of a *vihara* or meeting hall for monks. At the particularly large site of U-Thong, Boisselier (1968) excavated the remains of a Buddhist assembly hall, as well as three *stupas*. Fragments of the original stucco formed mythical *garudas*, that is eagles; *makaras*, a form of sea monster; and *nagas*, the sacred serpent of Hindu mythology. The degree to which

Buddhism took hold in central Thailand is likewise seen in the rendition of the wheel of the law at the site of Sa Morakod, the global symbol of this religion that represents its basic principles.

Proceeding from Chenla in an easterly direction up the coast of Vietnam, we encounter the remains of a once powerful group of early states known generically as Champa (Southworth 2000). The Chams were relatively recent arrivals along this shoreline, speaking an Austronesian language that sets them apart from other early states in South-east Asia. However, they too adopted Hinduism and Buddhism. This is seen at the major religious and ritual centre of My Son, where numerous brick shrines were constructed from the reign of King Bhadravarman in the late fourth century to at least the end of the eleventh century AD. As in Chenla, Buddhism was also favoured in parts of Chenla. The most impressive Buddhist site is known as Dong Duong, in a region known to the Chams as Amaravati. This site was probably built by King Jaya Indravarman in the late ninth century AD, and was essentially a temple site of the Mahayana branch of the religion. The hall of the Dong Duong monastery housed an impressively large statue of the Buddha, and a further statue depicts a *dharmapala*, or guardian of the law. Other sculptures, assembled after excavations at the site began in 1902, represent episodes in the life of the Buddha including the Buddha leaving his father's palace in his early quest for enlightenment.

6 THE KINGDOM OF ANGKOR

In the late eighth century, a great and charismatic leader known in history as Jayavarman II, set off on a great march from his capital on the left bank of the Mekong. This city, known today as Banteay Prei Nokor, has at its centre two massive brick shrines. His route took him up the course of the Mekong River, and then he struck out with his followers in a westerly direction that took him to the plains that lie between Cambodia's Great Lake and the Kulen uplands. He evidently defeated rival rulers during his migration, and in 802, in an esoteric Hindu ceremony at the site of Rong Chen, a temple high in Kulen Hills, he was proclaimed *Chakravartin*, or supreme leader on earth. Thus was founded the kingdom of Ankgor.

There can be few early civilizations that reveal through surviving buildings and texts the full force of their religion and ritual. For six centuries, Angkor was the centre of an illustrious state ruled by god-kings (Jacques and Freeman 1998). While we know little of Jayavarman II from contemporary accounts, and no buildings can be ascribed to his reign, we know a great deal about Indravarman I, his great nephew by marriage. This great king assumed power in 877 AD, and immediately set about constructing temple shrines at his capital of Hariharalaya just east of Angkor. One of these is known today as Preah Ko, the temple of the sacred ox. The other is called the Bakong. Preah Ko was originally known as Paramesvara, or supreme god. In this context, the supreme god was Siva. The complex was dedicated just two years after the king's accession. It is dominated by a platform foundation for six large brick shrines, some of which retain the original stucco. The inscriptions on the entrance portals tell us that the main shrine was dedicated to Jayavarman II, and those flanking it were for two of Indravarman's male ancestors. The three smaller temples that lie behind the front row were dedicated to the female consorts of these three men, Narendradevi, Prithivindradevi, and Dharanindradevi. There is no doubt that, linked with the Hindu pantheon, this temple was a constructed as an act of fealty to the kings ancestors, and for their worship.

The Bakong temple, dedicated in 881 AD, is the earliest temple pyramid of Angkor. It is entered, for the first time at Angkor, via a bridge flanked by the sacred naga snake, symbolizing the passage from the human world to the domain of the gods. Its massive sandstone blocks rise up through five stages to the platform summit, the first three of which were protected at the corners by elephant guardians. In 881, King Indravarman had an inscription carved which read 'In 881 AD, the king, like a god, dispenser of riches, has erected a *linga* named Indresvara here'. This name links that of the king with the supreme Hindu god Siva. Eight small sanctuaries placed uniformly round the base of the pyramid probably acknowledged the male and female ancestors of Indravarman, for the eastern set incorporates male figures on the exterior niches, while the western temples have females. The foundation text for this temple records that Indravarman 'erected eight lingas named by royal practice after the eight elements of Siva: earth, wind, fire, the moon, sun, water, ether and the sacrificer'.

The mention of water draws our attention to the Indratataka, a reservoir or *baray* positioned to the north of Hariharalaya. Fed by water from the Roluos River, the *baray* might well have symbolized the oceans that surrounded Mount Meru, the home of the Hindu gods. In one of his inscriptions, the king recorded that 'he made the Indratataka, mirror of his glory, like the ocean'. These constructions would have drawn on a large and dedicated labour force, and we are left in no doubt that sustaining villages in the Angkorian countryside were required to provide surplus food, cloth, and indeed all the essentials for the maintenance of the priesthood that fulfilled the daily rites of worship.

On the death of Indravarman in 889 AD, his son Yasovarman succeeded to the throne, and established his own capital 13 km to the west, naming it Yasodharapura, city of Yasovarman, protégé of glory. As one of his first acts, he had a new island temple constructed in the centre of his father's reservoir, known as Lolei, and had four shrines built for the worship of his father, maternal grandfather, his mother, and her mother. Then at Yasodharapura, he set in train the construction of a temple on the Bakheng Hill that surpassed both of his father's temples in size and grandeur, a temple formed to represent the five peaks of Mount Meru, home of the gods. To the west, he ordered the construction of a new reservoir that dwarfed in size the Indratataka. This reservoir was associated with the foundation of 100 *ashramas*, or retreats for ascetics to meditate and worship (Higham 2001).

From its earliest days therefore, the kingdom of Angkor had as its central focus, stone or brick temples representing the home of the gods, associated with the name of the sovereign. Over the ensuing century of the first dynasty of Angkor, further royal foundations sprang up, one of which, founded by Jayavarman IV in a remote location north-east of the traditional capital, reveals the speed with which a ritual and political centre could be constructed. This site, known today as Koh Ker, was formerly named Lingapura, City of the Linga. Founded in 928 AD, it was abandoned only two decades later. However, a massive 30-metre-high temple, the Prasat Thom dominates the site. Access entails the passage across a sacred naga bridge and by a single steep stairway that negotiates the seven tiers of this pyramid. At the top, stone garudas guard the platform on which would once have stood the sacred *linga*. Numerous subsidiary stone temples surround the central complex, covering an area of 35 km^2, some still containing their *linga*, and the stone conduit designed for the sacred water to flow through the temple wall to the outside world.

Rajendravarman, both the uncle and cousin of Jayavarman IV, returned the capital to Angkor and followed the established royal tradition of building his own temples, Pre Rup and the Eastern Mebon. Again, he linked his own name with that of Siva when naming his state *linga* Rajendrabhadesvara. The four subsidiary shrines at Pre Rup were dedicated to himself, to a Brahman ancestor, his aunt, and his immediate predecessor.

In about 1000 AD, there was a dynastic change, and under Suryavarman I, the Western Baray, the biggest reservoir at Angkor, was constructed. For long the purpose of these reservoirs was debated. Were they, in representing the oceans round Mount Meru, purely symbolic or did they have a more mundane function in providing irrigation water for the rice fields that were laid out below them? We now know that they were both, for the canal system issuing from the Western Baray has been identified. But the reservoirs at Angkor also had temples in the centre, where pilgrims could worship. When, in the late thirteenth century, a Chinese diplomat named Zhou Daguan visited Angkor, he described a huge bronze statue of the Buddha housed in the temple of this reservoir (Zhou Daguan 1993). He was wrong in his identification, because the remains of this statue have been found in 1936 and identified as being the Hindu god Visnu. By a complex siphon system, water from the reservoir was made to issue from the god's navel.

By now, the eleventh century, Angkor had few rivals in terms of the extent of its religious and ritual monuments, but this was only a prelude to the achievements of two kings, Suryavarman II and Jayavarman VII. In 1113 AD, we read that the venerable priest Divakarapandita anointed the former as sovereign. An inscription describes the king studying sacred rituals, celebrating religious festivals, and performing sacrifices to the spirits of his ancestors. The priest himself then undertook pilgrimages to the major provincial temples of the kingdom, to Wat Phu on the banks of the Mekong in Laos, where an ancient temple lay under a mountain, sacred due to the natural stone *linga* that dominated its summit. At the temple of Preah Vihear, commanding the heights of the Dang Raek range, he donated a golden image of a dancing Siva. Suryavarman was one of the greatest of Angkorian kings, and his temple mausoleum, known to us as Angkor Wat, is often described as the largest and finest religious monument ever built (Figure 30.2). Ringed by a massive moat and walls, it is reached by traversing a raised causeway flanked by sacred *naga* serpents. The central sanctuary rises in the form of five lotus-shaped towers, the central one designated to take the king's ashes when he went to live with the gods under his new name, Paramavisnuloka, 'He who has gone to live in the sacred world of Visnu'.

These towers are flanked by an ambulatory, the interior wall of which bears the longest set of stone reliefs in the world. These not only show us the king in state and at war, but also religious themes. One depicts the churning of the ocean of milk, in which the demons and gods are engaged in a tug of war in which the giant serpent Vasuki is rotated round Mount Mandara. By churning the cosmic ocean *amrita* the elixir of immortality is released.

Suryavarman was a follower of the god Visnu, but his kinsman Jayavarman VII, who came to the throne in 1181 AD, was a Mahayana Buddhist. He was also the greatest builder at

FIGURE 30.2 Angkor Wat was the temple-mausoleum of King Suryavarman II (r. AD 1113–1150). Its five stone towers, formerly probably gilded, represent the peaks of Mount Meru, home of the gods.

Angkor, responsible for numerous temples and the city of Angkor Thom. This city is entered across a causeway flanked by stone demons and gods pulling on a serpent, again representing the quest for the immortal elixir. In the centre of the city lies the Bayon temple, with its numerous stone heads gazing serenely over the city. These are thought to represent the king as a bodhisattva, or Buddhist saintly person bent on helping others. Two massive temples beyond the city walls were dedicated to the king's mother and father. Banteay Chmar, remotely located to the north-west, was dedicated to his crown prince (Figure 30.3). Tens of thousands of priests and other officiants were sustained in order to fulfil temple rites. Roads, hospitals, and rest houses were provided for pilgrims to visit and worship at the major temples across the kingdom.

The great stone faces of Jayavarman take one back to the painted image of a human face on a mortuary pot made at Ban Non Wat over 2,000 years earlier. Can we trace a thread of continuity over the generations that make up the history of South-east Asia, in which ancestors were venerated, even worshipped? The aura and mystique that surrounds Thai and Cambodian monarchies to this day suggest that this might well be the case.

FIGURE 30.3 Even in remote north-western Cambodia, King Jayavarman VII (r. AD 1181–1219) had a spectacular ritual complex constructed. Known as Banteay Chmar, the stone faces on the shrines represent the king as a Boddhisattva or Buddhist saint.

Suggested Reading

The evidence for prehistoric mortuary remains with ritual and religious implications is summarized in C. F. W. Higham, *Early Cultures of Mainland Southeast Asia* (Bangkok: River Books, 2002). Images of Dian bronzes can be seen in J. Rawson (ed.), *The Chinese Bronzes of Yunnan* (Cultural Relics Publishing House). Early religious beliefs in Cambodia are described by Michael Vickery in his book *Society, Economics and Politics in Pre-Angkor Cambodia* (Tokyo: The Centre for East Asian Cultural Studies for Unesco). Vittorio Roveda has published a detailed study of the religions of Angkor in *Images of the Gods: Khmer mythology in Cambodia, Laos & Thailand* (River Books, 2006). For a general description of Angkorian temples, see Claude Jacques and Philippe Lafond, *The Khmer Empire: Cities and sanctuaries* (River Books, 2006). Cham art and religions is covered in Emmanuel Guillon, *Cham Art: Treasures of the Da Nang Museum, Vietnam* (Thames and Hudson 2001).

References

Bentley, A. et al. 2007. 'Shifting gender relations at Khok Phanom Di, Thailand: Isotopic evidence from the skeletons', *Current Anthropology*, 48(2): 301–14.

Boisselier, J. 1968. *Nouvelles Connaissances Archaéologiques de la Ville d'U-Tong* (Bangkok).

——1969. 'Recherches Archéologiques en Thaïlände, II: Rapport sommaire de la mission 1965', *Arts Asiatiques*, XX: 47–97.

Glover, I. C. 1998. 'The role of India in the late prehistory of Southeast Asia', *Journal of Southeast Asian Archaeology*, 18: 21–49.

Higham, C. F. W. 2001. *The Civilization of Angkor* (London: Weidenfeld and Nicholson).

——2002. *Early Cultures of Mainland Southeast Asia* (Bangkok: River Books).

——and Higham, T. F. G. 2009. 'A new chronological framework for prehistoric Southeast Asia, based on a Bayesian model from Ban Non Wat', *Antiquity*, 83: 125–44.

——and Bannanurag, R. 1990. *The Excavation of Khok Phanom Di, I: The Excavation, Chronology and Human Burials* (London: The Society of Antiquaries of London and Thames and Hudson).

——and Thosarat, R. 2004. *The Excavation of Khok Phanom Di: Volume VII. Summary and Conclusions* (London: The Society of Antiquaries of London).

——and Kijngam, A. 2009. *The Origins of the Civilization of Angkor. Volume III. The Excavation Ban Non Wat, Introduction* (Bangkok: The Fine Arts Department of Thailand).

————2011. *The Origins of the Civilization of Angkor. Volume IV. The Excavation Ban Non Wat: The Neolithic Occupation* (Bangkok: The Fine Arts Department of Thailand).

Huang Ti and Wang Dadao 1983. 'Commentary on the plates' in Jessica Rawson (ed.), *The Chinese Bronzes of Yunnan* (London and Beijing: The Cultural Relics Publishing House), pp. 217–41.

Jacques, C. and Freeman, M. 1998. *Angkor: Cities and temples* (Bangkok: River Books).

Le Xuan Diem, Dao Linh Con, and Vo Si Khai 1995. *Van Hoa Oc Eo Nhung Kham Pha Moi* (Hanoi: Nha Xuat Ban Khoa Hoc Xa Hoi).

Moore, E. H. 2007. *Early Landscapes of Myanmar* (Bangkok: River Books).

Pelliot, P. 1903. 'Le Fou-Nan', *Bulletin de l'École Française d'Extrême Orient*, 2: 248–333.

Pham Huy Thong, Pham Minh Huyen, and Lai Van Toi (eds) 1990. *The Dong Son Drums in Viet Nam* (Ha Noi: The Viet Nam Social Science Publishing House).

Rispoli, F. 2008. 'The incised and impressed pottery style of mainland Southeast Asia: following the path of neolithization', *East and West*, 57 (1–4), 235–304.

Southworth, W. 2000. 'Notes on the political geography of Campa in Central Vietnam during the late 8th and early 9th centuries' in W. Lobo and S. Reimann (eds), *Southeast Asian Archaeology 1998* (Centre for South-East Asian Studies, University of Hull and Ethnologisches Museum, Staatliche Museum zu Berlin), pp. 237–44.

Vickery, M. 1998. *Society, Economics and Politics in Pre-Angkor Cambodia* (Tokyo: The Centre for East Asian Cultural Studies for Unesco).

Zhou D. 1993. *The Customs of Cambodia* (Bangkok: The Siam Society).

CHAPTER 31

HISTORICIZING COSMOLOGIES IN AUSTRALIA AND PAPUA NEW GUINEA

BRUNO DAVID

1 INTRODUCTION

FOR decades Anglophone researchers across the world have fretted at archaeological investigations of religion and ritual. In some circles, and influentially, religion and ritual were long sidelined as epiphenomena in the comprehension of social life and human beings, almost an irrelevance when trying to understand a people's history and social dynamism, which were supposedly best done through notions of environmental adaptation, economic rationalism, or maximizing/optimizing evolutionary processes. Yet what makes us who we are—and what makes cultural practices what they are—is precisely the kind of thing that a recognition of religion and ritual allows us to address: how the world is meaningful and how we understand it to be ordered (e.g. behaviourally, ethically, organizationally, socially) and to operate in this meaningfulness. Cosmological understandings locate us in a world imbued with meaning and guide us to live and act in specific ways. Hence Ian McNiven and his colleagues (McNiven et al. 2006: 13–14) have pointed out that while Lewis Binford (e.g. 1980), for example, recognized the presence of religious and ritual activities and sites among the Nunamiut of Anaktuvuk Pass in Alaska, he deemed religious and ritual sites to have marginal value for an understanding of cultural behaviours that purportedly revolved around ecologically motivated settlement-subsistence strategies. But:

> as Insoll (2004: 48) pointed out, this secular view is at odds with Nunamiut cosmology and shamanism. Binford stripped Nunamiut landscapes of their cosmological, symbolic and spiritual meaning and failed to mention 'shrines' and 'sacred sites' that clearly structured and mediated ecological relationships. This is an archaeology of place devoid of meaningful place and of meaningful emplacement, just as it is devoid of social experience and salience.
> [McNiven et al. 2006: 14]

It is those cosmological understandings, and the behavioural patternings that result from such understandings, that are the hallmark of religious experience and religious expression, if we understand religion to be about the mysterious ways of the world and how those ways affect our being. As David (2002a) has argued, an investigation of religion and ritual should aim to locate specific practices and understandings in their broader ontological or cosmological frameworks, for it is the latter that come to frame and give meaning to practice, and in the process shape experience. In this chapter, I review how archaeologists in Australia and Papua New Guinea (PNG) have historicized religion and ritual by considering the cosmologies in which they are located. While other archaeological attention has been given to religion and ritual—e.g. in trying to understand rock art and various sacred objects—it is in their historicization that archaeology has contributed its particular disciplinary abilities. The mappings of objects and places in documented or extrapolated social and cosmological contexts have been more widespread, both in archaeology and social anthropology.

In Australia and PNG, as in other parts of the world, the 1990s began to witness a shift in archaeological interest towards a concern with 'cosmologies', 'spiritscapes', and 'sacred geographies'. This came about some time after positivist (often foraging-based ecological) models had already begun to be questioned, and in the aftermath of both the postcolonial and 'social archaeology' turns of the early 1980s, in particular by Harry Lourandos (e.g. 1980, 1984, 1991) and his students (e.g. Barker 1995) and colleagues (e.g. Bowdler 1981; Thomas 1981). In Australia and to a lesser degree PNG (because archaeological research in PNG largely came to a standstill in the 1990s) this turn was significantly influenced by Indigenous critiques, as well as by overseas intellectual developments especially coming from Great Britain (e.g. Bender 1993; Hodder 1982; Shanks and Tilley 1987; Thomas 1993).

Since then, in many parts of the world investigations of past human engagements with the spiritual world have often taken place through an investigation of *monuments* thought to have commemorated or facilitated religious experience, such as residential places for religious elites, or places of religious performances and contemplation (e.g. temples, churches, shrines). At first impression, Australia and PNG lacked such permanent structures by which archaeologists could investigate religious and ritual pasts; in the case of Australia because it is commonly thought that Aboriginal people did not build religious installations, and in PNG because of the impermanency of wooden structures. However, archaeologists have begun to rethink such assumptions and to reconsider what constitutes 'constructed places' (often through closer integration of social anthropological findings; e.g. Godwin and Weiner 2006; Kearney and Bradley 2006; Langton and David 2004). In Australia, sacred places not only existed but were realized to be abundant, and included stone arrangements (e.g. O'Connor et al. 2007); sacred rock art by which the ancestral spirit beings metamorphosized into place (e.g. David et al. 1990, 1994; Flood 1997; Merlan 1989); sacred (and sometimes secret) ritual locations (e.g. David et al. 2009; Doring 2000), some of which were associated with locales of public agglomeration occupied during periods of ritual performance (e.g. Flood 1980; Smith 1988); stone quarries of high repute, imbued with sacred essences that enhanced the value of the stone points already present within the rocks and that were highly prized by neighbouring groups who attained them in ceremonial exchange cycles (e.g. Jones and White 1988); bark coffins in rock outcrops (e.g. L'Oste-Brown et al. 2002; McNiven and Russell 2002) or burials in earth mounds (e.g. Coutts et al. 1979), both of which marked into the future, for present and descendant generations, ancestral connections to place; and so-called 'natural' places of great cosmological significance, such as Ngarrabullgan in north-eastern Australia or Uluru in the arid centre (e.g. David and Wilson 1999; Layton 1986).

To allow such investigations to proceed, points of reference by which archaeological patternings could knowingly be related to religious or ritual activity have been needed. Such reference has invariably come from local ethnography. In all cases, one or the other of two general methods has been employed. The first, which we can conventionally refer to as the *direct ethnographic approach*, has taken aspects of local ethnography and applied it directly to the archaeological record without recourse to historical change (e.g. Sales 1992). An early example of this approach comes from Lake Mungo in western New South Wales, where in 1970 a late Pleistocene human cremation was reported, by ethnographic analogy signalling to the archaeologists more than 25 millennia of continuous tradition (Bowler et al. 1970). Because the Mungo I human remains were cremated, and partly because diet breadths were similar, Bowler et al. (1970: 58) concluded that 'a distinctively Australian culture was already established in the region when the Mungo Site was occupied some 25–32,000 years ago' (see Bowler et al. 2003 for a redating of the site). Flood (1989: 45) similarly hints that the Mungo I cremation practices were 'still in use among Australian Aborigines in the eighteenth and nineteenth centuries in some parts of eastern Australia and Tasmania', without having sufficient evidence to bridge the temporal gap that would allow an argument for spatial and temporal *continuity* in cultural practice as they relate to the disposal of the dead. The implicit assumption is that the similarities in diets and commonality of cremation practices more than 25,000 years ago and again during ethnographic times means continuity in cultural practice and care of the dead into the afterlife through time, without consideration of the possibility of cosmological change having taken place (a problem common to archaeological interpretations of the time).

Here history and cosmology are bereft of movement as the past becomes a clone of the present; as such the archaeological record does not in any substantial way reveal anything new about past lifeways; which in itself has left us with a conundrum: how do we investigate a religious past that could potentially have been different from that of ethnographic times? The answer has come through the second method, which attempts to historicize the present by gradually tracking back in time ethnographically known religious and ritual practices and cosmologies, in the process enabling archaeologists to identify discontinuities by which historical emergences could then be targeted and further explored. We have come to know this method as the *dual historical method* (David and McNiven 2004). World views, and with this religious experience, are treated as historical and emergent (as with all other aspects of culture), and it is the task of archaeology to explore this historical emergence and cultural dynamism. Explicitly or implicitly, this aim to historicize ethnography has formed the methodological cornerstone of most research on the archaeology of religion and ritual in Australia and PNG. It is this archaeological historicization of ethnographic cosmology and ritual that I focus upon in this chapter.

2 ABORIGINAL AUSTRALIA

Archaeological research into religion and ritual in Australia is still very much in its infancy. Only a handful of sporadic papers appeared prior to the beginning of the twenty-first century, although in the last few years interest has increased. This paucity of earlier concerted attention is surprising in many ways, for Australia has long been a stalwart of anthropological writings about Indigenous religion (e.g. Durkeim 1965; Stanner 1989;

Strehlow 1947), ritual (e.g. Morphy 1984), totemism (e.g. Spencer and Gillen 1927), ancestral beings and ancestral connections (e.g. Morphy 1991), and spirituality (e.g. Morphy 1984). However, the fact that archaeologists have not taken advantage of these considerable writings in the past is much a sign of the times, with positivist, ecological, and economic concerns having long predominated over more social or ontological/cosmological concerns until the 1980s, increasingly into the 1990s, when thinking on such matters began to change (in Australian archaeology, due to many factors but most noticeably to Harry Lourandos [e.g. 1980, 1984, 1991]; see also David et al. [2006]).

Until the 1990s, a few sporadic attempts were made to investigate the archaeology of religious sites. These were not, however, attempts to historicize religion or ritual themselves, but rather attempts to map cultural places usually in the context of settlement–subsistence modelling, or simply in the geographical mapping of cultural landscapes. Isabel McBryde (1974) was the first professionally trained archaeologist to target ritual structures in the form of stone arrangements, but at the time (and in the context of contemporary analytical techniques) these did not appear to possess sediments by which they could be dated. David Frankel (1982) was the first to attempt systematic internal examination and radiocarbon dating of ritual structures (in this case, an earthen *bora* ring of a kind reminiscent of ethnographically documented male initiation sites) near Sunbury in south-central Victoria. However, here the primary aim was not to systematically investigate the history of Aboriginal religious practices or ritual installations, but rather to demonstrate 'whether or not they [the Sunbury earthen rings] were of Aboriginal construction, and in order to define more clearly their nature and method of manufacture' (Frankel 1982: 89). Informed both by ethnography and by site contents, Frankel (1982: 96) concluded that 'there is no reason not to associate the set of circles at Sunbury with similar Aboriginal socio-religious activities, and most probably with initiation sites', without further exploring their implications for the history of *bora* rituals in the region. Other attempts to map and classify *bora* rings were subsequently undertaken in southern Queensland and northern New South Wales further to the north (in particular, see Satterthwaite and Heather, 1987), but to this day Frankel's excavations and radiocarbon dates at the Sunbury *bora* rings initiation site remains the only research of its kind in Australia.

2.1 The Dreaming

During the colonial period whence ethnographic documents first began to appear, across much of Australia Aboriginal groups understood the world to have attained its recent shape during a formative period known as the Dreaming (or Dreamtime). The Dreaming is not so much a period of time traceable to the past, as a mythic era of creation and transformation when numinous beings peopled the earth and gave each Aboriginal group its unique language, ritual paraphernalia, culture, lands, ancestry, and social connections. It is during the Dreaming that life forces emerged from the earth (and its waters), and when the various plant and animal species (e.g. emu) and cultural objects (e.g. firestick) attained their defining features. Through transformative acts, these species and objects often became the ancestral totemic beings of recent and present clans, and gave the earth its particular topography and toponymy enchaining each individual person to her or his ancestors through the land and the animals, plants, and items of material culture by which they trace their origins and ancestral connections (for apt anthropological expositions of the Dreaming, see Morphy 1996; Stanner 1965). Particular designs or design conventions (e.g. Morphy 1991; Munn 1986; Taçon 1987), colours (e.g. Morphy 1991; Taçon 1991, 1994, 1999) and 'mythical' personages (e.g. David et al. 1994), each with their own material and archaeologically traceable expressions, were given to people and to groups by the ancestral 'spirits' (see also Layton 1992). Also given to each group were the laws of the land and knowledge of the rituals required to be performed to ensure the world's continued order and health. Specific places were imbued with ancestral essences, and the particular affiliations that people had (and have) with those essences regulated how and where people could do things through the course of their lives (e.g. Morphy 1984, 1991; Taçon 1994). In this way social connections with place and the material world were enchained with sacred ancestral connections (for notions of enchainment, see Chapman 2008).

2.2 Historicizing the Dreaming

In part because the Dreaming (as we know of it from ethnography) is not so much a concrete period or moment of history as a 'mythical' process of transformation that shaped the world into recent times, popular commentators have often thought of it as a timeless and everlasting cultural expression. The Dreaming—and with this the Aboriginal groups who understood the world through the Dreaming—was thus seen to have a religious past, but not a religious history. We see this well even today in popular expressions expounding Aboriginal culture and the Dreaming as 'the oldest culture in the world' (see David [2002a] for a critique; see also the useful debate between Patrick Wolfe [1991] and Howard Morphy [1996]). However, such views give little recognition to the fact that during ethnographic times there was not one Dreaming but many, for each Aboriginal group recognized its own ancestry and had its own cosmological understandings, in some cases akin to that of neighbouring groups but in other cases very different (e.g. Keen 2004). For instance, Nicholas Peterson (1972: 23) notes that among the Warlpiri individuals recognized conception totems from other people's clan or moiety territories, whereas this was not the case among the Murngin. Or, in some parts of south-eastern mainland Australia 'great guardian-spirits' such as Baiame were recognized, but such omniscient beings did not occur in other places (Stanner 1965: 216).

Consequently, it would be a mistake to think of the ethnographically known Dreaming in the singular, for each group had its own religious views about the ways of the world. Furthermore, as is also apparent from the ethnographic record, these views were in a state of flux during the early colonial period, as is evident in the introduction and adoption of new 'religious' ideas and rituals (e.g. the spread of Molonga ceremonies across Australia between 1893 and 1918 [Mulvaney 1975]; or the introduction of new kinship systems with ancestral connections across arid and semi-arid Australia in the recent past [e.g. McConvell 1996]) and novel interpretations by particular groups. Consequently, the purported ahistoricity of the Dreaming promulgated by early commentators and many others since, and favoured by a broad range of alternative thinkers who look to Aboriginal Australia's 'otherness' in the hope or belief of finding life's essential answers and humanity's true original spiritual being (part of the primitivist project to which Aboriginal being has long been subjected in colonialist thinking—see Fabian 1983; Langton and David 2003), has been questioned through archaeological research aimed at exploring the historicity of Aboriginal life (e.g. David 2002a; McNiven and Russell 2005). In the process, the Dreaming itself has been used by archaeologists to question prevalent preconceptions about Aboriginal culture (and Aboriginal people) in popular culture (e.g. David 2002a; Langton and David 2003).

2.3 Art, the Spirits, and the Ancestors

The dual historical method was first engaged in Australia as a means to explore the antiquity of the Dreaming in one part of Aboriginal Australia, Wardaman country in the Northern Territory. Many Wardaman elders (by conventional Wardaman protocol, we cannot name individual deceased elders here) of the 1980s and 1990s had been brought up and taught by *their* elders the ways of the Dreaming, and understood the world to operate through it. Here Wardaman elders recalled their older kin painting and engraving in caves and rock shelters during the early twentieth century. These elders knew the Dreaming (*buwarraja*) meanings of specific artworks and sites (see Flood and David 1994; Flood 1997: 300–20 for details), while early anthropological writings documenting the creation of specific artworks relating to spirit-beings (e.g. the Lightning Brothers at Yiwarlarlay [see Arndt 1962]) complemented these more recent Aboriginal voices. An archaeology of the material expressions of Wardaman *buwarraja* symbolism, as expressed in the rock art, could thus shed light on the antiquity of ethnographically known Wardaman cosmology. With this in mind, Josephine Flood, Bruno David, and their colleagues, working together with Wardaman elders, systematically undertook detailed recordings of over 50,000 rock-art images from over 400 rock-art sites, recording the meanings of the art to the local clan elders and other Wardaman individuals (e.g. David et al. 1994; Flood and David 1994).

A broader body of past and contemporary anthropological research (e.g. Merlan 1989) allowed the art to be situated in its proper cosmological and cultural framework, so that the Dreaming was not somehow located as a spiritual world outside everyday life, but rather was understood to imbue all aspects of life, artistic practices included. It was this overarching cosmological framework known from ethnography that Flood and her co-workers aimed to historicize by systematically tracking back through archaeological excavation and radiocarbon dating specific Dreaming expressions. David (2002a) and David et al. (1994) thus concluded that Wardaman Dreaming, as we knew of it from ethnography, could be traced back in time some 900–1,400 years through its symbolic expressions, not thousands or tens of thousands of years as some public commentators were generally claiming. As David (2002a: 88) concluded:

> The late Holocene antiquity of Wardaman visual symbols implies a late Holocene antiquity for the graphic presencing of the ethnographically known Wardaman Dreaming. The fact that Wardaman symbols associated with the ethnographic Dreaming cannot be securely traced further back in time implies an epochal reworking of the open network of signs, as system of meaning, 900–1400 years ago.

This Wardaman research represents the first explicit application of the dual historical method to the archaeology of religion and ritual in Australia (although at the time the method was not named).

Further to the north, in western Arnhem Land, a similar attempt to explore the history of Aboriginal cosmologies was made by Paul Taçon et al. (1996) in their historicization of the

Rainbow Serpent, a major and powerful Dreaming being found across much of Australia (but with regionally varied significance). They began with ethnographic understandings of the Rainbow Serpent as it is understood to be in western Arnhem Land (north-central Australia), where it is intimately associated with flying foxes (both in the art and in oral traditions). Working their way backwards in time through a sequence of rock-art styles, and by systematically comparing the Rainbow Serpent's qualitative and metrical characteristics with those of various fauna, they noted that the earliest artistic manifestations of the Rainbow Serpent took on the form of pipefish. They also noted that 'Aboriginal creation stories reveal in great detail how the world was created by the Rainbow Serpent at a time of great transformations' (Taçon et al. 1996: 120), a period which they say corresponds well with the period around 4,000–6,000 years ago when the Yam Style of rock art which sees the birth of Rainbow Serpent art was in full operation.

In time, the Rainbow Serpent would change its appearance and undoubtedly also its symbolism, incorporating traits of other powerful fauna such as crocodiles and kangaroos, and most recently water buffalo. By tracking back in time the first manifestations of the Rainbow Serpent, and then exploring in the forward motion of time its transformations, Taçon et al. (1996) systematically historicized this important component of Aboriginal cosmology, in this case identifying 4,000–6,000 years ago as a major point of environmental, sociocultural, artistic, and cosmological change, one which eventually and through a series of further transformations led to the world of Aboriginal Australia that we have come to know from ethnography (see David 2002a for a critique). It is in this early Yam Style manifestation of the Rainbow Serpent that these authors see the birth of Dreaming beliefs that we can recognize through ethnography.

2.4 Sacred Places

David (2002a; David and Wilson 1999) also explored the antiquity of specific Dreaming attitudes to places, in this case by exploring the archaeology of the Djungan sacred mountain Ngarrabullgan in north-eastern Australia. Ngarrabullgan is an 18 km-long mesa which during ethnographic times was only rarely accessed by local Djungan people because of the presence of dangerous spirits ('devils') who made it its home (Figure 31.1). In the Dreaming, four 'devils' lived on and around Ngarrabullgan: Beerroo, Eekoo, Mooramully, and Barmboo. Eekoo was one of the most feared spirit-beings on the mountain, its home being a lake in the middle of the mesa. As Francis Richards (1926: 35) noted, 'Most sickness was attributed to the agency of these devils', and during ethnohistoric times people thus rarely ventured onto the mountain top. However, after undertaking archaeological excavations at all the known cultural sites possessing stratified deposits on the mountain, and a sample of sites off the mountain—a total of 15 caves and rock shelters (plus one cave without cultural evidence)—David and Wilson (1999; see also David 2002a) concluded that for thousands of years people had lived and/or used the mountain top until 600–700 years ago, when virtually all occupation ceased. David (2002a: 46) thus concluded that 'abandonment by the fourteenth century CE appears to have been mediated by the onset of a new system of signification that rendered the mountain inappropriate for habitation': it was then that the dangerous spirits Beerroo, Eekoo, Mooramully, and Barmboo as we know of them ethnographically began to make Ngarrabullgan their home, causing the Djungan to abandon the mountain as a residential space.

FIGURE 31.1 The sacred Djungan mountain of Ngarrabullgan, northern Australia.

2.5 Totemic Landscapes

Mike Smith (e.g. 1996, 2005; Smith et al. 1998; see also Ross and Davidson 2006) undertook intensive archaeological research in central Australia, asking a number of questions relating to the antiquity and history of occupation of the continent's arid core, focusing in particular on the subsistence (e.g. seed-based diets), exchange (e.g. ochre distribution networks), and territorial (e.g. establishment of totemic centres) strategies that enabled this extreme environment to be inhabited. He pointed out that specialized seed-grinding tools of a kind ethnographically known to have enabled the production of large quantities of staple foods to feed ritual gatherings had a limited antiquity not exceeding 3,000 years (Smith 1986). He also found that changes in rock art, and in the provenance of ochres used for the production of (often totemic) rock art, had taken place through time, in particular during the last 800 to 1,000 years. Smith (e.g. Smith 2005: 230–3; Smith et al. 1998) thus concluded that the Australian arid zone witnessed significant changes in occupational strategies and systems of land use, mediated through cognitive strategies by which territoriality and interregional (social) interactions could take place, late in the Holocene.

Bruno David (2002a) reviewed the archaeological excavations undertaken by Mike Smith (e.g. 1988) and his colleagues at Therreyererte (a Native Cat Dreaming place), Kweyunpe, Keringke (a Kangaroo Dreaming place), and Urre (a Grass Seed Dreaming place), four totemic centres in the arid zone, concluding that while there was fleeting evidence of occupation at some of these sites dating back to 3,600 years ago, the first signs of these sites' totemic significance, as expressed in ritual activity, did not appear until 1,400 years ago at Kwenyunpe, 800–1,000 years ago at Keringke and Urre, and 600 to 700 years ago at Therreyererte (David, 2002a: 60–1). Contrary to popular belief, the archaeology was used to argue that Aboriginal cosmology should be seen to be historical and emergent rather than fixed, originary, or essential.

Based on ethnography, he suggests that these strategic transformations involved 'the totemic referents' by which people connected with place and with others, for during ethnographic times people were connected with places and to each other through their totemic affiliations. Andree Rosenfeld and Mike Smith (2002: 103) followed this in greater detail in their analyses of rock art at the important occupational site of Puritjarra and surrounding areas, noting that 'archaeologists need to understand "the organisational relationships among *places*"' (Binford 1982). In Australian archaeology this approach has particular resonance because elaborate, religiously sanctioned relationships between people and place are one of the most distinctive features of Aboriginal Australia'. Following Layton (1992) who had 'suggested that... a shift to large "heraltic" motifs was linked with the development of contemporary clan totemism', they interpreted the major changes in rock-art conventions and major increases in intensities of site occupation during the last millennium (and in the last 800 years especially) as signalling shifts in ways of relating to place—specifically, the emergence of a new regional totemic geography (Rosenfeld and Smith 2002: 121). By examining changes in rock art, and in access to and use of places and resources, Rosenfeld and Smith were thus able to model changes in the way people strategized their existence through totemic affiliations in Australian deserts where connections between people and place were critical to survival.

2.6 Ancestral Connections: Stone Artefacts and Quarries

Rhys Jones and Neville White (1988) undertook ethnoarchaeological research at Ngilipitji, a stone quarry in the Northern Territory. While their research was focused on mapping the site, with a view to historicizing stone manufacturing technology, they also pointed out that Ngilipitji stone tools attained their great significance as trade items because the stone was imbued with magical qualities from the ancestral spirits of the Dreaming. In the process, these authors set up the possibility of archaeologically investigating aspects of the local religious and ritual past. They thus concluded that 'there are planes of understanding about Ngilipitji, its ritual role, and its mythology which transcend... utilitarian precepts... The ethnographic information can place such a system of production and exchange within a broader social, religious and intellectual context' (Jones and White 1988: 84). In a similar vein, Kim Akerman et al. (2002: 15) point out that in the Kimberley region of northern Australia 'stone-point production is linked with social organisation and particular moieties associated with certain classes of projectile points'. Here the ancestral heroes Wodoi and Tjungkun 'bequeathed the art of making such weapons to the ancestors of the Worora, Wunambal and Ngarinjin people of the North Kimberley' (Akerman et al. 2002: 17).

The quarries, stone artefacts, and moieties have Dreaming affiliations, and through these ancestral Dreamings particular individuals and groups have rights to access, work, and trade the stone tools (in this case, Kimberley points) from specific quarries. Therefore, patterns of change and continuity in the use of specific quarries imply not just economic rationality in raw-material provenance and use, but also changing relations between people and the ancestral spiritual affiliations that connect them with places and with the stone. While the religious and ritual dimensions of such connections, and of the underlying cosmological frameworks that prefigure them, remain to be archaeologically explored, like Jones and White at Ngilipitji, Akerman has set the foundation for the archaeological historicizing of ethnographically documented religious and ritual ways associated with stone quarrying and artefacts. John Bradley (2006) has done a similar service for cycad use among the Yanyuwa of north-central Australia, while Amanda Kearney and John Bradley (2006) have applied such logic to the archaeology of Yanyuwa sacred *kundawira* standing stones (conventionally known as 'cylcons' by archaeologists).

2.7 Other Approaches

Ian McNiven (e.g. 2003, 2008) points out that people engage with the sea's liminal qualities through ritual (because connections can be ritually made with the liminal and numinous). He points out that in Indigenous Australia 'ancient seascapes as spiritscapes can be accessed and historicized, in part, through archaeological analysis of places of ritual orchestration located strategically across tidal flats and the adjacent coastal zone' (McNiven 2008: 149, 154–5). Ritual orchestration enables us to better understand the significance of the sea and its place in religious experience and environmental comprehension. He thus explores the history of Indigenous relations with the sea through seaside ritual sites where spiritual forces were engaged.

Other approaches to the archaeology of religion and ritual have taken place from time to time in Australia, but none has seen sustained attention or impacts. For example, Kim Sales (1992) and Chris Chippindale et al. (2000) have argued for shamanistic practices, but ideas of shamanism have not assumed an influential role in Australian archaeology, and indeed most Australian archaeologists do not see shamanism to even have a role to play in the country. David (2002b, 2002c) has criticized the over-application of shamanistic models to world archaeology generally, and to Australia specifically, arguing instead for the exploration of each region's religious and ritual practices and cosmologies in their own terms, rather than through predefined (and often non-applicable) categories from abroad such as 'shamanism' (see also Ross and Davidson 2006: 308; Insoll 2004; see Eller 2007: 5–6 for an apt discussion of 'the problem of religious language').

In Tasmania, Antonio Sagona and his colleagues (Sagona 1994) attempted to research the archaeology of red ochre mining, in particular at the quarry site of Toolumbunner, 'to assess the deep-rooted human interest in red ochre' (Sagona 1994: xiii). The aims of this research were not so much to historicize Tasmanian religious or ritual practices or cosmologies, but rather to ask through ethnoarchaeology 'why humanity has been drawn unswervingly to this mineral for 300 millennia' (Sagona 1994: 10). They assumed that 'The basic symbolism of the colour red is comparable from one living culture to another' (through its association with blood), concluding that 'The persistence of the colour red in ritual behaviour of contemporary societies has given archaeologists a handle on the meaning of ochre in prehistoric contexts' (Sagona 1994: 153). However, and while the association of red (ochre) and blood is not without its own merits, the works of Morphy (1991) and others (e.g. Taçon 1991, 1999) has shown the socioculturally specific and historically emergent significance of colours (including red) in

Australia, and the need for archaeologists to systematically investigate and to historicize symbolic systems rather than to assume historical fixity and geographical commonality, as the symbolic systems are located in broader cosmological understandings which are themselves historically emergent.

Additionally, there have been numerous studies of rock art that have emphasized its religious and/or ritual dimensions (e.g. David and Wilson 2002; Layton 1992; Rosenfeld 2002; Ross and Davidson 2006; Taçon 1987, 1994). One such study, by Ian McNiven and Lynette Russell (2002), looks at how Aboriginal people in different parts of Australia have used depictions in sorcery (e.g. in resisting colonial invasion). While such research has usually mapped rock art across space and as social action, they have not, to this day, attempted to historicize sorcery art through systematic archaeological excavation or 'direct' dating of the art (presumably due to a paucity of temporal data).

3 TORRES STRAIT

Torres Strait consists of the islands between Cape York in northern Australia and the southern parts of PNG. Torres Strait Islanders are culturally and ancestrally different from Aboriginal peoples, and do not recognize themselves as Aboriginal. Nor are they Melanesian, islanders recognizing their own identities by island or island group (i.e. the people of Badu are Badulgal; those of Mua are Mualgal; those of Mabuyag are Goemulgal, after the ancestral village of Goemu on Mabuyag and so forth). In 1898, Alfred Haddon (1901–1935) led the world's first multidisciplinary anthropological expedition to Torres Strait, documenting in six volumes considerable details about Torres Strait Islander cultural practices and understandings and focusing on religious thought and ritual practices. It is this body of literature, along with present-day islander knowledge, that Ian McNiven (e.g. 2003, 2008; McNiven and Feldman 2003; McNiven and Wright 2008), Bruno David (e.g. David and Mura Badulgal Committee 2006; David et al. 2005, 2009), Joe Crouch (e.g. 2008), Liam Brady (e.g. Brady 2006, 2008), and Jeremy Ash (e.g. Ash and David 2008) have taken as the foundation for the archaeology of spiritscapes and religious experiences (including early missionary influences) which they have aimed to investigate.

Archaeological research on religion and ritual in Torres Strait has largely taken Haddon's anthropological records as a starting point upon which ritual sites and paraphernalia, and systems of cosmological organization (e.g. totemic networks) could be systematically characterized and historicized. In western Torres Strait, sacred ritual locations included the *kod* sites where males were initiated and the *aadhi* sacred objects and stories often associated with the *awgadh* (totems) were commemorated. McNiven (McNiven et al. 2008, in press) has undertaken detailed investigations on the small islet of Pulu where one of the most renowned, and most sacred, *kod* sites is found. Here he undertook excavations at a number of localized installations, including a large dugong bone mound and at the *aadhi* location where human heads taken during inter-island raids were hung, in an attempt to find out when the islet attained its ethnographically documented sacred significance. The excavations revealed a repeated temporal trend, with the cultural strata associated with the ethnographic ritual installations dating to the last 300–400 years in all parts of the site where radiocarbon dating was attempted. Prior to 300–400 years ago, he found evidence of an older village, but no evidence of the *kod* site. This timing corresponded well with the abandonment of Tigershark Rockshelter, an earlier nearby occupation site (McNiven et al. 2008). McNiven et al. (2008: 30) thus concluded that *kod* establishment at Pulu 'was probably associated with the transformation of the islet from a place of regular residential occupation to a restricted, formalised and highly controlled sacred landscape, as it remains today'.

One outcome of this research on Pulu concerns the dugong bone mounds themselves. At the time of initial archaeological investigation, such mounds remained somewhat enigmatic, for while dugong hunting was well known to be associated with ritual processes, only one other dugong bone mound site had previously been excavated (at Tudu to the east, in the year before the work at Pulu), and none had yet been analysed. A formal analysis of the excavated Pulu bone mound—a site known as Moegi Sibuy—revealed that such sites contained an overwhelming predominance of dugong ear and smashed rear skull bones. Dugongs possess highly sensitive hearing, and hunting today as in the past requires considerable stealth and know-how. But, as present-day islanders point out, it also requires a subliminal affinity with dugongs themselves and the maritime 'roads' along which they travel. This sensual affinity is what allows hunters to know the way of the dugong and allows the hunter and dugong to be drawn to each other, and thereby success in the hunt (see Manas et al. 2008). Based on his archaeological analysis of the excavated Pulu bones, together with knowledge revealed to him by knowledgeable (and in some cases elderly) islanders, and details of dugong physiology and ethology, Ian McNiven and Ricky Feldman (2003: 186-7) concluded that Moegi Sibuy represented a ritual installation by which dugong hunters practised hunting magic by communicating with dugongs through their ear bones, also known by islanders as 'radar bones' or 'wireless bones'. Subsequent archaeological research at other dugong bone mounds in the region indicated that while some such sites may be represented by only a few dugongs and little else (the smallest such excavated site—KN6—contains the remains of a minimum of seven dugongs; e.g. David and McNiven 2005), others such as the Dabangai Bone Mound contain the bones of some 10,000 dugongs (McNiven and Bedingfield 2008). These are clearly specialized sites, and all contain a significant over-representation of ear bones.

In the wake of McNiven and Feldman's (2003) identification of Pulu's dugong bone mounds as ritual sites associated with dugong hunting magic, David et al. (2009) undertook similar investigations at Koey Ngurtai, an isolated islet some 5 km south of Pulu. Here they found an assemblage of ritual sites reminiscent of the Pulu *kod* site. At Koey Ngurtai dugong bone mounds were also found (Figure 31.2), and after undertaking 50 archaeological excavations at various site types they found that here too the islet had become a specialized ritual centre (focused on dugong hunting magic) sometime between 350 and 550 years ago (with the first ritual site dating to sometime between 550 and 700 years ago, followed by a proliferation of ritual sites thereafter). As late nineteenth-century social anthropological details indicated that the Pulu *kod* was totemically arranged, McNiven et al. (2008) and David et al. (2009) concluded that Pulu and Koey Ngurtai signified not just shifts in ritual locations, but more broadly the commencement of new socio-religious institutions by which people could order their social and territorial land and seascapes.

Other ritual sites appear to have also developed in conjunction with the onset of ritual bone mounds and the *kod* sites at Pulu and Koey Ngurtai. While stone arrangements located in liminal places away from residential sites were clearly present well before dugong bone mounds (see David et al. 2004a), *Syrinx aruanus* (*bu*) shell arrangements (trumpet shell

FIGURE 31.2 Dugong bone mound KN17, Koey Ngurtai, Torres Strait.

arrangements) have an antiquity coinciding with that of the dugong bone mounds. Such sites are also located away from residential sites on various islands such as Badu in western Torres Strait (e.g. David et al. 2005), and are ethnographically known to have been consulted or strategically positioned across the landscape (e.g. in gardens) to ritually generate intended outcomes or to fulfil ritual obligations with the spirits (e.g. Haddon 1935: 357–8).

One site type with religious implications located within domestic space that has been investigated is a series of enigmatic mounds at the village site of Goemu on the island of Mabuyag (Ghaleb 1990; McNiven and Wright 2008). During ethnographic times, Goemu was recorded by Haddon (1904) to have been 'the settlement focus of the southeast district of the kaigas (shovel-nosed shark), waru (turtle) and umai (dog) totemic clans' and a centre for turtle-hunting rituals; it once contained 'a skull-house (kuiku-iut), a ceremonial kod (special men's area) and the wiwai turtle-hunting shrine' (McNiven and Wright 2008: 134). The presence of 95 discrete mounded middens at Goemu testified to the ritualized deposition of domestic products associated with family and clan feasting. Here 'midden mounding was a performative strategy that facilitated the management, containment and remembrance of the myriad symbolic values associated with the wide array of activities and social contexts represented by the items comprising these midden deposits', and referencing the ancestors signalled 'the formal and enduring ritualized architecture' of the village (McNiven and Wright 2008: 145). McNiven and Wright (2008: 144) concluded that 'Goemu village was a complex space where the boundary between domestic and ritual domains was negotiated, blurred and expressed materially through structured, formalised and patterned behaviours'. Radiocarbon dating suggests that ritual accumulation and marking at Goemu began around 500 years ago, contemporaneously (at an archaeological timescale) with the onset of ritual dugong bone mounds and distant *kod* sites at Pulu and Koey Ngurtai. The period after 300–500 years ago appears to have witnessed a reworking of ritual practices and the onset of the ethnographically recognized cosmological structures and their associated socio-spatial arrangements. The bigger question that has not yet been answered is what kind of religious and ritual practices took place beforehand, and how and why did they lead to the novel behaviours evident in the dugong bone mound, *bu* shell, and ethnographically recognizable *kod* sites.

4 PAPUA NEW GUINEA

Few archaeological studies in PNG have aimed to investigate religious or ritual practices, for most research was undertaken during the 1970s when questions of origins and notions of environmental adaptation were predominant within the discipline. However, Chris Ballard's (e.g. 1994) research is notable for bridging the gap between social anthropological concerns with meaningfully constituted social and sacred landscapes, and archaeological concerns hitherto focused on material objects (e.g. stone artefacts), economic adaptations, exchange relations, and environmental impacts (for impressive ethnoarchaeological concerns with social landscapes, in particular as represented in stone quarrying and objects of power in West Papua, see Pétrequin and Pétrequin 1993, 2006). Ballard's work has not so much targeted historicization as the mapping of Huli sacred geographies in the Southern Highlands, indicating that 'Distinguishing between the landscapes of belief within which historic agents acted and the social landscapes identified by external observers is an important step towards framing questions for archaeological research that can exploit the insights of both perspectives' (Ballard 1994: 130). Thus, for the Huli an important aspect of cosmological balance involves ongoing exchanges between the living and the ancestors through ritual performances that include the giving of pigs and pig fat to the spirits, 'in an attempt to maintain the stability of the universe and restore the fertility to the land' (Ballard 1994: 133). Exchange, notes Ballard (1994: 135), 'is characterised by enduring obligations', and these obligations apply to others and more so to ancestral and non-ancestral spirits who oversee the well-being of the land. A broad variety of objects routinely excavated by archaeologists are involved, including cuttings of pig meat, stone axes (both local and imported), ochre, and imported marine shells (some of which are important currency for payments of ritual performances). Huli sacred geography—the way Huli cosmology is encoded in the landscape—has implications for patterns of settlement, landscape modifications (e.g. deeply ditched pig droveways), land use, and the spatiality of exchange and ritual performance, each of which has archaeological potential.

More recently, David et al. (2008) worked among the Rumu where they investigated the history of clan-based approaches to the afterworld. The Rumu live in the mid-reaches of the Kikori River, parts of the southern lowlands of the Gulf Province. Here the thick rainforest is cut open by a network of rivers and streams by which both people and spirits travel from place to place. During ethnographic times, each Rumu clan possessed its own ossuary by which the spirits of recently deceased individuals travelled to their appropriate clan afterworld. However, archaeological excavations in caves and rockshelters on Himaiyu and Parua'uki clan lands revealed a shift from ossuaries containing individuals to those containing the remains of large numbers of people in centralized places. Radiocarbon dating and stratigraphic associations with various objects led these authors to suggest that late in the nineteenth century CE, with the onset of European colonialism, Rumu clans-people began to take the bones of their dead to communal ossuaries in response to increasingly centralized settlement locations often at some distance from traditional clan lands (the shifts in settlement locations were part of a novel process of government control and, to a lesser extent, missionization. These changes also caused a relaxation of the necessity for villages to be located away from major river systems as a means of protection from invading head-hunters—such as the Kerewo—from the south). The shifting location of ossuaries used by Rumu relatives to send the spirits of the dead to the clan afterworlds—among the Himaiyu, the clan ossuary of Rupo (Figure 31.3) from which the spirits of the dead travelled to their mysterious Hoimo—implies new and increasingly centralized cosmological configurations that themselves consolidated territorial relations at a time when clan members lived at some distance from their traditional clan lands. One implication of these results is that at times of social change and uncertainty people consolidate territory (David et al. 2008). The mortuary practices evident on Rumu lands suggest that one way of doing this is by establishing an ongoing history by reference to ancestral and sacred emplacements; that is, to create centres of activity legitimated by ancestral and/or sacred connections that confirm and strengthen claims to place.

Elsewhere, along the north coast of PNG, in the Aitape region of the Sepik coast, John Terrell and Esther Schechter (2007) have recently attempted to shed light on 3,300-year-old Lapita cosmologies by reference to complex symbolism shared between Lapita ceramics and ethnographic wooden platters by reference to the latter's ethnographic meanings. Here they found that the 'face' designs on Lapita ceramics are reminiscent of turtle designs found on ethnographic platters. The latter designs are known to relate to lores that explain the origins of the world and human procreation. Terrell and Schechter argue that in the Aitape region and nearby Ali Island, they 'have found a ceramic tradition on this coast that would appear to be historically derived from the ancient Lapita tradition' (Terrell and Schechter 2007: 82), and whose descendant (ethnographic) cosmological readings as documented in relation to wooden platters can be used to inform those more ancestral forms, at least as far as its key referents are concerned (in particular, the recognition of originary turtle ancestral stories).

5 CONCLUSIONS

Recent archaeological research in Australia and PNG has aimed to address not so much 'religion' or religious practices, but rather ontology, cosmology, pre-understanding, sacred geographies, and spiritscapes as well as ritual. The reason for this has often been explicit: while the notion of 'religion' expresses 'belief' about external spiritualities by which the earthly domestic world can then be lived, these other concepts begin with the notion that

FIGURE 31.3 The Himaiyu clan (Rumu) ossuary of Rupo, Papua New Guinea.

spirits and the sacred themselves imbue everyday earthly life and the way we understand the world to operate in human *and* numinous action. Avoiding a separation of religion from the domestic allows social land and seascapes to be explored as already engaged in a meaningfulness that from the onset sees the world as spiritual and engaging the numinous, rather than as material ecologies that are given meaning by 'supernatural' forces that are somehow outside the 'real' world. Thus, for example, Anne-Marie and Pierre Pétrequin (2006: 527) note for the island of New Guinea that 'we must insist that in New Guinea, most things we call "objects"—the greater part of which are manipulated by men in their quest for personal power or for its public confirmation—are more or less evident signs (in respect to secret knowledge) of the primordial forces of the ancient owners of the earth' (translation mine).

The manufacture of ground-edge axes, shell artefacts and the like is here founded on ancestral knowledge released to particular kin lineages by the 'mythical', originary ancestors upon their death at the hands of the first humans at the beginning of time. When stone is extracted from their sources, or when stone tools are made, for example, the events of the origin stories are reproduced in earthly life by the ritual specialists or by other knowledgeable lineage members, giving earthly truth to the mythical realm in the process. While this example relates specifically to the Wano and other groups of the highlands of New Guinea, it demonstrates well the inseparability of everyday action from cosmological understandings of where we come from and everyday cultural practice. An archaeological focus on ontology (how the world is understood to *be*); cosmology (how the world is understood to be, with a focus on its numinous qualities); pre-understanding (how the world is understood to be, explicitly reflecting on the hermeneutic process); sacred geographies (focusing on the sacred dimensions of life); and spiritscapes (focusing on numinous forces) are in many ways similar but differentially nuanced. What they all allow for is an exploration of meaning, a meaningfulness located not in evolutionary processes determined by notions of adaptation, economic growth or survival, but in the frames of reference by which individual groups have come to understand and experience their worlds. In Australia and PNG, such research has invariably attempted to historicize ethnography, in recent times through the dual historical method. And future potentials far outweigh what has already been achieved, with exciting prospects awaiting future archaeologists to historicize the kinds of meaningfulness already identified by social anthropologists and ethnoarchaeologists such as John Bradley, Kim Akerman, Anne-Marie and Pierre Pétrequin, Chris Ballard, and others and only touched upon in this chapter.

Acknowledgements

With many thanks to Alexandra Gartrell, Tim Insoll, Rachel MacLean, Ian McNiven, and June Ross for useful comments on an earlier draft of this paper.

Suggested Reading

Aboriginal Australia

The archaeology of religion and ritual in Australia has invariably begun with ethnographic understandings of Aboriginal worldviews and spiritual connections. Key readings on this theme are Bradley (2006), Doring (2000), Merlan (1989), Morphy (1984, 1991), Munn (1986), Peterson (1972) and Stanner (1965, 1989). In recent years, archaeologists have worked with Aboriginal elders to explore the archaeological potential of historicising Aboriginal religion, especially through ritual. Key readings include David (2002a), David et al. (1994), David and Wilson (1999), Gibbs and Veth (2002), McNiven (2005, 2008), McNiven and Russell (2002), Ross and Davidson (2006) and Taçon (1999). More than any other, Ian McNiven (e.g. 2003, 2005, 2008) has significantly contributed to an archaeology of seascapes as spiritscapes. A number of authors have explored the implications of historicizing Aboriginal religion for the decolonization of Aboriginality in contemporary society, in particular David (2002a), and McNiven and Russell (2005).

Torres Strait

Since the late 1990s, archaeological research in Torres Strait has focused on spiritscapes, e.g. David et al. (2009), David and Mura Badulgal Committee (2006), McNiven and Feldman (2003), McNiven and Wright (2008).

Papua New Guinea

Although research into the archaeology of religion and ritual is relatively new in PNG, approaches have been varied and focused on objects of power (Pétrequin and Pétrequin 1993, 2006), sacred ancestral and totemic connections (David et al. 2008), sacred geographies (Ballard 1994) and meaning and myth of enigmatic objects (Terrell and Schechter 2007).

References

AKERMAN, K., FULLAGAR, R., and VAN GIJN, A. 2002. 'Weapons and wunan: Production, function and exchange of Kimberley points', *Australian Aboriginal Studies*, 1: 13–42.

ARNDT, W. 1962. 'The interpretation of the Delamere lightning painting and rock engravings', *Oceania*, 32: 163–77.

ASH, J. and DAVID, B. 2008. 'Mua 22: Archaeology at the old village site of Totalai', *Memoirs of the Queensland Museum, Cultural Heritage Series*, 4: 451–72.

BALLARD, C. 1994. 'The centre cannot hold: Trade networks and sacred geography in the Papua New Guinea highlands', *Archaeology in Oceania*, 29: 130–48.

BARKER, B. 1995. 'The sea people: Maritime hunter-gatherers on the tropical coast—a late Holocene maritime specialisation in the Whitsunday Islands, central Queensland', unpublished PhD thesis, Department of Anthropology and Sociology, The University of Queensland, St. Lucia.

BENDER, B. 1993. 'Introduction: landscape—meaning and action', in B. Bender (ed.), *Landscape: Politics and perspectives* (Oxford: Berg), pp. 1–17.

BINFORD, L. R. 1980. 'Willow smoke and dogs' tails: Hunter-gatherer settlement systems and archaeological site formation', *American Antiquity*, 45: 4–20.

——1982. 'The archaeology of place', *Journal of Anthropological Archaeology*, 1: 5–31.

BOWDLER, S. 1981. 'Hunters in the highlands: Aboriginal adaptations in the eastern Australian uplands', *Archaeology in Oceania*, 16: 99–111.

BOWLER, J. M., JONES, R., ALLEN, H., and THORNE, A. G. 1970. 'Pleistocene human remains from Australia: A living site and human cremation from Lake Mungo, western New South Wales', *World Archaeology*, 2: 39–60.

——, JOHNSTON, H., OLLEY, J. M., et al. 2003. 'New ages for human occupation and climatic change at Lake Mungo, Australia', *Nature*, 421: 837–40.

BRADLEY, J. J. 2006. 'The social, economic and historical construction of cycad palms among the Yanyuwa' in B. David, B. Barker, and I. J. McNiven (eds), *The Social Archaeology of Australian Indigenous Societies* (Canberra: Aboriginal Studies Press), pp. 161–81.

BRADY, L. M. 2006. 'Documenting and analysing rock paintings from Torres Strait, NE Australia, with digital photography and computer image enhancement', *Journal of Field Archaeology*, 31: 363–79.

—— 2008. 'Symbolic language in Torres Strait, NE Australia: Images from rock art, portable objects and human scars', *Antiquity*, 82: 336–50.

CHAPMAN, J. 2008. 'Object fragmentation and past landscapes' in B. David and J. Thomas (eds), *Handbook of Landscape Archaeology* (Walnut Creek: Left Coast Press), pp. 187–201.

CHIPPINDALE, C., SMITH, C. B., and TAÇON, P. S. C. 2000. 'Visions of dynamic power: archaic rock-paintings, altered states of consciousness and "clever men" in western Arnhem Land (N.T.), Australia', *Cambridge Archaeological Journal*, 10(1): 63–101.

COUTTS, P. J. F., HENDERSON, P., and FULLAGAR, R. L. K. 1979. *A Preliminary Investigation of Aboriginal Mounds in North-West Victoria: Records of the Victorian Archaeological Survey* 9 (Melbourne: Ministry for Conservation).

CROUCH, J. 2008. 'Reading between the lands: Toward an amphibious archaeological settlement model for maritime migrations' in B. David and J. Thomas (eds), *Handbook of Landscape Archaeology* (Walnut Creek: Left Coast Press), pp. 131–40.

DAVID, B. 2002a. *Landscapes, Rock-art and the Dreaming: An archaeology of preunderstanding* (London: Leicester University Press).

—— 2002b. 'Review of J. L. Pearson's *Shamanism and the Ancient Mind: a cognitive approach to archaeology*', *Oceania*, 73: 81–2.

—— 2002c. 'Comment on Winkelman's "Shamanism and cognitive evolution"', *Cambridge Archaeological Journal*, 12: 88–9.

——, BARKER, B., and MCNIVEN, I. J. (eds) 2006. *The Social Archaeology of Australian Indigenous Societies* (Canberra: Aboriginal Studies Press).

——, CROUCH, J., and ZOPPI, U. 2005. 'Historicizing the spiritual: *bu* shell arrangements on the island of Badu, Torres Strait', *Cambridge Archaeological Journal*, 15: 71–91.

——, MCNIVEN, I., FLOOD, J., and FROST, R. 1990. 'Yiwarlarlay 1: Archaeological excavations at the Lightning Brothers site, Delamere station, Northern Territory', *Archaeology in Oceania*, 25: 79–84.

——, MC NIVEN, I., ATTENBROW, V., et al. 1994. 'Of lightning brothers and white cockatoos: Dating the antiquity of signifying systems in the Northern Territory, Australia', *Antiquity*, 68: 241–51.

——, MCNIVEN, I. J., MURA BADULGAL (TORRES STRAIT ISLANDERS) CORPORATION COMMITTEE, et al. 2004a. 'The Argan stone arrangement complex, Badu Island: Initial results from Torres Strait', *Australian Archaeology*, 58: 1–6.

——, MCNIVEN, I., BOWIE, W., et al. 2004b. 'Archaeology of Torres Strait turtle-shell masks: The Badu cache', *Australian Aboriginal Studies*, 1: 18–25.

——, PIVORU, M., PIVORU, W., et al. 2008. 'Living landscapes of the dead: Archaeology of the afterworld among the Rumu of Papua New Guinea' in B. David and J. Thomas (eds.), *Handbook of Landscape Archaeology* (Walnut Creek: Left Coast Press), pp. 158–66.

——, MCNIVEN, I. J., CROUCH, J., et al. 2009. 'Koey Ngurtai: The emergence of a ritual domain in Western Torres Strait', *Archaeology in Oceania*.

—— and MCNIVEN, I. J. 2004. 'Western Torres Strait Cultural History Project: research design and initial results' in I. J. McNiven and M. Quinnell (eds), *Torres Strait: Archaeology and material culture. Memoirs of the Queensland Museum, Cultural Heritage Series* 3: 199–208.

—— —— 2005. 'Archaeological survey and salvage programme of Koey Ngurtai, Torres Strait (Stage 2): final report', unpublished report to the Mura Badulgal (Torres Strait Islanders Corporation), Badu, Cultural Heritage Report Series 9, Programme for Australian

Indigenous Archaeology, School of Geography and Environmental Science, Monash University, Clayton.
DAVID, B. and MURA BADULGAL COMMITTEE 2006. 'What happened in Torres Strait 400 years ago? Ritual transformation in an island seascape', *Journal of Island and Coastal Archaeology*, 1: 123–43.
—— and WILSON, M. 1999. 'Re-reading the landscape: Place and identity in NE Australia during the late Holocene', *Cambridge Archaeological Journal*, 9: 163–88.
—— —— 2002. 'Spaces of resistance: Graffiti and Indigenous place markings in the early European contact period of northern Australia' in B. David and M. Wilson (eds), *Inscribed Landscapes: Marking and making place* (Honolulu: University of Hawai'i Press), pp. 42–60.
DORING, J. 2000. *Gwion Gwion: Secret and sacred pathways of the Ngarinyin Aboriginal people of Australia* (Köln: Könemann).
DURKHEIM, E. 1965. *The Elementary Forms of the Religious Life* (New York: The Free Press).
ELLER, J. D. 2007. *Introducing Anthropology of Religion* (London: Routledge).
FABIAN, J. 1983. *Time and the Other: How anthropology makes its object* (New York: Columbia University Press).
FLOOD, J. 1980. *The Moth Hunters: Aboriginal prehistory of the Australian Alps* (Canberra: Australian Institute of Aboriginal Studies).
—— 1989. *Archaeology of the Dreamtime: the story of prehistoric Australia and its people* (Sydney: Collins Publishers).
—— 1997. *Rock Art of the Dreamtime: Images of ancient Australia* (Sydney: Angus and Robertson).
—— and DAVID, B. 1994. 'Traditional systems of encoding meaning in Wardaman rock art, Northern Territory, Australia', *The Artefact*, 17: 6–22.
FRANKEL, D. 1982. 'Earth rings at Sunbury, Victoria', *Archaeology in Oceania*, 17: 89–97.
GHALEB, B. 1990. 'An ethnoarchaeological study of Mabuiag Island, Torres Strait, northern Australia', unpublished PhD thesis, Institute of Archaeology, University College London.
GIBBS, M. and VETH, P. 2002. 'Ritual engines and the archaeology of territorial ascendancy', Anthropology Museum, The University of Queensland, St Lucia, *Tempus*, 7: 11–19.
GODWIN, L. and WEINER, J. 2006. 'Footprints of the ancestors: The convergence of anthropological and archaeological perspectives in contemporary Aboriginal heritage studies' in B. David, B. Barker, and I. J. McNiven (eds), *The Social Archaeology of Australian Indigenous Societies* (Canberra: Aboriginal Studies Press), pp. 124–38.
HADDON, A. C. 1901–1935. *Reports of the Cambridge Anthropological Expedition to Torres Straits* (Cambridge: Cambridge University Press).
HODDER, I. 1982. *Symbols in Action: Ethnoarchaeological studies of material culture* (Cambridge: Cambridge University Press).
INSOLL, T. 2004. *Archaeology, Ritual, Religion* (London: Routledge).
JONES, R. and WHITE, N. 1988. 'Point blank: Stone tool manufacture at the Ngilipitji quarry, Arnhem Land, 1981' in B. Meehan and R. Jones (eds), *Archaeology with Ethnography: An Australian perspective* (Canberra: Research School of Pacific Studies, Australian National University), pp. 51–87.
KEARNEY, A. and BRADLEY, J. 2006. 'Landscapes with shadows of once living people: The *Kundawira* challenge' in B. David, B. Barker, and I. J. McNiven (eds), *The Social Archaeology of Australian Indigenous Societies* (Canberra: Aboriginal Studies Press), pp. 182–203.
KEEN, I. 2004. *Aboriginal Economy and Society: Australia at the threshold of colonisation* (Melbourne: Oxford University Press).

Langton, M. and David, B. 2003. 'William Ricketts Sanctuary, Victoria (Australia): Sculpting nature and culture in a primitivist theme park', *Journal of Material Culture*, 8: 145–68.

——2004. 'Art as social momentum: Coming into being in Yolŋu art', *Archaeological Review from Cambridge*, 19(1): 47–60.

Layton, R. 1986. *Uluru: An Aboriginal history of Ayers Rock* (Canberra: Australian Institute of Aboriginal Studies).

——1992. *Australian Rock-Art: A new synthesis* (Cambridge: Cambridge University Press).

L'Oste-Brown, S., Godwin, L., and Morwood, M. 2002. 'Aboriginal bark burial: 700 years of mortuary tradition in the Central Queensland Highlands', *Australian Aboriginal Studies*, 1: 43–50.

Lourandos, H. 1980. 'Change or stability? Hydraulics, hunter-gatherers and population in temperate Australia', *World Archaeology*, 11: 245–66.

——1984. 'Changing perspectives in Australian prehistory: A reply to Beaton', *Archaeology in Oceania*, 19: 29–33.

——1991. 'Palaeopolitics: resource intensification in Aboriginal Australia' in T. Ingold, D. Riches, and J. Woodburn (eds), *Hunters and Gatherers: History, evolution and social change* (New York: Berg), pp. 148–60.

McBryde, I. 1974. *An Archaeological Survey of the New England Region, New South Wales* (Sydney: University of Sydney Press).

McConvell, P. 1996. 'Backtracking to Babel: The chronology of Pama-Nyungan expansion in Australia', *Archaeology in Oceania*, 31: 125–44.

McNiven, I. J. 2003. 'Saltwater People: Spiritscapes, maritime rituals and the archaeology of Australian Indigenous seascapes', *World Archaeology*, 35: 329–49.

——2005. 'Ritual engines of the sea', *Ballarat Mechanics' Institute Journal*, 4(2): 23–31.

——2008. 'Sentient sea: seascapes as spiritscapes' in B. David and J. Thomas (eds), *Handbook of Landscape Archaeology* (Walnut Creek: Left Coast Press), pp. 149–57.

——and Bedingfield, A. C. 2008. 'Past and present marine mammal hunting rates and abundances: Dugong (*Dugong dugon*) evidence from Dabangai Bone Mound, Torres Strait', *Journal of Archaeological Science*, 35: 505–15.

——, Crouch, J., Weisler, M., et al. 2008. 'Tigershark Rockshelter (Baidamau Mudh): Seascape and settlement reconfigurations on the sacred islet of Pulu, western Zenadh Kes (Torres Strait)', *Australian Archaeology*, 66: 15–32.

——, David, B., and Barker, B. 2006. 'The social archaeology of Indigenous Australia' in B. David, B. Barker, and I. J. McNiven (eds), *The Social Archaeology of Australian Indigenous Societies* (Canberra: Aboriginal Studies Press), pp. 2–19.

——, ——, Goemulgau Kod, and Fitzpatrick, J. 2009, 'The Great Kod of Pulu: mutual historical emergence of ceremonial sites and social groups in Torres Strait, northeast Australia', *Cambridge Archaeological Journal* 19(3): 291–317.

——and Feldman, R. 2003. 'Ritually orchestrated seascapes: Hunting magic and dugong bone mounds in Torres Strait, NE Australia', *Cambridge Archaeological Journal*, 13: 169–94.

——and Russell, L. 2002. 'Ritual response: Place marking and the colonial frontier in Australia' in B. David and M. Wilson (eds), *Inscribed Landscapes: Marking and making place* (Honolulu: University of Hawai'i Press), pp. 27–41.

—— ——2005. *Appropriated Pasts: Indigenous peoples and the colonial culture of archaeology* (Walnut Creek, CA: AltaMira).

—— and Wright, D. 2008. 'Ritualised marine midden formation in western Zenadh Kes (Torres Strait)' in G. Clark, F. Leach, and S. O'Connor (eds), *Islands of Inquiry:*

Colonisation, seafaring and the archaeology of maritime landscapes, Terra Australis 29 (Canberra: Pandanus Press), pp. 133–47.
MANAS, J., DAVID, B., MANAS, L., et al. 2008. 'An interview with Fr John Manas', *Memoirs of the Queensland Museum, Cultural Heritage Series*.
MERLAN, F. 1989. 'The interpretive framework of Wardaman rock art: A preliminary report', *Australian Aboriginal Studies*, 2: 14–24.
MORPHY, H. 1984. *Journey to the Crocodile's Nest* (Canberra: Australian Institute of Aboriginal Studies).
—— 1991. *Ancestral Connections: Art and an Aboriginal system of knowledge* (Chicago: University of Chicago Press).
—— 1996. 'Empiricism to metaphysics: In defence of the concept of the Dreamtime' in T. Bonyhady and T. Griffiths (eds), *Prehistory to Politics: John Mulvaney, the humanities and the public intellectual* (Melbourne: Melbourne University Press), pp. 163–89.
MULVANEY, D. J. 1975. '"The chain of connection": The material evidence' in N. Peterson (ed.), *Tribes and Boundaries in Australia* (Canberra: Australian Institute of Aboriginal Studies), pp. 72–94.
MUNN, N. 1986. *Walbiri Iconography: Graphic representation and cultural symbolism in a central Australian Society* (Chicago: Chicago University Press).
O'CONNOR, S., ZELL, L., and BARHAM, A. 2007. 'Stone constructions on Rankin Island, Kimberley, Western Australia', *Australian Archaeology*, 64: 15–22.
PETERSON, N. 1972. 'Totemism yesterday: Sentiment and local organization among the Australian Aborigines', *Man*, 7: 12–32.
PÉTREQUIN, A.-M. and PÉTREQUIN, P. 2006. *Objets de Pouvoir en Nouvelle-Guinée: Approche Ethnoarchéologique d'un Système de Signe Sociaux—Catalogue de la donation Anne-Marie et Pierre Pétrequin* (Paris: Musée d'Archéologie Nationale de Saint-Germain-en-Laye).
PÉTREQUIN, P. and PÉTREQUIN, A.-M. 1993. *Écologie d'un Outil: la Hache de Pierre en Irian Jaya (Indonésie). Monographies du CRA* 12. Paris: CNRS.
RICHARDS, F. 1926. 'Customs and language of the western Hodgkinson Aboriginals', *Memoirs of the Queensland Museum* 8: 249–65.
ROSENFELD, A. 2002. 'Rock-art as an indicator of changing social geographies in central Australia' in B. David and M. Wilson (eds), *Inscribed Landscapes: Marking and making place* (Honolulu: University of Hawai'i Press), pp. 61–78.
—— and SMITH, M. A. 2002. 'Rock-art and the history of Puritjarra rock shelter, Cleland Hills, central Australia', *Proceedings of the Prehistoric Society*, 68: 103–24.
ROSS, J. and DAVIDSON, I. 2006. 'Rock art and ritual: An archaeological analysis of rock art in arid central Australia', *Journal of Archaeological Method and Theory*, 13: 305–41.
SAGONA, A. (ed.) 1994. *Bruising the Red Earth: Ochre mining and ritual in Aboriginal Tasmania* (Carlton: Melbourne University Press).
SALES, K. 1992. 'Ascent to the sky: A shamanistic initiatory engraving from the Burrup Peninsula, northwest Western Australia', *Archaeology in Oceania*, 27: 22–36.
SATTERTHWAITE, L. and HEATHER, A. 1987. 'Determinants of earth circle site location in the Moreton region, southeast Queensland', *Queensland Archaeological Research*, 4: 5–53.
SHANKS, M. and TILLEY, C. 1987. *Social Theory and Archaeology* (Cambridge: Polity Press).
SMITH, M. A. 1986. 'The antiquity of seedgrinding in arid Australia', *Archaeology in Oceania*, 21: 29–39.
—— 1988. 'The pattern and timing of prehistoric settlement in central Australia', unpublished PhD thesis, University of New England, Armidale.

——1996. 'Prehistory and human ecology in central Australia: an archaeological perspective' in S. R. Morton and D. J. Mulvaney (eds), *Exploring Central Australia: Society, the environment and the 1894 Horn Expedition* (Chipping Norton: Surrey, Beatty and Sons), pp. 61–73.

——2005. 'Desert archaeology, linguistic stratigraphy, and the spread of the Western Desert language' in P. Veth, M. A. Smith, and P. Hiscock (eds), *Desert Peoples: Archaeological perspectives* (Oxford: Blackwell), pp. 222–42.

——, FANKHAUSER, B., and JERCHER, M. 1998. 'The changing provenance of red ochre at Puritjarra rockshelter, central Australia: Late Pleistocene to present', *Proceedings of the Prehistoric Society*, 64: 275–92.

SPENCER, B. and GILLEN, F. 1927. *The Arunta: A study of a Stone Age people* (London: Macmillan).

STANNER, W. E. H. 1965. 'Religion, totemism, symbolism' in R. M. Berndt and C. H. Berndt (eds), *Aboriginal Man in Australia* (Sydney: Angus and Robertson), pp. 207–37.

——1989. *On Aboriginal Religion*, Oceania Monograph 36 (Sydney: University of Sydney).

STREHLOW, T. G. H. 1947. *Aranda Traditions* (Carlton: Melbourne University Press).

TAÇON, P. S. C. 1987. 'Internal-external: A re-evaluation of the 'x-ray' concept in western Arnhem Land rock art', *Rock Art Research*, 4: 36–50.

——1991. 'The power of stone: Symbolic aspects of stone use and tool development in western Arnhem Land, Australia', *Antiquity*, 65: 192–207.

——1994. 'Socialising landscapes: The long term implications of signs, symbols and marks on the land', *Archaeology in Oceania*, 29: 117–29.

——1999. 'All things bright and beautiful: The role and meaning of colour in human development', *Cambridge Archaeological Journal*, 9: 120–26.

——, WILSON, M., and CHIPPINDALE, C. 1996. 'Birth of the Rainbow Serpent in Arnhem Land rock art and oral history', *Archaeology in Oceania*, 31: 103–24.

TERRELL, J. E. and SCHECHTER, E. M. 2007. 'Deciphering the Lapita code: The Aitape ceramic sequence and late survival of the "Lapita face"', *Cambridge Archaeological Journal*, 17: 59–85.

THOMAS, J. 1993. 'The politics of vision and the archaeologies of landscape' in B. Bender (ed.), *Landscape: Politics and perspectives* (Oxford: Berg), pp. 19–48.

THOMAS, N. 1981. 'Social theory, ecology and epistemology: Theoretical issues in Australian prehistory', *Mankind*, 13: 165–77.

WOLFE, P. 1991. 'On being woken up: The Dreamtime in anthropology and in Australian settler culture', *Comparative Studies in Society and History*, 33: 197–224.

CHAPTER 32

PACIFIC AND NEW ZEALAND

PAUL RAINBIRD

1 INTRODUCTION

THE Pacific Ocean covers approximately a third of the total of the Earth's surface. Within this region of Oceania are tens of thousands of islands, ranging in size from New Guinea at 790,000 km^2, one of the world's largest, and the North and South islands of New Zealand (114,050 and 150,737 km^2 respectively), to myriad tiny islands and islets. Each of the islands and archipelagos of the Pacific have their mix of individual and shared histories, but historically they have been divided into the three groups of Melanesia, Micronesia, and Polynesia. Although in the nineteenth century, when these labels were established, they were based on a variety of distinctive characteristics relating to race, culture, and geography, in this chapter they should be regarded, unless otherwise indicated, as purely geographic terms. Melanesia incorporates the eastern half of New Guinea, politically divided with the western half part of Indonesia.

Despite some mid-twentieth-century claims to the contrary, it has been established that the islands have been settled in a west to east trajectory out of South-east Asia beginning at least 40,000 years ago, although beyond New Guinea, the Bismarck Archipelago, and the Solomon Islands, there is no evidence of settlement prior to 4,000 years ago, with the major islands in eastern and southern Polynesia settled in the last 1,500 to 800 years.

Archaeological research in the Pacific Islands is a twentieth-century phenomenon with only patchy coverage in Melanesia and Micronesia, and much more sustained research in Polynesia, this latter mostly through the auspices of the Bishop Museum in Honolulu. In Melanesia archaeology has been a very poor cousin in comparison to anthropological research. Richard Walter and Peter Sheppard (2006) note that apart from the Highlands of New Guinea very little archaeology has been studied in the inland areas of the larger islands, and where archaeology has taken place a fascination with the Lapita phenomenon (see below) means that a search for pottery and earliest sites has distracted archaeologists from examining, reporting, and surveying the rich surface archaeology; this is in contrast to such work in Polynesia since the 1920s. Research in Micronesia, in the late twentieth century and continuing, has tended to be led by governmental infrastructural, military, or tourism-related developments meaning that coverage can be described as patchy.

Given the history of archaeological research in Melanesia and Micronesia the archaeological study of ritual and religion has, for the most part, been incidental. In Polynesia the research has not been so ad hoc; indeed the surface archaeology of stone-built temple sites has provided both impetus and rich material for the archaeological surveys in these islands. Along with the standing remains there were also the vivid historical records from the late-eighteenth-century voyages of Captain James Cook and others that meant, along with local knowledge, that interpretation of such sites was easily achieved. These temples fitted neatly into the rise to social complexity expected in social evolutionary perspectives which saw the historically recorded Polynesian chiefdoms as exemplary markers of the chiefdom stage, while in the West the social sciences of the 1950s and 1960s established that the islanders of Melanesia were seen as exemplars of tribal societies at lower stages of social evolution without hereditary rank and unable to organize labour for temples and such like (see Christophe Sand 2002 for a valuable archaeological critique of this orthodoxy). Micronesia, with an apparent diversity of societies, resisted easy definition and was largely left out of these discussions in preference for the contrast between Melanesia and Polynesia.

As will be shown, the archaeology of ritual and religion is still in its infancy in Oceania, but much work has been done in the last twenty years to allow archaeologists to provide more subtle and anthropologically nuanced narratives on this topic. The chapter has been organized with the aim of making sense of the diversity of the material in both chronology, beginning with the area where Pleistocene settlement is attested, and geographically in relation to the tripartite division of Melanesia, Micronesia, and Polynesia.

2 NEAR OCEANIA

Evidence for the human colonization of New Guinea dates back to 40,000 years ago on the coast, with a rapid movement to the large islands of the Bismarck Archipelago. By 30,000 years ago there is environmental evidence to indicate that people had moved in to the valleys of Highland New Guinea and major trips by water to settle Manus and the northern end of the Solomon Islands occurred around 20,000 years ago. Site locations are both cave/rock shelters and open sites, but the archaeology of ritual and religion features little in discussion of this Pleistocene period in Pacific history; the literature is dominated by discussions of settlement, economy, and technology. Social issues are raised in relation to the evidence for long distance contacts at this period through finds of obsidian from New Britain sources moving to New Ireland and the translocation of animals from mainland New Guinea. These animals, particularly the Cuscus (*Phalanger orientalis*), a type of possum, are more normally discussed in economic terms as enhancing the subsistence potential of the tropical forests, rather than any human–animal social relations. Peter White (2004: 159), however, has recognized that these exotic animals may have also provided body parts for 'decoration, dress, as tools, and in ceremonies'—a welcome, but yet to be developed, instance of considering ritual in this period.

In the Holocene, from between 3,500 and 3,300 years ago, a new horizon marked by highly decorated pottery and other novel artefacts appears in the islands surrounding the Bismarck Sea. The suite of material culture found alongside Lapita pottery has led to the definition of a 'Lapita cultural complex' (e.g., Green 2003). However, any notion of the ritual or religion relating to this complex has not been at the forefront of discussion by Lapita archaeologists. In his book-length synthesis of the Lapita phenomenon Patrick Kirch (1997) opined that Lapita communities were 'house societies' (following Claude Lévi-Strauss) where components of the houses were 'ritual attractors' and these houses provided fundamental organizing significance for these people. Possibly related to this, the human face forms which have been found on decorated Lapita pottery may relate to 'ancestor rituals' taking place in the location of the ritual attractor of the house.

Despite the minimal development of an archaeology of ritual and religion, Walter and Sheppard (2006) have argued that the Lapita phenomenon, representing approximately 1,500 years of Melanesian history, has held a fascination for archaeologists of the region, which has held back the study of other periods and in particular the post-Lapita period that accounts for the last 1,500 to 1,000 years of Melanesian prehistory prior to European contact.

There have been a few notable studies of the post-Lapita period which have been aimed at elucidating the archaeology of ritual and religion. Projects of note have been conducted in the islands of the northern Massim region of Papua New Guinea. Work on Woodlark Island has led to a detailed study of stone arrangements there. These are extremely varied in character, but generally take the form of complex arrangements of 'room' type spaces surrounded by lines of spaced stones which can be up to 3 m in height. Simon Bickler (2006) found that the megalithic monuments were being constructed from at least 1,200 years up to 600/400 years ago. After this they were still being used to deposit burials in pots and caves were being used for the same purpose. The function of the stone arrangements was, at least in part, to mark inhumations; some evidence of a cosmological schema was identified through the identification of the monuments and burials being orientated in relation to the cardinal points. Some of the stone for the monuments was transported over several kilometres and morphological indications showed that the monuments were developed through accretion with additions to a primary burial and stone arrangement. Similar monuments have been noted on the islands to the west with stone from Woodlark Island moved over the sea for a distance of up to 200 km. Other studies of these megalithic monuments there have found a dearth of ethnographic or oral historical information to aid interpretation (Burenhult 2002; Winter 2003). This is in contrast to a study of stone monuments from a similar period in the Solomon Islands.

Commencing in 1996 the New Georgia Archaeological Survey has explored the Roviana Lagoon area of the western Solomon Islands. The survey has concentrated on the late period archaeological landscape dating to the last 700 years. The surface archaeology of this period is dominated by stone- and coral-built monumental structures many of which have been identified as shrines. Walter and Sheppard (2006) trace the development of the political, economic, religious, and ceremonial complex known historically as the Roviana chiefdom. When first encountered by Europeans this was regarded as a powerful chiefdom controlling an exchange and raiding network over a wide area, which became famed especially for their headhunting activities (Walter, Thomas, and Sheppard 2004). The shrines are variable in type, built of basalt or coral, often with stone table-like features, cobbled areas, and occasionally with associated stone ovens where offerings could be prepared. The shrines often held the skulls of ancestors and their broken possessions such as adzes and shell valuables. Late-nineteenth- and early-twentieth-century photos illustrate that wooden carvings had also been a feature of these shrines.

Oral, historical, and ethnographic evidence indicates that people drew the efficacy from the shines of ancestors who were particularly renowned for skills in particular activities, e.g. fishing or warfare. These shrines were active and often taboo to particular sectors of society. By the nineteenth century the barrier island of Nusa Roviana on the outer edge of the lagoon became the centre for ancestor and headhunting cults. On the highest parts of a central ridge of this island was located a fort divided into several enclosures by large walls within which are named shrines associated with particular ancestors, spiritual beings, and memorializing important historical events. People also lived in this fort, archaeologically attested by dozens of terraces and associated midden deposits, and this represents a compression of space, with people communing with the ancestors 'and perhaps even a blurring between the worlds of the ancestors and the living' (Thomas, Sheppard, and Walter 2001: 563).

3 LANDS OF THE LAPITA LANDFALLS

None of the island groups discussed in this section was settled by humans prior to the arrival of pottery using people between 3,300 and 2,900 years ago. Vanuatu and New Caledonia are large archipelagos within island Melanesia; Samoa and Tonga are in western Polynesia; Fiji straddles the divide between Melanesia and Polynesia.

Vanuatu is home to a remarkable cemetery dating to the earliest years of settlement, and which has finally provided some unambiguous evidence of Lapita period ritual practices. The site of Teouma on Efate has so far revealed 25 inhumations associated with large quantities of decorated Lapita pottery (Bedford, Spriggs, and Regenvanu 2006). Of particular note is that none of the burials has skulls in articulation; they all appear to have been removed after interment, some skulls have been replaced by shell rings or coral slabs. Only four adult skulls have been found at the cemetery and are all associated with rituals post-dating initial burial. Three were found together on the chest of a headless inhumation. The fourth skull was interred inside a ceramic vessel with a further vessel upturned and used as a lid. All of the evidence points to the curation of skulls, typical of many ethnographically recorded Oceanic societies, and that mortuary ritual was a multi-phased process.

Also from Vanuatu is the burial of a chief named Roy Mata. The reign of Roy Mata dates to around 400 years ago and in life he ruled the north of Efate; in death his body was taken to the small, uninhabited and arid island of Retoka. José Garanger (1982) excavated the burial site which was marked on the surface by two standing stones and a collection of conch shell trumpets (Figure 32.1). The excavation revealed an astonishing series of events.

Directly in front of the standing stones in a deep grave is the burial of Roy Mata, accompanied by a man and young woman, a further man and woman together as a couple, and a bundle burial. Around this grave was a compacted surface with broken shell ornaments, charred pig bones, and other features and objects interpreted as representing a dance ground where the ceremonies of interment took place. On top of this surface were placed eleven embracing couples with ten other individuals and several bundle burials interspersed. The men were lying on their backs in the apparent repose of sleeping, but the

FIGURE 32.1 Standing stones and conch shell trumpets marking the burial site of Chief Roy Mata on the taboo island of Retoka (Hat Island), Vanuatu.

women, holding their partners, were all in different positions. The logical interpretation has been that the inhumations represent people buried alive as self-sacrifices. The men may have been drugged with very strong *kava*, a stupefying liquid ethnographically forbidden to women. All except two of the inhumations were oriented towards the south-west, where according to local tradition is located the land of the dead. Similar chiefly burials are reported to have occurred in New Caledonia, although the rich archaeology of these islands, as with Fiji, has yet to establish the detail of ritual and religion there.

Tonga and Samoa have a wide range of monumental architecture, including star mounds of stone and earth, stone platforms, and burial mounds. Despite the rich collection of monumental architecture dating to the latest prehistoric phases an overview of west Polynesian material found that 'while ethnohistorical and traditional sources explicitly link the most recent use of monumental structures to leaders and chiefs . . . there have been few attempts to distinguish archaeologically the function of large mounds, and whether they were public buildings, burial sites, high status residences or had some other function' (Clark and Martinsson-Wallin 2007: 34). How, then, these sites are related to the archaeology of ritual and religion, as indeed some of these sites undoubtedly are, is still very much open to investigation.

Detailed investigation has taken place at the huge stone mound of Pulemelei in Samoa. It is estimated that this mound, rectangular in plan, has a volume of 17,000 m^3, and on the highest side the top terrace stands 12 m above the ground. The mound was constructed in several phases between 900 and 400 years ago and the investigators interpret the evidence as showing that ceremonial use of the site intensified in the most recent phase from 600 to 400 years ago (Martinsson-Wallin, Wallin, and Clark 2007). The evidence for this intensification is derived from a combination of the use of a large earth oven, the heightening of the mound to make activities on it invisible from the floor, the construction of two opposite entrance stairways centrally placed and marking the long east–west axis of the mound, along with many other stone ramps, pavements, and paths below the mound and marking out a spatially organized complex.

4 CENTRAL AND EASTERN POLYNESIA

The stone-built platforms, such as Pulemelei, in western Polynesia are of a type which can be related to ritual and religion in the archipelagos of central and eastern Polynesia. The linguistic correlates of these sites have been traced back to a shared ancestry in western Polynesia. Patrick Kirch and Roger Green (2001) found that amongst the shared words in Polynesia, and likely to have a deep ancestry, are *mana* and *tapu* (taboo) which are fundamental to Polynesian conceptualizations of the sacred. Put simply *mana* relates to the power of supernatural force, while *tapu* means prohibited, sacred, or under ritual restriction. Despite some variation in the names used for Polynesian ritual sites, Kirch and Green (2001: 254) identify components which are present across the region: (1) an open space for enacting ceremonies, variously elaborated into a formal courtyard; (2) attached to the courtyard some sort of god or spirit house (in eastern Polynesia this may be replaced by a raised platform or altar, commonly termed an *ahu*); and (3) posts, upright stones, or statues serving as symbolic representations/manifestations of ancestors or deities, situated around the perimeter or at one end of the courtyard, or in the god house (the statues are most famously elaborated as the *moai* on Rapa Nui).

Temples in central and eastern Polynesia are common features of the archaeological landscape. At Maeva village on Huahine, what was probably a settlement for the elite of society, has been estimated to have one *marae* (temple) for every 16 people (Wallin 2000).

Despite their ubiquity and the general understanding that together on an island they represent a sacred and symbolic landscape, little has been found regarding the location of each temple, which can be found on the edge of the sea or deep inland. An exception to this is the work by Matthew Campbell (2006) on Raratonga in the Cook Islands. Here, using a combination of archaeological, ethnographic, and archive evidence, Campbell was able to illustrate how the earliest *marae* of the island related to a unique prehistoric road which circled the island. This 'great' road, the *Ara Metua*, paved with coral and basalt and edged with stone, follows the route taken by the first founding ancestor. Ritual processions along this road memorialized the founding ancestor and passed up to 47 *marae* where further rituals could be enacted.

The Polynesian temples were built to serve an assortment of purposes and varied from small family shrines to vast complexes such as some of the *luakini heiau* in the Hawaiian islands (Figure 32.2). Thegn Ladefoged (1998) found that the spatial organization of these temples could be compared to that known for household clusters and individual houses, which indicated a common set of underlying principles predicated on ritual offerings and the performative aspects of the Hawaiian *kapu* system; a series of prescriptive rules of avoidance and etiquette in relation to sacred objects. People and objects were embedded in ritual and the household clusters and houses were also locations of shrines.

FIGURE 32.2 The restored *Hale O Lono Heiau* at Waimea Falls Park, Oahu, Hawai'i. The wooden replicas of oracle towers, mana house, and drum house have been reconstructed using historical evidence and the original post-holes.

Elsewhere in Hawai'i Kirch (2004) has analysed the orientations of the temple sites (*heiau*) in Kahikinui district of Maui finding that in the majority of cases they are in fact built with regard to cardinal directions and astronomical phenomena. In the study group all but one was orientated to one of three clusters with the directions of north, east-north-east, and east. Kirch found that three of the four major gods in the traditional Hawaiian pantheon had attributes that could be linked to these directions. Thus, temples with north orientations face the great soaring height of Mount Haleakala and were dedicated to Ku the deity linked to high mountains. The ENE cluster are orientated towards the rising of the star cluster of Pleiades, and it is known ethnohistorically that priests of the god Lono used the acronychal (sunset) rising of the Pleiades to announce the onset of the *Makahiki* season; a period of tribute collections and harvest celebrations. The final cluster, orientated in an easterly direction, could be related to the god Kane who is strongly associated with the sun and from these temples priests could have observed the progression of the sun throughout the year. Kirch (2004: 112) concludes that 'archaeologists may wish to pay more attention to the possibilities that ritual sites throughout the Polynesian archipelagos may frequently have been referentially orientated'.

5 MICRONESIA

In the second millennium AD, the people of the Marianas, today known as the Chamorro, began to construct groups of paired quarried limestone, sandstone, or basalt pillars, each supporting its own hemispherical capstone. These pillars, ranging in number between three and seven pairs, are known as *latte* stones and are unique to the Marianas. There is no evidence of *latte* stones prior to 900–1,000 years ago and they appear to have been in use when the Spanish arrived in 1521 AD. Historical reports confirm the interpretation that the majority of *latte* sets supported a wooden and roofed superstructure, which was the dwelling place for all or some of society (Russell 1998).

There is an extremely strong association between coastal *latte* sets and human burials with a regular pattern emerging of inhumations being placed between the paired stones and on the seaward side of the *latte* set. There are many examples of exhumation of parts of the skeleton; usually the skull and long bones. Historic documentation notes the keeping of skulls of ancestors for purposes of communication with dead relatives. Long bones, particularly of the lower limbs, were prized for fashioning into spearheads. Typical spearheads were manufactured in the form of harpoons with barbs, and likely played a role in fishing, although use in interpersonal violence has been recorded archaeologically.

On the northern islands of the Palau archipelago are located substantial terraced hillsides constructed on a monumental scale. In many cases, steep terraces cover complete hillsides and are often topped by a high-sided 'crown' at the peak (Figure 32.3). Pottery recovered from the construction fill of the terraces does not appear to relate to actual settlement on the terraces. Steve Wickler (2002) has proposed that construction dates to the period

FIGURE 32.3 Sculpted hillside of monumental terraces topped by a 'crown' feature, Imelik State, Palau.

between 2,000 and 800 years ago, with archaeological evidence pointing to multiple uses in agriculture, burial, boundary marking, defence, ceremony, social display, and as house platforms; replacing earlier simpler functional models of agriculture and/or defence. The complex use and symbolic potential of such undertakings surely reflect deeper early Palauan perspectives about landscape and experience and Sarah Phear (2007), in a detailed study through archaeological excavation, palaeoenvironmental analyses, and all other available sources, concluded that there was no evidence that they were built as fortifications or for agricultural purposes. Phear argues, compellingly, that the major modification of the landscape was in order to bring groups of people together in repetitive practices and in doing so acted to establish social cohesion and inclusiveness. These were ritual acts, and the earth of the terraces was not only filled with pottery, but also basalt cobbles and coral from the coast, which themselves may have come from special places and would have incorporated the ancestors into the newly constructed monuments. In excavation of the crown of Ngemeduu, evidence was found that some form of structure requiring post supports had been built, but this was not a house, as no domestic debris was recovered, and indeed it appears to have been short lived. Phear (2007: 135) proposes that it was built and removed 'as an act of "finishing" or "sealing" the ritual activities and elements of their meaning in the monument'. Phear's interpretation of the sculpted landscape of Palau would lead one to conclude that this must be the greatest materialization of sacred geography anywhere in the Pacific.

6 New Zealand

The two large islands which account for the majority of New Zealand (Aotearoa) are truly continental in scale and were first encountered by the ancestors of the Maori between 1,000 and 800 years ago. The archaeological evidence points to an east Polynesian source for the first settlers and one should expect evidence of ritual and religion similar to that for elsewhere in Polynesia. Certainly the word *marae* survives to describe Maori temple sites, but the stone platforms and terraces found elsewhere in Polynesia are not evident in New Zealand.

The earliest period of evidence for occupation of New Zealand is labelled the 'Archaic' and there is little evidence for ritual practice and religious beliefs in the material remains. The Maori *marae*, as open space for ceremonies and gatherings with an associated meeting house consisting of elaborate wooden carvings, both internal and external, are known only from the period of post-European contact. Ancestors feature strongly here and the physical structure of the meeting house symbolizes the body of an ancestral chief, with a carved face marking the head on the apex of the gable, the ridgepole marking the spine, and the rafters as ribs (Allen 1996).

The period between the Archaic and the European arrival, the 'Classic Maori' period, is dominated architecturally by the enclosures known as *pa*. These enclosures are most usually found on hilltops, but they are also found on top of coastal cliffs or surrounded by swamp. *Pa* have conventionally been interpreted as fortifications enclosing settlements, or on occasion for protecting storage pits containing sweet potatoes. The hilltop *pa* are dominant features of the landscape of North Island where the slopes have been sculpted into terraces, building platforms and areas for storage pits. Timber palisades completed the enclosures. As reviewed by Andrew Crosby (2004), in the absence of recognizable Polynesian-type *marae*, archaeologists have considered the possibility that rather than the key function of *pa* being for defence, they were the locations of *marae* spaces and temples, where the considerable effort in constructing these sites was a ritualized process and, as elsewhere in Polynesia at this time, ritual practices were being enacted in these places. This has best been considered so far for the *pa* in Pouerua (Sutton, Furey, and Marshall 2003). These were highly visible monuments with their presence creating a ritual landscape (Barber 1996) and, as Caroline Phillips and Matthew Campbell (2004: 103) opine, 'it was an inscription of *mana* on the landscape'. This interpretation of *pa* has the benefit of providing an explanation as to why monumental *marae* typical of Polynesia are not found in New Zealand as would have been predicted given the assumed origins of the Maori. However, many archaeologists in New Zealand remain to be convinced.

Richard Walter (2004) does not think that the *pa* should be equated with *marae*. He cites the archaeological evidence which does not, in his opinion, support such an interpretation and also argues for the uniqueness of the New Zealand situation in comparison to the rest of Polynesia. The archaeological remains can be argued either way, although the excavators at Pouerua admit there is nothing in the specific finds which would indicate a ritual interpretation, it is the spatial and earth-altering facets that indicate a ritual use. The uniqueness identified by Walter (2004: 144) is that the archaeology of New Zealand, and this is supported by oral tradition and historical accounts, is dominated by war and 'we have very little idea of how religion or ideology related to warfare, or how it was implicated in structuring socio-political systems. This is a significant divergence from the normal patterns of East Polynesian socio-political organisation, and it is a topic that deserves in-depth attention in relation to the archaeological record'.

7 Conclusion

The archaeology of ritual and religion is still in its infancy in the Pacific. There is, though, considerable potential especially considering the richness of the archaeology and ethnohistory for later prehistory. The New Georgia Archaeological Survey serves as a model to illustrate the importance of examining the more recent period in Melanesia's past. The use of an 'ethnographic archaeology' has integrated the rich archaeological remains with past and living history to provide insights not possible by maintaining disciplinary boundaries. For example, in Polynesia we know from ethnohistoric sources a certain amount about ritual practices at the temple sites (see Wallin 1998). With permission from traditional custodians it should be possible to examine practice and performance at these places, considering issues such as how might the use of chants, drums and conch-shell trumpets extend the range of the influence of these locales (e.g., Rainbird 2002; 2008). At a material level, what can the use of the selection of different stone tell us about the meanings inherent in temple construction and what can the use of coastal material at inland sites and vice versa tell us about the cosmological principles being addressed (e.g., Campbell 2006; also Rainbird 1996)? Post-processual approaches have yet to be widely applied to the archaeology of Oceania with potential for significant new studies to emerge.

The potential of rock art in identifying and understanding ritual landscapes is still in its infancy, and recording for many of the islands in the region is still in progress. Archaeological accounts of the region tend to ignore the rock art, which may be due to difficulties in dating the images (Wilson 2003). For Polynesia, Georgia Lee (1992: 200) noted that 'all serious enterprises were accompanied by religious activities to protect the populace from evil influences and to appeal to the gods through offerings and prayers. Carving on rocks, which themselves contained *mana*, was associated with such rites.' There is still much to do in this regard.

Finally, we should not deny that for much of the region establishing the basic chronology is still of vital importance. For example, there may still be a challenge to the orthodox understanding that Polynesian ritual architecture spread from west to east, with Rapa Nui (Easter Island) *ahu* currently pre-dating such monuments in the west (Anderson, Martinsson-Wallin, and Stothert 2007)—we may still need to consider the ancient influence of the Americas on Polynesian ritual and religion.

Suggested Reading

Kirch, P. V. 2000. *On the Road of the Winds: An archaeological history of the Pacific Islands before European contact* (Berkeley: University of California Press).

LILLEY, I. (ed.) 2006. *Archaeology of Oceania: Australia and the Pacific Islands* (Oxford: Blackwell).
RAINBIRD, P. 2004. *The Archaeology of Micronesia* (Cambridge: Cambridge University Press).
SPRIGGS, M. 1997. *The Island Melanesians* (Oxford: Blackwell).

REFERENCES

ALLEN, H. 1996. 'Horde and *hapū*: The reification of kinship and residence in prehistoric Aboriginal and Māori settlement organisation' in J. Davidson, G. Irwin, F. Leach, et al. (eds), *Oceanic Culture History: Essays in honour of Roger Green* (New Zealand Journal of Archaeology Special Publication), pp. 657–74.
ANDERSON, A., MARTINSSON-WALLIN, H., and STOTHERT, K. 2007. 'Ecuadorian sailing rafts and Oceanic landfalls' in A. Anderson, K. Green, and F. Leach (eds), *Vastly Ingenious: The archaeology of Pacific material culture in honour of Janet M. Davidson* (Dunedin: Otago University Press), pp. 117–33.
BARBER, I. 1996. 'Loss, change, and monumental landscaping: Towards a new interpretation of the Classic Maori emergence', *Current Anthropology*, 37: 868–80.
BEDFORD, S., SPRIGGS, M., and REGENVANU, R. 2006. 'The Teouma Lapita site and the early settlement of the Pacific Islands', *Antiquity*, 80: 812–28.
BICKLER, S. H. 2006. 'Prehistoric stone monuments in the northern region of the Kula Ring', *Antiquity*, 80: 38–51.
BURENHULT, G. (ed.) 2002. *The Archaeology of the Trobriand Islands, Milne Bay Province, Papua New Guinea. Excavation Season 1999*, BAR International Series 1080 (Oxford: BAR).
CAMPBELL, M. 2006. 'Memory and monumentality in the Rarotongan landscape', *Antiquity*, 80: 102–17.
CLARK, G. and MARTINSSON-WALLIN, H. 2007. 'Monumental architecture in West Polynesia: origins, chiefs and archaeological approaches' in H. Martinsson-Wallin (ed.), *Archaeology in Samoa: The Pulemelei investigations. Archaeology in Oceania*, 42 Supplement: 28–40.
CROSBY, A. 2004. 'Ritual' in L. Furey and S. Holdaway (eds), *Change Through Time: 50 years of New Zealand archaeology* (Auckland: New Zealand Archaeological Association Monograph 26), pp. 105–24.
GARANGER, J. 1982. *Archaeology of the New Hebrides*, trans. R. Groube (Sydney: Oceania Monograph 24).
GREEN, R. C. 2003. 'The Lapita horizon and traditions: Signature for one set of oceanic migrations' in C. Sand (ed.), *Pacific Archaeology: Assessment and prospects* (Nouméa: Service des Musées et du Patrimoine de Nouvelle-Calédonie), pp. 95–120.
KIRCH, P. V. 1997. *The Lapita Peoples: Ancestors of the oceanic world* (Oxford: Blackwell).
—— 2004. 'Temple sites in Kahikinui, Maui, Hawaiian Islands: Their orientations decoded', *Antiquity*, 78: 102–14.
—— and GREEN, R. C. 2001. *Hawaiki, Ancestral Polynesia: An essay in historical anthropology* (Cambridge: Cambridge University Press).
LADEFOGED, T. N. 1998. 'Spatial similarities and change in Hawaiian architecture: The expression of ritual offering and *kapu* in *luakini heiau*, residential complexes, and houses', *Asian Perspectives*, 37: 59–73.

LEE, G. 1992. *The Rock Art of Easter Island: Symbols of power, prayers to the gods*, Monumenta Archaeologica 17 (Los Angeles: The Institute of Archaeology, University of California).

MARTINSSON-WALLIN, H., WALLIN, P., and CLARK, G. 2007. 'The excavation of the Pulemelei site 2002-2004' in H. Martinsson-Wallin (ed.), *Archaeology in Samoa: The Pulemelei investigations. Archaeology in Oceania*, 42 Supplement: 41-59.

PHEAR, S. 2007. *The Monumental Earthworks of Palau, Micronesia*, BAR International Series 1626 (Oxford: BAR).

PHILLIPS, C. and CAMPBELL, M. 2004. 'From settlement patterns to interdisciplinary landscapes in New Zealand' in L. Furey and S. Holdaway (eds), *Change Through Time: 50 years of New Zealand archaeology* (Auckland: New Zealand Archaeological Association Monograph 26), pp. 85-104.

RAINBIRD, P. 1996. 'A place to look up to: A review of Chuukese hilltop enclosures', *Journal of the Polynesian Society*, 105: 461-78.

—— 2002. 'Making sense of petroglyphs: The sound of rock-art' in B. David and M. Wilson (eds), *Inscribed Landscapes: Marking and making place* (Honolulu: University of Hawaii Press), pp. 93-103.

—— 2008. 'The body and the senses' in B. David and J. Thomas (eds), *The Handbook of Landscape Archaeology* (Walnut Creek, CA: Left Coast Press), pp. 263-70.

RUSSELL, S. 1998. *Tiempon I Manmofo'na: Ancient Chamorro culture and history in the Northern Mariana Islands* (Saipan: Micronesian Archaeological Survey 32).

SAND, C. 2002. 'Melanesian tribes vs. Polynesian chiefdoms: Recent archaeological assessment of a classic model of sociopolitical types in Oceania', *Asian Perspectives*, 41: 284-96.

SUTTON, D., FUREY, L., and MARSHALL, Y. 2003. *The Archaeology of Pouerua* (Auckland: Auckland University Press).

THOMAS, T., SHEPPARD, P., and WALTER, R. 2001. 'Landscape, violence and social bodies: Ritualized architecture in a Solomon Islands society', *Journal of the Royal Anthropological Institute*, (n.s.) 7: 545-72.

WALLIN, P. 1998. *The Symbolism of Polynesian Temple Rituals*, The Kon-Tiki Museum Occasional Papers 4 (Oslo: The Kon-Tiki Museum).

—— 2000. 'Three special sites in East Polynesia' in P. Wallin and H. Martinsson-Wallin (eds), *Essays in Honour of Arne Skølsvold 75 Years*, The Kon-Tiki Museum Occasional Papers 5 (Oslo: The Kon-Tiki Museum), pp. 101-14.

WALTER, R. 2004. 'New Zealand archaeology and its Polynesian connections' in L. Furey and S. Holdaway (eds), *Change through Time: 50 years of New Zealand archaeology* (Auckland: New Zealand Archaeological Association Monograph 26), pp. 125-46.

—— and SHEPPARD, P. 2006. 'Archaeology in Melanesia: A case study from the Western Province of the Solomon Islands' in I. Lilley (ed.), *Archaeology of Oceania: Australia and the Pacific Islands* (Oxford: Blackwell), pp. 137-59.

——, THOMAS, T., and SHEPPARD, P. 2004. 'Cult assemblages and ritual practices in Roviana Lagoon, Solomon Islands', *World Archaeology*, 36: 142-57.

WHITE, J. P. 2004. 'Where the wild things are: Prehistoric animal translocation in the circum New Guinea archipelago' in S. Fitzpatrick (ed.), *Voyages of Discovery: The archaeology of islands* (Westport, CT: Praeger), pp. 147-64.

WICKLER, S. 2002. 'Terraces and villages: Transformations of the cultural landscape in Palau' in T. Ladefoged and M. Graves (eds), *Pacific Landscapes: Archaeological approaches in Oceania* (Los Osos, CA: Easter Island Foundation), pp. 63–96.

WILSON, M. 2003. 'Rock-art transformations in the western Pacific' in C. Sand (ed.), *Pacific Archaeology: Assessment and prospects* (Nouméa: Service des Musées et du Patrimoine de Nouvelle-Calédonie), pp. 265–84.

WINTER, O. 2003. 'Was there a Kula Ring before the Kula Ring?' in A. Karlström and A. Källén (eds), *Fishbones and Glittering Emblems: Southeast Asian archaeology 2002* (Stockholm: Museum of Far Eastern Antiquities), pp. 119–34.

CHAPTER 33

WALKING UPSIDE-DOWN AND BACKWARDS: ART AND RELIGION IN THE ANCIENT CARIBBEAN

PETER G. ROE

1 INTRODUCTION

THE Caribbean produced some of the most compelling art in the New World, particularly in the Greater Antilles (Bercht et al. 1997). It also witnessed the world's first ethnography since Tacitus, Friar Ramón Pané's (1498 [1999]) *An Account of the Antiquities of the Indians*, commissioned by Columbus. Based on his village experiences in eastern Hispaniola among the Taíno, it contains a wealth of first-hand information on the iconography and symbolism of a now vanished people's prehistoric art.

As Pané himself admitted, his account is not without its difficulties. He conflated three Amazonian–Guianan mythic cycles explaining the origin of women: the Wooden Bride, the Fruit Woman, and the Mermaid (Roe 1982). Other round, aquatic life forms also become 'mythic substitutes' for the Fish Woman in South America and the Caribbean, specifically Turtles and Frogs. 'She' did not even have to be female; a syphilitic male was impregnated via androcentric conception by the seminal, hallucinogen-laden mucus of his uncle's phallic nose (Arrom 1997). Depicted in ceramic effigies, *Deminán caracaracol* developed a swollen back 'hard as wood' (Figure 33.2a, c–d), which was opened like a tree by men with stone axes. Out emerged the Turtle Progenitrix (Figure 33.2f–h). The Frog Woman appears in a menhir petroglyphic frieze at the classic Taíno ball park at Caguana, Puerto Rico, a phallic-beaked, giant blue heron breaking her *vagina dentata*, thereby rendering her marriageable (Roe 2005). While Amazonian–Guianan mythology thus makes Pané's confused data intelligible (Alegría 1978; López-Baralt 1985), his text also highlights Antillean contributions, like the role of the syphilitic twin.

Living descendants cannot resolve these confusions because the Taíno largely disappeared 50 years after the conquest in the 'perfect storm' of introduced European diseases, warfare, ethnic relocation, slavery, and unfettered cruelty (Anderson-Córdova 2005). Yet modern ethnogenesis continues apace since some ex-patriate Puerto Ricans living in New York and elsewhere in the United States have started to auto-identify as 'Taíno' Indians (Haslip-Viera 1983), as has an island group (see <http://www.taino.org>), the 'Tribal Nation of Borikén', just as 'Neo-Taíno' art is an important emblematic badge of ethnicity in the Dominican Republic (Vega de Boyrie 1987) and Puerto Rico (whose native designation was *Borinquen*). (For reasons as to why the Spanish, North American, or African heritages of these islands are more problematic vis-à-vis the Taíno for ethnic self-definition see Roe and Hayward [2008].)

Chroniclers like Columbus (1493–4a, b, 1493, c.1496), Las Casas (1527a–c, c.1550), Martyr (c.1516, 1587) Oviedo y Valdéz (1535), and Pané; Caribbean archaeological artifacts; and ethnographic data from surviving South Amerindians, among whom the Taíno's ancestors, the Saladoids (Siegel 1989b), first set paddle to water in their journey into the Antilles in the sixth century BC, all help to reconstruct insular Arawak religion via its art.

2 First Settlers

The first people to arrive in the post-Pleistocene Caribbean, c.6000–4000 BC, long antedated these Taíno ancestors and came from a different region. They migrated from Belize in Mesoamerica, island-hopping in the then lower sea level from Yucatán to Cuba and Hispaniola (by-passing Jamaica). These Casimiroid foragers produced long flintknapped blades for projectile points, as well as ground stone and shell artefacts (Wilson 2007). The men hunted large Antillean ground sloths and other extinct fauna on land and sea. Their women gathered fruits and vegetables, and collected mussels. Little remains of their art and religion save curious tooth-, peg-, L- and ball-shaped ground-stone ceremonial objects (Figure 33.1b). An intricately carved wooden staff hints at social differentiation (a staff of authority? Figure 33.1c). A number of skulls arranged in a circle around the rest of the bones suggest attitudes toward the afterlife (Rouse 1992). Evolving through descendant cultures, these populations, the Guanahatabeys, endured in westernmost Cuba until European contact (arguments to the contrary notwithstanding, cf. Keegan 1989).

Cuban and Hispaniolan Casimiroid rock art (Dacal Moure and Manuel Rivero de la Calle 1996) presents a *horror vacui* of geometric cave pictographs: concentric circles, dots and straight lines in black and red. Entoptic images produced from altered states of consciousness, their geometric and repetitive, nested nature evokes both the egalitarian cast of Casimiroid society and a shamanic religion (Roe 2009).

The Casimiroids' fine ground and polished ceremonial artefacts attest to village specialists. Since these foragers had their pick of the best ecological settings, they cannot be compared with modern surviving foragers. Their societies were more complex than previously imagined, as in the Casimiroid descendants' possible independent invention of pottery and experimentation with plant domestication in Hispaniola and Puerto Rico (Keegan and Rodríguez Ramos 2007). This Archaic pottery is too fragmentary and rudimentary, however, to provide much data on decoration beyond simple incisions emulating basketry weaves.

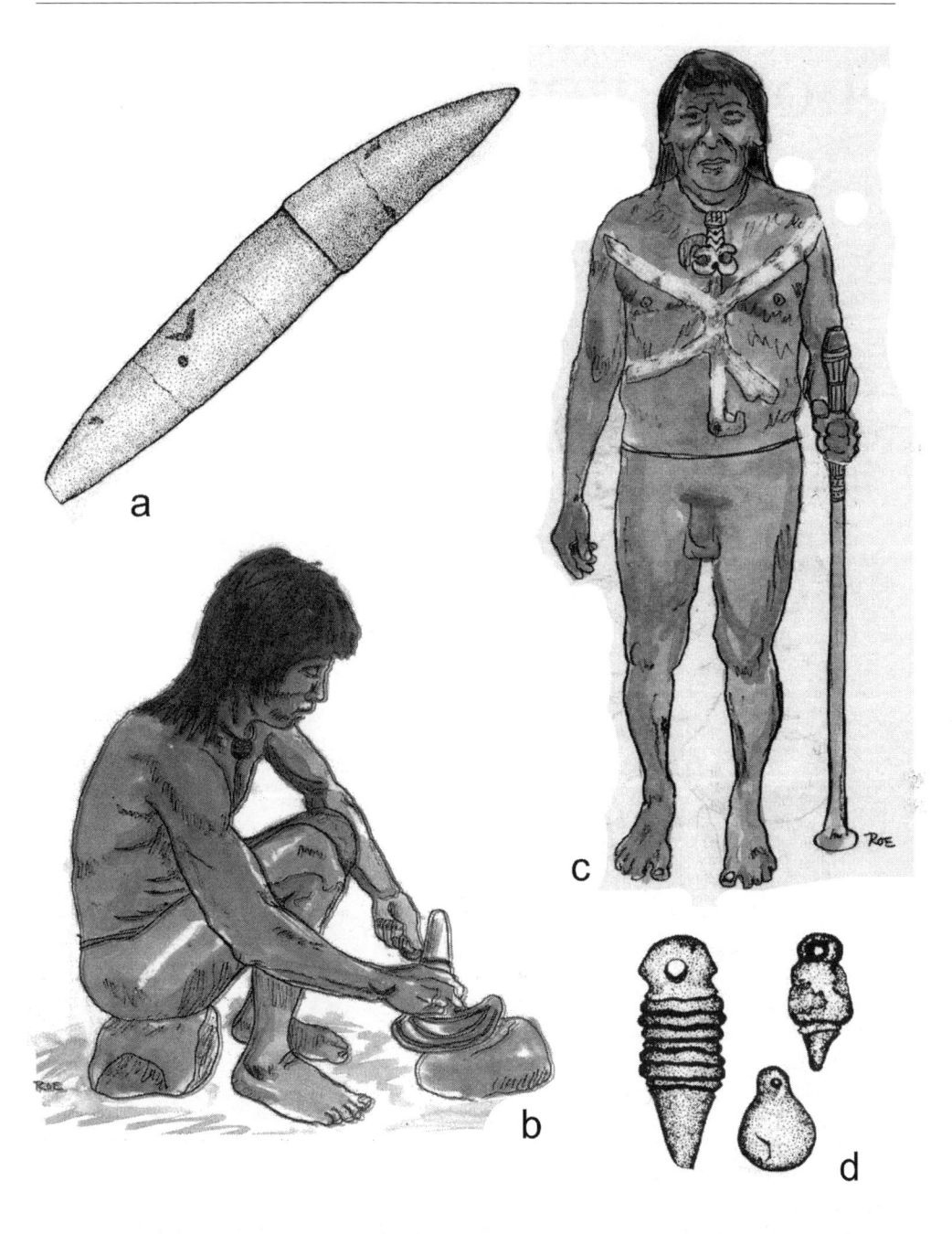

FIGURE 33.1 The art of the earliest Antilleans: Casimiroid and Ortoiroid. (a) A ceremonial knife (dagger?) 24 cm long, 4 cm wide, recovered from Ortoiroid contexts on the north coast of Puerto Rico, the Garrochales site, Arecibo; (b) A reconstruction of a Casimiroid man in Hispaniola working a unique L-shaped Couri culture ritual stone artefact (Rouse 1992: fig. 17f) by grinding and polishing; (c) A composite reconstruction of a Casimiroid man with body paint and a carved shell pendant. He carries a carved wooden staff of authority (?), probably from the Cayo Redondo culture; (d) Recovered ground and polished Ortoiroid amulets from the north coast of Puerto Rico: left and upper right from Los Caracoles Cave 2, 280 BC, lower right from the contemporary Angeles site.

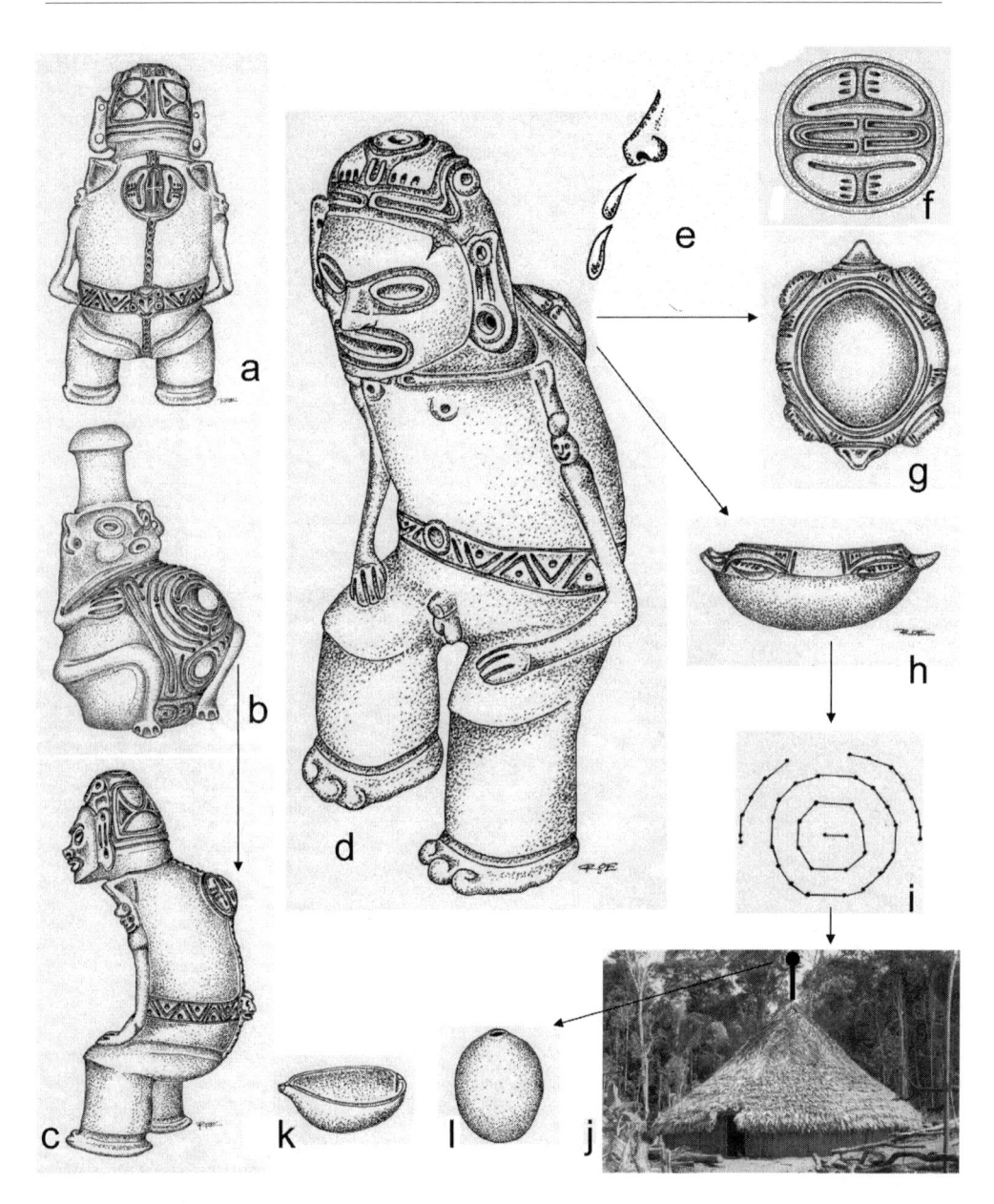

FIGURE 33.2 Androcentric gestation and portable wombs in Antillean art and religion. (a) A rear view of a standing ceramic anthropomorphic effigy figurine of *Deminán Caracaracol*, a Culture Hero Twin, from the Dominican Republic (Collection: National Museum of the American Indian, Smithsonian Institution, Catalog number 05/3753, height 40.6 cm) highlighting his dorsal eminence and its incised and excised design layout; (b) A Chican Ostionoid effigy bottle (Montás et al. 1985: 114) of a pregnant female from the Dominican Republic (Collection: Pierre Domino, 15.2 cm tall, 9.8 cm wide). Note the similarity of her protuberant belly with *Deminán*'s swollen dorsal womb; (c) A profile view of *Deminán* showing his dorsal eminence; (d) A three-quarter view of the hollow Taíno Ceramic figurine of *Deminán* with his 'hunchback' impregnation (Arrom 1997: fig. 50); (e) The phallic nose of

Other archaic populations reached the Caribbean from South America via the Lesser Antilles. These Ortoiroid people arrived in Trinidad at 6,000 BC and in Puerto Rico c.4,000 BC (Ayes Suárez 1990: 13), simultaneously with the Casimiroids in Hispaniola. The Straits of Mona formed a trading frontier between them. Large sites like La Angostura and Maruca demonstrate sedentism, as in Hispaniola, but reveal a less sophisticated material culture. Enigmatic comma-shaped and pointed ground stone artefacts (a dagger? Figure 33.1a) evoke ritual functions, carved stone amulets illustrate personal adornment (Figure 33.1d), while quartz crystals (Rouse 1992: fig. 18e) mirror religious practices. Those translucent, prismatic crystals (Roe 1985: pl. A4) remained treasured items in the succeeding Saladoid cultures, and persist as shamanic paraphernalia in the Guianas. Fock (1963: 31), on the Waiwai, for example, notes that a shaman's quartz crystals fall from heaven and access, once tobacco smoke is blown over them, the Father of Birds; Guss (1989: 243, n. 23), on the Ye'cuana, presents cognate data where shamans must travel to heaven to receive their quartz crystal healing stones, which are the elements inside his rattle. The quartz crystals are predictably regarded as embodying clarity and purity (ibid.: n. 29), and thus clean out the worms of contagion (ibid.: 148) as the rattle is shaken. They derive from the Sun's own crystals which were used to create the Culture hero *Wanadi* and the First People, and are symbolized by the colour white and its connotations of something 'uncontaminated'. Perhaps the semantic range of these crystals was somewhat similar in the ancient Caribbean. That may explain why they were traded between islands, thus anticipating later exchange networks for semi-precious stones, *cibas* (Cody 1993). Thus, the Ortoiroids also had a shamanic religion based on curing via altered states of consciousness.

FIGURE 33.2 (continued) the stingy maternal uncle, First Man *Bayamanaco*. He flung his *cohoba* hallucinogenic snuff-impregnated nasal mucus onto the back of his maternal nephew, *Deminán*, causing the latter's dorsal swelling and subsequent birth of the hapless nephew's female turtle offspring; (f) An enlargement of *Deminán*'s dorsal eminence showing a layout of a stylized turtle as seen in plain-view; (g) The first turtle Progenitrix born out of *Deminán*'s swollen back in the shape of a small Taíno turtle effigy bowl (17 cm long, 13 cm wide, 6 cm high) discovered in a cave (Cueva del Chivo) on the north coast of Puerto Rico, still charred from a ritual meal offering sustenance to the dead (Collection: Casa de la Cultura, Dorado, PR) as seen in plain-view; (h) A profile view of that incised and modelled-appliquéd turtle effigy bowl (tail reconstructed); (i) The post-mould outline of a late Saladoid communal hut, or *maloca*, from the Golden Rock site, St Eustatius, revealing a sea turtle outline with lateral curved wind-screens as leg paddles; (j) A panoramic shot of a Wawai maloca in Titkoñerï village on the Jatapuzin River, Brazil, as part of the *Centro de Investigaciones Indígenas de Puerto Rico* 1985 expeditions to the Waiwai under the direction of its curator, Dr Peter Roe, gourd finial highlighted; (k) A hollowed-out half gourd bowl of the sort mentioned as the womb of *Yayael*'s bones turned fish, its waters of parturition forming the sea in which they swim, all occasioned by *Deminán*'s oral greed; (l) A hollowed-out whole gourd of the sort used in a hut's central house-post finial.

3 HORTICULTURALISTS

These stingray-spine-tipped dart and *atlatl*-launcher-armed foragers proved formidable opponents for the intrusive Saladoid horticulturalists and ceramicists who arrived in Puerto Rico and Vieques around 400 BC. While the Ortoiroids, after putting up a stiff fight, retired to the interior in Puerto Rico, their Casimiroid counterparts across the Mona Straits held the Saladoids to a toe-hold in eastern Hispaniola (Roe 1991).

Relying upon their huge dugout canoes, defiant to winds and currents, these Antillean ceramic-making and horticultural Indians centred their culture-geographic areas on the straits between islands, not on the islands themselves as both the initial Lithic and Archaic peoples, and the later Europeans did. This resulted in the larger islands being divided in half by pre-Taíno times (600–1200 AD). Hispaniola alone retains that aboriginal division.

Continuities connect the initial Saladoids, via pre-Taíno, to the proto-historic Taíno in eastern Puerto Rico–the Virgin Islands. This supports the competitive exclusion of the Ortoiroids there and the *in situ* evolution of the eastern Taíno out of their ancestral Amazonian ancestors, aided by borrowing from the classic Taíno in western Puerto Rico–Mona Strait.

The Saladoid heritage is less clear in the west. Either via archaistic collecting from Saladoid middens, or by acculturation with Saladoid descendants, the Archaic populations contributed to Ostionan Ostionoid pottery (Keegan 2007), contemporary with the Elenan Ostionoid pottery to the east. The classic Taíno, 1200–1550 AD, represent these cultures' amalgamation.

Archaic descendants also left their mark on acculturating western Taíno cultures further to the west, hence the crudity of the Melliac and Lucayan pottery from western Hispaniola through to Jamaica (Atkinson 2006), eastern Cuba, and the Bahamas. Paradoxically, the similarity of Pané's texts to Amazonian–Guianan mythology vitiates any significant Archaic religious contributions. Of course, this is not a paradox at all if we take the ubiquitous South Amerindian pattern of differential male involvement with the supernatural coupled with wife capture (archaic women abducted via raiding by Saladoid-descendant warriors), which would produce precisely the pattern found: acculturation in the women's pottery, but no trace in the men's religious sphere.

The initial Saladoid migration headed directly for the Greater Antilles from the mainland of eastern Venezuela in two waves (Fitzpatrick 2006). The discoverer of the earlier wave, Chanlatte Baik, calls it 'Huecoid', from the eponymous site, La Hueca, Vieques (Chanlatte Baik and Narganes Storde 2005). Rouse, who defined the culture classifications from Venezuela through to the Bahamas, noted systematic similarities between La Hueca and the Saladoid series, albeit as a distinct style pertaining to a variant ethnic group within the Saladoid 'people', hence 'Huecan Saladoid' (Rouse 1992: 90). The other migrating ethnic group was 'Cedrosan Saladoid' (from Cedros, Trinidad). Their interrelationships are still debated. Their art and religion were similar, but not identical. Huecan pottery was a sloppy, but dynamic plastic-decorated ware, cross-hatched and modelled with a limited set of incised and punctuated designs filled with post-fire ochre crusting.

These serpentine geometric designs were based on the same elements and grammar as the Cedrosan Saladoid incisions, and the carinated and flanged vessel shapes were similar

(Roe 1989: fig. 29). Anthropomorphic *cohoba* inhalers, small restricted vessels with a bowl and dual nostril pipes (Roe 2004: fig. 7.3), as well as miniature stone grinders for the powder, illuminated Huecan religion. This hallucinogenic snuff (*Anadenanthera peregrina*), used throughout northern Amazonia, persisted until Taíno times in anthropomorphic Y-shaped inhaling tubes, snuffing trays, bowls, spoons, and tables (Rouse 1992: fig. 5d). Such paraphernalia allows animistic religions to contact spirit helpers for shamanic curing/bewitchment. Huecan animal familiars were bats (ghosts or ogres in the Caribbean and Amazonia, they appear on shallow carinated effigy bowls with asymmetrically pushed-in rims), as well as dogs decorating vertical-sided bowls. Large carnivores being absent on the islands, this introduced canine, also present in Cedrosan art, became a 'domesticated jaguar' (Roe 1995; Rodríguez López 2007) in body decoration (necklaces of perforated canines through to the Taíno), ceramic figurines, *adornos* (decorative rim lugs), woodcarving, and mythology.

Huecans also produced a miniature lapidary art in exotic jet, jadeite, carnelian, agate, green stone, and amethyst. Most of these artefacts are small perforated frog-effigy necklace elements (another natural icon from the impoverished insular fauna that endures into Taíno art). A feminine water-affiliated icon with fertility connotations, frog amulets also appear in long-distance prestige trade networks throughout Amazonia–Guianas (Boomert 1987).

The other lapidary icon, a profile vulture in jadeite with a prominent bill crest holding its nestling or a human trophy head in its claws, is equivocal. While it may be a condor from the Colombian or Venezuelan Andes, more likely it is the King Vulture from the South American lowlands. Its presence in Barrancoid ceramics from the lower Orinoco (there mislabelled as a harpy eagle, Oliver 2008: fig. 12.19) reinforces this lowland origin. In any event, the lizard and trophy head emphasize this large and colourful bird's fearsome raptor, not carrion-feeder, aspect. Using cognate South Amerindian mythic data (Roe 1982: 70–1), one could predict that the 'Ancient Eagle' King Vulture fed its young with human heads, and was therefore the icon of head-hunters.

This iconography implies ethnophysiological and magical notions, including the trophy skull as a 'portable bony womb' and its masculine appropriation of feminine fertility via an androcentric theory of procreation. This artefactual transformation (as trophy) of a naturefact (the skull) occurs via raiding one's enemies to magically harness their life force for game abundance (Roe 1991).

4 LATER SETTLERS

One of the ethnic groups these populations were probably raiding/trading with were their close cultural 'cousins', the more numerous Cedrosans, the other proto-Maipuran Arawak 'crab culture' (Rainey 1940). The Cedrosans arrived on the heels of the Huecan Saladoids and rapidly absorbed them, possibly via wife capture and trophy head-raiding. The long sequence of C-14 dates used to support Huecan persistence (Chanlatte Baik and Narganes Storde 2005: 92) likely results from bioturbation, myriad now-effaced land crab tunnels, because there is no evidence of stylistic change over a supposed 1,800 years of time, something unprecedented in world prehistory. A similarly improbably long series of dates without evidence of aesthetic evolution has been recorded for the Punta Candelero site on the eastern coast of Puerto Rico by Rodríguez López (1991), and is probably due to the same problem of mechanical mixture. Moreover, the proposed scenarios for peaceful cultural coexistence between the Huecans and the Cedrosans (Wilson 2007: 79–80) all derive from modern multicultural, stratified societies, and are therefore completely inappropriate to analogize with exclusionistic, prehistoric tribals.

Evidence for forced assimilation of the Huecans by the Cedrosans comes from site settlement patterns (isolated mounds being replaced by huge sheet middens) and ceramics, specifically the Cedrosan appropriation of Huecan cross-hatching, but much more finely executed. Along with polychrome pre-fire painting (white-on-red, with salmon, sometimes positive–negative), post-fire black resin crusting, and pattern smudging, this incision made Cedrosan pottery striking. WOR painting adorned 'campaniform' (bell-shaped) liquid food presentation bowls and plates. Complex silhouette liquid transport human effigy jars with appliquéd features materialized, as did elegant 'flying saucer' beer mugs and chalices, unique frog effigy stirrup-spout jars, and annular-based bird-effigy bowls. The latter highlighted birds as helpful intermediaries between the Sky World of the spirits and the Earth World of humans, a Guianan–Amazonian role. Cook pots manifested a milder campaniform shape, like their Huecan counterparts (Roe 1989: fig. 33).

Adornos, along with hollow ceramic figurines, depicted mainland fauna in realistic fashion, indicating that the Cedrosans remained in contact with South America. They also illustrated the Saladoid 'lateral view' to the world of the forest, and its plethora of animal spirits. Hollow painted human figurines recorded elaborate body painting, while incense burners, present also in the Lesser Antilles, suggest that tobacco smoke established 'ropes to heaven', as in Amazonia. Carved shell eye-pieces documented now-vanished wooden sculptural prototypes for much later Taíno idols.

Evidence for Cedrosan Saladoid trophy head-taking and raiding comes from human male frontal bones perforated as pectorals, the victim's visage incised–excised onto their surfaces. These ancient Cedrosan trophies formed the prototypes for flat Saladoid ceramic face effigy pendants, and persisted into 'Epi-Saladoid' Monserrate (600–800 AD). Ceramic and stone copies (Taíno *guaizas*) endured as icons of rank. The Taíno also used carved circular human skull bones as belt bosses (Keegan and Carlson 2008: fig. 33), underlining their religious appropriation of an enemy's life-force, and proving that they were less pacific than traditionally portrayed.

Other cultural differences between Huecan and Cedrosan assemblages highlighted their respective religious conceptions. No one has found a Huecan cemetery, whereas the Cedrosan site of Maisabel, Puerto Rico, revealed burials. It had a central plaza bereft of refuse surrounded by a circle of mounded middens behind large oblong communal huts, a South Amerindian lowland residential pattern. The extended- and fetal-position primary inhumations, as well as secondary bundle burials, often accompanied by funerary goods, were concentrated underneath the sacred central plaza (Siegel 1989a). Sometimes their ceramic offerings only included large sherds indicative that the 'dead' fragments would become intact in the afterlife to accompany the deceased to the Land of the Dead in the west. A variable pattern of burial orientation to the east, the land of rebirth, was consistent with such beliefs. This pattern continued in Epi-Saladoid sites like San Lorenzo, Puerto Rico, where otherwise intact vessels have their bottoms knocked out, ceremonially 'killed'.

Cedrosan design layouts illuminated their 'cultural epistemology' based on the same hallucinogen the Huecans used. Pané (1498 [1999]: 26, 52) remarked that the taking of *cohoba* produced visions of people walking about inverted and backwards. Many examples of this 'anatropic imagery' (vertical reflection) exist in the symmetry rules of Cedrosan art, particularly the inverted 'Occulate Being of the Hourglass', the key painted anthropomorph (Roe 1989: fig. 19). His skeletal round, staring eyes and exposed tooth row evoked the 'Eye Spirit' of the dead ancestors, the lowland South Amerindian permanent soul. Such inversions, and a 'dual-view' iconography, continued into pre-Taíno and Taíno art (Roe 2004).

5 ICONOGRAPHY AND SYMBOLISM

An important, and persistent, animal icon, from Saladoid to the Taíno, was the giant hawksbill sea turtle, the *carey*. Prized for its flesh and eggs, this impressive aquatic reptile gained religious importance. A rectangular turtle-effigy ceramic bowl (Figure 33.2g–h) in large, medium, small, and miniature sizes, decorated according to its phase, persisted, materializing in rock art (petroglyphs, cf. Roe 2005: fig. 8.6b; and pictographs, cf. ibid.: fig. 8.20j, or in a more stylized fashion, 8.23a, b), and in Taíno mythology.

The reason behind the turtle's religious prominence lay in the Amazonian form code and its androcentric theory of conception. The infant is the congealed product of repeated male ejaculations, reducing the female to a passive container into which the male actively 'constructs' the child, his 'artefact'. This explains ethnographic exotica like the *couvade* and male post-partum food taboos, while allowing men to iconically appropriate women's gestational powers. Congruent Guianan form codes envision males as long, linear, pointed, hard, and solid, versus females as short, round, hollow, and soft (Rivière 1969: 262, on the Cariban Trio). These oppositions cohere with the sexes' characteristic artefacts (male clubs, spears, darts, arrows and knives/female baskets, bags, gourds, pots, and baby slings), and project into their respective animal transforms: masculine carnivorous dogs, jaguars, and raptors, all possessing hard and pointed teeth, claws, talons and beaks/feminine soft and round-hollow vegetarian frogs, fish, and turtles, uniformly characterized by big mouths that devour whole. Frogs persisted from Saladoid to the Taíno Frog Lady of Caguana, *Atabey* the Water Goddess (Stevens-Arroyo 1988), as did turtles, both fresh (*jicotea*) and salt water (*carey*).

Such structural assignments, writ small in ceramic effigies, endure, writ large, in huts. The late Saladoid Golden Rock site, St Eustatius, revealed the ground plans of Saladoid circular communal huts ancestral to the Taíno *bohio*, including the wind screens that arched from their sides (Figure 33.2j). These edifices emulated the structure of the giant sea turtle, the curved screens mimicking their paddles. There are even more transparent sea-turtle effigies than huts in the Golden Rock site—see the rectangular work shed or meeting hut as reconstructed by Schinkel (1992: figs. 168–9).

The South American communal hut, the round *maloca* (Waiwai, Fig. 33.2; Ye'cuana), is similarly a hollow and soft (the thatch) feminine womb within which the social unit is reproduced via sexual congress, iconically represented by the erect and hard central house post as phallus. That non-structural member, brought in through the already constructed single doorway in transparent mimicry of intercourse, projects beyond the roof apex, capped, in a coital metaphor, by a hollow feminine gourd finial (Fig. 33.2l). The chronicler Oviedo y Valdés' drawings (Rouse 1992: fig. 4, top) show the same form of the hut complete with its gourd finials for both the Taíno *bohio* (the commoners' circular hut) and *caney* (the oblong chief's hut-temple). The femininity of the round hut, the gourd, the frog's round body, the turtle's hollow shell, and the turtle trays in which women offered food to guests all resonated in Caribbean mythic art.

As South Amerindian First Men copulate with round and hollow turtles, fish, frogs, and other aquatic 'containers', any similar object suffices. First Man (Shipibo) copulates with a gourd, out of whose broken shell the Magical Twins and other 'seed companions' emerge (forming the Pleiades and Orion). Pané (1498 [1999]: 14) records an isomorphic Taíno myth: First Man, *Yaya*, an anthropomorphic version of the Amazonian primordial Dragon, a stingy, withholding figure who must kill his own son, *Yayael*, to avoid the latter's patricide. Arrom (1989) suggests that *Yaya* is a batrachathrope and that identification would be consistent with a mythic substitution of the local frog amphibian for the Amazonian crocodilian. The son wants to steal his father's cultigens since the latter is unwilling to share them with humans. Practising secondary bundle burial, *Yaya* places *Yayael*'s bones in a calabash (Figure 33.2k) suspended from the ceiling of his hut, as per Taíno funerary custom witnessed by Columbus (Columbus 1492–3a: 170). The gourd functions as a masculine-appropriated womb, and like its Amazonian counterpart, falls, breaks and gives birth, in a forced caeserian section, not to twins, but to fish (*Yayael*'s transformed bones), its water of parturition forming their sea (Stevens-Arroyo 1988: 103). Comparative ethno-astronomical data (Roe 1993) suggests that this tale is really an astral myth that concerns the origin of horticulture, specifically manioc husbandry, the associated asterisms that herald it, as well as the origin of the meat (fish) that is eaten with it.

Yet twins still intrude. The cause of this productive calamity was the only named member, the hungry and careless *Deminán*, of the four (duplicated) Taíno Culture Heroes. Collapsing the nameless three into a single figure completes the dyad. Since the syphilitic sibling is foolish, driven by his appetites both sexual, hence his affliction, and gustatory, hence his function, he acts the mortal Younger Brother. The healthy collapsed twin thus becomes Elder Brother, the senior (brightest, first magnitude star) of the Pleiades, *Alcyone*. Syphilitic *Deminán*, via oral greed, caused the calabash to fall and break as the brothers raided *Yaya*'s food stuffs. This mutilated figure, the 'one-legged hunter' of the Amazon (Orion), confirms the identity of his murderous father, the withholding—hence irascible—Dragon, the Hyades. He is the reluctant bringer of manioc, a South American tradition (Rivière 1969: 260–1, on the trio) as old as its first civilization, Chavín, 3,000 years ago (Roe 1993; Roe and Roe 2010).

This new identification is supported by the inference that *Yúcahu*, the male deity of manioc and the sea (as *Yúcahu Bagua Maórocoti*), the son of *Atabey*, was in some sense *Yaya*'s inheritor (Robiou-Lamarche 2006: 87). Ethno- and archaeo-astronomical data aligns these most famous of South Amerindian's linked asterisms, since they rise along the ecliptic in that order: the Pleiades, then the pursuing Hyades (the 'V'-shaped jaws of the caymanic Dragon), and last, Orion, his mutilated victim. All are essential heralds of the rainy season that sustains manioc cultivation in Amazonia and the Caribbean. These deified asterisms help to decode three-pointers, sacred Antillean triangular objects.

Cedrosan *trigonolitos* recapitulated these gendered form connotations. While uniquely Caribbean, they do not appear in Huecan Saladoid, signalling a difference in religion and

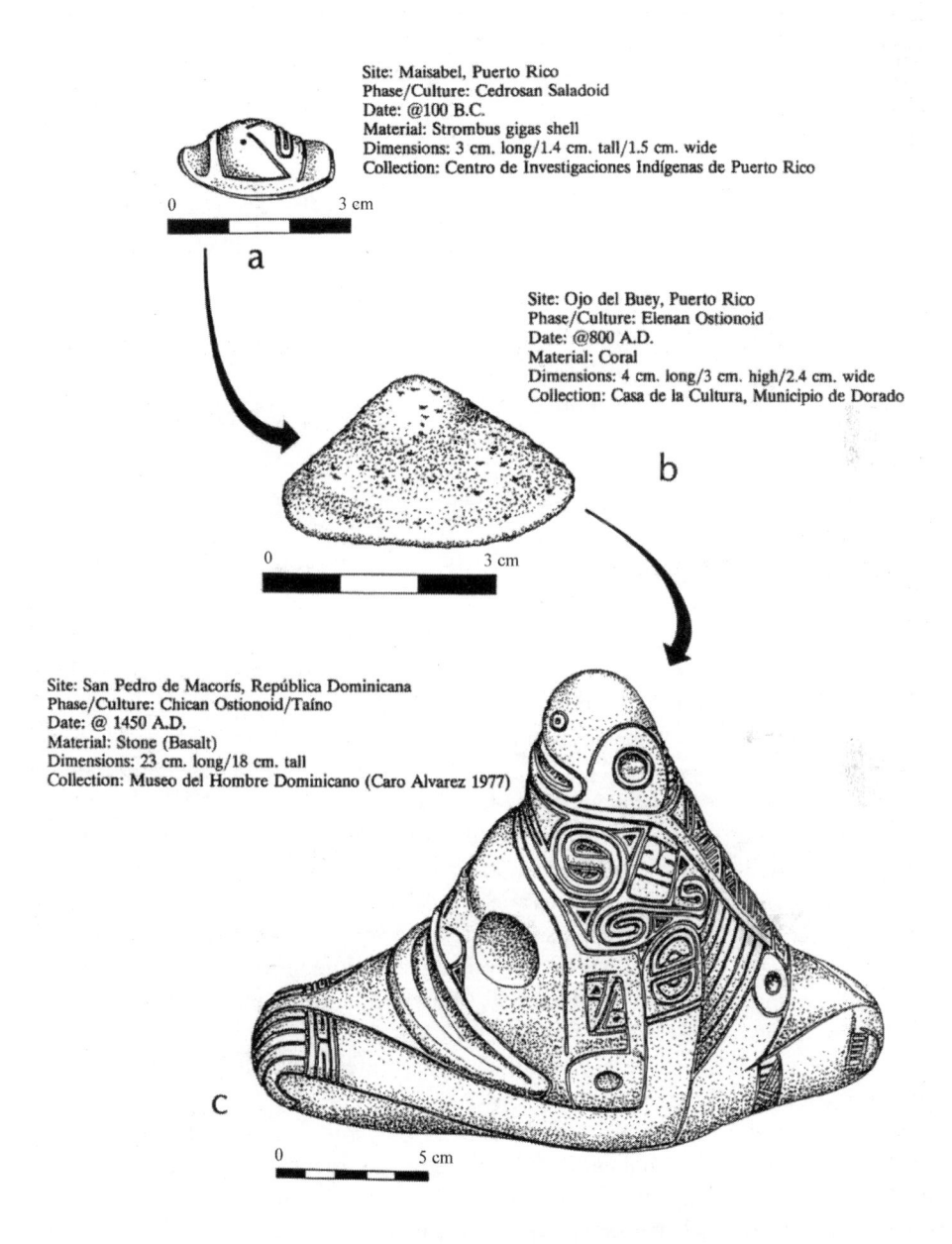

Site: Maisabel, Puerto Rico
Phase/Culture: Cedrosan Saladoid
Date: @100 B.C.
Material: Strombus gigas shell
Dimensions: 3 cm. long/1.4 cm. tall/1.5 cm. wide
Collection: Centro de Investigaciones Indígenas de Puerto Rico

a

Site: Ojo del Buey, Puerto Rico
Phase/Culture: Elenan Ostionoid
Date: @800 A.D.
Material: Coral
Dimensions: 4 cm. long/3 cm. high/2.4 cm. wide
Collection: Casa de la Cultura, Municipio de Dorado

b

Site: San Pedro de Macorís, República Dominicana
Phase/Culture: Chican Ostionoid/Taíno
Date: @ 1450 A.D.
Material: Stone (Basalt)
Dimensions: 23 cm. long/18 cm. tall
Collection: Museo del Hombre Dominicano (Caro Alvarez 1977)

c

FIGURE 33.3 The evolution of the three-pointer from Saladoid miniature art of personal presentation to Chican Ostionoid art of public power. (a) A miniature carved three-pointer with incised anthropomorphic upward-looking face, excavated by the *Centro de Estudios Avanzados de Puerto Rico y el Caribe*'s 1986 Field School at the Maisabel site under the direction of Dr Peter Roe; (b) A medium-sized plain three-pointer (*trigonolito*) found at the Ojo del Buey site, Dorado, Puerto Rico, by Hernán Ortíz, MA; (c) A monumental Chican Ostionoid (Taíno) three-pointer in the shape of a *Deminán* effigy from the Dominican Republic.

mythology. Carved to emulate the pointed sacred mountains of the islands, these three-pointers started small, fashioned from the tip of the central spire of the large *cobo*, or Queen Conch. This shell makes an admirable trumpet, the in-dwelling mollusc being also a good source of protein. It abounds in the turtle-grass meadows of the shallow waters within the sheltered semicircular embayments the Saladoids settled near. One of the earliest three-pointers was excavated at the site of Maisabel, Puerto Rico, in the high, well-drained soils good for manioc behind one such embayment. It bears a small, well-incised, upward-looking human face, an anthropomorphized mountain peak (Figure 33.3a).

Such exquisite artefacts form the prototypes for a continuous sequence of sacred portable sculptures passing through progressively larger, but generally plain (Figure 33.3b) pre-Taíno stone or coral skeuomorphs (retaining the shell's concave base), to the large, heavy, intricately incised Taíno stone *zemís*. One type (Figure 33.3c) embodies a crouching 'hunch-backed' figure with a little 'alter-ego' head at the tip of his dorsal eminence, *Deminán* and his swollen 'back womb'.

6 LATER DEVELOPMENTS

As these cultures settled into their new insular biome, perfecting their subsistence by shifting to molluscan and fish resources from the Saladoid terrestrially oriented 'crab cultures', their populations exploded and penetrated the interior, eliminating or absorbing most of the Archaic holdouts. Simultaneously, the small-scale, intricately decorated Saladoid 'personal presentation' material culture, emulative of an egalitarian tribal society, transitioned to the first inklings of hierarchy in a material culture of 'public power' evocative of incipient stratified chiefdoms (Roe 2004).

Despite increasing social complexity, pottery paradoxically *decreased* in elaboration. First the polychrome, cross-hatching and linear-incised Saladoid ware, with its complex silhouettes, died out, replaced by Monserratean monochrome painting and smudging, and then to just modelling and incision on simpler and less well executed pottery in succeeding Elenan and Ostionan Ostionoid periods (Lundberg 2007; Roe 1989: fig. 29). Technological devolution accompanied social evolution because earthenware pottery, available to all, expresses invidious social distinctions poorly. Also, the far-flung trade networks that supplied the many raw materials needed for elaborate pottery atrophied as cultures became regionally isolated (Hofman et al. 2007).

While these quotidian artefacts simplified, two monumental art media of local origin and sacred import appeared. Frontal and visible from greater distances, they were rock art and ball courts. Life-size pictographs and petroglyphs festooned the sacred solution caverns of the central cordillera, while petroglyphs encrusted boulders in the streams that descended from them. The rivers flowed toward the beach petroglyphs highlighting descent-group joint ownership of nearby freshwater fishing sites (Roe 2009). These horizontal eolinitic rock carvings featured 'wrapped ancestors' (erroneously called 'swaddled infants'), illustrating the practice of burying people tightly wrapped in their hammocks (Oliver 2005: 272–3; Roe 1997a: 155). Such lozenge-shaped bodies filled with net-like incisions, were portrayed in 'short-hand' cave pictographs as simple netted ovals held in the *behique*'s arms. He was the fasting shaman, purging himself with carved bone vomiting spatulas, and shaking carved wooden maracas. The *behique* acted as the purveyor of fertility between the dead ancestors, hence his skeletal depiction and inverted posture (Dávila y Dávila 2004: fig. 31; Roe 1997a: fig. 107), and their living descendants, hence his prominent erection, an Antillean–Amazonian death–life–death jungle continuum figure.

Petroglyphs added narrative via their syntactical positioning, yielding the Guianan 'Sun's Fish Trap' myth incised into the lithified strand of Maisabel beach (Roe 2005: fig. 8.6c–f). Such images invoked ancestral legitimacy while 'culturalizing' the landscape, marking it indelibly for ethnic groups, and the corporate descent groups within them, while staking out territory and resources.

Multiple-view and anatropic imagery continued to characterize the few ceramic modelled and appliquéd decorative lugs that survived (ibid.: fig. 8.4d–g). They included the ubiquitous *anolis* hut lizard, an Antillean 'mythic substitute' for the *terra firma* boa. These images of local fauna anticipated Chican Ostionoid (Taíno) pottery's elaborate shamanic play with images.

Pre-Taíno ball parks (*bateys*) emerged as public stages for the Antillean rubber-ball game (Alegría 1983). Early, simple rectangular open-ended Greater Antillean courts, lined with small human-head petroglyphs as boundary markers (Tibes, Puerto Rico), developed from the original plaza game brought from South America. These heads represented an increasing 'human-centric' iconography as ball parks became architectural stages for emergent hierarchy orchestrated by nobles (*nitaíno*). Later Elenan parks, like El Bronce (Puerto Rico), showcased giant free-standing menhirs carved with frontal full-body petroglyphs. They included the shark as a masculine Antillean icon, accompanied by a trophy head (Robinson 1985). These proto-*cacique* (chiefly) heads shifted attention from the visage, which everyone has, to the accoutrements of *cacical* office: large ear spools, necklaces, and elaborate feathered headdresses. The *cacique* was appropriating the shamanic role, assimilating the priest–temple–idol complex.

Elaborate wood, bone, shell, and stone carvings appeared with the classic Taíno, their eyes and teeth flashing with the 'hyper-animacy' (Roe 1997b) of shell and gold inlays, their bodies glistening black in *guayacán* wood (Helms 1987). Chroniclers likened *guayacán* to gleaming jet, endowing it with anti-syphilis properties. In animistic fashion, these trees offered themselves, as interpreted by the *behique*, for their artefactual transformation in exchange for cult observances (Saunders and Gray 1996). The elaborate wooden seats, *duhos*, the *caciques* sat upon were intricately carved. They were prevailingly anthropomorphic to emphasize hierarchy; literally an elite man sitting on a lesser reclining or prostrated commoner man (Ostapkowicz 1997: figs. 41, 44). Yet their bas-relief designs still betray anatropic and dual-view shamanic imagery (Roe 2004: fig. 7.14–15), revealing how these chiefly societies had not fully transcended egalitarianism.

Newly elaborated pottery, with double-stacked, biglobular vessels, bottles, oblong trays, and enduring turtle effigies, formed a second ceramic apogee, albeit just in plastic decoration (ibid.: fig. 7.9). While it was mass-produced by women, male artisans probably 'appropriated' the hollow, standing human ceramic effigies in archaistic emulation of the earliest Saladoid figurines. They portrayed sacred characters (*Deminán* with his swollen impregnated back, or *Itiba Cahubaba*, the 'bloody ancient mother' of the four twins).

The Taíno cosmos was a variant of the lowland South Amerindian layered triple worlds: Sky World (*Turey*) from which all light/bright items (like the imported copper–gold *tumbaga* alloy from Colombia, locally called *guanin*, a *cacical* prerogative), and beings (including Columbus himself (1492–3a: 170) descended, Earth World on which humans live, and a sub-aquatic Underworld fed by the rivers debouching out of solution caverns and flowing around petroglyph-decorated boulders to the sea. A 'water gyre' connected the night heavens to the rain clouds enshrouding the *cemízed* mountain peaks during the day. This stacked cosmos was tied together by the *axis mundi* armature of the giant Kapok World Tree, via its Guianan petrified tree 'World Rock' transform, Mount Cauta, in Hispaniola's central cordillera (Robiou-Lamarche 2006: 70; Siegel 1997: fig. 1)—compare its South Amerindian lowland ancestral prototype (Roe 1982: fig. 3). The Kapok is still revered in the Antilles.

The Taíno emerged from a sacred cave in mount Cauta (*Cacibajagua*, 'Cave of the Jagua'). This is the Genipap fruit (*Genipa americana*) with its indelible black dye used for body painting; the transformation of nature, the naked body, into culture = artistic designs. Their archaic enemies emerged from a lesser twin cave 'without value', *Amayaúa*. The sun and moon continued their voyages from the east, Land of Rebirth, emerging from the cave *Iguanaboína*, 'Iguana-boa', lair of the subterranean Underworld-associated reptiles. It travelled to the west, Land of the Dead, *Coaybay*. Nightly, the worlds reversed themselves, the cold, dark, damp Underworld arching overhead in the foaming Milky Way, the hot, bright daytime Sky World underfoot (Arrom 1997).

Night was full of dangerous and seductive ghosts, identified by lacking a belly button. They were the *Opía* bat transforms feeding on sweet fruits like *guayaba*, a local delectable = raw = hyper-natural food appropriate to such dangerous and seductive spirits. Mora Cavern, Puerto Rico, houses a microcosmic recapitulation of this triple-tiered macrocosmos. Vertically stratified, it is populated by the favoured dead, giant wrapped ancestral pictographs, elite-accessed in the central cavern. They are guarded, on each peripheral solution tube entrance, by commoner-accessible petroglyphs (Roe 2005: 312–25). Intentional dog burials and effigies continued from Saladoid times, this animal icon acting the Amazonian role of psychopomp. The four-footed dog-like *cemí Opiyelguobirán* fittingly dived into a lake upon the arrival of the Spanish with their new religion.

Taíno religion, called *zemísm* (*cemísm*) from the 'sweetness' of those ancestors (Oliver 1997), combined the animal spirits of their tribal Saladoid precursors with the 'departmental gods' of a now fully formed, two-tiered rank society. They included *Boínayel*, son of the female Great Serpent, a god of rain with Saladoid antecedents, represented with tear channels carved beneath his eyes in media ranging from sweating stalagtite sculpture to weeping wooden *cohoba* tables. The devastation of hurricanes (*Huracán*) involved the god of wind and rain, *Guataúba*; floodwaters (released terrestrial water), *Coatrisquie*; and *Guabancex* (whirlpools–rapids?); as well as a goddess of the water, *Atabey* or *Attabeira*, in her Amazonian Frog Woman guise. The staple crop flourished under a god of bitter manioc (*Yúcahu*) and his unleavened bread *cazabe*, and *Baibrama*, capable of regeneration like the tuber itself yet poisonous (disease-causing) if not properly propitiated. The stingy, hence irascible, old First Man, *Bayamanaco*, whose phallic nose ejaculated the *cohoba*-infused mucus that impregnated the back of his maternal nephew *Deminán* (Figure 33.2e) was its primordial withholding custodian as the Antillean anthropomorphic transformation of the South Amerindian Dragon (the Taíno were matrilineal [Keegan 2007] so the problematic authority relationship marked in myth ran from maternal uncle to nephew, not father to son), while a god of the dead, *Maquetaurie Guayaba*, emitted the sweetness of decay like his eponymous fruit.

These *cemís*, and others, were housed in the rectangular *caney* of the *cacique*, who now also took the hallucinogens, having fully usurped the power of the *behique* to augment his authority. He employed assistants with speaking tubes to make oracular pronouncements through orifices cut in the *cemí* idols to impress the commoner (*naboria*) worshippers in the temples (Las Casas 1527a) as in the boundary stones of the *batey* (Morse 1997: 40). The *cacique* had his ancestor depicted in a complex frieze as a feather-crowned, full-bodied dignitary seated on his *duho* (attired as the sun god?) on ball park menhir petroglyphs at Caguana, his consort (the *cacique*'s ancestress) next to, but below him, impersonating the water goddess/frog woman, together with her long-beaked bird (Oliver 2005: 269–72; Roe 2005: fig. 8.15).

The associated *batey* multiplied and hypertrophied in size and complexity, particularly at Caguana and the recently discovered one at Jacaná in Puerto Rico, and in eastern Hispaniola. These elaborate ball parks were oriented and organized as cosmic maps, 'sighting instruments' with archaeo-astronomic, calendric (solstitial/equinoctial), and star rising (the Pleiades–Hyades–Orion) alignments (Robiou-Lamarche 2006: 68). Growing huge along with their associated *bateys*, the three-pointers internally differentiated into several types, as did the stone rings, skeuomorphs of the original nock-in-trees hip-protectors via the 'elbow stone' stage. The latter became so enormous, in both gracile and massive forms, that they could no longer be worn in the game, being donned afterwards by the winners like the grossly enlarged belts of modern boxing champions. *Trigonolitos* fit into the collars' lozenge-shaped roughened areas (Walker 1997), forming a lashed, copulating pair.

Since the pointed 'upper earth' mountain-emulating *trigonolito* was male, placed 'above'—as in covering, a coital metaphor—the larger round and hollow body of the stone ring, often incised with ophidian ('lower earth') zig-zag design layouts appropriate to femininity, the ring represented *Atabey* (Robiou-Lamarche 2006: 66). The sky god and the earth–water goddess, so joined, guaranteed manioc fertility. Las Casas (1527a [1997]: 177) recorded that the three-pointers were buried (inserted) into the feminine *conuco* (ridged field plot). The pointed *trigonolito*'s association with the cassava tuber derives from the latter's phallic connotations in Amazonian cosmology. Manioc is long, tubular and pointed, a penis analogue; scraping it is analogous to the sex act; its milky expressed mash being equivalent to semen. It was brought to women sprouting from the tip of the phallic tail of their aquatic seducer cayman lover (Rivière 1969: 260–1). No wonder the Taíno god of manioc was male, despite gestating in the womb of the female earth goddess.

Antecedents to the *trigonolito* are widely spread from the Canelos Quichua of the Ecuadorian *Montaña* in the north-west Amazon (Whitten 1976: 19) to the Cariban groups (Akawaiyo and Waiwai) of the Guianas in the north-east (Yde 1965: 30). They are the cassava spirit stones similarly planted for manioc fertility and growth. South Amerindians regard the tubers as masculine, phallic icons, and the earth as feminine garden soil, hence the Cariban *Yuca* (manioc) mistress (Guss 1989: 29). In the Antilles this figure underwent a sex change, part of a pervasive pattern of the 'masculine appropriation' of feminine duties attending increased social stratification. 'She' became the male *Yúcahu*. The form code altered with that transformation, changing from the circular (feminine) shape of the *terra firma* river cobbles to the sharp three-pointer style of the Antilles. Such transformations are possible because, for Amerindians, manioc has both masculine and feminine connotations based on which aspect of the plant one views. While the long and thick tuber is a penis, the stalk's 'eyes', through which manioc vegetatively reproduces, are so many analogic vaginas (Kensinger 1975: 46–7, on the Cashinahua).

The cult of the ancestors continued in Taíno religion but now privileging those of the élite and the *caciques*. The first ancestor, *Mácocael*, turned to stone guarding the entrance to the ancestral cave of emergence, a mythic scene replicated in cave-flanking petroglyphs found in Hispaniola, Puerto Rico, and Cuba (Dacal Moure and Rivero de la Calle 1996: 46). Martyr (1997: 172) recorded woven cotton figures of seated humans, filled inside with what modern x-rays show were human skulls. These élite personages, as especially venerated ancestors (Siegel 1997: fig. 82), exemplified the equation, 'sequestered, whole human remains : ancestral relics :: portable artifacts of reduced human bone : war trophies' (Roe 1991).

The elite incorporated new materials (rhino horn and glass beads) brought by Europeans to construct 'trans-cultural' artefacts like the Pigorini 'Bead Baby'. Yet that skull reliquary retains the Amerindian pictorial dualistic Janus-headed life/death face, while its stubby cylindrical body carries Taíno-style, 'windowed' geometric design panels (Roe 1997b: fig. 1). Elaborate beaded belts with staring dog faces (ibid.: fig. 126), protective mascots, similarly hypertrophied the aboriginal masculine cotton belts, worn on the medial realm of men's 'cosmological bodies'. Thus, for a tragically short time the aboriginal religion persisted in beautiful, yet ephemeral, artefacts of 'cultural hybrid vigor' before disappearing forever.

While the main lineaments of Caribbean culture, history, and process are becoming clear there remains much to be done. The ceramic sequences, which in sherd form were the basis for the original area-wide chronological charts, need to be analysed in detail on a local level, particularly with an eye to reconstructing the 'cultural wholes' which were the intact pots that lived as prototypes in the minds of the ancient artisans. These sequences must then be correlated with other dimensions of material culture, like rock art and sculpture, again with an eye to reconstructing shifting style provinces and the cultures they reflect over time. Lastly, while the Greater Antilles (with the conspicuous exception of Haiti) are revealing an unexpected plethora of contesting ethnic groups and their archaeological phases, the modern linguistic and cultural divisions of the Lesser Antilles have hampered an overview of their role in the development of complex culture in the ancient Caribbean. Efforts to pull that material together are now going on and can only be encouraged further by the development of area-wide and linguistically accessible databases.

Further Reading

For a general summary of the prehistory of the Caribbean see Rouse (1992), and for a recent update that differs in perspective, by a younger scholar, see Samuel M. Wilson (2007). The 1997 volume edited by Wilson contains contributions by noted regional specialists on all of the prehistoric Caribbean. For the earliest horticultural–ceramicist arrivals in the Greater Antilles, with discussions by various experts, see Siegel's edited volume (1989b).

For a visually stunning compendium of the art and religion of the Taíno with authoritative chapters on all aspects of their culture see Bercht et al. (1997). An English translation of the first New World ethnography by Fray Ramón Pané (1498) on the Taíno can be read in Arrom's 1999 translation and a structuralist decoding of Taíno religion and mythology in

Antonio M. Stevens-Arroyo (1988). A regional perspective on the lowland South Amerindian myths reflected in Pané is found in Roe 1982, while Keegan (2007) explores myth and archaeology in the Bahamas.

Ricardo E. Alegría (1983) discusses the Antillean ballpark and game, the locus of much of the art. The art and archaeology of Cuba are covered in Moure and Rivero de la Calle (1996), that of Jamaica in Atkinson (2006), and of Puerto Rico in Siegel (2005). For a survey of the rock art of the Caribbean see Hayward, Atkinson, and Cinquino (2009). A veritable avalanche of recent studies are coming out from the University of Alabama Press that are also of interest (Curet 2005; Curet and Stringer 2010; Keegan and Carlson 2008; Rodríguez Ramos 2010).

References

ALEGRÍA, R. E. 1978. *Apuntes en torno a la mitología de los indios Taínos de las Antillas Mayores y sus orígenes suramericanos* (San Juan: Centro de Estudios Avanzados de Puerto Rico y el Caribe).
——1983. *Ball Courts and Ceremonial Plazas in the West Indies*, Yale University Publications in Anthropology No. 79 (New Haven: Department of Anthropology, Yale University).
ANDERSON-CÓRDOVA, K. F. 2005. 'The aftermath of conquest: The Indians of Puerto Rico during the early sixteenth century' in Peter E. Siegel (ed.), *Ancient Borinquen: Archaeology and ethnohistory of Native Puerto Rico* (Tuscaloosa: The University of Alabama Press), pp. 337–52.
ARROM, J. J. 1989. *Mitología y artes prehispánicas de las Antillas*, rev. edn (Mexico City: Siglo Veintinuno Editores).
——1997. 'The creation myths of the Taíno' in F. Bercht, E. Brodsky, J. A. Farmer, et al. (eds), *Taíno: Precolumbian art and culture from the Caribbean* (New York: Monacelli Press), pp. 68–79.
——(ed.) 1999. *An Account of the Antiquities of the Indians* (by Fray Ramón Pané, 1498), trans. Susan C. Griswold (Durham, NC: Duke University Press).
ATKINSON, L.-G. (ed.) 2006. *The Earliest Inhabitants: The dynamics of the Jamaican Taíno* (Kingston, Jamaica: University of the West Indies Press).
AYES SUÁREZ, C. M. 1990. 'El vestido y el adorno corporal entre los arcaicos de nuestro archipiélago', *Horizontes*, Febrero-Abril: 12–14.
BERCHT, F., BRODSKY, E., FARMER, J. A., et al. (eds) 1997. *Taíno: Pre-Columbian art and culture from the Caribbean* (New York: El Museo del Barrio and The Monacelli Press).
BOOMERT, A. (Arie). 1987. 'Gifts of the Amazons: "Green stone" pendants and beads as items of ceremonial exchange in Amazonia and the Caribbean', *Antropológica*, 67: 33–54.
CARO ALVAREZ, J. A. 1977. *Cemíes y trigonolitos* (Barcelona: Artes Gráficas Manuel Pareje).
CHANLATTE BAIK, L. A. and NARGANES STORDE, Y. M. 2005. 'Cultura La Hueca' in L. C. Baik and Y. Narganes Storde (eds), *Cultura La Hueca* (San Juan: Museo de Historia, Antropología y Arte, Universidad de Puerto Rico, Recinto de Río Piedras), pp. 10–55, 83–100.
CODY, A. 1993. 'Distribution of exotic stone artifacts through the Lesser Antilles: Their implications for prehistoric interaction and exchange' in A. Cummins and P. King (eds),

Proceedings of the Fourteenth Congress of the International Association for Caribbean Archaeology (St. Ann's Garrison, St. Michael, Barbados), pp. 204–26.

COLUMBUS, CHRISTOPHER 1492–3a [1989]. *Diario del primer viaje* [Original lost, only an extract made by Fray Bartolomé de Las Casas exists, facsimile edition by Carlos Sanz, Madrid, 1962], Appendices: 1 Christopher Columbus, Diary of the First Voyage [on the north-east coast of Cuba], trans. Susan C. Griswold, in F. Bercht, E. Brodsky, J. A. Farmer, et al. (eds), *Taíno: Precolumbian art and culture from the Caribbean* (New York: Monacelli Press), p. 170.

——1492–3b [1989]. *Diario del primer viaje* [Original lost, only an extract made by Fray Bartolomé de Las Casas exists, facsimile edition by Carlos Sanz, Madrid, 1962], Appendices: 1 Christopher Columbus, Diary of the First Voyage [on the north-west coast of Hispaniola], trans. Susan C. Griswold, in F. Bercht, E. Brodsky, J. A. Farmer, et al. (eds), *Taíno: Precolumbian art and culture from the Caribbean* (New York: Monacelli Press), p. 170.

——1493 [1989]. *Carta de Colón anunciando el descubrimiento del Nuevo Mundo, 15 de febrero-14 de marzo*, Barcelona, Pedro Posa, 1493 (Madrid 1956), Appendices: 1 Christopher Columbus, *Letter from Columbus Announcing the Discovery of the New World*, trans. Susan C. Griswold, in F. Bercht, E. Brodsky, J. A. Farmer, et al. (eds), *Taíno: Precolumbian Art and Culture from the Caribbean* (New York: Monacelli Press), pp. 170–1.

——c.1496 [1989]. 'The Admiral's Words' in Fernando Colombo (Ferdinand Columbus), *Historie del S.D. Fernando Colombo*, trans. Alfonso de Ulloa, Ch. 62, Venice, 1571, in F. Bercht, E. Brodsky, J. A. Farmer, et al. (eds), *Taíno: Precolumbian art and culture from the Caribbean* (New York: Monacelli Press), p. 171.

CURET, L. A. 2005. *Caribbean Paleodemography: Population, Culture History, and Sociopolitical Pressures in Ancient Puerto Rico* (Tuscaloosa: The University of Alabama Press).

——and STRINGER, L. M. *Tibes: People, Power, and Ritual at the Center of the Cosmos* (Tuscaloosa: The University of Alabama Press).

DÁVILA Y DÁVILA, O. 2004. *Arqueología de la Isla de la Mona* (San Juan: Editorial, Instituto de Cultura Puertorriqueña).

FITZPATRICK, S. M. 2006. 'A critical approach to 14C dating in the Caribbean: Using chronometric hygiene to evaluate chronological control and prehistoric settlement', *Latin American Antiquity*, 17(4): 389–418.

FOCK, N. 1963. *Waiwai: Religion and society of an Amazonian tribe*, Nationalmuseets Skrifter, Etnografisk Række, Ethnographic Series 8 (Copenhagen: National Museum).

GUSS, D. M. 1989. *To Weave and to Sing: Art, symbol, and narrative in the South American rain forest* (Berkeley and Los Angeles: The University of California Press).

HASLIP-VIERA, G. (ed.) 1983. *Taíno Revival: Critical perspectives on Puerto Rican identity and cultural politics* (Princeton: Markus Wiener Publishers).

HAYWARD, M., ATKINSON, L.-G., and CINQUINO, M. (eds) 2009. *Rock Art of the Caribbean* (Tuscaloosa: University of Alabama Press).

HELMS, M. W. 1987. 'Art styles and interaction spheres in Central America and the Caribbean: Polished black wood in the Greater Antilles' in R. D. Drennan and C. A. Uribe (eds), *Chiefdoms in the Americas* (New York: University Press of America), pp. 67–83.

HOFMAN, C. L., BRIGHT, A. J., BOOMERT, A., et al. 2007. 'Island rhythms: The web of social relationships and interaction networks in the Lesser Antillean Archipelago between 400 BC and AD 1492', *Latin American Antiquity*, 18(3): 243–68.

KEEGAN, W. F. 1989. 'Creating the Guanahatabey (Ciboney): The modern genesis of an extinct culture', *Antiquity*, 63: 373–9.

——2007. *Taíno Indian Myth and Practice: The arrival of the Stranger King* (Gainesville: University Press of Florida).

—— and CARLSON, L. A. 2008. *Talking Taíno: Caribbean natural history from a Native perspective* (Tuscaloosa: The University of Alabama Press).

—— and RAMOS, R. R. 2007. 'Archaic origins of the classic Tainos' in B. Reid, H. P. Roget, and A. Curet (eds), *Proceedings of the Twenty-First Congress of the International Association for Caribbean Archaeology*, I (The University of the West Indies, School of Continuing Studies, St. Augustine, Trinidad and Tobago), pp. 211–17.

KENSINGER, K. 1975. 'Studying the Cashinahua' in J. P. Dwyer (ed.), *The Cashinahua of Eastern Peru*, Studies in Anthropology and Material Culture No. 1 (Bristol: The Haffenreffer Museum of Anthropology, Brown University), pp. 9–85.

LAS CASAS, FRAY BARTOLOMÉ DE 1527a [1997]. *Apologética historia de las Indias*, Ch. 120: 'Concerning the idols worshipped by the Indians of the island of Hispaniola', Holographic manuscript, Muñoz Collection A-73, Madrid: Royal Academy of History, Appendix 3, Fray Bartolomé de Las Casas, trans. Susan C. Griswold, in F. Bercht, E. Brodsky, J. A. Farmer, et al. (eds), *Taíno: Precolumbian art and culture from the Caribbean* (New York: Monacelli Press), pp. 175–7.

—— 1527b [1997]. *Apologética historia de las Indias*, Ch. 166: 'Concerning the religion professed by the Indians of the island of Hispaniola', Holographic manuscript, Muñoz Collection A-73, Madrid: Royal Academy of History, Appendix 3, Fray Bartolomé de Las Casas, trans. Susan C. Griswold, in F. Bercht, E. Brodsky, J. A. Farmer, et al. (eds), *Taíno: Precolumbian art and culture from the Caribbean* (New York: Monacelli Press), pp. 177–9.

—— 1527c [1997]. *Apologética historia de las Indias*, Ch. 167: 'Concerning the fasts kept by the Indians of the island of Hispaniola and of Cuba in honor of their idols', Holographic manuscript, Muñoz Collection A-73, Madrid: Royal Academy of History, Appendix 3, Fray Bartolomé de Las Casas, trans. Susan C. Griswold, in F. Bercht, E. Brodsky, J. A. Farmer, et al. (eds), *Taíno: Precolumbian art and culture from the Caribbean* (New York: Monacelli Press), pp. 179–80.

—— c.1550 [1951]. *Historia de las Indias*, 3 vols. (Madrid, 1875), A. M. Carlo and L. Hanke (eds), Biblioteca Americana, Serie de Crónistas de México, nos. 15–17 (Mexico City: Fondo de Cultura Económica), trans. Weightman (New York: Harper & Row).

LÓPEZ-BARALT, M. 1985. *El mito taíno: Lévi-Strauss en las antillas* (Río Piedras: Ediciones Huracán).

LUNDBERG, E. R. 2007. 'A Monserrate component in the Virgin Islands in the context of inquiry into the Saladoid–Ostionoid transition' in B. Reid, H. P. Roget, and A. Curet (eds), *Proceedings of the Twenty-first International Congress for Caribbean Archaeology* (St Augustine: The University of the West Indies), pp. 338–46.

MARTYR, P. (a.k.a. Pietro Martire d'Anghiera, Pedro Mártir de Anglería) c.1516 [1964–5]. *Décades del Nuevo Mundo*, 2 vols., trans. A. M. Carlo (México, D.F.: José Porrúa e Hijos, Sucesores).

—— 1587 [1997]. *De Orbe Novo Petri Martyris Anglerii...Parisis, apud Gvillelmvm Avvary* MDLXXXVII, R. Hakluyt (ed.), Appendix 2, Pietro Martire d'Anghiera, trans. Susan C. Griswold, in F. Bercht, E. Brodsky, J. A. Farmer, et al. (eds), *Taíno: Precolumbian Art and Culture from the Caribbean* (New York: Monacelli Press), pp. 171–5.

MONTÁS, O., BORRELL, P. J., and MOYA PONS, F. 1985. *Arte Taíno* (Santo Domingo: Banco Central de la República Dominicana).

MORSE, B. F. 1997. 'The Salt River Site, St. Croix, at the time of the Encounter' in Samuel M. Wilson (ed.), *The Indigenous People of the Caribbean* (Gainesville: University Press of Florida), pp. 36–45.

Moure, R. D. and Rivero de la Calle, M. 1996. *Art and Archaeology of Pre-Columbian Cuba*, trans. Daniel H. Sandweiss (Pittsburgh: University of Pittsburgh Press).

Oliver, J. R. 1997. 'The Taino Cosmos' in Samuel M. Wilson (ed.), *The Indigenous People of the Caribbean* (Gainesville: University Press of Florida), pp. 140–53.

—— 2005. 'Proto-Taíno monumental *Cemís* of Caguana: A political–religious "manifesto"' in P. E. Siegel (ed.), *Ancient Borinquen: Archaeology and ethnohistory of Native Puerto Rico* (Tuscaloosa: The University of Alabama Press), pp. 230–84.

—— 2008. 'The archaeology of agriculture in ancient Amazonia' in H. Silverman and W. H. Isbell (eds), *Handbook of South American Archaeology* (New York: Springer), pp. 185–216.

Ostapkowicz, J. M. 1997. 'To be seated with "great courtesy and veneration": Contextual aspects of the Taíno Duho' in F. Bercht, E. Brodsky, J. A. Farmer, et al. (eds), *Taíno: Precolumbian art and culture from the Caribbean* (New York: Monacelli Press), pp. 56–67.

Oviedo y Valdéz, G. F. de 1535 [1959]. *Historia General y Natural de las Indias*, 5 vols, ed. Juan Pérez de Tudela, Biblioteca de Autores Españoles, vols. 117–22 (Madrid: Ediciones Atlas).

Pané, R., see Arrom 1999.

Rainey, F. G. 1940. *Porto Rican Archaeology*, Scientific Survey of Porto Rico and the Virgin Islands, vol. 18, pt. 2 (New York: New York Academy of Science).

Rivière, P. G. 1969. *Marriage among the Trio: A principle of social organization* (London: Oxford University Press).

Robinson, L. S. 1985. 'The stone row at El Bronce archaeological site, Puerto Rico' in L. S. Robinson, E. R. Lundberg, and J. B. Walker (eds), *Archaeological Data Recovery at El Bronce, Puerto Rico: Final Report, Phase 2*, Prepared for the United States Army Corps of Engineers, Jacksonville District, Ft Myers (Florida: Archaeological Services, Inc.), pp. I1–I12.

Robiou-Lamarche, S. 2006. *Mitología y religion de los Taínos* (San Juan: Editorial Punto y Coma).

Rodríguez López, M. 1991. 'Arqueología de Punta Candelero, Puerto Rico' in E. N. Ayubi and J. B. Haviser (eds), *Proceedings of the 13th International Congress for Caribbean Archaeology, Curaçao, Netherlands Antilles 1989*, Pt 2, Reports of the Archaeological-Anthropological Institute of the Netherlands Antilles No. 9 (Curaçao), pp. 605–27.

—— 1997. 'Religious beliefs of the Saladoid people' in S. M. Wilson (ed.), *The Indigenous People of the Caribbean* (Gainesville: University Press of Florida), pp. 80–7.

—— 2007. *Tras las huellas del perro indígena* (Hato Rey: Publicaciones Puertorriqueñas).

Rodríguez Ramos, R. 2010. *Rethinking Puerto Rican Precolonial History* (Tuscaloosa: The University of Alabama Press).

Roe, P. G. 1982. *The Cosmic Zygote: Cosmology in the Amazon Basin* (New Brunswick: Rutgers University Press).

—— 1985. 'A preliminary report on the 1980 and 1982 field seasons at Hacienda Grande (12 PSj7-5): Overview of site history, mapping and excavations' in *Comptes Rendu des Communications du Dixième Congrès International D' Études des Civilisations Précolombiennes des Petites Antilles, Fort-de-France, Martinique, 1983*, pp. 151–80, 206–24.

—— 1989. 'A grammatical analysis of Cedrosan Saladoid vessel form categories and surface decoration: Aesthetic and technical styles in early Antillean ceramics' in P. E. Siegel (ed.), *Early Ceramic Population Lifeways and Adaptive Strategies in the Caribbean*, BAR International Series (Oxford: BAR), pp. 267–382.

—— 1991. 'The best enemy is a killed, drilled, and decorative enemy: Human corporeal art (frontal bone pectorals, belt ornaments, carved humeri and pierced teeth) in pre-Colombian Puerto Rico', *Proceedings of the 13th International Congress for Caribbean Archaeology, Curaçao, Netherlands Antilles*, Pt 2, Reports of the Archaeological-Anthropological Institute of the Netherlands Antilles No. 9 (Curaçao), pp. 854–73.

——1993. 'The Pleiades in comparative perspective: The Waiwai *Shirkoimo* and the Shipibo *Huishmabo*' in C. Ruggles and N. Saunders (eds), *Astronomies and Cultures: Selected Papers from Oxford 3, International Conference on Archaeoastronomy* (Boulder: University Press of Colorado), pp. 296–328.

ROE, P. G. 1995. 'Eternal companions: Amerindian dogs from Tierra Firma to the Antilles' in R. E. Alegría and M. Rodríguez (eds), *Actas del Quintodécimo Congreso Internacional de Arqueología del Caribe* (San Juan, P.R.: Centro de Estudios Avanzados de Puerto Rico y el Caribe, La Fundación Puertorriqueña de las Humanidades and la Universidad del Turabo), pp. 155–72.

——1997a. 'Just wasting away: Taíno shamanism and concepts of fertility' in F. Bercht, E. Brodsky, J. A. Farmer, et al. (eds), *Taíno: Precolumbian art and culture from the Caribbean* (New York: Monacelli Press), pp. 124–57.

——1997b. 'The Museo Pigorini *Zemí*: The face of life/The face of death' in F. Bercht, E. Brodsky, J. A. Farmer, et al. (eds), *Taíno: Precolumbian art and culture from the Caribbean* (New York: Monacelli Press), pp. 164–9.

——2004. 'The ghost in the machine: Symmetry and representation in ancient Antillean art' in D. Washburn (ed.), *Embedded Symmetries: Natural and cultural* (Albuquerque: University of New Mexico Press), pp. 95–143.

——2005. 'Rivers of stone, rivers within stone: Rock art in ancient Puerto Rico' in P. E. Siegel (ed.), *Ancient Borinquen: Archaeology and ethnohistory of Native Puerto Rico* (Tuscaloosa: The University of Alabama Press), pp. 285–336.

——2009. 'The mute stones speak: Recent advances in recording, dating, and interpreting Antillean and northern South American rock art' in M. Hayward, L.-G. Atkinson, and M. Cinquino (eds), *Rock Art of the Caribbean* (Tuscaloosa: University of Alabama Press), pp. 198–239.

——and HAYWARD, M. 2008. 'Rock of ages: Rock art and ethnic identity in ancient and modern Puerto Rico' in I. D. Sanz, D. Fiore, and S. K. May (eds), *Archaeologies of Art: Time, place, identity* (Walnut Creek, CA: Left Coast Press, Inc.), pp. 51–77.

——and ROE, A. W. 2010. 'Riding the Cayman Canoe: The Iconography of Bats in Chavín Art', in J. Jones (ed.), *Adventures in Pre-Columbian Studies: Essay in Honor of Elizabeth P. Benson* (Washington, D.C.: The Anthropological Society of Washington, D.C.), pp. 50–74.

ROUSE, I. 1992. *The Taínos: The rise and fall of the people who greeted Columbus* (New Haven and London: Yale University Press).

SAUNDERS, N. J. and GRAY, D. 1996. 'Zemis, trees and spirits: Three Taíno carvings from Jamaica', *Antiquity*, 70(270): 801–12.

SCHINKEL, K. 1992. 'The Golden Rock features' in A. H. Versteeg and K. Schinkel (eds), *The Archaeology of St. Eustatius: The Golden Rock site*, Publication of the St Eustatius Historical Foundation No. 2; Publication of the Foundation for Scientific Research in the Caribbean Region, No. 131 (St Eustatius, Netherlands Antilles and Amsterdam: The St Eustatius Historical Foundation and the Foundation for Scientific Research in the Caribbean Region), pp. 143–212.

SIEGEL, P. E. 1989a. 'Site structure, demography, and social complexity in the early ceramic age of the Caribbean' in P. E. Siegel (ed.), *Early Ceramic Population Lifeways and Adaptive Strategies in the Caribbean*, BAR International Series 506 (Oxford: BAR), pp. 193–245.

——(ed.) 1989b. *Early Ceramic Population Lifeways and Adaptive Strategies in the Caribbean*, BAR International Series 506 (Oxford: BAR).

——1997. 'Ancestor worship and cosmology among the Taíno' in F. Bercht, E. Brodsky, J. A. Farmer, et al. (eds), *Taíno: Precolumbian art and culture from the Caribbean* (New York: Monacelli Press), pp. 106–11.

——(ed.) 2005. *Ancient Borinquen: Archaeology and ethnohistory of Native Puerto Rico* (Tuscaloosa: The University of Alabama Press).

STEVENS-ARROYO, A. M. 1988. *Cave of the Jagua: The mythological world of the Taínos* (Albuquerque: University of New Mexico Press).

VEGA DE BOYRIE, B. 1987. *Arte neotaíno*, Pamphlet (Santo Domingo, R.D.: Fundación Cultural Dominicana).

WALKER, J. B. 1997. 'Taíno stone collars, elbow stones, and three-pointers' in F. Bercht, E. Brodsky, J. A. Farmer, et al. (eds), *Taíno: Precolumbian art and culture from the Caribbean* (New York: Monacelli Press), pp. 80–91.

WHITTEN, N. E. JR 1976. *Sacha Runa: Ethnicity and adaptation of Ecuadorian Jungle Quichua* (Urbana, IL: University of Illinois Press).

WILSON, S. M. (ed.) 1997. *The Indigenous People of the Caribbean* (Gainesville: University Press of Florida).

——2007. *The Archaeology of the Caribbean* (Cambridge and New York: Cambridge University Press).

YDE, J. 1965. *Material Culture of the Waiwai*, Ethnographic Series 10 (Copenhagen: National Museum of Denmark).

CHAPTER 34

RECOGNIZING RELIGION IN MESOAMERICAN ARCHAEOLOGY
Maya

ROSEMARY A. JOYCE

1 MESOAMERICA DEFINED

MESOAMERICA is a culture-area construct recognizing shared practices among pre-Hispanic societies and traditional peoples descended from them in an area extending from Mexico to Honduras and El Salvador (Joyce 2004). Mesoamerican features cross pre-Hispanic political, social, and linguistic boundaries. They can be understood as products of historical relationships among neighbouring villages and towns. Among the defining features of Mesoamerica are ritual practices and beliefs.

Mesoamerican peoples kept count of time using multiple calendars (Rice 2004, 2007). Employing a base-20 number system, 18 periods of 20 days, with 5 additional nameless days formed a solar year of 365 days. This regulated ceremonies related to agriculture. A 260-day cycle of 13 periods of 20 days used ethnographically in some communities for divination served historically to commemorate birth dates and other anniversaries. Historical inscriptions recorded a single continuous count of days elapsed from a mythical origin point, in units of 20 days, 360 days, and multiples of 20 beyond this. Commemorations of the ending of these cycles, some explicitly referencing creation stories, were part of state religions. Cycles of lunar months, of the planet Venus, and a sequence of nine named nights were likely used to regulate the timing of other rituals.

The symbolic repetition of the numbers 4, 5, 7, 9, 13, and 20 is additional evidence of ritualization of otherwise mundane practices. Numbers were employed to record astronomical observations and projections, technologies for timing religious practice (Aveni 1980; Milbrath 2000). Numeration and astronomy assisted in planning spaces, including ball courts, observatories, and temples, through which religious practices were coordinated and systematically related to models of the cosmos (Carrasco 1998). Such architectural settings were sites where ritual performances, including dances, processions, games, and sacrifices took place.

Studies of Mesoamerican religion have liberally used documentary history from the sixteenth century to the present, and ethnographic studies beginning in the twentieth century, to identify beliefs that might have provided the context for meaning in pre-Hispanic religious practices documented through archaeological research. Historical continuity to contemporary societies is central to the definition of Mesoamerica, which takes shape over 3,000 years before European colonization began in the sixteenth century AD.

2 Historical Framework

In the Palaeoindian and Archaic periods (pre-1500 BC), populations were mobile and reliance on domesticated or cultivated plants was limited. With shifts to different strategies of subsistence in the Archaic period after c.8000 BC, more localized networks of people can be identified within the boundaries of what later would be Mesoamerica. This is the time of the earliest mortuary ritual known within these boundaries, the date of the earliest identifiable ritual space, and earliest definite use of special spaces, caves. Late in the Archaic period, several developments mark transitions to village life: increased sedentism; increased reliance on cultivated or domesticated plants; and the development of fired clay as a material medium. Site visibility increases with the spread of ceramics, the hallmark of the Formative (or Preclassic) period. Early Formative villages exist throughout the entire area by 1500 BC. Mortuary ritual is an evident focus of religion in these villages (Joyce 1999). Locally produced figurines in distinct styles representing human and animal images in fired clay are also interpreted as evidence of ritual and thus of religion (Cyphers 1993; Marcus 1998).

The last few centuries of the Early Formative period witness the development of a fully articulated religious iconography expressed in monumental stone sculpture at Mexican Gulf Coast Olmec archaeological sites, which were socially stratified towns (Clark 2004). Similar iconography is carved or incised on ceramic vessels from the central Valley of Mexico to Honduras (Pool 2007). After 900 BC, monumental stone sculpture with related imagery appears across the region. Jade and other green stones join or replace ceramic vessels as additional media for this iconography. Special architectural settings for the practice of ritual are created in many settlements. Unique places on the landscape, springs and caves, are sites of ritual practice (Ortíz and Rodríguez 1999; Stone 1992). Monumental sculpture, including bedrock engravings, marks other points on the landscape, likely also locales of ritual practice (Gillespie 1999; Grove 1999).

This rich visual and material culture is transformed by c.400 BC into a series of regional art styles (Guernsey 2006). Many ritual practices, including the construction of stepped terrace pyramids, burial below house floors and in pyramids, and marking of monumental settings by the placement of caches, persist. Writing is a key development in the Late Formative period. Ritual is a major topic of surviving texts. While all examples that have survived are on stone objects, there is every reason to suspect that a broader variety of textual media were in use, especially by the end of the Late Formative period (maximally 250 AD).

Between 200 BC and AD 250, political and economic factions compelled or persuaded large numbers of basic producers to support major public works projects, developing the great city of Teotihuacan in central highland Mexico (Sugiyama 2005), and dozens of smaller cities. With the emergence of routine urban life, state religion involving major temple building projects (Kowalski 1999), often with massive dedicatory deposits, including human offerings, coexisted with religion of everyday life: burial under or near houses, 'dedicatory' and 'termination' deposits in domestic structures, and continued or renewed use of figurines discarded in refuse or placed in burials or caches (Gonlin and Lohse 2007; Halperin et al. 2009; Mock 1998; Plunket 2002).

State and quotidian ritual and religion continued as parallel practices, employing a shared repertoire of ritual actions, with calendars forming a critical bridge between state and house. The shift from Classic to Postclassic political systems between 800 and 1200 AD accompanied the spread of cults whose practice linked political and social elites and distinguished them from the populations they ruled (Carrasco, Jones, and Sessions 2000). Attempts at suppression of visible aspects of everyday religious practice with the introduction of Roman Catholicism in the first half of the sixteenth century did not entirely destroy, but did modify, religious beliefs (Burkhart 1989; Gossen 1997). While presenting complexities beyond the scope of this chapter, the effects of colonization may be viewed not as the entire replacement of indigenous religious practices and understandings but as the introduction of a new lexicon and new spaces for ritual performance.

3 MESOAMERICAN BELIEFS

Creation mythology was recorded by Europeans and indigenous writers using the European script starting in the sixteenth century (Carrasco 1998). These narratives describe the creation of the earth in the midst of waters, and the imposition of order through the counting of days initiated by the first sunrise. The earth may be characterized as a living being, reptilian or saurian. The animation of the sun and the fertility of the earth are achieved through offering of blood or other substances to provide energy. Multiple cycles of creation and destruction of suns with different characteristics, or the replacement of a false sun with a legitimate one, are described.

Human beings come into existence as products of deliberate action by pre-existing supernatural beings, who shape successive attempts at humans out of a variety of substances (clay, wood) before finding that people of corn possess desired powers of speech and visual perception. Humans explicitly owe debts of commemoration and feeding to their predecessors. Supernatural beings need materials to provide energy, expect verbal acknowledgement, and require commemoration.

While these are colonial accounts, mythic narratives recorded in Classic Maya inscriptions and pre-Hispanic visual imagery are related. Pre-Hispanic sources may place more emphasis on actions initiating the current world: the placement of landmarks in sacred space, the first ritual bloodletting (Schele and Miller 1986), incense-burning (Bayles 2001), dances (Looper 2009), or recitations. Politically motivated pre-Hispanic images emphasize the repetition of ritual practices and their relationship to ensuring cycles of rain and plant growth. They represent ritual actors linked to supernatural beings in celestial or subterranean locales.

Based on such ethnographic, colonial, and pre-Hispanic sources, archaeologists make a number of assumptions about Mesoamerican thought. Mesoamerican calendars were used to coordinate rituals. Points in the daily and annual solar cycles orient layouts of sites and placement of settlements in landscapes. Mesoamerican peoples shared a concept of a 'layered universe' with at least three levels (celestial world, terrestrial world, underworld). The upperworld could be associated with the number 13 and the underworld with the number 9. Four world directions were universally recognized, often associated with colours. The four directions may be sides of the world, edges joined at inter-cardinal points. Five key spatial points orient the terrestrial plane: a centre point around which the four world directions are arrayed. Alternatively, four world directions may define a vertical plane, sunrise (east), zenith (up), sunset (west), nadir (down). The place of human beings in the cosmos varies depending on birth date, age, sexual status, and social position; differences sometimes associated with distinct supernatural beings. These and other Mesoamerican beliefs were reproduced through repeated actions timed by the seasonal calendar and the life cycles of humans.

4 Mesoamerican Ritual Practices

When Spanish colonizers entered Tenochtitlan, the capital city of the Mexica (Aztecs), children were being trained to memorize songs, play music, and dance as part of rituals (Burkhart 1997). Children training to be religious specialists were required to sweep sacred spaces. Adult ritualists employed calendars in divination, burned tree resins in ceremony, and offered the blood of animals and humans at shrines and temples. Mexica adults participated in ritual processions, dances, races, and games; witnessed human sacrifices at central temples; and offered dough images in neighbourhood ceremonies. Feasting and drinking was a central part of state and neighbourhood ceremony. In houses, recitation of speeches, singing, dancing, burning resins, drinking, and consuming special foods served to mark transitions over the life course from prenatal rituals through after-death commemoration of ancestors.

Early colonial texts describe Mesoamerican peoples destroying household objects in end-of-year ceremonies. Sacred objects, including human skeletal elements, were wrapped in cotton cloth or barkcloth, and carried in ritual procession (Guernsey and Reilly 2006). Bounded ritual spaces were enclosed. Objects and people were sacralized by painting with special pigments. Burning of natural rubber, producing black smoke, complemented the white smoke from copal tree resin (Stone 2002). Classic Maya inscriptions suggest the use of an even wider array of burned substances.

Specialized incense-burning vessels in Formative burials confirm this ritual act and formed part of mortuary ceremonies by 900 BC. Incense burners at Classic Teotihuacan featured composite images of humans and symbolic elements related to monumental art in temples (Berrin and Pasztory 1993; Sugiyama 2005). Disassembled censers were included in some burials. In Classic Maya city states, incense burners made in decentralized workshops were used in household ritual and deposited in architectural offerings and burials of nobles (Rice 1999). Incense burners with human and symbolic imagery remained part of Later Postclassic ritual practices as well. Examples of the materials burned have also been preserved. In an Early Formative spring at El Manatí, Mexico, rubber balls formed part of offerings (Ortíz and Rodríguez 1999). Bowls recovered from an anaerobic environment in a natural well, the 'Sacred Cenote' of Maya Chichen Itza, dating to the transition from

Classic to Postclassic, contained copal resin formed in balls and images (Coggins and Shane 1984).

Classic Maya texts suggest that burning was a sacralizing action (Stuart 1998). Burned materials, included broken objects, are commonly identified residues of ritual. The many burned and broken objects recovered from the Chichen Itza Cenote are prime examples (Coggins and Shane 1984). The deposition of selected broken and/or burned objects at moments of architectural remodelling in temples and domestic structures is the principal evidence for what are called dedicatory and termination rituals, especially but not solely in Classic Maya sites (Krochok 1991; Mock 1998). Such deposits are understood as indices of ritual actions including personal bloodletting; sacrifice of symbolically significant objects such as jade, marine shell, and obsidian that together reference cosmological planes; and orientation of the ritualist spatially to astronomical or landscape points. Dedicatory caches often incorporate green jade, and contrasting white and red shell, in ways that relate to the colour symbolism of the world directions.

The distinction between dedicatory and termination rituals is partly artificial; the termination of one version of a building (including battering and burning of imagery depicted on the building itself or associated monuments) may be immediately followed by renewal of the building, simultaneously associating deposits with termination and dedication. But the kinds of actions involved can be distinguished: breaking, burning, or overmarking objects, monuments, and buildings desacralizes them; placement of structured deposits containing elements indexing world levels, oriented directionally, emplaces ritual participants in space at particular marked points in time.

Other structured deposits, burials and caches, are also understood as evidence of ritual (e.g. Fitzsimmons 2009; Gillespie 2001, 2002; Joyce 1999; López Luján 2005; McAnany 1995). Burials and caches often incorporate serving vessels, some with confirmed traces of special foods such as chocolate. They may include jade, shell, and obsidian objects. Drawing a sharp distinction between burials and caches can be misleading, and it has been suggested they be considered together as 'earth offerings' (Becker 1993). Caches may include selected human skeletal elements, and burials may, as a result of multi-stage mortuary ritual, be left with few or no skeletal elements.

Household compounds are one focus of ritual practices (Gonlin and Lohse 2007; Plunket 2002). From the Formative period on, household rituals involved the use of clay figurines, 'incense burners', subfloor burial, and material placed during renovation of domestic structures either as part of termination rituals, dedicatory rites, or both. Household-trash deposits may contain similar materials, suggesting that the structured deposits we recognize are only a small reflection of the everyday practice of religion in domestic settings.

In most houses, burials and caches were simply placed below the floor. In houses of the wealthy or socially high-ranking, tombs and cache chambers could be constructed, and sometimes, separate shrines were built in the centre of house yards (patios) or on their eastern sides. Temples, sometimes constructed with nine terraces, can mark tombs of political leaders and their families. While these architectural contexts are radically different in size and degree of symbolic marking, as evidence for ritual and religion they exemplify the same kinds of beliefs and actions.

Specialized architectural complexes do provide evidence of additional religious beliefs and ritual practices. Imagery on courts used for ritual ball games at Classic period sites like Copan, Chichen Itza, and El Tajín explicitly associates these facilities with mythic narratives concerning celestial bodies, especially the sun (Scarborough and Wilcox 1991). Cache deposits placed in the alley and flanking spaces indicate that ball courts were sites of ritual practice, as do the residues of incense burning and feasting discarded around many ball courts. Some ball courts incorporate sweat baths. Found in domestic settings as well, sweat baths reflect the necessity of steam to some rituals, probably due to complex concepts about human personhood engaged in ritual.

5 Religion and the Living Person

Drawing heavily on historic and ethnographic materials, scholars working on Mexica, Zapotec, and Maya traditions have argued that Mesoamerican persons were understood to be composed of multiple physical and metaphysical substances, some recirculated from previous generations of kin, some dependent on co-participation in calendrical cycles, and some composed through everyday practices or invested through rituals (Houston, Stuart, and Taube 2006; Gillespie 2002; López Austin 1988; McKeever Furst 1995; Monaghan 2000). Mesoamerican persons received physical substances (flesh, blood, bone) from parents and via lifelong acts such as eating and sweat-bathing. A substantial part of mortuary ritual may have been directed to managing the disarticulation of human persons (Fitzsimmons 2009; Gillespie 2001, 2002; McAnany 1995). While less obvious archaeologically, other rituals were likely practised at transitions during the lifecourse to influence the formation of the person.

Figurines figured prominently in life-cycle rituals, including those related to pregnancy and birth, transition to adulthood, marriage, and death (Cyphers 1993; Halperin et al. 2009; Marcus 1998). Differences in frequencies of figurines over time, between, and within sites are consequently possible indicators of variation in ritual practices related to the life course. The importance of musical instruments in ritual, especially whistles and rattles, may be intimately connected with the way sound testifies to the presence of life breath (e.g. Ishihara 2008). Indeed, Classic Maya texts use the sign for 'breath' as the central element of expressions for 'death' (Houston, Stuart, and Taube 2006). Combinations of musical instrument and figurines that are common across Mesoamerica are especially likely ritual objects used in life-course rites (Healy 1988).

Early colonial Mexica texts document association through birth date of children with a shared fate or character articulated by ritual specialists using calendars, presumably perishable barkpaper or deerskin books like examples preserved in European archives. Ethnographic evidence demonstrates that in many Mesoamerican societies common birth date can result in different persons sharing metaphysical substances (Monaghan 2000). Ethnographically, this 'co-essential' relationship has been described as the person having a spirit companion, sometimes an invisible animal who appears in dreams or visions. The applicability of this concept to pre-colonial societies is supported by Classic Maya texts concerning beings called *wayab* (Houston and Stuart 1989). Depicted as an anthropomorphic animal, the *way* is identified with a historical human actor or mythological figure, who may be shown making a *way* appear through burning of blood- or rubber-spattered paper, or even transforming into the *way* in ritual dance. Researchers have argued that Formative period Gulf Coast Olmec sculptures depict related concepts, showing human–animal transformation (Reilly 1989).

Pre-Hispanic calendars thus located different persons in relation to each other through shared birthdates and links to metaphysical spirits. Such connections served to support divination and curing. Scholarly understanding of divination and curing relies heavily on both specific ethnographic analogies with Mesoamerican ethnography (e.g. Marcus and Flannery 1994), and general analogies with global literature on shamanism (Klein et al. 2002). There are multiple ethnographic cases, especially in Maya communities, of specialists who use indigenous calendrics and other ritual practices to guide people's actions. Contemporary indigenous names for such practitioners often incorporate references to vision. Some of these practitioners diagnose illness, often considered the result of violations of expectations of ancestors, and propose treatment, which may involve feeding ancestors or other spirits. Such contemporary traditional practices inform archaeological models of ritual specialists in villages assumed to have kept track of the calendar, provided information on the implications of birth dates, and cured physical and metaphysical illness.

Many deposits called caches could probably be considered evidence of the actions of such ritual specialists. Specific artefacts, particularly selected polished stones, identified as tools of village ritual specialists are included in some caches. Some figurines may have served in ritual practices of diviners or curers like contemporary Nahua-speaking people who cut paper to create vehicles to embody nature spirits (Sandstrom and Sandstrom 1986), or modern Lenca people who use unmodified bromeliads as spirit containers. In these cases, embodied spirits help both with maintaining health of individual people and that of agricultural fields. Ceramic vessels with modelled faces, called 'god pots' by the contemporary Lacandon Maya people who use them to burn resins, have a similar ritual character (McGee 1998). Through them, gods or ancestors can take part in ceremonies. While paper and unmodified plants might not preserve, let alone be recognized as evidence of ritual, in pre-Hispanic sites, ceramic vessels for incense burning, with and without figural elements, are widely reported.

6 Treatment of the Dead

Inhumation, while common, was often part of a complex sequence of mortuary treatment. Secondary burial of bundled bones and the placement of multiple individuals in multi-entry tombs or caves used as ossuaries are all known. Skeletal elements were extracted from burials, with crania being particularly likely to be missing from a burial, or to be found in skull caches, singly or in groups. Many burial sites were marked with low platforms (shrines), multi-terrace platforms (temples), or above-ground monuments with visual imagery and/or texts referencing burial and posthumous transformations. Cremation formed part of cycles of mortuary treatment, and may have been a preferred method of disposal of the dead in late pre-colonial societies. Early colonial texts tell us that there were simultaneous (or sequential?) practices of conserving at least some skeletal elements above ground in bundles.

Burials often incorporated objects. The dead body could be arrayed in ornaments, some of rare materials, which tend to vary by age and site or intra-site location, and secondarily by sex. This has been taken as an indication that at least in primary burial, the personal identity of the deceased remained associated with the physical body. Pottery vessels, including bottles and bowls with food residues, are evidence of provisioning of the dead, of mortuary meals for the living, or of feasts linking the survivors with the dead, reinforcing the idea that the buried person retained a degree of social agency. Local-style ceramic figurines are included in burials in many Formative period villages. Formative figurines are media for the representation of social differences specific to different sites, again suggesting that the dead person was still seen as socially relevant (Marcus 1998). In Classic period sites, especially Maya sites where indigenous texts are available, and where early colonial documents augment other evidence for Postclassic sites, it is absolutely clear that the dead were understood to continue to be engaged in the life of communities (Fitzsimmons 2009).

Scholars have argued that these burial treatments are material evidence of the development of ancestor cults (McAnany 1995). The deceased continued to be individually identifiable, at least for some period. In the case of multi-stage burial practices where the dead were eventually merged, for example in multi-burial tombs in Classic Oaxaca and Belize, or cave ossuaries in Formative Honduras and terminal Classic Chichen Itza, the individuality of the person may have been transformed into a corporate personhood, like the ancestral 'mothers–fathers' of Maya ethnography. Building tombs occupied by single individuals, covered (and thus made inaccessible for secondary mortuary behaviour) by temples, at many Classic Maya sites accompanied by monuments with historical inscriptions, singles out selected individuals as the potential apical ancestors of Classic lineage theory (McAnany 1995). Provision of shrines on platforms over such tombs or near them allowed continued commemoration of the individual or corporate ancestors, commemoration that centrally involved burning resin, described in at least one colonial text and in modern ethnographies as food for the dead.

7 Ritualization of Buildings and Settlements

Caves, springs, and natural rock formations served as part of wider landscapes referenced in ritual action (Prufer and Brady 2005; Stone 1995). Some scholars believe a clean, swept rectangular space framed by two lines of stones at Gheo Shih, Oaxaca, was already used for ball games by mobile Archaic period people (Rice 2007). The original excavators suggest it was a formal space for ritual dances (Marcus and Flannery 2005). Caves were definite sites of Archaic ritual, indicated above all by wall paintings (Stone 1995).

With the growth of sedentary settlements, built features add new ritualized spaces to the landscape. Even Early Formative villages included specialized architectural stages for ritual performance. Paso de la Amada, an early Mexican village, incorporated a ball court by 1400 BC (Clark and Hill 2001). Later ball courts were liminal spaces where two teams enacted or commemorated myths related to the recreation of celestial bodies and their movements and seasonal agricultural cycles (Scarborough and Wilcox 1991).

Olmec-style cave paintings, some in sites already in use during the Archaic, engraving of rock faces at places like Chalcatzingo and Chalchuapa, and placement of free-standing monumental sculptures outside settlements, served to demarcate peripheries of landscapes around settlements where the first temple platforms were constructed around 1000 BC

(Grove 1999; Stone 1992). Such pyramids stratified settlement space into zones further marked by placement of sculpted monuments that depicted mythological creatures or human actors interacting with ancestors and supernatural beings. At some sites, such as middle Formative La Venta, deposits of green stone, coloured clay, and other materials provide evidence of repeated episodes of ritual (Gillespie 2008).

In the new centres of the Formative period and their successors in Classic and Postclassic cities, multi-terrace platforms, oriented to cardinal directions or to horizon points marking the equinoxes and solstices (Aveni 1980), were foci of repeated acts of structured deposition, resurfacing and rebuilding. Astronomical orientations to the Pleiades were projected at Classic Teotihuacan through the orientation of the main avenue along which three great temples were placed. Building J, an irregular structure that forms part of Classic Monte Alban, was oriented to the appearance of the planet Venus. Many Classic Maya cities incorporated sets of buildings that allowed observation of solstice and equinox sunrises along the eastern horizon (Milbrath 1999). These and other astronomical orientations transformed the monumental architecture at the core of Mesoamerican sites into reiterations of cosmological order (Rice 2004). Associated with the same repertoire of ritual burning, offering of jade, shell, stone, and perishable materials, and burial of burned, broken objects, such larger community architectural foci translated ritual actions from the household scale to that of the city, state, and region.

8 State and Regional-Scale Religion

Large scale architectural centres were stages for political and social elites throughout Mesoamerica, where religion articulated with rulership (Gillespie 1999; Guernsey 2006; Guernsey and Reilly 2006; Krochok 1991; Schele and Miller 1986; Sugiyama 2005). The leaders of Gulf Coast societies in the Early Formative have been described as shaman-kings who used monumental art to advertise their ability to travel to other domains of existence, claiming a unique place as intermediaries between the people and collective or individual ancestors (Clark 2004; Reilly 1989). Visual images, pre-Hispanic texts, and early colonial documents describing ritual dances and calendrical ceremonies are identified as traces of shamanic rulership continuing in Classic and Postclassic period societies. While subject to intense critique (Klein et al. 2002), shamanic models call attention to the structuring of architectural spaces as performative stages for public rituals.

Placement of human burials in temples, especially common in Formative period and Maya Classic sites, leads to their interpretation as evidence of religion centred on worship of ancestral rulers (Fitzsimmons 2009; McAnany 1995). At other sites, similar buildings are interpreted as venues for worship of deities, many associated with natural forces such as wind, rain, the maize plant, or with astronomical bodies like the sun and moon. Documents written by sixteenth-century colonizers outline complex pantheons of deities, although debate continues about how well these writers represented the religions they were describing (Gillespie and Joyce 1998; Milbrath 2000; Taube 1992; Vail 2000).

The greatest convergence between colonial texts and archaeology is provided by excavations at the Templo Mayor ('great temple') of Tenochtitlan, the capital city of the Mexica (López Luján 2005). These produced repeated images of stereotyped anthropomorphic supernatural beings that can be identified using colonial documents. The Templo Mayor was divided into two sanctuaries, one dedicated to Tlaloc, god of rain, the other to Huitzilopochtli, patron deity of the Mexica, described as a sun god. Spanish writers describe these sanctuaries as regular sites of human sacrifices (Boone 1984). Colonial texts in the Nahuatl language outline a sophisticated theology behind human sacrifice, in which cycles of earthly processes required energy derived from blood to remain in motion. Each remodelling of the temple was accompanied by placement of structured deposits of human remains, animal bones, and other objects, some clearly models of the cosmos. The Templo Mayor was a site for interaction of living people with supernatural beings, including deceased leaders, and particularly, for actions ensuring these beings had necessary sources of energy, rather than a place for worship in the medieval Christian fashion.

Mexica state religious ceremonies were occasions to commemorate episodes in creation stories and state histories, through re-enactments by human actors, some acting as vehicles for named spirits the Spanish called gods (Boone 1989). Timed by the calendar, ball games, races, processions, dances, and feasts engaged the broader population in these pageants. Mock battles, exchanges of sarcastic speech and song, and human sacrifices recapitulated factional difference, from the level of the neighbourhood to the state, between men and women, subgroups within the city, and the city and its neighbours, allies, and enemies.

Architecture, records of mythology and ritual action in deciphered texts, and material traces of ritual practice suggest Postclassic and Classic state ritual was equally impressive. The main temple at Maya Chichen Itza, dating around AD 1000, is oriented so that on the spring equinox, the setting sun illuminates feathered serpents carved on balustrades of its northern stairway and makes them seem to undulate down to the ground (Milbrath 1999). The open space around this main temple can accommodate a quarter of a million people. The main street at Classic Teotihuacan in AD 400 was oriented so that the northern Pyramid of the Moon was placed under the seasonal appearance of the Pleiades in the night sky (Aveni 1980). Just south, the Pyramid of the Sun faces west, covering a human-modified cave system in the form of two crossing passages. Further south again, a third major pyramid was covered by modelled plaster depicting feathered serpents floating on red marine waters. Excavators have found that the construction of these pyramids included the mass burial of hundreds of human beings, dressed as warriors with their hands bound behind their back (Sugiyama 2005).

State religions also created connections between political elites at different sites. Regional variations on the iconography executed in monumental stone sculpture at Early Formative Gulf Coast Olmec settlements, and the execution of related imagery on bottles, bowls, jewellery, ritual axe blades, and (through the use of stamps and seals) on perishable materials including the human body, suggest that already rulers of Gulf Coast towns and leaders of villages elsewhere shared religious practices and beliefs that served at least in part to distinguish them from those they led or ruled (Clark 2004). In the transition from Classic to Postclassic polities, imagery of feathered serpents spread among ruling factions who adopted similar household pottery, wore newly developed metal objects, especially bells, and employed painters who depicted mythologies relating them to origin sites, executed in a common international ('Mixteca-Puebla') style (Carrasco, Jones, and Sessions 2000).

Religious coordination of ruling families across Mesoamerica was facilitated by pilgrimage to common sacred sites (Rice 2007). Early Spanish visitors witnessed pilgrimage to the shrine of Ix Chel at Postclassic Maya Cozumel. Later Spanish texts recorded Postclassic Maya histories of treachery when one noble family, on pilgrimage to then-abandoned Chichen Itza, was attacked.

Classic Maya inscriptions in the painted cave of Naj Tunich have been interpreted as evidence of pilgrimage by nobles (Stone 1995). It is possible that Classic Teotihuacan was a centre for pilgrimage visits by allied ruling families who returned to their home sites with regalia they reproduced locally, and with distinction from their connection to a sacred centre.

9 A Future for the Archaeology of Ritual and Religion in Mesoamerica

Archaeology of Mesoamerican religion today faces a central challenge: when we rely on accounts from the early colonial period, we interpret our archaeological materials through an early modern European lens. Using twentieth-century ethnography does not avoid this problem; it intensifies it, since contemporary traditional religions are colonial products as well. Until recently archaeologists have failed to investigate the five centuries of colonial history. New studies of colonial Catholicism highlight the importance of the church as a community structure, the flourishing of confraternities dedicated to the veneration of specific saints, and the rich material culture of Catholic cult. While describing these topics in detail is beyond the scope of this review, exploration of such historical passages will enable archaeologists to place the colonial documents, and modern ethnographies on which they rely, in relation to the archaeological sites that preceded them, producing a real historical account of the development of religion over the more than 4,000 years of the Mesoamerican tradition.

Suggested Reading

Monaghan (2000) provides an introduction to common features of religion evident in comparative ethnology. McKeever Furst's (1995) *Natural History of the Soul in Ancient Mesoamerica* is critical to understanding the metaphysical make-up of human beings. Carrasco (1998) provides an excellent overview of thinking on the relationship of architectural and spatial layouts and conceptions of cosmology and cosmogony. The relation of calendars and astronomy to cosmology has been re-examined by Rice (2004, 2007). Particularly influential studies of ball courts and ball games (Scarborough and Wilcox 1991), burial (McAnany 1995), dedication and terminal rituals (Mock 1998), and household ritual (Gonlin and Lohse 2007; Plunket 2002) provide introductions to the range of religious actions archaeologists have identified based on material evidence. Together, these studies provide the grounding for understanding the nature of the religious person and participation in religious practices across pre-Hispanic Mesoamerica. Burkhart (1989) is a critical study of the process of translation of religious concepts and ideas during the early colonial period.

REFERENCES

Aveni, A. F. 1980. *Skywatchers of Ancient Mexico* (Austin: University of Texas Press).

Bayles, B. 2001. 'Scaling the world trees: Ethnobotanical insights into Maya spiked vessels', *Journal of Latin American Lore*, 21: 55–78.

Becker, M. 1993. 'Earth offering among the Classic period lowland Maya: Burials and caches as ritual deposits' in M. J. I. Ponce de Leon and F. L. Perramon (eds), *Perspectivas Antropológicas en el Mundo Maya* (Girona: Sociedad Española de Estudios Mayas), pp. 45–74.

Berrin, K. and Pasztory, E. (eds) 1993. *Teotihuacan: Art from the City of the Gods* (San Francisco: Fine Arts Museums of San Francisco).

Boone, E. (ed.) 1984. *Ritual Human Sacrifice in Mesoamerica* (Washington, DC: Dumbarton Oaks).

——1989. *Incarnations of the Aztec Supernatural: The image of Huitzilopochtli in Mexico and Europe* (Philadelphia: American Philosophical Society).

Burkhart, L. 1989. *The Slippery Earth: Nahua-Christian moral dialogue in sixteenth-century Mexico* (Tucson: University of Arizona Press).

——1997. 'Mexica Women on the "Home Front": Housework and religion in Aztec Mexico' in S. Schroeder, S. Wood, and R. Haskett (eds), *Indian Women of Early Mexico* (Norman, OK: University of Oklahoma Press), pp. 25–54.

Carrasco, D. 1998. *Religions of Mesoamerica: Cosmovision and ceremonial centers* (Prospect Heights, IL: Waveland Press).

——, Jones, L., and Sessions, S. (eds) 2000. *Mesoamerica's Classic Heritage: From Teotihuacan to the Aztecs* (Boulder: University Press of Colorado).

Clark, J. E. 2004. 'The birth of Mesoamerican metaphysics: Sedentism, engagement, and moral superiority' in E. DeMarrais, C. Gosden, and C. Renfrew (eds), *Rethinking Materiality: The engagement of mind with the material world* (Cambridge: McDonald Institute for Archaeological Research, University of Cambridge), pp. 205–24.

—— and Hill, W. 2001. 'Sports, gambling, and government: America's first social compact?', *American Anthropologist*, 103: 331–45.

Coggins, C. C., and Shane, O. C. 1984. *Cenote of Sacrifice: Maya treasures from the sacred well at Chichen Itza* (Cambridge, MA: Peabody Museum of Archaeology and Ethnology, Harvard University).

Cyphers, A. 1993. 'Women, rituals, and social dynamics at ancient Chalcatzingo', *Latin American Antiquity*, 4: 209–24.

Fitzsimmons, J. 2009. *Death and the Classic Maya Kings* (Austin: University of Texas Press).

Gillespie, S. D. 1999. 'Olmec thrones as ancestral altars: The two sides of power' in J. E. Robb (ed.), *Material Symbols: Culture and economy in prehistory* (Carbondale: Center for Archaeological Investigations, Southern Illinois University), pp. 224–53.

——2001. 'Personhood, agency, and mortuary ritual: A case study from the ancient Maya', *Journal of Anthropological Archaeology*, 20: 73–112.

——2002. 'Body and soul among the Maya: Keeping the spirits in place' in H. Silverman and D. Small (eds), *The Space and Place of Death*, Archaeological Papers of the American Anthropological Association No. 11 (Washington, DC: American Anthropological Association), pp. 67–78.

——2008. 'History in practice: Ritual deposition at La Venta Complex A' in B. Mills and W. Walker (eds), *Memory Work* (Santa Fe, NM: School or Advanced Research Press), pp. 109–36.

Gillespie, S. D., and Joyce, R. A. 1998. 'Deity relationships in Mesoamerican cosmologies: The case of the Maya God L', *Ancient Mesoamerica*, 9: 1–18.

Gonlin, N. and Lohse, J. C. (eds) 2007. *Commoner Ritual and Ideology in Ancient Mesoamerica* (Boulder: University Press of Colorado).

Gossen, G. H. (ed.) 1997. *South and Meso-American Native Spirituality: From the cult of the feathered serpent to the theology of liberation* (New York: Crossroad).

Grove, D. C. 1999. 'Public monuments and sacred mountains: Observations on three formative period sacred landcapes' in D. Grove and R. Joyce (eds), *Social Patterns in pre-Classic Meosamerica* (Washington, DC: Dumbarton Oaks), pp. 255–99.

Guernsey, J. 2006. *Ritual and Power in Stone* (Austin: University of Texas Press).

——and Reilly III, F. K. (eds) 2006. *Sacred Bundles: Ritual Acts of wrapping and binding in Mesoamerica* (Barnardsville, NC: Boundary End Archaeology Research Center).

Halperin, C. Faust, K. A., Taube, R., et al. (eds) 2009. *Mesoamerican Figurines* (Gainesville: University Press of Florida).

Healy, P. 1988. 'Music of the Maya', *Archaeology*, 41: 24–31, 82.

Houston, S. and Stuart, D. 1989. 'The way glyph: Evidence for "co-essences" among the Classic Maya', *Research Reports on Ancient Maya Writing*, 30: 1–16.

Houston, S., Stuart, D., and Taube, K. 2006. *The Memory of Bones: Body, being, and experience among the Classic Maya* (Austin: University of Texas Press).

Ishihara, R. 2008. 'Rising clouds, blowing winds: Late Classic Maya rain rituals in the Main Chasm, Aguateca, Guatemala', *World Archaeology*, 40: 169–89.

Joyce, R. A. 1999. 'Social dimensions of pre-Classic Burials' in D. C. Grove and R. A. Joyce (eds), *Social Patterns in Pre-Classic Mesoamerica* (Washington DC: Dumbarton Oaks), pp. 15–47.

——2000. 'Girling the girl and boying the boy: The production of adulthood in ancient Mesoamerica', *World Archaeology*, 31: 473–83.

——2004. 'Mesoamerica: A working model for archaeology' in J. A. Hendon and R. A. Joyce (eds), *Mesoamerican Archaeology: Theory and practice* (Malden, MA: Blackwell), pp. 1–42.

Klein, C. F. Guzman, E. Mandell, C., et al. 2002. 'The role of shamanism in Mesoamerican art', *Current Anthropology*, 43: 383–419.

Kowalski, J. 1999. *Mesoamerican Architecture as a Cultural Symbol* (New York: Oxford University Press).

Krochock, R. 1991. 'Dedication ceremonies at Chichén Itzá: The glyphic evidence' in M. G. Robertson and V. M. Fields (eds), *Sixth Palenque Round Table, 1986* (Norman: University of Oklahoma Press), pp. 43–50.

Looper, M. 2009. *To Be Like Gods: Dance in ancient Maya civilization* (Austin: University of Texas Press).

López Austin, A. 1988. *The Human Body and Ideology: Concepts of the ancient Nahuas*, 2 vols. (Salt Lake City: University of Utah Press).

López Luján, L. 2005. *The Offerings of the Templo Mayor of Tenochtitlan* (Albuquerque: University of New Mexico Press).

McAnany, P. A. 1995. *Living with the Ancestors: Kinship and kingship in ancient Maya society* (University of Texas Press, Austin).

McGee, R. J. 1998. 'The Lacandon incense burner renewal ceremony: Termination and dedication ritual among the contemporary Maya' in S. B. Mock (ed.), *The Sowing and the Dawning: Termination, dedication, and transformation in the archaeological and ethnographic record of Mesoamerica* (Albuquerque: University of New Mexico Press), pp. 41–6.

McKeever Furst, J. L. 1995. *The Natural History of the Soul in Ancient Mesoamerica* (New Haven: Yale University Press).

Marcus, J. 1998. *Women's Ritual in Formative Oaxaca: Figurine-making, divination, death and the ancestors*, Memoir 33 (Ann Arbor: Museum of Anthropology, University of Michigan).

—— and Flannery, K. V. 1994. 'Ancient Zapotec ritual and religion: An application of the direct historical approach' in C. Renfrew and E. B. W. Zubrow (eds), *The Ancient Mind* (Cambridge: Cambridge University Press), pp. 55–74.

—— 2005. 'The radiocarbon dating of public buildings and ritual features in the ancient valley of Oaxaca', Foundation for Ancient Mesoamerican Studies, <http://www.famsi.org/reports/03006/>.

Milbrath, S. 1999. *Star Gods of the Maya: Astronomy in Art Folklore, and Calendars* (Austin: University of Texas Press)

—— 2000. *Star Gods of the Maya* (Austin: University of Texas Press).

Mock, S. B. (ed.) 1998. *The Sowing and the Dawning: Termination, dedication, and transformation in the archaeological and ethnographic record of Mesoamerica* (Albuquerque: University of New Mexico Press).

Monaghan, J. D. 2000. 'Theology and history in the study of Mesoamerican religions' in J. Monaghan (ed.), *Supplement to the Handbook of middle American Indians*, VI: *Ethnology* (Austin: University of Texas Press), pp. 24–49.

Ortíz, P., and del Carmen Rodríguez, M., 1999. 'Olmec ritual behavior at El Manatí: A sacred space' in D. Grove and R. Joyce (eds), *Social patterns in Pre-Classic Meosamerica* (Washington, DC: Dumbarton Oaks), pp. 225–54.

Plunket, P. (ed.) 2002. *Domestic Ritual in Ancient Mesoamerica*, Monograph 46 (Los Angeles: Cotsen Institute of Archaeology, UCLA).

Pool, C. A. 2007. *Olmec Archaeology and Early Mesoamerica* (New York: Cambridge University Press).

Prufer, K. M., and Brady, J. E. (eds) 2005. *Stone Houses and Earth Lords: Maya religion in the cave context* (Boulder: University Press of Colorado).

Reilly, F. Kent, III. 1989. 'The shaman in transformation pose: A study of the theme of rulership in Olmec art', *Record of the Art Museum, Princeton University*, 48: 4–21.

Rice, P. M. 1999. 'Rethinking Classic lowland Maya pottery censers', *Ancient Mesoamerica*, 10: 25–50.

—— 2004. *Maya Political Science: Time, astronomy, and the cosmos* (Austin: University of Texas Press).

—— 2007. *Maya Calendar Origins* (Austin: University of Texas Press).

Sandstrom, A. R. and Sandstrom, P. E. 1986. *Traditional Papermaking and Paper Cult Figures of Mexico* (Norman: University of Oklahoma Press).

Scarborough, V. L. and Wilcox, D. R. (eds) 1991. *The Mesoamerican Ballgame* (Tucson: University of Arizona Press).

Schele, L. and Miller, M. E. 1986. *The Blood of Kings* (Fort Worth: Kimbell Art Museum).

Stone, A. 1992. 'From ritual in the landscape to capture in the urban center: The recreation of ritual environments in Mesoamerica', *Journal of Ritual Studies*, 6: 109–32.

—— 1995. *Images from the Underworld: Naj Tunich and the tradition of Maya cave painting* (Austin: University of Texas Press).

—— 2002. 'Spirals, ropes, and feathers: The iconography of rubber balls in Mesoamerican art', *Ancient Mesoamerica*, 13: 21–39.

STUART, D. 1998. '"The fire enters his house": Architecture and ritual in Classic Maya texts' in S. Houston (ed.), *Function and Meaning in Classic Maya Architecture* (Washington, DC: Dumbarton Oaks), pp. 373–425.

SUGIYAMA, S. 2005. *Human Sacrifice, Militarism, and Rulership: Materialization of state ideology at the feathered serpent pyramid* (Cambridge: Cambridge University Press).

TAUBE, K. 1992. *The Major Gods of Ancient Yucatan*, Studies of Pre-Columbian Art and Archaeology No. 32 (Washington, DC: Dumbarton Oaks Research Library and Collection).

VAIL, G. 2000. 'Prehispanic Maya religion: Conceptions of divinity in Postclassic Maya Codices', *Ancient Mesoamerica*, 11: 123–47.

CHAPTER 35

AZTECS

MICHAEL E. SMITH

1 INTRODUCTION

BEGINNING with the first steps of Hernando Cortés on the Mexican mainland in AD 1519, outsiders have been both fascinated and repelled by the religious practices of the Aztecs. Elaborate monthly pageants brought thousands of people to the streets chanting and dancing to throbbing drums amidst the dense aromatic smoke of incense. Many of these ceremonies culminated in dramatic theatrical re-enactments of myths in which human victims had their hearts cut out at the top of pyramids. Early European writers about Aztec culture, especially the Spanish mendicant friars, were obsessed with native religion, and the number of pages they devoted to the topic in their books dwarfed their sections on economic or political topics. Fascination and revulsion with Aztec human sacrifice and other rituals continues today in both the scholarly literature and popular media.

Despite an extensive and rich body of historical documentation, key questions about Aztec religion and ritual have proven difficult or impossible for historians to answer. Perhaps the most publicly prominent of these is the extent of human sacrifice. Recently some 'experts' have proclaimed on television that they have proof that literally tens of thousands of victims were sacrificed at a single Aztec ceremony, while other 'experts' claim that human sacrifice was a myth invented by the conquering Spaniards and that the Aztecs were instead peaceful crystal-gazers.

The results of archaeological excavations and the analysis of museum collections of ritual objects are only now starting to contribute to knowledge about Aztec ritual. There has been a dominant tradition of scholarship on Aztec religion that largely ignored archaeology and ancient objects. That tradition began in the eighteenth century and was extended and codified in the seminal works of Eduard Seler (1990–8) in the late nineteenth century. Although Seler himself was interested in the material remains of Aztec ceremonies (see Figures 35.3 and 35.4 below), his followers generally limited themselves to historical sources. The dominant approach to Aztec religion is an example of what Lars Fogelin (2007) calls a 'structural approach' in that it focuses on symbolism and structure, relying primarily on written sources. The material culture that abounds in the ritual and mythological scenes in the codices was interpreted in isolation from the objects known from excavations and museum collections.

The two types of documents with the greatest information on Aztec religion are the writings of the Spanish friars after the conquest of the Aztecs (e.g., Sahagún 1950–82) and native painted ritual books called codices (e.g., Anders et al. 1993). These documents contain colourful enigmatic images of gods, myths, and ceremonies, with ample use of the 260-day ritual calendar.

The biggest archaeological blow to the structural approach to Aztec religion came from the discovery and excavation of the central temple of the Aztec capital Tenochtitlan starting in 1978. Scholars had known for centuries just where this temple (the 'Templo Mayor') lay buried under the centre of Mexico City. The 1978 discovery of a large stone relief led to exploratory excavations revealing that the preservation of the temple was much greater than had been thought. The Mexican government invested enormous resources in clearing the remains of the temple and its surrounding area. These excavations, directed by Eduardo Matos Moctezuma, uncovered hundreds of rich offerings under and around the Templo Mayor (López Luján 2005) and revealed much new architectural information.

The richness of the archaeological finds at the Templo Mayor had numerous beneficial affects on scholarship on Aztec ritual and religion. First, non-archaeologists started to take archaeological finds seriously. Ethnohistorians and historians of religion began to incorporate the results of the project into their accounts of Aztec religion. Second, members of the Templo Mayor project pursued detailed studies of documentary sources to aid in their interpretations of the material remains. Third, the excitement and energy associated with the Templo Mayor project strongly affected the larger context of central Mexican archaeology and stimulated new fieldwork. Although much of the new research followed the traditional, structural approach, the new primacy of archaeology led to a move toward what Fogelin calls a 'practice approach'—a 'focus on the ways that material remains can inform on the actions and experiences of past ritual participants' (Fogelin 2007: 56).

One unfortunate effect of the Templo Mayor project was that many writers interpreted the results as if they formed the totality of material evidence for Aztec ritual and religion. This tendency was particularly prevalent among historians of religion working within a structural approach. It was assumed that the social and religious patterns identified for the imperial capital applied equally well to other Aztec cities. A re-examination of archaeological data from Aztec city-state capitals, however, shows that in fact Tenochtitlan was quite different and that religion and ritual at other Aztec cities need to be examined in their own light (Smith 2008). In the remainder of this chapter I review the material culture of Aztec ritual and religion under four headings: temples and offerings, key deities, cult objects, and ceremonies. Because there is a massive literature of primary and secondary historical sources on Aztec religion (e.g. Graulich 1997; López Austin 1997), I concentrate primarily on archaeological materials; apart from the Templo Mayor, these remain poorly known today. Unless specifically noted, discussion focuses on Aztec state religion. Rather than limit the term 'Aztec' to the inhabitants of the imperial capital, as many authors do, I use the term to refer to the several million people living in highland central Mexico at the time of the Spanish conquest (Smith 2003).

2 Temples, Shrines, and Offerings

Compared to other Mesoamerican cultures such as the Maya, Aztec temples were relatively standardized in type and form (Smith 2008). Most Mesoamerican temples consisted of tall

FIGURE 35.1 Pyramid-temple with human sacrifice, from Fray Bernardino de Sahagún.

platforms or pyramids topped by one or more cult rooms reached by a stairway running up one side of the pyramid. The most powerful Aztec capitals had distinctive twin-temple pyramids in which the two cult rooms were reached by separate parallel stairways; the Templo Mayor of Tenochtitlan was of this form. The standard Aztec temple was the single-temple pyramid. Aztec pyramids were the settings for rituals of human sacrifice (Figure 35.1). The use of stone altars placed at the top of the stairs (in front of the cult rooms) made the sacrifices visible to anyone watching from the plaza below.

Each Aztec city had one or more patron deities whose cults were centred on the city's main temple. The two shrines on the Templo Mayor of Tenochtitlan, for example, were dedicated to Huitzilopochtli and Tlaloc. Other cities had different patron deities, but in most cases we lack information on their identities. A third Aztec temple type was the circular pyramid. In contrast to the variable patron deities of central temples, nearly all circular temples were dedicated to Ehecatl, god of the wind. Stone sculptures of Ehecatl

FIGURE 35.2 Row of small platforms at Teopanzolco.

have been recovered as offerings in several excavated circular temples. The ball court, where a version of the Mesoamerican ball game was played, was another important type of religious building in most cities.

One of the most distinctive features of the built environment in Aztec cities was the small stone platform or shrine (Figure 35.2). Although nearly all Mesoamerican cities had such platforms, in Aztec times these features proliferated and became important elements of urban design for the first time. The uses of some of these structures can be reconstructed, but most remain enigmatic. A few were bases for skull racks that displayed the crania of sacrificial victims, and others contained offerings of severed skulls and other goods. One prominent type was decorated with reliefs of skulls and crossed bones (no relationship to the Jolly Roger of pirate flags!), and these were probably settings where female curers propitiated a class of deity known as the tzitzimime (see below). Although many authors have employed Western interpretations of the skull motif as a symbol of death and doom, contextual analysis shows that to the Aztecs these elements symbolized life, fertility, and regeneration.

Aztec burials are very poorly known because so few have been excavated. Commoner burials in residential settings show a variety of body positions and are sometimes accompanied by ceramic vessels and other goods. The remains of children probably sacrificed to the deity Tlaloc have been recovered near large temples in Tenochtitlan and Tlatelolco. Written sources describe cremation as one type of body treatment, but very few cremated remains have been excavated. It seems likely that the Aztecs used cemeteries that have yet to be located. Other forms of buried offerings are best known from the Templo Mayor of Tenochtitlan, where a wide variety of very rich offerings were placed in stone chambers below floors and stairways (López Luján 2005). These include coral, fish and crocodile skeletons, stone sculptures, precious jewellery, censers, textiles, and many other goods.

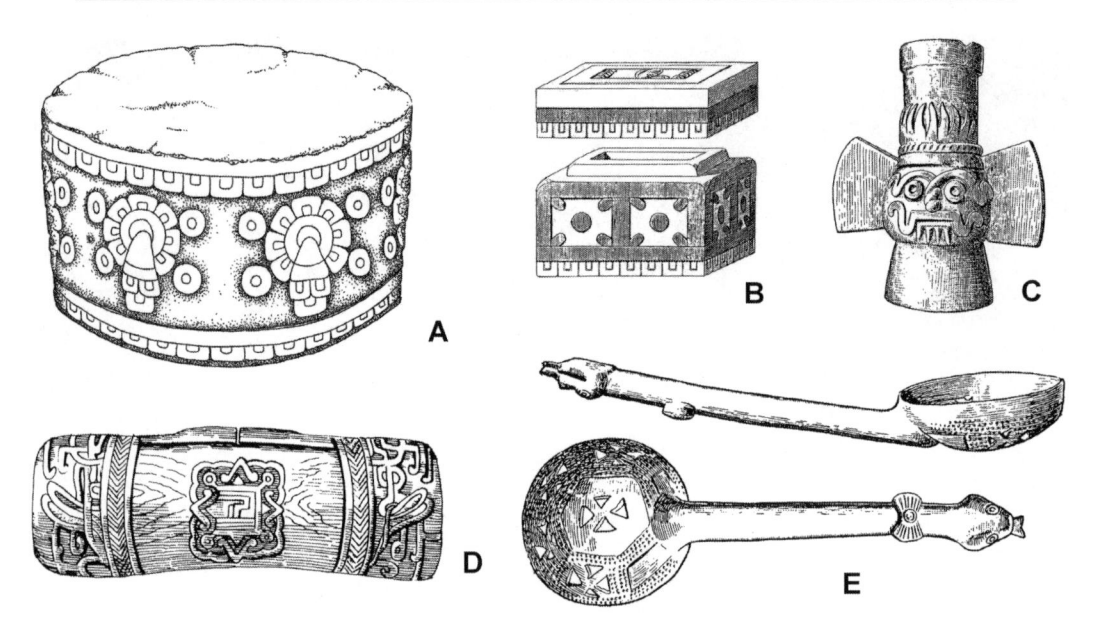

FIGURE 35.3 Large cult objects. A: sacrificial altar; B: stone box; C: ceramic brazier with Tlaloc effigy; D: wood slit-drum; E: ceramic censer. Object A is 71 cm across; the other objects are depicted with estimated relative sizes.

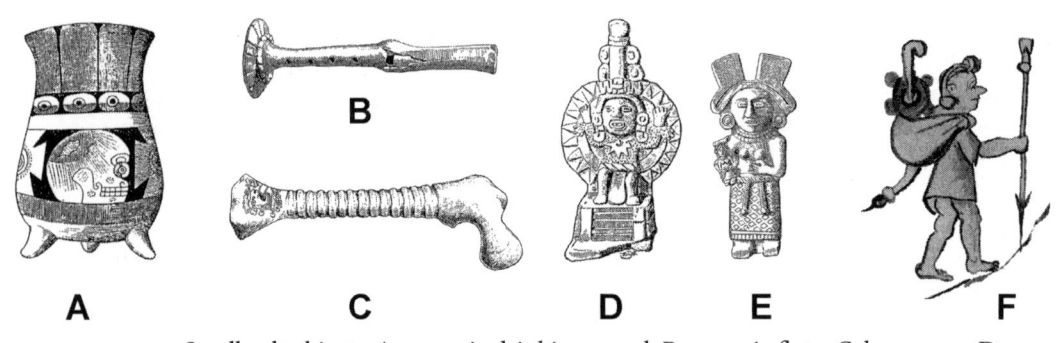

FIGURE 35.4 Small cult objects. A: ceramic drinking vessel; B: ceramic flute; C: bone rasp; D: ceramic figurine of Quetzalcoatl sitting on a temple; E: ceramic figurine of a woman with child; F: sacred bundle with smoking obsidian mirror from the Codex Azcatitlan. The height of object A is *c*.25 cm; the other objects are depicted with estimated relative sizes.

In the traditional, structural approach to Aztec religion, temples and shrines are interpreted almost exclusively for their symbolism and high-level meanings. This perspective was adopted by many scholars working on the Templo Mayor, for whom 'cosmovision' (religious cosmology) is a central concept (Carrasco 1999). Archaeologists, on the other hand, have tended to pursue a practice-based approach (Fogelin 2007) by emphasizing what Amos Rapoport (1990) calls the middle-level meanings of buildings and spaces. Aztec buildings and cities were carefully designed and built to communicate political messages about power, identity, memory, and status (Smith 2008), and the rituals that took place in and around these buildings were examples of what Kertzer (1988) calls political rituals (Brumfiel 2001). The static cosmovision concept of the structural approach ignores the social class divisions that were prominent in Aztec society and religion.

3 Cult Objects

Aztec religious ceremonies and activities employed a wide variety of cult objects. Within the traditional approach to Aztec religion, the cult objects depicted in the codices were analysed with little concern for their materiality; that is, they were rarely compared to actual objects from excavations or in museum collections. Instead, research focused on their indigenous names and symbolic associations. Recent work that has begun to address the materiality of these objects includes Berdan (2007) and Durand-Forest and Eisinger (1998). Figures 35.3 and 35.4 depict some of the major cult items. To emphasize the importance of museum collections, I use many of Seler's illustrations of artefacts in major European museums; most of these were initially published over 100 years ago.

3.1 Sculptures and Stone Objects

Stone sculpture, perhaps the major genre of Aztec art, has been studied from numerous perspectives. Although many or most anthropomorphic images probably represented deities or priests impersonating deities, the ways in which these objects were used in ceremonies remains poorly understood, in part because so few have been encountered in context. The uses of sacrificial altars, on the other hand, are much clearer. The example shown in Figure 35.3A was excavated at the base of a large circular temple at Calixtlahuaca and shows the potential of archaeological finds to provide information not present in the standard historical sources. Such sources are silent on the practice of human sacrifice at the circular temples of Ehecatl, whereas this altar points strongly to its occurrence. Smaller stone objects such as bowls and boxes with lids (Figure 35.3B) were used to hold the blood and hearts of sacrificial victims.

3.2 Braziers and Censers

Fire was an important part of Aztec ritual at many levels, from large state temples to the domestic hearth. Fires were kept burning in large ornate ceramic braziers at the major temples, and these iconographically complex and aesthetically pleasing objects have received considerable attention in exhibits of Aztec art. Smaller ceramic braziers, often with deity images (Figure 35.3C) are less well known but were probably more widespread in Aztec times. Various substances were added to the fire to produce smoke and aroma; these included rubber and the aromatic gum of the copal tree. Smaller censers were used in ceremonies in a variety of settings, from temples to homes. The most common form had a bowl with cut-out triangles at the end of a long, hollow handle with a modelled serpent heat at the opposite end (Figure 35.3E).

3.3 Complex Painted Ceramic Vessels

The finest Aztec ceramic ware consisted of serving vessels and deity effigy forms painted with bright colours on a white background (Figure 35.4A). These were made in a number of cities, of which Cholula was the best known. One Spanish conqueror wrote that the Mexica emperor Motecuhzoma insisted that his meals be served in Cholula polychrome vessels. By comparing the design fields and motifs on these vessels with the ritual codices scholars have identified some of the social and ceremonial contexts in which the vessels were used (Hernández Sánchez 2005; Pohl 2007). Although it is sometimes assumed that such vessels were used only by elites or in ceremonies, excavations of Aztec commoner houses typically uncover sherds from these objects. They were probably used in feasts to celebrate special occasions.

3.4 Musical Instruments

Music was an important part of Aztec ritual (Both 2002, 2005). The most common musical instrument was the ceramic flute (Figure 35.4B). Experimental analysis shows that these could play a number of scales and were not limited to a pentatonic scale as some authors have suggested. Many ceremonies involved flute music. In a major sacrifice to the god Tezcatlipoca, flutes were broken on the temple steps after they had been played (Figure 35.1). Numerous whole flutes have been recovered in offerings in Tenochtitlan, and broken fragments are not uncommon in domestic contexts. Two types of Aztec wood drum survive. Large upright hollow drums with skin heads provided loud music at public ceremonies, and smaller horizontal slit drums (Figure 35.3D) were probably used in a variety of contexts. Bone rasps were made by cutting shallow parallel grooves in human long bones (Figure 35.4C); these were used in various death-related ceremonies (Pereira 2005). Other musical instruments included conch shell trumpets, whistles, and various types of rattles.

3.5 Small Ceramic Figurines

Small fired clay models of people, gods, animals, plants, and temples were used in domestic ceremonies. Many whole figurines without context survive in museum collections, and excavations in residential contexts always recover numerous fragments. Most figurines were anthropomorphic in form. Costume elements show that some clearly depict deities (Figure 35.4D), whereas others show women and men without any obvious religious symbolism (Figure 35.4E). Some authors assume that all figurines must represent deities, leading to fruitless arguments about the correct classification of figurines that have no deity symbolism. A more likely explanation is that these were simply representations of people (Smith 2002) used in rites of curing and divination.

3.6 Special Items

Many other kinds of ceremonial objects are depicted in the ritual codices, but only a few have been identified in museum or fieldwork collections. Sacred bundles were of great importance, but little is known about their contents (Olivier 2006). Some apparently included obsidian mirrors (Figure 35.4F), a major item in the cult of the deity Tezcatlipoca. Mirrors were associated with smoke, and priests and diviners were thought to foresee the future by looking into the mirrors. Two forms of obsidian mirrors are found in museum collections today. Circular mirrors are common in the codices and probably served as Aztec cult items, whereas rectangular mirrors were not depicted before the Spanish conquest and may have been a Spanish colonial innovation.

4 THE ARCHAEOLOGY OF DEITIES

The Aztec conception of deity was complex and remains poorly understood. Although the Spanish friars wrote thousands of pages about Aztec gods, myths, and ceremonies, they obtained this information from laymen after the Spanish conquest; no Aztec priest ever explained religious concepts to a Western observer. Although the sources refer to literally hundreds of deities with individual names and attributes, scholars agree that most of these were avatars or transformations of one another. Deities were not anthropomorphic. They were viewed as supernatural spirits or forces that took material form when adorned with key elements of their costume. In this section I summarize information about the material culture associations of some of the key deities, particularly their temples and cult objects. Traditional structuralist scholarship has focused overwhelmingly on the symbolism and mythological roles of Aztec deities, and there is still much to learn about their cults and ceremonies from surviving material objects and depictions in codices.

4.1 Tezcatlipoca

Tezcatlipoca, patron of kings, was a powerful creator god. Dark and mysterious, he represents the closest thing to a 'high god' in Aztec religion. Tezcatlipoca has been studied more intensively than most Aztec deities, and as a result we have a much better understanding of his cult and its manifestations (Olivier 2003; Smith in preparation). The smoking mirror is the most important emblem and cult object of Tezcatlipoca; indeed his name means 'smoking mirror'. Unfortunately none of the obsidian mirrors in museum collections has a secure provenience. Ceramic flutes were another component of this cult. During the major annual Tezcatlipoca festival (called Toxcatl) priests and god impersonators paraded around the streets of the city playing the flute, and these were then broken on the pyramid steps during the sacrifice that concluded the festival (Figure 35.1). Archaeologists have yet to identify a temple dedicated to Tezcatlipoca, although many of the small platforms that filled the plazas of Aztec cities (Figure 35.2) were probably dedicated to this god.

4.2 Quetzalcoatl and Ehecatl

Quetzalcoatl, the 'feathered serpent', had a long history before Aztec times. His cult spread throughout Mesoamerica after the fall of Teotihuacan and this god's support became an important component of the legitimacy of kings. Quetzalcoatl helped create the world and people, and as the patron god of priests and learning he appears often in the ritual codices. One of Quetzalcoatl's avatars, Ehecatl, attained importance as the god of wind. This god preferred circular temples, reportedly because the lack of corners helped the flow of the wind. Quetzalcoatl and Ehecatl are among the major themes of Aztec stone sculpture, and small cult paraphernalia of the feathered serpent have been recovered in offerings at the Templo Mayor. These deities are also well represented in small ceramic figurines (Figure 35.4D).

4.3 Tlaloc

Tlaloc was an ancient central Mexican god of rain and fertility whose ancestral forms were prominent long before the Aztec period. Of the two gods worshipped at the Templo Mayor, the vast majority of the offerings were dedicated to Tlaloc and fertility. A wide variety of ceramic effigies of Tlaloc are known, including braziers both large and small (Figure 35.3C), crude offering vessels, and—in Templo Mayor offerings—some of the most finely made Aztec ceramic objects. In spite of Tlaloc's role in agricultural fertility, however, he is poorly represented among figurines and other objects of domestic ritual.

4.4 Huitzilopochtli

As the patron god of the Mexica people, Huitzilopochtli's image and bundle were carried on their migration to central Mexico. As the Mexica gained ascendancy in the Triple Alliance Empire, their scribes and priests burned the books of past peoples and promoted their patron god as an important and ancient creator god. One aspect of this process was the dedication of one of the two shrines on the Templo Mayor to Huitzilopochtli. Nevertheless, this deity is remarkable for his small number of images, offerings, and identifiable cult items.

4.5 Tzitzimime

The tzitzimime were female fertility deities invoked by curers, midwives, and other female religious practitioners. The skull and bones emblem was associated with the tzitzimime, and small altars decorated with this motif (see above) probably played a role in ceremonies that invoked these deities. The biases of the written record hamper our understanding of the tzitzimime more than other deities. The Spanish friars did not understand Aztec women and feared their ritual activities and powers. In their written accounts of Aztec religion, the friars transformed the tzitzimime deities from benevolent fertility deities to threatening and malevolent demons and causers of harm (Klein 2000). The proliferation of small platforms in public settings at Aztec cities (Figure 35.2) could represent an expansion of the public ceremonial role for midwives and curers during Aztec times (Smith 2008).

5 The Archaeology of Key Ceremonies

Public ceremonies are one of the best-known aspects of Aztec religion. Some of these elaborate celebrations were witnessed by Spanish conquerors, and they were strongly inscribed in the memories of the colonial Aztecs interviewed by the Spanish friars. One reason for the emphasis on ceremonies in both popular and scholarly writings is that many of them involved human sacrifice. These ceremonies have been extensively studied by scholars (e.g., Couch 1985; Graulich 1999), but their materiality remains understudied. In this section I first discuss the material manifestations of human sacrifice and then review some of the key Aztec ceremonies.

5.1 Human Sacrifice

Spanish descriptions of Aztec society contain extensive discussions of human sacrifice, and the practice is well represented in the codices. The Spanish sources, however, are heavily biased. The need to put an end to this custom was one of the prime rationalizations for the conquest of the Aztecs, and for this reason the Spanish writers almost certainly overstated the extent of sacrifice. This has led some modern authors to claim that the Spaniards invented the notion to make the Aztecs look bad, and that the Aztecs did not in fact practise sacrifice. Archaeological finds, however, demonstrate beyond a doubt that the Aztecs, like most ancient Mesoamerican cultures, did indeed sacrifice people. This practice was ancient and widespread in central Mexico. Unfortunately the archaeological evidence cannot yet reveal the frequency or intensity of Aztec human sacrifice. The notion that thousands of victims were dispatched at individual ceremonies, popularized by television documentaries and films like *Apocalypto*, is probably incorrect.

Rites of human sacrifice were part of a complex tapestry of myths and beliefs that have been extensively analysed and debated by specialists (Carrasco 1999; Graulich 1999). Key concepts include the sacredness of human blood, the idea that people owe a debt to the gods that must be repaid with blood and human lives, and the notion of a close relationship between life and death. In the process of creating the world and the first humans, some gods had been sacrificed and others undertook auto-sacrifice, the ceremonial letting of their blood (Klein 1987). If humans did not repay this debt with blood, the consequences would be dire.

Archaeological excavations have documented human sacrifice in central Mexico at least as early as the great Classic period (AD 100–600) metropolis Teotihuacan (Sugiyama 2004). In the Aztec period sacrificial offerings have been excavated at the Templo Mayor and other sites in the Basin of Mexico as well as in the nearby imperial provinces to the south and east of the Basin. The most direct evidence is osteological: offerings of decapitated crania with associated cervical vertebrae, crania with lateral perforations for hanging on skull racks, and cut marks on bones (Chávez Balderas 2007; Hernández Pons and Navarrete 1997; Pijoan and Mansilla Lory 1997; Pijoan et al. 1989). Some of the paraphernalia of sacrifice, including flint sacrificial knives and stone bowls and boxes for guarding blood and hearts (Figure 35.3B), have been excavated in offerings at the Templo Mayor of Tenochtitlan; these items are also found among the unprovenenced objects in many museum collections of Aztec materials. A number of sacrificial altars (Figure 35.3A) are known (Graulich 1998). These archaeological remains provide unambiguous evidence for Aztec human sacrifice, although we cannot yet judge the intensity of the practice from its material remains.

5.2 The Monthly ('Veintena') Ceremonies

The Aztec year was divided into 18 months of 20 days, and each month saw the performance of an elaborate ceremony; scholars call these the *veintena* ceremonies. The ceremonies lasted for several days and involved a series of actions: public rites in the centres of cities, processions through cities and the countryside, and offerings within people's houses. All sectors of society participated, usually in groups organized by residence, gender, occupation, or social class. Activities during the ceremony included music, dance, oration, feasting, offerings, and human sacrifice. Two lengthy descriptions of the veintena ceremonies survive (Durán 1971; Sahagún 1950–82), and these include paintings of the major events. A brief consideration of the activities carried out in the central plaza of a city during the ceremony of Tlacaxipeualiztli gives an idea of the material manifestations of the veintena ceremonies.

The central event of the Tlacaxipeualiztli festival, the culmination of several days of festivities, was the sacrifice of a victim to the god Xipe Totec ('Our lord with the flayed skin') on top of the main temple of the city. Afterwards the victim's body was flayed. At another point in the festival a gladiator sacrifice was carried out. In this rite the victim (a captured enemy warrior) was tied to a large circular stone altar and given mock weapons to battle experienced warriors with real weapons. Eventually the victim was overcome and killed, thereby ending the sacrifice. Upcoming victims lined up next to the skull rack. Priests paraded around the city centre playing conch-shell trumpets and ceramic flutes, while groups of nobles and commoners danced together with rattles. Most research on these ceremonies has emphasized their symbolism and meaning, but more recently scholars have expanded their perspectives to consider how the participants interacted with the built environment of the city centre (Smith 2008) and how the various ritual objects were used (Berdan 2007; Both 2002).

5.3 The New Fire Ceremony

The New Fire ceremony was celebrated every 52 years upon the completion of a major calendrical cycle. Aztec mythology predicted the destruction of the world at the end of a 52-year cycle, but left it unclear just which cycle was implicated. At the end of a cycle all fires were put out and people discarded their household goods. When it was clear that a new day was dawning (with a reprieve of 52 more years) a victim was sacrificed in the New Fire temple, a new fire was started, and from it fire was carried to all corners of the empire to celebrate the occasion. The New Fire temple (called Huixachtecatl), located at the top of a mountain near Tenochtitlan, has been excavated (Montero García 2002), but it has proven difficult to relate the findings to specific actions described in the documentary sources. On the other hand, ritual dumps at several sites can be associated with accounts of the discard of domestic objects every 52 years (Elson and Smith 2001).

Other important public ceremonies included the ball game and a series of state ceremonies focusing on the rites of life history and political history of rulers (Brumfiel 2001; Matos Moctezuma 1995).

5.4 Domestic Ritual

Spanish written sources have almost no information about Aztec domestic ritual. Most domestic ceremonies were performed by women, but the Spanish friars avoided speaking to native women and did not enter their houses (Burkhart 1997). All excavations of Aztec houses have uncovered broken fragments of ceramic figurines (Figures 35.4D and 35.4E) and censers of one form or another (e.g. Figure 35.3E). These two types of artefact point to distinct but overlapping domains of domestic religious practice (Smith 2002). The first domain includes objects and practices that replicate those of Aztec state religion. For example, the fragments of long-handled censers found in houses match precisely the whole censers recovered from offerings (Figure 35.3E) and depicted in the hands of priests in the codices. This correspondence suggests continuities between state and domestic rites.

The second domain of domestic ritual, focused on the use of ceramic figurines, was a women's world that only overlapped slightly with the state religion. Archaeological context and scattered historical references indicate that figurines were used by women for curing and divination. Figurines are rarely found in burials or offerings at temples, yet they are ubiquitous in domestic middens. Other cult objects recovered in household excavations include fragments of musical instruments and quartz crystals.

6 Conclusions and Future Directions

It is unlikely that Aztec archaeology will ever see another project as rich and influential as the Templo Mayor project. Nevertheless, archaeology has a key role to play as research on Aztec ritual and religion moves beyond the symbolic or structural interpretations (Fogelin 2007) of the dominant tradition of scholarship. In line with the more practice-oriented research of most archaeologists today, the next major advance will probably come from a more complete recognition of the materiality of Aztec ritual practice, and the analysis of that materiality in social terms. At the most basic level scholars need to match up four types of data: descriptions of ritual by the Spanish friars and others; depictions of gods and rituals in the codices; excavated finds from many different sites (not just the Templo Mayor); and the vast collections of unprovenanced Aztec objects that lie gathering dust in museums. Scholars have already made important starts in this area. Jacqueline de Durand-Forest and colleagues have begun a programme of systematic analysis of the material culture of the codices (Durand-Forest and Eisinger 1998; Durand-Forest et al. 2000), and other scholars have begun to bring together the textual data, codices, and archaeological finds (e.g. Berdan 2007; Klein 2000; López Luján 2005; Marcus 2007; Olivier 2003; Smith in preparation). Within this interdisciplinary approach to Aztec ritual and religion, archaeologists are increasingly playing the lead role, because of both their focus on material culture and materialization, and their role in uncovering new objects and contexts that extend knowledge beyond the relatively fixed corpus of written sources.

There are hundreds of thousands of Aztec objects curated in museum storerooms in Mexico, Europe, and the United States. Published catalogues exist for only a handful of these collections, and many museums simply have no idea of the content or extent of their Aztec collections. Yet this material can play several crucial roles in advancing scholarship on Aztec ritual and religion. These objects can be matched up with the written and pictorial sources as discussed above, and they help archaeologists interpret their fragmentary finds from excavations (Smith 2004).

A related theme in research on materiality is the spatial expression of Aztec rituals. An important volume edited by Davíd Carrasco (1991) initiated this line of analysis, and it continues with scholarship on the relationship between urban ceremonies and the built environment (Smith 2008) and studies of native maps (Boone 2000). As scholars begin to comprehend the places where rituals and processions took place, what buildings and open spaces were nearby, and what material objects were used, they will achieve a much richer understanding of Aztec ritual and religion.

Suggested Reading

The best overall descriptions of Aztec religion are the accounts of the Spanish friars, particularly the *Florentine Codex* of Fray Bernardino de Sahagún (1950–82) and Fray Diego de Durán's (1971) very readable account. Historians who have contributed most heavily to the secondary literature include David Carrasco (1991, 1999), Michel Graulich (1997, 1999), and Alfredo López Austin (1997). Most publications on the Templo Mayor are either technical reports or art books; the most useful scholarly synthesis are those of Eduardo Matos Moctezuma (1995) and Leonardo López Luján (2005, 2006).

References

ANDERS, F., JANSEN, M., and GARCÍA, L. R. 1993. *Códice Borgia: los templos del cielo y de la oscuridad: oráculos y liturgia*, Códices Mexicanos, V (Madrid, Graz, and Mexico City: Sociedad Estatal Quinto Centenario, Akademische Druck- und Verlagsanstalt, and Fondo de Cultura Económica).

BERDAN, F. F. 2007. 'Material Dimensions of Aztec Religion and Ritual' in E. Christian Wells and Karla L. Davis-Salazar (eds), *Mesoamerican Ritual Economy: Archaeological and ethnological perspectives* (Boulder: University Press of Colorado), pp. 245–300.

BOONE, E. H. 2000. *Stories in Red and Black: Pictorial histories of the Aztecs and Mixtecs* (Austin: University of Texas Press).

BOTH, A. A. 2002. 'Aztec flower flutes: The symbolic organization of sound in Late Postclassic Mesoamerica', *Orient-Archäologie*, 10: 279–89.

——2005. 'Music: Music and religion in Mesoamerica' in L. Jones (ed.), *Encyclopedia of Religion*, 2nd edn, IX (Detroit: Thomson-Gale), pp. 6266–71.

BRUMFIEL, E. M. 2001.'Aztec hearts and minds: Religion and the state in the Aztec Empire' in S. Alcock, T. N. D'Altroy, K. D. Morrison, et al. (eds), *Empires: Perspectives from archaeology and history* (New York: Cambridge University Press), pp. 283–310.

BURKHART, L. M. 1997. 'Mexica women on the home Front: Housework and religion in Aztec Mexico' in S. Schroeder, S. Wood, and R. Haskett (eds), *Indian Women of Early Mexico* (Norman: University of Oklahoma Press), pp. 25–54.

CARRASCO, D. (ed.) 1991. *To Change Place: Aztec ceremonial landscapes* (Boulder: University Press of Colorado).

——1999. *City of Sacrifice: The Aztec Empire and the role of violence in civilization* (Boston: Beacon Press).

CHÁVEZ BALDERAS, X. 2007. *Human Sacrifice and Mortuary Treatments in the Great Temple of Tenochtitlán*, Report to the Foundation for the Advancement of Mesoamerican Studies, Inc., <http://www.famsi.org/reports/05054/>

COUCH, N. C. C. 1985. *The Festival Cycle of the Aztec Codex Borbonicus*, BAR, International Series No. 270 (Oxford: BAR).

DURÁN, FRAY DIEGO. 1971. *Book of the Gods and Rites and the Ancient Calendar*, trans. Fernando Horcasitas and Doris Heyden (Norman: University of Oklahoma Press).

DURAND-FOREST, J. DE and EISINGER, M. (eds) 1998. *The Symbolism in the Plastic and Pictorial Representations of Ancient Mexico: A Symposium of the 46th International*

Congress of Americanists, Amsterdam 1988, Bonner Amerikanistische Studien XXI (Bonn: Holos).

DURAND-FOREST, J. DE, ROUSSEAU, E., CUCUEL, M., et al. 2000. *Los elementos anexos del Códice Borbónico*, trans. Edgar Samuel Morales Sales (Toluca: Universidad Autónoma del Estado de México).

ELSON, C. M., and SMITH, M. E. 2001. 'Archaeological deposits from the Aztec New Fire ceremony', *Ancient Mesoamerica*, 12: 157–74.

FOGELIN, L. 2007. 'The Archaeology of religious ritual', *Annual Review of Anthropology*, 36: 55–71.

GRAULICH, M. 1997. *Myths of Ancient Mexico*, trans. Bernard R. Ortiz de Montellano and Thelma Ortiz de Montellano (Norman: University of Oklahoma Press).

——1998. 'Sacrificial stones of the Aztecs' in J. de Durand-Forest and M. Eisinger (eds), *The Symbolism in the Plastic and Pictorial Representations of Ancient Mexico*, BAS, XXI (Bonn Bonner: Amerikanistische Studien), pp. 185–201.

——1999. *Fiestas de los pueblos indígenas: ritos aztecas, las fiestas de las veintanas* (Mexico City: Instituto Nacional Indígenista).

HERNÁNDEZ PONS, E. and NAVARRETE, C. 1997. 'Decapitación y desmembramiento en una ofrenda mexica del centro ceremonial de México-Tenochtitlan' in E. Hernández Pons (ed.), *La Antigua Casa del Marqués del Apartado: arqueología e historia* (Mexico City: Instituto Nacional de Antropología e Historia), pp. 73–107.

HERNÁNDEZ SÁNCHEZ, G. 2005. *Vasijas para ceremonia: iconografía de la cerámica tipo códice del estilo Mixteca-Puebla*, CNWS Publications (Leiden: Research School of Asian, African, and Amerindian Studies, Universiteit Leiden).

KERTZER, D. I. 1988. *Ritual, Politics, and Power* (New Haven: Yale University Press).

KLEIN, C. F. 1987. 'The Ideology of Autosacrifice at the Templo Mayor' in E. H. Boone (ed.), *The Aztec Tempo Mayor* (Washington, DC: Dumbarton Oaks), pp. 293–370.

——2000. 'The devil and the skirt: An iconographic inquiry into the pre-Hispanic nature of the tzitzimime', *Ancient Mesoamerica*, 11: 1–26.

KOLLMANN, J. 1895. 'Flöten und Pfeifen aus Alt-Mexiko in der ethnographischen Sammlung der Universität Basel' in *Mitteilungen aus der ethnographischen Sammlung der Universität Basel, I. Band, 2. Heft* (Basel/Leipzig: Carl Sallmann), pp. 45–81.

LÓPEZ AUSTIN, A. 1997. *Tamoanchan, Tlalocan: Places of mist*, trans. Bernard R. Ortiz de Montellano and Thelma Ortiz de Montellano (Boulder, CO: University Press of Colorado).

LÓPEZ LUJÁN, L. 2005. *The Offerings of the Templo Mayor of Tenochtitlan*, rev. edn, trans. Bernard R. Ortiz de Montellano and Thelma Ortiz de Montellano (Albuquerque University of New Mexico Press).

——2006. *La Casa de las Águilas: un ejemplo de arquitectura religiosa de Tenochtitlan* (Mexico City: Fonda de Cultura Económica, Conaculta, and Instituto Nacional de Antropología e Historia).

MARCUS, J. 2007. 'Rethinking ritual' in E. Kyriakidis (ed.), *The Archaeology of Ritual* (Los Angeles: Cotsen Institute of Archaeology), pp. 43–76.

MATOS MOCTEZUMA, E. 1995. *Life and Death in the Templo Mayor*, trans. Bernard R. Ortiz de Montellano and Thelma Ortiz de Montellano (Boulder: University Press of Colorado).

MONTERO GARCÍA, I. A. (ed.) 2002. *Huizachtepetl: geografía sagrada de Iztapalapa* (Mexico City: Delegación Iztapalapa).

NOGUERA, E. 1958. *Tallas prehispánicas en madera* (Mexico City: Editorial Guaranía).

OLIVIER, G. 2003. *Mockeries and Metamorphoses of an Aztec God: Tezcatlipoca, 'Lord of the Smoking Mirror'*, trans. Michel Bisson (Boulder: University Press of Colorado).

—— 2006. 'The sacred bundles and the coronation of the Aztec king in Mexico-Tenochtitlan' in J. Guernsey and K. F. Reilly, III (eds), *Sacred Bundles: Ritual acts of wrapping and binding in Mesoamerica*, Ancient America Special Publication, I (Barnardsville, North Carolina: Boundary End Archaeology Research Center), pp. 199–225.

PEREIRA, G. 2005. 'The utilization of grooved human bones: A reanalysis of artificially modified human bones excavated by Carl Lunholtz at Zacapu, Michoacán, Mexico', *Latin American Antiquity*, 16: 293–312.

PIJOAN, C. M. and LORY, J. M. 1997. 'Evidence for human sacrifice, bone modification and cannibalism in ancient Mexico' in D. L. Martin and D. W. Frayer (eds), *Troubled Times: Violence and warfare in the past* (Amsterdam: Gordon and Breach), pp. 217–40.

——, PASTRANA, A., and MAQUIVAR, C. 1989. 'El tzompantli de Tlatelolco: una evidencia de sacrificio humano' in C. Serrano and M. Salas (eds), *Estudios de antropología biológica* (Mexico City: Universidad Nacional Autónoma de México), pp. 561–83.

POHL, J. M. D. 2007. *Sorcerers of the Fifth Heaven: Nahua Art and Ritual of Ancient Southern Mexico*, PLAS Cuadernos, IX (Princeton, NJ: Princeton University Program in Latin American Studies).

RAPOPORT, A. 1990. *The Meaning of the Built Environment: A nonverbal communication approach*, rev. edn (Tucson: University of Arizona Press).

SAHAGÚN, FRAY BERNARDINO DE 1950–82. *Florentine Codex: General History of the Things of New Spain, 12 books*, trans. and ed. A. J. O. Anderson and C. E. Dibble (Santa Fe and Salt Lake City: School of American Research and the University of Utah Press).

SELER, E. 1990–8. *Collected Works in Mesoamerican Linguistics and Archaeology*, 6 vols., ed. Frank E. Comparato (Culver City, CA: Labyrinthos).

SMITH, M. E. 2002. 'Domestic ritual at Aztec provincial sites in Morelos' in P. Plunket (ed.), *Domestic Ritual in Ancient Mesoamerica*, Monograph, XLVI (Los Angeles: Cotsen Institute of Archaeology, UCLA), pp. 93–114.

—— 2003. *The Aztecs*, 2nd edn (Oxford: Blackwell Publishers).

—— 2004. 'Aztec materials in museum collections: Some frustrations of a field archaeologist', *Nahua Newsletter*, 38: 21–8.

—— 2008. *Aztec City-State Capitals* (Gainesville: University Press of Florida).

—— in preparation.'The archaeology of Tezcatlipoca' in E. Baquedano (ed.), *Tezcatlipoca: Trickster and supreme deity*.

SUGIYAMA, S. 2004. *Human Sacrifice, Militarism, and Rulership: The symbolism of the feathered serpent pyramid at Teotihuacan, Mexico* (New York: Cambridge University Press).

CHAPTER 36

INCA

KEVIN LANE

1 INTRODUCTION

> ... by animism I do not mean the theory of the soul in nature, but the tendency or impulse or instinct, in which all myth originates, to *animate* all things; the projection of ourselves into nature; the sense and apprehension of an intelligence like our own but more powerful in all visible things.
>
> (Hudson 1918 [1982]: 162)

> The animated world of the Andes evokes a vaster horizon than its occidental equivalent, each thing that possesses a function or a finality is animated so as to permit this function or finality: fields, mountains, rocks as well as people.
>
> [*El mundo animado de los Andes evoca un horizonte mucho más vasto que su equivalente occidental, cada cosa que posee una función o una finalidad es animada para permitir que se realice su función o su finalidad: las chacras, los cerros, las piedras así como los hombres.*]
>
> (Taylor 2000: 7, my translation)

> ... under the generic term *huaca*, Andean people meant the force that 'animated' what usually was inanimate; and this 'animation' manifested itself, firstly, through the ability to 'speak', to communicate with people.
>
> [... *con el término genérico huaca, los andinos indicaban la fuerza que animaba lo que comúnmente está inanimado; y esta animación se manifestaba, en primer lugar, a través de la facultad de hablar, de comunicarse con los hombres.*]
>
> (Curatola Petrocchi 2008: 17, my translation)

THIS chapter sets out to introduce and explain three underlying concepts underpinning Inca and Andean religion: animism (and anthropomorphism), oracular divination, and ancestor worship. Seeking to demonstrate how these worked within the evolution of Andean and, ultimately, Inca religion. Emerging from coeval highland religious traditions during the early Inca period, Inca religion was changing during the fifteenth century as a consequence of the experience of empire. The idea for this transformation of Inca religion was probably the effects of exposure to new ideas, from such well-organized cults as that of Pachacamac-Vichma and those of the Chimu Kingdom, along the central and northern coast respectively. This was manifested through the attempt by the Inca state to create a pan-Andean cult exalting the Sapa Inca (unique Inca) and the concomitant pantheon centred on the different aspects of the Viracocha deity—the Sun (Inti), Thunder (Inti-Illapa), and the Day (Punchao).

A series of specific problems arises in any consideration of a past culture's religion. This is especially so in the case of the Andes where no writing exists from the indigenous perspective at the moment of contact; *quipus*, a mnemonic 'writing' device on knotted strings, was unsuitable for long narratives (Urton 2003). The ethnohistoric accounts of Andean folklore, apart from some notable exceptions (de la Vega 1979 [1616]; see Guaman Poma de Ayala 1993 [1615]; Santa Cruz Pachacuti Yamqui 1927 [1613]; Yupanqui 2006 [1565–70]), have been written by Spaniards usually on official engagements, such as tribute or tabulation *visitas* or for the eradication of 'heathen' practices known as *Extirpacíon de Idolatrías* (Pillsbury 2008). Even the native writers of mixed birth or *mestizos* were born shortly before or just after the Spanish conquest and as such were already somewhat removed from the events and rituals that they describe. Garcilaso de la Vega (1539–1616), for instance, was writing at the end of his life, having left the Andes almost 50 years previously; he also wrote a highly partisan account. This bias arose from the fact that these learned *mestizo* chroniclers usually belonged to one or other of the Inca elite families known as *panacas*, thus embellishing the accounts of their particular forefathers.

The Spanish accounts, such as that of Juan de Betanzos (1996 [1557]), Sarmiento de Gamboa (1999 [1572]), Cieza de León (1995 [1554], 1996 [1554]) and Cobo (1979 [1653], 1990 [1653]) suffer from the prejudices and biases inherent in early colonial narratives. Many of these early authors did not know or understand what it was that they were describing, others pandered to a certain viewpoint or perspective. Sarmiento de Gamboa, for instance, was assigned by the authorities to investigate and discredit Inca claims to long-term suzerainty of large swathes of the Andean region. Nevertheless for all its problems the early documentary sources remains a crucial tool for disentangling the intricate web of native beliefs.

This is particularly true of the set of documents produced as a consequence of the *Extirpacíon de Idolatrías*. Known as the bastard child of the Spanish Inquisition (Duviols 2003: 48), the *Extirpacíon de Idolatrías* collected and collated native accounts of ritual practices and religion. In sum, all these accounts—indigenous, Creole, and Spanish—represent invaluable insights for understanding indigenous concepts of religion in the Andes. The work done by eminent ethnohistorians such as Maria Rostworowski de Diez Canseco, Gerald Taylor, Peter Gose, Pierre Duviols, and especially Tom Zuidema in this matter serves to show the importance of this source material in elucidating past Andean belief systems. Valuable as the work of these scholars has been, a major omission has been the lack of engagement with anthropological theory to elucidate the nature of Andean and Inca religion, especially the role of animism and anthropomorphism.

2 ANIMISM AND ANTHROPOMORPHISM

Pre-Hispanic Andean religion has been described as animistic in essence; but what in effect does this mean? Originally, animism was thought to represent the 'primitive' belief system common to 'primitive' tribal societies (Evans-Pritchard 1965; Tylor 1958 [1871]). Recent anthropological studies have revisited this theme contesting Tylor's 'primitive' label. Stringer (1999), for example, states that Taylor's use of phrases such as 'primitive', 'savage', or 'children' can only be understood under the epistemological concepts of the late nineteenth century.

Following from this, the scope of animism has been revised. No longer is animism understood to be a religion; indeed Tylor (1958 [1871]) himself acknowledged that animism is more a philosophy than a religion per se. Insoll (2004) makes the pertinent point that animism should be viewed as an element within a belief system and not necessarily as a whole religion. The approach here concurs with this observation noting that although largely animistic, Andean, and especially Inca religion cannot be viewed simply in these reductionist terms. Inca religion comprised animism embedded within a religion that also included a highly developed ancestor cult and oracular dimension.

Yet what is animism? Bird-David (1999: S79) notes that far from being a 'failed epistemology' or 'simple religion', animism represents the interaction or relatedness between people and animals or environments emphasizing the theme of nested relatedness within these relationships. This final point is crucial to any definition of animism. As she states, against '"I think therefore I am" stand "I relate, therefore I am" and "know as I relate"' (Bird-David 1999: S78). This definition highlights the concept of 'personhood' and belonging which is engendered through the animation and veneration of a given landscape. In animist traditions the 'gods', spirits, or manifestations inhabit and are represented actively in the world around them, opposing the separation that exists between the physical and the metaphysical in many Western religions.

Bird-David's linking of animism with anthropomorphism simplifies a more complex relationship. Stewart Guthrie (2001: 157) aptly describes the differences between these two terms, noting that:

> Animism ... is best defined as attributing characteristics of living things (e.g. sentience and spontaneous motion) to inanimate things and events, whereas anthropomorphism is best defined as attributing characteristics of humanity (e.g. language and symbolism) to non-human things and events, including other animals.

Guthrie (1993, 2001) therefore argues for a separation of the terms such that animals cannot be animistic being already animate; but they can nevertheless by anthropomorphized. This goes against the all-encompassing animist precepts espoused by Stringer (1999) and Hornborg (2006). Yet diminishing the scope of animism, such that anthropomorphism lies outside its definitional remit, supports the concept expressed by Insoll (2004) that animism is but one element within a religious belief structure. Nevertheless, it should be said that it is possible to both animate and anthropomorphize objects, a subject which we will return to when examining Andean and Inca religion.

In support of Bird-David, Ingold (2006) claims that animism in essence, is a means of *being* in the world, similar to the *relationality* expressed by Hornborg (2006). What is meant by this is that humans partake and relate in a world where all manner of objects and events are imbued with the logic of life, such that at its most extreme there is no division between subjects and objects, a veritable holistic living-in-the-world. Supporting this view, Bruno Latour (1993) argues that even in our modern, supposedly rigidly Cartesian, world we have not been able to shake this perennial animism, a fact noted by Gell (1998) in his theory on the agency of objects. In fact, Latour (1993) argues that in the modern world we seek to understand everything around us through the creation and maintenance of hybrids or quasi-objects that marry society, science, and nature in a new form of 'scientific' animism.

Somewhat cynically perhaps (and contra Boyer 1996), Guthrie (1993) suggests that animism and anthropomorphism are in effect a form of 'insurance policy'. Believing that something is alive or human-like can save you from unintended consequences; such as being eaten alive when the object you thought was a log turns out to be a crocodile. Essentially, underlying all these definitional variations is the constant that animism is always present, continuously alive, in movement (actual or perceived) and necessarily immediate, 'forever on the verge of the actual' (Ingold 2006: 12), and crucially that humans are an integral part of this process. It is this ascription of animism that is particularly important to the Andes.

3 HUACAS AND ORACLES

In the animistic Andes effectively the whole world was alive and intimately interrelated. Nevertheless, within this viewpoint there were aspects of the world which were more 'alive' than others. Central to this 'alive-ness' was the concept of *camac* (Taylor 2000; see also de Avila, 1999 [1598?]). As stated by Taylor (2000), the root of the word *camac* means 'to animate'. If the Andean environment was filled with *camac*, it was the *huacas* that best expressed this vitality through the act of 'talking'—oracular divination—through selected intermediaries (the *camasca*). The more powerful the *huaca*, concomitantly the more *camac* it had (Curatola Petrocchi 2008; Gose 1996).

This perception of life extended to the recently dead as well as to the living. Life and death in the Andes was a complex issue that comprised a series of stages between actual life and death (Salomon 1995). In death there was the possibility of the person becoming a good, locale-based *camaquen* ancestor or a bad, wandering shadow *upani* spirit that drifted aimlessly. It was the *camaquen* ancestor that became in turn revered and oracular—a *huaca* (Gose 1992).

It is through the concept of the *huaca* that Andean animism and anthropomorphism really comes through. Features in the landscape and ultimately the totality of the physical environment were represented by *huacas*. *Huaca* is a complex term that denotes a spirit or deity revealed as an object, feature, or happening such as mummy bundles, trees, and naturally occurring free-standing rocks or outcrops, as well as mountains, hills, rivers, springs, and literally all manner of physical manifestations, including rain, hail, lightning, thunder, and wind. Veneration of all of these deities and spirits was widespread and conducted in sanctuaries, temples, mortuary monuments, and natural locations such as lakes, spring heads, and caves. All these loci were also generically known as *huacas*. Effigy- or idol-objectified depictions of *huacas* were also common, but especially so when the physical manifestation of the spirit or deity was impossible, such as in the case of thunder for instance. The term *huaca* was also used for these representations. These idols came in many shapes and sizes, from carved stone, wood, dough, ashes, or precious mineral effigies through to common rocks and stones.

Nevertheless, at the root of the *huaca* concept was animation, its *camac*, reflected in communication: in essence the *huacas*' ability to impart wisdom and oracular divination. The relationship between people and *huacas* (and by implication the environment) was complex and in constant flux. Interaction with these physical manifestations of Andean, and Inca, animism had to be constantly negotiated through libation, consultation, worship, or even violence rendering some into kin and others into enemies (D'Altroy 2002). The centrality of *huacas* and oracular predestination within Andean society has been highlighted by MacCormack (1991) and Rostworowski (1988, 2002), and it has prompted Curatola Petrocchi (2008) to claim that Andean oracles can only be fully understood as a 'total social fact' (from Mauss 1990).

The power of a *huaca* derived from oracular predestination, its strength from the veracity of their divinations. Therefore a *huaca*'s power could wax and wane depending on their ability. Conquered people's *huacas* became subservient to the main *huaca* of the conqueror, so much so that the Incas held provincial oracles or *huacas* as hostages back in Cuzco. This allowed for the realignment of these *huacas* within the Cuzquenian ideology as well as subordinating these *huacas* under the central Inca cult. When these *huacas* were eventually returned to their places of origin they helped perpetuate the ascendency of the imperial cult. Another particularly powerful expression of *huaca* subjugation can be seen in the Capacocha ceremonies where children from the provinces were sacrificed to the Inca. These children were selected and came with their *huacas* to Cuzco where they were killed as a ritual of affirmation to Inca power. This ritual was also a forum whereby provincial *huacas* could negotiate with the principal Inca *huacas* residing in Cuzco (Schroedl 2008).

In the political sphere Andean oracles have been described as 'a form of political ventriloquism' (Gose 1996: 14). Indeed in the Andes, *huacas* functioned as a source of wisdom and information, without necessarily setting a moral standard, as well as serving as oracular entities. Generally, *huaca* oracles were a means by which rulers, in a segmentarily organized society, could listen to factional interests spoken through the medium of a founding ancestral hero or deity without the problem of a living rival (Gose 1996). This was especially important under the Incas given the multi-ethnic, and therefore multi-oracular, nature of their possessions (Ramírez 2008).

Finally, some *huacas* could disappear entirely; there is evidence to suggest that the eleventh Inca, Huayna Capac (AD 1493–1527), rationalized the system of *huacas* by declaring war against them and actually ridding the Inca Empire of a large number of them (Ramírez 2008). The Inca Atahualpa (AD 1532–3) destroyed the central Andean *huaca* oracle of Catequil because it had predicted that his brother Huascar would win the civil war that raged between them (MacCormack 1991). Similarly, Atahualpa destroyed Topa Inca's body (the tenth Inca, AD 1471–93, itself a *huaca* oracle), his attendant, and his descendants because of this *huaca*'s support for Huascar (Sarmiento de Gamboa 1999 [1572]).

4 GODS AND ANCESTORS

It is known that Inca cosmology shared many commonalities with that of other Andean ethnic groups, for besides a special cult to the Sun known as Inti, Inca religion was similar to other contemporary highland religions (Demarest 1981; McDowell 1992; Zuidema 2002).

This Andean pantheon included a certain number of 'gods', spiritual or natural entities and regional and local, real and fictitious, ancestor heroes also sometimes known as *mallquis*, founders of a lineage that were often hailed as conquerors (Rostworowski 1988). Generally it has been acknowledged that at the root of this religion lie ancestors, especially dead ones which nevertheless lived in the animated landscape of the Andes (Gose 1996; Salomon 1995). Although true, this is only a partial explanation of the complexity of Andean religion, not all deities were ancestors, although they were all oracular.

Death and ancestor worship is a constant theme throughout Andean religion and it is a complex issue especially regarding its role vis-à-vis ancestors and deities. As mentioned above, death in the Andes was not so much a finite episode but rather a transformational process or renewal and rebirth intimately tied to the Andean concept of the *pacarina* (Albornoz 1967 [1569]; Gose 1992). A *pacarina* is described as 'the destination of the deceased, also described . . . [as] a community's place of origin' (MacCormack 1991: 428); it defined the community it represented. *Pacarinas* were places of worship centred around veneration of ancestors and as such doubled as the origin point of communities or lineages. It was deities and *huacas* in their role as ancestors that were intimately linked with these community birthplaces.

A hierarchy of *pacarinas* existed from the local to the pan-regional through ancestors and perceived ties of kinship upwards towards the main ancestor of a particular group. Linking the various *pacarinas* was water, imaginary subterranean streams and rivers that returned the dead spirit to the source and back again in a ritual of re-affirmation of group identity and solidarity with the central or primary ancestor. New *pacarinas* could be established by a group taking part of the soil or water from a given *pacarina* to a new site, a concept similar to the idea of shrine-franchising developed by Insoll (2006). Death was the process by which humans became mummies and in certain cases acquired 'alive-ness' or *camac*, the first step in the process to becoming a bona fide ancestor hero or *mallqui* (see Salomon 1995 for a detailed description of the stages of death and return in the Andes).

Ancestors were not the only type of deified entity in existence in the Andes; aligned alongside proximate ancestors were also the original distant ancestor or creator-god. For instance, amongst the people of the Huamachuco region, one encounters the creator-god Ataguju and the primal ancestor Catequil; co-joined to Catequil is his companion aspect Piguerao, and Catequil's wife Mama Catequil (MacCormack 1991; Topic et al. 2002). This central Andean cosmological division presages many common themes in Andean religion, and indeed society. This is the idea of internal separation into unequal reciprocal divisions; in this case Catequil had a homologous counterpart in Piguerao but some deities were represented by two, three, or more aspects; Pariacaca, another central Andean deity had five aspects: Pariacaca, Churapa, Puncho, Pariacarco, and Sullca Illapa identified as his brothers (Astuhuamán 2008).

In the case of the Inca, these creator and ancestor deities were represented by Viracocha as the creator-god and Inti, the Sun, as the primary ancestor of the Inca royal lineage. Inti-Illapa, the Thunder God, was Inti's brother aspect as was Punchao, the Day; and Mama Quilla, the Moon, was Inti's wife (Demarest 1981). All four came together as part of a quadarchic cosmological organization and were worshipped jointly in the Coricancha, as well as individually. Nevertheless, Viracocha had less of a formalized, more distant, worship. The distance of creator-gods has been underlined by Sabine MacCormack (1991: 147): 'Andean ancestor gods, [were] a more distant presence', hence they were removed from the exigencies of daily cult and affairs, as these concerns were satisfied by ancestors and other local *huacas*.

Given the latent animism and anthropomorphism underlying ancestor worship in Andean religion it is hardly surprising that the relationship between deities tended to imitate life. The organization of the Andean supernatural confirmed many common social and cultural themes that existed in Andean society such that 'principal Andean *huacas* had kinship ties similar to those of the human inhabitants' (Rostworowski 1998: 346). This was shown in the often tortured relationships that existed between Andean deities, their concubines, wives, brothers, and sons. These were reflected in relationships where they lived, fought, died, resurrected, and procreated. A fine example of what Stewart Guthrie (1993: 3) has elegantly expressed in his statement 'man makes god in his own image'.

Within the cosmological hierarchy it was ancestor heroes or *mallquis*, referred to by the Spaniards as minor gods, that formed the most immediate type of deity with the most profuse number of *huacas* ascribed to these entities. Shared lineage and corporate identity was an important component of ancestral heroes and *mallquis*. A *mallqui* has been described as:

> ancestor mummies that belong to an *ayllu* [community], and sometimes to various groups unified by some type of reciprocity or kinship bonds.
>
> [*antepasados momificados pertenecientes a un ayllu, y a veces a varios grupos unidos por algún tipo de reciprocidad o de lazos de parentesco.*] (Rostworowski 1988: 14, my translation)

Alternatively, ancestor heroes are described as people who at some time either enacted large scale construction work, such as terracing and irrigation systems, or conquered new lands (Gose 1992: 488–9). In essence they are sometimes very similar; both were invoked as the heads of communities (*ayllu*) and both were venerated. The main distinction between the two was predominately one of hierarchical positioning within the cosmological order.

Ancestor heroes were normally mythical and had many of the characteristics associated with the larger creator-gods, or *huacas*, described in the deity section above. In a similar fashion to the major deities they were also responsible for the creation of people, albeit at a much more local scale. The pattern of veneration was also conducted in an almost identical form, through idol worship, sanctuaries, and sacred loci in the landscape. Again as between *mallqui* and ancestor heroes, the difference between ancestor heroes and major deities seems to have been one of scale. Ancestor heroes were located in small communities, forming the basis of belonging for groups of local *ayllu*. *Mallquis* were essentially dead founder ancestors; in this fashion they provided a much closer connection between the living community, the lived-in landscape and the past. *Mallquis* were usually thought to be direct descendants of deities or *huacas* (Salomon 1995). Not all dead people in a community became *mallquis* although other members of the lineage were added once deceased, providing a link between 'the recent dead and the heroic dead' (Salomon 1995: 322). As with *huacas*, a hierarchy of *mallquis* or lineages existed below the local minor deity or *huaca*.

An adjunct to the whole pantheon of deities were female entities; female deities had a more amorphous quality within Andean mythology. It is important to emphasize two in particular, the Pachamama (Earth Mother) and the Mamacocha (Mother Water), although others exist, including Mama Quilla (the Moon), K'uychi (the Rainbow), celestial constellations, and dark patches between these (see Urton [1981] for further examples). Apart from Mama Quilla, none of these important female entities seems to have been venerated directly in purpose-built shrines, although it is possible that small oratories existed.

Mama Quilla may have been venerated in Copacabana on the shores of Lake Titicaca (Rostworowski 1998). Garcilaso de la Vega (1979 [1616]: 116–17) recounts that Mama Quilla was also venerated in the Coricancha, the Inca Sun temple in Cuzco, in a separate room as the Sun's sister-bride. This concept of the female being venerated through, or in, the same place as the male might have pervaded much of Andean cosmology. Thus it is likely that the Pachamama, sometimes referred to as the wife of Pachacamac, the powerful *huaca* of the central Andean coast, was venerated to some extent within the large religious precinct of the site of Pachacamac. Female deities appear more often than not as mothers, wives, consorts, and sisters to male deities (Hernández Astete 2002; Rostworowski 1988). Nevertheless, veneration of the Pachamama was practised throughout the Andes (MacCormack 1991: 192).

If female deities have been given short shrift in the literature it is possible that this was as a consequence of both male bias on the part of the original Spanish chroniclers and because they predominantly occupied the lower moiety within Andean cosmological divisions (Hernández Astete 2002). Another common theme of many of these female deities is that they are often depicted as being manifest in important economic plants: Mama Sara was materialized in maize, Mama Acxo in potatoes and Mama Coca in coca, for instance (Rostworowski 1988: 72–3). It is possible, then, that female deities were of a slightly different type, less violent perhaps, more universal and more nurturing (Millones 1980). Their economic prowess, on the one hand, added to their geographical universality on the other, and probably occasioned a heightened level of offering and libations to these deities relative to their more geographically localized male counterparts.

5 Understanding Inca Religion

Along the path to empire the Incas claimed both the Pacific and Titicaca Lake as their maximal *Pacarinas*, linking their ancestors and creator-god Viracocha-Inti to them. This policy, akin to myth appropriation, had the dual purpose of restating Inca pre-eminence amongst other cultural groups, as direct descendants of the two largest most prestigious of *pacarinas*, whilst also subsuming all local *pacarinas* and, by association, all deities and *huacas* under the mantle of the Inca Sun cult (Demarest 1981; Sherbondy 1992). Likewise, the *ceque* system of radial lines linking shrines, *huacas*, and landscape to individual Inca lineages, was itself being exported to the empire. These probably usurped pre-existing pilgrimage routes that linked people and the living landscape, especially in the southern Andes (Zuidema 2002). The placement of an Inca Sun temple within the precincts of the powerful coastal oracle temple of Pachacamac also indicated the ascendency of the Inca Sun cult and Pachacamac-Vichma's relative abasement to Viracocha-Inti (Eeckhout 2004; Uhle 1903).

Yet, how different were the Inca in comparison to other cultures? The founding myths of Pariacaca (de Avila 1999 [1598?]; Salomon and Urioste 1991) and Pachacamac (Rostworowski 1992) also catalogue the defeat of earlier people and deities akin to that encountered by the Inca creator-god Viracocha in his defeat of the Chanka and their idols. Similarly, there is evidence to suggest that the Capacocha ceremony was not an innovation, having existed previously amongst the cultures of the north-central highlands (Zuidema 1989). The underlying indication seems to be that the Inca were not so much innovators, as collators of pre-existing *huacas*, rites, and rituals brought under their control and the cosmological suzerainty of Incan Viracocha-Inti deity.

Given the complexity of the various spirits, deities, and manifestations how then did the Andean religious system function? Essentially, *mallquis* formed the lowest echelon in the representational 'ladder' of veneration, followed in the cosmological order by the local *huaca*, through to major *huacas*. The relationship between the major *huacas* and the minor ones was usually one of parentage and kin association between the parent *huaca* and lesser deities. This had important repercussions for corporate cultural identity and was emphasized by the *mallquis* of *ayllus* that shared kinship ties at the *huaca* level being interpreted as brothers of each other (Salomon 1995).

Yet, all these divisions—deities, natural manifestations, and ancestral heroes—were not fixed. Many of these beings enjoyed a complex multilayering of complementary and contradictory identities in much the same way that communities and people did. A *mallqui* could be at the same time an ancestral hero and thus a local *huaca*, but it could also serve as an important oracle transcending the purely local. Catequil, in the northern highlands, was first and foremost the creator-god and common ancestor hero of the local people in his area in Huamachuco. But Catequil was also at the core of a larger regional cult centred in Cerro Icchal that established 'client' or franchise oratories across the land (Topic et al. 2002). This pattern correlates well with what we know of other major *huacas*: Pachacamac was venerated throughout the central coast and part of the highlands (Rostworowski 1992, 1998), Pariacaca enjoyed a similar status amongst the inhabitants of the central highlands (Astuhuamán 2005; de Avila 1999 [1598?]; Duviols 1997) and the Incan Viracocha in the southern cordillera (Demarest 1981).

As all of these entities, be they *mallquis* or *huacas*, were oracular, essentially their social status and power could be circumscribed according to how well they performed this and other duties, such as fertility, community protection, and conquest. Veneration of *huacas* and *mallquis* was constant and sometimes conducted at specific locations whilst at other times they were invoked in non-specific situations such as when a new field was placed under cultivation or a new house was built. This cosmological fluidity is important as it helps to trace the ways characteristically similar *huacas* could sometimes predominate over their immediate peers. Therefore, although the broad similarities between many of the larger *huacas* must have aided in the religious and physical assimilation of regional *huacas* that accompanied the expansion of the Inca Empire (Conrad and Demarest 1984), the Inca victory must in itself have cast doubt on the veracity and omnipotence of these regional *huacas* in the eyes of the populace. A similar crisis of cosmological confidence occurred with the coming of the Spaniards, as *huaca* predictions of imminent Spanish defeat proved singularly unfounded (MacCormack 1991).

Other than in the case of major oracles, such as Viracocha, Apurimác, and Pachacamac who had formalized temples, lands, and a hierarchically arranged organization of prelates, it is likely that for lesser-ranked and more local *huacas* there was no such formalized standing number of *huaca* retainers. Duviols (2003) has shown, in his compendium of idolatry persecutions in Cajatambo and Recuay from the seventeenth century, how the rank of priest, at the community level, was chosen from among the constituent communities.

Similarly, with land given over to the *huacas*, there seems to have been a more formalized division amongst the greater deities in the form of parcels which were worked by special retainers or communities for the purposes of feeding the major *huacas* and their attendants. This parcelling of land to deities saw its maximum expression under the Incas with the division of land to important *huacas* as well as to the different royal Inca *panacas* or lineages (Conrad and Demarest 1984; D'Altroy 2002; Rostworowski 1999); considering that the Incas portrayed themselves as deities in their own right this is not a surprising development. At the localized level the difficulty that the Spanish colonial authorities had in disentangling community from *huaca* lands (Aibar Ozejo 1968–9; Varón Gabai 1980) reflects much less clear-cut distinctions between these two (three if you include those of the Inca) types of land status. Probably most of the land and goods given over to the *huacas* were selected in a more informal manner; as and when local ritual practice necessitated them, rather than specifically allocated as part of an Inca state agenda, or as a specified donation to the major *huacas* (Gose 1992: 486). A strict division between lay and religious property did not exist in the Andean world, as it did in that of late medieval Spain (MacCormack 1991).

6 Conclusion

> There is no doubt that the Incas tied the origin of their own state and power to a direct relationship, of an oral order, between their ancestors and the *huacas* and to a whole series of other facts which were patently oracular.
>
> [... no cabe duda que los Incas hacían remontar el origen mismo de su Estado y de su poderío a una relación directa, de orden oral, entre sus ancestros y las huacas y a toda una serie de otros hechos patentemente oraculares.]
>
> (Curatola Petrocchi 2008: 19; my translation)

Inca and Andean religion then was essentially an ancestor focused animism projected through oracular divination, the roots of which were firmly within the *longue durée* of Andean religious tradition. As such this religion represented the totality of the landscape and environment as the stage, props, and cue to a veritable *dramatis personae* of manifestations, happenings, spirits, ancestors, and deities to which people related, combined, and interacted.

In this sense Inca religion was not particularly different to its contemporaries. In fact, evidence points to Inca religion, like the state, being probably in flux during the early sixteenth century. Given the short duration of the Inca Empire it is likely that imperial institutions had yet to crystallize and cohere into a more durable and rigid form (D'Altroy 2002). Inca religion therefore was still at a pre-state of development. This can be appreciated in the problems that Huascar, the twelfth Inca (AD 1527–32) had in curtailing the power of the *panacas* (households, lineages) of the 11 dead Incas that existed by the time of his reign. Some of these *panacas*, such as that of the ninth Inca, Pachacuti (AD 1438–71), owned vast amounts of property, were extremely powerful, and had a propensity to sometimes oppose the dictates of the ruling Sapa Inca (Conrad and Demarest 1984). The *panacas* were a throwback to the segmentary form of leadership that existed amongst many of the Late Intermediate period (AD 1000–1480) polities of the Andean highlands. In opposing them Huascar was going against a system that curtailed effective state and religious centralization.

Similarly, the Andes at this time enjoyed a plethora of local shrines and concomitant *huacas* that were but very loosely tied to the Inca central religion. This is amply demonstrated by the ease with which local groups abandoned the central Sun cult of the Incas (MacCormack 1991). The reason for this is not that it was an alien concept or cult as has been claimed (D'Altroy 2002); many of the essential components of the Viracocha-Inti cult were present in other great Andean creator-god cults, such as that of Pachacamac-Vichma and Ataguju-Catequil of the central coast and highlands respectively. Rather, the problem resides in the fact that the Incas just did not have enough time to consolidate their Sun cult at the apex of a cosmological hierarchy that included all these numerous local and regional cults. In the end, like the social, cultural, and economic ties that welded the empire together, their foundations proved to be too shallow to survive the coming Spanish onslaught.

Suggested Reading

On the Incas themselves the long article by Rowe (1946) still remains a classic, succinctly distilling a large amount of ethnohistoric information; for more recent compilations consult Rostworowski (1999), Zuidema (2005), and the outstanding Pärssinen (2003). An excellent general book that marries archaeological and ethnoarchaeological perspectives can be found in D'Altroy (2002). A closer perspective on the development of Cuzco and the rise of the Incas can be found in Bauer (2004), whilst Zuidema (1964) and Bauer (1998) set out to describe the complexities of the *ceque* system of ritual pilgrimage across the landscape; Duviols (1976) presents an important short introduction to the Capacocha ritual. Finally, Ogburn (2004) and Morris (1998) tackle the manner in which the Incas exported and imposed their religious and political authority.

References

Aibar Ozejo, E. 1968–9. 'La visita de Guaraz en 1558', *Cuadernos del Seminario de Historia*, 9: 5–21.

Albornoz, C. de 1967 [1569]. 'Instrucción para Descubrir todas las Guacas del Piru y sus Camayos y Haziendas', *Journal de la Société des Américanistes*, LVI(1): 8–39.

Astuhuamán, C. 2005. 'Los Otros Pariacaca; Oráculos, Montañas y Parentelas Sagradas' in M. Curatola (ed.), *Oráculos del Mundo Andino: 51° Congreso Internacional de Americanistas* (Lima: PUCP).

——2008. 'Los Otros Pariacaca; Oráculos, Montañas y Parentelas Sagradas' in M. Curatola Petrocchi and M. S. Ziółkowski (eds), *Adivinacion y oraculos en el mundo andino antiguo* (Lima: PUCP/IFEA).

Avila, F. de 1999 [1598?]. *Ritos y Tradiciones de Huarochirí*, 2nd edn (Lima: IFEA, Banco Central de Reserva Del Peru, Universidad Particular Ricardo Palma).

Bauer, B. S. 1998. *The Sacred Landscape of the Inca: The Cusco Ceque system* (Austin: University of Texas Press).

——2004. *Ancient Cuzco: The heartland of the Inca* (Austin: University of Texas Press).

BETANZOS, J. DE 1996 [1557]. *Narrative of the Incas* (Austin: University of Texas Press).
BIRD-DAVID, N. 1999. '"Animism" Revisited: Personhood, Environment, and Relational Epistemology', *Current Anthropology*, 40: S67–S91.
BOYER, P. 1996. 'What makes anthropomorphism natural: Intuitive ontology and cultural representations', *Journal of the Royal Anthropological Institute*, 2(1): 83–97.
CIEZA DE LEÓN, P. DE 1995 [1554]. *Crónica del Peru: Primera Parte* (Lima: Pontificia Universidad Católica del Peru/Academia Nacional de la Historia).
——1996 [1554]. *Crónica del Peru: Segunda Parte*, 3rd edn (Lima: Pontificia Universidad Católica del Peru/Academia Nacional de la Historia).
COBO, B. 1979 [1653]. *History of the Inca Empire* (Austin: University of Texas Press).
——1990 [1653]. *Inca Religion and Customs* (Austin: University of Texas Press).
CONRAD, G. W. and DEMAREST, A. A. 1984. *Religion and Empire: The dynamics of Aztec and Inca expansionism* (Cambridge: Cambridge University Press).
CURATOLA PETROCCHI, M. 2008. 'La función de los oráculos en el Imperio inca' in M. Curatola Petrocchi and M. S. Ziółkowski (eds), *Adivinacion y oraculos en el mundo andino antiguo* (Lima: PUCP/IFEA).
D'ALTROY, T. N. 2002. *The Incas* (Oxford: Blackwell).
DEMAREST, A. 1981. *Viracocha: The nature and antiquity of the Andean High God* (Cambridge, Massachussetts: Peabody Museum Press).
DUVIOLS, P. 1976. 'La capacocha: mecanismo y función del sacrifico humano, su proyección, su papel en la política integracionista y en la economía redistributiva del Tiwantinsuyu', *Allpanchis Phuturinqa*, 9: 11–57.
——1997. '¿Dónde estaba el santuario de Pariacaca?' in R. Varón Gabai (ed.), *Arqueología, Antropología e Historia en los Andes: Homenaje a María Rostworowski* (Lima: IEP).
——2003. *Procesos y Visitas de Idolatrías: Cajatambo, siglo XVII* (Lima: IFEA/PUCP).
EECKHOUT, P. (ed.) 2004. *Arqueología de la Costa Central del Perú en los Periodos Tardíos* (Lima: IFEA).
EVANS-PRITCHARD, E. E. 1965. *Theories of Primitive Religion* (Oxford: Clarendon Press).
GELL, A. 1998. *Art and Agency: An anthropological theory* (Oxford: Oxford University Press).
GOSE, P. 1992. 'Segmentary state formation and the ritual control of water under the Incas', *Comparative Studies in Society and History*, 35(3): 480–514.
——1996. 'Oracles, divine kingship and political representation', *Ethnohistory*, 43(1): 1–32.
GUAMAN POMA DE AYALA, F. 1993 [1615]. *Nueva Crónica y Buen Gobierno* (Lima: Fondo de Cultura Economica).
GUTHRIE, S. E. 1993. *Faces in the Clouds: A new theory of religion* (Oxford: Oxford University Press).
——2001. 'Rethinking animism', *The Journal of the Royal Anthropological Institute*, 7(1): 156–7.
HERNÁNDEZ ASTETE, F. 2002. *La Mujer en el Tahuantinsuyo* (Lima: PUCP).
HORNBORG, A. 2006. 'Animism, fetishism, and objectivism as strategies for knowing (or not knowing) the world', *Ethnos*, 71(1): 21–32.
HUDSON, W. H. 1918 [1982]. *Far Away & Long Ago: A childhood in Argentina* (London: Eland).
INGOLD, T. 2006. 'Rethinking the animate, re-animating thought', *Ethnos*, 71(1): 9–20.
INSOLL, T. 2004. *Archaeology, Ritual, Religion* (London and New York: Routledge).
——2006. 'Shrine franchising and the Neolithic in the British Isles: Some observations based upon the Tallensi, Northern Ghana', *Cambridge Archaeological Journal*, 16(2): 223–38.
LATOUR, B. 1993. *We Have Never Been Modern* (Cambridge, MA: Harvard University Press).

MacCormack, S. 1991. *Religion in the Andes: Vision and imagination in early colonial Peru* (New Jersey: Princeton University Press).

McDowell, J. H. 1992. 'Exemplary ancestors and pernicious spirits' in R. V. H. Dover, K. E. Seibold, and J. H. McDowell (eds), *Andean Cosmologies through Time: Persistence and emergence* (Bloomington: Indiana University Press).

Mauss, M. 1990. *The Gift: The form and reason for exchange in archaic societies* (London: Routledge).

Millones, L. 1980. 'La Religión Indígena en la Colonia' in Fernando Silva Santisteban (ed.), *Historia del Peru* (Lima: J. Mejía Baca).

Morris, C. 1998. 'Inka strategies of incorporation and governance' in G. M. Feinman and J. Marcus (eds), *Archaic States* (Santa Fe, New Mexico: School of American Research Press).

Ogburn, D. 2004. 'Dynamic display, propaganda, and the reinforcement of provincial power in the Inca empire', *Archaeological Papers of the American Anthropological Association*, 14(1): 225–39.

Pärssinen, M. 2003. *Tawantinsuyu: El estado Inca y su organización política* (Lima: IFEA/ Fondo Editorial de la Pontificia Universidad Católica del Perú/Embajada de Finlandia).

Pillsbury, J. (ed.) 2008. *Guide to Documentary Sources for Andean Studies, 1530–1900*, I–III (Norman: National Gallery of Art/University of Oklahoma).

Ramírez, S. E. 2008. 'Negociando el imperio: el estado inca como culto' in C. Caillavet and S. E. Ramírez (eds), *Bulletin de l'Institut Français d'Etudes Andines: Dinámicas del poder: historia y actualidad de la autoridad andina* (Lima: IFEA).

Rostworowski, M. 1988. *Estructuras Andinas del Poder: Ideología Religiosa y Politica* (Lima: IEP).

—— 1992. *Pachacámac y el Señor de los Milagros. Una trayectoria milenaria* (Lima: IEP).

—— 1998. 'Pachacamac and El Señor de los Milagros' in E. Hill Boone and T. Cummins (eds), *Native Traditions in the Postconquest World: A symposium at Dumbarton Oaks, 2nd through 4th October 1992* (Washington, DC: Dumbarton Oaks Research Library and Collection).

—— 1999. *History of the Inca Realm* (Cambridge: Cambridge University Press).

—— 2002. *Pachacamac* (Lima: IEP).

Rowe, J. H. 1946. 'Inca culture at the time of the Spanish conquest' in J. H. Steward (ed.), *Handbook of South American Indians*, Bureau of American Ethnography, Bulletin No. 143 (Washington, DC: Smithsonian Institution).

Salomon, F. 1995. '"The beautiful grandparents": Andean ancestor shrines and mortuary ritual as seen through colonial records' in T. D. Dillehay (ed.), *Tombs for the Living: Andean mortuary practices: A symposium at Dumbarton Oaks 12th and 13th October 1991* (Washington, DC: Dumbarton Oaks Research Library and Collection).

—— and Urioste, G. L. 1991. *The Huarochirí Manuscript: A testament of ancient and colonial Andean religion* (Austin: University of Texas Press).

Santa Cruz Pachacuti Yamqui, J. 1927 [1613]. 'Relación de Antiguedades deste Reyno del Piru' in F. de Santillán (ed.), *Historia de los Incas y Relación de su Gobierno por Juan Santa Cruz Pachacuti y el Lic* (Lima: Imprenta y Librería Sanmarti y Ca).

Sarmiento de Gamboa, P. 1999 [1572]. *History of the Incas*, Dover edition of the Hakluyt Society (1907) publication of *History of the Incas* by Pedro Sarmiento de Gamboa and *The Execution of the Inca Tupac Amaru* by Captain Baltasar de Ocampo (London: Dover Publications).

Schroedl, A. 2008. 'La Capacocha como ritual político. Negociaciones en torno al poder entre Cuzco y los curacas' in C. Caillavet and S. E. Ramírez (eds), *Bulletin de l'Institut*

Français d'Etudes Andines: Dinámicas del poder: historia y actualidad de la autoridad andina (Lima: IFEA).

SHERBONDY, J. E. 1992. 'Water ideology in Inca ethnogenesis' in R. V. H. Dover, K. E. Seibold, and J. H. McDowell (eds), *Andean Cosmologies through Time: Persistence and emergence* (Bloomington: Indiana University Press).

STRINGER, M. D. 1999. 'Rethinking animism: Thoughts from the infancy of our discipline', *The Journal of the Royal Anthropological Institute*, 5(4): 541–55.

TAYLOR, G. 2000. 'Camac, Camay y Camasca en el manuscrito quechua de Huarochirí' in G. Taylor (ed.), *Camac, Camay y Camasca* (Lima: IFEA/CBC).

TOPIC, J., LANGE TOPIC, T., and MELLY, A. 2002. 'Catequil: The archaeology, ethnohistory and ethnography of a major provincial Huaca' in W. H. Isbell and H. Silverman (eds), *Andean Archaeology*, I: *Variations in Sociopolitical Organization* (New York: Kluwer Press/Plenum Publishers).

TYLOR, E. B. 1958 [1871]. *Primitive Culture: Religion in primitive culture* (New York: Harper and Row).

UHLE, M. 1903. *Pachacamac: Report of the William Pepper, M.D., LL.D., Peruvian Expedition of 1896* (Philadelphia: University of Pennsylvania Press).

URTON, G. 1981. *At the Crossroads of the Earth and Sky: An Andean cosmology* (Austin: University of Texas Press).

—— 2003. *Signs of the Inka Khipu: Binary coding in the Andean knotted-string records* (Austin: University of Texas Press).

VARÓN GABAI, R. 1980. *Curacas y Encomenderos: Acomodamiento Nativo en Huaraz, Siglos XVI y XVII* (Lima: P. L. Villanueva Editor).

VEGA, G. DE LA 1979 [1616]. *The Incas: The royal commentaries of the Incas* (Lima: Librerias ABC).

YUPANQUI, T. C. 2006 [1565–70]. *History of How the Spaniards Arrived in Peru* (Indianapolis/Cambridge: Hackett Publishing Company).

ZUIDEMA, R. T. 1964. *The Ceque System of Cuzco: The social organization of the capital of the Inca* (Leiden: Brill).

—— 1989. 'Parentesco y culto a los antepasados en tres comunidades Peruanas: Una relación de Hernández Príncipe de 1622' in R. T. Zuidema (ed.), *Reyes y Guerreros* (Lima: Fomciencias).

—— 2002. 'Inca Religion: Its foundations in the central Andean context' in L. E. Sullivan (ed.), *Native Religions and Cultures of Central and South America* (New York and London: Continuum).

—— 2005. 'La Religión Inca', in M. M. Marzal (ed.), *Religiones Andinas* (Madrid: Editorial Trotta), 4: 89–113.

CHAPTER 37

MOCHE RELIGION

JEFFREY QUILTER

1 INTRODUCTION

MOCHE is a prehistoric archaeological culture: it is a conception of a suite of material remains of past human behaviour framed in the temporal dimension between AD 0 and 700 and in space in a series of desert valleys on the north coast of Peru. In that arid land, people had learned of and adapted to the benefits and dangers of living in a desert close to the Humboldt Current for more than 10,000 years by the time of Moche. They had mastered plant and animal domestication and irrigation agriculture and created one of the world's great maritime traditions. They had built large architectural complexes of stone and adobe for over 2,000 years. For slightly less time they had mastered the textile, ceramic, metal, and other arts. They had participated in the creation of religious systems that shared common features and one of these, Chavin, spread across the Peruvian landscape between *c*.700 and 200 BC collapsing to be succeeded by regional cults such as Moche. In the Early Intermediate period (*c*.200 BC–AD 800) when Moche flourished, different cultures followed their own religious traditions such as Nasca on the South Coast, and Recuay in the highlands.

Many Moche artefacts portray scenes which reasonably could be termed 'supernatural' in the common-sense use of the term and, therefore, related to 'religion'. These include depictions of creatures exhibiting mixtures of human and animal features, anthropomorphized animals, and other scenes such as *la danse macabre*. Most scholars, certainly most archaeologists, and most people in general would consider these as manifesting what we would recognize as religious acts such as rituals, and ideas such as deities and mythical heroes. Other than the fact that the Moche were masters of a distinctive style of representational art, the mixture of apparently quotidian and fantastic creatures is what makes the art style and culture fascinating for so many people.

2 INTERPRETING MOCHE RELIGION THROUGH ART AND ARCHAEOLOGY

Our current understandings of Moche religion have been shaped by the course of previous scholarship. Whether seen as diabolical or charming, the representational art of Moche ceramics, in particular, have drawn the attention of Europeans and local scholars. In the late nineteenth century the first serious archaeological studies were carried out at the great temple complex of the Huaca de la Luna, in the Moche Valley, by the German, Max Uhle (1913, 1915). Subsequently, both field archaeology and laboratory studies of collections increased awareness of the great amount of information available for study in painted and moulded Moche ceramics. In particular, Rafael Larco Herrera, who owned a large estate in the Chicama Valley—with the neighbouring Moche valley the 'heart' of Moche territory—conducted excavations, amassed a collection, published, and established a museum which drew scholars to study this culture.

Larco's activities took place between the 1930s and the 1960s. He and other scholars who wrote about the Moche understood the art to include both scenes of everyday life as well as depictions of deities. In the early 1970s, Christopher Donnan (1975, 1976, 1978) took a radically different approach to Moche art, however, in suggesting that all of the art reflected religious ideas. Thus, the depiction of a deer was not simply a representation of a wild animal or food source but was linked to concepts of royal hunting and of human sacrifice. Depictions of deer in the roles of warriors and prisoners helped to support this argument. Donnan also noted that there were certain stock scenes and variations of them depicting Moche deities interacting which he called themes. He saw these as equivalent to the tableau of religious figures commonly depicted on Christmas cards which exhibit key religious scenes (Birth of Jesus, Wise Men, Adoration of the Shepherds, etc.) and he advocated the Thematic Approach as a means to understand Moche religion (Figure 37.1).

The Thematic Approach substantially advanced understanding of the Moche by identifying key figures in the art which appear to have been principal deities in a Moche pantheon, and they were originally designated by letters, Figures 'A', 'B', 'C', 'D', etc. While Donnan, himself, never specifically identified these figures as gods, other scholars gave some of them names such as the Rayed Deity, the Goddess, and the Bird Deity (Figure 37.1). In addition, some or all of these figures were identified as consistently appearing in key themes: the Presentation Theme, the Burial Theme, and the Boat Theme. Beginning in the late 1980s, however, discoveries of high-ranking Moche elites buried in the costumes of some of these deities shifted scholarly attentions.

FIGURE 37.1 Roll out drawing from a Moche vessel of the Presentation Theme or Sacrifice Ceremony. The major figures were identified by Donnan as (from left to right) 'A' (holding cup and facing right), 'B', 'C', and 'D'. 'A' is sometimes referred to as the Rayed Deity or Warrior Lord, 'B' as the Bird Deity, and 'C' as the Goddess or Woman. After Donnan, 1976: 118, fig. 104a.

In particular, the 'Lord of Sipán' (Alva 1994, 2001; Alva and Donnan 1993) was dressed as the Rayed Deity while at the site of San José de Moro (Castillo 1993, 1996; Castillo and Donnan 1994) female burials were found costumed as the Goddess. Other lines of research confirmed that humans had dressed in costumes and performed ceremonies depicted in the art, including the consumption of the blood of sacrificed prisoners (Bourget 2001). These discoveries shifted interpretations from considering the mythological bases of Moche ritual to the rituals themselves and focusing on the art as portraying human actions and history.

Currently, students of Moche art are following multiple lines of evidence in interpreting Moche life and religion. Research at the Huaca de la Luna (Uceda 2001; Uceda et al. 1994), the Huaca Cao Viejo (Franco Jordán et al. 1994, 1996), San José de Moro (Castillo and Donnan 1994), Huancaco (Bourget 2004), and other sites have not only uncovered many artefacts and elaborate burials but also polychrome murals and friezes which have added to our understanding of rituals and religious ideas associated with them. So too, analyses of materials and production techniques, such as metals (Lechtmann 1996) and ceramic figurines (Russell and Jackson 2001) have expanded our knowledge of Moche religious ideas. In the interpretation of art, attempts have been made to link themes into longer mythic narratives (Castillo 1991; Quilter 1990, 1997; Golte 1994a) as well, while detailed studies of specific artistic traditions and sub-genres, such as schools of painters (Donnan and McClelland 1999) and portraiture (Donnan 2004) have been undertaken.

Although Moche as an art style and culture appears to have been radically transformed by AD 800, multiple lines of evidence suggest strong cultural continuities to and beyond the arrival of the Spanish in the sixteenth century. In addition, through time and space there appear to be commonly shared Andean ontological concepts which, used cautiously, may help in interpretation of ancient practices and beliefs.

Before reviewing some of the Moche religious concepts, deities, and rituals, it is worth considering issues of interpreting them in relation to different ideas of the political culture(s) which were related to them. Thirty years ago, in the 1970s, Moche was considered a relatively uniform phenomenon, distinguished by its distinctive art style which, it was assumed, was linked to an expansive state centred in the Moche Valley where the largest Moche pyramids (*huacas*) are located (Moseley 1983, 1992). Uniformity in space was matched by uniformity in time: a five-phase ceramic sequence, crucial for relative dating, originally developed by Larco, was believed to apply for the entire Moche region from Piura to the Nepeña Valley.

The intensive work at Moche sites following in the wake of the Sipán discoveries has begun to break down both the temporal and spatial uniformity of earlier times. At least two distinct Moche regions, one north of the Pampa de Paiján and one south of it, now are in evidence and the Larco sequence is not seen to apply to the northern Moche. Some scholars still see an expansive Moche state in the southern zone (Chapdelaine 2003). Increasingly, however, investigators are recognizing that the likely course of Moche politics and religion was complex and varied during the seven centuries or more of its existence. This raises issues of variability in Moche religion through time and space.

3 MOCHE RITUALS

Scholars differ regarding many aspects of Moche politics and religion but there is unanimity regarding a key ritual involving humans costumed as deities. Due to a combination of archaeological discoveries and iconographic studies, Walter Alva and Christopher Donnan

(1993) reinterpreted and renamed the Presentation Theme as the Sacrifice Ceremony. In brief, substantial evidence was marshalled that convinced scholars that the scene portrayed in art was enacted by costumed high-ranking Moche.

The rite consisted of the parading of naked, bound prisoners to a temple complex, slitting their throats, and collecting their blood in chalice-like goblets. The blood-filled cups were covered with small plates and presented by a file or group of costumed personages to an apparently higher-ranking individual who then, presumably, consumed the liquid. The personage receiving the cup is commonly the figure previously known as the Rayed Deity (because of the rays shown emanating from him) but renamed the Warrior Lord after the Sipán discoveries. The members of the entourage presenting the cup may vary in depictions but the Goddess and the Bird Deity are frequently portrayed, alone or with others.

The parading of prisoners, perhaps before an assembled crowd in temple plazas, appears to have preceded the sacrifice itself, judging by depictions on ceramics and large friezes at the Huaca de la Luna and the Huaca Cao Viejo. Who the prisoners were is a matter of some debate. Some scholars believe that they were residents of the same communities hosting the sacrifices, 'captured' in a ceremonial battle in which the outcome was predetermined. Others believe that the prisoners were taken in real battles.

Donnan (2010) suggests that other scenes in Moche art may be interpreted as ritual activities that precede the Sacrifice Ceremony. Although he previously saw themes (scenes) in relative isolation, he now sees a number of different depictions as linked together in what he refers to as the Warrior Narrative. This includes: warriors preparing for combat, one or more pairs of elite warriors fighting each other, the defeat of one of the warriors, their abuse (e.g. blows to the nose), the stripping of captives and the preparation of weapons, bundles of captured clothes and arms, and the parading of the bound naked prisoners to the place of sacrifice as noted above. This view assumes that Moche combat was ritual.

Previously, I (Quilter 1990, 1997) have suggested that a number of separate themes may be linked together to reconstruct a long segment of the central myth that was enacted in the Sacrifice Ceremony. In my view, the Sacrifice Ceremony as enacted by Moche priests was the recreation of a mythical event much as the celebration of the Eucharist or Mass is a re-enactment of the Last Supper of Jesus Christ. I have interpreted scenes of animated objects attacking humans through reference to early historical myths in the Andes that are also found throughout the New World as linked to ideas of a previous era of creation in which the world order was thrown out of joint. In this 'world turned upside down' the tables are turned as objects and animals normally subservient to humans rise up in rebellion against them. The revolt is headed by the Bird Deity and the Woman, perhaps also involving a human, but order is restored through the agency of the Rayed Deity. The original Presentation Theme or Sacrifice Ceremony was performed as penance by the defeated gods who lead the revolt although the trouble unleashed by them was not completely quelled. The Sacrifice Ceremony as performed by priests was a re-enactment of the mythical archetype to maintain world order. Donnan's view and mine are not necessarily mutually exclusive since rituals can be tied to many different interpretations and mytho-historical ideas.

Difficulties in interpretation lie in the palimpsest of archaeological sites and artefacts that are not always securely dated and in varying interpretations of art. For example, is the depiction of elaborately dressed warriors fighting in pairs, one-on-one, indicative of a particular style of combat or an artistic shorthand for combat between large armies consisting of varied ranks only the highest of which are shown in art?

As work has continued, it is now clear that there were several different kinds of sacrificial rites carried out by the Moche. At the Huaca de la Luna two major sacrificial forms were encountered. In one plaza, a number of apparent sacrificial victims, all males of prime military age, had been buried in a pit. Almost all bore evidence of cut marks in their thoracic vertebrae, suggesting that they had been killed in the manner shown in some versions of the Sacrifice Ceremony. In an adjacent plaza, however, the disarticulated skeletons of young males were found left exposed on the plaza floor with a curious associated practice of unfired clay portrait-like figurines smashed among some of them. This latter form of sacrifice has no clear representation in art unless some of the scenes of warrior combat refer to them. The use of unfired clay figurines smashed and left among the dead is not in evidence in the art, at all.

The degree to which archaeology confirms interpretations made from art as to the ritual practices varies. There are ceramic vessels that portray prisoners tied to scaffolds, but the only suggestion of this, archaeologically, is the presence of post-holes at archaeological sites that might have held such scaffolds. Individuals are also depicted in ceramics tied to posts with vultures pecking at their eyes. At Pacatnamú, vultures and stabbed victims who were possibly tied to posts have been found in archaeological contexts (Verano 1986; Rea 1986).

4 Religious Concepts and the Moche Pantheon

While the archaeological and art-historical tracing of sacrificial rites has been a fascinating scholarly adventure in the last two decades, the grisly facts of such rituals are unrelieved by identification of many pacific ceremonies. At the risk of ethnocentricism, the ferocity of turning fellow humans into disarticulated bones or, based on patterns of defleshed corpses, skeletons, held together by ligaments, displayed on temple parapets, is hard to comprehend. The only potential intellectual and emotional crutches on which the scholar or tourist might be able to lean are the provoking considerations on Aztec ontology offered by Inga Clendinnen (1991) and Davíd Carrasco (1999) for similarly brutal rites.

Attempting to outline the theology that supported the sacrificial rituals so clearly in evidence is difficult. There is substantial evidence to suggest that the Moche shared Inca and recent Andean concepts of dynamic, asymmetrical dualism (Burger and Salazar Burger 1993). The engine that drives the world consists of pairs of entities in a dynamic relationship in which one partner is slightly larger than the other but both are mutually dependent on each other. This kind of relationship may be in evidence in paired huaca complexes in the Moche and Chicama valleys and in the distribution of precious metals in graves, such as at Sipán, with silver placed on the burial's left side and gold on its right.

A more balanced dualism apparently is expressed in the form of the stirrup spout. Stirrup spout vessels were in use from very early times but favoured by the Moche (Figure 37.2). These vessels are awkward to fill or to pour from. Among the most carefully

FIGURE 37.2 A stirrup spout vessel depicting a fanged anthropomorphic deity showing the general features of a Moche high god. The distinct form of the dangling ear ornaments and the tubular, feline headdress may express one of many manifestations of a god or, perhaps, signal a distinct god different from other fanged anthropomorphs.

decorated of Moche pottery, it is quite likely that stirrup spout vessels served virtually no utilitarian purposes but were valued in and of themselves and for the symbolic imagery they displayed and concepts they expressed (Burger 1997: 29). The stirrup spout, itself, is an elegant expression of two things coming together to form one. This focus on the joining of two things finds expression today in the Quechua term *tinkuy* referring to the place where two things join, such as a seam in a piece of clothing or the meeting of two rivers (Harrison 1989). These are seen as places of spiritual power.

A number of scholars have noted that Andean epistemology is rooted in concepts of universal energy flows: just as water cycles from ocean, to clouds, to rain, to rivers, back to ocean again, so do other forces (Bastien 1978). Directionality may be present as soft, wet, bubbly babies gradually solidify in middle age to slowly harden as ancestor mummies in cave-shrines (Salomon 1995). Rocks and mountains are ancient ancestors transformed into ultimate hardness but they can rise up to aid Inca armies when necessary, according to the legend of the rise of Pachacuti, the founder of the Inca Empire.

If such views were held by the Moche we may be able to infer some of their understandings and constructions of their world. In the oases of their river valleys, they would have been acutely aware of the contrast between dry desert inertia and the flow of liquid fecundity. Rivers and irrigation systems derived from them were crucial in supporting life and major temples were often located at the crucial end points of such flows.

The striking and contrasting pairs in the physical world of the Moche seem to have been carried through in many expressions of the spiritual, such as dual huacas, and the paired use of gold and silver as mentioned above. But moving beyond a few examples, Moche scholars have yet to identify clear patterns of dualism in other important areas of human behaviour. We have no clear and consistent evidence of dual social organization, for example, and the variations in the representations of deities also shows unclear patterning.

While a pantheon of Moche gods has long been recognized, their ordering and ranking have proved a difficult undertaking. As early as 1931, Heinrich Ubbelohde-Doering recognized the Rayed Deity as did, subsequently, Gerdt Kutscher (1948, 1954) as a principal deity. About the same time, Larco Hoyle (1938, 1939) proposed a supreme deity which he called Ai-Apaec (Aiapaec). This term, 'creator', was taken from a dictionary written in 1644 (de la Carrera 1939) although we cannot be certain that the *muchik* language it recorded was spoken a thousand years earlier, in Moche times. It was virtually extinct by the mid-eighteenth century.

In more recent times, several scholars have proposed different identifications of Moche gods. As noted earlier, Donnan (1975) began by designating key figures in the Presentation Theme/Sacrifice Ceremony by letters and then later focused on these individuals as ritual officials. Elizabeth Benson (1972) distinguished between a high god, with a semi-circular headdress, and a lower-ranking god with a turban, fangs, and a snake-headed belt. Yuri Berezkin (1972, 1980) increased the number of deities, noting, for example, that there were two deities, distinguished by different headdresses, who each wear snake-headed belts. This number has now been increased to three by Baerbel Lieske (1992, 2001). Taking a different approach, Ann Marie Hocquenghem (1978, 1984, 1987) has used early Spanish chroniclers' accounts of Inca religion as frameworks by which to interpret Moche gods and rituals.

In the most thorough review, to date, of various theories of Moche deities, Krzystof Makowski (2003) confronts the difficulty of attempting to reconstruct a single pantheon of gods for people who may have shared common traditions but who lived over several hundred kilometres of coastline during seven or more centuries. Presuming that Moche communities were more likely independent, peer-polities than under a single centralized government, Makowski reasonably suggests that, similar to the ancient Greeks, the Moche shared a common pantheon but varied in their favour of particular gods.

Makowski (2003: 353) suggests that there is a consensus among scholars on the identification of four distinct gods. These are personages: (1) with a conical hat surrounded by rays (the Rayed Deity); (2) with a semi-circular, fan-like decorated headdress usually with two plumes extending from it, shown between (and often holding) two large serpents; (3) with a bicephalic serpent belt, commonly accompanied by a dog and an iguana (Aiapaec of Larco); (4) with a headdress of serpents and ocean waves with Cupsinique- (Coastal Chavin-)borrowed facial features. To these could be added the Goddess (Donnan's 'Priestess').

There is perhaps less consensus than Makowski proposes, even though the four deities he cites are frequently shown in art. The key question is how many gods we are viewing. As Makowski himself points out, only when we can view more than one deity in the same scene, such as the Presentation Theme, can we be relatively confident that one god is distinct from others. Some scholars make fine distinctions. For example, a commonly displayed figure is standing, facing forward, knees bent, with fangs, and wearing double-holed ear spools. In one hand he holds a crescent-bladed knife (sometimes referred to as an Inca *tumi*) and in the other, a decapitated head. This figure is commonly known as the *Decapitador* (Decapitator) God. A figure identical in all features except that the weapon held is not a tumi but a chisel-like instrument (found archaeologically, at Sipán) presumably used for cutting into jugular veins for tapping blood, is sometimes referred to as a different god, the *Degollador* (Throat Slitter).

The key features of Aiapaec, Decapitator, Throat Slitter, and the Rayed Deity are the same and few in number (Figure 37.2). The greatest artistic emphasis is devoted to the face both in terms of its frequency of representation and in attention to its features. The visage is anthropomorphic with prominent fangs being the only clearly non-human trait. When the deity is shown in a standing, front-facing mode, it often is distinct in sporting double ear ornaments or, alternatively, ears rendered with the upper part and lobe shown in the same shape and size.

All other details can vary considerably, such as clothing, headdress, and other regalia. To complicate matters further, one variant of this figure (if it is a single deity) has distinctive lines on the cheeks and forehead. This character has been seen as a separate deity, sometimes known as 'Wrinkle Face'. The same, similar, or a suite of related figures is interpreted as a culture hero and dubbed *Quismique* by Jürgen Golte (1994b).

Thus, in addition to controlling spatial and temporal variability, scholars attempting to define the Moche pantheon are confronted with formal variability as well. Which aspects of costume and auxiliary features (secondary figures, costume details, weapons, etc.) are significant and which are expressions of artistic licence or similar relatively unimportant variability? How many gods are represented in the apparent distinctions of the Rayed Deity, Decapitator, Throat Slitter, or Wrinkle Face and other characters?

To complicate the picture even more, there are examples of ceramics representing quotidian objects, such as manioc roots, capped with the face of Wrinkle Face. How are we to interpret this? It could be part of a myth but we have no other reference to any such story. Alternatively, it could represent an animistic conception in which manioc is conceived to contain a spirit. The possibility that there were different, somewhat separate religious traditions is also another issue which has not been fully considered, as well. At Cerro Mayal, in the Chicama Valley, excavations at a ceramic workshop uncovered thousands of fragments of moulds and discarded castings of clay figurines. Most of the figures represented do not appear to share the iconography shown on fancier pottery or temple walls. A Little Tradition of common folk, in contrast to the Great Tradition of temple cult, may be represented in these fragments although the ceramics were being made at a ceremonial centre presumably controlled by elites.

Donnan (1975) tells of a myth recorded in early colonial times of a hermit who said that as the lice multiplied on his body so would the people of the region increase their numbers. Examples of Moche ceramics depicting seated men with lice or sometimes small people on their bodies suggest that the tale was told a thousand years before it was written down. The story has the flavour of local legend rather than the credo of a state religion. Similarly, examples of ceramics depicting shamanic curers and the continuance of similar practices today, suggest that a strong tradition of folk beliefs and practices existed in ancient times and continue in various ways.

5 Art Programmes and Political Change

The use of large polychrome murals and friezes in prominent public places offers us opportunities to consider the form and possible content of Moche politico-religious ideology. How Moche huaca centres were situated in relation to what was surely a complex web of social sectors with differing interests is uncertain. It is clear, however, that other than irrigation systems, the greatest amount of collective labour in the Moche world was concentrated in the construction of temple complexes and the support of the cadres of priests and other officials who officiated at them. So too, as the most elaborate and high status burials found in the lands of Moche are costumed as gods, it is reasonable to infer that priestly roles were key components of the highest levels of Moche political power.

The best-preserved and most exposed public art in the lands of Moche is at the Huaca de la Luna (Figure 37.3) where the entire decorative programme of the front of the huaca is exposed as well as most of the interior rooms. There is no obvious patterning in the sequencing of the friezes of successive terraces. The lowest terrace shows victorious warriors parading bound, naked prisoners, an event that may have actually taken place in front of this frieze. The next row up appears to show human officials holding hands as if to cordon off the march of prisoners below them. The next terrace up shows a spider-like creature with a tumi and decapitated human head. Next is a deity with caught fish. There follows a curl-snout monster also with a decapitated head. The next level combines an access ramp (below a snake, above, warriors) and to the right a monster deity head. The uppermost level exhibits the Decapitator Deity.

Although a full analysis of these friezes cannot be offered here, a few observations may be made. If the snake and marching warriors are ignored as artistic solutions to fill in the long triangular walls produced by the rising access ramp, then the terraces may be grouped into three thematic sectors. The two lowest (prisoner march and officials) concern human affairs: the capture of prisoners for sacrifice and bringing them to the place of sacrifice. The three middle terraces (arthropod, fisher-god, curl-snout monster) show supernatural characters

FIGURE 37.3 Artistic rendering of how the Huaca de La Luna may have appeared at the height of its development, c.500–700 AD. The friezes discussed in the text were on the terraced walls facing the large plaza.

who, like the warriors below, are aggressive captors. The upper two terraces show iconic deities with the Decapitator at the top, emphasizing the main thematic motif of prisoner capture.

Inside the huaca, various walled patios show a relatively simple motif of rhomboids with the head of Aiapaec in the centre surrounded by stylized catfish which, as freshwater denizens of canals, are symbolically associated with agriculture. Both inside and outside, the multiple layers of construction that occurred through time at Huaca de la Luna show that almost identical artistic programmes were repeated as the temple grew. Only slight variations of the interior Aiapaec rhomboids and the earlier use of murals and later employment of friezes on the exterior seem to be relatively significant, though overall, minor.

In the neighbouring Chicama Valley, the Huaca Cao Viejo's exterior walls were painted in solid colours (red, yellow, and white) throughout much of its use. In the last major building phase, however, the Huaca de la Luna programme was adopted and followed very closely. Shortly after this, the Huaca Cao Viejo was abandoned and, very likely, trouble also visited the Huaca de la Luna. This late adoption of the Moche frieze programme at the Chicama site suggests some kind of political expansion or alliance, closely associated with distinctive religious practices. The subsequent cessation of site use suggests that whatever strategy was followed was not successful.

While there was continuity in ritual and major religious themes throughout the centuries of Moche culture there appear to have been shifts in emphasis in its final years. Pottery decoration changed to include smaller and more numerous figures filling spaces on painted pottery. Alan Cordy-Collins (1977, 1990) has suggested an increase in maritime themes in late Moche art, perhaps tied to the growing importance of the trade in *Spondylus princeps* shells, the closest source of which for the Moche were the warm waters of Ecuador. Some deities, such as the Owl Deity, likely seen as a warrior god, also appear to increase in popularity, perhaps due to increasingly unstable social conditions.

Why Moche collapsed is unclear but it seems safe to say that a system in which major political leaders costume themselves as gods leaves little tolerance for failure. The seamless combination of political and religious leadership would have meant that once the supporting populace withdrew support of one aspect the entire system would have collapsed. Succeeding cultures influenced by new configurations of power and belief from the southern Peruvian highlands (Wari) and Bolivia (Tiwanaku), may have separated the religious from the political more sharply than the Moche.

6 CONCLUSIONS

From the mid-1970s to the mid-2000s Moche studies have undergone tremendous advances, especially by the data from the Sipán excavations and subsequent research at the huaca sites. It is the power of the combination of information from field archaeology and the detailed study of iconography that has allowed scholars to identify rituals, priestly roles, deities, and to speculate on larger matters of religious creeds.

Scholars wishing to make sense of any aspect of the Moche are now confronted with a surfeit of riches in terms of great amounts of data. At the same time, however, a full engagement with theoretical and methodological tools to make sense of the site reports, catalogues of pottery, and other materials, remains to be accomplished. The Moche archaeological culture—the collection of artefacts and facilities—is often reified as an ethnic or political unit. As noted previously, there does appear to have been a close association of politics and religion but how political endeavours were articulated with religious practice within a constellation of competing social sectors is only just beginning to be addressed (see Quilter and Castillo 2010). These investigations are complicated by reconsiderations of the basic ceramic chronology, first developed by Larco, on which Moche studies relied for almost half a century.

As research continues many other aspects of Moche religious beliefs and practices are coming to light which remain to be fully integrated into the views of them developed to date. For example, Steve Bourget (2006) has recently presented an extensive argument that Moche erotic pottery vessels and, indeed, much of Moche art is associated with concepts of the transformation of the dead into ancestors. At the Huaca Cao Viejo and the Huaca de la Luna the identical artistic programmes of the temple facades, late in Moche times, included the creation of elaborate friezes which depict complex scenes of figures interacting (Franco Jordán and Vilela Puelles 2003) (Figure 37.4). Some of the figures shown can be linked to known iconography but others cannot and the entire scene has no direct relationship to well known Moche religious themes. As a final example, a large, carved wooden sculpture which portrays a simple human figure was found ceremonially interred in a room at Huaca

FIGURE 37.4 The complex theme frieze as found at Huaca Cao Viejo. Sections of the polychrome frieze have eroded over time. A human figure with large crown appears repeatedly suggesting that this may be a key figure in the events portrayed.

Cao Viejo (Franco Jordán and Vilela Puelles 2003: 75). This brings to mind that the holiest of Inca images, in the most sacred temple in Cuzco, were portrayals of Inti, the Sun God, in human form as was also the case in the sanctum sanctorum at the pilgrimage site of Pachacamac, near Lima. Perhaps at the heart of Moche religion, the ultimate deity also was interpreted in human form. All of these recent finds suggest that there is much more to Moche religion than we currently know but also offer the possibility that we will learn much more in the future.

REFERENCES

ALVA, W. 1994. *Sipán* (Lima: Cervecería Backus y Johnston, S.A.).
—— 2001. 'The royal tombs of Sipán: Art and power in Moche society' in J. Pillsbury (ed.), *Moche Art and Archaeology in Ancient Peru* (Washington, DC: National Gallery of Art), pp. 223–45.
—— and DONNAN, C. B. 1993. *The Royal Tombs of Sipán* (Los Angeles: Fowler Museum of Cultural History).
BASTIEN, J. W. 1978. *Mountain of the Condor* (St. Paul: West Publishing Company).

Benson, E. P. 1972. *The Mochica: A Culture of Peru* (New York and Washington: Praeger Publishers).

Berezkin, Y. 1972. 'Mitologiya Mochika (Pieru)', *Sovitskaya Arkheologiya* 4: 171–92.

—— 1980. 'An Identification of Anthropomorphic Mythological Personages in Moche Representations', *Ñawpa Pacha* 18: 1–26.

Bourget, S. 2001. 'Rituals of sacrifice: Its practice at Huaca de la Luna and its representation in Moche iconography' in J. Pillsbury (ed.), *Moche Art and Archaeology in Ancient Peru* (Washington, DC: National Gallery of Art), pp. 89–109.

—— 2004. *A Case of Mistaken Identity? The Moche presence in the Viru Valley*, Paper presented at the 69th Annual SAA Meeting, Montreal (see e-paper at <www.anthro.umontreal.ca>).

—— 2006. *Sex, Death, and Sacrifice in Moche Religion and Visual Culture* (Austin, TX: University of Texas Press).

Burger, R., and Salazar Burger, L. 1993. 'The Place of Dual Organization in Early Andean Ceremonialism: A Comparative Review', in L. Millones and Y. Onuki (eds), *El Mundo Ceremonial Andino* (Tokyo: Senri Ethnological Series No. 37), pp. 97–116.

Burger, R. L. 1997. 'Life and the afterlife in pre-Hispanic Peru: Contextualizing the masterworks of the Museo Arqueológico Rafale Larco Herrera' in K. Berrin (ed.), *The Spirit of Ancient Peru: Treasures from the Museo Arqueológico Rafale Larco Herrera* (New York: Thames and Hudson and the Fine Arts Museums of San Francisco), pp. 21–32.

Carrasco, D. 1999. *City of Sacrifice: The Aztec Empire and the role of violence in civilization* (Boston, MA: Beacon Press).

de la Carrera, F. 1939 [1644]. *Arte de la Lengua Yunga*, ed. R. A. Altieri (Tucumán: Instituto de Antropología).

Castillo, L. J. 1991. 'Narrations in Moche iconography', a paper submitted to the Archaeology Program at the University of California, Los Angeles, in partial fulfillment of the requirements for the degree of Master of Arts.

—— 1993. 'Prácticas funerarias, poder e ideología en la sociedad Moche tardía: el proyecto arqueológico San José de Moro', *Gaceta Arqueológica Andina*, 23: 61–76.

—— 1996. *La tumba de la sacerdotisa de San José de Moro*, Exhibition Catalogue (Lima: Centro Cultural de la Pontificia Universidad Católica del Perú).

—— and Donnan, C. B. 1994. 'La ocupación moche de San José de Moro, Jequetepeque' in S. Uceda and E. Mujica (eds), *Moche: Propuestas y Prospectivas. Actas del Primer Coloquio sobre la Cultura Moche (Trujillo, 12 a 16 de abril de 1993) Travaux de l'Institute Francais d'Etudes Andines* 79 (Lima: Universidad de La Libertad, Trujillo, Instituto Francés de Estudios Andinos and Asociación Peruana para el Fomento de las Ciencias Sociales), pp. 93–146.

Chapdelaine, C. 2003. 'La ciudad de Moche: urbanismo y estado' in Santiago Uceda and Elias Mujica (eds), *Moche: Hacia el Final del Milenio. Actas del Segundo Coloquio sobre la cultura Moche (Trujillo, 1 al 7 de agosto de 1999)* (Lima: Universidad Nacional de Trujillo and Pontificia Universidad Católica del Perú), pp. 247–85.

Clendinnen, I. 1991. *Aztecs: An interpretation* (Cambridge: Cambridge University Press).

Cordy-Collins, A. 1977. 'The Moon is a Boat! A study in iconographic methodology' in A. Cordy-Collins and J. Stern (eds), *Pre-Columbian Art History: Selected readings* (Palo Alto, California: Peek Publications), pp. 421–34.

—— 1990. 'Fonga Sidge, Shell Purveyor to the Chimu Kings' in M. E. Moseley and A. Cordy-Collins (eds), *The Northern Dynasties: Kingship and statecraft in Chimor* (Washington, DC: Dumbarton Oaks Research Library and Collection), pp. 393–418.

Donnan, C. B. 1975. 'The Thematic Approach to Moche iconography', *Journal of Latin American Lore*, 1(2): 147–62.

——1976. *Moche Art and Iconography*, Latin American Studies 33 (Los Angeles: Latin American Center, University of California).

——1978. *Moche Art of Peru: Pre-Columbian symbolic communication* (Los Angeles: Museum of Cultural History, University of California, Los Angeles).

——2004. *Moche Portraits from Ancient Peru* (Austin, TX: University of Texas Press).

——2010. 'Moche state religion: A unifying force in Moche political organization' in J. Quilter and L. J. Castillo (eds), *New Perspectives on Moche Political Organization* (Washington, DC: Dumbarton Oaks Research Library and Collections).

—— and McClelland, D. 1996. 'Los descubrimientos arqueológicos en la Huaca Cao Viejo, Complejo "El Brujo"', *Arkinka*, 1(5): 82–94.

—— ——1999. *Moche Fineline Painting* (Los Angeles: Fowler Museum of Cultural History, University of California, Los Angeles).

Franco Jordán, R., Gálvez Mora, C., and Vásquez Sánchez, S. 1994. 'Arquitectura y decoración Mochica en la Huaca Cao Viejo, Complejo El Brujo: Resultados Preliminares', in S. Uceda and E. Mujica (eds), *Moche: Propuestas y Prospectives. Actas del Primer Coloquio sobre la Cultura Moche (Trujillo, 12 a 16 de abril de 1993). Travaux de l'Institut Français d'Etudes Andines* 79 (Trujillo: Instituto Francés de Estudios Andinos; and Asociación Peruana para el Fomento de las Ciencias Sociales), pp. 147–80.

—— —— ——1996. 'Los descubrimientos arqueológicos en la Huaca Cao Viejo, Complejo 'El Brujo', *Arkinka* 1(5): 82–94.

Franco Jordán, R., and Vilela Puelles, J. V. 2003. 'Aproximaciones al calendrio ceremonial Mochica del complejo El Brujo, valle de Chicama' in S. Uceda and E. Mujica (eds), *Moche: Propuestas y Perspectivas*, vol. 1 (Lima: Universidad Nacional de Trujillo y Pontifícia Universidad Católica del Perú), pp. 383–423.

Golte, J. 1994a. *Iconos y Narraciones: La reconstrucción de una sequencia de imágenes Moche* (Lima: Instituto de Estudios Peruanos).

——1994b. *Los Dioses de Sipán II: La Rebelión Contra el Dios Sol* (Lima: IEP ediciones).

Harrison, R. 1989. *Signs, Songs, and Memory in the Andes: Translating Quechua language and culture* (Austin: University of Texas Press).

Hocquenghem, A. M. 1977. 'Les représentations de chamans dans l'iconographie mochica', *Ñawpa Pacha* 15: 117–21.

——1978. 'Les combats mochicas: Essai d'interprétation d'un matériel archéologique à l'aide de l'iconologie, de l'ethnohistorie et de l'ethnologie', *Baessler Archiv, Neue Folge* 26: 125–57.

——1984. *El orden andino* (Berlin: Latinamericanische Institut, Freie Universität).

——1987. *Iconografía Mochica* (Lima: Pontificia Universidad Católica del Perú, Fondo Editorial).

Kutscher, G. 1948. 'Religion und Mythologie der frühen Chimu (Nord-Peru)', *XXVIIIth International Congress of Americanists*: 621–31.

——1954. 'Nordperuanische Keramik. Figürlich verzierte Fefässe der Früh Chimu/Cerámica del Perú Septentrional. Figuras ornamentals en vasijas de los Chimúes antiquos', *Monumenta Americana* 1 (Berlin: Geb. Mann Verlag).

Larco Hoyle, R. 1938. *Los Mochicas*, Tomo I (Lima: Casa Editora La Crónica y Variedades).

——1939. *Los Mochicas*, Tomo II (Lima: Empresa Editorial Rimac S.A.).

Lechtmann, H. 1996. 'Cloth and metal: The culture of technology' in E. Hill Boone (ed.), *Andean Art at Dumbarton Oaks*, I (Washington, DC: Dumbarton Oaks Research Library and Collections), pp. 33–44.

Lieske, B. 1992. *Mythische Erzählungen in den gefäßmalereien der altperuanischen Moche-Kultur. Versuch einer iknographischen Rekonstrucktion* (Bonn: Holos Verla).

LIESKE, B. 2001. *Göttergestalten der altperuanischen Moche-Kultur. Veröffentlichung der Projekgruppe Iknographie an Lateinamerika* (Berlin: Institut der Freien Universität).
MAKOWSKI HANULA, K. 2003. 'La deidad suprema en la iconografía mochica, cómo definirla?', in S. Uceda and E. Mujica (eds), *Moche: Hacia el Final del Milenio. Actas del Segundo Coloquio sobre la cultura Moche (Trujillo, 1 a 7 de agosto de 1999)* (Trujillo and Lima: Universidad Nácional de Trujillo and Pontificia Universidad Católica del Perú), pp. 343–82.
MOSELEY, M. E. 1983. 'Central Andean civilizations' in J. Jennings (ed.), *Ancient South Americans* (San Francisco: W. H. Freeman and Company), pp. 179–239.
——1992. *The Incas and their Ancestors: The archaeology of Peru* (London: Thames and Hudson).
QUILTER, J. 1990. 'The Moche revolt of the objects', *Latin American Antiquity*, 1(1): 42–65.
——1997. 'The narrative approach to Moche iconography', *Latin American Antiquity*, 8(2): 113–33.
——and CASTILLO, L. J. *New Perspectives on Moche Political Organization* (Washington, D.C.: Dumbarton Oaks Research Library and Collection).
REA, A. M. 1986. 'Black Vultures and Human Victims: Archaeological Evidence from Pacatnamu' in C. B. Donnan and G. A. Cock (eds), *Pacatnamu Papers*, Volume I (Los Angeles: Museum of Cultural History, University of California), pp. 139–44.
RÉGULO, F. J., MORA, C. G., and SÁNCHEZ, S. V. 1994. 'Arquitectura y decoración Mochica en la Huaca Cao Viejo, Complejo El Brujo: Resultados Preliminares' in S. Uceda and E. Mujica (eds), *Moche: Propuestas y Prospectivas. Actas del Primer Coloquio sobre la Cultura Moche (Trujillo, 12 a 16 de abril de 1993) Travaux de l'Institute Francais d'Etudes Andines 79* (Lima: Universidad de La Libertad, Trujillo; Instituto Francés de Estudios Andinos; and Asociación Peruana para el Fomento de las Ciencias Sociales), pp. 147–80.
——and PUELLES, J. V. 2005. *El Brujo: El Mundo Mágico y Religioso Mochica y El Calendario Ceremonial* (Trujillo, Peru: Minkaperu).
RUSSELL, G. S. and JACKSON, M. A. 2001. 'Political Economy and Patronage at Cerro Mayal, Peru' in J. Pillsbury (ed.), *Moche Art and Archaeology in Ancient Peru* (Washington, DC: National Gallery of Art), pp. 159–75.
SALOMON, F. 1995. 'The Beautiful Grandparents' in T. Dillehay (ed.), *Tombs for the Living: Andean Mortuary Practices* (Washington D.C.: Dumbarton Oaks Research Library and Collection), pp. 247–81.
UBBELHOHDE-DOERING, H. 1931. 'Altperuanische Gefässmalereien. Tiel 2', *Marburger Jahrbuch für Kunstwissenschaft* 6 (Marburg).
UCEDA CASTILLO, S. 2001. 'Investigations at Huaca de la Luna, Moche Valley: An example of Moche religious architecture' in Joanne Pillsbury (ed.), *Moche Art and Archaeology in Ancient Peru* (Washington, DC: National Gallery of Art), pp. 47–67.
——, MORALES, R., CANZIANI, J., et al. 1994. 'Investigaciones sobre la arquitectura y relieves policromos en Huaca de la Luna, valle de Moche' in S. Uceda and E. Mujica (eds), *Moche: Propuestas y Prospectivas. Actas del Primer Coloquio sobre la Cultura Moche (Trujillo, 12 a 16 de abril de 1993) Travaux de l'Institute Francais d'Etudes Andines 79* (Lima: Universidad de La Libertad, Trujillo; Instituto Francés de Estudios Andinos; and Asociación Peruana para el Fomento de las Ciencias Sociales), pp. 251–303.
UHLE, M. 1913. 'Die Runinen von Moche', *Journal de la Société des Amereicanistes de Paris*, 10: 95–117.
——1915. 'Las ruinas de Moche', *Boletín de la Sociedad Geográfica de Lima*, 30(3–4): 57–71.
VERANO, J. W. 1986. 'A Mass Burial of Mutilated Individuals at Pacatnamu' in C. B. Donnan and G. A. Cock (eds), *Pacatnamu Papers*, Volume I (Los Angeles: Museum of Cultural History, University of California), pp. 117–38.

CHAPTER 38

NORTH AMERICA
Pueblos

KELLEY HAYS-GILPIN

1 INTRODUCTION

THE archaeology of Pueblo religions connects material evidence for ritual practice with ethnography and ethnohistory. Pueblo people still live where their ancestors did when Spanish explorers first entered what is now the Southwestern United States in 1540, and traditional religions are still practised. Archaeological evidence suggests that Pueblo religion emerged around AD 600 as kin-group-based ritual practice focused on maize agriculture; experienced regional differentiation over the next 800 years; and coalesced in elaborate calendars of labour-intensive sequences of ritual performances by AD 1400. Spanish missionization challenged Pueblo religion in the seventeenth and eighteenth centuries. United States government-sponsored 'salvage ethnography' and archaeology of the nineteenth century initiated intense scrutiny by outsiders that is only now giving way to intellectual sovereignty and community control over public presentation of information about Pueblo religion and histories.

Exploration of evidence for over 1400 years of Pueblo religion reveals some apparent contradictions: today's elaborate ritual calendar helps maintain an ideology of gender complementarity and economic egalitarianism, but ritual practice is directed by gerontocracies of mostly male religious leaders. Ideology of peaceful accommodation of ethnic diversity has been punctuated by conflicts that include the 1680 Pueblo Revolt against Spanish rule, and roles for warriors and occasional episodes of violence are integral parts of Pueblo religion. Pueblo ritual and iconography have clear affinities to those of Mesoamerica, but Pueblo interpretations and uses are localized and diverse. These contradictions can be understood in terms of Pueblo philosophy's deliberate cultivation of heterodoxy; non-hierarchical ideologies based in dynamic, interpenetrating, alternating dualities and the concept of reciprocity between humans and the spirit world; and in the migration histories of ancestral kin groups and historical relationships among ritual societies, dual social and ritual divisions, and distinct communities that speak different languages but cultivate long-term ritual and economic exchanges.

Investigating Pueblo religion is also fraught with contradictions. In Pueblo thought, knowledge should only be shared with those who have earned rights to and responsibilities for knowledge; academics believe that knowledge should be freely shared. Pueblo religious knowledge is deliberately distributed among different kin, community, and ritual society (sodality) groups; in the Pueblo view, cross-cultural comparisons and generalizations favoured by anthropologists are not appropriate uses of ritual knowledge. Pueblo and academic philosophers alike understand that contradictions are unavoidable, and indeed underlie all creative acts. I therefore understand that what I write here will satisfy neither audience, but hope that this review will at least stimulate critique of past and current research.

2 Pueblos

Pueblo communities in New Mexico and Arizona are fighting language-loss, but have members who still speak native languages in which key religious concepts and metaphors are embedded. The Hopi language belongs to the Uto-Aztecan family. Tiwa, Tewa, and Towa belong to the Kiowa-Tanoan family. Zuni and Keresan are language isolates. In spite of linguistic diversity, all the Pueblos share history as village-dwelling farmers whose economy depended on cultivating maize, beans, squash; hunting wild game; and keeping domesticated dogs and turkeys. They also share certain aspects of cosmology, philosophy, and ritual practices that focus on maize, rain, ancestors, health, hunting (and formerly warfare), and earth stewardship. They hold in common many symbols and ritual practices with other indigenous North American and Mesoamerican cultures, and partake of a pan-Mesoamerican maize-based cosmology that probably spread when early farmers brought domesticated maize out of its Mexican homeland.

Joe Sando, a member of Jemez Pueblo, notes that no Pueblo language has a word for religion, but all Pueblos value knowledge of spiritual life, beliefs, and practices that permeate every aspect of life and determine human relationships with the natural world. Pueblo religion's 'basic concern is continuity of a harmonious relationship with the world in which man lives. To maintain such a relationship between the people and the spiritual world, various societies exist, with particular responsibilities for weather, fertility, curing, hunting, and pleasure or entertainment of the people' (Sando 1976: 22). All Pueblos maintain an elaborate ritual calendar whose components focus on 'prayerful requests for an orderly life, rain, good crops, plentiful game, pleasant days, and protection from the violence and vicissitudes of nature' (Sando 1976: 23).

Pueblo philosophy and ritual practice generally concern the dynamic relationship between order and chaos, the role of humans in reciprocal relationships between this world and the spirit world, and a vocabulary of symbols and metaphors that facilitate communication of human intentions to denizens of the spirit world. Important concepts that are sometimes given material form and thus can be discerned in the archaeological record include upward emergence from the underworld(s); conflation of maize and humans (e.g. corn guardians, maidens, and mothers); association of all water with a horned or feathered serpent; marking seasonal solar movements; division of the year into two seasons marked by particular symbols and activities; identification of ancestors, clouds, cotton, rain, and katsinas (ancestral spirit beings); and the importance of four directions and central places, colour symbolism, migration, and pilgrimage. Overarching questions for archaeologists are how this complicated system of ritual practice came to be, and what past ritual roles and practices have ceased to be.

3 History of Research

To learn about past religions, archaeologists rely on iconography and material evidence for cosmology and ritual behaviour. Pueblo ethnography is very rich, but using it appropriately has been problematic for archaeologists (Dozier 1970b; Ware 2001). To help make sense of the material record, we look for ethnographic parallels. But agricultural intensification, migrations and population aggregations, the Spanish entrada and missionization, American westward expansion, and the reservation system have impacted Pueblo land-base, demography, and religion. Ethnographies and documentary records have their own biases. And known ritual activity is not always obvious in the material record. Evidence for katsina performance, such as images in rock art and pottery (Figure 38.1), is highly visible, but no material evidence for past ritual clowning has survived, and evidence for the activities of medicine societies is sparse. We cannot reconstruct thoughts, songs, prayers, or performances, but we do find prayer sticks and other offerings, ritual regalia such as shell jewellery, fetishes, and figurines, and ritual spaces—kivas, great kivas, plazas, and shrines.

Pueblo archaeology and ethnology began in the late nineteenth century as government-sponsored attempts to salvage information about indigenous peoples and places from anticipated extermination of indigenous lifeways by Euroamerican colonization. The Smithsonian Institution dispatched anthropologists to the Pueblos to collect objects and information. Some (e.g. Mathilda Coxe Stevenson [1887, 1904]) acted like the outsiders they were, and others (e.g. Frank Hamilton Cushing [Green 1979]) tried to become insiders. Elsie Clews Parsons' *Pueblo Religion* (1939) is still a productive mine of useful information, although many Pueblo scholars view her work as too broad and sometimes inaccurate.

Mid twentieth century ethnography and archaeology largely followed structural-functionalist approaches, and focused on links between social and economic structures and systems. Julian Steward (1937, 1955) argued that sound historical reconstruction has to take economy and ecology into account. He associated architectural units that included kivas with social units he equated with matrilineal clans. Likewise, Fred Eggan (1950) viewed ritual and religion in terms of social integrative functions.

Archaeology of the 1970s–80s also emphasized social integration and economic redistribution of resources (Lipe and Hegmon 1989). A few explored ritual and symbolic meanings, prompted by clear description of Pueblo cosmology by Alfonso Ortiz, an ethnologist and member of San Juan Pueblo, in *The Tewa World* (1969). For example, John Fritz (1978) suggested that Pueblo Bonito's (c.AD 870–1130) elaborate architectural symmetry encoded Puebloan ideology of complementary dualisms, such as the Tewa Winter and Summer moieties. Richard Ford linked Tewa ritual to exchange with Comanches, Utes, and Apaches, who supplied many items used in 'proper ritual apparel' including ochre pigments, bison heads and hair, shell, and parrot feathers (1972a: 42). He also addressed ceremonial food redistribution (1972b), and the ritual and ecological roles of separate strains of pure-coloured

FIGURE 38.1 Katsina images on pottery and rock art, fourteenth century. Top left: Jeddito Black-on-yellow bowl design with Tsakwayna katsina face and banding line with 'breath gate'. Top right: Jeddito Black-on-yellow bowl with katsina face and butterflies. Lower left: Glaze I yellow bowl from Pecos Pueblo. Lower Right: Talpa Black-on-white bowl fragment from T'aitöna, an ancestral Taos site.

maize (1980), which are adaptive aspects of Pueblo rituals. Due to the central ritual metaphor that 'corn is our Mother', Ford called for identification of evidence of ritual uses of maize in the archaeological record (1994). Past ritual uses and symbolic meanings of cotton (associated with clouds and rain) and cotton textiles (symbols of ritual leadership), datura (a hallucinogen), tobacco, and other ritually important plants, animals, and birds also have been explored (Huckell and VanPool 2006; Potter 2000, 2002; Webster and Loma'omvaya 2004).

As interest in religion increases, so has critical thinking about method and theory for discerning how religion and ritual behaviours are manifested archeologically. William Walker (1995; Walker et al. 2000) advocated tracing the life histories of objects and structures used in ritual activities. Ritual closure rites that involved placing offerings in kivas, then deliberately burning and filling the structures, can then be distinguished from fires caused by accidents or raids. Closure rites might have been occasioned by the death of an important ritual leader or in preparation for migration.

The archaeology of Pueblo religion in the 1990s was dominated by debates about origins and functions of the katsina religion (or katsina cult), and about links between ritual knowledge and leadership, power, feasting, warfare, and other forms of violence (discussed below). Archaeological theory diversified in the 1990s, and so did the profession. The Southwest always has been accessible to women archaeologists and anthropologists in a male-dominated profession, but relatively few women became full-time archaeologists until the 1980s. A number of Pueblo scholars became anthropologists as early as the 1960s, but few studied archaeology until the 1990s. Diversification of theoretical approaches and of the workforce has introduced feminism and gender studies into the study of Pueblo religion, as well as the study of praxis, performance, and audience, metaphor theory, and increased attention to ethnography and traditional histories.

Since passage of the Native American Graves Protection and Repatriation Act in 1990, archaeologists regularly consult with tribal governments about research and cultural resource management projects. Recognition of tribal sovereignty and the rights of communities to control acquisition and distribution of knowledge resulting from archaeological activities has increased. Most archaeology done in the Puebloan region today is applied work, such as data-recovery done prior to infrastructure development, support for land and water claims, documentation of Traditional Cultural Properties (a term created by the National Park Service to include shrines, plant gathering areas, springs, and other kinds of important places), determining cultural affiliation as required for repatriation of objects and human remains, and helping educators develop local history curricula.

Tribal cultural preservation programmes and museums are setting their own research and education agendas. Pueblo individuals, communities, and governmental entities disagree on what kinds of information should be shared outside the community, and different factions within communities often debate this issue. Although there are some basic commonalities among Pueblos, and archaeologists can make some generalizations about Pueblo religion in the past, differences among Pueblos are part of what makes Pueblo religion flexible and long-lived. What can be said, and how much can be said, by way of interpretation of meanings and specific ritual practices and histories must be constrained by the ethics of working with the history of living traditions whose survival depends in part on appropriate transmission of privileged knowledge across generations (see Brandt 2002). Yet many understand the need to counter Western culture's 'primitivist' assumptions and explain to the rest of the world that Pueblo religion is just as sophisticated, complex, coherent, and effective as any of the world's major religions.

4 Diverse Community Histories and Archaeological Affiliations

Each of the extant Pueblo communities has its own unique history of migration and aggregation of people from different regions and language groups. Each is descended in part from local populations who were present in the Southwest for over 10,000 years, and in part from immigrants, some of whom probably migrated from as far away as Mexico over the last 5,000 years. Continuities in iconography, pottery technology, oral traditions, and subterranean ritual structures called kivas link historic Pueblos with prehistoric sites throughout the Colorado Plateau (the high desert of northern Arizona, southern Utah, south-western Colorado, and north-western New Mexico). In the early twentieth century, archaeologists called this culture area 'Anasazi', from a Navajo word meaning 'ancient enemies' or 'ancient non-Navajos' (Walters and Rogers 2001). Today, Pueblo people prefer indigenous terms, or the generic 'Ancestral Puebloans'. Other archaeologically defined village farming cultures of the Colorado Plateau and mountains and deserts to the south and west contributed to Puebloan religion and ancestry. Mogollon, Mimbres, Casas Grandes, Salado, and Hohokam cultures should properly receive much more attention than this short chapter allows. Pueblo religion, then, draws on a large source area with diverse ecological niches, languages, and ritual practices. What follows is an attempt to establish the antiquity and continuity of Pueblo religion, and to highlight a few of the important transitions in this historical trajectory.

5 BASKETMAKER BEGINNINGS

A recognizable pattern for later Pueblo religion emerged in the Basketmaker III period, *c.*AD 500–750. Mobile farmers who appear to have practised a shamanistic ritual tradition (Cole 1989) began to live in clusters of pithouses, sometimes surrounding large community structures known as Basketmaker great kivas. Some great kivas are associated with rock

FIGURE 38.2 White Mound Black-on-white bowl fragment from NA8939, a pithouse village site near Houck, Arizona. Female dancers with butterfly hair whorls alternate with possibly male dancers wearing a single horn or feather. Associated tree-ring dates *c.*AD 800.

art depictions of masks and processions (Hays-Gilpin 2000b; Robins and Hays-Gilpin 2000). Basketmakers of this era grew beans as well as maize and squash, made pottery, and domesticated turkeys. Social organization based on matrilineal descent groups probably developed in this era. Ritual practices and iconography that show direct continuity into the present day include a distinctive hairstyle known as 'butterfly hair whorls' associated with the Pueblo girls' puberty corn-grinding ceremony. Rock art depictions of butterfly hair whorls date as early as AD 200 in Canyon de Chelly, north-eastern Arizona (Hays-Gilpin 2002, 2004). In the seventh and eighth centuries, painted pottery bowls depicting lines of dancers holding hands appear in several regions; some of the dancers wear butterfly hair whorls. Hopi cultural experts recognize this dance today (Cordell 1997: 250) (Figure 38.2). Other examples of iconography and ritual objects that first appear in this period and reappear later include flutes and images of flute players, elaborate twined sandals, burden baskets, the 'line break' or 'life's pathway' motif in basketry and pottery designs (Hays-Gilpin 2008), bird imagery (Robins and Hays-Gilpin 2000), prayer feathers, and pipes for smoking tobacco. Clay figurines representing women and burden baskets are frequent in this period (Morss 1954), but the female images apparently did not continue into later times.

6 KIVAS, KIN, AND RITUAL SODALITIES

During the pithouse-to-pueblo transition in many parts of the northern Ancestral Pueblo area in the AD 800s, some pithouses were converted to ritual use as kivas. As dependence on maize agriculture increased and seasonal mobility decreased, habitation and storage shifted to above-ground structures. Kivas are one of the most archaeologically salient indicators of Pueblo religion (Figure 38.3), although they probably were not used exclusively for ritual (Lekson 1988). 'Protokivas', deep pithouses with some features of kivas, appear early in Pueblo I (AD 750–900), and structures most archaeologists would agree were kivas are present by at least the Pueblo II period (AD 900–1100). Kivas are subterranean structures with a hearth and one or more distinctive features that may include an elbow-shaped ventilator with an upright deflector slab on the floor in front of the vent opening, benches, pilasters, foot drums, niches, a southern or south-eastern recessed area, and usually a sipapu—a small hole in the floor that according to Pueblo people today represents the original place of emergence from the underworld to this world (Lipe and Hegmon 1989; Smith 1990). According to the traditions of Acoma Pueblo, Iatiku, the primordial mother of the Acomas, explained how to build the first kiva. Called 'underworld house' in ceremonial language, each kiva represents the place where Acoma ancestors lived with the corn mothers in the underworld prior to emergence (Stirling 1942: 18–20). Though different pueblos vary in the details evident, kivas generally embody connections between this world and the underworld, present and past, humans and ancestors (Ortman 2008).

Archaeological discussion has focused on what kinds of social units built and used kivas (Ware and Blinman 2000). For functionalists such as Steward and Eggan, kivas evolved early but clan sodalities and their ceremonies waited to appear until they had large villages to integrate. In contrast, Ware suggests that the clan-ceremony-sodality-kiva complex, including medicine societies, may date to the Basketmaker III–Pueblo I transition (c.AD 700) (Ware 2002: 98).

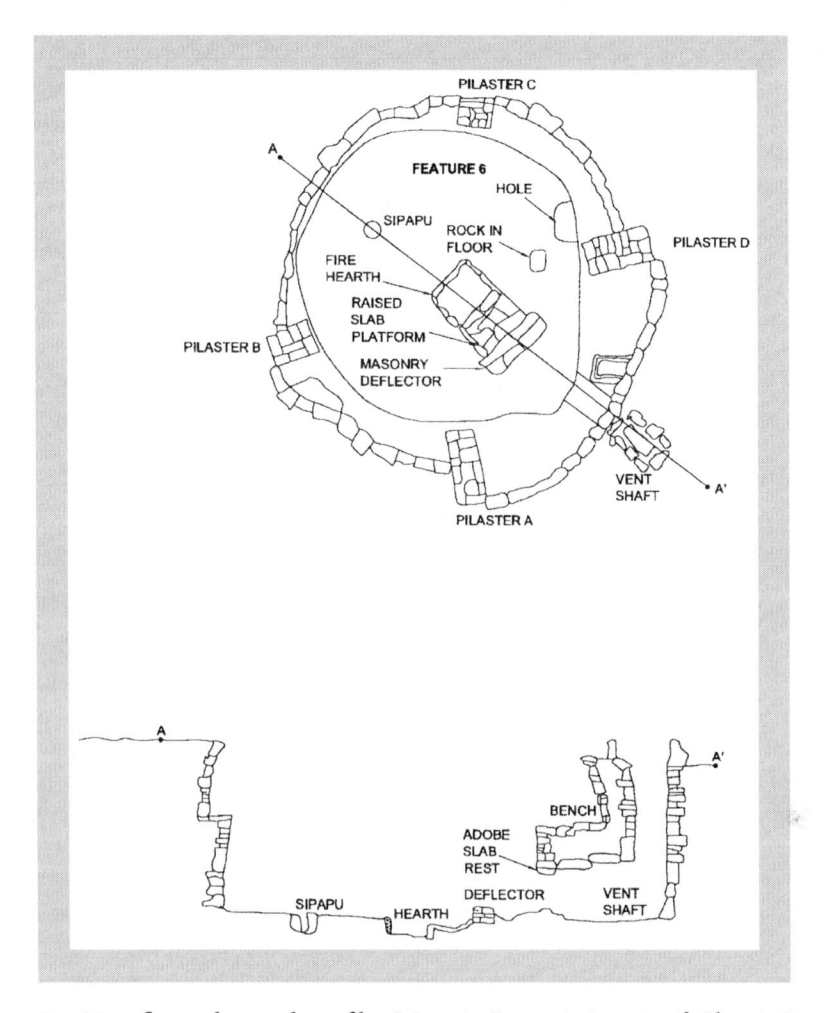

FIGURE 38.3 Kiva floor plan and profile. LA2578, Feature 6, west of Chaco Canyon in McKinley County, New Mexico, late Pueblo II period, c.AD 1050–1100. This kiva was about 4 m diameter and 1.8 m deep. Note the Sipapu (symbolic emergence place) northwest of the hearth. The ventilator complex to the south-east allows the kiva to breathe like a living being, as well as providing fresh air to its human inhabitants. This small unit pueblo site also had masonry rooms that would have housed one or two families.

In the northern Ancestral Puebloan world, kivas were paired with subterranean mealing rooms, where women would have spent many hours each day grinding corn for both ritual and domestic uses (Mobley-Tanaka 1997). Historically, grinding and other food-preparation activities were part of women's devotional activities, complementary to men's weaving and, perhaps, painting. A formalized space for women's corn-grinding paired with a kiva suggests that female ritual roles centred on preparing special foods were also formalized at this time.

Ritual activities were probably not confined to kivas and mealing rooms. In both south-western Colorado and northern Arizona, elevated frequencies of broken redware pottery bowls (imported from one production area in south-eastern Utah) at sites with kivas, compared to sites without, suggests that residential units with kivas hosted potluck-like feasts (Blinman 1989; Plog 1989). In larger Puebloan communities, the relatively simple Basketmaker great kivas became more formal and probably served as venues for ritual performance attended by members of large communities of dispersed-unit pueblos.

Settlement pattern and ethnographic evidence indicates that between the eighth and ninth centuries, sodalities may have been detached from kin organizations in the east, but not in the west (Ware 2002: 102–6). This process paved the way for more complicated and larger-scale ritual organization in the eastern Ancestral Pueblos, most notably in and around Chaco Canyon.

7 THE CHACO RITUALITY

The most elaborate ritual activities and spaces in the Puebloan world appear in Chaco Canyon in north-western New Mexico in the Pueblo II period (*c.*AD 900–1130). The canyon has larger-than-usual earlier communities, but population, or at least buildings, increased dramatically around AD 900. Chaco's inhabitants, and perhaps visiting pilgrims, constructed massive multi-storied pueblos known as great houses, with numerous kivas, great kivas, and plazas. Great house architecture was characterized by limited access to internal spaces such as storage rooms and blocked-in kivas. Kantner concludes that, 'in many ways, Chacoan religious structures provided a mixed message, with the monumental, highly visible, but spatially confined great houses fronted by large great kivas and expansive plaza areas' (2006: 37). Two of the largest great houses, Pueblo Bonito and Chetro Ketl, contained storerooms with unusually elaborate artefacts, including effigy vessels, copper bells imported from west Mexico, polished stone celts called tchamahias, sandal-shaped stone tablets, pottery models of burden baskets, wooden staffs, remains of macaws imported from Mexico, mosaic ornaments, arrows, pigments, painted wooden flowers and birds, and prayer sticks (Judd 1954; Mathien 2003; Neitzel 2003; Pepper 1920; Vivian et al. 1978). A cliff-face amphitheatre (Loose 2008), platform mounds, plazas, and great kivas indicate facilities for public performances in which the elaborate and sometimes exotic artefacts would have been displayed.

A network of roadways, ramps, and staircases extends far outside the canyon and links, or at least points to, prominent landscape features (Roney 1992). Road segments and buildings align with cardinal directions, solstices and equinoxes, and possibly lunar events. On solstices and equinoxes, daggers of light pierce shadowed spiral petroglyphs in simple observatories. These features indicate concern with marking and perhaps controlling time (Farmer 2003; Malville 2004; Stein et al. 1997). Phenomenological investigation of Chacoan landscape and built environment suggests a microcosm of the Pueblo cosmos, with buildings, roadways, and vistas that emphasize relationships between earth and sky, seen and unseen, and movements of sun and seasons (van Dyke 2008). Kivas were apparently remodelled at intervals and pottery cylinder jars, a vessel form that is found only in some great houses, were apparently scraped down and repainted, suggesting periodic world renewal rites (Crown and Wills 2003). Residue analysis of cylinder jar fragments has yielded traces of chocolate, an important ritual drink in Mesoamerica. Inhumations easily interpreted as high-status ritual leaders in rooms in the oldest sections of Pueblo Bonito support linking leadership and priesthood; two clusters of individuals, from two biologically distinct familial groups, were somewhat taller and healthier than individuals buried in small sites in the canyon. They were accompanied by large numbers of turquoise beads and ornaments, prayer stocks, carved wands, cylinder jars, pigments, and other 'fancy' items (Akins 2003).

Ritual performances and priest-leaders must have been important organizing factors in the relationships that prevailed among Chacoan great houses inside the canyon and between the Chaco Canyon 'core' and its 'outlier' great house communities throughout the San Juan Basin and beyond, but few agree on details (Judge 1989). Was Chaco a pilgrimage centre for ritual activity or a political–economic centre; was the Chaco core self-supporting, or did it depend on importing food? If so, did Chaco export ritual? Because no ethnographic models seem to fit Chaco, the term 'rituality' has been proposed to describe a society in which leadership was based on ritual knowledge and authority, and the ability to organize access to farmland, water, trade goods, construction labour, large-scale public ritual performances, and transmission of esoteric knowledge (Yoffee, Fish, and Milner 1999).

8 Migration and Reorganization

Pueblo historians identify the Pueblo III period, c.AD 1130–1300, as the 'migration period'. Twelfth-century population movements resulted in increased variations in ritual architecture and iconography, and in episodic violence in some areas. In what had been the greater Chacoan sphere of influence, some Chacoan features survive in various combinations. Monumentality and organizational consistency decreases, and buildings show an increase in public accessibility compared to Chaco structures (Kantner 2006: 43). Pueblo ritual practice apparently retained concerns with ancestral connections, seasonal cycling, the movement of celestial bodies, and the concept of emergence and a layered universe but expressed these concepts in new ways. For example, wall murals in thirteenth-century multi-storied towers in Mesa Verde cliff-dwellings seem to depict horizon lines punctuated by mountains, earth, and sky, in which textile designs, perhaps representing clouds, appear (Brody 1991; Newsome 2005).

In contrast to Pueblo Bonito's group burials of apparent high-status ritual leaders, burials of priestly leaders in later periods are fewer, and individual. The most elaborate is the 'Burial of the Magician', discovered beneath the floor of a room in Ridge Ruin, a late twelfth-century masonry pueblo with features of a post-Chaco great house near Flagstaff (McGregor 1943). An adult male was entombed with pigments, arrow points, bone awls and tubes, carved wooden sticks, crystals, sucking tubes, painted baskets, 25 pottery vessels, and ornaments of turquoise, jet, argillite, and marine shell. Clearly a high-status individual, he was likely a priest. Around 1940, Hopi elders consulted about the assemblage verified that the man would have served as a leader of a ritual sodality that, until the late nineteenth century, performed a ceremony designed to strengthen warriors and the performance involved 'sleight of hand' feats and stick-swallowing.

Many historic pueblos have dual alternating social and ritual divisions, and material evidence for these may appear earliest in Pueblo Bonito's paired plazas and great kivas (Fritz 1978), and in the two hereditary groups evident in the high-status mortuary remains there (Akins 1986: 140). Evidence for dual divisions in the Pueblo III period, when present at all, varies. Architectural layout, kiva forms, and access routes in Mug House, a thirteenth-century Mesa Verde cliff dwelling, suggests that the village's ritual and social organization was divided in two spatially delineated parts (Rohn 1971: 39–40). Dual divisions did not always occur within what archaeologists identify as one village, and some eastern Pueblo migration traditions describe paired communities that travelled together but settled on opposite sides of a river (as at Taos Pueblo today). Two kinds of short-lived but large plaza-oriented pueblo communities appear in late thirteenth-century settlements of the El Morro valley, between present-day Zuni and Acoma. Round roomblocks located on valley floors near arable land have an unusually large number of water birds in their faunal assemblage. Square roomblocks located on mesas and ridge tops have a high proportion of raptors in their faunal assemblages and evidence for communal hunting and feasting. These seemingly separate settlements may have been integrated into a dual alternating social and ritual system based on oppositions between summer, agriculture, and feminine-gendered concepts and activities vs. winter, hunting, and masculine-gendered concepts and activities (Potter 2002; Potter and Perry 2000). Later, in the 1300s and 1400s, these short-lived dual organizations came to reside together in larger, more stable, long-term settlements, where we find them today.

Though archaeologists interpret dual divisions and sodality membership as integrative mechanisms that help deflect conflict, evidence for violence is particularly frequent for the Pueblo III period, an era punctuated by severe droughts and depopulation of entire regions. In some areas, villages were sited in defensible locations, and osteologists have identified injuries and deaths likely due to violence. Human remains in some sites include evidence for what some have tactfully termed 'processed human bone'—bones deliberately broken into fragments, burned, and perhaps boiled in pots (LeBlanc 1999: 169–76). Ritual cannibalism, acts of war, and witch execution have all been proposed as explanations, but because evidence varies considerably, interpretations should—and do—vary as well (Chamberlin 2006; Darling 1998; Dongoske et al. 2000; Nichols and Crown 2008; Walker 1998).

9 REGIONAL ICONOGRAPHIES, LOCAL VARIATIONS

The Pueblo world as we know it from historic records and contemporary experience coalesces in fourteenth-century settlement clusters that extend along the Rio Grande from the Chama Valley and Taos south to the Salinas Pueblos; and from the Albuquerque area west along the Rio Puerco of the East, Rio Puerco of the West, Zuni River, and Little Colorado River up to the Hopi Mesas in the west. In this Pueblo PIV time period, $c.$AD 1300–1540, multi-storied plaza-oriented villages dominate the architectural record. Representational imagery, including birds, flowers, butterflies, serpents, katsinas, and designs derived from cotton textiles dominate rock art, kiva murals, and painted pottery (Brody 1991; Hill and Hays-Gilpin 1999).

Large settlements south of the Colorado Plateau, in the area often termed 'Salado', are also part of the broad pattern of shared community organization, ritual practice, and iconography that continues to the present day. Iconography of Salado and western Pueblo polychrome pottery beginning around AD 1300 includes abstract images of birds and serpents rendered in red, black, and white replace bichrome geometric designs. Crown (1994) associates this imagery with rituals focused on earth, fertility, sky, and rain, and terms the complex the 'Southwestern Regional Cult'. Polychrome bowls with similar imagery, but locally distinct colour schemes, appear all over the Pueblo world after 1300. Large brightly coloured bowls, enhanced by shiny glaze paints in the Zuni and Rio Grande Pueblos, suggest that public contexts for feasting— likely associated with ritual performances in plazas—increased in both the western Pueblo and Rio Grande areas (Mills 2004; Spielmann 1998). Feasts and katsina performances likely had a great deal to do with forming community identities (Eckert 2008) and defining contrasts and competition (Chamberlin 2006; Plog and Solometo 1997) with neighbouring pueblos.

Links between ritual sodalities and leadership roles continue to appear in mortuary contexts. At Grasshopper Pueblo, with 500 rooms in the early 1300s, about half of adult men were buried with one of four distinctive objects that may have signified sodality membership: *Glycymeris* shell pendants, *Conus* shell tinklers, bone hairpins, and clusters of arrowheads. Only one individual, a 40–45-year-old male, had all four items in abundance, as well as a painted wand and a bone rasp (Reid and Whittlesey 1999: 126–32).

Gender roles appear to have narrowed and specialized in some parts of the Pueblo world, especially in the eastern Pueblos, around AD 1300. Women's group-grinding rooms disappear in the east and diminish in the west. Shrines probably associated with women's activities surround a Pueblo III-period ancestral Taos site, but not later villages. Paradoxically, feminine imagery such as flowers, corn maidens, and stone figurines representing women increase in Pueblo IV ritual contexts. Male priests may have recruited ritual power from the realm of actual female praxis and reinvested it in masculine religious ideology (Fowles 2005; Hill and Hays-Gilpin 1999).

10 Katsinas, Calendars, and Conflict

Depictions of spirit beings known as katsinas in most pueblos appear as early as AD 1300 in rock art, painted pottery, and kiva murals associated with growing plaza-oriented villages throughout the Pueblo world (Schaafsma 1994). In present-day katsina practice, initiated men personate the spirit beings responsible for bringing rain and all good things; transformation in part effected with masks (Ladd 1994; Tedlock 1994: 171), more sensitively termed 'katsina friends' (Hieb 1994: 26). Early western Pueblo katsina depictions in pottery and rock art usually show only faces, and are much simpler than Rio Grande images which often show the whole body (Figure 38.1). Katsina religion may have spread north from the southern Rio Grande area, as suggested by rock art (Schaafsma 1994), or it may have coalesced in the rectangular kivas and village plazas of early-fourteenth-century villages in the Upper Little Colorado River region (Adams 1991, 1994). Or similar movements may have begun in several areas and merged through migration and aggregation. Both areas may have hosted Mimbres migrants, who left southwest New Mexico in the mid-1100s. At the peak of Mimbres population and intense mortuary ritual c.AD 1000–1130, Mimbres potters had depicted ritual subjects (Brody 2004), some of which prefigure katsina-related iconography. Mimbres imagery in turn shares themes with Mesoamerican iconography

(Thompson 1994), and most acknowledge at least distant Mesoamerican origins or influences on katsina religion (see especially Schaafsma and Schaafsma 1974).

The development and spread of katsina religion likely involved exchange of local versions of the 'Southwestern Regional Cult', reinterpretations of old and new icons from many areas, and new innovations (Hays-Gilpin 2006). For example, contemporary Pueblo ritual dress, especially katsina regalia, includes items from both southern and northern traditions that were blended through large-scale migrations in the late thirteenth through fifteenth centuries (Teague 2000; Webster and Loma'omvaya 2004). By the mid-1400s, Rio Grande-style katsina imagery appears in kiva murals, rock art, and painted pottery in the Hopi area (Hays-Gilpin and LeBlanc 2007; Schaafsma 1994, 2000, 2007a). Katsina religion is portable across the landscape and language groups and helps integrate large communities by initiating all community members (or all males, as is the case today everywhere but Hopi).

The assumption that the katsina religion has always served an integrative function for large, aggregating villages whose component parts had disparate migration histories and perhaps spoke distinct languages (i.e. Adams 1991), has been challenged with iconographic and ethnographic associations between some katsinas and weapons, shields, scalps, and warriors (Plog and Solometo 1997). Fifteenth-century kiva murals (Brody 1991; Dutton 1963; Hibben 1975; Smith 1952; Schaafsma 2007b) and rock art (Schaafsma 2000) depict warriors and weapons, some associated with katsinas. The early katsina religion, then, might have had roles in conflict, boundary negotiation, and asserting distinct community identities.

By the late AD 1400s, the number of inhabited Pueblo villages decreased. Large areas were depopulated as Pueblo populations aggregated into the areas they inhabit today. Some suggest population declined due to European-introduced diseases spreading in advance of Spanish explorers, or droughts that made dry farming difficult. But consolidation of the Pueblo ritual calendar might also have provided a 'pull' factor to draw members into participation in katsina religion, a variety of sodalities, and feasting events that would have redistributed food among participants.

11 MISSIONS, REVOLT, AND RENEWAL

Spaniards arrived in the Pueblo world in 1540 and began to establish colonies and missions in 1598. Up to this point, all evidence points to Pueblo religion as additive, not exclusionary. New sodalities were adopted; new katsinas appeared. In contrast, Franciscan priests expected their Pueblo hosts to practise only Catholicism and punished those who practised native religion. Yet Pueblo people continued to practise their religion in secret (Polingyouma 2008). In the 1680 Pueblo Revolt, they successfully removed Spaniards from their Pueblo communities. By 1696, the Pueblos of New Mexico were back under Spanish rule, but the Hopi villages were never re-conquered.

Little archaeology of religion has been done in settlements of the Mission, Revolt, and Reconquest periods. Catholic missions at several now-depopulated villages have been excavated (Hayes 1974; Ivey 1998; Montgomery et al. 1949; Vivian 1979; Toulouse 1949). Evidence from architecture, pottery, rock art, mural painting, oral histories, and documentary evidence suggest that Pueblo people and Spanish priests did not successfully separate the traditional and Catholic religions, but each accommodated and in some cases tried to subvert the other in sometimes subtle ways. For example, pre-mission glaze-painted pottery in the Rio Grande Pueblos depicted birds, katsinas, and other important religious imagery. In the mission period, potters invented a glaze paint that became runny upon firing, obscuring their traditional designs. They painted crosses to satisfy the priests, but used forms that signified dragonflies and birds in their own iconography (Mobley-Tanaka 2002). Zuni potters reduced native religious symbols such as katsinas on their pottery in the seventeenth century and resorted to textile and feather motifs which certainly had ritual importance but were less obvious to their oppressors (Mills 2002: 94). After the Revolt, bird and prayer feather designs reappeared on Pueblo pottery in many areas, but the Pueblos did not reject all Spanish influences. They kept Spanish-introduced livestock and crops, and some Spanish-style bird and flower designs (Liebmann 2002: 137).

This well-documented and well-remembered episode in Pueblo history offers archaeologists a new way to think about relationships between ritual and violence hinted at in the archaeological record of earlier periods. Most Pueblo ritual is about managing order and disorder at some level. Ritual clowning parodies bad behaviour on the part of community members. Parodies of neighbouring ethnic groups are also frequent in Pueblo ritual performance. Witchcraft rumours and actions taken against witches escalate enforcement of good behaviour and stress differences between the good-hearted and the evil-hearted.

In Pueblo thought, purification sometimes calls for violence. In 1700, following the village of Awat'ovi's decision to allow Spanish friars to re-establish the mission that had been destroyed in the Pueblo Revolt, members of other Hopi villages attacked. On the basis of ethnology, ethnohistoric records, and traditional histories describing destruction of previous worlds and villages, Peter Whiteley (2002) concludes that destruction of Awat'ovi was a process or purification and world renewal. The attackers in effect eliminated threats of witchcraft and Spanish return but rescued Awat'ovi's ritual sodalities and replanted them in their own villages by adopting sodality leaders and incorporating their ceremonies into the Hopi ritual calendar. Thus violence is sometimes part of a continuum of ritual actions that are necessary to keep the world in balance, and the Western separation of sacred and secular blurs, as it always does in the Pueblo world.

12 CONCLUSION

The biggest challenge faced right now by archaeologists and Pueblo communities alike is how to work together productively and respectfully. Ultimately, 'preserving' Pueblo religion is the responsibility of the Pueblo communities (Suina 2002: 16) and not of anthropologists, who at best, can offer assistance if invited. Can methods and theories developed by archaeologists from outside the Pueblo world assist Pueblo people with writing detailed long-term histories, documenting land claims and use-rights to shrines, plant-gathering areas, and other sacred places, and establishing cultural affiliation for repatriation of human remains, funerary objects, and sacred objects in museums and private collections? Or must Pueblo scholars invent new ways to meet these goals? Can archaeologists productively and respectfully continue to study the functions and organizational structures of Pueblo religion? How should archaeology of Pueblo religion, or any other archaeology done in Ancestral Pueblo places, proceed? Rina Swentzell, an architectural historian and member of Santa Clara Pueblo, writes:

With the belief that places [like houses] are alive, Pueblo people visit the old ruins to breathe in the strength of the place and of 'those who have gone on before.' . . . That is why we must think and move carefully wherever we go, because we become one with the place and, therefore, influence its spiritual quality. [Swentzell 1993: 144]

Suggested Reading

Foundations of archaeology of Puebloan religion rest on abundant ethnographic research, especially that of the Bureau of American Ethnology, Smithsonian Institution. Recent works that link traditional histories with archaeological evidence include Teague (1993) and Whiteley (1998). Ethnologies and histories by members of Pueblo communities include Dozier (1970a), Kuwanwisiwma (2004), Ladd (1994), Nequatewa (1967), Ortiz (1969, 1972), Sando (1976), Swentzell (1993, 2001), and Yava (1978). For recent history of the archaeology of Pueblo religion, see *Religion in the Prehispanic Southwest* (VanPool et al. 2006) and the *Southwest Symposium* series (Hegmon 2000, Mills 2004, Schlanger 2002, Webster and McBrinn 2008). Ritual structures and spaces are addressed in *The Architecture of Social Integration in Prehistoric Pueblos* (Lipe and Hegmon 1989). Essential topics include foodways, feasting, and maize ritual (Adams 1991; Blinman 1989; Bohrer 1994, 1995; Eckert 2008; Ford 1972b, 1980, 1994; Mills 2004; Mobley-Tanaka 1997; Ortman 1998; Plog 1989; Potter 2000, 2002; Potter and Perry 2000; Spielmann 1998); gender and ritual practice (Fowles 2005; Hays-Gilpin 2000a, 2000b, 2004, 2007, 2008; Robins and Hays-Gilpin 2000), the katsina religion (Adams 1991; Plog and Solometo 1997; Schaafsma 1994; Sekaquaptewa and Washburn 2004, 2006); ritual landscapes (Anschuetz 2005, van Dyke 2008); and archaeoastronomy (Farmer 2003, Malville 2004, Stein et al. 1997). For connections between Pueblos and Precolumbian Mexico, begin with Braniff et al. (2001), Fields and Zamudio-Taylor (2001), Riley (2005), Schaafsma (1999, 2001), Taube (2000, 2001), and Thompson (1994, 2004).

References

Adams, E. C. 1991. *The Origin and Development of the Pueblo Katsina Cult* (Tucson: University of Arizona Press).
——1994. 'The kachina cult: a western Pueblo perspective' in P. Schaafsma (ed.), *Kachinas in the Pueblo World* (Albuquerque: University of New Mexico Press), pp. 35–46.
Akins, N. J. 1986. *A Biocultural Approach to Human Burials from Chaco Canyon, New Mexico*, Reports of the Chaco Center No. 9 (Santa Fe: National Park Service, U.S. Department of the Interior, Branch of Cultural Research).
——2003. 'The burials of Pueblo Bonito' in J. E. Neitzel (ed.), *Pueblo Bonito: Center of the Chacoan world* (Washington, DC: Smithsonian Books), pp. 94–106.
Anschuetz, K. F. 2005. 'Landscapes as memory: Archaeological history to learn from and live by' in M. Hegmon and B. S. Eiselt (eds), *Engaged Anthropology: Research essays on North American archaeology, ethnobotany, and museology: Papers in honor of Richard I. Ford* (Ann Arbor: Museum of Anthropology, University of Michigan Press), pp. 52–72.

BLINMAN, E. 1989. 'Potluck in the protokiva: Ceramics and ceremonialism in Pueblo I villages' in W. D. Lipe and M. Hegmon (eds), *The Architecture of Social Integration in Prehistoric Pueblos*, Occasional Papers of the Crow Canyon Archaeological Center, 1 (Cortez, Colorado: Crow Canyon Archaeological Center), pp. 113–24.

BOHRER, V. 1994. 'Maize in Middle American and Southwestern United States agricultural traditions' in S. Johannesson and C. Hastorf (eds), *Corn and Culture in the Prehistoric New World* (Boulder: Westview Press), pp. 469–512.

——1995. 'The where, when, and why of Corn Guardians' in H. Wolcott Toll (ed.), *Soil, Water, Biology, and Belief in Prehistoric and Traditional Southwestern Agriculture*, New Mexico Archaeological Council Special Publication 2 (Albuquerque: New Mexico Archaeological Council), pp. 361–8.

BRANDT, E. 2002. 'The climate for ethnographic/ethnohistoric research in the Southwest' in S. H. Schlanger (ed.), *Traditions, Transitions, and Technologies: Themes in Southwestern archaeology* (Boulder: University Press of Colorado), pp. 113–26.

BRANIFF, B., CORDELL, M., GUTIÉRREZ, E., et al. 2001. *La Gran Chichimeca: el lugar de las rocas secas* (Mexico City: CONACULTA).

BRODY, J. J. 1991. *Anasazi and Pueblo painting* (Santa Fe: School of American Research Press).
——2004. *Mimbres Painted Pottery*, rev. edn (Santa Fe: School of American Research Press).

CHAMBERLIN, M. A. 2006. 'Symbolic conflict and the spatiality of tradition in small-scale societies', *Cambridge Archaeological Journal*, 16: 39–51.

COLE, S. J. 1989. 'Iconography and symbolism in Basketmaker rock art' in J. S. Day, P. D. Friedman and M. J. Tate (eds), *Rock art of the Western Canyons* (Denver: Denver Museum of Natural History and the Colorado Archaeological Society), pp. 59–85.

CORDELL, L. 1997. *Archaeology of the Southwest*, 2nd edn (New York: Academic Press).

CROWN, P. L. 1994. *Ceramics and Ideology: Salado polychrome pottery* (Albuquerque: University of New Mexico Press).

——and WILLS, W. H. 2003. 'Modifying pottery and kivas at Chaco: Pentimento, restoration, or renewal?', *American Antiquity*, 68(3): 511–32.

DARLING, A. 1998. 'Mass inhumation and the execution of witches in the American Southwest', *American Anthropologist*, 100: 732–52.

DONGOSKE, K. E., MARTIN, D. L., and FERGUSON, T. J. 2000. 'Critique of the claim of cannibalism at Cowboy Wash', *American Antiquity*, 65: 179–90.

DOZIER, E. P. 1970a. *The Pueblo Indians of North America* (New York: Holt, Rinehart, and Winston).

——1970b. 'Making inferences from the present to the past' in William A. Longacre (ed.), *Reconstructing Prehistoric Pueblo Societies* (Santa Fe: School of American Research Press), pp. 202–13.

DUTTON, B. P. 1963. *Sun Father's Way: The kiva murals of Kuaua, A Pueblo ruin, Coronado State Monument, New Mexico* (Albuquerque: University of New Mexico Press).

DYKE, R. VAN 2008. *The Chaco Experience: Landscape and ideology at the center place* (Santa Fe: School of Advanced Research Press).

ECKERT, S. L. 2008. *Pottery and Practice: The expression of identity at Pottery Mound and Hummingbird Pueblo* (Albuquerque: University of New Mexico Press).

EGGAN, F. 1950. *Social Organization of the Western Pueblos* (Chicago: University of Chicago Press).

FARMER, J. D. 2003. 'Astronomy and ritual at Chaco Canyon' in J. E. Neitzel (ed.), *Pueblo Bonito: Center of the Chacoan world* (Washington, DC: Smithsonian Books), pp. 61–71.

Fields, V. and Zamudio-Taylor, V. (eds) 2001. *The Road to Aztlan: Art from a mythic homeland* (Los Angeles: Los Angeles County Museum of Art).

Ford, R. I. 1972a. 'Barter, gift, or violence: An analysis of Tewa intertribal exchange' in E. N. Wilmsen (ed.), *Social Exchange and Interaction*, Anthropological Papers No. 46 (Ann Arbor: Museum of Anthropology, University of Michigan), pp. 21–45.

——1972b. 'An ecological perspective on the Pueblos' in Alfonso Ortiz (ed.), *New Perspectives on the Pueblos* (Albuquerque: University of New Mexico Press), pp. 1–17.

——1980. 'The color of survival', *Discovery*, 1–80: 17–29.

——1994. 'Corn is our mother' in S. Johannesson and C. Hastorf (eds), *Corn and Culture in the Prehistoric New World* (Boulder: Westview Press), pp. 513–25.

Fowles, S. 2005. 'Our father (our mother): Gender ideology, praxis, and marginalization in Pueblo religion' in M. Hegmon and B. Sunday Eiselt (eds), *Engaged Anthropology: Research essays on North American archaeology, ethnobotany, and museology: Papers in honor of Richard I. Ford* (Ann Arbor: University of Michigan Press), pp. 27–51.

Fritz, J. 1978. 'Paleopsychology today: Ideational systems and human adaptation in prehistory' in C. Redman, M. J. Berman, E. V. Curtin, et al. (eds), *Social Archeology: Beyond subsistence and dating* (New York: Academic Press), pp. 37–59.

Green, J. (ed.) 1979. *Zuñi: Selected writings of Frank Hamilton Cushing* (Lincoln: University of Nebraska Press).

Hayes, A. C. 1974. *The Four Churches of Pecos* (Albuquerque: University of New Mexico Press).

Hays-Gilpin, K. 2000a. 'Gender ideology and ritual activities' in P. L. Crown (ed.), *Women and Men in the Prehispanic Southwest: Labor, power, and prestige* (Santa Fe: School of American Research Press), pp. 91–135.

——2000b. 'Gender constructs in the material culture of seventh century Anasazi farmers in northeastern Arizona' in M. Donald and L. M. Hurcombe (eds), *Gender and Material Culture: Representations of gender from prehistory to the present* (Hampshire, UK: Macmillan), pp. 31–44.

——2002. 'Wearing a butterfly, coming of age: A 1500 year old Pueblo tradition' in K. A. Kamp (ed.), *Children in the Prehistoric Puebloan Southwest* (Salt Lake City: University of Utah Press), pp. 196–210.

——2004. *Ambiguous Images: Gender and rock art* (Walnut Creek, CA: AltaMira).

——2006. 'Icons and ethnicity: Hopi painted pottery and murals' in C. S. VanPool, T. L. VanPool, and D. A. Phillips Jr (eds), *Religion in the Prehispanic Southwest* (Walnut Creek, CA: AltaMira), pp. 67–80.

——2007. 'Beyond mother earth and father sky: Sex and gender in ancient Southwestern visual arts and ethnography' in T. Insoll (ed.), *The Archaeology of Identities: A Reader* (London: Routledge), pp. 154–74.

——2008. 'Life's pathways: Geographic metaphors in protohistoric Puebloan material culture' in L. Webster and M. McBrinn (eds), *Archaeology without Borders: Contact, commerce, and change in the U.S. Southwest and Northwestern Mexico* (Boulder: University Press of Colorado), pp. 257–70.

——and LeBlanc, S. 2007. 'Sikyatki style in regional context' in Polly Schaafsma (ed.), *New Perspectives on Pottery Mound Pueblo* (Albuquerque: University of New Mexico Press), pp. 109–36.

Hegmon, M. (ed.) 2000. *The Archaeology of Regional Interaction: Religion, warfare, and exchange across the American Southwest and beyond* (Boulder: University Press of Colorado).

Hibben, F. C. 1975. *Kiva Art of the Anasazi* (Las Vegas, Nevada: KC Publications).

HIEB, L. A. 1994. 'The meaning of *katsina*: Toward a cultural definition of "person" in Hopi religion' in P. Schaafsma (ed.), *Kachinas in the Pueblo World* (Albuquerque: University of New Mexico Press), pp. 23-33.

HILL, J. H. and HAYS-GILPIN, K. 1999. 'The flower world in material culture: An iconographic complex in the Southwest and Mesoamerica', *Journal of Anthropological Research*, 55: 1-37.

HUCKELL, L. and VANPOOL, C. 2006. '*Toloatzin* and shamanic journeys: Exploring the ritual role of sacred Datura in the prehistoric Southwest' in C. S. VanPool, T. L. VanPool, and D. A. Phillips Jr (eds), *Religion in the Prehispanic Southwest* (Walnut Creek, CA: AltaMira), pp. 147-64.

IVEY, J. E. 1998. 'Convento kivas in the missions of New Mexico', *New Mexico Historical Review*, 73: 121-52.

JUDD, N. S. 1954. *The Material Culture of Pueblo Bonito*, Smithsonian Miscellaneous Collections, CXXIV (Washington, DC: Smithsonian Institution).

JUDGE, W. J. 1989. 'Chaco Canyon—San Juan Basin' in L. S. Cordell and G. J. Gumerman (eds), *Dynamics of Southwest Prehistory* (Santa Fe: School of American Research Press), pp. 209-61.

KANTNER, J. 2006. 'Religious behavior in the post-Chaco years' in C. S. VanPool, T. L. VanPool, and D. A. Phillips Jr (eds), *Religion in the Prehispanic Southwest* (Walnut Creek, CA: AltaMira), pp. 31-51.

KUWANWISIWMA, L. J. 2004. '*Yupköyvi*: The Hopi story of Chaco Canyon' in D. G. Noble (ed.), *In Search of Chaco: New approaches to an archaeological enigma* (Santa Fe: School of American Research Press), pp. 41-7.

LADD, E. J. 1994. 'The Zuni ceremonial system: The kiva' in P. Schaafsma (ed.), *Kachinas in the Pueblo World* (Albuqueque: University of New Mexico Press), pp. 17-21.

LEBLANC, S. A. 1999. *Prehistoric Warfare in the American Southwest* (Salt Lake City: University of Utah Press).

LEKSON, S. H. 1988. 'The idea of the kiva in archaeology', *Kiva*, 53(3): 213-34.

——1999. 'Was Casas a Pueblo?' in C. F. Schaafsma and C. L. Riley (eds), *The Casas Grandes World* (Salt Lake City: University of Utah Press), pp. 84-92.

LEVY, J. E. 1992. *Orayvi Revisited: Social stratification in an 'egalitarian' society* (Santa Fe: School of American Research Press).

LIEBMANN, M. J. 2002. 'Signs of power and resistance: The (re)creation of Christian imagery and identities in the Pueblo revolt era' in R. W. Preucel (ed.), *Archaeologies of the Pueblo Revolt: Identity, meaning, and renewal in the Pueblo world* (Albuquerque: University of New Mexico Press), pp. 132-44.

LIPE, W. D., and HEGMON, M. (eds) 1989. *The Architecture of Social Integration in Prehistoric Pueblos*, Occasional papers of the Crow Canyon Archaeological Center No. 1 (Cortez, Colorado: Crow Canyon Archaeological Center).

LOOSE, R. W. 2008. 'Tse'Biinaholds'a Yalti (Curved rock that speaks)', *Time and Mind: The Journal of Archaeology, Consciousness and Culture*, 1: 31-49.

LYONS, P. D. 2003. *Ancestral Hopi Migrations*, Anthropological Papers of the University of Arizona No. 68 (Tucson: University of Arizona Press).

MCGREGOR, J. C. 1943. 'Burial of an early American magician', *Proceedings of the American Philosophical Society*, 86(2): 270-98.

MALVILLE, J. M. 2004. 'Sacred time in Chaco Canyon and beyond' in D. G. Noble (ed.), *In Search of Chaco: New approaches to an archaeological enigma* (Santa Fe: School of American Research Press), pp. 86-92.

MATHIEN, J. 2003. 'Artifacts from Pueblo Bonito: One hundred years of interpretation' in J. E. Neitzel (ed.), *Pueblo Bonito: Center of the Chacoan world* (Washington, DC: Smithsonian Books), pp. 127–42.

MILLS, B. J. 2002. 'Acts of resistance: Zuni ceramics, social identity, and the Pueblo Revolt' in R. W. Preucel (ed.), *Archaeologies of the Pueblo Revolt: Identity, meaning, and renewal in the Pueblo world* (Albuquerque: University of New Mexico Press), pp. 85–98.

——(ed.) 2004. *Identity, Feasting, and the Archaeology of the Greater Southwest* (Boulder: University Press of Colorado).

MOBLEY-TANAKA, J. L. 1997. 'Gender and ritual space during the pithouse to Pueblo transition: Subterranean mealing rooms in the northern Southwest', *American Antiquity*, 62: 437–48.

——2002. 'Crossed cultures, crossed meanings: The manipulation of ritual imagery in early historic Pueblo resistance' in R. W. Preucel (ed.), *Archaeologies of the Pueblo Revolt: Identity, meaning, and renewal in the Pueblo world* (Albuquerque: University of New Mexico Press), pp. 77–84.

MONTGOMERY, R. G., SMITH, W., and BREW, J. O. 1949. *Franciscan Awatovi: The excavation and conjectural reconstruction of a 17th-century Spanish mission establishment at a Hopi Indian town in northeastern Arizona* (Cambridge, MA: Harvard Peabody Museum of Archaeology and Ethnology).

MORSS, N. 1954. *Clay figurines of the American Southwest: With a description of the new Pillings find in northeastern Utah and a comparison with certain other North American figurines* (Cambridge, MA: Harvard Peabody Museum of Archaeology and Ethnology).

NEITZEL, J. D. 2003. 'Artifact distributions from Pueblo Bonito' in J. E. Neitzel (ed.), *Pueblo Bonito: Center of the Chacoan World* (Washington, DC: Smithsonian Books), pp. 107–26.

NEQUATEWA, E. 1967. *Truth of a Hopi: Stories relating to the origin, myths and clan histories of the Hopi* (Flagstaff, Arizona: Northland Press).

NEWSOME, E. 2005. 'Weaving the sky: The Cliff Palace Painted Tower', *Plateau*, 2(2): 28–41.

NICHOLS, D. and CROWN, P. (eds) 2008. *Social Violence in the Prehispanic American Southwest* (Tucson: University of Arizona Press).

ORTIZ, A. 1969. *The Tewa World: Space, time, being, and becoming in a Pueblo society* (Chicago: University of Chicago Press).

——1972. 'Ritual drama and the Pueblo worldview' in A. Ortiz (ed.), *New Perspectives on the Pueblos* (Albuquerque: University of New Mexico Press), pp. 135–61.

ORTMAN, S. 1998. 'Corn grinding and community organization in the Pueblo Southwest, AD 1150–1550' in K. A. Spielmann (ed.), *Migration and Reorganization: The Pueblo IV period in the American Southwest*, Arizona State University Anthropological Research Papers 51 (Tempe: Arizona State University), pp. 165–92.

——2008. 'Architectural metaphor and Chacoan influence in the northern San Juan' in L. D. Webster and M. E. McBrinn (eds), *Archaeology without Borders: Contact, commerce, and change in the U.S. Southwest and Northwestern Mexico* (Boulder: University Press of Colorado), pp. 227–56.

PARSONS, E. C. 1939. *Pueblo Religion* (Chicago: University of Chicago Press).

PEPPER, G. 1920. *Pueblo Bonito*, Anthropological Papers of the American Museum of Natural History, XXVII (New York: American Museum of Natural History).

PLOG, S. 1989. 'Ritual, exchange, and the development of regional systems' in W. D. Lipe and M. Hegmon (eds), *The Architecture of Social Integration in Prehistoric Pueblos*, Occasional Papers of the Crow Canyon Archaeological Center 1 (Cortez, Colorado: Crow Canyon Archaeological Center), pp. 143–60.

PLOG, S. and SOLOMETO, J. 1997. 'The never-changing and the ever-changing: The evolution of western Pueblo ritual', *Cambridge Archaeological Journal*, 7(2): 161–82.

POLINGYOUMA, E. 2008. 'Awatovi: A Hopi history' in H. Davis (ed.), *Remembering Awatovi: The story of an archaeological expedition in northern Arizona, 1935–1939* (Cambridge, MA: Harvard Peabody Museum of Archaeology and Ethnology), pp. xv–xviii.

POTTER, J. M. 2000. 'Pots, parties, and politics: Communal feasting in the American Southwest', *American Antiquity*, 65: 471–92.

——2002. 'Community, metaphor, and gender: Technological changes across the Pueblo III to Pueblo IV transition in the El Morro Valley, New Mexico' in S. H. Schlanger (ed.), *Traditions, Transitions, and Technologies: Themes in Southwestern archaeology* (Boulder: University Press of Colorado), pp. 332–49.

——and PERRY, E. M. 2000. 'Ritual as a power resource in the American Southwest' in B. J. Mills (ed.), *Alternative Leadership Strategies in the Prehispanic Southwest* (Tucson: University of Arizona Press), pp. 60–78.

REID, J. J. and WHITTLESEY, S. 1999. *Grasshopper Pueblo: A story of archaeology and ancient life* (Tucson: University of Arizona Press).

RILEY, C. L. 2005. *Becoming Aztlan: Mesoamerican influence in the greater Southwest, AD 1200–1500* (Salt Lake City: University of Utah Press).

ROBINS, M. and HAYS-GILPIN, K. 2000. 'The bird in the basket: Gender and social change in basketmaker iconography' in P. F. Reed (ed.), *Foundations of Anasazi Culture: The basketmaker–Pueblo transition* (Salt Lake City: University of Utah Press), pp. 231–47.

ROHN, A. 1971. *Mug House, Mesa Verde National Park, Colorado,* Archeological Series No. 7D (Washington, DC: National Park Service).

RONEY, J. R. 1992. 'Prehistoric roads and regional integration in the Chacoan system' in D. E. Doyel (ed.), *Anasazi Regional Organization and the Chaco System*, Anthropological Papers No. 5, Maxwell Museum of Anthropology (Albuquerque: University of New Mexico), pp. 123–31.

SANDO, J. S. 1976. *The Pueblo Indians* (San Francisco: The Indian Historian Press, American Indian Educational Publishers).

SCHAAFSMA, P. 1994. 'The prehistoric katsina cult and its origins as suggested by Southwestern rock art' in P. Schaafsma (ed.), *Kachinas in the Pueblo World* (Alburquerque: University of New Mexico Press), pp. 63–79.

——(ed.) 1994. *Kachinas in the Pueblo World* (Albuquerque: University of New Mexico Press).

——1999. 'Tlalocs, Kachinas, sacred bundles, and related symbolism in the Southwest and Mesoamerica' in C. F. Schaafsma and C. L. Riley (eds), *The Casas Grandes World* (Salt Lake City: University of Utah Press), pp. 164–92.

——2000. *Warrior, Shield, and Star: Imagery and ideology of Pueblo warfare* (Santa Fe: Western Edge Press).

——2001. 'Quetzalcoatl and the horned and feathered serpent of the Southwest' in V. M. Fields and V. Zamudio-Taylor (eds), *The Road to Aztlan: Art from a mythic homeland* (Los Angeles, Angeles County Museum of Art), pp. 138–49.

——2007a. 'The Pottery Mound murals and rock art' in P. Schaafsma (ed.), *New Perspectives on Pottery Mound Pueblo* (Albuquerque: University of New Mexico Press), pp. 137–66.

——2007b. *New Perspectives on Pottery Mound Pueblo* (Albuquerque: University of New Mexico Press).

—— and SCHAAFSMA, C. F. 1974. 'Evidence for the origins of the Pueblo Kachina cult as suggested by Southwestern rock art', *American Antiquity*, 39: 535–45.

SCHLANGER, S. H. (ed.) 2002. *Traditions, Transitions, and Technologies: Themes in Southwestern archaeology* (Boulder: University Press of Colorado).

SEKAQUAPTEWA, E. and WASHBURN, D. 2004. 'They go along singing: Reconstructing the Hopi past from ritual metaphors in song and image, *American Antiquity*, 69(3): 457–86.

—— 2006. 'Metaphors of meaning in mural paintings, pottery, and ritual song', *Plateau*, 3(1): 26–47.

SMITH, W. 1952. *Kiva Mural Decorations at Awat'ovi and Kawaika-a*, Reports of the Awat'ovi Expedition No. 5, Papers of the Peabody Museum of American Anthropology and Ethnology Papers of the Peabody Museum of American Anthropology and Ethnology, XXXVII (Cambridge, MA: Harvard University Press).

—— 1990. 'When is a kiva?' in R. H. Thompson (ed.), *When is a Kiva? And other questions about Southwestern archaeology* (Tucson: University of Arizona Press), pp. 59–75.

SPIELMANN, K. A. 1998. 'Ritual influence on the development of Rio Grande Glaze A ceramics' in K. A. Spielmann (ed.), *Migration and Reorganization: The Pueblo IV period in the American Southwest*, Arizona State University Anthropological Research Papers 51 (Tempe: Arizona State University), pp. 253–61.

STEIN, J., SUITER, J. E., and FORD, D. 1997. 'High noon in Old Bonito: Sun, shadow, and the geometry of the Chaco complex' in B. H. Morrow and V. B. Price (eds), *Anasazi Architecture and American Design* (Albuquerque: University of New Mexico Press), pp. 133–48.

STEVENSON, M. C. 1887. 'The religious life of the Zuni child' in *Fifth annual report of the Bureau of American Ethnology for the years 1883–1884* (Washington, DC: Smithsonian Institution), pp. 533–55.

—— 1904. 'The Zuni Indians: Their mythology, esoteric fraternities, and ceremonies', *Twenty-third Annual Report of the Bureau of American Ethnology* (Washington, DC: Smithsonian Institution), pp. 3–634.

STEWARD, J. 1937. 'Ecological aspects of Southwestern society', *Anthropos*, 32: 87–104.

—— 1955. *Theory of Culture Change: The methodology of multilinear evolution* (Urbana: University of Illinois Press).

STIRLING, M. 1942. *Origin Myth of Acoma, and Other Records*, Bureau of American Ethnology Bulletin 135 (Washington, DC: Smithsonian Institution).

SUINA, J. H. 2002. 'The persistence of the corn Mothers' in R. W. Preucel (ed.), *Archaeologies of the Pueblo Revolt: Identity, meaning, and renewal in the Pueblo world* (Albuquerque: University of New Mexico Press), pp. 212–16.

SWENTZELL, R. 1993. 'Mountain form, village form: Unity in the Pueblo world' in S. Lekson (ed.), *Ancient Land, Ancestral Places: Paul Logsdon in the Pueblo Southwest* (Santa Fe: Museum of New Mexico Press), pp. 139–47.

—— 2001. 'Centers in the Pueblo world' in V. M. Fields and V. Zamudio-Taylor (eds), *The Road to Aztlan: Art from a mythic homeland* (Los Angeles: Los Angeles County Museum of Art), pp. 310–17.

TAUBE, K. 2000. 'Lighting celts and corn fetishes: The Formative Olmec and the development of maize symbolism in Mesoamerica and the American Southwest' in J. Clark and M. Pye (eds), *Olmec Art and Archaeology in Mesoamerica* (Washington, DC: National Gallery of Art), pp. 297–337.

TAUBE, K. 2001. 'The breath of life: The symbolism of wind in Mesoamerica and the American Southwest' in V. M. Fields and V. Zamudio-Taylor (eds), *The Road to Aztlan: Art from a mythic homeland* (Los Angeles: Los Angeles County Museum of Art), pp. 102–23.

TEAGUE, L. S. 1993. 'Prehistory and the traditions of the O'Odham and Hopi', *Kiva*, 58: 435–54.

——2000. 'Outward and visible signs: Textiles in ceremonial contexts' in M. Hegmon (ed.), *The Archaeology of Regional Interaction: Religion, warfare, and exchange across the American Southwest and beyond* (Boulder: University of Colorado Press), pp. 421–47.

TEDLOCK, D. 1979. 'Zuni religion and world view' in A. Ortiz (ed.), *The Southwest*, Handbook of North American Indians, IX (Washington, DC: Smithsonian Institution), pp. 499–508.

——1994. 'Stories of Kachinas and the dance of life and death in P. Schaafsma (ed.), *Kachinas in the Pueblo World* (Alburquerque: University of New Mexico Press), pp. 161–74.

THOMPSON, M. 1994. 'The evolution and dissemination of Mimbres iconography in P. Schaafsma (ed.), *Kachinas in the Pueblo World* (Albuquerque: University of New Mexico Press), pp. 93–105.

——2004. 'Pre-Columbian Venus: Celestial twin and icon of duality. *Tolatzin* and shamanic journeys: Exploring the ritual role of sacred Datura in the prehistoric Southwest' in C. S. VanPool, T. L. VanPool, and D. A. Phillips Jr (eds), *Religion in the Prehispanic Southwest* (Walnut Creek, CA: AltaMira), pp. 165–83.

TITIEV, M. 1944. *Old Oraibi: A study of the Hopi Indians of Third Mesa*, Papers of the Peabody Museum of American Archaeology and Ethnology, Harvard University, II(1) (Cambridge, MA: Harvard University Press).

TOULOUSE, J. H. JR 1949. *The Mission of San Gregorio de Abó: A report on the excavation and repair of a seventeenth-century New Mexico mission*, Monographs of the School of American Research No. 13 (Albuquerque: University of New Mexico Press).

VANPOOL, C. S., VANPOOL, T. L., and PHILLIPS D. A. JR (eds) 2006. *Religion in the Prehispanic Southwest* (Walnut Creek, CA: AltaMira).

VIVIAN, G. 1979. *Gran Quivira: Excavations in a 17th-Century Jumano pueblo*, Archaeological Research Series No. 8 (Washington, DC: National Park Service).

VIVIAN, R. G., DODGEN, D. N., and HARTMANN, G. H. 1978. *Wooden Ritual Artifacts from Chaco Canyon, New Mexico*. Anthropological Papers of the University of Arizona 32 (Tucson: University of Arizona Press).

WALKER, W. 1995. 'Ceremonial Trash?' in J. M. Skibo, W. H. Walker, and A. E. Nielson (eds), *Expanding Archaeology* (Salt Lake City: University of Utah Press), pp. 67–79.

——1998. 'Where are the witches of prehistory?', *Journal of Archaeological Method and Theory*, 5(3): 245–308

——, LAMOTTA, V. M., and ADAMS, E. C. 2000. 'Katsinas and kiva abandonment at Homol'ovi: A deposit-oriented perspective on religion in Southwest prehistory' in M. Hegmon (ed.), *The Archaeology of Regional Interaction: Religion, Warfare, and Exchange across the American Southwest and Beyond* (Boulder: University Press of Colorado), pp. 341–60.

WALTERS, H. and ROGERS, H. C. 2001. 'Anasazi and "Anaasází": Two words, two cultures', *Kiva*, 66: 317–26.

WARE, J. 2001. 'Chaco social organization: A peripheral view' in L. S. Cordell, W. J. Judge, and J. Piper (eds), *Chaco Society and Polity: Papers from the 1999 Conference*, Special Publication 4 (Albuquerque: New Mexico Archaeological Society), pp. 79–93.

——2002. 'Descent group and sodality: Alternative Pueblo social histories' in S. H. Schlanger (ed.), *Traditions, Transitions, and Technologies: Themes in Southwestern archaeology* (Boulder: University Press of Colorado), pp. 94–112.

——and BLINMAN, E. 2000. 'Cultural collapse and reorganization: Origin and spread of Pueblo ritual sodalities' in Michelle Hegmon (ed.), *The Archaeology of Regional Interaction: Religion, warfare, and exchange across the American Southwest and beyond* (Boulder: University Press of Colorado), pp. 381–409.

WEBSTER, L. and LOMA'OMVAYA, M. 2004. 'Textiles, baskets, and Hopi cultural identity' in B. J. Mills (ed.), *Identity, Feasting, and the Archaeology of the Greater Southwest* (Boulder: University Press of Colorado), pp. 74–92.

——and MCBRINN, M. 2008. *Archaeology without Borders: Contact, commerce, and change in the U.S. Southwest and Northwestern Mexico* (Boulder: University Press of Colorado).

WHITELEY, P. M. 1998. *Rethinking Hopi Ethnography* (Washington, DC: Smithsonian Institution Press).

——2002. 'Re-Imagining Awat'ovi' in R. W. Preucel (ed.), *Archaeologies of the Pueblo Revolt: Identity, meaning, and renewal in the Pueblo world* (Albuquerque: University of New Mexico Press), pp. 147–66.

YAVA, A. 1978. *Big Falling Snow: A Tewa-Hopi Indian's life and times and the history and traditions of his people*, ed. and annotated H. Courlander (New York: Crown Publishers).

YOFFEE, N., FISH, S. K., and MILNER, G. 1999. 'Communidades, ritualities, chiefdoms: Social evolution in the American Southwest and Southeast' in J. E. Neitzel (ed.), *Great Towns and Regional Polities in the Prehistoric American Southwest and Southeast*, Amerind Foundation Publication (Albuquerque: University of New Mexico Press), pp. 261–71.

CHAPTER 39

NORTH AMERICA
Eastern Woodlands

VERNON JAMES KNIGHT

1 INTRODUCTION

THE Eastern Woodlands of North America is among the best-documented archaeological regions of the world. Here, Native American cultural chronology is traced from the terminal Pleistocene to the present, and there is a relatively abundant and continuous archaeological record of indigenous ritual and religion across this span. By Eastern Woodlands, we refer to the culture area east of the prairie Plains in North America and south of the eastern Subarctic, inhabited in pre-contact times principally by speakers of Algonquian, Iroquoian, Muskogean, and Siouan languages.

2 CHRONOLOGICAL FRAMEWORK

Eastern Woodlands chronology is conventionally divided into five stages that emphasize changes in subsistence and settlement characteristics. The Palaeoindian stage (*c.*9500–8000 BC) marks the entry of first peoples bearing a sophisticated Upper Pleistocene hunting technology into the region at the close of the last global Ice Age and the beginning of the Holocene epoch with its modern pattern of climatic fluctuation. The Archaic stage (*c.*8000–500 BC) featured the thoroughgoing adaptation of bands of hunter-gatherer-fishermen to eastern forests and rivers. In the latter part of the stage as population increased, bands became larger, more territorially restricted and more sedentary. In some areas broad-spectrum harvesting of plant foods led to the initial domestication of local plants, while heavy container technologies including pottery and stone bowl manufacture were introduced. The Woodland stage (*c.*500 BC–1000 AD) saw the initial appearance of permanent villages, as domestic gardening and pottery manufacture became ubiquitous and distinctions in social prestige became more apparent. During the Mississippian stage (*c.*1000–1600 AD) intensive agriculture based on corn and squash helped to underwrite the political unification of towns into small-scale chiefdoms featuring permanent social hierarchies. With the arrival of European explorers and then settlers in the sixteenth and seventeenth centuries, chiefly hierarchies collapsed due to the combined weight of several disruptive factors including Old World epidemic diseases. Surviving indigenous peoples adapted in several ways to the European-introduced pressures of the Historic stage (c.1600 AD–present), either by coalescing into large state-like war confederacies (e.g., the Iroquois), by steadfastly maintaining features of traditional social hierarchy (e.g. the Natchez), or by re-forming as communities of missionized Christians (e.g. the Apalachee).

3 Eastern Woodlands Ritual Traditions

Features of religious ritual and cult evolved in concert with changes in other features of social life from the small-scale, mobile bands of the Palaeoindian times to the hierarchical political chiefdoms of the Mississippian stage. Within this evolution there appeared several ritual traditions which, once introduced, endured and which together lend this culture area much of its special character. In what follows I will discuss several of the more important of these ritual traditions as seen in the archaeological record. Before proceeding, however, it will be worthwhile to comment on the possible connections of these traditions to Mesoamerica.

As recently as the 1960s, it was common to assume that many of the religious features of the prehistoric Eastern United States, including the plan of ceremonial centres, pyramidal mounds, and high-art styles, were derivative, having been introduced by direct contact with Middle American societies in Mexico (e.g., Caldwell 1958; Ford 1969; Willey 1966). However, in the light of newer and much more abundant data, what now stands in bolder relief is the relative isolation of the Eastern United States, not only from Mesoamerica to the south but also from societies of the Puebloan Southwest. Evidence of direct contact among these, while it does exist, is extraordinarily rare. Instead, many resemblances that were once seen as evidence of specific intrusions of Mesoamerican beliefs and practices are now seen as convergent or parallel developments, arising from an ancient stratum of common beliefs (Webb 1989). For example, Mississippian-stage religious art, much of which was once thought to be directly inspired from Mesoamerica, is in reality unmistakably distinct in both style and subject matter from anything to the south. Such recognitions have forced Eastern Woodlands archaeologists to look more closely at the antiquity of local cultural traditions as key elements in later emergent forms. There remains some debate, in that some scholars (e.g. Hall 1997, 2006) interpret trait resemblances as revealing a steady trickle of southern contacts. However, most specialists would now concur with White and Weinstein who conclude that 'there was no sustained contact between the Southeast and Mesoamerica, only sporadic contact through the centuries, with fundamental ideological similarities between the regions originating in deeper time and perhaps sustained by those sporadic contacts' (2008: 260).

4 Ritual Use of Exaggerated Weapons

Among the most ancient and enduring ritual traditions of the indigenous Eastern United States is the use of symbolic weaponry whose size, delicacy, material of manufacture, and craftsmanship are outside the bounds of any weapons that might have been actually used.

Often these exaggerated faux-weapons saw final use as grave accompaniments, but ethnohistoric texts from the area reveal a variety of ritual arenas in which such objects were deployed. Such texts suggest not only the use of these props in the pragmatic supplication of spirits for success in hunting, warfare, and games, but also the commemoration of mythic combat among supernaturals during creation times.

Exaggerated weaponry appears as early as late Palaeoindian times, where oversized, expertly crafted, unused bifaces made of non-local chert were crafted in shapes mimicking ordinary Dalton-style dart points. These oversized points, measuring 8–18 cm in length, occur in flexed cemetery burials in Arkansas together with other grave goods (Morse 1997). Later, in the Archaic stage, comparable oversized chert bifaces were used in a variety of regional settings, including cemeteries of the Red Ocher mortuary complex of the upper Midwest (Ritzenthaler and Quimby 1962). Characteristic bifaces of the Red Ocher complex are called turkey-tail knives, which are broad leaf-shaped forms with small notches for hafting at one end. Robert Hall (1983) has suggested that turkey-tail knives were used as bull-roarers and as talismans by individuals in vision quests.

Moving forward in time to the Mississippian stage, we again find exaggerated weaponry too fragile for use in actual combat, and by now largely associated with social and political elites. The forms are several. They include wood-handled axes with delicate copper blades, monolithic axes (skeuomorphs for wood-handled stone axes, where blade and handle are carved from a single stone), enormous 'hypertrophic' axe heads, flaked chert sword-form knives of extraordinary length and delicacy, copper-clad wooden knives, and flaked stone eccentrics in the form of maces and raptor claws (Brown 1996; Lewis and Kneberg 1958; Pauketat 1997). There are clear continuities of some of these forms into the Historic stage, including coppers in the form of axe blades, now divorced from their handles and of even larger size (42–53 cm in length), found from Ontario to Alabama (Fox 2004). In the eighteenth century, the Creek Indians of Tukabatchee town venerated such objects as gifts from the Master of Breath, where they were confined to bundles under the care of priests (Figure 39.1). They were still held as sacred in the early twentieth century (Howard 1968). Mace-form objects of Mississippian times also seem to have persisted into the post-contact era in the form of the Creek *atassa*, a notched wooden implement symbolizing a war club. In the eighteenth century, atassas embellished the rooflines of buildings marginal to Creek square grounds, where they were said to represent victories against rivals during violent inter-town ball games. Smaller atassas were given to young males during naming ceremonies, and among the Apalachee, they adorned their central ball pole whose symbolism celebrated the mythic victories of the thunder deity (Hann 1988; Howard 1968; Swanton 1928). Brookes (1997) envisions a line of direct cultural continuity from oversized flaked stone knifes used ceremonially in the middle Archaic Benton culture of the Deep South about 4200 BC, through much later Mississippian-stage sword-like forms of chert probably used theatrically in dances, to oversized knife-like atassas still used today in square ground dances among the Creeks.

5 Earthen Mound-Building

Thousands of prehistoric earthworks have been reported for the Eastern United States. As these came to the attention of early antiquarians, their makers came to be known as the 'Mound-builders'. This term is no longer used, as it masks the fact that the earthworks were

FIGURE 39.1 Sheet copper 'Tukabatchee plate', a ceremonial artefact in the form of an exaggerated axe blade, early seventeenth century, eastern Alabama. Maximum length 58.3 cm.

built by numerous ethnolinguistic groups, they occur in a wide variety of forms, they had many different uses, and perhaps most importantly, they were built over a period of some six millennia. Nonetheless it may be said that earthen mound-building generically is one of those traits that lend distinctiveness to Eastern Woodlands ritual practices.

5.1 Archaic Stage Mounds

The earliest known sites bearing deliberately constructed earthen mounds are middle Archaic in age, dating to as early as 3400 BC. Among these, the classic locus is Watson Brake in Louisiana, consisting of an oval arrangement of eleven conical mounds connected by an earthen ridge about 1 m high and 280 m in diameter. The tallest mound of the group rises to a height of 4.5 m. Limited excavations by Saunders and his colleagues (Saunders et al. 1997) confirm that these are not burial mounds. Instead they appear to commemorate earlier living surfaces found beneath them. The largest of the Archaic mound centres is the famous Poverty Point site, also in Louisiana, which dates to c.1600 to 600 BC. Poverty Point is a ceremonial centre featuring a symmetrical layout of six concentric semicircular earthen ridges with an outside diameter of 1.2 km. The ridges were used as living surfaces. There are also several conical and flat-topped earthen mounds at Poverty Point, the largest of which is an enormous T-shaped construction approximately 21 m tall which ranks among the largest mounds in North America. The uses of these mounds are uncertain, but their formal design and construction by semi-sedentary hunter-gatherer-fishermen has provided fertile ground for rethinking the social and political capabilities of non-food producers in naturally abundant environments (Gibson 2000).

5.2 The Burial Mound Tradition

Dome-shaped or conical earthen mounds used specifically for burial became commonplace during the Woodland stage. Such mounds may be thought of as monumentalized cemeteries. They often appear in groups, which suggest the separate burial facilities of segmentary societies. In the types of ritual practices responsible for these monuments, Hall (1997) sees parallels in ethnohistorically described Eastern Woodlands communal feasts of the dead, adoption rituals, and world-renewal ceremonies.

While outwardly similar in their morphology, some burial mounds were accretional and were added to over long periods of use, while others were of a single-ceremony type, raised in one or two major episodes over an important tomb, a flat-ground cemetery, a low earth platform, a mortuary crypt, or a dismantled charnel house (Brown 1979; Sears 1958). Many such mounds include additional interments intrusive into their completed surfaces. Burial mounds range in size from only a metre or so tall containing only a few human interments, to much larger structures such as Mound A at the Crooks site in Louisiana, which held an astounding 1,159 interments in a mound 5.5 m tall and 26 m in diameter (Ford and Willey 1940). While the earliest florescence of the burial mound tradition was no doubt the mortuary complex in the Ohio River valley of c.400 BC–AD 100 called Adena in the older literature (Webb and Snow 1974; the Adena concept is now somewhat in disfavour [Brown 2005; Clay 2005]), the tradition spread vigorously in later Woodland times, continued in more modest expressions through the Mississippian stage, and lasted even into post-contact times where early Historic stage burial mounds containing European trade goods are known, especially from Florida and coastal Georgia (Smith 1956). Effigy mounds in the shapes of birds and mythic 'water panthers' were a late Woodland speciality of the Upper Midwest and are usually found in groups.

5.3 The Platform Mound Tradition

While occasional flat-topped mounds were built by Archaic stage peoples, as at Poverty Point, their uses are not known. It was not until the Woodland stage that platform mounds became a regular feature of larger ceremonial centres. Woodland platform mounds were usually rectangular in plan (less commonly circular) with flattened summits. Certain examples, situated at one end of the earliest permanent villages in the Eastern Woodlands, share a number of features. They were built up episodically, as new layers of earth, often using specially coloured clays, were added to the older surfaces. Their summits feature dense scatters of post-holes, perhaps indicating the scaffolding of goods. Some posts were monumentally large, featuring specially dug ramps for their insertion and extraction; these may have been marker poles of some sort. These mound summits also show small pits, hearths, and sheet middens containing abundant animal bone, sherds of specially decorated or foreign pottery, and miscellaneous exotica. In all, it appears that Woodland platform mounds were raised as a ritual process, often by host groups who used their summits for the preparation and display of goods for feasting (Knight 2001).

While Woodland-stage platform mounds seldom had roofed buildings on their summits, later Mississippian-stage platform mounds often had crowded arrangements of roofed buildings and walled enclosures on them. These mound-top buildings, framed by wooden poles, conformed to several architectural patterns and had a number of uses including elite residences, lineage houses, council houses, and temples. Mississippian mounds were arranged in tangent to specially prepared plazas that served as communal spaces, although the mounds themselves were often walled off at the bases and summits, limiting access (Lewis et al. 1998; Lindauer and Blitz 1997). Larger examples were in excess of 18 m tall and were equipped with earthen ramps with wooden steps ascending to their summits. Major Mississippian towns generally had one mound dominant in size over the others (Figure 39.2); this mound supported the paramount chief's residence. The largest of all Mississippian platforms, Monks Mound at the great Cahokia site in Illinois, rises 30 m high above the adjacent plaza and covers just shy of 7 ha at the base (Pauketat 2004). Its summit has four distinct terraces of different elevations.

Like their Woodland predecessors, Mississippian mounds were built up by increments, each enlargement featuring the dismantling and renewal of the summit structures. This was a process of ritual renewal at a communal level. Based on ethnohistoric accounts of the meaning of mounds in Eastern Woodlands mythology and beliefs, mounds were treated as icons symbolic of the four-quartered Earth Island and related concepts. Their renewal (and consequent enlargement), which completely buried the older mound on both flanks and summit with a fresh covering of compacted clay, was a form of world-renewal ceremony. Analogues can be found among the communal purification ceremonies of the historic Creeks, during whose annual green corn ceremony small mounds and embankments to this day are built up from the accretions of old polluted earth swept from the square ground (Knight 1989).

FIGURE 39.2 Moundville, a large Mississippian ceremonial centre featuring platform mounds arranged around a central plaza, western Alabama, c.AD 1200–1500.

5.4 Ceremonial Centres and Earthen Enclosures

Presaged by mound centres like Watson Brake and Poverty Point built by Archaic-stage peoples, their Woodland-stage descendants built elaborate mounded landscapes combining multiple earth embankments, dome-shaped burial mounds, and occasionally platform mounds. In some cases, as at the Kolomoki site in Georgia (Pluckhahn 2003), these centres coincided with densely settled permanent villages, the first true villages of the Eastern Woodlands. In other cases they were vacant ceremonial centres serving a dispersed populace, having only a 'caretaker' resident population.

The most spectacular of these are the middle Woodland Hopewell ceremonial centres of Ohio, which feature embankments forming precise geometric enclosures of conjoined circles, squares, ellipses, and octagons, with dome-shaped burial mounds within. Most have long since vanished since they were first recorded in the nineteenth century, but a few have survived, such as the conjoined octagon and circle at Newark, Ohio preserved by the Moundbuilders Country Club golf course. The original complex, of which the preserved embankments are only a part, covered more than ten km^2 (Lepper 2004). There is some evidence that Ohio Hopewell centres were interconnected across long distances by artificial causeways lined by earth embankments.

These Ohio Hopewell geometric enclosures were vacant ceremonial centres and places of pilgrimage, some oriented with reference to an astronomy of celestial objects. Excavated structures outlined by post-hole patterns found within enclosures such as Seip-Pricer, Edwin Harness, and Mound City were special-function charnel houses, yielding feasting pits, clay-lined crematory basins, and deposits of finely crafted artefacts. The scale of some of these ritual structures and the size and quantity of the mortuary offerings indicates participation by large numbers of people in cult activity (Greber 1996; Seeman 1979, 2004).

6 Ancestor Shrines

A major component of Mississippian and early Historic cult practice at ceremonial centres was the ancestor shrine, generally located on a platform mound (Brown 2001). These shrines or temples were dedicated to the distinguished lineages of elite families and their supernatural connections, and often included seated statues representing lineage founders. Such statues of stone or wood often occur in matched pairs, male and female (Figure 39.3). Mound-top shrines recorded during the post-contact era also served as burial places for the honoured dead, loci for sacred fires tended by priests in veneration of the solar deity, reliquaries for power-imbued objects, storehouses of wealth, and repositories for war trophies (DePratter 1991). Good reports of excavations of mound-top temples are available for both the Mississippian and the Historic stage. Examples include, for the Mississippian, the Angel site in Indiana (Black 1967), and for the Historic, the Grand Village of the Natchez (the Fatherland site) in Mississippi (Neitzel 1965).

7 Use of Tobacco

Tobacco use, predominantly by means of pipe smoking, is a prominent and ubiquitous aspect of ancient ritual practice in the Eastern Woodlands. The introduction of tobacco appears to be bound up with shamanic practices that date from remote periods in which very small scale societies were the norm. Shamanic practices are implicated, for example, in such paraphernalia as Archaic-stage tubular forms similar to the sucking tubes used by shamanic healers. Tobacco itself, however, dates no earlier than the middle Woodland stage in this region, where it was quickly adopted into a pre-existing smoking complex involving non-nicotian plants smoked in tubular stone pipes. Tobacco's appearance coincides with, and no doubt provoked, a great elaboration of smoking pipes of stone. The prototypical Hopewellian smoking pipe is the platform pipe, so called because it has a flattened stem from which the bowl protrudes at the midway point. Pipe bowls often were elaborately carved into animal forms, principally birds, aquatic mammals, and frogs. These avian or aquatic animal figures almost invariably faced the smoker virtually nose to nose; it is plausible that the animals depicted were spiritual aids to shamanic trancing (Brose et al. 1985). The species used, *Nicotiana rustica*, has more nicotine than the modern commercial

FIGURE 39.3 Paired male and female ancestor shrine figures, Etowah site, northern Georgia, Mississippian, c.AD 1325–75.

product and is strong enough to produce altered states of consciousness, even hallucinations, if ingested in large doses (von Gernet 1995). During Historic times the rise of smoke and its transfer by means of breath were (and still remain) metaphors for communication with unseen spirits, and there is little doubt that this general idea is an ancient one.

During the Mississippian stage there is further evidence of shamanic activity stimulated by tobacco smoking, particularly in large sculpted stone and pottery pipes that seem to depict shamans in trancing postures. Communication with spirits is also indicated by elaborately carved pipe bowls depicting human-form deity figures and a variety of beneath-world zoomorphic supernaturals. With the advent of modern archaeobotanical fine-screen recovery methods, it has become possible to identify charred tobacco seeds. Many, for example, have been found in contexts associated with Mississippian stone shrine figures at the Sponemann site near Cahokia (Parker 1992).

Despite this evidence of individual use of tobacco in trancing, there is also evidence from Mississippian times of the adaptation of tobacco smoking to more communal forms of ritual. Small pipes of clay with perishable reed stems became common at this time. In the post-contact era, tobacco smoking was central to such key rituals as the calumet dance of the Mississippi Valley, which was essentially an elaborate greeting protocol combined with a ritual adoption of guests by host communities (Lankford 2008). Von Gernet (1995) argues that even in the Historic stage, when tobacco smoking had been popularized to the point of being a ubiquitous (and certainly non-hallucinatory) feature of ordinary indigenous life, it nonetheless never lost its original cognitive association as a vehicle for communicating with the spirit world.

While underscoring the key role of tobacco smoking in Eastern Woodlands ritual practice, we should not overlook the ancillary role played by other stimulants. While neither alcoholic beverages nor peyote use diffused prehistorically into the Eastern Woodlands, charred seeds of jimson weed (*Datura stramonium*), a strong intoxicant and hallucinogen, have been found in the context of a small shrine on the outskirts of the great Mississippian centre of Cahokia (Emerson 1997). Use of jimson weed is also historically documented among Virginia and North Carolina Algonquian peoples, and may once have been more widespread.

8 Iconography

Prehistoric indigenous Eastern Woodlands ritual was enacted using a variety of display goods, especially of marine shell, sheet copper, and exotic stone. These objects reveal a rich array of representational art, especially during artistic florescences in the middle Woodland and Mississippian stages. There have been relatively recent advances in their interpretation of these images, as shown especially in the articles contained in two recent books: *Hero, Hawk, and Open Hand: American Indian art of the ancient Midwest and South* (Townsend and Sharp 2004), and *Ancient Objects and Sacred Realms: Interpretations of Mississippian iconography* (Reilly and Garber 2007).

Middle Woodland Hopewell representations overwhelmingly focus on animal forms, often rendered in such accurate detail that the species depicted are readily identifiable. Prominent among these are water birds, falcons, ducks, dogs, beavers, otters, frogs, panthers, wolves, and bears. These subjects suggest human relations to animal spirit helpers. Humans, when depicted, are sometimes costumed as bears, panthers, or deer, evoking the social importance of shamans as intercessors with the spirit world in Hopewell religious life (Seeman 2004).

Much more study has been devoted to later Mississippian iconography. In the first place it has been possible to identify Mississippian cosmograms engraved on circular gorgets (pendants) whose imagery reflects the layered cosmos (sky, earth, and beneath world) known to Historic-stage Eastern Woodlands peoples (Lankford 2004, 2007). Leaders at some of the major mound sites seem to have had special relationships with either the celestial or the netherworld, based on the imagery of personal adornment. It has been increasingly recognized that much of the human and zoomorphic imagery in Mississippian art depicts mythic scenes, especially myths that chartered social statuses (Keyes 1994; Knight et al. 2001). For example, progress has been made in interpreting 'birdman' images on copper and shell by analogy to Siouan myths referring to ancient heroes whose accomplishments celebrate the triumph of life over death (Brown 2007). Previously the same images were commonly viewed as depictions of mortal humans costumed as 'falcon dancers' and interpreted in the light of Muskogean rather than Siouan beliefs and rituals. Such fundamental myths as the Twins who undergo earthly trials later to become celestial weather powers found their way into Mississippian art (Steponaitis et al. 2011). Rock art and cave art reveal similar emphases on mythic subject matter (Diaz-Granados 2004). In contrast to Woodland zoomorphic images, Mississippian zoomorphs much more commonly depict otherworld beings, often composite creatures such as the beneath-world horned serpent or the underwater panther/rattlesnake/bird.

Rather than focusing on religious features supposedly common to Mississippian religion in a generic sense, current research has emphasized the distinguishable media, styles, motifs, and thematic content found in different parts of the Mississippian world, relating their distinct iconographies and religious institutions to the different political histories of specific major chiefdoms and ethnolinguistic groups in each area (Cobb and King 2005; Steponaitis and Knight 2004).

9 TRENDS AND FUTURE DIRECTIONS

Since William Sears's optimistic assessment of the possibilities for investigating prehistoric religious systems in the Eastern Woodlands nearly 50 years ago (Sears 1961), important progress has indeed been made, especially since the decade of the 1980s when many researchers became more sanguine about the 'recovery' of prehistoric religious life. Indeed, it has been possible to escape the confines of the ethnographic present to begin the task of constructing a history of indigenous religious traditions in this area. This is an elaborate history that tracks closely with the evolution of societies from small, egalitarian bands through segmentary societies through politically organized agricultural chiefdoms. It continues through the disruptions of European conquest and colonization, and incorporates indigenous beliefs and practices of the present day.

This history builds on an ancient basal stratum of shamanic practice by individual ritual specialists and healers, a tradition onto which tobacco smoking was evidently grafted as a medium for trancing. As populations became more sedentary and socially differentiated, religious cults became diversified and elaborated. In Woodland times we find evidence not merely of individual shamanic practice but also of formalized cults of world renewal, feasting, and mortuary practices organized by increasingly communal social segments and ritual organizations, carried out within formal ritual spaces on increasingly grand scales. With the political consolidation of Mississippian chiefdoms, we begin to see an additional layer of cults devoted to mythic chartering of elite social positions and to the veneration of ancestors in mound-top shrines devoted to this purpose. Many such cults did not survive the European onslaught intact. Some of the most finely crafted art in copper, marine shell, and stone of the Mississippian stage were emblemic of mythic chartering of elite cult complexes. With growing complexity, distinct regionalization of beliefs and practices is increasingly apparent.

With the realization that there is no single Hopewellian nor Mississippian religion, but rather, assemblages of cults at different scales (Brown 1985; Knight 1986) that developed in parallel, a much more subtle appreciation of Eastern Woodlands religious practice is beginning to emerge. One outcome is the deconstruction of such venerable concepts as the Southeastern Ceremonial Complex (a.k.a. the Southern Cult), a concept that inferred pan-regional unity of religious beliefs and practices in Mississippian times. That concept has recently been discarded by some, this author included (Knight 2006), as one that is not merely outmoded but that detracts from understanding Mississippian art styles, religious paraphernalia, and cult practices as locally constituted within the broader streams of shared cosmology and social evolution.

The events of sixteenth- and seventeenth-century European contact and consequent depopulation were decisive for Eastern Woodlands societies. As disjunctions in religious beliefs and practices were inevitable across this span, 'upstreaming' from ethnohistoric sources dating from the eighteenth century onward to interpret practices several centuries removed must be done with methodological rigour. There are undeniable long-term continuities across this divide which demand that ethnohistorical sources and present-day practices be understood in their contexts. Yet, as elsewhere, precisely how and when to engage this information in the interpretation of past practices is the most pressing issue for future research.

SUGGESTED READING

See also James A. Brown's 'The archaeology of ancient religion in the Eastern Woodlands' (1997), Charles Hudson's *Elements of Southeastern Indian Religion* (1984), and my own 'Ceremonialism until AD 1500' in the *Handbook of North American Indians: Southeast* (2004). For a general introduction to the Eastern Woodlands culture area, its mounds, ceremonial spaces, and a sampling of its religious paraphernalia, see George Milner's *The Moundbuilders: Ancient peoples of Eastern North America* (2004). This source discusses the Archaic mound centres of Watson Brake and Poverty Point. For the latter, see also Jon L. Gibson's *The Ancient Mounds of Poverty Point: Place of rings* (2000). For Ohio Hopewell, see Christopher Carr and D. Troy Case (eds), *Gathering Hopewell: Society, ritual, and ritual interaction* (2005). Good, abundantly illustrated discussions of Woodland and Mississippian stage ceremonial centres, ritual, and religious artefacts can be found in two edited volumes: David S. Brose, James A. Brown, and David W. Penney (eds), *Ancient Art of the American Woodland Indians* (1985), and Richard F. Townsend and Robert V. Sharp (eds), *Hero, Hawk, and Open Hand: American Indian Art of the ancient Midwest and South* (2004). For the most recent work on Mississippian iconography see F. Kent Reilly and James F. Garber (eds), *Ancient Objects and Sacred Realms: Interpretations of Mississippian iconography* (2007). Robert L. Hall has sensitively interpreted many features of prehistoric Eastern Woodlands ritual and religious paraphernalia in the light of ethnographic realities in his book *An Archaeology of the Soul: North American Indian belief and ritual* (1997).

REFERENCES

BLACK, G. A. 1967. *Angel Site: An archaeological, historical, and ethnological study*, 2 vols. (Indianapolis: Indiana Historical Society).
BROOKES, S. O. 1997. 'Aspects of the middle Archaic: The Atassa' in Charles H. McNutt (ed.), *Results of Recent Archaeological Investigations in the Greater Mid-South*, Occasional Paper No. 18 (Memphis: Anthropological Research Center, University of Memphis), pp. 55–70.

BROSE, D. S., BROWN, J. A., and PENNEY, D. W. (eds) 1985. *Ancient Art of the American Woodland Indians* (New York: Harry N. Abrams).

BROWN, J. A. 1979. 'Charnel houses and mortuary crypts: Disposal of the dead in the middle Woodland period' in D. Brose and N. Greber (eds), *Hopewell Archaeology: The Chillicothe Conference* (Kent, Ohio: Kent State University Press), pp. 211–19.

——1985. 'The Mississippian period' in D. S. Brose, J. A. Brown, and D. Penney (eds), *Ancient Art of the American Woodland Indians* (New York: Harry N. Abrams), pp. 93–145.

——1996. *The Spiro Ceremonial Center: The Archaeology of Arkansas Valley Caddoan Culture in Eastern Oklahoma*, 2 vols., Memoirs of the Museum of Anthropology No. 29 (Ann Arbor: University of Michigan Press).

——1997. 'The Archaeology of ancient religion in the Eastern Woodlands', *Annual Review of Anthropology*, 26: 465–85.

——2001. 'Human Figures and the Southeastern ancestor shrine' in P. Drooker (ed.), *Fleeting Identities: Perishable material culture in archaeological research* (Carbondale: Southern Illinois University Press), pp. 76–93.

——2005. 'Reflections on taxonomic practice' in D. Applegate and R. C. Mainfort Jr (eds), *Woodland Period Systematics in the Middle Ohio Valley* (Tuscaloosa: University of Alabama Press), pp. 111–19.

——2007. 'On the identity of the birdman within Mississippian period art' in F. K. Reilly III and J. F. Garber (eds), *Ancient Objects and Sacred Realms: Interpretations of Mississippian iconography* (Austin: University of Texas Press), 56–106.

CALDWELL, J. R. 1958. *Trend and Tradition in the Prehistory of the Eastern United States*, Memoir 88, American Anthropological Association, Scientific Papers, X (Springfield: Illinois State Museum).

CARR, C. S. and CASE, D. TROY (eds) 2005. *Gathering Hopewell: Society, ritual, and ritual interaction* (New York: Springer-Verlag).

CLAY, R. B. 2005. 'Adena: Rest in Peace?' in D. Applegate and R. C. Mainfort Jr (eds), *Woodland Period Systematics in the Middle Ohio Valley* (Tuscaloosa: University of Alabama Press), pp. 94–110.

COBB, C. R., and KING, A. 2005. 'Re-inventing Mississippian tradition at Etowah, Georgia', *Journal of Archaeological Method and Theory*, 12: 167–93.

DEPRATTER, C. B. 1991. *Late Prehistoric and Early Historic Chiefdoms in the Eastern United States* (New York: Garland Press).

DIAZ-GRANADOS, C. 2004. 'Marking stone, land, body, and spirit: Rock art and Mississippian iconography' in R. F. Townsend and R. V. Sharp (eds), *Hero, Hawk, and Open Hand: American Indian art of the ancient Midwest and South* (Chicago: The Art Institute of Chicago), pp. 139–49.

EMERSON, T. E. 1997. *Cahokia and the Archaeology of Power* (Tuscaloosa: University of Alabama Press).

FORD, J. A. 1969. 'A comparison of formative cultures in the Americas: Diffusion or the psychic unity of man', Smithsonian Contributions to Anthropology XI (Washington, DC: Smithsonian Institution).

——and WILLEY, G. R. 1940. *Crooks Site: A Marksville period burial mound in La Salle Parish, Louisiana*, Anthropological Study No. 3 (New Orleans: Department of Conservation, Louisiana Geological Survey).

FOX, W. A. 2004. 'The north–south copper axis', *Southeastern Archaeology*, 23: 85–97.

GERNET, A. VON 1995. 'Nicotian dreams: The prehistory and early history of tobacco in Eastern North America' in J. Goodman, P. E. Lovejoy, and A. Sherratt (eds), *Consuming Habits: Drugs in history and anthropology* (Oxford: Routledge), pp. 67–87.

GIBSON, J. L. 2000. *The Ancient Mounds of Poverty Point: Place of rings* (Gainesville: University Press of Florida).

GREBER, N. 1996. 'A commentary on the contexts and contents of large to small Ohio Hopewell deposits' in P. J. Pacheco (ed.), *A View from the Core: A synthesis of Ohio Hopewell archaeology* (Columbus: The Ohio Archaeological Council), pp. 150–72.

HALL, R. L. 1983. 'A pan-continental perspective on Red Ocher and glacial kame ceremonialism' in R. C. Dunnell and D. P. Grayson (eds), *Lulu Linear Punctated: Essays in honor of George Irving Quimby*, Anthropological Papers 72 (Ann Arbor: University of Michigan Museum of Anthropology), pp. 74–107.

——1997. *An Archaeology of the Soul: North American Indian belief and ritual* (Urbana: University of Illinois Press).

——2006. 'The enigmatic Copper Cutout from Bedford Mound 8' in Douglas K. Charles and Jane Buikstra (eds), *Recreating Hopewell* (Gainesville: University Press of Florida), pp. 464–74.

HANN, J. H. 1988. *Apalachee: The land between the rivers*, Ripley P. Bullen Monographs in Anthropology and History 7 (Gainesville: University Press of Florida).

HOWARD, J. H. 1968. *The Southeastern Ceremonial Complex and Its Interpretation*, Memoir No. 6 (Columbia, Missouri: Missouri Archaeological Society).

HUDSON, C. 1984. *Elements of Southeastern Indian Religion*, Iconography of Religions 10 (Leiden: Brill).

KEYES, G. 1994. 'Myth and Social History in the Early Southeast' in P. B. Kwachka (ed.), *Perspectives on the Southeast: Linguistics, archaeology, and ethnohistory* (Athens: University of Georgia Press), pp. 106–15.

KNIGHT, V. J. JR 1986. 'The Institutional Organization of Mississippian Religion', *American Antiquity*, 51: 675–87.

——1989. 'Symbolism of Mississippian mounds' in G. A. Waselkov, P. H. Wood, and T. Hatley (eds), *Powhatan's Mantle: Indians in the Colonial Southeast* (Lincoln: University of Nebraska Press), pp. 279–91.

——2001. 'Feasting and the emergence of platform mound ceremonialism in Eastern North America' in M. Dietler and B. Hayden (eds), *Feasts: Archaeological and ethnographic perspectives on food, politics, and power* (Washington, DC: Smithsonian Institution Press), pp. 311–33.

——2004. 'Ceremonialism until AD 1500' in R. Fogelson (ed.), *Handbook of North American Indians: Southeast* (Washington, DC: Smithsonian Institution Press), pp. 734–41.

——2006. 'Farewell to the Southeastern ceremonial complex', *Southeastern Archaeology*, 25: 1–5.

——, BROWN, J. A., and LANKFORD, G. E. 2001. 'On the subject matter of Southeastern ceremonial complex art', *Southeastern Archaeology*, 20: 129–41.

LANKFORD, G. E. 2004. 'World on a string: Some cosmological components of the Southeastern ceremonial complex' in R. F. Townsend and R. V. Sharp (eds), *Hero, Hawk, and Open Hand: American Indian art of the ancient Midwest and South* (Chicago: The Art Institute of Chicago), pp. 207–17.

——2007. 'Some cosmological motifs in the Southeastern ceremonial complex' in F. K. Reilly III and J. F. Garber (eds), *Ancient Objects and Sacred Realms: Interpretations of Mississippian iconography* (Austin: University of Texas Press), pp. 8–38.

——2008. *Looking for Lost Lore: Studies in folklore, ethnology, and iconography* (Tuscaloosa: University of Alabama Press).

LEPPER, B. T. 2004. 'The Newark earthworks: Monumental geometry and astronomy at a Hopewellian Pilgrimage Center' in R. F. Townsend and R. V. Sharp (eds), *Hero, Hawk, and Open Hand: American Indian art of the ancient Midwest and South* (Chicago: The Art Institute of Chicago), pp. 73–81.

LEWIS, R. B., STOUT, C., and WESSON, C. B. 1998. 'The design of Mississippian towns' in R. B. Lewis and C. Stout (eds), *Mississippian Towns and Sacred Spaces: Searching for an architectural grammar* (Tuscaloosa: University of Alabama Press), pp. 1–21.

LEWIS, T. M. N. and KNEBERG, M. 1958. *Tribes that Slumber: Indians of the Tennessee region* (Knoxville: University of Tennessee Press).

LINDAUER, O. and BLITZ, J. H. 1997. 'Higher Ground: The archaeology of North American platform mounds', *Journal of Archaeological Research*, 5: 169–207.

MILNER, G. R. 2004. *The Moundbuilders: Ancient peoples of Eastern North America* (London: Thames and Hudson).

MORSE, DAN F. 1997. *Sloan: A Paleoindian Dalton cemetery in Arkansas* (Washington, DC: Smithsonian Institution Press).

NEITZEL, R. S. 1965. *Archaeology of the Fatherland Site: The grand village of the Natchez*, Anthropological Papers, LI, Pt 1 (New York: American Museum of Natural History).

PARKER, K. E. 1992. 'Archaeobotany' in D. K. Jackson, A. C. Fortier, and J. A. Williams (eds), *The Sponemann Site 2: The Mississippian and Oneota occupations*, American Bottom Archaeology FAI-270 Site Reports, XXIV (Urbana: University of Illinois Press), pp. 305–24.

PAUKETAT, T. R. 1997. 'Specialization, political symbols, and the crafty elite of Cahokia', *Southeastern Archaeology*, 16: 1-15.

—— 2004. *Ancient Cahokia and the Mississippians* (Cambridge: Cambridge University Press).

PLUCKHAHN, T. J. 2003. *Kolomoki: Settlement, ceremony, and status in the Deep South, AD 350 to 750* (Tuscaloosa: University of Alabama Press).

REILLY, F. K., III and GARBER, J. F. (eds) 2007. *Ancient Objects and Sacred Realms: Interpretations of Mississippian iconography* (Austin: University of Texas Press).

RITZENTHALER, R. E. and QUIMBY, G. I. 1962. 'The Red Ocher culture of the Upper Great Lakes and adjacent areas', *Fieldiana Anthropology*, 36: 243–75.

SAUNDERS, J. W., MANDEL, R. D., SAUCIER, R. T., et al. 1997. 'A mound complex in Louisiana at 5400–5000 years before present', *Science*, 277: 1796–9.

SEARS, W. H. 1958. 'Burial Mounds on the Gulf Coastal Plain', *American Antiquity* 23: 274–84.

—— 1961. 'The Study of Social and Religious Systems in North American Archaeology', *Current Anthropology*, 2: 223–46.

SEEMAN, M. F. 1979. 'Feasting with the dead: Ohio Hopewell charnel house ritual as a context for redistribution' in D. Brose and N. Greber (eds), *Hopewell Archaeology: The Chillicothe Conference* (Kent, Ohio: Kent State University Press), pp. 39–46.

—— 2004. 'Hopewell art in Hopewell places' in R. F. Townsend and R. V. Sharp (eds), *Hero, Hawk, and Open Hand: American Indian art of the ancient Midwest and South* (Chicago: The Art Institute of Chicago), pp. 57–71.

SMITH, H. G. 1956. *The European and the Indian: European–Indian contacts in Georgia and Florida*, Florida Anthropological Society Publications No. 4 (Gainesville: Florida Anthropological Society).

STEPONAITIS, V. P. and KNIGHT, V. J. JR 2004. 'Moundville art in historical and social context' in R. F. Townsend and R. V. Sharp (eds), *Hero, Hawk, and Open Hand: American Indian art of the ancient Midwest and South* (Chicago: The Art Institute of Chicago), pp. 167–81.

——, ——, LANKFORD, G. E., et al. 2011. 'Iconography of the Thruston Tablet' in G. E. Lankford, F. K. Reilly III and J. F. Garber (eds), *Visualising the Sacred. Cosmic Visions, Regionalism and the Art of the Mississippian World* (Austin: University of Texas Press).

SWANTON, J. R. 1928. 'Social organization and social usages of the Indians of the Creek Confederacy', *42nd Annual Report of the Bureau of American Ethnology 1924–1925* (Washington, DC: Smithsonian Institution), pp. 23–472.

TOWNSEND, R. F., and SHARP, R. V. 2004. *Hero, Hawk, and Open Hand: American Indian Art of the Ancient Midwest and South* (Chicago: The Art Institute of Chicago).

WEBB, M. C. 1989. 'Functional and historical parallelisms between Mesoamerican and Mississippian cultures' in Patricia Galloway (ed.), *The Southeastern Ceremonial Complex: Artifacts and analysis* (Lincoln: University of Nebraska Press), pp. 279–93.

WEBB, W. S. and SNOW, C. E. 1974. *The Adena People* (Knoxville: University of Tennessee Press).

WHITE, N. M. and WEINSTEIN, R. A. 2008. 'The Mexican connection and the Far West of the U.S. Southeast', *American Antiquity*, 73: 227–77.

WILLEY, G. R. 1966. *An Introduction to American Archaeology*, I: *North and Middle America* (Englewood Cliffs, New Jersey: Prentice-Hall).

CHAPTER 40

THE RELIGIOUS SYSTEM OF THE NORTHWEST COAST OF NORTH AMERICA

ROY L. CARLSON

1 INTRODUCTION

The Northwest Coast (NWC) of North America is a narrow strip of green coniferous forest sandwiched between the Pacific Ocean on the west and the Coast–Cascade–Cordilleran mountain ranges on the east, that stretches from the Alaska Panhandle south to north-west California. Large rivers linking the coastal cultures with those of the continental interior provided the basis—preserved and stored salmon—for the economic surplus that allowed the aboriginal societies to evolve from nomadic fisher-folk to seasonally sedentary villagers with monumental art, a ranked society, and complex ceremonialism approaching that of food producers in other parts of the world. The hinterland, the Columbia-Fraser Plateau, is sometimes grouped with the NWC as part of a larger culture area based on exploiting the anadromous salmon. The basic religious system of both areas was based on animism, the belief in spirits, and shamanism, the application of spirit power by specialists to resolving problems of both good and evil. Ritualists, who recited formulaic speeches on specified occasions such as the first salmon ceremony, were also common. Spirits were everywhere and permeated all actions. By promoting the development of an extensive oral literature as well as ceremonialism and graphic arts the belief in spirit power gave life to what could otherwise have been a mundane existence. These activities reinforced the belief in the power of spirits that in itself served as a social control while providing retrospective explanations for observed or imagined phenomena.

The ethno-historic database on NWC religion is considerable and documents many variations among the ethnic groups who occupied this area, although there are wide gaps in knowledge partly as a result of population decimation by introduced diseases during the proto-historic and early historic periods, and partly because of the impact of aggressive Christianity. Spanish, English, and Russian explorers in the late eighteenth century provided the earliest written records, and numerous ethnographers documented the cultures of the late nineteenth and early twentieth centuries. Village autonomy was the rule and villages were both cross-cut and linked by kinship networks rather than by any overriding civil or religious authority. Religion is not a concept indigenous to the native peoples of the NWC who viewed supernatural phenomena in the context of everyday life and death and periodic ceremonies rather than as an all-encompassing abstraction. In many ways Tlingit religious beliefs and practices provide the best analogues for interpreting the evidence for prehistoric NWC religion. The reasons for this are partly because of the nature and extent of the ethnographic data collected, but I think mostly because the Tlingit retained more of the older system that had declined in the Coast Salish region where it originated. Philip Drucker (1950, 1951, 1955), who did ethnographic research with a number of different NWC ethnic groups, characterized their religious beliefs as lacking systematization of beliefs on creation, deities, and cosmology, as entertaining the possibility of lifelong assistance from a guardian spirit, and combining beliefs in immortality of certain species with rituals that would ensure their return. Some groups had a vague notion of a remote supreme being. Extensive coverage and bibliography of NWC cultures can be found in Suttles (1990). A summary of highly varied opinions on the relationship of NWC art to religion and society is given in Jonaitis (1986: 141–9).

Archaeological evidence of religion is dependent upon discovery of material expressions of beliefs and practices. The rich material culture of the ethnohistoric period was only rarely executed in any medium other than perishable wood, horn, hide, and fibre. Edifices, such as the Yuquot whaling shrine (Jonaitis 1999), are rapidly reclaimed by the forces of nature. Certain burials may reflect particular religious beliefs; an adult female covered with quartz crystal and obsidian chips, and another buried face down accompanied by a bone pendant in the form of a spotted toad or salamander have been interpreted as shaman burials (Hickock et al. 2010). The following types of material remains are found archaeologically and offer clues to past religious behaviour: rock art; tools, spoons, bowls, pipes, pendants, and weapons of stone, bone or antler bearing representational motifs. A few wooden examples have survived in waterlogged sites.

The period preceding contact with Europeans in the late eighteenth century is now known from archaeological excavations spanning the previous 13,000 years although direct evidence of religious beliefs and practices only becomes known in the Middle period after 6,000 years ago. In the paragraphs that follow the ethnographic data with some reference to prehistoric materials is first summarized and is then followed by chronological presentation of the archaeological data. Differences in the dates given here from those in some of the sources referenced result from calibration and rounding off of the radiocarbon dates so they approximate BC–AD calendar dates.

2 Religious Beliefs

During the ethnohistoric period there were three general beliefs found throughout the NWC that transcended local and individual variations, and for which there is archeological evidence: spirit power, transformation, and regeneration.

2.1 Spirit Power

Boas (1966) indicates spirits were potentially present in all natural phenomena although most spirit power came from animals, ancestral humans, and mythological monsters rather than from inanimate objects. For example, the Nuu-chah-nulth chief, Maquinna, while hosting the Malaspina expedition in 1792 retired to a special cubicle to commune with his spirit helper whose anthropomorphic image was painted on the interior wall (Grunfeld 1988: 277). Spirits that empowered individuals are usually called 'guardian spirits' although they were more enablers than protectors in that they provided power for skills in specialist activities including curing by the shaman. Collins (1974: 144–205) gives a detailed description of both lay and shamanic spirits used by the Coast Salish speaking Skagit.

Undecorated perforated canine teeth from animals are found in several regions of the NWC by 4000 BC and may be indicators of individual spirit power. More specific evidence is found beginning about 2000 BC when images showing skeletal parts and prominent tongues (Figure 40.1) have been discovered. After that date representations of birds or animals are found on some tools such as leisters (Figure 40.2) where the representation of a great blue heron can be taken to mean that the owner of this implement possessed spirit power for fishing. Prominent tongues found on ritual objects and in rock art throughout much of the NWC are probably indicators of the belief that the tongue was the locus of spirit power, although ethnographic information on the meaning of this motif is limited to the Tlingit (Krause 1885: 197). The most widespread ethnographic object with this motif is the raven rattle (Gould 1973) where transference of spirit power via the tongue, sometimes with the assistance of what is called a frog (but was originally a toad?), is shown graphically. The various images found in rock art are also indicators of beliefs in spirit power as are the occasional stone or bone effigies of humans and animals. The belief in spirit power is still firmly entrenched among NWC native peoples. For example, the Tlingit firmly believe in shamanic spirits even though there have been no practising Tlingit shamans for over 50 years (Dauenhauer and Dauenhauer 1989).

2.2 Transformation

The clues to the presence of transformation beliefs are masks and images that are part human and part animal. The transformation of humans into birds or animals and vice versa runs throughout NWC mythology and ceremonialism. Even with the central Coast Salish whose ancestors were humans, the myths abound with other transformation stories particularly of beings turned to stone (Mohs 1987). In some societies such as the Bella Coola (McIlwraith 1948), the ancestors in their descent from the sky removed their bird or animal costumes to reveal their human form, whereas in others the means of transformation is unspecified. Some masks with both human and animal attributes indicate transformation in progress. Elaborate wooden masks with hinged parts that opened and closed to reveal different inner and outer images were employed particularly among the Kwakwakawakw (Waite 1982). Raven was the most common trickster-transformer on the northern NWC whereas other beings occupied this role elsewhere.

The earliest archaeological evidence for transformation beliefs dates to 2000 BC and consists of effigies of masks carved on the handles of spoons (Figures 40.1 and 40.3) used for feeding the ancestors (Carlson 2005: 48–57).

FIGURE 40.1 Fragmentary antler spoon-handle with an image of a humanoid mask with a protruding tongue surmounted by two fish-form forehead masks or frontlets from the Pender Canal site, Coast Salish region, dating to 2000 BC. The images are all open in the back indicating they are masks.

FIGURE 40.2 Bone point from a leister incised with the image of a great blue heron indicating spirit power for fishing dating to the Marpole phase, c.AD 1, Whalen Farm site, Coast Salish region.

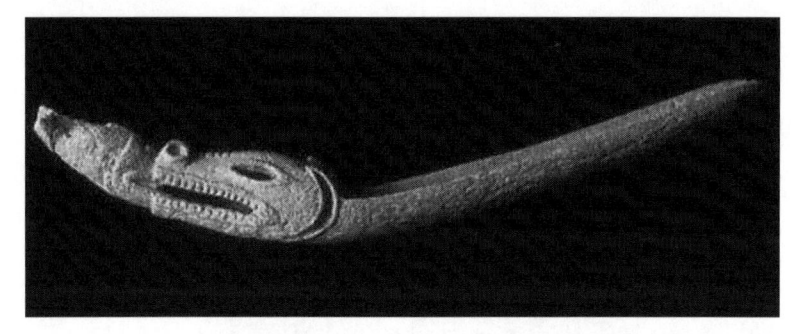

FIGURE 40.3 Spoon made of antler with the image of a mask of a sea-wolf confronting a rockfish dating to 2000 BC from the Pender Canal site. The sea-wolf image is hollow and open on the lower surface indicating it is the image of a mask. This spoon was used for feeding the ancestors.

2.3 Regeneration

Regeneration is based on the belief that the life force of living beings resides in the bones and is regenerated from the bones. The need to treat the bones of fish and animals with respect in order to ensure their rebirth runs throughout NWC mythology. This belief is documented extensively in regard to salmon that return every year from their home under the sea, are caught and dried or eaten, and their bones returned to the water or burned so that they can be regenerated and come back for harvest in succeeding years (Gunther 1928: 150–5). Regeneration from bone was also applied to humans, at least among the Tlingit (Kan 1989: 50–2, 309), and was probably present at one time from at least the Columbia River to the northern end of the NWC judging from the representations of bones in petroglyphs and on ritual paraphernalia from this entire region. Regeneration from bone is part of the initiation process in Siberian and Eskimo shamanism (Eliade 1964: 59–63). Ritual death and rebirth as part of shamanic and secret society initiations and the vision quest is widely reported for the NWC (Benedict 1923; Castile 1945: 411; Drucker 1940; Jilek and Jilek-AALL 2000; Kennedy and Bouchard 1983: 86; McIlwraith 1948, I: 661–7). The portrayal of ribs, backbones, and joint marks on humans and animals is found both ethnographically and archaeologically throughout the NWC north of the Columbia River and clearly relates to the belief in regeneration that is best articulated among the Tlingit (Kan 1989; de Laguna 1972: 761–2; Jonaitis 1986; Wardwell 1996). Strong's (1945) speculation that skeletal elements in the artwork of the lower Columbia River evidenced presence of a ghost cult related to historic period disease-induced depopulation ignores the considerable time depth and widespread distribution of skeletal imagery on the NWC, Alaska, and Siberia.

3 Religious Practices

3.1 Spirit Quest

The quest for spirit help by fasting in remote areas in order to obtain a vision and a familiar spirit was undertaken in all regions by the shaman, and by lay people in the Salish region of both the NWC and Plateau where everyone was expected to seek a guardian spirit. To the south on the Oregon coast the quest was present but very weak (Barnett 1955: 197). North of the Coast Salish region among the Kwakwakawkw spirit power was obtained by initiation into one of the secret societies (Benedict 1923: 12–14; Drucker 1940) and this may have been the case further north among the Tlingit, Haida, and Tsimshian where lay people did not undertake a vision quest (Drucker 1950: 235), although every Tlingit is reported to have his own guardian spirit (Krause 1885: 199). Coast Salish adolescents sought guardian spirits and such experiences were sometimes recorded as rock art as were shamanic experiences (Hill and Hill 1974). The only archaeological evidence for the spirit quest other than rock art are cairns and walls of stones in remote areas that have no obvious utilitarian function (Caldwell and Carlson 1954), and match descriptions of spirit quest behaviour found mostly among Plateau peoples, but also among the Lower Chinook (Ray 1942: 237).

3.2 Shamanism

The shaman, usually male, was present in all NWC societies and could both cure disease and cause misfortune. He usually had multiple spirit helpers. Among the Tlingit, but not other ethnic groups, masks represented the shaman's spirit helpers. Everywhere sickness was attributed to either spirit intrusion or soul loss. Sucking or massage removed the intrusive spirit. The Coast Salish engaged in a particular soul loss recovery ceremony in which a group of shaman canoed to the land of the dead to recover the wandering soul (Waterman 1930). Many rock art sites are reported as recording shamanic experiences (Hill and Hill 1974), and the occasional artefact found archaeologically such as small stone or bone worms (Borden 1983: fig. 8:6) could represent the intrusive spirit displayed by the shaman after its removal from the patient. Shamanic images comparable to those found as rock art are recovered from archaeological sites and help date the rock art (Carlson 1993). The symbols of regeneration—ribs and backbones—are associated with shamanic rebirth. Shamans' burials were sometimes treated differently according to the ethnographies and bone pendants, some stone bowls, and stone pipes are probably shamanic equipment. Images of snakes, spotted toads, and salamanders found archaeologically represent shamanic spirit helpers. The well-known bone soul-catcher has not yet been found in a datable archeological context.

3.3 Ceremonialism

The winter months after the salmon runs ceased and winter food supplies had been stored and dried were the times of abundant ceremonialism including *rites de passage*, potlatches, spirit dances, and secret-society performances using masks and rattles and other paraphernalia. Direct archaeological evidence for these activities is very limited although the presence of ritual spoons used to feed the dead strongly suggests presence of the memorial potlatch by 2000 BC, the most widespread type of potlatch on the coast (Birket-Smith 1967). There is one prehistoric effigy of carved antler showing a masked dancer with a bird rattle (Figure 40.4). While potlatches and the erection of totem poles are usually treated as secular occasions promoting the social rank of individuals or kin groups, there is an underlying belief in ancestral encounters with spirits both in family crests and in the stories accompanying the origin and display of such crests.

FIGURE 40.4 Image of a masked dancer with a bird rattle from the Marpole site dating c.1 AD. This image is part of a comb with the tines broken and missing.

3.4 Feeding the Ancestors

Different methods were used to feed the dead ancestors by different NWC societies. Among the Kwakwakawakw and Coast Salish (Barnett 1955), who still practise this custom today, food was sent to the spirit world by burning, whereas among the Tlingit the use of ritual spoons by participants in the memorial potlatch symbolized feeding the ancestors (Victor-Howe 2007). Archaeological expressions of feeding the ancestors consist of burials from the Pender Canal site with spoons at the mouth or nearby, or with clam shell bowls in the hand or near the face, or with food remains such as fish bones in or near the mouth, or in other words actual rather than symbolic feeding the dead. The fact that human skeletons during this same period are found intentionally buried in middens replete with food remains—shellfish, fish, bird, and mammal bones—may be an indication that humans were buried there because these remains would also be regenerated in the land of the dead for use as food (Carlson 1999: 44).

4 THE EARLY PERIOD

Very little is known about the earliest inhabitants of the NWC in the period between 13,000 and 4000 BC (Carlson and Magne 2008). From the Alaska Panhandle south to the Strait of Juan de Fuca, the earliest peoples are known by the presence of lithic industries using leaf-shaped and weakly shouldered chipped stone knives and points, and only slightly later by microblades. Both industries are known earlier in arctic Alaska and northeast Asia. These peoples were maritime fishers and hunters, but also employed specialized techniques for taking bears in their dens. South of the Strait of Juan de Fuca the earliest people are known by the scattered presence of fluted points that belong to the widespread Clovis culture of the continental interior. The Clovis peoples were inland hunters and gatherers capable of taking mammoths and other large land mammals.

Archaeological data bearing on the religious beliefs of these earliest peoples is almost non-existent. Clovis fluted points are examples of superb workmanship in chipped stone, above and beyond that required to make serviceable weapons, applied to choice raw materials usually a brilliant agate, chert, or obsidian. They are sometimes found in caches suggesting ritual burial. The closest cache to the Northwest Coast is at East Wenatchee just east of the Cascade Mountains (Mehringer and Foit 1990). The points themselves suggest wealth and status based on hunting prowess and a belief system related to the successful hunting of large land mammals. A similar belief system but with a maritime flavour was probably present among the coastal peoples. The widespread distribution of animism and shamanism in northern Asia and throughout the New World suggests that these belief systems were part of the cultural inventory of the earliest migrants, although it is only in younger periods that direct evidence has been found.

5 THE MIDDLE PERIOD

Evidence for human presence is considerably more abundant after 2000 BC. Those patterns of culture above and beyond subsistence that typify the ethnohistoric period have their roots at this time and aspects of religion and ceremonialism related to ethnographic practices begin to appear. The cradle for this development is the Fraser River and protected waterways in and around the adjacent offshore islands. In this coastal region there are three sequent cultural phases—Mayne or Charles, Locarno Beach, and Marpole—that occupy the time period between 2000 BC and AD 400 from which most of the data on pre-contact Northwest Coast religion comes (Borden 1983; Carlson 1996, 1999, 2005). Presence of the communal fish trap on the lower Fraser by 2700 BC (Eldridge and Acheson 1992) indicates that preservation and storage of the annual salmon harvests that provided the economic surplus necessary for cultural elaboration was already present. Models of past climate indicate stability during the period from about 2000 BC to AD 400, the period of development and elaboration of the religious system, followed by a sharp change at the end of that period (Carlson 2008).

The earliest evidence for the Northwest Coast religious system comes from the Pender Canal site (DeRt 2) in the Gulf Islands just off the mouth of the Fraser River (Carlson 2005, 1999; Carlson and Hobler 1993). This site consists of the higher elevation remnants of the burial area belonging to what was once a village destroyed by rising sea levels and construction of a ship canal. The remains of 150 individuals and fragments of many others were excavated. Carved spoons made of elk antler were found directly associated with five adult female burials, and fragments of an additional four spoons that probably came from disturbed burials, were found. Two additional spoons from the site are in the collections of the Royal BC Museum. The earliest burial with a spoon dates to 2148±320 cal BC and the youngest to 1551±250 cal BC. Three spoons were found at the mouths of the skeletons and one near the face. Bowls consisting of a valve of the large horse clam were found with nine additional burials including adult females, adult males, and children. One stone bowl in the shape of a fish was found near one burial. It is probable that spoons made of wood and other food containers of basketry or wood accompanied many of the other burials.

Veneration of the ancestors by gifts of food is the basis for not only the memorial potlatch, but is the universal ingredient of all potlatches of the historic period. Feasting is a mechanism whereby individuals or kin groups could achieve status and higher rank than their peers (Hayden 1995). Judging from the status symbols such as the variety of labrets that appear in the period 2000 BC to 1000 BC this process was well underway. Once rank became hereditary, rather than achieved, the sociological basis for inheritance of spirit power such as is found in the ethnographically known secret societies was present, and may have occurred during this period.

Images carved on the handles of the Pender spoons are as follows: masks of sea wolf, mountain goat, two humanoids with ear spools, two fish, one bird; joint marks on one humanoid and three salamanders; ribs on two salamanders; protruding tongues on one humanoid and three salamanders; external backbones on one rockfish and one salamander; three eagle(?) effigies; two owls; and one spoon handle with zigzags (lightning?) and geometric feather motifs terminating in a neck with the head missing (thunderbird?). These spoons are illustrated in Carlson (1999: 48–57; 2005: 39–46).

These images indicate that the fundamentals of NWC religious belief including spirit power (human, animal, bird effigies, protruding tongues), regeneration (ribs, backbones, joint marks), and transformation (masks) were present by 2000 BC in the Coast Salish region, and that practices involving feeding the ancestors and ceremonialism using masks were present. These beliefs and practices probably continued in this region through the end of the Marpole phase.

Much of the evidence for subsequent religious behaviour in the Coast Salish region between 1000 BC and the end of the Marpole phase about AD 300–500 can be found in Borden (1983) and consists of the following: a cache of spoons from the Musqueam site dating to 600 BC of the same type as those at Pender; mask effigies, ribbed figures, and human and animal effigies from the Marpole site; and a miniature human skull from the Locarno Beach site. This skull and a miniature bird monster mask, also dating to about 600 BC, from the Crescent Beach site (Carlson 2005: fig. 9) have analogues with ethnographic secret-society paraphernalia. The development probably late in this period of masked seated human figures of stone holding a bowl bearing various images including snakes, spotted toad, salamanders, and prominent ribs and backbones indicate their use by the shaman. Some of these stone figures are wearing shaman's crowns (Keddie 2003). Effigies on tools such as carving knives and fish spears are indicative of guardian spirits giving power to their owners for these tasks.

Spotted toads and salamanders are probably indicators of shamanic beliefs. The NWC has long been characterized as an area in which hallucinogens were not employed to induce visions. Such is probably not actually the case (Wihr 1993). Dall (1881: 111) reported that the shaman receives either poison or the power to produce evil effects from the 'frog', and several Tlingit shaman's masks show a 'frog' in the mouth of the shaman (see Frontispiece in Wardwell 1996) that may represent the slime-sucking shaman inducing a trance. The raven rattle of the northern NWC frequently shows the 'frog' as the intermediary in the transfer of spirit power from one being to another. Gerry Duodoward, a contemporary Tsimshian carver-of-raven-rattles, advised me that the 'frog' is an intermediary in the transfer of spirit power. What is probably meant here is not a frog, but the spotted toad. There are only toads (*Bufo boreas*) on the Queen Charlotte Islands and (until recent introductions) these are far more common than frogs on the adjacent northern NWC mainland (Carl 1966: 17). The skins of toads and salamanders secrete hallucinogenic bufotenins (McNamee 1994: 1697) whereas the skin of frogs does not. Salamanders (*Aneides ferreus*) are very clearly shamanic as they are identified on Coast Salish power boards used in the soul recovery ceremony (Waterman 1930). The only recorded instance of what may be a salamander-sucking shaman is a Nuu-chah-nulth shaman who sucked on the tongue of a 'lizard' during curing rites (Drucker 1951: 199). Many ethnographic references to frogs and lizards should probably be to toads and salamanders.

The early presence of complex transformation masks is suggested by a three-dimensional carving on the handle end of a wooden spear thrower dated AD 335 (Fladmark et al. 1987; Carlson 2005: fig. 11) that depicts a human face surmounted by a massive headdress representing a sea monster, probably a sea-wolf, or at least a human with his alter ego.

All of the preceding data comes from the Coast Salish region centred on the Fraser River and adjacent islands and coast, and it is clear that this region is the heartland for the elaboration of the NWC religious system from simpler beginnings. The quantity and quality of meaningful art in this region begins earlier and exceeds that of all other coastal regions during the period 2000 BC–AD 400. It is probable that this art and the religious meanings that accompanied it spread from this region to elsewhere on the coast where some aspects are found in later archaeological deposits.

There are some evidences of religious beliefs on other parts of the NWC at this time period, 2000 BC–AD 400, but they are not as early nor are they found in the same quantity. At the waterlogged Hoko River site on the border between Salish and Nuu-chah-nulth territory, belted kingfishers on a wooden mat creaser, and animal heads with protruding harpoon points (Croes 1995: 169, 175) may represent spirit power of their owners. To the south on the Oregon coast several effigies dating 700 BC–AD 400 include effigies of an owl, humans, and other birds on hafts for stone tools and an isolated eye on a digging stick handle (Connolly 1992), and may represent the same.

On the northern coast beginning 2500 BC (MacDonald 1983) art is primarily geometric with one example of what may be a spirit helper in the form of a human face on the haft of a carving knife. By 1200 BC concretions showing incised ribs, joint marks, and backbones appear and continue into later periods, and the raven makes his only appearance as a stone pendant about 1000 BC. By AD 1 an art form that does not appear on the southern coast—the stone club with phallic and biomorphic figures usually of long beaked birds, but also of humans and fish—makes its appearance. A cache of these clubs was found upriver on the Skeena at Hagwilget (Duff 1963) and while the dating of this cache is uncertain, an early simple club of this type was found in deposits at Prince Rupert dating about AD 1. These images probably mark spirit power for war, but could be family crests, or indeed both. There was probably an evolution from images of personal spirit power to family crests as rank and prestige became more and more important, but when this occurred is uncertain.

6 Late Period

Other than a shift from burial in middens to exposure of the dead in rock-shelters, trees, or grave houses that typifies the entire NWC, the Late period, AD 400 to European contact in the late 1700s differs little from the Middle period except in the Coast Salish region. This shift in burial practices might coincide with a change in actual feeding of the dead to sending food to the land of the dead by burning. On the northern coast (MacDonald 1983) polished slate mirrors presumably used by the shaman in spirit communication are added to the religious paraphernalia, and the classic northern NWC art style of intricate interlocked human and animal figures contorted to fit available space comes into being. Other customs established during the Middle period continued.

Data from the Kwakwakawakw/Nuxalk region of the central coast are limited, although it seems probable that the secret societies were now in existence there. While long-beaked bird masks are known earlier in the Coast Salish region, a small antler plaque with incised depictions of two bird-monster masks (Figure 40.5) that look like specific Kwakwakawakw forms has been dated AD 1442 (Carlson 2005: fig. 8).

In the Coast Salish region about AD 400 there was a decline in art forms (Borden 1983) probably related to climate change that resulted in reduction of the salmon surplus leading to a more dispersed settlement pattern and fewer specialists in art and religion (Carlson 2008). Pipes for smoking appear early in this period. Some are in the same styles as the earlier human figure bowls and indicate smoking has entered the realm of shamanic cures. Other new religious artefacts are large anthropomorphic pendants (Carlson 1983: figs 7:2, 11:14) made of elk antler that look like they are meant to be suspended on the chest as with Siberian examples, and are probably the equivalent of shaman's dolls.

The small pox epidemic of 1782–3 reduced the Coast Salish population by two-thirds and possibly as much as nine-tenths (Harris 1997: 18). This event may have been instrumental in the rise of a new religion, the Sxwayxwey, the dominant religious expression of the central Coast Salish during the ethnohistoric period. Unlike other primary ceremonies the Sxwayxwey was first and foremost a cleansing rite (Suttles 1983) and employed a distinctive mask and type of rattle.

FIGURE 40.5 Small antler plaque with incised images of two bird masks back to back from southern Vancouver island dating AD 1442. These images closely resemble secret-society Hamatsa masks.

The most complete evidence for religion during the late pre-contact period comes from the fortuitous preservation of wooden objects at the Makah village of Ozette on the northwest corner of the state of Washington. The village was covered by a mudslide in the early 1700s, and excavations have provided a wealth of information from normally perishable materials (Daugherty and Friedman 1983). Images of owls, humanoids, whales, dogs or wolves, sea monsters, and thunderbirds, and an effigy of a whale saddle made of wood inlaid with sea otter teeth, provide a glimpse of religious beliefs at that time period that are actually very similar to the first ethnographic data acquired more than a century later (Swan 1870). Ozette was a village of whalers. This site is a testament as to what has been lost regarding art and religion over the centuries.

7 CONCLUSIONS

Archaeology provides impoverished glimpses of religious beliefs and practices of the past that are, however, part of patterned human thought and behaviour of the period in which they occurred, and when interpreted using ethnographic analogy in areas such as the NWC with its strong evidence of cultural continuity, can elicit a model of the development of the religious system as has been presented in the preceding pages. This model assumes the presence of the belief in spirit power among the earliest inhabitants from which evolved more complex beliefs and practices that first appeared in the archaeological record about 2000 BC. At that time skeletal imagery indicates the belief in ritual death and regeneration that is basic to both shamanic and secret society initiations. Also present at this time are masks of humans and animals indicating transformation beliefs, images of spirit helpers, and burials that demonstrate the custom of feeding the ancestors. Through time these beliefs and practices were elaborated in the Coast Salish region centred on the Fraser River as societies expanded in size and complexity, and these elaborations continued spreading to adjacent regions of the NWC even after they declined in the Coast Salish region itself where there was a regression to simpler forms and a change to an emphasis on cleansing rituals.

SUGGESTED READING

BENEDICT, R. F. 1923. *The concept of the guardian spirit in North America*, Memoirs of the American Anthropological Association No. 29 (Menasha).
CARLSON, R. L. (ed.) 1983. *Indian Art Traditions of the Northwest Coast* (Burnaby, BC: Archaeology Press).
——2005. 'Images of precontact Northwest Coast masks', *American Indian Art Magazine*, 30 (2): 48–57.
HOPPAL, M. and VON SADOVSZKY, O. (eds) 1989. *Shamanism Past and Present* (Budapest: Istor Books).
DRUCKER, P. 1940. 'Kwakiutl dancing societies', *University of California Anthropological Records*, 2(6): 201–230.
JONAITIS, A. 1976. *Art of the Northern Tlingit* (Seattle: University of Washington Press).
KAN, S. 1989. *Symbolic Immortality* (Washington DC: Smithsonian Institution Press).
SUTTLES, W. (ed.) 1990. *Handbook of North American Indians*, VII: *Northwest Coast* (Washington DC: Smithsonian Institution Press).
WARDWELL, A. 1996. *Tangible Visions* (New York: The Monacelli Press).

REFERENCES

BARNETT, H. G. 1955. *The Coast Salish of British Columbia* (Westport, Connecticut: Greenwood Press).
BENEDICT, R. F. 1923. *The Concept of the Guardian Spirit in North America*, Memoirs of the American Anthropological Association No. 29 (Menasha).
BIRKET-SMITH, K. 1967. *Studies in Circumpacific Culture Relations I. Potlatch and Feasts of Merit*, Det Kongelige Danske Videnskabernes Selskab Historsk-fiilosofiske Meddelelser 42(3) (Copenhagen: Munksgaard).
BOAS, F. 1966. *Kwakiutl Ethnography*, ed. H. Codere (Chicago and London: The University of Chicago Press).
BORDEN, C. E. 1983. 'Prehistoric art of the lower Fraser region' in R. L. Carlson (ed.), *Indian Art Traditions of the Northwest Coast* (Burnaby, BC: Archaeology Press), pp. 131–66.
CALDWELL, W., and CARLSON, R. L. 1954. 'Further documentation of stone piling during the Plateau Vision Quest', *American Anthropologist*, 56: 441–2.

CARL, C. G. 1966. *Amphibians of British Columbia* (Victoria: British Columbia Museum Handbook 2).

CARLSON, R. L. (ed.) 1983. *Indian Art Traditions of the Northwest Coast*. (Burnaby, BC: Archaeology Press).

——1993. 'Content and chronology of Northwest Coast (North America) rock art' in J. Steinbring, A. Watchman, P. Faulstich, et al. (eds), *Time and Space* (Melbourne: AURA Occasional Publication 8), pp. 7–12.

——1996. 'The later prehistory of British Columbia' in R. L. Carlson and L. Dalla Bona (eds.), *Early Human Occupation in British Columbia* (Vancouver: University of British Columbia Press), pp. 215–26.

——1999. 'Sacred sites on the Northwest Coast of North America' in B. Coles, J. Coles, and M. S. Jorgensen (eds), *Bog Bodies, Sacred Sites and Wetland Archaeology* (Exeter: Warp Occasional Paper 12, Department of Archaeology, University of Exeter), pp. 39–46.

——2005. 'Images of precontact Northwest Coast masks', *American Indian Art Magazine*, 30(2): 48–57.

——2008. 'The rise and fall of Native Northwest Coast cultures', *Journal of North Pacific Prehistory*, II, (Madrid: The University Book).

——and HOBLER, PHILIP M. 1993. 'The Pender Canal excavations and the development of Coast Salish culture' in K. Fladmark (ed.), *Changing Times: British Columbia archaeology in the 1980s* (Vancouver: BC Studies 99), pp. 25–52.

——and MAGNE, M. P. R. (eds) 2008. *Projectile Point Sequences in Northwestern North America* (Burnaby, BC: Archaeology Press).

CASTILE, G. P. (ed.) 1985. *The Indians of Puget Sound* (Seattle: University of Washington Press).

COLLINS, J. M. 1974. *Valley of the Spirits* (Seattle: University of Washington Press).

CONNOLLY, T. 1992. 'Human Responses to Change in Coastal Geomorphology and Fauna on the Southern Northwest Coast: Archaeological Investigations at Seaside Oregon', *University of Oregon Anthropological Papers* 45: 1–198.

CROES, D. R. 1995. *The Hoko River Archaeological Site Complex* (Pullman: Washington State University Press).

DALL, W. H. 1881. 'On masks, labrets, and certain Aboriginal customs', *Annual Report of the Bureau of American Ethnology*, III: 67–202.

DAUENHAUER, N. M. and DAUENHAUER, R. 1989. 'Treatment of shaman spirits in contemporary Tlingit oratory' in M. Hoppal and O. von Sadovszky (eds), *Shamanism Past and Present*, Pt 2 (Budapest: Istor Books), pp. 317–30.

DAUGHERTY, R. and FRIEDMAN, J. 1983. 'An introduction to Ozette art' in R. L. Carlson (ed.), *Indian Art Traditions of the Northwest Coast* (Burnaby, BC: Archaeology Press), pp. 183–98.

DRUCKER, P. 1940. 'Kwakiutl dancing societies', *University of California Anthropological Records*, 2(6): 201–30.

——1950. 'Cultural element distributions XXV: Northwest Coast', *University of California Anthropological Records*, 9(3): 157–294.

——1951. 'The northern and central Nootkan tribes', *Bureau of American Ethnology Bulletin*, 144.

——1955. *Indians of the Northwest Coast* (Garden City, NY: McGraw-Hill for the American Museum of Natural History).

DUFF, W. 1963. 'Stone Clubs from the Skeena River Area', *Annual Report of the BC Provincial Museum for 1962*: 2–12.

ELDRIDGE, M., and ACHESON, S. 1992. 'The antiquity of fish weirs on the Southern Coast: A response to Moss, Erlandson, and Stuckenrath', *Canadian Journal of Archaeology*, 16: 112–16.

ELIADE, M. 1964. *Shamanism* (London: ARKANA Penguin Group publishers).

FLADMARK, K. R., NELSON, D., BROWN, T., et al. 1987. 'AMS dating of two wooden artifacts from the Northwest Coast', *Canadian Journal of Archaeology*, 11: 1–12.

GOULD, J. C. 1973. 'The Iconography of the Northwest Coast Raven Rattle'. Unpublished Master's thesis, University of British Columbia, Vancouver.

GRUNFELD, F. V. 1988. *Catalogo El Ojo del Totem* (Centro Cultura de la Villa, Madrid and Museu Ethnologic Barcelona).

GUNTHER, E. 1928. 'A further analysis of the First Salmon Ceremony', *University of Washington Publications in Anthropology*, 2(5): 129–73.

HARRIS, C. 1997. *The Resettlement of British Columbia* (Vancouver: University of British Columbia Press).

HAYDEN, B. 1995. 'Pathways to power: Principles for creating socioeconomic inequalities' in T. D. Price and G. M. Feinman (eds), *Foundations of Social Inequality* (New York: Plenum), pp. 15–86.

HICKOCK, A. W., WHITE, W., RECALMA-CLUTESI, K., et al. 2010. 'Mortuary evidence of Coast Salish shamanism?', *Canadian Journal of Archaeology*, 34(2): 240–64.

HILL, B. and HILL, R. 1974. *Indian Petroglyphs* (Saanichton, BC: Hancock House Publishers).

JILEK, W. G. and JILEK-AALL, L. 2000. 'Shamanic symbolism in the revived ceremonials of the Salish nation of the Pacific Northwest', *Shaman*, 8(1): 3–34.

JONAITIS, A. 1986. *Art of the Northern Tlingit* (Seattle: University of Washington Press).

——1999. *The Yuquot Whalers' Shrine* (Seattle: University of Washington Press).

KAN, S. 1989. *Symbolic Immortality* (Washington and London: Smithsonian Institution Press).

KEDDIE, G. 2003. 'A new look at Northwest Coast stone bowls' in R. L. Carlson (ed.), *Archaeology of Coastal British Columbia: Essays in honour of Professor Philip M. Hobler* (Burnaby, BC: Archaeology Press), pp. 165–74.

KENNEDY, D. and BOUCHARD, R. 1983. *Sliammon Life, Sliammon Lands* (Vancouver: Talonbooks).

KRAUSE, A. 1885. *The Tlingit Indians*, trans. Erna Gunther (Seattle: University of Washington Press).

LAGUNA, F. DE 1972. *Under Mt. St. Alias: History and culture of the Yakutat Tlingit* (Washington DC: Smithsonian Contributions to Anthropology VII).

MACDONALD, G. 1983. 'Prehistoric Art of the Northern Northwest Coast' in R. L. Carlson (ed.), *Indian Art Traditions of the Northwest Coast* (Burnaby, BC: Archaeology Press), pp. 99–121.

MCILWRAITH, T. F. 1948. *The Bella Coola Indians* (Toronto: University of Toronto Press).

MCNAMEE, D. 1994. 'Eye of newt, toe of frog', *The Lancet*, 344: 1696–7.

MEHRINGER, P. J. and FOIT, F. F. 1990. 'Volcanic ash dating of the Clovis Cache at East Wenatchee', Washington', *National Geographic Research*, 6(4): 495–503.

MOHS, G. 1987. 'Spiritual sites, ethnic significance, and native spirituality: The heritage and heritage sites of the Sto:lo Indians of British Columbia', unpublished MA thesis, Department of Archaeology, Simon Fraser University, Burnaby.

RAY, V. 1942. 'Culture element distribution: Plateau', *Anthropological Records*, 8:2 (Berkeley: University of California).

STRONG, W. D. 1945. 'The occurrence and wider implications of a "Ghost Cult" in the Columbia River suggested by carvings in wood, bone, and stone', *American Anthropologist*, 47: 244–61.

SUTTLES, W. 1983. 'Productivity and its constraints: A Coast Salish case' in R. L. Carlson (ed.), *Indian Art Traditions of the Northwest Coast* (Burnaby, BC: Archaeology Press), pp. 67–88.

——(ed.) 1990. *Handbook of North American Indians*, VII: *Northwest Coast* (Washington DC: Smithsonian Institution).

SWAN, J. G. 1870. 'Indians of Cape Flattery', *Smithsonian Contributions to Knowledge*, 16(8): 1–106.

VICTOR-HOWE, A.-M. 2007. *Feeding the Ancestors* (Cambridge, MA: Peabody Museum Press, Harvard University).

WAITE, D. 1982. 'Kwakiutl transformation masks' in Z. Mathews and A. Jonaitis (eds), *Native North American Art History* (Palo Alto, California: Peek Publications), pp. 137–56.

WARDWELL, A. 1996. *Tangible Visions* (New York: The Monacelli Press).

WATERMAN, T. T. 1930. 'The Paraphernalia of the Duwamish "Spirit-canoe"', *Indian Notes and Monographs* 7(2–4) (New York: Museum of the American Indian Heye Foundation).

WIHR, W. S. 1993. '"You toad-sucking fool": An inquiry into the possible use of bufotenine by Northern Northwest Coast shamans', *Northwest Anthropological Research Notes*, 29(1): 51–9.

CHAPTER 41

RITUAL AND ARCHAEOLOGICAL VISIBILITY IN THE FAR NORTHEAST OF NORTH AMERICA

BRIAN S. ROBINSON

1 INTRODUCTION

THE Far Northeast of North America, from Maine to Labrador, was occupied by hunter-gatherer societies into recent times. Ritual themes influenced the visibility of archaeological materials and spatial patterns, to the degree that major cultural traditions of the Early Holocene remained undetected until interrelated technological and ritual patterns were recognized. Burial ritual provides bright nodes of visibility between 8500–3500 radiocarbon years BP during the so-called Archaic period. Greater continuity with recent Algonquian traditions in the last 3,000 years allows better understanding of more diverse ritual contexts, influencing perceptions of continuity and change that are the basis of archaeological interpretation and of concern to modern descendents. Emphasis is placed on varied scales of patterning, preservation contexts, modern interests, and the profound influence that ritual may have on archaeological visibility.

Ritual is often used to signify highly formalized and repetitive behaviour that is non-utilitarian (Brück 1999), lacking 'any practical relationship between the means one chooses to achieve certain ends' (Bell 1997: 46). This outsider-perspective has obvious problems, but it does set limits that help frame the selection of topics. Put more positively, ritual activities are performed to achieve certain ends that are most meaningful in particular cultural contexts and belief systems (Brück 1999: 327). Although, recovering precise meaning is problematic in the absence of historical texts or applicable oral traditions, the contexts of contrasting rituals may be strongly expressed at different scales and locations on the landscape. The definition of ritual as 'highly formalized and repetitive' demands attention whenever we are looking for organization in the archaeological record.

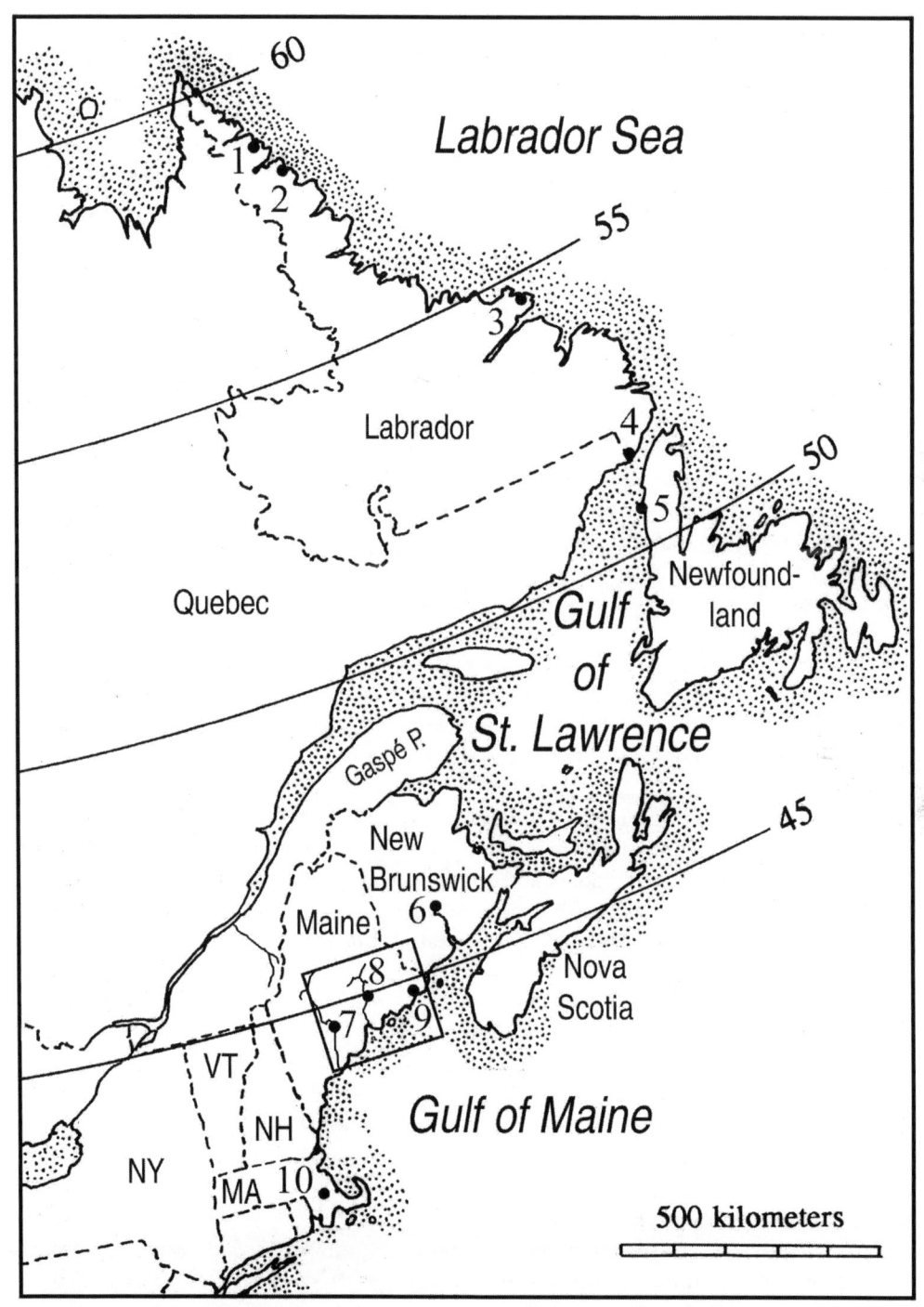

FIGURE 41.1 Regional map of the Far Northeast with places referred to in the text. The left side of the inset box (for Figure 41.2) is at the western side of the Maritime Peninsula, which includes Maine, New Brunswick, Nova Scotia and the Gaspé Peninsula. (1) Ramah Bay, (2) Nulliak Cove, (3) Rattlers Bight, (4) L'Anse Amour on the Straight of Belle Isle, (5) Port au Choix, (6) Cow Point site on the St John River, (7) Kennebec River, (8) Indian Island on the Penobscot River, (9) Machias Bay, (10) Wapanucket site.

The Far Northeast (between 44 to 59 degrees north latitude) is a region of extensive lake and river systems in the south, tundra to the north, and varied marine environments along the coast (Fitzhugh 1975; Sanger and Renouf 2006). Hunter-gatherers from the region are now represented by the Labrador Inuit (Eastern Eskimo); the Innu (Montagnais-Naskapi) of Quebec and Labrador; and the Wabanaki of the Maritime Peninsula of Maine, New Brunswick, Nova Scotia, and the Gaspé Peninsula of Quebec (Figure 41.1). The Wabanaki confederacy currently consists of four tribes, the Penobscot, Passamaquoddy, Maliseet, and Micmac. With the exception of the Inuit, the recent cultures speak Algonquian languages and share similar origin stories (Goddard 1978; Speck 1935: 54).

During the Archaic period, the Moorehead phase ('Red Paint People') and the Maritime Archaic tradition were first defined by highly visible burial components (Bourque 1995; Moorehead 1922; Tuck 1976; Willoughby 1935: 16). In normative culture-history frameworks, highly visible aspects of culture are often used to represent culture areas. Alternatively, archaeologists have focused on the interrelationship of different cultural subsystems, each having somewhat different sets of rules and codes, with burial traditions (Sanger 1973: 107), technological systems (Robinson 1992: 95), and ceramic styles (Petersen and Sanger 1991) presented as potentially separate systems in which no single trait dominates cultural models (Clarke 1978: 35). One of the lessons of ritual research is the degree to which material manifestations may change from hallmarks of identity to invisibility, requiring the fullest range of variables to approach better understandings.

Regional expressions of Archaic period mortuary patterns are discussed here from Labrador, Newfoundland, and the Maritime Peninsula. Elements of ritual practice and direct trade link the most distant parts of the ritual horizon across a straight-line distance of 1,800 km. Less emphasis is placed on more western areas including the St Lawrence River and Great Lakes region, in particular the enigmatic Laurentian tradition (Chapdelaine and Clermont 2006: 203; Cox 1991; Funk 1988) although these are important players in broader interaction spheres. Three ritual topics are addressed for the later Ceramic (or Woodland) period (3000–400 BP), drawing on Algonquian oral traditions and historical documents for sources of meaning. The three overlapping topics are: (1) burial ritual, social aggregation and feasting; (2) petroglyphs and shamanism; and (3) hunting rituals and the treatment of animal bone.

2 ORIGINS

The earliest occupants of the Far Northeast are fluted-point using Palaeoindian groups from *c.*11,000 BP, contemporary with northern tundra and glacial ice of the Younger Dryas cold period (Borns et al. 2004; Spiess et al. 1998). Continuity between Palaeoindian and Archaic period occupants is perceived in Labrador and the Canadian Maritimes, largely based on triangular projectile point styles during the Early Archaic period (8500–6500 BP) (Pintal 2006: 119). Continuity is possible in the Gulf of Maine region but there is also dramatic change. Sharp contrasts in technology between northern New England and the better known Southeastern projectile point sequences (Anderson et al. 1996; Coe 1964; Dincauze 1976) delayed recognition of northern cultural components, resulting in a perceived occupation hiatus spanning 5,000 years between the Palaeoindian and Late Archaic periods (Peterson and Putnam 1992; Sanger 2006: 230). The strongly visible sequence of related projectile point styles of the Southeast are effectively absent from the Gulf of Maine Archaic tradition (Petersen 1991; Robinson 1992). During the Middle Archaic period (8000–6000 BP) the two contrasting technological traditions coexist on either side of the Kennebec River drainage in Maine, with little overlap in assemblage content (Hamilton and Mosher 2000; Sanger 2006: 231).

The origins of the Gulf of Maine Archaic and Early Maritime Archaic traditions in the Far Northeast are almost immediately accompanied by instances of burial elaboration from Labrador to southern New England. This was first recognized in southern Labrador, at L'Anse Amour. A child of about 12 years old was found in a stone cist, 1.6 m below the surface of an 8 m-wide rock mound, with unexpectedly early radiocarbon dates of 7530 ± 140 and 7255 ± 80 BP (Tuck 1978: 68). This is part of a pattern of large individual boulder mounds located directly on the coast in Labrador and Quebec that extend through the Late Archaic period (Fitzhugh 2006: 57; Pintal 2006: 114).

Earlier burial sites were excavated in southern New England that were only recently recognized to be from the Early Archaic period (Robinson 2001, 2006). The earliest of these, Wapanucket Feature 206, is dated to 8600 BP and consists of a formal cemetery with at least eleven stone-lined cist burials (Robbins 1968; Robinson 2006). Three formal cremation cemeteries from southern New England date before 8400 BP, the earliest manifestation of a 5,000-year mortuary tradition culminating in the Moorehead burial tradition of Maine. Among the specialized artefact forms are high proportions of stone gouges and whetstones, the latter elaborated into long ground stone rods. Maurice Robbins (1968: 78) suggested a straightforward meaning for these artefact classes in burial context. If gouges and the tools to sharpen them were used in boat-making, then boat transportation must have been important in the realm of the dead. The high frequency and important symbolic position of gouges and whetstones throughout the 5,000-year mortuary tradition makes this a plausible interpretation.

Other elements of meaning apparently control the selection of bone and stone for tool-making. In Early Archaic period cremation cemeteries, bone tools were cremated with the dead, while stone tools are included in secondary deposits, unburned (Robinson 2006). Ground stone tools such as the elaborately finished full-channelled gouges appear to be early stone copies of bone prototypes. Different preferences for bone and stone artefacts in death rites may account for the absence of stone projectile points for hunting in the Gulf of Maine Archaic tradition (Robinson and Ort 2011). Ritual factors affecting the selection of raw materials for tools may drastically influence the visibility of utilitarian artefact classes and, in turn, the visibility of broad cultural traditions.

3 REGIONAL SCALE VISIBILITY: LATE ARCHAIC PERIOD FLORESCENCE (5000–3800 BP)

Throughout the Far Northeast, regional continuity in technology and mortuary ritual form long, if intermittently visible, traditions. Between about 5000 to 3800 BP all regions show a marked increase in mortuary organization based on the number, size and location of burial sites, although not obviously in terms of social status. Each region has unique visible aspects of ritual organization, contributing evidence of local identity and broad interaction.

3.1 The Labrador Maritime Archaic Tradition

The coasts of Labrador and northern Newfoundland emerged during much of the Holocene as relative sea level dropped, preserving earlier occupations on a series of raised beaches. The long tradition of individual boulder mounds is associated with these beaches. There was also greater use of stone in house construction north of the tree line in Labrador, increasing the visibility of domestic activities. Long houses up to 100 m in length were divided into 20 to 25 segments in the Late Archaic period (Fitzhugh 1985: 88). Individual rooms provide the context for identifying domestic rituals in the form of abundant pendants of soapstone at Nulliak Cove and Rattlers Bight, including engraved and perforated pendants and small plummets (Fitzhugh 1985: 98). The soapstone pendants are abundant in domestic contexts but absent from nearby burial mounds. In contrast, native copper pendants occur in burial contexts but not in houses (Fitzhugh 1985: 98). It has been suggested that the system of domestic and burial pendants may cross-cut the Far Northeast including plummets in mortuary contexts and perhaps accounting for the elaboration of utilitarian fishing weights in domestic sites (Fitzhugh 1985; Robinson 2006).

More direct evidence of ritual selection in mortuary and domestic contexts is found in the extensive use and trade of Ramah chert from northern Labrador to Maine in the Late Archaic period (Figure 41.1). Ramah chert is a translucent quartzite that comes from a dramatic source:

> Some of the most accessible and highest quality chert at Ramah is to be obtained along the walls of a prominent glacial cirque carved into the mountain massif on the north side of Ramah Bay... The chert-bearing deposits are reached by following a stream that drains the cirque. The final approach to the quarry bowl passes through a dramatic band of iron rich rocks that have stained the streambed and surrounding rocks a brilliant blood red. Here the narrow stream valley is at its most constricted point with sheer cliffs rising on both sides. The symbolic pairing of the red-ocher-stained rocks with the source for the material with which the most sacred practice—the killing of animals—was intimately associated must have figured significantly in the telling of the story. [Loring 2002: 184]

The extensive use of Ramah chert for hunting weapons and burial ritual during the Late Labrador Maritime Archaic was intensified during the Rattlers Bight phase ($c.$3600–4000 BP, Fitzhugh 2006: 58). At this time, intrusive Palaeoeskimo (Pre-Dorset) settlers from the north had surrounded the Ramah chert quarries on the coast, while Rattlers Bight people retained a foothold or enclave at the quarries (Fitzhugh 2006: 63). During the Middle Moorehead burial tradition ($c.$4000 BP), Ramah chert points and knives became a standard inclusion in burial contexts in Maine, in the style of the Rattlers Bight phase. Finished artefacts were transported from the source up to 1,800 km in a straight line or 2,400 km by way of the Strait of Belle Isle from the source. The emphasis on specific materials in the context of life and death rituals may mirror the distinction between bone and stone in the Early Archaic period.

3.2 The Newfoundland Maritime Archaic Tradition

Newfoundland provides another distinct centre of mortuary ritual, with close links to both Labrador and Maine. Most evidence of this southern branch of the Maritime Archaic in Newfoundland dates between 5500–3200 BP (Renouf and Bell 2006: 5). Here the cemeteries are few in number, but the Port au Choix site on the west coast is among the largest and best preserved, yielding a wealth of bone artefacts, effigies, and the bones of selected animal species (Tuck 1976). Abundant remains of sea birds are found with caribou, seal, walrus and whale bone. 'Seal claws, fox teeth and jaws, caribou incisors, the bills, and other bones of numerous species of birds, all have specific parallel uses among northern peoples as hunting charms' (Tuck 1976: 92). Numerous bird effigies were found along with the bones of 30 bird species. 'Judging from the common occurrence of bird bills, and especially of bird bills still attached to the skull, it seems that bird skins were made into pouches into which were put various magical objects—stones, bones and so on' (Tuck 1976: 69). Among three distinct clusters of graves, bird remains provide the strongest contrast between clusters, with 238 great auk bills found in 8 to 10 graves from Group C (the largest group), while over half of the gull bones came from Group A (the smallest group, Tuck 1976: 68, 94). One explanation is that different species of birds signified different family groups (Tuck 1976: 95). However, recent DNA analysis resulted in revised sex attributions, suggesting that gull and auk among other birds may have sex and/or status associations (Jelsma 2006: 90). Correct sex determination is one critical factor, raising the issue of other important social factors that are far less visible.

Large sample sizes are often needed to establish statistically significant relationships, but rarity (such as the killer whale effigy in burial 27 or the apparent cloak with 200 attached great auk bills and a second killer whale effigy in burial 35A) is often interpreted to represent special status. These are among the standard interpretive problems associated with symbolic analysis. The stone and bone artefacts at Port au Choix show differences and specific overlaps with those of Maine and Labrador (Bourque 1995: 230; Fitzhugh 2006: 61). As with the Moorehead burial tradition, the Port au Choix cemetery is situated near abundant seasonal resources, but focused on seal rather than anadromous fish (Renouf and Bell 2006: 13; Spiess 1992: 169). Port au Choix provides a spectacular window, limited by its near uniqueness.

3.3 The Moorehead Burial Tradition on the Gulf of Maine

Cemeteries of the Moorehead burial tradition (Sanger 1973: 107) in Maine and New Brunswick lack bone preservation, with the exception of the Nevin site in Blue Hill, Maine (Byers 1979). The large number of sites and artefacts documented over the last century provide the basis for regional analysis, revealing evidence of social and cultural organization at the scale of changing cemetery location on the landscape (Robinson 2001, 2006). The cemeteries are often placed on high landforms separate from occupation sites, with multiple small burial pits, copious use of red ochre, and specialized burial artefact types (Bourque 1992: 26; Moorehead 1922; Robinson 1996a; Sanger 1973: 101, 107; Smith 1948). Continuity in mortuary symbolism is implied from the Early Archaic period (8500 BP), but the period after about 5,200 years ago witnessed greater use of formal cemeteries

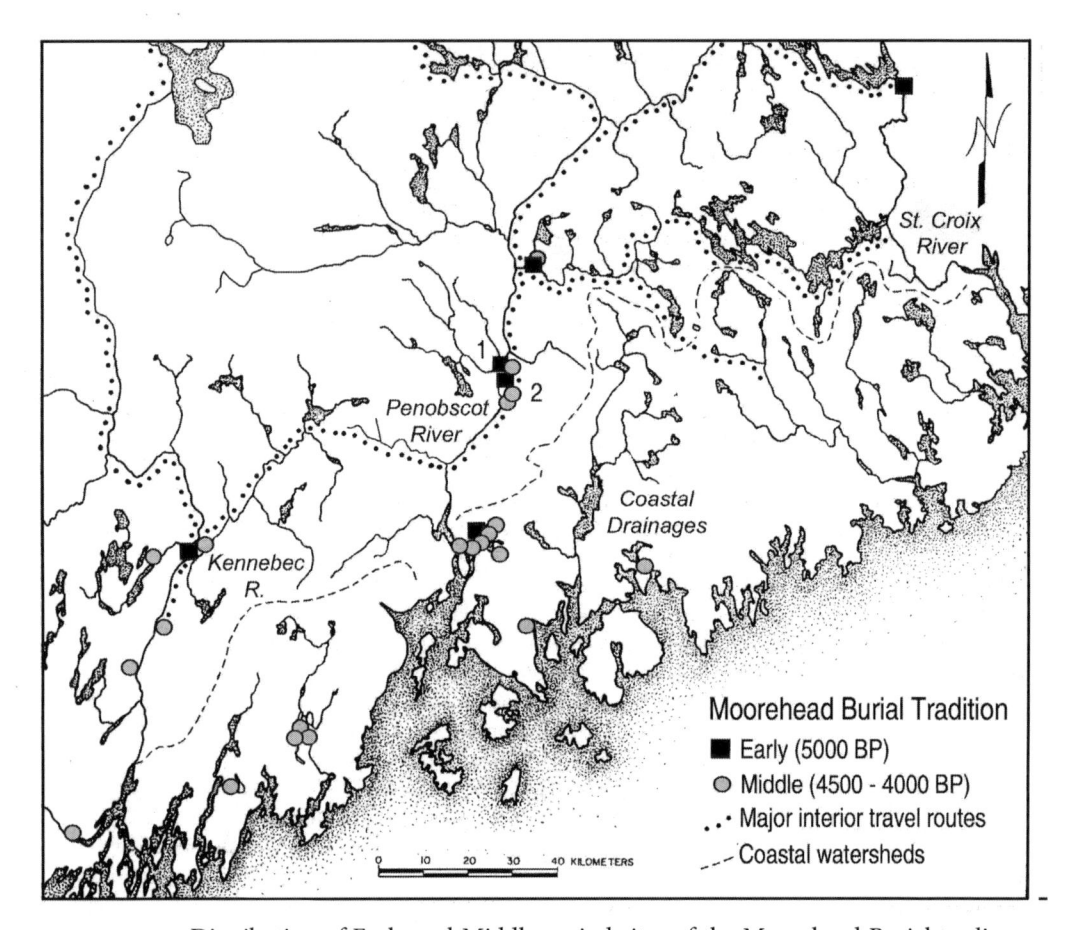

FIGURE 41.2 Distribution of Early and Middle period sites of the Moorehead Burial tradition, showing interior travel routes and the watershed boundary of smaller coastal rivers. (1) Hathaway site, Early Moorehead burial tradition, (2) Oak Hill site on Indian Island, Middle Moorehead burial tradition.

(specialized burial places). At present 34 formal cemeteries are attributed to three periods between 5200–3800 BP, with some cemeteries spanning more than one period.

Several factors associated with the Moorehead burial tradition make it particularly suitable for regional analysis. The fixed locations of maritime resources provide contrasting adaptive zones between the coast and the interior. Although coastal and interior population differences are common anthropologically, evidence of specialized coastal and interior populations in the Gulf of Maine is a comparatively recent development (Petersen 1996; Sanger 1996; Robinson 1996b). Major rivers in the Gulf of Maine flow from upland lake basins, providing numerous interior portage routes and networks of communication (Figure 41.2; Cook 1985: 3). The modern Wabanaki on the Gulf of Maine is a confederacy of four tribes that communicated through these waterways and along the coast (Wabanaki Program of the American Friends Service Committee 1989: D1–D21). Cemeteries of the

Moorehead burial tradition are distributed within the area of this communication and subsistence network.

Maritime adaptations are an important part of the territorial organization. In contrast to the focus on caribou and seal on the coast of Labrador and Newfoundland, warmer environments on the Gulf of Maine in the Late Archaic supported populations of white-tailed deer and swordfish as the largest and most abundant prey (Bourque 1995; Spiess and Lewis 2001). Harpoon foreshafts and bayonets with hexagonal cross-sections made from swordfish sword are part of the inventory of the Moorehead phase (Byers 1979; Bourque 1995: 51). Ground slate bayonets resembling those of swordfish sword may be part of the tradition of adapting bone prototypes to ground stone forms. The long, slender bayonets made from slate (Figure 41.3j) are thought to be too fragile to be practical. Their symbolic function is emphasized by carefully incised designs that are usually restricted to one side, with that side facing up in the graves (Sanger 1973: 52).

Despite the maritime focus, the cemeteries are located exclusively near anadromous fishing sites, on or near fresh water. Anadromous fish (especially alewife and shad) move from salt to fresh water to spawn (Saunders et al. 2006) providing abundant predictable resources. The cemetery locations are interpreted as spring aggregation sites, placing burial ritual more in the context of feasting and permanent gathering places, than as proxies for occupation sites. Fishing sites with different landscape associations were selected at different times depending on the scale and distribution of social groups involved. Systematic changes in location mark potential changes in social context (Robinson 2001, 2006).

The Early Moorehead burial tradition, with only six formal cemeteries, is one of the most highly structured burial patterns in the Far Northeast, both in terms of specific locations on the landscape, and specialized use of raw materials for mortuary artefacts (Moorehead 1922: 50; Robinson 1996a). Five of the six Early period sites (83 per cent) are located on access routes between major interior river systems and the coast (Figure 41.2). Four cemeteries (66 per cent) are at major waterfalls that obstruct the main channel of the river. At least two of these are situated immediately above well-known portage routes that all travellers had to confront when moving between the coast and interior. Cemeteries of this period are like signposts at major geographical obstructions.

Artefacts of the Early Moorehead tradition are specialized forms often made of uniform material types. The most abundant artefact type (the gouge, Figure 41.3d) is made from a variety of volcanic tuff that is believed to be from a single source, transported to all known cemeteries and representing up to 95 per cent of the gouges at the Hathaway Site (Snow 1969). Long perforated whetstones (Figure 41.3a) are in the tradition of long stone rods originating in the Early Archaic period. Atlatl weights or bannerstones, one of the most elaborated and long-lived ritual artefacts in the Archaic period of Eastern North America (Sassaman 1996), are rare in the entire Far Northeast, but occur in at least four of the six Early Moorehead tradition cemeteries, with five of seven specimens made from stones that are two-toned, or half light and half dark stones (Figure 41.3b and c; Robinson 1996a). The overall impression from landscape patterns is one of a highly specialized burial context involving a small proportion of the society, at centralized points of access on each major river system.

There is a distinct change in regional distribution from the Early to the Middle Moorehead burial tradition (Figure 41.2). Although the mid-river locations on major waterways

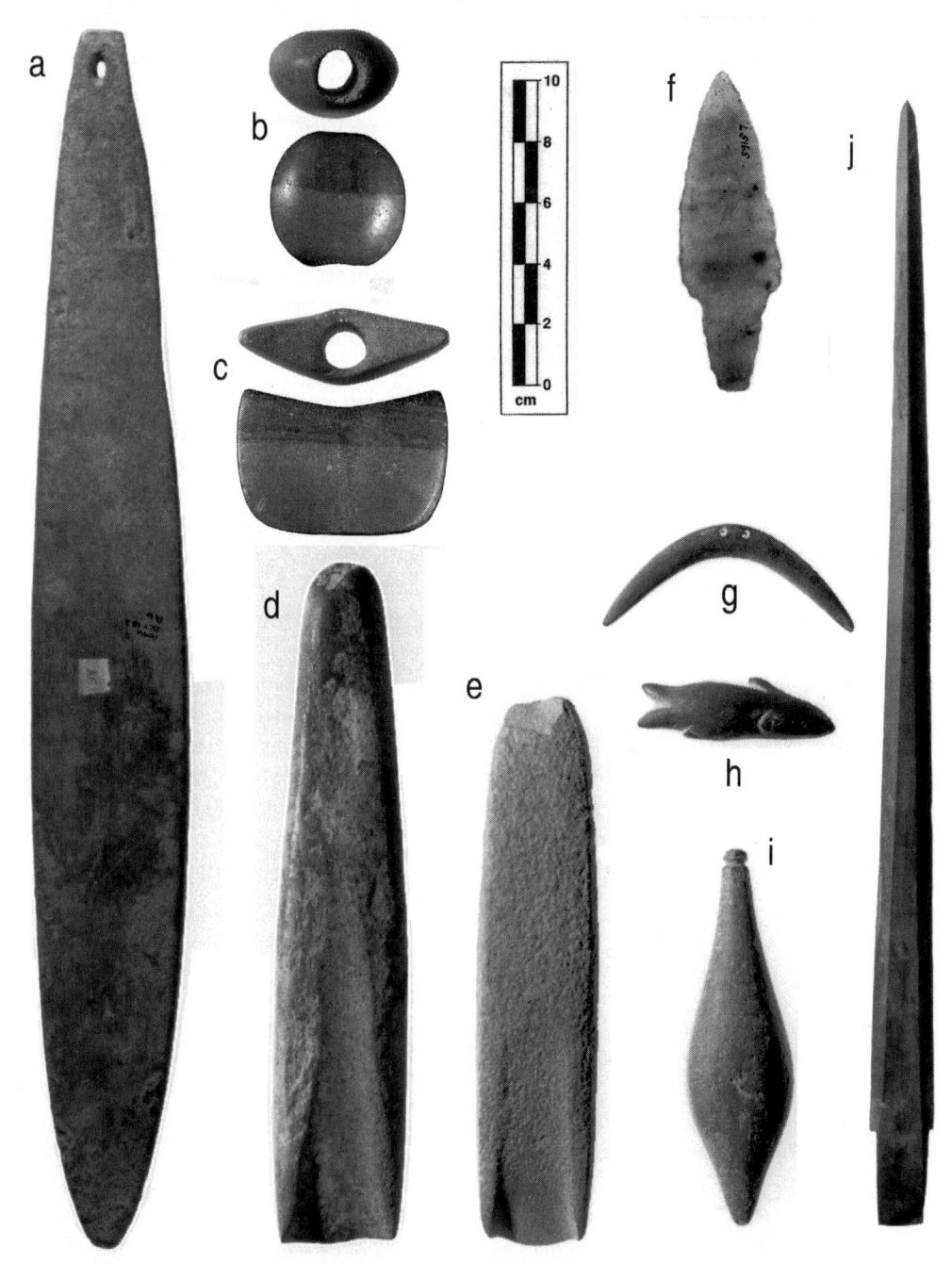

FIGURE 41.3 Artefacts of the Early (a–d), Middle (e–h), and Late (j) Moorehead burial tradition: perforated whetstone (a); bannerstones (b and c); gouges (d and e); Ramah chert biface (f); crescent (g); effigy fish (h); plummet (i); ground slate bayonette (j).

are not completely abandoned, the majority of Middle period sites are not located at river obstructions, but rather at tributary and pond outlets with 57 per cent (12/21) located on short coastal river drainages, clustered within a coastal territory. Middle period sites are more abundant and have larger numbers of individuals (up to 60 and perhaps many more in badly disturbed sites, Moorehead 1922: 36). If an analogy from the single Late period site with skeletal preservation applies (with 5 females, 7 males, and 15 children and infants), the cemeteries may have had a cross-section of age and sex groups (Byers 1979; Shaw 1988: 59, 62). Stone effigies (including plummets) are introduced in the Middle period with birds, mammals, and fish among more abstract forms (Figure 41.3h; Bourque 1995: 52; Moorehead 1922: fig. 39), a reflection of animal symbolism evident with good bone preservation at Port au Choix. Among the three time periods, Middle period cemeteries are: (1) the most abundant; (2) restricted to the smallest region in the central Gulf of Maine; and (3) involved in the most extensive transport of Ramah chert from Labrador (Bourque 1994).

Although all of the cemeteries are at anadromous fishing locations interpreted as spring aggregation sites, contrasting landscape associations, cemetery characteristics and artefact variability suggest a change in social context represented at the gatherings. Taken together, Early period sites are located toward the interior boundary of the cemetery distribution (Figure 41.2) and occur at a time when there is the most evidence and debate about contrasting interior and coastal cultures involving the Laurentian tradition and little known coastal manifestations (Bourque 1995: 242; Cox 1991; Sanger 2006: 237; Robinson 1996b). I have interpreted the change in cemetery location from the Early to Middle Moorehead burial tradition as a change from aggregation in a boundary context between interior and coastal populations, to aggregations of smaller social groups within the coastal territory, perhaps kin groups (Robinson 2001, 2006).

With the potential that different cemetery locations may represent different social groups, changes in mortuary artefacts and symbolism are given another interpretive platform. Do changes in artefact types represent simple change through time, or do they represent changing scales of social identity, from societies in a boundary context to family symbols or totems at sub-cultural levels? This is a complex and fascinating topic that requires the quantification of artefact types in a wide variety of contexts (Robinson 2001, 2006). For example, between the Early and Middle Moorehead burial tradition, large perforated whetstones of the Early Moorehead burial tradition (Figure 41.3a) disappear and are replaced by equally large proportions of stone plummets (Figure 41.3i; Robinson 2006). Up to 1,000 years later at the Late period Cow Point site, in New Brunswick, this pattern is reversed with plummets in an earlier component replaced by perforated and notched whetstones in the later component (Sanger 1973). At the same time the greenstone that dominated Early period gouges, was reintroduced in the Late period (Poole and Turay 1973). This set of relationships, if properly understood, could provide an important historical signature for social relations. Plummets, at the same time, have variable roles in broader contexts, in Labrador, New York, Maine, and southern New England, suggesting that they are a ritually influenced artefact class, sometimes employed as utilitarian fishing weights and sometimes reserved for ritual contexts (Robinson 2001, 2006). Taken together, I suggest that ritual functions influenced the selection of raw material and form of projectile points, gouges, whetstones and plummets, among a variety of more specialized forms. Similar efforts in multiple regions, for example Southeastern North America (Sassaman

1996), provide a variety of avenues to explore social and cultural boundary phenomena and interaction at increasingly large scales.

About 3800 BP the Moorehead burial tradition is interrupted in Maine by another technological and mortuary pattern known as the Susquehanna tradition, with origins to the south, providing the leading candidate for a migration in Northeast prehistory (Bourque 1995; Sanger 2006: 241). Controversy and many questions remain as to the nature of contacts, interaction, and continuity. The intrusion extends partly into the Far Northeast, weakening but present on the St Croix River at the border of Maine and New Brunswick, with apparent ripple effects beyond (Black 2000; Deal et al. 2006: 265; Sanger 2008). The strong connections to the south dissipate after 400–800 years and the character of the Far Northeast as an interaction sphere is resumed.

In the Far Northeast, burial ritual has played a particularly large role in our understanding of Archaic period archaeology, with some of the earliest formal cemeteries in North America. Like the earlier Late Palaeoindian Sloan Cemetery in Arkansas (Morse 1997), enduring traditions developed around essentially permanent ritual areas, in the midst of mobile economic and settlement patterns.

4 Ritual Themes on the Gulf of Maine, the Last 3,000 Years

Broadly in eastern North America, the Woodland period (c.3000–400 BP) is associated with increasingly complex ritual developments such as the Early Woodland Adena and Middle Woodland Hopewell interaction spheres. These particular manifestations are centred in the Midwest but with far-reaching relations that also represent a transition between hunting and gathering and increasingly agricultural economies (Milner 2004). Midwestern mortuary ritual had dramatic extensions into the Northeast (Vermont, Heckenberger et al. 1990), and the Far Northeast (New Brunswick, Turnbull 1976) and the scale of intrusion and apparent connections to ritual centres may reflect an evolutionary scale of increasing complexity. But these ritual intrusions are rare in the Far Northeast and largely limited to the Early Ceramic (or Early Woodland) period, with much left to learn about regional cultural manifestations beyond the spread of the earliest pottery (Blair 2004; Robinson 2003). Here I focus on the Gulf of Maine, where Ceramic period mortuary elaboration is little known, but where greater continuity with Algonquian traditions extends the range of interpretation. Keeping with the theme of archaeological visibility, three topics are addressed and compared to earlier Archaic period archaeological evidence of ritual: (1) burial practices, feasts and gathering places; (2) petroglyphs and shamanism; and (3) hunting rituals and treatment of animal bones.

4.1 Burial Practices, Feasts, and Gathering Places

The large number of Ceramic period coastal shell middens increases preservation of organic materials greatly compared to earlier times. Subsistence and settlement patterns are much better known, but despite preservation of bone on the coast there are relatively few burials in coastal shell middens on the Maritime Peninsula, suggesting an avoidance of burial in domestic areas. Occasional Ceramic period burials were reported during the excavation of Archaic period cemeteries over the last century (Willoughby 1935: 26–9; Moorehead 1922: 46). Re-excavation of the Hathaway site (Early Moorehead burial tradition, Figure 41.2) revealed a complex series of burial episodes including large 'fire-holes' interpreted as burials from the Ceramic period, but without artefacts (Snow 1975). Why is so little known about Ceramic period burials compared to the Archaic period? Recognition and different levels of archaeological attention are major problems.

While documenting a sand pit that marked the previous location of a Late Moorehead burial tradition cemetery (the Erkkila site) in Warren, Maine, renewed sand-pit operations exposed a series of very large pits, some with layers of fire-cracked boulders and compressed tubes of partly burned logs (Robinson 1996c). Although excavation was limited and most deposits were only recorded in profile on the sand pit walls, the site yielded what were identified as nine large Middle Ceramic period burial pits (1700 BP), before the knoll was destroyed. Bone was absent except for a small area of tooth enamel and degraded cranial fragments protected beneath a rock slab. Only one artefact was recovered from the whole area, a copper bead on a knotted piece of cordage. No occupation remains of the time period were identified, supporting the interpretation that this was an isolated formal cemetery on the same landform as the Late Archaic period Erkkila site. The inclusion of large burned rocks that were heated elsewhere and partly burned pine logs (apparently green when burned) suggests smoke and steam were important parts of the ceremony. The near absence of artefacts, presence of burned layers and fire-cracked rock, and the separation from occupation sites suggests that many such features go unrecognized or are interpreted as storage or fire pits.

Although still poorly recognized, the combined evidence suggests that between 1700 to 1000 BP and perhaps more recently, burials were sometimes placed on the same kind of landscape features as during the Moorehead burial tradition, associated with anadromous fishing sites and quite probably with seasonal gatherings. In contrast to the Late Archaic period, burial pits of the Middle Ceramic period are often much larger with more episodes of activity (burning, burial, burning, occasional re-entry and reburning). The pits are more complex but they are devoid of artefacts to the degree that certain materials (stone and pottery) seem to be intentionally excluded. Native copper beads or pendants are known in at least four cases, and in one case copper beads were associated with 32 shark teeth including one from a Great White shark (Snow 2006: 18).

Burial ceremonies during the Ceramic period occurred, at least in part, at seasonal aggregation sites. The homeland of the modern Penobscot Nation is situated at one of these locations on Indian Island just above the Old Town Falls on the Penobscot River. This island was used for centuries for seasonal gatherings and ceremonies, including the induction of Penobscot chiefs or governors. Governor John Aitteon and Lieutenant-Governor John Neptune were inducted into office on September 19, 1816, with necessary and formal participation of delegates from the St John Maliseet and Passamaquoddy tribes. The ceremony was described in some detail, with all the caveats associated with outsider perspectives (Eckstorm 1980: 113; Williamson 1832: 495):

> More than three hours were consumed in these ceremonies; which were succeeded by a feast already preparing. Two fat oxen, slaughtered and severed into pieces, were roasting; rice, beans, and garden vegetables were boiling; and bread-loaves and crackers were abundant. If

the cookery, neatness and order, were unworthy of modern invitation; the defects were counterbalanced by the hearty invitations and welcomes, with which all the visitants equally with the natives, were urged to become partakers, both of the repast and of the festive scenes. [Williamson 1832: 498]

Although by 1816 the feast featured oxen and garden vegetables, the importance of the anadromous fishery is well documented at this location, particularly at a small rocky island called Shad Island above Old Town Falls and just below Indian Island. 'This island is extremely well situated for the shad fishing which fish the Indians depend upon in a great measure for their subsistence' (Letter from the Penobscot Tribe to General Blake, cited in MacDougall 1995: 62). After 1797, the island became the focus of decades of legal and social conflict between the Penobscots and the newly settled Euro-Americans who valued Shad Island for the footing of dams, cutting off the fishway (Pawling 2007: 17). Two hundred years later 'The Penobscot River Restoration Project' has raised $25 million toward the removal of three dams 'as part of an unprecedented project to reopen spawning grounds for Atlantic salmon and other fish species'. Partners in the project include the Penobscot Nation, landowners, six conservation groups, and seven state and federal agencies (Miller 2008: A1, A6).

Indian Island is one of several major anadromous fishing locations on the Penobscot River, the importance of which varied with the context of social gatherings. The chiefs ceremony of 1816 represents the diversity of activities at such feasts, perhaps akin to the variety of activities 5,000 years ago when burial in the formal cemetery was part of the occasion. Four major Moorehead burial tradition cemeteries occur within 700 m of Indian Island, the largest of which, Oak Hill, was used for hundreds of years and was located on a rise just behind the historic gathering place. Anadromous fishing sites provided one important setting for social gatherings. Another place, interpreted as a trade fair during the Late Ceramic period, occurred on the tip of a maritime peninsula on east side of Penobscot Bay (Bourque and Cox 1981). Gathering places may have been the most permanent base among seasonally mobile people.

4.2 Petroglyphs and Shamanism

Burial rituals probably employed specialized ritual practitioners, in what appear to be highly standardized rituals at seasonal gatherings. Another kind of ritual practitioner becomes visible in the Ceramic period, perhaps 3,000 years ago with the introduction of petroglyphs into the Gulf of Maine. Pecked human/spiritual/animal figures on bedrock persist for thousands of years but are concentrated in small areas such as Machias Bay in Eastern Maine and on one ledge in the Kennebec River. In Machias Bay, the historical territory of the Passamaquoddy tribe, the latest petroglyphs include seventeenth-century single-masted sailing ships with rigging, bow sprit, and sterncastle (Hedden 2002).

The petroglyphs are a prolific symbol system practised widely enough that interpretation from direct historical accounts of other Algonquian tribes, such as the Great Lakes Ojibwa (Schoolcraft 1851–7), can be combined with historical and oral accounts of the Wabanaki to understand specific meanings. Mark Hedden, who has spent 30 years documenting petroglyphs of Maine, attributes some of them specifically to vision quests among Algonquian shamans, or in dialect variations in Penobscot and Passamaquoddy, *m'teoulin or medo'win*.

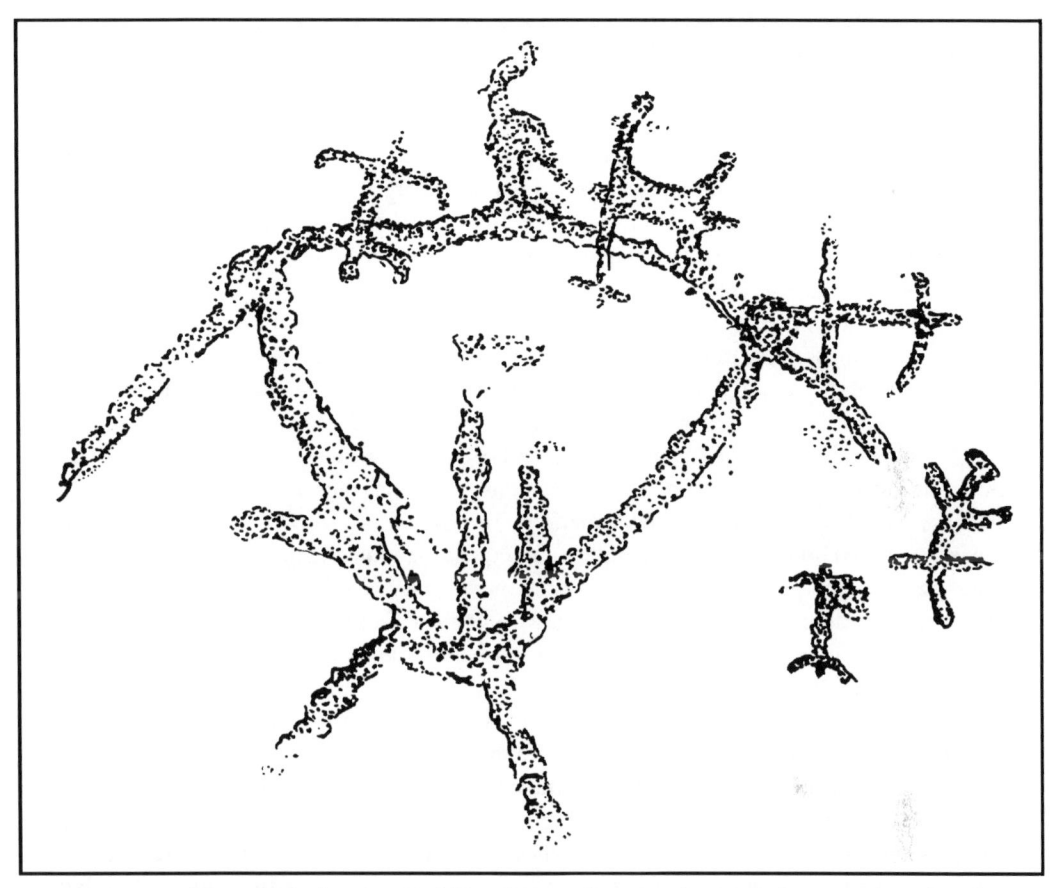

FIGURE 41.4 Petroglyph showing bird-like shaman figure and spirit helpers attributed to the Shaking Tent ceremony.

In 1893, Joseph Nicolar described the spiritual power received while in a trance (Nicolar 2007: 151). The activities may be conducted secretly or accompanied by public displays at seasonal gatherings (Hedden 2004: 337, 338). Unlike the effigies associated with Archaic period burials, petroglyphs include many human and/or spirit forms some of which can be specifically identified.

One of the most famous Wabanaki shamans is Lieutenant-Governor John Neptune referred to above. Eckstorm (1980: 27) provides a dramatic account of how Neptune's shamanistic role was hidden from Euro-Americans throughout his active life. One of Neptune's performances as a shaman was told in 1914 by Clara Neptune. The account resembles petroglyphs from Machias Bay (Figure 41.4; Hedden 1983: 2). In Eckstorm's (1980: 36) description:

> It was a long story about his calling his spirits to help him . . . She described his making a little house of interwoven branches and going inside. He had a little fire. Then they heard noises like wings (she did not use the words 'wings,' but imitated the noise and the motion). Then those outside the house saw the sides of the little hut bulge in places and some one, looking through a crack, saw the Old Governor sitting by his fire, and several, perhaps half a dozen 'what you find

em under old boat and in fork of tree' standing up around the fire. I worked some time to make out what she meant and then made sure they were the small spotted salamanders, not uncommon here. The fire she said, had made them come out of the wood he was burning and the Governor was talking with them. That is, they were his familiar spirits.

This event is associated with the Shaking Tent ceremony which often represents a response to a specific crisis at any time of the year, practised widely among Algonquians from the Great Lakes to Labrador and Maine (Hedden 2004: 338). The historical accounts provide specific meanings to some petroglyphs and changing meanings over time have been inferred for petroglyphs spanning 3,000 years.

At Machias Bay, the practitioners picked a strictly coastal canvas for their work, at the edge of land and sea. On the upper Kennebec River, at Emden, a ledge projecting into the river was used, the special research focus of Penobscot researcher Michael Sockalexis. The nineteenth-century Micmac petroglyphs at Kejimkujik Lake in Nova Scotia are on the shores of an interior lake (Lenik 2002: 19). All of these places have suitable rock surfaces, but all such surfaces are not used. The petroglyphs at Machias Bay are so concentrated that the choice of location begs for an explanation. Over 250 petroglyphs spanning a thousand years are located on one ledge, with outer submerged ledges having figures dating approximately 2,500 years ago (Hedden 2004). Passamaquoddy historian, Donald Soctomah, calls it 'a place of communication', which would be appropriate to the needs of a shaman for private or public performance (personal communication, June 10, 2008).

In eastern Maine, petroglyphs are situated on a landscape with Passamaquoddy place names that are intelligible to Native speakers providing further insights into the Passamaquoddy homeland (Sanger et al. 2006; Soctomah 2004). The major petroglyph site in Machias Bay was returned to the Passamaquoddy in a ceremony in 2006. As a direct link with their own spiritual past, they have formed the Maluhsi-hikon Petroglyph Foundation for research and for exploring ways to educate, build respect for, and preserve their heritage. One of the most practical and respectful efforts to preserve the fragile intertidal petroglyphs is removal of shoes while walking on the rock surface.

The spiritual connection between the modern Wabanaki and the petroglyph traditions influences the manner in which the sites are interpreted to the public, as well as the potential for preservation and study. One of the perpetual problems of recent centuries has been individuals leaving their own initials on the rock for posterity, sometimes defacing the earlier petroglyphs. While this may be an understandable and even innocent practice in the great scheme of changing traditions, it is more obviously desecration when the petroglyphs are presented as active sacred sites, and when preservation of unique aspects of cultural heritage is a source of pride to Native and non-Native communities. These concerns directly influence educational interests, cultural values, and preservation of heritage sites.

4.3 Hunting Rituals and the Treatment of Animal Bones

I have suggested that different ritual treatment of bone and stone in the Early Archaic period may be one of the reasons that flaked stone projectile points were excluded from the Gulf of Maine Archaic tradition between 8,500 to 6,000 years ago. Good preservation at the Late Archaic period burial site at Port au Choix in Newfoundland demonstrates the abundant use of animal bone in ritual contexts at that time. The special treatment of animal bone is one of the more widespread and tenacious of practices among Algonquians, associated with a variety of special human/animal relationships including the hunters respect for the animals. Joseph Nicolar recorded for the Wabanaki that the first 'spiritual men' were instructed: 'Teach them also never to abuse the spirit of the animals. You may kill the animal and eat his flesh but never abuse the spirit of it, because if you do abuse the spirit of the animal he will never come to your calling' (Nicolar 2007 [1893]: 152).

Respect for the animal's spirit took different forms. Speck recorded for the Innu (or Naskapi) of Subarctic Canada that 'it becomes a religious obligation for the righteous-minded hunter' to skin beaver with a scraper made from the leg bone of a bear because 'the slain beaver feels satisfaction in having its pelt removed with the leg-bone skinning tool' (Speck 1935: 216–17). It is a widespread belief among the Innu (Montagnais/Naskapi) Cree, and Wabanaki that it is disrespectful for dogs to feed on game animals (Sanger 2003: 31, Tanner 1979: 166). Bones were sometimes burned, hung in trees or disposed of in the water to keep them from dogs. The Mistassini Cree suspend the bones of 'bear, beaver, caribou and certain species of birds and fish in trees . . . Only hare, certain mustelids, ptarmigan/grouse and some fish species were fed to the dogs' all of which influenced the distribution of bone around the occupation site (Gordon 1980: 92).

Sanger (2003: 33) observed in the Gulf of Maine that little burned bone was recovered from coastal shell middens, and that gnaw marks attributed to dogs were common. Although bone preservation is poor on the interior, hearths with abundant burned bone are sufficiently common to suggest a different disposal pattern and potential for a cosmological approach to the identification of coastal versus interior groups and belief systems (Sanger 2003: 33). Rituals of respect may be universal among hunter-gatherers, with contrasting rituals traceable through time, perhaps starting with specialized treatment of bone and stone in the Early Archaic period in the Gulf of Maine.

The potential to identify specialized treatment of animal bone use is mostly limited to coastal shell middens where good bone preservation provides a more comprehensive range of selective processes. Current research through the University of Maine and the Passamaquoddy petroglyph project is directed, in part, to finding relationships between the treatment of animal bone and closely associated animal petroglyphs, both implicating ritual hunting practices as a subset of broader religious and subsistence activities. The near absence of human remains from coastal shell middens in eastern Maine provides important evidence that human burial was separated from domestic space, emphasizing multiple ritual places linked at a regional scale. The visibility of spiritual domains afforded by good preservation of faunal remains and associated petroglyphs is precariously situated within a few metres of high tide, subject to rising sea level, artefact collecting, and coastal development. Preservation efforts are potentially enhanced by the integration of academic and sacred concerns.

5 CONCLUSIONS

Ritual as a category is often ambiguous and eclectic, focusing on things that may at first appear 'odd' from an outsider's point of view. But as such we have to double our efforts to understand them. This is of value whether our goal is to understand particular cultural traditions, or to identify what we should count if our interests are economic or demographic. Either way, 'the subtleties and complexities of ritual will require definition on a case-by-case basis' (Insoll 2004: 12). The Archaic period traditions of the Far Northeast are more visible when elaborated burial customs and domestic structures provide the spatial structure to discern social and ritual context. With the combination of archaeology and oral tradition from later times, three domains of ritual practice were discussed here, each identifiable in archaeological contexts, each with different spatial characteristics, and all potentially coexisting in the same cultural systems. Identification and integration of such domains contributes to better understanding of how ritual activities shape what we see in the archaeological record.

Acknowledgements

I thank Timothy Insoll and Rachel Maclean for the invitation to contribute to this volume. I thank Mark Hedden, David Sanger, and Ann Surprenant, as well as Bonnie Newsom, Penobscot Tribal Historic Preservation Officer, and Donald Soctomah, Passamaquoddy Tribal Historic Preservation Officer, for reading and comments on the paper. Funding for current research on coastal shell middens and petroglyphs comes from a Maine Academic Prominence Initiative (MAPI) grant for the UM archaeological field school, and the National Park Service for 'Comprehensive Land-use Planning for the Passamaquoddy Machias Bay Petroglyph Sites' (directed by D. Soctomah). I am of course responsible for errors and inadequacies.

Suggested Reading

The Archaic of the Far Northeast (Sanger and Renouf 2006) provides recent research on early cultural manifestations addressed above. An early account of ritual and religion by Penobscot author Joseph Nicolar (2007), *The Life and Traditions of the Red Man*, was recently reprinted. Adrian Tanner's (1979) *Bringing Home Animals* is a detailed account of Cree (Algonquian) religion, especially related to respect for animal spirits. Mark Hedden's 2004 article addresses shamanism and the rock art of Machias Bay, Maine.

References

Anderson, D. G., O'Steen, L. D., and Sassaman, K. E. 1996. 'Environmental and chronological considerations' in D. G. Anderson and K. E. Sassaman (eds), *The Paleoindian and Early Archaic Southeast* (Tuscaloosa: University of Alabama Press), pp. 3–15.
Bell, C. 1997. *Ritual: Perspectives and Dimensions* (New York: Oxford University Press).
Black, D. W. 2000. 'Rum Beach and the Susquehanna tradition in the Quoddy region, Charlotte County, New Brunswick', *Canadian Journal of Archaeology*, 24: 89–105.

BLAIR, S. 2004. 'Pihcesis Ajemseg: The Maritime Woodland at Jemseg' in S. Blair (ed.), *Wolastoqiyik Ajemseg: The people of the Beautiful River at Jemseg*, II: *Archaeological Results*, Manuscripts in New Brunswick Archaeology No. 36E (Fredericton: New Bruswick Archaeological Services), pp. 251–76.

BORNS, H. W. JR., DONER, L. A., DORIAN, C. C., et al. 2004. The deglaciation of Maine, U.S.A' in J. Ehlers and P. L. Gibbard (eds), *Quaternary Glaciations: Extent and chronology, Part II: North America* (Amsterdam: Elsevier), pp. 89–109.

BOURQUE, B. J. 1992. *Prehistory of the Central Maine Coast*, PhD dissertation, Harvard University, 1971 (New York: Garland Publications).

—— 1994. 'Evidence for prehistoric exchange on the Maritime Peninsula' in T. G. Baugh and J. E. Ericson (eds), *Prehistoric Exchange Systems in North America* (New York: Plenum Press), pp. 23–46.

—— 1995. *Diversity and Complexity in Prehistoric Maritime Societies: A Gulf of Maine perspective* (New York: Plenum Press).

—— and Cox, S. L. 1981. 'Maine State Museum investigation of the Goddard site', *Man in the Northeast*, 22: 3–27.

BRÜCK, J. 1999. 'Ritual and rationality: Some problems of interpretation in European archaeology', *European Journal of Archaeology*, 2(3): 313–44.

BYERS, D. S. 1979. *The Nevin Shellheap: Burials and observations*, Papers of the R. S. Peabody Foundation for Archaeology 9 (Andover: The Foundation, Phillips Academy).

CHAPDELAINE, C. and CLERMONT, N. 2006. 'Adaptations, continuity and change in the Middle Ottawa Valley: A view from the Morrison and Allumettes Island Late Archaic sites' in D. Sanger and M. A. P. Renouf (eds), *The Archaic of the Far Northeast* (Orono: University of Maine Press), pp. 191– 219.

CLARKE, D. 1978. *Analytical Archaeology*, 2nd edn, rev. Bob Chapman (London: Methuen and Co. Ltd).

COE, J. L. 1964. *The Formative Cultures of the Carolina Piedmont* (Philadelphia: Transactions of the American Philosophical Society, New Series 54(5)).

COOK, D. S. 1985. *Above the Gravel Bar: The Indian canoe routes of Maine* (Milo, Maine: Milo Printing Company).

Cox, S. L. 1991. 'Site 95.20 and the Vergennes phase in Maine', *Archaeology of Eastern North America*, 19: 135–61.

DEAL, M., RUTHERFORD, D., MURPHY, B., et al. 2006. 'Rethinking the Archaic sequence for the Maritime provinces' in D. Sanger and M. A. P. Renouf (eds), *The Archaic of the Far Northeast* (Orono: University of Maine Press), pp. 253–307.

DINCAUZE, D. F. 1976. *The Neville Site: 8000 years at Amoskeag*, Peabody Museum Monographs 4 (Cambridge, MA: Harvard University Press).

ECKSTORM, F. H. 1980 [1945]. *Old John Neptune and Other Maine Indian Shamans*, A Marsh Island Reprint (Orono: University of Maine Press).

FITZHUGH, W. W. (ed.) 1975. 'Papers from a symposium on Moorehead and Maritime Archaic problems in Northeastern New England, held at the Smithsonian Institution, February 27–March 2, 1974', *Arctic Anthropology*, 12(2).

—— 1985. 'The Nulliak pendants and their relation to spiritual traditions in Northeast prehistory', *Arctic Anthropology*, 22(2): 87–109.

—— 2006. 'Settlement, social and ceremonial change in the Labrador Maritime Archaic' in D. Sanger and M. A. P. Renouf (eds), *The Archaic of the Far Northeast* (Orono: University of Maine Press), pp. 47–81.

FUNK, R. E. 1988. 'The Laurentian concept: A review', *Archaeology of Eastern North America*, 16: 1–42.

GODDARD, I. 1978. 'Eastern Algonquian languages' in Bruce G. Trigger (ed.), *Northeast*, Handbook of North American Indians, XV (Washington, DC: Smithsonian Institution), pp. 70–7.

GORDON, D. 1980. 'Reflections on refuse: A contemporary example from James Bay, Quebec', *Canadian Journal of Archaeology*, 4: 83–97.

HAMILTON, N. D. and MOSHER, J. P. 2000. 'Rumford Falls: A Holocene cultural sequence in Northwestern Maine', Report on file, Maine Historic Preservation Commission, Augusta.

HECKENBERGER, M. J., PETERSEN, J. B., BASA, L., et al. 1990. 'Early Woodland period mortuary ceremonialism in the Far Northeast: A view from the Boucher cemetery', *Archaeology of Eastern North America*, 18: 109–44.

HEDDEN, M. 1983. Cover, *Maine Archaeological Society Bulletin*, 23(2): 2.

—— 2002. Contact period petroglyphs in Machias Bay, Maine', *Archaeology of Eastern North America*, 30: 1–20.

—— 2004. 'Passamaquoddy Shamanism and rock art in Machias Bay, Maine' in C. Diaz-Granados and J. R. Duncan (eds), *The Rock Art of Eastern North America* (Tuscaloosa: The University of Alabama Press), pp. 319–43.

INSOLL, T. 2004. *Archaeology, Ritual, Religion* (London: Routledge).

JELSMA, J. 2006. 'Three social status groups in Port au Choix: Maritime Archaic mortuary practices and social structure' in D. Sanger and M. A. P. Renouf (eds), *The Archaic of the Far Northeast* (Orono: University of Maine Press), pp. 83–103.

LENIK, E. 2002. *Picture Rocks: American Indian rock art in the Northeast Woodlands* (Hanover: University Press of New England).

LORING, S. 2002. 'And they took away the stones from Ramah: Lithic raw material sourcing and Eastern Arctic archaeology' in W. W. Fitzhugh, S. Loring, and D. W. Odess (eds), *Honoring our Elders: A history of Eastern Arctic archaeology*, National Museum of Natural History, Arctic Studies Center, Contributions to Circumpolar Anthropology 2 (Washington DC: Smithsonian Institution), pp. 163–85.

MACDOUGALL, P. M. 1995. *Indian Island, Maine: 1780 to 1930*, PhD dissertation, History Department, University of Maine, Orono.

MILLER, K. 2008. 'River Trust to buy dams on Penobscot', *Bangor Daily News* (Bangor, Maine), 22 August 2008, p. A1.

MILNER, G. R. 2004. *The Moundbuilders: Ancient peoples of Eastern North America* (London: Thames and Hudson Ltd).

MOOREHEAD, W. K. 1922. *A Report on the Archaeology of Maine*, Department of Anthropology, Phillips Academy (Andover: AMS Press).

MORSE, D. F. (ed.) 1997. *Sloan: A Paleoindian Dalton cemetery in Arkansas* (Washington: Smithsonian Institution Press).

NICOLAR, J. 2007. *The Life and Traditions of the Red Man*, ed. A. Kolodny from the original of 1893 (London: Duke University Press).

PAWLING, M. A. P. (ed.) 2007. *Wabanaki Homeland and the New State of Maine: The 1820 journal and plans of survey of Joseph Treat* (Amherst: University of Massachusetts Press, in conjunction with the Penobscot Indian Nation, Indian Island, Maine).

PETERSEN, J. B. 1991. *Archaeological Testing at the Sharrow Site: A deeply stratified Early to Late Holocene cultural sequence in Central Maine*, Occasional Publications in Maine Archaeology 8 (Augusta: Maine Historic Preservation Commission).

PETERSEN, J. B. 1996. 'Fiber industries from Northern New England: Ethnicity and technological traditions during the Woodland period' in James B. Petersen (ed.), *A Most Indispensable Art: Native Fiber Industries from Eastern North America* (Knoxville: The University of Tennessee Press), pp. 101–19.

—— and PUTNAM, D. E. 1992. 'Early Holocene occupation in the Central Gulf of Maine region' in Brian S. Robinson, J. B. Petersen, and A. K. Robinson (eds), *Early Holocene Occupation in Northern New England*, Occasional Publications in Maine Archaeology 9 (Augusta: Maine Historic Preservation Commission), pp. 13–61.

—— and SANGER, D. 1991. 'An Aboriginal ceramic sequence for Maine and the Maritimes' in M. Deal and S. Blair (eds), *Prehistoric Archaeology in the Maritimes: Past and present research* (Fredericton: Council of Maritime Premiers), pp. 121–78.

PINTAL, J. Y. 2006. 'The Archaic sequence of the St Lawrence Lower North Shore, Quebec' in D. Sanger and M. A. P. Renouf (eds), *The Archaic of the Far Northeast* (Orono: University of Maine Press), pp. 105–38.

POOLE, W. H. and TURAY, M. 1973. 'Lithological description of artifacts, Cow Point Site, New Brunswick, Appendix 2' in D. Sanger (ed.), *Cow Point: An Archaic cemetery in New Brunswick*, Archaeological Survey of Canada Paper 12 (Ottawa: National Museum of Man), pp. 153–74.

RENOUF, M. A. P. and BELL, T. 2006. 'Maritime Archaic site locations on the Island of Newfoundland' in D. Sanger and M. A. P. Renouf (eds), *The Archaic of the Far Northeast* (Orono: University of Maine Press), pp. 1–46.

ROBBINS, M. 1968. *An Archaic Ceremonial Complex at Assawompsett* (Attleboro: Massachusetts Archaeological Society).

ROBINSON, B. S. 1992. 'Early and Middle Archaic period occupation in the Gulf of Maine region: Mortuary and technological patterning' in B. S. Robinson, J. B. Petersen, and A. K. Robinson (eds), *Early Holocene Occupation in Northern New England*, Occasional Publications in Maine Archaeology 9 (Augusta: Maine Historic Preservation Commission), pp. 63–116.

—— 1996a. 'A regional analysis of the Moorehead burial tradition: 8500–3700 BP', *Archaeology of Eastern North America*, 24: 95–148.

—— 1996b. 'Projectile points, other diagnostic things and culture boundaries in the Gulf of Maine Region', *The Maine Archaeological Society Bulletin*, 36(2): 1–24.

—— 1996c. 'The Erkkila site: Later Archaic and Middle Ceramic period cemeteries in Warren, Maine', Report submitted to the Maine Historic Preservation Commission, Augusta.

—— 2001. *Burial Ritual: Groups and boundaries on the Gulf of Maine: 8600–3800 BP*, PhD dissertation, Anthropology Department, Brown University, Providence, RI.

—— 2003. 'Population Fluctuation, Climatic Events, and Culture History in the Northeast: Review of Fiedel', *The Review of Archaeology*, 24(1): 56–61.

—— 2006. 'Burial ritual, technology, and cultural landscape in the Far Northeast: 8600–3700 BP' in D. Sanger and M. A. P. Renouf (eds), *The Archaic of the Far Northeast* (Orono: University of Maine Press), pp. 341–81.

—— and ORT, J. C. 2011. 'Paleoindian and Archaic Period Traditions: Particular Explanations from New England', in K. E. Sassaman and D. H. Holly, Jr. (eds), *Hunter–Gatherer Archaeology as Historial Process*, Amerind Studies in Archaeology (Tucson: University of Arizona Press), pp. 209–26.

SANGER, D. 1973. *Cow Point: An Archaic cemetery in New Brunswick*, Archaeological Survey of Canada Paper 12 (Ottawa: National Museum of Man).

——1996. 'An analysis of seasonal transhumance models for pre-European State of Maine', *Contributions to the Archaeology of Northeastern North America, The Review of Archaeology* (Salem: Peabody Essex Museum), 17(1): 54–8.

——2003. 'Who lived in pre-European Maine?: A cosmology approach to social patterning on the landscape', *Northeast Antrhopology*, 66: 29–39.

——2006. 'An introduction to the Archaic of the Maritime Peninsula: The view from Central Maine' in D. Sanger and M. A. P. Renouf (eds), *The Archaic of the Far Northeast* (Orono: University of Maine Press), pp. 221–52.

——2008. 'Discerning regional variation: The Terminal Archaic period in the Quoddy region of the Maritime Peninsula', *Canadian Journal of Archaeology*, 32(1): 1–42.

——and RENOUF, M. A. P. (eds) 2006. *The Archaic of the Far Northeast* (Orono: University of Maine Press).

——, PAWLING, M., and SOCTOMAH, D. 2006. 'Passamaquoddy homeland and language: The importance of place' in J. Kerber and J. Watkins (eds), *Cross Cultural Collaboration* (Lincoln: University of Nebraska), pp. 314–28.

SASSAMAN, K. 1996. 'Technological innovations in economic and social contexts' in K. Sassaman and D. Anderson (eds), *Archaeology of the Mid-Holocene Southeast* (Gainsville: University of Florida Press), pp. 57–74.

SAUNDERS, R., HACHEY, M. A., and FAY, C. W. 2006. 'Maine's diadromous fish community: Past, present, and implications for Atlantic salmon recovery', *Fisheries*, 37(11): 537–47.

SCHOOLCRAFT, H. R. 1851–1857. *Historical and Statistical Information Respecting the History, Condition and Prospects of the Indian Tribes of the United States*, 6 vols. (Philadelphia: Lippincott, Gambo and Co).

SHAW, L. 1988. 'A biocultural evaluation of the skeletal population from the Nevin site, Blue Hill, Maine', *Archaeology of Eastern North America*, 16: 55–71.

SMITH, B. L. 1948. 'An Analysis of the Maine Cemetery Complex', *Bulletin of the Massachusetts Archaeological Society*, 9(2–3): 20–71.

SNOW, D. R. 1969. 'A Summary of Excavations at the Hathaway Site in Passadumkeag, Maine, 1912, 1947 and 1968', Ms. on file, Department of Anthropology, University of Maine, Orono.

——1975. 'The Passadumkeag Sequence', *Arctic Anthropology*, 12(2): 46–59.

——2006. 'Recollecting Maine archaeology, 1966–1970', *Maine Archaeological Society Bulletin*, 46(2): 15–20.

SOCTOMAH, D. G. 2004. *Landscapes, Legends & Language of the Passamaquoddy People: An interactive journey in the land of the Passamaquoddy*, CD, Skicin Records and Passamaquoddy Historic Preservation Office, Pleasant Point, Maine.

SPECK, F. G. 1935. *Naskapi: The savage hunters of the Labrador Peninsula* (Norman: University of Oklahoma Press).

SPIESS, A. 1992. 'Archaic period subsistence in New England and the Atlantic provinces' in B. S. Robinson, J. B. Petersen, and A. K. Robinson (eds), *Early Holocene Occupation in Northern New England*, Occasional Publications in Maine Archaeology 9 (Augusta: Maine Historic Preservation Commission), pp. 163–85.

——and LEWIS, R. 2001. *The Turner Farm Fauna: 5000 years of hunting and fishing in Penobscot Bay, Maine*, Occasional Publications in Maine Archaeology 11 (Augusta: The Maine State Museum, The Maine Historic Preservation Commission and The Maine Archaeological Society).

——, WILSON, D., and BRADLEY, J. W. 1998. 'Paleoindian occupation in the New England–Maritimes region: Beyond cultural ecology', *Archaeology of Eastern North America*, 26: 201–64.

TANNER, A. 1979. *Bringing Home Animals: Religious Ideology and Mode of Production of the Mistassini Cree Hunters*, Memorial University of Newfoundland, Social and Exonomic Studies No. 23 (New York: St Martin Press).

TUCK, J. A. 1976. *Ancient People of Port au Choix: The Excavation of an Archaic Indian Cemetery in Newfoundland*, Newfoundland Social and Economic Studies 17 (St John's: Institute of Social and Economic Research, Memorial University of Newfoundland).

——1978. 'Archaic burial ceremonialism in the "Far Northeast"' in W. E. Englebrecht and D. Grayson (eds), *Essays in Northeastern Archaeology in Memory of Marion E. White*, Occasional Publication in Northeastern Anthropology 5 (Rindge, NH: Franklin Pierce College), pp. 67–77.

TURNBULL, C. J. 1976. 'The Augustine site: A mound from the Maritimes', *Archaeology of Eastern North America*, 4: 50–62

WABANAKI PROGRAM OF THE AMERICAN FRIENDS SERVICE COMMITTEE 1989. *The Wabanakis of Maine and the Maritimes: A resource book about Penobscot, Passamaquoddy, Maliseet, Micmac and Abenaki Indians*, 2002 edn (Philadelphia: Wabanaki Program of the American Friends Service Committee).

WILLIAMSON, W. D. 1832. *The History of the State of Maine: From its first discovery, AD 1602, to the separation, AD 1820, inclusive*, I (Hollowell: Glazier, Masters & Co).

WILLOUGHBY, C. C. 1935. *Antiquities of the New England Indians*, Peabody Museum of American Archaeology and Ethnology (Cambridge, MA: Harvard University Press).

PART IV

RELIGION AND CULT OF THE OLD WORLD

CHAPTER 42

PREHISTORIC RELIGIONS IN THE AEGEAN

COLIN RENFREW

1 Introduction

THE religions of the prehistoric Aegean have been studied and discussed more than those of most areas where the archaeological record is (or rather was until the decipherment of the Linear B script) unassisted by intelligible texts. In the early days of study, until the mid-twentieth century, the period was sometimes regarded simply as a prelude to the Classical world. And the texts of the Classical authors, especially those claiming to write about the early past, were often taken as an inevitable and authoritative starting point. This situation gradually changed with the accumulation of archaeological data which could reasonably be regarded as indicative of religious, or at least of ritual practice. These came first in Minoan Crete, from the 'palaces' and the 'peak sanctuaries' as well as cave sites, from the beginning of the twentieth century onwards. Building upon the discoveries of Sir Arthur Evans and others in Crete, Martin Nilsson extended the picture to the Greek mainland with his study of the 'Minoan–Mycenaean' religion (Nilsson 1950 [1927]). The picture was later transformed, however, by substantive discoveries such as the shrines at the Mycenaean centres of Mycenae and Tiryns, and the Late Bronze Age sanctuaries at Aghia Irini on the Cycladic island of Kea and at Phylakopi on Melos.

These and numerous other relevant discoveries have allowed a critical re-assessment of the evidence, encouraged for the end of the Late Bronze Age by the decipherment of the 'Minoan' Linear B script and hence of the study of the archives of the Mycenaean palaces (including the archive of the Mycenaean period at Knossos in Crete), with their tantalizing references to what may be interpreted as offerings and the occurrences within them of names which by the Classical period are those of deities.

As in other areas of the study of early religions, the subject is beset with methodological problems, not least in the problem of deciding what is properly to be termed 'religious' in those cases where the archaeological record documents what may reasonably be regarded as ritual practice, with public performance and the practice of feasting. The religious component often cannot easily be distinguished from activities which are certainly to be regarded as social, but which might not be focused upon the divine. There are problems of definition here.

As in most areas of the study of early religion, much has been written in earlier decades where, without detailed critical or theoretical analysis, scholars came to share received views whose foundations do not bear detailed examination today. Yet it is these views which underlie much of the discussion which still continues. It is necessary first to recognize and characterize some of these traditions of thought.

2 Traditions of Scholarship

Several traditions of thought, emerging mainly in the nineteenth century, still underlie much that is written today about the early Aegean religions. This is true despite the wealth of evidence uncovered during the remarkably energetic and fruitful archaeological explorations of the twentieth century, notably in Crete and southern Greece. But it is fair to say that the results of those excavations were often interpreted within the existing frameworks of thought, which at that time had little empirical foundation. That was perhaps inevitable, but it has to be recognized clearly if fresh interpretation is to become possible. Several significant influences can be recognized.

2.1 Matriarchy and the Great Earth Mother Goddess

Already in 1861 the Swiss anthropologist Johann Jakob Bachofen in his book *Mutterrecht* ('Mother Right': Bachofen 1861) identified 'matriarchy' as an early stage of social and religious development, preceding a further supposedly universal stage of patriarchy. Although his views are generally rejected today, Bachofen's writing influenced Marx and Engels. His ideas also had a particular resonance for students of Aegean prehistory, where human sculptural representations ('figurines') are a notable feature of the neolithic period. Although some of these are male and many lack explicit sexual attributes, many of them can indeed be recognized as female, and were widely taken to exemplify the concept of matriarchy. Many later writings (e.g. Gimbutas 1989, 1996) can be seen to lie in this tradition of thought, despite the demonstration by Ucko (1968) that it lacks a secure empirical basis (see Goodison and Morris 1998). The finds by Mellaart (1967) at the neolithic site of Çatalhöyük in central Turkey have often been taken to support the view of the alleged Anatolian Mother Goddess.

Lewis Henry Morgan's *Ancient Society* (Morgan 1877), upon which Karl Marx and Friedrich Engels drew heavily in their studies of early societies, was strongly influenced by Bachofen's four phases of cultural evolution, of which the second was matriarchy. The concept of such seemingly 'natural' stages of development has overshadowed and indeed undermined much subsequent evolutionary thinking.

2.2 Indo-European Replacement Theories

Replacement models for the 'Coming' of the Greeks to the Aegean have overshadowed and continue to overshadow many considerations of the early Aegean religions. The notion that there was an overarching and early Indo-European religious structure and mythology is still central to the field of Indo-European studies (Mallory 1989). Indisputably the Greek language belongs to the Indo-European language family, and the religion of the Classical Greeks is commonly regarded as 'Indo-European', although surprisingly few of the Olympian deities have a clear Indo-European etymology. The majority of historical linguists still assume that an early form of the Greek language arrived in Greece during the Bronze Age, and consequently that there was a shift from a non-Indo-European to an Indo-European belief system at that time. The possibility of a longer continuity in development is therefore excluded on a priori grounds. These are not based upon the archaeological data but on assumptions of linguistic replacement (see Renfrew 1987). An alternative view, regarding developments in cult practice through time as a series of more local transformations, has been proposed (Renfrew 1985: 431–41).

2.3 The Mycenaean Tree and Pillar Cult

One of the great pioneers in the study of prehistoric Aegean religious thought was Sir Arthur Evans. He was one of the first to study carefully the iconography of the prehistoric Aegean, even before the beginning of his excavations at Knossos in 1899. His 'The Mycenaean Tree and Pillar Cult' (1901) was a brilliant study of the data available at that time, although the material reviewed was mainly from Crete (the term 'Minoan', which Evans himself later popularized, not yet being in general use). His later work naturally centred upon what became known as 'Minoan' Crete—Crete in the Bronze Age. It developed the ideas of his 1901 paper, which was itself naturally influenced by the prevalent ideas of the nineteenth century, including those of Bachofen. Evans advocated the concept of a great mother goddess, sometimes accompanied by a youthful male consort. These ideas were his interpretation of the iconography, including figurines, wall paintings, and sealstones, which since his excavations has formed the basis for the study of Minoan religion.

2.4 The 'Minoan–Mycenaean' Religion

In 1927 the Swedish scholar Martin Nilsson first published his great work *The Minoan–Mycenaean Religion and its Survival in Greek Religion* that brought together in a comprehensive way the available archaeological and iconographic evidence. One of its great merits was to give due weight to the evidence from mainland Greece, and it rightly emphasized some of the continuities between the religious practices of the Bronze Age and those of the Greek world of the Iron Age. Inevitably, though, the perspective was radically changed a quarter of a century later by the demonstration by Ventris and Chadwick (1973) that the Myceaneans wrote and presumably spoke an early form of the Greek language. This served to strengthen rather than weaken many of Nilsson's conclusions, but it called into question many earlier assumptions. The archaeological discoveries of the later twentieth century did however make the apparent religious unity of the Late Bronze Age Aegean seem questionable (Renfrew 1981), emphasizing local traditions more strongly.

It is against these traditions of scholarship that a reassessment of the prehistoric religions of the Aegean will soon be needed. It will have to be based, however, on a more rigorous consideration of the nature of the available evidence than was generally exercised in the studies undertaken during the twentieth century, and a recognition of the varieties of religious practices in question (D'Agata et al. 2008).

3 Towards a Framework for the Archaeology of Cult Practice

A central problem in the study of early religions is that the belief systems of their practitioners do not reveal themselves to us directly in the activities of those believers and hence in the archaeological record, or at least only do so if they were set down in writing or made somehow explicit in such iconographic representations as may survive. The Linear B tablets of the Later Bronze Age present many difficulties in interpretation (see below). Moreover the prehistoric Aegean does not offer monumental structures on a grand scale which immediately reveal themselves as 'temples', such as are seen in Sumer or Egypt, or indeed in Classical Greece from the Archaic period onward.

The problems in the undertaking were discussed in Chapter 1 of *The Archaeology of Cult* (Renfrew 1985), although that analysis did not sufficiently address some of the difficulties. The first question to be faced is what one means by 'religion'. Some like Durkheim (1915) followed by Geertz (1966) have emphasized the social aspect, the shared practices of a community or 'church'. But these scholars have tended to avoid the central issue of the supernatural: that most religions are oriented towards transcendental forces or powers (often regarded as deities). Different approaches are possible (see Wright 1995; Insoll 2004; Marcus 2007), as discussed elsewhere in this volume. I find it convenient to follow the definition of religion proposed by Spiro (1966: 96): 'an institution consisting of culturally patterned interaction with culturally postulated superhuman beings'.

In the discussion in *The Archaeology of Cult* a number of features of sacred ritual were suggested by which such ritual practices might be recognized in the archaeological record (Renfrew 1985: 18–26, see Renfrew 1994). These included the systematic use of attention-focusing devices, and the special effects of the liminal zone between the terrestrial and the supernatural when religion is practised. One of those effects is the supposed presence of transcendent forces or beings which are often given symbolic focus. This imagined or experienced presence is often accompanied by practices of participation and offering by the cult celebrants. This analysis allowed the proposal of some 20 or so 'correlates'—features which may often appear in the archaeological record as an indication of the practice of cult. From the Middle Bronze Age of Minoan Crete around 2000 BC special locations or 'peak sanctuaries' are documented which have widely been accepted as locations for cult practice, mainly on the basis of the offerings which were left at them. From the Late Bronze Age, around 1300 BC, shrines have been identified at the place centres of Mycenae and Tiryns on the Greek mainland and at a rural location on Methana, as well as at the urban site of Phylakopi on the Cycladic island of Melos. In general, however, special places which can plausibly be identified as shrines or sanctuaries are rare in the prehistoric Aegean, and inferences about religious ritual generally have to be based upon iconographic representations (figurines, wall paintings in the late bronze age, seal stones etc.) for which very varying interpretations can be offered.

3.1 Recent Developments

Recently, however, several different arguments on the functioning of ritual in relation to material culture have been put forward. They agree that the distinction between religious ritual (focused, that is upon transcendent power, as defined above) and secular ritual (where the ritual practice is not directed towards supernatural agencies) is not always clear (Kyriakidis 2005; Renfrew 2007). For the Neolithic period, Chapman (2000) and Bailey (2005) have outlined arguments which would deny to the numerous terracotta figurines found their role as the representation of deities. For the Early Bronze Age marble figures of the Cyclades, discussed below, Hoffman (2002) and Hendrix (2003) put forward arguments for repeated ritual use, which certainly counter the view that they were produced solely for funerary rituals. And for the Later Bronze Age peak sanctuaries of Crete, Kyriakidis (2005) has argued for rituals of an 'institutional' nature so as to call into question the view that the rituals practised there were focused upon deities. Similarly the recent development of interest in feasting in the prehistoric Aegean (Wright 2004; Hitchcock et al. 2008) may invite a social rather than a religious interpretation. The boundary between secular ritual and religious ritual, if there is one, has become increasingly hard to identify.

In a brief survey of this kind the focus is inevitably upon the areas and periods where relevant materials have been found. For the Bronze Age, this implies mainly the Minoan and Mycenaean worlds along with the Cycladic islands. The evidence in the eastern Aegean (including the Anatolian coast) and in the north (Thessaly, Macedonia, and Thrace) is much less rich iconographically during the Bronze Age and for them a synthetic summary would be difficult at present.

4 Before the Bronze Age

The Palaeolithic and Mesolithic periods of Greece are not yet richly represented in the archaeological record. Despite some earlier but unsubstantiated claims, no indications of cave art have been found, nor have human representations (figurines) been reported. It is not until the period of the early farmers, the Neolithic, that small terracotta (and sometimes stone: Evans and Renfrew 1968) representations of the human figure are found. Such finds are well represented in the early Neolithic of Anatolia and in much of South-east Europe. As noted earlier they have often been taken to imply religious ritual and belief (Gimbutas 1989, 1996). Their identification with a supposed Great Earth Mother goddess was effectively questioned by Ucko (1968). In a wide-ranging study Talalay (1993) explored the much wider range of possible explanations for their production and use, including their possible function as toys or as educational devices. Often they are found broken, and Chapman (2000; also Chapman and Gaydarska 2006) has developed an interesting theory of 'enchainment'—the deliberate breakage of such figurations, and the exchange of the fragments creating social linkages. In this way networks of personal relationships are created or reinforced between those partaking in the exchange. The analysis suggests that rather than having a religious significance, the figurines operated to construct personal relations or identities. Douglass Bailey (2005) has also recently regarded the Neolithic and chalcolithic figurines of Greece and the Balkans as operating in a social rather than a religious context.

The problem in the Greek Neolithic is ultimately one of context. For although small assemblages of figurines have sometimes been found together in a manner suggestive of ritual practice, there are few good contexts of association within buildings which might present stronger grounds for inference.

5 THE EARLY BRONZE AGE

With the Early Bronze Age of the Aegean, from around 3200 BC, the practice of systematic burial in cemeteries becomes widespread. Already at Late Neolithic Kephala on Kea (Coleman 1977) there are burials in cist graves, built out of small stones, with accompanying grave goods. The Early Cycladic cultures were first recognized from their extensive cemeteries of cist graves (Tsountas 1898; Renfrew 1972; Doumas 1977). The grave goods sometimes contain marble vessels and, during the developed Early Cycladic period (Early Cycladic II, around 2500 BC) are sometimes accompanied by the characteristic folded-arm figurines of marble (Renfrew 1969; Getz-Preziosi 1987).

The Early Helladic mainland has less conspicuous cemeteries than the Cyclades, and the richer sites sometimes show Cycladic influence. Minoan Crete, however, has a range of religious customs, which includes the construction of quite ambitious buildings to contain the dead and their accompanying grave goods. The best known are the round tombs of the Mesara plain (Xanthoudides 1924; Branigan 1970). There are abundant indications of ritual practices, not least in the repertoire of well-made vessels of fine stone which often accompany the dead (Warren 1969). In north Crete, for instance at Mochlos, the burial chambers are rectangular, and the grave foods offer the best indications we have of Minoan craft production, in pottery, stone, metal, and ivory.

There are, however, no buildings for which a strong claim for dedicated use as a sanctuary can be claimed. So most arguments for ritual practice are focused upon the iconography which is observed in pottery, terracotta, and stone. Just a few finds come from settlements: there is a fine anthropomorphic vessel from Myrtos Phournou Koriphi, but most are in the tombs. Cycladic figurines and their local imitations are found at Archanes and some of the Mesara sites. But if there is religious ritual at this time in Crete, it seems mainly associated with the dead.

Until recently, the same observation could be made for the Cyclades, where most finds of the marble folded-arm figurines came from the Cycladic cemeteries, although many in the world's museums, being the product of looting, lack a secure provenance (Gill and Chippindale 1993; Thimme and Getz-Preziosi 1977). Just a few are almost life-sized, although sadly none of them comes from a properly recorded archaeological context. Some of these figures have traces of painted decoration, with indications of eyes, of hair and sometimes of what seem facial tattoos or face paint. Recent studies (Hoffman 2002; Hendrix 2003) indicate that these figures or effigies must have been painted on several different occasions. It has been suggested, therefore, that they were not made primarily for funerary use, but were carried in ritual processions on a number of different occasions, perhaps associated with rites of passage (e.g. marriage) of those persons associated with them.

The site of Dhaskalio Kavos on Keros has yielded hundreds of fragments of such figurines, deliberately smashed before deposition (Renfrew et al. 2007; Renfrew et al. 2008; Sotirakopoulou 2005), along with broken pottery and marble vessels. The lack of joins suggests that they were broken elsewhere—which opens the possibility of some interpretation following Chapman's 'enchainment' hypothesis (2000). The context is clearly a ritual one, and must have involved ritual deposition of these special (and broken) materials brought from a number of islands. These are the first indications of what seems to be regional ritual activity in the Aegean. And in this instance there seems to be no direct connection with the burial of the dead, although the rites of passage perhaps being commemorated could include funerary ones.

Open to debate, however, is the subject of the figuration represented in the characteristic folded-arm form. It is notable that by the Early Bronze Age the clay figurines, so common during the Neolithic period, have almost disappeared. The marble figurines are now mainly found in the Cyclades, with some outliers in Crete. Is this a deity, certainly female in many cases, represented in a well-defined form and position? Or could this simply be a stylized version of the human figure made for these ritual ceremonials? Aspects of the iconography have been considered by Goodison (1989), but plausible arguments can be made both for the secular and the divine interpretations. Certainly these are the most notable figurations that we have from the Early Bronze Age, and it is tantalizing that no workshops where they were made have yet been found.

6 Minoan Religion

It is in the Middle Minoan period of Crete, from around 2100 BC, that what have been termed 'cave sanctuaries' and 'peak sanctuaries' are found. These are not primarily burial places. They are however characterized by considerable quantities of symbolic 'offerings' and can reasonably be regarded as locations of cult activity. But, as Kyriakidis (2005) has argued, while the evidence for ritual activity is compelling, the inference that it was devoted towards supernatural beings (i.e. deities), and thus cult activity (as defined above) is not always so clear. Many interpretations of Minoan religion are possible (Marinatos 1993).

In the cave sanctuaries considerable quantities of pottery, terracotta animal figurines and sometimes bronze objects are found (Watrous 1996). The Arkalochori cave had numerous bronze weapons as well as double axes, and the Kamares Cave produced wonderful Middle Minoan pottery. At the same time peak sanctuaries—cult centres near the summit of hills (not usually mountain peaks)—are found, with human terracotta figurines and sometimes stone 'tables of offerings' with Linear A inscriptions. The sanctuaries at Petsopha in East Crete and Iouktas near Knossos go back to the beginning of the Middle Minoan period and later at Iouktas a substantial building was constructed.

The palaces of the Neopalatial period (from 1700 BC) with their courts and their ashlar masonry and frescoes were no doubt used for a number of rituals, some of which are indeed depicted on the frescoes, including the practice of bull leaping. To identify specific locations as the locus for cult practice is however more difficult, although well-paved areas in some rooms, lying below the level of the floor, the so-called 'lustral basins' have been so considered by some scholars. The most readily identifiable location dates in fact from the

Post-Palatial period (Late Minoan IIIB, around 1400 BC): the 'Shrine of the Double Axes'. It may be described as a bench sanctuary (Gesell 1985: no. 37) and is very small (1.5 m x 1.5 m) with a series of finds including stuccoed clay 'horns of consecration', between which was a round socket designed to hold a double axe. A female figurine was found between the two pairs of 'horns' and a male figurine with a dove was found nearby.

This is one of the few cases, and a late one, where what can be identified as a shrine can be recognized *in situ* in a Minoan palace. Gesell, understandably, identifies the Throne Room Complex to the west of the Central Court at Knossos, with its lustral basin (Gesell 1985: no. 34) as a shrine, but the sceptic could argue that the rituals no doubt practised there were secular rather than religious. More convincing perhaps is the collection of cult objects found in the Vat Room deposit (including faience figurine fragments) going back to the Middle Minoan IA period. But it is difficult to identify any specific location in the palaces of Crete (other than the late 'Shrine of the Double Axes') as a temple or even as an altar.

It is indeed only after the end of the palaces, in the Post-Palatial period, that a series of rather clearer shrines can be recognized (including the Shrine of the Double Axes at Knossos, noted above), for instance at Gournia (Hawes 1908: 47; Gesell 1985: no. 10) and at Gazi (Marinatos 1937). They are small buildings with low benches and with other paraphernalia, and in particular with bell-shaped terracotta representations of the Minoan Goddess with Upraised Arms (see Alexiou 1958)—five of these were found at Gazi. The repeated finding in Crete (also, for instance, at Karphi) of a room with an effigy or effigies in this specific form and in association with symbols elsewhere depicted in a context of expressive action, seem a firm indication of religious ritual.

Another find of considerable importance is the painted sarcophagus from the site of Aghia Triadha (Long 1974), again produced after the end of the palace period. It is decorated on the exterior with painted scenes, including the sacrifice of a bull, seen in association with representations of the 'horns of consecration' and of the double axe. Since this is a sarcophagus, the rituals depicted are likely to be funerary, but the association of objects makes a religious association likely.

It is indeed in the rich iconography of Minoan Crete, on sealstones as well as on wall paintings (Immerwahr 1990) that the full wealth of the Minoan cultic repertoire becomes clear. These repeat and supplement the main motifs already observed in the cave and peak sanctuaries—the horns of consecration, the double axes etc. Yet the palaces and settlements offer very few convincing cases of sanctuaries until the Post-Palatial period, after 1350 BC. Then, as noted above, shrines apparently dedicated to the 'Minoan Goddess with Upraised Arms' are found.

7 The Late Bronze Age in the Cyclades Before 1350 BC

There are few finds indicative of cult practice on the Greek mainland until a comparatively late period in the Mycenaean world, during the Late Helladic III period, after 1400 BC. There are materials of iconographic interest in the Shaft Graves at Mycenae around 1600 BC, and strong Minoan influence can be seen at this time (Renfrew 1998) but it is not until later, in the shrines at Mycenae and Tiryns (discussed below), that materials are found in what may be interpreted as a cult context. There are, however, two very interesting finds from the Cyclades during the earlier part of the Late Bronze Age.

The first of these is at the Late Cycladic settlement of Akrotiri on Thera, destroyed (and the wall paintings preserved) in the catastrophic eruption of the Thera volcano. The date is still a matter of dispute among scholars, but it can certainly be situated during the Late Minoan IA period, probably during the sixteenth century BC, during the heyday of the Minoan places.

At Akrotiri, one particular building complex known as Xeste 3 attracts attention. The rooms of the building are well preserved, and one contains a remarkable wall painting (Doumas 1992) which has been carefully restored. Many of the wall paintings at Akrotiri are notable for their vitality, and for the activities which they depict. The most notable, however, is special in that it depicts what can only be regarded as a goddess, seated upon a throne, and receiving offerings of crocuses from attendant ladies. The divine status of this goddess seems assured by the winged mythic beast (griffin) which attends her (Laffineur 2001; Laffineur and Hägg 2001). Just as in some religious depictions in the Near East, the accompaniment of mythical beasts (sphinxes, harpies, winged griffins) seems a clear indication of the presence of the Other World. The lustral area in the same room is reminiscent of those of the contemporary palaces of Crete. But at Akrotiri the explicit nature of the wall painting seems to make clear that these were not simply social rituals that were practised but ceremonies undertaken in honour of, or in presence of, the divine. The case is persuasive that the building complex of Xeste 3 had a cultic purpose.

The other Cycladic case is impressive also, but in a different way. This is the 'temple' at Ayia Irini, on the island of Kea. Here the excavator J. L. Caskey found a complex of six rooms, measuring 23 m x 6 m, with the remains of some 50 fragmentary terracotta figures, varying in height between 70 cms and life-size. These were female, with prominent bare breasts (a form already familiar in Minoan iconography). They have been interpreted (Caskey 1981, 1986), mainly on the basis of their number, as attendants of a deity, rather than as representations of the deity herself. It is difficult to fault the arguments deployed that this constitutes one of the most impressive indications of prehistoric cult practice in the Aegean. But more detailed interpretation must await the full publication of the architecture and the finds.

8 THE LATE BRONZE AGE OF GREECE AND THE CYCLADES AFTER 1350 BC

The small shrines of Post-Palatial Crete have long been known, but the sanctuaries of Mycenaean Greece are a more recent discovery. The most significant is that of Mycenae. The cult centre at Mycenae has been discussed in various publications by Mylonas (1972, 1977). Following the criteria discussed above, our interest focuses upon the 'Temple' and the adjoining Room with the Idols, and the neighbouring Room with the Fresco (Taylour 1970; Moore 1988; Moore and Taylour 1999). The Temple at Mycenae is a building comparable in scale to the West Shrine at Phylakopi (see below), some 10 m long, again with a smaller room behind, the Room with the Idols. Along the wall facing the entrance door was a cult bench at one end of which stood a figure and a small table of offerings. More terracotta figures were found in the room behind. These human figures generally lack definite indications of sex, and none of them can positively be identified as male. They are, however, what most securely identifies the cult functions of the 'Temple'.

At Tiryns there is a series of what have been identified as small shrines in the Lower Town (Kilian 1981). Again, a distinguishing feature was a bench on which terracotta figures were placed. The Tiryns shrines date to the Late Helladic IIIC period, around 1150 BC, the time following the destruction of the Temple at Mycenae.

At the site of Phylakopi on Melos a shrine or sanctuary has been uncovered (Renfrew 1985) with several features resembling those of Mycenae and Tiryns, not least the presence of a terracotta wheel-made figure which may well be the representation of a deity. She was found in a storeroom behind the West Shrine. With a height of 45 cm 'The Lady of Phylakopi' is much smaller than the 1.2-metre-high terracotta figures at Ayia Irini, there recognized as 'attendants', but it has been suggested that she is the effigy of a deity. In a smaller East Shrine (5 m x 3 m) numerous small terracotta figurines were found, some 10 cm high and of a kind familiar from the Mycenaean world in the standard 'Phi' and 'Psi' forms (so called from the Greek letters approximating to the shape of the figures with their arms upraised). In the context of the sanctuary at Phylakopi, in view of the other finds, these can be identified with confidence as of religious significance, a conclusion not always certain at other sites where the context of discovery is sometimes unclear or ambiguous. The West Shrine at Phylakopi and its two storerooms contained the wheel-made 'Lady of Phylakopi' and a number of wheel-made bull figures, as well as smaller figurines, including two of terracotta which were undoubtedly male. Such male representations are rare in the Mycenaean world. But at Phylakopi they were accompanied by two small (22 cm) bronze figurines of a striding male with one arm held high, in what in the Near East is known as the 'Smiting God' posture.

The evidence from Phylakopi is broadly in harmony with that from Mycenae and Tiryns, and is backed up by other finds from mainland Greece: that in the Late Bronze Age, after about 1400 BC, there emerged cult practices involving the use of smaller than life-sized terracotta effigies, along with much smaller terracotta figures of animals, and smaller human figurines. These are the most persuasive indications of cult practice. But there is a rich iconography in the wall painting of the palaces (Immerwahr 1990), in the sealstones (Krzyszkowska 2005) and in the gold finger rings (Niemeier 1990) which can plausibly be associated with such practices. The body of material is increasing all the time through archaeological exploration. The discovery of these shrines or sanctuaries should make possible the development of more secure interpretations of such iconography than was possible for Nilsson (1950) writing in the middle of the twentieth century, before the principal sanctuaries now known had been discovered.

8.1 The Evidence of the Tablets

Since the decipherment of Linear B, the Mycenaean tablets from the palace of Pylos, as well as those from Knossos in the late period of its Mycenaean reoccupation, have offered the hope of insights into Mycenaean religion (Chadwick 1985). But since the tablets are mainly occupied with economic accounting, the relevant entries take the form of the record of offerings made to named entities. Their divine status is established mainly by recognizing these names as close to those of divine personages in Classical times. One of the most frequent named is Potnia (= 'mistress'), and Zeus and Poseidon have been recognized among the entries from both places. But as Bendall (2007: 3) points out: 'What is being stated is... that, in the barest sense *po-se-da-o-ne* was used by speakers of Mycenaean Greek to refer to a deity. What exactly they conceived of as "Poseidon", what his attributes and associations were, are separate questions.' At the moment there are few if any direct links between the epigraphic evidence of the tablets at Pylos or Thebes or Knossos and the artefactual evidence for the practice of religion at these sites.

8.2 The Transition to the Iron Age

Before the decipherment of the Minoan Linear B script, when it was still possible to imagine that the 'Coming of the Greeks' took place at the end of the second millennium BC, during the so called 'Dark Ages', one could imagine that the Greek religion of Classical times was in some ways the product of that incoming migration of people. That is no longer the position, and significant continuities can now be seen in what we know of religious practice across the intervening period. This was the view formulated by Nicholls (1970), and it has been reinforced by the finds at the Phylakopi sanctuary (Renfrew 1985: 440) where the male figurines in terracotta and bronze anticipate those of the geometric and Archaic periods. An impressive series of finds at the important Minoan peak sanctuary at Syme (Lebessi and Muhly 1987, 2003) is likewise indicative of continuity. That the emergence of the religion of Classical Greece was a transformation effected upon a Mycenaean base rather than an introduction from elsewhere now seems clear (Morgan 1996). This is of course supported by the evidence of the tablets, noted above.

9 CONCLUSIONS AND OVERVIEW

The material evidence bearing upon the Aegean religions is very rich, but it is geographically and chronologically patchy. For the Neolithic, the evidence of the figurines is widespread, but the extent to which their significance is 'religious' is open to debate. For the Early Bronze Age, funerary rituals are richly documented in Early Minoan Crete, and the iconography of the folded-arm figures in the Cyclades may well be indicative of religious practices. For the Middle Bronze Age, it is only in Crete that the cave and peak sanctuaries indicate rituals which the symbolic evidence from later periods suggests may already have been religious in nature. The indications from the Minoan palaces of the Later Bronze Age are still open to differing interpretations. It is only with the 'temple' at Ayia Irini on Kea and the evidence from the wall painting at the building complex of Xeste 3 on Thera, around 1500 BC that we find persuasive indications of cult observances which are clearly directed towards deities. Subsequently in the Later Bronze Age, Crete, the Cyclades, and Mainland Greece all give evidence of shrines and sanctuaries testifying to the practice of a religion or to religions. This is reflected in the Mycenaean Linear B tablets, although they do little to clarify it.

There are numerous indications in all three areas of continuities across the so-called 'dark ages' between the Bronze Age and Greece of the first millennium BC. However the religion of the Olympian gods which then emerges is a rather different one, soon taking a standard form in such writers as Homer and Hesiod. It seems syncretistic, with numerous outside influences, but neither then nor at any other period since the early Neolithic does one have the impression of major and determinant external influence. It seems possible instead to see the Aegean religions as undergoing a series of transformations, the faiths of each period building upon those of the preceding one.

The good news in Aegean archaeology is that new evidence is coming to light all the time, and often finds in one area are able to offer insights into the interpretation of those in another. There are grounds for hoping that in a few more years Nilsson's *The Minoan-Mycenaean Religion* (Nilsson 1950) will be superseded by a successor work which will exploit in the same way the rich iconography now becoming available from a range of finds and which will be able to take more account of the rich regional variability and diversity of the time.

Suggested Reading

The traditional treatment on prehistoric religions in the Aegean remains Nilsson's classic work *The Minoan–Mycenaean Religion* (Nilsson 1950), although a different and more critical approach was advocated by Renfrew in *The Archaeology of Cult* (Renfrew 1985). The impact of the decipherment of the Linear B tablets can be gauged in the paper by Chadwick (1985) and the recent monograph by Bendall (2007). Important evidence from Akrotiri on Thera, from Mycenae, from Tiryns, from Phylakopi on Melos, etc. is reviewed in the edited volume *POTNIA: Deities and Religion in the Aegean Bronze Age* (Laffineur and Hägg 2001).

References

ALEXIOU, S. 1958. 'I Minoiki thea meth'upsomenon cheiron', *Kretika Chronika*, 12: 179–299.

BACHOFEN, J. J. 2006 [1861]. *Das Mutterrecht [Mother Right: A study of the religious and juridical aspects of gynecocracy in the Ancient World]* (New York: Edwin Mellen Press)

BAILEY, D. W. 2005. *Prehistoric Figurines: Representation and corporeality in the Neolithic* (London: Routledge).

BENDALL, L. M. 2007. *Economics of Religion in the Mycenaean World* (Oxford: Oxford University School of Archaeology).

BRANIGAN, K. 1970. *The Tombs of Mesara* (London: Duckworth).

CASKEY, M. E. 1981. 'Ayia Irini, Kea: The terracotta statues and the cult in the temple' in R. Hägg and N. Marinatos (eds), *Sanctuaries and Cults in the Aegean Bronze Age* (Stockholm: Swedish Institute in Athens), pp. 127–35.

——1986. *Keos II, 1: The Temple at Ayia Irini: The Statues* (Princeton: American School of Classical Studies at Athens).

CHADWICK, J. 1985. 'What do we know about Mycenaean religion' in A. Morpurgo Davies and Y. Duhoux (eds), *Linear B: A 1984 survey* (Louvain: Institut de Linguistique), pp. 191–202.

CHAPMAN, J. 2000. *Fragmentation in Archaeology: Peoples, places and broken objects in the prehistory of South Eastern Europe* (London: Routledge).

——and GAYDARSKA, B. 2006. *Parts and Wholes: Fragmentation in prehistoric context* (Oxford: Oxbow).

COLEMAN, J. E. 1977. *Keos 1. Kephala: A Late Neolithic settlement and cemetery* (Princeton, NJ: Princeton University Press).

D'AGATA, A. L., VAN DE MOORTEL, A., and RICHARDSON, M. M. (eds) 2008. *Archaeologies of Cult: Essays on Ritual and Cult in Crete*, Hesperia Supplement 42 (Athens: American School of Classical Studies).

DOUMAS, C. 1977. *Early Bronze Age Burial Habits in the Cyclades*, Studies in Mediterranean Archaeology 48 (Göteborg: Paul Åström).

——1992. *The Wall Paintings of Thera* (Athens: Thera Foundation).

DURKHEIM, E. 1915. *The Elementary Forms of Religious Life* (London: Allen and Unwin).

EVANS, A. J. 1901. 'The Mycenaean tree and pillar cult and its Mediterranean relations', *Journal of Hellenic Studies*, 21: 99–204.

EVANS, J. D. and RENFREW, C. 1968. *Excavations at Saliagos near Antiparos*, British School at Athens Supplementary V (London: British School at Athens).

GEERTZ, C. 1966. 'Religion as a cultural system' in M. Banton (ed.), *Anthropological Approaches to the Study of Religion*, A.S.A. Monographs 3 (London: Tavistock).

GESELL, G. C. 1985. *Town, Palace and House Cult in Minoan Crete* (Göteborg: Paul Åstroms Förlag).

GETZ-PREZIOSI, P. 1987. *Sculptors of the Cyclades: Individual and tradition in the third millennium BC* (Ann Arbor, MI: University of Michigan).

GILL, D. and CHIPPINDALE, C. 1993. 'Material and intellectual consequences of esteem for Cycladic figures', *American Journal of Archaeology*, 97: 602–73.

GIMBUTAS, M. 1989. *The Language of the Goddess* (London: Thames and Hudson).

——1996. *The Goddesses and Gods of Old Europe* (London: Thames and Hudson).

GOODISON, L. 1989. *Death, Women and the Sun: Symbolism of regeneration in early Aegean religion*, Institute of Classical Studies Bulletin Supplement 53 (London: University College London).

——and MORRIS, C. 1998. 'Beyond the 'Great Mother': The sacred world of the Minoans' in L. Goodison and C. Morris (eds), *Ancient Goddesses: The myths and the evidence* (London: British Museum Press), pp. 113–33.

HAWES, H. B. 1908. *Gournia, Vasiliki and other Prehistoric Sites on the Isthmus of Hierapetra, Crete* (Philadelphia: American Exploration Society).

HENDRIX, E. A. 2003. 'Painted Early Cycladic figures: An exploration of context and meaning', *Hesperia*, 72: 405–46.

HITCHCOCK, L. A., LAFFINEUR, R., and CROWLEY, J. (eds) 2008. *DAIS: The Aegean feast (Aegaeum 29)*, Proceedings of the 12th International Aegean Conference (Liège and Austin, TX).

HOFFMAN, G. L. 2002. 'Painted ladies: Early Cycladic II mourning figures?', *American Journal of Archaeology*, 106: 525–50.

IMMERWAHR, S. A. 1990. *Aegean Painting in the Bronze Age* (University Park: Pennsylvania State University Press).

INSOLL, T. A. 2004. *Archaeology, Ritual, Religion* (London and New York: Routledge).

KILIAN, K. 1981. 'Zeugnisse mykenischer Kulatausübung in Tiryns' in R. Hägg and N. Marinatos (eds), *Sanctuaries and Cults in the Aegean Bronze Age* (Stockholm: Paul Åstroms Förlag), pp. 49–58.

KRZYSZKOWSKA, O. 2005. *Aegean Seals: An introduction* (London: Institute of Classical Studies).

KYRIAKIDIS, E. 2005. *Ritual in the Aegean: The Minoan peak sanctuaries* (London: Duckworth).

——. 2001. 'Seeing is believing: Reflections on divine imagery in the Aegean Bronze Age' in R. Laffineur and R. Hägg (eds), *POTNIA: Deities and religion in the Aegean Bronze Age, Aegaeum* 22 (Liège and Austin, TX), pp. 387–92.

LAFFINEUR, R. and HÄGG, R. (eds) 2001. *POTNIA: Deities and religion in the Aegean Bronze Age, Aegaeum* 22 (Liège and Austin, TX).

LEBESSI, A. and MUHLY, P. 1987. 'The sanctuary of Hermes and Aphrodite at Syme, Crete', *National Geographic Research*, 3(1): 102–13.

—— —— 2003. 'Ideology and cultural interaction: Evidence from the Syme sanctuary, Crete', *Cretan Studies*, 9: 95–103.

LONG, C. R. 1974. *The Haghia Triadha Sarcophagus*, Studies in Mediterranean Archaeology 41 (Göteborg: Paul Åstroms Förlag).

MALLORY, J. P. 1989. *In Search of the Indo-Europeans: Language, Archaeology and Myth* (London: Thames and Hudson).

MARCUS, J. 2007. 'Rethinking ritual' in E. Kyriakidis (ed.), *The Archaeology of Ritual* (Los Angeles: Cotsen Institute of Archaeology), pp. 43–76.

MARINATOS, N. 1993. *Minoan Religion: Ritual, Image and Symbol* (Columbia: University of South Carolina Press).

MARINATOS, S. 1937. 'Ai minoikai theai tou Gazi', *Archaeologike Ephemeris*, 1937: 278–91.

MELLAART, J. 1967. *Çatal Hüyük: A Neolithic town in Anatolia* (London: Thames and Hudson).

MOORE, A. 1988. 'The large monochrome figures from Mycenae: The problem of interpretation' in E. B. French and K. A. Wardle (eds), *Problems in Greek Prehistory* (Bristol: Bristol Classical Press), pp. 219–28.

—— and TAYLOUR, W. D. 1999. *The Temple Complex (Well Built Mycenae: The Helleno-British excavations within the Citadel at Mycenae 1959–1969)*, Fascicule 10 (Oxford: Oxbow).

MORGAN, C. A. 1996. From palace to polis? Religious developments on the Greek mainland during the Bronze Age/Iron Age transition' in P. Hellström and B. Alroth (eds), *Religion and Power in the Ancient Greek World* (Uppsala: Ubsaliensis S. Academiae), pp. 27–57.

MORGAN, L. H. 1877. *Ancient Society, or Researches in the Lines of Human Progress from Savagery through Barbarism to Civilisation* (London: Macmillan).

MYLONAS, G. E. 1972. *The Cult Centre at Mycenae* (Athens: Academy of Athens).

—— 1977. *Mycenaean Religion, Temples, Altars and Temene* (Athens: Academy of Athens).

NICHOLLS, R. V. 1970. 'Greek votive statuettes and religious continuity c.1200–700 BC' in B. F. Harris (ed.), *Auckland Classical Essays Presented to E. M. Blaiklock* (Auckland: Auckland University Press), pp. 47–57.

NIEMEIER, W.-D. 1990. 'Cult scenes on gold rings form the Argolid' in R. Hägg and G. C. Nordquist (eds), *Celebrations of Death and Divinity in the Bronze Age Argolid* (Stockholm: Paul Åstroms Förlag), pp. 165–70.

NILSSON, M. 1950 [1927]. *The Minoan–Mycenaean Religion and its survival in Greek Religion*, 2nd edn (Lund: Biblo and Tannen).

RENFREW, C. 1969. 'The development and chronology of the Early Cycladic figurines', *American Journal of Archaeology*, 73: 1–32.

—— 1972. *The Emergence of Civilisation: The Cyclades and the Aegean in the third millennium BC* (London: Methuen).
—— 1981. 'Questions of Minoan and Mycenaean cult' in R. Hägg and N. Marinatos (eds), *Sanctuaries and Cults in the Aegean Bronze Age* (Stockholm: Paul Åstroms Förlag), pp. 27–33.
—— (ed.) 1985. *The Archaeology of Cult: The Sanctuary at Phylakopi*, British School at Athens Supplementary XVIII (London: Thames and Hudson).
—— 1987. *Archaeology and Language: The puzzle of Indo-European origins* (London: Jonathan Cape).
—— 1994. 'The archaeology of religion' in C. Renfrew and E. Zubrow (eds), *The Ancient Mind: Elements of Cognitive Archaeology* (Cambridge: Cambridge University Press), pp. 47–54.
—— 1998. 'Word of Minos: The Minoan contribution to Mycenaean Greek and the linguistic geography of the Bronze Age Aegean', *Cambridge Archaeological Journal*, 8(2): 239–62.
—— 2007. 'The archaeology of ritual, of cult and of religion' in E. Kyriakidis (ed.), *The Archaeology of Ritual* (Los Angeles: Cotsen Institute of Archaeology).
——, DOUMAS, C., MARANGOU, L., et al. (eds) 2007. *Keros, Dhaskalio Kavos: The Investigations of 1987–8*, McDonald Institute Monographs (Cambridge: McDonald Institute for Archaeological Research).
——, PHILANIOTOU, O., BRODIE, N., et al. 2008. 'Keros: Dhaskalio and Kavos, Early Cycladic stronghold and ritual centre', Preliminary report of the 2006 and 2007 excavation seasons, *Annual of the British School at Athens*, 102: 1–33.
SOTIRAKOPOULOU, P. 2005. *The 'Keros Hoard': Myth or reality?* (Athens: N. P. Goulandris Foundation).
SPIRO, M. E. 1966. 'Religion: Problems of definition and explanation' in M. Banton (ed.), *Anthropological Approaches to the Study of Religion*, A.S.A. Monographs 3 (London: Tavistock), pp. 85–126.
TALALAY, L. 1993. *Deities, Dolls and Devices: Neolithic figurines from Franchthi Cave, Greece* (Bloomington: Indiana University Press).
TAYLOUR, W. D. 1970. 'New light on the Mycenaean religion', *Antiquity*, 44: 260–80.
THIMME, J. and GETZ-PREZIOSI, P. (eds) 1977. *Art and Culture of the Cyclades in the Third Millennium BC* (Chicago, IL: University of Chicago Press).
TSOUNTAS, C. 1898. 'Kykladika', *Archaiologike Ephemeris*: 137–212.
UCKO, P. J. 1968. *Anthropomorphic Figurines of Predynastic Egypt and Neolithic Crete* (London: Andrew Szmidla).
VENTRIS, M. and CHADWICK, J. 1973. *Documents in Mycenaean Greek* (Cambridge: Cambridge University Press).
WARREN, P. M. 1969. *Minoan Stone Vases* (Cambridge: Cambridge University Press).
WATROUS, L. V. 1996. *The Cave Sanctuary of Zeus at Psychro: A study of extra-urban sanctuaries in Minoan and Early Iron Age Crete*, Aegaeum 15 (Liège: Aegaeum).
WRIGHT, J. C. 1995. 'The archaeological correlates of religion: Case studies in the Aegean' in R. Laffineur and W.-D. Niemeier (eds), *POLITEIA: Society and State in the Aegean Bronze Age* (Liège), pp. 341–8.
—— 2004. 'A survey of evidence for feasting in Mycenaean society' in J. C. Wright (ed.), *The Mycenaean Feast*, Hesperia 73:2 (Princeton: The American School of Classical Studies at Athens), pp. 13–58.
XANTHOUDIDES, S. 1924. *The Vaulted Tombs of Mesara* (London: Hodder and Stoughton).

CHAPTER 43

ANCIENT GREECE

JULIA KINDT

If the archaeologist cannot account for his data then his claims to be able to produce history of any sort must seem exceedingly thin. If the historian cannot produce a history which accounts for such major changes in the material world then he must seriously face up to the question of just what it is that his history purports to describe and account for: is the history gleaned from written sources not after all the history of a world but the history of a fiction of the world?

Robin Osborne (1989: 318)

Archaeology is cultural history or it is nothing.

Ian Morris (2000: 3)

1 GENERAL CONSIDERATIONS

THE study of ancient Greek religion is one of the most vibrant and rapidly developing branches of classical scholarship with an increasing number of monographs and articles being published on the topic each year. Within this dynamic area of scholarly interest, however, the need to integrate the archaeological evidence better into historically oriented scholarship on ancient Greek religion is arguably the most serious challenge currently facing the field. Material remains, when they are included at all, too frequently serve as a mere illustration of features of Greek religion derived from the study of Greek literature.

While most historically oriented works still take literary texts as their point of departure in the conceptualization of Greek religious beliefs and practices, there is an increasing awareness of the need to bring the material evidence into the picture (e.g. Dignas 2002; Price 1999). But while it has often been noted that material remains are still not sufficiently integrated into the study of Greek religion, classical scholars struggle to find meaningful ways in which to consider different types of data. As a result, some students of ancient Greek religion now consciously problematize the challenges scholars face when attempting to include the material record and seek strategies to overcome them (e.g. Hägg 1992; Morris 2000; Osborne 1994).

The absolutely crucial nature of an integrated approach to even a very basic understanding of Greek religion, however, becomes obvious as soon as we take into account the fact that many rural shrines and religious institutions are only known to us from epigraphic and archaeological evidence.

But the material record offers more than just an additional set of data. To find ways of integrating different types of evidence is a necessary and desirable, albeit difficult, exercise because the material record raises major questions that provide an important check for concepts of Greek religion derived from the literary sources. Used in a conceptual way, the material record can help classical scholarship to overcome some of the problems and unhelpful distinctions that trouble current research in the field.

2 TYPES OF EVIDENCE

The items revealed as relevant for the study of Greek religion by classical archaeology are numerous and encompass different types of evidence, ranging from individual objects and artefacts to the (architectonic) structures of religious space and inscriptions. Every type of evidence poses its own challenges for the student of ancient Greek religion and should be assessed in its own right first before it is used to contextualize other data, in particular information derived from the literary evidence. If used carefully, the material record is able to shed light on important dimensions of ancient Greek religion, which might otherwise remain unnoticed.

Amongst the individual artefacts, dedicatory offerings of various kinds form a large group. In particular *kouroi* and *korai* (sculptures in the form of boys and girls) and tripods have been found in large numbers throughout the Greek world—sometimes as part of burial arrangements (see Richter 1968, 1988). As manifestations of religious practices that 'made sense' to those involved in them, these and other cult objects enable the student of ancient Greek religion to connect the invisible with the visible dimensions of ancient Greek religion and belief with practice. The material record hence helps to correct tendencies in current scholarship, which focus too much on religious agency and sideline belief and the personal dimension of ancient Greek religion.

Coins, vases, reliefs, sculptures, and figurines of gods and goddesses offer an elaborate variety of iconographical depictions of the Greek gods and their 'circulation' in everyday life. These representations of the Greek pantheon visualize the dynamic and polyvalent fabric of ancient Greek religion like no other group of evidence—and hence challenge the scholarly tendency to draw up too static images of divine representation based on the literary evidence. Representations of Greek divinity refer to a mythological background that is in itself flexible. They are all statements made in the 'language' of religion and hence should not be reduced to the smallest common denominator of a mythological masternarrative (see Goldhill and Osborne 1994: 1–11).

Curse tablets, amulets and animal remains offer an important insight into the sacrificial and cult activity of ordinary people, including those who were not part of the sociopolitical elites. As evidence they suggest a more pluralistic understanding of Greek religion as a symbolic medium for contradictory, even conflicting (power-) discourses. Such evidence for unauthorized or elective religious activity has also triggered an ongoing debate on how we define religion, in particular concerning the distinction frequently made between religious practice and magical practice (see Kindt 2009; Bremmer 2010; see Graf 1997 for a comprehensive introduction to the debates concerning magic, see also Parker 1995 on the relationship between orphism and polis religion).

In addition to individual artefacts, however, classical archaeology has been enormously successful in revealing altars, temples and the spatial and architectonic structures of Greek religion more generally. Archaeological surface survey is a promising technique, which allows us to get an insight into the topography of sacred landscapes, both rural and urban (e.g. Stageira, see *Archaeological Reports* (48) 2001–2: 77–9). Surprisingly few religious items have been found in excavations of private houses but the archaeology of the *oikos* is still in its early days and more excavations are likely to yield better results (for some recent works in this area see Nevett 2001; Bradley and Nevett 2005).

Finally, we have a very large number of inscriptions related to things sacred, which were found all over the Greek world. Most of these inscriptions are sacred laws organizing individual cults (for a recent collection see Lupu 2005). Through these inscriptions we can gain an insight into the economic side of Greek religion and the administration of religious cults (see Dignas 2002). There are, however, also inscriptions reporting the outcome of oracle consultations, revealing a personal side of ancient Greek religion, which is frequently neglected in scholarship on 'official' Greek religion (e.g. *Bulletin de Correspondance Hellenique* 80 (1956): 550 concerning an oracle consultation about childbirth).

The personal dimension of Greek religion is also tangible in the *Derveni papyrus* published in full in 2006 in a critical edition by Kouremenos, Passássoglou, and Tsantsanoglou (see also the preliminary edition by Betegh 2004). The papyrus has triggered an increased awareness of the existence of mystery religions, in particular Orphism. It is an important source for the study of ancient Greek religion not least because it shows in what ways Orphism is and is not like official (polis) religion. Particularly interesting about the materiality of the papyrus is also the very fact that its abstract content was placed in a burial context.

Examination of the important contribution the material evidence can make to the study of Greek religious beliefs and practices shows how unproductive the scholarly preoccupation with the literary evidence is. The reasons for this self-inflicted restriction, however, are manifold and are to a significant extent rooted in the historical relationship between ancient history and classical archaeology.

3 THE EMERGENCE OF A DISCOURSE

From an interdisciplinary point of view, the most puzzling aspect of classical archaeology as a discipline is, perhaps, its long and far-reaching separation from other archaeologies. Until relatively recently classical archaeology was grounded in the notion of *Altertumswissenschaft* (the interdisciplinary study of antiquity) as a joint effort of recovering the ancient (Greek and Roman) past rather than being related to the archaeology of other cultures and societies. As a result, the archaeology of Greece and Rome remained closely tied to classical philology while other archaeologies evolved mostly as a branch of anthropology (see Whitley 2001 for an accessible outline of the history of Greek archaeology).

The archaeology of Greece maintained for long a distinctly historicist profile born out of Romanticism and an antiquarian interest in the past. With the foundation of various national schools at Athens during the second half of the nineteenth century and the organization of excavations at famous sites like Olympia and Delphi ('big digs'), classical archaeology underwent a process of increasing professionalization. Its ultimate objective, however, remained the 'celebration' of Hellenism through Greek 'art' (on this see Morris 1994).

Until the 1970s traditional Classical archaeology was centred mainly on the collection, description, and classification of material remains. The interpretation of these remains, however, was considered largely outside the scope of the archaeological profession. From a more historically oriented point of view, it was hence tempting to see classical archaeology as a mere *Hilfswissenschaft* (supplementary discipline). Archaeology was able to provide the student of the ancient world with a further set of data to master, but was fundamentally unable to make a methodological contribution to the study of Greek culture and society. Archaeology was not considered capable of changing (let alone correcting) the kind of questions historians of the ancient world tended to ask.

The strict disciplinary boundaries between ancient history, on the one hand, and classical archaeology, on the other, translated directly into the forms and conventions of academic publishing. In particular the (still existing) tendency of classical archaeologists to publish findings of one genre (e.g. votives) from one or different sites together is of limited help for the ancient historian interested in writing the cultural history of Greek ritual and religion (e.g. Beazley 1956; Boardman 1970; and, more recently, Clairmont 1993).

In the last 30-odd years, however, the two disciplines have moved much closer together. Ancient historians and classical archaeologists have begun to overcome the difficulty of finding a common language. Crucial paradigm changes have initiated a fundamental redefinition of the relationship between the disciplines. A variety of scholars has pioneered a trend that seriously challenges traditional Classical archaeology and has helped shape a new archaeology of Greece.

This development was driven by an interest in social change and larger societal processes, a 'turn' towards the context of finds which made the new archaeology of Greece compatible with the themes and interests of social history. To mention just a few names that inaugurated this change in paradigm: Colin Renfrew at Cambridge, for example, pursued the study of the Aegean Bronze Age as a social and contextual archaeology (e.g. Renfrew 1972; also Barrett and Halstead 2004.). In his acclaimed Melos survey and in other similar projects Renfrew used intensive surface survey to generate quantifiable data, which he interpreted as indicators for diachronic processes of social change, in particular of state formation. In his important study of the sanctuary at Phylakopi, Renfrew has significantly advanced the study of the archaeology of cult (Renfrew 1985). In abstracting from his case study, Renfrew has outlined the very parameters of research into ritual space and its different material manifestations. Despite its merits, however, the over-schematic checklist approach adopted here has sometimes proven too rigid to do justice to the variety of sanctuaries and other cult places in the Greek world.

Anthony Snodgrass, another Cambridge scholar, likewise took an interest in explaining the processual character of Greek state formation. In a sophisticated quantitative analysis of grave deposits Snodgrass demonstrated a steep increase in population during the eighth century BC, a demographic change he considered to be at the heart of the emergence of the Greek polis during the same period (Snodgrass 1980).

Renfrew, Snodgrass, and other like-minded scholars deviated strongly from traditional Classical archaeology. Their investigative focus and their research methods aligned their work more closely with larger trends within the archaeological profession, in particular with processual archaeology and comparative world-archaeology. Both scholars expanded the evidence considered worthy of scholarly attention to include not only high art but also everyday items of human activity and both applied quantitative methods to 'read' the evidence. With the work of scholars like Renfrew and Snodgrass, classical archaeology turned from a largely descriptive science to an explanatory discipline, from a branch of philology to a branch of anthropology.

As a result, the historical discipline can no longer see classical archaeology as simply providing another, supplementary (and thus ultimately negligible) set of data. These days both disciplines apply their different methodologies to a similar end: that of uncovering the full spectrum of Greek culture and society and tracing the distinct discourses of Greek (self-) representation, which pervade all cultural productions. There is currently no single interpretative paradigm which dominates the communication between the two disciplines, but there are various perspectives and approaches around which an interdisciplinary discourse has evolved.

In the field of religion, these approaches have centred on a variety of themes and problems: various students of Snodgrass, for example, have further developed his socio-contextual approach towards the archaeology of Greece. Some of them have explicitly connected this with an interest in the material evidence for religious beliefs and practices. Ian Morris, for instance, has challenged Snodgrass's methods to research demographical developments. In *Burial and Ancient Society* he argued that the number of grave sites cannot provide a direct indicator for changes in demography for there were certain ideologies regulating burial practices in Athens and elsewhere (Morris 1987). Catherine Morgan, in turn, has extended Snodgrass's interest in Greek state formation by exploring various processual changes in the sociopolitical and religious landscapes of Greece (Morgan 1990; Morgan 1994; see also Morgan and Whitelaw 1991). Susan Alcock has further developed Snodgrass's investigative focus to study the development of Greece during the Roman period, including the role of cults and extra-urban sanctuaries (see Alcock 1993).

A different and productive strand of discourse that in many ways supplements and extends social and contextual archaeology began with the introduction of structuralism into classical art history by Herbert Hoffmann (Hoffmann 1977). The arguably most persuasive account of structuralism in the archaeology of Greek ritual and religion, however, is a product of the Paris School. *A City of Images* is a sophisticated account of the iconographic semantics of Attic vase painting (Bérard et al. 1989). Although the subtitle of the English translation has, curiously, lost the religious dimension inherent in the French original, this work examines a variety of contexts relevant to the archaeology of ritual and religion, including (but not limited to) representations of sacrifice, festivals, and the Greek gods. Structuralism also shaped the debates around François de Polignac's influential work on the development of the polis as a religious community during the Archaic period (de Polignac 1991, see below).

The increasing emphasis on images that was so skilfully pursued in *A City of Images* and elsewhere, however, is also representative of a larger interest in problems of representation and in religion as a symbolic system. Material artefacts are now frequently seen as providing a way into previously hidden structures of symbolic meaning. Scholarly attention is now directed towards detecting the hidden layers of meaning included in religious symbols and to the role of the viewer in symbolic representation (e.g. Osborne 1988; Osborne 1994). A recent example is Judith Barringer's investigation of the exterior decorations of the temple of Zeus at Olympia (Barringer 2005). She has argued that the sculptural elements of the pediments and metopes of the temple should be considered together and placed in their Olympic context: rather than being reminders of hubris and justice as the traditional view has it, these sculptures supported and promoted the much more positive aspects of competitive achievement and Olympic glory.

But despite such promising starting points for a comprehensive study of ancient Greek ritual and religion, there is still considerable ground to cover before a truly integrated perspective that draws upon all types of evidence is reached. The fundamental methodological division between the disciplines is still maintained by the way in which students of the ancient world are trained in research of a kind which qualifies them for a future career in both ancient history and classical archaeology. Truly interdisciplinary programmes, such as the *Ancient History and Mediterranean Archaeology Group* at the University of California at Berkeley, remain rare.

Significant obstacles also challenge the teaching of ancient Greek religion as an interdisciplinary subject that draws on both the literary and the material evidence. Although there is now a considerable interest in a perspective towards Greek religion which encompasses different classical disciplines, the major study tools available for the student of Greek religion still reflect the earlier conceptual gap between a historically oriented work based mainly on the literary record and disciplines focusing on other types of evidence. A Greek equivalent for the acclaimed sourcebook *Religions of Rome* by Beard, which includes epigraphic and material evidence alongside literary sources within its thematic sections has recently been published (see Kearns 2010).

There are also a few new and exciting encyclopaedic tools available to researchers in the field which are structured thematically and which draw on different types of evidence. The *Lexicon Iconographicum Mythologiae Classicae* (*LIMC*) for example, focuses on the pictorial representation of individual gods. The *Thesaurus Cultus et Rituum Antiquorum* (*ThesCRA*) offers a comprehensive account of cult activity. Such projects are as much a result of the growing interest in integrated perspectives towards Greek religion as they provide a starting point for future research in the field interested in integrating different types of evidence.

4 Areas of Current Debate

The emergence of a genuine discourse between classical archaeology and historically oriented scholarship on ancient Greek religion provides the background against which current debates take shape. Four particularly promising fields of scholarly inquiry currently involve a re-evaluation of the material record in the light of a more integrated approach towards the evidence: the phenomenology of sacred space, the functionality of the Greek temple, the role of sacrifice and feasting, and the use of votive offerings. These areas show a general tendency to move away from the mere description of material remains towards embracing questions of their 'agency'. Questions of how architectonic structures and other cultic material objects 'act' in and interact with their surroundings feature largely in current works in the field without, however, necessarily assuming any degree of intentionality. In addition, classical archaeologists now frequently draw on concepts developed in social anthropology to evaluate the material remains of ancient Greek religion—the result of the classical discipline's new view of itself as a part of the interdisciplinary study of culture.

4.1 The Functionality of Form: The Greek Temple

While classical archaeology has focused for long on the description of material remains such as the Greek temple, a vibrant area of current research now looks at the architectonic structures of ancient Greek religion in functional rather than strictly formal terms. Scandinavian scholars at Uppsala and Stockholm in particular have pioneered this promising area of current inquiry. More recently, however, scholarly interest in the functionality of form has become absolutely mainstream in research on Greek sanctuaries. Today, most scholars involved in excavating and publishing a sanctuary consider how form translates into function and vice versa.

Classical scholars now explore how the physical characteristics of the Greek temple (its distinctive shape and size and its architectonical composition) are linked to its various social and religious functions. The subdivisions within the interior of Greek temples, for example, are used as an indicator of their function; research on temples now includes their role as places of economic activity rather than as venues for secret rituals (Hollinshead 1999). The essays collected by Nanno Marinatos and Robin Hägg (1993) provide a good example of how widespread the interest in the function of Greek sanctuaries has become particularly in the Anglo-American world. The study brings together contributions from classical archaeologists (Catherine Morgan, Helmut Kyrieleis) and ancient historians (Walter Burkert). It shows the variety of ways in which classical scholars currently use the functionality of form as an interpretative paradigm to trace, for example, the historical development of sanctuaries in different parts of the Greek world.

4.2 The Phenomenology of Sacred Space

Beyond individual architectonic structures there is now a larger interest in the form and function of Greek sacred space. Arguably the most influential (and most criticized) study of Greek sacred space is François de Polignac's *Naissance de la cité grecque* (published in English as *Cults, Territory and the Origin of the Greek City State* [de Polignac 1984]). As a student of both Snodgrass and Vernant, de Polignac combined an interest in Greek state-formation with a structuralist conceptualization of sacred space.

The point of departure of de Polignac's study is essentially phenomenological: why are Greek sanctuaries where they are? Writing against the prevailing notion of the time that the emergence of the city was primarily a process of increasing political institutionalisation, de Polignac argues that between the late ninth and early seventh centuries BC, the Greek city came to define itself first and foremost as a religious community. For this purpose, de Polignac conceptualizes the Greek sacred landscape as a bipolar geometrical plane, in which the polis identity was shaped in a dynamic tension between sanctuaries situated at the centre and periphery.

De Polignac's provocative study has triggered a lively debate challenging his somewhat simplifying overall argument, correcting him in detail, and extending his investigative focus. Alcock and Osborne's (1994) jointly edited volume is not only representative of the kind of questions that have emerged from de Polignac's work. It is also a wonderful example of how productive the collaboration between ancient history and classical archaeology is for research on the archaeology of Greek religion and ritual. In the course of this ongoing debate, de Polignac himself has extended his strictly bipolar synchronicity to a more chronologically and geographically differentiated picture of Greek state formation (see de Polignac 1991 [1984], 2009).

In response to de Polignac, there is considerable scholarly interest in evaluating the role of the polis in relation to other units of collective identity (see e.g. 'panhellenism' in Scott 2010: 250–73). The prevailing view now seems to be that the polis offered an alternative model of sociopolitical identification that continued to coexist with other forms of identity, such as the *ethne*. Such scholars as Jonathan Hall (1997) and Catherine Morgan (2003) now depict religious identity as part of local and ethnic identities.

Within a wider interdisciplinary context, there is currently a variety of productive lines of inquiry that expand the phenomenological approach by considerably complicating the concept of sacred space itself. In particular, scholars of prehistory are asking questions of considerable relevance to classical scholarship in the field. Conceptualizations of sacred space in scholarship on prehistory include (and sometimes even start from) the point of view of the individual moving through it (Tilley 1994, 2004); these conceptualizations also include the unaltered features of natural landscapes alongside the study of settlement and monumental architecture (Bradley 1998, 2000). The potential for future research resulting from such new and productive lines of inquiry is extensive. How do institutions like the Delphic oracle capitalize on the features of their stunning natural surroundings? To what extent do processions constitute a sacred space 'on the move' that defines itself through the tension between individual and collective, participant and observer?

4.3 The Role of Sacrifice and Feasting

Communal sacrifice was arguably the most significant way in which the Greeks sought to establish meaningful relationships with the gods. Various occasions virtually demanded a sacrifice, including, but not only, warfare, the celebration of festivals, and the consultation of oracles. While the Greeks sometimes sacrificed vegetarian products (fruits, honey, vegetables), blood sacrifice was standard, and within this category the sacrifice of an ox rated most highly. Significantly, ancient Greek blood sacrifice almost always involved feasting, that is the communal consumption of the sacrificial meat.

For several decades now, blood sacrifice has been a key area of interest in the interdisciplinary study of religions (for some influential studies see Hubert and Mauss 1981 [1964], Girard 1977 [1972]). In particular, with the works of Walter Burkert and Jean-Pierre Vernant, classical scholarship has contributed significantly to this ongoing interdisciplinary effort (Burkert 1983 [1972]; Detienne and Vernant 1989 [1979]). These scholars hold opposing positions concerning the societal function of ancient Greek blood sacrifice. Burkert interprets the communal act of killing from a sociobiological point of view, arguing that it controlled yet allowed an important human skill that goes all the way back to the hunter-gatherer society, hence creating cohesion between those involved. Vernant, for his part, lays the interpretative stress on the subsequent feasting and argues that it is the communal consumption of meat that creates group solidarity.

Most recently, however, the impasse between the two positions has somewhat dampened scholarly interest in this area of inquiry.

The archaeological evidence might be able to help in its revival. If used in a conceptual way it can reveal frequently neglected aspects of sacrifice and feasting. Besides the rich literary record available to scholars working in this area, there is plenty of archaeological evidence for sacrifice and feasting. Both practices are variously depicted on Greek pottery (e.g. Bérard et al. 1989: 53–70; Etienne and Le Dinahet 1991). Feasting scenes also feature in Cretan and Aegean frescos. Moreover, classical archaeology has revealed the spatial and material traces of sacrifice and feasting, including altars, bones, and other organic residues, as well as various ceramic pieces designed for the consumption of food and drink, such as kraters and drinking vessels. In addition, inscriptions include various laws regulating the ritual killing of livestock and its subsequent consumption (e.g. Lupu 2003).

A common problem of the interpretative models developed by Burkert and Vernant is that they offer a largely ahistoric explanation for both practices. Their interpretations trace all forms of sacrifice and feasting back to the same synchronic model. Current archaeological research, however, has considerably complicated this static picture by differentiating between individual regions and by tracing changes in feasting habits over time. To give just two examples, a case study of Mycenean feasting habits during the Middle and Late Bronze Age has revealed the way in which these practices reflect the complex palace hierarchy (Wright 2004); and the archaeological evidence is also able to complicate our picture of Homeric drinking rituals: the existence of different chronological layers means that they should not be pieced together in a simple composite picture (Sherratt 2004).

The obvious next step would be to find ways to place such interesting results within a larger sociocultural framework. Perhaps conceptual guidance might again emerge from current studies in social anthropology. Various scholars working at the intersection of ethnography and archaeology (both ancient and modern) are currently pursuing the study of feasting as a central and universal cultural practice (e.g. Dietler and Hayden 2001). These studies offer a reflective and systematic approach towards feasting and reveal the variety of ways in which scholars currently conceptualize it as a deeply social practice at the intersection of economics, religion, society, and power. The questions posed by ethnoarchaeologists (and the concepts they develop in response) may prove invaluable for classical scholarship on ancient Greek religion: what is the link between feasting as a social and a ritual practice? To what extent can feasts serve as 'ritual theatres for the cultural construction and transformation of value'? (Dietler and Hayden 2001: 17).

4.4 Votive offerings

While blood sacrifice is a temporary and ultimately destructive offering to the gods, votive offerings constitute lasting and visible monuments of human reference to the divine. Votives included any material offering or dedication made voluntarily to a god or goddess, which is not a sacrifice (a dedication for consumption) or a tax. Votives were made for a variety of reasons: to appease a divinity, in thanksgiving after the successful granting of a wish or recovery from a severe disease, and in support of prayer and supplication. There are several contexts in which votive offerings feature particularly prominently, such as warfare, childbirth, and other transitional moments in life, such as marriage or retirement from manual labour. Because of the many situations in which they were used and the various functions they fulfilled, a variety of objects could serve as votive offerings. The spoils of war and other prestige objects such as tripods were obvious choices. But votive offerings also included locks of hair (some real, some in form of stone reliefs), tools of trade, masks, representations of limbs and (at healing sanctuaries), other body parts, and, in particular, virtually thousands of little figurines and statues.

Scholarship on votive offerings directly reflects the larger developments in both disciplines as sketched above. Early works were mainly interested in collecting, systematizing, and describing the evidence available to the student of ancient Greek religion (Rouse 1902). More recent research, however, has chosen a narrower yet more ambitious focus, advancing the interpretation of votive offerings. The form of votives (in particular, recurrent iconographical motifs) is now related to their function in order to reveal votive religion as an important aspect of Greek personal religion (e.g. van Straten 1981). In order to research the function of votive offerings they are now increasingly placed in their respective sociocultural and religious contexts (e.g. Linders and Nordquist 1987; Scott 2010). Anthropomorphic votive figurines for example are now researched in relation to the cult image of the divinity to which the votive was offered (Alroth 1989). Despite the diversity of their outlooks, such works exemplify a trend towards researching regional similarities and differences and a strong awareness of the importance of the historical and situational contexts for the interpretation of votive offerings.

As James Whitley (2006) has recently pointed out, some scholarly works make a fundamental qualitative distinction between different types of votive offerings. Some votives, such as the famous 'peplos *kore*' from the Athenian acropolis, have become central pieces in the reconstruction of the chronology of Greco-Roman art history. As such, they were subjected to a form of analysis that treated them as reflective of an aesthetic realm ultimately separate from its social and cultural contexts. In contrast, other, more mundane objects were frequently labelled as expressions of 'popular' (folk) religion and have received much less scholarly attention. It has recently been suggested that this notion of art is a product of the Enlightenment and ultimately foreign to Greek thought; material artefacts should hence be related not only to the individual artists who created them, but also to patrons, viewers, and the institutions of Greek culture and society more generally (Tanner 2006).

One of the most ingenious and productive trends in classical scholarship is currently concerned with establishing the very modes and modalities of Greco-Roman visuality (e.g. Goldhill and Osborne 1994; Elsner 2007). By bringing together texts and objects that explore how material artefacts were perceived in the ancient world, classical scholars have sought to establish the existence of a specific religious gaze (Elsner 2007). This ritual-centred visuality is developed alongside, and in exchange with, the naturalism of classical mimesis. But in contrast to it, the religious way of viewing is oriented towards the ritual significance of material artefacts. If applied to the study of votives, this conceptualization of the religious visuality might provide a way of reintegrating the aesthetic dimension of dedications back into their religious context. If combined with the literary evidence on religious dedications and their perception in Greco-Roman antiquity (e.g. Pausanias), the study of votive offerings could establish itself at the forefront of a truly interdisciplinary study of ancient Greek religion that draws on both the literary and the material evidence.

5 CONCLUSION

There are now a variety of promising areas of current debate, which pursue the study of ancient Greek religion and ritual as a truly interdisciplinary effort, grounded in both the literary and the material evidence. As a result, classical scholarship has come to realize that the archaeology of the sacred is, in many ways, central to our understanding of ancient Greek religious beliefs and practices. Both literary texts and material artefacts are cultural products. Research that conceptualizes archaeology as cultural history and scholarship that acknowledges that cultural history has a strong material dimension will hence yield further insights not only into the nature and fabric of ancient Greek religion, but into the society which practised it.

SUGGESTED READING

Whitley (2001) is an excellent introduction to the archaeology of Greece, including (but not limited to) the archaeology of the sacred. Morris (2000) has the most explicit formulation of the scope and methods of archaeology as cultural history. Osborne (1988) and Osborne (1994) are excellent examples of how the material evidence can be used to shed light on social and cultural contexts. Bérard et al. (1989) and the essays collected in Gordon (1981) demonstrate the interpretative powers of French structuralism applied to the iconographic 'texts' (vases) and literary texts respectively. De Polignac (2009) is a revised formulation of his influential approach to the study of sanctuaries in the Greek sacred landscape (see also de Polignac 1991, Alcock and Osborne 1994).

REFERENCES

ALCOCK, S. E. 1993. *Graecia Capta: The landscapes of Roman Greece* (Cambridge: Cambridge University Press).
—— and OSBORNE, R. (eds) 1994. *Placing the Gods: Sanctuaries and sacred space in ancient Greece* (Oxford: Clarendon Press).
ALROTH, B. 1989. *Greek Gods and Figurines: Aspects of the anthropomorphic dedications* (Uppsala: Almqvist and Wiksell).
BARRETT, J. C. and HALSTEAD, P. (eds) 2004. *The Emergence of Civilisation Revisited* (Oxford: Oxbow Books).
BARRINGER, J. 2005. 'The Temple of Zeus at Olympia, Heroes, and Athletes', *Hesperia* 74: 211–41.
BEARD, M., NORTH, J., and PRICE, S. (eds) 1998. *Religions of Rome*, 2 vols. (Cambridge: Cambridge University Press).
BEAZLEY, SIR J. D. 1956. *Attic Black-Figure Vase Painters* (Oxford: Clarendon Press).
BÉRARD, C., BRON, C., DURAND, J.-L., et al. 1989. *A City of Images: Iconography and society in ancient Greece* (Princeton: Princeton University Press); trans. from the French orig., *La Cité des images: religion et société en Grèce antique* (Paris, 1984).

BETEGH, G. 2004. *The Derveni Papyrus: Cosmology, theology, and interpretation* (Cambridge: Cambridge University Press).

BLACKMANN, D. 2001. 'Archaeology in Greece 2001–2002', *Archaeological Reports* 48: 1–115.

BOARDMAN, SIR J. 1970. *Archaic Greek Gems: Schools and artists in the sixth and early fifth centuries BC* (London: Thames and Hudson).

BRADLEY, A. and NEVETT, L. (eds) 2005. *Ancient Greek Houses and Households: Chronological, regional and social diversity* (Philadelphia: University of Philadelphia Press).

BRADLEY, R. 1998. *The Significance of Monuments: On the shaping of human experience in Neolithic and Bronze Age Europe* (London: Routledge).

—— 2000. *An Archaeology of Natural Places* (London: Routledge).

BREMMER, J. 2010. '*Manteis*, Magic, Mysteries and Mythography: Messy Margins of *Polis* Religion?', *Kernos* 23: 13–25.

BURKERT, W. 1983. *Homo Necans: The anthropology of ancient Greek sacrificial ritual and myth* (Berkeley: de Gruyter); trans. P. Bing from the German orig., *Homo Necans: Interpretation altgriechischer Opferriten und Mythen* (Berlin, 1972).

CLAIRMONT, C. 1993. *Classical Attic Tombstones*, 8 vols. (Kilchberg: Akanthus).

DETIENNE, M. and VERNANT, J.-P. 1989. *The Cuisine of Sacrifice among the Greeks* (Chicago: University of Chicago Press); trans. P. Wissing from the French orig., *La cuisine du sacrifice en pays grec* (Paris: Gallimard, 1979).

DIETLER, M. and HAYDEN, B. (eds) 2001. *Archaeological and Ethnographic Perspectives on Food, Politics, and Power* (Washington: Smithsonian Institution Press).

DIGNAS, B. 2002. *Economy of the Sacred in Hellenistic and Roman Asia Minor* (Oxford: Oxford University Press).

ELSNER, J. 2007. *Roman Eyes: Visuality and subjectivity in art and text* (Princeton: Princeton University Press).

ETIENNE, R. and LE DINAHET, M. (eds) 1991. *L'Espace sacrificiel dans les civilisations méditerranéennes de l'antiquité: actes du colloque tenu à la Maison de l'Orient, Lyon, 4–7 juin 1988* (Paris: Boccard).

GIRARD, R. 1977. *Violence and the Sacred* (Baltimore: Johns Hopkins University Press); trans. P. Gregory from the French orig., *La violence et le sacré* (Paris, 1972).

GOLDHILL, S. and OSBORNE, R. (eds) 1994. *Art and Text in Ancient Greek Culture* (Cambridge: Cambridge University Press).

GORDON, R. (ed.) 1981. *Myth, Religion and Society: Structuralist essays by M. Detienne, L. Gernet, J.-P. Vernant and P. Vidal-Naquet* (Cambridge: Cambridge University Press).

GRAF, F. 1997. *Magic in the Ancient World* (Cambridge, MA: Harvard University Press); trans. F. Philip from the French orig., *Idéologie et pratique de la magie dans l'antiquité gréco-romaine* (Paris, 1994).

HÄGG, R. 1992. 'Cult Practice and Archaeology: Some Examples from Early Greece', *SIFC*, 10: 79–95.

HALL, J. 1997. *Ethnic Identity in Greek Antiquity* (Cambridge: Cambridge University Press).

HOFFMANN, H. 1977. *Sexual and Asexual Pursuit: A Structuralist Approach to Greek Vase Painting* (London: Royal Anthropological Institute).

HOLLINSHEAD, M. B. 1999. '"Adyton", "Opisthomos", and the Inner Room of the Greek Temple', *Hesperia*, 68: 189–218.

HUBERT, H. and MAUSS, M. 1981. *Sacrifice: Its nature and function* (Chicago: University of Chicago Press); trans. W. Halls from the French orig., *Essai sur la nature et le fonction du sacrifice* (Paris, 1964).

Kearns, E. 2010. *Ancient Greek Religion: A Sourcebook* (Malden: Wiley-Blackwell).
Kindt, J. 2009. 'Polis Religion—A Critical Appreciation', *Kernos* 22: 9–34.
Kouremenos, T., Passássoglou, G. M., and Tsantsanoglou, K. (eds) 2006. *The Derveni Papyrus: Edited with Introduction and Commentary* (Florence: L. S. Olschki).
Linders, T. and Nordquist, G. (eds) 1987. *Gifts to the Gods: Proceedings of the Uppsala Symposium 1985* (Uppsala: Almqvist and Wiksell).
Lupu, E. 2003. 'Sacrifice at the Amphiareion and a fragmentary sacred law from Oropos', *Hesperia*, 72: 321–40.
——2005. *Greek Sacred Law: A collection of new documents* (Leiden: Brill).
Marinatos, N. and Hägg, R. N. (eds) 1993. *Greek Sanctuaries: New approaches* (London: Routledge).
Morgan, C. 1990. *Athletes and Oracles: the Transformation of Olympia and Delphi in the Eighth Century BC* (Cambridge: Cambridge University Press).
——1994. 'The Evolution of a Sacral Landscape', in J. Ober (ed.) *Athenian Legacies: Essays on the Politics of Going on Together*. (Princeton: Princeton University Press), pp. 69–91.
——2003. *Early Greek States beyond the Polis* (London: Routledge).
——and Whitelaw, C. 1991. 'Pots and Politics: Ceramic Evidence for the Rise of the Argive State', *AJA* 95: 79–108.
Morris, I. 1987. *Burial and Ancient Society: The rise of the Greek city-state* (Cambridge: Cambridge University Press).
——1994. 'Introduction' in I. Morris (ed.), *Classical Greece: Ancient Histories and Modern Archaeologies* (Cambridge: Cambridge University Press), pp. 3–7.
——2000. *Archaeology as Cultural History: Words and things in Iron Age Greece* (Malden, MA: Blackwell).
Nevett, L. 2001. *House and Society in the Ancient Greek World* (Cambridge: Cambridge University Press).
Osborne, R. 1988. 'Death revisited, death revised: The death of the artist in Archaic and Classical Greece', *Art History*, 11: 1–15.
——1989. 'A crisis in archaeological history? The seventh century BC in Attica', *ABSA*, 84: 297–322.
——1994. 'Archaeology, the Salaminioi, and the politics of sacred space in Archaic Attica' in S. Alcock and R. Osborne (eds), *Placing the Gods: Sanctuaries and Sacred Space in Ancient Greece* (Oxford: Clarendon Press), pp. 143–60.
Parker, R. 1995. 'Early Orphism' in A. Powell (ed.), *The Greek World* (London: Routledge), pp. 483–510.
Polignac, F. de 1991. *Cults, Territory, and the Origin of the Greek City State* (Chicago: University of Chicago Press); trans. J. Lloyd from the French orig., *La Naissance de la cité grecque: cultes, espace et société* (Paris, 1984).
——2009. 'Sanctuaries and festivals' in H. van Wees and K. Raaflaub (eds), *Blackwell Companion to Archaic Greece* (Oxford: Blackwells), pp. 427–43.
Price, S. 1999. *Religions of the Ancient Greeks* (Cambridge: Cambridge University Press).
Renfrew, C. 1972. *The Emergence of Civilization: The Cyclades and the Aegean in the third millennium BC* (London: Methuen).
——1985. *The Archaeology of Cult: The sanctuary at Phylakopi* (London: Thames and Hudson).
Richter, G. M. A. 1968. *Korai, Archaic Greek Maidens: A Study of the Development of the Kore in Greek sculpture* (London: Phaidon Publishers).

——1988. *Kouroi: Archaic Greek Youths: A Study of the Development of the Kouros Type in Greek Sculpture* (New York: Hacker Art Books).
Rouse, W. H. D. 1902. *Greek Votive Offerings: An Essay in the History of Greek Religion* (Cambridge: Cambridge University Press).
Scott, M. *Delphi and Olympia: The Spatial Politics of Panhellenism in the Archaic and Classical Periods* (Cambridge: Cambridge University Press).
Sherratt, S. 2004. 'Feasting in Homeric epic', *Hesperia*, 73: 301–37.
Snodgrass, A. 1980. *Archaic Greece: The age of experiment* (London: Phaidon Press).
Spencer, N. 1995. 'Heroic time: Monuments and the past in Messenia, Southwest Greece', *Oxford Journal of Archaeology*, 14: 277–92.
Straten, F. T. van 1981. 'Gifts for the gods' in H. S. Versnel (ed.), *Faith, Hope and Worship: Aspects of religious mentality in the ancient world* (Leiden: Brill), pp. 65–151.
Tanner, J. 2006. *The Invention of Art History in Ancient Greece* (Cambridge: Cambridge University Press).
Tilley, C. 1994. *A Phenomenology of Landscape: Places, Paths, and Monuments* (Oxford: Berg).
——2004. *The Materiality of Stone: Explorations in Landscape Phenomenology*, I (Oxford: Berg).
Whitley, J. 2001. *The Archaeology of Ancient Greece* (Cambridge: Cambridge University Press).
——2006. 'Classical art and human agency: A tale of two objects in fifth-century Greece' in *ΓΕΝΕΘΛΙΟΝ: Αναμνηστικός Τόμος για την Συμπλήρωση Είκοσι Χρόνων Λειτουργίας του Μουσείου Κυκλαδικής Τέχνής*, 227–36.
Wright, J. 2004. 'A survey of evidence for feasting in Mycenaean society', *Hesperia*, 72: 133–78.

CHAPTER 44

ETRUSCAN RITUAL AND RELIGION

TOM RASMUSSEN

1 INTRODUCTION

IN the ancient Mediterranean world, ritual and religion were not add-ons to human existence but an intrinsic part of daily living. This seems to have been especially true of Etruscan society. *Les plus religieux des hommes* was the title given to a conference held in 1992 on Etruscan religion, and the phrase was not invented for the occasion but are the words of the Roman historian Livy, from whom we get a good deal of relevant information. This brings us straight to a serious problem in studying the topic. Livy was writing during the reign of the emperor Augustus, by which time the Etruscans had been under Roman rule for more than two centuries and an independent Etruria was but a very distant memory. Cicero, another important source, was a generation earlier than Livy, but many other key informants are of the later Roman Empire and Byzantine periods, all of them writing about a society of long before their time, that belonged essentially to the period of the tenth to first centuries BC. Moroever, few of these writers knew anything about the Etruscan language, while few of the earlier sources that they quote go back earlier than the first century BC.

Exactly when the non-Indo-European-speaking Etruscans first emerged in central Italy is at present not known, but their heartland was the area between the Tyrrhenian sea and the Arno and Tiber Rivers. This territory was divided between a number of separate, independent states, but which were linked to each other by social, cultural, and, especially, religious ties (Rasmussen 2005). Several sources speak of a league of twelve cities (in Latin the *duodecim populi*) which met regularly at the *fanum* (sanctuary) of Voltumna. Two pieces of information about it we learn from a very late Roman inscription: it was presided over by an annually elected priest, and the sanctuary was somewhere in the region of Volsinii (Orvieto). At present the best candidate for its location is a site at Campo della Fiera outside that city.

Early approaches at understanding Etruscan cult and religion, which go back to the eighteenth century, were confined to listing and discussing the relevant Greek and Latin sources. Only in the last century did the available archaeological material begin to be taken into consideration (e.g. Ross Taylor 1923), and in the latter part of it attention was also given in earnest to the iconography of figurative art works, of which many were specifically produced for sanctuary and funerary use. In the meantime, understanding of the Etruscan language, which is written in a basically Greek alphabet, has gained greater precision (Bonfante and Bonfante 2002); most inscriptions, of which there are many thousands (Rix 1991) beginning c.700 BC, can be read with little difficulty. Some of the longer ones—including the longest of all which is written on linen later used for wrapping an Egyptian mummy now in Zagreb Museum—have specifically to do with liturgy and cult practice, and these do pose problems mainly of vocabulary. It is now generally recognized that the way forward is to give equal focus to all three types of evidence: the monuments and their archaeological context, the many relevant inscriptions, and what the ancient (non-Etruscan) sources have to say on the subject.

There are many basic elements concerned with the sacred which the Etruscans shared with other Mediterranean peoples such as the Greeks. For example, their cult activities took place in carefully laid out sanctuaries to various gods, which were situated both within the urban environment and also in the countryside beyond (Colonna 1985). In the latter case, their siting may have had a political as well as a religious motive, affirming the extent of the territory of the controlling city. Sanctuaries might have one or more temples or none at all. An altar was essential, and animal sacrifice was common. The evidence for human sacrifice is controversial and it seems not to have been a regular practice. Votive offerings were in various forms including pottery, sculpture, figurines, or anatomical models of body parts.

Other elements are quite distinctive, however, especially the tradition surrounding the figure of Tages (Richardson 2008). The name is Latin, but behind it must lie an Etruscan name such as Tarchies. The Etruscans possessed a body of written doctrine, now mostly lost but known to the Romans as the *Etrusca disciplina*, that was supposed to go back to a divine teacher. Tages, who sprang up from a plough furrow with the stature of an infant but the features of an adult, proclaimed this wisdom to a large audience that included leaders from all over Etruria. That the setting for the event should have been Tarquinia, one of the largest and oldest Etruscan cities, seems appropriate: here is the site of one of the biggest temples (the Ara della Regina), as well as a recently excavated sanctuary where the focal point seems to have been the burial of a small child with cranial abnormalities suggestive of epilepsy (which in the ancient world was associated with trance-like and revelatory states). We know of no large-scale Etruscan secular literature, but the sacred books of the *disciplina* were divided into sections on, among other topics, divination and the afterlife, on the interpretation of lightning, and on rituals connected with the founding of cities and sacred places (Jannot 2005: 3–16).

2 DIVINATION

We may obtain a flavour of these texts from the lengthy 'thunder (brontoscopic) calendar' that survives in a Greek translation but the original of which is thought to go back to the Tagetic writings (Turfa 2006). For example, for 23 February: 'If it thunders, it threatens deformity for men but destruction for birds'; for 23 April: 'If it thunders, it signifies a rain helpful for the sprouting time.' Not surprisingly for any ancient society, many of the worries concerning the future are to do with health and with crop fertility. Lightning, too, needed careful evaluation. Different shapes and colours of lightning offered different meanings, and it mattered greatly where it appeared in the sky and where on the ground it struck. Being an adept at understanding the laws of lightning was not, to the Etruscan mind, such a far cry from being able to produce it, to draw lightning down from the sky, and we hear of occasional claims that people were able to do this.

On the subject of lightning the Roman writer Seneca (*Quaestiones Naturales* 2.32.2) is particularly revealing: 'We think that because clouds collide, lightning is emitted; but they [the Etruscans] believe that clouds collide in order that lightning may be emitted. They are convinced that . . . these things occur because they are meant to reveal the future'. The close observation of natural phenomena is a priestly concern that one also finds in the ancient Near East and Mesopotamia, but the Etruscans always went beyond pure observation to interpretation: the natural world, and the cosmos, were not randomly arranged but organized by the gods in accordance with a system of signs that, correctly understood, could unveil the future. It is a system that embraced not only virtually all aerial phenomena, such as the flight of birds and the calls they emitted, but also all life on earth. Anything out of the ordinary (e.g. birth defects), or that occurred unexpectedly (e.g. meteors) was a clue concerning the gods' will.

Another approach to divination was to examine the entrails of sacrificed animals, especially the liver of sheep. This art of haruspicy also has very close correlations with Mesopotamian practice where the animal liver (and sometimes the lungs and other organs) was examined for similar purposes. Focus was on the liver presumably because it is not only the largest internal organ but also because its surface is particularly responsive to changes in the overall health of the animal. A healthy liver was good, any sign of disease bad; and that is probably as far as Mesopotamian (and Greek) practitioners went. But the Etruscans saw the liver in cosmic terms—as a reflection of the sky above, different parts of which were 'inhabited' by different gods. One of the most famous of all Etruscan artefacts is a life-size bronze model of a sheep's liver (van der Meer 1987), found near Piacenza in 1877, its upper surface divided into many compartments with the name of a god inscribed in each (Figure 44.1). A breakthrough in understanding the object came, some generations ago, when its upper surface was shown to bear a close resemblance to a description of the sky in 16 parts by the late Roman writer Martianus Capella (1.45–61); this is the same number as the compartments on the outer rim of the model. The 16 parts of the Etruscan sky are also mentioned by earlier writers such as Cicero, but it is only Martianus who connects each of the regions to one or more gods. The Roman names of several of Martianus' gods have some correlations with those on the liver, others are more difficult to compare with it, but it is generally agreed that his text, though laden with later quasi-philosophical embellishments, goes back to an original Etruscan treatise.

The precise orientation of the regions of the Etruscan sky in terms of north, south etc., is supplied in a brief passage by Pliny (2.55.143). Moreover the locations of a number of gods listed in Martianus to a certain extent match their positions on the rim of the liver, sufficiently to make it clear that the gods of good omen and those of ill omen were on opposite sides of the heavens (roughly, east and west respectively). There are others in his list that correspond to some of the names in the liver's inner compartments. The sky, then, is not an undifferentiated area, nor is the surface of the liver—which, if held in correct relation to it, was made to yield relevant information about the will of specific gods,

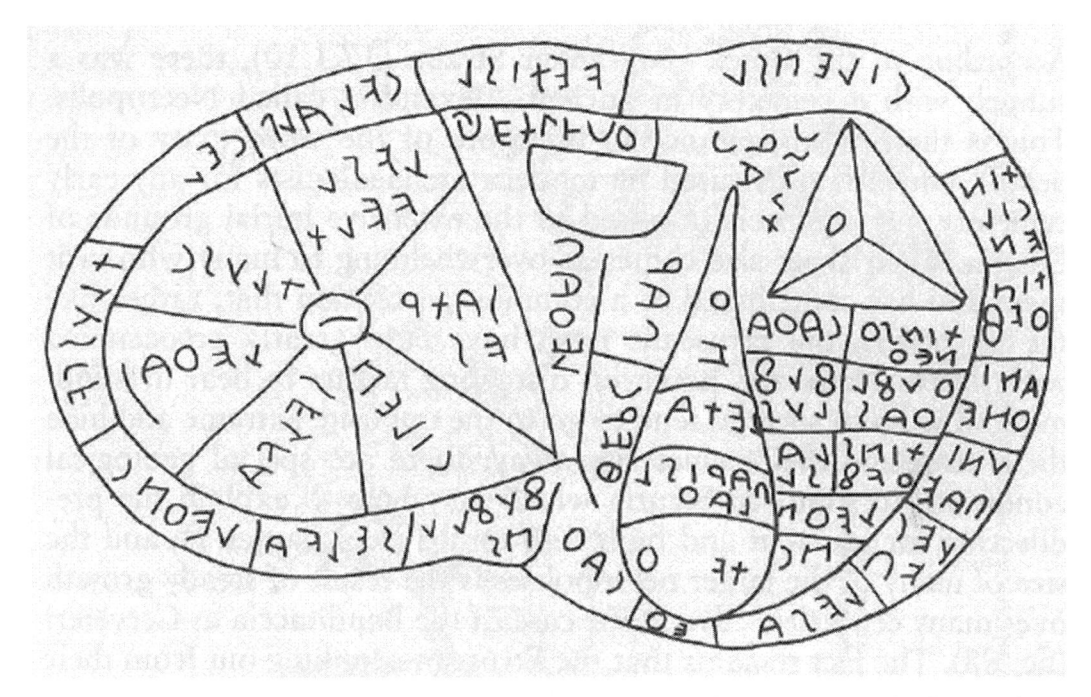

FIGURE 44.1 Drawing of upper surface of bronze liver from Piacenza, third–second century BC.

through close observation of the position of any blemishes or other striking features on its surface.

The practice of liver examination is shown on a number of Etruscan monuments, notably engraved mirrors. Recently it has been shown that illustrations of prophecy and divination of other kinds are commonplace both on mirrors and other artefacts with figurative decoration, in scenes where they had not been noticed before (de Grummond 2000); indicative factors include the stance of the diviner (often with one foot resting on a rock), facial expression, bodily gesture, and hair dishevelled or standing on end. The Romans were also interested in—almost obsessed by—techniques of divination, especially in the revelatory potential of abnormal events (*ostenta*), and not only did they learn much from their skilled neighbours but they also looked up to the Etruscans as the master practitioners, employing their experts on a regular basis through the period of the empire.

3 THE GODS

Because Etruscan civilization did not develop in a hermetically sealed environment but enjoyed prolonged contact with the Greeks and, closer to home, the Romans, some Etruscan deities in consequence were given names derived from Greek and Roman gods, and certain of the deities developed iconographies familiar from Greek depictions. The naming of gods, in the ancient world generally, is often fluid and the same god may be called different names from locality to locality and from one era to another. The reason for the adoption of Greek iconography is presumably because the Greek gods were part of such an enormously rich mythology, which was enjoyed and retold in different ways in the various centres of Etruria. The list of gods that follows is only very partial:

ETRUSCAN	GREEK	ROMAN
Aita, Calu	Hades	Pluto
Ap(u)lu	Apollon	Apollo
Aritimi, Artumes	Artemis	Diana
Cel	Gaia	Tellus
Fufluns, Pacha	Dionysus	Bacchus, Liber
Laran	Ares	Mars
Men(e)rva	Athena	Minerva
Nethuns	Poseidon	Neptunus
Sethlans	Hephaistos	Vulcanus
Phersipnei	Persephone	Proserpina
Thesan	Eos	Aurora
Tin(ia)	Zeus	Jupiter
Turan	Aphrodite	Venus
Turms	Hermes	Mercurius
Uni	Hera	Juno
Usil	Helios	Sol

These are some of the more commonly mentioned gods, and included are some cosmic and underworld deities. Where there is a close Greek name one can assume that it is the origin of the Etruscan name (for example, Apollo/Apulu), and on the Roman side this may also be sometimes true (the origin of the name Menrva, for example, is usually thought to be Roman). More confusingly, although the gods of the tripartite list can be regarded as counterparts in the different cultures, they are by no means exact equivalents. This is not surprising as many Greek gods each have numerous different aspects and hence were given different titles or epithets; this is equally true of Etruscan gods, and one would hardly expect a precise match in each case.

But there are differences also in the quintessential characters and powers of the gods. Eos, goddess of the dawn and beloved of Homer and other poets, was not the object of cult-veneration in Greece, but her Etruscan counterpart Thesan had major temples dedicated to her (as at Pyrgi). Tinia, unlike Zeus, was not the only god capable of hurling lightning, there were others who could do this, such as Menrva (as seen on mirror engravings); and although Tinia could throw three different kinds of lightning, according to Seneca he had to consult with other major gods before issuing the two more destructive kinds; he does not always appear to be all-powerful, and unlike the mature, bearded Zeus, he is sometimes depicted as youthful and beardless. His consort Uni may be shown young too, as well as naked, unlike the matronly Hera, and famous inscriptions from Pyrgi equate her (rather than Turan) with the Near Eastern love-goddess, Astarte. In the Phoenician world, Astarte was the object of devotion in the form of sacred prostitution, and G. Colonna, excavator of the Pyrgi sanctuary, has very likely identified a row of small chambers on the site as the location where it was practised.

Roman sources insist that the most powerful Etruscan god was called Vertumnus (or Vortumnus). The relationship of this god to Tinia is often discussed; presumably they were one and the same. The name also has close similiarities with the female deity Voltumna, at whose sanctuary the 'twelve Etruscan peoples' regularly met. The sexual ambiguity of Vertumnus–Voltumna, which is confirmed by descriptions of this god by Roman poets, extends more generally to other deities. Many minor gods and even major ones such as Aritimi can be portrayed in art as of either sex. Deities may also be duplicated, and both major and minor gods may be shown twice or thrice in the same scene, sometimes bearing different epithets. In general it seems as if gender and number were relatively unimportant, and this may hark back to an early period when the gods were conceived as non-anthropomorphic powers and spirits.

4 Sanctuaries

One of the earliest structures within the urban site of Roselle is a sacred precinct of mud-brick enclosing a square building and, within that, a circular chamber. Of a similar period (seventh century) is the sacred building 'Beta' at Tarquinia (Bonghi Jovino and Chiaramonte Treré 1997), the site of the child burial already mentioned; this simple rectangular structure was divided into two rooms, one containing a large altar, where blood and drink offerings were diverted by a channel to a nearby natural cleft. Soon after completion this too was surrounded by a precinct wall, here of stone. Such early sanctuaries, set up in the heart of, or surrounded by, settlement areas and presumably at the behest of centralized authority, are one of several indications that urbanization was well underway in Etruria by the mid-seventh century.

Etruscan religion did not require monumental temples and cult statues. These arose in the sixth century, partly as a result of Greek influence. But the standard Vitruvian 'Tuscanic' temple has columns (usually wooden) only at the front, rather than an all-round colonnade, as had the Belvedere temple at Orvieto, for example (Figure 44.2); Etruscan sculpture, however, followed Greek conceptions of deities (especially of the 'Olympian' gods) quite closely. Of the cult requirements at the sanctuary what was of most importance was the demarcation of the sacred area by a precinct wall, and the altar, which from the sixth century was always open-air. The Portonaccio sanctuary outside the walls of Veii shows the kinds of structures that a large-scale sacred site could offer the worshipper (Figure 44.3). In addition to the temple (A) and altar (F) there was a sacred pool (B) fed by rock-cut water tunnels (*cuniculi*), and porticoed buildings (G, H) to house votive offerings. The rectangular structure (I) is now thought to be a shrine dedicated to Menrva. Modest shrines, often without roofs, seem to have been common. There were several at the Pyrgi sanctuary (Colonna 2006): one of them, divided into two chambers, was dedicated to the goddess Cavtha, most likely a solar goddess, and to Suri (who is equated with Aplu in

FIGURE 44.2 View of present remains of Belvedere temple, Orvieto, fifth century BC.

his underworld aspects), and there were also individual shrines here to these two gods. A large sanctuary such as Pyrgi could accommodate a plethora of gods: in addition to Cavtha and Suri, the two major temples were dedicated to Thesan and Uni-Astarte. At the Portonaccio sanctuary Aplu was clearly important as well as Menrva.

The identities of the gods in their sanctuaries are often made clear by votive offerings recovered, especially when these include inscriptions. At Pyrgi, Cavtha could be honoured with gold jewellery. More frequently found are objects of bronze, including major sculpture. The famous bronze Chimaera in Florence Archaeological Museum with a dedicatory inscription on its leg to Tinia suggests, from its finding place, that there was a sanctuary to the god at Arezzo. But many votives are small-scale and/or of inexpensive materials: little bronze or terracotta figurines of human or animal forms, and pottery which is sometimes in miniature format. Votives might be objects used in daily life or they could be made specially for the sanctuary ritual. To remove the objects from circulation and to show that they were for the gods' use alone they might be deliberately broken or 'killed'. Beneath the entrance of shrine 'Beta' at Tarquinia were found three votive bronzes: an axe head, a long musical horn and a round embossed shield both of which had been carefully folded and buckled.

Anatomical votives, usually of terracotta, are especially prevalent from the fourth century onwards (Turfa 1986), and it would appear that many if not most gods (e.g.

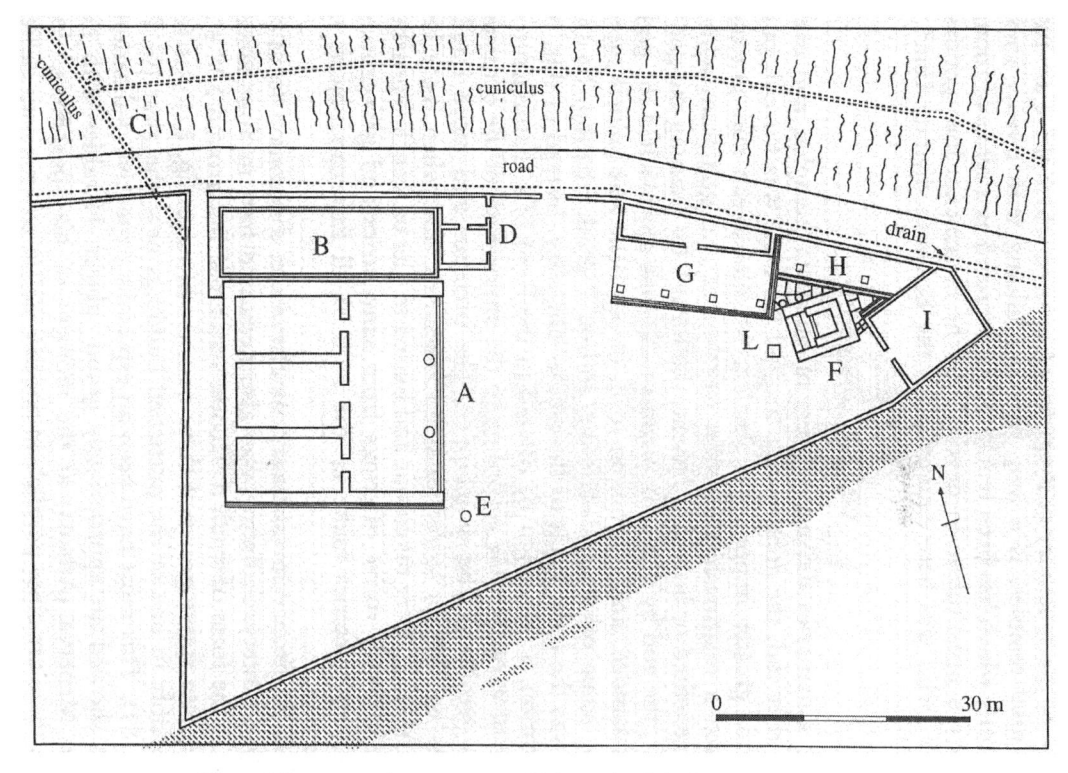

FIGURE 44.3 Plan of Portonaccio sanctuary, Veii, end of sixth century BC.

Artumes, Menrva) encompassed healing aspects. All manner of human body parts may be included: hands, feet, ears, eyes, breasts, intestines, genital organs. Like the Brontoscopic Calendar, they reveal much anxiety about health issues, but whether the dedications were made before or after healing is difficult to know. Models of swaddled babies are also common in these assemblages, and again one cannot be sure whether they signify a wish for the future or a successful outcome. It is probably no mere coincidence that production and dedication of anatomical terracottas in central Italy intensifies soon after the cult of the Greek healing god Asklepios was introduced in Rome in the early third century.

5 DEATH RITUAL AND THE AFTERLIFE

Considering the effort that was expended on the planning and construction of tombs and cemeteries, it is clear that provision for the dead was an important Etruscan concern. In southern Etruria, where cemeteries were excavated into the soft volcanic rock, the more elaborate tombs are of one or more chambers which were not only filled with grave goods of great variety but which also featured carved or painted decoration on their interior walls. The Etruscans believed in an afterlife but our knowledge about it is derived mainly from the imagery of the tombs and the artefacts found within them, also from the carved burial containers (sarcophagi, ash-urns) of stone and terracotta in which the dead were frequently buried.

Burial ritual, concerning such basic matters as cremation and inhumation, varied in different parts of the country and at different periods. But even where inhumation predominated cremation was sometimes reserved for individuals of high rank. A ritual meal seems to have been consumed, judging by tomb finds of pottery hearths containing carbonized food remains (Barbieri 1987: 166–7). Funeral games may also have been staged, and the sports depicted—chariot-racing, boxing, and so forth—on the walls of painted tombs may show them, or may be a (less costly) fictive substitute for the real thing.

The experiences that the dead needed to go through were no doubt fully described in the Book of the Dead (*Libri Acheruntici*) of the *Etrusca disciplina*. Many tombs are so well equipped with crockery and the utensils of daily life, or their painted or sculpted equivalents, that the final destination of the deceased might be thought to be the tomb itself. But the liminal transference to another world was visualized in terms of entry through a monumental doorway (Serra Ridgway 2000: 310), and beyond it the journey to reach the underworld is shown in different ways. Crossing the sea or a stretch of water is often envisaged and almost certainly explains the model terracotta boats found in early Iron Age tombs from the ninth century and later. But a journey overland on horseback or by horse-drawn wagon or chariot is also commonly depicted, and it would seem that both land and water had to be crossed.

The great door needed to be guarded and in one instance it is by a female demon, Vanth, carrying a key, but elsewhere she appears in many guises. Equally ubiquitous is Charu(n), who also is sometimes depicted as a plurality, and who wields a heavy mallet probably for knocking the bolts of the door into place. He clearly takes his name from Charon, the Greek ferryman of the dead; Charun too, despite his hideous facial features, is essentially harmless, his mallet rarely being used in anger but more simply symbolizing the finality of death. The Etruscans have a rich demonology (Herbig 1965), and the various personages that comprise it, female and male, are often marked out with the addition of wings. Despite their sometimes threatening appearance and attitudes the main function they perform seems to be to act as guides for the deceased, though the Vanths have a tendency to act and dress like Greek Furies, even taking part in the fighting in battle scenes.

The underworld itself is not represented until the fourth century BC and later, and how we assess the Etruscans' understanding of it is complicated by its depiction in Greek (Homeric) terms. The atmosphere and details, however, are quite un-Greek. So Aita/Hades wears a wolf-head cap, of local significance, and his consort Phersipnei/Persephone has snakes in her hair; long-dead Greek heroes may also be present but accompanied by demons. Greek monsters such as three-headed Cerberus may be in attendance but counter-balanced by Etruscan snake-legged beings. In these settings grand banquets take place, with members of the family taking part including the recently deceased and ancestors of the distant past. The mood may be sombre—painted tombs show dark infernal clouds hanging in the background—but the food is sumptuous. The essential message here is one of reunion and the strength of the family—precisely what is highlighted later in Roman funerary art.

Early Etruscan funerary scenes of banqueting, celebration, music, and dancing contain few overt references to the underworld; but the standard mode of representing the dead on their sarcophagi and ash-urns is as banqueters reclining on their couches, and frequently there is a depiction in the tomb of the door to the underworld. This is not strictly a door of no return. It may be opened to allow previous generations of the deceased to exit the underworld to greet those who have recently died as they are guided towards it. Logically that meeting place ought to be the tomb chamber itself, and hence the tomb might be thought of as being inhabited from time to time, which may also help to explain why banqueting vessels are placed there in such abundance. Just as the votive dedications at sanctuaries were for the gods' sole use so the goods deposited in tombs were for the dead alone to enjoy; consequently the reflecting surfaces of bronze mirrors or the bodies of amphorae might have *suthina* ('for the tomb') scratched on them in large letters (de Grummond 2009).

Given the emphasis placed on the importance of the family, it should be of little surprise that there is considerable evidence of ancestor worship in Etruria. Altars and shrines were frequently set up adjacent to tombs, especially to the larger tumuli, and there are examples at Cortona, San Giuliano, and Vulci. At the latter site and at Grotta Porcina there are stepped theatral areas for performances in honour of the tomb occupants, while at Cerveteri one chamber of a tomb featured a row of rock-cut chairs occupied by terracotta statuettes, presumably representations of ancestors, seated in front of stone tables as if at a perpetual banquet. This is an early tomb (seventh century), of an era before the reclining banqueting pose was adopted in the early sixth century.

It is difficult to construct a single narrative of death and the afterlife that would satisfactorily account for all the material remains and iconographic details of the Etruscan burial sites, and it may be mistaken to try to do so. Beliefs and ideas about such a momentous, and also personal, subject are invariably fluid, and during the many centuries of Etruscan civilization older and newer ideas were likely to form a multilayered amalgam. To attempt to explain the later iconography of a demon-inhabited underworld, modern commentators have frequently resorted to interpretations in terms of the Greek mystery cults of Orpheus, Dionysus, and Demeter. Of these figures the most important in Etruria was Dionysus (Etruscan Fufluns), but more as god of revelling than of mysteries, while his satyr followers were thought also to have prophetic powers. The Greek mystery religions separated initiates from the ignorant and promised them a better afterlife: they alone would know the correct path to follow to the underworld and would also avoid tortures and punishments that might await those who were not in the god's favour. But the idea of a journey that the deceased must undertake is a very old one in Etruria; nor is there any division of the saved and the damned in Etruscan funerary imagery, and the only punishments in evidence are reserved for figures of Greek mythology.

6 FATE AND THE ETRUSCAN NATION

Just as the span of each person's life was determined by the gods, so—and this is a peculiarly Etruscan notion—was the length of time that the nation itself was permitted to survive (Barker and Rasmussen 1998: 93). The sources here are again Roman, though clearly going back to Etruscan texts, and many details remain obscure. The nation (Latin *nomen etruscum*) had ten Great Generations (*saecula*) allotted to it, and the duration of each was determined according to the longest lifespan of any individual within it. The longest one recorded is 123 years, and some actual dates are given for some of the later ones; from which we can calculate that the whole Etruscan enterprise lasted from the tenth century to some time after the murder of Julius Caesar in 44 BC—which in archaeological and historical terms happens to make not unreasonable sense. Two issues complicate the matter: first, individual cities may have had their own schema of saecula; secondly, the collation of data seems to have been recorded late in Etruscan history. In fact the duration of the first four saecula gives every indication of having been invented long after the event, each one lasting exactly 100 years. Nevertheless, as inexorably in the later centuries the Etruscans succumbed to Roman power and culture, the conviction that their days were numbered according to cosmic laws must inevitably have coloured their view of the whole process in a fatalistic way.

7 Conclusions and Future Prospects

The old way of relying heavily on Roman and Greek sources and using them as the sole point of departure, even when they have no connection with Etruscan texts, is increasingly giving way to a more archaeological approach. Much progress has been made in recent years by confronting the material remains and the imagery head-on with minimal recourse to explanations via external influences. Etruscan religion is not Greek religion or Roman religion in modified form, and can and should be explained on its own terms and without all the Greek and Roman terminology that is often used. Moreover, although the Etruscans were very interested in Greek mythology, there does exist a real Etruscan mythology which can, but only with much patient observation, be extricated from it. Future progress is also very likely to be moulded by new discoveries. For example, two of the most recent finds of painted tombs, at Tarquinia (Tomb of the Blue Demons) and at Sarteano near Chiusi, made in 1985 and 2003 respectively, have provided vital new information about the underworld journey (Steingräber 2006: 163–82, 215–20); while the third-longest Etruscan inscription, a bronze tablet from Cortona which had been folded and ritually put out of use, was discovered in 1992 and published in 1999. The study of Etruscan cult and religion has, therefore, a constantly shifting dynamic.

Further Reading

A number of key studies have appeared in the last few years. Jannot (2005) is a good introduction to the whole area. De Grummond and Simon (2006) is multi-authored, and includes a history of scholarship as well as a presentation of relevant ancient texts both in the original language (Greek, Latin) and in translation. De Grummond (2006) assesses the evidence for Etruscan mythology from iconographic sources, and some of this ground is also surveyed in Bonfante and Swaddling (2006); while various aspects of ritual are discussed in Gleba and Becker (2009). For continental scholarship there is the wide-ranging series of papers in Gaultier and Briquel (1997). Finally, for discussion and exegesis of many pertinent inscriptions see Bonfante and Bonfante (2002).

REFERENCES

Barbieri, G. (ed.) 1987. *L'alimentazione nel mondo antico: gli etruschi* (Rome: Istituto Poligrafico e Zecca dello Stato).

Barker, G. and Rasmussen, T. 1998. *The Etruscans* (Oxford: Blackwell).

Bonfante, G. and Bonfante, L. 2002. *The Etruscan Language: An Introduction*, 2nd edn (Manchester: Manchester University Press).

Bonfante, L. and Swaddling, J. 2006. *Etruscan Myths* (London: British Museum Press).

Bonghi Jovino, M. and Chiaramonte Treré, C. 1997. *Tarquinia: testimonianze archeologiche e ricostruzione storica: scavi sistematici nell'abitato: campagne 1982–1988 (Tarchna 1)* (Rome: 'L'Erma' di Bretschneider).

Colonna, G. (ed.) 1985. *Santuari d'Etruria* (Milan: Electa).

——(ed.) 2006. 'Sacred architecture and the religion of the Etruscans' in N. T. De Grummond and E. Simon (eds.), *The Religion of the Etruscans* (Austin, TX: University of Texas Press), pp. 134–68.

Gaultier, F. and Briquel, D. (eds) 1997. *Les Étrusques, les plus religieux des hommes* (Paris: La documentation française).

Gleba, M. and Becker, H. (eds) 2009. *Votives, Places and Rituals in Etruscan Religion. Studies in honour of Jean MacIntosh Turfa* (Leiden: Brill).

Grummond, N. T. de 2000. 'Mirrors and manteia: themes of prophesy on Etruscan mirrors' in M. D. Gentili (ed.), *Aspetti e problemi della produzione degli specchi figurati etruschi* (Rome: Aracne), pp. 27–67.

——2006. *Etruscan Myth, Sacred History, and Legend* (Philadelphia: University of Pennsylvania Press).

——2009. 'On mutilated mirrors' in M. Gleba and H. Becker (eds), *Votives, Places and Rituals in Etruscan Religion: Studies in honour of Jean MacIntosh Turfa* (Leiden: Brill), pp. 171–82.

——and Simon, E. (eds) 2006. *The Religion of the Etruscans* (Austin, TX: University of Texas Press).

Herbig, R. 1965. *Götter und Dämonen der Etrusker* (Mainz: Philipp von Zabern).

Jannot, J.-R. 2005. *Religion in Ancient Etruria* (Madison: University of Wisconsin Press).

Meer, L. B. van der 1987. *The Bronze Liver of Piacenza* (Amsterdam: J. C. Gieben).

Pfiffig, A. J. 1975. *Religio etrusca* (Graz: Akademische Druck).

Rasmussen, T. 2005. 'Urbanization in Etruria' in R. Osborne and B. Cunliffe (eds), *Mediterranean Urbanization* (Oxford: Oxford University Press), pp. 71–90.

Richardson, J. H. 2008. 'A note on the myth of Tages', *BABESCH*, 83: 107–9.

Rix, H. 1991. *Etruskische Texte*, I–II (Tübingen: Gunter Narr Verlag).

Ross Taylor, L. 1923. *Local Cults in Etruria* (Rome: American Academy in Rome).

Serra Ridgway, F. R. 2000. 'The tomb of the Anina family. Some motifs in late Tarquinian painting' in D. Ridgway et al. (eds) *Ancient Italy in its Mediterranean Setting: Studies in honour of Ellen Macnamara* (London: Accordia Research Institute), pp. 301–16.

Steingräber, S. 2006. *Abundance of Life: Etruscan wall painting* (Los Angeles: J. Paul Getty Museum).

Turfa, J. M. 1986. 'Anatomical votive terracottas from Etruscan and Italic sanctuaries' in J. Swaddling (ed.), *Italian Iron Age Artefacts in the British Museum* (London: British Museum Publications), pp. 205–13.

——2006. 'The Etruscan brontoscopic calendar' in N. T. De Grummond and E. Simon (eds), *The Religion of the Etruscans* (Austin, TX: University of Texas Press), pp. 173–90.

CHAPTER 45

EGYPT

ANNA STEVENS

1 Introduction: The Egyptians and their World

THE first traces of ancient Egyptian culture emerged in the Nile Valley towards the end of the fourth millennium BC. These developed into a civilization that was to remain intact for over 3,000 years (Table 45.1) until eventually obscured by infusions of Hellenistic Greek culture, Christianity, and the effects of the Arab conquest of Egypt in AD 641. In part, this longevity of cultural cohesion can be attributed to the effectiveness of Egypt's ritual framework (cf. Shafer in Shafer 1997: 21).

Most people today are broadly familiar with ancient Egypt, or at least with certain royal figures and monuments: Tutankhamun, Cleopatra, the Giza pyramids. For most Egyptians such individuals and institutions were peripheral to their experiences. Life was acted out in a small mud-brick house in a rural village or in the more urbanized environment of a city, and was heavily tied to the land. Many people died young, after leading difficult lives (Baines 1991: 135–7). Social position was closely connected with occupation, and the small upper strata of society were dominated by high officials, whose working lives were centred upon supporting the king in his role as the administrative, religious, and military head of the land (Silverman 1995).

The Egyptian conception of their universe was complex, and to some extent changeable, but was in a basic sense tripartite, comprising the heavens, earth, and the underworld (Allen 2003). Humans shared the universe with several other orders of being, amongst whom the gods, the dead, and a group known as *akhu* were especially prominent. They occupied a continuum of existence, and a degree of transformation between orders was possible (Lloyd 1989: 121–2); the desire after death for the average person was to become an *akh*, or transfigured dead at one with the gods of the afterlife. Communication between humans and divine beings was crucial because the relationships between them were those of mutual dependence. Divinities had the power to manipulate the affairs of the living in both a positive and negative way, but at the same time had a need for sustenance. Through ritual action and words of power, known as *heka*, humans could influence divinities and also their own situation within the cosmos (Lloyd 1989: 122). The king had a distinct role as

Table 45.1 Chronological List of the Ancient Egyptian Periods: Scholars deal with the great depth of time encompassed by ancient Egyptian history by dividing it into a series of dynasties, following the writings of the third-century-BC priest Manetho, and grouping these according to several broad periods. (After Shaw 2000: 479–83 and Kemp 2006: 14)

Predynastic period (c.5300–3000 BC)
Early Dynastic period (c.3000–2686 BC), Dynasties 1–2
Old Kingdom (2686–2160 BC), Dynasties 3–8
First Intermediate period (2160–2055 BC), Dynasties 9–mid-11
Middle Kingdom (2055–1650 BC), Dynasties mid-11–13/14
Second Intermediate period (1650–1550 BC), Dynasties 15–17
New Kingdom (1550–1069 BC), Dynasties 18–20
Third Intermediate period (1069–664 BC), Dynasties 21–25
Late period (664–332 BC), Dynasties 26–30, including 1st Persian period (Dynasty 27) and 2nd Persian period (Dynasty '31')
Ptolemaic period (332–30 BC)
Roman period (30 BCE–395 AD)
Egypt ruled by Byzantium (395–641 AD)
Arab conquest of Egypt (641 AD)

intermediary between the gods and humankind and could himself possess divine attributes, although his divinity was not static and did not obscure his mortal origins (Silverman 1991: 58–87; 1995).

A mythological framework helped to explain the universe, in which six key chronological events can be recognized (Pinch 2004): pre-creation, in which the universe was in a state of chaos; the formation of the world and its inhabitants, often conceptualized as taking place on a mound of earth that rose from the primeval waters; the reign of the sun god; a period of direct rule by other deities; rule by semi-divine kings (history); and the return to chaos. Preventing the latter required the upkeep of *maat*, or cosmic and universal order (Hornung 1992: 131–45; Teeter 1997). This was achieved largely by keeping the gods satisfied, primarily by tending and making offerings to them via their cult statues housed in temples (Figure 45.1). Because the Egyptians held two conceptions of time, linear time and cyclical time, creation happened both once in the distant past but also every morning with the rising of the sun (Hornung 1992: 49). The world was in a continual, but necessary, state of tension between the forces of order and chaos.

The pervasive image of ancient Egyptian religion is one shaped by temples and tombs, in which upholding *maat* and attaining and maintaining an afterlife were predominant concerns. The centrality of ritual, especially exchange-based forms of communication, can be stressed. Temple cult, in particular, was one of ritual obligation. As Meskell (2004: 69) notes, 'the words "image" and "cult" point to the very heart of Egyptian religion'. If we want to paint a picture of Egyptian religion in broad brush-strokes, this is a reasonable view, although it is a perspective acquired largely from formal contexts and based on religion conceived with a view to perpetuity. It is also unclear how relevant it is for the

FIGURE 45.1 Alternative means of creating sacred space. At the top, a view of the Temple of Hathor at Dendera, dating largely to the Ptolemaic period. Many of the devices used to set ritual apart from the mundane are best expressed in temple architecture, particularly the use of myth and dualism—open and closed, solar and chthonic, hidden and revealed. Progression through the temple complex brought a transition from open courts into enclosed spaces as the floor level simultaneously rose and the roof level lowered. In this way the sanctuary, positioned at the furthest end of the temple, recalled the mythical 'mound of creation'. Below is a hypothetical reconstruction of the Early Dynastic landscape at the site of Coptos. Excavation in 1894 revealed fragments of colossal limestone figures of the god Min, carved probably just before Dynasty 1. Drawing on evidence for the use of 'standing stones' at other sacred sites, of this and later periods, Kemp (2006: 129; also Kemp, Boyce, and Harrell 2000) reconstructs the colossi as an '[a]rc of guardian figures surrounding a central feature of interest', the latter shown as a mound (which was revealed during excavation) with a simple hut shrine (of which no trace has been found).

earliest phases of Egyptian history when the source material is limited (to such an extent that the possibility of an aniconic tradition cannot be ruled out [Kemp 2006: 118]).

Within Egyptology, ritual is usually viewed as a part of religion; it is certainly most visible now within the context of formal religion. Ascertaining how far ritual existed exclusive of religion depends in part on how we define these realms (cf. Bell 1997: 94). Many ancient

Egyptian rituals had a clear mythological or cosmological explanation. Others, in lacking this, can be considered chiefly social rites, although they often involved recourse to magic or medical spells, or the intercession of divinities and spirits whose remit was everyday concerns. Although not the focus of the discussion here, a very broad definition of ritual might also find much in Egyptian society to classify as secular rites, particularly in the context of reinforcing status or event. Sources such as elite tomb scenes convey a world in which social distinctions were marked and important, and in which there was a well-developed 'sense of occasion', aspects that could be reinforced by the selection of costume, insignia and posture. It is not clear how strongly performance-based these selection processes were, but as strategies for differentiation they take at least a step towards 'ritualization' (Bell 1992).

2 Sources for the Study of Ritual and Religion

Research into Egyptian religion and ritual is driven largely by textual sources, which tend to be richest from the New Kingdom onwards. Funerary texts, largely spells designed to assist the deceased in their transition to the afterlife, are one important source, with a continuous history of copying, editing, and fresh composition starting in the Fifth Dynasty. Since the word, both written and spoken, was considered efficacious in this world and the next, these texts were themselves ritual tools. Many magico-medical spells intended for everyday use also survive (e.g. Borghouts 1978). In part, these outline the practice of religion, and so provide a fruitful context for interaction with archaeology (e.g. Szpakowska 2003). They also draw attention to ephemeral items used in religion that are rarely recognizable archaeologically, some so elaborate and unusual that we might doubt whether they ever existed other than in the imagination. Otherwise, written sources extend to such genres as mythological texts, hymns, offering formulae and prayers, 'instruction' literature, biographical texts, so-called Dream Books and Calendars of Lucky and Unlucky Days, and occasionally private letters (e.g. Assmann 1999; McDowell 1999: 91–126; 2001; Baines 2002). In seeking to elucidate belief frameworks from these, Egyptologists need to deal with the fact that the Egyptians were more accepting of multiple truths than later societies and did not always require a linear or a written narrative. There were several different versions of the creation myth, for instance (Hornung 1992: 39–54). In a similar fashion, images and substances were often rich in symbolism, usually multivalent (Wilkinson 1992, 1994).

Iconographic evidence takes the form largely of tomb and temple decoration, and the scenes on ritual objects such as stelae. As with the word, the image was considered efficacious (Hornung 1992: 34), and the two often functioned as one. By far the most common ritual scene, that of offerings being made to the gods or the deceased, showed that religious obligations were being perpetually fulfilled, whilst scenes on temple walls could be intimately connected with the rituals conducted nearby (Arnold 1962; David 1981). Occasionally images of divinities shown in wall reliefs themselves served as cult images, either by design or public appropriation, particularly those on temple walls and gateways (Teeter

FIGURE 45.2 A small sample of ritual objects, sourced from New Kingdom sites but broadly representative of material found in other periods. Bottom left: limestone stela of a priest named Yamen originally set up in a small shrine beside the elite burial of Maya and Meryt at Saqqara. Yamen, wearing panther-skin robes, offers liquid libations and incense to Osiris and to the deceased couple using purpose-made vessels, whilst offerings are piled on portable stands (after Raven 2001: pl. 28). Bottom right: a scene from the tomb of the official Horemheb showing the rite of 'breaking of the red pots' (after Martin 1989, pl. 123). The remaining material is from the site of Amarna: a group of pottery figures of foreigners found in the Central City, possibly the remnants of execration rites (obj. 33/34; after Pendlebury 1951, pl. LXXVIII.3), pieces of amuletic jewellery in the form of the domestic deity Bes, an anthropoid bust probably connected with ancestor worship, a crocodile, and the sacred *wedjat*-eye (obj. 30/784, 34801, 34128; the crocodile design is from an unnumbered mould), and a portable limestone offering table (obj. 37678).

1997: 4–5; Brand 2007). These are a good illustration of how iconography can bridge the gap between text and archaeology.

The Egyptians also used a rich and varied material framework to support their religious beliefs and practices (Figure 45.2). Archaeology makes a great deal of this accessible, although variably so. Generally material from funerary and temple contexts is more accessible than that from settlements. The latter, traditionally situated along the alluvial flood plain, have suffered particularly from environmental degradation connected with the annual flooding of the Nile, and from overbuilding. More specific trends are the predominance of mortuary monuments amongst exposed pre-New Kingdom ritual architecture, and the near absence for all periods of surviving settlements that were not regional towns.

Archaeologists also have to deal with the reality that excavation in Egypt began as treasure hunting. Early-nineteenth-century antiquarians were attracted especially to temples and elite cemeteries in their search for museum-quality objects, which set the tone for much work to follow. Towards the end of the nineteenth century, an interest began to emerge in the use of material culture to reconstruct everyday life, and attention turned slowly to settlement sites and non-elite cemeteries. These expeditions were often successful in producing a record of sites that have now suffered looting or been lost to urban growth and agriculture. Unfortunately, given the often cursory recording standards of the day and how large-scale excavations commonly were (Shaw 1999), the legacy is a number of important sites that are now largely 'worked over' and a mass of objects with limited context, often dispersed to public and private collections worldwide. Moves to make public collections accessible via online databases (e.g. MacDonald, McKeown, and Quirke 2000) are an important development.

Today, cemetery- and temple-based research is still prominent, but fieldwork in Egypt covers a wider range of themes and approaches. Current priorities include the production of a fuller record of the archaeology of the Delta; exploration of the desert landscapes and oases; and the filling-in of gaps in the record of settlements, temples and shrines. At the same time, the development of a scholarly tradition that uses material culture as the basis for studying Egyptian religion and ritual, and draws its inspiration as much from modern and pre-historical material-cultures studies as it does from ancient texts, is still very much in its infancy.

3 RITUAL GENRES

The remainder of this chapter takes three ritual genres that are particularly well expressed in archaeological material—rites of exchange and communion, rites of affliction, and rites of passage—as a means of conveying further the character of the source material and some prominent directions of research. These by no means cover the full set of known Egyptian rituals, which is extensive, and extends to calendrical and commemorative rites, rites of feasting and festivals, and political rites: the full spectrum of genres, with the exception of rites of fasting, that are typical of clearly defined religious traditions (Bell 1997: 93–137). All were important in the Egyptian context, and can be in part recovered archaeologically. As is often the case, there was considerable blurring of boundaries between ritual genres: offering rites are common to all genres, for example, rites of affliction frequently accompany rites of passage, and many mortuary rituals associated with the transition to the afterlife seem to have paralleled aspects of birth and childhood, and rituals undertaken at these times (Roth 1992; 1993; Roth and Roehrig 2002).

3.1 Rites of Exchange and Communion

Making offerings was the fundamental ritual action, common to temple, mortuary, and domestic settings. Offerings were usually consumables and other perishables—liquid libations were particularly popular and incense indispensable—but could also take the form of more robust items, as already noted.

3.1.1 Formal Exchange at Temples

Temple cult had as its central ritual the daily offering to the cult image. The focus of the rite was the clothing of the statue and presentation to it of food, wine, and beer, accompanied by symbolic gestures and words (Fairman 1954: 178–81; David 1981). The offerings were sourced mainly from temple-owned agricultural land and related resources. In a practice known as the 'reversion of offerings', attested for most of Egyptian history, the goods offered could be redistributed to the public (Haring 1997)—clearly a key to the effectiveness of Egyptian ritual structure. Priests and temple staff claimed priority in receiving reversion offerings, to the extent that these could amount to a salary. Others could access them by making donations to the temple, especially of land and produce (e.g. Morkot 1990), although quite how far these benefits spread into the broader community is unclear.

One site where an attempt has been made to match this practice with the archaeological record is Amarna (Kemp 1994; 1995: 33–4; also Kemp and Garfi 1993: 50–65; see Figure 45.3). This is the location of the ancient city of Akhetaten, which served briefly as Egypt's capital in the late second millennium BC. The city's founder, king Akhenaten, is remembered for his 'heretic' attempts to promote his own divinity and the cult of a single solar deity, the Aten, above all others (Hornung 1999). For archaeologists Amarna provides by far the largest exposure of ancient settlement anywhere in Egypt, offering something close to a true 'cityscape' that includes much of the original urban setting of its temples. The largest ritual arena was the Great Aten Temple, which now survives in a denuded state. The temple enclosure was enormous, and contained around 1,820 offering tables (Kemp 1995: 33), a striking illustration of the tendency in Egyptian religion towards redundancy. Scenes in officials' tombs show these tables heaped with offerings, especially joints of meat, bread, incense, and plants. On the ground, state-run bakeries and spaces for the storage of wine and meat production can be identified not far from the temple. In part, these probably stocked Akhetaten's temples, pointing to major state involvement in this practice. They may also have supplied the main royal palace, located nearby, reflecting the overlapping roles of palace and temple in ancient Egypt (Kemp 1994, 1995: 34). We can make an informed guess that goods sent to the temple were eventually distributed amongst the city's occupants, perhaps after being laid out on the offering tables (Kemp 1995: 33–4). Much more work is needed on how the goods circulated around the city, which may be especially viable through the study of faunal evidence, generally an underutilized source in the study of religion (see Payne 2006, 2007 and Legge 2010 for preliminary work).

The Great Aten Temple demonstrates another aspect of temple offering: scope for donation by the elite of items such as statues and furnishings, probably the origin of a set of metal vessels found beneath the sanctuary floor (Pendlebury 1951: 10, 12, 188–9, pl. LX.5–

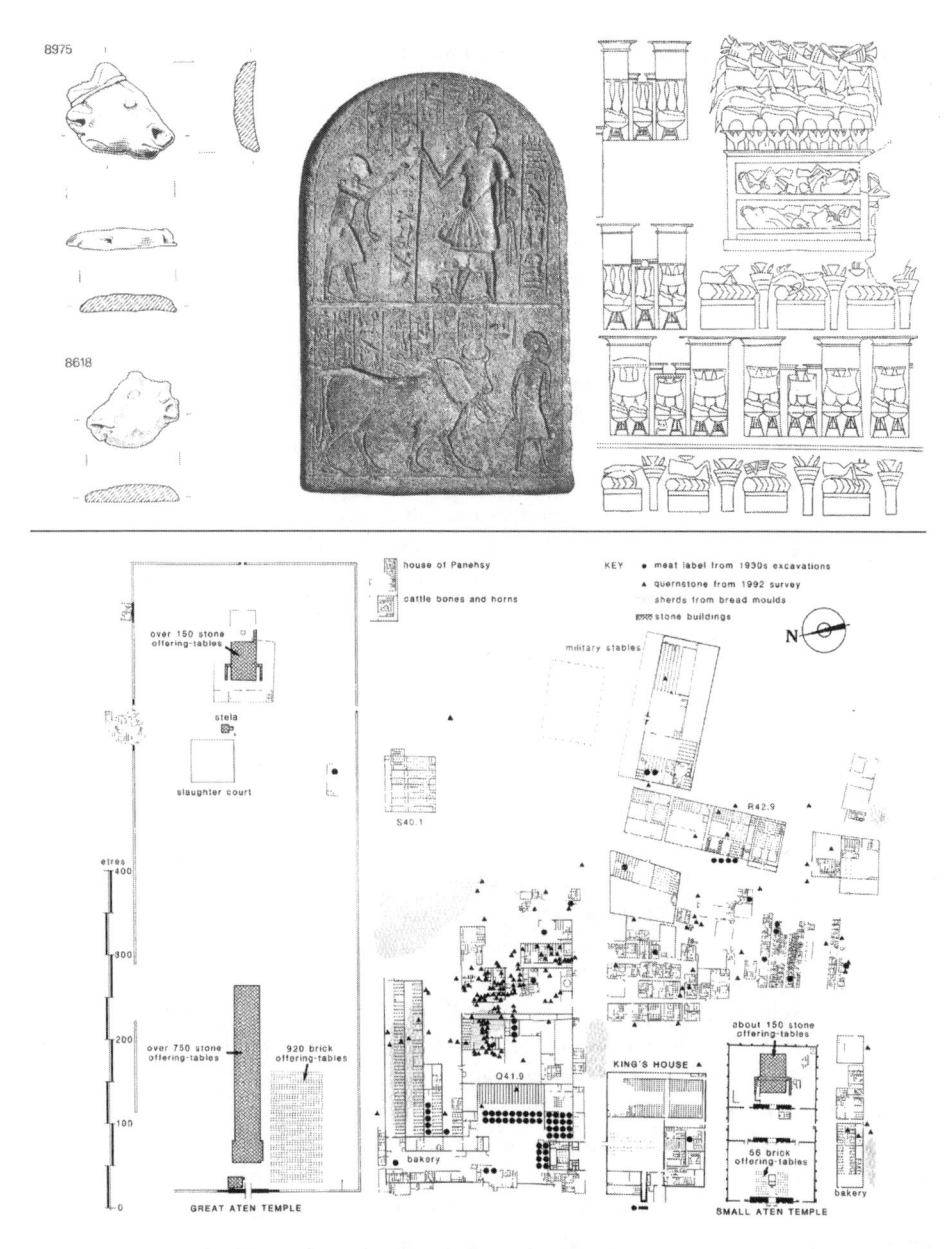

FIGURE 45.3 Anticlockwise from bottom: plan of the Great Aten Temple at Amarna and adjacent areas for food production and storage (after Kemp 1994: fig. 14.4); a scene from the Amarna tomb of the official Meryra showing offering tables in the temple piled with food and incense (after Davies 1903, pl. XXVIII); a stela donated at the tomb of the official Any showing the presentation of an ox in the context of his mortuary cult (after Davies 1908, pl. XXI); and small faience plaques in the shape of bovine heads of a type commonly found amongst houses, perhaps used in offering rites (after Boyce 1995, fig. 2.23).

8, fig. 25; Kemp 1995: 35, fig. 2). A further mode of contact—the provision of private mortuary cults—might be documented in a small stela donated at the Amarna tomb of the official Any. The stela shows the donor, a scribe called Nebwawi, leading an ox that has been fattened-up for offering, whilst brief inscriptions mention the king's involvement in preparing Any's burial (Davies 1908: 10, pl. XXI; Corteggiani 1987: 108–9). One viable interpretation of the scene is that it shows Nebwawi presenting the ox at the Great Aten Temple or a similar institution. This is one potential context in which the tomb scenes of temple offerings, the offering spaces attested archaeologically at the temples, and the realities of religious conduct overlapped. People may have acquired specially fattened cattle, from private supplies (for which see Kemp 1994: 143–5) or a centralized stock, and have them slaughtered in the presence of, and so offered to, the Aten in order that the king granted an associate an afterlife. Some of the meat could have been redistributed to the tomb or in household shrines as offerings. In this way, concerns regarding the dead may have bridged the gap between state and popular interests at Akhetaten, often held to have been in conflict. Sites such as Amarna also offer the chance to write archaeologies of religion that are integrated contextually, and so move beyond the tendency towards subdivision (state religion, private religion, funerary religion, etc.) that underlies much writing on past religion.

3.1.2 Votive Offerings

Whilst layers of reciprocal obligation appear to have accompanied much formal donation to temples, something closer to spontaneous engagement seems to underlie the practice of votive offering at temples and shrines that occurs sporadically across Egyptian history (Kemp 1995: 36). Surviving deposits of votives offer an approach to the personal concerns that drove religious conduct and to the changing role of temples as outlets for public cult. As a general trend, the deposits seem to reflect an increase in such behaviour over time, but it is important not to stress too linear a development here. The deposits, and the periods in which they are absent, are difficult to position in a single cohesive narrative.

The earliest substantial deposits date from the Early Dynastic period into the Old Kingdom, and are a particularly important source on the role of the temple at this time. A model in which the early votives reflect largely elite contact with temples is usually thought to best fit the cultural milieu of the time (Baines 1991: 173). The site of Elephantine in Egypt's south offers a well-recorded set (Dreyer 1986), but there are many others (Wilkinson 2001: 269–72, 306–20; Kemp 2006: 112–35). The composition of the deposits varies. Often they comprise groups of small figurines and models, but some include obviously high-status ceremonial and ritual items such as palettes and mace heads. A long tradition of enquiry accompanies these items, which are also known beyond temple caches, particularly as sources for the emergence of the Egyptian state, and the role of ritual therein (e.g. Petrie 1953; Wengrow 2001).

After a considerable hiatus, the next peak in votive offerings occurs during the Eighteenth Dynasty. Whilst there are few excavated shrines of the intervening period, and votive material is not unheard of at these (Pudleiner 2001), the Eighteenth Dynasty deposits do seem to represent a genuine increase in the practice, although some see the donors still as a small and largely elite group (Baines 1991: 180). The deposits appear especially at shrines and temples to the goddess Hathor and related deities, where they seem often to have been donated to address concerns relating to female fertility (Pinch 1993), but are also known elsewhere, such as the provincial shrine to the jackal god Wepwawet at Asyut (Munro 1962). A favoured offering at the Asyut shrine was stelae that range greatly in scale and quality, some being little more than small, possibly undecorated, plaques. A much greater variety of offerings appears at Hathor shrines, but again showing a range in quality, to include inscribed statues, decorated textiles, amulets and pieces of jewellery, figurines, unworked pebbles, and many other items (Baines 1991: 180–3; Pinch 1993; Kemp 1995: 27–9).

Votive offering on a mass scale appears again in the archaeological record from the Third Intermediate period, proliferating in the Late period onwards. Bronze vessels and statuettes, usually of divinities and animal manifestations thereof, were donated in large numbers at shrines across Egypt (Roeder 1937; Hill 2001). The god Osiris was particularly popular, and inscriptions indicate that the donations were often propelled by concerns for eternal life. Most votive bronzes were discovered as caches in the early days of Egyptian archaeology and recorded only briefly before being dispersed to museum collections. Most caches are difficult to interpret, therefore, as cohesive assemblages. Fortunately, they have also been uncovered during more recent controlled excavations, including at the Sacred Animal Necropolis at Saqqara (Nicholson and Smith 1996).

The bronzes overlap broadly with the appearance of such necropolises, where thousands of animal mummies have been excavated in cemeteries and subterranean catacombs (Kessler 1986, 1989, 1998; Ikram 2005). They, and the bronzes, belong in the context of a growth in the attribution of oracular powers to divine animals, and concurrently of such practices as incubation and dream interpretation to communicate with divinities. There is considerable divergence of scholarly opinion on the origin of the animal mummies, however. A common view is that they were originally donated by the public at shrines for deities to whom the animals were often sacred, and subsequently cached in necropolises (Ikram 2005). An alternative theory holds that the practice often represents the burial of animals who died within temple precincts, often sacred animals that had lived in the temple and were used within temple rituals and ceremonies (advocated especially by Kessler 1989; Kessler and Nur el-Din 2005).

3.1.3 Approaching Domestic Offering Rites

In domestic contexts, rites of exchange and communion are best attested not in offerings themselves but in installations and objects that facilitated such rites. Most of the material comes from houses of the New Kingdom and later, which have been the most thoroughly investigated. But it is likely that these rites were occurring in domestic contexts prior to this time, to judge from finds of portable spouted offering tables and trays, and offering stands within earlier houses (Petrie 1891: 11, pl. VI; Adams 1998; Smith 2003: 128–9; Szpakowska 2008: 133–6). Images at least of 'domestic' divinities and perhaps the house owner (as living person or as deceased) were probably being erected as focal points of veneration (e.g. Mace 1921; Arnold 1996).

Domestic altars proper, best known from the New Kingdom, often took the form of an elevated mud-brick platform with a projecting set of stairs or ramp, although others were simple nondescript pedestals; domestic ritual did not always use displays of grandeur to create otherness. At some sites, stone slabs set into the floors might have been designed to receive liquid libations (Spence 2007). A very rare instance where evidence of cult has been found in connection with a domestic altar occurs at Askut, an Egyptian fortress in Nubia (Smith 1993; 1995; 2003). Here, a small mud-brick altar was constructed around the beginning of the New Kingdom in the courtyard of a private house. It took the form of a low mud-brick platform fronting a niche with modelled cornice (Figure 45.4). When excavated, the niche still contained a limestone stela—a fairly standard Egyptian stela on which the partially legible text comprised largely an offering formula to a man named Meryka, shown seated and receiving offerings. The platform of the altar sloped down to a pottery drain positioned above a series of buried pots. The altar was clearly designed to receive and drain liquid libations, perhaps the cause of some of the wear to its surface. Holes in the platform suggest it incorporated a wooden canopy or similar to enclose the stela niche. The courtyard location of the altar may have drawn attention to it in a semi-public domain, and perhaps taken advantage of people entering and leaving the house to draw the cult into personal routines. It is very rare, in fact, that a space seems to have been set aside exclusively for cult in the home, which we might read as a sign of its embeddedness within domestic life—although we cannot be certain of this.

Smith (2003: 133) contrasts the Askut altar with what seems to be an earlier shrine at the same site, which took the simpler form of a rectangular niche set into a wall above a low bench. He observes that the elaboration of the later shrine may represent a growth in 'personal piety' at Askut. The development of this aspect of religion, usually understood as direct contact with gods and personal experience of them (Baines 1991: 173), has been a prominent theme of Egyptological research, spawned mostly by New Kingdom texts in which it is more immediately apparent than in earlier sources (Baines 1991: 172–86; Assmann 1999). We might also ask whether the Askut shrine reflects growing ritualization of domestic religion, or more specifically increasing formalization of rites of exchange and communion in a domestic setting—which may have gone hand in hand with an intensification of personal closeness to divinities.

3.2 Rites of Affliction

Rites of affliction are strongly attested in the Egyptian context, particularly in magico-medical spells that address such concerns as protection against harmful animals, disease and illness (often given an otherworldly source), deceased persons, and the evil eye. Treatment usually required a combination of words, carefully selected objects or ingredients, and actions and gestures that could include burial, burning, breaking, making loud noises, encircling, sealing, and knot-tying (Ritner 1993; Pinch 2006: 76–89; Wendrich 2006). Often these actions were intended to contain or destroy hostile forces, but their purpose was heavily context-dependent.

Communities included individuals skilled in treating affliction by magico-medical means, who were often attached to temples (Gardiner 1917; Baines 1987: 93–4; Quack 2002; Pinch 2006: 47–60). Such figures and their actions are documented almost exclusively in textual sources. An 1896 excavation of a Thirteenth Dynasty tomb at Thebes, however, revealed what seems to be the toolkit of a 'chief of mysteries' (Quibell 1898: 3–4, pl. 3; Bourriau 1988: 110–27), whilst a study of female figurines from the Temple of Mut at Luxor has concluded that they were the remnants of healing rituals conducted by temple personnel on behalf of the public (Waraksa 2007). An important role of archaeology in

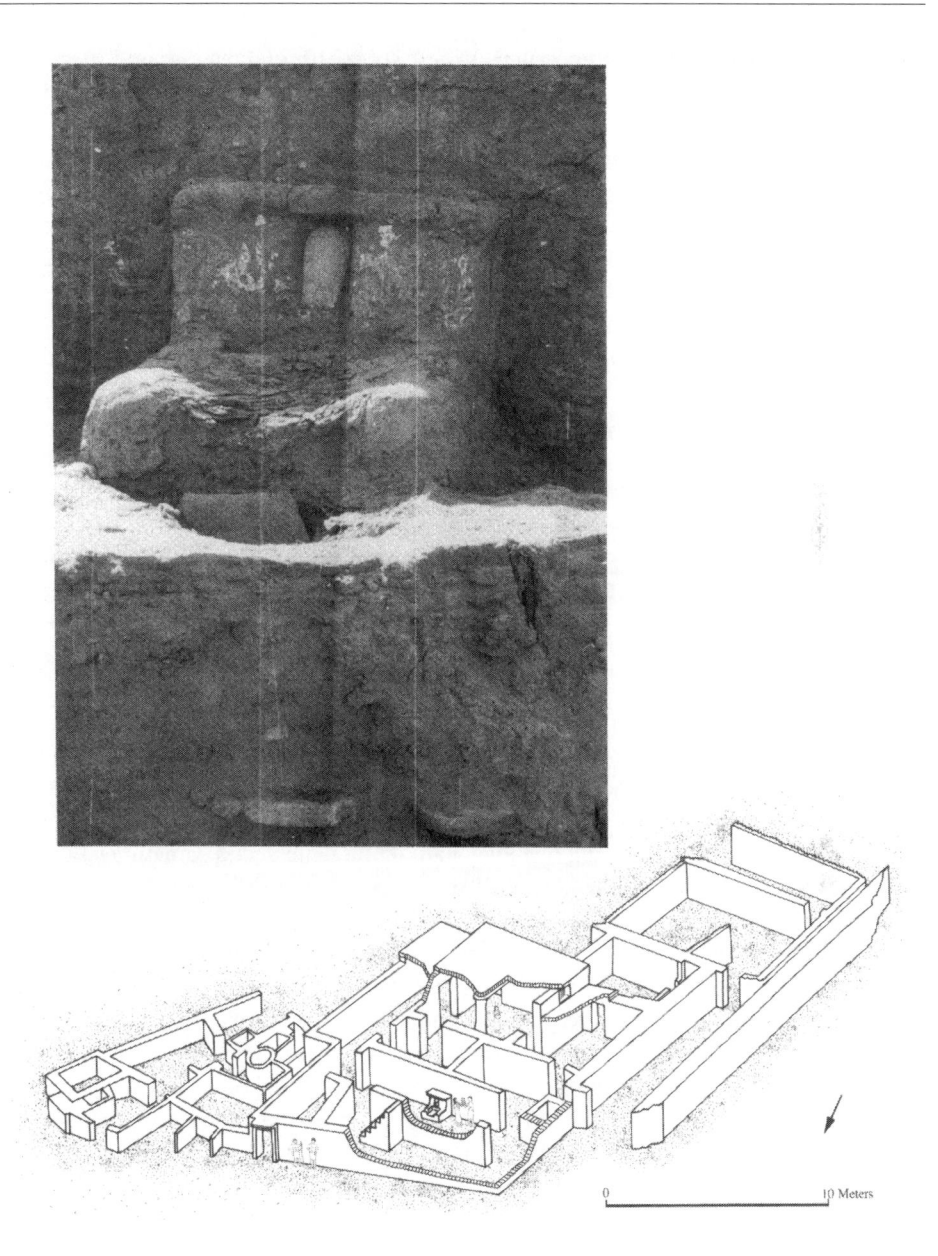

FIGURE 45.4 The shrine for Meryka at Askut: a photograph of the shrine as found, with stela still in place (note the layers of floor build-up in the excavator's cut in the foreground), and a hypothetical reconstruction of the house showing the courtyard location of the shrine.

this context is to test how far actions such as these spread beyond temples and specialized practitioners, in light of the influential view that Egyptian religious knowledge was deliberately restricted to the elite (Baines 1990: 6–10).

One remarkable discovery, in a late-fifth-century-BC house at Tell el-Muqdam, was of several figurines sealed in the lower parts of the walls (Redmount and Friedman 1994, 1997). The figurines take the form of erotic figures (usually males with enormous phalli), but also animals, horse-and-rider figurines and a possible image of a woman giving birth. The excavators noted that all of the figurines 'were incomplete or broken in some way, but were placed carefully, one by one and never in groups, at various points—usually corners and abutments—within the first above-ground course of the wall' (Redmount and Friedman 1997: 63). The deposits suggest a tradition of domestic foundation offerings, far better known from state cult buildings (Montet 1964; Weinstein 1973; Rossi 2004: 148–73). The house, and by extension its occupants, was the focus of protection, a level of concern otherwise known mainly in magic spells (Jankuhn 1972; Borghouts 1978, 15, 82–3, nos. 15, 121). Unfortunately there is no way of ascertaining, from the archaeology alone, whether the house owner oversaw the rite or commissioned a specialist practitioner. Nor are the layers of meaning that accompanied the selection of the figurine types immediately apparent.

3.2.1 *Temple Cult as Rite of Affliction*

Egyptian temple cult itself embraced a form of community-wide rite of affliction, often pre-emptively maintaining balance but at other times focusing on destroying evil or addressing specific hardships. One ritual, documented both in tomb and temple inscriptions and archaeologically, focused on foreigners, who were considered a source of chaos and magical disruption to the universe. Cursing formulae naming foreigners, and sometimes Egyptian criminals and the deceased, were inscribed on jars and anthropomorphic figurines and disabled by such means as breakage and burial, whilst wax figures were burnt (Posener 1975; Willems 1990: 46–8; Wimmer 1993; Ritner 1993: 136–42). Most surviving execration deposits have been recovered from cemeteries, placing the ritual within the private domain (Baines 2007: 8). But the largest deposit yet found originates from the Egyptian fortresses at the Nubian site of Mirgissa. Here, a large pit contained 7,000 inscribed potsherds and other items that included three figurines and a dismembered body, the only clear case of actual human sacrifice accompanying the rite (Ritner 1993: 153–80). At another of the Nubian fortresses, at Buhen, a group of hippopotamus skulls were excavated near the Middle Kingdom Temple of Horus, perhaps a rare archaeological survival of a rite in which the king harpooned a hippopotamus, an animal associated with Seth, the main god of chaos (Säve-Söderbergh 1953; Smith 1979: 72).

It is no coincidence that such rites appear in Egyptian occupied territories abroad. These were liminal zones (as were cemeteries) in which threats to Egypt and Egyptians were magnified. Even the practice of conducting foreign correspondence from within Egypt itself may have required counteractive measures, to judge from the excavation at Amarna of broken figurines of foreigners in the general vicinity of the building where cuneiform tablets (the Amarna Letters) documenting exchanges between the Egyptian court and Near Eastern kings and dignitaries were stored (Pendlebury 1951: 118, pl. LXXVIII.3; and Figure 45.2).

3.3 Rites of Passage

Finally, rites of passage are most visibly represented in archaeological and other source material in connection with death and, to a lesser extent, birth. Although the Egyptians conceived of life as being divided into stages, or forms, which included the afterlife, evidence of rituals accompanying life transitions has otherwise proven obscure. Allowing for the inevitable incompleteness of the source material, it has been speculated that lives, particularly of females, were not as punctuated with marked or symbolic transition points as we might assume (Meskell 2002: 89–90). Male circumcision was practised, but probably never widespread (Meskell 2002: 87–8; also Roth 1991: 72), whilst female circumcision is known only in texts from the Ptolemaic period and possibly later (Baines 1991: 144, note 59; Huebner 2009). There is no clear evidence for a marriage ceremony, although rituals involving naming and hair cutting may have taken place during childhood (Baines 1991: 144). It is tempting to interpret finds of mud balls containing human hair as remnants of hair-cutting rites (e.g. Crompton 1916), partly in light of modern ethnographic accounts of childhood rituals that involved the cutting of hair, which was sometimes buried in a ball of clay (Blackman 1927: 86; Ayrout 1968: 132).

3.3.1 Birth and Life

The moment of birth itself is rarely represented, but magico-medical rites were undoubtedly prominent at this time. One set of spells was said over amuletic bricks on which the mother squatted during delivery (Roth and Roehrig 2002, 19–33; and Wegner 2002 for an excavated example), whilst groups of buried placenta and birthing equipment excavated at the New Kingdom village of Deir el-Medina have also been suggested as the remnants of birthing rituals (Bruyère 1937: 11; Meskell 2002: 71, 81). After birth, the mother and child probably entered a period of seclusion, which may have included purification rituals. The main source here is a group of New Kingdom ostraca showing women, sometimes with infants, in vine-draped arbours (Brunner-Traut 1955: 24; Pinch 1993: 219–20), whilst a period of seclusion of 14 days is listed in a Middle Kingdom papyrus (Papyrus Westcar: Lichtheim 1975: 221). A related rite was the probable seclusion of women during menstruation, implied in a New Kingdom text (Wilfong 1999; Meskell 1998: 235–7; 2002: 90).

Efforts to identify 'seclusion spaces' in the archaeological record (e.g. Kemp 1986: 25; Meskell 1998: 235–7) have proven inconclusive, although a feature of settlement remains generally is the prominence of objects with protective imagery, often connected with childbirth and the care of children, such as amulets of the composite lion–hippopotamus–crocodile goddess Taweret, or the leonine dwarf Bes (Figure 45.2). Such figures also appear occasionally on domestic altars and wall paintings (Bruyère 1939; Kemp 1979, 2009), which probably served in part to form a protective backdrop to everyday life. This material, along with votive deposits to the goddess Hathor, has been a favoured source for gender-based approaches to religion, which have done much to explore the relationship between females and fertility concerns, but not extended far beyond this (although see Meskell 1998; 2002: 110–21).

3.3.2 Death, Burial, and the Afterlife

Egyptian mortuary rituals were concerned both with death and burial, and with the continued upkeep of the deceased. They are known through funerary texts, representations in tombs and on cult equipment, and burials themselves. Ideally the body was embalmed, a process that included the ritual placement of amulets on the body, burning of incense and recitation of spells (Ikram and Dodson 1998). The excavation of unmummified human remains at non-elite cemeteries, however, shows that for most this ceremony was probably abridged, or abandoned completely. Individuals buried at a non-elite cemetery under excavation at Amarna, for example, are showing no clear signs of deliberate mummification (see Kemp 2005: 22–3; 2007; Ambridge and Shepperson 2006; Dolling 2007, 2008). The funerary rituals that followed were directed largely towards enabling the deceased to complete the perilous journey to the afterlife. The Opening of the Mouth ceremony, undertaken from at least the Old Kingdom, was central here (Fischer-Elfert 1998). Designed to animate the body and render the deceased capable in the next world, it involved purification, censing, anointing, incantation, and touching ritual items to various parts of the body. At the Amarna cemetery, mummification may have been forgone but a version of this ritual may have been retained for at least one individual, with a small adze, an implement connected with this ceremony, recovered from the grave of a juvenile (Dolling 2008: 31). Another distinctive funeral ritual was the 'breaking of the red pots' in which vessels were broken at tombs, probably to keep at bay evil forces lurking at the boundaries of the ordered world (Borchardt 1930; van Dijk 1985; 1993: 173–88; Figure 45.2). Similar rites are recorded in temple contexts.

Following burial, rituals for the maintenance of the deceased consisted mainly of making offerings of food and drink, communal feasting and acts of remembrance such as pronouncing the deceased's name. Part commemorative, part rite of affliction, in helping propitiate the afterlife such activities can also be considered a form of ongoing rite of passage. So fundamental was this aspect of the mortuary cult—the maintenance of the dead in the world of the living—that its development has been suggested as one of the driving forces behind the emergence of the Egyptian state, in prompting developments in ritual architecture and bureaucracy (Wengrow 2006: 266–8).

Ideally, it seems, maintenance of the deceased took place at the gravesite. Offerings to the dead and feasting are documented in the archaeological record of cemeteries, particularly in deposits of pottery (e.g. Seiler 1995). But at the Amarna cemetery, again, a somewhat different picture of usage is emerging. So far, work has revealed the cemetery, at least in parts, to be crowded with little space between burials, few of which seem to have had markers by which their occupants could be identified. Whilst something more like community-level commemoration may have taken place, perhaps on the adjacent open ground, this is nonetheless raising questions of how far the cemetery served as a ritual arena beyond interment. The hope for most at Amarna was probably to be remembered in other ways: perhaps through temple offerings, and certainly in domestic ancestor cults. The latter are particularly well attested in stelae, statues, and amulets that show private individuals usually thought to be deceased (although this is not always made explicit) from Amarna and other sites and mainly of New Kingdom date (Demarée 1983; Keith-Bennett 1981; Friedman 1985; Keith in press; Figure 45.2).

This is the context of the Meryka shrine at Askut discussed above, a particularly interesting case because of the depth of time it represents. Stratigraphic and ceramic evidence suggest that some kind of shrine existed on this spot for over 300 years, with Meryka himself worshipped for several generations: his stela seems to have been manufactured some 200 years before the shrine was abandoned (Smith 2003: 129). Perhaps Meryka was still living when the stela was first built, the stela beginning life as a monument to a figure of local importance, and becoming a cult image after his death. Egyptian religion was concerned largely with conditions in the present and future, but at Askut domestic ancestor cults seem to have perpetuated memory of the past in a familial context. Such links may have had added significance to this expatriate community, and perhaps also a legitimizing function to their circumstances. Archaeological evidence that the shrine was an active ritual space and not simply a background memorial is important because performance, in conjunction with the erection of memorials, seems to be a particularly effective means of perpetuating memory (Meskell 2004: 64).

4 CONCLUSIONS

Given the long history of archaeology in Egypt, it is unrealistic to expect that future excavation will expand greatly the range of material evidence available for the study of religion—although we can certainly anticipate data that has been more closely provenanced than in the past, and the addition of more environmental material. One of the main contributions of archaeological research into religion is in building profiles of ritual according to social, contextual, or temporal bases. Execration and foundation rituals provide a strong basis for such research in Egypt. Another is to supply ideas and terms that originate within more theoretical archaeological writing that is not necessarily connected with ancient Egypt at all. There is much scope for the continuation of such lines of enquiry. These often highlight the strength of material evidence in elucidating non-elite and non-formal experiences of religion which, as often from the ancient world, are not expressed strongly in Egyptian textual or iconographic sources.

A related path of enquiry is to seek something of the 'actuality' of religion, both in testing the reality of non-material sources but also in the sense of repopulating religion with people and positioning it in a real-life setting. Such aims have particular resonance in the Egyptian context because of the strong tendency towards idealism in text and representation, whilst the belief in the efficaciousness of the word and image sees religion at times almost reaching a stage where it is played out apart from people in texts and images themselves. This might be achieved by further positioning the material evidence for religion alongside that of other activities (e.g. Smith 2003), and considering how everyday activity patterns, including religious performance, are reflected in the layout and organization of settlements. Life-history approaches remain very relevant, and further engagement with the concept of ritualization is likely to be beneficial. The task of challenging the view from elite tombs that has come to represent the standard image of Egyptian mortuary religion is a clear priority (Richards 2005: 49–54), as is that of reintegrating the religious landscapes of tomb, temple, house, and so on.

A further goal is to formulate approaches to material culture that are both specific to ritual and religion within the Egyptian context, and contribute to the ways in which we conceptualize these realms. The broad division of religion into ritual and belief that underlies much archaeological discourse, for example, does not comfortably accommodate such forms of conduct as the wearing of amulets or use of protective paintings and reliefs that are strongly attested in the Egyptian source material. This is especially the case if we understand ritual to involve an element of action. Indeed, this fundamental division of religion into belief and practice can only be taken so far in Egypt where ritual, as a means of making religion effective, is not optional, at least in the world of temple cult. The archaeology of ritual and religion in Egypt is as much the archaeology of problem solving, lifestyle, performance, experience, and faith.

Acknowledgements

I am most grateful to Professor Barry Kemp for his comments on a draft of this chapter.

Suggested Reading

A key text is Kemp's (2006) overview of ancient Egyptian society in which archaeological material is brought to the fore and religion is a recurrent theme. For Egyptian religion generally see the volume edited by Shafer (1991), and similarly that on temples (Shafer 1997). Also on temples and temple cult, the conference proceedings edited by Quirke (1997) and Dorman and Bryan (2007) provide an up-to-date source. The key source on foundation deposits at temples is Weinstein (1973); see also Rossi (2004: 148–73). The nature of early temples is a prominent research theme (Kemp 1995: 41–5; Kemp, Boyce, and Harrell 2000; Kemp 2006: 111–35; O'Connor 1992; Seidlmayer 1996), as is the role of smaller private chapels (Bomann 1991; Weatherhead and Kemp 2007). Wegner's (2007) excavation report on the Mortuary Temple of Senwosret III is a good introduction to the realities of excavation at temple sites. For the Early Dynastic and Old Kingdom votive material, the excavation report by Dreyer (1986) is a starting point (see also Kemp 2006), whilst the standard reference for New Kingdom votives at Hathor shrines is Pinch (1993). On the religious roles of animal mummies see Ikram (2005).

For tombs and mortuary practice see Ikram and Dodson (1998), Dodson and Ikram (2008), Assmann (2003), and Grajetski (2003), amongst others; Richards (2005) focuses especially on material remains, and Wengrow (2006) on the role of mortuary religion in the emergence of the Egyptian state.

Phenomenological approaches to the study of sacred space, including that beyond buildings proper, are rare, but see Donohue (1992), Richards (1999), O'Connor (1982; 1989; 1997), and Meskell's (2002) work on New Kingdom social life. Syntheses of religious material from Middle and New Kingdom settlement sites include: Friedman (1994), Meskell (1998), Smith (2003: 124–35), Quirke (2005), Stevens (2006), and Szpakowska (2008: 128–49), and Weiss (2009).

On ancient Egypt generally, see the volumes edited by Shaw (2000) and Wilkinson (2007).

References

Adams, M. 1998. 'The Abydos Settlement Site Project: Investigation of a major provincial town in the Old Kingdom and First Intermediate period' in C. J. Eyre (ed.), *Proceedings of the Seventh International Congress of Egyptologists* (Leuven: Peeters), pp. 19–30.

Allen, J. P. 2003. 'The Egyptian concept of the world' in D. O'Connor and S. Quirke (eds), *Mysterious Lands* (London: UCL Press), pp. 23–30.

Ambridge, L. and Shepperson, M. 2006. 'South Tombs cemetery, 2006', *Journal of Egyptian Archaeology*, 92: 27–37.

Arnold, D. 1962. *Wandrelief und Raumfunktion in ägyptischen Tempeln des Neuen Reiches* (Berlin: Bruno Hessling).

Arnold, F. 1996. 'Settlement remains at Lisht-North' in M. Bietak (ed.), *Haus und Palast im alten Ägypten* (Wien: Verlag der Österreichischen Akademie der Wissenschaften), pp. 13–21.

Assmann, J. 1999. *Ägyptische Hymnen und Gebete*, 2nd edn (Freiburg/Göttingen: Universitätsverlag/Vandenhoeck and Ruprecht).

—— 2001. *The Search for God in Ancient Egypt*, trans. D. Lorton (Ithaca: Cornell University Press).

—— 2003. 'The Ramesside tomb and the construction of sacred space' in N. Strudwick and J. H. Taylor (eds), *The Theban Necropolis: Past, present and future* (London: British Museum Press), pp. 46–52.

Ayrout, H. H. 1968 (2005 reprint). *The Egyptian Peasant* (Cairo: The American University in Cairo Press).

Baines, J. 1987. 'Practical religion and piety', *Journal of Egyptian Archaeology*, 73: 79–98.

—— 1990. 'Restricted knowledge, hierarchy, and decorum: Modern perceptions and ancient institutions', *Journal of the American Research Center in Egypt*, 27: 1–23.

—— 1991. 'Society, morality, and religious practice' in B. E. Shafer (ed.), *Religion in Ancient Egypt: Gods, myths, and personal practice* (Ithaca: Cornell University Press), pp. 123–200.

—— 2002. 'Egyptian letters of the New Kingdom as evidence for religious practice', *Journal of Ancient Near Eastern Religions*, 1: 1–31.

—— 2007. 'Displays of magic in Old Kingdom Egypt' in K. Szpakowska (ed.), *Through a Glass Darkly: Magic, dreams and prophecy in ancient Egypt* (Swansea: The Classical Press of Wales), pp. 1–32.

Bell, C. 1992. *Ritual Theory, Ritual Practice* (Oxford: Oxford University Press).

—— 1997. *Ritual Perspectives and dimensions* (Oxford: Oxford University Press).

Blackman, W. S. 1927 (2000 reprint). *The Fellahin of Upper Egypt* (Cairo: American University in Cairo Press).

Bomann, A. 1991. *The Private Chapel in Ancient Egypt: A study of the chapels in the workmen's village at El Amarna with special reference to Deir el Medina and other sites* (London: Kegan Paul International).

Borchardt, L. 1930. 'Bilder des "Zerbrechens der Krüge"', *Zeitschrift für Ägyptische Sprache und Altertumskunde*, 64: 12–16.

Borghouts, J. 1978. *Ancient Egyptian Magical Texts* (Leiden: Brill).

Bourriau, J. 1988. *Pharaohs and Mortals: Egyptian Art in the Middle Kingdom* (Cambridge: Cambridge University Press).

Boyce, A. 1995. 'Report on the 1987 excavations. House P46.33: The finds' in B. J. Kemp (ed.), *Amarna Reports*, VI (London: Egypt Exploration Society), pp. 44–136.

Brand, P. 2007. 'Veils, votives, and marginalia: the use of sacred space at Karnak and Luxor' in P. F. Dorman and B. M. Bryan (eds), *Sacred Space and Sacred Function in Ancient*

Thebes, Studies in Ancient Oriental Civilization 61 (Chicago: Oriental Institute of the University of Chicago), pp. 51–83.

BRUNNER-TRAUT, E. 1955. 'Die Wochenlaube', *Mitteilungen des Deutschen Archäologischen Instituts, Abteilung Kairo*, 3: 11–13.

BRUYÈRE, B. 1937. *Rapport sur les fouilles de Deir el Médineh (1934–1935), Deuxième Partie* (Cairo: Institut Français d'Archéologie Orientale).

——1939. *Rapport sur les fouilles de Deir el Médineh (1934–1935), III: Le village, les décharges publiques, la station de repos du col de la Vallée des Rois* (Cairo: Imprimerie de l'Institut Français d'Archéologie Orientale).

CORTEGGIANI, J.-P. 1987. *The Egypt of the Pharaohs at the Cairo Museum* (London: Scala Books).

CROMPTON, W. M. 1916. 'Two clay balls in the Manchester Museum', *Journal of Egyptian Archaeology*, 3: 218.

DAVID, A. R. 1981. *A Guide to Religious Ritual at Abydos* (Warminster: Aris and Phillips).

DAVIES, N. DE G. 1903. *The Rock Tombs of El Amarna, I: The Tomb of Meryra* (London: Egypt Exploration Society).

——1908. *The Rock Tombs of El Amarna, V: Smaller Tombs and Boundary Stelae* (London: Egypt Exploration Society).

DEMARÉE, R. 1983. *The ꜣḫ iḳr n Rꜥ-stelae: On ancestor worship in ancient Egypt* (Leiden: Nederlands Instituut voor het Nabije Oosten).

DIJK, J. VAN 1985. 'Zerbrechen der roten Töpfe' in W. Helck, E. Otto, and W. Westendorf (eds), *Lexikon der Ägyptologie*, VI (Wiesbaden: Otto Harrassowitz), pp. 1389–96.

——1993. *The New Kingdom Necropolis of Memphis*, Historical and Iconographical Studies (Groningen: Rijksuniversiteit).

DODSON, A. and IKRAM, S. 2008. *The Tomb in Ancient Egypt* (London: Thames and Hudson).

DOLLING, W. 2007. 'South Tombs Cemetery' in B. Kemp, 'Tell el-Amarna, 2006–7', *Journal of Egyptian Archaeology*, 93: 21–56.

——2008. 'South Tombs Cemetery' in B. Kemp, 'Tell el-Amarna, 2007–8', *Journal of Egyptian Archaeology*, 94: 13–31.

DONOHUE, V. A. 1992. 'The goddess of the Theban mountain', *Antiquity*, 66: 871–85.

DORMAN, P. F. and BRYAN, B. M. (eds) 2007. *Sacred Space and Sacred Function in Ancient Thebes*, Studies in Ancient Oriental Civilization 61 (Chicago: Oriental Institute of the University of Chicago).

DREYER, G. 1986. *Elephantine VIII. Der Tempel der Satet: Die Funde der Frühzeit und des Alten Reiches*, Deutsches Archäologisches Institut, Abteilung Kairo, Archäologische Veröffentlichungen 39 (Mainz: Phillip von Zabern).

FAIRMAN, H. W. 1954. 'Worship and festivals in an Egyptian temple', *Bulletin of the John Rylands Library, Manchester*, 37: 165–203.

FISCHER-ELFERT, H.-W. 1998. *Die Vision von der Statue im Stein: Studien zum Altägptischen Mundöffnungsritual*, Schriften der philosophisch-historischen Klasse der Heidelberger Akademie der Wissenschaften 5 (Heidelberg: Carl Winter, Universitätsverlag).

FRIEDMAN, F. 1985. 'On the meaning of some anthropoid busts from Deir el-Medina', *Journal of Egyptian Archaeology*, 71: 82–97.

——1994. 'Aspects of domestic life and religion' in L. H. Lesko (ed.), *Pharaohs Workers: The villagers of Deir el-Medina* (New York: Cornell University Press), pp. 95–117.

GARDINER, A. H. 1917. 'Professional magicians in ancient Egypt', *Proceedings of the Society of Biblical Archaeology*, 39: 31–44.

GRAJETSKI, W. 2003. *Burial Customs of Ancient Egypt: Life in death for rich and poor* (London: Duckworth).

HARING, B. 1997. *Divine Households: Administrative and economic aspects of the New Kingdom royal memorial temples in western Thebes* (Leiden: Nederlands Instituut voor het Nabije Oosten).

HILL, M. 2001. 'Bronze statuettes' in D. B. Redford (ed.), *The Oxford Encyclopedia of Ancient Egypt* (Oxford: Oxford University Press), pp. 203-8.
HORNUNG, E. 1992. *Idea into Image: Essays on ancient Egyptian thought*, trans. E. Bredeck (New York: Timken).
—— 1999. *Akhenaten and the Religion of Light* (Ithaca: Cornell University Press).
HUEBNER, S. R. 2009. 'Female circumcision as a *rite de passage* in Egypt—continuity through the millennia?', *Journal of Egyptian History* 2: 149-71.
IKRAM, S. (ed.) 2005. *Divine Creatures: Animal mummies in ancient Egypt* (Cairo: The American University in Cairo Press).
—— and DODSON A. 1998. *The Mummy in Ancient Egypt: Equipping the dead for eternity* (Cairo: American University Press).
JANKUHN, D. 1972. *Das Buch 'Schutz des Hauses' (s3—pr)* (Bonn: Rudolf Habelt Verlag).
KEITH, J. L. in press. *Anthropoid Busts of Deir el Medineh and Other Sites and Collections* (Cairo: Institut Français d'Archéologie Orientale).
KEITH-BENNETT, J. 1981. 'Anthropoid busts: II. Not from Deir el Medineh alone', *Bulletin of the Egyptological Seminar*, 3: 43-72.
KEMP, B. J. 1979. 'Wall paintings from the workmen's village at el-'Amarna', *Journal of Egyptian Archaeology*, 65: 47-53.
—— 1986. 'Report on the 1985 excavations: Work inside the walled village' in B. J. Kemp (ed.), *Amarna Reports III* (London: Egypt Exploration Society), pp. 1-33.
—— 1994. 'Food for an Egyptian city' in R. Luff and P. Rowley-Conwy (eds), *Whither Environmental Archaeology?* (Oxford: Oxbow), pp. 133-53.
—— 1995. 'How religious were the ancient Egyptians?', *Cambridge Archaeological Journal*, 5: 25-54.
—— 2005. 'Tell el-Amarna', *Journal of Egyptian Archaeology*, 91: 15-27.
—— 2006 (rev. edn). *Ancient Egypt: Anatomy of a Civilization* (London: Routledge).
—— 2007. 'The orientation of burials at Tell el-Amarna' in Z. Hawass and J. Richards (eds), *The Archaeology and Art of Ancient Egypt: Essays in honor of David B. O'Connor* (Cairo: Supreme Council of Antiquities Press), pp. 21-31.
—— 2009. 'A wall painting of Bes figures from Amarna', *Egyptian Archaeology* 34: 18-19.
——, BOYCE, A., and HARRELL, J. 2000. 'The colossi from the early shrine at Coptos in Egypt', *Cambridge Archaeological Journal*, 10: 211-42.
—— and GARFI S. 1993. *A Survey of the Ancient City of el-'Amarna* (London: Egypt Exploration Society).
KESSLER, D. 1986. 'Tierkult' in W. Helck, E. Otto, and W. Westendorf (eds), *Lexikon der Ägyptologie*, VI (Wiesbaden: Otto Harrassowitz), pp. 571-87.
—— 1989. *Die Heiligen Tiere und der Konig*, I (Wiesbaden: Otto Harrassowitz).
—— 1998. *Tuna el-Gebel*, II: *Die Paviankultkammer G-C-C-2* (Hildesheim: Gerstenberg).
—— and ABD EL HALIM NUR EL-DIN. 2005. 'Tuna al-Gebel: Millions of ibises and other animals' in S. Ikram (ed.), *Divine Creatures: Animal mummies in ancient Egypt* (Cairo: The American University in Cairo Press), pp. 120-63.
LEGGE, A. J. 2010. 'The mammal bones from Grid 12', in B. Kemp and A. Stevens (eds), *Busy Lives at Amarna: Excavations in the Main City (Grid 12 and the House of Ranefer, N49. 18). Volume I: The Excavations, Architecture and Environmental Remains* (London: Egypt Exploration Society and Amarna Trust), pp. 445-52.
LICHTHEIM, M. 1975. *Ancient Egyptian Literature*, I: *The Old and Middle Kingdoms* (Berkeley: University of California Press).
LLOYD, A. B. 1989. 'Psychology and society in the ancient Egyptian cult of the dead' in W. K. Simpson (ed.), *Religion and Philosophy in Ancient Egypt*, Yale Egyptological Studies 3 (New Haven: Yale Egyptological Seminar), pp. 117-33.

MacDonald, S., McKeown, R., and Quirke, S. 2000. 'Opening the stable door: New initiatives at the Petrie Museum of Egyptian archaeology', *Archaeology International* 4 (London: Institute of Archaeology), UCL, pp. 57–9.

McDowell, A. G. 1999. *Village Life in Ancient Egypt: Laundry lists and love songs* (Oxford: Oxford University Press).

Mace, A. 1921. 'The Egyptian Expedition 1920–1921. I: Excavations at Lisht', *Bulletin of the Metropolitan Museum of Art*, 16: 5–19.

Martin, G. T. 1989. *The Memphite Tomb of Horemheb Commander-in-Chief of Tut'ankhamun*, I (London: Egypt Exploration Society).

Meskell, L. 1998. 'An archaeology of social relations in an Egyptian village', *Journal of Archaeological Method and Theory*, 5(3): 209–43.

—— 2002. *Private Life in New Kingdom Egypt* (Princeton: Princeton University Press).

—— 2004. *Object Worlds in Ancient Egypt: Material biographies past and present* (Oxford: Berg).

Montet, P. 1964. 'Le rituel de fondation des temples égyptiennes', *Kêmi*, 17: 74–100.

Morkot, R. 1990. 'Nb-mꜣꜥt-Rꜥ-United-With-Ptah', *Journal of Near Eastern Studies*, 49: 323–37.

Munro, P. 1962. 'Einige Votivstelen an Wp wꜣwt', *Zeitschrift für Ägyptische Sprache und Altertumskunde*, 88: 48–58.

Nicholson, P. T. and Smith, H. S. 1996. 'The sacred animal necropolis at north Saqqara', *Journal of Egyptian Archaeology*, 82: 8–11.

O'Connor, D. 1982. 'Cities and towns' in E. Brovarski, S. K. Doll, and R. E. Freed (eds), *Egypt's Golden Age: The art of living in the New Kingdom 1558–1085 BC* (Boston: Museum of Fine Arts), pp. 17–25.

—— 1989. 'City and palace in ancient Egypt', *Cahiers de Recherches de l'Institut de Papyrologie et d'Égyptologie de Lille*, 11: 73–87.

—— 1992. 'The status of early Egyptian temples: An alternative theory' in R. Friedman and B. Adams (eds), *The Followers of Horus: Studies dedicated to Michael Allen Hoffman 1994–1990* (Oxford: Oxbow), pp. 83–98.

—— 1997. 'The elite houses of Kahun' in J. Phillips (ed.), *Ancient Egypt, the Aegean, and the Near East: Studies in honour of Martha Rhoads Bell* (San Antonio: Van Siclen Books), pp. 389–400.

Payne, P. 2006. 'Recovering animal bone at the house of the High Priest Panehsy' in B. Kemp, 'Tell el-Amarna, 2005–6', *Journal of Egyptian Archaeology*, 92: 21–56.

—— 2007. 'Re-excavation at the Amarna house of Panehesy', *Egyptian Archaeology*, 30: 18–20.

Pendlebury, J. D. S. 1951. *The City of Akhenaten*, III: *The Central City and the Official Quarters*, 2 vols. (London: Egypt Exploration Society).

Petrie, W. M. F. 1891. *Illahun, Kahun and Gurob: 1889–1890* (London: D. Nutt).

—— 1953. *Ceremonial Slate Palettes* (London: British School of Archaeology in Egypt/Bernard Quaritch).

Pinch, G. 1993. *Votive Offerings to Hathor* (Oxford: Griffith Institute).

—— 2004. *Egyptian Mythology: A guide to the gods, goddesses and traditions of ancient Egypt* (Oxford: Oxford University Press).

—— 2006. *Magic in Ancient Egypt*, rev. edn (London: British Museum Press).

Posener, G. 1975. 'Ächtungstexte' in W. Helck, E. Otto, and W. Westendorf (eds), *Lexikon der Ägyptologie I* (Wiesbaden: Otto Harrassowitz), pp. 67–9.

Pudleiner, R. 2001. 'Hathor on the Thoth Hill', *Mitteilungen des Deutschen Archäologischen Instituts, Abteilung Kairo*, 57: 239–45.

Quack, J. F. 2002. 'La magie au temple', *La magie en Égypte: Actes du colloque organize par le Musée du Louvre les 29 et 30 septembre 2000* (Paris: Louvre), pp. 41–68.

Quibell, J. 1898. *The Ramesseum* (London: Bernard Quaritch).

Quirke, S. 1997. *The Temple in Ancient Egypt: New discoveries and recent research* (London: British Museum Press).

—— 2005. *Lahun: A town in Egypt 1800 BC, and the history of its landscape* (London: Golden House Publications).

RAVEN, M. 2001. *The Tomb of Maya and Meryt, II: Objects and Skeletal Remains* (London/ Leiden: Egypt Exploration Society/National Museum of Antiquities Leiden).

REDMOUNT, C. and FRIEDMAN, R. 1994. 'The 1993 field season of the Berkeley Tell el-Muqdam Project: Preliminary report', *Newsletter of the American Research Center in Egypt*, 164: 1–10.

—— —— 1997. 'Tales of a Delta site: The 1995 field season at Tell el-Muqdam', *Journal of the American Research Center in Egypt*, 34: 57–83.

RICHARDS, J. E. 1999. 'Conceptual landscapes in the Egyptian Nile Valley' in W. Ashmore and B. Knapp (eds), *Archaeologies of Landscape: Contemporary perspectives* (Oxford: Blackwell), pp. 83–100.

—— 2005. *Society and Death in Ancient Egypt: Mortuary landscapes of the Middle Kingdom* (Cambridge: Cambridge University Press).

RITNER, R. K. 1993. *The Mechanics of Ancient Egyptian Magical Practice* (Chicago: Oriental Institute of the University of Chicago).

ROEDER, G. 1937. *Ägyptische Bronzewerke* (Glückstadt: J. J. Augustin).

ROSSI, C. 2004. *Architecture and Mathematics in Ancient Egypt* (Cambridge: Cambridge University Press).

ROTH, A. M. 1991. *Egyptian Phyles in the Old Kingdom* (Chicago: Oriental Institute of the University of Chicago).

—— 1992. 'The *psš-kf* and the "Opening of the Mouth": A ritual of birth and rebirth', *Journal of Egyptian Archaeology*, 78: 57–80.

—— 1993. 'Fingers, stars, and the "Opening of the Mouth": The nature and function of the *nṯrwj*-blades', *Journal of Egyptian Archaeology*, 79: 57–79.

—— and ROEHRIG, C. 2002. 'Magical bricks and the bricks of birth', *Journal of Egyptian Archaeology*, 88: 121–39.

SÄVE-SÖDERBERGH, T. 1953. *On Egyptian Representations of Hippopotamus Hunting as a Religious Motif* (Uppsala: C. W. K. Gleerup).

SEIDLMAYER, S. J. 1996. 'Town and state in the early Old Kingdom: A view from Elephantine' in J. Spencer (ed.), *Aspects of Early Egypt* (London: British Museum Press), pp. 108–27.

SEILER, A. 1995. 'Archäologisch fassbare Kultpraktiken in Grabkontexten der frühen 18. Dynastie in Dra' Abu el-Naga/Theben' in J. Assmann, E. Dziobek, H. Guksch, and F. Kampp (eds), *Thebanische Beamtennekropolen: Neue Perspektiven archäologischer Forshung Internationales Symposion Heidelberg 9.–13.6.1993* (Heidelberg: Heidelberger Orientverlag), pp. 185–203.

SHAFER, B. E. (ed.) 1991. *Religion in Ancient Egypt: Gods, myths, and personal practice* (Ithaca: Cornell).

—— (ed.) 1997. *Temples of Ancient Egypt* (London: I.B.Tauris).

SHAW, I. 1999. 'Sifting the spoil: Excavation techniques from Peet to Pendlebury at el-Amarna' in A. Leahy and J. Tait (eds), *Studies on Ancient Egypt in Honour of H. S. Smith* (London: Egypt Exploration Society), pp. 273–82.

—— (ed.) 2000. *The Oxford History of Ancient Egypt* (Oxford: Oxford University Press).

SILVERMAN, D. P. 1991. 'Divinity and deities in ancient Egypt' in B. E. Shafer (ed.), *Religion in Ancient Egypt: Gods, myths, and personal practice* (Ithaca: Cornell University Press), pp. 7–87.

—— 1995. 'The nature of Egyptian kingship' in D. O'Connor and D. P. Silverman (eds), *Ancient Egyptian Kingship* (Leiden: Brill), pp. 49–92.

SMITH, H. S. 1979. 'Part II: Archaeological commentary' in W. B. Emery, H. S. Smith, and A. Millard (eds), *The Fortress of Buhen: The archaeological report*, Egypt Exploration Society Forty-Ninth Excavation Memoir (London: Egypt Exploration Society), pp. 21–105.

SMITH, S. T. 1993. 'The house of Meryka at Askut and the beginning of the New Kingdom in Nubia' in G. Zaccone and T. di Netro (eds), *Sesto congresso internazionale di egittologia*, II (Turin: Società Italiana per il Gas p. A.), pp. 497–509.

——1995. *Askut in Nubia: The economics and ideology of Egyptian imperialism in the second millennium BC* (New York: Kegan Paul International).

——2003. *Wretched Kush: Ethnic identities and boundaries in Egypt's Nubian Empire* (London: Routledge).

SPENCE, K. 2007. 'A contextual approach to ancient Egyptian domestic cult: The case of the "lustration slabs" at el-Amarna' in D. A. Barrowclough and C. Malone (eds), *Cult in Context: Reconsidering ritual in archaeology* (Oxford: Oxbow), pp. 285–92.

STEVENS, A. 2006. *Private Religion at Amarna: The material evidence* (Oxford: Archaeopress).

SZPAKOWSKA, K. 2003. 'Playing with fire: Initial observations on the religious uses of clay cobras from Amarna', *Journal of the American Research Center in Egypt*, 40: 43–53.

——2008. *Daily Life in Ancient Egypt: Recreating Lahun* (Oxford: Blackwell).

TEETER, E. 1997. *The Presentation of Maat: Ritual and legitimacy in ancient Egypt* (Chicago: Oriental Institute of the University of Chicago).

WARAKSA, E. 2007. 'Female figurines from the Mut precinct: Context and ritual function', PhD Dissertation, Johns Hopkins University.

WEATHERHEAD, F. and KEMP, B. J. 2007. *The Main Chapel at the Amarna Workmen's Village and its Wall Paintings* (London: Egypt Exploration Society).

WEGNER, J. 2002. 'A decorated birth-brick from South Abydos', *Egyptian Archaeology*, 21: 3–4.

——2007. *The Mortuary Temple of Senwosret III at Abydos* (New Haven: Peabody Museum of Natural History of Yale University and University of Pennsylvania Museum of Archaeology and Anthropology).

WEINSTEIN, J. 1973. 'Foundation Deposits in Ancient Egypt', PhD dissertation, University of Pennsylvania.

WEISS, L. 2009. 'Personal religious practice: house altars at Deir el-Medina', *Journal of Egyptian Archaeology* 95: 193–208.

WENDRICH, W. 2006. 'Entangled, connected or protected? The power of knots and knotting in ancient Egypt' in K. Szpakowska (ed.), *Through a Glass Darkly: Magic, dreams and prophecy in ancient Egypt* (Swansea: The Classical Press of Wales), pp. 243–69.

WENGROW, D. 2001. 'Rethinking "cattle cults" in early Egypt: Towards a prehistoric perspective on the Narmer Palette', *Cambridge Archaeological Journal*, 11: 91–104.

——2006. *The Archaeology of Early Egypt: Social transformations in north-east Africa, 10,000 to 2650 BC* (Cambridge: Cambridge University Press).

WILFONG, T. 1999. 'Menstrual synchrony and the "Place of women" in ancient Egypt. Oriental Institute Museum Hieratic Ostracon 13512' in E. Teeter and J. A. Larson (eds), *Gold of Praise: Studies in honour of Professor Edward F. Wente* (Chicago: University of Chicago Press), pp. 419–34.

WILKINSON, R. H. 1992. *Reading Egyptian Art: A hieroglyphic guide to ancient Egyptian painting and sculpture* (London: Thames and Hudson).

——1994. *Symbol and Magic in Egyptian Art* (London: Thames and Hudson).

WILKINSON, T. A. H. 2001. *Early Dynastic Egypt* (London: Routledge).

——(ed.) 2007. *The Egyptian World* (London: Routledge).

WILLEMS, H. 1990. 'Crime, cult and capital punishment (Mo'alla Inscription 8)', *Journal of Egyptian Archaeology*, 76: 27–54.

WIMMER, S. 1993. 'Neue Aechtungstext aus dem Altem Reich', *Biblische Notizen*, 67: 87–101.

CHAPTER 46

ROME
Imperial and Local Religions

RICHARD HINGLEY

1 INTRODUCTION

By the early third century BC, the city of Rome had taken control of most of mainland Italy and, by the middle of the first century BC, its territories surrounded the Mediterranean Sea and incorporated Gaul (France). The Emperor Augustus (31 BC–AD 14) pushed back the frontiers to the Rhine and Danube, and his successor Claudius began the conquest of Britain in AD 43 (Figure 46.1). The empire was divided into a large number of provinces, each of which was governed by its own provincial governor, a senior imperial official (Wacher 1987). This chapter explores the evidence for ritual and religion in Italy and the Western Roman Empire, focusing on the period from the first century BC to the third century AD. The evidence for the Eastern empire contrasts with that for the West (for a recent summary, see Rives 2007: 54–88), but is not addressed here. The rise of Christianity from its first-century origin as a persecuted religion to its role as the dominant religion of the empire by the fourth century is also not addressed.

Much of the available information for Roman religion derives from the writings of classical authors (Feeney 1998) and, while these texts cannot be ignored, this chapter explores the archaeological evidence for the religious cults of Italy, Iberia, Gaul, Germany, and Britain, including inscriptions, statues and cult sites. The variety of religious experiences and the evidence for the less wealthy are also addressed.

2 DEFINITIONS

The problems of terminology, meaning, and context that affect studies of religion in archaeology are directly relevant to the study of Roman religion (Insoll 2004: 6–8; Rives 2007: 4). The source for the English word 'religion' is the Latin noun *religio*, which means an obligation to the divine (Rives 2007: 13–4). With the rise of Christianity in the late fourth century AD, *religio* came be connected directly with a coherent set of beliefs that focused on

FIGURE 46.1 The Western Roman Empire, showing major sites mentioned in the text.

an individual deity (ibid.; Insoll 2004: 6). The dichotomy that is often drawn between religious and non-religious behaviour did not exist in a clearly defined manner for the societies of the Roman Empire, since religious beliefs were bound up with everyday life. In addition, ideas about the gods were not tied in closely with the types of attitudes to morality and ethical behaviour associated with certain religions such as Judaism, Christianity, and Islam (Feeney 1998: 3, 13).

The word 'cult', derived from the Latin *cultus*, is used here to identify the various practices of worship (Rives 2007: 23). Classical textual sources contain vital information about the beliefs that lay behind ritual, or cult, activities, but objects and structures uncovered through archaeological excavation also provide important information. Such items are very common in urban and rural contexts throughout the Roman Empire, indicating the fundamental significance of religion to human life, action, and identity (Rives 2000: 245). Information derived from temples, images of gods, inscriptions, and ritual deposits provide evidence for a variety of cults. Relatively humble people created some of the archaeological information, and its use enables a study of religion that is not entirely focused upon the elite perspectives that tend to dominate classical writings. The focus of much past study of state religion and elite architecture means that evidence for the religious activities of the less wealthy requires emphasis.

Fundamentally, there were many different conceptions of the divine in the Roman Empire, ideas that erode any coherent idea of a single Roman religion (Rives 2007: 5). The inspirations and desires of diverse groups, both in Rome and across the empire, were far too complex to be incorporated into a single set of religious beliefs. There was no one form of religion in the Roman Empire, but highly variable regional cults and practices based partly upon the traditions of particular peoples. At the same time, a degree of uniformity was created among these local religious practices, resulting from the actions of Roman officials in the provinces and the manner in which provincial societies were assimilated into the empire (Whittaker 1997); a process which enabled a significant degree of continuity in religious beliefs.

3 A State Religion: Unifying Centralizing Aspects of Roman Religion

Denis Feeney (1998: 1) writes of Roman religion as 'a range of cultural practices, interacting, competing, and defining each other in the process'. He also stressed (ibid.: 4) that the obsessive writings about tradition in Roman culture obscure the dynamic nature of the ways in which the people of the city of Rome responded to centuries of experience of new peoples. Roman religion was an active part of a Roman imperial culture that was transformed through its role in the extension of imperial domination across the empire (Whittaker 1997). This section focuses upon the contribution of religions to the creation and maintenance of imperial unity, through an exploration of the extent to which various provincial peoples were drawn into a relatively unified empire (Woolf 1998; Hingley 2005).

James Rives defines a 'normative' official imperial and urban cult that, while recognizable to certain elite groups across the empire (2000: 246), was, at the same time, hybrid in nature. The creation of this imperial religion was a matter 'of finding and creating common ground between different traditions, resulting from ... the need to get along' (ibid.). Across the extremely extensive area that, by the first century AD, was incorporated into the empire, people needed a common language and culture in order to communicate and identify themselves, and religion formed a significant part of this commonality. In Rives' account, this religion is defined through an exploration of the traditional cults of the city of Rome and by addressing the attitude of the Roman authorities toward the religion of the other people with whom they came into contact during the expansion of the empire in the late first millennium BC and early first millennium AD.

3.1 Rome

Religion in the city of Rome was based upon a group of traditional practices, cults that were thought to establish contacts between mortals and gods with the aim of winning divine favour and securing peace and political stability (Ferguson 1987a: 750). Significant practices included prayer and sacrifice (Rives 2007: 23–8). Prayers were requests to a particular god for help and were often associated with offerings, sometimes to be given to the god once the request was granted. The offerings varied from the everyday to the valuable: for example, a flower, cake, altar, statue, or war booty (Ferguson 1987a: 750; Rives 2007: 24). Blood sacrifices were particularly common and these could vary from a single small animal to a full-grown bull, often performed on an altar in front of a temple (Rives 2007: 25). These cult practices were common across most of the empire (ibid.: 27). Evidence for ritual practice derived from textual sources, inscriptions, and offerings suggests that people felt an ability to communicate with and influence a wide variety of divinities and also that certain deities had special powers and properties. The main deities of the Roman pantheon were highly influenced by Greek religious practice (for the complexity of the relationship, see Feeney 1998: 7–8, 68), but there was no bounded and stable set of religious beliefs (ibid.: 68–9).

Divine support was important for the individual but also for the state and, as a result, the rulers of Rome ensured that rituals of prayer and offering established a permanent relationship with between the community and particular divinities (for the interrelationship of 'public' and 'private' religion; Feeney 1998: 6). To this end, representatives of the community, magistrates, and priests, established public cults focused on shrines in the city, where regular performances of sacrifices and rituals were conducted (Rives 2000: 253). The gods for which important public cults were established were felt to have a particularly close relationship with the Roman state; an important temple to Jupiter Optimus Maximus, Juno, and Minerva was built on the Capitoline Hill in Rome (Ferguson 1987a: 750–1), but there was a multitude of other deities (Rives 2007: 15–21). As time went on, various divinities became incorporated into the cult practices conducted in Rome and across the empire (Rives 2007: 137–41). A cult site could comprise an altar, but most significant cults focused on temples, which became increasingly monumental and elaborate and which housed the cult statue together with offerings made to the god. The Capitoline Hill was the 'inner stronghold and cult-centre of Rome', alongside the Palatine Hill, another area 'replete with sanctity' (Ferguson 1987a: 756–7). Major temple complexes and other religious structures across these areas and throughout the city of Rome were rebuilt in monumental fashion by the first emperor, Augustus, in order to symbolize the unity of the state with the deities.

Significant annual rituals took place on fixed dates and the religious calendar of the city of Rome has been reconstructed from a number of surviving calendars; these indicate that at least 45 major festivals occurred each year. These rituals aimed to seek and observe the signs that indicated the approval or disapproval of the gods and to ensure that the right steps were taken to ensure their support (Ferguson 1987a: 750). The ceremonies were presided over by priestly officers, derived from the powerful families of Rome, who competed for significant roles.

Private individuals also required the support of the gods and personal prayers and offerings were made, for instance for recovery from an illness or for success in love. Some deities had particular functions, such as Venus, who was associated with love and Mercury who was identified with trade. Personal and public religion were not closely connected and, in general, public authorities did not concern themselves with the private beliefs and practices of individuals, although certain cults were banned from time to time for specific reasons, particularly when these demanded a degree of commitment and obedience that provided an alternative to public religion or where they threatened the control of the Roman authorities (Rives 2000: 256–8; examples include Christianity and druidic beliefs in Britain and Gaul).

3.2 The Empire

Indigenous elites in the territories conquered by Rome responded to a Roman cultural and religious initiative and, as such, a search for a pure 'Roman' religion and contrasting indigenous (Celtic, Germanic, or Iberian) beliefs is unrealistic. 'State' and indigenous religions did not form two independent aspects of the religious experience of the Roman empire, since the empire expanded and consolidated itself through the incorporation and (at least partial) assimilation of the societies that it subsumed (Woolf 2001). At the same time, however, the local experiences and personal histories of communities incorporated into the empire were significant for the religious practices they adopted. Local religious identities tell us much about the histories and regional cultures of the communities drawn into the empire and also about those people who moved within the empire, including traders, soldiers, and imperial officials.

Roman culture is often seen as having been incorporative of others and it was partly because of the open character of Roman religious beliefs that it was possible to assimilate elites across the Mediterranean and Northern Europe into a single imperial state. The conquest of new peoples clearly demonstrated that the gods favoured the Romans. The administrative elite of Rome appear to have been extremely effective at incorporating local elite groups across much of the empire into the structure that maintained the empire (Whittaker 1997), but it also appears that these groups were not required to adhere strictly to a clearly defined body of cult practices (Rives 2000: 259).

Whittaker (1997: 143) has explored the 'long history of imperialism woven into the ideological structure of Roman religion', defining the idea that local cults were colonized through the act of incorporation. Whether the creation of a degree of religious uniformity was centrally directed and intentional or was a matter of choice on the part of indigenous elites is, however, an issue that is the subject of considerable debate (Webster 1997: 166; Whittaker 1997: 148, 152–5; Woolf 1998). The willing adoption by provincial elites of aspects of the state religion was probably directly encouraged by Roman officials (Whittaker 1995:

21). Roman religious practices, as in the worship of the major gods of Rome during the late Republican era and the cult of the emperor from the time of Augustus, became common in the provinces.

During the expansion of Rome across Italy during the latter first millennium BC, entire populations of some cities were given Roman citizenship. Roman religious calendars have been found in some centres, and colonies often featured a temple to the Capitoline Triad at their urban core (Rives 2000: 259). These communities often maintained the worship of their own gods, combining Roman traditions with indigenous worship, adding new religious beliefs to pre-existing traditions (ibid.: 260). Elsewhere, the cult of local deities continued and was transformed under Roman rule. A vast array of gods and goddesses are attested by altars and inscriptions that date to the end of the first millennium BC and first three centuries AD, occurring in their thousands across the Roman Empire (Rives 2001). The Roman authorities had no need to ban or limit the worship of these gods, since they were fundamental to local identities and provided no conflict with the worship of the Roman deities (Rives 2000: 261).

Alongside a general encouragement of the conversion of local cults into a more recognizably Roman form, there were strong pressures to adopt certain aspects of Roman religion throughout the empire (Rives 2000: 261–2; see Whitaker 1997: 154–5 for some of the mechanisms employed), particularly once Augustus had come to power. As Rives has argued (ibid.: 262), religion played a key role in defining civic identity and structuring powerful alliances at a local level; it also provided an excellent way to forge political ties between local communities and Rome. Local elites could use religion to advance their interests both within their local communities and with influential imperial officials (Whittaker 1997: 154–5). In the West this was accomplished by adopting Roman cults and by making local cults appear more Roman, while across the empire there was more of a focus on links that were forged through the figure of the emperor (Rives 2000: 262).

The most evident sign of imperial influence is provided by emperor-worship (Ferguson 1987b), a range of cults that drew upon the emperor as a source of imperial unity (Rives 2007: 148). The Romans had a long history of sacred kingship and both Julius Caesar and Augustus were declared gods after their deaths. Elements of divine status had been granted to both during their life times, but the historical concern of the Roman elite with kingship and the problematic association of oriental divine kingship made deification a dangerous precedent for both rulers (Ferguson 1987b: 766–70). The 'Divine Augustus' was admitted among the gods of the state in AD 23.

In the provinces, the deification of the emperor was less problematic. Augustus' successor, Tiberius, authorized the local urban community at Tarraco (Taragona, Spain) to build a temple to Divine Augustus in Tarracononsis, where a major sanctuary for the worship of the emperor developed (Figure 46.2). After AD 15, an elaborate complex of buildings, including a circus, amphitheatre and two fora, was constructed (Keay 2003), following a monumental pattern that characterized urban centres elsewhere in the empire (Whittaker 1997: 149). Comparable imperial cult centres developed at places such as Lyon in Gaul (Fishwick 1999) and Camulodunum in Britain, where they served as the meeting places of provincial councils. The cult of the emperor was promoted by imperial officials but its success was a result of its value to members of the provincial elite. The cults enabled these people to pursue their own local interests through the adoption and adaptation of core elements of a Roman culture suited to the creation and display of power and status within

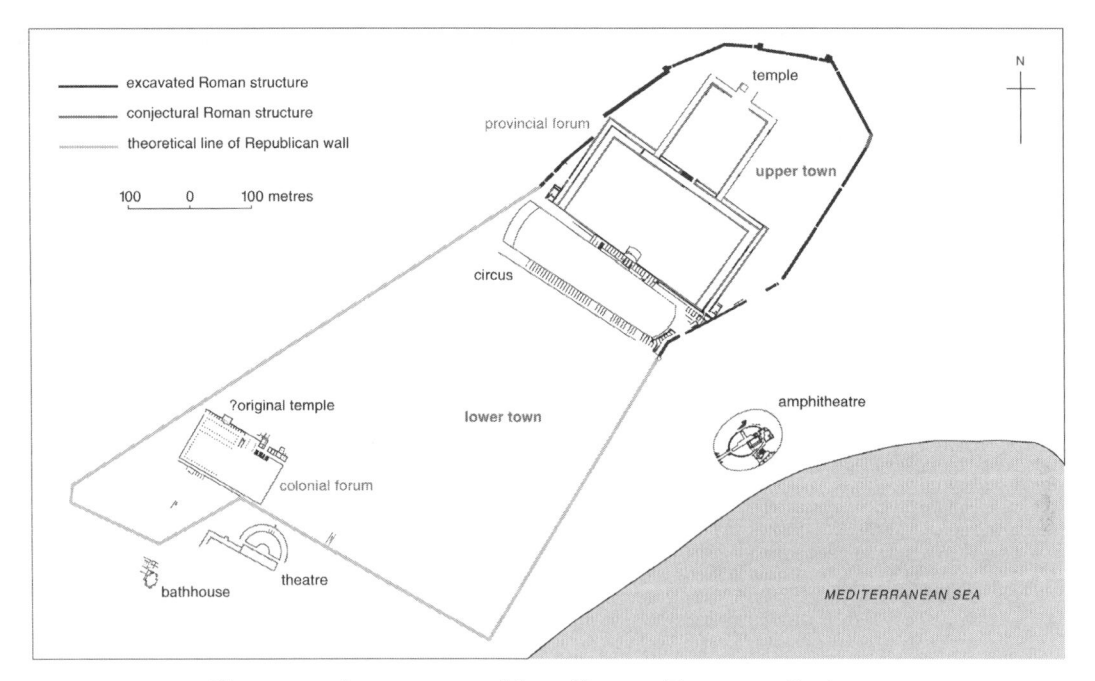

FIGURE 46.2 The centre of emperor-worship at Tarraco, Tarragona, Spain.

their own communities. The cults at such centres provided important opportunities for members of the indigenous elite to take powerful positions that related to the spirit of the emperor and to compete as patrons of the towns (Woolf 1998: 40). The power of the imperial cult in Iberia, Gaul, and Britain suggests a degree of uniformity of practice, but it is also clear that the emperor cults varied from place to place (Rives 2007: 149).

Emperor-worship also spread far more widely through the provision of statues of Augustus and later emperors in many cities (for other examples of the ever-present status of the emperor, see Whittaker 1997: 149–51). Across the frontier regions of the empire, soldiers took a direct role in emperor-worship, making annual vows to the reigning emperor (for soldiers and religion, see Rives 2007: 138–9). This was part of the way in which military solidarity was created (James 1999: 16–17). Military units throughout the frontier regions of the Western Empire also dedicated a vast number of inscriptions both to Roman and local gods, indicating the hybrid nature of religious experiences across the empire. One example is the cult of Coventina on Hadrian's Wall in England. This goddess or water nymph was a local spirit, although her cult is not attested prior to the Roman period. She was worshipped through the making and displaying of altars and a considerable collection of cult objects and offerings was found in a well close to the site of her sacred spring.

As a result of the spread of Roman religious practices, local elites and soldiers adopted elements of Roman religion into their existing religious traditions, modifying both to create new and variable traditions (Rives 2000: 269). The creation of a relative coherency for Roman culture meant that there were centralizing tendencies leading to religious convergence, as elite groups within the provinces vied with each other to attract the patronage of visiting Roman officials and administrators (Hingley 2005: 74–5); this took place, however, alongside the incorporation of local traditions.

4 THE DIVERSITY OF RELIGIOUS EXPERIENCES: GAUL AND BRITAIN

The evidence for religion and cults in Gaul, Germany and Britain is very rich (Rives 2007: 77) and includes extensive information derived from cult sites, inscriptions, and statues. Jane Webster (Webster 1995: 157) has argued that the process of *interpretatio Romana* was an instrument of Roman imperialism by which an alien deity was superimposed on a classical one, constituting the imposition of one dominant (Roman) belief system on another (see Rives 2007: 143). The term *interpretatio Romana* is derived from the classical author Tacitus' *Germania* (43, 3) and relates to the fact that the world of native gods was described and reconceptualized mainly in Roman terms by attributing a Latin name to a native god or goddess (Derks 1998: 81). An example is the deity Sulis Minerva, who was worshipped at the Roman sacred and medicinal baths at Bath in Britain. Sulis is the indigenous name for a goddess who was identified with the classical deity Minerva and many further examples are attested.

Webster (1997) argues that this imposition of Latin titles onto indigenous deities projects the power-relations behind Roman imperial control. In many accounts this process of synthesis has been viewed as requiring very little explanation, since the incorporation of indigenous religions into the Roman system is usually thought to have created a 'happy marriage' of religious beliefs, derived from an imperial strategy of pragmatic benign accommodation and an indigenous desire for assimilation (ibid.: 165). Such an accommodation appears to be indicated, for example, through the twinning of Roman and Celtic deities such as Lenus Mars in the frontier region of Germany (see below) and Sulis Minerva at Bath.

Yet Webster has argued forcefully that this process of accommodation, evident in a range of religious expressions (including inscriptions, imagery, and religious architecture) was neither natural nor benign. The introduction of Roman state religion—official cults and emperor-worship—may have been embraced only by certain privileged sectors of the provincial populations, such as the urban elite, wealthy landowners (Webster 1997: 166), and soldiers, while others continued to worship their gods in more traditional ways. An important aspect of such an imposition is the process by which elements of newly modified cults may have been contested by peoples across the empire. Examples addressed by Webster include the druidic challenge to Rome in Britain and Gaul (ibid.: 167–9; 1999), armed acts of resistance often led by elite groups which resulted in the serious suppression of native religious practices by the Roman state. Relations of power are also to be seen in the 'happy marriage' scenes involving a Roman male deity and a Celtic female partner, which may be an allegory of Roman domination over colonized peoples, clearly symbolized by marriage scenes of Mercury and Rosmerta (Webster 1997). In such religious practices, it may be possible to reconstruct the politics of the imposition of Roman religion together with the critical responses of indigenous peoples to the new relations of power that these actions entailed.

Another way of exploring the issues addressed by Webster is to suggest that certain elements of classical belief and practice helped to transform indigenous beliefs, but that the polytheism of Roman religion enabled indigenous peoples to assimilate themselves into a hybrid Roman culture in ways that allowed them to maintain aspects of their own religious beliefs without a substantial loss of identity (Rives 2000: 269–71). Perhaps the flexibility of these assimilatory practices enabled peoples from across the social spectrum to adapt their practices to suit their own needs and aspirations (Hingley 2005), drawing on ideas of past identity at the same time that they partly assimilated themselves. Taking such a perspective, it is possible that even fairly humble and poor members of provincial populations adopted relevant aspects of a broader Roman religious identity. In Britain, the evidence of curse tablets from temple sites, thin sheets of lead alloy that bear a written curse in Latin, may indicate that the writing of curses, a Roman tradition, spread to relatively lowly rural peasants as it served a particular function in their lives (Mattingly 2004: 20).

The hybrid character of religious practices is evident in the associated architecture of the numerous cult sites found across the landscapes of the provinces of Gaul, Germany, and Britain (Derks 1998: 82–3; Woodward 1992). Ton Derks' study of Gaul and Germany (1998: 82–91) indicates 2,000 votive inscriptions distributed across a fairly restricted geographical area, dedicated to a variety of gods and goddesses. A cluster of inscriptions relating to local gods who were associated with Mars occurs in the area of Trier. The native names for this god vary across this region, but it has been suggested that the prevalence of the name Lenus Mars indicates that this god was the main deity of the *civitas* (or people) named the Treveri (Derks 1998: 96). This study also identified more than 300 cult places spread across this territory (ibid.: 131).

Numerous cult places in the pre-Roman and Roman periods would have been in the open, including hill-tops, dense woodlands, caves, springs, rivers, and brooks, where the rituals were conducted (Brunaux 1988: 41–4; Derks 1998: 136–8). In some cases, extensive areas of the landscape may have held ritual significance, as suggested, for instance, by the common votive offerings deposited on the margins of the Cambridgeshire Fenlands in England (Rogers 2007). Often the open-air cult sites and temple complexes are marked by the discovery of large numbers of coins and brooches which were left to the gods as votive offerings (Woodward 1992: 66–80). Many of these cult places did not witness the construction of substantial buildings during the Roman period, but temples were constructed on some sites. Often these monumentalized cult sites developed from pre-Roman sanctuaries (Brunaux 1988: 11–3; Derks 1998: 170–1; Woodward 1992: 19–30). As elsewhere in the empire, archaeological attention has focused on the most monumental and impressive temple complexes, while less monumental and open-air cult places have been comparatively ignored. The buildings on these sites and the cults that were celebrated differed from the forms of worship that occurred prior to the Roman conquest, although changing religious practices clearly built upon pre-existing cults. Roman assimilation transformed local cults, creating new forms of architecture and religious practice.

The temples that developed in the urban centres across the Roman West were often substantial and monumental. Rural temples were sometimes equally impressive stone-built structures. The three main types of temple in Gaul, Britain, and Germany constituted the classical, the Gallo-Roman and the single-room types (Derks 1998: 145; Woodward 1992:

31–47). Classical temples were broadly comparable to the main temple structures in the city of Rome (Figure 46.3); these were also built in major towns across the empire and, on occasions, in rural settings. The Gallo-Roman temple is a distinct form, usually square in shape and with a central *cella* (room for the god) and surrounding ambulatory, such as at the Roman temple complex at Emple in the Netherlands (Derks 1998: 149–51). In some parts of the Roman West, less monumental temples and shrines have been excavated, often consisting of a small single room, which can be circular or rectangular. Sometimes these were far less 'Roman' in form, as at Heybridge (Essex) where the shrine was an earth and timber circular structure set within an irregular ditched enclosure (Atkinson and Preston 1998). Modest shrines of this form were probably very common across the Western Empire, representing local cult sites where relatively humble farmers and traders visited their gods to make offerings and request assistance.

At Emple, Heybridge, and elsewhere, the shrine or temple building was sited within a *temenos*, or sacred enclosure. Ritual activities in these enclosures focused on the temple building in the centre (Woodward 1992: 47–50). In well-examined cases, the temple and *temenos* were often located in the centre of an extensive cult-focused settlement with a variety of structures such as guesthouses, bathhouses, and theatres for religious festivals. Examples of rural religious complexes include Ribemont-sur-Ancre in France (Brunaux 1988: 16–21) and Frilford in England (Kamash et al. 2006). At both of these sites the theatres

FIGURE 46.3 The Maison Carée in Nimes, France, a classical temple.

and other buildings indicate that substantial numbers of people attended the festivities at these places, presumably at significant times of the year.

It is evident from recent work in Britain that religious and ritual activity was not confined to clearly defined cult places. The deposition of significant objects in particular locations on many settlements and at Roman forts suggests that people were depositing items both within and also at the edges of their own domestic environments, in pits, ditches, and in banks (see Hingley 2006 for a particular case study involving iron items). These practices of deposition continued a tradition that originated during the Iron Age (Hill 1995) and may often represent the cult activities and beliefs of farmers rather than members of the urban elite. Where relevant work has been undertaken overseas (e.g. Martens 2007), comparable information has been found and these everyday acts of offering occurring outside defined cult sites require more serious attention from scholars across the Roman world.

5 Conclusion

This chapter has stressed the considerable variety in the religious activity of people across the Western Roman Empire. Much of the impressive monumental evidence for temples both in Rome and the Roman cities of the empire relates to the structures of power through which the imperial and provincial rulers operated in their own localities. Religion acted as an important means for creating and maintaining local relations of power and imperial solidarity. Roman state religion, the worship of the Capitoline Triad, and emperor-worship cemented relations of power across the empire. The character of Roman religion was, however, sufficiently open and flexible to enable people of differing status from across the empire to be incorporated. Certain groups were marginalized and persecuted (Christians), or destroyed (druids), because of their perceived threat to the state but, on the whole, imperial religion was remarkably tolerant of different beliefs.

Across the western provinces religious cults developed in highly variable forms, incorporating traditional (pre-Roman) beliefs in complex ways and modifying them to create a new world of imperial unity. Spreading traditions, such as the representation of gods in stone and the new practice of writing dedicatory inscriptions on stone and lead, appear to have drawn many people into cult practices that may be defined as broadly Roman in character. Nevertheless, the politics of imperial control are vital to the ways in which people were assimilated. The creation of imperial unity drew people into new ways of life, but in ways that marginalized the poor and powerless, while not necessarily suppressing their opportunities for religious expression. Expressions of religious identity enabled the poor to communicate their beliefs and aspirations through acts of worship that have left physical traces, including the occurrence of curse tablets, the construction of relatively modest shrines, and the deposition of items within cult sites and in special locations within settlements and the landscape. In contrast to Britain and Gaul, where cult sites of a less monumental and less directly Roman form have, on occasions, been explored, most excavation in Italy and the Mediterranean area has focused upon the study of monumental classical religious architecture. The impressive buildings of Roman cities provide important information about Roman religion but local cults indicate the flexibility of Roman religious practices.

SUGGESTED READING

Rives's article (2001) provides a thoughtful introduction to the topics covered in this chapter, while his recent book (Rives 2007) addresses topics which are covered here in brief, including the meaning of certain fundamentally important terms such as religion and cult. Feeney (1998) explores the textual evidence for Roman religion, while Ferguson's article (1987b) provides the most useful introductory account of emperor worship. For the evidence from particular provinces, Brunaux (1988) addresses the pre-Roman evidence from Gaul, Derks (1998) provides a very detailed account of the Roman information from north Gaul and Germany, while Woodward (1992) addresses the evidence for Britain.

REFERENCES

ATKINSON, M. and PRESTON, S. J. 1998. 'The Late Iron Age and Roman settlement at Elms Farm, Heybridge, Essex', *Britannia*, 29: 885–110.
BRUNAUX, J. L. 1988. *The Celtic Gauls: Gods, rites and sanctuaries* (London: Seaby).
DERKS, T. 1998. *Gods, Temples and Ritual Practices: The transformation of religious ideas and values in Roman Gaul* (Amsterdam: Amsterdam University Press).
FEENEY, D. 1998. *Literature and Religion at Rome* (Cambridge: Cambridge University Press).
FERGUSON, J. 1987a. 'Classical religions' in J. Wacher (ed.), *The Roman World*, II (London: Routledge), pp. 749–65.
——1987b. 'Ruler worship' in J. Wacher (ed.), *The Roman World*, II (London: Routledge), pp. 766–84.
FISHWICK, D. 1999. 'Coinage and cult: The provincial monuments at Lugdunum, Tarraco, and Emerita' in G. M. Paul and M. Ierardi (eds), *Roman Coins and Public Life under the Empire*, E. Togo Salmon Papers II (Ann Arbor: The University of Michigan Press), pp. 95–121.
HILL, J. D. 1995. *Rituals and Rubbish in the Iron Age of Wessex*, BAR British 242 (Oxford: BAR).
HINGLEY, R. 2005. *Globalising Roman Culture: Unity, diversity and empire* (London: Routledge).
——2006. 'The deposition of iron objects in Britain during the later prehistoric and Roman periods', *Britannia*, 37: 213–59.
INSOLL, T. 2004. *Archaeology, Ritual and Religion* (London: Routledge).
JAMES, S. 1999. 'The community of the soldiers' in P. Baker (ed.), *TRAC 98: Proceedings of the Eighth Annual Theoretical Roman Archaeology Conference Leicester 1998* (Oxford: Oxbow), pp. 14–25.
KAMASH, Z., GOSDEN, C., and LOCK, G. 2006. *The Vale and Ridgeway Project: Excavations at Marcham/Frilford 2006: Interim report*, <http://www.arch.ox.ac.uk/research/research_projects/?a=2503>

KEAY, S. 2003. 'Recent archaeological work in Roman Iberia', *Journal of Roman Studies*, 93: 146–211.

MARTENS, M. 2007. 'Creating order in waste: Structured deposition in Roman Tienen, Belgium' in R. Hingley and S. Willis (eds), *Roman Finds: Context and theory* (Oxford: Oxbow), pp. 150–5.

MATTINGLY, D. 2004. 'Being Roman: Expressing identity in a provincial setting', *Journal of Roman Archaeology*, 17: 5–25.

RIVES, J. 2000. 'Religion in the Roman world' in J. Huskinson (ed.), *Experiencing Rome: Culture, identity and power in the Roman Empire* (London: Routledge), pp. 245–76.

—— 2001. 'Civic and religious life' in J. Bodel (ed.), *Epigraphic evidence: Ancient history from inscriptions* (London: Routledge), pp. 118–37.

—— 2007. *Religion in the Roman Empire* (London: Routledge).

ROGERS, A. 2007. 'Beyond the economic in the Roman Fenland: Reconsidering land, water, hoards and religion' in A. Fleming and R. Hingley (eds), *Prehistoric and Roman Landscapes: Landscape history after Hoskins* (Macclesfield: Windgather), pp. 113–30.

WACHER, J. (ed.) 1987. *The Roman World*, 2 vols. (London: Routledge).

WEBSTER, J. 1995. 'Interpretatio: Roman word power and the Celtic gods', *Britannia*, 26: 153–61.

—— 1997. 'A negotiated syncretism: Readings on the development of Romano-Celtic religion' in D. Mattingly (ed.), *Dialogues in Roman Imperialism: Power, discourse, and discrepant experiences in the Roman Empire*, Journal of Roman Archaeology Supplementary Series No. 23 (Portsmouth, RI), pp. 165–84.

—— 1999. 'At the end of the world: Druidic and other revitalization movements in post-conquest Gaul and Britain', *Britannia*, 30: 1–20.

WHITTAKER, C. 1995. 'Integration of the early Roman West: The example of Africa' in J. Metzler, M. Millett, N. Roymans, et al. (eds), *Integration in the Early Roman West: The role of culture and ideology* (Luxembourg: Musée National d'Histoire et d'Art No. 4), pp. 19–32.

—— 1997. 'Imperialism and Culture: The Roman initiative' in D. Mattingly (ed.), *Dialogues in Roman Imperialism: Power, discourse, and discrepant experiences in the Roman Empire*, Journal of Roman Archaeology Series No. 23 (Portsmouth, RI), pp. 143–64.

WOODWARD, A. 1992. *Shrines and Sacrifice* (London, Batsford).

WOOLF, G. 1998. *Becoming Roman: The origins of provincial civilization in Gaul* (Cambridge: Cambridge University Press).

—— 2001. 'The Roman cultural revolution in Gaul' in S. Keay and N. Terrenato (eds), *Italy and the West: Comparative issues in Romanization* (Oxford: Oxbow), pp. 173–86.

CHAPTER 47

MALTESE PREHISTORIC RELIGION

CAROLINE MALONE AND SIMON STODDART

1 Introduction

THE small Mediterranean archipelago of Malta holds some of the best-preserved material remains of prehistoric religion in Europe (Figure 47.1). The rich potential of the parent limestone bedrock and the lack of alternative building material privileged stone construction. Over the course of time, this stone construction became increasingly more elaborate, and between 3600 BC and 2400 BC, substantial stone monuments were first constructed, and then maintained, for primarily ritual purposes. Their construction was a profound statement of Maltese identity expressed through religion, since such constructions have no close parallel and, apart from examples from Sardinia, no similar level of elaboration in the Mediterranean. The dating of these earliest monuments makes them some of the earliest substantial stone monuments in the world, although monumental shrines have been more recently found in the northern Mesopotamia region (Schmidt 2006) of earlier date. After the abandonment of these ritual structures at about 2400 BC, and a certain amount of reuse for different purposes, there followed a different dolmen—purely burial—tradition in the Bronze Age that can be closely connected to contemporary developments in Puglia, Italy.

2 The History of Research

In common with other major megalithic constructions in Europe, the megalithic constructions of Malta were noticed at an early date (Evans 1971: 3–5). The first definite mention of a Maltese temple is in the seventeenth century (Abela 1647). In the course of the late eighteenth century and early nineteenth century, Malta became an important focus of the Grand Tour, principally by British travellers (Angas 1842; Brydone 1790; Burton 1838; Cockburn 1815; Davy 1842; Stoupe 1780). The more observant of these began to record the impressive megalithic structures. The most important of these early records is that of Jean

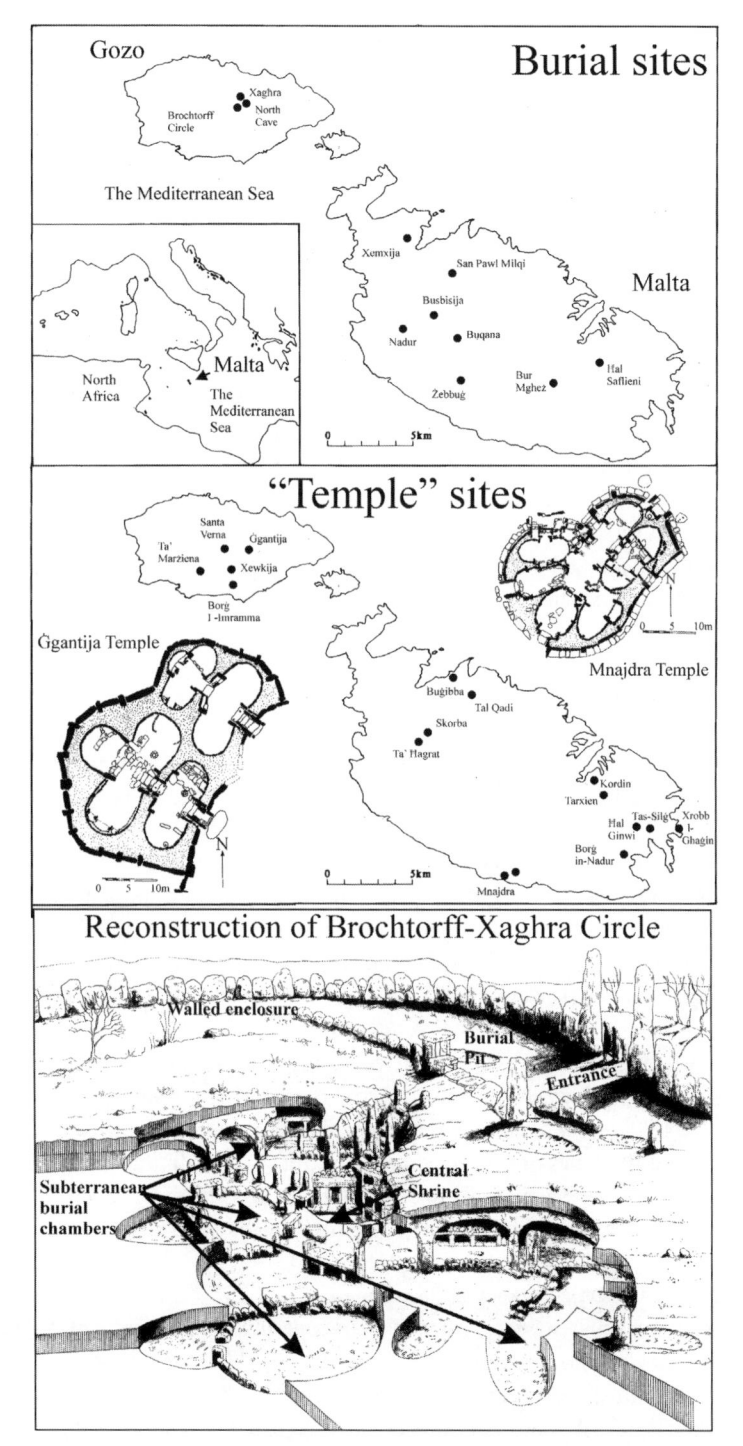

FIGURE 47.1 Map of Malta showing main temple and burial sites, with plans of typical 'temples' (Ġgantija and Mnajdra) and reconstruction of the Brochtorff-Xagħra Circle funerary site.

Houel who was the engraver to King Louis of France (Houel 1782-87). In a curious link to the study of some of the prominent prehistoric monuments of Wessex in south-western England, Colt Hoare (1817) was another early visitor.

Excavation of these monuments is recorded at least by the 1820s, in some cases by local administrators. It is known that Ġgantija was excavated in 1827, the nearby burial monument of the Brochtorff Circle at Xagħra at much the same time, Ħaġar Qim in 1839, and Mnajdra in 1840. Records were, however, relatively scant and it is only through the good fortune of the presence of an artist such as de Brocktorff (Grima 2004a), or of a chaplain from a passing ship, or in some cases more detailed descriptions (Vance 1842) that any understanding of the original condition of excavated monuments is known to us today. More systematic work had to await the investigations of Caruana at the end of the century (Caruana 1882; 1886; 1896a; 1896b).

Notice of these monuments, however, did not signify full recognition of their antiquity. The monuments were invariably dated to later periods, most notably the Phoenicians, by analogy with civilizations considered capable of such elaborate constructions. In fact the dating of these monuments has invariably remained a problem, since dry-stone construction can lack the clear stylistic form of classical antiquity and militates against easy stratigraphy. Subtleties such as sealed floors within the megalithic structures were only recognized later.

Work has been undertaken by scholars to unravel the sociological context of these explorations (Leighton 1989). Prehistoric monuments appeared early in artistic renderings but then took second place when other topics became more favoured (Sant Cassia 1993). Furthermore, in the early depictions, the local people are closely connected with their monuments, whereas later in the colonial period there appears to be a relative alienation (Grima 2004a).

The recognition of the relative antiquity of these monuments was only definitively achieved in the early twentieth century (Mayr 1901; 1908). These publications coincided with a reawakening of fieldwork on megalithic remains by Tagliaferro (Tagliaferro 1910, 1911a, 1911b, 1912) and Magri. The latter scholar tragically died before he could adequately record his work at the underground megalithic funerary construction of Ħal Saflieni (Briffa 2002-3).

These achievements were, however, dwarfed by the work of Zammit who as director of the museum of archaeology from 1904 to 1935 transformed Maltese archaeology. On appointment, he first rescued, as best he could, the understanding of the excavations of Ħal Saflieni without the notes of the excavator (Zammit 1908-9; Zammit 1910; Zammit 1925; 1928; Zammit et al. 1912). Even more importantly he directed the excavation of the one megalithic structure, Tarxien, where—until recently—we have an adequate understanding of its spatial organization (Zammit 1915-16, 1916, 1916-17, 1918-20, 1930). Furthermore, Zammit took steps to invite colleagues from Malta (Tagliaferro 1910) and beyond (Ashby et al. 1913; Murray 1923-9) to work with him in uncovering the megaliths of Malta, leading to a great expansion of knowledge from a range of sites. The records created by Zammit were of such a standard that they are now being further investigated to extract the full interpretative potential (Anderson and Stoddart 2007; Barrowclough 2007; Malone and Stoddart in preparation).

Synthesis of this new information took longer. The work of Ugolini (Ugolini 1934) was until recently damned because of its connection with Fascist Italy and the rather elaborate schemes placing Malta at the centre of a Mediterranean civilization. Grandiose reconstructions of the monuments were undertaken at a similar time by Ceschi (1939). However, more recently, Ugolini's interpretative analysis of the spatial organization of the megalithic structures has been highlighted and shown to be highly innovative (Pessina and Vella 2005; Vella 2007). Nevertheless, the main levels of synthesis have been achieved more recently by a matching of material culture to structures, and thus to relative dating (Evans 1971; Renfrew 1973) and then popularized (Cilia 2004). The original synthesis of culture history (Evans 1953) was modified by the use of radiocarbon at the excavation of Skorba (Trump 1966) and elsewhere, and then calibrated (Renfrew 1972) to produce the framework that essentially still exists today.

In more recent times the main fieldwork has been undertaken on the two megalithic funerary complexes of the Brochtorff Circle at Xagħra and the Ħal Saflieni monument. The first was a relatively large Anglo-Maltese project which uncovered some 220,000 human skeletal parts in the midst of an underground megalithic-cum-cave complex, in association with art and animal bones (Malone et al. 2009; Stoddart et al. 1993). This has proved to be complementary to the understanding of the Ħal Saflieni complex whose bones were almost entirely lost after excavation, but which was recently partly reinvestigated prior to conservation and reopening of the monument to the public (Pace 2000).

3 THE HISTORICAL DEVELOPMENT OF MALTESE MEGALITHS

A principal characteristic of the Maltese megaliths is the relationship between subterranean megalithic monuments and above-ground megalithic monuments. Two of the most impressive megalithic monuments are mortuary structures below ground. The first (Ħal Saflieni) is a construction where the megalithic element is the globigerina bedrock itself. This site bears a clear stylistic similarity to the form and structure of the famous upstanding megalithic structures of Ġgantija, Mnajdra, Ta' Ħaġrat, and Ħaġar Qim. The second (Brochtorff Circle at Xagħra) is a natural cave system within the coralline bedrock where globigerina limestone megalithic blocks have been imported to megalithize a natural setting.

This relationship of form has been developed into an evolutionary framework broadly from the simple and underground to the complex and overground back to the complex and underground (Evans 1959). The discoveries of lobe-shaped chambered tombs at Żebbuġ (Baldacchino and Evans 1954) and Xemxija (Evans 1971) in the Żebbuġ and Ġgantija periods respectively were interpreted as the precursors of the simpler versions of the lobe-shaped monuments above ground. Megalithic structures above ground were interpreted as developing from simple trefoil structures in the Mgarr phase to clusters of monuments in the Ġgantija phase (3600–3000 BC) and multiple-lobed elaborately decorated structures in the Tarxien phase (3000–2400 BC). The stratigraphy of this sequence has been broadly tested by excavation of the multiple floors of the monuments, but the phasing of the dry-stone walling is more difficult to establish. The final stage of this evolutionary development is the transfer of the complex surface architecture to the subterranean funerary domain. The phasing is difficult to establish at Ħal Saflieni because of the lack of analysed stratigraphy. However, at Brochtorff Circle at Xagħra, the vast majority of the evidence is Tarxien period, which does tend to confirm the dating of this final phase of elaboration.

There is also probably a sub-history of each monument. Both known mortuary structures and a number of the above ground megalithic structures had a foundation in the Żebbuġ phase (4100–3800 BC) which survives as pockets within or under the main structure (Bonanno et al. 1990). Most known monuments have most probably been left in the form that the practices of the elaborate Tarxien developed them, which makes it difficult to understand the intervening period of Ġgantija. Furthermore, in a number of cases, most notably that of the Brochtorff Circle at Xagħra, there is the potential for a deliberate and conscious closure of the monument at the end of its use. In this case, the recovery of objects from the monuments may represent more this closure of ritual than a frozen understanding of the living rituals themselves, a point that will be referred to again below.

4 The Maltese Temples

The term *temple* has been deliberately avoided as a terminology until this moment. The surface megalithic structures of the Maltese islands are generally given the nomenclature temple (Stroud 2007). At first sight this may seem an anachronistic imposition from a classical past. However, the term *templum* from its Etruscan and Roman usage, precisely connotes that sense of place which a visit to a Maltese megalithic structure confirms. Furthermore, of all prehistoric societies, it is the Maltese that appears to develop the profound sense of formal difference between three contexts of daily practice: the domestic (or at least some aspects), the interment of the dead (subterranean mortuary megalithic structures), and the rituals of the living (above ground temples).

4.1 The Structures of Maltese Temples

The structures of the Maltese temples combine a number of distinctive features: monumentality, axial symmetry, an external concave façade, and internal-lobed and generally concave stone structures. The 'temple' is immediately recognizable as a repeated regular form, albeit with variations across the 30 plus examples recorded. These repeated structural features come together to give an indication of the types of liturgy which might have been practised over several centuries between around 3500–2400 BC. The axial nature of the monument directs the eye from the entrance over slightly rising ground to a central focal apse and is clearly theatrical in design and intent. The external façade and the narrow monumental entrance distinguish the outside of the monument from the inside. The control of that opening (as suggested by rope or closure holes) would permit theatrical revelation to those outside, controlled by those performing inside the recesses of the monument. The lobed spaces grant opportunities for off-stage activities partly within the sight of observers, the display of objects and the enactment of ritual action, but also providing deeper areas of secrecy and privacy. The full experience of this liturgical potential requires both a personal presence (Tilley and Bennett 2004) and a systematic scientific analysis of the internal space (Anderson and Stoddart 2007; Malone 2007a and 2007b). The fixed furniture included display benches; shelves and recesses in the walls; recesses in the ground and libation holes; and thresholds and screens, which added to the complexity of the internal space and were enhanced by the movable presence of liturgical objects (see below) as well as textured, patterned, and coloured surfaces.

Within the canon of these features, the Maltese temples offer some distinctive variation and it is worth identifying some of the ways the temples differ. There are differences in monumentality; the numbers of individual temples clustered together; and their aesthetic appearance which are related partly to constructional material, partly to their individual setting, and partly, unfortunately, to their state of preservation.

The four temples at Tarxien have left the best knowledge of spatial organization thanks to a higher level of excavation records. The original vertical scale of the monument is difficult to measure since it has been truncated by agricultural activity, but the relatively intact façade of the most westerly structure measures some 30 m across, and nearly 3 m high. The general reconstruction scheme suggests that the five-apse temples were initially built in a sequence from east to west (Tx E, Tx Cent, and Tx S), until finally a six-apse temple (Tx SE) was inserted into the space between the two most westerly examples and interconnected to the third through a north-east apse. However, other sequences might suggest that Tx S was the final flourish of building, constructed rapidly and with poorer materials, but a high level of internal decoration, whilst the middle temple structure was rebuilt on the base of an earlier structure (Cilia 2004: 64; Evans 1971: 137). As with all the temples investigated, Tarxien metamorphosed through many forms over its long life.

The three temples of Mnajdra are arranged around a small curvilinear court that measures some 30 m across at its greatest extent. The southern temple is a small trefoil structure. The middle temple is a larger four-apsed structure. The final lower temple has two main apses whereas the inner apses are subdivided and reach some 5 m in height.

The two temples of Ġgantija on Gozo are the most monumental that survive. The full double curvilinear façade is more than 40 m across and the façade can be reconstructed to have reached some 10 m in height. All this monumentality is enhanced by the coralline limestone from which the monument is constructed. The southern five-apse temple appears to have been constructed first and the four-apse north temple added at a later date, although all within the Ġgantija phase.

The main temple at Ħaġar Qim and three adjacent building groups present a very different pattern. The main temple cluster consists of at least two conjoined temple structures (and in-filled spaces) with at least five entrances from different points that lack the axial directionality of most other temple structures. A principal concave façade does survive to the south-east and this measures some 20 m across with the highest single stone reaching 6 m in height (although care must be taken since it is difficult to calculate the extent of restoration). Other temple layouts, such as Skorba, Ta' Ħaġrat, and Borġ in-Nadur are far more fragmentary, and not suitable for detailed analysis.

Some work has been done on the mobilization of manpower and the constructional techniques of the Maltese temples. Estimates of the mobilization of manpower suggest that the construction of the temples was well within the capacity of agricultural societies on the islands (Clark 2004). Early analysis of the temples appeared to suggest that they were, at least in part, open to the sky. More recent analysis, in part echoing the earlier work of Ceschi, now suggests that it was quite within the capability of the builders and the stability of the monuments to be completely roofed in stone (Torpiano 2004). This interpretation appears to be supported by small contemporary models of temples showing roofs, and by the subterranean roofing skeomorph of Ħal Saflieni.

4.2 Artefacts from Maltese Temples

The Maltese temples have provided a rich repertoire of artefacts that include representations of the human form, representations of animals, axe amulets, large stone bowls, and richly decorated ceramics (Figure 47.2).

The representations of the human form are some of the richest components of the liturgical furniture from the Temple Culture and range across a variety of forms (Evans 1971; Malone 1998; 2008; Malone and Stoddart in preparation; Stoddart and Malone 2008; Vella 2005). In general terms the 'classic' figures (traditionally and erroneously named 'mother goddesses') conform to a principle of sexual ambiguity and corpulence (Malone et al. 1995), often decorated with distinctive pleated skirts. A second group are far more linear in form, with elaborate hair/headdress and pleated skirts. A third group include schematic monstrous and pathological figures of small scale. In specific terms these different groups are distinct in terms of scale and material.

At the largest scale, there is a truncated standing figure found in the west temple at Tarxien, first right-hand apse, which must originally have been 2 m high. This figure was carved from limestone and was clearly static, architecturally placed in a hierarchical relationship with the observer. Two smaller standing figures, in the order of 1 m high and also made of limestone, have been discovered at Ħaġar Qim (a pair) and at Tas Silġ. These could be manoeuvred into position, but could not have been easily manipulated in the liturgy. A smaller class of mainly seated figures, also made of limestone, in the order of 20–40 cm in height have been mainly found at Ħaġar Qim. These could easily be moved into new positions (wear to their bases attests this suggestion) and they also permitted the manipulation of changeable heads, with puppet-like strings threaded through the neck. At this scale, there is an overlap of use of materials. At least three standing figures with pleated skirts, originally as much as 60 cm in height and made out of baked clay, were found in the temple of Tarxien. These were moulded around a straw armature and appear to have been remodelled several times.

The largest class of figurative representation is much smaller (less than 10 cm in size) and almost always made out of baked clay. Fewer of these representations have been found in temples compared with those found elsewhere, but this may reflect the techniques employed in excavation. Nevertheless examples have been found at Ħaġar Qim and Tarxien. In addition, a range of heads of corresponding scale, have been found at a number of temple sites including Tarxien, Mnajdra, and Ħaġar Qim.

A further class of find is provided by a particular part of the male human body. The phallus in single or multiple form has been found principally at Tarxien. These are generally small scale. Other similar-sized objects have been found at Tal-Qadi, Mnajdra, and Ġgantija. In addition, the Ġgantija temple contained a large phallic stone of about 1 m high.

Animal representation is generally found in the form of two-dimensional relief. The most prominent examples are at Tarxien where there is a line of ovicaprines and a pig in the first apse on the left and a pig/piglets and two bulls in an inner recess on the right beyond. A fish relief is represented at the temple of Buġibba.

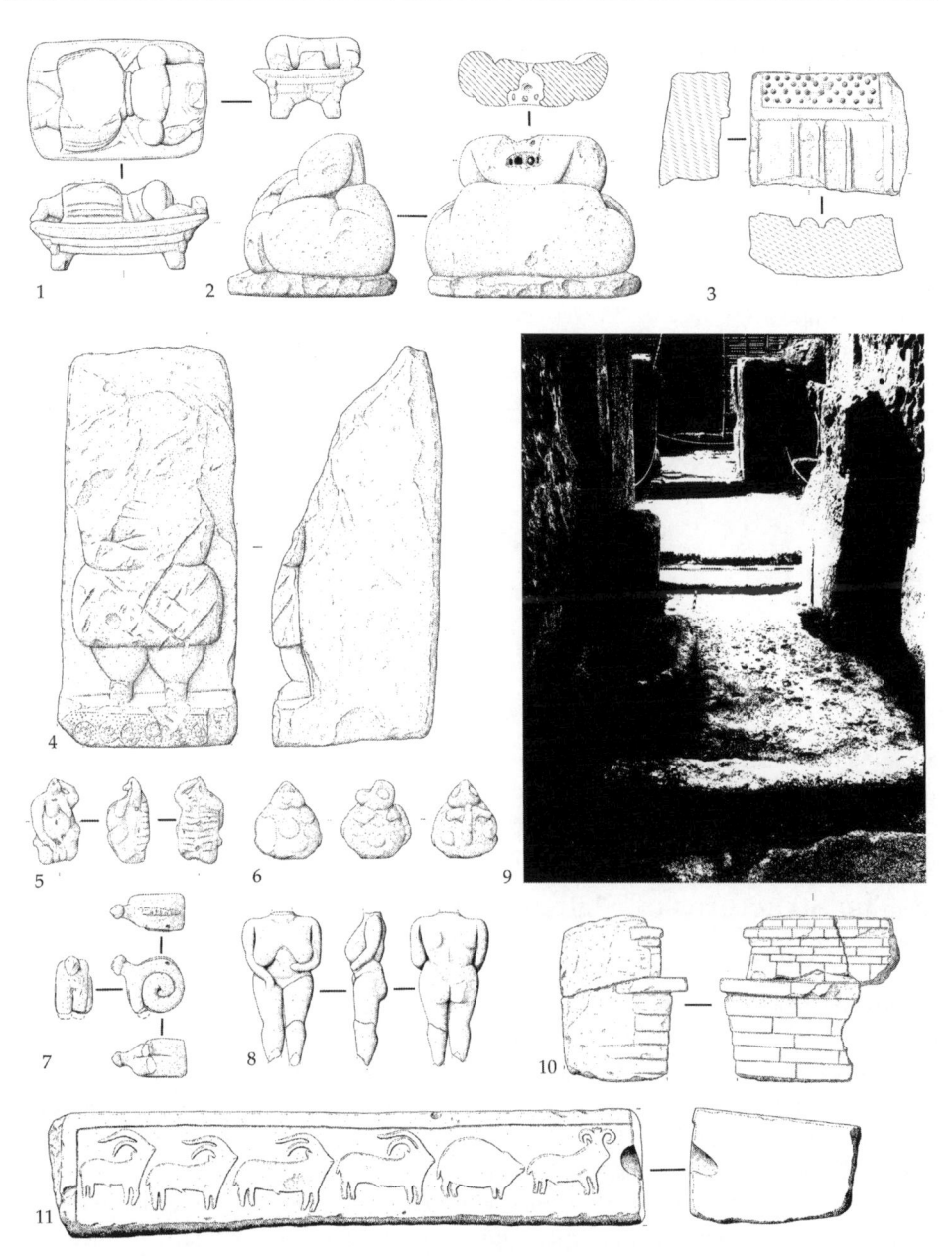

FIGURE 47.2 Examples of liturgical furniture from temples and funerary sites. (1) Terracotta sleeping bed figure, Ħal Saflieni (SP1001, 4 cm × 9 cm × 5.6 cm); (2) Stone figure with movable head, Ħaġar Qim (QS14, 23.5 cm); (3) Stone 'phallic' shrine fragment, Tarxien (TS18, 16 × 14.5 cm); (4) Stone statue recovered from Tas Silġ (122 cm); (5) Terracotta grotesque figure, Tarxien (TP1001, 7 cm); (6) Terracotta 'turtle', Mnajdra (MnP1011, 7.2 cm); (7) Terracotta 'snail', Brochtorff-Xaghra Circle (BR800, 37 cm × 35 cm); (8) Terracotta 'Venus', Ħaġar Qim (QP1000, 12.9 cm); (9) Photograph of southern temple access into Ġgantija showing thresholds and libation trough; (10) Stone model of temple, Tarxien (TS13, 19.2 cm); (11) Stone frieze of male animals from S Temple, Tarxien (once 2.3 m × 22 cm × 30 cm).

Other notable finds from the temples include liturgical furniture. Stone bowls appeared in great numbers suggesting that ritual largesse was part of the practices undertaken in prehistoric times. Feasting is further suggested by the presence of animal bones, in one case secreted into a hidden altar recess at Tarxien. Portable altars occur in a number of temples. Fire is suggested by the presence of circular receptacles on the ground with signs of burning. Washing is indicated by the presence of large stone bowls and troughs. Another prominent feature was the storage or caching of sacred objects, including stone axes and pierced, reduced, and sacralized axe amulets, figurines, statues and other 'valuables'.

The movable liturgical objects were combined with the complexities of the liturgical space to produce a theatrical effect. The scenes could be changed and the *dramatis personae* altered with great impact by the ritual specialists engaged in the temple ritual. All the senses—sight, smell, hearing, and even taste—would have been involved in a sensual experience that involved many sounds, smells, and colours.

5 Maltese Funerary Megalithic Structures

The funerary megalithic structures below ground provided a mirror image of the structures above ground. In the funerary context, the megalithic construction was mainly residual rather than constructional. Only two underground megalithic structures have been discovered, so it is more difficult to generalize, but they both clearly belong to the same megalithic conceptual tradition.

5.1 The Structures of Maltese Funerary Megalithic Structures

Two funerary megalithic structures have been discovered: Ħal Saflieni (Astley 1914; Pace 2004; Tagliaferro 1910) on the larger island of Malta and the Brochtorff Circle at Xagħra on the island of Gozo (Malone et al. 2008). The first is closely associated with the megalithic structures of Tarxien and Kordin. The second is closely associated with the megalithic structures of Ġgantija and Santa Verna.

The Ħal Saflieni represents the pure form of the residual megalithic monument. In other words, the globigerina limestone bedrock was excavated to create a three-dimensional representation of an underground megalithic complex. This extraordinary architectural effect was achieved on three vertical levels, converging on a central area where the megalithic effect of trilithons and corbelled roof was fully realized. The effect was a deep, dark structure where eleven thresholds had to be crossed to reach the deepest of seventy locales some 10 m below the ground. Some of these locales were open ceremonial spaces, including the central megalithic focus; others were cubicles for the reception of human remains.

The Brochtorff Circle at Xagħra occupies an intermediate position between the fully constructed megalithic structures above ground and the fully excavated megalithic structure of Ħal Saflieni below ground. The below-ground structure is based on a natural cave system which was enhanced by the addition of megalithic features both to fill the centre of cavities and to mark the edges and transitions of caves. The back of one inner cave had an upright phallic megalith. This composite megalithic architecture was then filled with human remains and liturgical furniture in an elaborate and structured manner (Stoddart 2007). Above ground, the site was enclosed with a megalithic circle that had its formal entrance framed by two megalithic uprights on the east side facing the Ġgantija temple.

5.2 The Finds from Maltese Funerary Megalithic Structures

The liturgical furniture of funerary sites overlaps considerably with that of the temples. The two major differences in the funerary context are the overwhelming presence of human remains and the smaller scale of the objects. Portability of both human remains and ritual objects is the key feature of the finds which had to be transported below ground via tortuous access.

Human representation is one key feature of the finds. Only two representations are of reasonable size. A globigerina limestone standing figure from Ħal Saflieni is almost 40 cm high and a much broken standing figure from the Brochtorff Circle at Xagħra might have approached 1 m in height. All other finds were in the order of centimetres in size, generally made of clay and representing single individuals or parts of individuals, sometimes of very schematic form. In the case of the grouping of objects from the sacristy shrine at the Brochtorff Circle at Xagħra the size was at the upper end of the range but portability was still prominent. This ritual cache comprised in one case three seated figures on a couch, and in the other six schematic figurines, a human head on a stand, a male pig on a stick, and a human head on a double-legged support. Similarly, the two cases of prone figures on couches from Ħal Saflieni, in this case made out of clay, are readily portable. At the smallest end of the scale there is a set of human heads from the Brochtorff Circle at Xagħra carved onto individual animal phalanges, of up to 3.5 cm long.

Small-scale three-dimensional representation of animals is another feature of the finds from funerary megalithic structures. Apart from a baked clay snail with a human head from the Brochtorff Circle at Xagħra, the main repertoire has been found at Ħal Saflieni. These mainly take the form of pendants representing birds and a range of animals, or are representations modelled in clay of reptiles and fish.

A further class of material from megalithic funerary structures are ceramic bowls. Although it is difficult to quantify these precisely, they appear to be less frequent than on temple sites. Only 14 complete bowls were found from the Brochtorff Circle at Xagħra, although as many as 400 could have been present if the full weight of the ceramics is taken into account. In any case the number is considerably less than the minimum number of individuals (800 plus) buried at the site.

A further set of items can be considered personal ornaments. Only the recent study of the Brochtorff Circle at Xagħra permits a statistical study of these finds (Malone et al. 2008) where some 1,000 items have been found. Of these 850 are made of shell; 57 bone, ceramic, and stone; 41 are axe pendants from outside the Maltese islands; and 45 are pseudo-anthropomorphic bone pendants, dating principally from before the megalithic period (that is Żebbuġ). Chert and flint objects may be more utilitarian in nature. The 267 pieces of flint-chert from the Brochtorff Circle at Xagħra are represented by a limited range of forms, principally large knife-scrapers, small scrapers, regular blades, irregular waste flakes with occasional working and retouch, and waste chips.

6 The Landscape Setting of Maltese Temple Culture

The original interpretation of the landscape setting of the Maltese megaliths was that they formed the central focus of hierarchical groups or chiefdoms (Renfrew 1973). More recently, the clustering of temples into groups, and groups of clusters around a mortuary monument, has suggested a more internally competitive social organization (Bonanno et al. 1990). Further work using Geographical Information Systems has suggested that the temples provided portals between the Mediterranean and the island world accessed along natural routeways (Grima 2004b; Grima 2005; Grima 2007) and that megalith funerary structures provided portals between life and death (Malone et al. 2008). The Maltese islands have dramatic natural topography with prominent ridges and flat-topped plateaux, but the location of temples rarely seems to take full visual advantage of these places. Instead, the arrangement of the monumental clusters seems to be organized more in relation to natural features such as routes or springs, and to each other. Notions of east and west, sunrise, sunset, and the surrounding sea and heavens may well have been significant in layout. These are particularly shown in the mortuary sites, where access seems to be from the east or west, in comparison to the broadly southern, SE–SW directions of the main corridors of the temples (Malone 2007b).

7 The Religion and Cosmology of Maltese Megalithic Monuments

The landscape setting of the Maltese monuments appears to map onto a corresponding cosmology (Stoddart 2002, 2007) (Figure 47.3). The funerary megalithic structures located below ground belonged to the world of the dead in the lowest cosmological level. The temples located above ground belonged to the world of the living in the middle cosmological level. The sky, the location of stars and ancestors (in distant Sicily), formed the uppermost cosmological level. Cosmological analysis has also been undertaken of the internal organization of the temples, envisaging them as a mapping of the place of Malta in the Mediterranean onto an idealized reconstruction in the form of the temple itself (Grima 2001).

The religion that lay behind the Maltese megalithic structures is difficult to reconstruct in its entirety. Ideas of mother goddesses (Gimbutas 1991) have generally been replaced by concepts of identity (Robb 2001), and regeneration and celebration of the cycle of life (Stoddart 2007). Recent research has shown that there are clear underlying structuring principles behind the layout out of the temples and their liturgy into left and right, sinister and favoured, and possibly in the posture of some of the figures where right hands are extended (Malone 2007b). The categorization of animal and human representation is also graphic and potentially suggestive of cosmological beliefs. Birds (models or amulets or shown in relief on pottery), domestic mammals (associated with food vessels or relief panels in temples), and cold-blooded subterranean or reptilian creatures (mostly modelled or in

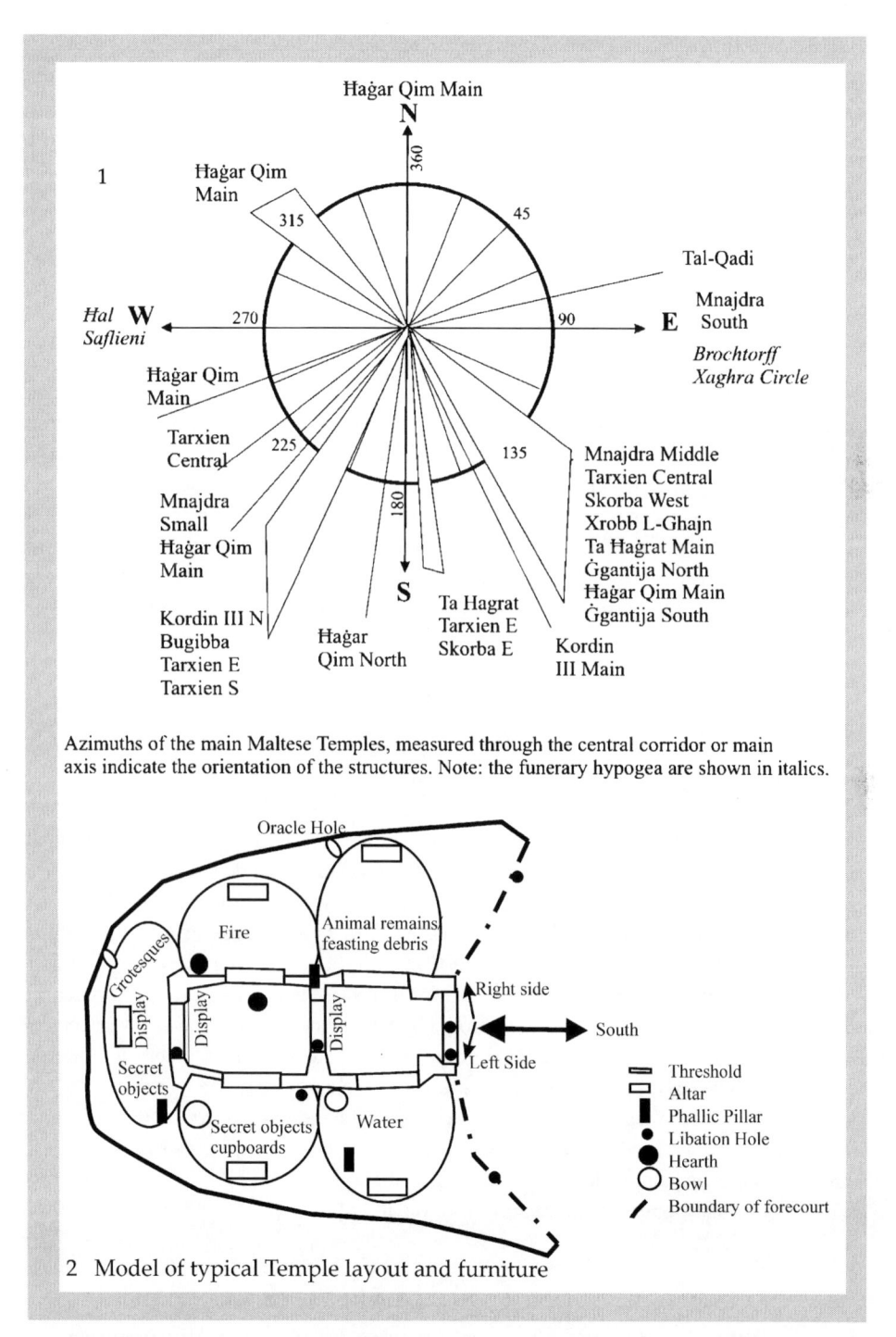

FIGURE 47.3 The cosmology of prehistoric Malta. (1) Azimuth directions of main corridors in temples and hypogea (Brochtorff Xagħra Circle and Ħal Saflieni); (2) Schematic plan of temple layout, showing typical positions of furniture and architectural features; (3) Cosmological model for early Malta.

3. Model for the celestial–cosmological world of early Malta

LEVEL	DEFINITION	OCCUPANTS	MATERIAL CULTURE	IMAGES
UPPER	Celestial	Exotic ancestors/divine	Stars, exotic materials	Birds, ancestors
MIDDLE	Mundane	The living	Temples, houses	Figurative, mammals
LOWER	Spirits	The dead	Mortuary complexes	Cold blooded

FIGURE 47.3 (Continued)

architectural relief) form a rich and varied zoo of images. The birds could echo the mass migrations that feature on Malta, and signal changing seasons, or travel between different cosmological levels. The cold-blooded creatures are rich with ideas of metamorphosis, cold, death, sea, and so on. Human representation, in comparison, is always modelled in the round, unless so abbreviated and schematic that they are suggested in phallic shrines. The prone bed and the standing, clothed, and ornamented figures all imply a variety of symbolic activities, gestures, and status and, together with the richness of the architectural space and these contained artefacts, permit an unprecedented insight into a prehistoric religion.

8 The Ending of the First Megalithic Tradition

The Tarxien period elaboration of the megalithic tradition came to a close in about 2400 BC as revealed by the latest radiocarbon dating from the Brochtorff Circle at Xagħra (Malone et al. 2008). The reasons behind this ending may have been simply the preordained closure of a ritual cycle in a manner that has been noted in closure of a number of other megalithic traditions from Wessex (Piggott 1962) to Anatolia (Schmidt 2006). Alternatively, or perhaps interacting with this reasoning, doubts about the efficacy of the religion, possibly influenced by ecological change, or even external demographic movements, may have influenced the prehistoric Maltese to bring the tradition to a close. In two instances, there is potential evidence of iconoclasm directed against the prehistoric religion. A human figure at Tas Silġ may have suffered its damage at a later date (Vella 1999), but a figure of similar dimensions at Brochtorff Circle appears to have been damaged during the late Tarxien period, since some of its fragments were well embedded in the Tarxien stratigraphy. If this interpretation is correct, then it was the practitioners of the religion who instituted its own completion.

9 Conclusions: An Italian Endnote

The final megalithic note on Malta is one that connects to peninsular Italy. In the full Bronze Age, a tradition of dolmen construction appeared in Malta (Evans 1956). The date and form of these dolmen are closely related to a similar development in the Puglia region of peninsular Italy. No burials have been definitively found associated with these dolmen in Malta, but this is most probably a product of their severely eroded condition. These new megalithic structures appear to form a new cultural tradition, completely distinct in date, form, and scale from all that preceded them in Malta. The most probable explanation is that these new structures were employed to display the dead in a particular orientation (Hoskin 2001) to a new cosmological structure.

Suggested Reading

David Trump's general guidebook to early Malta is very useful, *Malta: An archaeological guide*, 2nd rev. edn (Valletta: Progress Press, 2000) as is his 2002 *Malta: Prehistory and temples (Malta's living heritage)* (Malta: Midsea Books). Barrowclough and Malone's 2007 *Cult in Context* (Oxford: Oxbow), provides many useful papers that focus on the issues of ritual and religion in early Malta. Cilia's 2004 beautifully illustrated volume, *Malta before History: The world's oldest free-standing stone architecture* (Malta: Miranda) is a comprehensive introduction.

References

Abela, G. F. 1647. *Della descrittione di Malta, Isola nel Mare Siciliano, con le sue Antichità ed altre notizie* (Malta: P. Bonacota).

Anderson, M. and Stoddart, S. K. F. 2007. 'Mapping Cult Context: GIS applications in Maltese temples' in D. Barrowclough and C. A. T. Malone (eds), *Cult in Context* (Oxford: Oxbow), pp. 41–4.

Angas, G. F. 1842. *A Ramble in Malta and Sicily, in the autumn of 1841* (London: Smith, Elder and Co).

Ashby, T., Bradley, R. N., Peet, T. E., et al. 1913. 'Excavations in 1908–11 in various megalithic buildings in Malta and Gozo', *Papers of the British School at Rome*, 6(1): 1–126.

Astley, H. J. D. 1914. 'Notes on the Hypogeum at Ħal Saflieni, Malta', *Journal of the Royal Anthropological Institute*, 44: 394–6.

Baldacchino, J. G. and Evans, J. D. 1954. 'Prehistoric tombs near Żebbuġ, Malta', *Papers of the British School at Rome*, 22 (n.s. 9): 1–21.

Barrowclough, D. 2007. 'Putting cult in context: Ritual, religion and cult in temple-period Malta' in D. Barrowclough and C. A. T. Malone (eds), *Cult in Context* (Oxford: Oxbow), pp. 45–53.

Bonanno, A., Gouder, T., Malone, C., et al. 1990. 'Monuments in an island society: The Maltese context', *World Archaeology*, 22(2): 190–205.

Briffa, J. M. 2002–3. 'New light on Fr Magri's exploration of the Hypogeum: Notes from correspondence with the British Museum', *Malta Archaeological Review*, 6: 41–6.

Brydone, P. 1790. *A Tour through Sicily and Malta in a series of letters to William Beckford Esq. of Somerly in Suffolk from P. Brydone, F.R.S. in two volumes* (London: Printed for A. Steahan and T. Cadell, in the Strand).

Burton, N. 1838. *Narrative of a voyage from Liverpool to Alexandria: touching at the island of Malta, and from thence to Beirout in Syria; with a journey to Jerusalem, voyage from Jaffa to Cyprus and Constantinople and a Persian journey from Constantinople, through Turkey, Wallachia, Hungary, and Prussia, the town of Hamburgh in the years 1836-7* (Dublin: John Yates).

Caruana, A. A. 1882. *Report on the Phoenician and Roman Antiquities in the Group of the Islands of Malta* (Malta: Government Printing Office).

—— 1886. *Recent Further Excavations of The Megalithic Antiquities of 'Hagiar-Kim' Malta, executed in the year 1885, under the direction of Dr. A. A. Caruana* (Malta: Government Printing Office).

—— 1896a. 'Further great stones, Gozo, explored in 1893', *The Archaeological Journal*, 53: 140–3.

—— 1896b. 'Further megalithic discoveries and explorations in the islands of Malta during 1892 and 1893, under the governorship of Sir Henry A. Smyth KCMG', *The Archaeological Journal*, 53: 26–45.

Ceschi, C. 1939. *Architettura dei templi megalitici di Malta* (Roma: Casa Editrice Fratelli Palombi).

Cilia, D. (ed.) 2004. *Malta before History: The world's oldest free-standing stone architecture* (Malta: Miranda).

Clark, D. 2004. 'Building logistics' in D. Cilia (ed.), *Malta before History* (Malta: Miranda), pp. 367–77.

Cockburn, G. 1815. *A voyage to Cadiz and Gibraltar, up the Mediterranean to Sicily and Malta: in 1810 and 11 including a description of Sicily and the Lipari islands and an excursion in Portugal* (London: Printed for J. Harding, 36 St James Street and M. N. Mahon, Dublin).

Colt Hoare, R. 1817. *Recollections Abroad, During the Year 1790: Sicily and Malta* (Bath: Richard Cruttwell).

Davy, J. 1842. *Notes and Observations on the Ionian Islands and Malta: With some remarks on Constantinople and Turkey, and on the system of quarantine as at present conducted* (London: Smyth, Elder and Co.).

Evans, J. D. 1953. 'The prehistoric culture sequence of the Maltese archipelago', *Proceedings of the Prehistoric Society*, 19: 41–94.

—— 1956. 'The dolmens of Malta and the origins of the Tarxien cemetery culture', *Proceedings of the Prehistoric Society*, 22: 85–101.

—— 1959. *Malta*, Ancient Peoples and Places (London: Thames and Hudson).

—— 1971. *The Prehistoric Antiquities of the Maltese islands: A survey* (London: Athlone Press).

Gimbutas, M. 1991. *The Civilization of the Goddess: The world of old Europe* (New York: HarperCollins Publishers).

Grima, R. 2001. 'An iconography of insularity: A cosmological interpretation of some images and spaces in the Late Neolithic Temples of Malta', *Papers from the Institute of Archaeology*, 12: 48–65.

—— 2004a. *The Archaeological Drawings of Charles Fredrick de Brochtorff* (Malta: Midsea Books Ltd and Heritage Malta).

—— 2004b. 'The landscape context of megalithic architecture' in D. Cilia (ed.), *Malta Before History* (Malta: Miranda), pp. 327–45

—— 2005. *Monuments in Search of a Landscape: The landscape context of monumentality in Late Neolithic Malta*, Unpublished PhD Dissertation, University of London.

Grima, R. 2007. 'The cultural construction of the landscape in Late Neolithic Malta' in D. Barrowclough and C. A. T. Malone (eds), *Cult in Context* (Oxford, Oxbow), pp 35–40.
Hoskin, M. 2001. *Tombs, Temples and their Orientation: A new perspective on Mediterranean prehistory* (Bognor Regis: Ocarina Press).
Houel, J. P. L. L. 1782–87. *Voyage pittoresque des isles de Sicile: de Malte et de Lipari, où l'on traite des antiquités qui s'y trouvent encore; des principaux phénomènes que la nature y offre; du costume des habitans, & de quelques usages* (Paris : Imprimerie de Monsieur).
Leighton, R. 1989. 'Antiquarianism and Prehistory in West Mediterranean Islands', *The Antiquaries Journal*, 69(II): 183–204.
Malone, C. A. T. 1998. 'God or goddess: The temple art of ancient Malta' in L. Goodison and C. Morris (eds), *Ancient Goddesses: The myths and the evidence* (London: The British Museum Press), pp. 148–63.
——2007a. 'Structure, art and ritual in a Maltese temple' in D. Barrowclough and C. A. T. Malone (eds), *Cult in Context* (Oxford, Oxbow), pp. 23–34.
——2007b. 'Access and Visibility in Prehistoric Malta' in M. Pomeroy-Kellinger and I. Scott (eds), *Recent Developments in the Research and Management at World Heritage Sites* (Oxford: Oxbow), pp. 15–25.
——2008. 'Metaphor and Maltese art: Explorations in the Temple Period', *Journal of Mediterranean Archaeology*, 21.1: 81–109.
——and Stoddart, S. K. F. in preparation. 'Explorations into the conditions of spiritual creativity in prehistoric Malta: Catalogue and study of figurative art from ancient Malta in context'.
——, and Townsend, A. 1995. 'The landscape of the island goddess? A Maltese perspective of the central Mediterranean', *Caeculus (Papers on Mediterranean Archaeology, Archaeological Institute, Groningen University)*, 2: 1–15.
——, Trump, D. et al. (eds) 2008. *Mortuary Ritual in Prehistoric Malta: The Brochtorff Circle excavations (1987–1994)* (Cambridge: McDonald Institute).
Mayr, A. 1901. 'Die vorgeschichtlichen Denkmäler von Malta', *Abhandlungen der Königlich Bayerischen Akademie der Wissenschaften*, 21: 645–721.
——1908. *The Prehistoric Remains of Malta*, trans. Marchioness of Milford Haven (Private circulation).
Murray, M. A. 1923–9. *Excavations in Malta*, 3 vols. (London: B. Quaritch).
Pace, A. (ed.) 2000. *The Ħal Saflieni Hypogeum 4000 BC–2000 AD* (Malta: National Museum of Archaeology).
——2004. *The Ħal Saflieni Hypogeum. Paola* (Sta Venera, Malta: Heritage Books–Heritage Malta).
Pessina, A. and Vella, N. 2005. *Un archeologo italiano a Malta. Luigi Maria Ugolini. An italian archaeologist in Malta* (Sta Venera, Malta: Midsea Books–Heritage Malta).
Piggott, S. 1962. *The West Kennet Long Barrow* (London: HMSO).
Renfrew, A. C. 1972. 'Malta and the calibrated radiocarbon chronology', *Antiquity*, 46(182): 141–4.
——1973. *Before Civilisation* (London: Jonathan Cape).
Robb, J. 2001. 'Island identities: Ritual, travel and the creation of difference in Neolithic Malta', *European Journal of Archaeology*, 4(2): 175–202.
Sant Cassia, P. 1993. 'The discovery of Malta: Nature, culture and ethnicity in 19th century painting (review article)', *Journal of Mediterranean Studies*, 3: 354–77.
Schmidt, K. 2006. *Sie bauten die ersten Tempel. Das rätselhafte Heiligtum der Steinzeitjäger* (Munich: C. H. Beck Verlag).
Stoddart, S. K. F. 2002. 'The Xagħra shaman?' in G. Carr and P. A. Baker (eds), *New Approaches to Medical Archaeology and Medical Anthropology: Practitioners, practices and patients* (Oxford: Oxbow Books), pp. 125–35.

—— 2007. 'The Maltese death cult in context' in D. Barrowclough and C. A. T. Malone (eds), *Cult in Context* (Oxford: Oxbow), pp. 54–60.
——, BONANNO, A., GOUDER, T., et al. 1993. 'Cult in an island society: Prehistoric Malta in the Tarxien period', *Cambridge Archaeological Journal*, 3(1): 3–19.
—— and MALONE, C. A. T. 2008. 'Changing beliefs in the human body in prehistoric Malta 5000–1500 BC', in D. Boric and J. Robb (eds), *Past Bodies. Body-centred Research in Archaeology* (Oxford: Oxbow), pp. 19–28.
STOUPE, J. G. A. 1780. *A tour through Sicily and Malta in a series of letters to William Beckford of Suffolk from P. Brydone* (Paris: J. G. A. Stoupe).
STROUD, K. 2007. 'Of giants and deckchairs: Understanding the Maltese megalithic temples' in D. Barrowclough and C. A. T. Malone (eds), *Cult in Context* (Oxford: Oxbow), pp. 16–22.
TAGLIAFERRO, N. 1910. 'The prehistoric pottery found in the hypogeum at Ḥal Saflieni, Casal Pawla, Malta', *Annals of Archaeology and Anthropology*, 3(1–2): 1–21.
—— 1911a. 'On the pottery lately found at Hagiar Kim and Mnaidra', *Archivum Melitense (Journal of the Malta Historical and Scientific Society)*, 1(3): 61–4.
—— 1911b. 'Prehistoric burials in a cave at Bur Meghez, near Mqabba, Malta', *Man*, 11: 147–50.
—— 1912. 'Prehistoric burial in a cave at Bur Meghez, near Mqabba, Malta', *Archivum Melitense (Journal of the Malta Historical and Scientific Society)*, 1 (1910–12) (7 (September 1912)): 143–9.
TILLEY, C. Y. and BENNETT, W. 2004. *The Materiality of Stone: Explorations in landscape phenomenology* (Oxford: Berg).
TORPIANO, A. 2004. 'The Construction of the Megalithic Temples' in D. Cilia (ed.), *Malta before History: The world's oldest free-standing stone architecture* (Malta: Miranda), pp. 347–65.
TRUMP, D. H. 1966. *Skorba: Excavations carried out on behalf of the National Museum of Malta. 1961–3*, Research Reports of the Society of Antiquaries of London 22 (London: Society of Antiquaries).
UGOLINI, L. M. 1934. *Malta. Origini della Civiltà Mediterranea* (Roma: La Libreria dello Stato).
VANCE, J. G. 1842. 'Description of an ancient temple near Crendi, Malta', *Archaeologia*, 29: 227–40.
VELLA G. I. 2005. *The Human Form in Neolithic Malta* (Malta: Midsea Books Ltd).
VELLA, N. C. 1999. '"Trunkless legs of stone": Debating ritual continuity at Tas-Silġ, Malta' in A. Mifsud and C. Savona-Ventura (eds), *Facets of Maltese Prehistory* (Malta: The Prehistoric Society of Malta), pp. 225–39.
—— 2007. 'From cabiri to goddesses: Cult, ritual and context in the formative years of Maltese archaeology' in D. Barrowclough and C. A. T. Malone (eds), *Cult in Context* (Oxford: Oxbow), pp. 61–71.
ZAMMIT, T. 1908–9. *Annual Report of the Curator of the Valletta Museum for the financial year 1909.*
—— 1910. *The Ḥal-Saflieni Prehistoric Hypogeum at Casal Paula, Malta. (The Small Objects and the Human Skulls found in the Ḥal-Saflieni Prehistoric Hypogeum, etc.) First report* (Malta: Government of Malta).
—— 1915–16. 'The Ḥal-Tarxien Neolithic Temple, Malta', *Archaeologia*, 67: 127–44.
—— 1916–17. 'Second Report on the Ḥal-Tarxien Excavations, Malta', *Archaeologia*, 68: 263–84.
—— 1918–20. 'Third Report on the Ḥal-Tarxien excavations, Malta', *Archaeologia*, 70: 179–200.
—— 1925. *The Ḥal-Saflieni Hypogeum 'Casal Paula-Malta': A short description of the monument with plan and illustrations* (Valletta: Giov. Muscat).
—— 1928. *The Neolithic Hypogeum at Ḥal-Saflieni, Casal Paula-Malta* (Valletta: Empire Press).
—— 1930. *Prehistoric Malta: The Tarxien temples* (Oxford and London: Oxford University Press).
——, PEET, T. E., and BRADLEY, R. N. 1912. *The Small Objects and the Human Skulls Found in the Ḥal-Saflieni Prehistoric Hypogeum at Casal Paula, Malta*, Second report (Valletta).

CHAPTER 48

MESOPOTAMIA

MICHAEL SEYMOUR

1 Introduction

THE term 'ancient Mesopotamia' refers to the land of the Tigris and Euphrates valleys, including all of Iraq as well as parts of modern Turkey and Syria, to several millennia of written history and to several further millennia of social, economic, cultural, and religious life prior to writing's first appearance in the region. This chapter concentrates on the literate, urban world of the late fourth to late first millennium BC, a span beginning roughly with the emergence of the first cities and ending with the gradual decline in the importance of native Mesopotamian gods during the Achaemenid Persian period (539–323 BC).

From the emergence of the world's first cities in Mesopotamia and the appearance of the world's earliest known writing there by c.3300 BC we see societies organized around large temple and palace institutions with extensive bureaucracies and priesthoods. More intimate, personal religion and ritual practice flourished alongside these large institutions at all times; however, while evidence does exist for these aspects of ancient religious life, our archaeological, textual, and iconographic data are undeniably biased toward the large institutions and their practices.

Many features of religious life varied greatly over the long period addressed here. Even the 'sacred marriage', an important ritual known from several cities through which the Sumerians renewed their bonds with the gods, vanishes in later Mesopotamia. Studies of historical change in Mesopotamian religion constitute some of the most important theoretical work in the field, and with a view to the comparative aims of the present volume the final part of the chapter focuses on this history of interpretation and research.

2 Data

The data available to Mesopotamian archaeologists on religion and ritual fall into three broad categories: texts, iconography, and archaeology.

2.1 Texts

Because of the practice of writing on clay tablets an enormous quantity and diversity of textual material from ancient Iraq has survived into the present; so much, indeed, that a key limitation in our knowledge stems principally from a shortage of Assyriologists—philologists with the specialist knowledge necessary to read, translate, and analyse the ancient sources. Nevertheless, 150 years of patient research has yielded incredible results, and texts relevant to many aspects of religious life are now available, albeit clustered in certain times and locales. Best known are the literary texts, all of which give us some insight into religious beliefs: Gilgamesh, the Descent of Inanna to the Underworld, the Babylonian Creation Epic, and Atra-hasis, to name a few. Alongside these is a wealth of hymns and prayers, oracles, divination literature, and magical texts, as well as more prosaic documents revealing details of the economic life and workings of temple institutions and the roles of priests and kings in ritual practice. It should thus be noted that in the study of ancient Mesopotamia 'theory' is as much a matter of literary criticism and theory as the application of archaeological or anthropological ideas and models (for a recent consideration in the context of Sumerian literature, see Black 1998).

2.2 Iconography

Though perhaps less abundant than texts, there is nevertheless much source material for the study of religious imagery available to us from the ancient Mesopotamian world. From the researcher's point of view the most important medium is glyptic. Cylinder and stamp seals carved in stone are highly varied and survive in quantity; they therefore form the mainstay of our knowledge on ancient Mesopotamian iconography (Figure 48.1). The representational content of their designs underwent substantial change over time, and to some extent this development has fed into synthetic theories on religious history (discussed below). More commonly, seals have proven crucial in understanding the meaning and significance of the vast array of symbols and associations in Mesopotamian visual culture (Black and Green 1992; Collon 2005). Green (1997) outlines some of the correlations between mythology as expressed in texts and in Mesopotamian art, while Lambert (1997) and Postgate (1994a) consider some of the problems involved in making such identifications.

Other visual sources include sculpture, temple, and palace decoration including relief carvings and some painting, as well as many votive objects. No cult statue of a god is known to have survived from any ancient Mesopotamian temple, and indeed it is quite possible that a complete example never will be found (see below). Their images can be seen in other art forms, however, and when combined with textual sources some impression of these central visual features of ancient Mesopotamian religion can be gleaned. It is interesting to note some reluctance to represent the highest members of the pantheon in quite the same direct way as other gods. Enlil is held in texts to be terrible to look upon, and in art tends to be represented simply by the divine symbol of a horned headdress (on divine images see Ornan 2005).

2.3 Archaeology

Both the above categories, of course, are themselves archaeological. In this context, however, 'archaeology' typically refers particularly to the study of ancient architecture and to the

FIGURE 48.1 Cylinder seals feature an enormous variety of iconography relating to divinities, mythology and ritual practice. This famous example shows several of the major gods with their attributes. In the centre of the seal impression the sun god Shamash rises between two mountains. Flanking him are the figures of Ishtar and Ea, the former winged and armed, the latter identified by the streams flowing from his shoulders and the presence of his double-faced attendant Usimu. All the figures wear the horned caps reserved for divinities in ancient Mesopotamian art. Probably from Sippar, *c.*2300 BC. © Trustees of the British Museum.

evidence for the use and deposition of material culture in ritual and religious contexts. In the former category we are once again well-resourced: much is known of the layouts of important religious buildings in many times and places within ancient Iraq. In the latter case we have perhaps been less fortunate. Many of the major excavations in Iraq were conducted at a very early date, and recording was consequently poor by modern standards. Compounding this problem, the near impossibility of conducting field research in Iraq since 1990 has greatly limited the application of new techniques of scientific analysis in the Mesopotamian heartland.

3 THE PANTHEON

3.1 The Gods

By the time, in the mid-third millennium BC, that we first encounter quantities of detailed religious texts, all of southern Iraq (known to its inhabitants as 'the Land of Sumer and Akkad' or simply 'the Land') shared an enormous and complex pantheon in which syncretism between Sumerian and Semitic (Akkadian) gods was already evident through their dual names (e.g. Sumerian Utu/Akkadian *Shamash*, the sun god). There is no reason to see this shared religious culture as a natural or inevitable state of affairs, since the many city states of the period were not only religiously distinct but to an extent defined by religious differences: a city's patron deity was a major part of that city's identity; moreover the city's major shrine would house a cult statue in which the god was at some level considered to be embodied. In such a context it is remarkable not only that all the gods of other cities were recognized, but that to some degree their genealogical relations and major deeds seem to have been widely agreed.

The dominant positions of the major gods appear to have remained relatively stable over millennia. When changes do occur they may reflect mortal politics: in later periods Enlil is supplanted by Marduk, patron deity of the great city of Babylon, as most powerful of the gods, a change in the universal order enshrined in the Babylonian Creation Epic known as *Enuma elish*. An/*Anu*, god of the sky, was always the father of the gods and nominal head of the pantheon, but seems to have been a distant entity, rarely endowed with characteristics of action or decision.

It can be argued that although superficially quite stable, the pantheon can be seen to change more substantially over time in practical terms. This evolution involves not so much the removal of gods—for Mesopotamia's vast and increasingly cosmopolitan pantheon remained supremely inclusive—but rather changes in the focus given to specific deities within it (most notably the syncretism of Sumerian and Semitic gods [Foster 2007: 170] and a reduction in the number of female divinities in later periods, some being combined into single deities, others recognized as consorts of male gods) and changes in their perceived roles (Jacobsen 1976).

Henotheism, the favouring of one god within a pantheon, is evidenced by the quantity of literature attributing, in apparently contradictory fashion, divine supremacy to many different gods. Some explanation for the phenomenon is to be found in the psychology of religious feeling and experience:

> We might consider such an attitude as only a too-human example of that *captatio benevolentiae* that underlies almost obligatorily all requests for service: flatter the one from whom one seeks to obtain a favour, to ensure his positive response. But it is clear that we must see more than that; there is a true necessity in the religious sentiment not to disperse one's energies over a multitude of objects but to project oneself entirely onto one single personality, not in principle, but in fact. [Bottéro 2001: 42–3]

Beyond this argument, rooted in the very personal question of one's experience of the divine, a clue may be found in the gods' hierarchical arrangement (which mirrored that of human society [Lambert 1975]). The role of personal gods seems frequently to have been to petition the major gods on behalf of their adherents. Again we are struck by the extent to which the heavenly order mirrors that on Earth. A frequently depicted subject in early second-millennium cylinder seals is the presentation of an individual to a major deity by an attendant god, and perhaps it is here that we are most clearly presented with some clue as to the order which for the ancient Mesopotamians themselves structured prayer and devotion. Most importantly our impression is of a supremely flexible polytheism, a structure under which the concept of the jealous god appears to have possessed little traction. Perhaps only in the exceptional, highly politicized cases of Ashur and Marduk can we at times see a tension parallel to, and resulting from, the long-running contest for political pre-eminence between the lands of Assyria and Babylonia (von Soden 1994: 182).

4 INSTITUTIONS

4.1 The Temple

Until relatively recently the proto-literate and early literate societies of southern Iraq were widely held to have been temple-states, in which priests or priest-kings sat at the top of polities whose economies were run entirely from temple institutions (Postgate 1994b: 109, citing the example of Childe 1954). This view is no longer tenable, but the role of temples as centres of worldly as well as spiritual power is in no doubt. Temples' functions included the management of large amounts of land, and a role in storage and redistribution of resources and 'social services' in the community. They functioned alongside palace institutions centred on the power of kings, but to term these two parallel organizations 'religious' and 'secular' is to misrepresent both the economic functions of the temple and the ritual and religious responsibilities of kings.

The characteristics of temple architecture changed considerably over the centuries (for an overview see Frankfort 1996). One development was that of raised platforms, leading by the end of the third millennium BC to the appearance of ancient Mesopotamia's most distinctive architectural form, the ziggurat. These stepped temple-towers consisted of solid mud-brick, sometimes encased in baked brick and perhaps coated in a white lime slip. The top level of the ziggurat held a temple, access to which was highly restricted. The names of the temples themselves are known from lexical lists and other documents (compiled in George 1993). Perhaps the most famous of all was E-sag-ila, the 'House whose Top is High', the great temple of Marduk in Babylon, with its associated ziggurat E-temen-anki, the 'Foundation Platform of Heaven and Earth.'

From an archaeological perspective, one of the most enticing aspects of ancient Mesopotamian religion is the extent to which the divine world was not only reflected but frequently *manifested* materially. From the mid-third millennium BC—and probably earlier—the gods were provided with literal houses for temples, and even with physical bodies in cult statues.

4.2 The Role of the King

Although possessed also of corporate decision-making bodies, Mesopotamian city states (and later empires) were ruled exclusively by kings. For the Uruk period we still habitually refer to 'priest-kings' when discussing images of male figures, clearly leaders of some sort, engaged in religious activities such as those pertaining to the sacred marriage. The distinction between 'kings' and 'priest-kings' is meaningful, however, only in that it reflects our uncertainty as to the particular political roles played by the figures represented in fourth-millennium-BC art; it does not mean that we imagine later Mesopotamian kings to have played a less important role in ritual and religion.

Deification of kings was rare, but not unknown. The first clear example of the practice is Naram-Sin of Akkad, whose famous victory stela depicts him wearing the horned cap normally reserved only for the gods. While the practice was not common, neither does it seem to have attracted censure. A king's subjects were, in any case, prepared to accept that his power was in some sense divinely ordained, and that as his people's representative his relationship to the gods was very different from that of his subjects: divine or otherwise he represented a step on the chain that led from ordinary people's lives, through intermediaries, to the great gods.

Two rituals, widely separated in time, illustrate something of the king's 'connecting' role. The first, the Sumerian 'sacred marriage' ceremony, known from late third- and early second-millennium texts in certain cities but in some form probably much older and more widespread (Cooper 1993), saw the king (as the shepherd god Dumuzi) uniting and 'lying with' a goddess (Inanna), sometimes through the human representative of a priestess. The marriage both ensured agricultural abundance for the coming year and renewed the community's ties to the gods, ensuring prosperity for the king and the people (Kramer 1969; Cooper 1997: 86). In the Neo-Babylonian period (sixth century BC) similar ties were emphasized in Babylon's New Year Festival with the celebration of Marduk's triumph over the forces of chaos (see below). The absence of the king from Babylon, however, meant disaster, and the festival could not be conducted without his presence (see *The Persian Verse Account of Nabonidus*, Pritchard 1969: 312–15; Beaulieu 1989: 4).

4.3 Priests and Officials

Temples employed large numbers of personnel, engaged in a wide variety of roles. Some of these remain obscure, but it is possible to define three broad groups of temple staff: 'cultic', 'administrative', and 'domestic' (Sigrist 1984: 160; Postgate 1994b: 126–7). We must again take account, however, of the lack of any meaningful division between 'secular' and 'religious' roles: the work of many craftsmen and others who would fall under the domestic heading had cultic significance, while it is surely a mistake to imagine 'administrative' personnel as subsidiary to the core cultic business of the temple. Some temple posts were prebends: they could be bought and even inherited (Charpin 1986: 260–9). Often these positions were part-time, shared up to the point where an individual's responsibilities might run to only a few days in the year, perhaps even less.

One exceptional cultic position was that of the high-priestess of the moon god Nanna/ *Sin* at Ur. In the late third and second millennia this post was regularly held by the daughter of the king, and the practice was still sufficiently remembered that Nabonidus of Babylon could revive it in the mid-sixth century BC. It has been suggested that 'Queen' Pu-abi from the famous Royal Graves of Ur (*c*.2600–2400 BC) was perhaps one such high-priestess, although this hardly begins to explain the strange character of these unique burials (Woolley 1934, 1982; Pollock 1991). More certainly, a holder of this post is the first named female author known in the world: Enheduanna, daughter of Sargon of Akkad in the late third millennium BC (Winter 1987; Frayne 1993: 35–9).

5 Ritual Practice

5.1 Material Gods: Cult and the Cult Statue

The cult statue was not merely a portrait of the divinity—it was the god's very incarnation (Hallo 1983; Hurowitz 2003). Underlining this point, one recent study (Bahrani 2003) has argued that the very term for 'image'/'representation', *salmu*, cannot be understood only as equating to the potential for mimesis, but rather 'has the potential of becoming an entity in its own right, a being rather than a copy of a being' (Bahrani 2003: 124–5). This embodiment does not mean that the image could be said to contain or constitute a god in a manner analogous to the ties between human body and identity (however these latter are themselves conceived). Rather a god was simultaneously immanent in a cult statue or statues (some gods having temples and statues in multiple cities), in those forces of nature with which they were associated (Enlil with air and the wind, for example), and finally in some more distant, omniscient, and omnipresent form (Jacobsen 1987a; Selz 1997: 183; Pollock

1999: 186). Nonetheless, the cult statue could be said to contain a combination of (and to modern eyes perhaps a tension between) material and divine qualities. One case in point is the god's need for food. There is a functional aspect to this practice in drawing food to the temple for internal and external distribution, but there remains here a practice involving non-material elements that were nevertheless tied to physical objects in some fundamental way. In what sense did the god 'eat' of food offerings?

The statue would require constant attention and maintenance: to be housed, clothed, and entertained (Winter 1992). The deity's needs at times extended further, in the desire, for example, to visit another god. With physical bodies and homes on Earth, it was possible for such divine journeys, too, to be enacted in the material world. Literary texts describing visits by one god to another, the giving of gifts and requests for assistance, reflect a tradition in which cult statues could be transported to another city in order to visit the temples and statues of other gods. Perhaps the most famous example of a statue's journey is that of Marduk at the Babylonian New Year Festival (Black 1981). A first millennium BC text details the necessary rituals to be performed by priests at appropriate times, and the path taken by Marduk out of the city and to the *akitu* (New Year) temple (Cohen 1993: 400–53; Pongratz-Leisten 1994).

Inevitably, the god's materialization in the form of the cult statue created scope for its defilement by enemies. This, however, was not the greatest danger. Rather than vandalizing a god it was common practice for the victorious enemy instead to abduct the cult statue. This was a matter of grave consequence for the city concerned, but many texts and even one Assyrian relief show that the practice was employed frequently (Potts 1997: 191). The act of carrying away a city's god was emblematic of the city having lost that god's protection, support, and favour. This concept of divine will, rather than that of the god's weakness or inability to prevent disaster, was the framework within which the abduction was understood, and indeed conquerors were often careful to position themselves in inscriptions as agents of the gods of the conquered (Kuhrt 1987, 1995: 580, 602).

There is no surviving example of a cult statue from ancient Mesopotamia. The principal reason for this absence is that the materials from which the statues were made were either valuable, recyclable, or subject to organic decay: a wooden core overlaid with precious metals, set with imported stones and clothed in rich fabrics would stand little chance of surviving for the archaeologist to uncover (Figure 48. 2). Fragments in stone and metal that probably formed parts of cult statues have been found, though the best sources for the statues' appearance remain the many representations of the gods in art.

5.2 Personal Devotion and Votives

One of our few windows onto the everyday religious practices of ordinary people is provided by the survival of large numbers of simple, often mass-produced votives, from the eye-idols of the Uruk period to terracotta plaques showing deities and divine symbols (Moorey 1975, 2001; Stone 1993). Less ambiguous are votive statues (Figure 48.3), often inscribed with details of their exact purpose (on sculpture in the round see Frankfort 1996: 45–66). Eye-idols, consisting of two large 'eyes' sat on a simple rectangular 'body', and thus far found only at the Syrian site of Tell Brak, were probably a precursor to these, and seem from their pared-down form to have been intended to look upon the god constantly on behalf of the petitioner (later votives, such as the famous

FIGURE 48.2 Although mud-brick temple architecture survives and much has been excavated, many of the materials used in temples' decoration and furnishing have perished or been recycled. Surviving large examples of metalwork such as this are rare. This 60-cm-high statue of a bull, whose copper surface was originally laid over a wooden core, was one of four found at the temple of the goddess Ninhursag at the site of al-'Ubaid. From Tell al-'Ubaid, c.2500 BC. © Trustees of the British Museum.

Early Dynastic statues from Tell Asmar—ancient Eshnunna—also have emphasized and sometimes greatly enlarged eyes). Later, elaborate statues of kings dedicated to the gods had the important secondary function of representing the piety and other virtues of the king, and in this respect contrast with the anonymity or sense of corporate identity represented by the eye-idols.

As well as major temples, Mesopotamian cities contained large numbers of smaller shrines. At Ur, Sir Leonard Woolley discovered niches in houses, again dating to the Old Babylonian period, which he interpreted as household altars intended for personal devotion (Woolley 1976). The temple was not primarily a site of communal worship: its inner chambers were accessible to few, and its principal function was to provide housing and the fulfilment of earthly requirements for the god (Oppenheim 1964: 181–2; Pollock 1999: 178). Another surviving residue of religion outside the temple and palace environments is to be found in personal names, which were normally structured as short prayers. It has been suggested that the varying frequency with which different gods are invoked in personal names gives a more accurate picture of changing religious practice than the orientations of the major temples, which were always devoted to a relatively small, stable group of deities at the head of the pantheon.

FIGURE 48.3 Votive statues, often inscribed, were set up in temples to pray on behalf of their donors. Male and female worshippers are represented; in this case a woman clasps her hands in the pious gesture typical of the statues. From Tello (ancient Girsu), c.2500 BC. © Trustees of the British Museum.

This use of personal names to access religion is only one example of prosopography in the field. The importance and potential of this approach in the study of (particularly) non-elite life in ancient Mesopotamia is increasingly recognized, and recent publications stress its usefulness for future work (van de Mieroop 1999: 89–92). Increasing digitization of texts should greatly aid research of this kind, and indeed has already allowed the production of resources such as *Prosopography of the Neo-Assyrian Empire* (Parpola et al. 1998–2002). Much as personal names provide useful data, however, the personal (in the sense of individual, private) aspect of religion even outside the large institutions should not be overstressed. A recent study argues that 'family religion' is perhaps a more appropriate term than 'personal religion', since in general individual, family and local religious practices are so strongly related as to amount to much the same thing (van der Toorn 1996: 3).

5.3 Omens and Divination

Divination and the study of ominous phenomena were a central preoccupation of ancient Mesopotamian scholarship. The business of divination was normally centred on the person of the king (and through him the fortunes of the polity), although in the later first millennium BC predictions for individuals do appear. The means of predicting the future were several: astrology (Britton and Walker 1996; Rochberg 2004), dream-interpretation (Butler 1998), and extispicy (the study of a sacrificed animal's organs) (Jeyes 1989) were three crucial categories. Here it is important simply to note the underlying premise: that the material world contains (perhaps consists of) meaningful signs that can be decoded to reveal the future and the will of the gods.

5.4 Magic

Disease was understood to originate in supernatural forces, and hence was treated primarily by magical means. Amulets and apotropaic devices survive, as do texts describing many magico-medical treatments (Scurlock 2006). The source of disease could be a demon, ghost, evil spirit, or dangerous animal, but could also stem from the 'hand of a god', whose reasons for inflicting the illness might remain incomprehensible to the sufferer, since the gods themselves were capricious. Only in the second millennium BC does illness as a divine punishment for sin emerge explicitly (Cunningham 1997).

5.5 Death and Burial

Practices surrounding the treatment of the dead vary considerably across time and space, and although some spectacular discoveries have been made we arguably do not have a full or clear picture of burial practices for any period in Mesopotamia. A striking problem is the relative lack of burials for many periods. Where cemeteries or other grouped burials are found they produce samples that often seem highly unrepresentative of population in terms of age and sex ratios. These factors strongly suggest the existence of burial practices as yet unidentified by archaeologists (such as burial in very remote locations) or of practices that are archaeologically invisible (such as disposal of the dead by water).

Although highly elaborate burials are rare it is clear that the dead did need to be propitiated. Burials under house floors are of particular interest in this regard, although again little is understood of this practice. The most common surviving grave goods are ceramic vessels suggesting provision of food and drink for the deceased, while in some exceptional cases—famously the recently excavated royal tombs at Qatna in Syria—there is strong evidence for banquets held by the living. Early second-millennium BC texts describe a ritual called *kispu* in which the living visited the realm of the dead (i.e. a tomb chamber) to eat with the deceased, and it is thought that the tombs at Qatna represent a very similar tradition. Without the proper attention the ghosts of deceased family members could cause problems for the living. Dealing with these malign spirits was an important branch of magic, and as with driving out illness many exorcistic spells survive.

6 Cosmology

Mesopotamian myths of cosmogony vary, but do share a common pool of material including the personalities and behaviours of major gods, a great flood, and the creation of humankind to serve the gods. Certain aspects of this creation mythology have links to Genesis, most famously the story of the Flood and its single human survivor. In some Mesopotamian accounts the Flood is sent by Enlil, who is irritated by the noise humanity is making. After the Flood the solution arrived at by the gods is the invention of death as a means to limit the human population. With death came the afterlife, a bleak place in which material comforts buried with the individual, or remembrance by loved ones, might provide some slight respite, but where real pleasure was impossible, where 'Dust is their food, clay their bread' (*The Descent of Ishtar to the Underworld*, after Dalley 2000: 155).

In the late second millennium the story of creation was consciously revised in order to explain Marduk's recently achieved primacy among the gods. The Babylonian Epic of Creation describes Marduk's battle against chaos, represented as Tiamat, the ancestral sea. Marduk's victory in this epic conflict was commemorated annually as part of Babylon's New Year festival, perhaps playing a role similar to the by-now defunct sacred marriage as humanity's means of reaffirming its compact with the gods.

In most accounts, humanity is created from clay in order to serve the gods. The broad view of history seems to have been degenerative, with the world of the gods giving way to that of mortals via a long chain of ancestral kings. The first kings are given reigns of many thousands of years, these numbers gradually reducing to match the mortal span of more recent, historical rulers. The standard presentation defied the reality of city states and multiple kings: in the king lists reigns do not overlap and kingship passes from one city to another. In the third millennium the title King of Kish seemed to indicate some superiority or power of arbitration over other kings (though certainly not genuine overlordship), but the reality is nonetheless impossible to reconcile with the model of a single, continuous monarchy.

Various documents give us information on cosmic geography and the shape of the universe. The most important is the so-called Babylonian Map of the World (Horowitz 1998: 20–42). The parallels with a modern map are limited: the sixth century BC drawing contains a schematic representation of the known world (centred on Babylon, the point at which Earth was tied to the heavens), but at its edges, beyond a great encircling river, are regions in which dwell monsters and legendary figures such as Uta-napishti, the survivor of the Flood and possessor of eternal life. Older documents make clear that the groundwater, of which Enki/Ea was god, was conceived as a great freshwater sea beneath the land, below which lay the underworld.

The single most important work of literature from ancient Mesopotamia is the Babylonian Epic of Gilgamesh, an extended narrative that has become perhaps the only ancient Mesopotamian text to be widely read by non-specialists. The poem's principal theme is the acceptance of human mortality. Gilgamesh, the legendary king of Uruk, defeats all enemies, even the fearsome monster Humbaba, but cannot overcome death. His search for eternal life takes him all the way to Uta-napishti, the one mortal to have been granted eternal life, but ultimately he succeeds only in learning that life is short, and that his time spent attempting to achieve immortality has been wasted. Gilgamesh has attracted, and continues to attract, considerable scholarly attention; the most important recent contribution being the new translation and commentary of George (2003; see also Maier 1997; George 1999; Dalley 2000: 39–153). Other recent work has explored the theme of sexuality in the poem (Cooper 2002; Ackerman 2005).

7 THE WIDER PICTURE: SYNTHESIS AND ANALYSIS

Theories of ancient Mesopotamian religion greatly predate any such thing as Mesopotamian archaeology. The polytheistic world of the Babylonians and Assyrians was presented as one doomed to destruction even in the Bible, and in European models of history from the Enlightenment onward was seen as a necessary but early step in the spiritual progress of humanity. This notion, and the models of historical progress upon which it depends, have only relatively recently been substantially challenged, and it is unsurprising that a perception of ancient Mesopotamian religion as a less morally developed precursor to the monotheistic religions has been so potent (e.g. Rogers 1908; Albright 1940). More recently the problem facing scholars has been to develop a new narrative in which the contribution of Mesopotamian religion in world history is recognized without reinforcing this linear evolutionary picture (Kohl 1989: 244–5).

To no small extent it was religion that prompted much early exploration of ancient sites in the Middle East, including Iraq (Chavalas 2002; Larsen 1989a, 1989b; Kucklick 1996). Early European travellers to the area attempted to identify the Tower of Babel, while the first major excavations in Iraq aimed at (and ultimately succeeded in) uncovering ancient Nineveh (Larsen 1996; Russell 1997: 17–51). In general, pre-archaeological scholarship took for granted the fidelity of the Old Testament sources. While this approach led to errors, it also provided the keys to the very distant world of ancient Mesopotamian history. An unexpected consequence of this exploration was the further discovery of a society—and even more surprisingly a vast body of literature—much earlier than any known through the Bible. The study of Sumerian language and civilization in the twentieth century revealed a religious world quite distant from that of the Old Testament.

The matter of a relationship between biblical and ancient Mesopotamian texts became general knowledge in England in the 1870s with George Smith's remarkable 'Flood tablet' discoveries (Meyer 1997: 39). The academic and theological questions arising from this relationship would shape theories of Mesopotamian religion for at least the next half-century, and indeed remain relevant today. Smith's discoveries were well received, perhaps because nineteenth-century British attitudes to the Old Testament, opposed to the critical treatments that had emerged in France and Germany, were sufficiently robust to accommodate the Flood tablet (although George Rawlinson, brother of the Assyriologist Henry, expressed concerns at where such enquiries might lead [Chavalas 2002: 27]). The flashpoint, however, came as late as 1902. With recently commenced German excavations in Mesopotamia proving a great success and Near Eastern studies in royal favour, the Assyriologist Friedrich Delitzsch was to deliver a series of three high-profile lectures on the theme of *Babel und Bibel*. These lectures proved enormously controversial (Lehmann 1994; Larsen 1995; Bohrer 2003: 286–7). Delitzsch effectively put a case against treating the Old Testament as revelation, emphasizing Babylonian origins and even suggesting that the Babylonian material might in some ways be morally superior. This assertion of Babylonian primacy conflicted with a general view that the Mesopotamian texts served as handmaiden to the Old Testament whose purpose was to confirm in a vivid way the truth of historical material in the Bible (Foster 2007: 207).

Delitzsch was not alone in his view. At around the same time as the *Babel–Bibel* crisis Hugo Winckler became the most prominent exponent of a movement known as pan-Babylonianism. Pan-Babylonianism asserted that all of the world's major religions had their origins in a single astral religion of ancient Mesopotamia. It is true that certain stars were associated with gods. The epithet 'astral religion', however, is highly misleading (rather, Bottéro [2001: 212–18] argues that such a religion develops regionally in the Mediterranean and Middle East in the last centuries BC), as is the simplistic idea of Mesopotamia as the fountainhead of all the world's major religions: this latter is perhaps the result of a unilinear modern paradigm in which 'historical significance' meant essentially significance to a single narrative of man's progress. In this sense pan-Babylonianism can be understood as the consequence of a system that of its nature *sought* a single ancestral religion (early syntheses on Mesopotamian religion by Jastrow (1898) and Rogers (1908) show a similar tendency). At the same time it was also a bullish response to the low import accorded Assyriology by traditional theologians and biblical specialists in Germany and Europe more widely (Chavalas 2002: 32). Gradually, however, the desire for a major stake in biblical studies was succeeded by a desire for independence from it. That Winckler's ideas lost their appeal over time is owed not only to the development of a more nuanced understanding of historical influence between religions, but also to an increasingly concerted desire to approach the religious life of ancient Mesopotamia on its own terms and for its own sake.

The best-known statement on ancient Mesopotamian religion is the great Assyriologist A. Leo Oppenheim's warning that 'a Mesopotamian religion should not be written' (Oppenheim 1964: 172). Oppenheim was profoundly sceptical of the capacity for the available data and interpretative theory to bring modern researchers close to the personal experience of religion in which ancient individuals were involved. He emphasized the indirect nature of the available evidence, arguing in effect that all archaeologists and Assyriologists had available to them were the fragmentary and inadequate material trappings of a now vanished spiritual experience. He also contended that the polytheistic breadth, openness, and fluidity of ancient Mesopotamian religion was simply so far removed from the narrowness and intensity of monotheistic religion as to make the conceptual gulf dividing them too vast to bridge (cf. Bottéro's view on henotheism, quoted above). These feelings are reflected in the title of his book from which the quote is drawn: *Ancient Mesopotamia: Portrait of a dead civilisation*.

Oppenheim's view might surprise researchers in other archaeological fields, whose data are rarely so rich as those available for the study of ancient Mesopotamia. Since he wrote, however, the success which more anthropological processual and post-processual approaches have met in the study of prehistoric religious practices at least suggests that such pessimism is no longer entirely justified. If there is a good reason in the Mesopotamian data for not making the attempt, it is perhaps that they are so rich that the many nuances they reveal over a wide spectrum of times, places, and social contexts are difficult—perhaps, indeed, impossible—to reconcile into a clear overall picture. We are perhaps in a stronger position to conduct micro-history than to build grand narratives, and this is also a part of Oppenheim's point. It is a genuine constraint, but hardly an adequate justification for avoiding larger-scale studies. Archaeological interpretation requires frequent shifts between scales of analysis and a preparedness to synthesize and take broad positions on the available data. Without such top-level assessment the detachment of material remains from human experience that concerned Oppenheim becomes something of a self-fulfilling prophecy.

To address the second point, the stress placed by Oppenheim on a great conceptual gulf between polytheistic and monotheistic religion is astute in its encouragement to the reader (whatever their own religious beliefs) to consider the difficulty and importance of empathy in considering the spiritual and emotional centre of an ancient religion. Whether it is truly possible to achieve such empathy, however, is a secondary issue. The methodological question should be, is it the purpose of an archaeology of religion to make the attempt? If the answer is negative the result is arguably not an archaeology of religion at all, but one only of ritual and of mythological texts. To produce a meaningful archaeology of religion the expert thus has a right, and perhaps an obligation, to offer some tentative synthetic view based on existing knowledge, however imperfect.

Bold and constructive attempts have been made to understand Mesopotamian religion on a large scale, most importantly Thorkild Jacobsen's classic history of Mesopotamian religion *The Treasures of Darkness* (Jacobsen 1976; see also Jacobsen 1987a). In this work Jacobsen attempted to identify and explain historical change in Mesopotamian religion in terms not only of practice but of meaning. He made frequent reference to the human experience of the numinous (religious awe), and to the changing relationships between mortal and god he saw in what he argued was the gradual rise of 'personal religion' in the second millennium BC. Today the interpretations are less clear-cut, but Jacobsen's attempt to synthesize and explain the data framed key questions that have catalysed the study of Mesopotamian religion ever since.

Jacobsen argued that a change could be perceived whereby divinities that in the earliest Sumerian world were rooted in and resemble natural forces and were conceptualized as 'providers' would later come to resemble earthly 'kings' and finally, with the rise of what might be termed personal religion, 'parents'. The thesis of a transition from gods as natural forces to gods as anthropomorphized rulers has since won general agreement (Foster 2007: 170, though see Lambert 1990 for an argument that Sumerian gods are conceived anthropomorphically from the start). The particular conclusions Jacobsen draws are less important here, however, than his establishment of the principle that in ancient Mesopotamian religion we see a process of transformation whereby the same gods may have been understood and related to in different ways and at different times. From here it is a very small step to the recognition that this variation must equally be possessed of a social dimension: the differences between priest, king, and commoner in this respect surely amounted to more than a difference in sheer quantity of names and mythologies known, just as the differences between lay and clerical understanding of religion do in our own time. The religion that survives in texts is principally of the more scholarly form.

Jacobsen's philosophical approach stands in contrast to the earlier work of Samuel Noah Kramer, also one of the key figures in the decipherment of the Sumerian language and who can be credited with consciously introducing Sumerian literature into comparative mythology (Kramer 1944). Kramer took a resolutely worldly perspective, breathing life into his subjects as prosaic individuals not fundamentally different to people in the present. His great popular work, *History Begins at Sumer* (Kramer 1961), exemplifies the approach, taking a long list of Sumerian 'firsts' and emphasizing their similarity to activities and behaviours that we see every day. The negative side of this otherwise highly empathetic and even sympathetic perspective was a reluctance to infer structuring religious or cosmological principles from the literature, leading Kramer to the conclusion that 'The Sumerians failed to develop a systematic philosophy in the accepted sense of the word' (Kramer 1961: 118). Jacobsen's work took a very different view.

The most recent broad synthesis is that of Jean Bottéro (2001). In addressing historical change Bottéro focuses on the shift from a predominantly 'Sumerian' religion in which the world of the gods closely mirrored that of their earthly subjects, to a 'Semitic' one in which the supreme gods were less anthropomorphized and more distant from human experience. He acknowledges, however, that since these two strands are already somewhat intertwined by the time literary texts appear in the mid-third millennium BC, and since at no point is either seen to be operating exclusively, their disentanglement is a complex and problematic matter.

8 CONCLUSIONS

One key aim for future work in the study of Mesopotamian religion is the greater integration of archaeological, iconographic, and textual data. Until now syntheses on religion have been based very largely on textual sources, but the potential for these to be informed by archaeological and social anthropological perspectives is increasingly recognized (Potts 1997: 185–207; Pollock 1999: 173–95). Current projects making cuneiform materials more widely available in transliteration and translation will facilitate this and other research. Comparative mythology and work on the relationships between ancient Mesopotamian and biblical texts will certainly remain an important theme, yet the aims and character of this work have changed dramatically over the discipline's history and will surely continue to do so. From a theoretical perspective the greatest challenge will remain high-level interpretation, and it is to be hoped that new research focused on questions of identity and personal experience will continue to build on Jacobsen's and Bottéro's attempts to understand the epistemological and ontological underpinnings of ancient Mesopotamian religious life.

A final aim, in this as in all aspects of Mesopotamian archaeology, is the resumption of excavation and survey within Iraq itself. Huge problems exist and there is no imminent prospect of foreign excavation teams operating in Iraq, but at the time of writing the Iraq State Board of Antiquities and Heritage was once again conducting work at several sites, while travel and training programmes run by foreign institutions have allowed Iraqi and non-Iraqi scholars to resume collaboration following the virtual isolation of Iraqi academics during the 1990s.

Further Reading

The most important overviews of ancient Mesopotamian religion are those of Bottéro (2001) and Foster (2007). For Mesopotamian history more broadly see Kuhrt 1995; van de Mieroop (2004). The changing political and religious geography of ancient Mesopotamia is explained by Roaf (1990); for general surveys of the archaeology of Iraq see Postgate (1994b); Pollock (1999); Matthews (2003) and with specific application to the archaeology of religion and ritual Potts (1997: 185–207). Pollock (1999: 173–95) deals with the issue of ideology in the archaeology of Mesopotamian religion, while Ross (2005) addresses similar issues for iconographic data. Key introductions to Mesopotamian art are Collon (1995) and Frankfort (1996); the latter also introduces changing temple architecture, while Black and Green (1992) offer a survey of iconography and symbolism and Gunter (1990) an examination of contexts of artistic production. For cylinder seals see Collon (2005). There is a growing corpus of ancient Mesopotamian literature available in accessible English translation, the bulk of which is relevant to religion: Dalley (2000); McCall (1990); Black et al. (2004); George (1999); Foster (2005); Pritchard (1969); Jacobsen (1987b). All of these contain some introduction to the literature and other explanatory material. For method and theory in textual analysis see Black (1998); Black et al. (2004), Michalowski (1996). For the integration of textual and iconographic evidence see Postgate (1994a); Lambert (1997); Zimansky (2005). For Mesopotamian magic see Abusch and van der Toorn (1999). For the archaeology of death and burial see Alster (1980); Crawford (1991: 103–23); Jonker (1995).

References

Abusch, T. and van der Toorn, K. (eds) 1999. *Mesopotamian Magic: Textual, historical and interpretative perspectives: Ancient magic and divination 1* (Groningen: Styx).

Ackerman, S. 2005. *When Heroes Love: The ambiguity of Eros in Gilgamesh and David* (New York: Columbia University Press).

Albright, W. F. 1940. *From the Stone Age to Christianity* (London: Oxford University Press).

Alster, B. (ed.) 1980. *Death in Mesopotamia: XXVIe Rencontre Assyriologique Internationale* (Copenhagen: Akademisk Forlag).

Bahrani, Z. 2003. *The Graven Image: Representation in Babylonia and Assyria* (Philadelphia: Pennsylvania University Press).

Beaulieu, P.-A. 1989. *The Reign of Nabonidus, King of Babylon 556–539 BC*, Yale Near Eastern Researches 10 (New Haven: Yale University Press).

Black, J. A. 1981. 'The New Year Ceremonies in Ancient Babylonia: "Taking Bel by the hand" and a cultic picnic', *Religion*, 11: 39–59.

——1998. *Reading Sumerian Poetry* (London: Athlone Press).

——and Green, A. 1992. *Gods, Demons and Symbols of Ancient Mesopotamia: An illustrated dictionary* (London: British Museum Press).

——, Cunningham, G., Robson, E., and Zolyomi, G. 2004. *The Literature of Ancient Sumer* (Oxford: Oxford University Press).

Bohrer, F. N. 2003. *Orientalism and Visual Culture: Imagining Mesopotamia in nineteenth-century Europe* (Cambridge: Cambridge University Press).

BOTTÉRO, J. 2001. *Religion in Ancient Mesopotamia*, trans. T. L. Fagan (Chicago and London: Chicago University Press).
BRITTON, J. and WALKER, C. B. F. 1996. 'Astronomy and Astrology in Mesopotamia' in C. B. F. Walker (ed.), *Astronomy before the Telescope* (London: British Museum Press), pp. 42–67.
BUTLER, S. 1998. *Mesopotamian Conceptions of Dreams and Dream Rituals*, Alter Orient und Altes Testament 258 (Münster: Ugarit-verlag).
CHARPIN, D. 1986. *Le Clergé d'Ur au siècle d'Hammurabi (XIXe –XVIIIe siècles av. J.-C.)*. École pratique des Hautes Études, IVe section, II, Hautes Études orientales, vol. 22 (Geneva and Paris: Droz Librairie).
CHAVALAS, M. W. 2002. 'Assyriology and biblical studies: A century and a half of tension' in M. W. Chavalas and K. L. Younger (eds), *Mesopotamia and the Bible: Comparative explorations*, Journal for the Study of the Old Testament Supplementary Series No. 341 (London: Sheffield Academic Press), pp. 21–67.
CHILDE, V. G. 1954. *What Happened in History*, 2nd edn (Harmondsworth: Penguin).
COHEN, M. E. 1993. *The Cultic Calendars of the Ancient Near East* (Bethesda: CDL Press).
COLLON, D. 1995. *Ancient Near Eastern Art* (London: British Museum Press).
——2005. *First Impressions: Cylinder seals in the ancient Near East*, 2nd edn (London: British Museum Press).
COOPER, J. S. 1993. 'Sacred marriage and popular cult in early Mesopotamia' in E. Matsushima (ed.), *Official Cult and Popular Religion in the Ancient Near East* (Heidelberg: Carl Winter), pp. 81–96.
——1997. 'Gendered sexuality in Sumerian love poetry' in I. L. Finkel and M. J. Geller (eds), *Sumerian Gods and their Representations*, Cuneiform Monographs 7 (Groningen: Styx), pp. 85–97.
——2002. 'Buddies in Babylonia: Gilgamesh, Enkidu and Mesopotamian homosexuality' in I. Tzvi Abusch (ed.), *Riches Hidden in Secret Places: Ancient Near Eastern studies in memory of Thorkild Jacobsen* (Winona Lake: Eisenbrauns), pp. 73–86.
CRAWFORD, H. 1991. *Sumer and the Sumerians* (Cambridge: Cambridge University Press).
CUNNINGHAM, G. 1997. *'Deliver me from evil': Mesopotamian incantations 2500–1500 BC*, Studia Pohl, Series Maior 17 (Rome: Pontificio Istituto Biblico).
DALLEY, S. M. 2000. *Mesopotamian Myths*, rev. edn (Oxford: Oxford University Press).
FOSTER, B. R. 2005. *Before the Muses: An anthology of Akkadian literature* (Bethesda: CDL Press).
——2007. 'Mesopotamia' in John R. Hinnels (ed.), *A Handbook of Ancient Religion* (Cambridge: Cambridge University Press), pp. 161–213.
FRANKFORT, H. 1996. *The Art and Architecture of the Ancient Orient*, ed. M. Roaf and D. Matthews, 5th edn (New Haven and London: Yale University Press).
FRAYNE, D. R. 1993. *Sargonic and Gutian Periods (2334–2113 BC)*, The Royal Inscriptions of Mesopotamia: Early Periods, II (Toronto: University of Toronto Press).
GEORGE, A. R. 1993. *House Most High: The temples of ancient Mesopotamia* (Eisenbrauns: Winona Lake).
——1999. *The Epic of Gilgamesh* (London: Penguin).
——2003. *The Babylonian Gilgamesh Epic: Introduction, critical edition and cuneiform texts*, 2 vols. (Oxford: Oxford University Press).
GREEN, A. 1995. 'Ancient Mesopotamian religious iconography' in Jack M. Sasson (ed.), *Civilizations of the Ancient Near East*, 4 vols. (New York: Charles Scribner's Sons), pp. 1837–56.

——1997. 'Myths in Mesopotamian art' in I. L. Finkel and M. J. Geller (eds), *Sumerian Gods and their Representations*, Cuneiform Monographs 7 (Groningen: Styx), pp. 135–58.

GUNTER, A. C. (ed.) 1990. *Investigating Artistic Environments in the Ancient Near East* (Washington, DC: Arthur M. Sackler Gallery, Smithsonian Institution).

HALLO, W. 1983. 'Cult statue and divine image: A preliminary study' in W. Hallo, J. Moyer, and L. Purdue (eds), *Scripture in Context*, II: *More Essays on the Comparative Method* (Winona Lake: Eisenbrauns), pp. 1–17.

HOROWITZ, W. 1998. *Mesopotamian Cosmic Geography* (Winona Lake: Eisenbrauns).

HUROWITZ, V. A. 2003. 'The Mesopotamian god image, from womb to tomb', *Journal of the American Oriental Society*, 123(1): 147–57.

JACOBSEN, T. 1976. *The Treasures of Darkness: A history of Mesopotamian religion* (New Haven: Yale).

——1987a. 'The graven image' in P. Miller Jr, P. Hanson, and S. Dean (eds), *Ancient Israelite Religion: Essays in honour of Frank Moore Cross* (Philadelphia: Fortress), pp. 15–32.

——1987b. *The Harps that Once...: Sumerian poetry in translation* (New Haven and London: Yale University Press).

JASTROW, M. 1898. *The Religion of Babylonia and Assyria* (London and New York: Putnam's).

JEYES, U. 1989. *Old Babylonian Extispicy: Omen texts in the British Museum* (Istanbul and Leiden: Nederlands Instituut voor het Nabije Oosten (NINO)).

JONKER, G. 1995. *The Topography of Remembrance: The dead, tradition and collective memory in Mesopotamia*, Studies in the History of Religions, Numen Book Series 68 (Leiden: Brill).

KOHL, P. L. 1989. 'The material culture of the modern era in the ancient Orient: Suggestions for future work' in D. Miller, M. Rowlands, and C. Tilley (eds), *Domination and Resistance* (London: Unwin Hyman), pp. 240–5.

KRAMER, S. N. 1944. *Sumerian Mythology: A study of spiritual and literary achievement in the third millennium BC* (Philadelphia: The American Philosophical Society).

——1961. *History Begins at Sumer*, 2nd edn (London: Thames and Hudson).

——1969. *The Sacred Marriage Rite: Aspects of Faith, Myth and Ritual in Ancient Sumer* (Bloomington and London: Indiana University Press).

——1983. *Le mariage sacré à Sumer et à Babylone*, trans. J. Bottéro (from S. N. Kramer, 1969. *The Sacred Marriage Rite: Aspects of faith, myth and ritual in ancient Sumer*) (Bloomington and London: Indiana University Press).

KUCKLICK, B. 1996. *Puritans in Babylon: The ancient Near East and American intellectual life 1880–1930* (Princeton: Princeton University Press).

KUHRT, A. 1987. 'Usurpation, conquest and ceremonial: From Babylon to Persia' in D. Cannadine and S. Price (eds), *Rituals of Royalty: Power and ceremonial in traditional societies* (Cambridge: Cambridge University Press), pp. 20–55.

——1995. *The Ancient Near East c.3000–330 BC* (London and New York: Routledge).

LAMBERT, W. G. 1975. 'The cosmology of Sumer and Babylon' in C. Bleecker and M. Loewe (eds), *Ancient Cosmologies* (London: Allen and Unwin), pp. 42–65.

——1990. 'Ancient Mesopotamian gods: Superstition, philosophy, theology', *Revue de l'histoire des religions*, 207: 115–30.

——1997. 'Sumerian gods: Combining the evidence of texts and art' in I. L. Finkel and M. J. Geller (eds), *Sumerian Gods and their Representations*, Cuneiform Monographs 7 (Groningen: Styx), pp. 1–10.

LARSEN, M. T. 1989a. 'Orientalism and the ancient Near East' in M. Harbsmeier and M. T. Larsen (eds), *The Humanities Between Art and Science: Intellectual developments 1880–1914* (Copenhagen: Akademisk Forlag), pp. 181–202.

LARSEN, M. T. 1989b. 'Orientalism and Near Eastern Archaeology', in D. Miller, M. Rowlands, and C. Tilley (eds), *Domination and Resistance* (London: Unwin Hyman), pp. 229–239.
—— 1995. The 'Babel–Bible' controversy and its aftermath' in J. M. Sasson (ed.), *Civilisations of the Ancient Near East*, 4 vols. (New York: Charles Scribner's Sons), pp. 95–106.
—— 1996. *The Conquest of Assyria: Excavations in an antique land, 1840–1860* (London and New York: Routledge).
LEHMANN, R. G. 1994. *Friedrich Delitzsch und der Babel–Bibel Streit* (Freiburg: Universitätsverlag).
LEICK, G. 1994. *Sex and Eroticism in Mesopotamian Literature* (London and New York: Routledge).
MCCALL, H. 1990. *Mesopotamian Myths* (London: British Museum Press).
MAIER, J. (ed.) 1997. *Gilgamesh: A reader* (Wauconda, Illinois: Bolchazy-Carducci).
MATTHEWS, R. 2003. *The Archaeology of Mesopotamia: Theories and Approaches* (London and New York: Routledge).
MEYERS, E. M. 1997. 'History of the field: An overview' in E. M. Meyers (ed.), *The Oxford Encyclopedia of Archaeology in the Near East* (Oxford: Oxford University Press), pp. 37–42.
MICHALOWSKI, P. 1996. 'Sailing to Babylon, reading the Dark Side of the Moon' in J. S. Cooper and G. M. Schwartz (eds), *The Study of the Ancient Near East in the 21st Century: Proceedings of the Albright Centennial Symposium* (Winona Lake: Eisenbrauns), pp. 177–94.
MIEROOP, M. VAN DE 1999. *Cuneiform Texts and the Writing of History* (London and New York: Routledge).
—— 2004. *A History of the Ancient Near East ca. 3000–323 BC* (Oxford: Blackwell).
MOOREY, P. R. S. 1975. 'Terracotta plaques from Kish', *Iraq*, 37: 79–99.
—— 2001. *Idols of the People: Miniature images of clay in the ancient Near East* (Oxford: Oxford University Press for The British Academy).
OPPENHEIM, A. L. 1964. *Ancient Mesopotamia: Portrait of a dead civilisation* (Chicago: University of Chicago Press).
ORNAN, T. 2005. *The Triumph of the Symbol: Pictorial representation of deities in Mesopotamia and the biblical image ban*, Orbis Biblicus et Orientalis 213 (Fribourg: Academic Press/ Göttingen: Vandenhoeck and Ruprecht).
PARPOLA, S., RADNER, K., BAKER, H. D., and WHITING, R. M. (eds) 1998–2002. *The Prosopography of the Neo-Assyrian Empire*, 3 vols, The Neo-Assyrian Text Corpus Project (Helsinki: University of Helsinki).
POLLOCK, S. 1991. 'Of priestesses, princes, and poor relations: The dead in the Royal Cemetery of Ur', *Cambridge Archaeological Journal*, 1: 171–89.
—— 1999. *Ancient Mesopotamia: The Eden that never was* (Cambridge: Cambridge University Press).
PONGRATZ-LEISTEN, B. 1994. *Ina Sulmi Irub. Die Kulttopographische und ideologische Programmatik der akitu-Prozession in Babylonien und Assyrien im I. Jahrtausend v. Chr* (Mainz: Philipp von Zabern).
POSTGATE, J. N. 1994a. 'Text and figure in ancient Mesopotamia: Match and mismatch' in C. Renfrew and E. B. W. Zubrow (eds), *The Ancient Mind: Elements of cognitive archaeology* (Cambridge: Cambridge University Press), pp. 176–84.
—— 1994b. *Early Mesopotamia: Society and economy at the dawn of history* (London and New York: Routledge).
POTTS, D. T. 1997. *Mesopotamian Civilisation: The material foundations* (Ithaca: Cornell University Press).

Pritchard, J. B. 1969. *Ancient Near Eastern Texts Relating to the Old Testament*, 3rd edition (Princeton: Princeton University Press).

Roaf, M. 1990. *Cultural Atlas of Mesopotamia and the Ancient Near East* (New York: Facts on File).

Rochberg, F. 2004. *The Heavenly Writing: Divination, horoscopy and astronomy in Mesopotamian culture* (Cambridge: Cambridge University Press).

Rogers, R. W. 1908. *The Religion of Babylonia and Assyria, Especially in its Relations to Israel* (New York: Eaton and Main).

Ross, J. C. 2005. 'Representations, reality, and ideology' in S. Pollock and R. Bernbeck (eds), *Archaeologies of the Middle East: Critical perspectives* (Oxford: Blackwell), pp. 327–50.

Russell, J. M. 1997. *From Nineveh to New York* (New Haven and London: Yale University Press).

Scurlock, J. 2006. *Magico-Medical Means of Treating Ghost-induced Illnesses in Ancient Mesopotamia*, Ancient Magic and Divination 3 (Leiden: Brill/Styx).

Selz, G. J. 1997. '"The holy drum, the spear and the harp": Towards an understanding of the problems of deification in the third millennium in Mesopotamia' in I. L. Finkel and M. J. Geller (eds), *Sumerian Gods and Their Representations*, Cuneiform Monographs 7 (Groningen: Styx), pp. 167–213.

Sigrist, M. 1984. *Les* Sattukku *dans l'Ešumeša durant la période d'Isin et Larsa*, Bibliotheca Mesopotamica 11 (Malibu: Undena Publications).

Soden, W. von 1994. *The Ancient Orient: An introduction to the study of the ancient Near East* (Grand Rapids: William B. Eerdmans).

Stone, E. C. 1993. 'Chariots of the gods in old Babylonian Mesopotamia (c.2000–1600 BC)', *Cambridge Archaeological Journal*, 3(1): 83–107.

Toorn, K. van der 1996. *Family Religion in Babylonia, Syria and Israel: Continuity and change in the forms of religious life* (Leiden: Brill).

Winter, I. 1987. 'Women in public: The Disk of Enheduanna, the beginning of the office of *En*-Priestess, and the weight of visual evidence' in J.-M. Durand (ed.), *La femme dans le Proche-Orient antique* (Paris: Éditions Recherche sur les Civilisations), pp. 189–201.

——1992. '"Idols of the King": Royal images as recipients of ritual action in ancient Mesopotamia', *Journal of Ritual Studies*, 6: 13–42.

Woolley, C. L. 1934. *Ur Excavations*, II: *The Royal Cemetery* (London and Philadelphia: British Museum Press and Pennsylvania University Museum).

——1976. *Ur Excavations*, VII: *The Old Babylonian period* (London: British Museum Press).

——1982. *Ur of the Chaldees: The final account*, rev. and updated by P. R. S. Moorey (London: Herbert Press).

Zimansky, P. 2005. 'Archaeology and texts in the ancient Near East' in S. Pollock and R. Bernbeck (eds), *Archaeologies of the Middle East: Critical perspectives* (Oxford: Blackwell), pp. 308–26.

CHAPTER 49

RETRIEVING THE SUPERNATURAL
Ritual and Religion in the Prehistoric Levant

MARC VERHOEVEN

1 INTRODUCTION

This chapter deals with ritual and religion in the Palaeolithic and Neolithic of the Levant, consisting of Israel, the Palestinian Territories, Lebanon, Jordan, and Syria. The objective is to present a chronological overview of indications of ritual and religion, as well as an account of approaches, as exemplified by current work on (1) Neolithic religion, (2) the so-called skull cult, and (3) feasting.

The Middle Palaeolithic evidence will be briefly discussed, but we shall largely be concerned with the Upper Palaeolithic (45,000–20,000 cal. BP), Epipalaeolithic (20,000–12,000 cal. BP) and the Neolithic (12,000–7,300 cal. BP). The Early and Middle Epipalaeolithic is represented by the Kebaran; the Late Epipalaeolithic by the Natufian. The subsequent Neolithic consists of the Pre-Pottery Neolithic A (PPNA), the Pre-Pottery Neolithic B (PPNB) and the Late (Pottery) Neolithic periods. The various key sites mentioned are depicted in Figure 49.1. The identification of ritual is based on the concept of framing as introduced in chapter 9.

2 THE SEQUENCE

2.1 Palaeolithic

Middle and Upper Palaeolithic sites in the Levant only provide few clues with regard to ritual and religion. In principle, human burials are the main source of evidence. About 25 probable burials (see Belfer-Cohen and Hovers 1992) of both morphologically archaic humans (resembling Neanderthals) and modern humans are known from the Middle Palaeolithic, such as at Qafzeh, Skhul, and Kebara cave in the southern Levant and Dederiyeh in western Syria. From Upper Palaeolithic and Kebaran sites in the Levant,

1	Çayönü	▲	13	'Ain Mallaha	+	
2	Domuztepe	▼	14	Hayonim Cave and Terrace	+	
3	Nevali Çori	▲	15	Ein Gev I	×	
4	Göbekli Tepe	■▲	16	Ohalo II	×	
5	Sabi Abyad	▼	17	Qafzeh	⚘	
6	Jerf el-Ahmar	■	18	Kfar Hahoresh	▲	
7	Mureybet	+■▲	19	Skhul	⚘	
8	Dederiyeh	⚘+	20	Nahal Oren	+■	
9	Qermez Dere	■	21	El-Wad	+	
10	Aswad	▲	22	Kebara Cave	⚘×	
11	Ramad	▲	23	Neve David	+	
12	Beisamoun	▲	24	Wadi Hammeh 27	+	
25	'Ain Ghazal	▲				
26	Jericho	+■▲▼				
27	'Ain Sakhri	+				
28	Kharaneh IV	×				
29	Nahal Hemar	▲				

⚘ Middle Palaeolithic
× Kebaran
+ Natufian
■ Pre-Pottery Neolithic A
▲ Pre-Pottery Neolithic B
▼ Late Neolithic

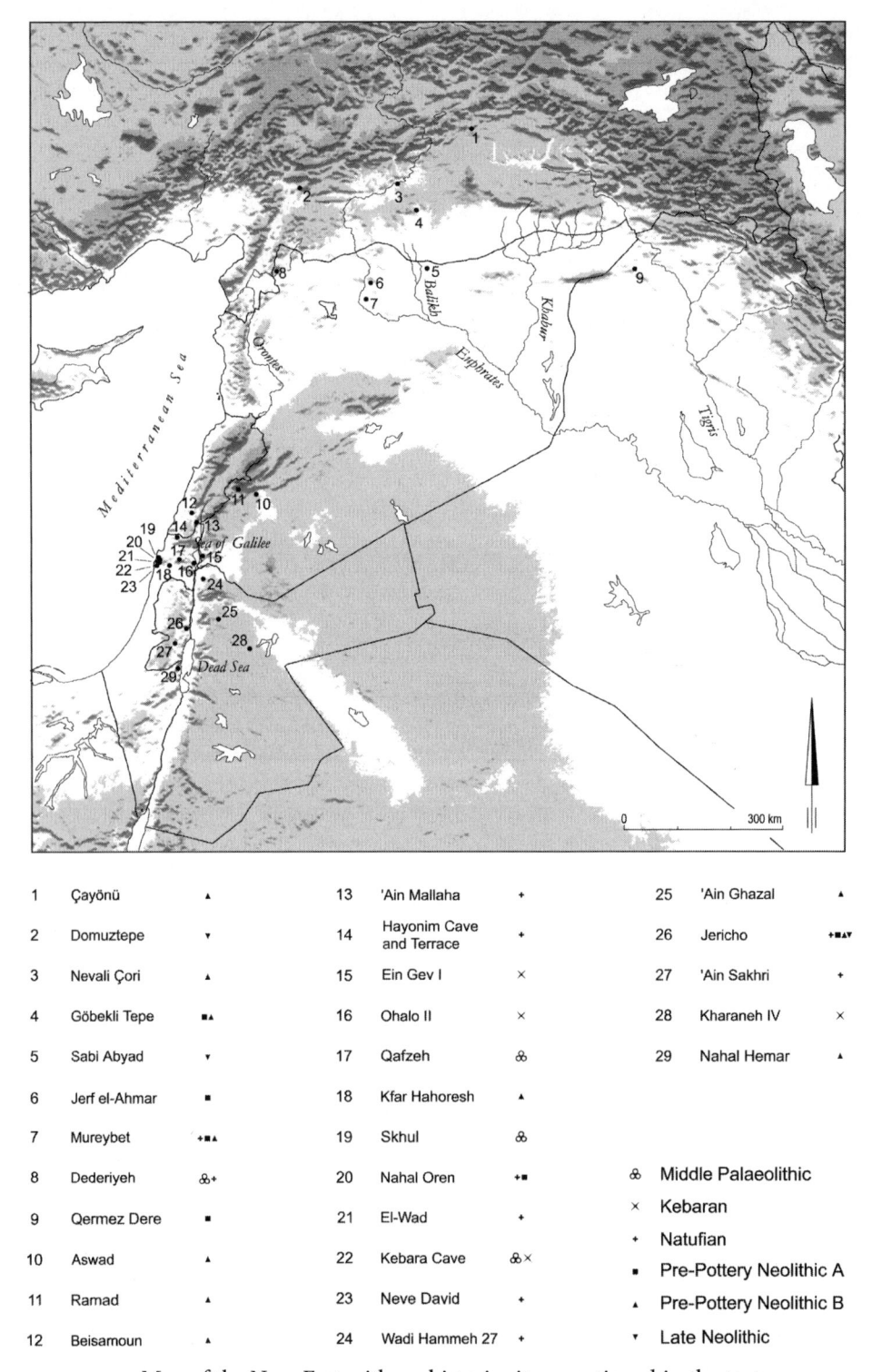

FIGURE 49.1 Map of the Near East with prehistoric sites mentioned in the text.

however, only very few burials are known. Skeletal remains from Ohalo II, Ein Gev I, and Neve David provide the main evidence. The burials are mostly primary, with the skeletons in flexed positions. Burial gifts mainly consisted of domestic tools. At Neve David three mortars were found in a male burial; one of the mortars covered the skull, another lay between the legs. The burial in Ein Gev I was spatially related to pestles, a mortar, and a hearth. The scarcity of burials does not seem to reflect unfavourable circumstances of preservation, indicating that burial in habitation sites was uncommon and suggesting a highly mobile hunting-gathering way of life in this period. Like burials, decorated objects, which might be indicative of a concern with the supernatural, are very rare, mostly consisting of incised stones and none of them associated with burials (Gilead 1998; Goring Morris and Belfer-Cohen 2002, 2003).

2.2 Natufian

Burials become very common in the Natufian. Natufian people are often referred to as 'complex hunter-gatherers', as in some areas (the Mediterranean zone of the southern Levant) they lived in villages consisting of oval and round houses for extended periods of time. Moreover, here they partly subsisted from the harvesting of wild cereals in natural stands (e.g. Delage 2004; Bar-Yosef and Valla 1991).

Typically, the dead were buried in communal burial grounds (e.g. El-Wad, with more than 100 burials), but burials were also present in and between houses (e.g. Hayonim Cave, Mallaha, El-Wad, Wadi Hammeh 27). There is a large variety of mortuary practices: burials are primary or secondary, single or multiple, and body position ranges from extended, to flexed, to semi-flexed (Belfer-Cohen and Hovers 1992; Byrd and Monahan 1995). Some burials have burial gifts, others not, and no association between age, sex, and such gifts has been noted. The burial of humans and domesticated dogs at Mallaha and Hayonim Terrace is the first evidence of a bond that lasts until today (Ronen 2004; Valla 1998).

From the Natufian there are also indications of the special, possibly ritual use of specific buildings. At Mallaha, for instance, one of the largest buildings (structure 131) seems to have been purposely situated on clusters of burials. The floors of other buildings at this site were marked by conspicuous configurations with a probably ritual and religious significance, such as an isolated human skull near a hearth and the attachment of gazelle horncores to human skulls. Other possible indications for Natufian ritual and religion are small figurines of animals and occasionally humans, including a limestone figurine of a mating couple from Wadi Khareitoun ('Ain Sakhri), decorated sickle hafts, and bone and stone objects with engraved abstract patterns (Belfer-Cohen 1991).

2.3 Pre-Pottery Neolithic A

The PPNA represents the first phase of the Neolithic. Sites are quite rare, but it is clear that the symbolic and ritual role of buildings, particularly houses, was intensified. For instance, skulls and horncores of wild cattle or aurochs are repeatedly associated with houses, often 'buried' in benches or walls, such as at Jerf el Ahmar and Mureybet near the Euphrates in Syria (e.g. Cauvin 2000; Ibáñez 2008). Manipulation of human skulls, which started in the Late Natufian, also increased. For instance, at Jerf el Ahmar a deposit of three human skulls was found in the remains of an exterior oven. Skull deposits in houses at other PPNA sites also betray ritual activities. Apart from these probably house(hold)-related rituals, there are indications of communal ritual practices. For example, at Jerf el Ahmar a number of large subterranean round buildings have been found that were probably used for storage, meetings, and rituals. They were supplied with stone benches, engraved friezes and, probably, wall paintings. Apart from triangles, humans and birds of prey were depicted. Another building was completely burned (presumably deliberately set on fire) and besides a human skull, a decapitated human skeleton with outstretched arms was found on the floor of the central room (Stordeur 2000). New discoveries at other PPNA sites, such as at Göbekli Tepe in south-eastern Anatolia, where many circular stone buildings were associated with decorated sculpture, some of which (the T-shaped pillars) of megalithic proportions (Schmidt 2006, 2007), also indicate the importance of symbolism and ritual in the PPNA.

PPNA burials are often single, without skulls. Burial gifts are virtually absent. The graves are generally found under house floors. In Mureybet (phase III), for instance, a female skull and long bones were buried under a small basin-shaped hearth, the rest of the skeleton was interred outside the house. Figurines are stylized representations of portions or all of human bodies. Sex or gender is sometimes clearly indicated (phalli, vulvae, breasts), but can be omitted as well (Kuijt and Chesson 2005). Abstract engraved designs, such as zig-zag lines, on stones have been noted at different sites.

2.4 Pre-Pottery Neolithic B

The PPNB is the period of increased sedentism, craft specialization, and the domestication of plants and animals. It is also well known for spectacular evidence with regard to ritual and religion. It is probably true to say that the PPNB was marked by a—material at least—preoccupation with the supernatural. The key features of this are: (1) special, ritual buildings; (2) various kinds of burials, including decapitated skeletons; (3) skull caches; (4) plastered skulls; (5) symbolic human–animal relations including therianthropic sculpture; (6) large statuary; (7) human and animal figurines; and (8) the use of horncores (especially of cattle) in domestic buildings, ritual buildings, and burials. Two Levantine sites that stand out with respect to these indications are 'Ain Ghazal and Kfar HaHoresh.

'Ain Ghazal is a large settlement near Amman in Jordan dating from the Middle to the Final PPNB (or PPNC). A number of buildings at this site are marked by special shapes (apsidal or circular), interior features (plastered hearths, basins, 'altars', subfloor channels), and painting. Due to their distinctiveness, these structures are generally interpreted as ritual buildings (e.g. Rollefson 2000). The second class of probable ritual objects is represented by two caches containing respectively 26 and 7 large (up to 90 cm high) anthropomorphic statues, including two-headed busts, made of lime plaster. Both caches were found beneath the floors of houses that had been abandoned long before the statues were buried. Fragments of comparable plaster statues have also been recovered from Jericho and Nahal Hemar. The relatively large size of these statues suggests that they were meant to be visible from a distance and perhaps used in public ceremonies. The burial record at 'Ain Ghazal is represented by about 120 human interments. Various types of burials can be distinguished, including those of decapitated and flexed skeletons. Human skulls without the rest of the skeleton, belonging to adults as well as to children, were also recovered. Apart from skulls, the plaster remains (the 'faces') of three plastered skulls were found in a cache. Finally, large numbers of animal figurines and around 40 human—mostly female—clay figurines were recovered. Most of the animal figurines represent cattle, the other species are sheep/ goats and equids. The discovery of some bovine figurines with flint bladelets in their bodies, as well as the fact that the large majority of them were headless and probably deliberately decapitated, suggests that some figurines served 'magical' purposes (Rollefson 2000).

Kfar HaHoresh is a small site located in northern Israel dating from the Early to the Late PPNB. Only a few clear indications for habitation have been found; the site is especially known for its astonishing variety and complexity of burial practices. In fact, the site was probably a mortuary centre, given that in all the areas of excavation quite unusual and spectacular remains of funeral ceremonies have been encountered (e.g. Eshed et al. 2008; Goring-Morris 2000; but see Garfinkel 2006). At least 70 individuals have been buried at the site. Many of the burials are either missing skeletal parts or have been supplied with other bones, human as well as animal. An example of this concern with establishing relations between humans and animals is a well-preserved human plastered skull, which was found just above a complete but headless gazelle carcass. Another fascinating therianthropic context is represented by a pit in which mostly human long bones had been intentionally arranged in such a manner that when viewed from above they depicted an animal in profile (possibly a wild boar, an aurochs, or a lion: Figure 49.2). An illustration of mortuary relations between different humans is the recovery of two headless adult burials, one with a headless infant cradled in its arms. 'Above and around them numerous postcranial bones, some in partial articulation, and mandibles representing another 13 individuals were found in an oval arrangement around the periphery of the pit' (Goring-Morris 2008: 1908). Manipulation of human skulls is further indicated by the finds of more than a dozen isolated skulls, including three plastered skulls, as well as evidence for *in vivo* deformation of some skulls.

Based on an analysis of ritual and symbolism at 'Ain Ghazal, Kfar HaHoresh and other sites, I have proposed (Verhoeven 2002a) that PPNB ritual and ideology was marked by four basic so-called structuring principles: (1) *communality*, as many PPNB rituals seem to be marked by public display (such as ritual buildings, statues, masks, *stelae*); (2) *dominant symbolism*, indicating the use of highly visual, powerful, and evocative symbols (e.g. statues); (3) *human–animal linkage*, denoting the physical and symbolical attachment of humans with animals (such as seen at Kfar HaHoresh); (4) *vitality*, referring to fertility, sexuality (e.g. female figurines); and (5) *life force*, the vital power which principally resides in the head (e.g. skull manipulation).

2.5 Late Neolithic

The Late Neolithic was marked by the intensification and spread of agriculture (including pastoralism) and sedentism, as well the introduction of pottery. There are a number of examples which point to a continuation of PPNB ritual traditions in the Late Neolithic. Dramatic indications for ritual such as found in the PPNB, however, are much rarer. Burials and figurines, typologically varying according to region and period, are the most common indications of ritual practices. It seems that many rituals in this period were marked by *domesticity*, referring to a generally domestic, secluded and private kind of ritual practice, probably mainly related to individuals and households (Verhoeven 2002b). However, there is also evidence for rituals at the community level. For instance, at Tell Sabi Abyad I in

FIGURE 49.2 Depiction of an animal (boar, aurochs, or lion?) in profile made from human and gazelle bones found at the PPNB burial site Kfar HaHoresh in Israel. (Photo: Nigel Goring-Morris).

northern Syria a mortuary ritual related to two persons consisted of the display of a series of large creatures made of clay, as well as the apparent intentional conflagration of a settlement (Verhoeven 2000). Manipulation of human skulls, including plastering, has been found at a few Late Neolithic sites in Iraq and Anatolia (e.g. Köşk Höyük: Bogonofsky 2005) and, as we shall see below, indications for feasting and dancing also point to collective rituals.

3 APPROACHES

From the above it appears that the main indications for ritual and religion used by most Near Eastern prehistorians are: (1) burials, (2) decorated objects (e.g. incised stones and ornaments), (3) 'special' buildings, (4) 'special' deposits, (5) human and animal figurines, (6) statues, (7) masks, (8) monoliths, and (9) wall and floor paintings. Most likely, these categories are used in many other parts of the world as well for retrieving the supernatural. But how do Near Eastern prehistorians deal with ritual and religion?

In general terms, before c.1995, in many studies that in one way or another dealt with prehistoric ritual and religion, (1) ritual and religion were not acknowledged, or not clearly defined; (2) symbolism largely stood for ritual and religion; (3) there was a rather strict separation between the religious and the profane; (4) the wealth of data from social anthropology on ritual and religion was largely ignored or applied in a non-critical manner; (5) interpretations were largely according to the processual paradigm and were mostly (a) 'common sense', (b) functionalist, or (c) cognitive; (6) many contributions tended to be descriptive, rather than interpretative. Moreover, given the extremely rich and promising indications of prehistoric ritual and religion in the Levant, remarkably few detailed studies about these issues appeared.

In recent years, however, this has changed and—although much works still needs to be done—ritual and religion have come to the fore as important research topics. This is probably due to the exciting new discoveries of one or more of the supposed indications of ritual and religion indicated above. Many archaeologists are faced with fascinating material that needs to be dealt with in a rigorous fashion. Moreover, there seems to be a growing awareness of not only the necessity, but also the possibility of dealing with ritual and religion (e.g. Gebel et al. 2002; Hodder 2010; Kuijt 2000; Rollefson 2000; Schmidt 2006), presumably brought about by the growing number of studies about it in general. This, and the retrieval of new data, promises to make the study of ritual and religion in the Levant, in fact in the entire Near East, a very fruitful subject of investigation. The following sections provide examples.

4 NEOLITHIC RELIGION

A milestone in the study of prehistoric religion in the Levant is Cauvin's *Religions néolithiques de Syro-Palestine* of 1972. The ideas presented in that study were further developed in his influential *Naissance des divinités, naissance de l'agriculture. La révolution des symboles au Néolithique* of 1994 (published in English in 2000). His main thesis is that the real Neolithic revolution was not the domestication of plants and animals, but a restructuring of human psycho-cultural capacities: Cauvin argues for a revolution of symbols which resulted in the invention of religion. Based on the ideas of Rousseau and Hegel, he regards religion as an alienation, as indicated by a projection of supernatural divine personalities. This alienation, then, reshaped human cognition, as it made the mind suitable and effective for increasing manipulations of the surrounding, external, world. This would all have started in the PPNA, in which there was a proliferation of the human image, as testified by the appearance of skull caches, decorated skulls, female figurines, statues, and masks. Moreover, from the beginning of the PPNA skulls of aurochs complete with horns (*bucrania*) were used in houses. Focusing on the female figurines and the bucrania, Cauvin argues that Neolithic ideology was centred around the cult of the woman and the bull. About the woman he writes: 'she was not only a "fertility symbol" but a genuine mythical personality, conceived as a supreme being and universal mother, in other words a goddess who crowned a religious system which one could describe as "female monotheism"' (Cauvin 2000: 32). In this system, the bull represents the male (see also e.g. Guilaine 2003; and Hodder 2001 for a critique).

Recently Watkins has further developed Cauvin's ideas (e.g. Watkins 2004, 2005, 2008). Like Cauvin, his point of departure is that the beginning of the Near Eastern Neolithic was a period of major cognitive and symbolic transformations, indicated by the 'explosion of symbolism' starting in the PPNA. It is argued that Upper Palaeolithic people were animistic and had vague and unspecific ideas about the supernatural. This would have changed drastically with the supposed rise in population levels and the related onset of sedentism in the Natufian. Life in these 'permanent' villages would have engendered social stress and the need to create physical as well as material boundaries between, for example, public and private and different spaces with the settlements. The signification of ideas and concepts in terms of material symbols would have been part of a systematization of the surrounding world. The oppositions that were part and parcel of domestic life, then, would have been the basis for further, symbolic, oppositions. The most important of these was the distinction between the profane and sacred world. Religion, then, was born in the Neolithic. It is further argued that these religious ideas remained powerful, easy to remember, and easy to transmit due to people's ability to codify messages in material symbols (so-called external symbolic storage).

5 THE SKULL CULT

Perhaps one of the most intriguing aspects of prehistoric ritual and religion in the Levant is the physical and symbolic manipulation of human skulls (including crania)—as a shorthand, often termed the skull cult. This ritual practice, this living with the dead, started in the (Late) Natufian, continued in the PPNA, intensified in the PPNB, and was practiced occasionally in the Late Neolithic. It was first recognized in Kenyon's excavations in Jericho (Kenyon 1957). Since then examples have been encountered at many sites distributed over a vast geographical area in the Near East, stretching from the Levant in the west (Aswad, Ramad, Nahal Hemar, Beisamoun, Kfar HaHoresh, Jericho, and 'Ain Ghazal) to the Anatolian Taurus foothills in the north (Nevali Çori, Çayönü) and the plains of Iraq in the east (Qermez Dere).

The evidence consists of skull removal, skull caching, skull decoration, and skull deformation. Perhaps most intriguing are the decorated skulls, some 70 of which were found at the Levantine sites mentioned above. By means of, for example, plaster, collagen, paint, and cowrie shells as eyes, these skulls were probably meant to portray the deceased. The decorated skulls are of males, females, and children, without a significant bias to either age or sex (Bonogofsky 2001). The modelled skulls, most often grouped together in caches, stem from different contexts, including abandoned houses (above and below floors), courtyards, and a cave (Nahal Hemar). They are often associated with other human remains, including unplastered skulls (even of neonates) and headless skeletons. Typically, a complete 'life cycle' of Neolithic manipulated skulls consisted of: (1) burial of corpse, usually under the floor of a house; (2) opening of the grave and removal of the skull; (3) possible selection for decoration; (4) use and display; (5) disposal, most often burial, of the skull.

Recent fieldwork at Tell Aswad near Damascus in Syria has provided fascinating evidence with regard to the skull cult. The excavations have revealed two funeral areas located at the periphery of the settlement zone (Stordeur 2003; Stordeur and Khawam 2007). Both areas are dated to the Middle or Late PPNB, but they are stratigraphically separated, hence their designations as respectively the early and late burial ground. Interestingly, both areas were founded by means of deposits of plastered skulls. The skull cache in the early burial ground consisted of two pairs of modelled skulls, arranged in a

FIGURE 49.3 Cache of plastered skulls which founded the 'late burial ground' at PPNB Tell Aswad in Syria (Photo: Laurent Dugué. Excavations at Tell Aswad, directed by D. Stordeur, Mission El Kowm-Mureybet Ministère Affaires Etrangères France).

semi-circle, along the edge of a circular pit. The remaining part of the pit was used for a further ten burials, including the headless skeleton of an adult, as well as the complete skeleton of a young child. The burials were covered by a low earthen mound surrounded by small basalt slabs. The skull cache in the late burial ground consisted of four plastered skulls, a plaster 'face' without skull, a lower jaw, and the unplastered skull of a child. Contrary to the early burial ground, subsequent burials were located above—and not in—the pit. The four plastered skulls were grouped around the child's skull (see Figure 49.3). Three of the skulls were attached to each other by lumps of loam. The skulls were painted with red ochre and, apart from the large and crude ears, have realistic and fine facial features. Like all plastered skulls from Aswad, the eyes are closed. As yet, the gender of the skulls is unknown.

Most authorities agree that the evidence for removal of the skull after burial, the fact that jaws are often left in the headless burials, and the near absence of marks of violence, make it unlikely that the skulls and burials had to do with head hunting. It is commonly assumed, then, that the skull cult was related to a veneration of the ancestors. In this view, the skulls of (important) ancestors may *pars pro toto* have influenced the lives of their relatives (e.g. Bienert 1991). Kuijt (2000) has in this respect argued that rituals related to ancestors served to integrate communities in times of stress, that may have appeared due to the economic and social changes of the new Neolithic way of life. Moreover, ritual would have been a means to consolidate authority and a way of creating intergenerational memory in early agricultural communities (Kuijt 2002, 2008). It is indeed likely that the display and caching of human skulls is indicative of a ritual and religious role of ancestors, but recent research seems to point out that there may have been more dimensions. Based on a series of meticulous analyses of plastered skulls and their contexts, Bonogofsky (e.g. 2003) concludes that the recovery of modelled skulls of males, females, and children, their presence in different contexts, and the occasional presence of burial gifts indicates that the skulls probably had different functions and meanings, including the promotion of fertility (see also Fletcher et al. 2008; Meskell 2008). Indeed, in my view, largely based on an analysis of ethnographically documented examples of skull manipulation (see also Aufderheide 2009; Bonogofsky 2006b), human skulls, plastered as well as unplastered, were especially honoured because they were the seat of so-called life force. This denotes a vital energy or power residing in the head, which could be used to ensure fecundity and prosperity to persons, plants, and animals (Verhoeven 2002a).

6 FEASTING AND DANCING

In recent years there has been growing interest in the social and ritual role of feasting in both anthropology and archaeology (see e.g. Dietler and Hayden 2001; Dietler, Ch. 13, this volume). With regard to the prehistoric Near East, Hayden's theory of domestication, which holds that the emergence of agriculture was brought about by competitive feasting in Natufian communities (Hayden 1990), is one of the first studies on the role of feasting. Here we shall be concerned with some examples from later prehistory (see e.g. Schmandt-Besserat 2001 for feasting in historic periods in the Near East).

In a detailed analysis, based on ethnographically informed archaeological 'signatures' of feasting, Twiss (2008) has assessed the evidence for feasting in the Pre-Pottery Neolithic of the southern Levant. Her 'common aspects of feasting' which may result in material correlates are: consumption of large quantities of food and/or drink; consumption of an unusually wide variety of foods; consumption of rarely-eaten and/or symbolically important foods; culinary emphasis on large animals; consumption of domesticated animals; consumption of alcohol; use of special locations; performances in public rituals; displays of wealth and/or status; special serving paraphernalia; and the production/display of commemorative items. The analysis suggests that there is an increase in both the frequency and scale of feasting from the Early to the Late PPNB, with a decrease in the final PPNB (the PPNC). Departing from the view that feasts are contexts for both competition and integration, these results are linked to socio-economic transformations. It is argued that as the scale and complexity of society grew, competition increased, making integration an important issue. As population agglomeration lessened towards the end of the period, feasting declined as well. A particularly interesting suggestion is that the apparent intensification of cattle feasting, as indicated by bucrania, may have contributed to their adoption as domesticates.

An example of PPNB cattle feasting is provided by Kfar HaHoresh. Here, the so-called *Bos* pit probably contained the remains of a funerary feast (Goring-Morris and Horwitz 2007). Apparently, the bones of eight aurochs were deposited in this pit after their meat had been consumed. The pit was then covered by a human burial, which was plastered over. After a while, the skull was removed. Interestingly, the aurochs skulls were also absent. The estimated amount of meat consumed (*c.*500 kg), reinforces the claim that Kfar HaHoresh served as a regional mortuary centre (see above).

As our final example, Garfinkel (2003) has concerned himself with the analysis of dancing in Neolithic and Chalcolithic village communities in the Near East. His conclusions are based upon an extended study of (probable) depictions of dancing on stone (e.g. rock art), walls and floors and especially decorated pottery from some 170 sites. It is suggested that the earliest evidence for the dancing motif comes from Pre-Pottery Neolithic sites in the form of incised stone slabs and floor paintings. In the subsequent early Late Neolithic the motif becomes more common, mostly appearing as applied plastic decoration on pottery vessels. It is argued that in later Neolithic periods (especially the Samarra and Halaf cultures) dance motifs are quite common, and occur over a large area (see also Nieuwenhuyse 2007; contra Helwing 2003). Various styles are evident, including naturalistic, linear, and geometric. With regard to interpretation, Garfinkel takes a cognitive approach, which is not unlike that of Cauvin (2000) and Watkins (2005), in which the significance of dancing is related to the Neolithic revolution. He argues that the beginnings of agriculture involved a cognitive revolution concerning the relationships between work investment and its final product, referring to the agricultural cycle. Through dancing at scheduled agricultural ceremonies and festivals communities transmitted messages to themselves (cf. Leach 1976: 45) with regard to the tasks at hand. Moreover, 'The high supernatural powers also become involved in the process, as the circle of dance is the actual place where contact is made between this and the other world' (Garfinkel 2003: 82).

7 BOUNDARIES, DOMESTICATION, AND THE SUPERNATURAL

As we have seen, many researchers have suggested that the prominence of ritual in the Pre-Pottery Neolithic was related to the advent of agriculture and sedentism, more specifically to the establishment of physical and subsequently social boundaries, as well as divisions between the sacred and profane.

However, with regard to the latter, while the sacred was indeed foregrounded, there is substantial evidence that boundaries between the sacred and profane were transgressed, rather than clearly established. There are many indications of both the physical and symbolic linking of people, animals, and the supernatural in the Pre-Pottery Neolithic (Verhoeven 2004; see also Boyd 2004). Moreover, while social boundaries were probably indeed established and negotiated through ritual, I argue that there also was a 'deeper' psychological reason for the importance of ritual and religion in the Pre-Pottery Neolithic. An important aspect of living and working together—sedentism, craft specialization, and agriculture—was the accumulation and elaboration of material culture. Due to this materialization, coupled with the cultivation of plants and control of animals, i.e. domestication in the widest sense, people must have become increasingly aware of their manipulating and creative powers. The dominance of material and most likely religious symbolism can be regarded, then, as a conscious attempt to even manipulate the supernatural world, in order to better deal with the social and economic changes. The decline of such symbolism at the end of the PPNB and in the subsequent Late Neolithic might be due to the fact that people had become used to the agricultural way of life, and thus had less need for such intensive supernatural intervention.

8 Conclusion

As we have seen, there are many indications of ritual and religion in the prehistoric periods of the Levant. In fact, these ancient communities probably cannot be properly understood without reference to what they believed. A number of recent detailed and high-quality studies, such as the few briefly summarized in this chapter, are promising in this regard. The strength of many of these analyses is the meticulous attention to data, as well as the contextualization of it. Included in some of these studies, or based on them, there are also more generalizing and interpretative accounts, dealing with the prominence, structure, meaning, function, and transformation of ritual and religion in certain periods and/or regions. Clearly, more work needs to be implemented, but if this 'two-track approach' can be continued and intensified, ritual and religion of the prehistoric Levant will become as important as they once were.

Acknowledgements

First of all, I would like to thank Tim Insoll for giving me the opportunity to write a chapter in this volume. Moreover, his editorial comments improved the paper. Rachel MacLean is also thanked for her work in this regard. I am greatly indebted to Nigel Goring-Morris and Danielle Stordeur for providing illustrations and publications. Many thanks are also due to Sofie Debruyne, Olivier Nieuwenhuyse, and Trevor Watkins, who helped with literature as well. Jenny Wagstaffe of Oxford University Press made all the necessary arrangements for publishing this contribution. Ans Bulles corrected the English text and Mikko Kriek made Figure 49.1.

Suggested Reading

Although there are many articles dealing with aspects of prehistoric ritual and religion in the Levant, there are as yet very few syntheses. Some exceptions with regard to Neolithic ritual and religion are Cauvin (2000), Verhoeven (2002a), and Watkins (2005). A collection of case studies of Neolithic ritual is presented in Gebel et al. (2002). Bonogofsky (2006a) is a good overview of the skull cult, while Kuijt (2000) deals with its social function. Twiss (2008) is a fine paper on prehistoric feasting in the southern Levant.

REFERENCES

AUFDERHEIDE, A. C. (ed.) 2009. *Overmodeled Skulls* (Duluth: Heide Press).
BAR-YOSEF, O. and VALLA, F. R. (eds) 1991. *The Natufian Culture in the Levant* (Ann Arbor: International Monographs in Prehistory).
BELFER-COHEN, A. 1991. 'Art items from layer B, Hayonim Cave: A case study of art in a Natufian context' in O. Bar-Yosef and F. R. Valla (eds), *The Natufian Culture in the Levant* (Ann Arbor: International Monographs in Prehistory), pp. 569–88.
—— and HOVERS, E. 1992. 'In the eye of the beholder: Mousterian and Natufian burials in the Levant', *Current Anthropology*, 33(4): 463–71.
BIENERT, H. D. 1991. 'Skull cult in the prehistoric Near East', *Journal of Prehistoric Religion*, 5: 9–13.
BONOGOFSKY, M. 2001. *An Osteo-archaeological Examination of the Ancestor Cult during the Pre-Pottery Neolithic B Period in the Levant* (Ann Arbor: University Microfilms International).
—— 2003. 'Neolithic plastered skulls and railroading epistemologies', *Bulletin of the American Schools of Oriental Research*, 331: 1–10.
—— 2005. 'A bioarchaeological study of plastered skulls from Anatolia: New discoveries and interpretations', *International Journal of Osteoarchaeology*, 15: 124–35.
—— 2006a. 'Cultural and ritual evidence in the archaeological record: Modeled skulls from the ancient Near East' in M. Georgiadis and C. Gallou (eds), *The Archaeology of Cult and Death* (Budapest: Archaeolingua), pp. 45–69.
—— (ed.) 2006b. *Skull Collection, Modification and Decoration*, BAR International Series 1539 (Oxford: BAR).
BOYD, B. 2004. 'Agency and landscape: Abandoning the "nature/culture" dichotomy in interpretations of the Natufian and the transition to the Neolithic' in C. Delage (ed.), *The Last Hunter-gatherers in the Near East*, BAR International Series 1320 (Oxford: BAR), pp. 119–36.
BYRD, B. F. and MONAHAN, C. M. 1995. 'Death, mortuary ritual, and Natufian social structure', *Journal of Anthropological Archaeology*, 14(3): 251–87.
CAUVIN, J. 1972. *Religions néolithiques de Syro-Palestine* (Paris: Libraire d'Amérique et d'Orient, Jean Maisonneuve).
—— 2000. *The Birth of the Gods and the Origins of Agriculture*, trans. T. Watkins (Cambridge: Cambridge University Press).
DELAGE, C. (ed.) 2004. *The Last Hunter-gatherers in the Near East*, BAR International Series 1320 (Oxford: BAR).
DIETLER, M. and HAYDEN, B. (eds) 2001. *Feasts: Archaeological and ethnographic perspectives on food, politics and power* (Washington: Smithsonian Institution Press).
ESHED, V., HERSHKOVITZ, I., and GORING-MORRIS, A. N. 2008. 'A re-evaluation of burial customs in the Pre-Pottery Neolithic B in light of paleodemographic analysis of the human remains from Kfar HaHoresh, Israel', *Paléorient*, 34: 91–103.
FLETCHER, A., PEARSON, J., and AMBERS, J. 2008. 'The manipulation of social and physical identity in the Pre-Pottery Neolithic', *Cambridge Archaeological Journal*, 18: 309–25.
GARFINKEL, Y. 2003. *Dancing at the Dawn of Agriculture* (Austin: University of Texas Press).
—— 2006. 'The burials of Kfar HaHoresh: A regional or local phenomenon?', *Journal of the Israel Prehistoric Society*, 36: 109–16.
GEBEL, H. G. 2002. 'Walls: Loci of forces' in H. G. K. Gebel, B. D. Hermansen, and C. H. Jensen (eds), *Magic Practices and Ritual in the Near Eastern Neolithic*, Studies in Early Near Eastern Production, Subsistence, and Environment 8 (Berlin: Ex Oriente), pp. 119–32.

——, Hermansen, B. D., and Jensen, C. H. (eds) 2002. *Magic Practices and Ritual in the Near Eastern Neolithic*, Studies in Early Near Eastern Production, Subsistence, and Environment 8 (Berlin: Ex Oriente).

Gilead, I. 1998. 'The foragers of the Upper Paleolithic period' in T. E. Levy (ed.), *The Archaeology of Society in the Holy Land* (London: Leicester University Press), pp. 124–40.

Goring-Morris, A. N. 2000. 'The quick and the dead: The social context of aceramic Neolithic mortuary practices as seen from Kfar Hahoresh' in I. Kuijt (ed.), *Life in Neolithic Farming Communities: Social organization, identity, and differentiation* (New York: Kluwer Academic/Plenum Publishers), pp. 103–35.

——2008. 'Kefar Ha-Horesh' in E. Stern (ed.), *The New Encyclopedia of Archaeological Excavations in the Holy Land*, V (Jerusalem: Israel Exploration Society & Biblical Archaeology Society), pp. 1907–9.

——and Belfer-Cohen, A. 2002. 'Symbolic behaviour from the Epipaleolithic and Early Neolithic of the Near East: Preliminary observations on continuity and change' in H. G. K. Gebel, B. D. Hermansen, and C. H. Jensen (eds), *Magic Practices and Ritual in the Near Eastern Neolithic*, Studies in Early Near Eastern Production, Subsistence, and Environment 8 (Berlin: Ex Oriente), pp. 67–79.

——————2003. 'Structures and dwellings in the Upper and Epi-Paleolithic (*ca*42–10 K BP) Levant: Profane and symbolic uses' in O. Soffer, S. Vasil'ev, and J. Kozlowski (eds), *Perceived Landscapes and Built Environments: The cultural geography of Late Paleolithic Eurasia*, BAR International Series 1122 (Oxford: BAR), pp. 65–81.

——and Horwitz, L. K. 2007. 'Funerals and feasts during the Pre-Pottery Neolithic B of the Near East', *Antiquity*, 81: 902–19.

Guilaine, J. 2003. *De la vague à la tombe: la conquête néolithique de la Méditerranée* (Paris: Seuil).

Hayden, B. 1990. 'Nimrods, piscators, pluckers, and planters: The emergence of food production', *Journal of Anthropological Archaeology*, 9: 31–69.

Helwing, B. 2003. 'Feasts as a social dynamic in prehistoric Western Asia: Three case studies from Syria and Anatolia', *Paléorient*, 29(2): 63–86.

Hodder, I. 2001. 'Symbolism and the origins of agriculture in the Near East', *Cambridge Archaeological Journal*, 11: 107–12.

——2010. *Religion in the Emergence of Civilization: Çatalhöyük as a case study* (Cambridge: Cambridge University Press).

Ibáñez, J. J. (ed.) 2008. *Le site néolithique de Tell Mureybet (Syrie du Nord): en hommage à Jacques Cauvin*, BAR International Series 1843 (Oxford: BAR).

Kenyon, K. 1957. *Digging up Jericho* (London: Ernest Benn).

Kuijt, I. 2000. 'Keeping the peace: ritual, skull caching and community integration in the Levantine Neolithic' in I. Kuijt (ed.), *Life in Neolithic Farming Communities: Social organization, identity, and differentiation* (New York: Kluwer Academic/Plenum Publishers), pp. 137–63.

——2002. 'Reflections on ritual and the transmission of authority in the Pre-Pottery Neolithic of the southern Levant' in H. G. K. Gebel, B. D. Hermansen, and C. H. Jensen (eds), *Magic Practices and Ritual in the Near Eastern Neolithic*, Studies in Early Near Eastern Production, Subsistence, and Environment 8 (Berlin: Ex Oriente), pp. 81–90.

Kuijt, I. 2008. 'The regeneration of life: Neolithic structures of remembering and forgetting', *Current Anthropology*, 49(2): 171–97.

——and Goring-Morris, N. 2002. 'Foraging, farming, and social complexity in the Pre-Pottery Neolithic of the southern Levant: A review and synthesis', *Journal of World Prehistory*, 16: 361–440.

—— and CHESSON, M. 2005. 'Lumps of clay and pieces of stone: Ambiguity, bodies, and identity as portrayed in Neolithic figurines' in S. Pollock and R. Bernbeck (eds), *Archaeologies of the Middle East: Critical perspectives* (Malden: Blackwell), pp. 152–83.

LEACH, E. R. 1976. *Culture and Communication: The logic by which symbols are connected* (Cambridge: Cambridge University Press).

MESKELL, L. 2008. 'The nature of the beast: curating animals and ancestors at Çatalhöyük', *World Archaeology*, 40(3): 373–89.

NIEUWENHUYSE, O. 2007. *Plain and Painted Pottery: The rise of Late Neolithic ceramic styles on the Syrian and Northern Mesopotamian plains* (Turnhout: Brepols).

ROLLEFSON, G. O. 2000. 'Ritual and social structure at Neolithic 'Ain Ghazal' in I. Kuijt (ed.), *Life in Neolithic Farming Communities: Social organization, identity, and differentiation* (New York: Kluwer Academic/Plenum Publishers), pp. 163–90.

RONEN, A. 2004. 'Why was the dog domesticated?' in C. Delage (ed.), *The Last Hunter-gatherers in the Near East*, BAR International Series 1320 (Oxford: BAR), pp. 153–60.

SCHMANDT-BESSERAT, D. 2001. 'Feasting in the ancient Near East' in M. Dietler and B. Hayden (eds), *Feasts: Archaeological and ethnographic perspectives on food, politics and power* (Washington: Smithsonian Institution Press), pp. 391–403.

SCHMIDT, K. 2006. *Sie bauten die ersten Tempel: das rätselhafte Heiligtum der Steinzeitjäger* (München: C. H. Beck).

—— 2007. 'Die Steinkreise und die Reliefs des Göbekli Tepe' in C. Lichter (ed.), *Vor 12.000 Jahren in Anatolien: die ältesten Monumente der Menschheit* (Stuttgart: Theiss), pp. 83–96.

STORDEUR, D. 2000. 'Jerf el Ahmar et l'émergence du néolithique au Proche Orient' in J. Guilaine (ed.), *Premiers paysans du monde* (Paris: Éditions Errance), pp. 33–60.

—— 2003. 'Des crânes surmodelés à Tell Aswad de Damascène (PPNB Syrie)', *Paléorient*, 29(2): 109–16.

—— and KHAWAM, R. 2007. 'Les crânes surmodelés de Tell Aswad (PPNB Syrie): premier regard sur l'ensemble, premières réflexions', *Syria*, 84: 5–32.

TWISS, K. C. 2007. 'The Neolithic of the southern Levant'. *Evolutionary Anthropology*, 16: 24–35.

—— 2008. 'Transformations in an early agricultural society: Feasting in the southern Levantine Pre-Pottery Neolithic', *Journal of Anthropological Archaeology*, 27: 418–42.

VALLA, F. R. 1998. 'The first settled societies: Natufian (12,500–10,200 BP)' in T. E. Levy (ed.), *The Archaeology of Society in the Holy Land* (London: Leicester University Press), pp. 169–87.

VERHOEVEN, M. 2000. 'Death, fire and abandonment: Ritual practice at Late Neolithic Tell Sabi Abyad, Syria', *Archaeological Dialogues*, 7(1): 46–83.

—— 2002a. 'Ritual and ideology in the Pre-Pottery Neolithic B of the Levant and south-east Anatolia', *Cambridge Archaeological Journal*, 12(2): 233–58.

—— 2002b. 'Transformations of society: The changing role of ritual and symbolism in the Pre-Pottery Neolithic B and Pottery Neolithic periods in the Levant and south-east Anatolia', *Paléorient*, 28(1): 5–14.

—— 2004. 'Beyond boundaries: Nature, culture and a holistic approach to domestication in the Levant', *Journal of World Prehistory*, 18(3): 179–282.

WATKINS, T. 2004. 'Building houses, framing concepts, constructing worlds', *Paléorient*, 30: 5–23.

—— 2005. 'The Neolithic revolution and the emergence of humanity: A cognitive approach to the first comprehensive world-view' in J. Clarke (ed.), *Archaeological Perspectives on the Transmission and Transformation of Culture in the Eastern Mediterranean*, Levant Supplementary Series, II (Oxford: Council for British Research in the Levant & Oxbow Books), pp. 84–8.

—— 2008. 'Supra-regional networks in the Neolithic of Southwest Asia', *Journal of World Prehistory*, 21(2): 139–71.

CHAPTER 50

IRAN

DANIEL POTTS

1 INTRODUCTION

WITH a surface area roughly four times the size of France and diverse topography consisting of deserts, mountains, narrow coastal plains, landlocked basins, and inter-montane valleys, Iran has never been culturally homogeneous. Any survey of the archaeology of ritual and religion in Iran must therefore contend with both the cultural diversity of the area and the enormous variations in religious traditions attested, depending on the chronological period one is studying. For present purposes, Iran is defined in the minimalist sense as the modern Islamic Republic of Iran, not in the maximalist sense of 'greater Iran', which extended deep into the Caucasus and Central Asia, incorporating areas well outside the boundaries of present day Iran at various points in the pre-Islamic past. The boundaries of Iran have always been porous, however, and not all religious praxis within ancient Iran can be considered indigenous. By the late fourth millennium BC, if our understanding of certain divine symbols is correct, non-local deities were being worshipped at Iranian sites, and this phenomenon persisted over the course of the next 3,500 years.

Some non-local religions (Judaism, Christianity), though practised in ancient Iran, are excluded here because of space limitations. Manichaeism, too, is not discussed for, although bound up both politically and culturally with Iran, its most classic expressions were found outside of the country. Zoroastrianism, on the other hand, although most probably of non-Iranian origin, is included since it was so important from the first millennium BC to the coming of Islam and beyond. For convenience, the evidence will be treated in chronological order under the rubrics, rituals, sites, objects, and representations.

2 RITUALS

In the absence of written sources, the identification of rituals in the prehistoric past must necessarily remain speculative. Possible prehistoric representations (see below) are known as early as the late fourth millennium BC, but the nature of the rituals involved is impossible to determine. By the mid-third millennium BC south-western Iran was culturally dominated by the Elamites, but they in turn were often subject to strong Mesopotamian influence throughout their history and, at times, political hegemony (in Khuzestan), particularly during the period c.2500–2000 BC. The first names of deities in the region appear in a Sumerian list from Abu Salabikh where the names ᵈlugal-NIM, literally 'ᵍᵒᵈking (of) Elam' and ᵈnin-šušinak, literally 'ᵍᵒᵈlord (of) Susa', occur. Each is qualified by the use of the *dingir* sign, a star-like, prepositional determinative used only for divine names. The Sumerogram NIM denoting 'high' (a reference to the elevation of the Iranian Plateau in contrast to the low-lying Mesopotamian plain), was the standard shorthand designation for Elam in Sumerian and later Akkadian sources, while ᵈnin-šušinak anticipates the name Inšušinak, the chief deity of Susa and the Susian pantheon in later times (Potts 1999: 87).

Elamite religion was polytheistic and Sumerian, Akkadian and later Elamite texts contain the names of over 200 deities (Vallat 1998: 335), some of whom were originally Mesopotamian (e.g. Adad, Belet-Ali, Ea, Inanna, Nabu, Ninhursag, Šala, and Sin). The majority of deities worshipped in south-western Iran were presumably Elamite (though some of these may have been non-Elamite and non-Mesopotamian deities worshipped by other indigenous peoples in Iran who have left us no written records). During the Iron Age the Aramaean god Hadad and the Urartian god Haldi were worshipped at Bukan in Kurdistan (Eph'al 1999; Teixidor 1999).

In addition to specific deities, other aspects of religious praxis were adopted from Mesopotamia, such as divination practices, using an animal liver (extispicy), attested by the fifteenth to fourteenth century BC at Susa, Haft Tepe, and Chogha Pahn (Biggs and Stolper 1983). The presence of in-ground, individual inhumations in all periods would also suggest the existence of rituals associated with death and burial, though these cannot be reconstructed on the basis of evidence excavated to date.

By the Achaemenid period (539–331 BC) we have evidence of the practice of a new religion, unrelated to any traditions attested in Iran during the preceding centuries. With the arrival of the Iranian-speaking peoples (Medes, Persians) on the Iranian Plateau by c.1000 BC, a religious tradition variously known as Indo-Iranian or Old Iranian, according to some scholars (e.g. Koch 1977; Malandra 1983), appeared. Given that the date (and even existence) of this religion's eponymous prophet, Zoroaster, is hotly disputed (contrast Boyce 1988; Gnoli 1980; or Skjærvø 2005), the date at which we can speak of Zoroastrianism, as a modified form of Old Iranian religion, reflected in the holy books of the *Avesta*, is very difficult to say. Some scholars have suggested that the early Achaemenids, although worshipping the Indo-Iranian deity Ahura Mazda, were not yet Zoroastrians (e.g. Gray 1929; Koch 1977; Malandra 1983), whereas Skjærvø has argued that the Old Persian royal inscriptions from the time of Darius I (522–486 BC) onward contain enough specific allusions (not quotations) to the teachings of Zoroaster as expressed in the Gathas, the oldest part of the Avesta, even if they do not mention the prophet by name, that we are justified in considering Darius I and his descendants Zoroastrians (Skjærvø 2005).

Avestan *daēnā-*, Middle Persian *dyn, d'yn*, meant generally 'religion', but in some contexts it is better understood as a 'set of spiritual qualities of any given individual' (Skalmowski 1982: 225). Zoroastrianism is a dualistic religion that turned the Old Iranian distinction between truth (*ta*) and falsehood (*drugh/draugha*) into a battle between the 'wise lord' Ahura Mazda and the followers of the lie. Zoroastrianism stresses 'good thoughts, good words, good deeds'. Chosen by Ahura Mazda as his first human sacrificer,

Zoroaster fought against the Evil Spirit, Angra Maniiu or Ahriman and his accomplices, the *daēvas*, 'old' or 'other gods' (Skjærvø 2005: 55).

Zoroastrianism, however, evolved through time and most of what we know comes from literature produced after the Islamic conquest, or from the Sasanian period (*c.*AD 224–642). A great deal of scholarship has been produced trying to sift the various elements of the religion and produce a chronology of its theological development. The charting of change and development in Zoroastrian religious ritual over time is, however, problematic, largely because of the complex history of textual transmission (de Jong 1999).

In his inscriptions on the rock face at Bisotun near Kermanshah in western Iran Darius I identified Ahura Mazda as 'the god of the Iranians' and immediately thereafter referred to 'the other gods who are' (Stronach 1984: 487). Slightly later texts from Persepolis give us a good idea of who those other gods were. Non-Iranian deities receiving offerings at Persepolis included Adad, 'Earth' (^{AŠ}KI^{MEŠ}), Halma, Humban, Irdanapirrurtiš, Išpandaramattiš, Mariraš, Minam, Mišdušiš, Nabbazabba, Nah, Napiriša, Narišanka, Pirdakamiya, Šetrabattiš, Šimut, Turme/a, or simply 'the gods' (Henkelman 2008: 519–56). Most often these deities, as well as Auramazda (Ahura Mazda), were mentioned in the context of a priest (^{AN}*la-an-li-ri-ra* 'oblator' refers to the officiant who performed the ^{AN}*la-an*, a general term for 'oblation' [Henkelman 2008: 181–304]; other officiants included the *šatin* [cultic expert], *haturmakša, makuš*, and *pirramadda* [ibid.: 208]) receiving livestock (sheep, goat), grain, flour, fruit, beer, and wine for these offerings (Henkelman 2008: 209). The Elamite term ^{AN}*la-an* for 'oblation', which occurs 81 times in 5,623 available Persepolis texts was qualified as either *gal* (El.), literally 'ration', or *daušam/daušiyam* (Old Persian), literally 'offering' (Henkelman 2008: 211; cf. Razmjou 2004). Some texts record the allotment of livestock for the *šip*-feast and the *anši*-feast in honour of a specific deity or 'the gods' at several sites, including Cyrus the Great's capital, Pasargadae (Henkelman 2008: 549–50).

Although sacrifices were normally daily or monthly, the allocations of commodities to be used in them were often made on an annual basis (Henkelman 2008: 210). At least two Old Persian month names (and their Elamite equivalents) in the Achaemenid royal inscriptions refer specifically to offerings, viz. Bāgayādi (month 7) and Āçiyādiya (month 9), meaning roughly '[pertaining to the] worship of god/(the) gods' and 'fire worship/worship by the fire/sacrifice in or before the fire', respectively (Schmitt 2003: 30–2). Later, each day in each month of the Zoroastrian calendar was 'entitled to a god or related to religious concepts' (Basello 2002: 17; on the Zoroastrian calendar see also Tavernier 2005: 358–60).

Blood sacrifice (*yaz-*), normally the sacrifice of animals, was a well-attested part of early Zoroastrianism (Benveniste 1964: 46; Boyce 1966: 105; de Jong 2002: 128) and although it has often been said that Zoroaster rejected it, this is debated. For example, the *drōn* ritual involved consumption of sacrificial meat and tasting of a cake (de Jong 2002: 128). Herodotus described a sacrifice performed to a god by a layman:

> he leads the victim to a clean spot, and invokes the god, usually having his tiara decked with myrtle. He that sacrifices is not permitted to pray for blessings for himself alone; but he is obliged to offer prayers for the prosperity of all the Persians... When he has cut the victim into small pieces, and boiled the flesh, he strews under it a bed of tender grass, generally trefoil, and then lays all the flesh upon it; when he has put everything in order, one of the Magi standing by sings an ode concerning the origin of the gods, which they say is the incantation; and without one of the Magi it is not lawful for them to sacrifice. [1.132]

Strabo also noted that:

> the Persians do not erect statues or altars, but offer sacrifice on a high place ... with earnest prayer they offer sacrifice in a purified place, presenting the victim crowned; and when the Magus, who directs the sacrifice, has divided the meat the people go away with their shares, without setting apart a portion for the gods, for they say that the god requires only the soul of the victim and nothing else; but still, according to some writers, they place a small portion of the caul [the omentum, a fatty membrane surrounding the internal organs of sheep, pigs, cows, etc.] upon the fire. [*Geog.* 15.3.13].

This latter practice has been compared with the later Zoroastrian sacrifice of the *andom* ('limb/part') to the fire (*ātaš-zōhr*) (Boyce 1966: 107–8).

Strabo also observed, 'But it is especially to fire and water that they offer sacrifice. To fire they offer sacrifice by adding dry wood without the bark and by placing fat on top of it; and then they pour oil upon it and light it below, not blowing with their breath, but fanning it; and those who blow the fire with their breath or put anything dead or filthy upon it are put to death' (*Geog.* 15.3.14). He also described animal sacrifices to water, 'placing pieces of meat on myrtle or laurel branches, the Magi touch them with slender wands and make incantations, pouring oil mixed with both milk and honey, though not into fire or water, but upon the ground; and they carry on their incantations for a long time, holding in their hands a bundle of slender myrtle wands', i.e. the *barsom* bundle, a standard element in Zoroastrian cult performance depicted in glyptic, reliefs, and coins, and attested in the *Avesta* (Calmeyer 1975: 12). A separate description by Strabo of Magi in Cappadocia, though geographically outside of Iran, is nonetheless relevant to a study of early Zoroastrianism. In Cappadocia the Magi entered the fire temple, 'And there, entering daily, they make incantations for about an hour, holding before the fire their bundle of rods and wearing round their heads high turbans of felt, which reach down over their cheeks far enough to cover their lips' (*Geog.* 15.3.15).

Scholars have often invoked Artaxerxes II's (404–359 BC) inscriptions at Hamadan (A^{2}Ha) and Susa (A^{2}Sa), in which Ahura Mazda, Anahita, and the Zoroastrian divinity of contracts, Mithra, are mentioned, as marking a departure in Achaemenid religion (Lecoq 1997: 269). Although Artaxerxes II's predecessors never listed the three deities together, Mithra was already known as a theophoric element in many personal names in both the Elamite and the Aramaic texts at Persepolis (Hallock 1969: 732–3; Gershevitch 1970: 192; Duchesne-Guillemin 1971: 29; Mayrhofer 1973; Schmitt 1991: 117–18). Following Alexander the Great's conquest of the Achaemenid Empire, Greek deities or amalgams of Greek and Iranian deities were worshipped (e.g. Boyce 1975: 100–1; Boyce and Grenet 1991: 44). These are attested archaeologically at, for example, Bisotun (reclining Heracles relief and Greek inscription) near Kermanshah; Karafto cave in Kurdistan (Greek inscription); the *frataraka* temple at Persepolis, with inscribed dedications to Zeus Megistos, Athena Basileia, Apollo, Artemis and Helios (Wiesehöfer 1994: 72); and Masjid-e Soleiman (statuary found at excavated temples) (Potts 1999: 371–82). Strabo noted that 'the Persians ... regard[ing] the heavens as Zeus; and they also worship Helios, whom they call Mithras, and Selene and Aphrodite, and fire and earth and winds and water' (*Geog.* 15.3.13). It has been suggested that, during the Sasanian period, 'an "official" form of Zoroastrianism, untainted by elements that were felt to be of Hellenistic origin', was officially promulgated (Kreyenbroek 1991: 143). In addition to advocating a 'pure' form of Zoroastrianism, the religious zealot *magus* Kirdir was active in suppressing Hinduism, Buddhism, Manichaeism, Judaism, and Nestorian Christianity in Iran during the third century AD (Gignoux 1991; Pourshariati 2008: 327–34).

Turning briefly to funerary rituals, eschatological texts from Susa of mid-second millennium BC date show that the chief deity Inšušinak served as the judge, Išnikarab as the 'Weigher' of the soul of the deceased, and Lagamar as the devil's advocate (Henkelman 2008: 61). Zoroastrianism differed in proscribing in-ground burial, which was theoretically taboo because of a dread of polluting the earth. Instead, Zoroastrians were meant to expose the deceased, so that the flesh could be removed by birds of prey, and then inter the bones in an ossuary, often a rock-cut niche (Boyce 1988: 21). Nevertheless, the large number of in-ground burials from the first millennium BC and later suggests heterodoxy, a large proportion of non-Zoroastrians amongst the population of Iran, or both.

3 SITES

Temples to some of the many deities attested in cuneiform texts are known at over a dozen sites including Tol-e Bormi, Chogha Pahn East, Chogha Pahn West, Chogha Zanbil, Deh-e Now, Susa, Tappeh Deylam, Tappeh Gotvand, Tappeh Horreeye, and KS [Khuzestan Survey] 937, all of which are in Khuzestan; and Tal-e Malyan, Tol-e Peytul, and Tol-e Spid in Fars. In most cases, however, their existence is attested only through the discovery of stamped or inscribed bricks mentioning a particular religious structure, not through a completely excavated building. A varied vocabulary in Elamite (El.) for these structures suggests the existence of different types of shrines, including temples (El. *siyan*) within larger building complexes (El. *kizzum*), 'high temples' (El. *kukkunum*) built on raised platforms or stepped terraces (El. *zagratume/ziqqurrat*) (Figure 50.1), temples in groves or gardens (El. *siyan husame/husani*), temples particularly associated with procreation (El. *aštam*), subterranean sacred places (or tombs under temples? *haštu*), and the enigmatic *kumpum kiduya* and *suhter* (Potts 2009: 54–60). Many inscribed bricks record restorations undertaken by Elamite rulers generations after the original construction of a shrine (Malbran-Labat 1995). A number of building types attested in the inscribed bricks and inscriptions from Choga Zanbil (*c*.1400–1200 BC) in Khuzestan are associated with specific deities (e.g. *kuten*-house of Napiriša; *hunin*-temple of Hišmitik and Ruhurater; *kinin*-temple of Šimut and Bēlet-āli; *likrin*-temple of Inšušinak, etc.) but to date have not been clearly elucidated (Potts 2009: 61–2). It has been suggested that a late fourth-millennium-BC building excavated in the ABC area at Tal-e Malyan in Fars was a temple (Wasilewska 1991) but this has not generally found acceptance. An Iron Age shrine, distinguished by the large number of votive offerings found in it, was excavated at Surkh Dum in Luristan (*c*.800 BC) (Schmidt, Van Loon, and Curvers 1989).

The slightly later mud-brick Central Temple at Nush-i Jan in central western Iran (seventh–sixth century BC), in an area later identifiable as lying within Media, has given rise to considerable discussion. The shape of the building may be described as a stepped-cruciform, roughly 16 m × 16 m at its widest points. An 85-cm-tall mud-brick altar with a square upper surface (1.41 m × 1.41 m), in the centre of which was a fire bowl *c*.23 cm in diameter, was located in the west side of the central space. The shallow fire bowl would not

FIGURE 50.1 The ziggurat of Choga Zanbil.

seem to have been conducive to permanent, Zoroastrian-style fires and their large accumulations of ash.

This rather small structure was tower-like and preserved to a height of 8–10 m. This building has commonly been associated with the Medes, though not with 'classical' Zoroastrianism. One feature of particular interest was the fact that it was carefully filled in with an estimated 300 m^3 of shale, to the full height of the building. In addition, certain doorways were bricked up (Stronach and Roaf 2007). That this was a ritual act seems clear, but as the excavators noted, 'We are left to wonder... if the filling of the central temple was indeed a complete end in itself, or if a prior plan to raise an important new building on this key part of the site was in the end abandoned before it could be implemented; or if, from the start, the purpose of the Filling had been to create an elevated "sacred space" for a new form of outdoor worship' (Stronach and Roaf 2007: 213; cf. Boucharlat 1984: 122–4).

Herodotus famously stated of the Persians, 'it is not their practice to erect statues, or temples, or altars... because, as I conjecture, they do not think the gods have human forms, as the Greeks do' (to the extent that the only overtly religious symbol in Achaemenid art is the presumed figure of Ahura Mazda hovering in a winged sun-disk, itself an ancient symbol attested in Egypt, Assyria, Anatolia, etc. [Root 1979: 148, n. 54], this is true, for anthropomorphic statues of deities from the Achaemenid period are unknown). Rather, Herodotus said, 'they are accustomed to ascend the highest parts of the mountains, and offer sacrifice to Jupiter... They sacrifice to the sun and moon, to the earth, fire, water, and the winds' (1.131). This was virtually paraphrased by Strabo (*Geog.* 15.3.13) who added, 'and with earnest prayer they offer sacrifice in a purified place'. Strabo also noted, 'And to water they offer sacrifice by going to a lake or river or spring', taking care that no blood (from the sacrificial animal) should pollute the water source (*Geog.* 15.3.14). The references in Herodotus and Strabo to sacrifices to rivers are indeed confirmed by the Persepolis fortification texts which contain references to five different rivers (Henkelman 2008: 539–41). Water continued to be significant much later as well. The fact that the Elamite rock relief at Kurangun (Potts 2004) and 24 out of 38 known Sasanian rock reliefs in Iran were sited near water can hardly be coincidental (Callieri 2006: 342).

Speaking of the Magi in Cappadocia (which had been part of the Achaemenid empire for two centuries), Strabo wrote, 'They also have *Pyraetheia*, noteworthy enclosures; and in the midst of these there is an altar, on which there is a large quantity of ashes and where the Magi keep the fire ever burning' (*Geog.* 15.3.15; cf. Boucharlat 1984: 121). This sounds very much like a description of an entire functional complex consisting of: (1) the sacred fire, referred to as 'most holy fire', the son of the supreme deity Ahura Mazda, 'whose corporeal manifestation was flames', used by Ahura Mazda as the male factor in the creation of both humankind and the beneficent members of the animal kingdom (Macuch 2003), the smoke of which was thought to purify; (2) the fire altar (*takht-e ātaš/ātašdān*); (3) the fire precinct (*ātašgāh*), where 'fires burn on fire altars or in fire pits'; and (4) the fire temple (*ātaškada*) of later Zoroastrianism (Choksy 2007: 230–1; for an exhaustive study of the terminology of fire and fireplaces, and their occurrence in toponyms, see Eilers 1974).

A unique building dated on internal grounds to the sixth–fifth centuries BC, interpreted as a temple, was excavated at Dahan-e Ghulaiman in Seistan (Scerrato 1966). This nearly square building of baked brick (53.2 m × 54.3 m) had a large, internal courtyard (28.9 m × 27.8 m) in which three rectangular altars stood. Each altar had a depression in the upper surface, assumed to have been for the fire. The excavator has suggested that the three altars may have been intended for Ahura Mazda, Mithra and Anahita (Scerrato 1966: 17; cf. Schippmann 1971: 56; Boucharlat 1984: 132–3). Literary references to temples of Bel, Athena, and Artemis in the Elamite highlands during the second century BC may relate to some of the sites in northern Khuzestan like Shami, Tang-i Butan, Tang-i Sarvak (unexcavated), or Bard-e Nechandeh (excavated) in the Bakhtiari mountains, but the names undoubtedly mask native Elamite or Iranian deities (Guépin 1965–6; Potts 1999: 382–3). It has been suggested that a large, square, semi-subterranean stone building with a water channel running around its perimeter at Bishapur in Fars was an Anahita temple (Schippmann 1971: 151; Bier 1985: 1009–10) but this is unconfirmed by epigraphic or literary evidence.

Kuh-e Khwaja (second–first century BC) in Seistan is often considered the earliest true fire temple in Iran (Kaim 2004: 323). The altar is located in the centre of a small square pavillion known as a *chahār tāq* (New Persian, 'four arches', supporting a domed roof or *gumbad*) (Ghanimati 2000). Although not all buildings with the characteristic dome and four arches of the *chahār tāq* type, were fire temples (Huff 1995), this was the principal form taken by most fire temples from the third century AD onwards, and many unexcavated, freestanding ruins of this type exist across Iran (Schippmann 1971; Boucharlat 1985). Excavated pre-Islamic examples include the temples at Bandian and Tureng Tepe, in north-eastern Iran, and at Takht-e Suleiman, in Azerbaijan (north-western Iran).

In the Sasanian period holy fires were ranked and these ranks continue to be retained by modern Zoroastrians (Choksy 2007: 252). Only the 'victorious fires' were required to burn continuously; fires of lesser rank were allowed to burn themselves out. Takht-e Suleiman was the site of one of the most important 'victorious fires' in ancient Iran, *Ādur Gušnasp*. The identification was confirmed by the discovery there of clay stamp seal impressions with the legend 'chief magus of the residence of *Ādur Gušnasp*' (Humbach 1967; Choksy 2007: 249).

4 OBJECTS

By analogy with much later periods, anthropomorphic and zoomorphic baked-clay figurines may have been used in rituals associated with childbirth, healing, hunting, etc. Both types of figurines appear in Iran from the aceramic Neolithic (after $c.7500$ BC, e.g. at Chogha Bonut, Ali Kosh, Ganj Dareh) onwards and are found in most periods (Alizadeh 2003: 67–8; Daems 2004; Spycket 1992; Martinez-Sève 2002; Boucharlat and Haerinck 1994). Anthropomorphic statues of deities (e.g. Narundi) are attested at Susa as early as the late third millennium BC.

Haoma, an intoxicating drink made from a plant (Taillieu 1997), was consumed in early Zoroastrian ritual. In addition to literary (de Jong 2002: 129) and epigraphic evidence for this (Bowman 1970), green chert and marble mortars, pestles, plates, and trays found during the Persepolis excavations, are thought by some scholars to have been used to make *haoma* (Bowman 1970: 44–55). That the objects were manufactured, handed over to officials of the treasury and used in a 'crushing ceremony' is explicitly stated in some Aramaic notes written in ink directly on these objects but their role in a *haoma* ceremony remains conjectural (Levine 1972: 72).

Of particular relevance to the perceived elevation of Anahita noted above is the testimony of the early third-century-BC Babylonian astronomer Berossus, according to whom Artaxerxes II erected statues of Anahita at 'Babylon, Susa, Ecbatana [the Median capital, modern Hamadan], among the Persians and Bactrians, and from Damascus to Sardis [capital of Lydia in western Asia Minor]' (Clement of Alexandria, *Protrepticus* 5.65.4; cf. Brosius 1998: 227; Tavernier 2005: 360). The significance of this has been debated for generations and has given rise to a large amount of speculation (Frye 1984: 172; for Anahita in the early Sasanian period, see Chaumont 1958). If true, then it suggests that the aniconism of the Persians described by Herodotus had certainly changed, though whether this was due to internal theological developments or to external influences is impossible to say.

One of the most prominent artifact types associated with Zoroastrianism is the fire altar itself (Houtkamp 1991). This most often took the form of a stepped pedestal supporting a column which in turn held the actual basin in which the fire burned. If, following Herodotus, the earlier Persians had no temples (cf. Boyce 1975), then it is possible that a limestone platform at Pasargadae, capital of Cyrus the Great, founder of the Persian empire, may have functioned as an open-air fire altar (Stronach 1978: figs. 70–1; Boucharlat 1984: 126; Choksy 2007: 237–8 and fig. 3). The fact that a second limestone feature, a block or small platform with a small staircase attached, is located some metres to the south, and that both were located within a walled precinct (though possibly of later date according to the excavator), has led some scholars to suggest, by analogy with representations of Achaemenid kings on their grave reliefs (see below), that the 'king or magus climbed to the top of the southern plinth, faced the northern plinth which bore a fire altar with flame, and performed devotions facing Zoroastrianism's main icon' (Choksy 2007: 238).

Free-standing stone columns represent another type of altar support, assuming a portable fire bowl was set on the upper surface. Examples of uncertain date are known from various sites in Fars, such as Naqš-e Rustam (Stronach 1966: 219–20), and at Shimbar in Khuzestan, and may have been used for open-air ceremonies (Choksy 2007: 240, 245). West of the main, carved face of Naqš-e Rustam are two altars with a square fire bowl in the upper surface, hewn out of the living rock in the form of a small building with four arched sides, reminiscent of the later *chahār tāq*-type fire temple (Choksy 2007: figs. 7a–b).

5 Representations

Late prehistoric (c.3400–3000 BC) cylinder-seal impressions from Susa (Hole 1983) and Choga Mish (Alizadeh 2003) display a number of scenes which may depict rituals. These include a file of males with arms raised above the head, processing left with stylized trees in the background (Alizadeh 2003: pl. 144D); a file of males processing right, each of whom, apart from one who holds his left arm aloft, carries an object (staff/sceptre, spouted ceramic vessel, unidentifiable vertical object [Alizadeh 2003: pl. 152D]); and scenes of people and animals near a building with niched decoration which, by analogy with Mesopotamian religious architecture, could be identified as a temple (Alizadeh 2003: pl. 154A–B). One seal impression shows the gatepost identified in Mesopotamian iconography as the symbol of the Sumerian goddess Inanna (Alizadeh 2003: pl. 154A) whom we know from epigraphic evidence was worshipped at Susa. In view of the close ties between Khuzestan and southern Mesopotamia at the end of the fourth millennium BC, there is every reason to adopt the same identification in this case. A niched, multi-storey building with mounted horns is, by analogy with the ziggurat of Susa described in the Assyrian accounts of Assurbanipal's campaign against Elam in 647 BC (the shining bronze horns of which he says he broke off), a stepped platform surmounted by a temple (Amiet 1987; Potts 1990, 1999: 284).

Statuary in Mesopotamian style depicting a standing male holding a kid, as well as wall-plaques used to decorate the walls of temples, are known from Susa in the mid-third millennium BC (Amiet 1966: 174–9, 191). Scenes on south-east Iranian cylinder seals of late third-millennium-BC date, showing complex iconography involving deities and mortals as well as animals and enclosures of various sorts, may depict ritual or may be mythological in character (Amiet 1998, 2007: 72–4). By this time the originally Mesopotamian convention of indicating deities by horned headgear had been adopted in the glyptic and statuary of the Elamite world (south-western Iran) and was widely employed throughout the second and early first millennium BC (Amiet 1992).

Achaemenid royal tomb reliefs, such as those of Darius I and Xerxes I at Naqš-e Rustam, depict the king standing on a stepped platform, opposite a fire altar consisting of a fire bowl or basin supported by a column-like shaft on top of a stepped plinth. As noted above, these have been compared with free-standing examples of limestone at Pasargadae (Boyce 1988: 28). Generally similar-looking altars are found on the reverses of all Sasanian kings. These are either flanked by two attendants/priests or, in some cases, by the king and a deity. In some cases the deity emerges from the flames. Depictions of the raised hand (Middle

Elamite through Sasanian) and the bent forefinger (Parthian and Sasanian) as gestures of worship and reverence for deities are attested from the second millennium BC onwards, particularly on coins and rock reliefs (Choksy 1990a; 1990b: 204–5).

Rock reliefs in western Iran shed light on ritual and religion as well. The early second-millennium-BC relief at Kurangun, in western Fars, shows what appears to be a ritual scene involving Elamite deities, variously identified as Ea = Inšušinak = Napiriša and Kiririša, with worshippers, high above the Fahliyan River (Potts 2004). Animal sacrifice, involving officiants and associated musicians, is shown on the rock relief of Hanni at the open-air sanctuary of Kul-e Farah (de Waele 1989). The post-Achaemenid reliefs at Sakavand and Dokkan-e Da'ud, near Kermanshah, depict a male, usually interpreted as a fire priest (*magus*), standing with upraised hands before a stepped altar (Choksy 2007: 244). By the Sasanian period images of investiture were common, occurring in 10 out of 28 known Sasanian rock reliefs (Kaim 2009: 403). Given that Ahura Mazda bestowed kingship on the Achaemenid kings, the god was most probably the most significant actor in the investiture ceremony (Figure 50.2) which, therefore, must be considered as much a religious as a royal/political ceremony (cf. Callieri 2006: 345; for the site of the Sasanian investiture ritual, see Chaumont 1964). Unusually, the investiture of Ardashir II (379–83 AD) by Mithra, holding a barsom bundle in one hand and a beribboned diadem in the other, rather than Ahura Mazda, may be depicted on one of the rock reliefs at Taq-i Bustan, near Kermanshah, though this remains controversial (Frye 1978: 207).

FIGURE 50.2 The investiture of Ardashir I (*c.*AD 240), left, by Ahura Mazda, right, at Naqsh-e Rustam.

6 CONCLUSIONS

Iran's religions have left an indelible mark on the material culture and landscape of the region. Despite a wealth of written documentation from the Bronze Age onwards, however, many questions remain unanswered as a result of the fact that the sources either do not address matters of religious praxis (as in the case of the Bronze Age and much of the Iron Age) or they post-date the periods of greatest concern (as in the case of the Avestan and other sources on Zoroastrianism) and cannot therefore be projected back onto situations that may have obtained during the Achaemenid, Parthian, and Sasanian eras. New insights into Avestan and Zoroastrian problems are unlikely to be garnered through the discovery of new sources, and enough cuneiform sources have been discovered from the earlier periods to dampen any optimism about the chances of finding texts that actually discuss religious praxis. Nevertheless, archaeological discoveries are being made all the time in Iran and the body of evidence is steadily growing. An awareness of Iran's rich religious heritage is a *sine qua non* for all who wish to interpret and derive the maximum benefit from those new discoveries. Finally, given the complexity of Iranian iconography in various media (seals, reliefs, architectural decoration, ceramics, stone vessels), it is likely that many new insights will emerge in years to come from an improved understanding of this rich universe of forms.

SUGGESTED READING

For Elamite religion in all periods, see Vallat (1998) and Potts (1999). For the religious practices at Persepolis during the reign of Darius I see Henkelman (2008). For the Old Persian inscriptions see Lecoq (1997). A very good introduction to Zoroastrianism and its principal texts and tenets is provided by Malandra (1983). For Zoroastrian practices as transmitted by Greek and Latin sources see de Jong (1997). There are many entries on religious matters and individual deities in the *Encyclopaedia Iranica*. Gray (1929) is still very useful. For the evolution of Zoroastrianism through time, see Mary Boyce's *A History of Zoroastrianism* (Leiden: Brill) but note that the specialist literature on the Avesta and Zoroastrianism more generally contains widely diverging views on many topics dealt with here.

REFERENCES

ALIZADEH, A. 2003. *Excavations at the Prehistoric Mound of Chogha Bonut, Khuzestan, Iran: Seasons 1976/77, 1977/78, and 1996* (Chicago: Oriental Institute Publication 120).
AMIET, P. 1966. *Elam* (Auvers-sur-Oise: Archée Éditeur).
—— 1987. 'Temple sur terrasse ou forteresse?', *Revue d'Assyriologie*, 81: 99–104.
—— 1992. 'Tiares élamites', *Studi Micenei ed Egeo-Anatolici*, 30: 257–65.
—— 1998. 'Déesses et reines d'Élam', *Ancient Civilizations from Scythia to Siberia*, 5: 4–11.

—— 2007. 'L'âge des échanges inter-iraniens' in G. Ligabue and G. Rossi-Osmida (eds), *Sulla Via delle Oasi* (Florence: Il Punto), pp. 64–87.

BASELLO, G. 2002. 'Elam and Babylonia: The evidence of the calendars' in A. Panaino and G. Pettinato (eds), *Ideologies as Intercultural Phenomena* (Milan: Univ. of Bologna and IsIAO), pp. 13–36.

BENVENISTE, E. 1964. 'Sur la terminologie iranienne du sacrifice', *Journal Asiatique*, 252: 45–58.

BIER, C. 1985. 'Anāhīd iv. Anāhitā in the arts', *Encyclopaedia Iranica*, 1: 1009–11.

BIGGS, R. D. and STOLPER, M. W. 1983. 'A Babylonian omen text from Susiana', *Revue d'Assyriologie*, 77: 155–62.

BOUCHARLAT, R. 1984. 'Monuments religieux de la Perse achéménide: État des questions' in G. Roux (ed.), *Temples et sanctuaires* (Lyon: Travaux de la Maison de l'Orient 7), pp. 119–35.

—— 1985. '*Chahar taq* et temple du feu sasanide: Quelques remarques' in J.-L. Huot, M. Yon, and Y. Calvet (eds), *De l'Indus aux Balkans: Recueil à la mémoire de Jean Deshayes* (Paris: Éditions Recherche sur les Civilisations), pp. 461–78.

—— and HAERINCK, E. 1994. 'Das ewig-weibliche: Figurines en os d'époque parthe de Suse', *Iranica Antiqua*, 29: 185–99.

BOWMAN, R. A. 1970. *Aramaic Ritual Texts from Persepolis* (Chicago: Oriental Institute Publications 91).

BOYCE, M. 1966. '*Ātaš-zōhr* and *āb-zōhr*', *Journal of the Royal Asiatic Society 1966*: 100–18.

—— 1975. 'Iconoclasm among the Zoroastrians', in J. Neusner (ed.), *Christianity, Judaism and other Greco-Roman Cults: Studies for Morton Smith at Sixty* (Leiden: Brill), pp. 93–111.

—— 1988. 'The religion of Cyrus the Great' in A. Kuhrt and H. Sancisi-Weerdenburg (eds), *Achaemenid History III* (Leiden: Nederlands Instituut voor het Nabije Oosten), pp. 15–31.

—— and GRENET, F. 1991. *A History of Zoroastrianism*, III: *Zoroastrianism under Macedonian and Roman Rule* (Leiden: Handbuch der Orientalistik), 1/8/1/2/2.

BROSIUS, M. 1998. 'Artemis Persike and Artemis Anaitis' in M. Brosius and A. Kuhrt (eds), *Achaemenid History XI* (Leiden: Nederlands Instituut voor het Nabije Oosten), pp. 227–38.

CALLIERI, P. 2006. 'Water in the art and architecture of the Sasanians' in A. Panaino and A. Piras (eds), *Proceedings of the 5th Conference of the Societas Iranologica Europæa held in Ravenna, 6–11 October 2003*, I: *Ancient and Middle Iranian Studies* (Milan: Mimesis), pp. 339–49.

CALMEYER, P. 1975. 'Barsombündel im 8. und 7. Jahrhundert v. Chr', in *Wandlungen: Studien zur antiken und neueren Kunst Ernst Homann-Wedeking gewidmet* (Waldsassen: Stiftland-Verlag), pp. 11–15.

CHAUMONT, M. 1958. 'Le culte d'Anāhitā à Staxr et les premiers Sassanides', *Revue de l'Histoire des Religions*, 153: 154–75.

—— 1964. 'Où les rois sassanides étaient-ils couronnés?', *Journal Asiatique*, 252: 59–75.

CHOKSY, J. K. 1990a. 'Gesture in ancient Iran and Central Asia I: The raised hand', *Iranica varia: Papers in honor of Professor Ehsan Yarshater* (Leiden: Acta Iranica 30), pp. 29–37.

—— 1990b. 'Gesture in ancient Iran and Central Asia II: Proskynesis and the bent forefinger', *Bulletin of the Asia Institute*, 4: 201–7.

—— 2007. 'Reassessing the material contexts of ritual fires in ancient Iran', *Iranica Antiqua*, 42: 229–69.

DAEMS, A. 2004. 'On prehistoric human figurines in Iran: Current knowledge and some reflections', *Iranica Antiqua*, 39: 1–31.

DUCHESNE-GUILLEMIN, J. 1971. 'Die Religion der Achämeniden', *Acta Antiqua Academiae Scientiarum Hungaricae*, 19: 25–35.

EILERS, W. 1974. 'Herd und Feuerstätte in Iran' in M. Mayrhofer and H. Guntert (eds), *Antiquitates Indogermanicae: Studien zur Indogermanischen Altertumskunde und zur Sprach- und Kulturgeschichte der indogermanischen Völker, Gedenkschrift für Hermann Güntert zur 25. Wiederkehr seines Todestages am 23. April 1973* (Innsbruck: Innsbrucker Beiträge zur Sprachwissenschaft 12), pp. 307–38.

EPH'AL, I. 1999. 'The Bukān Aramaic inscription: Historical considerations', *Israel Exploration Journal*, 49: 116–21.

FRYE, R. N. 1978. 'Mithra in Iranian archaeology' in *Études mithriaques* (Leiden: Acta Iranica 17), pp. 205–11.

—— 1984. 'Religion in Fars under the Achaemenids' in *Orientalia J. Duchesne-Guillemin emerito oblata* (Leiden: Acta Iranica 23), pp. 171–8.

GERSHEVITCH, I. 1970. 'Iranian nouns and names in Elamite garb', *Transactions of the Philological Society 1969*: 165–200.

GHANIMATI, S. 2000. 'New perspectives on the chronological and functional horizons of Kuh-e Khwaja in Sistan', *Iran*, 38: 137–50.

GIGNOUX, P. 1991. *Les quatre inscriptions du mage Kirdīr* (Leuven: Studia Iranica Cahier 9).

GNOLI, G. 1980. *Zoroaster's Time and Homeland: A study on the origins of Mazdeism and related problems* (Naples: Istituto Universitario Orientale Series Minor 7).

GRAY, L. H. 1929. *The Foundations of the Iranian Religions* (Bombay: K. R. Cama Oriental Institute Publication 5).

GUÉPIN, J. P. 1965–6. 'A contribution to the location of *Ta Azara*, the chief sanctuary of Elymais', *Persica*, 2: 19–26.

HALLOCK, R. T. 1969. *Persepolis Fortification Tablets* (Chicago: Oriental Institute Publications 92).

HENKELMAN, W. F. M. 2005. 'Animal sacrifice and "external" exchange in the Persepolis Fortification Tablets' in H. D. Baker and M. Jursa (eds), *Approaching the Babylonian Economy: Proceedings of the START Project Symposium held in Vienna, 1–3 July 2004* (Münster: Alter Orient und Altes Testament 330), pp. 137–65.

—— 2008. *Achaemenid History XIV: The other gods who are: Studies in Elamite-Iranian acculturation based on the Persepolis fortification texts* (Leiden: Nederlands Instituut voor het Nabije Oosten).

HOLE, F. 1983. 'Symbols of religion and social organization at Susa' in T. C. Young Jr, P. E. L. Smith, and P. Mortensen (eds), *The Hilly Flanks and Beyond: Essays on the prehistory of southwestern Asia presented to Robert J. Braidwood, November 15, 1982* (Chicago: Studies in Ancient Oriental Civilization 36), pp. 315–31.

HOUTKAMP, J. 1991. 'Some remarks on fire altars of the Achaemenid period' in J. Kellens (ed.), *La religion iranienne à l'époque achéménide, Actes du Colloque de Liège 11 décembre 1987* (Gent: Iranica Antiqua Supplement 5), pp. 23–48.

HUFF, D. 1995. 'Beobachtungen zum Čahartaq und zur Topographie von Girre', *Iranica Antiqua*, 30: 71–92.

HUMBACH, H. 1967. 'Ātur Gušnasp und Takht i Suleimān' in G. Wiessner (ed.), *Festschrift für Wilhelm Eilers: Ein Dokument der internationalen Forschung zum 27. September 1966* (Wiesbaden: Harrassowitz), pp. 189–90.

JONG, A. DE 1997. *Traditions of the Magi: Zoroastrianism in Greek and Latin literature* (Leiden: Brill).

—— 1999. 'Purification in absentia: On the development of Zoroastrian ritual practice' in J. Assmann and G. G. Stroumsma (eds), *Transformations of the Inner Self in Ancient Religions* (Leiden: Brill), pp. 301–29.

—— 2002. 'Animal sacrifice in ancient Zoroastrianism: A ritual and its interpretations' in A. I. Baumgarten (ed.), *Sacrifice in Religious Experience* (Leiden: Studies in the History of Religions 93), pp. 127–48.

—— 2005. 'The contribution of the Magi' in V. S. Curtis and S. Stewart (eds), *Birth of the Persian Empire* (London: I.B.Tauris), pp. 85–99.

KAIM, B. 2004. 'Ancient fire temples in the light of the discovery at Mele Hairam', *Iranica Antiqua*, 39: 323–37.

—— 2009. 'Investiture or mithra: Towards a new interpretation of so called investiture scenes in Parthian and Sasanian art', *Iranica Antiqua*, 44: 403–15.

KELLENS, J. 2002. 'L'idéologie religieuse des inscriptions achéménides', *Journal Asiatique*, 290: 417–64.

KOCH, H. 1977. *Die religiösen Verhältnisse der Dareioszeit: Untersuchungen an Hand der elamischen Persepolistäfelchen* (Wiesbaden: Göttinger Orientforschungen III/4).

KREYENBROEK, P. 1991. 'On the shaping of Zoroastrian theology: Aši, Vərəθraγna and the promotion of the Aməša Spəṇtas' in P. Bernard and F. Grenet (eds), *Histoire et cultes de l'Asie centrale préislamique: Sources écrites et documents archéologiques* (Paris: Éditions du Centre Nationale de la Recherche Scientifique), pp. 137–45.

LECOQ, P. 1997. *Les inscriptions de la Perse achéménide* (Paris: Gallimard).

LEVINE, B. A. 1972. 'Aramaic texts from Persepolis', *Journal of the American Oriental Society*, 92: 70–9.

MACUCH, M. 2003. 'On the treatment of animals in Zoroastrian law' in A. van Tongerloo (ed.), *Iranica selecta: Studies in honour of Professor Wojciech Skalmowski on the occasion of his seventieth birthday* (Turnhout: Silk Road Studies VIII), pp. 167–90.

MALANDRA, W. W. 1983. *An Introduction to Ancient Iranian Religion* (Minneapolis: University of Minnesota Press).

MALBRAN-LABAT, F. 1995. *Les inscriptions royales de Suse: Briques de l'époque paléo-élamite à l'Empire néo-élamite* (Paris: Éditions de la Réunion des Musées Nationaux).

MARTINEZ-SÈVE, L. 2002. *Les figurines de Suse: De l'époque néo-élamite à l'époque sassanide* (Paris: Réunion des Musées Nationaux).

MAYRHOFER, M. 1973. *Onomastica persepolitana: Das altiranische Namengut der Persepolis-Täfelchen* (Vienna: Sitzungsberichte der Österreichischen Akademie der Wissenschaften, phil.-hist. Kl. 268).

POTTS, D. T. 1990. 'Notes on some horned buildings in Iran, Mesopotamia, and Arabia', *Revue d'Assyriologie*, 84: 33–40.

—— 1999. *The Archaeology of Elam: Formation and transformation of an ancient Iranian state* (Cambridge: Cambridge University Press).

—— 2004. 'The numinous and the immanent: Some thoughts on Kurangun and the Rudkhaneh-e Fahliyan' in K. von Folsach, H. Thrane, and I. Thuesen (eds), *From Handaxe to Khan: Essays presented to Peder Mortensen on the occasion of his 70th birthday* (Aarhus: Aarhus University Press), pp. 143–56.

—— 2009. 'Elamite temple building' in M. Boda and J. R. Novotny (eds), *From the Foundations to the Crenellations: Essays on temple building in the ancient Near East and Hebrew Bible in honour of Richard Ellis* (Münster: Alter Orient und Altes Testament), pp. 49–70.

POURSHARIATI, P. 2008. *The Decline and Fall of the Sasanian Empire: The Sasanian-Parthian confederacy and the Arab conquest of Iran* (London: I.B.Tauris).

RAZMJOU, S. 2004. 'The lan ceremony and other ritual ceremonies in the Achaemnid period: The Persepolis fortification tablets', *Iran*, 42: 103–17.

ROOT, M. C. 1979. *The King and Kingship in Achaemenid Art* (Leiden: Acta Iranica 19).

SCERRATO, U. 1966. 'Excavations at Dahan-i Ghulaman (Seistan, Iran): First preliminary report', *East and West*, 16: 9–30.

SCHIPPMANN, K. 1971. *Die iranischen Feuerheiligtümer* (Berlin: de Gruyter).

SCHMIDT, E. F., VAN LOON, M., and CURVERS, H. H. 1989. *The Holmes Expedition to Luristan* (Chicago: Oriental Institute Publication 108).

SCHMITT, R. 1991. 'Name und Religion: Anthroponomastisches zur Frage der religiösen Verhältnisse des Achaimenidenreiches' in J. Kellens (ed.), *La religion iranienne à l'époque achéménide*, Actes du Colloque de Liège 11 décembre 1987 (Gent: Iranica Antiqua Supplement 5), pp. 111–35.

—— 2003. *Meno-logium Bagistano-Persepolitanum: Studien zu den altpersischen Monatsnamen und ihren elamischen Wiedergaben* (Vienna: Sitzungsberichte der Österreichischen Akademie der Wissenschaften, phil.-hist. Kl. 705).

SKALMOWSKI, W. 1982. 'Some remarks on Avestan DAĒNĀ-' in J. Quagebeur (ed.), *Studia Paolo Naster oblata*, II (Leuven: Orientalia Lovaniensia Analecta 13), pp. 223–9.

SKJÆRVØ, P. O. 2005. 'The Achaemenids and the *Avesta*' in V. S. Curtis and S. Stewart (eds), *Birth of the Persian Empire* (London: I.B.Tauris), pp. 52–84.

SPYCKET, A. 1992. *Les figurines de Suse*, I: *Les figurines humaines, IVe-IIe millénaires av. J.-C* (Paris: Mémoires de la Délégation Archéologique en Iran 52).

STRONACH, D. 1966. 'The Kūh-i-Shahrak fire altar', *Journal of Near Eastern Studies*, 25: 217–27.

—— 1978. *Pasargadae* (Oxford: Clarendon Press).

—— 1984. 'Notes on religion in Iran in the seventh and sixth centuries BC' in *Orientalia J. Duchesne-Guillemin emerito oblata* (Leiden: Acta Iranica 23), pp. 479–90.

—— and ROAF, M. 2007. *Nush-i Jan I: The major buildings of the Median settlement* (Leuven: Peeters).

TAILLIEU, D. 1997. 'The sauma controversy after 1968', *Orientalia Lovaniensia Periodica*, 28: 43–54.

TAVERNIER, J. 2005. 'Reflections on the origin and the early history of Tīr' in W. H. Van Soldt (ed.), *Ethnicity in Ancient Mesopotamia: Papers read at the 48th Rencontre Assyriologique Internationale, Leiden, 1–4 July 2002* (Leiden: Nederlands Instituut voor het Nabije Oosten), pp. 356–71.

TEIXIDOR, J. 1999. 'L'inscription araméenne de Bukān, relecture', *Semitica*, 49: 117–21.

VALLAT, F. 1998. 'Elam vi. Elamite religion', *Encyclopaedia Iranica*, 8: 335–42.

WAELE, E. DE 1989. 'Musicians and musical instruments on the rock reliefs in the Elamite sanctuary of Kul-e Farah (Izeh)', *Iran*, 27: 29–38.

WASILEWSKA, E. 1991. 'To be or not to be a temple? Possible identification of a Banesh period temple at Tall-i Malyan, Iran' in L. de Meyer and H. Gasche (eds), *Mésopotamie et Elam* (Ghent: Mesopotamian History and Environment Occasional Publication 1), pp. 144–52.

WIESEHÖFER, J. 1994. *Die 'dunklen Jahrhunderte' der Persis: Untersuchungen zu Geschichte und Kultur von Fārs in frühhellenistischer Zeit (330–140 v. Chr.)* (Munich: C.H. Becks'sche Verlagsbuchhandlung).

CHAPTER 51

....

ANATOLIA

....

KARINA CROUCHER

1 INTRODUCTION

....

THIS chapter addresses Anatolia during the Neolithic, a time-span covering approximately 5,000 years, and a geographical region broadly covering modern-day central and southern Turkey (Figure 51.1). The period is traditionally divided up chronologically into timespans which broadly correspond to those of the Levant. These are, the Pre-Pottery Neolithic (PPN), which is further subdivided into the Pre-Pottery Neolithic A (PPNA) (*c*.10,000–8550), and Pre-Pottery Neolithic B, which is itself further subdiviced into early, middle and late: EPPNB (*c*.8550–8100), MPPNB (*c*.8100–7300), the LPPNB (*c*.7300–6750), and the Pre-Pottery Neolithic C (PPNC) (*c*.6750–6300). This is followed by the Pottery Neolithic (PN), which includes the subdivisions of 'Hassuna' and 'Samarra' (until *c*.6000), and 'Halaf' (*c*.6000–5200) periods. The 'Halaf' is a period which is also often termed 'Chalcolithic' rather than 'Neolithic', further demonstrating some of the problems with our categorizations. However, it should be noted that the categorizations are our own modern ones and will not have been entities perceived by the people and societies we are studying. Consequently, many of the themes and strands of evidence also relate to a broader study of the 'Near East', including the regions of ancient Levant and Mesopotamia (modern-day Syria, Iraq, Jordan, Cyprus, Israel and Palestine, and into Iran). This chapter will begin by outlining the background to the study of ritual and religion in the prehistory of the region. This will be followed by three case studies; Çayönü Tepesi, Domuztepe, and Göbekli Tepe, through which new approaches to the archaeology of ritual and religion will be discussed.

The sites chosen here include features ranging from the small to large-scale: Domuztepe with its Death Pit, containing the disarticulated and further fragmented remains of around 40 people; Göbekli Tepe, a mountain-top site displaying monumental stone pillars, sculptures, and shrines; and Çayönü Tepesi, with its communal architecture and 'special buildings', including the Skull Building, which contained the remains of over 450 people. Whilst these sites have been selected due to their range of evidence, including mortuary practices, architecture, and monumentality, they are chosen from a backdrop of sites displaying ritual behaviour, the most notable of which include Çatalhöyük (Hodder 2006b), with its tightly packed architecture featuring reliefs, sculptures, and a plastered skull; Pınarbaşı (Baird in press), with animal bones encased in plaster; Nevalı Çori, a site

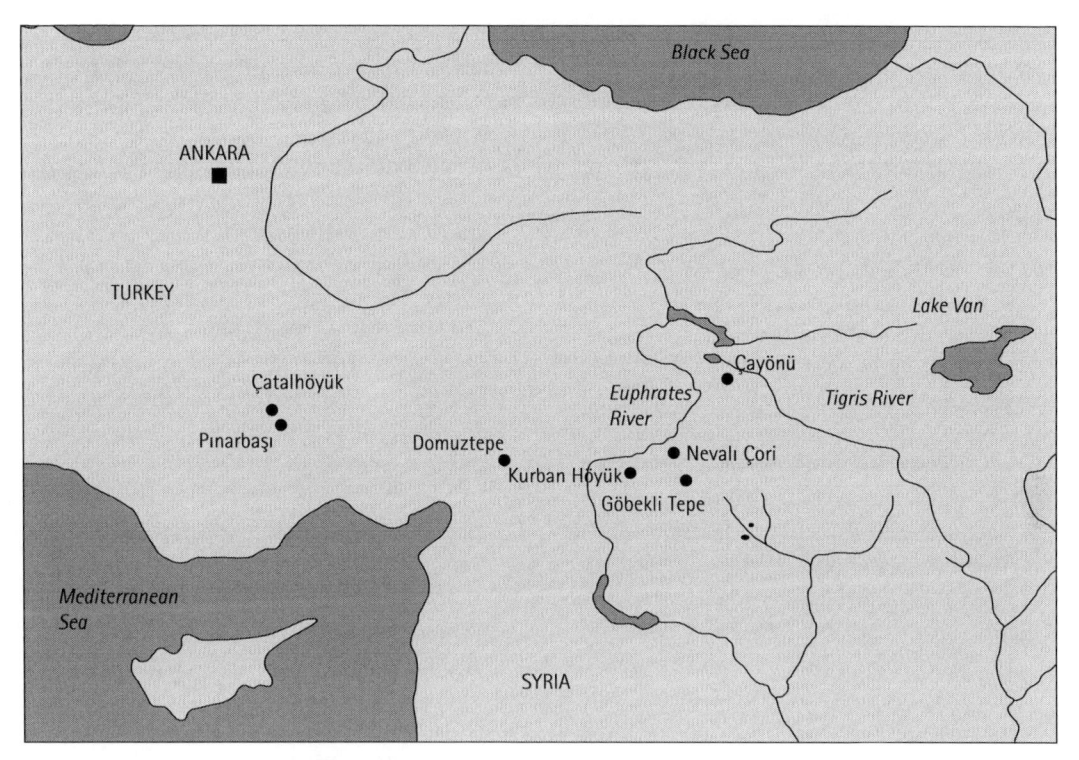

FIGURE 51.1 Map of ancient Anatolia and sites discussed.

featuring 'cult buildings' and spectacular sculptures (Hauptmann 1987, 1990, 1999), and numerous sites containing mortuary evidence, figurines, special architecture, cranial modification, and human–animal burials.

2 BACKGROUND

Traditionally, study in the region, including that of ritual and religion, has been dominated by the use of large-scale patterns and frameworks, with cultural groups related to increasingly sedentary behaviour, domestication, and agriculture, and increasing complexity and social stratification (see for example Roaf 1996; Matthews 2000; Charvát 2002; Kuijt and Goring-Morris 2002: 362; Bar Yosef 2008; Ozdogan 2008, and used more critically in Matthews 2003: 64) These studies have provided a framework for managing the interpretation of the vast quantities of excavated material derived from the Near East. However, problems arise when the frameworks used in the present are taken too literally and understood to represent actual entities in the past, an approach arising from the culture-historic background of research in the region (see Campbell 1992, 1998; Croucher and Campbell 2009; Watkins 1998 for a more in-depth discussion of these issues).

Related to the use of chronological and culture–historic frameworks (an approach which still dominates much of Near Eastern research), has been the prioritization of the study of hierarchies and social stratification, with research often focused towards the search for the development of social complexities. This is carried into many areas of study (such as architecture, mortuary practice, trade and exchange), with studies searching for evidence of either growing social stratification, or a lack of it as evidence for egalitarianism. Likewise, evidence of ritual behaviour is directly related to social stratification, whether arguing for egalitarianism, or the development of hierarchies in both Anatolia and the Levant, through ritual specialization (e.g. Schmidt 2005; Özdoğan 2004; Goring-Morris 2000; Hauptmann 1999; Kuijt and Goring-Morris 2002; Kuijt 2000, 2008; Verhoeven 2002a, 2002b, 2002c; see also Hole 2000 for a more critical approach). For instance, Hauptmann (1999: 65) describes the ritual architecture of Çayönü, Nevalı Çori, and Göbekli Tepe as resulting from the change from hunting to gathering and 'differentiated societies', which 'clearly demonstrate steps developmental to a central organization in which the trade or barter of an elite class was restricted to sites with cult facilities' (1999: 82).

Whilst such approaches have been extremely valuable in the development of the discipline, they can be argued today to create an oversimplified picture of the past. In reality, when such large-scale frameworks are analysed for details, it becomes apparent that there are as many differences as similarities; the evidence is clearly not sympathetic to this approach. A case in point is Çatalhöyük in central Anatolia, dating to around 7400–5400 BC, where interpretations place this village site in a problematic situation—the site is large, around 13.6 ha, with an estimated population of 5–10,000 people (Orbasli and Doughty 2004). The houses, accessed via their rooftops, were crammed tightly together, with little evidence of specialization, hierarchy, or an elite. A site of this size might be expected to produce evidence of specialization, an elite, and large communal areas, rather than the evidence for a fairly even distribution of labour and resource (Balter 1998). However, the site does reveal evidence of rich symbolic and artistic actions, including shrine areas, plastered features, bucrania, wall-paintings, figurines, and burials, focused on particular houses, described as 'history houses' (Hodder 2009). Cauvin (2000: 238) has discussed the concepts of goddess and bull cults as being strengthened by imagery at Çatalhöyük (see also Gimbutas 1981, 1982, 1991, 2001; and Mellaart 1967 for discussions about the 'Mother Goddess'), a concept developed by Forest (1994), who draws on these to discuss male/female binary oppositions (Voigt 2000: 254; see Balter 2005 and Hodder 2006b for discussions of mother goddess and bull symbolism at Çatalhöyük and issues surrounding it, and Rountree 2007). Along with goddess and bull cults has been a broader perception of a 'cult of skulls' or skull cult. The Skull Cult has its roots in the Levantine PPNB, with plastered skulls recovered from sites including Jericho, 'Ain Ghazal, Kfar HaHoresh and Tell Aswad (see Verhoeven, ch.49, this volume). Recent excavations have extended this phenomenon into Anatolia, with plastered skulls recovered from Köşk Höyük (Özbek 2009), and one skull, that of an adult male, buried in the arms of an adult female at Çatalhöyük (Hodder and Farid 2004; Hodder 2006b). Such plastered skulls were originally believed to venerate elder, male ancestors (Cauvin 1994, 2000; Kenyon 1957; Bienert 1991; Wright 1988); however, recent analysis has revealed that many plastered skulls were children and females (Bonogofsky 2004), suggesting that were these related to ancestors, the 'ancestor' category was not one limited to the elder male image (Fletcher et al 2008).

Such ritual behaviour is traditionally related to subsistence and changing social complexity, argued by some to be the result of, and enabled by, a 'symbolic revolution', where changes in mind and beliefs were facilitated and accompanied by agriculture and the rise of the 'Neolithic'. Cauvin (1994, 2000) has suggested that a change in mentality occurred during the Neolithic, evidenced by these large-scale 'cults', leading to domestication and exploitation of the environment, and thus a different concept and perspective of the landscape and resources.

Parallels and trends in subsistence, organization and rituals are analysed between sites and across geographical regions in the Near East, with direct relationships sought between ritual and social organization; Kuijt (2002: 88) anticipated that 'archaeologists, prehistorians, and anthropologists, will develop new insights into the specific links between ritual, magic, and Neolithic social organization'. However, that a unity of meaning existed behind such traits is debatable (Christensen and Warburton 2002: 164), and recent literature has been critical of the concept of such 'cults', discussing their representation of the present, rather than necessarily their reality in the past (Meskell 1995; Hamilton 2000; Daems 2008; Croucher 2008; Gatens 1994; Bonogofsky 2004, 2005, 2006; Conkey and Tringham 1995; see also Talalay 2004).

Research by Hodder (1987, 1990) in the late 1980s and early 1990s discussed Çatalhöyük's place in the adaption to agriculture and domesticity, with changing perceptions of notions such as 'domestic' and 'wild' (categories which are now often contested in anthropological and archaeological research, i.e. Descola and Pálssen 1996; Ingold 2000 [esp. chs. 3 and 5]; Boyd 2004). More recently, long-term changes in daily practice, which created and embedded social memory, have been credited with enabling the social conditions for changes in subsistence and economies, the use of which would also have supported the interests of dominant social groups (Hodder and Cessford 2004: 36). Refreshingly however, interpretations are moving away from focusing on social stratification, as the rich archaeological data at Çatalhöyük lends itself to a variety of other avenues of interpretation, including investigation into art and representation, human–animal relationships and people's engagements with the landscape (e.g. Russell and Düring 2010; Twiss 2006; Russell and Meece 2005; Hodder 1999, 2004, 2006).

Çatalhöyük has also been instrumental in changing methodological approaches, influenced by theoretical developments necessitating a detailed and contextual approach (Lucas 2001; Hodder 2000, 1996). A change in archaeological practice has involved greater interaction between excavators and specialists, and highlighted the role and value of interpretation at the 'trowel's edge', as well as greater engagement and involvement with the public, including making data immediately available via the project website. Obviously, however, challenges still remain; the changed approach takes time to implement, and with the quantities of data generated by excavation of a Neolithic Anatolian site (see Campbell 2008b), Near Eastern archaeology faces methodological challenges in both excavation and post-excavation analysis which differ vastly from those faced by archaeologists excavating Neolithic sites in many other parts of the world.

So, what is the way forward if we are to move beyond hierarchy and the aim of attempting to tie into the traditional chronological and typological frameworks? Building on the foundations of this existing valuable research, new avenues can now be explored. Through the following case studies, alternative approaches will be discussed, including investigating alternative attitudes and approaches to the body, and the way it is treated in both life and death. This includes relationships between people, the living and the dead, and with animals, material culture and the environment, and a move away from the dichotomy of ritual vs domestic, investigating how the spheres of ritual and domestic are intimately entwined, rather than separated. As Lewis-Williams and Pearce (2005: 79) rightly suggest, ritual activities, whilst serving to hold together communities, are not practiced explicitly for this purpose in itself, but for reasons and motives in their own rights. However, Lewis-Williams and Pearce (2005: 81–2) return this argument back to status and hierarchy, rejecting the notion that rituals 'cement social relationships', and arguing instead that 'the practices and the architectural structures in which they were performed probably point to social discriminations, to a hierarchical society in which an emerging elite manipulated surplus wealth and controlled what could and could not be seen'.

It is inevitable that power relationships and hierarchies were being disputed and played out at these sites; as argued eloquently by Christensen and Warburton (2002: 170), even primates have hierarchies and power structures; however, these are not always demonstrated in ways we expect or would recognize archaeologically, i.e. through determining characteristics such as material wealth, architecture, or grave goods and mortuary practices. If we can accept that inevitable power relationships were inherent, we can begin to look beyond their search, instead examining other avenues of research. For instance, the relationships between the living and the dead, between people and animals, their interactions with material culture and the landscape, and inherently, their rituals, beliefs, and actions.

3 ÇAYÖNÜ TEPESI: THE SKULL BUILDING

Çayönü Tepesi is situated in the Diyarbakır region of south-east Anatolia, and was occupied from around 9400–6900 BC. Previous publications relating to Çayönü have understandably focused on either its architectural features (demonstrating uniformity in the architectural phases across the site, from the earliest PPNA and 'Round Building sub-phase', to the late PPNC and 'Large Room Building sub-phase'), or on its subsistence (with a shift from hunter-gathering to agriculture) (Redman 1983: 189; Özdoğan and Özdoğan 1998; Özdoğan 1999; Schirmer 1990). The focus of this current case study will be on the Skull Building, a building which contained the remains of at least 450 people, predominantly represented by skulls (see also Özdoğan and Özdoğan 1998; Croucher 2005, 2006).

The Skull Building was originally constructed in at least five phases (for a detailed account of the architecture, see Schirmer 1990; Özdoğan 1999). Of the earliest Skull Building (BM1), only the northern, apsidal area survived. Skulls had been placed on the floor area, as well as in pits which contained disarticulated bones of both humans and aurochs, with one pit additionally containing some primary human burials (Schirmer 1990: 379–81; Özdoğan 1999: 47). Following a period of disuse, the Skull Building was rebuilt to the same alignment, and continued throughout the remainder of its life to be rebuilt to the same plan and orientation (BM2a–c). That the orientation of the Skull Building remained constant, contrasts with the remainder of the architecture on the site, which changed its design and orientation through phases of rebuilding.

Within the Skull Building, there remained a distinction in the architecture throughout its lifetime, with the northern part of the structure constructed of stone, and separated from the plastered southern area by a step, and later by standing stones, and finally by a wall with door openings (Figure 51.2); the interior space was clearly delineated, and would have dictated movement, access, and the experience of being within the building. It is from the northern area of the building that the majority of the human remains have been recovered. Cellar rooms were initially dug into the soil beneath the northern section of the Skull

ANATOLIA 831

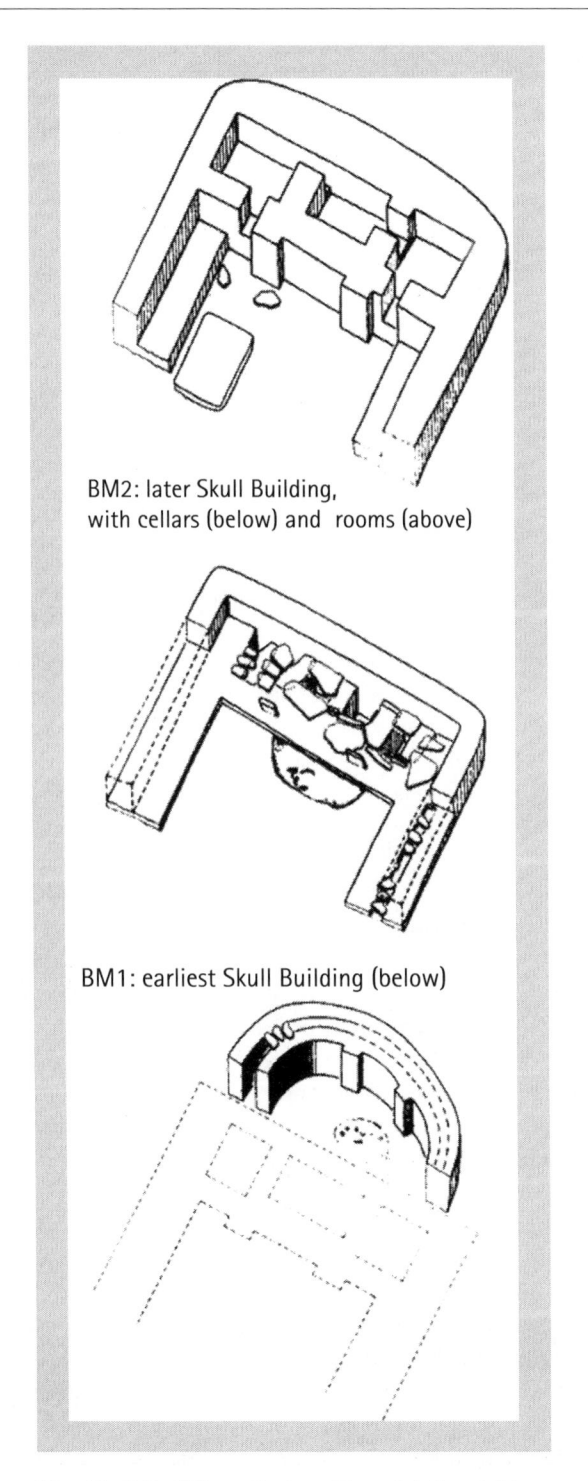

BM2: later Skull Building,
with cellars (below) and rooms (above)

BM1: earliest Skull Building (below)

FIGURE 51.2 Plan of the Skull Building, Çayönü Tepesi (after Schirmer 1990: Fig. 12).

Building. Into the most western cellar had been placed over 90 skulls, arranged in rows in a north–south direction, and facing east or west, belonging to both males and females, aged between 18–50 (Özbek 1992; Özdoğan 1991). The skulls were accompanied by piles of long bones, which had been deliberately stacked (Özbek 1992; Özdoğan 1991: 4). Other cellar contents were less ordered, although often contained many layers of skulls. The eastern cellar contained jumbles of human bones, and in the lower level of one cellar had been placed an articulated leg. There was also a complete primary burial of a female, aged 45–50 and of poor health, placed in a flexed position at the bottom of one of the cellars (Özdoğan 1991: 5, 1999: 51).

Human remains were also placed in rooms constructed above the cellars in the northern section of the Skull Building. Most were skulls of males and females of all ages, predominantly with their mandibles. Analysis of the remains by Özbek (1988: 129) has demonstrated that the skulls were placed in the Skull Building over a considerable time span; they were not deposited at the same time. They represent the results of repeated actions over a long period of time.

In contrast to the northern part of the building, which was kept distinct, and around which movement and access would have been restricted, the southern area was much more open in nature, with benches around the interior walls of the building. A highly polished stone slab, measuring 2 m^2 and 10 cm deep, was recovered from within the southern area of the building. Intriguingly, blood crystals were retrieved, both from the slab, and from the distal end of a large, 20-cm-long blade made of black flint (Wood 1998: 764). Analysis of the blood crystals revealed that the source was 9,000-year-old human haemoglobin, with blood from sheep and aurochs (Loy and Wood 1989; Wood 1998).

This evidence is unsurprisingly taken to be indicative of sacrifice, as by Lewis-Williams and Pearce (2005: 81–2), who argue for evidence of a social elite exercising control through religious belief; 'it seems likely that the elite controlled transition to spirit realms by means of sacrifice: they had the power to send people, whether sacrificed children, specially selected individuals or captives, in to the other world and, by effecting such cosmological and supernatural transitions, to benefit the living'. However, whilst undoubtedly sacrifice is an option suggested by the evidence, this certainly is not the only interpretation, and should not be taken to be conclusive; the blood may be reflective of cutting up of bodies soon after death (rather than the cause of death), and evidence of attached vertebrae, which Lewis-Williams and Pearce argue (particularly in relation to Jericho, but within the same frame of argument as Çayönü) as evidence of decapitation whilst alive, could equally relate to post-mortem practice. Additionally, the skeletal remains at Çayönü display a lack of violence, and no evidence of a violent cause of death (Özdoğan 1991: 6). Whatever the case, the possibility does raise questions and debates which go beyond status and hierarchy, such as about concepts of life and death, relationships between the living and the dead, concepts of whole and fragmented bodies, and the place of the dead in the lives of the living.

What we see in the Skull Building is, I would argue, a site of transition; the building is in a liminal location in the site, outside of the main living and activity areas—an area of the site which remains separated throughout the site's duration. In both earlier and later periods the dead were buried whole, in pits, or more commonly beneath house floors (usually in the northern end of the building, as indeed is the case within the Skull Building). However, during the period of use of the Skull Building we see a change, with the dead brought to this location for whatever processing took place; deposition for some, and perhaps movement and circulation for others. Interestingly, contemporary with the Skull Building are other remains recovered from across the site of secondary burials and bones, especially jaw and cranio fragments (Özdoğan 1999: 47); perhaps this is indicative of a movement or circulation of remains of the deceased. That there was also a lack of post-cranial remains recovered from the Skull Building (Özdoğan 1991: 2) may support this possibility, with no clear evidence at present as to the fate of the remainder of the bodies belonging to the owners of the skulls recovered from within the Skull Building.

The evidence shows changing concepts of the way the dead should be dealt with—from primary inhumation, to disarticulation and secondary burial, and selection of particular parts of the body, mainly the skulls and long bones. Clearly this necessitates a much closer physical relationship with the dead, involving the tactile and sensory processes of chopping and fragmenting. The evidence suggests that negotiations were taking place in people's relationships with the deceased body, and with the realm of the dead. And undoubtedly the beliefs underpinning these actions and processes permeated everyday life.

We additionally see the comparable treatment of animals and humans within the Skull Building. Not only is there the evidence of aurochs and sheep blood on the knife and stone slab, but additionally the Skull Building contained numerous aurochs bones, most commonly skulls and horns, with the human remains. The interment of animal bones with human remains is also seen in the earlier BM1 structure, in the pits containing disarticulated bones. There are additional examples from elsewhere at Çayönü, including a dog burial, boar skull and human male interred together (Özdoğan 1999: 47), and the placement of human bones marking the closure of buildings (Özdoğan and Özdoğan 1998: 590). Associations continue with a deliberate deposition of four mandibles from large, wild pigs in the south-west cell of a Cell Building (Redman 1983: 192), and from another, the lower jaw and tusks of a boar had been carefully placed over two burials (Özdoğan 1999: 52).

It is feasible that conceptions of animals were far removed from our own, not viewed as products to be owned and consumed (as is our experience in the modern west), but rather viewed as being akin to humans (Ingold 1988, 1996; Howell 1996; Willis 1994 [and chapters within]; Midgley 1983; Arhem 1996). Such debates are seen more commonly in the study of the British Neolithic, where relationships between animals and people have been more readily explored (Jones and Richards 2002; Levy 1995; Ray and Thomas 2002). Clearly the archaeological material of the British Neolithic differs greatly from that of the Near East; nevertheless such research provides a useful insight into alternative approaches to human–animal relationships (see Boyd forthcoming).

With both humans and animals, it seems that realms of death were brought into the lives of the living in a tangible manner, necessitating the living to process and deal with the remains of the deceased, in contrast to our experiences in the modern west where death has become sanitized and removed from everyday life (Croucher and Campbell 2009; see also Insoll 2007). And such experiences were apparently common to the inhabitants of the site of the next case study, Domuztepe.

4 Domuztepe: The Death Pit

Domuztepe's Death Pit relates to a later period than the Skull Building, dating to the Late Pottery Neolithic, around 5500 cal. BC. (Campbell et al. 1999; Carter et al. 2003; Campbell and

Carter in preparation; Campbell 2008a). Domuztepe is a large, 20-ha. site situated in the south east of Turkey, in the Kahramanmaraş region. The Death Pit measured c.3 m in diameter, and contained the disarticulated and further fragmented remains of around 40 people, along with remains of cattle and dog in association with the human remains (Kansa and Campbell 2004).

The human remains were highly processed, evidencing cutting, chopping, and apparent signs of butchery (Gauld and Oliver forthcoming; Campbell 2002, 2007–8; Kansa et al. 2009); the evidence suggests a very tactile relationship in dealing with the remains of the deceased, involving chopping and butchering, and it seems, possibly consumption of the deceased (Gauld and Oliver forthcoming). However, rather than being viewed with the repulsion often surrounding cannibalism, the remains may indicate compassion and respect for the deceased, examples of which are well documented ethnographically (Conklin 2001; White 1992; Spencer and Gillen 1904: 548; Howitt 1904: 457, 470; Poole and Porter 1983: 15–16; Strathern 1982: 125; Bloch and Parry 1982: 9; Hertz 1960: 32; see also discussions of cannibalism within Turner and Turner 1999; Rawson 1999). As well as the disarticulation of the human body, we also see fragmentation of material culture, including a piece of pottery which had been sliced through prior to firing (Irving and Heywood 2005). It also appears that human remains were curated and circulated (Campbell et al. 1999: 402–3), including an example where a piece of a human skull was recovered from a deposited pottery vessel (Campbell 2005: 4, 2007–8). Such practices demonstrate the physical and tactile processing of the dead (Croucher and Campbell 2009; Croucher 2010/11), of people, animals, and material culture. Certain people and species of animals were transformed and potentially consumed in prominent funerary events of disarticulation, eating, and burial.

5 GÖBEKLI TEPE

The site of Göbekli Tepe in the Urfa region of south-east Turkey is probably one of the most enigmatic sites in the region excavated to date, revealing reliefs of anthropomorphic forms and a wide array of animals carved onto megalithic limestone pillars of monumental size, arranged in enclosures. The site is still under excavation, consequently, much remains to be learnt and revealed, and final interpretation must be put on hold. However, a discussion of ritual in the region would be incomplete without mention of the site.

Göbekli Tepe is situated in a remote mountain location, on a limestone ridge, northeast of Urfa (Schmidt 2006). There are two pre-historic phases of activity, with Layer III, the earliest so far uncovered, dating to the PPNA/EPPNB. The layer above, Layer II, is slightly younger, dating to the EPPNB/MPPNB, and features comparable, but smaller, enclosures. The enclosures of both levels lack fireplaces, ovens, and other suggestions of domestic activity, which combined with the monolithic art has led to the interpretation of the site as a 'ritual centre'. There appears to be a shift in style, with the earlier Layer III enclosures containing fewer human and mostly animal depictions, with a greater emphasis on human representations in the later Layer II enclosures (Schmidt 1999: 14, 2002: 24, 2005; Stordeur 2005). Whilst recent excavations are beginning to reveal an older, nucleus tell, at Göbekli, the interpretation of the shrine area as a 'ritual centre' remains unchanged (Klaus Schmidt pers. comm.).

The enclosures usually contain 12 pillars, characteristically T-shaped. In 2003, 39 *in situ* pillars had been revealed. The space within the enclosures is delineated by up to 12 megaliths, interconnected by walls and stone benches. The pillars towards the centre of the enclosures are reported to be larger and of finer quality, with greater attention paid to the surfaces and decoration (Schmidt 1999: 12, 2003: 4). The pillars themselves are 3–5 m in height, and weigh about 10 tons each. One example, measuring 7 m in length, has been found at a nearby quarry site (Schmidt 1998: 4).

Geophysical survey has revealed that the complex contains at least 20 enclosure areas, with an estimation of over 200 pillars (Schmidt 2003: 5). The pillars already excavated display a range of images and depictions, including snakes, wild cattle, bucrania, cranes, boars, ducks, crocodiles, foxes, gazelle, wild ass and other quadrupeds (many of which are life-size), insects and spiders, as well as geometric shapes, including 'H' shapes (Schmidt 1999: 12, 2003: 4, 2004: 103).

As well as the art on the monoliths, other forms have also been found, including small stone figurines (Schmidt 2003: 3) and animal sculptures (Schmidt 2004: 97). Additionally, limestone plates have been recovered, with a channel running between the rim and centre, and usually six small drillings had been made on the plate; their exact purpose remains unknown, other than suggestions that they were related to offerings (Schmidt 2004: 99). Aside from the pillars already discussed, other stonework has been recovered, such as a large limestone ring measuring 60 cm in diameter, and a U-shaped monolithic limestone entrance (Schmidt 2005: 17, figs. 5–6).

As the site is still under excavation, interpretation is limited. However, it is accepted that the site's focus was 'ritual' in nature, rather than a settlement site (Schmidt 2004: 103). It is additionally suggested that the site itself may have been fundamental in the shift to agriculture, and brought about the accumulation of the people required to construct the site (Schmidt 1999: 14; 2002: 25; Lewis-Williams and Pearce 2005: 33). The interpretations of the ritual site indicate again the dominance of interpretations relating to status and hierarchy, with Schmidt suggesting that the labour involved is 'indicative of a complex, hierarchical social organization and a division of labour involving large numbers of people' (2004: 103).

An alternative approach to the evidence is taken by Lewis Williams and Pearce (2005: 125, 157), who discuss the site of Göbekli as being a location where religious experiences and altered states of consciousness may have been experienced, with the animal carvings probably related to myths and with certain parallels between entering rock-cut crypts and moving between spirit realms. However, this is ultimately tied back into status, with the site being used by elite leaders 'extending their influence beyond the village level' (Lewis-Williams and Pearce 2005: 81). This evidence is related to hierarchy and status, although Lewis Williams and Pearce (2005: 42) also discuss other factors, considering beliefs as much more integrated into daily lives, and proposing uses of the site as pertaining to religious experiences.

Many of the reliefs, which would have taken considerable time to carve, were partially obscured or built over, suggesting their creation was more significant than purely long-term viewing. Also, there appears to be very little evidence of a hierarchical arrangement of images, without a clear focal point or area of 'best view' (McBride forthcoming), perhaps suggesting movement through the structures, rather than secluded access. If this is the case, then interpretations around hierarchy become more complex, especially as some enclosures would have been able to hold around 90 people (McBride forthcoming), suggesting that whilst there may have been some restrictions to access, they may not have been as prohibitive as some interpretations suggest.

Themes that can be considered from the evidence at Göbekli include human–animal relationships—do the depictions suggest a different categorization of animals? Or the role of performance, where the actual events taking place may have involved dancing and chanting or music, perhaps taking place at night with flickering light, not to mention the performance involved in the very placing and carving of the stones. Although it is difficult to draw firm conclusions about Göbekli Tepe due to the ongoing excavation status of the site, it is clear that the intent to move such monumental pieces of stone, and place and carve them at the site, represents significant social commitment and effort. Perhaps, much as has been argued in relation to Stonehenge (Richards 2004), the construction of the site was as important as its final completion and use, with communal events and purpose in constructing the site, perhaps bringing together groups from across the landscape, with significance also attached to the source of the stones and those that carried and carved them.

As well as the effort in moving the stones, the additional food and resources needed to accompany the construction must also be considered; clearly this was not just a matter of labour and crafts persons, but additionally would have required food, water, fire, and other resources in what must have been a significant event in the lives of the participants, perhaps structuring their lives around the construction of the monument. Again we begin to see how ritual is not separated from everyday life, but rather, is often an integral part of it.

Finally, the closure of the site should be considered. The enclosures were taken out of use and were filled in using an estimated 300–500 m^3 of settlement debris, rather than sterile soil (Schmidt 2003: 7). The source of the debris is unknown at present. This must have been a huge undertaking, again requiring labour and resources, likely to have been a significant event in the lives of the people participating, taking this enigmatic site out of use and rendering it buried on a mountainside for millennia.

6 CRANIAL MODIFICATION

Through the examples considered we can see the uses of the body and performance in ritual events in varying ways, including through mortuary practices, with the fragmentation and circulation of the deceased, consumption of the body, as well as representations of bodies, people, and animals. There are examples of bodily decoration in the region dating to the ninth millennium BC and earlier on the central Anatolian plateau (Baird in press), suggesting that the body was a site for display and adornment, constructing and communicating identities. The use of the body in performatory contexts can also be seen through cranially modified skulls excavated from the region, leading to discussions of display and identity. Examples have been recovered from Çayönü (Theya Molleson, pers. comm.), Kurban Höyük (Alpagut 1986), and recent excavations at Hakemi Use (Tekin 2005). Cranial modification is a result of the head being bound during infancy, whilst still soft and malleable. This dictates the growth of the cranium in particular ways, depending on the type of binding practiced. The effects of this can be quite dramatic, causing the head to be either elongated or broadened, often with very visual implications (Molleson and Campbell 1995; Daems and Croucher 2007). Whilst this chapter has focused on moving beyond discussions of elites and hierarchy, it seems that the practice of cranial modification was not universal, and selection was made about the persons whose skulls were modified in this manner, perhaps suggesting some kind of social status, kin group, or other factor determining group membership, especially as the decision would need to have been made during a child's infancy (Daems and Croucher 2007; Croucher 2008; Fletcher et al. 2008).

Whilst it is difficult to fully understand the practice during prehistoric times, it does seem apparent that the body was closely related to displays of identity, portraying aspects of identity visually through bodily manipulation and decoration. The practice is brought into the everyday realms of ritual, as whatever beliefs dictated that the practice took place (social, economic, or spiritual perhaps), the outcome was manifested in everyday life, through the practices of binding the skull, and most likely enhancing it throughout life with hairstyle and head ornament, as appears to be depicted on pottery decoration. A sherd of pottery from Domuztepe and a comparable example from Sabi Abyad (Akkermans 1989; fig. iv) appear to show the figures displayed in what seems to be dance (Campbell 2008), perhaps marking the various rituals associated with the passing of life, time, seasons, or communal events. Performance brought together the realms of ritual and belief into everyday lives, as bodies were manipulated and displayed, both through life and in death, and used to communicate beliefs and identities.

7 Conclusions

Whilst research in the region has traditionally been dominated by large-scale approaches, cultural groups, concepts of various cults, and ritual activity related to equality, hierarchy, or social complexity, there are alternative ways of viewing the evidence. The wealth of archaeological material provides real opportunities for studying concepts of the body and identity, and can reveal insights into people's relationships with the deceased and concepts of life and death. It can also suggest how perceptions of the body were changing, and how identities were constructed, reflected, and communicated through bodily treatment during life, and into death. We can also see how people interacted with their environments, and the importance of animals, plants, and the world around them, in ways more meaningful than being related simply to subsistence and resource, with material culture perhaps signifying more about relationships and identity than about productivity, trade, and technology. Concepts of circulation, fragmentation, and discard may play a role, relying on contextual and interpretative approaches, revealing alternative attitudes to life, death, and the body (Croucher 2010/11; Croucher in press).

It is evident that a simplistic, linear, developmental approach is limited; instead complexities should be recognized and included in interpretations. Through using both the small and large scale, a more detailed and nuanced impression of the past can be gained. Approaches which examine the small-scale are becoming increasingly prominent and offer new insights into the past, complementing existing, larger-scale approaches which examine regional patterns and trends. For instance, recent research at Çatalhöyük has provided small-scale analyses of human–animal relations (Russell and During 2009), and understandings of health and work in the past (Molleson et al 2005; Molleson 2007). At Domuztepe, analyses of the Death Pit are providing new understandings of consumption and funerary activity (Kansa et al 2009; Croucher and Campbell 2009), and at neighbouring sites in north Mesopotamia, new interpretations of the role of plants and communal activities are emerging from Jerf el-Ahmar (Stordeur and Willcox 2010; Asouti and Fuller forthcoming), and understandings of the role of pottery (Nieuwenhuyse 2010) and whiteware (Nilhamn in press) at Sabi Abyad are providing a picture of the symbolic roles of otherwise 'mundane' materials. Such interpretations remain evidence-based, rather than being formulated purely theoretically—this balance of theory and data is integral to a study of the past. It is through such approaches that the study of the wealth of archaeological material reveals theoretically informed interpretations that are grounded in real data, offering exciting and new interpretations about the enigmatic evidence available to us.

Acknowledgements

I would like to thank Douglas Baird, Stuart Campbell, Suellen Gauld, Alexis Mcbride, Theya Molleson, and Klaus Schmidt for discussing their unpublished material, as well as the AHRC for doctoral funding, research from which has contributed to this paper, and the British Academy for funding my postdoctoral research. Thank you also to Tim Insoll and Rachel Maclean for inviting me to contribute to this volume, and to Alexandra Fletcher for commenting on this chapter; any errors are, of course, my own.

Suggested Reading

For excavation reports of some of the most prominent sites in the region, see Arsebük et al. (1998), Özdoğan and Basgelen (1999, in press), and Belli (2001). General overviews of archaeology in the region include Sagona and Zimansky (2009), Matthews (1998), Gérard and Thissen (2002), and Özdoğan (1995). For those wanting to focus on mortuary practice, Campbell and Green (1995) is still the main source of reference, shortly to be joined by Croucher (in press). For a summary of ritual activity that links PPN Anatolia to the rest of the Near East, see Stordeur 2010; Goring-Morris 2005; Goring-Morris and Belfer-Cohen 2010. I would also point readers towards recent work by Boyd (2002, 2004) and Jones (2009), which has used alternative approaches in interpreting Levantine and Cypriot material respectively, comparable to those discussed in this present chapter.

References

Alpagut, B. 1986. 'The human skeletal remains from Kurban Hoyuk (Urfa Province)', *Anatolica*, 13: 149–74.
Arhem, K. 1996. 'The cosmic food web: Human-nature relatedness in the Northwest Amazon' in P. Descola and G. Palsson (eds), *Nature and Society: Anthropological perspectives* (London and New York: Routledge), pp. 185–204.

ARSEBÜK, G., MELLINK, M., and SCHIRMER, W. (eds) 1998. *Light on Top of the Black Hill* (Istanbul: Ege Yayinlari).
BAIRD, D. in press. 'Pınarbaşı; From Epipalaeolithic camp-site to sedentarising village in central Anatolia' in M. Özdögan and N. Basgelen (eds), *The Neolithic in Turkey: New excavations, new discoveries* (Istanbul: Arkeoloji v Sanat Yayinlari).
BALTER, M. 1998. 'Why settle down? The mystery of communities', *Science*, 282 (5393): 1442–5.
——2005. *The Goddess and the Bull: Çatalhöyük: An Archaeological journey to the dawn of civilization* (New York: Free Press).
BAR-YOSEF, O. 2008. 'Farming, herding, and the transformation of human landscapes in Southwestern Asia' in B. David and J. Thomas (eds), *Handbook of Landscape Archaeology* (Walnut Creek: Left Coast Press), pp. 315–27.
BELLI, O. (ed.) 2001. *İstanbul University Contributions to Archaeology in Turkey (1932–2000)* (Istanbul: İstanbul Üniversitesi).
BIENERT, H. D. 1991. 'Skull cult in the prehistoric Near East', *Journal of Prehistoric Religion*, 5: 9–23.
BLOCH, M. and PARRY, J. 1982. *Death and the Regeneration of Life* (Cambridge: Cambridge University Press).
BONOGOFSKY, M. 2003. 'Neolithic plastered skulls and railroading epistemologies', *Bulletin of the American Schools of Oriental Research*, 331: 1–10.
——2004. 'Including women and children: Neolithic modeled skulls from Jordan, Israel, Syria and Turkey', *Near Eastern Archaeology*, 67(2): 118–19.
——2005. 'A bioarchaeological study of plastered skulls from Anatolia: New discoveries and interpretations', *International Journal of Osteoarchaeology*, 15(2): 124–35.
BONOGOFSKY, M. 2006. 'Complexity in context: Plain, painted and modelled skulls from the Neolithic Middle East' in M. Bonogofsky (ed.), *Skull Collection, Modification and Decoration*, BAR International Series 1539 (Oxford: BAR), pp. 15–28.
BOYD, B., 2002. 'Ways of eating/ways of being in the Later Epipalaeolithic (Natufian) Levant' in Y. Hamilakis, M. Pluciennik, and S. Tarlow (eds), *Thinking Through the Body: Archaeologies of corporeality* (New York: Kluwer/Plenum), pp. 137–52.
——2004. 'Agency and landscape: abandoning the nature/culture dichotomy in interpretations of the Natufian' in C. Delage (ed.), *The Last Hunter-gatherer Societies in the Near East*, BAR International Series 1320 (Oxford: BAR), pp. 119–36.
——forthcoming. *Beyond Bones: Towards a Social Archaeology of Human Animal Relations* (Cambridge: Cambridge University Press).
CAMPBELL, S. 1992. 'The Halaf period in Iraq: Old sites and new', *Biblical Archaeologist*, 55: 182–7.
——1998. 'Problems of definition: The origins of the Halaf in north Iraq' in M. Lebeau (ed.), *Subartu IV, I: Landscape, Archaeology, Settlement* (Brussels: Brepols Publishers), pp. 39–52.
——2005. 'Domuztepe 2004 excavation season', *Anatolian Archaeology*, 10: 4–5.
——2007–8. 'The dead and the living in Late Neolithic Mesopotamia' in G. Bartoloni and M. G. Benedettini (eds), *Sepolti tra i vivi. Evidenza ed interpretazione di contesti funerari in abitato*, Atti del Convegno Internazionale (Università degli Studi di Roma 'La Sapienza' 26–9 Aprile 2006).
——2008a. 'Feasting and dancing: Gendered representation and pottery in Later Mesopotamian Prehistory' in D. Bolger (ed.), *Gender Through Time in the Ancient Near East* (Oxford: AltaMira), pp. 53–76.
——2008b. 'Publishing Çatalhöyük: multivocality in action?', *Antiquity*, 82: 497–500.

CAMPBELL, S. and CARTER, E. (eds) forthcoming. *Prehistoric Domuztepe*, I (Los Angeles: Monumenta Archaeologica).
——, CARTER, E., HEALEY, E., ANDERSON, S., KENNEDY, A., and WHITCHER, S. 1999. 'Emerging complexity on the Kahramanmaraş Plain, Turkey: The Domuztepe Project 1995-1997', *American Journal of Archaeology*, 103: 395-418.
——and GREEN, A. (eds) 1995. *The Archaeology of Death in the Ancient Near East* (Oxford: Oxbow Books).
——, CAMPBELL, S., and GAULD, S. 2003. 'Elusive complexity: New data from late Halaf Domuztepe in south central Turkey', *Paléorient*, 29(2): 117-33.
Çatalhöyük website: <http://www.catalhoyuk.com/bibliography.html>.
CAUVIN, J. 1994. *The Birth of the Gods and the Origins of Agriculture*, trans. T. Watkins (Cambridge: Cambridge University Press).
——2000. 'The symbolic foundations of the Neolithic revolution in the Near East' in I. Kuijt (ed.), *Life in Neolithic Farming Communities: Social organisation, identity, and differentiation* (New York: Kluwer Academic/Plenum Publishers), pp. 235-52.
CHARVÁT, P. 2002. *Mesopotamia before History* (London and New York: Routledge).
CHRISTENSEN, L. B. and WARBURTON, D. A. 2002. 'Theories, definitions and goals: Obstacles and openings for the understanding of Neolithic ritual' in H. G. K. Gebel, B. D. Hermansen, and C. H. Jensen (eds), *Magic Practices and Ritual in the Near Eastern Neolithic*, Studies in Early Near Eastern Production, Subsistence, and Environment 8 (Berlin: Ex Oriente), pp. 163-73.
CONKEY, M. W. and TRINGHAM, R. E. 1995. 'Archaeology and the goddess: Exploring the contours of feminist archaeology' in D. C. Stanton and A. J. Stewart (eds), *Feminisms in the Academy* (Michigan: Ann Arbor), pp. 199-247.
CONKLIN, B. 2001. *Consuming Grief* (Texas: University of Texas Press).
CROUCHER, K., 2005. 'Queerying Near Eastern Archaeology', *World Archaeology*, 37(4): 609-19.
——2006. 'Death, display and performance: A discussion of the mortuary remains at Çayönü Tepesi, southeast Turkey' in M. Georgiadis and C. Gallou (eds), *Archaeology of Cult and Death* (Budapest: Archaeolingua Publications), pp. 11-44.
——2008. 'Ambiguous genders, altered identities: Alternative interpretations of figurine and mortuary evidence from the 'PPNB'-'Halaf' periods' in D. Bolger (ed.), *Gender through Time in the Ancient Near East* (Oxford: AltaMira), pp. 21-52.
——2010/11. 'Tactile engagements: The world of the dead in the lives of the living' in M. Benz (ed.), *The Principle of Sharing: Segregation and construction of social identities at the transition from foraging to farming* (Berlin: Ex Oriente).
——in press. *Death and Dying in the Neolithic Near East* (Oxford: Oxford University Press).
——and CAMPBELL, S. 2009. 'Dying for a change? Bringing new senses to Near Eastern Neolithic mortuary practice' in S. Tereny, N. Lyons, and J. Kelly (eds), *Que(e)rying Archaeology: The proceedings of the 30th annual Chacmool Conference, Calgary* (Calgary: Archaeological Association of the University of Calgary).
DAEMS, A. 2008. 'Evaluating patterns of gender through Mesopotamian and Iranian human figurines: A reassessment of the Neolithic and Chalcolithic industries' in. D. Bolger (ed.), *Gender through Time in the Ancient Near East* (Oxford: AltaMira), pp. 77-118.
——and CROUCHER, K. 2007. 'Cranial Modification in Ancient Iran', *Iranica Antiqua*, 42: 1-21.
DESCOLA, P. and PÁLSSEN, G. (eds) 1996. *Nature and Society: Anthropological perspectives* (London and New York: Routledge).

FLETCHER, A., PEARSON, J., and AMBERS, J. 2008. 'The manipulation of social and physical identity in the Pre-Pottery Neolithic', *Cambridge Archaeological Journal*, 18(03): 309–25.

FOREST, J. D. 1994. 'Towards an interpretation of the Çatal Höyük reliefs and wall paintings', *1993 YiliAnadolu Mediniyetleri Müzesi Konferanslari* (Ankara: Museum of Anatolian Civilizations), pp. 118–36.

GATENS, M. 1994. 'The dangers of a woman-centred philosophy' in Polity Press (ed.), *The Polity Reader in Gender Studies* (Cambridge: Polity Press), pp. 93–107.

GAULD, S. and OLIVER, J. forthcoming. 'Human remains at Domuztepe' in S. Campbell and E. Carter (eds), *Prehistoric Domuztepe*, I (Los Angeles: Monumenta Archaeologica).

GÉRARD, F., and THISSEN, L. (eds) 2002. *The Neolithic of Central Anatolia* (Istanbul: Ege Yayinlari).

GIMBUTAS, M. 1981. 'Vulvas, breasts and buttocks of the Goddess Creatress: Commentary on the origins of art' in G. Buccellati and C. Speroni (eds), *The Shape of the Past*, Studies in Honour of Franklin D. Murphy (Los Angeles, CA: UCLA Institute of Archaeology), pp. 19–40.

—— 1982. *The Goddesses and Gods of Old Europe* (Los Angeles: University of California Press).

—— 1991. *The Civilization of the Goddess: The world of Old Europe* (San Francisco, CA: Harper).

—— 2001. *The Language of the Goddess* (London: Thames and Hudson).

GORING-MORRIS, A. N. 2000. 'The quick and the dead: The social context of aceramic Neolithic mortuary practices as seen from Kfar HaHoresh' in I. Kuijt (ed.), *Life in Neolithic Farming Communities: Social organisation, identity, and differentiation* (New York: Kluwer Academic/Plenum Publishers), pp. 103–30.

—— and BELFER-COHEN, A. 2010. 'Different ways of being, different ways of seeing... Changing worldviews in the Near East' in B. Finlayson and G. Warren (eds), *Landscapes in Transition* (Oxford: Oxbow), pp. 9–22.

HAMILTON, N. 2000. 'Concepts of sex and gender in figurine studies in prehistory' in M. Donald and L. Hurcombe (eds), *Representations of Gender from Prehistory to the Present* (London: Macmillan Press Ltd), pp. 17–30.

HAUPTMANN, H. 1987. 'Nevali Çori', *Anatolian Studies*, 37: 206–7.

—— 1990. 'Nevali Çori', *American Journal of Archaeology*, 94: 127.

—— 1999. 'The Urfa region' in M. Özdögan (ed.), *Neolithic in Turkey* (Istanbul: Arkeoloji ve Sanat Yay), pp. 65–86.

HERTZ, R. 1960 [1907]. *Death and the Right Hand* (Aberdeen: Cohen and West).

HODDER, I. 1987. 'Contextual archaeology: An interpretation of Catal Hüyük and a discussion of the origins of agriculture', *Bulletin of the Institute of Archaeology (London)*, 24: 43–56.

—— 1990. *The Domestication of Europe: Structure and contingency in Neolithic societies* (Oxford: Blackwell).

—— (ed.) 1996. *On the Surface: Çatalhöyük 1993–1995*, British Institute of Archaeology at Ankara Monograph 22 (London and Cambridge: British Institute of Archaeology at Ankara and McDonald Institute for Archaeological Research).

—— 1999. 'Symbolism at Çatalhöyük' in J. Coles, R. Bewley, and P. Mellars (eds), *World Prehistory: Studies in memory of Grahame Clark*, Proceedings of the British Academy 99 (Oxford University Press), pp. 177–91.

—— (ed.) 2000. *Towards Reflexive Methods in Archaeology: The example at Çatalhöyük*, British Institute of Archaeology at Ankara Monograph 28 (London and Cambridge: British Institute of Archaeology at Ankara and McDonald Institute for Archaeological Research).

—— 2004. 'Women and men at Çatalhöyük', *Scientific American*, 290: 66–73.

HODDER, I. 2006. 'The spectacle of daily performance at Çatalhöyük' in T. Inomata and L. S. Coben (eds), *Archaeology of Performance: Theaters of power, community, and politics* (Lanham: AltaMira), pp 81–102.
—— 2006b. *The Leopard's Tale: Revealing the mysteries of Çatalhöyük* (New York: Thames & Hudson).
—— 2009. 'An archaeological response', *Paléorient*, 35 (1): 109–11.
—— and CESSFORD, C. 2004. 'Daily practice and social memory at Çatalhöyük', *American Antiquity*, 69(1): 17–40.
—— and FARID, S. 2004. *Season Review, Çatal News* 11. http://www.catalhoyuk.com/newsletters/11/index.html. Accessed August 2010.
HOLE, F. 2000. 'Is size important? Function and hierarchy in Neolithic settlements' in I. Kuijt (ed.), *Life in Neolithic Farming Communities: Social organisation, identity, and differentiation* (New York: Kluwer Academic/Plenum Publishers), pp. 191–210.
HOWELL, S. 1996. 'Nature in culture or culture in nature' in P. Descola and G. Palsson (eds), *Nature and Society: Anthropological perspectives* (London and New York: Routledge), pp. 127–44.
HOWITT, A.W. 1904. *The Native Tribes of South-east Australia* (London: MacMillan and Co. Ltd).
INGOLD, T. 1988. 'Introduction' in T. Ingold (ed.), *What Is an Animal?* (London: Unwin Hyman), pp. 1–16.
—— 1996. 'Growing plants and raising animals: An anthropological perspective on domestication' in D. R. Harris (ed.), *The Origins and Spread of Agriculture and Pastoralism in Eurasia* (London: UCL Press), pp. 12–24.
—— 2000. *The Perception of the Environment: Essays in livelihood, dwelling and skill* (London and New York: Routledge).
INSOLL, T. 2007. *Archaeology. The Conceptual Challenge* (London: Duckworth).
IRVING, A. and HEYWOOD, C. 2005. 'The ceramics from the "Death Pit" at Domuztepe: Conservation and analysis', *Anatolian Archaeology*, 10: 6.
JONES, A. and RICHARDS, C. 2002. 'Animals into ancestors: Domestication, food and identity in Late Neolithic Orkney' in M. Parker Pearson (ed.), *Food, Culture and Identity in the Neolithic and Bronze Age*, BAR International Series 1117 (Oxford: BAR), pp. 45–52.
JONES, P. L. 2009. 'Considering Living-Beings in the Aceramic Neolithic of Cyprus', *Journal of Mediterranean Archaeology*, 22(1): 75–99.
KANSA, S. W. and CAMPBELL S. 2004. 'Feasting with the dead? A ritual bone deposit at Domuztepe, south eastern Turkey (c.5550 cal. BC)' in S. Jones O'Day, W. van Neer, and A. Ervynck (eds), *Behaviour behind Bones: The zooarchaeology of ritual, religion, status and identity* (Oxford: Oxbow), pp. 2–13.
——, GAULD, S., CAMPBELL, S., and CARTER, E. 2009. 'Whose bones are those? Preliminary comparative analysis of fragmented human and animal bones in the "Death Pit" at Domuztepe, a Late Neolithic settlement in southeastern Turkey', *Anthropozoologica*.
KENYON, K. 1957. *Digging up Jericho* (London: Ernst Benn).
KUIJT, I. 2000. 'Keeping the peace: Ritual, skull caching, and community integration in the Levantine Neolithic' in I. Kuijt (ed.), *Life in Neolithic Farming Communities: Social organisation, identity, and differentiation* (New York: Kluwer Academic/Plenum Publishers), pp. 137–62.
—— 2002. 'Reflections on ritual and the transmission of authority in the Pre-Pottery Neolithic of the Southern Levant' in H. G. K. Gebel, B. D. Hermansen, and C. H. Jensen (eds), *Magic Practices and Ritual in the Near Eastern Neolithic*, Studies in Early Near Eastern Production, Subsistence, and Environment 8 (Berlin: Ex Oriente), pp. 81–90.

——2008. 'The Regeneration of Life: Neolithic Structures of Symbolic Remembering and Forgetting', *Current Anthropology*, 49(2): 171–97.
——and GORING-MORRIS, N. 2002. 'Foraging, farming, and social complexity in the Pre-Pottery Neolithic of the Southern Levant: A review and synthesis', *Journal of World Prehistory*, 16(4): 361–440.
LEVY, T. 1995. 'Animals good to think: Bronze Age Scandinavia and Ohio Hopewell' in K. Ryan and P. J. Crabtree (eds), *The Symbolic Role of Animals in Archaeology* (Philadelphia: MASCA), pp. 9–19.
LEWIS-WILLIAMS, D. and PEARCE, D. 2005. *Inside the Neolithic Mind: Consciousness, cosmos, and the realm of the gods* (London: Thames and Hudson).
LOY, T. and WOOD, A. R. 1989. 'Blood residue analysis at Çayönü Tepesi, Turkey', *Journal of Field Archaeology*, 16: 451–60.
LUCAS, G. M. L. 2001. *Critical Approaches to Fieldwork: Contemporary and historical archaeological practice* (London: Routledge).
MCBRIDE, A. forthcoming. *The emergence of Neolithic corporate groups in the Near East* (Liverpool: University of Liverpool).
MATTHEWS, R. 1998. *Ancient Anatolia* (London: British Institute of Archaeology at Ankara).
——2000. *The Early Prehistory of Mesopotamia 500,000 to 4,500 BC* (Brepols: Turnhout).
——2003. *The Archaeology of Mesopotamia: Theories and approaches* (Routledge: London).
MELLAART, J. 1967. *Çatal hüyük: A Neolithic town in Anatolia* (London).
MELLINK, M. 1992. 'Archaeology in Anatolia', *American Journal of Archaeology*, 96: 119–50.
MESKELL, L. M. 1995. 'Goddesses, Gimbutas and new age archaeology', *Antiquity*, 69: 74–86.
——1998. 'Oh my goddess! Archaeology, sexuality and ecofeminism', *Archaeological Dialogues*, 5(2): 126–42.
MIDGELY, M. 1983. *Animals and Why They Matter: A journey around the species barrier* (Georgia: University of Georgia Press).
MOLLESON, T. 2007. 'Times of stress at Çatalhöyük' in M. Faerman, L. K. Horwitz, T. Kahana, and U. Zilberman, (eds), *Faces from the Past: Diachronic patterns in the biology of human populations from the Eastern Mediterranean* (Oxford: Archaeopress, BAR), pp. 140–50.
——ANDREWS, P., and BOZ, B. 2005. 'Reconstruction of the Neolithic people of Çatalhöyük' in I. Hodder (ed.), *Inhabiting Çatalhöyük: reports from the 1995–99 seasons.* (Cambridge: McDonald Institute for Archaeological Research / British Institute of Archaeology at Ankara), pp. 279–300.
——and CAMPBELL, S. 1995. 'Deformed skulls at Tell Arpachiyah: The social context' in S. Campbell and A. Green (eds), *Archaeology of Death in the Ancient Near East* (Oxford: Oxbow Monograph 51), pp. 45–55.
ORBASLI, A. and DOUGHTY, L. 2004. 'TEMPER 2004: Catalhoyuk management plan', <http://www.catalhoyuk.com/smp/index.html>.
ÖZBAŞARAN, M. 1998. 'The heart of a house: The hearth. Aşıklı Höyük, a pre-pottery Neolithic site in central Anatolia' in G. Arsebük, M. J. Mellink, and W. Schirmer (eds), *Karatepe'deki Isik/Light on top of the Black Hill* (Istanbul: Ege Yayinlari), pp. 555–66.
ÖZBEK, M. 1988. 'Culte des cranes humains a Çayönü', *Anatolica*, 15: 127–37.
ÖZBEK, M. 1992. 'The human remains at Çayönü', *American Journal of Archaeology*, 96: 373.
——2009. 'Remodeled human skulls in Köşk Höyük (Neolithic age, Anatolia): a new appraisal in view of recent discoveries', *Journal of Archaeological Science*, 36(2): 379–86.
ÖZDOĞAN, A. 1999. 'Çayönü' in M. Özdoğan (ed.), *Neolithic in Turkey* (Istanbul: Arkeoloji ve Sanat Yay), pp. 35–63.

ÖZDOĞAN, M. 1991. 'An anthropological approach to the people of Çayönü', *93rd Annual Meeting of the Archaeological Institute of America*, Chicago. Dec. 1991.

ÖZDOĞAN, M. 1995. 'Neolithic in Turkey: The status of research' in *Readings in Prehistory: Studies presented to Halet Cambel* (Istanbul, Graphis Pub.), pp. 41–59.

——2004. 'Definitions, Perceptions, and Borders.' *Neo-Lithics* 1/04: 41–2.

——2008. An Alternative Approach in Tracing Changes in Demographic Composition in J. P. Bocquet-Appel and O. Bar-Yosef (eds), *The Neolithic Demographic Transition and its Consequences*, pp. 139–78.

——and BASGELEN, N. (eds) 1999. *Neolithic in Turkey: The cradle of civilization* (Istanbul: Arkeoloji ve Sanat Yay), pp. 35–63.

————(eds) in press. *The Neolithic in Turkey: new excavations, new discoveries* (Istanbul: Arkeoloji v Sanat Yayinlar).

——and ÖZDOĞAN, A. 1998. 'Buildings of cult and the cult of buildings' in G. Arsebük, M. J. Mellink, and W. Schirmer (eds), *Karatepe'deki Isik/Light on top of the Black Hill* (Istanbul: Ege Yayinlari), pp. 581–93.

POOLE, F. and PORTER, J. 1983. 'Cannibals, tricksters, and witches: Anthropophagic images among Bimin-Kuskusmin' in P. Brown and D. Tuzin (eds), *The Ethnography of Cannibalism* (Washington: Society for Psychological Anthropology), pp. 6–32.

RAWSON, C. 1999. 'Unspeakable rites: Cultural reticence and the cannibal question', *Social Research*, 66(1): 1–131.

RAY, K. and THOMAS, J. 2002. 'In the kinship of cows: The social centrality of cattle in the earlier Neolithic of southern Britain' in M. Parker Pearson (ed.), *Food, Culture and Identity in the Neolithic and Bronze Age*, BAR International Series 1117 (Oxford: BAR), pp. 37–44.

REDMAN, C. L. 1983. 'Regularity and change in the architecture of an early village' in T. C. Young, P. E. L. Smith, and P. Mortensen (eds), *The Hilly Flanks and Beyond* (Chicago: Oriental Institute of the University of Chicago), pp. 189–206.

RICHARDS, C. 2004. 'Rethinking the great stone circles of Northwest Britain' in *Orkney Archaeological Trust* <http://www.orkneydigs.org.uk/DHL/PAPERS/cr/index.html>.

ROAF, M. 1996. *Cultural Atlas of Mesopotamia and the Ancient Near East* (Oxford: Facts on File).

ROUNTREE, K. 2007. 'Archaeologists and Goddess Feminists at Çatalhöyük: An Experiment in Multivocality', *Journal of Feminist Studies in Religion*, 23(2): 7–26.

RUSSELL, N., and DÜRING, B. S. 2010. 'Worthy is the lamb: a double burial at Neolithic Çatalhöyük (Turkey)', *Paléorient*, 32(1): 73–84.

——and MEECE, S. 2005. 'Animal Representations and Animal remains at Çatalhöyük' in I. Hodder (ed.), *Çatalhöyük Perspectives: Reports from the 1995–99 seasons* (Oxford: McDonald Institute Monographs/British Institute of Archaeology at Ankara), pp. 209–30.

SAGONA, A., and ZIMANSKY, P. 2009. *Ancient Turkey* (London: Routledge).

SCHIRMER, W. 1990. 'Some aspects of building at the "Aceramic-Neolithic" settlement of Çayönü Tepesi', *World Archaeology*, 21(3): 363–87.

SCHMIDT, K. 1998. 'Beyond daily bread: Evidence of Early Neolithic ritual from Göbekli Tepe', *Neo-Lithics*, 2(98): 1–5.

——1999. 'Boars, ducks, and foxes: The Urfa Project 99', *Neo-Lithics*, 3(99): 12–15.

——2002. Göbekli Tepe, southeastern Turkey: The seventh campaign, 2001', *Neo-Lithics*, 1(02): 23–5.

——2003. 'The 2003 campaign at Göbekli Tepe (southeastern Turkey)', *Neo-Lithics*, 2(03): 3–8.

——2004. 'Göbekli Tepe excavations 2004', *Kazi Sonuçlari Toplantisi*, 28(2): 97–110.

——2005. '"Ritual Centers" and the Neolithisation of Upper Mesopotamia', *Neo-Lithics*, 2(05): 13–21.
——2006. *Sie bauten die ersten Tempel: Das rätselhafte Heiligtum der Steinzeitjäger* (München: Beck).
SPENCER, B. and GILLEN, F. J. 1904. *The Northern Tribes of Central Australia* (London: MacMillan and Co. Ltd).
STRATHERN, A. 1982. 'Witchcraft, greed, cannibalism and death: Some related themes from the New Guinea Highlands' in M. Bloch and J. Parry (eds), *Death and the Regeneration of Life* (Cambridge: Cambridge University Press), pp. 111–33.
TALALAY, L. E. 2004. 'Heady business: Skulls, heads and decapitation in Neolithic Anatolia', *Journal of Mediterranean Archaeology*, 17(2): 139–63.
TEKIN, H. (2005). 'Hakemi Use: a new discovery regarding the northern distribution of Hassunan/Samarran pottery in the Near East', *Antiquity*, 79 (303): Article number 79008, http://antiquity.ac.uk/ProjGall/tekin/.
TURNER, C. G. II and TURNER, J. A. 1999. *Man Corn: Cannibalism and violence in the prehistoric American Southwest* (Salt Lake City: University of Utah Press).
TWISS, K. C. 2006. 'A modified boar skull from Catalhoyuk', *American Schools of Oriental Research*, 342: 1–12.
VERHOEVEN, M. 2002a. 'Ritual and ideology in the Pre-Pottery Neolithic B of the Levant and Southeast Anatolia', *Cambridge Archaeological Journal*, 12(2): 233–58.
——2002b. 'Ritual and its investigation in prehistory' in H. G. K. Gebel, B. D. Hermansen, and C. H. Jensen (eds), *Magic Practices and Ritual in the Near Eastern Neolithic*, Studies in Early Near Eastern Production, Subsistence, and Environment 8 (Berlin: Ex Oriente), pp. 5–42.
——2002c. 'Transformations of society: The changing role of ritual and symbolism in the PPNB and the PN in the Levant, Syria and south-east Anatolia', *Paléorient*, 28(1): 5–14.
VOIGT, M. M. 2000. 'Çatal Höyük in context: Ritual at Early Neolithic sites in central and eastern Turkey' in I. Kuijt (ed.), *Life in Neolithic Farming Communities: Social organisation, identity, and differentiation* (New York: Kluwer Academic/Plenum Publishers), pp. 253–93.
WATKINS, T. 1998. 'Centres and Peripheries: The beginnings of sedentary communities in north Mesopotamia' in M. Lebeau (ed.), *Subartu IV, I: Landscape, Archaeology, Settlement* (Brepols, Brussels), pp. 1–11.
WHITE, T. 1992. *Prehistoric Cannibalism: At Mancos 5MTUMR-2346* (Princeton University Press).
WILLIS, R. (ed.) 1994. *Signifying Animals: Human meaning in the natural world* (London: Routledge).
WOOD, A. R. 1998. 'Revisited: Blood residue investigations at Çayönü, Turkey' in G. Arsebük, M. J. Mellink, and W. Schirmer (eds), *Karatepe'deki Isik/Light on top of the Black Hill* (Istanbul: Ege Yayinlari), pp. 763–4.
WRIGHT, G. 1988. 'The severed head in earliest Neolithic times', *Journal of Prehistoric Religion*, 2: 51–6.

CHAPTER 52

OLD NORSE AND GERMANIC RELIGION

ANDERS ANDRÉN

1 THE TEXTUAL BACKGROUND

OLD Norse religion is the conventional name of the religious traditions in Scandinavia before the conversion to Christianity in the tenth and eleventh centuries. Sometimes this tradition is included in the broader concept Germanic religion, designating religious traditions in the Germanic-speaking world as a whole. In present-day Germany, the Netherlands, northern Belgium, and England these religious traditions successively disappeared with the Christian conversion in the seventh, eighth, and ninth centuries (de Vries 1970; Simek 1993, 2003; DuBois 1999; Steinsland 2005; cf. Nilsson 1996; Müller-Wille 1997; Carver 2003).

Although runic writing was used in northern Europe since about AD 200 (Odenstedt 1990; Fischer 2005;), the pre-Christian religion was above all based on ritual practice and oral traditions (Gunnell 1995), which means that almost all written accounts of the religious traditions are external, written either by Christians referring back to their pagan past or by foreigners in ethnographical perspectives. Old Norse religion is the best-documented version of Germanic religion, due to the rich and varied Icelandic literature. The mythological world is summarized in a poetic survey (*Snorri's Edda*) from the early thirteenth century by the Icelandic chieftain and poet Snorri Sturlusson (1179–1241). Several mythological poems, probably from the time of the conversion, are also preserved in the *Poetic Edda*, which was written down and edited in the early thirteenth century. Sometimes references are made to the pagan past in the Icelandic sagas from the thirteenth and fourteenth centuries. The Danish historian Saxo Grammaticus has also written extensively about Scandinavia's pagan past in his Danish history (*Gesta Danorum*) from the early thirteenth century. Besides, descriptions of Scandinavian ritual practice are known from accounts by the Arabic geographer Ibn Fadlan (922) and by three German historians, Rimbert (*c.*870), Thietmar of Merseburg (*c.*1010) and Adam of Bremen (*c.*1075) (de Vries 1970; Clover and Lindow 1985; Beck and Andersson 1992; Simek 1993, 2003; Steinsland 2005).

In the Frisian, Saxon, and Anglo-Saxon regions of Northern Europe, references to some of the gods, goddesses, and heroes, known from the Icelandic tradition, are made in texts as well as in a few place names. Above all, the German poem *Nibelungenlied* and the Anglo-Saxon poem *Beowulf* have many links to Old Norse religion. A background for using the term Germanic religion is also found in the description of the barbarians outside the Roman Empire in *Germania*, written by the the Roman historian Tacitus in AD 98. In some cases the names as well as the desciptions of the divinities and the rituals found in *Germania* can be related to the later Icelandic tradition (de Vries 1970; Simek 1993, 2003).

1.1 History of Research

All the written accounts about Old Norse and Germanic religion have meant that research has long since been carried out by historians, philologists, place-name scholars, literary scholars, historians of religion, and archaeologists in an interdisciplinary field of research. The modern study of Old Norse and Germanic religion started in the Romantic period in the first decades of the nineteenth century, with a recognition that the gods and goddesses represented a non-Christian religion and an alternative northern heritage to the dominant classical tradition in Europe at that time (de Vries 1970; Clunies Ross and Lönnroth 2001; Raudvere et al. 2005). However, since the main sources for this pagan tradition are medieval Christian texts, the recurring issue has been how pagan the sources are. Are the texts only Christian interpretation of a pagan past, as a kind of 'fantasy religion', or do the narratives contain elements based on a pagan reality? Historians, philologists, and literary scholars tend to be more sceptical (Clover and Lindow 1985; Meulengracht Sørensen 1993; Janson 1998), whereas place-name scholars, historians of religion, and archaeologists usually are more positive, combining the scanty written accounts with other sources (Vikstrand 2001; Steinsland 2005; Andrén et al. 2006).

The Romantic background to the study of Old Norse and Germanic religion means that research has often been framed by nationalism, underlining the northern, non-Christian and non-classical origin of the religious tradition. In the nineteenth and early twentieth centuries many of the gods and goddesses were depicted in sculptures and painting, and gave their names to streets, squares, journals, and private firms in many parts of Northern Europe (Allzén 1990; Roesdahl and Meulengracht Sørensen 1996). The narratives of the northern gods have also been a recurring source of inspiration for artists. Wagner used the *Nibelungenlied* as inspiration for his opera *The Ring*, whereas Tolkien created his own universe in *The Lord of Rings* from his extensive knowledge of Germanic religion (Arvidsson 2007). During the 1930s and 1940s elements of Germanic religion were overtly misused by the pan-Germanic movement in Nazi Germany. Still today, several small right-wing groups use symbols, names, and references from Old Norse and Germanic religion (Raudvere et al. 2001; Gregorius 2006; Janson 2006). Due to the political misuse in Nazi Germany, research on Old Norse and Germanic religion nearly disappeared after the Second World War. Only in the last decades has a new scholarly interest been clearly visible again, often combined with an attempt to reconquer and redefine a politically contested field of research.

1.2 Outline of Mythology and Rituals

According to *Snorri's Edda* and the *Poetic Edda* the world was created from an original emptiness called *Ginnungagap* in which the primodial giant *Ymir* was shaped from ice and fire. Ymir was the ancestor of the first giants and dwarfs, and the first gods were sons of a giantess. They killed Ymir and built the world from its body. Finally the gods created humans from two tree trunks. The fully created world was inhabited by various creatures living in different parts of *Midgard* ('The middle world'). Apart from humans there were gods of two families (*Vanir* and *Æsir*), giants, dwarfs, elves, different kinds of goddesses of fate, and several different death realms. The Vanir included the gods *Njordr* and *Freyr* and the goddess *Freya*, which were connected to fertility, water, bogs, and the underworld. Among the many *Æsir* were the sky god *Tyr*, the thunder god *Thor*, the god of hunting and skiing *Ullr*, and the wise high god and warrior god *Odin*, who was a very complex divinity with shamanistic traits.

Around the whole world the Midgard serpent was twined. In the middle of the world, and surrounded by nine worlds, stood a world tree, sometimes called *Yggdrasill*. The world tree, with its crown, trunk and roots, materialized the connection between heaven, world, and underworld. At the base of the world tree was the spring or well of destiny, knowledge, and memory. By its side lived the goddesses of fate *Urdr*, who sometimes appeared as three aspects of time, spinning the threads of human destiny. This, in many respects, ideal world collapsed in large-scale wars between the gods and the giants, leading to the destruction of the world in *Ragnarök* ('final destiny of the gods'). However, after *Ragnarök* a new world emerged, indicating a circular worldview (de Vries 1970; Simek 1993, 2003; Clunies Ross 1994, 1998; Schjødt 1999; Lindow 2001; Steinsland 2005).

The mythological world described here is first and foremost based on Scandinavian sources, but the concepts of all the major supernatural powers are found in other Germanic languages, too. The names of three gods (Tyr, Odin, and Thor) and one goddess (Frigga) are also found in the early Germanic translation of the Roman weekdays, based on the Roman divinities Mars, Mercury, Jupiter, and Venus. According to Tacitus the Germanic high god was called Mercury and the Germanic war god was called Mars, which according to the translation of the weekdays should represent Odin and Tyr. Tacitus also mentioned a fertility goddess or 'mother Earth' called *Nerthus*, which is a cognate to the Scandinavian god *Njord*. Apart from these direct references, the names of the sky god Tyr and the protogiant Ymir also indicate vast connections in time and space. Tyr is a cognate of Greek Zeus and Roman Jupiter as well as Sanskrit Dyas and Baltic Dievas, whereas Ymir is etymologically related to Sanskrit Yama (de Vries 1970; Simek 1993).

The mythological narratives are full of different supernatural powers, but only a handful of them seem to have been ritually important for people living in the centuries before the Christian conversion. According to sacral place names in mainland Scandinavia the most important ritual divinities were the three *Vanir*-divinities and the four *Æsir*-gods mentioned above. Special rituals for elves and disir (goddesses of fate) are mentioned in texts and known from a few place names (Brink 2001; Vikstrand 2001). Whether giants and dwarfs were parts of rituals is disputed, but not totally impossible (Steinsland 1986).

Written descriptions of rituals and ritual specialists are often vague, but there is enough information from many different sources to suggest a spectrum from large public rituals taking place at specific intervals, sometimes every ninth year, to small private rituals going on more regularly. Descriptions, as well as different concepts connected to rituals, indicate killing animals, sacrificing blood, boiling meat, and drinking. Human sacrifices are mentioned at special occasions, but it is unclear whether this could have been connected with punishment or prisoners of war (Green 1998; Näsström 2002; Steinsland 2005; Steinsland and Vogt 1981; cf. Düwel 1985).

Concepts as well as personal names and place names indicate that both men and women could be ritual specialists. Since some ruling families began to claim divine descent from the fifth and sixth centuries onwards, several rulers also acted as ritual specialists. Some ritual terms emphasized people who had special skills in remembering, speaking, reading, seeing, and transforming things (Green 1998; Sundqvist 2002, 2007). A special dimension of ritual practice was the Old Norse form of divination or *sejdr*, when a person was supposed to leave his or her body in the disguise of an animal. Many scholars see *sejdr* as an Old Norse form of Eurasian shamanism, but the character and background for the shamanistic traits in *sejdr* are much disputed (Strömbäck 1935; Hedeager 1997; Price 2002; Raudvere 2002; Solli 2002).

2 ARCHAEOLOGY OF OLD NORSE AND GERMANIC RELIGION

Archaeology has played a varying role in the study of Old Norse and Germanic religion. The first comprehensive investigation of Old Norse religion was made by the Danish archaeologist Henry Petersen in 1876 (Petersen 1876). In many cases archaeology has been reduced to a means of illustrating phenomena already known from written documents. However, in the last decades, archaeology has begun to play a more active role in this field. Questions of temporal change, spatial and social variation, foreign influences and hybridization, as well as new aspects of mythology, cosmology, and ritual practice have been raised (Andrén et al. 2006).

2.1 Mythology and Cosmology

The narrative form of Icelandic mythology was highly complex skaldic poetry, with metaphors in several layers, with unusual word orders and with sound associations binding the words and verses together (Clunies Ross 2005). Several scholars have pointed to the contemporary animal art as an analogue form of expression, with animals binding the ornaments together and with more or less hidden humans and animals recalling the hidden meaning of the metaphors. Animal art was used from the early fifth century until the twelfth century in many parts of Northern Europe (Johansen 1979; Hedeager 1997; Andrén 2000; Høilund Nielsen and Vellev 2002; Domeij Lundborg 2006).

The content of the complex mythological world that is known to us from the Icelandic sources can in some cases be related to material culture dated to the centuries before the Christian conversion. The best parallels to the Icelandic texts are large picture stones dated to the ninth and tenth centures on the island of Gotland. Images of Odin on his eight-legged horse Sleipner can be identified as well as images of the smith Völund (Wayland the Smith),

FIGURE 52.1 The picture stone from Ardre on Gotland, dated to about AD 800. On top of the stone is a scene with Odin on his eight-legged horse Sleipner, probably approaching Valhall, where a valkyrie (female warrior) is holding a drinking cup. In the middle panel is a representation of the story of Wayland the smith, who has just decapitated two royal sons in his smithy, and is fleeing in the disguise of a bird.

which are also known from the Anglo-Saxon Frank's casket (Figure 52.1). Probably, several representations of the well-known narratives around Sigurd Fafnisbani are attested on some of the largest and best-executed picture stones on Gotland. Apart from the Gotlandic picture stones, several Swedish runestones from the eleventh century also contain images related to the Icelandic narratives (Lindquist 1941–2; Buisson 1976; Andrén 1993).

Although Odin was depicted on Gotlandic picture stones, the gods and goddesses were above all represented via figurines, amulets, pendants, fibulas, and images on weapons. Many images of Odin can be reasonably well identified on golden bracteates from the fifth and sixth centuries, as well as on helmets and other weapons from the seventh century onwards. Predominantly, he is depicted as a rider, with a spear and his two ravens who collected news from all over the world. In a few cases it is especially marked that one of Odin's eyes was blind. An early golden bracteate from Östergötland dated to the fifth century probably depicts the sky god Tyr, when he puts his hand in the mouth of the wolf Fenrir (Hauck et al. 1985-9). The thunder god Thor is largely represented through his attribute, the hammer Mjölnir. Silver pendants of Thor's hammer are well known in the whole of Scandinavia during the ninth, tenth, and eleventh centuries. In central Sweden iron neck-rings with small hammers and sickles are also common in cremation graves during the same period. Also Thor's hammer is depicted on some runestones, and a few runestone-texts from the tenth century end with invocations to Thor (Staecker 1999). A small bronze figurine of a seated man with a large phallus from Rällinge in Södermanland, from the ninth-tenth centuries, can probably be a representation of the fertility god Freyr. Similarly, a silver pendant of a woman with an enormous necklace from Aska in Östergötland dated to the ninth century can be reasonably interpreted as an image of the fertility goddess Freya, with her famous necklace Brisingamen, which in the Anglo-Saxon tradition is known as Brosinga Mene (Arbman 1936).

Although the attributions of the divine images always will be provisional (Price 2006), it is remarkable that no images dated before AD 400-550 have been convincingly identified with divinities known from the Icelandic tradition (cf. van der Sanden and Capelle 2001). A similar iconographical shift can be followed in the Gotlandic picture stones. The images on the early monuments from AD 200-550 seem to refer to other mythological narratives, centred around a solar myth (Gelling and Davidson 1969). This has led some archaeologists to propose a drastic change to a new Æsir-religion in the fifth and sixth centuries, centred around the high god Odin (Hedeager 1997). However, if the interpretation of Tacitus' account of Mercury (Odin), Mars (Tyr), and Nerthus (Njord/Njärd) is correct, some of the main gods must have existed in Northern Europe already in the first century AD (Simek 1993, 2003). Therefore another, more plausible, explanation of the pictorial shift in the fifth and sixth centuries is that the character of gods, and consequently the stories about them, changed (Kaliff and Sundqvist 2004). This explanation can be futher supported by the fact that animal art, as an analogue form to the skaldic poetry, was created in the early fifth century. Before this period not only the content but also the narrative form of the divine stories must have been different.

A higher degree of long-term continuity can be traced for more formalized representations of the northern cosmology. The world tree, as well as the idea of Midgard itself, were expressed through material culture in specific formalized ways. I have argued that three-pointed stone-settings ('tricorn'), often with a monolith stone or a wooden post in the centre, can be interpreted as representations of the world tree, with its trunk and three roots. Three-pointed stone-settings are dated from the first century AD until the tenth century, and they are found in Sweden and Norway. Many of them are found as single monuments in the centre of large burial grounds. Some of them are cremation graves whereas others, only containing charcoal, may have been the sites of the cremations (Andrén 2004). A variation of the same theme can be rings of large stones, sometimes with a monolith in the middle. These monuments can be regarded as a model of Midgard itself, with the world tree in the middle surrounded by many worlds. The number of stones is usually uneven, and most common are seven or nine stones, recalling the nine worlds surrounding the world tree. These monuments mark out cremation graves from the first centuries BC until about AD 700. They are found in Norway, Sweden, eastern Denmark, and northern Germany (Andrén 2006).

Similar ideas can also be traced in the layout of some ringforts from the period AD 200–650 on the island of Öland. The best example is the ringfort at Ismantorp, built around AD 200 (Figure 52.2). In the middle of the fort was a triangular place with a small house and a large post, representing the world tree. Around the centre were about 95 houses inside a large stone wall with nine gates, again representing the nine worlds around the world tree. In this case Old Norse cosmology was inscribed into a military order, in the same way as Roman cosmology was represented in contemporary Roman fortresses (Andrén 2006). It is worth underlining that these cosmological symbols transgress the iconographic shift of divine representations in the fifth and sixth centuries, and can be followed back at least a few centuries BC. This continuity speaks in favour of more successive changes of the divine figures and their character rather than a drastic introduction of a new religion.

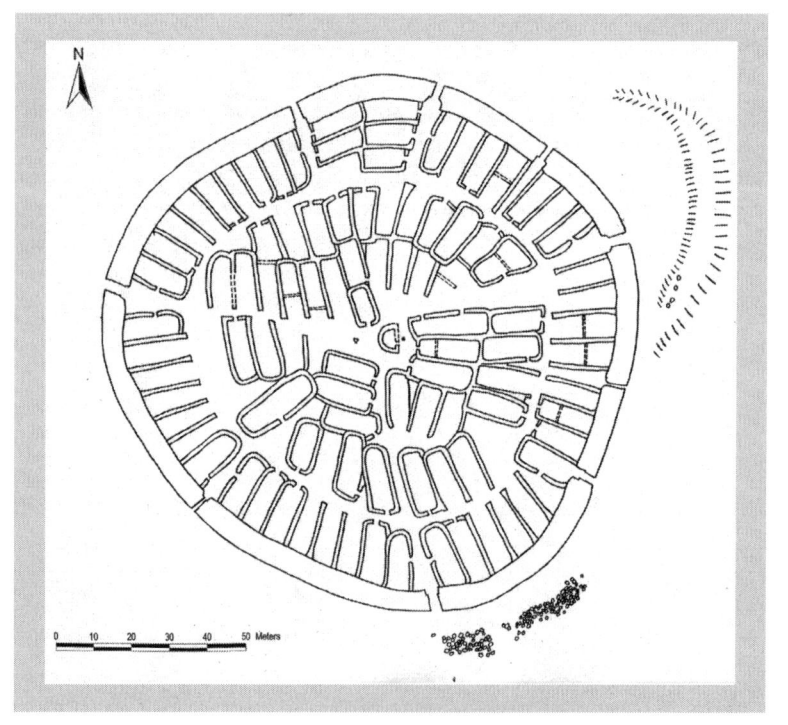

FIGURE 52.2 Plan of the ring-fort at Ismantorp on Öland, which was used temporarily between AD 200–650. The site consists of a large stone wall with nine gates, about 95 houses, and a central triangular place with a small house and a large post. The layout of the ring-fort can be interpreted as a large scale representation of Old Norse cosmology, with the world tree in the middle of the world, surrounded by nine worlds.

2.2 Rituals

In contrast to the literary background of mythology and cosmology, the primary source for rituals and ritual sites is to a large extent archaeology. Written sources are very vague about rituals, whereas the material remains of ritual sites can be continuously investigated. Besides, Old Norse and Germanic religion had no holy scripture, but was basically a ritually and orally performed tradition. At the time of the conversion it was called *forn sidr*—that is, 'the old custom' or 'the old way of living', clearly emphasizing the ritual aspects of that tradition. Consequently, archaeology has a very central role in understanding the ritual basis of Old Norse and Germanic religion, very much in line with current ritual theory (Bell 1992; Humphrey and Laidlaw 1994).

It is well known that wetlands and lakes were the classical ritual sites in many periods of North European prehistory. Small-scale deposits of objects were made in the Neolithic as well as the Bronze Age (Stjernquist 1997; Müller-Wille 1999). However, it was not until the fifth to third centuries BC that large-scale deposits occured, with everyday objects, animals, or weapons. One example of a site with everyday objects is the small lake Käringsjön ('Hage Lake') in Halland, with deposits from the first four centuries AD (Carlie 1998). On the edge of the shore were wooden platforms, beside which pots containing food and drink were deposited as well as offerings such as bunches of flax, stones wrapped in bast rope, and various wooden tools. The little lake has been interpreted as a site for seasonal rituals, probably performed by women only, and addressed to fertility divinities such as disir and female elves.

An example of large-scale deposits including weapons is provided by Skedemosse on Öland (Hagberg 1967a, 1967b). Huge quantities of animals, humans, weapons, and gold objects were thrown into this shallow lake from the fifth century BC until the tenth century AD. Although only fractions of the lake have been excavated, remains of a total of 38 young and old people of both sexes have been found, along with 100 horses, 80 cattle, 60 sheep and goats, 15 pigs, and 7 dogs. On several occasions during the period AD 200–500, many destroyed weapons and seven gold rings were also deposited in the lake. The name of the site may refer to horse races and stallion baiting, underlining the significance of horses and their slaughter. The weapon deposits in Skedemosse had many contemporary parallels in Southern Scandinavia. The best-known site is Illerup ådal in central Jutland, where an estimated 10,000 weapons were deposited on just one occasion around AD 200 (Ilkjær 2000; Jørgensen et al. 2003). These large scale weapon deposits were clearly inspired by the contemporary Roman triumphs, where weapons from vanquished armies were displayed in the same way and deposited in sanctuaries (Andrén 2007). After about AD 500 the large-scale wetland deposits disappeared, but rituals on a smaller scale continued along lakes and rivers until the eleventh century (Zachrisson 2004a).

Less is known about rituals on dry land, but some sites have been discovered in the last few decades. At Lunda (meaning 'grove') in Södermanland a small hill representing the grove has been found close to a contemporary settlement (Andersson 2006; Andersson and Skyllberg 2008). On the hill burnt bones of domesticated animals, above all piglets, burnt clay, pieces of resin, as well as unburnt beads, knives, and arrowheads were spread from the second century BC until the tenth century AD. A lone tree could also be the focus of rituals, as is shown by a root found on Frösö ('island of Freyr') in Jämtland (Hildebrandt 1989). At the foot of a large birch were bones of bear, elk, and red deer, but also pigs, sheep/goats, and cattle deposited in the ninth and tenth centuries. The birch can be interpreted as a sacrificial tree, representing the world tree at the centre of the world.

Ritual deposits were often relatively well demarcated through natural boundaries, such as lakes, bogs, or hills. But there are also sacral place names indicating that a particularly holy site could be marked off by ropes (*vébönd*) and known as a *vé* or 'sanctuary'. At Ullevi in Östergötland, one such site from the period 400 BC–AD 400 has been excavated (Nielsen 2005). The site consists of an irregular rectangular area, demarcated with posts and connected with a contemporary settlement by a paved road. Inside the enclosure about 40 hearths and cooking pits have been found, with burnt and unburnt bones from domesticated animals. The demarcated area and the name of the place show that this was a local 'sanctuary' to the god Ullr.

For a long time it has been disputed whether ritual buildings existed in Old Norse religion (Olsen 1966; McNicol 1997). However, the last 20 years have witnessed a virtual archaeological breakthrough in the study of cult houses and their spatial contexts. Above all ritual buildings have been found in 'central places', with political, religious, judicial, and mercantile functions. To date around 20 central places are known from Denmark, central Sweden, and probably southern Norway. The largest central places, which were highly complex, cover areas up to 50 ha. Many of them have general sacral names, such as Gudme ('Home of Gods'), Vä ('Holy Place'), and Helgö ('Holy Island'). In several cases the layout of the central places seems to have referred to Old Norse world views, thus combining cosmology with rituals (Hårdh and Larsson 2002; Hedeager 2002; Jørgensen 2002; Zachrisson 2004b).

Only two of the central places, Lejre on Sjælland and Uppsala in Uppland, are known from written sources from the tenth and eleventh centuries. Both are described as royal seats with large-scale sacrifices every ninth year, including human sacrifices (Hultgård 1997; Ljungkvist 2006; Niles et al. 2007). The longest continuity can be traced in Uppåkra in Skåne which functioned from the second century BC until the end of the tenth century AD (Larsson and Hårdh 2003). Many of the other central places were established around AD 200, although their importance varied through time. Most of them lost their central functions at the Christian conversion, and were replaced by new Christian cities in the tenth and eleventh centuries.

Important elements in these central places were very large halls with ritual traces and in some cases specific ritual buildings beside the halls. The best-known example comes from Uppåkra, where a small but solid and probably tall house stood on a platform in the middle of the settlement. The house was first built in the third or fourth centuries and later rebuilt eight times until around 800 when it was replaced by another kind of building. It was surrounded by animal bones from large-scale slaughter, and by destroyed weapons placed in a circle around the house. Inside the house, many objects with ritual associations have been found, such as gold foil figures, two large iron rings, a large glass bowl and a gilded silver 'chalice' with decoration in animal art (Larsson 2004; cf. Ratke and Simek 2006). Another example of a ritual building, from the eighth to the tenth centuries, has been found at Borg in Östergötland. It was a small log building, with a paved yard and a bare rock in front of the house. The yard contained traces of iron forging, and huge quantities of bones from domestic animals, above all boars and sows, that were deposited in different parts of the yard. Along the bare rock about a hundred iron amulets in the shape of fire-steels were deposited (Nielsen 1997). Ritual buildings seem to have been introduced in Scandinavia in the third, fourth, and fifth centuries. They were probably modelled after early Christian churches in the Roman Empire, which represented a similar change in use of ritual space, from open air rituals around altars to indoor rituals (Andrén 2007). The new ritual buildings in Scandinavia must also be seen as important parts of political and religious change at that time (Fabech 1991). These changes led to ruling families claiming divine descent as well as the development of new narrative traditions around the gods and goddesses, which became the historical background for the Icelandic literature.

Apart from rituals at demarcated cult sites, people's everyday lives were ritualized in a way that we only partly can recognize. These rites were in large measure a matter of transforming people and things. The rituals were primarily part of the actual transformation, although they could sometimes also refer to the divine powers and the cosmology. Through different rites of passage seen via archaeology people continousely changed their identity. The clearest rites of passage are the burials (Müller-Wille 1970; Näsman 1994; Artelius and Svanberg 2005). There were significant variations in mortuary practice during the whole Iron Age. The dead could be buried in pits, wooden coffins, wooden chambers, boats, or stone cists. The dead could also be cremated, and the burnt bones could be left lying at the site of the pyre, buried in pits, placed in pots and kegs, or partly spread outside the burial grounds. Occasional very richly furnished graves were filled with objects, pots of food and drink, and sacrificed animals, while others contained only remains of the dead person's dress, and many had no finds other than the bones of the deceased. The graves could be invisible, with no external markers, or clearly manifested through burial mounds or stone settings and standing stones in various geometrical figures. Most people were buried in burial grounds, but solitary graves are also known. Different mortuary practices show distinct ritual diversity between different regions (Svanberg 2003a, 2003b). This indicates that Old Norse religion from a ritual perspective must be regarded as a series of partly overlapping traditions, differing in space and social context.

Everyday rituals were not only associated with humans but also with the transformation of material culture, such as iron production, bronze-casting, goldsmithing, weaving, leather crafts, and building of houses. In recent years several archaeological studies have focused on these issues (Burström 1990; Carlie 2004; Gansum 2004; Falk 2006; Heide 2006), especially in respect to iron production. As in many other cultures refinement of iron has been perceived as an adjustment of an already created world, which meant that smiths had to master rituals that controlled the powers of the world (Haaland 2004; Barndon 2006). Ritualized transformation might explain why specialized smithwork often appears at cult sites, why a blast nozzle could have mythological motifs, why human bones were used to make steel and why iron slag can be found in graves in some parts of Scandinavia.

Ritual specialists are known from Icelandic texts, runic inscriptions, personal names, and place names, but they are hard to find through material culture. The best attempts to recognize ritual specialists are in regard to women connected with *sejdr*. Through detailed descriptions of their appearance it has been possible to point out a series of graves from the ninth–tenth centuries, where women were buried with iron staffs and other specific objects, such as the claws of wild animals (Price 2002; Heide 2006). Some scholars point towards a Saami shamanistic origin of *sejdr*, whereas others underline a much greater time-depth, because graves with shamanistic traits are found already in the Bronze Age (Kaul 1998).

3 WIDER PERSPECTIVES IN TIME AND SPACE

Old Norse and Germanic religion has predominantly been discussed in relation to the archaeology of the Iron Age in Northern Europe, i.e. 500 BC–AD 1000. Possible links to rituals and iconography in Bronze Age Scandinavia (1700–500 BC) is much more disputed, but not totally unreasonable. The iconographical world of rock carvings and bronze objects coincides spatially with the much later sacral place names. Recently a specific Scandinavian Bronze Age religion has been outlined, centred around the daily cycle of the sun and the twin motif of men, warriors, riders, or horses (Randsborg 1993; Kaul 1998; 2004). This religion is supposed to disappear around 500 BC at the end of the Bronze Age. However, there seems to be an overlap since some of the Bronze Age symbols, such as the wheel cross, is known from later on. Besides the solar cycle and the twin motifs are clearly present on the early picture stones on Gotland during the third to fifth centuries AD. Even in the early thirteenth century AD, Snorri can describe how the sun was drawn over heaven by a horse, in a way very similar to the the famous sun chariot from Trundholm, dated to the fifteenth century BC (Gelling and Davidson 1969).

The best way to interpret these long-term traits is to regard Old Norse religion as a cultural patchwork, without any common origin (Andrén 2007). Instead, the tradition can be viewed as consisting of varying elements, introduced as part of social strategies at different periods and influenced from different regions. Some general elements, such as the role of the sun and shamanism, may go back to the early Bronze Age, with inspiration from the east Mediterranean as well as the circumpolar region. Other elements such as an ordered cosmology and large-scale wetland deposits may go back to the Iron Age, possibly inspired by the Mediterranean world and above all the Roman Empire. Ritual buildings, divine figures, and skaldic poetry, however, were introduced when aristocratic families began to claim divine descent. They were part of a new political landscape during the Migration period, when large-scale transformation of the late Roman Christian world occured in many parts of Europe. Finally, some aspects of northern paganism may be viewed as reactions against the Christian mission from the ninth century onwards.

Several promising archaeological issues regarding Old Norse religion have been raised in recent years. They concern long-term perspectives as well as cultural and religious interactions and hybridizations. Other new areas to consider are further investigations of rituals and ritual sites, from which new results are obtained nearly every year. In the future not only the layout of the sites and the rituals in general will be studied, but also the social, regional, and seasonal aspects of rituals and their elements.

SUGGESTED READING

The most comprehensive survey of Old Norse and Germanic religion based on written sources and place names is still de Vries (1970), although the general perspectives and most references to archaeology are outdated. More recent overviews are those of Clunies Ross (1994, 1998); DuBois (1999); Lindow (2001); Simek (2003); and Steinsland (2005), although their references to archaeology are fairly limited. For the moment no comprehensive survey of the archaeology of Old Norse and Germanic religion exists, since the archaeological breakthrough of the last decades has not been properly summarized. Instead, important archaeological aspects of the study of Old Norse and Germanic religion are found in archaeological reports, articles and monographs on specific issues (for instance Nielsen 1997; Carlie 1998; Ilkjær 2000; Jørgensen 2002; Price 2002; Larsson 2004; Zachrisson 2004b; Artelius and Svanberg 2005; Andrén et al. 2006; Andersson and Skyllberg 2008).

REFERENCES

ALLZÉN, B. 1990. *Tid för vikingar: Vikingatid lanseras i nordisk konst*, Malmö Museers årsbok 1990 (Malmö: Malmö museer).
ANDERSSON, G. 2006. 'Among trees, bones and stones: The Sacred Grove at Lunda' in A. Andrén, K. Jennbert, and C. Raudvere (eds), *Old Norse Religion in Long-term Perspectives: Origins, changes, and interactions*, Vägar till Midgård 8 (Lund: Nordic Academic Press), pp. 195–9.
—— and SKYLLBERG, E. (eds) 2008. *Gestalter och gestaltningar: Om tid, rum och händelser på Lunda* (Stockholm: Riksantikvarieämbetet).
ANDRÉN, A. 1993. 'Doors to other worlds: Scandinavian death rituals in Gotlandic perspectives', *Journal of European Archaeology*, 1: 33–56.
——2000. 'Re-reading embodied texts: An interpretation of rune-stones', *Current Swedish Archaeology*, 8: 7–32.
——2004. 'I skuggan av Yggdrasil: Trädet mellan idé och realitet i nordisk tradition' in A. Andrén, K. Jennbert, and C. Raudvere (eds), *Ordning mot kaos: Studier av nordisk förkristen kosmologi*, Vägar till Midgård 4 (Lund: Nordic Academic Press), pp. 389–430.
——2006. 'A world of stone: Warrior culture, hybridity, and Old Norse cosmology' in A. Andrén, K. Jennbert, and C. Raudvere (eds), *Old Norse Religion in Long-term Perspectives. Origins, changes, and interactions*, Vägar till Midgård 8 (Lund: Nordic Academic Press), pp. 33–8.
——2007. 'Behind *Heathendom*: Archaeological studies of Old Norse religion', *Scottish Archaeological Journal*, 27(2): 105–38.
——, JENNBERT, K., and RAUDVERE, C. (eds) 2006. *Old Norse Religion in Long-term Perspectives: Origins, changes, and interactions*, Vägar till Midgård 8 (Lund: Nordic Academic Press).
ARBMAN, H. 1936. *Människoframställningar i vår forntida konst*, Ur Statens historiska museums samlingar 4 (Stockholm: Statens historiska museum).
ARTELIUS, T. and SVANBERG, F. (eds) 2005. *Dealing with the Dead: Archaeological perspectives on prehistoric Scandinavian burial ritual* (Stockholm: Riksantikvarieämbetet and Statens Historiska Museum).
ARVIDSSON, S. 2007. *Draksjukan: Mytiska fantasier hos Tolkien, Wagner och de Vries*, Vägar till Midgård 11 (Lund: Nordic Academic Press).
BARNDON, R. 2006. 'Myth and metallurgy: Some cross-cultural reflections on the social identity of smiths' in A. Andrén, K. Jennbert, and C. Raudvere (eds), *Old Norse Religion in Long-term Perspectives: Origins, changes and interactions*, Vägar till Midgård 8 (Lund: Nordic Academic Press), pp. 99–103.

BECK, H. and ANDERSSON, T. (eds) 1992. *Germanische Religionsgeschichte: Quellen und Quellenprobleme*, Ergänzungsbände zum Reallexikon der germanischen Altertumskunde 5 (Berlin and New York: de Gruyter).

BELL, C. M. 1992. *Ritual Theory, Ritual Practice* (Oxford and New York: Oxford University Press).

BRINK, S. 2001. 'Mythologizing Landscape: Place and Space of Cult and Myth' in M. Strausberg, O. Sundqvist, and A. van Nahl (eds), *Kontinuitäten und Brücke in der Religionsgeschichte. Festschrift für Anders Hultgård zu seinem 65. Geburtstag am 23.12.2001*, Ergänzungsbände zum Reallexikon der Germanischen Altertumskunde 31 (Berlin and New York: de Gruyter), pp. 76–112.

BUISSON, L. 1976. *Der Bildstein Ardre VIII auf Gotland. Göttermythen, Heldensagen und Jenseitsglaube der Germanen im 8. Jahrhundert n. Chr.* Abhandlungen der Akademie der Wissenschaften in Göttingen. Philologisch-Historische Klasse, Dritte Folge Nr. 102 (Göttingen: Vandenhoeck and Ruprecht).

BURSTRÖM, M. 1990. 'Järnframställning och gravritual: En strukturalistisk tolkning av järnslagg i vikingatida gravar i Gästrikland', *Fornvännen*, 85: 261–71.

CARLIE, A. 1998. 'Käringsjön: A fertility sacrificial site from the Late Roman Iron Age in south west Sweden', *Current Swedish Archaeology*, 6: 17–37.

——2004. *Forntida byggnadskult: Tradition och regionalitet i södra Skandinavien*. Arkeologiska undersökningar, Skrifter 57 (Stockholm: Riksantikvarieämbetet).

CARVER, M. (ed.) 2003. *The Cross Goes North: Processes of Conversion in Northern Europe, AD 300–1300* (Woodbridge: York Medieval Press).

CLOVER, C. J. and LINDOW, J. (eds) 1985. *Old Norse-Icelandic Literature: A critical guide* (Ithaca: Cornell University Press).

CLUNIES ROSS, M. 1994. *Prolonged Echoes: Old Norse myths in a medieval northern society*, I: *The Myths*, The Viking Collection 7 (Odense: Odense University Press).

——1998. *Prolonged Echoes: Old Norse myths in a medieval northern society*, II: *The Reception of Norse Myths in Medieval Iceland*, The Viking Collection 10 (Odense: Odense University Press).

——2005. *A History of Old Norse Poetry and Poetics* (Cambridge: Brewer).

——and LÖNNROTH, L. 2001. 'Den fornnordiska musan: Rapport från ett internationellt forskningsprojekt' in C. Raudvere, A. Andrén, and K. Jennbert (eds), *Myter om det nordiska: Mellan romantik och politik*, Vägar till Midgård 1 (Lund: Nordic Academic Press), pp. 23–58.

DAVIDSON, H. R. E. 1964. *Gods and Myths of Northern Europe* (Harmondsworth: Penguin).
——1969. *Scandinavian Mythology* (London: Hamlyn).

DOMEIJ LUNDBORG, M. 2006. 'Bound animal bodies: Ornamentation and skaldic peotry in the process of Christianization' in A. Andrén, K. Jennbert, and C. Raudvere (eds), *Old Norse Religion in Long-term Perspectives: Origins, changes, and interactions*, Vägar till Midgård 8 (Lund: Nordic Acamedic Press), pp. 39–44.

DUBOIS, T. 1999. *Nordic Religions in the Viking Age* (Philadelphia: University of Pennsylvania Press).

DUMÉZIL, G. 1973. *Gods of the Ancient Northmen* (Berkeley: University of California Press).

DÜWEL, K. 1985. *Das Opferfest von Lade: Quellenkritische Undersuchungen zur germanische Religionsgeschichte*, Wiener Arbeiten zur germanischen Altertumskunde und Philologie 27 (Vienna: K. M. Halosar).

FABECH, C. 1991. 'Samfundsorganisation, religiøse ceremonier og regional variation' in C. Fabech and J. Ringtved (eds), *Samfundsorganisation og Regional Variation: Norden i romersk jernalder og folkevandringstid*, Jysk Arkæologisk Selskabs Skrifter 27 (Århus: Aarhus Universitetsforlag), pp. 283–303.

FALK, A.-B. 2006. 'My home is my castle: Protection against evil in medieval times' in A. Andrén, K. Jennbert, and C. Raudvere (eds), *Old Norse Religion in Long-term Perspectives: Origins, changes, and interactions*, Vägar till Midgård 8 (Lund: Nordic Acamedic Press), pp. 200–5.

FISCHER, S. 2005. *Roman Imperialism and Runic Literacy: The Westernization of Northern Europe (150–800 AD)*, Aun 33 (Uppsala: Department of Archaeology and Ancient History).

GANSUM, T. 2004. 'Jernets fødsel og dødens stål: Rituell bruk av bein' in Å. Berggren, S. Arvidsson, and A.-M. Hållans (eds), *Minne och myt: Konsten att skapa det förflutna*, Vägar till Midgård 5 (Lund: Nordic Academic Press), pp. 121–55.

GELLING, P. and DAVIDSON, H. R. E. 1969. *The Chariot of the Sun and other Rites and Symbols of the Northern Bronze Age* (London: Dent).

GRÄSLUND, B. 1993. 'Folkvandringstidens Uppsala: Namn, myter, arkeologi och historia', *Kärnhuset i riksäpplet. Upplands fornminnesförening och hembygdsförbunds årsbok. Uppland*, 1993: 173–208.

GREEN, D. H. 1998. *Language and History in the Early Germanic World* (Cambridge: Cambridge University Press).

GREGORIUS, F. 2006. 'The "Allgermanische Heidnische Front" and Old Norse religion' in A. Andrén, K. Jennbert, and C. Raudvere, (eds), *Old Norse Religion in Long-term Perspectives. Origins, changes, and interactions*, Vägar till Midgård 8 (Lund: Nordic Acamedic Press), pp. 389–92.

GUNNELL, T. 1995. *The Origins of Drama in Scandinavia* (Cambridge: Brewer).

HAALAND, R. 2004. 'Technology, transformation and symbolism: Ethnographic perspectives on European iron working', *Norwegian Archaeological Review*, 37: 1–19.

HAGBERG, U. E. 1967a. *The Archaeology of Skedemosse, I: The Excavations and Finds of an Öland Fen, Sweden* (Stockholm: Almqvist and Wiksell International).

——1967b. *The Archaeology of Skedemosse, II: The Votive Deposits in the Skedemosse Fen and their Relation to the Iron Age Settlement on Öland, Sweden* (Stockholm: Almqvist and Wiksell International).

HÅRDH, B. and LARSSON, L. (eds) 2002. *Central Places in the Migration and Merovingian Periods: Papers from the 52nd Sachsensymposium, Lund, August 2001*, Uppåkrastudier 6 and Acta Archaeologica Lundensia, Series in 8°, No. 39 (Stockholm: Almqvist and Wiksell International).

HAUCKE, K., AXBOE, M., DÜWEL, K., et al. 1985–9. *Die Goldbrakteaten der Völkerwanderungszeit: Ikonographischer Katalog 1–3*. Münstersche Mittelalterschriften 24: 1–3.

HEDEAGER, L. 1997. *Skygger af en anden virkelighed. Oldnordiske myter* (Copenhagen: Samleren).

——2002. 'Scandinavian "Central Places" in a cosmological setting' in B. Hårdh and L. Larsson (eds), *Central Places in the Migration and Merovingian Periods: Papers from the 52nd Sachsensymposium, Lund, August 2001*, Uppåkrastudier 6 and Acta Archaeologica Lundensia, Series in 8°, No. 39 (Stockholm: Almqvist and Wiksell International), pp. 3–18.

HEIDE, E. 2006. 'Spinning seidr' in A. Andrén, K. Jennbert, and C. Raudvere (eds), *Old Norse Religion in Long-Term Perspectives: Origins, Changes, and Interactions* (Vägar till Midgård 8 (Lund: Nordic Academic Press).

HILDEBRANDT, M. 1989. 'Frösö kyrka byggd på hednisk grund?' in O. Hemmendorff (ed.), *Arkeologi i fjäll, skog och bygd 2: Järnålder och medeltid*, Fornvårdaren 24 (Östersund: Jämtlands läns museum), pp. 153–66.

HØILUND NIELSEN, K. and VELLEV, J. (eds) 2002. 'Nordeuropæisk dyrestil 400–1100 e. Kr.' *Hikuin*, 29.

HULTGÅRD, A. (ed.) 1997. *Uppsala-kulten och Adam av Bremen* (Nora: Nya Doxa).

HUMPHREY, C. and LAIDLAW, J. 1994. *The Archetypal Action of Ritual: A theory of ritual illustrated by the Jain rite of worship* (Oxford: Clarendon Press).

ILKJÆR, J. 2000. *Illerup Ådal: Et arkæologisk tryllespejl* (Moesgård: Moesgård Museum).

JANSON, H. 1998. *Templum nobilissimum: Adam av Bremen, Uppsalatemplet och konfliktlinjerna i Europa kring år 1075*, Avhandlingar från Historiska institutionen i Göteborg 21 (Gothenburg: Department of History).

——2006. 'The organism within: On the construction of non-Christian Germanic nature' in A. Andrén, K. Jennbert, and C. Raudvere (eds), *Old Norse Religion in Long-term Perspectives: Origins, changes, and interactions*, Vägar till Midgård 8 (Lund: Nordic Academic Press), pp. 393–8.

JOHANSEN, A. B. 1979. *Nordisk dyrestil: Bakgrunn og opphav*, AmS-skrifter 3 (Stavanger: Arkeologisk museum i Stavanger).

JØRGENSEN, L. 2002. 'Kongsgård – kultsted – marked. Overvejelser omkring Tissøkompleksets struktur og funktion' in K. Jennbert, A. Andrén, and C. Raudvere (eds), *Plats och praxis: Studier av nordisk förkristen ritual*, Vägar till Midgård 2 (Lund: Nordic Academic Press), pp. 215–47.

——, STORGAARD B., and GEBAUER THOMSEN, L. (eds) 2003. *Sejrens triumf: Norden i skyggen af det romerske imperium* (Copenhagen: Nationalmuseet).

KALIFF, A. and SUNDQVIST, O. 2004. *Oden och Mithraskulten: Religiös ackulturation under romersk järnålder och folkvandringstid*, Occasional Papers in Archaeology 35 (Uppsala: Department of Archaeology and Ancient History).

KAUL, F. 1998. *Ships on Bronzes: A study in Bronze Age religion and iconography 1–2* (Copenhagen: National Museum).

——2004. *Bronzealderens religion: Studier af den nordiske bronzealders ikonografi* (Copenhagen: Det kongelige nordiske oldskriftselskab).

LARSSON, L. (ed.) 2004. *Continuity for Centuries: A ceremonial building and its context at Uppåkra, southern Sweden*, Uppåkrastudier 10 and Acta Archaeologica Lundensia, Series in 8°, No. 48 (Stockholm: Almqvist and Wiksell International).

——and HÅRDH, B. (eds) 2003. *Centrality—regionality: The social structure of southern Sweden during the Iron Age*, Uppåkrastudier 7 and Acta Archaeologica Lundensia, Series in 8°, No. 40 (Stockholm: Almqvist and Wiksell International).

LINDOW, J. 2001. *Handbook of Norse Mythology* (Santa Barbara, CA: ABC-Clio).

——, LÖNNROTH, L., and WEBER, G. W. (eds) 1986. *Structure and Meaning in Old Norse Literature: New approaches to textual analysis and literary criticism*, Viking Collection 3 (Odense: Odense University Press).

LINDQVIST, S. 1941-2. *Gotlands Bildsteine* (Stockholm: Kungliga Vitterhets, Historie och Antikvitetsakademien).

LJUNGKVIST, J. 2006. *En hiar atti rikR: Om elit, struktur och ekonomi kring Uppsala och Mälaren under yngre järnåldern*, Aun 34 (Uppsala: Department of Archaeology and Ancient History).

MCNICOL, J. 1997. *Plasseringen av de første kirkene i Norge i forhold til de hedenske kultstederne. En historiografisk studie omfattende tiden etter 1830*, Kults skriftserie 98 (Oslo: Norges forskningsråd).

MEULENGRACHT SØRENSEN, P. 1993. *Fortælling og ære: Studier i islændingesagaerne* (Århus: Aarhus universitetsforlag).
MÜLLER-WILLE, M. 1970. 'Bestattung im Boot: Studien zu einer nordeuropäischen Grabsitte', *Offa*, 25–6.
——(ed.) 1997. *Rom und Byzanz im Norden: Mission und Glaubenswechsel im Ostseeraum während des 8.–14. Jahrhunderts*, I–II, Akademie der Wissenschaften und der Literatur, Mainz. Abhandlungen der Geistes- und Sozialwissenschaftlichen Klasse, Jahrgang 1997: 3, I–II (Stuttgart: Franz Steiner Verlag).
——1999. *Opferkulte der Germanen und Slawen*, Archäologie in Deutschland, Sonderheft (Stuttgart: Theiss).
NÄSMAN, U. 1994. 'Liv och död: Sydskandinaviska grav- och offerriter från 200 till 1000 e. Kr.' in J. P. Schjødt (ed.), *Myte og ritual i det førkristne Norden* (Odense: Odense Universitetsforlag), pp. 73–94.
NÄSSTRÖM, B.-M. 2002. *Blot: Tro och offer i det förkristna Norden* (Stockholm: Norstedts).
NIELSEN, A.-L. 1997. 'Pagan cultic and votive acts at Borg: Expression of the central significance of the farmstead in the Late Iron Age' in H. Andersson, P. Carelli, and L. Ersgård (eds), *Visions of the Past: Trends and traditions in Swedish medieval archaeology*, Lund Studies in Medieval Archaeology 19 and Riksantikvarieämbetet, Arkeologiska undersökningar, Skrifter 24 (Stockholm: Almqvist and Wiksell International), pp. 372–92.
——2005. 'Under Biltema och Ikea: Ullevi under 1500 år' in A. Kaliff and G. Tagesson (eds), *Liunga. Kaupinga. Kulturhistoria och arkeologi i Linköpingsbygden*, Arkeologiska undersökningar, Skrifter 60 (Stockholm: Riksantikvarieämbetet), pp. 204–35.
NILES, J. D., CHRISTENSEN, T., and OSBORN, M. (eds) 2007. *Beowulf and Lejre* (Tempe, AZ: Arizona Center for Medieval and Renaissance Studies).
NILSSON, B. (ed.) 1996. *Kristnandet i Sverige. Gamla källor och nya perspektiv*, Sveriges Kristnande, Publikationer 5 (Uppsala: Lunne böcker).
ODENSTEDT, B. 1990. *On the Origin and Early History of the Runic Script: Typology and graphic variation in the older Futhark*, Acta Academiae Regiae Gustavi Adolphi 59 (Uppsala: Kungliga Gustav Adolfs Akademien for svensk folkkultur).
OLSEN, O. 1966. 'Hørg, hov og kirke: Historiske og arkæologiske vikingetidsstudier', *Aarbøger for nordisk Oldkyndighed*, 1965: 1–307.
PETERSEN, H. 1876. *Om nordboernes gudedyrkelse og gudetro i hedenold: En antikvarisk undersøgelse* (Copenhagen: Reitzel).
PRICE, N. S. 2002. *The Viking Way: Religion and war in Late Iron Age Scandinavia*, Aun 31 (Uppsala: Department of Archaeology and Ancient History).
——2006. 'What's in a name?' in A. Andrén, K. Jennbert, and C. Raudvere (eds), *Old Norse Religion in Long-Term Perspectives: Origins, Changes, and Interactions*, Väger till Midgård 8 (Lund: Nordic Academic Press), pp. 179–183.
RANDSBORG, K. 1993. 'Kivik: Archaeology and iconography', *Acta Archaeologica*, 64(1): 1–147.
RATKE, S. and SIMEK, R. 2006. '"Guldgubber": Relics of pre-Christian law rituals?' in A. Andrén, K. Jennbert, and C. Raudvere (eds), *Old Norse Religion in Long-term Perspectives: Origins, changes, and interactions*, Vägar till Midgård 8 (Lund: Nordic Academic Press), pp. 259–66.
RAUDVERE, C. 2002. 'Trolldomr in Early Medieval Scandinavia' in B. Ankarloo and S. Clark (eds), *Witchcraft and Magic in Europe* (London: Athlone), pp. 73–172.
——, ANDRÉN, A., and JENNBERT, K. (eds) 2001. *Myter om det nordiska: Mellan romantik och politik*, Vägar till Midgård 1 (Lund: Nordic Academic Press).

Raudvere, C., Andrén, A., and Jennbert, K. (eds). 2005. *Hedendomen i historiens spegel: Bilder av det förkristna Norden*, Vägar till Midgård 6 (Lund: Nordic Academic Press).

Roesdahl, E. and Meulengracht Sørensen, P. (eds) 1996. *The Waking of Angatyr: The Scandinavian past in European culture*, Acta Jutlandica 71:1, Humanities Series 70 (Århus: Aarhus University Press).

Sanden, W. van der and Capelle, T. 2001. *Immortal Images: Ancient anthropomorphic wood carvings from Northern and Western Europe* (Silkeborg: Silkeborg Museum).

Schjødt, J. P. 1999. *Det førkristne Norden: Religion og mytologi* (Copenhagen: Spektrum).

Simek, R. 1993. *Dictionary of Northern Mythology* (Cambridge: Brewer).

——2003. *Religion und Mythologie der Germanen* (Darmstadt: Wissenschaftliche Buchgesellschaft).

Solli, B. 2002. *Seid: Myter, sjamanisme og kjønn i vikingenes tid* (Oslo: Pax).

Staecker, J. 1999. 'Thor's Hammer: Symbol of Christianization and political delusion', *Lund Archaeological Review*, 1999: 89–104.

Steinsland, G. 1986. 'Giants as recipients of cult in the Viking Age?' in G. Steinsland (ed.), *Words and Objects: Towards a dialogue between archaeology and history of religion* (Oslo: Norwegian University Press; Oxford: Oxford University Press), pp. 212–22.

——2005. *Norrøn religion: Myter, riter, samfund* (Oslo: Pax).

——and Vogt, K. 1981. '"Aukinn ertu Uolse ok vpp vm tekinn": En religionshistorisk analyse av Volsathattr i Falteyarbok', *Arkiv för nordisk filologi*, 96: 87–106.

Stjernquist, B. 1997. *The Röekillorna Spring: Spring-cults in Scandinavian prehistory*, Acta Regiae Societatis Humaniorum Litterarum Lundensis 82 (Stockholm).

Strömbäck, D. 1935. *Sejd: Textstudier i nordisk religionshistoria*, Nordiska texter och undersökningar 5 (Stockholm: Gebers; Copenhagen: Levin and Munksgaard).

Sundqvist, O. 2002. *Freyr's Offspring: Rulers and religion in ancient Svea society*, Historia religiorum 21 (Uppsala: Acta Universitatis Upsaliensis).

——2007. *Kultledare i fornskandinavisk religion*, Occasional Papers in Archaeology 41 (Uppsala: Department of Archaeology and Ancient History).

Svanberg, F. 2003a. *Decolonizing the Viking Age*, I, Acta Archaeologica, Series in 8° No 43 (Stockholm: Almqvist and Wiksell International).

——2003b. *Decolonizing the Viking Age, II: Death Rituals in South-East Scandinavia AD 800–1000*, Acta Archaeologica Lundensia, Series in 4° No 24 (Stockholm: Almqvist and Wiksell International).

Turville-Petre, E. O. G. 1964. *Myth and Religion of the North* (London: Weidenfeld and Nicolson).

Vikstrand, P. 2001. *Gudarnas platser: Förkristna sakrala ortnamn i Mälarlandskapen.* Studier till en svensk ortnamnsatlas 17 (Uppsala: Kungliga Gustav Adolfs Akademien för svensk folkkultur).

Vries, J. de 1970. *Altgermanische Religionsgeschichte*, I–II, Grundriss der germanischen Philologie 12: I–II (Berlin: Gryuter).

Zachrisson, T. 2004a. 'Hynevadsfallet och den kulturella mångfalden: Om depositioner i strömmande vatten i Södermanland' in A. Åkerlund (ed.), *Kulturell mångfald i Södermanland* (Nyköping: Länsstyrelsen i Södermanlands län), pp. 18–33.

——2004b. 'The holiness of Helgö' in H. Clarke and K. Lamm (eds), *Excavations at Helgö 16: Exotic and sacral finds from Helgö* (Stockholm: Kungliga Vitterhets, Historie och Antikvitetsakademien), pp. 143–75.

CHAPTER 53

PRE-CHRISTIAN PRACTICES IN THE ANGLO-SAXON WORLD

MARTIN WELCH

1 INTRODUCTION

RELIGION and religious practices were indissoluble aspects of life and death within Anglo-Saxon society. They provided an inbuilt function of the world view of its peoples before the acceptance of Christianity in England between the late sixth century and the late seventh century AD. Fertility rites, shamanism, and belief in ghosts and spirits, ancestor-worship, and gods liable to intervene actively in the affairs of the living, appear to be the chief components. We can only hope to understand such belief systems and practices by examining the entire range of archaeological and written evidence available to us (Price 2002: 26).

Their legacy survives in the four weekdays named after Germanic deities (*Tīw* for Tuesday, *Woden* Wednesday, *Thunor* Thursday, and *Frigg* Friday). In the early eighth-century *De temporum ratione*, Bede describes religious festivals associated with months from a pagan calendar (*De mensibus anglorum*). Thus *Solmanoth* (February) saw 'cakes' offered to gods; successive months were dedicated to the goddesses *Rheda* (March) and *Eostre* (April); *Halegmonath* (September) was a holy month probably linked to harvesting and *Blotmanoth* (November) sees the annual slaughter of livestock. Whether the maintenance of such a calendar helps to prove the existence of a priesthood is a moot point (Campbell 2007: 68). Regnal lists and genealogies recorded for Anglo-Saxon kings by Christian clergy in the seventh and eighth centuries contain the names of gods now transformed back into ancestors. *Woden* holds the place of honour in every one of these, except for the East Saxon list, which gives that role to *Seaxneat*. He is the same *Saxnot* listed together with *Thunor* and *Woden* as gods to be abjured in a ninth-century baptismal vow taken by the converted Old Saxons in north Germany (Turville-Petre 1964: 100). Other gods appear as royal ancestors such as the fertility deity *Ingui* in Bernicia (North 1997: 42–8) and a pairing of horse gods *Hengest* and *Horsa* as well as *Æsc* in Kent (Brooks

1989: 58–64). It seems probable that kings performed a sacral role, hence the importance of first converting them.

2 BEDE, ALDHELM, AND EDDIUS STEPHANUS AS SOURCES

Contemporary Christian commentators, such as Bede or the author of the *Life of St Wilfrid*, usually writing in Latin rather than a vernacular language, provide our primary written source material. They leave an impression that pre-Christian worship of unnamed deities took place in holy places and involved sacrifices on altars and the foretelling of events. They are referred to as pagans, derived from Latin *pagani*, the country folk whose beliefs are contrasted in Roman thinking with the Christian orthodoxy of urban populations. The Old English equivalent was *hæðen*, perhaps derived from Gothic *haiþno*, and the Old Norse equivalent is *heiðinn*. Both pagan and heathen carried pejorative overtones matching concerns expressed repeatedly in ecclesiastical texts that remote communities covertly followed pre-Christian practices (Wilson 1992: 37–8).

Bede uses Latin *fanum*, usually translated as a shrine, when describing pre-Christian religious sites, rather than a term that might imply a roofed building, such as Latin *templum* or Greek *temenos* (e.g. *HE* I.30 and 32, II.10, 11, 13 and 15). These *fana* are dedicated to the worship of devils (*cultus daemonum*) and contained idols (*idoli*) and altars (*altare* and *arula*), but we are nowhere told whether these were covered or open-air structures. For example, Rædwald of the East Angles placed a newly acquired Christian altar in a *fanum*, yet retained the small altar (*arula*) on which he sacrificed to other gods there (*HE* II.15). Presumably different gods could be worshipped on appropriate occasions in such a setting. His descendent Ealdwulf, the ruler of the East Angles between 663/4 and 713, remembered seeing this *fanum* as a boy. This implies it had survived for several decades after Rædwald's death (sometime after 616). A bit more helpful is the account of the desecration of a *fanum* at *Gudmunddingaham* associated with the conversion of the Deiran ruler Edwin in the mid-620s (*HE* II.13). Almost certainly located at Goodmanham on the edge of the Yorkshire Wolds, its name seems to be a post-conversion one and we never learn the 'heathen' original. We read that the common folk were gathering there for a religious festival and the desecrator was a 'priest' (*pontifex*) with the unique name of Coifi. He mounted a stallion (rather than a mare), belted on a sword, rode to the *fanum* and cast a spear into it.

The banning of iron weapons during religious ceremonies is recorded in the first century AD for the annual progress of a wagon containing the image of a mother-earth goddess (*Terra Mater*) named as Nerthus (*Germania* 40). In fact Nerthus may have been the male counterpart to the *Terra Mater* with the name being cognate with the Norse god Njrðr (North 1997: 11). Another relevant account in Norse literature relates to a temple dedicated to *Freyr* in Iceland (Campbell 2007: 68; Davidson 1964: 101–2). A weapon ban suggests that fertility rites took place at Goodmanham, which probably originated in the Bronze Age, if not still earlier with the first European farmers. While doubtless a skilled warrior could throw a spear through the open doorway of a modest, roofed, wooden building, it is easier to envisage a spear flying over or through an open gate of an unroofed structure defined by a ditch and palisade or a hedge. Bede states that this *fanum* possessed associated enclosures (*saeptum*) and everything, including the idols, proved flammable. A letter written by Aldhelm in the 680s describes *fana profana* as containing crude pillars (*ermula cruda*) of a snake and a stag that were formerly worshipped (Lapidge and Herren 1979: 160–1). This implies either timber or stone pillars, presumably with animal or phallic ornamentation (Blair 1995: 2–3).

A controversial reading of Bede's account proposes that Coifi was no pagan priest, but rather Bishop Paulinus intervening directly and that 'Coifi' describes his episcopal headgear (North 1997: 323–40). The only other contemporary reference to a pagan priest (*sacerdos*) appears in the *Life of St Wilfrid*. Eddius describes the 'priest' as standing on a high mound aiding local pagans (*pagani*) who were attacking Wilfrid's ship when it ran aground off the West Sussex coast (Eddius, trans. Colgrave 1985: 27–9: ch. 13). In appropriate Old Testament style, the 'priest' is killed by a slingshot from the ship for urging on the wreckers and the ship escapes on the tide in the nick of time. This 'priest' is also referred to as a *magus* here and is a rather different individual to Coifi and seems to be a shaman or male witch (Old Norse *seiðmaðr*) seeking magically to assist the attackers and confound the defenders of the ship from his elevated position (North 1997: 333). A shaman-like priest (*sacerdos*) dressed in women's clothing is described by Tacitus (*Germania* 43) and can be matched in later Norse sources (North 1997: 49–51; Price 2002: 62–5, 122–4).

Elsewhere Bede refers to the sacrifice of oxen (*HE* I.30) and a possible example of human sacrifice in pre-Christian Sussex (*HE* IV.13). Towards the end of a famine caused by an extended drought, groups of 40 or 50 South Saxon men took to throwing themselves off cliffs or into the sea. Bede attributes these suicides to sheer desperation of emaciated individuals, but they might well represent voluntary mass sacrifice to appease particular gods. Augury is also a practice mentioned by Bede in association with pagan *fana* in the time of Eadbald king of Kent (*HE* II.11) and remained a matter of concern for clergy there much later in the seventh century (Theodore's *Penitential*; Haddan and Stubbs 1871: 190; Wilson 1992: 37).

3 Place-Name Evidence

Surviving English place names incorporate the names of the same gods featured in our weekdays. The most common is *Woden*, as in Woodnesborough (Kent) and Wansdyke (Wiltshire). He is also known by his by-name of Grim, as in *grimes dic* (dated 956), now Grimsdyke (Wiltshire). *Thunor* is again fairly popular, as in Thundersley (Essex), but the identifications of *Tīw* and *Frigg* with places such as Tysoe (Warwickshire) and Freefolk (Hampshire) are regarded as more controversial (Hines 1997: table 12–1, figs. 12–1a and 1b; Wilson 1992: 11–16, fig. 2). Then there are place names in *ēs* or *ōs* as in Easewrithe Hundred (Sussex) and Easole (Kent) that refer to an unspecified god. These names relating to gods are associated either with man-made features in the landscape, such as a burial mound or barrow (*hlæw* or *beorg*), or with natural elements, including extensive landscape features such as a wood or grove (*lēah*), an area of open land (*feld*), a spur (*hōh*), a pool (*mere*), a valley, etc. The nature names and especially those in *lēah* are sometimes seen as more authentic (e.g. Hines 1997: 386) because they match references by Tacitus to earlier Germanic worship in groves (*Germania* 7, 9, 10, 39, and 43).

Of the two Old English names for a shrine, that in *hearg* was used in a Mercian English translation of Bede's *Historia Ecclesiastica* as the equivalent for Bede's *fanum* (Meaney 1995: 31–5; Wilson 1992: 6–11). Harrow in Middlesex is derived from *hearg* and typically such a place name occupies a hilltop as here, while its Old Norse equivalent *horgr* describes a heap of stones as a place of sacrifice. Such a site can belong to a tribal group for the *Gumeningas* own the Middlesex Harrow (Charter dated 767: *gumeninga hergae*). A *wig* or *wēoh* as in Wye (Kent) or Weedon (Buckinghamshire) represents a different type of site, perhaps a wayside shrine as typically they are located close to a road or trackway (Wilson 1992: 8–10, fig. 1). A *wēoh* might be personal property, as with the now-lost *Cusanwēoh*, and perhaps Cusa and his heirs exercised priestly functions there (North 1997: 333).

Interestingly the names of gods are never combined with *hearg* or *wēoh*, so perhaps more than one god could be worshipped in them. Other place names refer to a special tree, a wooden post or pillar, such as *bēam* in Bampton (Oxfordshire) or *stapol* in Staploe (Cambridgeshire). Perhaps words used in later Old English texts to describe a Christian cross, notably *rōd*, *trēow*, and *bēam* imply that the earliest crosses were viewed by Anglo-Saxons as equivalents to their own earlier sacred wooden markers (Blair 2005: 186 and 227). Then names in *heafod* can refer to the heads of humans, animals (both domesticated and wild) and birds, as in Manshead and Swineshead. Decapitated heads may indeed have been mounted on stakes at such places (Meaney 1995: 30–1), though carved or painted images might have been substituted later. Bede's account of the dismemberment of Oswald's corpse after battle and the display of his head and hands on stakes suggests an offering to the war god who had granted the Mercian Penda victory over his Christian Bernician rival (*HE* III.12).

4 Idols, Cult Sites, Sacrifices, and Offerings in Scandinavia and Germany

We have to cross the North Sea to the continental and Scandinavian homelands of the Anglo-Saxons to find surviving wooden figures used as idols. These date to the Roman period and have been recovered from former pools or lakes that have become peat-bogs. Typically they are very crude, often simple modifications of tree branches as with the female idols from Foerlev Nymølle and Rebild Skovhuse, a bearded male figure with a semi-erect phallus from Broddenbjerg and another from Spangeholm Fen, all in Denmark (Glob 1971: 126–8, pls; Behm-Blancke 1976: Taf. 54a). An open-air shrine by a wooden trackway in Lower Saxony produced stylized two-dimensional wooden figures, again both male and female, at Wittemoor in Wesermarsch (Behm-Blancke 1976: 373, Abb. 101–2, Taf. 21; Hayen 1971: Abb. 15–16).

In central Germany multiple wooden idols have been recorded from the open-air cult sites at Oberdorla near Mühlhausen and Possendorf near Weimar (Behm-Blancke 1976: 369–71, Abb. 100, Taf. 52; Seyer 1983: Taf. 40a). Phallic-shaped items, sexless idols, and female figures were associated with the remains of both human and animal sacrifices including dogs. Wagon parts also occur in several Scandinavian bog deposits, notably the complete pair of wagons from Dejbjerg in Jutland (Krüger 1976: Taf. 19). These allow us to envisage the cult wagon containing the Earth-Mother image described by Tacitus (*Germania* 40). Well-preserved waterlogged human remains represent either sacrifices or punishments as described by Tacitus (*Germania* 9, 12, 19, 39, and 40). These practices seem to be in decline by the Migration period in north Germany and Scandinavia. Although individuals who had been strangled, had their throats slit, or been drowned were typically located in liminal situations, this seems to relate to boundaries between life and death and between settled farmland and more marginal landscapes (Hines 1989b: 196).

War booty, particularly of weapons, sometimes including entire ships, as well as horses and other equipment, feature in other lake deposits here during the Roman Iron Age. Examples occur in Jutland at Thorsbjerg and Nydam, but once again these disappear during the Migration period with the last examples belonging to the early sixth century at Illerup and Kragehul. It is probable that large used-weapon deposits represent equipment captured from defeated warbands and armies. Analysis of individual deposits excavated to modern standards at Ejsbøl-North and Illerup has confirmed that these are coherent assemblages. They match the gift-exchange practices that bound a warlord to his *comitatus* by rewarding loyal service both past and future with gold and weapons (Bazelmans 1999). The gods could be bound similarly into obligations to continue to favour a lord and his heirs by receiving their full share of the spoils. The battles were not necessarily located close by, for these lakes were typically reused on three or four separate occasions within the period between the second and fourth centuries AD. Rather the booty was transported and often ritually 'killed' to prevent its immediate reuse (Hines 1989a and 1989b: 194–7).

Changes take place around the beginning of the fifth century. For example at Ejsbøl a fifth-century hoard of finely crafted cast buckle and belt fittings, clasps, and scabbard fittings in gilded silver or copper alloys (Ejsbøl-South) was recovered a few metres south of the mid-fourth-century weapon and horse-gear deposit representing a defeated warband (Ejsbøl-North). Similar collections of high-quality military belt sets and weapon fittings occur in the same century with the Nydam II find and at Sjörup (Skåne, Sweden) and significantly none of these show evidence of battle use. They seem to be offerings made by a smaller elite warrior group at a local religious centre. By the mid-fifth century such male belt and military equipment hoards form only part of a much wider range of items found in individual votive deposits. These include dress fittings normally worn by women including brooches and small pendants, the latter typically made of gold. They represent a duplication or extension of dress assemblages found in female burials elsewhere, including Anglo-Saxon England and arguably can be interpreted as 'grave substitutes' (Hines 1989b: 197–9). We can also find animal sacrifices, especially involving horses accompanied by bridle and other harness mounts (Hines 1989b: 197).

Place names help us locate major cult centres here. One of the best known has been located at Gudme inland from a beach market at Lundeborg (Fyn). Its name is derived from Old Norse *goðheim* and means the home of gods. Since 1833 Gudme has produced a series of magnificent gold and silver hoards that start in the third–fourth centuries and continue on up to the eleventh–twelfth centuries (Hedeager 2002; Nielsen et al. 1994). We cannot be sure that it was called *goðheim* before the Viking Age, but there is no doubt that significant wealth was being deposited here from the late Roman Iron Age onwards. Hoard II here contained large numbers of small ornamented sheet-metal gold disc pendants of the fifth to sixth centuries (bracteates) associated elsewhere with female costume. This hoard came from the fill of an internal load-bearing post within a timber building establishing a relationship between cult activity in the building and the sacrifice of gold to the gods

(Petersen 1994: 34–5, fig. 12). Bracteates were created as cult symbols from melted-down Roman gold coinage and began as Scandinavian copies of fourth-century medallions portraying the emperor wearing a diadem. The Scandinavian portraits take on the attributes of a god, most probably *Woden* (*Óðin*) accompanied by creatures, signs, and symbols such as a bird, a swastika, or a star. Runic letters sometimes replace the Latin inscriptions of the Roman medallions. It has been argued that where we can relate such images to Roman iconography, we can then attempt to establish their meaning in Germanic mythological terms (Hauck 1994; Axboe 1994).

In the region of Skåne (south-west Sweden) the partially excavated settlement of Uppåkra represents the pre-Christian precursor of Lund. A 'sacred house' there first excavated in 2001 measures 13 m × 6.5 m with three entrances and four substantial post-holes (Larsson 2002: 25–8, fig. 4; Hårdh 2002: 46, fig. 8). A deposit of two sixth-century vessels (a glass bowl and an elaborately decorated metal-footed beaker) had been placed under its floor as offerings, while the fills of the western pair of internal post-holes contained gold foils representing human figures (*Guldguber*). Such foils first appear in the later sixth century continuing on into the Viking period and amongst them was a representation of a naked male figure wearing only a collar and a waist belt (Larsson 2002: figs. 7–10). There were also dies for making more foils that typically depict well-dressed women presenting drinking vessels.

5 IMAGES AND ICONOGRAPHY IN ANGLO-SAXON ENGLAND

As yet no wooden figures have been recorded in England to match the Scandinavian and German idols. The nearest we have is a ceramic three-dimensional seated male figure on an urn lid from the mixed-rite cemetery at Spong Hill (Norfolk). This may well represent a god, probably *Woden* on his throne from which he could see across all the worlds (Hills 1980: pl. VIII; Wilson 1992: fig. 51). A similar carved wooden seat was excavated from a waterlogged ship burial at Fallward in Lower Saxony (Schön 1999: 80–1, colour plate) and there are Viking Age miniature silver pendants depicting such chairs. The pendants come from the graves of women who probably practised *seiðr* rituals and one such pendant from Hedeby (Schleswig-Holstein) depicts pairs of birds and two wolf-like creatures along its arms emphasizing the connection to *Óðin* (Drescher and Hauck 1982: Taf. XXIII). From Finglesham (Kent) grave 138 there is a miniature three-dimensional cast pendant depicting a human head that might conceivably represent the head of *Mímir* consulted by *Óðin* and from grave 95 comes a depiction on a buckle plate of a near-naked warrior carrying two spears wearing similar headgear to that on the pendant (Hawkes 1982; Hawkes et al. 1965; Hawkes and Grainger 2006: figs. 2.102 and 2.117). A small gold disc pendant from a necklet made up of pendants at Riseley, Horton Kirby (Kent), again presumably represents cult practices as it depicts a long-bearded man holding a snake in each hand (Hawkes 1982; Hawkes et al. 1965: 21–2, fig. 3). All three of these Kentish examples date to the seventh century and thus post-date by a considerable margin the late sixth-century conversion of its kingdom (Welch 2007).

Also produced in the early seventh century are various items of fine metalwork bearing iconography from the Sutton Hoo first ship burial in Suffolk. One of the easier examples to read are the helmet plates depicting a mounted warrior riding down another fallen warrior (Marzinzik 2007). While the main figure appears triumphant with his spear raised over arm, the fallen man stabs the horse with his sword putting the horseman into danger. Meanwhile a miniature figure is aiding the mounted hero by supporting his spear and it seems that divine aid will protect this warrior through the dangers and confusions of battle and take him to *Woden*'s hall if he dies in combat. This particular scene recurs on other contemporary helmets from Swedish boat burials and from a disc brooch in south-west Germany, enabling us to compare and contrast different variant versions (Hawkes et al. 1965).

Returning to pottery cremation containers, it is commonplace to find on them ancient Indo-European religious symbols such as swastikas, often identified with Thunor (Wilson 1992: 142–64). Stamps depicting rows of animals, including horses, also occur, but the clearest example is a freehand incised scene on an urn from Caistor-by-Norwich. This depicts a rowing boat identified with a mythical ship made from the nails of dead men (*Naglfar*) and a much larger wolf-like creature presumed to be *Fenrir* depicted at *Ragnork* (Myres and Green 1973: 118, 180, fig. 44; Wilson 1992: 153–4, fig. 48). Stamped or incised runic inscriptions also feature on pottery vessels and some of these seem to represent incantations. Runes incised on sword fittings may well have had a protective function, but runes were also used to identify the makers or the owners of an item and should not automatically be assumed to have a magical or religious function.

6 HUMAN AND ANIMAL SACRIFICES

Although bog-finds of human remains have been recorded at Lindow (Cheshire) for the pre-Roman Iron Age period, as yet no post-Roman Anglo-Saxon equivalents have been identified. The possibility of wives sacrificing themselves to accompany their husband in his grave has been explored and others being buried alive has been considered (Harman et al. 1981). It has been suggested that a fully dressed woman buried face-down with a stone placed over the small of her back in grave 41 at Sewerby (Yorkshire) was being punished for causing the death of a younger woman buried below her in grave 49 (Hirst 1985), but many commentators remain unconvinced. Still more controversial is the interpretation of a young woman, seemingly buried naked at Kingsworthy (Hampshire), as a rape victim punished by being buried alive (Hawkes and Wells 1975). The limitations of such evidence have been commented on and it has been argued that the only convincing argument for human sacrifice in an archaeological context would require the presence of animal remains as well (Carver 2005: 315–59). The burial of a horse with its harness in the same grave or in an adjacent grave to a warrior burial, as at Eriswell, Lakenheath (Suffolk) is more straightforward. Sometimes the horse is not directly associated with a particular grave, while on other occasions only the horse head is present, as occurs at Springfield Lyons (Essex). Horse sacrifice seems to be a minority practice in England and is far more common across northern Germany and Scandinavia. A set of pits filled with horses surrounded the burial mound of Childeric, the last pagan king of the Franks c.481–2 at Tournai (Belgium), which provides one of the best examples close to England

(Müller-Wille 1996: Abb. 145–7). Horses are only one of the domestic species present, together with some wild animals on cremation pyres (Bond 1996). Their presence probably had a ritual aspect as well as making a social statement and it should be noted that cremation was very much a pagan burial practice that was unacceptable to the Christian Church.

7 VOTIVE OFFERINGS

Large-scale weapon offerings have not been found in England, but significant numbers of weapons including spears, swords, seaxes, and shield fittings have been recovered from rivers including the Thames (Bradley and Gordon 1985). It has been noted that the proportions of particular spear shapes found in rivers are different from those recovered from contemporary graves (Hines 1997: 380–1) and it is improbable that these can be explained by weaponry from graves being eroded into rivers. Interestingly the practice seems to include weapon types manufactured as late as the ninth–tenth centuries and also involves precious metal fittings from high-status weapons such as two-edged swords. The possibility that quite a few find spots of bracteates in central and eastern England were votive offerings of individual bracteates or small groups of them rather than disturbed grave deposits needs to be borne in mind (Hines 1989b: 198). Much more research needs to be undertaken in this direction, but it seems that a pale reflection of practices found in Southern Scandinavia was present here (C. Behr pers. comm.).

8 SANCTUARIES OR SHRINES AND FURNISHED BURIALS IN ANGLO-SAXON ENGLAND

Three excavated sites now provide us with insights into the appearance of Bede's *fana* with the best known occurring in the western sector of the settlement at Yeavering (Northumberland). This was identified with a seventh-century royal *villa* described by Bede (*HE* II.14). Most commentators have accepted its excavator's case for identifying the rectangular, roofed, timber building D2 as a pagan temple (Hope-Taylor 1977: 97–102, 158–61; Blair 1995; Meaney 1995: 29). Although built on the scale of a normal house with a pair of opposed doorways set in the middle of its long walls, uniquely the first building here had been encased by a second slightly larger version. Both possessed standing earth-fast timber walls when the structure was destroyed by fire. There were numerous non-functional postholes within the building which might have supported altars and there was a pit containing ox skulls set within the inner wall. So it seems that D2 was too important to demolish when its foundations weakened, hence its encasement and the reason that cattle were sacrificed here. It was further argued that other structures around the building reflected advice given by Pope Gregory to Mellitus in Canterbury as to how to convert a pagan temple to Christian worship without destroying it (Bede, *HE* I.30). It should be noted that cattle bones without any skulls were recorded in the nearby area to the north of building D3 (Hamerow 2006: 7; Hope-Taylor 1977: 103–8). If D2 was a temple, it might represent the creation of a pagan equivalent to the earliest missionary churches or else an equivalent to the sacred house at Uppåkra. A short distance away were the remains of an open-air structure described as the Western Ring-Ditch, which combined a circular ditch with a square fenced structure imposed over it (Hope-Taylor 1977: 108–16). This seems to have been the hub of pre-Christian cult activities here (Blair 1995: 16–17, fig. 11 and 2005: 54–7) and may well represent the precursor of D2.

The other two locations revealed similar circular and rectangular structures at Slonk Hill (Sussex) and Blacklow Hill (Warwickshire) and are probably *hearg* sites. They can be attributed securely to the early Saxon period through the presence of burials accompanied by an iron knife. It was a female inhumation at Slonk Hill, but the size and form of the knife or seax found with one of two burials on Blacklow Hill will only be established when its final excavation report is published (Blair 1995: 16–18, figs. 11–12; Wilson 1992: 64–6, fig. 20). The Blacklow Hill site has both an inner and an outer enclosure, though the hollows recorded across the outer area are more likely to be the remains of a modern tree plantation than Anglo-Saxon sacrificial pits (A. Reynolds pers. comm.). Scepticism can also be expressed concerning the antiquity of grooves running downhill from the outer boundary, but there is no reason to doubt that this had been a major Anglo-Saxon shrine. Blair catalogued a significant number of other sites sharing such combinations of square and circle ditches. Some of these were associated directly with burials datable to the Iron Age, the Roman period, and subsequent periods, both within Britain as well as in pre-Roman Gaul. His conclusion is that the specifically Anglo-Saxon sites belong to a long-established tradition for sacred sites to be constructed with such features within Britain. As yet, however, no equivalents have been identified from the Anglo-Saxon continental homelands, but that does not mean that they do not exist.

9 MALE 'PRIESTS' AND FEMALE WITCHES

Yeavering has also produced a possible burial of a priest, though the excavator presented it as a royal surveyor (Hope-Taylor 1977: 67–9, 200–3, figs. 25 and 94; Meaney 1985: 19–21; Wilson 1992: 176, fig. 56). The individual in grave AX cannot be sexed, aged, or dated securely, but was accompanied by a goat's skull by the feet and by a long wooden staff with elaborate crosspieces with metal-cap ends. As reconstructed in the report, however, this staff cannot have functioned effectively as a Roman surveying instrument (or *groma*). It has been suggested that this might represent a priestly staff, but to date it appears to be unique as an object. Females buried in Viking-Age Scandinavia and on the Isle of Man who are argued to be practitioners of *seiðr* are typically accompanied by a staff (Price 2002), but these look very different compared to the Yeavering 'staff'. A reference in Tacitus to a male priest dressed in women's clothing (*Germania* 43) has led to the suggestion that individuals buried in female costume, but identified as definitely male by biological anthropologists, might represent such priests in Anglo-Saxon England. The most frequently cited example is the individual in Portway, Andover (Hampshire), grave 9 (Cook and Dacre 1985: 25–6, 56, figs. 30 and 44). We should retain an open mind here, however, allowing that the sexing of skeletal remains is not an exact science and that there is some degree of error even where the bone material is well preserved which most often it is not.

Turning to female burials, many women are accompanied by one or more items that can be considered amuletic (Meaney 1981). These can be made from natural materials, such as fossils; the teeth, claws, or tusks of animals or birds; and shells. Cowries imported via the Mediterranean world seem likely to be associated with female fertility and childbirth. Other amulets are manufactured, commonly worn as pendants around the neck or in bags and purses. Small silver disc pendants with a central raised boss seem to imitate the form and decoration of shields and presumably magically protected the wearer in a similar manner to a warrior's buckler. Much the same range of items can be found in Scandinavia and Germanic Europe implying a common range of superstitious beliefs and practices. In a modern analysis we might choose to separate superstition and magic from religion, but it is quite plausible that the Anglo-Saxons recognized no such distinction, as they formed part of the same cosmological world view.

The ornament on metalwork introduced from Scandinavia in the fifth and sixth centuries can reflect beliefs linked to particular cults. Thus the boar that features on Style II metalwork is probably linked to the Vanir fertility gods, predatory birds to *Óðin*'s raven and eagle and the snake again to *Óðin* or *Woden* as in the Riseley pendant described above (Speake 1980). Quadrupeds in Style I can be ambiguous, looking like an animal from one angle, but portraying a side view of a human face when turned through 90 degrees (Leigh 1984). These animal-men (*Tiermenschen*) may well reflect shamanistic beliefs that some humans can enter a trance and leave their bodies, often travelling in animal or bird form. The wearers of brooches with such ambiguous animal ornament sometimes combined them with Scandinavian type gold bracteates, while other items of continental Frankish origin might be suspended from their waists. Rock crystal balls in silver slings and silver jewelled sieve spoons found in some of the richest sixth-century Kentish graves are likely to have had magical properties and functions as well as being status symbols (Welch 2007). Such women may well have played a leading role in the cult activities of their society (Behr 2000).

Finally a woman buried with a set of miniature copper-alloy pendants imitating the form of buckets and various other unusual items at Bidford-on-Avon (Warwickshire) has been identified as a 'cunning woman' or witch (Dickinson 1993). She perhaps represents the equivalent of the Viking-Age women in Scandinavia considered to be exponents of *seiðr* on the basis of their grave furnishings (Price 2002). The bucket pendants represent the female role of the hostess in Germanic society and here may either have been sewn onto or have formed part of the contents of a bag found under the body of this woman. They are only one component of a burial assemblage that stands out as very unusual and likely to have belonged to a woman with special powers.

10 CONCLUSIONS

Although our understanding of Anglo-Saxon pre-Christian religion from written sources and from place names is partial and far from complete, archaeology is beginning to reveal more. Comparative studies have allowed us to start to make sense of excavated cult sites in Northumberland, Sussex, and Warwickshire in their landscape context (Blair 1995). Similarly the analysis of the animal art, symbolism, and iconography on metal artefacts is throwing new light on other aspects of the religious beliefs of these peoples (Behr 2000). There is much more to do, but at least we seem to be making significant progress now.

Addendum

Since this chapter was submitted, the discovery of a very large hoard of gold and silver fittings, from swords, seaxes, helmets, and other weaponry, during July 2009 in Staffordshire may well require some revision of statements made in it. It is possible that this hoard, probably representing battle trophies from one or more campaigns, is a votive offering, dedicated by a pagan warlord such as the Mercian King Penda to a god or gods before the middle decades of the seventh century. Alternatively, if the Christian crosses and the Latin inscribed fitting with a biblical text belong to a significantly later period within the seventh century or the early eighth century, and this has yet to be determined with certainty, this hoard would presumably have been buried instead with the intention of recovery and the recycling of its bullion by manufacture as new fittings and jewellery. Either way, this is the first time we have recovered a hoard within England that is remotely comparable to those found across Scandinavia in the pre-Viking period.

Suggested Reading

The most accessible general introduction to the range of evidence for pre-Christian Anglo-Saxon religion is David Wilson's *Anglo-Saxon Paganism*, while for the related Nordic religions and their earlier Germanic origins Hilda Ellis Davidson's *Gods and Myths of Northern Europe* remains a classic. For a different interpretation of the literary evidence that seeks to correct the apparent dominance of Woden and draw our attention to the importance of the gods of the Vanir and in particular Ingui in seventh-century England, see Richard North's *Heathen Gods in Old English Literature*. John Blair has explored the archaeological evidence for the physical appearance of pagan shrines in the periodical *Anglo-Saxon Studies in Archaeology and History* 8, 1995, 1–28 and Tania Dickinson the burial evidence for women with magical and/or religious skills in a volume edited by Martin Carver entitled *In Search of Cult*. Finally, Morten Axboe has published a useful study of gold bracteates which bear religious scenes in a volume entitled *Brakteatstudier* (Copenhagen 2007). This has an extensive English summary and provides a good introduction to iconographic studies for this period.

References

Axboe, M. 1994. 'Gudme and the Gold Bracteates' in P. O. Nielsen, K. Randsborg, and H. Thrane (eds), *The Archaeology of Gudme and Lundeborg* (Copenhagen: Copenhagen University Academic Press), pp. 68–77.

Bazelmans, J. 1999. *By Weapons Made Worthy: Lords, retainers and their relationship in Beowulf* (Amsterdam: Amsterdam University Press).

Bede 1969. *Historia Ecclesiastica Gentis Anglorum*, trans. B. Colgrave and R. A. B. Mynors (Oxford: Larendon Press).

Behm-Blancke, G. 1976. 'Kult und Ideologie' in B. Krüger (ed.), *Die Germanen. Geschichte und Kultur der germanischen Stämme in Mitteleuropa*, I: *Von den Anfängen bis zum 2. Jahrhundert unserer Zeitrechnung* (Berlin: Akademie Verlag), pp. 351–73.

Behr, C. 2000. 'The origins of kingship in early medieval Kent', *Early Medieval Europe*, 9: 25–52.

BLAIR, J. 1995. 'Anglo-Saxon pagan shrines and their prototypes', *Anglo-Saxon Studies in Archaeology and History*, 8: 1–28.
——2005. *The Church in Anglo-Saxon Society* (Oxford: Oxford University Press).
BOND, J. M. 1996. 'Burnt offerings: Animal bone in Anglo-Saxon cremations', *World Archaeology*, 28(1): 76–88.
BRADLEY, R. and GORDON, K. 1985. 'Human skulls from the river Thames', *Antiquity*, 62: 503–59.
BROOKS, N. 1989. 'The creation and early structure of the kingdom of Kent' in S. Bassett (ed.), *The Origins of Anglo-Saxon Kingdoms* (Leicester: Leicester University Press), pp. 55–74.
CAMPBELL, J. 2007. 'Some considerations on religion in early England' in M. Henig and J. Tyler-Smith (eds), *Collectanea Antiqua: Essays in memory of Sonia Chadwick Hawkes*, BAR International Series 1673 (Oxford: Archaeopress), pp. 67–73.
——and ANDERSON, S. 1999. 'RAF Lakenheath Saxon cemetery', *Current Archaeology*, 163 (XIV.7): 244–50.
CARVER, M. 2005. *Sutton Hoo: A seventh-century princely burial-ground and its context* (London: British Museum Press).
COOK, A. M. and DACRE, M. W. 1985. *Excavations at Portway, Andover 1973–1975* (Oxford: Oxford University Committee for Archaeology).
DAVIDSON, H. R. E. 1964. *Gods and Myths of Northern Europe* (Harmondsworth: Penguin Books).
——1992. 'Human sacrifice in the Late Pagan period in North Western Europe' in M. Carver (ed.), *The Age of Sutton Hoo* (Woodbridge: Boydell Press), pp. 331–40.
DICKINSON, T. M. 1993. 'An Anglo-Saxon "cunning woman" from Bidford-on-Avon' in M. Carver (ed.), *In Search of Cult* (Woodbridge: Boydell Press), pp. 45–54.
DRESCHER, H. and HAUCK, K. 1982. 'Götterthrone des heidnischen Norden', *Frühmittelalterliche Studien*, 16: 237–301.
EDDIUS, STEPHANUS 1985. *The Life of Bishop Wilfrid*, ed. and trans. B. Colgrave (Cambridge: Cambridge University Press).
FABECH, C. 1994. 'Reading society from the cultural landscape: South Scandinavia between sacral and political power' in P. O. Nielsen, K. Randsborg, and H. Thrane (eds), *The Archaeology of Gudme and Lundeborg* (Copenhagen: Copenhagen University Academic Press), pp. 169–83.
GLOB, P. V. 1971, *The Bog People: Iron-Age man preserved*, trans. R. Bruce-Mitford (London: Paladin).
HADDAN, A. W. and STUBBS, W. 1871. *Councils and Ecclesiastical Documents Relating to Great Britain and Ireland*, III (Oxford: Clarendon Press).
HAMEROW, H. 2006. '"Special deposits" in Anglo-Saxon Settlements', *Medieval Archaeology*, 50: 1–30.
HÅRDH, B. 2002. 'Uppåkra in the Migration and Merovingian periods' in B. Hårdh and L. Larrson (eds), *Central Places in the Migration and Merovingian Periods* (Stockholm: Almqvist and Wiksell International), pp. 41–54.
HARMAN, M., MOLLESON, T., and PRICE, J. L. 1981. 'Burials, bodies and beheadings in Romano-British and Anglo-Saxon cemeteries', *Bulletin of the British Museum Natural History (Geology)*, 35: 145–88.
HAUCK, K. 1994. 'Gudme als Kultort und seine Rolle beim Austausch von Bildformularen der Goldbrakteaten' in P. O. Nielsen, K. Randsborg, and H. Thrane (eds), *The Archaeology of Gudme and Lundeborg* (Copenhagen: Copenhagen University Academic Press), pp. 78–88.

HAWKES, S. C. 1982. 'The archaeology of conversion: Cemeteries' in J. Campbell (ed.), *The Anglo-Saxons* (London: Phaidon), pp. 48–9.

——, DAVIDSON, H. R. E., and HAWKES, C. 1965. 'The Finglesham Man', *Antiquity*, 39: 17–32.

—— and GRAINGER, G. 2006. *The Anglo-Saxon Cemetery at Finglesham, Kent* (Oxford: Oxford University School of Archaeology).

—— and WELLS, C. 1975. 'Crime and Punishment in an Anglo-Saxon Cemetery?', *Antiquity*, 49: 118–22.

HAYEN, H. 1971. 'Hölzerne Kultfiguren am Bohlenweg XLII (1p) im Wittemoor (Gemeinde Berne, Landkreis Wesermarsch)', *Die Kunde*, N. F. 22: 88–123.

HEDEAGER, L. 2002. 'Scandinavian "central places" in a cosmological setting' in B. Hårdh and L. Larrson (eds), *Central Places in the Migration and Merovingian Periods* (Stockholm: Almqvist and Wiksell International), pp. 3–18.

HILLS, C. 1980. 'Anglo-Saxon Chairperson', *Antiquity*, 54: 52–4.

HINES, J. 1989a. 'The military context of the *adventus Saxonum*: Some continental evidence' in S. C. Hawkes (ed.), *Weapons and Warfare in Anglo-Saxon England* (Oxford: Oxford University Committee for Archaeology), pp. 25–48.

—— 1989b. 'Ritual hoarding in Migration-period Scandinavia: A review of recent interpretations', *Proceedings of the Prehistoric Society*, 55: 193–205.

—— 1997. 'Religion: The limits of knowledge' in J. Hines (ed.), *The Anglo-Saxons from the Migration Period to the Eighth Century: An ethnographic perspective* (Woodbridge: Boydell Press), pp. 375–410.

HIRST, S. 1985. *An Anglo-Saxon Inhumation Cemetery at Sewerby, East Yorkshire* (York: York University Archaeological Publications).

HOPE-TAYLOR, B. 1977. *Yeavering: An Anglo-British centre of early Northumbria* (London: HMSO).

KRÜGER, B. (ed.) 1976. *Die Germanen. Geschichte und Kultur der germanischen Stämme in Mitteleuropa*, I: *Von den Anfängen bis zum 2. Jahrhundert unserer Zeitrechnung* (Berlin: Akademie Verlag).

LAPIDGE, M. and HERREN, M. 1979. *Aldhelm: The prose works* (Cambridge: D. S. Brewer).

LARSSON, L. 2002. 'Uppåkra—Research on a Central Place: Recent excavations and results' in B. Hårdh and L. Larrson (eds), *Central Places in the Migration and Merovingian Periods* (Stockholm: Almqvist and Wiksell International), pp. 19–30.

LEIGH, D. 1984. 'Ambiguity in Anglo-Saxon Style I art', *Antiquaries Journal*, 64: 34–42.

MARZINZIK, S. 2007. *The Sutton Hoo Helmet* (London: British Museum).

MEANEY, A. L. 1981. *Anglo-Saxon Amulets and Curing Stones*, BAR British Series 96 (Oxford: BAR).

—— 1985. 'Bede and Anglo-Saxon Paganism', *Parergon*, New Series 3: 1–29.

—— 1995. 'Pagan English sanctuaries, place-names and hundred meeting-places', *Anglo-Saxon Studies in Archaeology and History*, 8: 29–42.

MÜLLER-WILLE, M. 1996. 'Königtum und Adel im Spiegel der Grabfunde' in A. Wieczorek et al. (eds), *Die Franken Wegbereiter Europas* (Mannheim: Verlag Philipp von Zabern), pp. 206–21.

MUNKSGAARD, E. 1984. 'Bog Bodies: A brief survey of interpretations', *Journal of Danish Archaeology*, 3: 120–23.

MYRES, J. N. L. and GREEN, B. 1973. *The Anglo-Saxon Cemeteries of Caistor-by-Norwich and Markshall, Norfolk* (London: Thames and Hudson).

NIELSEN, P. O., RANDSBORG, K., and THRANE, H. (eds.) 1994. *The Archaeology of Gudme and Lundeborg* (Copenhagen: Copenhagen University Academic Press).

NORTH, R. 1997. *Heathen Gods in Old English Literature* (Cambridge: Cambridge University Press).

PETERSEN, P. V. 1994. 'Excavations at sites of treasure trove finds at Gudme' in P. O. Nielsen, K. Randsborg, and H. Thrane (eds), *The Archaeology of Gudme and Lundeborg* (Copenhagen: Copenhagen University Academic Press), pp. 30–40.

PRICE, N. S. 2002. *The Viking Way: Religion and war in Late Iron Age Scandinavia* (Uppsala: Uppsala University).

SCHÖN, M. D. 1999. *Feddersen Wierde, Fallward, Flögeln: Archäologie im Museum Burg Bederkesa, Landkreis Cuxhaven* (Bad Bederkesa: Museum Burg Bederkesa).

SEYER, R. 1983. 'Kunst und Ideologie' in B. Krüger (ed.), *Die Germanen. Geschichte und Kultur der germanischen Stämmein Mitteleuropa*, II: *Die Stämme und Stammesverbände in der zeit vom 3. Jahrhundert bis zur Herausbildung der politischen Vorherrschaft* (Berlin: Akademie Verlag), pp. 248–69.

SPEAKE, G. 1980. *Anglo-Saxon Animal Art and its Germanic Background* (Oxford: Oxford University Press).

TACITUS 1999. *Germania*, trans. J. B. Rives (Oxford: Clarendon Press).

TURVILLE-PETRE, E. O. G. 1964. *Myth and Religion of the North: The religion of ancient Scandinavia* (London: Weidenfeld and Nicolson).

WELCH, M. 2007. 'Anglo-Saxon Kent' in J. H. Williams (ed.), *The Archaeology of Kent to AD 800* (Woodbridge: Boydell Press), pp. 187–248.

WILSON, D. 1992. *Anglo-Saxon Paganism* (London: Routledge).

CHAPTER 54

THE ARCHAEOLOGY OF BALTIC RELIGIONS

TÕNNO JONUKS

1 INTRODUCTION

BALTIC countries have traditionally been treated separately in religious studies and the current approach—to look at Estonia, Latvia, and Lithuania as one unit—is exceptional. It is clear that the Baltic countries should not be treated as one entity and for historical, religious, and especially for reasons of different sources, all three areas should be covered separately. But as the methodologies and theoretical approaches have been very similar throughout the history of research, the current approach is justified. The following focuses on archaeological studies, leaving the folk religion from the near past, which is based on oral tradition and which has dominated over the archaeological approach, less represented. Also no descriptions of Baltic mythology, based on medieval and modern written sources, will be presented as these can be easily found elsewhere (e.g. Gimbutas 1968; Greimas 1992).

2 THE BACKGROUND

Several essential areas meet in the Baltic. On the one hand the linguistic background is important: in the southern part the Baltic languages (Latvian, Lithuanian, and extinct Prussian) which belong to the Indo-European languages dominate, as a result of which the southern Baltic has been looked at as one entity. In the northern part there is the Balto-Finnic Estonian language together with the almost extinct Livonian (Figure 54.1). The linguistic background has brought along the creation of different, wider frameworks in which religions are studied. Therefore the Baltic people have been associated with the Indo-European cultural sphere, and Baltic religion and mythology have been integrated into several wider studies by European scholars (e.g. Puhvel 1989; Dumézil 1952). In contrast,

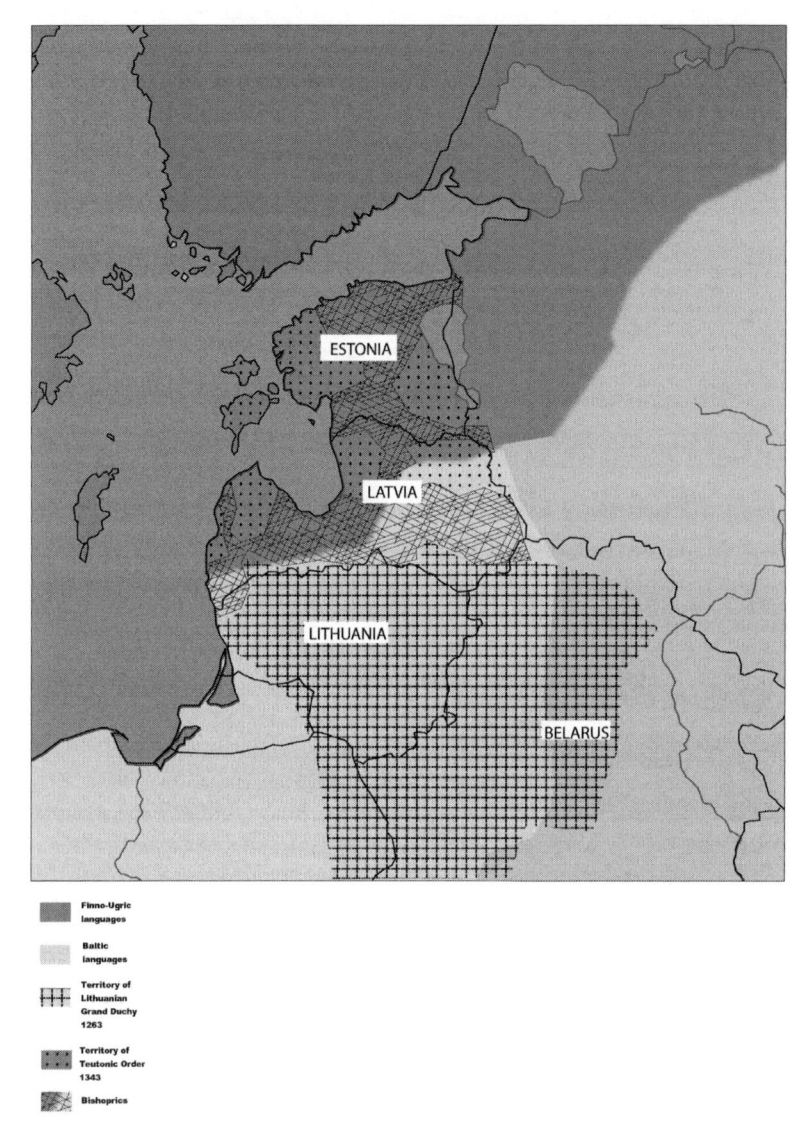

FIGURE 54.1 Map of the Baltic countries showing linguistic areas, Lithuanian Grand Duchy, Territory of Teutonic Order, Bishoprics and contemporary borders.

Estonia has traditionally been treated together with Finland and in the wider cultural space with the Finno-Ugric people in northern Russia and these religions appear comparatively rarely in pan-European studies. In addition, very specific topics are represented, for example soul, power, etc., especially in Estonia (see Loorits 1949), which makes it difficult to regard these studies in a wider geographical frame.

Beside the linguistic differences all three countries have different historical backgrounds. Since the beginning of human habitation at c.12,000–11,000 BC various archaeological cultures and micro areas have been discerned in the area, some of which can be followed even nowadays. But Christianization during the twelfth–fourteenth centuries AD has been of major importance, especially considering its impact on the sources of religion. Baltic countries were the last to be involved in the Christian Ecumene in Europe. Estonia and northern Latvia, conquered by the Danish and German crusaders by 1227, were subjected to new administrative structures, partly to new nobility, and officially to new religion. This differed from the rest of Northern Europe where Christianization took place mostly from the same linguistic and cultural background, but Estonia and Latvia were Christianized from outside. On one hand this obviously influenced the formation of written sources; on the other hand the strange official religion, which remained essentially in a foreign language for centuries, contributed to the preservation of pre-Christian phenomena through the medieval and modern period. A different situation developed in Lithuania where by the thirteenth century the core of the future Lithuanian Grand Duchy was formed (Figure 54.1), and where paganism was recognized as the official religion. Thus only as late as 1387 did the Grand Duke Jogaila accept Catholicism. The presence of such a late heathenism and the developing interest in the pagan past during the Renaissance meant that the majority of written documents on pagan religion, its mythology, and rituals are largely concerned with Lithuania, although these were not recorded by pagans themselves (Vėlius 1996).

However, despite differences the area also has many similarities. Throughout the twentieth century, when (pre)historic religions have been academically studied, the Baltic countries have shared a similar history and dominating ideologies. Thus their histories of research, methodologies, and theoretical approaches can be compared. The sources are very similar as well—in each country oral tradition has been dominant, all medieval written sources about past religion were recorded by non-native speakers, and archaeological material has only been utilized relatively recently. It is also characteristic of all three countries that the native language has been favoured in writing about religion, including its archaeology, which makes it difficult to incorporate these studies into wider discussions.

3 History of Research

Interest in the pagan past was first aroused during the Renaissance, especially in Lithuania, where the pagan past was only a few centuries distant. However, these were only solitary attempts and the actual *studying* of past religions started during the Enlightenment in the eighteenth century. Despite their naivety and romanticism, these treatments, where several theoretical and methodological standpoints can be followed, clearly concern pre-Christian religion. Following the example of German philosopher and folklorist J. G. Herder oral tradition was preferred and direct analogy was employed according to which the life of past people could be studied on the basis of contemporary folklore and ethnographic description. A characteristic feature of the period was also the use of *interpretatio antiqua* and the study of mythology instead of religion. The latter involved raising classical Mediterranean mythology as a standard and was a dominating methodology in the eighteenth century (Burton and Richardson 1975: 302). It led to several attempts where systematic and complicated constructions were presented, starting with creation myths and ending with eschatology, despite the obvious lack of available sources, especially in Estonia. Although these eighteenth- and nineteenth-century constructions of pantheons have been criticized, it should be remembered that according to the methodology of the time it would have been impossible to study mythology in any other way than on the basis of the Mediterranean example.

In the nineteenth century, on the basis of national romantic movements, a systematic collection of folklore started in the Baltic countries. This has created a corpus of texts, which has been used to study and interpret religion. But it also brought along a major discrepancy. Earlier studies, based on the medieval and early modern chronicles and other written sources, treated Estonia, Latvia, Prussia, and also Lithuania, as a single uniform area with a pagan people. From the nineteenth century, when different language affinities were stressed and native-language folklore became the dominant source, the manner of research changed. Since then Latvia and Lithuania have been studied together, whereas Estonia has been treated separately or together with Finland, especially in relation to mythology. During the last decades of the nineteenth century, systematic survey of archaeological sites started, where in addition to graves, hill forts, and hoards, holy places from folk religion were also recorded (e.g. Jung in Estonia, Bielenstein in Latvia, Pokrovskiy and Tarasenka in Lithuania [Lang 2006; Urtāns 2008; Vaitkevičius 2004]).

Despite the importance and widespread use of allusions to pre-Christian religions in the nineteenth- and the early twentieth-century national ideologies, it did not attract the interest of archaeologists, even despite some remarkable studies (e.g. Šturms 1946). One of the reasons for this is that the popular collection of folklore and large quantity of notes on religion allowed folklorists and mythologists to create overall narratives and offer systematic reconstructions about past religions. In the case of Estonia the wide use of ethnographic parallels from the Finno-Ugric peoples of Russia became equally important (Loorits 1949; Paulson 1971), and in Latvia–Lithuania similarities with Indo-European mythologies were stressed (Biezais 1961; Gimbutas 1968; Greimas 1992). This tradition remained dominant almost until the end of the twentieth century, and the differences between religions in one area were ignored. The latter has been stressed in the critique of the studies of religion more widely (Rydving 2006: 317). So the studies of scholars were mainly focused on mythologies and the symbolic meanings of myths, known from oral and written sources. In addition, local archaeological sites and finds offered little material for religious interpretations and as the picture that was offered by folklorists and mythologists fitted well with the concept of archaeologists about the past, the need for archaeological interpretations was absent. So archaeology was only used to prove or illustrate the concepts offered by other disciplines (cf. Insoll 2004: 37).

Only from the second part of the twentieth century did archaeologists start to pay more attention to past religions, despite the ideological context of scientific atheism which condemned religious studies. In Estonia the first studies concentrated on Stone Age beliefs (L. Jaanits), cup-marked stones (V. Lõugas) and offering springs (T. Tamla). After the 1990s when access to the publications and approaches of western theoretical archaeology was gained, religion became more recognized. In addition to Christianization (Mägi 2002; Valk 2003), the concept of holiness, as well as the use of stone graves as communication sites, were all discussed (Lang 1999, 2000). Studies about medieval and early modern rural burials in Estonia were also completed in which interpretation was based on local oral tradition (Valk 2001, 2006). A different situation was evident in Latvia, where already in the 1970s systematic archaeological excavations were started at different holy places, e.g. stones, springs, etc. (Urtāns 1988). Traditionally Stone Age religion in Latvia (Loze 1995) has been an important topic, but during the last few years new studies about holy places have occurred (Urtāns 2008; Laime 2009). Some attention has also been paid in Estonia and Latvia to stone axes with shaft-holes and their possible religious background. As these have been found in different contexts, both a general protective meaning as well as a more specific interpretation associated with thunder and thunderbolts have been used to help interpret them (Vasks 2003; Johanson 2009 and references therein). In contrast, Lithuanian archaeology of religion has been more connected with mythology and the majority of studies have been published about periods or topics where such an approach is possible. Natural holy places (V. Urbanavicius, V. Daugudis, V. Vaitkevičius, see below), Stone Age religions (A. Butrimas, M. Iršenas), the symbolic meaning of amber and its use for magical purposes (Rimantiene 1980; Bliujiene 2007), etc. have all been studied. Religion has also been discussed in several other studies, especially in relation to burials and death culture.

4 THEORETICAL STANDPOINTS

Throughout the twentieth century, religious studies in the Baltic countries have been mostly empirical, presenting the results of excavations, describing, classifying and cataloguing, and at the same time interpretations have been seldom made and theoretical standpoints little considered. Traditionally an ahistorical approach which focuses on a single phenomenon has also been favoured (Insoll 2007: 141). Different studies have been isolated and religion has not been seen as an entity where different phenomena interact. This approach has recently been criticized and a more historical approach has been suggested, where religion is discussed by periods and according to sources from this period (Usačiovaitė 2006; Jonuks 2005, 2009a). Formerly, as a result of the ahistorical approach, past religions were considered linear, with single phenomena or its remains preserved throughout medieval and modern Christianity and represented in contemporary folk religion and folklore.

Thus all non-Christian phenomena, or that not derived from official Christianity, have, without any discussion, been connected to pre-Christian religion. Within such a framework all non-Christian religious loans or developments during the Christian era have been excluded. This is particularly important as there is a lack of a discussion about medieval Catholicism and its connection with folk religion. If changes in religions over time have been discussed, two classical factors have been stressed: first, changes in economy, together with differences between hunter-fisher-gatherers and agricultural religions; and second, language-based ethnic relations where the invasion of Indo-Europeans with their new religion and domination over proto-Indo-European or Finno-Ugric people was seen as important. Such a periodization of religions means that as the majority of population of the Baltic countries remained rural until the twentieth century it implicitly gave a formal justification to use twentieth-century agrarian folklore to interpret the past since the Late Bronze Age, when agriculture became dominant.

This was done even despite the changed social structures and radically altered burial customs, and without mentioning the intervening 3,000 years.

In the only clearly formulated theoretical approach in the Baltic countries—archaeo-mythology—Marija Gimbutas has been the most important figure. This school has had more influence on the studies of religion of the Balts and less so in Estonia. According to the language-based theory of M. Gimbutas (1968, 1989), Europe was originally settled by pre-Indo-European matriarchal culture, from where chthonic goddesses connected with fertility—Žemyna, Laima, and Ragana—were absorbed into later Baltic religions. This later (3000–2500 BC) became dominated by a militant Indo-European strata associated with male gods, Dievs, Perkunas, Kalevelis, and Velnias, and interpreted as forming paganism as we know it. As Gimbutas has stressed, it was not a process where one layer was replaced by another, but rather represents an intertwining of the two, and this has given further justification to the use of contemporary folklore for studying old beliefs, as motifs from earlier layers have been preserved.

Characteristic of this school is the wide use of folklore sources, which have been combined with archaeology in trying to associate different stages with different dates. But the resulting understanding of the development of religion is again linear—to one religion a new layer has been deposited, then another, and Christianity forms the last one; while reversing the process and peeling off the newer layers of folklore we could study the original religion. Despite stressing the importance of archaeology and using its sources to a greater extent than any other school in the Baltic countries, studies of archaeo-mythology are still based upon folklore and archaeology has only been used selectively. The greater part of archaeological material which could not be reconciled with folklore has been left out and many phenomena of past religions have thus not been discussed as they cannot be compared with folklore.

5 SOURCES

As the religious source material from the Baltic countries is relatively poor, a rich variety of different sources have been used, with three being dominant—medieval and early modern written documents, nineteenth- and twentieth-century oral tradition and toponyms, and archaeological material.

5.1 Written Sources

Written sources from the Middle and Modern Ages have been the most extensively used. Beside chronicles and travelogues, these also include church visitation reports, juridical documents and witch trial protocols that have been used for studying pre-Christian religion. Even though the majority of data pertaining to religious history in the Baltic countries has been amassed since the nineteenth century (e.g. Mannhardt 1936; Vėlius 1996), the interpretation of this material has remained until very recently in a state of relative methodological naivety. For the most part, the data found in chronicles and official documents have been seen as direct evidence of religious practices without taking into account their inner ideological and rhetorical codes (Tamm and Jonuks in press). Hence, the only reports that are available are written by strangers to the language, religion, and culture, and in several cases their hostility towards the described religion and their bearers is stressed.

The earliest chronicles which are also the most valuable for studying pre-Christian religion are the thirteenth- and fourteenth-century ones, and these were written down in the context of mission (e.g. the Chronicle of Henry of Livonia, the Livonian Rhymed Chronicle). They stress the difference between pagan countries and the Christian world, thus giving legitimacy to the Crusade. After the end of active Christianization, descriptions become shorter and more stereotypic, stressing universal pagan *topos* like the worship of sun, moon, trees, stones etc. by local peasants.

The main problem in using the written sources has been the lack of source criticism. Texts have been seen as ethnographic descriptions of local people and the role of the scribe as well as the purpose of writing has not been considered. Of course, it does not mean that all of the descriptions should be considered as misinterpretations by foreigners, but a more careful approach to them than has so far been adopted is clearly necessary.

5.2 Folklore

Folklore has been most widely utilized in Estonia and Latvia. This was because the oral tradition was seen as indigenous and authentic and was thus preferred over the chronicles written down by foreigners, a process occurring since the nineteenth-century national awakening (see Putelis 1997; Jonuks 2009a). On the other hand the reason could also be the scarcity of written sources when compared with the living folk religion. The concept of religion and folklore as principally stable and unchangeable influenced and contributed to the use of folklore. Thus the dating of the subjects of the oral tradition never became a research topic. This in turn has influenced the whole understanding of folklore and throughout the history of its use mostly archaic elements have been stressed and the dynamism or changing nature of folklore has been a secondary issue. Instead, in using folklore as a source for interpreting (pre)historic religions it should be noticed that folklore is a living cultural tradition, which changes and develops together with the society which bears it.

The consideration that folklore is constantly dynamic and changes together with its host society gives a new perspective on folklore as a source. At this point the dating possibilities of folklore are important. Among folklorists it is generally accepted that folkloric motifs are difficult to date, and it is impossible to present any exact dates. Nevertheless, such attempts, even speculations, should be considered valuable, since via dates it would be possible to place folkloric motifs in chronological context and thereby observe the functioning of the motifs in a more complete religious picture. As long as we avoid placing folkloric motifs in chronological context, their use to study the distant past as well as the period preceding their documentation, i.e. primarily the nineteenth century, cannot be justified by any means.

In addition to folklore narratives, place names including the words connected with sacredness have been used with the purpose of locating ancient holy places. These include, in addition to the Estonian *hiis*, the Latvian and Lithuanian *elks*, and *alkas*, meaning 'holy place', also the terms for offering-, holy-, church-, healing- etc. (Straubergs 1960; Urtāns 1993, 2008; Vaitkevičius 2004, 2006; Valk 2007a). In addition to locating holy places according to folklore, etymologies of *hiis* and *elks/alkas* have been discussed (Vaitkevičius

2003; Jonuks 2009b and references therein). It is also interesting to note the difference in the spread of toponyms—in the territory of the Baltic languages and mythology multiple toponyms linked with gods (Jānis, Māra, Laima, Perkūnas, etc.) are represented while in Estonia only single examples, connected with the thunder god Uku, are known. Probably such a difference in the distribution of place names also indicates differences in pre-Christian religion, which is even more important as besides the rich Baltic pantheon we know only one Estonian pre-Christian god by name—Tharapita (Sutrop 2004).

5.3 Archaeological Sources

As there are few archaeological sites or materials that can be directly associated with religion a lack of discussion can also be observed. Thus the way of studying the Baltic material fits well into the wider East European tradition where emphasis has been placed upon publication and description but where interpretation has been left out (for a critique of such approaches see Bailey 2005) or, where interpretation is included, it has been done in a naive way through transferring modern folk-beliefs on to the Stone Age. Traditionally burial places have been most used to interpret past religion but here the dominating way is to interpret religion through social relationships. It is clear that it is not possible to separate religion, ritual, and social systems and to study one without the other can be problematic, but in these interpretations religion has been either ignored or used in a vulgar, Marxist way, as one possibility of manifesting social positions. Another important problem is also the highly symbolic nature of archaeological material and the lack of direct 'narrative' sources. The majority of ornament was probably made on artefacts for aesthetic purposes without wider symbolic meaning. However, different symbolic meanings, mostly connected with astral symbolism, have been ascribed to the swastika, cross, and lunula (Simniškytė 2002; Vaska 2003; Zemītis 2003). Only from the Viking Age are there more pendants in the form of animals, birds etc. For example, Audrone Bliujienė (1999) has tried to find features of the World Tree concept known from Baltic mythology on jewellery. According to this interpretation a three-part vertical (heaven, earth, underworld) and a four-part horizontal (north–south–east–west) axis can be seen, where ornament based on the numbers three or four can be found. But such mythological approaches to ornament remains only a single example (see also Vaska 2006). Such a highly symbolized character of archaeological material brings difficulties in interpretation and has caused a scarce use of archaeology or the style where only very general and universal interpretations (e.g. a ring as a symbol of the sun) have been offered but which are not helpful in studying past religions.

6 Religious Sites and Natural Holy Places: An Archaeological Perspective

In regard to the religious archaeological sites, many studies have focused on stones that have been considered holy for different reasons. Cup-marked stones have predominantly been investigated in Estonia, and a variety of interpretations have been presented; from the connection of cup marks with forging to the archaeo-astronomical interpretation of cup-marks as a stellar map. The two dominant interpretations associate cup marks with either death- or fertility cults (Tvauri 1999; Lang 2007). In addition, new and alternative interpretations have been presented, that the cup marks on stones function as a ritualizing tool (Vedru 2002). It seems, however, that the understanding of cup marks as the outcome of different traditions (cf. Kaliff 1997) will gradually be more widely accepted. The stones with bigger depressions, artificial form, or without marking but with associated folklore, have unfortunately remained unstudied in Estonia but have been the subject of research in Latvia–Lithuania (Urtāns 1992; Daugudis 1995). It is remarkable that often no oral tradition is associated with stones with big conical or flat-bottomed depressions or with stones of cylindrical form, although according to excavations their dating is relatively late, from the sixteenth–eighteenth centuries AD. However, sometimes pottery and charcoal dated to the first millennium AD have also been found in association with them (Daugudis 1995: 135). The majority of holy stones lack associated material, which makes it difficult to place them into a chronological framework. In contrast to Estonian cup-marked stones where interpretations emphasize the symbolic, the big depressions found on the stones in Latvia and Lithuania have gained more ritualistic interpretations, connected with rituals of fire or collecting holy water from the depressions.

During the past couple of decades natural holy places have gained much attention from archaeologists, although actual excavations have seldom been done (Urtāns 1988, 2008; Vaitkevičius 2004; Jonuks 2009b; Valk 2007b). In Latvia and Lithuania the archaeological study of these sites started prior to the Second World War (Tarasenka 1923; Šturms 1946). The current situation regarding these sites is best in Lithuania, where catalogues by area have been published (Vaitkevičius 1998, 2006), whilst an overview has been published of Semigallia in Latvia (Urtāns 2008), and in Estonia the general inventory of holy sites is being planned. It is again characteristic of the Baltic countries that the research remains at a descriptive level and most of the studies focus on localizing and describing the sites rather than interpreting them. As some kind of classification is necessary holy places have mostly been divided according to their geomorphologic features (hills, springs, rivers, fields, etc.). Since the 1990s the term *mythical place* has started to be used in Latvia and Lithuania, but the term is more content-related and implies that all we know about these sites is that they are connected with legend/myth (stories about giants etc.) and no 'cultic' activity should be connected with them.

Since the beginning of the academic study of these sites a single common feature has been looked for which has caused different places in the landscape to be considered holy (e.g. Šturms 1946). In such treatments the anomaly of places has been stressed—springs running towards the east 'against the sun' (Vaitkevičius 2004: 45), standing stones, dominating hills, and other features which look strange in a particular landscape (Figure 54.2). Heiki Valk (2007c) has also recently suggested the importance of the role of energetic fields and the anomaly of vegetation caused by it (branches of trees growing upwards or downwards etc.) as a characteristic of holy places.

A common similarity of all Baltic countries exists in relation to the sources concerning holy sites, with the domination of oral tradition and toponyms (Urtāns 2008; Vaitkevičius 2004; Jonuks 2007). In addition to these, historical records have also been used in order to begin to consider the time before the recording of oral tradition. It is also common to the holy sites of the Baltic countries that associated archaeological features (finds, cultural layer etc.) are missing and it is difficult if not impossible to study sites by 'classical' archaeological

FIGURE 54.2 Holy hill of Tõrma in north Estonia.

methods. This has caused a situation where, despite the importance of holy sites being stressed, these have not been excavated, and according to mainstream opinion such excavations are unlikely to be effective. Such an approach has remained regardless of several contrary examples. For instance, several reports of stray finds (coins, jewellery, other items) dating to a long period from the Viking Age to the twentieth century are known from Estonian holy places (Jonuks in press), whilst the best example from Latvia is perhaps the Zebrene *Elka kalns* (Idol hill) (Urtāns 2006) where archaeological research started in the 1860s. Also in Lithuania small excavations have been conducted on some hills or other holy sites (Vaitkevičius 2004 and references therein). With reference to these holy sites a possible feature that could be studied by archaeological methods must be stressed—fences that might have once surrounded the sites. Fences known from folklore have been studied both in Zebrene in Latvia (Urtāns 2006) as well as in Paluküla in Estonia (Jonuks in press); however, the interpretation of the results remained ambiguous.

Rare finds and deficient research methodology hinders the dating of holy sites more precisely. Whenever it has been necessary to offer a more exact date than 'ancient', it has been suggested that sites may have been considered holy for centuries and millennia but without any proper supporting argument. The majority of non-Christian holy sites have been dated from the end of the first millennium through to the beginning of the second millennium AD, i.e. to the period immediately preceding the acceptance of Christianity, which would appear to be logical. However, several stones with artificial depressions, dated to the sixteenth to eighteenth centuries, do not fit this chronology. So it should be stressed that the term 'natural holy place' includes a variety of different sites, some of which have a long tradition of use, but others should be dated only to the near past (especially regarding healing stones, offering sites at single farmsteads, etc.).

In addition to the differences in dating holy sites, their character has been described as different and diverse rituals, numbers of participants, as well as the size of the accompanying hinterland have all been suggested (see Vaitkevičius 2004: 49ff.). The 'smallest' unit could be considered holy stones, sacred trees, etc., which are connected with single farmsteads and the religious background to which are linked rituals and offerings associated with a particular family. Second, holy sites connected to whole villages possess a somewhat wider meaning with communal rituals being conducted in addition to personal rituals. The third level includes sites with the greatest significance and which have been distinguished as political centres with regional, interregional, or intertribal meaning, and which are connected to central places and hill forts (Šturms 1946; Urtāns 2008; Vaitkevičius 2004).

The latter years have brought interest in the topic of cultic places next to natural holy sites. The antique authors' descriptions of Germans and Balts, who used forests and groves for sacrifices instead of temples, are widespread, although both written, as well as archaeological data, exists on temples and god-figures from Latvia and Lithuania (Vėlius 1996: 72ff.). The majority of such open ritual areas with their post-holes, fire pits, putative roofed houses, etc. which have been interpreted as the remains of sanctuaries, have been studied in Latvia and Lithuania (Gimbutas 1968; Daugudis 1995; Vaitkevičius 2004: 3; Smirnova 2006 and the references therein). A slightly different but broadly similar site has also been identified in Estonia, in Tõnija on Saaremaa (Mägi 2001, 2005). Such constructions have been dated mostly to the first millennium AD or slightly earlier. The majority are associated with graves and thus they have been associated with death cultures and accompanying transition rituals have been suggested to have taken place there. A few cases of possible Stone Age holy sites are also known, localized beside waterbodies and originally marked with wooden posts or figures (Butrimas 2000).

7 CONCLUSIONS AND DIRECTIONS OF FUTURE RESEARCH

Considering the increasing interest in studies about religion during the past few years in the Baltic countries, especially by younger students, new studies and interpretations can be expected. Most certainly the wide use of different sources should be continued but a more source-critical approach is necessary. So far, source criticism has been used predominantly for medieval and modern texts; however, folklore notes have been used more haphazardly and their dating or different interpretive possibilities have hardly been discussed. A more critical approach towards sources would probably allow seeing a more diverse picture of past religions and will probably also exclude naïve interpretations where sources from different periods and topics have simply been mixed together. Discussions about the interaction between Christianity and medieval and modern folk religion have been rather simple as well. As Christianity has often been considered merely a new religious layer beside the conservative folk religion, the changes and developments in the latter have not been discussed, resulting in separate studies of Christianity and folk religion. Treating them together would offer new perspectives, some 'ancient' motifs may turn out to be Christian, and folk religion will become more alive.

However, the most important aspect in future studies should be a more historical approach. Studies so far, that have often focused on single phenomena and emphasized the stability and conservativeness of folklore as the main source of analogy, have supported the treatment of religion as ahistorical. Instead, through looking at several phenomena together in time and studying their relationships, a more complete picture of a past religion that is more dynamic will appear. Only then will the religions of the Baltic countries during the past 10,000 years be more fully understood.

Suggested Reading

The few studies that exist on the archaeology of religion in the Baltic countries have largely been published in native languages; it is therefore difficult to offer a comprehensive list for the international reader. This noted, studies utilizing a traditional approach include: Gimbutas (1968, 1989); Greimas (1992); Biezais (1961); Loorits (1949); Paulson (1971), and several recent publications are available focusing upon holy places: Vaitkevičius (2004); Urtāns (2008); Jonuks (2009b) and sacred stones: Urtāns (1992); Daugudis (1995), reflecting the main topics of research on the archaeology of religion in the Baltic States. About recent studies of methodology and theoretical approach see Jonuks (2005, 2009a).

References

BAILEY, D. 2005. *Prehistoric Figurines: Representation and corporeality in the Neolithic* (London: Routledge).
BIEZAIS, H. 1961. *Die Gottesgestalt der Lettischen Volksreligion*, Acta Universitatis Uppsaliensis. Historia Religionum 1 (Stockholm, Göteborg, Uppsala: Almqvist and Wiksell).
BLIUJIENE, A. 1999. *Vikingų epochos kuršių papuošalų ornamentika*, Lietuvos Istorijos Institutas (Vilnius: Diemedis).
——2007. *Lietuvos priešistorės gintaras*, Klaipėdos Universiteto Baltijos Regiono Istorijos ir Archaeologijos Institutas (Vilnius: Versus Aureus).
BUTRIMAS, A. 2000. 'Human figurines in Eastern-Baltic Prehistoric Art' in A. Butrimas (ed.), *Prehistoric Art in the Baltic Region* (Vilnius: Vilnius Academy of Fine Art), pp. 93–105.
DAUGUDIS, V. 1995. 'Die Eisenzeitliche Kultstätten in Litauen', *Archaeologia Baltica*, 1: 121–46.
DUMÉZIL, G. 1952. *Les Dieux des Indo-Europeens* (Paris: Presses Universitaires de France).
FELDMAN, B. and RICHARDSON, R. D. 1975. *The Rise of Modern Mythology 1680–1860*, (Bloomington: Indiana University Press).
GIMBUTAS, M. 1968. *The Balts* (New York, Washington: Praeger).
——1989. 'The Pre-Christian religion of Lithuania' in *La cristianizzazione della Lituania. Pontificio comitato di sceinze storiche. Atti e documenti 2* (Libreria editrice Vaticana: Città del Vaticano), pp. 13–25.
——1991. *The Civilization of the Goddess: The world of old Europe* (New York: Harper Collins).

GREIMAS, A.J. 1992. *Of Gods and Men: Studies in Lithuanian mythology*, trans. M. Newman (Bloomington and Indianapolis: Indiana University Press).
INSOLL, T. 2004. *Archaeology, Ritual, Religion* (London: Routledge).
—— 2007. '"Natural" or "human" spaces? Tallensi sacred groves and shrines and their potential implications for aspects of Northern European prehistory and phenomenological interpretation', *Norwegian Archaeological Review*, 40(2): 138–58.
JOHANSON, K. 2009. 'The changing meaning of "thunderbolts"', *Folklore: Electronic journal of folklore*, 42: 129–74.
JONUKS, T. 2005. 'Archaeology of religion—Possibilities and prospects', *Estonian Journal of Archaeology*, 9(1): 32–59.
—— 2007. 'Holy groves in Estonian religion', *Estonian Journal of Archaeology*, 11(1): 3–35.
—— 2009a. *Eesti muinasusund*, Dissertationes archaeologiae Universitatis Tartuensis 2 (Tartu: University of Tartu Press).
—— 2009b. '*Hiis*-sites in the Research History of Estonian Sacred Places', *Folklore: Electronic journal of folklore*, 42: 23–44.
—— in press. '*Hiis*-sites in the Parishes of Rapla and Juuru', *Estonian Journal of Archaeology*.
KALIFF, A. 1997. *Grav och kultplats: Eskatologiska föreställningar under yngre bronsålder och äldre järnålder i Östergötland*, Aun, 24 (Uppsala University, Department of Archaeology).
LAIME, S. 2009. 'The sacred groves of the Curonian Ķoniņi: Past and present', *Folklore: Electronic journal of folklore*, 42: 67–80.
LANG, V. 1999. 'Kultuurmaastiku luues. Essee maastiku religioossest ja sümboliseeritud korraldusest', *Eesti Arheoloogia Ajakiri*, 3(1): 63–85.
—— 2000. 'Keskusest ääremaaks: Viljelusmajandusliku asustuse kujunemine ja areng Vihasoo-Palmse piirkonnas Virumaal', *Muinasaja teadus*, 7.
—— 2006. 'The History of Archaeological Research (up to the late 1980s)' in V. Lang and M. Laneman (eds), *Archaeological Research in Estonia 1865–2005*, Estonian Archaeology 1 (Tartu: Tartu University Press), pp. 13–40.
—— 2007. *The Bronze and Early Iron Ages in Estonia*, Estonian Archaeology 3 (Tartu: Tartu University Press).
LOORITS, O. 1949. 'Grundzüge des Estnischen Volksglaubens, 1', *Skrifter utgivna av Kungl. Gustav Adolfs Akademien för folklivsforskning*, 18: 1.
LOZE, I. 1995. 'Late Neolithic burial practices and beliefs in Latvia', *Archaeologija Baltica*, 1: 33–42.
MÄGI, M. 2001. 'Probable cult site beside the Tõnija *tarand*-grave on the island of Saaremaa' in *AVE Arheoloogilised välitööd Eestis/Archaeological Fieldworks in Estonia 2000* (Tallinn: Muinsuskaitseamet), pp. 48–55.
—— 2002. *At the Crossroads of Space and Time: Graves, changing society and ideology on Saaremaa (Ösel), 9th–13th centuries* AD, CCC papers, 6 (Tallinn)
—— 2005. 'Mortuary houses in Iron Age Estonia', *Estonian Journal of Archaeology*, 9(2): 93–131.
MANNHARDT, W. 1936. *Letto-Preussische Götterlehre*, Magazin der Lettisch-Literärischen Gesellschaft XXI (Riga).
PAULSON, I. 1971. *The Old Estonian Folk Religion* (Bloomington: Indiana University; The Hague: Mouton).
PUHVEL, J. 1989. *Comparative Mythology* (Baltimore: Johns Hopkins University Press).
PUTELIS, A. 1997. 'Folklore and Identity: the Situation of Latvia', *Folklore: Electronic journal of folklore*, 4: 61–76.
RIMANTIENĖ, R. 1980. *Šventoji II: Pamarių kultūros gyvenvietės* (Vilnius: Mokslas).

RYDVING, H. 2006. 'Constructing religious pasts: Summary reflections' in L. B. Mortensen (ed.), *The Making of Christian Myths in the Periphery of Latin Christendom (c. 1000-1300)* (Copenhagen: Museum Tusculanum Press, University of Copenhagen), pp. 315-21.

SIMNISKYTE, A. 2002. 'Roman period metal half-moon shaped pendants with knobs in eastern Baltic region', *Archaeologia Baltica*, 5: 95-122.

SMIRNOVA, M. 2006. 'Pole constructions in open air ritual areas of the northern Sambian coast in the first millennium AD', *Archaeologia Baltica*, 6: 58-67.

STURMS, E. 1946. 'Die Alkstätten in Litauen', *Contributions of Baltic University*, 3: 1-36.

STRAUBERGS, K. 1960. 'Latviešu kultavietu vārdi' in E. Hauzenberga-Sturma (ed.), *In honorem Endzelini* (Chicago: Čikāagas baltu filologu kopa), 138-48.

SUTROP, U. 2004. 'Taarapita: The great god of the Oeselians', *Folklore: Electronic journal of folklore*, 26: 27-64.

TAMM, M. and JONUKS, T. in press. 'Religious practices of the Estonians in the Medieval Written Sources (11th-15th centuries)' in M. Kõiva (ed.), *Mythologia Uralica* (Suomen Kirjallisuuden Seura; Hungarian Academy of Sciences).

TARASENKA, P. 1923. 'Alko akmenys Trakų apskrityje', *Kultūra*, 1: 25-34.

TVAURI, A. 1999. 'Cup-marked stones in Estonia', *Folklore: Electronic journal of folklore*, 11: 113-69.

URTĀNS, J. 1988. *Yazicheskiye kultoviye pamiatniki na territoriyi Latviyi* (Leningrad: Akademiya Nauk SSSR).

—— 1992. 'Cylindrical ritualistic stones with cup-mark in Latvia', *Journal of Baltic Studies*, XXIII(1): 47-56.

—— 1993. 'Velna vārds Latvijas vietās un vietvārdos', *Latvijas Vēsture*, 11: 55-61.

—— 2006. 'Cult hill *Zebrenes Elka kalns* in Semigallia' in E. Usačiovaitė (ed.), *Senovės baltų kultūra. Gamta ir religija*, Kultūros, Filosofijos ir Meno Institutas (Vilnius: Versus Aureus), pp. 94-109.

—— 2008. *Ancient Cult Sites of Semigallia. Zemgales senās kulta vietas*, CCC papers 11 (Riga: Nordik).

USACIOVAITE, E. 2006. 'Dėl senosios baltų religijos tyrinėjimo metodų' in E. Usačiovaitė (ed.), *Senovės baltų kultūra. Gamta ir religija*, Kultūros, Filosofijos ir Meno Institutas (Vilnius: Versus Aureus), pp. 14-63.

VAITKEVICIUS, V. 1998. *Senosios Lietuvos šventvietės. Žemaitija* (Vilnius: Diemedis).

—— 2003. *Alkai. Baltų Šventviečių Studija*, Lietuvos Istorijos Institutas (Vilnius: Diemedis).

—— 2004. *Studies into the Balt's Sacred Places*, BAR International Series 1228 (Oxford: John and Erica Hedges Ltd).

—— 2006. *Senosios Lietuvos šventvietės. Aukštaitija* (Vilnius: Diemedis).

VALK, H. 2001. *Rural Cemeteries of Southern Estonia 1225-1800 AD*, CCC papers, 3 (Visby and Tartu: University of Tartu Press).

—— 2003. 'Christianisation in Estonia: A process of dual-faith and syncretism' in M. Carver (ed.), *The Cross Goes North: Processes of conversion in Northern Europe, AD 300-1300* (York: Woodbridge), pp. 571-9.

—— 2006. 'Cemeteries and ritual meals: Rites and their meaning in the traditional Seto worldview' in A. Andrén, K. Jennbert, and C. Raudvere (eds), *Old Norse Religion in Long-Term Perspectives: Origins, changes, and interactions*, Vägar till Midgård 8 (Lund: Nordic Academic Press), pp. 141-6.

——2007a. 'Archaeology, oral tradition and traditional culture' in V. Lang and M. Laneman (eds), *Archaeological Research in Estonia 1865–2005*, Estonian Archaeology 1 (Tartu: Tartu University Press), pp. 311–16.

——2007b. 'Looduslikud pühapaigad kui muistised: arheoloogia vaatenurk' in H. Valk and A Kaasik (eds), *Looduslikud pühapaigad. Väärtused ja kaitse*, Õpetatud Eesti Seltsi Toimetised XXXVI. Maavalla Koda (Tartu Ülikool: Tartu), pp. 135–70.

——2007c. 'Choosing holy places', *Journal of Roman Archaeology*, 67(1): 201–12.

VASKA, B. 2003. 'Solar and lunar symbols in medieval archaeological material from Latvia (13th–17th century)' in I. Loze (ed.), *Art, Applied Art and Symbols in Latvian Archaeology*, Humanities and Social Sciences, Latvia 2(39) (Riga: University of Latvia), pp. 96–117.

——2006. 'Baltu pasaules modeļa atspoguļojuma iespējamās paralēles folklorā un arheoloiskajā ornamentā', *Kultūras krustpunkti*, 3: 91–112.

VASKS, A. 2003. 'The symbolism of stone work-axes (based on material from the Daugava Basin)', *Archaeologia Lituana*, 4: 27–32.

VEDRU, G. 2002. 'Maastik, aeg ja inimesed' in V. Lang (ed.), *Keskus—tagamaa—ääreala: Uurimusi asustushierarhia ja võimukeskuste kujunemisest Eestis*, Muinasaja teadus, 11 (Ajaloo Instituut: Tallinn), pp. 101–22.

VELIUS, N. 1996. *Baltų religijos ir mitologijos šaltiniai. Nuo seniausių laikų iki XV a. Pabaigos*, I (Vilnius: The Science and Encyclopedia Publishers).

ZEMĪTIS, G. 2003. 'The swastika in Latvian archaeological material' in I. Loze (ed.), *Art, Applied Art and Symbols in Latvian Archaeology*, Humanities and Social Sciences, Latvia 2(39) (Riga: University of Latvia), pp. 141–9.

PART V
ARCHAEOLOGY OF WORLD RELIGIONS

CHAPTER 55

THE ARCHAEOLOGY OF RITUAL AND RELIGION IN ANCIENT ISRAEL AND THE LEVANT, AND THE ORIGINS OF JUDAISM

AARON A. BURKE

1 INTRODUCTION

THERE has been no shortage of attempts to interpret the archaeological evidence for the rituals and religion of the Canaanites and Israelites over the last century (see Suggested Reading). Although in recent years studies in the archaeology of Israelite religion have begun to consider new questions and issues such as the role of women in Israelite religion and the existence of multiple traditions of Israelite religious practice, the results of many of these approaches remain fairly predictable. The greatest limitations of such studies have been the result of their overwhelming reliance on the use of the Hebrew Bible for interpreting Canaanite religious traditions and the varied conclusions that can be drawn from the archaeological evidence for Israelite religion. Studies of Israelite and Canaanite ritual and religion have, therefore, quite often engaged in circular argumentation with a reliance on the Hebrew Bible to interpret Canaanite religion and vice versa. Since ritual pertains to customs of regular occurrence, in this context pertaining to religious practices, this treatment of the origins of Israelite religion will address the places, artefacts, and symbols associated with what may be identified as the ideal type that characterized ritual and religious practices of the Israelites as they developed from their predecessors, the Amorites and Canaanites. In light of the limits of space it is perhaps most important to begin by articulating a discrete framework for interpreting the archaeological evidence that has contributed to our understanding of the development of Israelite ritual and religion, and hence to the origins of Judaism. Because of the general recognition by scholars of the Hebrew Bible and the archaeology of Israel that the term Judaism is reserved for reference to the Jewish religion during the Second Temple period (c.520 BC to AD 70), the reader is referred to Chapter 56, 'The Archaeology of Judaism from the Persian Period to the Sixth Century AD', for these later developments. This chapter therefore addresses the development of Amorite and Canaanite religion through the end of Israelite religion, namely, the destruction of the First Temple in 586 BC.

1.1 Ethnic Terms

To begin with, it is necessary to define the ethnic terms that must be employed in this chapter to distinguish between the related rituals and religious practices of Amorites, Canaanites, Israelites, and Jews after the destruction of the First Temple. While these are certainly not all of the groups relevant to a discussion of the evolution of Canaanite and Israelite cult, these groups are those that significantly shaped the development of Israelite religion and provide a context for the consideration of the origins of Judaism. Nevertheless, to some extent, it is impossible not to make reference to discoveries related to the religion of Israel's neighbours during the Iron Age (c.1200–500 BC), which include the Phoenicians, Ammonites, Moabites, and Edomites, all of which can be included under the umbrella of Iron Age cults that continued Canaanite traditions. Virtually nothing is known, however, of Aramean cult practices, which were also most likely an outgrowth of earlier Amorite cult practices. The term Amorite is employed here to distinguish the cult practices of the inhabitants of the Levant (western Syria, Lebanon, Israel, the Palestinian territories, Jordan, and the Sinai) during the period prior to the emergence of Israel no later than the mid-thirteenth century BC. (For the primary historical text, demonstrating the emergence of Israel during the thirteenth century BC, see the Merneptah Stele in Hallo 2000.) The earliest phase that can be identified with Amorite religion extends from the beginning of the nineteenth century BC to the end of the thirteenth century BC, while the later phase, which we may identify with Canaanite religion, continues its development from the Iron Age through the early classical period and, in effect, parallels the development of Israelite religion, which for the reasons discussed in this work must be considered an outgrowth of Canaanite religion. Thus, both Canaanite and Israelite religions of the first millennium BC trace their origins to Amorite ritual and religious practices of the second millennium BC. It is possible to identify so-called 'ideal types' (i.e. standard patterns of ritual practice) in the archaeological evidence for Amorite ritual and religion during the second millennium BC that persist in the archaeology of Israelite religion (which also continue in early Judaism) and provide an important starting point for the consideration of Israelite ritual and religion.

1.2 Relevant Texts

The foregoing distinction between Amorite and Israelite religious traditions of the second and first millennia BC presumes a familiarity with the textual corpora of these traditions, which introduces the first major challenge to the study of the archaeology of Amorite, Canaanite, and Israelite cults. In this respect it is a long-established scholarly tradition to regard these texts as artefacts in and of themselves. That these texts are widely recognized as artefacts is clearly supported by their archaeological contexts. On the one hand, a corpus of cult and ritual texts written in Ugaritic on clay tablets, which were found in the so-called 'priest's house' at Ugarit in Syria and date to the end of the Late Bronze Age (c.1200), provide the primary framework for understanding Ugaritic religion (Wyatt 1999). On the other hand, the Hebrew Bible (Old Testament among Christians), a collection of etiological stories, religious law, royal history, prophetic writings, and wisdom literature written in Hebrew and Aramaic which appear to have been canonized c.AD 90, serve as the starting point for our understanding of Israelite religion. The discovery of the Dead Sea Scrolls in the late 1940s provides the strongest basis for the recognition of these texts as archaeological artefacts. However, archaeological discoveries, such as the Ketef Hinnom inscription dated to the late seventh century, tomb inscriptions, and a handful of other monumental inscriptions, lend support not only for the historical context of the Hebrew Bible and its recognition as an archaeological artefact but also the veracity of many details it records concerning the religion, culture, and history of Israel. Despite the usefulness of such corpora, both the Ugaritic texts and Hebrew Bible reflect limited phases in the development of their respective religious traditions, and they can provide only a few points of data within approximately 2,000 years of development in these religious traditions. For this very reason, therefore, archaeology continues to play a critical role in our interpretation of the relationship and the development of these traditions.

1.3 Archaeological Approaches

In light of the large corpus of archaeological data that exists for understanding Amorite and Israelite religions, and the fact that such textual corpora exist by which it is possible to check our interpretations, an historical–archaeological approach to the development of Israelite religion remains fundamental. In pursuing such an approach it is imperative that the aforementioned texts serve as data for the periods from which they derive, while attempting to avoid the circular argumentation that has plagued the study of the archaeology of Israelite religion. This circular argumentation usually begins with the assumption that Israelite ritual and religion is sufficiently well understood from biblical texts and later interpreters, and archaeology serves merely to illuminate this understanding. A second assumption is that Israelite religion primarily constituted a singular system of beliefs and practices, despite the fact the texts record considerable conflict within Israelite society concerning what was to be identified as acceptable, orthodox, or mainstream. With such assumptions in mind the archaeological evidence from the Bronze Age (i.e. prior to 1200 BC) in the Levant has only served to buttress interpretations of Israelite religion as reconstructed from the text of the Hebrew Bible. Nevertheless, to accurately understand the relationship between earlier Amorite religious traditions and later Israelite traditions during the first millennium BC it is essential to understand the origins and evolution of Amorite religious traditions during the second millennium BC independent of first millennium trajectories that grow out from it, which include both Israelite and Canaanite religions. The fact that this has only rarely been the case is underscored by the wholesale lack of a comprehensive archaeological analysis of Amorite religion without reference to Israelite religion.

For nearly every category of archaeological evidence that must be discussed in connection with the development of Israelite religion, its antecedents are to be found in the archaeological record of the Amorite and Canaanite (Amorites of the southern Levant) inhabitants of the Middle and Late Bronze Ages (c.1900–1200 BC) in the Levant. The evidence represented by the archaeological remains includes temples and shrines, idols (e.g. statues and figurines), altars, cult paraphernalia (e.g. cult stands, ritual vessels), standing stones (*massebôt*) and stele, votives and offerings, amulets, and tombs and cemeteries (royal and non-royal). The correlations are, however, more than those that are shared by ancient Near Eastern religions in general; the correlates are both categorical and functional. As is the case for the Iron Age, the material culture of Bronze Age ritual and religion can be divided into archaeological evidence, on the one hand, of state or tribal cult and, on the other hand, for personal piety. Nevertheless, it is important to remember that, while such distinctions are helpful for categorizing the evidence, there is little support for the suggestion that religious views expressed in personal piety were qualitatively different than, or perceived to be in direct conflict with, those expressed at the level of the state or tribe. Simply put, insofar as these two categories were distinguished in antiquity, they are recognized as having met different needs: on the one hand, the needs of the state, and on the other, societal and individual needs.

2 STATE CULT

Given the evidence for the establishment of large territorial kingdoms during the Middle Bronze Age (Burke 2008), it is appropriate to begin with the archaeological evidence for state cult during this period, which is associated with the establishment of Amorite dynasties. In the archaeological record state cult is particularly conspicuous in two forms of evidence: monumental temples and the royal mortuary cult. The most conspicuous evidence for state cult and ritual during the Middle and Late Bronze Age consisted of monumental temples of a single type, which are often identified as migdôl or tower temples (Figure 55.1; Mazar 1990: 211–12). This temple construction features an *in antis* plan, which based on the width of the walls probably supported a multi-storey structure (i.e. tower-like in appearance). This building type finds its precursor among so-called Antentempels of the mid-third millennium from northern Mesopotamia in the region to the east of the Euphrates bend (Akkermans and Schwartz 2003: 251). The cultural and temporal relationship between these two temple types, which are attested in neighbouring regions (northern Mesopotamia and the northern Levant), is now demonstrated at the northern Levantine site of Ebla, where a large migdôl temple dated to the last quarter of the third millennium BC has recently been identified. As the earliest example of this temple type it now appears that it is contemporary with the Antentempel type known in eastern Syria. During both the Middle and Late Bronze Age the migdôl-style temple was constructed throughout the Levant at sites such as Tilmen Höyük, Ugarit, Alalaḫ, Ebla, Hazor, Megiddo, Shechem, Tel Kitan, and Haror (Mazar 1992), and it is widely accepted that this temple style was the basis for the plan of several early Iron Age temples (e.g. 'Ain Dara, Aleppo, Shechem) including the first Israelite temple, which according to the Book of Kings was built in Jerusalem during the tenth century BC (1 Kings 6: 1).

Aside from the fact that this temple type serves as evidence of political and cultural complexity, the cultic and ritual significance of these temples is that they were considered the dwellings of the chief deity or deities of the communities in which they were located. While there is a limited amount of evidence for the statues of the deities (e.g. Ugarit, Megiddo, Hazor), which were probably located at the rear of these temples (and thus

| Ebla | Alalakh VII | Alalakh VI | Megiddo X |
Temple D

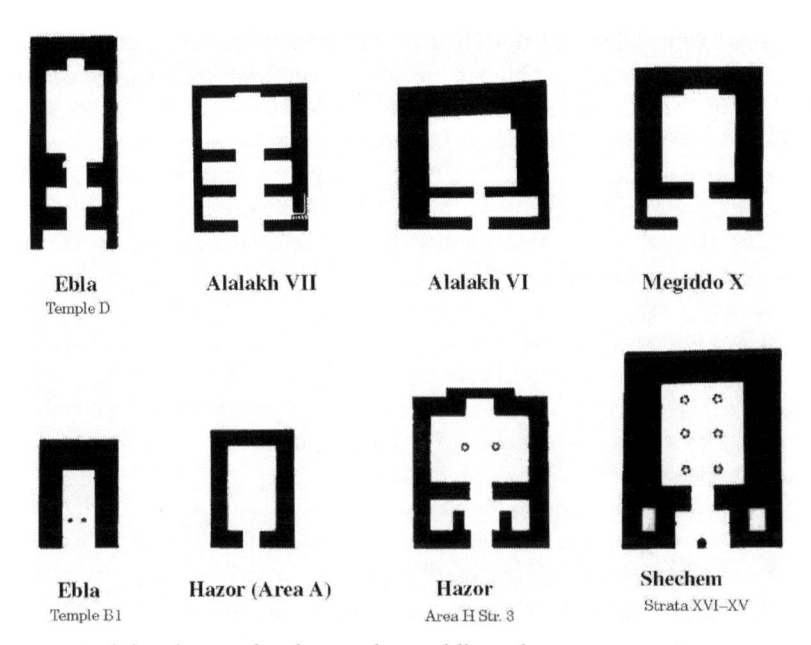

| Ebla | Hazor (Area A) | Hazor | Shechem |
Temple B1 · Area H Str. 3 · Strata XVI–XV

FIGURE 55.1 Migdôl-style temples during the Middle and Late Bronze Ages.

identified by archaeologists as the 'holy of holies', as with the first Israelite temple), the correlation between the iconography of these statues and the Ugaritic texts that describe the physical appearance of some Canaanite divinities suggests the identification of the venerated deities as most likely Baʿal or possibly El; Dagon is suggested as the second deity for which a migdôl temple at Ugarit was constructed. It is quite clear that these temples were constructed primarily for the chief Canaanite deities and not for every deity venerated by the city's inhabitants. While more than 300 divinities are attested in the Ugaritic texts from Late Bronze Age Ugarit, only two migdôl-style temples were constructed within the city. The pattern is similar, therefore, to that prevalent in Mesopotamia, where individual cities identified themselves as the subjects of a chief divinity, despite the existence of a pantheon that often included the chief gods of neighbouring kingdoms. By and large, in the Levant the chief deity appears to have been a manifestation of the Amorite deity Baʿal-Hadad, while the worship of other major Amorite and Canaanite gods such as El, Dagon, Reshef, and Astarte/Anat was less prominent. For example, the so-called 'Ceremonial Palace' (Bonfil and Zarzecki-Peleg 2007; Ben-Tor 2008) that stands alone on the acropolis at Hazor and should be identified as a migdôl-style temple writ large (as argued primarily by Sharon Zuckerman), appears on the basis of the identification of a large metal statue to have been a temple to Baʿal or Hadad. Smaller temples at Hazor in Area A and located in the lower city in Areas C, F, and H, probably served the cultic needs of non-royal residents of the city in their veneration of the city's chief deity as well as the other major Canaanite deities worshipped at Hazor.

While the veneration of the chief Canaanite gods through the construction of centrally located migdôl-style temples during both the Middle and Late Bronze Age is a well-established observation, the cultural significance of this precedent is often inadequately acknowledged in discussions of Iron Age cult in ancient Israel. In short, it appears that

Amorite rituals and religious traditions that were centred around such temples during the Middle and Late Bronze Age established the ideal type to which Iron Age cult aspired, as among the Israelites. This pattern is not, however, one that can be borne out solely by the archaeological record, but rather requires a reliance on textual data, primarily from the Hebrew Bible since the first Israelite temple cannot be archaeologically reconstructed. The pattern described in the bible which is probably normative for Iron Age states in the Levant, as characterized by the description of the construction of the Israelite temple for Yahweh (who is characterized as the sole god of Israel by the biblical writers), is effectively identical: the largest example of a temple *in antis* was built within the capital city for the divinity that was intended to serve as the focal point of religious worship for the nation. Although smaller temples to other Canaanite deities are not preserved, it is again the biblical authors themselves who reveal that shrines were dedicated to these deities (e.g. II Kings 18: 4 and 23: 1–25) and an abundance of ritual paraphernalia suggest the reality of this scenario (see discussion below).

The consensus that has emerged around discussions of ancient Israelite religions leaves, therefore, ample room for the recognition of similarities between Israelite and earlier Amorite cults. Cult among Iron Age Levantine states was, for example, characterized by similarly diverse pantheons, which were largely made up of Canaanite deities already attested in Late Bronze Age sources, with a similar tendency toward the placement of emphasis on the veneration of a chief deity. Alongside the identification of Yahweh, for example, as the chief deity of Israel, biblical texts as well as ostraca (inscribed potsherds) permit the identification of Hadad, Molech, Kemosh, Qaus, and Ba'al as the chief divinities of the Aramaeans, Ammonites, Moabites, Edomites, and Canaanites (Phoenicians), respectively, with widespread acknowledgement that the 'sun, moon, and stars', all of which are identifiable as manifestations of Canaanite deities (i.e. Šapšu, Yariḫu, Šaḫru, Šalimu), persisted to be venerated by the populations of Israel and Judah. None of this should be surprising, however, since for nearly two decades emphasis has been placed on the continuity of material culture and social customs that existed from the end of the Late Bronze Age into the Early Iron Age with the emergence of Israel. Thus, it may be asserted that a proclivity for politically entrenched henotheism marks the archaeological (and historical) record of the Levant from the Middle Bronze Age through the Iron Age, and that the shifting boundaries of the political territories under the 'hegemony' of principal deities reflected the political shifts that Levantine states underwent over more than 1,500 years. Smaller temples, especially during the Middle Bronze Age, marked lesser political centres and probably served as local focal points of worship of chief deities. This trend persisted in the Iron Age with the identification of alternate, although usually smaller, centres of worship such as Arad in Judah (Figure 55.2), and the establishment of multiple sanctuaries in the northern kingdom of Israel at Tel Dan and Bethel (I Kings 12: 28–33). Thus, the principle of the central role played by veneration of the kingdom's chief deity was retained from the Bronze Age through the Iron Age.

Royal mortuary practices comprise the second manifestation of state cult in Levantine society. The existence of an Amorite royal cult during the Middle Bronze Age can be substantiated by the archaeological evidence for the burial complexes of Amorite kings. Perhaps the clearest evidence of the practices associated with the royal cult are to be found at Qatna, where a large burial complex (Figure 55.3) was recently discovered below the late Middle Bronze Age and Late Bronze Age palace (Pfälzner 2007: 55–9). The large complex

FIGURE 55.2 Arad temple, Late Iron Age.

consisted of a long corridor leading to a vertical shaft that gave access to a large central chamber, which was flanked by benches on all sides. This room provided ample evidence of ritual feasting, which included a large quantity of animal bones below the benches and a variety of feasting vessels that the excavators suggest may be connected with *kispum* rituals, as they are known in Mesopotamia. Opposite the entrance and in the left and right walls of the central chamber were entrances leading to three adjoining chambers, which served as the place of interment for the kings, and undoubtedly other members of Qatna's royal household. Although the findings derived from the discovery of the royal tomb at Qatna are quite remarkable for what they reveal concerning the burial practices of Amorite kings during the Middle Bronze Age, what is more remarkable is the fact that rituals associated with Amorite royal burial customs reflect the burial practices of Amorite communities throughout the Levant, which can be discussed within the context of popular cult and the relationship of these practices to later Iron Age burial customs.

3 POPULAR CULT

From the start of the Middle Bronze IIB (*c*.1700 BC) and throughout the Late Bronze Age the burial customs of Amorites and Canaanites consisted largely of family tombs dug into the bedrock, often constructed below the house (Gonen 1992b) or, if extramurally located,

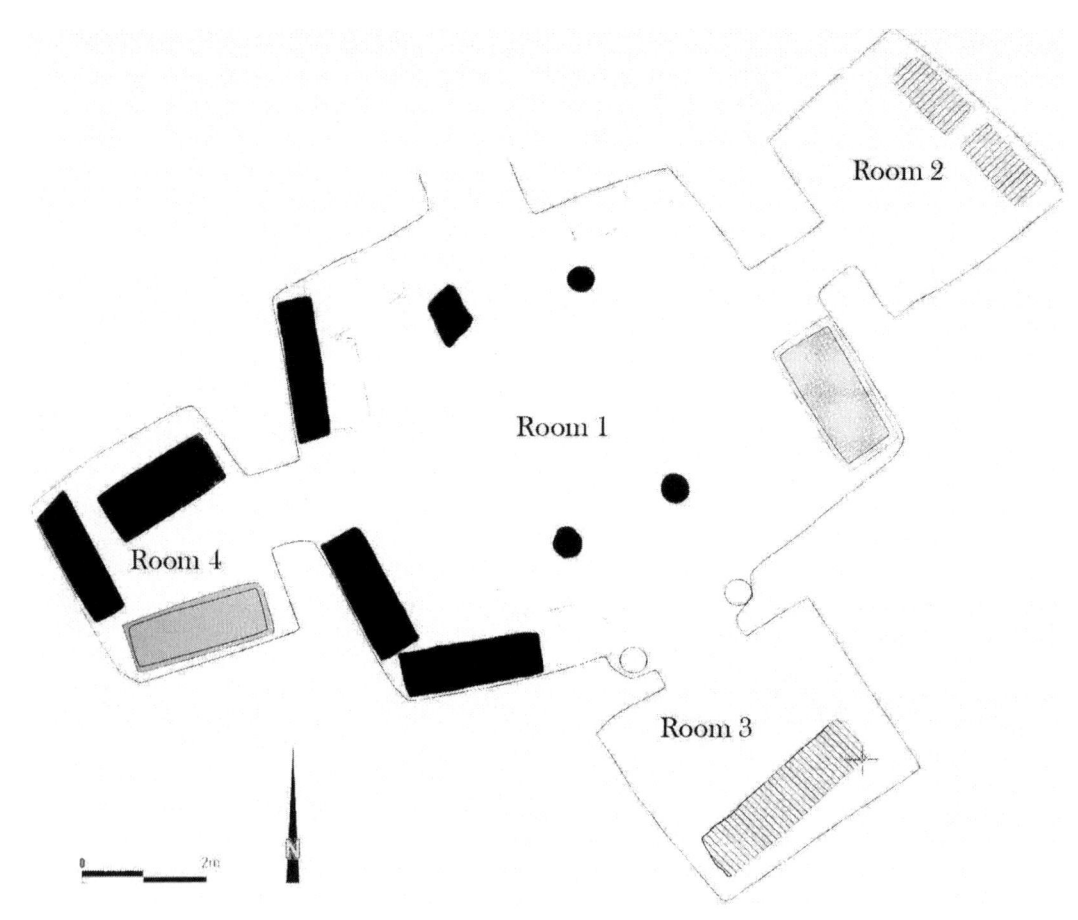

FIGURE 55.3 Plan of the Royal tomb of Qatna. Stone benches in black, sarcophagai in grey, and hatched wooden installations.

cut into a hillside adjacent to the city (Mazar 1990: 213–14; Gonen 1992a). Such large communal tombs, which are known to have served extended patrimonial households, functioned for many generations, and in many instances continued to be used throughout the Late Bronze Age. For the most part, deviations from this burial practice reflect local adaptations to environmental conditions rather than substantive ideological or religious differences across the Levant. This is most clearly demonstrated by the Amorite burials of the late Middle Bronze Age (MB IIC, c.1640–1530 BC) excavated at Avaris in the eastern delta of Egypt (Bietak 1991) where mudbrick cists were constructed above ground. A similar strategy was, in fact, adopted during this period in the southern Levant in what appears to have been an attempt to accommodate additional burials in cemeteries after they had largely achieved their maximum size (e.g. Tell el-'Ajjul, Jericho, Ashkelon). Offerings made within these tombs, although varied in their ornate character and thus suggesting a differentiation in social rank, are remarkably consistent for much of the population (e.g. Baker 2006). They often consist of foodstuffs contained in storage jars, small juglets that may have held perfumes or drink offerings, imported Cypriot and Aegean wares probably bearing expensive perfumes and unguents, and a 'leg of lamb' served on a platter. Scarabs, amulets, and jewellery often adorned the body, but whether these were intended for a religious and/or decorative function can rarely be determined.

The ideal type of Levantine burial practice continued during the Iron Age throughout the southern Levant including in Israel and Judah. Although we possess no clear evidence of Iron Age royal burials belonging to the kings of Israel and Judah, references as in I Kings 2: 10 indicate that these burial practices were far more akin to Amorite and Canaanite burial practices, especially since Judean kings, for example, appear to have been interred within the city and below the palace. The remainder of the population, probably largely as a result of physical constraints on space within the city (although ritual purity is invoked in biblical tradition; Leviticus 19: 11–16), engaged in burial outside of the city walls in adjacent hillsides, which reflects the continuation of a tradition of extramural burial begun during the Middle Bronze Age.

Although during the Iron Age the construction of the finest of these tombs took on an unprecedented level of care for architectural detail (Bloch-Smith 1992), the ideal type remained: a central subterranean tomb complex intended for an extended family, featuring a central room off which smaller chambers opened to accommodate individual family members (Barkay 2000). Even though by the Iron Age there is no direct archaeological evidence for feasting in connection with the burial rites, following the deposition and decomposition of the body, the bones were similarly gathered within special repositories within the tomb, often below the benches upon which bodies could be laid. As during the Bronze Age, also during the Iron Age, the character of the burials varied among social strata as well as in proximity to the capital city, Jerusalem. Nevertheless, like their Amorite and Canaanite antecedents burials included ceramic vessels (presumably with their contents), amulets, and other items suggesting a range of interpretations from preparation and adornment of the body after death to the continuation of earlier beliefs about the needs of the individual in the afterlife. Given the range of Israelite religious perspectives that existed (as indicated in the biblical tradition), it is also likely that a range of interpretations concerning these practices persisted among Israelites and Judeans.

4 EVIDENCE FOR PARTICIPATION IN RITUAL

In addition to the evidence of popular cult that is attested among the burial customs discussed above, other lines of evidence suggest ritual activity on a local level beginning in the Middle Bronze Age and continuing through the Iron Age. Female cult figurines, usually identified with the Canaanite female goddesses Asherah or Astarte, are found throughout these periods, beginning with a large collection of metal figurines during the Middle and Late Bronze Ages (Negbi 1976: 60–105). Although they reveal changing styles of production, ceramic examples of these figurines (Kletter 1996) reveal what may have been the focus of female participation in Canaanite cult and the retention of such practices among many Israelites during the Iron Age. Shrines in veneration of Ba'al are also attested on the basis of metal figurines of the Middle and Late Bronze Ages (Negbi 1976: 8–59) and bull figurines from the Middle Bronze Age (Stager 2006, 2008) to the Iron I period (Mazar 1999), with the adoption of the iconography of Baʿal for the chief deities within Iron Age pantheons, as attested for Yahweh in the biblical texts.

Equally important within personal veneration of Canaanite deities throughout the Bronze and Iron Age is the existence of a number of ritual items and vessels of limited production that are found in domestic contexts or otherwise removed from monumental temple complexes. Among these are ceramic model shrines (Muller 2002; Ziffer and Kletter 2007). These indicate the appearance of temples and shrines during these periods but also verify the identification of the deities venerated within them through the use of symbols associated with the different deities. Although exactly how these models functioned is unknown, they may have served as stand-ins for cult centres that could not be regularly visited by many individuals. Indeed the challenges posed for making ritual pilgrimages are illustrated by the traditional pilgrimages to Jerusalem reportedly made by Israelites during the Iron Age, a practice that was continued during the Second Temple period.

Objects of personal adornment also revealed aspects of individual religious conviction, although to what extent these reflected or were used in ritual activity is impossible to determine. During the end of the Middle, and throughout the Late Bronze Age, pendants adorned the bodies of buried females (McGovern 1985). The consistent depiction of a female goddess, not unlike the ceramic figurines, with emphasis on breasts and the pubic area (and adopting Egyptian artistic tradition associated with Hathor) suggest the identification of the goddess with Asherah or Astarte. A shift towards aniconism may be suggested in the absence of such pendants and the dearth of images of Baʿal during the Iron Age in Israel, as in the absence of any unequivocal evidence for the identification of iconography or statuary associated with Yahweh.

That throughout the Bronze and Iron Ages individuals burned incense and made personal sacrifices to their gods is suggested by incense stands and ritual vessels. While many exemplars of these are likely to have been metal and thus have not survived, a variety of painted vessels from the Middle and Late Bronze Ages serve as likely candidates for use in ritual, as also suggested by their contexts. These include bichrome ware of the late Middle Bronze and early Late Bronze Age (Epstein 1966) with a range of animal motifs that correlate with Canaanite deities: the bull (Baʿal), bird or dove (Asherah), fish (Lotan/Leviathan), and disc-wheel (Šapšu/Šemeš), and vessels decorated with various motifs, such as the tree-of-life throughout the Late Bronze Age (Amiran 1970: 161–5). In addition to ceramic cult stands, ritual vessels of the Iron Age include *kernoi*, circular ceramic rings with attached cups and spouts, the function of which is entirely enigmatic (Amiran 1970: 302–6). Ceramic incense stands were also accompanied by horned altars, which make their appearance in ancient Israel during the Iron Age continuing the tradition of burning incense to the gods, as depicted in Egyptian reliefs showing besieged Canaanite cities during the Late Bronze Age.

5 Conclusions

If any trends present themselves as characteristic of Israelite ritual and religion during the Iron Age, these are most evident by contrasting Israelite cult with that of the Amorites and Canaanites. Such an approach reveals that, at the level of state cult, limited change is evident in the archaeological record, with increased centralization as perhaps the most evident change during the Iron Age. This occurred principally with nearly exclusive construction of monumental temples within capital cities such as Jerusalem during the Iron Age. Nevertheless, shrines and smaller temples, which may reflect attempts to retain local access to the central cult, continued to be built in keeping with the visibility of state cult that was characteristic during the Middle and Late Bronze Ages. Increased efforts to centralize cult may have contributed to the proliferation of artefacts associated with personal piety, such as cult stands, female goddess figurines, and ceramic cult vessels that are not described as part of orthodox Israelite religion in the Hebrew Bible.

Suggested Reading

Levantine archaeology (Steiner and Killebrew forthcoming; Mazar 1990; Stern 2001; Ben-Tor 1992); Israelite religion (Albertz 1992; Miller 2000); archaeology of Canaanite and Israelite religion (Zevit 2001; Nakhai 2001; Dever 2005); Canaanite myths (Cross 1973); Ugaritic religious texts: (1) Baʻal cycle (Pardee 1997b), Kirta epic (Pardee 1997c), and ʻAqhatu cycle (Pardee 1997a), (2) Ugaritic cult ritual texts (Pardee 2002), and technical discussions concerning the Canaanite sacrificial system, see del Olmo Lete (1999).

References

Akkermans, P. M. M. G. and Schwartz, G. M. 2003. *The Archaeology of Syria: From complex hunter-gatherers to early urban societies (ca.16,000–300 BC)* (Cambridge: Cambridge University Press).

Albertz, R. 1992. *A History of Israelite Religion in the Old Testament Period*, I: *From the Beginnings to the End of the Monarchy* (Louisville, KY: Westminster John Knox).

Amiran, R. 1970. *Ancient Pottery of the Holy Land: From its beginnings in the Neolithic period to the end of the Iron Age*, English edn (Piscataway, NJ: Rutgers University Press).

Baker, J. L. 2006. 'The Funeral Kit: A newly defined Canaanite mortuary practice based on the Middle and Late Bronze Age tomb complex at Ashkelon', *Levant*, 38: 1–31.

Barkay, G. 2000. 'Excavations at Ketef Hinnom in Jerusalem' in H. Geva (ed.), *Ancient Jerusalem Revealed* (Jerusalem: Israel Exploration Society), pp. 85–106.

Ben-Tor, A. 1992. *The Archaeology of Ancient Israel* (New Haven: Yale University Press).

——2008. 'The "White Building" is a temple: Response to Bonfil and Zarzecki-Peleg', *IEJ*, 58: 94–9.

Bietak, M. 1991. *Tell el-Dabʻa V: Ein Friedhofsbezirk der Mittleren Bronzezeitkultur mit Totentempel und Siedlungsschichten*, Denkschriften Der Gesamtakademie IX (Vienna: Österreichischen Akademie der Wissenschaften).

Bloch-Smith, E. 1992. *Judahite Burial Practices and Beliefs about the Dead*, JSOT/ASOR Monograph Series 7 (Sheffield: JSOT).

Bonfil, R. and Zarzecki-Peleg, A. 2007. 'The palace in the upper city of Hazor as an expression of a Syrian architectural paradigm', *BASOR*, 348: 25–47.

BURKE, A. A. 2008. *'Walled Up to Heaven': The evolution of Middle Bronze Age fortification strategies in the Levant*, Studies in the Archaeology and History of the Levant 4 (Winona Lake, IN: Eisenbrauns).

CROSS, F. M. 1973. *Canaanite Myth and Hebrew Epic: Essays in the history of the religion of Israel* (Cambridge, MA: Harvard University Press).

DEVER, W. G. 2005. *Did God Have a Wife? Archaeology and folk religion in ancient Israel* (Grand Rapids, MI: Eerdmans).

EPSTEIN, C. 1966. *Palestinian Bichrome Ware*, Documenta et monumenta Orientis antiqui 12 (Leiden: Brill).

GONEN, R. 1992a. *Burial Patterns and Cultural Diversity in Late Bronze Age Canaan*, American Schools of Oriental Research Dissertation Series (Winona Lake, IN: Eisenbrauns).

—— 1992b. 'Structural Tombs in the Second Millennium BC' in A. Kempinski and R. Reich (eds), *The Architecture of Ancient Israel: From the prehistoric to the Persian periods* (Jerusalem: Israel Exploration Society), pp. 151–60.

HALLO, W. W. (ed.) 2000. *The Context of Scripture*, II: *Monumental Inscriptions from the Biblical World* (Leiden: Brill).

KLETTER, R. 1996. *The Judean Pillar-Figurines and the Archaeology of Asherah*, BAR International Series 636 (Oxford: Tempus Reparatum).

McGOVERN, P. E. (ed.) 1985. *Late Bronze Palestinian Pendants: Innovation in a cosmopolitan age*, JSOT/ASOR Monograph Series 1 (Sheffield: JSOT).

MAZAR, A. 1990. *Archaeology of the Land of the Bible 10,000–586 BCE*, 1st edn, Anchor Bible Reference Library (New York: Doubleday).

—— 1992. 'Temples of the Middle and Late Bronze Ages and the Iron Age' in A. Kempinski and R. Reich (eds), *The Architecture of Ancient Israel: From the prehistoric to the Persian Periods* (Jerusalem: Israel Exploration Society), pp. 161–87.

—— 1999. 'The "Bull Site" and the "Einun Pottery" reconsidered', *PEQ*. 131: 144–8.

MILLER, P. D. 2000. *The Religion of Ancient Israel* (Louisville, KY: Westminster John Knox Press).

MULLER, B. 2002. *Les «maquettes architecturales» du Proche-Orient: Mésopotamie, Syrie, Palestine du IIIe au milieu du Ier millénaire av. J.-C.*, Bibliothèque archéologique et historique 160 (Beirut: Institut Français d'Archéologie du Proche-Orient).

NAKHAI, B. A. 2001. *Archaeology and the Religions of Canaan and Israel*, ASOR Books 7 (Boston: American Schools of Oriental Research).

NEGBI, O. 1976. *Canaanite Gods in Metal* (Tel Aviv: Tel Aviv University).

OLMO LETE, G. DEL 1999. *Canaanite Religion: According to the liturgical texts of Ugarit* (Bethesda, MD: CDL).

PARDEE, D. 1997a. 'The "Aqhatu" Legend' in W. W. Hallo and K. L. Younger (eds), *The Context of Scripture*, I (Leiden: Brill), pp. 343–56.

—— 1997b. 'The Ba'lu Myth' in W. W. Hallo and K. L. Younger (eds), *The Context of Scripture*, I (Leiden: Brill), pp. 241–85.

—— 1997c. 'The Kirta Epic' in W. W. Hallo and K. L. Younger (eds), *The Context of Scripture*, I (Leiden: Brill), pp. 333–43.

—— 2002. *Ritual and Cult at Ugarit*, Writings from the Ancient World Series, Society of Biblical Literature 10 (Atlanta: Scholars).

PFÄLZNER, P. 2007. 'Archaeological investigations in the royal palace at Qatna' in D. M. Bonacossi (ed.), *Urban and Natural Landscapes of an Ancient Syrian Capital:*

Settlement and Environment at Tell Mishrife/Qatna and in Central-Western Syria, Studi Archeologici su Qatna 1 (Udine: Universitaria Udinese), pp. 29–64.

STAGER, L. E. 2006. 'The House of the Silver Calf of Ashkelon' in E. Czerny, I. Hein, H. Hunger, et al. (eds), *Timelines: Studies in honour of Manfred Bietak*, II, Orientalia Lovaniensia Analecta 149 (Leuven: Peeters), pp. 403–10.

——2008. 'The Canaanite silver calf' in L. E. Stager, J. D. Schloen, and D. M. Master (eds), *Ashkelon 1: Introduction and Overview (1985–2006)*, Final Reports of The Leon Levy Expedition to Ashkelon 1 (Winona Lake, IN: Eisenbrauns), pp. 577–80.

STEINER, M. L. and KILLEBREW, A. E. forthcoming. *The Oxford Handbook of the Archaeology of the Levant (ca. 8000–332 BCE)* (Oxford: Oxford University Press).

STERN, E. 2001. *Archaeology of the Land of the Bible*, II: *The Assyrian, Babylonian, and Persian Periods (732–332 BCE)*, 1st edn, Anchor Bible Reference Library (New York: Doubleday).

WYATT, N. 1999. 'The Religion of Ugarit' in W. G. E. Watson and N. Wyatt (eds), *Handbook of Ugaritic Studies*, Handbuch der Orientalistik 39 (Leiden: Brill), pp. 529–85.

ZEVIT, Z. 2001. *The Religions of Ancient Israel: A synthesis of parallactic approaches* (New York: Continuum).

ZIFFER, I. and KLETTER, R. 2007. *In the Field of the Philistines: Cult furnishings from the Favissa of a Yavneh temple* (Tel Aviv: Eretz Israel Museum).

CHAPTER 56

THE ARCHAEOLOGY OF JUDAISM FROM THE PERSIAN PERIOD TO THE SIXTH CENTURY AD

JAMES F. STRANGE

1 JUDAISM IN THE PERSIAN PERIOD

IN 539 BC Cyrus the Great conquered Babylon and ruled an empire that included Judea, now known as 'Yehud'. According to the Cyrus Cylinder and Ezra (1: 2–4), he allowed subjugated peoples to return to their ancestral homes and defeated deities to be returned to their ruined sanctuaries. Cuneiform clay tablets of the Persian period have appeared in excavations at Gezer and in Hadid, about 35 km north-west of Jerusalem. The combined testimony of these cuneiform tablets with the Cyrus cylinder and Ezra suggests that there was indeed a new, presumably Jewish population in Yehud (Judea) from Assyria.

Ezra reports that Sheshbazzar was 'the prince of Judah' (Ezra 1: 8) and 'governor of Judah' (Ezra 5: 14). It is impossible to test via excavation the assertion in Ezra 5: 16 that Sheshbazzar 'laid the foundation of the House of Yahweh which is in Jerusalem'. Some have interpreted 'House of Yahweh' as a reference to the outdoor sacrificial altar, not necessarily to the Temple. The returnees reinstituted sacrifices from the first day of the month of Tishri, apparently in 538 BC.

Archaeological evidence for the new province of 'YHD' or 'Yᵉhûd' includes seal impressions marked 'Yᵉhûd' on jar handles of the sixth century BC found in Mizpah in the north, Jericho in the east, En-Gedi in the south, Gezer in the west, and in Jerusalem. In the capital city not only have excavators found the Yehud seal impressions on jar handles, but have also found clay bullae (seal impressions on clay pellets) with Jewish names of officials, such as Hananiah and Ahzai. Minute silver coins (15 mm in diameter) stamped with the name 'YHD' in Hebrew letters appear in Jerusalem itself, south of Jerusalem, and in a few nearby localities in the fifth century BC. These coins bear images of a lily, an Athenian owl, and even Athena. Since the Jewish cult favoured aniconism, these coins are often interpreted as representing religious syncretism. Yet the coin inscriptions are in a palaeo-Hebrew script.

Furthermore the lily was a decorative feature of the First (Solomon's) Temple and its ceremonial vessels (I Kings 7: 19). Therefore the lily may be understood as a Jewish religious symbol, though theories of symbol in archaeology comprise a thorny issue (Gimbutas 1992, 1997; Talalay 1999; Robb 1998; Emerton 1999).

The archaeological remains assigned with confidence to the Persian period reveal a complex, agrarian society, though with a population much smaller than the earlier period. In fact theoretical debates on method in calculating the number of persons that can live on an acre range from 80 to 200 per acre. These will give widely different estimates of ancient populations in Persian Yehud.

2 JUDAISM IN THE HELLENISTIC PERIOD

Persian domination of Yehud came to a sudden end with the conquests of Alexander the Great, especially the conquest of Judea in 332 BC. From this date forward Judea became the battleground between the Seleucid kings at Damascus and the Ptolemies of Egypt, quartered at Alexandria.

At the time of Nehemiah, the governor of Judea, Sanballat, was in conflict with the Samaritans over the issue of who was allowed to worship at the Temple in Jerusalem. The historical and social conflict yields a prediction that archaeological excavation should tend to confirm or disconfirm the Jewish/Samaritan split. Excavations on Mt Gerizim north of Jerusalem establish that there was an extensive Samaritan cult practiced there. The Samaritans were strongly critical of the Temple cult in Jerusalem according to Josephus and the New Testament. Another group, namely the Essenes, dated their withdrawal from Jerusalem to 390 years after the captivity in Babylon, or 197 BC (Damascus Document, col. I.6–7). This date places them in the reign of the Seleucid King Antiochus III the Great. He and his successors arguably bring about huge changes in Jerusalem, including supporting the Jewish priesthood. Excavations at Qumran suggest that this, the main site of the aforementioned Essenes, was first occupied about 125 BC or during the reign of John Hyrcanus I. Thus at this time there came to be the official cult in Jerusalem, a second Jewish group at Samaria (the Samaritans) strongly critical of the Jerusalem Temple, and a third at Qumran. Current theories of religion stress variation within the cult, and archaeological theories of cult tend to do the same (Kleibrink et al. 2004; Mazar 1982; Bell 1997).

Early Hellenistic, bronze coins from Judea continue the Persian types listed above, but the name of the province is now spelled 'Yehudah' in palaeo-Hebrew letters. These coins copy Ptolemaic coins and therefore feature the head of Ptolemy I and his wife Bernice I or a bird with head turned backwards. Yet by the time of John Hyrcanus I (134–104 BC) there are a dozen types of small, bronze coins (about 15 mm in diameter) from this province, but without human or divine images. These coins most commonly feature the lily and anchor or two cornucopias with a pomegranate between them. A five-line inscription in palaeo-Hebrew in a wreath reads 'John the High Priest and Council of the Jews'. The lack of forbidden images, the use of palaeo-Hebrew writing, and the titles used on the coins tend to support the hypothesis that the coin symbols represent a revitalization of Judaism in this period.

In this period there is a strong Diaspora presence in Egypt and Greece. Greek inscriptions from structures called a *proseuché* ('place of prayer') appear in Egypt as early as Ptolemy and Bernice (*CPJ* 3.1532a)—perhaps Ptolemy III Euergetes and Bernice II (married about 246 BC). Some inscriptions actually mention a '*proseuché* of the Jews'. Current theories are that the Egyptian *proseuché* is the same institution as the Judean *synagogé* ('gathering') (Levine 2005; Flesher 2001; Horbury and Noy 1992). The earliest synagogue building is from the Greek island of Delos and was first built in the second century BC, but came into Jewish use about 88 BC. Its form and Greek inscriptions are thoroughly eastern Greek, but scholars interpret the references to the 'highest God' as monotheistic. Yet two Greek inscriptions from the site mention offerings to the temple 'on Holy Mount Gerizim', which would make the worshippers Samaritans. One of the dedicatory inscriptions on an inscribed base also contained the Greek word *proseuché* for the name of the building. The earliest excavated synagogues in Judea appear at approximately the same period. These include the synagogues excavated at Modi'in (built after 150 BC), Herodian Jericho (first century BC), Shuafat (first century BC), and Gamla (after about 50 BC).

The Theodotos inscription concealed in a cistern in Jerusalem about 70 AD suggests the presence of a synagogue building founded in the Hellenistic Period. The synagogue is a non-priestly and non-sacrificial institution in ancient Judaism. The challenge is to understand the building as 'sacred space' in some coherent sense, because these earliest structures are virtually without decorations or symbols recognized in the repertoire of ancient Jewish art.

In late Hellenistic Galilee, Jewish ritual baths very similar to those in Jerusalem appear in a fortress at Sepphoris and at Gamla in the Golan Heights. The ritual bath or *miqveh* appears to be a marker of concern with ritual cleanliness, as is the manufacture and use of chalk stone vessels (not subject to uncleanliness in Jewish law). Tombs of this period continue the burial traditions of the past, but some begin to adopt Hellenistic monumental forms. The issue of 'Hellenization' of Judaism is the focus of a protracted debate, both in the theoretical arena and in textual and artifact studies (Grabbe 1992; Hengel 1974, 1980, 1989; Bowersock 1990; Levine 1998).

3 Judaism in the Early Roman Period

The historical narrative to explain the imposition of Roman rule on Judea is too long to recite here. It is enough to relate that the Roman General Ptolemy entered Jerusalem by invitation of the locals in 63 BC. Shortly it was clear that Rome had no ambitions to abandon this corridor between Europe and Africa, but to retain it for themselves as part of the province of Syria.

The ruler who leaves the strongest imprint on the historical and archaeological record is Herod the Great, friend of Octavian and son of an Idumean father and a Nabatean mother. He is remembered as a despot, but also as a builder. Many of his projects are still the objects of archaeological investigation: the Temple in Jerusalem; the founding of the city and harbour of Caesarea; the refounding of Samaria as Sebasté; the renovation or establishment of palaces at Jerusalem, Masada, Jericho, Duk, Herodium (his burial place),

Betharamatha, Sepphoris, Ascalon, Hyrcania, Alexandrium, and Machaerus, the last east of the Dead Sea.

The construction of the 'Second Temple' by Herod the Great was a major religious, economic, and political act. Its beauty was proverbial. It secured the ascendancy of the priesthood, i.e. the Sadducees, who were thereby elevated in status because of the new, enhanced status of the new Temple.

It is politically impossible to excavate within the Temple platform today, but explorations around the south and south-west sides of the Temple Mount have disclosed a network of streets, drains, and buildings that suggest extensive infrastructures for the main Temple complex (Stern et al. 2008: 1801–11; Geva 1994, 2000). These would include tunnels for entrance and egress of the priesthood (preserving cultic cleanliness), the broad steps on the south side that led to the entrances and exits to the Temple Mount, and the presence of ritual baths in one building near the south stairs. The presence of extensive ritual-bathing facilities tends to confirm hypotheses of ritual cleanliness before entry into the Temple courts by at least some of the population. In these same areas extensive destruction is documented archaeologically that is most easily dated to, and identified with, the devastation by Titus in 70 AD.

Some hypotheses about the siting of the Temple and its courts may be tested by inspection of certain clues on the Temple Mount including built walls, types of masonry, and types of mortar. A vertical 'seam' in the masonry on the east wall of the Temple Mount near its south end suggests a major enlargement of the Temple Mount after the time of Ezra and Nehemiah, most likely by Herod the Great.

It is clear that Judaism was primarily a temple religion before 70 AD. On the other hand, lay worship and learning centres are also found, namely, synagogues. Those found continue in use at Modi'in, Herodian Jericho, Shuafat, and Gamla, but there is also evidence of such structures from Qiryat Sefer (early first century AD), Herodium or Herodion (66–71 AD), Capernaum (first century AD), Magdala, and Horvat Etri (late first century AD). The excavators have interpreted these buildings as synagogues because of the similarity of these buildings in plan to later such buildings with Greek, Hebrew, and Aramaic inscriptions that identify them as synagogues.

From the rabbis, most notably from Mishnah Megilla, it is possible to deduce that a 'synagogue' in the legal sense means a gathering of ten men for the purpose of declamation of Torah. This legislation regulates Torah reading, recitation of the *Shema*, raising the hands in the priestly benediction, passing before the ark to lead in worship or the *Amidah* (the synagogue liturgy), concluding Torah reading by reading from a prophet, and related matters in the synagogue. These could take place anywhere, but the sages appear to assume that they will take place in a building also called a 'synagogue' (*bet knesset*). The sages do not specify an architectural character for this edifice.

Stone vessels are attested archaeologically from Judea to Samaria and north and east to Galilee and the Golan heights (Magen 2002; Deines 1993; Cahill 1992). In fact, these soft, chalkstone vessels are so closely identified with ritual cleanliness that they have become virtual markers for archaeologists for a Jewish presence. These are often turned on lathes and range from small bowls or cups to large standing vessels such as are mentioned in John 5. One type of chalkstone vessel shows prominent marks from having been shaved vertically by a knife. Often these have two handles. In the past they were identified as 'measuring cups' (Magen 1994a, 1994b), but they are now understood to be vessels used in ritual, perhaps in washing of the hands, a Jewish ritual mentioned many times in ancient texts. These stone vessels suggest a lively concern with ritual purity, as in the case of ritual baths. This would be purity of the object, including purity of vessels rendered pure when needed by immersion in water in large, standing, chalkstone vessels.

Family tombs are the norm in ancient Israel before the Persian period, and the same idea appears in the Roman period. Families often own a tomb in the village or town cemetery. Open courtyards cut down into bedrock feature a staircase for access to the tomb openings. Stones cover the doorways. The plan of the tomb is ordinarily a rectangular chamber with a slot about a metre or more wide cut into the floor so that one can stand without bumping one's head. The entrance to the tomb is usually a square opening about 1.5–2 Roman feet square and located at about the height of the waist of a person standing outside. One closes the tomb from outside by pushing a large, cut stone in front of and against the opening or by rolling a flat, cylindrical stone in front of the opening so that the rolling stone sat in a shallow slot of its own. Inside the tomb there are special openings cut into the chamber walls about the length of a human body for simple inhumation. Bodies were prepared for burial by the family who washed them and provided them with a woollen or linen shroud, both attested in archaeological remains and in ancient literary sources (Bloch-Smith 2002; Gittlen 2002; Hachlili 2005; Hallote and Dee 2001; Kloner and Zissu 2003; Rahmani 1994a).

Great burial monuments are also known from the early Roman period. These may feature façades cut to resemble ornate buildings with decoration in low relief of pomegranates, citrons, acanthus leaves, and other floral motifs. A stone, pyramid-shaped or other monument may appear on top. This monument is called a *nephesh*, the Hebrew word for person or soul.

In the Roman period hardly anyone is buried with any significant jewellery, clothing, or other adornment. One may find bronze 'costume jewellery' on bodies or frit earrings, but hardly ever silver or gold. In fact, so common is simple burial that it suggests a hypothesis that there was an ideology or theology of burial that excludes adorning the dead for afterlife. Adornment is for the living.

Very occasionally the names of the dead appear above the burial slot (called a '*kokh*' among archaeologists, using the ancient Hebrew word for 'place'). The name, if it appears, is written in informal letters in Greek, Hebrew, or Aramaic for the family, usually scratched or even written with a finger that has been dipped in mud from the winter rains. For example one may read 'Joanna daughter of Ya'akov' (Rahmani 1994b; Hachlili 1988), though the spelling may vary. Epitaphs are known, but they are not so common.

One unique feature of Jewish burial in the Roman period is the practice of reburial in soft, chalkstone bone boxes or ossuaries. One year after inhumation in the family tomb the bones may be gathered and placed in an ossuary and the ossuary returned to the tomb. These boxes are cut by hand, and some are decorated with two rosettes laid out by compass on one side with some other emblem like a column between the rosettes. The lid is custom cut, either shaped like a peaked roof or rounded. Sometimes more than one individual's bones are reburied in an ossuary, even if only one name occurs on the outside—as in 'Yohanan the son of Haggai' (Strange 1975; Geraty 1975). Interpreters have suggested ideological and theological ideation behind this practice, even perhaps a belief in resurrection (Meyers 1971; Rahmani 1972; 1981a, 1981b, 1982a, 1982b). Whatever the practice means, it may at least illustrate a practice enshrined in the sentence, 'He was gathered to his people (forefathers)', as in Gen. 25: 8 (Abraham), Gen. 25: 17 (Ishmael), Gen. 35: 29 (Isaac), Gen. 49: 29 (Jacob), and others.

Ossuary reburial ceases in Judea, as far as excavation can show, with the destruction of Jerusalem and the flight of the priestly classes to Galilee. Reburial in ossuaries seems to move to Galilee after 70 AD, where it is found also during the second century AD. Ossuaries in Galilee are also made of both stone and clay, departing from the customary and simple chalkstone boxes of Jerusalem.

Pilgrimage to the holy city of Jerusalem is an ancient duty according to the Torah (Deut. 16: 16 and Exodus 23: 17). Is there archaeological evidence of such pilgrimage? One of the most common lamps in the first century repertoire are the 'Herodian lamps', which have a wheel-turned body, a central hole in the body, and an added nozzle with knife carved and bow shaped or spatulated nozzles. Recent trace-element analysis of clays has suggested that most of the first-century-AD Herodian lamps discovered at Jewish sites in the Galilee originated in Jerusalem (Adan-Bayewitz et al. 2008). That is, neutron-activation analysis of the lamps shows that they are manufactured from the clays in and around Jerusalem. At mainly gentile sites such as Dor in the north, Herodian lamps are almost all of local, northern manufacture from Galilean clay beds. Therefore careful examination of materials from the Galilee yields a hypothesis that first-century pilgrimage to Jerusalem is detectable in the archaeological remains of lamps brought back from the holy city.

In 70 AD the loss of the Temple to the Roman forces under Titus was as heavy a blow as could possibly be imagined. As long as the Temple stood, there was no reason to elevate synagogues or rabbinic schools to similar status, as there was no cult associated with the synagogue. But for synagogues of the second century and later it is hard to miss that about half of them have facades that point to Jerusalem and the ruins of the Second Temple.

In terms of some theories of religion (Kyriakidis 2007; Renfrew 2007; Turner 1982), one might predict that the loss of the Temple, with no prospect of rebuilding it, set the stage for transfer of elements of the Temple cult to the synagogue. In 135 AD the complete refounding of Jerusalem as a pagan centre tends to support the idea that, not only would the synagogue increase in importance among Jews in Galilee, Samaria, and Judea, but that enclaves of Jews in Judea and Galilee would be embattled by the pressures of reinvigorated pagan religions.

Excavators of Jewish sites have often found important artefacts that bear images or symbols commonly interpreted as elements drawn from Judaism. This practice is entirely predictable, given modern theories of religion. For example, common household lamps might bear an image of a menorah, which is an item from the ritual. In fact, the menorah occurs so commonly on lamps and other everyday items, particularly after 70 AD, that some scholars understand it to be the Jewish symbol *par excellence*. On the other hand the menorah is known on only one coin type in the first century BC, namely on a lepton of Herod's enemy Mattathias Antigonus.

Other Jewish coins are well known, though it is a question precisely what is a Jewish coin. In any case the symbols and depictions on coins of Jewish rulers may surprise the researcher. Theories of symbol in archaeology are legion (Robb 1998; Hodder 2008; Tilley 1999; Jones 2002), but it is seldom that theories of symbol predict successfully what the archaeologist will find. This is also true of Jewish coins. The first coins issued by a Jewish ruler are coins about 14–15 mm in diameter depicting a lily, a double cornucopia, and a pomegranate between the cornucopias. The name of King John Hyrcanus I (134–104 BC) and his title as High Priest is given in palaeo-Hebrew letters within a wreath: 'Yehohanan the High Priest and the Council of the Jews'. Sometimes 'Head of' is inserted before 'the Council' (Hendin 2001; Meshorer 2001). The lily and pomegranate are apparently borrowed from the Israelite cult, where they appear on the capitals of the two main columns (named Joachin and Boaz) which stood at the entrance of the Temple. This borrowing of First Temple decorations suggests that the lily and pomegranate were understood to be clear, public symbols for the Temple and its cult.

Another symbol on Hasmonean coins is the anchor, which appears both upside down and right side up on different issues. This appearance on the coins of Jewish rulers is usually understood as borrowing an emblem from the reigning east Greek culture. The anchor was already known in Greek Seleucid coinage and stood for Seleucid maritime powers. After the Jews threw off Seleucid hegemony, the symbol appropriately passed to the former underdogs. It appears on coins of Alexander (Yannai, 103–76 BC), Herod the Great (40–4 BC), and Herod Archelaus, eldest son of Herod the Great and himself 'Ethnarch' rather than 'king' (4 BC–6 AD).

One of the most easily recognized symbols on Hasmonean coinage is the star, which appears on coins of Alexander Jannaeus. Jannaeus is borrowing from Greek and other non-Jewish neighbours. He sometimes places a diadem around the star, which was already recognized as a symbol of royalty in Hellenistic circles. Some scholars connect the star on his coins with the 'star out of Jacob' prophecy in Numbers 24: 27 (Hendin 2001).

The palm branch or palm tree became a recognizable Jewish symbol as early as the reign of John Hyrcanus I, when a palm branch appeared on the obverse of a lepton, and a lily appeared on its reverse with the palaeo-Hebrew inscription. On a coin of Alexander Jannaeus a very realistic palm branch appears with the lily also on the reverse. The name of the king is found in Hebrew letters on the obverse: 'Yehonatan the King'. The palm branch occurs also on coins of Herod the Great, Herod Antipas, Herod Agrippa II (56–95 AD). Finally the palm tree or palm branch occurs on coins of several procurators, which suggests that they give expression to the Roman idea that the proper symbol for the defeated nation is also the palm tree or palm branch: Coponius (6–9 AD), Marcus Ambibulus (9–12 AD), Valerius Gratus (15–26 AD), Antonius Felix (52–9 AD), and Porcius Festus (59–62 AD).

The parade example of the use of the palm tree or branch as a Jewish symbol is given to Jewish coins of the First Revolt against Rome (66–73 AD) and to Roman 'Judea Capta' coins. In the first instance these coins are usually understood to give expression to Jewish nationalism and religious feelings. There are many symbols from the cult, but the palm tree with seven branches and with clusters of fruit appears on a type of year 'four and one-half'. The inscription on the obverse reads 'For the redemption of Zion'. On the reverse one sees an ethrog with a lulav on either side, the symbols of the Festival of Tabernacles mentioned above. A half-shekel of year four shows three palm branches on the obverse and a wreath of palm branches on the reverse. Other examples with palm tree or palm branch occur in Second Revolt Coins (132–5 AD).

Roman Judea Capta coins or Judea Devicta coins, on the other hand, appear to display the Roman idea that the palm tree represents the defeated province best. These coins were minted under the emperors Vitellius (69 AD), Vespasian (69–79 AD), Titus (79–81 AD), Domitian (81–96 AD), and Nerva (96–8 AD). The one such coin of Nerva bears the legend FISCI IUDAICI CALVMNIA SVBLATA ('The insult of the Jewish Tax has been removed'). The elevation of the synagogue from a simple gathering place to sacred space became visible in developing Jewish art, in the emergence of specific internal furniture such as the synagogue ark for storage of scrolls, and the heightening of internal decorations in the form of mosaic floors.

Archaeological theories of religion give reason to predict that the synagogue, with heightened importance, will gradually develop its own rich art, including carvings in the round of eagles and lions; elaborate mouldings on lintels, doorposts, and windows; but also garlands, palm fronds, flowers, birds, and other artistic motifs carved into the stonework (Fine 2005; Hachlili 1988; Levine 2000; Strange 2003; Olsson and Zetterholm 2009). In fact this is the picture of the development of the synagogue as the main structure in a Jewish village or town until the seventh century AD.

4 Late Roman Judaism

There seems to be a proliferation of synagogues built beginning the mid-third century AD. After two devastating revolts against Rome, Judaism appears to be recovering. Communities were growing and required new worship and instructional facilities. Such buildings also accord well with theories of social change in which constructing public buildings amounts to a demonstration of social cohesion and social identity by Jews during otherwise uncertain times.

Often synagogues of the mid-third century and later feature a facade with three portals. This is reminiscent of the southern triple-gate entry into the Temple Mount. The columns on the interior of the synagogue may also be an allusion to the Second Temple, as may low-relief decorations. Galilean synagogues of the mid-third century often reveal an orientation of the facade on Jerusalem. This feature will become virtually a norm in later synagogues. Furthermore, the synagogue was erected in the middle of town and sometimes even shares walls with other structures, such as houses. The building is prominent in terms of its location, size, workmanship, and building materials. These ideas correlate well with current theories of the importance of the synagogue both for worship and as a village or town community centre. The functionality of the synagogue appears also in contemporary Jewish texts that mention activities besides worship and study. This helps us to understand references to eating in synagogues, whether forbidden in a text like the Tosephta Megillah 2: 18 or assumed in an earlier inscription, the Theodotus inscription in Jerusalem, which lauds Theodotus for building the synagogue 'for the reading of the Law and for teaching the commandments; furthermore, the hostel, and the rooms, and the water installation for lodging strangers from abroad'. Hospitality for the stranger, so entrenched in ancient Jewish documents, likely includes food.

These third-century synagogues of the north are devoid of Jewish symbols on the outside, but they are beautifully and carefully built. The best examples are from Khirbet Shema', Meron, Gush Halav, Nabratein, Bar'am, Chorazim, Qatsrin (Golan Heights), and Horvat 'Ammudim. In the south such buildings are seen at Susiya, Eshtemoa, 'Ein Gedi, and Ma'on. In the late third century one sees a development of decoration to include a Menorah on the outside entrance, as at Khirbet Shema', and a menorah inside a wreath on the lintel of the synagogue at Nabratein.

Another step in the development of the synagogue as a building more devoted to declamation of Torah and instruction and less like that of a community centre is found in archaeological remains of synagogue floors of the fourth century and later. Synagogue mosaic floors of the fourth to sixth centuries often divide the floor into two or three panels. The last panel opposite the entrance(s) will often show symbols of furniture borrowed from the Second Temple, including two menorahs on either side of a Torah ark, but also with recumbent lions, incense shovels, bound branches of the myrtle, palm, willow, and ethrog branches (the 'lulab'), and the citron (the 'ethrog', fruit of the tree), and shofars or rams' horns. These four species of trees are used in the Festival of Tabernacles ('Sukkoth', see Lev. 23: 40). The triangular pediment of the ark as depicted in various mosaic floors has also been excavated as a piece of stone furniture (an *immobilium*) in a fourth-century synagogue at Nabratein and likely other sites.

Archaeological theory predicts that a religious artefact, like religion itself, does not remain 'pure', but is always influenced by its culture (Durkheim 2001; Kyriakidis 2007; McCauley and Lawson 2007). This is true of the late Roman synagogues, at least nine of which feature the zodiac in their floors, complete with Helios driving his quadriga or four-horse chariot in the central circle. The ancient craftsmen named the signs of the zodiac in Hebrew, and in at least one case (Sepphoris, sixth century AD), named the corresponding Hebrew month. Often the circle of the zodiac is depicted in a square, and the four corners of the square bear the names for the four seasons in Hebrew. Depictions of four women's faces represent the seasons. Also at Sepphoris the two solstices are named in Greek, as are the two equinoxes. This tends to confirm the hypothesis that the zodiac in the synagogue is really a calendar.

Certain norms for art changed with the advancing development of Jewish art. For example, the low-relief decorations on the Temple of Herod the Great did not contain any representations of animals, humans, or divine beings. But we have already seen that the zodiac became a recognizable motif in synagogue art in the Late Antique period. The zodiac contains animals: goat, bull, crab, lion, fishes, scorpion. There are also human figures: twins, Virgo, sometimes Aquarius as a boy, or Sagittarius as a man, or the scales as a man with scales in his hand. Finally there are chimeras: Capricorn (goat and cetan) and sometimes Sagittarius as half man, half horse. Theories of accommodation to the dominant Greco-Roman culture of the eastern Mediterranean allow for such changes.

The main alternative to Judaism in fourth-century Judea and later was Christianity. Archaeological and social theories of religion predict that religions may begin borrowing from one another as they come into close contact (Faraone and Obbink 1997; Spiro 1966; Hoppe 1994; Meyers, Kraabel, and Strange 1976; Meyers, Strange, and Meyers 1981; Meyers, Meyers, and Strange 1990), but most of the borrowing goes from the dominant religion to the dominated. This sway of Christian art over Jewish art is visible in synagogue floors at places such as Beth Alpha and Sepphoris. At Beth Alpha the main panel one sees at one's feet when entering from the main entrance is a depiction of what Jews called the *Akeda* or Binding of Isaac. This scene, called in Christian circles 'the Sacrifice of Isaac' shows all the elements of the story with Hebrew inscriptions at strategic places identifying the figures. To the left one sees two servants and a loaded ass. In the centre is a ram with his horns hung in a bush. To the right of the ram Abraham stands with a knife in his right hand and Isaac in his left. To the extreme right one sees the altar with fire upon it. In the top centre one sees a hand emerging from a cloud, and, inscribed in Hebrew, the instruction 'Do not extend [your hand]', a citation from Genesis 22: 12. A similar example of the dominance of the church is that synagogues also adopt certain architectural features, such as the apse and the chancel screen, from church architecture.

SUGGESTED READING

APPLEBAUM, S. and NEUSNER, N. (1989). *Judaea in Hellenistic and Roman Times: Historical and archaeological essays*, Studies in Judaism in Late Antiquity 40 (Leiden: Brill).
EDWARDS, D. R. and MCCOLLOUGH, C. T. (1997). *Archaeology and the Galilee: Texts and contexts in the Graeco-Roman and Byzantine periods*, South Florida Studies in the History of Judaism (Atlanta: Scholars Press).
HACHLILI, R. (1988). *Ancient Jewish Art and Archaeology in the Land of Israel*, Handbuch der Orientalistik 7. Kunst und Archaeologie (Leiden: Brill).
——(1998). *Ancient Jewish Art and Archaeology in the Diaspora*, Handbook of Oriental Studies/Handbuch Der Orientalistik (Leiden: Brill).
LEVINE, L. I. (2000). *The Ancient Synagogue: The first thousand years* (New Haven: Yale University Press).
MAGNESS, J. (2002). *The Archaeology of Qumran and the Dead Sea Scrolls* (Grand Rapids: Eerdmans).
MEYERS, E. M. and STRANGE, J. F. (1981). *Archaeology, the Rabbis, and early Christianity* (Nashville: Abingdon Press and London; SCM Press).
RICHARDSON, P. (2004). *Building Jewish in the Roman East* (Waco, TX: Baylor University Press).

REFERENCES

ADAN-BAYEWITZ, D., WIEDER, M., ASARO, F., and GIAUQUE, R. D. 2008. 'Preferential distribution of lamps from the Jerusalem area in the Late Second Temple period (late first century BCE to 70 CE)', *Bulletin of the American Schools of Oriental Research*, 350 (May): 37–85.
BELL, C. 1997. *Ritual: Perspectives and dimensions* (Oxford: Oxford University Press).
BLOCH-SMITH, E. 2002. 'Death in the Life of Israel' in Barry M. Gittlen (ed.), *Sacred Time, Sacred Place: Archaeology and the religion of Israel* (Winona Lake: Eisenbrauns).
BOWERSOCK, G. W. 1990. *Hellenism in Late Antiquity* (Ann Arbor: University of Michigan Press).
CAHILL, J. M. 1992. 'Chalk Vessel Assemblages of the Persian/Hellenistic and Early Roman Periods' in A. De Groot and D. T. Ariel (eds), *City of David Excavations, Final Report III*. Qedem 33 (Jerusalem), pp. 190–274.
DEINES, R. 1993. *Jüdische Steingefäße und pharisäische Frömmigkeit* (Tübingen: J. C. B. Mohr).
DURKHEIM, É. 2001. *The Elementary Forms of the Religious Life*, trans. C. Cosman (Oxford: Oxford University Press).
EMERTON, J. A. 1999. 'Yahweh and his Asherah: The goddess or her symbol?', *Vetus Testamentum*, 49(3): 315–37.
FARAONE, C. A. and OBBINK, D. 1997. *Magika Hiera: Ancient Greek magic and religion* (Oxford: Oxford University Press).

FINE, S. 2005. *Art and Judaism in the Greco-Roman World: Toward a new Jewish archaeology* (Cambridge: Cambridge University Press).

FLESHER, P. V. M. 2001. 'Prolegomenon to a theory of early synagogue development' in A. J. Avery-Peck and J. Neusner (eds), *Judaism in Late Antiquity*, Pt Three: *Where We Stand: Issues and debates in ancient Judaism*, IV: *The Special Problem of the Synagogue* (Leiden: Brill), pp. 121–54.

GERATY, L. T. 1975. 'A thrice repeated ossuary inscription from French Hill, Jerusalem', *Bulletin of the American Schools of Oriental Research*, 219 (Oct.): 73–8.

GEVA, H. (ed.) 1994. *Ancient Jerusalem Revealed* (Jerusalem: Israel Exploration Society).

——2000. *Ancient Jerusalem Revealed: Expanded Edition: Excavations 1993–99* (Jerusalem: Israel Exploration Society).

GIMBUTAS, M. 1992. *Die Ethnogenese der europäischen Indogermanen* (Innsbruck: Institut für Sprachwissenschaft der Universität Innsbruck, Innsbrucker Beiträge zur Sprachwissenschaft, Vorträge und kleinere Schriften 54).

——1997. *The Kurgan Culture and the Indo-Europeanization of Europe*, Selected articles from 1952 to 1993. *Journal of Indo-European Studies* monograph 18 (Washington, DC: Institute for the Study of Man).

GITTLEN, B. M. (ed.) 2002. *Sacred Time, Sacred Place: Archaeology and the religion of Israel* (Winona Lake: Eisenbrauns).

GRABBE, L. 1992. *Judaism from Cyrus to Hadrian* (Minneapolis: Fortress).

HACHLILI, R. 1988. *Ancient Jewish Art and Archaeology in the Land of Israel*, Handbuch der Orientalistik 7: Kunst und Archaeologie (Leiden: Brill).

——2005. *Jewish funerary Customs and Rites in the Second Temple Period*, Supplement to the Journal for the Study of Religion 94 (Leiden: Brill).

HALLOTE, R. S. and DEE, I. R. 2001. *Death, Burial and Afterlife in the Biblical World* (Chicago: Ivan R. Dee).

HENDIN, D. 2001. *Guide to Biblical Coins*, 4th edn (New York: Amphora Books).

HENGEL, M. 1974. *Judaism and Hellenism*, 2 vols. (London: SCM; Philadelphia: Fortress).

——1980. *Jews, Greeks and Barbarians: Aspects of the Hellenization of Judaism in the pre-Christian period* (Philadelphia: Fortress; London: SCM).

——1989. *The 'Hellenization' of Judaea in the First Century after Christ* (London: SCM).

HODDER, I. 2008. *Symbols in Action*, New Directions in Archaeology (Cambridge: Cambridge University Press).

HOPPE, L. 1994. *The Synagogues and Churches of Ancient Palestine* (Collegeville, MN: The Liturgical Press).

HORBURY, W. and NOY, D. 1992. *Jewish Inscriptions of Greco-Roman Egypt* (Cambridge: Cambridge University Press).

JONES, A. 2002. *Archaeological Theory and Scientific Practice* (Cambridge: Cambridge University Press).

KLEIBRINK, M., JACOBSON, J. K., and HANDBERG, S. 2004. 'Water for Athena: Votive gifts at Langaria', *World Archaeology*, 36(1): 43–67.

KLONER, A. and ZISSU, B. 2003. *The Necropolis of Jerusalem in the Second Temple Period* (Jerusalem: Yad Izhak Ben Zvi and the Israel Exploration Society) [Hebrew].

KYRIAKIDIS, E. 2007. 'Archaeologies of ritual' in E. Kyriakidis (ed.), *The Archaeology of Ritual*, Cotsen Advanced Seminar 3 (Los Angeles: Cotsen Institute of Archaeology), pp. 289–308.

LEVINE, L. I. 1998. *Judaism and Hellenism in Antiquity: Conflict or confluence* (Seattle: University of Washington Press).

—— 2000. *The Ancient Synagogue: The first thousand years* (New Haven: Yale University Press).

—— 2005. *The Ancient Synagogue: The first thousand years*, 2nd edn (New Haven: Yale University Press).

McCauley, R. N. and Lawson, E. T. 2007. 'Cognition, religious ritual, and archaeology' in E. Kyriakidis (ed.), *The Archaeology of Ritual*, Cotsen Advanced Seminar 3 (Los Angeles: Cotsen Institute of Archaeology), pp. 209–54.

Magen, Y. 1994a. 'The stone vessel industry during the Second Temple period' in *Purity Broke out in Israel*, Catalogue, The Reuben and Edith Hecht Museum (Haifa: University of Haifa), pp. 7–28.

—— 1994b. 'Jerusalem as a center of the stone vessel industry during the Second Temple period' in H. Geva (ed.), *Ancient Jerusalem Revealed* (Jerusalem: Israel Exploration Society; Washington, DC: Biblical Archaeology Society), pp. 244–56.

—— 2002. *The Stone Vessel Industry in the Second Temple Period*, I: *Excavation at Hizma and Jerusalem Temple Mount* (Jerusalem: Israel Antiquities Authority).

Mazar, A. 1982. 'The "Bull Site": An Iron I open cult place', *Bulletin of the American Schools of Oriental Research*, 247: 27–42.

Meshorer, Y. 2001. *A Treasury of Jewish Coins from the Persian Period to Bar Kokhba* (Jerusalem: Yad ben-Zvi Press; Nyack, NY: Amphora).

Meyers, E. M. 1971. *Jewish Ossuaries: Reburial and rebirth* (Rome: Biblical Institute Press).

——, Kraabel, A.T., and Strange, J. F. 1976. *Ancient Synagogue Excavations at Khirbet Shema, Upper Galilee, Israel 1970–1972*, Annual of the American Schools of Oriental Research, XLII (Cambridge: American Schools of Oriental Research).

—— and Meyers, C. L. (with Strange, J. F.) 1990. *Excavations at the Ancient Synagogue of Gush Halav* (Winona Lake, IN: Eisenbrauns).

——, Strange, J. F., and Meyers, C. L. 1981. *Excavations at Ancient Meiron, Upper Galilee, Israel, 1971–72, 1974–75, 1976* (Cambridge, MA: American Schools of Oriental Research).

Olsson, B. and Zetterholm, M. (eds) 2003. *The Ancient Synagogue from its Origins until 200 CE: Papers Presented at an International Conference at Lund University, October 14–17, 2001*. Coniectanea Biblica, New Testament Series 39 (Stockholm: Almqvist & Wiksell International).

Rahmani, L.Y. 1972. 'A bilingual ossuary-inscription from Khirbet Zif', *Israel Exploration Journal*, 22(2–3): 113–16.

—— 1981a. 'Ancient Jerusalem's funerary customs and tombs, Part One', *Biblical Archaeologist*, 44 (Summer 1981): 171–7.

—— 1981b. 'Ancient Jerusalem's funerary customs and tombs, Part Two', *Biblical Archaeologist*, 44 (Fall 1981): 229–35.

—— 1982a. 'Ancient Jerusalem's funerary customs and tombs, Part Three', *Biblical Archaeologist*, 45 (Winter 1982): 43–53.

—— 1982b. 'Ancient Jerusalem's funerary customs and tombs, Part Four', *Biblical Archaeologist*, 45 (Spring 1982): 109–19.

—— 1994a. '*Ossuaries* and *Ossilegium* (Bone-Gathering) in the late Second Temple period' in H. Geva (ed.), *Ancient Jerusalem Revealed* (Jerusalem: Israel Exploration Society), pp. 191–205.

—— 1994b. *A Catalogue of Jewish Ossuaries in the Collection of the State of Israel* (Jerusalem: Israel Antiquities Authority and Israel Academy of Sciences and Humanities).

Renfrew, C. 2007. 'The archaeology of ritual, of cult, and of religion' in E. Kyriakidis (ed.), *The Archaeology of Ritual*, Cotsen Advanced Seminar 3 (Los Angeles: Cotsen Institute of Archaeology), pp. 109–22.

Robb, J. E. 1998. 'The archaeology of symbols', *Annual Review of Anthropology*, 27: 329–46.

Spiro, M. E. 1966. 'Religion: Problems in definition and explanation' in M. Blanton (ed.), *Anthropological Approaches to the Study of Religion*, A.S.A. Monographs 3 (London: Tavistock), pp. 85–126.

Stern, E., Geva, H., Paris, A., and Aviram, J. (eds) 2008. *The New Encyclopedia of Archaeological Excavations in the Holy Land*, V: *Supplementary Volume* (Jerusalem: Israel Exploration Society and the Biblical Archaeology Society).

Strange, J. F. 1975. 'Late Hellenistic and Herodian ossuary tombs at French Hill, Jerusalem', *Bulletin of the American Schools of Oriental Research*, 219 (Oct 1975): 39–67.

—— 2003. 'Archaeology and the Synagogue to 200 CE' in A. Runesson, D. D. Binder, and B. Olsson (eds), *The Ancient Synagogue from Its Origins until 200 CE*, Papers Presented at an International Conference at Lund University, October 14–17, 2001 (Leiden: Brill), pp. 37–62.

—— 2009. 'Archaeology and religion' in G. Kalantzis and T. F. Martin (eds), *Studies on Patristic Texts and Archaeology: If these stones could speak...: Essays in honor of Dennis Edward Groh* (Lewiston: The Edwin Mellen Press), pp. 163–87.

Talalay, L. E. 1999. 'Review of M. Gimbutas, *Living Goddesses*', *Bryn Mawr Classical Review*, 10 May 1999.

Tilley, C. 1999. *Metaphor and Material Culture* (Oxford, Malden, MA: Blackwell Publishers).

Turner, V. 1982. *From Ritual to Theatre: The human seriousness of play* (New York: Performing Arts Journal Publications).

CHAPTER 57

ARCHAEOLOGY OF HINDUISM

NAMITA SUGANDHI AND KATHLEEN MORRISON

1 Defining the Archaeology of Hinduism

It is a difficult and complicated matter to identify and interpret the archaeological remains associated with the Hindu religion. Hinduism cannot be defined as a singular codified system, but instead must be understood as a heterogeneous amalgam of beliefs and practices that vary widely across both space and time. As such, there is no simple or universally agreed upon definition of 'Hinduism', and any attempt to synthesize the archaeological record of Hinduism is sure to be controversial (Bhan 1997).

Interpretations of the origins of Hinduism have spanned the transcendental to the colonial. It is a religion which has developed and transformed over millennia, incorporating regional, foreign, and shared 'pan-Indic' traditions, many of which exist up until the present day. The earliest material evidence for Hinduism is found in the Indo-Gangetic divide during the mid-first millennium BC, and in the succeeding centuries these traditions spread to incorporate the entire Indian subcontinent, eventually reaching South-east Asia during the first millennium AD. These traditions are associated with Vedic and Puranic Hinduism, but their systems of ritual practice and iconographic representation have roots which reach back thousands of years.

In one of the first comprehensive overviews of the archaeology of early Hinduism, Chakrabarti (2001) states three major points. The first is that an organized Brahmanical framework developed only after the advent of the textual record, which dates from approximately the sixth century BC, or the beginning of what is known as the Early Historic period in South Asian chronology. Consequently, much of the archaeology of what is manifestly early Hinduism may be considered logocentric, in that it attempts to correlate material traces and artefacts with references in early literature and epigraphic records. Once ritual practice shifted decisively toward temple-focused forms of worship in the first millennium CE, archaeological and art-historical research on architecture and iconography becomes a powerful source of evidence for both orthodox and alternative forms of religious practice in both the public and private spheres.

However, Chakrabarti also notes that 'individual components' of Hinduism may be linked to ritual practices and beliefs that date to earlier pre- and proto-historic time periods (2001: 58). This relates to his second point, which concerns the continuity of Hindu sacred space over time. Much research tracing long term continuities has focused on the descriptive and formal analysis of material culture and written records, which allows a long-term perspective on the development of styles and literature, but says little about the actual practices of Hinduism and their considerable transformations over time in different regional and individual contexts. An archaeological perspective which focuses on practice, as well as the wider social context of objects, offers a unique view through which to examine the dynamic mass of beliefs and practices that characterize the Hindu religion.

An archaeological interpretation that situates religious practice within its wider sociocultural and economic setting is demonstrated by Chakrabarti's third point, which looks to pilgrimage networks as significant components of the economic and social relationships connecting different parts of South Asia to one another, and to the world beyond. Early Historic and prehistoric patterns of interregional and foreign interaction are certainly reflected in the diversity of traditions that characterize Hindu practice and representation. This is often typified as a fusion of regional and local 'folk' customs with wider 'Pan-Indic' Brahmanical traditions. Further syncretism may be marked between various orthodox Hindu traditions and heterodox religions such as Buddhism and Jainism, and links to more-foreign Zoroastrian, Scythian, and Greek traditions are also distinct, particularly in the iconographic and epigraphic styles of the north-west.

2 Categories of Evidence

In terms of material culture, there are numerous categories of evidence which may be examined in the study of Hindu practices as they developed over time. Evidence for ritual activity can be inferred through the study of structures such as platforms, altars, shrines and larger temple complexes. In addition to these types of constructions, smaller portable objects such as figurines, coins, seals, and ritual vessels and instruments attest to a diversity of enduring religious traditions in both public and private contexts (Ghosh 1989). The material consideration of these structures and objects may be further encompassed within a broader reflection of sacred space across the Hindu landscape. Across the Indian subcontinent, sacred rivers, hills, mountains and other localities may be marked by shrines, inscriptions or other evidence for ritual activity, and may also figure in the literary record of Hinduism (Eck 1981). In this way, particular cities such as Mathura, Varanasi, and Tirupati are also recognized as sacred locations in traditions that link urban settlements and textual references in a historical geography of Hinduism which continues up until the present day.

In addition to the study of ritual practice and space, the study of material culture also contributes a considerable amount to our understanding of the Hindu pantheon of divinities and its elaboration over time. It is not until the second half of the Early Historic period (c.first–fifth century AD) that a systematic iconographic tradition developed which can be identified with deities associated with Puranic Hindusim. The latter centuries of this period also mark a transformation from earlier Vedic elite practices of sacrifice towards more popular traditions of worship and devotion, and a consequent shift in material culture. Earlier representations of divinities found in prehistoric and proto-historic contexts are sometimes linked to Vedic figures such as Rudra and Ushas, but are also thought to prefigure later forms of Hindu gods and goddesses known from Puranic and Epic literature such as Vishnu, Siva, Brahma, Lakshmi, Durga, and Saravati, as well as many of their numerous avatars, and other minor deities such as Nagas, Yakshas, and Yakshinis. Many of these deities are also associated with local cultic gods and goddesses, who over time were either absorbed or marginalized by orthodox Brahmanical Hinduism and its iconographic conventions.

3 EARLY EVIDENCE

Examples of built platforms and small shrine-shaped objects have been cited as evidence for early ritual practice during the Upper Palaeolithic (tenth to ninth millennia BC) at sites such as Baghor in central India, but it is not until the development of Neolithic farming communities during the fourth–third millennia BC that more definitive evidence of religious symbolism is seen. The earliest evidence is found in the region of Baluchistan, where terracotta female figurines have been recovered at sites such as Mehrgarh (Ardeleanu-Jansen 2002). These early agricultural communities are linked to the emerging traditions of the Indus civilization, which flourished from the mid-third to late second millennia BC with a geographical scope stretching from Saurashtra to the Iranian borderlands (Possehl 2002). Since the discovery of the Indus civilization (also known as the Harappan civilization) in the early twentieth century, many have attempted to link evidence for ritual activity at Indus sites with later Hindu practices. Although several points of possible convergence have been noted between the Indus civilization and later Hindu forms of religious practice and representation, these connections are vague and often hotly contested by specialists (Atre 2002).

Female terracotta figurines found at Indus sites are often associated with a broader tradition of Mother Goddess worship, and are thought to have symbolized creativity, fertility and birth (Bhardwaj 2004). These figurines are linked to later female images that display a more consistent iconography such as the goddess with five–ten *āyudhas* (weapons) in her headdress, and the *lājja-gaurī*, frequently depicted as headless and posed in a squatting position. However, these more identifiable images are not seen until much later, from the first century BC onwards, and any connection to the earlier Indus figurines remains speculative. Male figures depicted on seals found at Indus sites have been categorized as 'Proto-Śivas', referring to their yoga-like posture and ithyphallic nature. This image is also depicted with a buffalo-horned headdress and is frequently surrounded by wild animals such as elephants, tigers, and rhinos (Figure 57.1). This has led some to identify this figure with the god *Śiva* as *Mahayogi* (Master of Yoga) and also as the Vedic *Rudra* in the form of *Pasupati* (Lord of Beasts). However as several scholars have pointed out (Sullivan 1964; Srinivasan 1983), such direct links are somewhat tenuous, and the connection between the Indus horned deity and the Śiva images of later Puranic Hinduism remains ambiguous. Nevertheless, there are some suggestions for the existence of a cult of human sexuality in the Indus civilization, as depicted by *linga*-type phallic objects and ring stones at sites such as Mohenjo-Daro, Harappa, and Surkotada (Ghosh 1989).

FIGURE 57.1 Sealing from Indus stamp-seal showing the so-called 'Proto Śiva' figure with horned headdress.

In addition to the representation of deities and their aniconic forms, evidence for ritual practice during the Indus civilization has also been interpreted from various architectural elements. A noteworthy feature of Indus urban centres is the marked absence of monumental architecture, religious or otherwise. One exception to this is the Great Bath complex at Mohenjo-Daro, which lies on the elevated 'citadel' above the lower town. In general, water is believed to have played an important role in the ideology of the Indus civilization, as evidenced by the extensive bathing and drainage facilities found at many Indus settlements, and this perhaps can be regarded as a predecessor to later Hindu practices of ceremonial ablutions and the construction of tanks and wells at many temple complexes (Possehl 2002).

Other proposed ritual structures associated with Indus Civilization include 'fire-altars'. These small ash and debris filled pits have been identified at sites such as Kalibangan, Rakhigarhi, Lothal, and Navdatoli. A definitive identification of these 'fire-altars' as ritual features has yet to be made, and suggestions that these structures may be correlated with sacrificial structures depicted in Vedic literature have become entangled in debates concerning the nature of society during the centuries following the decline of the Indus civilization, and the origins of 'Vedic' culture.

The origins and nature of 'Vedic' society are the subject of much controversy in both politics and historical scholarship. Archaeologically, there is little in the material record that can be identified as 'Vedic', though a marked shift from earlier Indus traditions is certainly seen. In general, most scholars characterize the late-second through mid-first millennia BC in north India and the north-west territories as a time of disintegrating urban traditions, and the emergence of pastoral communities associated with groups of Indo-European language speakers who gradually migrated into the Indian subcontinent during the second millennium BC (Thapar 2000 [1983]). This is in contrast to the view that there was no Indo-European migration and all developments in South Asia were of indigenous origin—for both groups archaeological arguments have become closely linked to contemporary politics.

Archaeologically, the period following the decline of the Indus civilization is characterized by a number of regional cultures, largely defined by ceramic types, such as the Malwa and Jorwe of central and western India, and other Chalcolithic 'cultures' of the Middle and Lower Gangetic Plains. Terracotta figurines found at many of these sites suggest a continuation of regional cults worshipping mother goddesses, phallic icons, and cattle. North India and the north-west territories are associated with a 'Painted Grey Ware' culture that is sometimes controversially related to a 'Vedic' society. However, the development of Vedic traditions should not be regarded as a specific 'culture' per se, but rather as a gradual accumulation of ritual practices and belief systems that integrated ideological aspects from many different regions. The composition of the earliest Vedic *samhita* verses are conventionally dated to the second half of the second millennium BC, but material evidence of Vedic ritual practices and representations are not seen until much later, during the latter half of the first millennium BC.

The Early Historic period begins during the mid-first millennium BC—in north India and it is conventionally dated to approximately 600 BC, while in the south it begins about three centuries later. This was a period that saw not only the crystallization of *Brahmana* Hindu norms and practices (as well as those of many other 'heterodox' or *Sramana* sects), but also the re-emergence of urbanism, complex political formation, and a general intensification of interregional interaction and long-distance networks. As suggested by the term 'Early Historic', this is the time associated with the earliest literary traditions in India, beginning with the wide corpus of Vedic prose compositions that include the *Brahmanas*, *Aranyakas*, and *Upanishads*. These early texts are not found in any extant form until the second millennium AD, but later manuscripts are presumed to derive from a long line of copies that may date back to the earliest centuries of the Early Historic period. This earliest literary corpus, categorized as *shruti* ('what is heard'), gradually expanded to include *smrti* texts ('that which is to be remembered'), and *shastra* texts which served as explanatory treatises for a wide variety of subjects.

Included in these genres are the *Puranas*, the *Mahabharata*, and *Ramayana* epics, and various *Agama*, *Darsana*, and *Dharmasastra* texts (Dimock et al. 1974). This literature represents the remarkably varied canonical body of early Hinduism, but it must be remembered that existing versions most certainly went through a significant amount of revision and loss over time. Thus it is quite difficult to definitively correlate archaeological evidence for religious practice with textual references that may be uncertain in terms of both chronology and origin. Similarly, it is also a complicated matter to identify the social manifestation of Hindu caste ideology without relying heavily on textual or ethnographic records (Boivin 2005). Although, some settlement evidence attests to the stratified nature of early Indian society and the existence of occupational communities, there is very little in the archaeological record that definitively demonstrates a social hierarchy based on concepts of ritual purity or a distinction between upper-caste *arya* groups and low-caste *dasas*.

Nevertheless, the material record of the Early Historic period attests to the development of rich and diverse traditions of religious artistic expression, as seen in architecture, sculpture, numismatic records, seals and epigraphic evidence. In the early centuries AD, Buddhism was more politically favoured than Hinduism, based on epigraphic evidence as well as architectural remains of stupas, *viharas*, and monastic complexes. Indeed, the rock-cut Buddhist 'cave' temple provided the structural model for slightly later Hindu temples made in the same mode and, sometimes, in the same locations. Both, clearly, built on a history of wooden structures, as is evident from, for example, the forms of structurally unnecessary 'beams' cut out of what is often referred to as the living rock. While Buddhism and Jainism were explicitly formulated in response to Hinduism, the distinction between traditions was not always rigid. Yaksha images, for example, are common on Buddhist reliefs. Still later, the Buddha would be taken in as an avatar of Vishnu, despite (or perhaps because of) the aggressive suppression of Buddhism in the Middle period and its eventual disappearance from the country of its birth.

What Michaels (2004: 32) refers to as the period of 'Preclassical Hinduism' (200 BC–300 AD) marked the re-emergence of Vedic–Brahmanic Hinduism from the heterodox challenges, a restoration movement that, he notes, was accompanied by the compilation of the two great epics, the *Ramayana* and the *Mahabharata*, even though these refer to much earlier periods. This revival was not so much a return to the past as a new synthesis of belief and practice. Some of the more egalitarian impulses of Buddhism appear to have been eroded, and both descent and ritual purity emerged or re-emerged as concerns of some parts of society. Although these kinds of changes would have had material consequences, this has to date not been much investigated archaeologically. This is unfortunate, as the epigraphic record suggests significant changes, including change in practices of religious donation. At many Buddhist religious centres such as Sanchi, thousands of inscriptions record small donations from craftspeople, merchants, and other non-elite members of society, including a significant number of women (Dehejia 1992). In contrast, by the Middle periods, religious prestation had become a privilege of the elite, wielded with great energy in the building of political power and alliances as well as devotion.

In this 'Preclassical' era, too, shifts in devotional practices created very clear archaeological signatures. At least iconographically, Vedic deities were virtually replaced by Siva and Vishnu in their various forms, as well as by goddesses in various forms. Temple-based forms of worship, if established by this time, did not leave us architectural remains, but archaeological evidence from sites such as Mathura provide tantalizing evidence for the establishment of what would become stable long-term cult centres. Mathura, an important early city on the Gangetic plain, was occupied from at least the 'Painted Grey Ware' period or Early Iron Age, though the Early Historic and into the fourth century AD. This location, famed now for its proximity to Brindavan, the traditional birthplace of the god Krishna (an incarnation of Vishnu), has seen significant long-term excavation as well as sustained art-historical research. From the first few centuries BC, Mathura was a cosmopolitan place where Jains, Hindus, and Buddhists lived together. Srinivasan (1989) argues that Mathura became a regional centre of Vaisnavism beginning around the second century AD, identifying a large number of coins, images, and reliefs with figures from the Vaishnava Bhagavata movement, though many of iconographic attributes of Vishnu known from later periods were not found in the Mathura assemblage.

The diverse array of 'folk' deities and practices such as the worship of Nagas or snakes, are clearly evident in this period, as well as later ones. For example, Shaw documented large sculpted Nagas placed atop the embankments of the Early Historic reservoirs she documented all around the site of Sanchi, an important Buddhist monastic centre, arguing that these large images are contemporaneous with the reservoirs themselves (Shaw 2000). Smaller objects such as miniature votive tanks arguably used for religious purposes are also found in many excavated contexts.

Pollock (1996: 197) has argued that the expansion of Sanskrit in the first few centuries AD across the large region from Afghanistan to Bali, was the product of a pan-regional cultural and conceptual order, his 'Sanskrit Cosmopolis'. Though not associated with any unitary political order or sweeping religious movement, this transformation was certainly accompanied by state formation throughout this vast region and, until the beginning of the Middle period (around AD 1000) when the so-called vernacular languages emerged as literary and religious vehicles, the widespread use of Sanskrit certainly also must have facilitated religious as well as literary communication across a vast area.

4 THE MIDDLE PERIODS

While the Middle Periods (1000–1600 AD) saw the decline and, in many cases, the active suppression of Buddhism, Jainism continued to be important, especially in some regions such as Gujarat and Karnataka. Perhaps the most striking transformation in the ritual landscape of Hindu South and South-east Asia during these centuries was the establishment and institutionalization of temple-based worship. While early stone temples such as the sixth-century Vishnu temple in Deogarh, Bihar, and the seventh-century Durga temple at Aihole, Karnataka (Figure 57.2), constitute important models for later structures, the Early Middle period saw a virtual explosion of temple construction across the entire Hindu world. In part, this change was associated with shifts in devotional practice toward more

FIGURE 57.2 Seventh-century Durga temple at Aihole, Karnataka. The apsidal form recalls Buddhist structures; Ray (2004) has argued that both traditions employed existing architectural forms rather than one being influenced by the other.

FIGURE 57.3 Sixteenth-century Vijayanagara temple complex dedicated to Tiruvengalanatha, a form of Vishnu. This late Vijayanagara temple was classified as a city in its own right; its form borrows heavily from earlier Chola imperial styles.

'personal' and, to some extent, more congregational styles of worship carried out in public or semi-public structures such as temples. This shift is exemplified by the Bhakti movement, a series of schools of thought emphasizing personal love of god, at least some of which also espoused a more egalitarian social ideology (Veluthat 1987).

Despite the existence of many transregional as well as local traditions of religious hymns, poems, and scholars, distinct regional styles of temple architecture and sculpture can be identified. In some cases, these styles clearly carried very specific political messages which could be asserted through architectural emulation. For example, Michell (1994) has noted that the sixteenth-century Vijayanagara kings, at a moment of imperial expansion, adopted Chola imperial temple forms virtually wholesale, despite the thousands of kilometres and hundreds of years separating the two polities (Figure 57.3). In general, there is a rich architectural and art-historical literature on Hindu temples, which also find ample mention in historical documents of various kinds. Among the latter are tens of thousands of inscriptions, carved both into 'books' made of copper plates as well as into stone. The latter may be inscribed into temple walls or gates or, often, onto monumental slabs set up in temples, villages, fields, and other locations. While historical analysis of the content of these texts has been the most common approach, the archaeologists Morrison and Lycett (1994, 1997) have shown both how a quantitative analysis of inscription content can reveal unexpected patterns and how the physical context of inscriptions is related to their content, indicating the limits of study based only on temple inscriptions.

Middle period temples ranged widely in size from small shrines to vast walled complexes approaching the size of small cities. Temples could control large landholdings, and often invested their considerable wealth in agriculture and craft production. Large temples maintained occupational specialists such as priests, dancers, and scholars and also ran kitchens in which both public feasts and private meals were prepared. Detailed architectural documentation has been carried out for many temple complexes, though studies of

FIGURE 57.4 Chola king as devotee, Tiruchirapalli. Just rule was closely linked to patronage of religious institutions such as Hindu temples.

artefacts or plant remains are generally lacking. This is unfortunate since, for example, temple kitchens would provide outstanding contexts for the study of changing food practices and should be quite amenable to archaeological study. Pilgrimage, too, became important in the Middle period, and both regional residential mobility, amply documented historically though generally with a low level of specificity, as well as shorter-term mobility could be studied using archaeological tools such as strontium isotope analysis. The regional movement of specialist-produced objects, including sculptures, musical instruments, and other paraphernalia of worship is another important area of study (Figure 57.4). An important metallurgical analysis of Chola bronze sculptures by Srinivasin (2004) stands as an example of the potential contribution of archaeology to the study of religion in this period. Srinivasin's work not only pinpointed specific bronze-working workshops, but also showed that the famous Shiva Natraj 'dance of bliss' was actually an earlier Pallava innovation, rather than tenth-century Chola as had usually been believed.

As noted, temples were often closely associated with claims to just rule, and temple patrons included local leaders, merchant groups, and royal personages, all of whom documented their largesse in lithic and copper plate inscriptions and in sculpted donor portraits. As early as the seventh and eighth centuries, some temple complexes were built to make grand imperial gestures, such as the Bubaneshwar temple in Orissa or the Mahabalipuram complex in Tamil Nadu. The political and economic roles of Hindu temples have been widely discussed though only a few archaeological studies explicitly address these aspects. One of the most comprehensive combinations of iconographic, architectural, and archaeological research is the analysis of thousands of structures and images in and around the city of Vijayanagara by Verghese (2000), who convincingly documents religious shifts across more than 300 years in this huge imperial city. Verghese's material analysis reveals in great detail some of the patterns long noted by historians such as Stein (1978), who described a pattern of assimilation of local gods and goddesses

FIGURE 57.5 Fifteenth- or sixteenth-century Naga carved on boulder outcrops in rural area near the abandoned imperial city of Vijayanagara, in southern India. Note that this image is still in worship.

into more orthodox Hindu pantheons across the Middle periods. Similarly, in a study of the large-scale transformation of sacred space occasioned by the construction and reconstruction of temples, gates, and roads at Vijayanagara, Wagoner (1991) has shown how both the natural world and the built environment were made to reflect changing religious practices from worship of a local river goddess to her displacement by Shiva and her domestication to Parvati, Shiva's more docile wife, as well as connected claims to political authority. Were there information on artefacts, portable votive objects, food residues, and other archaeological information from these same locales, one can only imagine how much richer these analyses could be.

Although most research has been directed toward large temple complexes, some attention has been paid to smaller shrines and isolated sculptures and their integration into regional landscapes (Figure 57.5). Such landscape-based approaches show a great deal of promise in documenting the broad range of religious practices of the Middle periods and integrating religious practice with broader questions about social and political life. Further, regional-scale studies can isolate patterns not easily found in texts. For example, Morrison (2008) noted that in the region outside the city of Vijayanagara and especially in areas far from any evidence of government authority, worship of Shiva and the Goddess (Devi) predominated, even to the extent that Vishnu temples built during the imperial era were later transformed into Shiva or Goddess shrines. Building on a detailed analysis of local temples by Patil (1992), Morrison also documented the religious significance of Vijayanagara reservoirs in this region, part of an overall pattern of significance for water and water features that apparently has an extremely long history in this region. Reservoir sluice gates, for example, often contain images of the goddess Lakshmi as well as other images associated with temple doorways; she has argued that reservoirs were meant to represent temples themselves as well as to evoke the eternal ocean that encircles this earth.

Temples and, to a lesser extent, inscriptions and images dominate the archaeological scholarship on Middle period Hinduism. However, the realm of personal and family devotion remains a critical understudied area of work. Objects of personal devotion such as the small Shiva Lingas worn by Lingayat groups in the south and tiny clay or stone images of Nandi (the bull, vehicle of Shiva) are found in both excavated and surface contexts (e.g. Narasimaiah 1992), yet to date there has been no systematic study of such objects nor has there yet been much work on household shrines, which presumably were common across all of South Asia, as they are today. Many personal practices, too, such as vegetarianism and the avoidance of specific foodstuffs, have both religious and social associations and these would certainly be amenable to archaeological analysis.

5 CONCLUSIONS

While archaeological analysis of religious belief and practice is never straightforward, the record of that broad and diverse category that falls under the rubric of Hinduism has left us a rich material record. While research has been dominated by the rich iconography and styles of sculptures, bronzes, and other images as well as by the imposing Hindu temples and temple complexes, a great deal remains to be done on the more quotidian remains of personal devotion and practice that are manifest in, for example, household shrines, objects of personal devotion, broad landscapes of fields, villages, and sacred spaces, and even the bodily practices of diet, dress, and family.

SUGGESTED READING

For an introduction to the archaeology of Hinduism see Dilip Chakrabati's 2001 article, 'The archaeology of Hinduism', the 2004 article by Nayanjot Lahiri and Elizabeth Bacus, 'Exploring the archaeology of Hinduism', and Michaels' 2004 volume, *Hinduism, Past and Present*. Harappan religion and archaeology are discussed by Atre (2002), Hindu temples by Michell (1988) and early Hindu shrines by Ray (2004). Michael Willis (2009) examines the early development of Hinduism focusing upon the site of Udayagiri in central India and Verghese (2000) presents a selection of essays on the now-ruined city of Vijayanagara, capital of the fourteenth–seventeenth century AD south Indian Vijayanagara Empire.

REFERENCES

ARDELEANU-JANSEN, A. 2002. 'The terracotta figurines from Mohenjo-Daro: Considerations on tradition, craft and ideology in the Harappan civilization (*c*.2400–1800 BC)' in S. Settar and R. Korisettar (eds), *Indian Archaeology in Retrospect*, II: *Protohistory: Archaeology of the Harappan civilization* (New Delhi: Indian Council of Historical Research and Manohar), pp. 205–22.

ATRE, S. 2002. 'Harappan religion: Myth and polemics' in S. Settar and R. Korisettar (eds), *Indian Archaeology in Retrospect*, II: *Protohistory: Archaeology of the Harappan civilization* (New Delhi: Indian Council of Historical Research and Manohar), pp. 185–204.

BHAN, S. 1997. 'Recent trends in Indian archaeology', *Social Scientist*, 25(1–2): 17–32.

BHARDWAJ, D. 2004. 'Problematizing the archaeology of female figurines in north-west India' in H. P Ray and C. M. Sinopoli (eds), *Archaeology as History in Early South Asia* (New Delhi: Indian Council of Historical Research and Aryan Books International), pp. 481–504.

BOIVIN, N. 2005. 'Orientalism, ideology and identity: Examining caste in South Asian archaeology', *Journal of Social Archaeology*, 5(2): 225–52.

CHAKRABARTI, D. 2001. 'The archaeology of Hinduism' in T. Insoll (ed.), *Archaeology and World Religion* (London: Routledge), pp. 33–60.

DEHEJIA, V. 1992. 'The Collective and Popular Basis of Early Buddhist Patronage: Sacred Monuments, 100 BC–AD 250' in B. Stoler Miller (ed.), *The Powers of Art: Patronage in Indian Culture* (Delhi: Oxford University Press), pp. 35–45.

DIMOCK, E. C., GEROW, E., NAIM, C. M., et al. 1974. *The Literatures of India: An introduction* (Chicago: The University of Chicago Press).

ECK, D. L. 1981. 'India's *Tīrthas*: "Crossings" in sacred geography', *History of Religions*, 20(4): 323–44.

ELGOOD, H. 2004. 'Exploring the roots of village Hinduism in South Asia', *World Archaeology*, 36(3): 326–42.

GHOSH, A. (ed.) 1989. *An Encyclopaedia of Indian Archaeology* (New Delhi: Munshiram Manoharlal Publishers Pvt. Ltd).

LAHIRI, N. and BACUS, E. A. 2004. 'Exploring the archaeology of Hinduism', *World Archaeology*, 36(3): 313–25.

MICHAELS, A. 2004. *Hinduism, Past and Present* (Princeton: Princeton University Press).

MICHELL, G. 1988. *The Hindu Temple: An Introduction to its meanings and forms* (Chicago: University of Chicago Press).

——1994. 'Revivalism as the imperial mode: Religious architecture during the Vijayanaganara period' in C. B. Asher and T. R. Metcalf (eds), *Perceptions of South Asia's Visual Past* (Delhi: AIIS, Swadharma Swarjya Sangha, and Oxford & IBH Press), pp. 187–97.

MORRISON, K. D. 2008. *Daroji Valley: Landscape history, place, and the making of a dryland reservoir system*, Vijayanagara Research Project Monograph Series (Delhi: Manohar Press).

——and LYCETT, M. T. 1994. 'Centralized power, centralized authority? Ideological claims and archaeological patterns', *Asian Perspectives*, 33(2): 312–53.

————1997. 'Inscriptions as artifacts: Precolonial South India and the analysis of texts', *Journal of Archaeological Method and Theory*, 3(3–4): 215–37.

NARASIMAIAH, B. 1992. *Metropolis Vijayanagara: Sigificance of remains of citadel* (Delhi: Book India Publishing Co.).

PATIL, C. S. 1992. *Temples of Raichur and Bellary Districts, Karnataka, 1000–1325 AD* (Mysore: Directorate of Archaeology and Museums).

POLLOCK, S. 1996. 'The Sanskrit cosmopolis, 300–1300 CE: Transculturation, vernacularization, and the question of ideology' in J. E. M. Houben (ed.), *Ideology and the Status of Sanskrit: Contributions to the history of the Sanskrit language* (New York: Brill), pp. 197–247.

POSSEHL, G. L. 2002. *The Indus Civilization: A contemporary perspective* (Oxford: AltaMira).

RAY, H. P. 2004. 'The archaeology of sacred space: Introduction' in H. P. Ray and C. M. Sinopoli (eds), *Archaeology as History in Early South Asia* (New Delhi: Indian Council of Historical Research and Aryan Books International), pp. 350–75.

Shaw, J. 2000. 'Sanchi and its archaeological landscape: Buddhist monasteries, settlements and irrigation works in central India', *Antiquity*, 74: 775–6.

Srinivasan, D. M. 1983. 'Vedic Rudra-Śiva', *Journal of the American Oriental Society*, 103(3): 543–56.

——1989. 'Vaishnava art and iconography at Mathura' in D. M. Srinivasan (ed.), *Mathura: The Cultural Heritage* (New Delhi: Manohar), pp. 383–92.

Srinivasin, S. 2004. 'Shiva as "cosmic dancer": On Pallava origins for the Nataraja bronze', *World Archaeology*, 36(3): 432–50.

Stein, B. 1978. 'Temples in Tamil country, 1350–1750 AD', in B. Stein (ed.), *South Indian Temples* (New Delhi: Vikas), pp. 11–45.

Sullivan, H. P. 1964. 'A re-examination of the religion of the Indus civilization', *History of Religions*, 4(1): 115–25.

Thapar, R. 2000 [1983]. 'The Archaeological Background to the Agnicayana Ritual', in *Cultural Pasts: Essays in early Indian history* (New Delhi: Oxford University Press), pp. 336–66.

Veluthat, K. 1987. 'The temple base of the Bhakti movement in south India' in K. M. Srimali (ed.), *Essays in Indian Art, Religion, and Society* (Delhi: Munshiram Manoharlal), pp. 151–9.

Verghese, A. 2000. *Archaeology, Art and Religion: New perspectives on Vijayanagara* (New Delhi: Oxford University Press).

Wagoner, P. B. 1991. 'Architecture and mythic space at Hemakuta Hill: A preliminary report' in D. V. Devaraj and C. S. Patil (eds), *Vijayanagara Progress of Research 1984–1987* (Mysore: Directorate of Archaeology and Museums), pp. 142–8.

Willis, M. D. 2009. *The Archaeology of Hindu Ritual: Temples and the establishment of the gods* (Cambridge: Cambridge University Press).

CHAPTER 58

BUDDHISM

ROBIN CONINGHAM

1 INTRODUCTION

IN 1854 Alexander Cunningham published the first comprehensive study of a Buddhist complex, Sanchi in central India. Recording his excavation and survey of the hilltop site three years previously, Cunningham set the standard for future Buddhist scholars by studying the complex's history alongside detailed observations of its landscape, plans and elevations of the main monuments and key finds, including inscriptions and sculpture (Cunningham 1854). Later, as India's first Director-General of Archaeology, Cunningham applied this rigour to studies of other Buddhist sites such as Bharhut in 1879 and Mahabodhi in 1892 and realized his earlier suggestion that 'it is hoped that the...Directors will...open the numerous Topes (*stupas*)...and to draw up a report on all the Buddhist remains...A work of this kind would be of more real value for the ancient history of India than the most critical and elaborate edition of the eighteen Puranas' (Cunningham 1854: x–xi). His contribution to the development of Buddhist archaeology is clear when one compares the systematic nature of his Sanchi report with the later ones produced by John Marshall for the monuments at Sanchi (1940) and Taxila (1951). However, as the field of Buddhist research has expanded, studies have increasingly focused on the examination of individual traits. This is not to detract from the excellence of the scholarship involved in producing syntheses like Mitra's *Buddhist Monuments* (1971) or from the value of published reports of single monastic sites such as Prematilleke's study of Alahana Perivena (1982), but to recognize that this process has not resulted in a balanced corpus of Buddhist scholarship.

This imbalance has, as noted elsewhere (Coningham 1998, 2001), resulted in an environment where textual scholarship has achieved such a predominant role that it is possible for one scholar to suggest that 'Buddhist art, inscriptions and coins...cannot be understood without the support given by the texts. Consequently, the study of Buddhism needs first of all to be concentrated on the texts' (de Jong 1975: 14–15) and another to date the Gautama Buddha without addressing the nature of the archaeological evidence (Gombrich 1996)—a far deviation from Cunningham's request of 1854 for fieldwork rather than critical editions! Indeed, such is the reliance on texts, that it is possible to accuse many archaeologists of allowing research to be 'dominated by textually based scholars or by historians of art or architecture, relegating archaeologists to a solitary role of primary producer, not venturing further than the description of excavated remains' (Coningham 1998: 122).

In my reviews of the archaeology of Buddhism in 1998 and 2001, I noted that the rematerialization of Buddhism had not yet begun and that many scholars were still ignoring the benefits which could be brought to their research by articulating with archaeological resources. However, in the intervening years, a series of studies have begun to readdress that balance, ranging from Fogelin's study of Buddhist ritual presentation and the use and manipulation of space (2003), Hammarstrand's review of 'a Microarchaeology of Buddhism' in 2007 to the interdisciplinary analysis of wider Buddhist landscapes (Coningham et al. 2007; Shaw 2000; Fogelin 2006). The following sections will review our current understanding of Buddhist archaeology, its monuments and landscapes, developing the key theme of this chapter—the need to place monuments within their immediate and wider landscapes and the need to reconstruct the social and economic roles they played.

2 THE LIFETIME OF THE BUDDHA

Rather than reiterating the narrative of the Buddha's life (Coningham 2001; Dutt 1962; Mitra 1971), or discussing the inadequacies of our understanding of his birth or death dates (Bechert 1995; Coningham 2001), or location of his childhood home (Coningham 2001), this section will provide the context for the growth and spread of Buddhism. The individual known as the Buddha, or enlightened one, was born in the Terai, near the foothills of the Himalayas. Named Gautama Siddhartha, he was the son of King Suddhodana of Kapilavastu, ruler of the Shakya clan, and Queen Mayadevi, daughter of the neighbouring king of Devadaha. He was born in a period of rapid change as the more powerful of the ancient *Mahajanapadas* or states of northern India absorbed their weaker neighbours (Erdosy 1995: 115). Thus the armies of Kosala defeated the *Mahajanapada* of Kasi and their king, Vidudabha, destroyed Kapilavastu, and massacred the Buddha's own clan even during his lifetime. Another developing power was the state of Magadha, which would later reduce Kosala and emerge as the sole ruler of the Ganges Valley by the fourth century BC (Allchin 1995a: 187).

This period, known as the *matsya-nyaya*, or the maxim of the fish in which larger fish devour smaller ones and are themselves eaten, also saw the emergence of fortified cities such as Rajagriha, the capital of Magadha, demonstrating their rulers' abilities to attract population as well as focus labour on the construction of ramparts (Coningham 1995b: 69). In addition to these major geopolitical changes within the plains of the Ganges, other transformations were occurring with the growth of guilds of merchants and craftsmen trading from the new cities (Thapar 1984, 2000, 2002). Engaged in commerce, their activities and influence were accelerated by the development of stamp seals and coinage, allowing the exchange of consumables for non-consumables. As the mercantile elites had no wish to endure their low position within the caste rank of purity, they began to move their patronage from the traditional practitioners, the priestly *Brahmins*, to the growing numbers of casteless *sramanas*, or renounceant seekers, who were examining issues of rebirth, cause and effect, and the overcoming of the weaknesses of the physical body (Akira

1998: 16). By the time of Gautama's enlightenment, there were five other charismatic heterodoxical teachers who were beginning to gather large numbers of disciplines and patrons, including Gosaliputra of the Ajivikas and Mahavira of the Jains (Akira 1998: 17).

Whilst there were many similarities between the *dhamas*, or spiritual cultures, of the main *sramana* sects, the Buddha and his disciplines were differentiated by their regulations which directed them to live as a community for three months during the monsoon season in a rain-retreat. These annual congregations were formally configured within fixed boundaries and helped transform the new sect of wanderers into the sedentary communal order known as the *Sangha* (Dutt 1962: 54–7). A second feature which accelerated this process was the development of the *Sangha*'s *Vinaya* or framework of monastic discipline (Horner 1957; Dhirasekera 1982; Dutt 1962: 74–7), which allowed the community to be self-governing and offered a 'constitutional guarantee for corporate existence' (Dutt 1962: 81). The contents of the *Vinaya* and the *Suttas*, or Buddha's sayings, were confirmed in the presence of the *Sangha* at the First Buddhist Council soon after his final transformation, the *mahaparinirvana*. The presence of such a framework resulted in state protection for members of the *Sangha* and state protection for properties and privileges donated to it and, in this way, the temporary structures for wandering *sramanas* were to develop into vast monastic estates.

According to the Buddhist Pali canon, which includes the *Vinaya*, the Buddha attracted many patrons during his travels within the Ganges plain including rulers, merchants, and farmers demonstrating the breadth of the appeal of his teachings. The temporal holdings of the *Sangha* began at this time with recorded donations of a monastery by a physician in the city of Rajagriha, a mango grove by a courtesan in the vicinity of Sravasti, and four retreats at Kausambi donated by bankers and a wood-carver (Mitra 1971: 8). These were later augmented by the Buddha himself who advised the *Sangha* that the four great sites of pilgrimage were to be Lumbini, where he was born; Bodhgaya, where he achieved enlightenment; Sarnath, where he preached the first sermon of his *Dharma*; and Kusinagara, where he underwent his *Mahaparanirvana* (Mitra 1971: 8–9). From these modest origins, Buddhism spread throughout South Asia to become the dominant heterodox sect by the third century BCE although none of its early structures have survived. Indeed, the first recognizable archaeological horizon of Buddhist structures dates to the third century BC and comprise a series of brick or stone-built stupas and shrines at Sarnath, Taxila, Vaisali, and Sanchi as well as enlarged caves at Rajgir and in Sri Lanka (Allchin 1995b; Coningham 2001).

This distinct 'horizon' coincides with the advent of monumental royal patronage as represented by the presence of inscribed pillars at key sites of Buddhist pilgrimage. Erected by the Mauryan Emperor Asoka, the pillar at Lumbini records that Asoka worshipped at the site because the Buddha was born there and that he erected a stone wall and pillar to commemorate his visit (Allchin 1995b). According to Buddhist tradition, Asoka is a key figure because he also held the Third Buddhist Council, expelling 80,000 heretical monks, and opened up seven of the *stupas* containing the Buddha's corporeal remains and rededicated the relics in 84,000 stupas throughout India (Mitra 1971: 9). Whether the *dharma* noted on Asoka's inscriptions was the same as the Buddha's teachings is uncertain (Coningham and Manuel 2009), we know from his inscriptions that he went on a pilgrimage of the Buddhist natal landscape erecting walls, pillars, and a stupa (Coningham 2001), and even inscribed warnings at monasteries stating that monks or nuns causing dissention should be expelled. This is not, of course, to suggest that Buddhism was a dynastic religion as Asoka is also thought to have donated a rock-cut cave to the Ajivika sect (Allchin 1995b: 247) and others have argued he was more dedicated to imperial expansionism, even by ritual entrainment. Considering the latter, even Kanishka, identified by tradition as the convenor of the Fourth Buddhist Council, was not adverse from utilizing images of Hellenistic, Indic, and Iranian divinities on his coinage in recognition of the different ethnic and religious affiliations of his subjects (Coningham and Manuel 2009).

3 BUDDHIST MONUMENTS

As noted above, the earliest properties of the *Sangha* were clustered in the vicinity of Rajagriha, Sravasti, and Kausambi as well as the four major sites associated with the life of the Buddha (Mitra 1971: 8–9). The exact nature of these early Buddhist structures is not known but the *Vinaya* identified the presence of *Avasas* in the countryside, constructed by members of the *Sangha*, and *Aramas* in the vicinity of cities, maintained by donors. It also advised that the former should not overlap with one another and that their limits should be demarked by natural boundaries (Dutt 1962: 55–7). There are no traces of these early structures but three major monument types are attributed to this early phase: the *stupa*, the *griha*, and the *vihara*.

The *stupa* is the most recognizable and resilient Buddhist monument, comprising a solid mound of brick, stone, or clay usually erected over relics. It is one of the earliest Buddhist monuments as it is recorded that ten *stupas* were raised over the divisions of the Buddha's corporeal remains, the ashes and the urn in which they were gathered (Mitra 1971: 7). Although most of these early monuments were subsequently remodelled or opened in order to reallocate their contents, one was excavated outside the city of Vaisali in 1958. Built over one of the original divisions of relics, the *stupa* was a small mound of clay with a height of 3 m and a diameter of 8 m (Coningham 2001: 72). These clay monuments were all enlarged by brick and form part of the very noticeable brick and stone 'horizon' which is often associated with the Emperor Asoka. Although only one *stupa* can be categorically attributed to Asoka, that of the Kanakamuni Buddha as recorded on his Nigali Sagar pillar (Coningham 2001: 240), the uniformity of construction at Taxila, Sarnath, Vaisali, and Sanchi suggests a programme of patronage in order to facilitate 'Mauryanization' (Coningham and Manuel 2009; Smith 2005). Indeed, these *stupas* were all hemispherical domes set on terraced drums and crowned with a spire of stone umbrellas (Mitra 1971: 24) and built in stone or brick, dependent on local availability.

The *stupa* cult spread across Asia and began to manifest regional characteristics, most notably in Sri Lanka where a series of *stupas* over 100 m in height were constructed at the cities of Anuradhapura (Figure 58.1) and Polonnaruva (Coningham 1999, 2001), but also in Myanmar and South-east Asia where pagodas or tiered platforms were built. Patterns of donation also altered as individual kings erected Anuradhapura's monumental *stupas* whilst hundreds of lesser donors built small votive *stupas* crowding the monastic courtyards of Gandhara in the north. Not only was there differentiation in *stupa* style and size, but also in contents. The Pali canon records that *saririka* stupas were to be erected over corporeal relics of the Buddha and his disciples, *paribhogika stupas* over objects used by the

FIGURE 58.1 The great *stupa* of the Jetavana monastery in the ancient Sri Lankan city of Anuradhapura stands over 160 m high and was built in the third century AD.

Buddha, *uddesika stupas* at sites associated with the Buddha's life (and former lives), as well as votive *stupas* at sites of pilgrimage for merit (Mitra 1971: 21–2). It is also possible that *stupas* were designed to perform other functions; for example, housed in simple stone vaults, some Sri Lankan *stupa* relics were sealed in elaborately decorated chambers and designed to represent the universe and thus the Buddha's centrality within it (Paranavitana 1946: 21). These characteristics notwithstanding, there are still many complexities associated with the function and attribution of *stupas* and in many cases we cannot be certain which of the 20 of the Buddha's predecessors is commemorated, to which of the four categories of content the *stupa* belongs, and whether the *stupa* is Buddhist or Jain (Coningham 2001: 74).

The *Griha* or sanctuary is the second category of monuments most commonly used to identify the presence of a Buddhist complex. As in the case of the *stupa*, we have very little idea of the character of the pre-Mauryan *griha* but the Mauryan horizon provides evidence of brick-built sanctuaries close to the site of Asokan pillars as at Sanchi and Sarnath (Allchin 1995b: 244). At the latter, an oblong hall with an apsidal end was constructed directly west of the pillar but circular *grihas* are associated with Mauryan patronage at Bairat (Piggott 1943). What is clear from this formative period, is that the apsidal-ended *griha* was not an architectural form restricted to Buddhist practice as a number of rock-cut chambers with apsidal ends are also associated with Mauryan patronage and appear to have been dedicated to the Ajivika sect (Huntington 1975). Indeed, in her review of Buddhist monuments, Mitra suggests that 'there is no difference in the treatment of Buddhist, Jaina and Brahmanical temples' (Mitra 1971: 52). Whilst some early *grihas* were clearly focused on *stupas* at their apsidal ends, as at Bairat, it is anticipated that a number were also dedicated to Bodhi-trees. Difficult to identify (Bandaranayake 1974: 49), the presence of carvings of such monuments at the early *stupa* of Bharhut, suggest that they were not uncommon. S*tupa*-focused *grihas* continued to be one of the key Buddhist monuments and spread across South Asia and we are fortunate to have a series of well-preserved rock-cut examples at Ajanta and Karla (Brown 1956: xix) which encapsulate vernacular timber styles. However, the earlier focus on *stupas* was steadily replaced by the Buddha image, a process well recorded within the valley of Nagarjunakonda (Sarkar 1962: 73; Coningham 2001: 87), and the *griha* was to undergo a process of giganticism to meet the extremes of Paharpur in Bengal in the eighth century AD and Angkor Thom in Cambodia four centuries later.

As noted above, the *Vihara* or monastic residence (see Figure 58.2) is the earliest monument to have been donated to the *Sangha*, although we have little evidence of pre-Mauryan construction. The identification of the Jivakarama monastery at Rajgir is conjectural only and its dating is far from clear (Allchin 1995b: 246) and there is no evidence to suggest that it was even a monastery. That such structures were commonly used for Buddhist veneration by the first and second century BC is suggested by the carved friezes of Bharhut, which depict huts and fenced shrines within a compound (Brown 1956: 16; Mitra 1971: plate 13). Soon after the transmission of Buddhism to the island of Sri Lanka, over 1,000 *viharas* were dedicated between the third and first century BC but these consisted of single—or clusters of—natural rock-shelters made habitable with the cutting of a drip ledge over the opening (Coningham 1995a). This individual focus is also found at the

FIGURE 58.2 The monastic residence, or *vihara*, at Mohra Moradu in the Taxila Valley of Pakistan was built between the fourth and fifth centuries AD and is quadrangular in form with individuals cells arranged around a central court.

Dharmarajika monastery at Taxila where the earliest residential structures appear to have taken the form of a set of cells fronted by a verandah (Marshall 1951: 246). However, by the second century BC patrons in the Deccan replaced individual chambers with a rock-cut format with three rows of cells opening onto a central court which itself was accessed through a facade in the cliff face (Mitra 1971: 33). This model spread throughout south Asia during the first half of the first millennium AD. It may denote a major shift in the relationship between Sangha and laity as suggested by Marshall (1951: 246) but it is also possible to draw similarities between the compound plans of urban merchants, as at Bhita (Marshall 1912), and the new monastic plans.

Notwithstanding the above survey, there were a number of other structures at monastic complexes, some built in brick or stone but others in perishable materials (Coningham 2001: 71). Regional transformations are also apparent, especially in the form of Buddhist giganticism, whether of the Damila *stupa* of Polonnaruva, or the *griha* and *vihara* court of Paharpur, and even within regions there are clear chronological transformations. For example, portable relics become the focus of devotion in Sri Lanka as the veneration at the static *stupas* of the cities of Anuradhapura and Polonnaruva became unviable due to the worsening political position of the Sinhala state in the eleventh century AD (Coningham 2001: 84). There are also divisions apparent even within city environments and Carrither's separation of the modern Sri Lankan *Sangha* into those attached to villages and cities and those located in forests (1983) maps well against ancient Sri Lankan *vihara* types. Indeed, the ornate orthodox monasteries within Anuradhapura's sacred city compare starkly with the isolated western monasteries whose only decoration is of ornate *vihras* carved on urinals, suggesting a self-evident contestatory discourse (Coningham 2001: 87). Finally, note should also be made of pilgrimage to the sites of significance without major monuments, such as *Sri Pada*, or the Buddha's footprint in Sri Lanka, as not only do such sites draw other denominations but are also landmarks in the landscape.

4 Buddhist Landscapes

When investigating the development of Buddhist monasticism in South Asia, it is clear that there is very little agreement amongst scholars as to the physical and spiritual roles of such establishments. Indeed, as Fogelin has demonstrated (2006: 52), some academics have interpreted the role of monasteries as isolated retreats with limited links with laity (Brown 1956), others as arenas for competition amongst patrons (Thapar 2002), an integral part of trade infrastructure (Morrison 1995, Ray 1994), or as agricultural facilitators (Heitzman 1984). Fogelin's attempt to attribute one (or more) of these roles to the Early Historic monastery of Thotlakonda reached the conclusion that there was a focus on isolation but that it was tempered by economic and ritual interactions with local lay communities (Fogelin 2006: 195–7). Undertaking a similar survey of Sanchi's landscape, Shaw has produced a different interpretation underlining the importance of monumental intervisibility and the physical prominence of stupas as a way of protecting the relics within (2000: 27). As both studies were based on limited surface surveys without excavation, it could be argued that both lack the finer chronological, environmental, and artefactual resolution necessary for detailing the relationship between their selected monumental Buddhist clusters and their surrounding landscapes. In the summer of 2008, such a programme was completed in the hinterland of Anuradhapura linking the ancient Sri Lankan capital to its rural communities, both secular and religious. Intensely surveying over 96 km^2, the Anuradhapura (Sri Lanka) Project recorded over 835 archaeological sites, 13 of which were excavated (Coningham et al. 2006, 2007).

Anuradhapura is one of Asia's great Buddhist pilgrimage sites and although its sacred role has never been lost, the original function of many of its monuments and structures became confused. The early investigation of the city and its sacred ring of monasteries was haphazard but later generations of scholars, such as Hocart (1924) and Paranavitana (1950), systematically studied the site and integrated it with the island's historical texts, identifying many of the monuments and their patrons. This framework laid, it was possible for scholars such as Bandaranayake (1974) and Silva (1988) to study the developmental sequences of its monumental monasteries and record shifts in cult practice. This work was augmented in the 1980s and 1990s with a programme of excavations in the city's monasteries (Ratnayake 1984; Wickramagamage 1984) and publication of the first artefact sequences from the secular core of Anuradhapura—the Citadel (Coningham 1999, 2006). With a view to understand the relationship between the city and its monasteries with both lay and religious communities in its hinterland, Coningham and Gunawardhana organized a team of archaeological scientists, archaeologists, and geo-archaeologists to redirect focus from the city to its hinterland by incorporating and analysing all archaeological sites there, whether monumental monasteries or villages.

As noted above, this comprehensive landscape approach led to the recording of over 800 sites in Anuradhapura's hinterland, of which the most numerous are ceramic scatters and monastic sites. Over half of the sites encountered on transect survey were ceramic scatters covering less than 25 m^2. Excavation and auger coring at a sample suggest that they are less than 0.2 m thick and the presence of post-holes suggests construction in perishable materials. With a notable absence of the fine wares, semi-precious stone, glass, and metal associated with the sequence of the Citadel (Coningham 2006), we have identified them as short-lived 'peripatetic villages engaged in *chena* (slash-and-burn) agriculture' (Coningham et al. 2007: 707). Of these shallow ceramic scatters, there are only two which might be attributed the title of town on the grounds of size and artefactual record, Rajaligama and Siyambalawewa, although both are dwarfed by the 100 ha Citadel. The former was 25 km south of Anuradhapura and comprised a scatter of 6 ha. Excavations and auger cores at the site failed to identify a depth of more than 0.3 m; however, it had an enhanced artefactual assemblage dating to the third century BC including imported Rouletted Ware, bone, and glass.

The second site, Siyambalawewa, is located on the banks of the Malwattu Oya some 13 km north of Anuradhapura. Close to an ancient annicut and ford across the river, it consisted of a shallow scatter of sherds covering an area of 3.5 ha centred on a unique configuration of four clusters of undressed stone pillars. The presence of an Early Brahmi inscription on one of the pillars again suggests the establishment of a higher-order settlement, but its shallow sequence suggests rapid abandonment. In tandem, this corpus of scatters suggest the presence of mobile communities with little or no access to the city, or its exotic and monumental materials, as well as what may be considered to have been a short-lived attempt to regulate the landscape from Anuradhapura (2007: 717). In contrast, our second most numerous category of site, monastic, is typified by the presence of monumental structures, inscriptions and exotic imports. For example, the site of Veheragala had a 3-metre-deep sequence of brick, tile, and stone as well as finds of glass and bone. These were augmented by imported Northern Black Polished Ware and Rouletted Ware, all providing a chronology stretching from the third century BC to the eleventh century AD—a sequence paralleled by the great monasteries of Anuradhapura and its Citadel (Coningham et al. 2007).

This pattern led the project team to suggest in 2007 that, in the absence of higher-order settlements, monasteries 'played a dual role of religious and secular administrators' (Coningham et al. 2007: 717). This overlap of roles was not uncommon in the Kandyan Kingdom and British administrators legally recognized such establishments through the nineteenth-century Buddhist Temporalities Ordinance (Karunananda 2006). Whilst this term, Buddhist Temporality, avoids some of the unfortunate connotations associated with our earlier use of 'theocratic landscape', our working model was that the city's surrounding landscape of villages and rural communities was not centrally regulated by the state through higher-order settlements and royal officials but through a network of *viharas*, closely linked to the great monasteries of the city rather than the throne (Coningham et al. 2007: 717). Although we are still examining the exact nature and chronology of the relationship between the different categories of monasteries and secular settlements through the excavated artefactual record, our model is supported by the research of Malini Dias who has identified a pattern of increasing grants of royal land to monasteries within Anuradhapura's hinterland (2001). The earliest inscriptions of the region record the donation of rock-shelters to the *Sangha* in the third century BC (Coningham 1995a), but this was later augmented by the donation of agricultural resource, such as the Palu Makiccava inscription of King Gaja Bahu I (r. AD 177–99) who created a reservoir and presented it to the monks at the Thuparama *vihara* of Anuradhapura, some 16 km away (*Epig. Zey.* I: 211).

As Dias notes, this pattern of haphazard allocation was succeeded by an intensified period of dedication as recorded by the corpus of pillar inscriptions erected between AD 800 and 1200 (2001: 151). These inscriptions confirm the donation of land, and often associated rights, to a Buddhist institution and name the royal donor, the location of the land and even the identity of the witnesses present at the time of its erection (*Epig. Zey.* II: 5). Such donations were not merely devotional but also had ramifications for the future management of the land as they also granted what Dias refers to as immunities (2001: 154). King Udaya I's (r. AD 952–63) pillar at Noccipotana, for example, directs that the following immunities were granted 'district headmen, and keepers of (district) records shall not enter; enforcers of customary rules shall not enter; carts, oxen, labourers, and buffaloes shall not be appropriated; labourers shall not be impressed for river-work; those who have come for asylum shall not be arrested' (*Epig. Zey.* II: 8). Often accompanied by carvings of the sun, moon, dog, and crow, the message was clear: the donation was to last as long as the universe and those who ignored the dedication would be reborn as scavengers. The *Culavamsa* records that when King Udaya III (r. AD 935–8) pursued officials into the Topovana monastery precinct and had them executed: 'the people in the town (of Anuradhapura) and country and the troops became rebellious like the ocean stirred by wild storms' (*Cul.* 53:16).

This demonstrates that these pillars record far more than an alienation of resource from the state, rather an alienation of jurisdiction. The effect of such a policy is clear from Dias' perspective, 'a plausible suggestion for this (practice) is that lands and villages in the territories beyond the control of the central authority were given to the monasteries to bring some control over them... This way the monastic institutions became the landed intermediary between the central political authority and the people' (2001: 115). The centralized control of the *Sangha* over such temporalities is also made clear by the pillar inscriptions with the Ataviragollava pillar recording that King Dappula V (r. AD 991–1003) granted immunities to the village of Velangama which belonged to the Jetavana monastery of Anuradhapura (*Epig. Zey.* II: 48). It is also clear that this alienation of land was accompanied by an alienation of product and surplus as illustrated by the record that the village of Kolayunu was to contribute an annual tithe of oil for the lamps in Anuradhapura's Abhayagiri monastery in the tenth century AD (*Epig. Zey.* II: 19)—firmly linking the hinterland to the centre.

5 CONCLUSIONS AND NEW PERSPECTIVES

This link between Anuradhapura's urban and rural monasteries suggests a centralizing function in the landscape far beyond those entertained by other scholars, and is certainly absent within Fogelin (2006) and Shaw's interpretations (2000). Indeed, it is tempting to suggest that the epigraphic and settlement data support a hypothesis that, after the state failed with its attempts at Early Historic centralization, the *viharas* of Anuradhapura filled the vacuum through the deployment of temporalities within the landscape. When Dias suggested that 'territories beyond the control of the central authority were given to the monasteries to bring some control over them' (2001: 115), she also implied that there was a central strategy using monasteries as agents for colonization and incorporation. It is interesting to note that the potential of monasteries as community catalysts did not go unnoticed during the 1940s re-colonization of the north central province of Sri Lanka. For example, a number of new agricultural settlements founded by D. S. Senanayake were granted to volunteers drawn from many different regions around the island. Planned around a central core which included a monastery, villagers confirm that community affiliation was reinforced by the communal act of building the *vihara* and that its first incumbent played a critical role in forming the settlement's identity (Piyasena pers. comm.).

This is not to suggest that all land colonization or incorporation was state-sponsored and again contemporary examples may be presented. As described by one of its managers, Herman Gunaratna, the Sri Lankan Mahaweli development programme of the 1980s sought to develop and allocate irrigated land in unoccupied areas of the eastern provinces of the island with communities from more densely populated areas (1988: 22). Although occupied by less than 90 people per km^2, the engineers investigating the Maduru Oya basin were surprised to find evidence of ancient monasteries as they built new dams and annicuts in the jungle, leading some to suggest that 'Maduru Oya was thus sanctified with these sacred historical findings' (1988: 51). In response to what was perceived to be the unhindered encroachment of new plots by illegal Tamil settlers, the incumbent of the regional *Vihara*, the Rev. Matara Kithalagama Sri Seelalankara Thero, announced the distribution of 'temple' land in early August 1983 (1988: 70). Within a month, thousands of landless people gathered at his temple and were led to Maduru Oya by chanting monks where they appropriated over 2,400 ha of government land. When requested by the government to return home, the incumbent stated that 'he had a right to do this as these lands according to ancient records, belong to the Dimbulagala Maha Vihara and that he will not vacate these areas' (1988: 89).

This colonizing role, whether sponsored or unsponsored, is notably beyond that traditionally attributed to Buddhist monasteries in the past (Fogelin 2006) but the applicability of this model throughout the Early Historic and medieval Buddhist world is, of course, less certain. For example, it might not match against the presence of the centralized state as reconstructed from Erdosy's survey of the hinterland of the *Mahajanapada* of Vatsa with its postulated tiers of higher order settlements (1988). However, it is not necessary to possess the wealth of Sri Lanka's epigraphic and textual evidence or the strength of its archaeological record to hypothesize such an application. The distinct pattern of clusters of monasteries within the Vale of Peshawar and the Swat and Dir valleys to its north, raise the possibility that temporalities may also have ordered more peripheral landscapes in Gandhara during the period of Kushan hegemony. This, in turn, raises the fascinating possibility that monasteries in South Asia were responses to particular social, economic, and physical environments—a possibility which would favourably compare with some of the theories advanced for the role of early English monasteries (Bond 2004). In conclusion, whilst traditional architectural and textual studies of Buddhist monasteries have concentrated on monasteries as isolated monuments, often as places of reflection or asceticism, recent landscape projects highlight the potential for focusing on monasteries as active and integral temporalities within the social and economic landscape of urban and rural communities, whose incumbents, in select environments, could exercise greater authority and presence than that of secular rulers.

Suggested Reading

There are a number of useful historical narratives of the emergence and development of Buddhism ranging from the works of Gombrich (1996) and Akira (1998) to Dutt's classic of 1962, but these are somewhat over-reliant on textual sources. A corpus of more critical case studies by Schopen (1997), Dias (2001), and Fogelin (2003) has, however, revealed a far more flexible relationship between Buddhist practice and scriptural precept.

For the study of the development of all periods of South Asian Buddhist architecture, Debla Mitra's survey of 1971 remains the key review, although Brown's (1956) reconstructions of individual monuments and sites provides a more vivid feel of how Buddhist sites may have looked. Both are now considerably out of date but are, as yet, without substitute.

A useful foil to these architectural and textual studies are the archaeological reviews which provide a broader social, economic, and cultural context. These range from the overviews by Allchin, Erdosy, and Coningham in the 1995 *Archaeology of Early Historic South Asia* and Romila Thapar's 2002 volume to the study of individual themes, such as Ray's masterful investigation of the relationship between maritime trade and the spread of Buddhism (1994).

Finally, there are a growing number of scholars who are critically evaluating our current understanding of the development of Buddhism through systematic archaeological survey and, in some cases, excavation as exemplified by the work of Coningham et al. (2007), Shaw (2000), and Fogelin (2006). This work, in parallel with the critical case studies cited above, forms a key development in the necessary 'rematerialization of Buddhist studies as identified by Coningham in 1998 and 2001.

REFERENCES

AKIRA, H. 1998. *A History of Indian Buddhism: From Sakyamuni to early Mahayana*, trans. P. Groner (Delhi: Motilal Banarsidass).
ALLCHIN, F. R. 1995a. 'Early cities and states: Beyond the Ganges Valley' in F. R. Allchin (ed.), *The Archaeology of Early Historic South Asia* (Cambridge: Cambridge University Press), pp. 123–51.
——1995b. 'Mauryan architecture and art' in F. R. Allchin (ed.), *The Archaeology of Early Historic South Asia* (Cambridge: Cambridge University Press), pp. 222–73.
BANDARANAYAKE, S. D. 1974. *Sinhalese Monastic architecture* (Leiden: Brill).
BECHERT, H. 1995. 'Introductory essay: The dates of the historical Buddha' in H. Bechert (ed.), *When Did the Buddha live?* (Delhi: Sri Satguru Publications), pp. 11–36.
BOND, J. 2004. *Monastic Landscapes* (Stroud: Tempus).
BROWN, P. 1956. *Indian Architecture: Buddhist and Hindu periods* (Bombay: D. B. Taraporevala Sons and Co.).
CARRITHERS, M. 1983. *The Forest Monks of Sri Lanka* (Delhi: Oxford University Press).
CONINGHAM, R. A. E. 1995a. 'Monks, caves and kings', *World Archaeology*, 27: 266–81.
——1995b. 'Dark age or continuum?' in F. R. Allchin (ed.), *The Archaeology of Early Historic South Asia* (Cambridge: Cambridge University Press), pp. 54–74.
——1998. 'Buddhism "rematerialised" and the archaeology of the Gautama Buddha', *Cambridge Archaeological Journal*, 8: 121–6.
——1999. *Anuradhapura, I: The Site* (Oxford: Archaeopress).
——2001. *The Archaeology of Buddhism* in T. Insoll (ed.), *Archaeology and World Religion* (London: Routledge), pp. 61–95.
——2006. *Anuradhapura, II: The Artefacts* (Oxford: Archaeopress).
——, GUNAWARDHANA, P., ADIKARI, G., et al. 2006. 'The Anuradhapura (Sri Lanka) Project: The hinterland (phase II) preliminary report of the first season', *South Asian Studies*, 22: 55–64.
——, GUNAWARDHANA, P., MANUEL, M. J., et al. 2007. 'The state of theocracy: Defining an early medieval hinterland in Sri Lanka', *Antiquity*, 81: 699–719.
——and MANUEL, M. J. 2009. 'The early empires of South Asia: 323 BC–500 AD' in T. Harrison (ed.), *The World's Greatest Empires* (London: Thames and Hudson), pp. 42–63.
Culavamsa 1928. Trans. W. Geiger (London: Pali Text Society).
CUNNINGHAM, A. 1854. *The Bhilsa Topes or Buddhist monuments of Central India* (London: Smith and Elder).
——1879 (1962). *The Stupa of Barhut* (Varanasi: Indological Book House).
——1892 (1998). *Mahabodhi or the Great Buddhist Temple under the Bodhi Tree at Buddha-Gaya* (New Delhi: Munshiram Manoharlal).

Dhirasekera, J. 1982. *Buddhist Monastic Discipline: A study of its origin and development in relation to the Suttas and Vinaya Pitakas* (Dehiwala: Buddhist Cultural Centre).
Dias, M. 2001. *The Growth of Buddhist Monastic Institutions in Sri Lanka from Brahmi Inscriptions* (Colombo: Archaeological Survey of Sri Lanka).
Dutt, S. 1962. *Buddhist Monks and Monasteries of India* (London: George Allen and Unwin).
Epigraphia Zeylanica, I. 1912. Trans. De Zilva M. Wickremasinghe (Colombo: Archaeological Survey of Ceylon).
Epigraphia Zeylanica, II. 1927. Trans. De Zilva M. Wickremasinghe (Colombo: Archaeological Survey of Ceylon).
Erdosy, G. 1988. *Urbanisation in Early Historic India* (Oxford: BAR).
——1995. 'City states of north India and Pakistan at the time of the Buddha' in F. R. Allchin (ed.), *The Archaeology of Early Historic South Asia* (Cambridge: Cambridge University Press), pp. 99–122.
Fogelin, L. 2003. 'Ritual presentation in early Buddhist religious architecture', *Asian Perspectives*, 42(1): 129–54.
——2006. *Archaeology of Early Buddhism* (Lanham: AltaMira).
Gombrich, R. 1996. *How Buddhism Began: The conditioned genesis of the early teachings* (Atlantic Highlands, NJ: Athlone Press).
Gunaratna, H. H. 1988. *For a Sovereign State* (Ratmalana: Sarvodaya Publishers).
Hammarstrand, L. 2007. 'Emptiness and form: A microarchaeology of Buddhism' in P. Cornell and F. Fahlander (eds), *Encounters, Materialities, Confrontations: Archaeologies of social space and interaction* (Newcastle: Cambridge Scholars Press), pp. 123–49.
Heitzman, J. 1984. 'Early Buddhism: Trade and empire' in K. Kennedy and G. Possehl (eds), *Studies in the Archaeology and Paleopathology of South Asia* (New Dehli: Oxford University Press), pp. 21–37.
Hocart, A. M. 1924. *Anuradhapura* (Colombo: Archaeological Survey of Ceylon).
Horner, I. B. 1957. *The Book of Discipline (Vinya-Pittaka)* (Oxford: Pali Text Society).
Huntington, J. C. 1975. 'The Lomas Rishi: Another look', *Archives of Ancient Art*, 28: 34–56.
Jong, J. W. de 1975. 'The study of Buddhism: problems and perspectives', *Studies in Indo-Pacific Art and Culture*, 4: 7–30.
Karunananda, U. K. 2006. *Nuwaralawiya and the North Central Province under British Administration 1833–1900* (Kelaniya: University of Kelaniya).
Marshall, J. H. 1912. 'Excavations at Bhita', *Annual Reports of the Archaeological Survey of India*, 1911–12: 29–94.
——1951. *Taxila* (Cambridge: Cambridge University Press).
——, Foucher, A., and Majumdar, N. G. 1940. *The Monuments of Sanchi* (Delhi: Archaeological Survey of India).
Mitra, D. 1971. *Buddhist Monuments* (Calcutta: Sahitya Samsad).
Morrison, K. 1995. 'Trade, urbanism and agricultural expansion', *World Archaeology*, 27: 203–21.
Paranavitana, S. 1946. *The Stupa in Ceylon* (Colombo: Archaeological Survey of Ceylon).
——1950. *Anuradhapura* (Colombo: Archaeological Survey of Ceylon).
Piggott, S. 1943. 'The earliest Buddhist shrines', *Antiquity*, 17: 2–6.
Prematilleke, P. L. 1982. *Alahana Perivena: First excavation report* (Colombo: Central Cultural Fund).
Ratnayake, H. 1984. *Jetavanarama Vihara Project: First archaeological and excavation report* (Colombo: Central Cultural Fund).

Ray, H. P. 1994. *Winds of Change* (New Delhi: Oxford University Press).
Sarkar, H. 1962. 'Some aspects of the Buddhist monuments at Nagarjunakonda', *Ancient India*, 16: 65–84.
Schopen, G. 1997. *Bones, stone and Buddhist monks* (Honolulu: University of Hawaii).
Shaw, J. 2000. 'The sacred landscape' in M. Willis (ed.), *Buddhist Reliquaries from Ancient India* (London: British Museum Press), pp. 27–38.
Silva, R. 1998. *Religious Architecture in Early and Medieval Sri Lanka* (Druk: Krips Repro Meppel).
Smith, M. 2005. 'Networks, territories and the cartography of ancient states', *Annals of the Association of American Geographers*, 95(4): 832–49.
Thapar, R. 1984. *Lineage to State: Social formations in the mid-first millennium BC in the Ganga Valley* (New Delhi: Oxford University Press).
—— 2000. *History and Beyond: interpreting early India* (New Delhi: Oxford University Press).
—— 2002. *Early India: From the origins to AD 1300* (Berkeley: University of California Press).
Wickramagamage, C. 1984: *Abhayagiri Vihara Project: First archaeological and excavation report* (Colombo: Central Cultural Fund).

CHAPTER 59

CHRISTIANITY

SAM TURNER

1 INTRODUCTION

THE archaeology of Christianity extends across almost 2,000 years and for the last 500 is truly global in scope. Even during the Middle Ages, a traveller might encounter Christian communities from China to Ireland, and from the Arctic to East Africa. This short chapter cannot hope to describe satisfyingly archaeological research into these societies and their rich material cultures. Instead, it is limited to providing a brief overview of archaeological approaches to Christianity and to outlining some potentially fruitful avenues for future research and discovery. As such it is divided into two sections. The first section sketches the nature of Christianity's global archaeology in terms of the buildings, monuments and material culture produced by Christian communities. It briefly considers some previous archaeological approaches to this material and how both digging and writing can be influenced by archaeologists' own social contexts. With this in mind, the second section looks at some ways archaeologists might approach Christianity today. It emphasizes Christian archaeology's potential for illuminating the lives of past communities not only within but also beyond the church building or cemetery, and suggests engaging with themes from modern archaeological theory that might enliven our research agendas and enrich our interpretations.

2 THE ARCHAEOLOGY OF CHRISTIANITY

Ever since its first emergence, Christian archaeology has been an avowedly interdisciplinary subject. By definition, this is a historical archaeology: literacy has played a prominent role in the life of Christian communities since the outset. The reader of a book like W. H. C. Frend's *The Archaeology of Early Christianity: A history* (1996) is left in no doubt as to the lasting value of archaeologists' discoveries for fields such as epigraphy and New Testament studies. The huge range of historical, literary, theological, architectural, and artistic studies that necessarily interact with Christian archaeology can seem bewildering, without even considering the relevant sub-disciplines of archaeology itself. These interdisciplinary perspectives undoubtedly bring great richness, for example by helping archaeologists of Christianity to place the phenomena they record and interpret at the local scale fully in the flow of world history. Even so, they are also associated with certain risks. The archaeology of Christianity is a highly fragmented subject both regionally and chronologically, and despite the generally growing interest in periods such as Late Antiquity and the European Reformation (Bowersock et al. 1999; Gaimster and Gilchrist 2003; Jäggi and Staecker 2007) scholars of 'adjacent' eras are often unaware of each other's research.

A more serious problem for all historical archaeologists is that their research agendas have frequently been assembled in response to the demands of other disciplines (Trigger 2006: 504–5). There is no doubt that archaeological methods and interpretations can and must cast light on many questions of interest to different constituencies (Bergquist 2001: 182–3), but archaeologists should not forget to ask 'archaeological' questions of all the assembled data too (e.g. Harlow and Smith 2001; Carver 2008: 221). Sometimes the overwhelming quantity of material that must be recorded has militated against this, not least where it is assigned a particularly high value by one discipline or another: thus the Byzantine frescos of many Aegean churches are better analysed than the ancient buildings that contain them. There are long and honourable traditions of producing *corpora* of Christian buildings, monuments, and art that provide reference materials for archaeologists of Christianity (e.g. Krautheimer et al. 1937–77; Cramp 1984; *Premiers monuments* 1995–8), but the scope of modern archaeology is greater than just understanding the material culture of societies: it aims to analyse and interpret the societies that created the material too. Archaeologists of Christianity must ensure that their interpretative endeavours keep pace with their work in recording and publishing the evidence (for a good example see Edwards 2007).

2.1 Churches and Monasteries

Understandably, the first focus for archaeologists of Christianity has been churches, from the greatest cathedrals to the humblest chapels. A rich heritage of research has helped elucidate the chronology and history of these buildings, which have been central to Christian societies for worship, as meeting places, the expression of patronage and political power, and for burial and commemoration. In the urban centres the modern roots of Christian archaeology lie in the Renaissance, for example with the excavations below St Peter's in Rome during the replacement of Constantine's basilica (Frend 1996: 16–17). The great churches of Rome and other major cities like Istanbul and Jerusalem preserve a massive quantity of standing and buried remains (Krautheimer 1983; Mainstone 1988; Carpiceci and Krautheimer 1995, 1996; Biddle 1999). In common with most churches, the continuous use of cathedrals over many centuries has left vestiges from many periods (as revealed by excavations like those of Geneva or York: Bonnet 1993; Philips and Heywood 1996). Archaeological studies can relate expansion or contraction and changing arrangements of space and decoration to social, religious, and ideological change in different eras (Gilchrist 2005). Though scholars have often placed particular emphasis on elucidating the earliest phases of church buildings, remains from all periods can be analysed using archaeological methods.

Monastic centres of medieval Europe like Cluny in Burgundy (Baud 2003) or the famous Cistercian houses of northern England (Coppack 1998) have also proved important quarries for archaeologists, who have not only explored their churches and monastic accommodation, but also their industrial and agricultural infrastructures (e.g. Platt 1969; Carver 2004; McEarlean and Crothers 2007). Even in the European later Middle Ages, the different religious orders built and inhabited a diversity of monastic settlements, from urban friaries to remote hermitages (Gilchrist 1995). In earlier and later periods the term 'monastery' is applied to an even greater range of settlements: the sprawling complexes of the Egyptian desert (Pareich 2004) contrast strikingly with the tiny island monasteries of western Ireland (White Marshall and Walsh 2005; Ó Carragáin and O'Sullivan 2008), the mountain-top settlements of Ethiopian Orthodox monks (Finneran 2003: 142–4), or the fiercely fortified monasteries of the Tur Abdin (Bell 1913).

From Late Antiquity onwards most of the Christian faithful lived in the country rather than the town, and hundreds of thousands of rural churches were built across Europe and the Mediterranean as foci for their devotions. In Europe many of these sites are still occupied by a church which preserves physical remains of its medieval past (Figure 59.1; Morris 1989). Elsewhere, as in much of North Africa and parts of the eastern Mediterranean, thousands of churches were built but later abandoned, providing a fabulous resource for archaeologists of Christianity (Frend 1996; Caseau 1999). Since the rise of non-conformity and European colonialism, churches and chapels of many denominations have been built all over the world, their great variety and varied fates providing archaeological testimony to the aspirations, means, and methods of different missions and communities (e.g. Lane 1999; Stell 2002).

2.2 Church Art, Sculpture, and Portable Objects

Archaeological excavation and survey of church buildings is complemented by studies of church art, sculpture, and portable objects. The painted decoration inside and outside churches takes many forms, from frescos to textual quotations. Archaeologists have often interpreted changing schemes of decoration in terms of major movements in church history. So, for example, the layers of painted plaster in early Byzantine churches are often dated on the basis of the presence or absence of figural painting, commonly believed to relate to the rise and defeat of iconoclasm (Cormack 2000). In Late Antiquity, bold floor mosaics enlivened church interiors with geometric or didactic schemes; in Byzantium, glittering wall mosaics presented Christ and the saints, or commemorated rulers and donors. Coloured glass put decorative schemes in the windows, whose size, shape, or position might be modified over time to create different effects depending on the demands of liturgy and theology (e.g. Cramp 2005, 2006; James 1996, 2006). These concerns also shaped the internal space of churches, which might be divided at different times by curtains or screens in wood or stone such as the richly carved and painted medieval rood-screens of south-west England or the altar-screens of northern Spain in the early Middle Ages (Dodds 1990: 53–4; Godoy Fernández 1995; Gerstel 2007).

In many Christian traditions, carved or sculpted decoration brought figurative or abstract embellishment to churches, exemplified by the west fronts of medieval buildings like Wells Cathedral (Sampson 1998) or Notre Dame la Grande, Poitiers. Carved crosses could mark significant points within monastic and other ecclesiastical enclosures (Harbison 1992; Ó Carragáin 2005; Orton et al. 2007). Christian sculpture is also found far beyond

FIGURE 59.1 The early medieval church of St Vinçenç d'Obiols, Catalonia, Spain. The church is surrounded by rock-cut burials, now exposed.

the bounds of the church and its precincts. In Byzantium, apotropaic crosses were deployed to protect important monuments like the aqueducts that ensured Constantinople's water supply (Crow et al. 2008). Crosses in early medieval Britain or runestones in conversion-period Scandinavia carried Christian iconography and text out into the wider landscape (Edwards 1999; Turner 2006a; Jansson 1987).

The liturgy itself required particular items, and liturgical objects like chalices and patens are commonly found in medieval European burials (Gilchrist and Sloane 2005: 160–5). Reliquaries elaborated with precious stones and metals were made to house the remains of saints (Youngs 1989). Particular objects came to represent pilgrimage to particular places, like Egyptian St Menas flasks (Finneran 2003: 87–8) or scallop shells, linked in the Middle Ages with Santiago de Compostela. In the wider community, Christian iconography influenced the decoration of many ordinary artefacts, from everyday ceramics or metal vessels stamped with crosses to devices worked into jewellery or woven into cloth (e.g. Hayes 1972; Maguire 1990; Petts 2003).

2.3 Burials

The other major category of evidence used by archaeologists of Christianity comes from Christian burial grounds. Contrary to the image of Christian burials as plain, unfurnished, and regimented, scholars have shown that even in periods like the later Middle Ages considerable diversity was normal (Gilchrist and Sloane 2005). Exceptional examples, like the burial of St Cuthbert from Durham cathedral, preserve not only bones but also vestments and personal effects (e.g. his gold pectoral cross and fine imported silks; Battiscombe 1956; Bonner et al. 1989); more normally, Christian burials include occasional dress items such as pins, rings, or buttons. The nature of the graves themselves also varies widely, from elaborately carved Late Antique sarcophagi or late medieval tombs to simple burials in wooden coffins or shrouds. Christian communities also buried their dead in many different kinds of locations, from the Catacombs of ancient Rome and the dense clusters around early medieval saints' graves to humble country burial plots far from any church (Stephenson 1978; Sapin 1999; Young 1999; Blair 2005). Finally, the buried bones themselves give archaeologists rich information on topics ranging from diet and disease to family relationships and the geographical origins of the people in the cemetery (Mays et al. 2007; Gilchrist and Sloane 2005: 202–13).

2.4 The Materials of the Archaeology of Christianity

These, then, have been the basic materials of the archaeology of Christianity: buildings, settlements, art and material culture, the remains of people, and their burials. Archaeologists of Christianity have been largely concerned—ostensibly at least—with the description and quantification of the massive body of evidence bequeathed by two Christian millennia. There can be no question that this work is vital and must continue, not least because excavation and discovery provide the life-blood of archaeology, the raw excitement at the trowel's cutting edge. But this has never been the whole story: all archaeologists are enmeshed in the particular political and social contexts of their times, and those studying the remains of Christian cultures are no exception. Right from the start the archaeology of Christianity has also been about politics, sectarianism, and indeed personal belief. William Frend describes how Severanus, editor in 1634 of Bossio's *Roma Sotteranea* and a faithful servant of Catholic orthodoxy, was intent on showing that the early Christian catacombs were untainted by pagan, schismatic, or heretical use (Frend 1996: 15–16).

In the nineteenth century imperial ambitions were sometimes linked explicitly to archaeological expeditions: archaeologist and government agent were not uncommonly one and the same person. The extraordinary life of British explorer and diplomat Gertrude Bell shows how archaeological fieldwork could still be a useful preparation for high politics in the early twentieth century (Figure 59.2; Ousterhout and Jackson 2008). Two brief but interesting examples show how religion, nationalism, and archaeology could be intertwined. A graphic example is provided by the life of C.-M. A. Lavigerie, described by Frend as a 'sort of ecclesiastical Cyril Rhodes' (Frend 1996: 65–73). Lavigerie studied early church history in Paris, becoming a professor at the Sorbonne and later archbishop of Algiers and then cardinal. Through his excavations in Algeria and Tunisia he aimed not

FIGURE 59.2 The church at Çanli Kilise, Turkey, photographed by Gertrude Bell, July 1907 (www.gerty.ncl.ac.uk). Recent research has shown that many Anatolian churches, formerly thought to be monastic, lay at the heart of Christian settlements (Ousterhout 2006).

only to add prestige to French scholarship, but also to expose Christian foundations on which he could build a new Catholic, French North Africa. He constructed new churches on early Christian sites like the acropolis of Carthage, and contrary to government policy launched missions aimed at converting African Muslim populations.

For Lavigerie, early Christian archaeology was an important tool to be used in support of both missionary work and the extension of France's imperial power. Less extreme is the case of V. E. Nash-Williams, who in 1950 published his illustrated corpus of early medieval stone sculpture entitled *Early Christian Monuments of Wales*. As well as being a prominent Cardiff archaeologist, Nash-Williams was a dedicated Anglican and a member of the Governing Body of the Church in Wales. It has been suggested that early medieval inscribed stones were particularly appealing to him as potential evidence for links between early Welsh Christianity and the eastern Mediterranean, because this would obviate the need to find direct influence from Rome, the seat of Catholicism (Knight 2007: 132). If so, Nash-Williams' research agenda was also significantly influenced by his political and religious beliefs.

3 CHRISTIANITY AND THE ARCHAEOLOGY OF COMMUNITIES

The worlds of Lavigerie and Nash-Williams are now gone forever, but like them today's archaeologists remain embedded in their own times and places. However much they strive for objectivity, all scholars are influenced by the agendas of their peers, and by the political, social, and economic contexts of the world in which they pursue their research (H. Williams 2005). Archaeological writing on ethnicity and migration in post-Roman Europe provides a classic example, with scholars' estimates of the number of migrants swinging from tiny trickles to massive invasions, to some degree apparently in response to contemporary world events (Härke 2007). Equally linked to modern political realities are certain trends in research on Europe's Atlantic coast, where the search for universal 'Celtic' traits in early Christian Irish or British societies has been largely abandoned in favour of more topical questions about individualism and communalism or international links and local identity (see James 1999; Herring 2006;).

Most archaeologists today are interested in writing social archaeologies rather than national ones. In terms of the archaeology of religion this might mean investigating not only how and where people worshipped, but also how particular religious contexts influenced changing relationships between individuals and groups. Shifting theoretical priorities are an important feature of the scholarly landscape, and as well as renewing the impetus for enquiry they can add new layers to the wealth of existing interpretations and perhaps even help to ensure that scholarship keeps pace in a broader sense with the concerns of society. Archaeologists of Christianity can engage with changing priorities by asking new 'archaeological' questions to develop richer interpretations of both existing and newly discovered sites and objects (for a theoretically oriented discussion of relevant themes, see Gardner 2007: 35–51). In the rest of this chapter, I will highlight a handful of issues and research themes that relate particularly to putting people and communities at the heart of the archaeology of Christianity.

First, it is worth considering the relationship between religious belief and everyday life. In the intellectual culture of post-Enlightenment Europe, it is normal to regard the sacred and the secular as separate spheres (Insoll 2004: 15–16). The archaeology of Christianity has been much studied by Western European scholars, and this separation has naturally been perpetuated in their work. As already noted, this work has focused primarily on churches and church complexes, sacred art, and burials, and these elements have often been considered quite separately from other archaeological data on neighbouring settlements and their economy, agriculture, and so on. Nevertheless, archaeologists should not assume that past or even present Christian communities would understand a similar division. Paul Lane has noted that in modern African societies belief in a Christian God does not necessarily imply acceptance of Western European cultural values (Lane 2001: 149). Even in many parts of rural Europe the separation of religion and everyday life is a modern phenomenon: Hamish Forbes's study of the Methana peninsula in Greece shows how Orthodoxy permeated every level of social and domestic life until very recently (Forbes 2007).

Prehistorians' work on ethnographic and archaeological data has shown that understanding cosmologies can be crucial to appreciating how people relate to and shape their surroundings. At the level of the individual house (Boivin 2000), the ritual monument (Richards 1996), or indeed the whole landscape (Snead and Preucel 1999), religious beliefs and ideologies can affect every aspect of people's daily lives. Whilst the extent to which this applies may vary in different places and times (Insoll 2004: 17–18), archaeologists must be aware that Christian beliefs could fully permeate and shape communities. Thus in Greek villages the sign of the cross was raised over the threshed crops, and made over the dough prepared for bread (Halstead and Jones 1989; Forbes 2007: 348–9). Icons stood not only on the iconostasis of the church, but also in niches in the houses of villagers; as Juliet du Boulay was told, 'what is a house without icons? A shelter for animals' (du Boulay 1974: 54) (Figure 59.3). Byzantine houses and settlements in the eastern Mediterranean also contained icons and crosses worn on fabrics or carved above doors and thresholds (Maguire 1990; Mitchell 2008; see also the *Life* of St Mary the Younger; Laiou 1996: 206, 265). At a broader scale, Christian ideology deeply affected perceptions of the landscape itself. Monuments like churches or icon-stands served to focus the divine presence in particular areas (Nixon 2006; Forbes 2007), but on a wider scale the perception of different zones of land-use could also be linked to religious ideology. Demons lurked beyond the safe confines of the Greek village (du Boulay 1974: 51–5); in Northern Europe, the cultivated land around the settlement provided safe refuge for people and animals after nightfall (Roymans 1995). Medieval monastic founders made much out of their supposed isolation and spiritual exposure in such 'desert' lands, even though detailed studies suggest their situations were sometimes rather more comfortable than they admitted (Wickham 1990; Menuge 2000).

Phenomenological approaches developed in archaeology can help us to move beyond binary sacred/secular divisions by highlighting the power of perception in the creation of space and community (Tilley 2004; Brück 2005). From this perspective, objects, people, and places are not simply either sacred or profane: instead, sacredness is created in perception through practice. So for different groups, different sacred objects and places can be valued in different ways. An important emerging theme is to understand how objects, monuments, and places sanctified through religious practice were perceived and used by different religious communities. This could open many new avenues for research in the archaeology of Christianity, not least in contexts where Christians coexisted with other religious communities (e.g. with pagans in fourth-century Rome: Christie 2006: 80–112; with Muslims and Jews in medieval Spain: Dodds 1990; Remensnyder 2000). For example, Late Ottoman 'popular' religious practice presents a range of religious ambiguities between Christianity and Islam that are sometimes bewildering to modern secular observers (Hasluck 1929). The application of phenomenological or related approaches could help us understand how Christian communities perceived and modified their environments and in turn how their Muslim or Jewish neighbours related to them (see Baer 2004).

If religion shaped the perception of landscape, even the most 'mundane' of economic activities might be accompanied by specific rituals, like the blessing of prepared ground or newly planted crops from modern Greece to Anglo-Saxon England (du Boulay 1974; Blair 2005). The link between religion and landscape lends another aspect to landscape archaeology, and understanding the relationships between settlement patterns and sacred sites becomes important. It can be argued, for example, that the location of churches in settlements or the wider landscape could have a range of meanings, relating not only to religious ideas but also social and political realities. In fourth-century Rome, the great Christian sites of St Peter's, St John Lateran, and Santa Croce in Gerusalemme were not

FIGURE 59.3 Ruined post-medieval house in the village of Rachi, Naxos, Greece. Niches in the far wall probably once held icons.

established at the heart of the ancient city, but close to gates or beyond the walls. This might suggest that though Christianity was now tolerated, the Roman emperors were unwilling to disrupt the traditional pagan core of the city and risk alienating the senatorial classes (Christie 2006: 98–107). By contrast, in middle Saxon England important churches were commonly sited close to royal centres amidst the richest agricultural land, reflecting the close relationship that developed between royal power and churches in the seventh and eighth centuries (Turner 2006b). Whereas splendid medieval churches occupied central locations in medieval English villages, humble post-medieval non-conformist chapels were often sited on waste ground, in back plots, or buildings converted from other purposes (Morris 1989: 424–5). At other times churches were deliberately isolated in moor, marsh, desert, sea, or mountain, perhaps because their users sought spiritual distance (Baumer 2006: 111–15) or because their role was to 'conquer' wilderness country for the faith (Altenberg 2003). Understanding why churches were sited in certain places can help us understand the roles of Christianity in everyday life.

Spatial and chronological scales are important issues here. The archaeology of Christianity can be studied in relation to different types of communities at (and across) various scales. At the level of the household, certain rooms and activities may have had stronger religious associations. Beyond individual buildings or complexes, links between churches and local landscapes can be studied through various types of archaeological survey (e.g. Bowes et al.

2006; Ó Carragáin 2003). The spatial analysis of churches can reveal aspects of their role as foci for communal devotions (Stocker and Everson 2006), but can also show how different people might have accessed or used buildings differently based on status or gender, for example in nunneries and cathedral precincts (Gilchrist 1994; 2005; Richardson 2003); in early Byzantine churches (Clark 2007); or medieval and post-medieval English churches (Graves 2000; Giles 2007). Other aspects of community relations can also be accessed through church archaeology: for example, the location of burials or tombs within the church or graveyard might reflect wealth, social status or patronage (Duval 1988; Mytum 2004), and the act of burial in a certain place could itself help create new scales of community (Treffort 1996).

At the regional or international level, changing political and economic communities of the social elite could shape religious practice and church form. The archaeology of Christianity often allows scholars insights into the ways large-scale processes affected people in the localities (e.g. Handley 2003 on burial epitaphs in the post-Roman West; Hodges 1995 on the monastery of San Vincenzo al Volturno in Carolingian Europe; O'Keeffe 2007 on the European Romanesque). Pilgrimage and the visiting of shrines at particular times created travelling communities on geographical and temporal scales that ranged from purely local to very long-distance. Some churches or chapels might only be frequented by a few visitors on its annual saint's feast day, whereas others became the constant focus of mass devotion; some chapels were just for the people of the parish, whereas great pilgrimage churches attracted travellers from all over the Christian world. Fairs and markets linked to saint's days created opportunities for social and economic interactions beyond everyday networks (Pestell 2005), and along established pilgrim routes particular infrastructures served the needs of long-distance communities, from churches and hostels to the tracks themselves (Webb 1999; Foss 2002).

The archaeology of Christianity is certainly important in understanding how religious belief helped shape the lives of past communities. But faith and religious ideology can also be linked to the construction and expression of cultural and political identities and interpreted in terms of power, conflict, and resistance. The pursuit of Christian religious orthodoxy or dominance has undoubtedly led to extensive conflict in the past. When this has been linked to significant political power, persecution, warfare, destruction, and (re-)construction could result, sometimes creating a legacy of distinctive archaeological remains. The Crusader archaeology of Europe and the Mediterranean provides a good illustration, with castles, churches, monasteries, and rural settlements from France to the Holy Land part of its heritage (e.g. Pringle 1992; 1998). Christian foci might be established on the sites of earlier places of worship as a means of establishing and asserting cultural and political power, like the churches that replaced temples as the power of Christianity grew in Late Antique cities (Bayliss 2004) and early modern Central America (Hanson 1995). In late medieval Spain Muslim places of worship were deliberately converted into churches rather than demolished and rebuilt in order to emphasize the victory of the Christian powers; the same strategy may have been intentionally employed by the Spanish Conquistadors when they turned temples into churches in sixteenth-century Mexico (Remensnyder 2000). The use of Christianity in European empire-building was mentioned above in relation to Lavigerie and French North Africa, and deliberate attempts to impose religious practice or express power through Christian monuments were made in many parts of the world, as in India by the Portuguese and subsequently the British (e.g. Baumer 2006: 237–9; Scarre and Roberts 2005). Nevertheless, the practice and experience of European colonialism was far from monolithic, and the archaeology of different communities shows how they were affected by and reacted to the imposition or introduction of Christianity (e.g. Lane 1999).

Major political and religious transformations like the Reformation deeply affected local practice and the ability of ordinary people to continue their traditional modes of worship. The changes reflected in the replacement of images with texts in sixteenth- and seventeenth-century churches also affected developments in the domestic sphere and everyday life, and to understand them better we need to study both together (Finch 2007). Archaeologists can study how people resisted and negotiated such changes. In post-Reformation households that remained Catholic, services and devotions were often maintained at great personal risk (R. Williams 2005). Though bound by the ties of long years of devotion, these parishioners and families were not merely locked into their habitual practices, but instead were exercising communal and personal choices in the face of powerful external change. Likewise, archaeological evidence from settlements in Southern Africa shows that modern Tswana communities consciously preserved aspects of their pre-colonial culture and adapted Christian practices to suit them: here colonizer and colonized entered into a dialectical relationship, particularly in their material culture (Reid et al. 1997; see also Webster 1997).

Similar negotiations in conversion-period northern Europe have been the focus of much archaeological research, though little scholarly agreement (Carver 2002; Blair 2005: 53–4; Hoggett 2007). Burial practices in this region changed significantly over an extended period spanning the conversion, but it remains unclear exactly how they related to Christianity. In common with much post-processual scholarship (Insoll 2004: 76–7), many early medievalists now prefer to downplay religious affiliations and important studies have concentrated on social and political explanations of burials rather than religious ones (e.g. Effros 2002; Williams 2006). Nevertheless, belief and religious practice played important roles in constructing early medieval identities (Geake 1997; Carver 1998, 2005). Depending on people's ability to exercise their own choices, variations from place to place might result from resistance or subversion as much as some form of syncretism in practice or belief (Pluskowski and Patrick 2003; for a North American example, see Graham 1998).

4 CONCLUSIONS

One of the most useful lessons to emerge from the twentieth-century debates between different schools of archaeological theorists is surely that taking a range of different perspectives on any given problem provides the richest and most satisfying range of answers. This 'multivocality' not only allows different groups to contribute more fully to debates (Trigger 2006: 515–16), but also helps reflect the complexity of the past. Just as now, people in the past saw things differently depending on their background and context; just like people today, people in the past argued, disagreed, and dissented (Little 2007: 136–72). Struggles for power between groups and individuals found expression in religious ideologies and practices; Christianity was no exception, with an impressive range of denominations even for a world religion. We know well from documentary sources that sectarianism with its attendant divergences in practice and belief has been alive throughout the Christian era; archaeology can help us understand how the lives of communities shaped and were touched by such differences.

Summing up another review of this subject, Paul Lane wondered whether archaeologists could contribute anything more than a 'parallel history' of Christianity when faced with religious people who placed little value on the kind of Western scientific knowledge they were creating (Lane 2001: 176). Fundamentalist and 'fideistic' archaeologies which aim to prove the veracity of biblical events certainly exist (Insoll 2004: 60–1; Trigger 2006: 547). There is little opportunity for debate if their proponents refuse to accept the possibility of other perspectives, though we might observe that similar difficulties can also arise in the academic sphere when archaeological interpretations are hard to reconcile with other historical texts.

Nevertheless, religious ideas and doctrines change over time, and many believers welcome engagement with ideas based on archaeological research (Bergquist 2001). In any case, researching the nature and impact of religions is not the sole prerogative of the faithful, and it is not necessary to have faith to create genuine insights. Even where the aims of Christian congregations and archaeologists are not entirely congruent, useful results can emerge from research projects: the rich heritage of Christianity provides an outstanding body of data that can be approached in very many different ways. Encouraging multivocality (either amongst academics or in the community more widely) is not the same as taking an extreme relativist position where one view is just as valid as any other: the interpretations emerging from different people's stances can still be compared and evaluated in relation to social, cultural, and religious beliefs (Moreland 2001: 117–18). By engaging with archaeological themes like the few mentioned above (and see Insoll 2004: 146–50), archaeologists can contribute to debate about the nature of Christianity and its impact on past societies. It seems likely they will also create insights that are useful in understanding the possible roles of religion today and in the future.

Acknowledgements

I am grateful to Jim Crow, Chris Fowler, Mark Jackson, and David Petts for helpful discussions and references.

Further Reading

A classic introduction to early Christian archaeology is Frend (1996), who provides many further references to relevant standard works, conference proceedings, and North Africa. Krautheimer (1983) and Brown (2003) provide orientation and context for this period, and Webb (2001) gives a brief guide to sites in Rome. Byzantine churches and art are introduced by Krautheimer (1986) and Cormack (2000); for medieval Western Europe see in general Conant (1959), Stalley (1999), and O'Keeffe (2007); *Naissance* (1991) and the volumes (15 to date) of the *Topographie chrétienne des cités de la Gaule* (e.g. Gauthier 1986) (for France); Taylor and Taylor (1965) and Blair (2005) (for England). For Africa, see Finneran (2003); and for Asia, Baumer (2006). Cramp (2005 and 2006) (Wearmouth and Jarrow) and Hodges (1993 and 1995), and Bowes et al. (2006) (San Vincenzo al Volturno) provide case studies of excavations at particular monasteries. For stone sculpture, see e.g. Cramp (1984) and the subsequent volumes in the British Academy's *Corpus of Anglo-Saxon Stone Sculpture*, Redknap and Lewis (2007) and Edwards (2007); and for burials see Gilchrist and Sloane (2005). For Britain, Blair and Pyrah (1996) gives overviews of all periods of church archaeology. For churches as part of broader landscapes, see Morris (1989), and more recently Ó Carragáin (2003), Pestell (2004), Stocker and Everson (2006), Nixon (2006), and Turner (2006b). Some papers on periods of transformation in Europe from archaeological and/or interdisciplinary perspectives are available in Brogiolo and Ward-Perkins (1999) (Late Antiquity), Carver (2003) (conversion period), Gaimster and Gilchrist (2003), and Jäggi and Staecker (2007) (Reformation). A few examples of recent, theoretically informed discussions from various perspectives are Gilchrist (1994, 2005); Graves (2000); and Giles (2007).

References

ALTENBERG, K. 2003. *Experiencing Landscapes: A study of space and identity in three marginal areas of medieval Britain and Scandinavia* (Stockholm: Almqvist and Wiksell).
BAER, M. 2004. 'The great fire of 1660 and the Islamization of Christian and Jewish space in Istanbul', *International Journal of Middle East Studies*, 36: 159–81.
BATTISCOMBE, C. F. (ed.) *The Relics of St Cuthbert* (Oxford: Dean and Chapter of a Durham Cathedral).
BAUD, A. 2003. *Cluny: un grand chantier medieval au cœur de l'Europe* (Paris: Picard).
BAUMER, C. 2006. *The Church of the East: An illustrated history of Assyrian Christianity* (London: I.B.Tauris).
BAYLISS, R. 2004. *Provincial Cilicia and the Archaeology of Temple Conversion*, BAR International Series 1281 (Oxford: Archaeopress).
BELL, G. 1913. *The Churches and Monasteries of the Tûr 'Abdîn and Neighbouring Districts* (Heidelberg: C. Winter's Universitätsbuchhandlung).
BERGQUIST, A. 2001. 'Ethics and the archaeology of world religions' in T. Insoll (ed.), *Archaeology and World Religion* (London: Routledge), pp. 182–92.
BIDDLE, M. 1999. *The Tomb of Christ* (Stroud: Sutton).
BLAIR, J. 2005. *The Church in Anglo-Saxon Society* (Oxford: Oxford University Press).
——and PYRAH, C. (eds) 1996. *Church Archaeology: Research directions for the future*, CBA Research Report 104 (York: Council for British Archaeology).
BOIVIN, N. 2000. 'Life rhythms and floor sequences: Excavating time in rural Rajasthan and Neolithic Çatalhöyük', *World Archaeology*, 31(3): 367–88.
BONNER, G., ROLLASON, W., and STANCLIFFE, C. (eds) 1989. *St Cuthbert, his Cult and his Community to AD 1200* (Woodbridge: Boydell).
BONNET, C. 1993. *Les fouilles de l'ancien groupe épiscopal de Genève (1976–1993)* (Geneva: Cahiers d'archéologie genevoise I).
DU BOULAY, J. 1974. *Portrait of a Greek Mountain Village* (Oxford: Oxford University Press).
BOWERSOCK, G., BROWN, P., and GRABAR, O. (eds) 1999. *Late Antiquity: A guide to the Postclassical world* (Cambridge, MA: Belknap Press of Harvard University Press).
BOWES, K., FRANCIS, K., and HODGES, R. 2006. *Between Text and Territory : Survey and excavations in the Terra of San Vincenzo al Volturno* (London: British School at Rome).
BROGIOLO, G. and WARD-PERKINS, B. (eds) 1999. *The Idea and Ideal of the Town between Late Antiquity and the Early Middle Ages*, Transformation of the Roman World 4 (Leiden: Brill).

BROWN, P. 2003. *The Rise of Western Christendom*, 2nd edn (Oxford: Blackwell).
BRÜCK, J. 2005. 'Experiencing the past? The development of a phenomenological archaeology in British prehistory', *Archaeological Dialogues*, 12(1): 45–72.
CARPICECI, A. and KRAUTHEIMER, R. 1995. 'Nuovi dati sull'antica basilica di San Pietro in Vaticano. (Parte I)', *Bolletino d'Arte*, 93–4 (anno lxxx, serie vi): 1–70.
——1996. 'Nuovi dati sull'antica basilica di San Pietro in Vaticano. (Parte II)', *Bolletino d'Arte*, 95 (anno lxxxi, serie vi): 1–84.
CARVER, M. 1998. 'Conversion and politics on the eastern seaboard of Britain: Some archaeological indicators' in B. Crawford (ed.), *Conversion and Christianity in the North Sea World* (St Andrews: University of St Andrews), pp. 11–40.
——2002. 'Reflections on the meanings of monumental barrows in Anglo-Saxon England' in S. Lucy and A. Reynolds (eds), *Burial in Early Medieval England and Wales* (Leeds: Society for Medieval Archaeology), pp. 132–43.
——(ed.) 2003. *The Cross Goes North: Processes of conversion in Northern Europe, AD 300–1300* (Woodbridge: Boydell).
——2004. 'An Iona of the east: The early-medieval monastery at Portmahomack, Tarbat Ness', *Medieval Archaeology*, 48: 1–30.
——2005. *Sutton Hoo: A seventh-century princely burial ground and its context* (London: British Museum Press).
——2008. 'Archaeology, monasticism and *Romanitas* in northern Britain', *Antiquity*, 82: 220–2.
CASEAU, B. 1999. 'Sacred landscapes' in G. Bowersock, P. Brown, and O. Grabar (eds), *Late Antiquity: A guide to the Postclassical world* (Cambridge, MA: Belknap Press of Harvard University Press), pp. 21–59.
CHRISTIE, N. 2006. *From Constantine to Charlemagne: An archaeology of Italy AD 300–800* (Aldershot: Ashgate).
CLARK, D. 2007. 'Viewing the liturgy: A space syntax study of changing visibility and accessibility in the development of the Byzantine church in Jordan', *World Archaeology*, 39(1): 84–104.
CONANT, K. 1959. *Carolingian and Romanesque Architecture, 800–1200* (Harmondsworth: Penguin).
COPPACK, G. 1998. *The White Monks: The Cistercians in Britain, 1128–1540* (Stroud: Tempus).
CORMACK, R. 2000. *Byzantine Art* (Oxford: Oxford University Press).
CRAMP, R. 1984. *Corpus of Anglo-Saxon Stone Sculpture*, I: *County Durham and Northumberland*, 2 parts (Oxford: British Academy/Oxford University Press).
——2005. *Wearmouth and Jarrow Monastic Sites*, I (London: English Heritage).
——2006. *Wearmouth and Jarrow Monastic Sites*, II (London: English Heritage).
CROW, J., BARDILL, J., and BAYLISS, R. 2008. *The Water Supply of Byzantine Constantinople*, Journal of Roman Studies Monograph 21 (London: Society for the Promotion of Roman Studies).
DODDS, J. 1990. *Architecture and Ideology in Early Medieval Spain* (University Park, PA: Pennsylvania State University Press).
DUVAL, Y. 1988. *Auprès des saints corps et âme. L'inhumation* ad sanctos *dans la chrétienté d'Orient et d'Occident du IIIe au VIIe siècle* (Paris: Études Augustiniennes).
EDWARDS, N. 1999. 'Viking-influenced sculpture in north Wales: Its ornament and context', *Church Archaeology*, 3: 5–16.
——2007. *A Corpus of Early Medieval Inscribed Stones and Stone Sculpture in Wales*, II: *Southwest Wales* (Cardiff: University of Wales Press).

EFFROS, B. 2002. *Caring for Body and Soul: Burial and the afterlife in the Merovingian world* (University Park, PA: Pennsylvania State University Press).
FINCH, J. 2007. 'Sacred and secular spheres: Commemoration and the practice of privacy in Reformation England' in C. Jäggi and J. Staecker (eds), *Archäologie der Reformation. Studien zu den Auswirkungen des Konfessionswechsels aud die materielle Kultur* (Berlin: Walter de Gruyter), pp. 195–210.
FINNERAN, N. 2003. *The Archaeology of Christianity in Africa* (Stroud: Tempus).
FORBES, H. 2007. *Meaning and Identity in a Greek Landscape: An archaeological ethnography* (Cambridge: Cambridge University Press).
FOSS, C. 2002. 'Pilgrimage in medieval Asia Minor', *Dumbarton Oaks Papers*, 56: 129–51.
FREND, W. 1996. *The Archaeology of Early Christianity: A history* (London: Geoffrey Chapman).
GAIMSTER, D. and GILCHRIST, R. (eds) 2003. *The Archaeology of Reformation 1480–1580* (Leeds: Society for Post-Medieval Archaeology).
GARDNER, A. 2007. *An Archaeology of Identity: Soldiers and society in late Roman Britain* (Walnut Creek, CA: Left Coast Press).
GAUTHIER, N. 1986. *Province ecclésiastique de Trèves (Belgica Prima)*, Topographie chrétienne des cités de la Gaule des origines au milieu du VIIIe siècle, I (Paris: de Boccard).
GEAKE, H. 1997. *The Use of Grave-Goods in Conversion-Period England, c.600–c.850*, British Archaeological Reports British Series 261 (Oxford: John and Erica Hedges).
GERSTEL, S. (ed.) 2007. *Thresholds of the Sacred: Architectural, art historical, liturgical and theological perspectives on religious screens, East and West* (Washington DC: Dumbarton Oaks).
GILCHRIST, R. 1994. *Gender and Material Culture: The archaeology of religious women* (London: Routledge).
——1995. *Contemplation and Action: The other monasticism* (London: Leicester University Press).
——2005. *Norwich Cathedral Close: The evolution of the English cathedral landscape* (Woodbridge: Boydell and Brewer).
——and SLOANE, B. 2005. *Requiem: The medieval monastic cemetery in Britain* (London: Museum of London Archaeology Service).
GILES, K. 2007. 'Seeing and believing: Visuality and space in pre-modern England', *World Archaeology*, 39(1): 105–21.
GODOY FERNÁNDEZ, C. 1995. *Arqueología y liturgia. Iglesias hispánicas (s. IV–VIII)* (Barcelona: Universitat de Barcelona).
GRAHAM, E. 1998. 'Mission archaeology', *Annual Review of Anthropology*, 27: 25–62.
GRAVES, P. 2000. *The Form and Fabric of Belief: An archaeology of lay experience of religion in medieval Norfolk and Devon*, British Archaeological Report British Series 311 (Oxford: Archaeopress).
——2007. 'Sensing and believing: Exploring worlds of difference in pre-modern England: A contribution to the debate opened by Kate Giles', *World Archaeology*, 39(4): 515–31.
HALSTEAD, P. and JONES, G. 1989. 'Agrarian ecology in the Greek islands: Time stress, scale and risk', *Journal of Hellenic Studies*, 109: 41–55.
HANDLEY, M. 2003. *Death, Society and Culture: Inscriptions and epitaphs in Gaul and Spain, AD 300–750*, BAR International Series 1135 (Oxford: Archaeopress).
HANSON, C. 1995. 'The Hispanic horizon in Yucatan: A model of Franciscan missionization', *Ancient Mesoamerica*, 6: 15–28.

HARBISON, P. 1992. *The High Crosses of Ireland: An iconographical and photographic survey*, 3 vols. (Bonn: Romisch-Germanisches Zentralmuseum, Forschungsinstitut für Vor- und Frühgeschichte, Monographie Band 17).
HÄRKE, H. 2007. 'Ethnicity, race and migration in mortuary archaeology: An attempt at a short answer', *Anglo-Saxon Studies in Archaeology and History*, 14: 12–18.
HARLOW, M. and SMITH, W. 2001. 'Between feasting and fasting: The literary and archaeobotanical evidence for monastic diet in Late Antique Egypt', *Antiquity*, 75: 758–68.
HASLUCK, F. 1929. *Christianity and Islam under the Sultans* (Oxford: Oxford University Press).
HAYES, J. 1972. *Late Roman Pottery* (London: British School at Rome).
HERRING, P. 2006. 'Cornish strip fields' in S. Turner (ed.), *Medieval Devon and Cornwall: Shaping an ancient countryside* (Macclesfield: Windgather Press), pp. 44–77.
HODGES, R. (ed.) 1993. *San Vincenzo al Volturno*, I (London: British School at Rome).
——1995. 'San Vincenzo al Volturno and the plan of St Gall' in R. Hodges (ed.), *San Vincenzo al Volturno, II: The 1980–86 Excavations, Part 2* (London: British School at Rome), pp. 153–75.
HOGGETT, R. 2007. 'Charting conversion: Burial as a barometer of belief?', *Anglo-Saxon Studies in Archaeology and History*, 14: 28–37.
INSOLL, T. 2004. *Archaeology, Ritual, Religion* (London: Routledge).
JÄGGI, C. and STAECKER, J. (eds.) 2007. *Archäologie der Reformation. Studien zu den Auswirkungen des Konfessionswechsels aud die materielle Kultur* (Berlin: Walter de Gruyter).
JAMES, E. 1996. *Light and Colour in Byzantine Art* (Oxford: Oxford University Press).
——2006. 'Byzantine glass mosaic tesserae: Some material considerations', *Byzantine and Modern Greek Studies*, 30(1): 29–48.
JAMES, S. 1999. *The Atlantic Celts: Ancient people or modern invention?* (London: British Museum Press).
JANSSON, S. 1987. *Runes in Sweden* (Stockholm: Royal Academy of Letters, History and Antiquities, Central Board of Antiquities).
KNIGHT, J. 2007. 'The historical and archaeological contexts' in M. Redknap and J. Lewis (eds), *A Corpus of Early Medieval Inscribed Stones and Stone Sculpture in Wales, I: South-east Wales and the English border* (Cardiff: University of Wales Press), pp. 131–8.
KRAUTHEIMER, R. 1983. *Three Christian Capitals: Topography and politics* (Berkeley: University of California Press).
——1986. *Early Christian and Byzantine Architecture*, 4th edn (New Haven, CT: Yale University Press).
——, CORBETT, S., FRANKL, W., et al. 1937–77. *Corpus Basilicarum Christianorum Romae I–IV* (Vatican City: Pontificio Istituto di Archeologia Cristiana).
LAIOU, A. 1996. 'The life of St Mary the Younger' in A.-M. Talbot (ed.), *Holy Women of Byzantium: Ten saints' lives in English translation* (Washington, DC: Dumbarton Oaks), pp. 239–89.
LANE, P. 1999. 'Archaeology, Nonconformist missions and the "colonisation of consciousness" in southern Africa c.1820–1900' in T. Insoll (ed.), *Case Studies in Archaeology and World Religion*, BAR S755 (Oxford: Archaeopress), pp. 153–65.
——2001. 'The archaeology of Christianity in global perspective' in T. Insoll (ed.), *Archaeology and World Religion* (London: Routledge), pp. 148–81.
LITTLE, B. 2007. *Historical Archaeology: Why the past matters* (Walnut Creek, CA: Left Coast Press).

McErlean, T. and Crothers, N. 2007. *Harnessing the Tides: The early medieval tide mills at Nendrum Monastery, Strangford Lough* (Belfast: The Stationery Office).

Mainstone, R. 1988. *Hagia Sofia: Architecture, structure, liturgy of Justinian's Great Church* (London: Thames and Hudson).

Maguire, H. 1990. 'Garments pleasing to God: The significance of domestic textile designs in the early Byzantine period', *Dumbarton Oaks Papers*, 44: 215–24.

Mays, S., Harding, C., and Heighway, C. 2007. *Wharram XI: The churchyard*, A Study of Settlement on the Yorkshire Wolds XI (York: University of York Department of Archaeology).

Menuge, J. 2000. 'The foundation myth: Yorkshire monasteries and the landscape agenda', *Landscapes*, 1(1): 22–37.

Mitchell, J. 2008. 'Keeping the demons out of the house: The archaeology of apotropaic strategy and practice in late antique Butrint' in L. Lavan, E. Swift, and T. Putzeys (eds), *Objects in Context, Objects in Use, Material Spatiality in Late Antiquity*, Late Antique Archaeology 5 (Leiden: Brill), pp. 273–313.

Moreland, J. 2001. *Archaeology and Text* (London: Duckworth).

Morris, R. 1989. *Churches in the Landscape* (London: Dent).

Mytum, H. 2004. *Mortuary Monuments and Burial Grounds of the Historic Period* (New York: Kluwer Academic/Plenum).

Naissance 1991. *Naissance des arts chretiens: atlas des monuments paleochretiens de la France* (Paris: Ministère de la Culture et de la Communication).

Nixon, L. 2006. *Making a Landscape Sacred: Outlying churches and icon stands in Sphakia, Southwestern Crete* (Oxford: Oxbow).

Ó Carragáin, E. 2005. *Ritual and the Rood: Liturgical images and the Old English poems of the* Dream of the Rood *Tradition* (London: British Library).

Ó Carragáin, T. 2003. 'A landscape converted: Archaeology and early church organisation on Iveragh and Dingle' in M. Carver (ed.), *The Cross Goes North: Processes of conversion in Northern Europe, AD 300–1300* (Woodbridge: Boydell), pp. 127–52.

—— and O'Sullivan, J. 2008. *Monks and Pilgrims in an Atlantic Landscape*, I: *Archaeological Survey and Excavations* (Cork: The Collins Press).

O'Keeffe, T. 2007. *Archaeology and the Pan-European Romanesque* (London: Duckworth).

Orton, F. and Wood, I., with Lees, C. 2007. *Fragments of History: Rethinking the Ruthwell and Bewcastle monuments* (Manchester: Manchester University Press).

Ousterhout, R. 2006. *A Byzantine Settlement in Cappadocia* (Washington, DC: Dumbarton Oaks).

—— and Jackson, M. 2008. 'Editors' preface' in W. Ramsay and G. Bell, *The Thousand and One Churches*, With newly digitized original images from Newcastle University and University of Pennsylvania Museum Archives (first published 1909) (Philadelphia, PA: University of Pennsylvania Museum of Archaeology and Anthropology), ix–xxxvii.

Pareich, J. 2004. 'Monastic landscapes' in W. Bowden, L. Lavan, and C. Machado (eds), *Recent Research on the Late Antique Countryside* (Leiden: Brill), pp. 413–47.

Pestell, T. 2004. *Landscapes of Monastic Foundation: The establishment of religious houses in East Anglia c.650–1200* (Woodbridge: Boydell).

—— 2005. 'Using material culture to define holy space: The Bromholm Project' in A. Spicer and S. Hamilton (eds), *Defining the Holy: Sacred space in medieval and early modern Europe* (Aldershot: Ashgate), pp. 161–86.

PETTS, D. 2003. 'Votive deposits and Christian practice in late Roman Britain' in M. Carver (ed.), *The Cross Goes North: Processes of conversion in Northern Europe, AD 300–1300* (Woodbridge: Boydell), pp. 109–18.

PHILIPS, A. and HEYWOOD, B. 1996. *From Roman Basilica to Norman Minster: Excavations at York Minster*, I (London: Royal Commission on Historical Monuments).

PLATT, C. 1969. *The Monastic Grange in Medieval England: A reassessment* (New York: Fordham University Press).

PLUSKOWSKI, A. and PATRICK, P. 2003. '"How do you pray to God?" Fragmentation and variety in early medieval Christianity' in M. Carver (ed.), *The Cross Goes North: Processes of conversion in Northern Europe, AD 300–1300* (Woodbridge: Boydell), pp. 29–57.

Premiers monuments. 1995–8. *Les premiers monuments chrétiens de la France.* 3 vols. (Paris: Picard Éditeur/Ministère de la Culture).

PRINGLE, D. 1992. *The Churches of the Crusader Kingdom of Jerusalem: A corpus*, I (Cambridge: Cambridge University Press).

——1998. *The Churches of the Crusader Kingdom of Jerusalem: A corpus*, II (Cambridge: Cambridge University Press).

REDKNAP, M. and LEWIS, J. 2007. *A Corpus of Early Medieval Inscribed Stones and Stone Sculpture in Wales*, I: *South-east Wales and the English border* (Cardiff: University of Wales Press).

REID, A., LANE, A., SEGOBYE, L., et al. 1997. 'Tswana architecture and responses to colonialism', *World Archaeology*, 28(3): 370–92.

REMENSNYDER, A. 2000. 'The colonization of sacred architecture: The Virgin Mary, mosques, and temples in medieval Spain and early sixteenth-century Mexico' in S. Farmer and B. Rosenwein (eds), *Monks and Nuns, Saints and Outcasts: Religion in medieval society* (Ithaca: Cornell University Press), pp. 189–220.

RICHARDS, C. 1996. 'Monuments as landscape: Creating the centre of the world in late Neolithic Orkney', *World Archaeology*, 28(2): 190–208.

RICHARDSON, A. 2003. 'Corridors of power: A case study in access analysis from medieval England', *Antiquity*, 77: 373–84.

ROYMANS, N. 1995. 'The cultural biography of urnfields and the long-term history of a mythical landscape', *Archaeological Dialogues*, 2(1): 2–24.

SAMPSON, J. 1998. *Wells Cathedral West Front: Construction, sculpture and conservation* (Stroud: Sutton).

SAPIN, C. 1999. 'Architecture and funerary space in the early Middle Ages' in C. Karkov, K. Wickham-Crowley, and B. Young (eds), *Spaces of the Living and the Dead: An archaeological dialogue*, American Early Medieval Studies 3 (Oxford: Oxbow), pp. 39–60.

SCARRE, C. and ROBERTS, J. 2005. 'The English cemetery at Surat: Pre-colonial cultural encounters in western India', *Antiquaries Journal*, 85: 250–91.

SNEAD, J. and PREUCEL, R. 1999. 'The ideology of settlement: Ancestral Keres landscapes in the northern Rio Grande' in W. Ashmore and B. Knapp (eds), *Archaeologies of Landscape* (Oxford: Blackwell), 169–97.

STALLEY, R. 1999. *Early Medieval Architecture* (Oxford: Oxford University Press).

STELL, C. 2002. *An Inventory of Nonconformist Chapels and Meeting Houses in Eastern England* (Swindon: English Heritage).

STEPHENSON, J. 1978. *The Catacombs: Rediscovered monuments of ancient Christianity* (London: Thames and Hudson).

STOCKER, D. and EVERSON, P. 2006. *Summoning St Michael: Early Romanesque towers in Lincolnshire* (Oxford: Oxbow Books).

TAYLOR, H. and TAYLOR, J. 1965. *Anglo-Saxon Architecture*, 2 vols. (Cambridge: Cambridge University Press).

TILLEY, C. 2004. *The Materiality of Stone: Explorations in landscape phenomenology* (Oxford: Berg).

TREFFORT, C. 1996. *L'église carolingienne et la mort* (Lyon: Presses Universitaires de Lyon).

TRIGGER, B. 2006. *A History of Archaeological Thought*, 2nd edn (Cambridge: Cambridge University Press).

TURNER, S. 2006a. 'The Christian landscape: Churches, chapels and crosses' in S. Turner (ed.), *Medieval Devon and Cornwall: Shaping an ancient countryside* (Macclesfield: Windgather Press), pp. 24–43.

—— 2006b. *Making a Christian Landscape: The countryside in early medieval Cornwall, Devon and Wessex* (Exeter: University of Exeter Press).

WEBB, D. 1999. *Pilgrims and Pilgrimage in the Medieval West* (London: I.B.Tauris).

WEBB, M. 2001. *The Churches and Catacombs of Early Christian Rome: A comprehensive guide* (Brighton: Sussex Academic Press).

WEBSTER, J. 1997. 'Necessary comparisons: A post-colonial approach to religious syncretism in the Roman provinces', *World Archaeology*, 28(3): 324–38.

WHITE MARSHALL, J. and WALSH, C. 2005. *Illaunloughan Island: An early medieval monastery in County Kerry* (Bray, Co. Wicklow: Wordwell Books).

WICKHAM, C. 1990. 'European forests in the early middle ages: Landscape and land clearance', *Settimane di Studio del Centro Italiano di Studi sull'Alto Medioevo*, 36: 479–545.

WILLIAMS, H. 2005. 'Review article: Rethinking early medieval mortuary archaeology', *Early Medieval Europe*, 13(2): 195–217.

—— 2006. *Death and Memory in Early Medieval Britain* (Cambridge: Cambridge University Press).

WILLIAMS, R. 2005. 'Forbidden sacred spaces in Reformation England' in A. Spicer and S. Hamilton (eds), *Defining the Holy: Sacred space in medieval and early modern Europe* (Aldershot: Ashgate), pp. 95–114.

YOUNG, B. 1999. 'The myth of the pagan cemetery' in C. Karkov, K. Wickham-Crowley, and B. Young (eds), *Spaces of the Living and the Dead: An archaeological dialogue*, American Early Medieval Studies 3 (Oxford: Oxbow), pp. 61–85.

YOUNGS, S. 1989. *The Work of Angels: Masterpieces of Celtic metalwork, 6th–9th Centuries* AD (London: British Museum).

CHAPTER 60

ISLAM

ANDREW PETERSEN

1 INTRODUCTION

ONE of the problems in investigating the archaeology of Islam as a religion is that the whole of society is permeated with the religion and in many ways it is difficult to disassociate any aspect of life from the religion. Although this may be the case with other world religions, this is particularly the case with Islam where there has really been no resolution of the question of leadership of the Muslim community since the death of the Prophet Muhammad. Within this short review of Islamic archaeology the term religion has thus been interpreted quite broadly to include most aspects of the Muslim past although issues particularly pertaining to religion and worship have been emphasized. In the first part of this chapter the historiography of Islamic archaeology is examined initially from a European point of view and then from a Muslim point of view. In the second half a number of significant themes within the subject are reviewed whilst the conclusions point the way to further research themes.

2 HISTORIOGRAPHY

In a sense there are two separate historiographies of Islamic archaeology, one which is primarily European and secular and the other which is indigenous and developed within a context of Muslim traditions. The majority of published works and major excavations belong to the European secular tradition, even if occasionally the practitioners were Muslim, and as such this has become the dominant narrative. However the reaction against Orientalism inspired by Edward Said (Said 1978) and the increasing importance of religious approaches to the humanities have meant that archaeology carried out by Muslims or within the Muslim tradition has acquired renewed significance.

2.1 European Secular Tradition

The study of Islamic archaeology can be seen as a branch of historical archaeology in the sense that both the religion and culture were formed within the context of written historical texts. Therefore any considerations of historiography must take into account the development of historical studies of Islam as well as the development of archaeology as a complementary or alternative way of looking at the Muslim past.

Although many scholars in medieval Europe knew Arabic for the purposes of studying ancient Greek texts this interest was primarily of a scientific nature and there is little evidence of interest in Islamic culture and history for its own sake. However, from the sixteenth century a number of factors led to an increasing academic and popular interest in Islam both as a religion and as a culture (Holt 1957: 445–7). One of these factors was the religious schism between the Roman Catholic and Protestant churches which from a Protestant point of view saw Islam as a potential ally. Another factor was the increasing international trade which meant that European merchants were increasingly coming into contact with, and even living in, Muslim countries. A third factor is the increasing interest in collecting all forms of knowledge as a way of developing a scientific and cultural understanding of the world. In England academic interest in Muslim history began with the establishment of two professorships in Arabic, one at Cambridge (1632) and one at Oxford (1636). Of particular importance was Edward Pocoke, the first Laudian Professor of Arabic at Oxford, who translated and commented on a number of Arabic works on Muslim history. The significance of Pococke and other early historians of Islam is that they provided the basic outlines which still form the parameters for most contemporary discussions of Muslim history and its archaeology.

The origins of the study of Muslim material culture or archaeology are much later and initially at least were quite far removed from the study of history. Two main strands have been identified in the early study of Islamic archaeology; these are an intellectual interest in the history of fine arts and, secondly, the growth of Orientalism (Vernoit 1997). The fine-arts approach tried to place Islamic art within a classification system that had little to do with the culture that produced it. Orientalism had first been used as a term in France in the eighteenth century and came to mean both a system of knowledge and a form of representation which described the Orient (principally the Muslim Middle East) as essentially different from and inferior to Europe. The Orientalist interest in Islamic antiquities was concerned with exoticism and favoured strangeness and mystery over social context. Neither of these approaches was particularly suited to investigating Islamic culture within an historical framework and both placed more emphasis on aesthetic appearance and exotic value than on the physical and cultural context of an object or monument. In this sense Islamic archaeology lagged behind that of many other areas and cultures in part because as a medieval culture it was regarded as too recent and also because those carrying out the investigations were generally non-Muslim and often had a disdainful view of both the religion and the culture (see e.g. Said 1978: 229).

As a result of its Orientalist origins the most intensively investigated areas of Islamic archaeology are the Near East and North Africa. In these regions the excavation of ancient and classical sites often resulted in large quantities of later (Islamic) period remains being uncovered. Although the Islamic remains were not the primary interest of the excavators, the bright colours of the glazed pottery combined with the intricacy and complexity of the designs attracted the interest of art collectors and art historians. For example, excavations at the classical sites of Ephesus, Baalbak, and Miletus recovered large quantities of Islamic material which could not be ignored. In addition to scientific excavations there was an increasing number of uncontrolled excavations aimed at recovering material for the art market. Prominent examples include the nineteenth-century robber trenches dug within the remains of ancient Raqqa in Syria by 'peasants in search of the now celebrated Rakkah ware' (Bell 1911: 59–60, cited in Vernoit 1997: 5).

Another well-known example is the ancient city of Rayy in modern Iran which was exploited on an almost industrial scale with pottery, glass, and metalwork recovered as well as silks which were plundered from graves (Vernoit 1997: 5 n. 37). Such actions encouraged responsible museums and organizations to carry out scientific fieldwork and extend legislative protection to these sites. Thus by the end of the nineteenth century, expeditions specifically concerned with Islamic antiquities were organized. Possibly the earliest of these was the excavation of Samarqand carried out in 1885 by Russian archaeologists following on from the conquest of what is now Uzbekistan in 1866 (Rogers 1974: 51). One of the most significant developments for Islamic archaeology was the establishment of the Committee for the Conservation of Arab Art in Cairo in 1881. This was followed in 1884 by the founding of the Museum of Arab Art in Cairo which remains the world's oldest Museum of Islamic Art. In 1912 the Museum carried out its first excavations at Fustat under the directorship of the Egyptian archaeologist 'Ali Baghat, bringing to an end the illegal excavations which had destroyed a large part of the site (Vernoit 1997; Kubiak 1987).

The introduction of railways into the Middle East in the early years of the twentieth century opened up the region for foreign archaeologists who carried out excavations at a number of major Islamic sites, the most important of which was Herzfeld's expedition to Samarra in Iraq between 1911 and 1914 (Herzfeld and Sarre 1923–48). During the twentieth century a series of excavations at major sites established a coherent body of knowledge which enabled Islamic archaeology to move away from its origins in art history and 'Oriental Studies'. Prominent figures in the development of the field included Max Van Berchem who initiated a monumental series on Arabic inscriptions, Gertrude Bell who published a monograph on the Abbasid palace of Ukhaydir (Bell 1914) as well as founding the Iraq Museum, and K. A. C. Creswell who established a basis for the study of Islamic architecture with his two-volume study, *Early Muslim Architecture* (Cresswell 1932). By the late twentieth century, as Islamic archaeology became more aligned with mainstream archaeology, the research focus shifted away from monumental sites and the acquisition of museum pieces towards less well known, often anonymous, sites (e.g. Khirbet Faris) designed to answer specific regional questions. Another development of the late twentieth century was an expansion in the geographical scope of Islamic archaeology beyond the Near East in particular into areas such as Central Asia and sub-Saharan Africa.

2.2 Indigenous/Muslim Tradition

The Muslim tradition of archaeology is much more difficult to discuss, both because in one sense, as we will see, it is much earlier than the European secular tradition and also because it is rarely discussed in a secular academic context. The earliest references to archaeology within the Muslim tradition come from the Qur'an and relate to the remains of older civilizations from the *Jahiliyya* (Age of Ignorance). One of the most famous examples relates to some people who fell asleep in a cave and woke up sometime later. When the people went into the nearest town they tried to buy some food but found their currency was unrecognized because it was hundreds of years old. Other examples include references to ancient cities such as Madain Salih which was a city punished by God because the people refused to believe evidence sent by the Prophet Salih (Qur'an *Sura* xi, 64–71 and *Sura* vii, 77). If we move from the Qur'an to medieval Arabic authors we can see explanations and references to ancient monuments which reveal a sophisticated view of the pre-Islamic past. For example, the medieval Egyptian writer Abu Jafar al-'Idrissi complained about the destruction of ancient Egyptian monuments and called for their preservation basing his argument on the actions of the Prophet Muhammad's companions. Of particular interest is the writing of 'Abd al-Latif al-Baghdadi (1162–1231) who wrote a book on Egypt which included a section devoted to ancient monuments. Although a devout Muslim 'Abd al-Latif had a deep respect for the learning of the ancients and their monuments (Richter-Bernberg 2007). In a statement which seems remarkably sophisticated and intelligent he summarizes the reason for preserving ancient monuments as follows:

> Antiquities should endure as markers of a remote epoch and reminders of the ages since elapsed. They will serve as witness to the revealed scriptures for the venerable Koran mentions them and their people; thus by seeing them, narration becomes experience and tradition is verified... They indicate something of the forebears' circumstances and conduct, the ampleness of their learning and the clairvoyance of their notions. [al-Latif Baghdadi, trans. Richter-Bernberg 2007: 365]

However, not all writers were so rational in their approach, thus the twelfth-century Andalucian Ibn Jubayr wrote that the dome of the Umayyad mosque in Damascus was built with divine assistance. Another way in which medieval Islamic society dealt with the material remains of the past is through the discovery of sacred sites which might then be converted into Muslim shrines (Petersen 1999). Throughout Syria and Palestine there are a series of shrines which incorporate the excavated remains of both pre-Islamic and early Islamic periods. However the best-documented examples of how Muslims dealt with the material remains of their own past relate to the holy cities of Mecca (Figure 60.1) and Medina. Possibly the earliest account of what might be called Islamic archaeology in practice concerns the destruction and rebuilding of the Ka'ba (the black cube at the centre of Mecca) by Ibn Zubayr in 683 AD. The event is recorded by a number of authors and includes the discovery of earlier foundations beneath the Ka'ba which were interpreted as the remains of the original structure built by Abraham. Another discovery was a basket of green stones excavated in the ground beneath the *hijr* (inner enclosure) and interpreted as the tomb of Ishmael. Also during this process the Black Stone at the corner of the Ka'ba was removed and examined by a team of learned scholars who measured, examined, and described the object before handing it back for incorporation into the new structure (Peeters 1994: 62–4).

By the nineteenth century, there was a convergence of the archaeological techniques developed by Europeans and Muslims interested in the past. Thus in the nineteenth century an Imam carried out archaeological excavations at Zafar, the ancient Himaryite capital in Yemen. At the Ottoman imperial capital Osman Hamdi was appointed director of the Archaeological Museum in 1884 and carried out his own excavations at a number of sites including Sidon in present day Lebanon.

FIGURE 60.1 Sixteenth-century ceramic tile in Rustem Pasha Mosque (Istanbul, Turkey) depicting the Ka'ba in Mecca—the holiest shrine in Islam.

3 MAJOR SITES AND THEMES

A number of themes may be identified within Islamic archaeology which help to define it as an area of enquiry. These may be summarized as follows: (i) palaces and centres of power, sites such as the Umayyad Palaces, Samarra; (ii) Indian Ocean trade major sites, such as Siraf, Shanga, Mantai, and Qalhat; (iii) cities and urban life and relevant sites such as Fustat, Ramla, and Merv; (iv) rural and environmental studies; and (v) mosques and religious sites.

3.1 Palaces and Centres of Power

Until recently the emphasis of Islamic archaeology has been on the major political sites with a focus on political elites rather than the rural peasantry who will have formed the majority of the population (see Insoll 1999: 60–92, esp. 61, 90–2). One of the first groups of monuments to attract scholarly attention are the so called Desert Castles or Umayyad palaces which are to be found predominantly in the desert regions of modern Jordan and

Syria. The isolated location and luxurious decoration of many of these buildings suggest that they were used by a princely elite composed of members of the Umayyad dynasty which ruled during the seventh and eighth centuries AD. From the point of view of the archaeology of religion these buildings are of interest because they represent a lifestyle that does not conform with the expected norms of Islam. For example, al-Walid's palace (Khirbat al-Mafjar) in the Jordan valley is built around a magnificent bath house decorated with voluptuous figural statuary as well as having pools and fountains which used wine instead of water (Hamilton 1959, 1988).

If we move from the palaces of eighth-century Syria to those of ninth-century Iraq, significant changes are visible. Unfortunately the remains of the early Abbasid palace at Baghdad has yet to be located though literary accounts suggest a scale of grandeur and magnificence which make the earlier Umayyad palaces appear provincial. In the ninth century, the Abbasid rulers moved out of Baghdad to Samarra, a new city the bulk of which was made up of vast palaces. Excavation of these palaces shows a level of luxury equivalent to that of the Umayyads though with important differences—although there is some evidence of wine consumption there is less figural imagery and the first appearance of an abstract form of decoration which was to become common in Islamic art (Herzfeld and Sarre 1923–48; Northedge 2008). Also of interest in terms of religion are the two mosques which dominate the remains of Abbasid Samarra. The first of these, the Great Mosque, comprises a massive rectangular enclosed area with a 60-metre-high spiral minaret at the *qibla* (southern end). The second mosque, the mosque of Abu Dulaf replicates this design but is built on a smaller scale and also with the spiral minaret. Both mosques are built next to palaces with a doorway leading into the mosque from behind the *mihrab* (Petersen 1998: 249–51). In other words the remains give the impression of the (Abbasid) caliph as a semi-divine figure who would appear in front of the masses of troops and officials who were the only other residents of this vast city complex.

3.2 Indian Ocean Trade

One of the problems with the European secular study of the history of Islam is that the focus has been on the major dynasties and political centres (for a criticism of this view see Insoll 1999). This view sees Islam as a religion of empires with religion and culture spread by military conquest. However since the 1970s there have been a growing number of archaeological projects looking at long-distance trade within the Indian Ocean and beyond which present a different view of Islamic civilization (for an overview see Pearson 2003: 62–112). Major projects include excavations at the port of Siraf in Iran (Whitehouse 1970), the trading settlement of Mantai in Sri-Lanka (Carswell and Prickett 1984), and a series of excavations in East Africa including Kilwa (Chittick 1974), Manda (Chittick 1984), Shanga (Horton 1996), Zanzibar, and Pemba. The written historical evidence for these settlements is very limited and in some cases virtually non-existent yet the remains identified by archaeology indicate a sophisticated Muslim maritime culture spread over a large area including many ethnicities, languages, and traditions unified by a religious code with Arabic as the *lingua franca*. Each of the settlements excavated contained pottery and other finds traded over huge distances; thus the port of Manda in Kenya had fired bricks imported from Sohar in Oman as well as pottery from the Persian Gulf, India, and China

(Chittick 1984). The fourteenth-century Moroccan writer Ibn Battuta gives some idea of how this civilization functioned and thus he was able to travel from Tangier in Morocco to China remaining within an international Muslim community.

3.3 Cities and Urban Life

Islam is often characterized as an urban religion based on the fact that it was developed in the Arabian cities of Mecca and Medina (Yathrib). Although of course this view is exaggerated and there are many components of the religion and culture which relate either to nomadic or rural life, cities remain one of the most significant symbols of Muslim life. In consequence, the archaeology of cities has become one of the most contentious issues within the study of Muslim culture. One of the main issues is whether the transition from late Roman/Byzantine to Muslim rule in Syria and North Africa should be regarded as a period of decline, continuity, or progress. Related to this discussion is the idea developed first in North Africa that Muslim cities have certain characteristics which make them different from and inferior to cities of the Classical world or medieval and later Europe. Characteristics which were said to be typical of Muslim cities included a non-orthogonal plan (i.e. not laid out on a grid), dark narrow streets, cul-de-sacs, absence of large, public spaces and generally cramped living conditions (for a discussion of these issues see Petersen 2005: 3–6).

This view was developed largely by comparing the medieval cities of Algeria or Morocco with planned French colonial new cities forgetting that many European cities were also unplanned chaotic and crowded (see, for example, Engels' description of nineteenth-century Manchester in *The History of the English Working Classes*). The impact of these views on archaeology meant that when ancient cities of the Middle East were excavated there was an assumption that the transition from the Late Antique period to the Islamic period would show a decline. Thus the encroachments of shops onto main thoroughfares, subdivision of larger houses, and changing street patterns were seen to be a result of the change to Arab Muslim rule. However recent archaeological research has called these assumptions into question, firstly by showing that many of these changes pre-dated the Muslim conquest, secondly by showing that similar changes took place in Europe where there was no Muslim presence, and thirdly that these changes may equally denote a thriving privatized economy (see e.g. Pentz 1992; Petersen 2005; Walmsley 2007).

Against this background there have been some major archaeological excavations of Muslim cities which have helped to give some definition to the concept of Islamic urbanism. For the purposes of this chapter three examples will be discussed. Probably the first Muslim urban area to be excavated was at Fustat which was an inner-city suburb of medieval Cairo. Excavations at Fustat have been carried out over the greater part of a century and have revealed a flourishing cosmopolitan settlement of predominantly middle- and working-class people living in courtyard houses (Kubiak 1987). The archaeological information has been supplemented by detailed historical information from the Cairo Geniza documents, a synagogue archive, providing a very detailed picture of urban life that included Jews and Christians as well as Muslims.

If we move to Palestine, the city of Ramla near modern Tel Aviv presents an example of a city founded by Muslim Arabs in the early eighth century (712 AD). Although archaeological work has been more restricted than at Fustat the main features of the city's development are now fairly clear (Petersen 2000, 2001, 2005: 95–102). The city started as a development around a palace and congregational mosque with an aqueduct bringing water to a number of underground cisterns. The early city appears to have had a regular orthogonal layout with building covering an area of several square miles. During the eleventh century the city suffered from an earthquake and invasions culminating in the Crusader occupation. With the return to Muslim rule in the late twelfth century the layout of the city was radically altered—instead of a widely spaced development, settlement was concentrated in one quarter around the Crusader church which was converted to a mosque whilst the former congregational mosque was left isolated within a vast graveyard. The other notable feature of the late medieval city was the large number of neighbourhood mosques, the majority of which were built around the tombs of warriors (*shahid*) and holy men. Both the increasing density of settlement and the proliferation of small mosques is a characteristic feature of the change from early Islam to the medieval period and probably indicating a less-centralized approach to religion.

The third example is the city of Merv, located in the newly independent country of Turkmenistan though historically part of the eastern region of Iran known as Khurassan. Like Fustat, Merv was one of the first Islamic sites to be investigated due to its historical significance and location on the ancient silk road. Although Merv existed before the Islamic period and dated back to Selucid times (third century BC) a new city was built by the Seljuk rulers in the eleventh century, dominated by the mausoleum of Sultan Sanjar. One of the notable features of the Seljuk city, Sultan Kala, is that the street plan was laid out on a grid pattern with Sanjar's mausoleum at the centre. Although there are few structures standing within the city, the whole area is enclosed by walls standing up to 8 m high. As with medieval Ramla, religious buildings are mostly built around the tombs of holy men representing different Sufi brotherhoods (for an overview see Herrmann 1999).

3.4 Rural and Environmental Studies

For reasons already stated, Islamic archaeology has tended to concentrate on towns and major sites and consequently little attention has been paid to smaller settlements and human interaction with the environment. More recently, however, this has begun to change partly because of the increased number of rescue excavations and partly because there has been a growing awareness that the majority of Muslims in the past lived in a rural environment. One of the first studies to look at the archaeology of rural landscape was the survey of the Diyala basin in Iraq carried out by Robert Adams in the late 1950s which looked at long-term settlement and land-use patterns (Adams 1965). More recent studies of rural life in the Muslim world include the Khirbat Faris Project which was centred on the excavation of a small medieval and Ottoman-period village in present-day Jordan (McQuitty 2005). Although the settlement does not appear in historical documentation, it was clearly inhabited during the Islamic period (630 AD to 1800s) and was of some significance to the economy of the Karak region in Jordan. Other studies of the agricultural economy include studies of the fortified granaries in Morocco and their relationship to local villages (De Meulemester 2005).

Environmental sampling in Islamic archaeology was suggested as long ago as the late nineteenth century by Jacques De Morgan while excavating at Susa in Iran although it has not become commonplace until the late 1990s. Significant discoveries in this field include the identification of cotton production in medieval Merv and coffee consumption at Kush in eastern Arabia during the twelfth–thirteenth centuries. Environmental sampling can be of particular use in detecting the extent to which Muslim dietary rules and traditions are observed, for example eating pork or the consumption of alcohol (cf. Insoll 1999: 93–107).

3.5 Mosques and Religious Sites

The archaeological study of religious sites in Islam may be divided into two main categories, the first comprises the holy sites of Mecca, Medina, and Jerusalem whilst the second includes shrines, mosques, and related buildings throughout the Muslim world. Mecca, Medina, and Jerusalem have a specific status because they are mentioned in the Qur'an and therefore their investigation and any interpretations are dominated by religious considerations. This does not mean that differing interpretations are not permitted but rather that any archaeological findings must be considered secondary to religious belief. Whilst this may appear anathema to any processual archaeologist, it should also be self-evident that the results of archaeological investigations are unlikely to change a 1,400-year-old belief system. Against this background it is no surprise that most archaeological work connected with these holy sites has been of a theoretical nature and has been primarily concerned with documenting the history of structures in the holy cities since the advent of Islam. Nevertheless, theoretical and architectural studies of these buildings (as distinct from excavation) have been of considerable value in the study of the development of Muslim society. For example, the first mosque was Muhammad's house in Medina (now known as the Prophet's Mosque) which comprised a rectangular area covered with a roof of palm trunks and a courtyard. Studies of this mosque based on texts and architectural evidence have shown how the building was adapted to the growing demands of the new religion (Sauvaget 1947; Petersen 1998: 182–4).

If we now look at the second, wider field of mosques outside the holy cities, the field of enquiry and range of questions becomes much wider. One of the areas in which archaeology can make a particularly significant contribution concerns the construction and development of early mosques. At its simplest a mosque comprises a rectangular open area with a niche (*mihrab*) aligned towards Mecca (the *qibla*). Some of the earliest mosques so far encountered are of this type and numerous examples have been excavated and studied in the deserts of Arabia, Syria, and Palestine. Interesting theories about the origins of Islam have been based on these simple structures. For example, an Israeli study makes the unlikely suggestion that the early mosques of the Negev Bedouin evolved out of structures devoted to a stella cult based on the incorporation of a large stone used to mark the *qibla* (direction of prayer) (Avni 1994). Other studies have shown how mosques were incorporated into the structure of towns; thus at Shivta in the Negev (Israel) a small mosque was built into the courtyard of a church which was evidently still in use (Petersen 2005: 63). At Jerash in Jordan a large mosque was built at the main crossroads of the city indicating a considerable degree of continuity and confidence on the part of the new Muslim rulers (Walmsley and Damgaard 2005).

One of the most intriguing aspects of Islamic archaeology is the almost ubiquitous presence of shrines built around the tombs of holy men (e.g. warriors [*shahid*], Sufis, imams, or prophets [see Figure 60.2]) despite the universal condemnation of this practice in Muslim religious texts. Many of these shrines are extremely elaborate and the veneration of these figures is often very intense showing a marked departure from more formal

FIGURE 60.2 Pilgrims progress around the fourteenth-century tomb of Najm al-Din Kubra at the ancient city of Kunya Urgench south of the Aral Sea in northern Turkmenistan.

constructions of Islam. Palestine has a particularly rich collection of shrines which articulate the hilly landscape around Jerusalem, Hebron, and Nablus. Recent studies have shown how these shrines often incorporate pre-Islamic features of the landscape adding to a sense of local continuity (e.g. Petersen 1999).

The Hajj (pilgrimage) routes which converge on Mecca like a giant spider's web represent a more formal version of Muslim sacred geography (Petersen 1995). In addition to these major routes there are also pilgrimages associated with Shia holy places, in particular Najaf, Kufa, and Mashad which indicate an alternative religious orthodoxy. Archaeological studies of these routes may include not only the roadside facilities but also natural and ancient features which fed into the religious experience of those taking part in the pilgrimage.

4 THEORETICAL CONSIDERATIONS

Islam is the youngest of the major world religions and as such the archaeology of Muslim societies is still developing both in terms of discoveries and theoretical positions. In view of these considerations and the fact that Islam is the fastest-growing religion it is likely that the archaeology will be very different in the twenty-first century from its beginnings in the nineteenth and twentieth centuries when it was dominated by European Orientalists and art connoisseurs. The most significant change is likely to be the growing importance of religion both in interpretation and selection of sites and themes for investigation. This of course reflects wider changes both within Islamic societies and within the world as a whole where a secular view of the world is no longer taken for granted. One of the by-products of this development will be an increasing geographical scope—whereas in the past Muslim archaeology was considered as the medieval archaeology of the Near East, its scope is now widening to include regions such as South-East Asia, sub-Saharan Africa (e.g. Insoll 2003) and any other areas where Islam has been adopted even as a minority religion (e.g. Petersen 2008).

At the end of the twentieth century, Tim Insoll's book *The Archaeology of Islam* (1999) indicated that Islamic archaeology had become firmly established as an area of legitimate archaeological enquiry. Perhaps more importantly, Insoll's book argued that the focus of the subject should be firmly grounded in an understanding of the religion and religious traditions of Islam rather than seeing the religion either as monolithic and unchanging or as of no significance. In reply, Donald Whitcomb has argued that instead of looking specifically at Islam as a religion we should be looking at an 'Islamicate' society—in other words a community where Islam may be the religion of the majority but where other religions and religious traditions also have their influence (Whitcomb 2005). The difference between these two views is not necessarily fundamental and may be regarded as a question of emphasis rather than contradiction. In any case, what seems clear is that the focus of Islamic archaeology is moving away from objects and buildings towards Muslim society itself.

For the future, there are four major theoretical areas of enquiry which need to be investigated which may be summarized as follows: (1) Muslim religious attitudes to archaeology and the past; (2) definition of the legitimate scope of an archaeology of Islam (i.e. is this just a study of Islam as a religion or as a culture); (3) problems of archaeological practice (i.e. what should happen to human remains recovered from an archaeological site, what should happen to excavated pig bone, can a mosque be excavated to reveal an earlier structure, Muslim or otherwise?); (4) questions of interpretation. Is it possible for archaeological evidence to conflict with accepted religious tradition? Should an archaeologist excavating an Islamic site be Muslim in order to understand the 'true' nature of what is being found? The archaeology of Islam in the twenty-first century thus offers interesting challenges.

Further Reading

For an overview of Islamic archaeology in practice, see the series of articles in the journal *Antiquity* 304 (2005). Another good source of articles dealing with Islamic architecture and archaeology is the journal *Muqarnas* published by the Agha Khan Foundation for Architecture.

For a discussion of the early study of Arabic history in Britain see Holt's 1957 study of the seventeenth-century scholar, Edward Pococke, whilst Edward Said's seminal work *Orientalism* (1978) provides a context and critical framework to British, European, and American interest in the Arabic and Islamic world. For a history of the study of Islamic material culture in Britain and Europe see Rogers (1974), Vernoit (1997), and Petersen (2008). A good example of the early study of Islamic architecture can be found in the works of Gertrude Bell including *From Amurath to Amurath* (1911) and *Palace and Mosque at Ukhaidhir* (1914). Probably the most influential and important book for Islamic archaeology and architecture is Creswell's monumental two-volume study, *Early Islamic Architecture* (1932–69) which formed a prologue to his other main work, the two-volume *The Muslim Architecture of Egypt* (1952).

For an indication of some medieval Muslim attitudes to the Islamic and pre-Islamic past, see the study by Richter-Bernberg (2007) which deals with an often neglected area of Arabic literature. Peeters' (1994) study of the Hajj is a compilation of mostly Arabic and Muslim texts which give an insight into the development and archaeology of the Haram in Mecca. For a discussion of the archaeology of the Syrian and Iraqi Hajj routes see Petersen (1995).

Important studies of palaces include Gertrude Bell's study of Ukhaidhir (1914) mentioned above, as well as Robert Hamilton's studies of Khirbat al-Mafjar (1959, 1988). Creswell also devotes considerable space to discussions of palaces in his studies of early Islamic architecture (1932–69). For an introduction to the archaeology and history of the Indian Ocean see Pearson (2003) and for specific sites and areas see Chittick (1974, 1984) and Horton (1996). There are many books and articles which discuss Islamic cities; useful studies relating to specific cities are Fustat (Kubiak 1987), Samarra (Northedge 2008), Ramla and other cities in Palestine (Petersen 2005), Merv (Hermann 1999), and Buraimi (Petersen 2009).

Wilkinson's study of *Near Eastern Landscapes* provides a context and includes useful sections on Islamic period land use. For examples of regional and rural studies see Adams' (1965) pioneering study of the Diyala Plain in Iraq and De Meulemeester's discussion of rural Moroccan agriculture (2005). The long-awaited publication of the Khirbat Faris Project in Jordan will provide one of the most comprehensive studies of rural life from the pre-Islamic period to the nineteenth century (in the meantime see McQuitty 2005).

For a general introduction to mosques see Petersen (1998: 195–7) and Insoll (1999: 26–59) and for a recent example of mosque archaeology see reports on the excavation of the Jerash mosque (Walmsley and Damgaard 2005) and a more art historical approach to the Great Mosque of Damascus (Flood 2001).

Insoll's book *The Archaeology of Islam* (1999) marks the emergence of Islamic archaeology into the mainstream of archaeological research whilst the collection of essays published by Whitcomb, under the title *Changing Social Identity with the Spread of Islam* (2005), provides an introduction to different points of view. For an indication of possible future directions see my recent discussion of Islamic archaeology in Britain (Petersen 2008).

REFERENCES

ADAMS, R. M. 1965. *Land behind Baghdad: A history of settlement in the Diyala Plains* (Chicago and London: University of Chicago Press).

AVNI, G. 1994. 'Early mosques in the Negev highlands: New evidence on the Islamic penetration of southern Palestine', *Bulletin of the American Schools of Oriental Research*, 294: 83–100.

BELL, G. 1911. *From Amurath to Amurath* (London).

——1914. *Palace and Mosque at Ukhiadhir: A study in early Mohammedan architecture* (Oxford: Oxford University Press).

CARSWELL, J. and PRICKETT, M. 1984. 'Mantai (1980): A preliminary investigation', *Ancient Ceylon*, 5: 3–80.

CHITTICK, H. 1974. *Manda: Exacavations at an island port on the Kenya Coast*, British Institute in Eastern Africa, Memoir No. 9 (Nairobi: British Institute in Eastern Africa).

——1984. *Manda: Excavations at an island port on the Kenya coast*, British Institute in Eastern Africa, Memoir No. 9 (Nairobi: BIEA).

CRESWELL, K. A. C. 1932. *Early Islamic Architecture*, 2 vols. (Oxford: Oxford University Press).

——1952. *The Muslim Architecture of Egypt*, 2 vols. (Oxford: Oxford University Press; repr. 1978, New York: Hacker Books).

DONKOW, I. 2004. 'The Ephesus excavations 1863–1874, in the light of the Ottoman legislation on antiquities', *Anatolian Studies*, 54: 109–17.

FLOOD, F. B. 2001. *The Great Mosque of Damascus: Studies in the making of an Umayyad visual culture* (Leiden: Brill).

HAMILTON, R. 1959. *Khirbat al-Mafjar: An Arabian mansion in the Jordan Valley* (Oxford: Oxford University Press).

——1988. *Walid and his Friends: An Umayyad Tragedy*, Oxford Studies in Islamic Art 2 (Oxford: Oxford University Press).

HERRMANN, G. 1999. *Monuments of Merv: Traditional Buildings of the Karakum* (London: The Society of Antiquaries of London).

HERZFELD, E. and SARRE, F. 1923–48. *Die Ausgrabungen von Samarra* (Berlin and Hamburg).

HOLT, P. M. 1957. 'The study of Arabic historians in seventeenth century England: The background and the work of Edward Pococke', *Bulletin of the School of Oriental and African Studies, University of London*, 19(3): 444–55.

HORTON, M. (1996). *Shanga: A Muslim community on the East African coast*, British Institute in Eastern Africa, Memoir No. 14 (Nairobi: BIEA).

INSOLL, T. 1999. *The Archaeology of Islam* (Oxford: Blackwell).

——2003. *The Archaeology of Islam in Sub Saharan Africa* (Cambridge: Cambridge University Press).

KUBIAK, W. 1987. *Al-Fustat: Its foundation and early development* (Cairo: American University in Cairo Press).

MCQUITTY, A. 2005. 'The rural landscape of Jordan in the seventh to nineteenth century: The Karak Plateau', *Antiquity*, 304: 327–38.

MEULEMEESTER, J. DE 2005. 'Granaries and irrigation: Archaeological and ethnological investigations in the Iberian peninsula and Morocco', *Antiquity*, 304: 609–15.

NORTHEDGE, A. 2008. *Historical Topography of Samarra*, Samarra Studies 1 (London: British School of Archaeology in Iraq and Max Van Berchem Foundation).

PEARSON, M. 2003. *The Indian Ocean* (London: Routledge).

PEETERS, F. E. 1994. *The Hajj: The Muslim pilgrimage to Mecca and the holy places* (New Jersey: Princeton University Press).

PENTZ, P. 1992. *The Invisible Conquest: The ontogenesis of sixth and seventh century Syria* (Copenhagen: National Museum of Denmark).

PETERSEN, A. D. 1995. 'The archaeology of the Syrian and Iraqi Hajj routes', *World Archaeology*, 26(1): 47–56.

——1998. *Dictionary of Islamic Architecture* (London and New York: Routledge).

——1999. 'The archaeology of Muslim pilgrimage and shrines in Palestine' in T. Insoll (ed.), *Case Studies in Archaeology and World Religion: The proceedings of the Cambridge Conference*, BAR International Series 755 (Oxford: Archaeopress).

Petersen, A. D. 2000. 'Preliminary report on the topographic survey of Ramla 1997 and 1999', *Levant*, 32: 97–9.
—— 2001. 'Interim report on geophysical and surface surveys of Ramla 1999', *Levant*, 33: 1–6.
—— 2005. *The Towns of Palestine under Muslim Rule*, BAR International Series 1381 (Oxford: Archaeopress).
—— 2008. 'Islamic archaeology in Britain: Recognition and potential', *Antiquity*, 82(318): 1080–92.
—— 2009. 'Islamic urbanism in eastern Arabia: The case of the al-'Ain/Buraimi Oasis', *Proceedings of the Seminar for Arabian Studies*, 39: 307–20.
Richter-Bernberg, L. 2007. 'Past Glory and Present Ignorance. 'Abd al-Latīf al-Baġdādī on 'Ayyūbid Egypt', in U. Vermeulen and K. D'hulster (eds), *Egypt and Syria in the Fatimid, Ayyubid and Mamluk Eras V*, Orientalia Lovaniensia Analecta 169: 349–68.
—— 2008. 'Past glory and present ignorance: 'Abd al-Latif al-Bagdadi on "Ayyubid Egypt"' in U. Vermeulen and K. D'Hulster (eds), *Egypt and Syria in the Fatimid, Ayyubid and Mamluk Era*, V (Leuven: Peeters), pp. 349–68.
Rogers, J. M. 1974. *From Antiquarianism to Islamic Archaeology* (Cairo: Instituto Italiano di Cultura per la R.A.E.).
Said, E. 1978. *Orientalism* (London: Penguin).
Sauvaget, J. 1947. *La Mosquée Omeyyade de Medine. Études sur les origins architecturales de la mosque et de la basilique* (Paris: Geuthner).
Vernoit, S. 1997. 'The rise of Islamic archaeology', *Muqarnas*, 14: 1–10.
Walmsley, A. 2007. *Early Islamic Syria*, Duckworth Debates in Archaeology (London: Duckworth).
—— and Damgaard, K. 2005. 'The Umayyad congregational mosque at Jarash in Jordan and its relationship to early mosques', *Antiquity*, 304: 362–78.
Whitcomb, D. (ed.) 2005. *Changing Social Identity with the Spread of Islam*, Oriental Institute Seminars Number 1 (Chicago, IL: Oriental Institute of the University of Chicago).
Whitehouse, D. 1970. 'Siraf: A medieval port on the Persian Gulf', *World Archaeology*, 2(2): 141–58.
Wilkinson, T. J. 2003. *Near Eastern Landscapes* (Tuscon: University of Arizona Press).
Wright, H. T. 2007. *Early State Formation in Central Madagascar: An archaeological survey* (Ann Arbor: Memoirs of the University of Michigan).

PART VI

ARCHAEOLOGY OF INDIGENOUS AND NEW RELIGIONS

CHAPTER 61

SHAMANISM

NEIL PRICE

1 Introduction: Shamanism (un)Defined

SHAMANISM has been a contested topic in the history of ritual and religious experience since the first Western observations of the phenomenon, made in Siberia by Elizabethan English explorers in the mid-1500s and Russian exiles a century later (Hutton 2001). In the twenty-first century, its very existence is still a matter of debate and constant redefinition, as controversial as ever. At the same time, there is no doubt of its continued relevance to the study of spirituality, witnessed not least in the Neo-Shamanic movements discussed elsewhere in this volume (Blain, Ch. 63). Recent decades have seen a resurgence in archaeological studies of shamanism, as the increasing general awareness of traditional religions has been matched by a corresponding expansion of research into ancient faiths, belief systems, and spiritual practices. But what actually *is* shamanism?

As Rydving (1987: 186–7) has observed, 'historians of religion sometimes have a tendency to talk as if "shamanism" were something concrete, thereby forgetting that it only exists as an abstraction and a concept in the brains of its students'. This abstraction came only gradually into being during the period from the late seventeenth to the late nineteenth centuries, as Siberia was traversed by missionaries, political refugees (often highly educated intellectuals), Tsarist agents, and European travellers. Over the years, more and more stories were brought back of the intriguing beliefs and practices to be found among the tribal peoples there: from the Nenets, Mansi, Khanty, Ngansan, and Enets of the Uralic group around the Yamal peninsula, the Ob and Yenisei river basins, and the north Siberian coast; the Turkic-speaking Dolgan and Yakut (or Sakha) on the lower Lena; the Tungusic-Manchurian peoples of central Siberia, including the Even and the Evenki; and the Yukaghir, Chukchi, Koryak, and Itelmen of eastern Siberia and the Pacific coast, amongst many others.

The tales told by these early voyagers were startling, and aroused intense interest from St Petersburg to London. A fragmentary picture emerged of an 'ensouled world' in which everything was alive, and filled with spirits—animals, natural features, even what to Western eyes were inanimate objects. To such beings could be linked almost every aspect of material life: sickness and health, the provision of food and shelter, success in hunting, the fortunes of sex, and the well-being of the community. The maintenance of good

FIGURE 61.1 The shamanic dilemma in archaeology: Prehistoric rock carvings such as these from Siberia show astonishing parallels with shaman costumes photographed by early ethnographers, but does the one 'prove' the antiquity of the other, and how secure are our definitions? The relationship between these and other material expressions of spiritual practice is far from straightforward. Carvings from (1) Oglakhty, Middle Yenisei River, (2) Middle Yenisei River, (3) Mokhsogolokh-Khaja, Middle Lena River.

relationships with these spirits was thus of crucial importance, and the most striking of the travellers' stories concerned the special individuals who took charge of this. These people were seen to attain what we would now call altered states of consciousness, in order to send out their souls to communicate with these beings, to enlist their aid or bind them to their will, sometimes even to engage them in combat. The operative sphere of these people,

FIGURE 61.2 Photograph of an Altai shaman, early 1920s.

whom the Evenki called *šaman*, was revealed as a world of mediation, of negotiation between the realm of human beings and the adjacent, occasionally coincident, planes of existence in which dwelt the gods, the spirits of nature, and the souls of the dead. The complex variety of equipment used in these ceremonies was also described: the strange headgear, hats crowned with antlers and fantastic arrangements of wood or leather; jackets hung with jingling amulets, adorned with fur, feathers, and even the whole bodies of animals; the garments covered with bronze figures, bells and hundreds of long straps; the masks and veils; the effigies and figurines; and above all, the drums.

Some of this data was published and widely discussed in scholarly circles, and during the eighteenth century the Evenk concept of the *šaman* was taken up in Russian as a useful collective for the similar figures that were encountered from one tribe to another across the region (a process charted in Flaherty 1992: 21–66). The indigenous Siberians had no written language, and the phonetic constructions used to record these concepts was soon normalized via Russian to the Western European languages, creating the more conventional 'shaman'. We may note that the Evenki pronounced the word with the accent on the second syllable, 'sha-márn', but the alternative forms of 'shár-man' or 'sháy-man' are now equally common. The term has also been taken up as a verb, in an attempt to render a similar indigenous use of the appropriate regional terms—thus in the secondary literature one can often read of a shaman 'shamanizing'. The term *šaman* seems to have literally meant 'one who is excited, moved or raised', but also has connotations of hard work, tiredness as a result of exertion, and other aspects of ritual effort. Among the Tungus-speaking peoples there were other variants, such as *hamman* and *samman*, but in general each of the Siberian peoples had their own terms for the equivalent in their respective cultures.

At first, there were few that associated these individuals, and the role that they played within their communities, with 'religion' in the sense of an organized system of worship. The notion of shaman*ism* as a collective pattern of belief arose first when the Christian missions began to seriously target the Siberian peoples for conversion, and thus sought to identify a pagan faith towards the overthrow of which they could concentrate their efforts. In his book *Shamans: Siberian spirituality and the Western imagination* (2001), Ronald Hutton has charted this 'creation' of shamanism, providing a contextualized discussion of why shamanism has been interpreted in different ways at different times.

This question as to the exact nature of shamanism has been central to shamanic studies from the very beginning. Already in 1853, the Finnish scholar Castrén challenged the idea that shamanism could be described as a religion rather than as a pattern of behaviour, and this debate continued throughout the late 1800s when the first major Russian works on the subject appeared. By the beginning of the twentieth century, this social, psychological, and arguably religious phenomenon was already the subject of an established body of literature (this period of early research is summarized and fully referenced in Hultkrantz 1998).

Similar practices had earlier been described from other parts of the northern hemisphere, for example among the Sámi, but it was not until the early 1900s that the beliefs of other circumpolar arctic and subarctic cultures began to be specifically—though tentatively—described in terms of shamanism. This development was largely due to the remarkable Jesup North Pacific Expedition, launched from the American Museum in New York in 1897, with the objective of analysing early contacts between Siberia and Alaska, and in the hope of illuminating the possible Asian origins of the Native American peoples. Six years of fieldwork undertaken by multiple teams around the North Pacific rim resulted in a series of massive English-language volumes which greatly eased the link to Siberia in Western research (the impact of the expedition is best explored through Krupnik and Fitzhugh 2001; Kendall and Krupnik 2003).

Through the early twentieth century the notion of shamanism spread slowly in North America, being applied to the 'medicine-men' of First Nations peoples, but even here the definitions common in Siberia were being adapted to local circumstances (e.g. Dixon 1908). Although shamanism was widely adopted as a psychological and psychiatric concept in the years between the world wars, as Hultkrantz has noted, 'it is difficult to find surveys of [non-Russian] shamanism before 1950' (1998: 61). There were, however, many foreigners working on the Siberian material, and Finnish researchers were particularly active. Until the fall of the Soviet Union, or at least the late 1980s, the division between Western and Eastern studies of shamanism was almost total.

There were many attempts to explain what shamanism was, or what caused it. Soviet scholars sought its origins in a particular concentration of power and shifting control of production, with an additional emphasis on medical interpretations often based on notions of mental illness. The explanation of shamanism as due to a kind of 'arctic hysteria' induced by cold and deprivation was adopted with enthusiasm in Soviet Russia, where it became fundamental in the policies of suppressing this perceived threat of independent thought and spiritual allegiance. The erotic elements of shamanic practice were stressed by several authors, and numerous detailed accounts of what anthropologists would now call spirit possession were collected not only from Siberia but also among the Inuit in Greenland and the peoples of arctic North America. Discussions of this phenomenon were relatively free from racist overtones in the early twentieth century, but by 1939 when Ohlmarks published his work on shamanism, the notion of arctic hysteria had become ethnocentric and made to stand for the perceived primitivism of the 'lower races' that underpinned so much of the pseudo-science of the time. Under the Soviet regime, the shaman as a kind of ultimate arctic hysteric joined the idea of the shaman as mentally unbalanced psychopath as the preferred conclusion of 'scientific' reports.

Long into the twentieth century the twin poles of discussion revolved around the definition of shamanism as either a 'primitive religion' or part of one—the crucial point being whether it was a self-contained system or a component in a larger pattern of belief. Terminologies were as inconsistent then as now, with a plethora of vaguely articulated concepts such as 'religio-magic' and 'preanimism'. However, even in some of the earliest studies it was clear that shamanism was also perceived as a view of reality over and above the specifics of its rituals. As Banzarov put it in writing about the Mongolian shamanism known as the 'Black Faith', it could be defined as 'a certain primitive way of observing the outer world—Nature—and the inner world—the soul' (1891: 4f., translated from the Russian). This debate continues today.

2 THE SHAMANIC FRAME

The concept of shamanism progresses through three phases in its transition from the religion of indigenous peoples to its employment by academics, and this trajectory provides the key to its validity as a category of spiritual phenomena. At the first level, which has only separate indigenous terminologies, this kind of belief system quite simply provides a cartography of reality in the cultures concerned. At the second level is the lexical process by which aspects of these indigenous beliefs are transformed into an anthropological concept—from the *šaman* and other similar figures to the notion of sham*anism*, as we have seen above. At the third level is the stipulative application of this concept, adapted and interpreted according to circumstance and definition.

Shamanism as an anthropological category is thus entirely invented, and in a sense the word means no more or less than what those who use it decide. However, despite the impression given by some of its critics, shamanism is not all things to all people, and the difficulties of exact definition are actually to be embraced. The situation has been summarized by Daniel Ogden in his studies of magic in the ancient world, when he criticizes those who 'confuse the attempt to give final definition to an abstract concept, ancient or modern, which is self-evidently impossible, with the delineation of a coherent core of source-material for study' (2008: 3). Like these academic enquiries into the nature of early magic, the study of shamanism has also become similarly fetishized—by both advocates and critics—in a manner that strangely departs from and obscures the evident facts of ancient spirituality that lie at its heart.

Seen in this way, the use of shamanism as an analytical tool and a comparative vocabulary is no more controversial than any of the other academic categories ('ritual', 'sacred', 'holy', etc.) which have been coined to give meaningful shape to the intangibles of belief and which have also been the subject of continuous debate for centuries. So long as we understand the implications and frames of reference involved, then shamanism provides us with a useful terminology for describing patterns of ritual behaviour and spiritual beliefs found in strikingly similar form across much of the arctic and subarctic regions of the world. The essential question is whether we can truly speak of shamanism beyond the circumpolar sphere.

It is here that we enter a broader framework of interpretation, which moves outward from Siberia and the circumpolar region on a sliding scale of inclusion to embrace shamanistic traits in the ritual practices of South America, Oceania, Africa (particularly controversially), and ultimately the globe. Four scales of geo-cultural reference are found in shamanic studies, representing three different perspectives on these belief systems:

- the Evenki and some of the Tungus-speaking peoples
- Siberia
- the circumpolar region: Siberia, North-east Asia, the North Pacific, (sub)arctic North America, Greenland, northern Fenno-Scandia, and the White Sea
- the entire globe.

The first level is exclusive, culturally specific to those peoples who actually employ the word *šaman*, and has no comparative focus. When the latter is introduced at the second level, a major paradigm shift comes with the acceptance of the shamanic concept as a research tool. The Siberian framework differs from that of the circumpolar region only by degree, as they both incorporate shamanism as an anthropological category within areas of cultural continuity. The most controversial shift comes between the third and fourth levels, because a global platform transforms shamanism from a culturally situated belief system into a generalizing manifestation of human neuropsychology expressed in localized cultural forms.

Given the wide-ranging nature of the topic it is impossible to provide full examples of all its manifestations, but we can nonetheless illustrate the breadth of the field through a series of brief case studies focusing upon the key aspects of ancient shamanic belief systems that have been explored through archaeology. In so doing, we can simultaneously examine the relative claims of the four-stage shamanic framework.

3 COGNITIVE ARCHAEOLOGY AND SHAMANIC ORIGINS: THE EARLIEST 'RELIGION'?

In essence, shamanism constitutes nothing less than a particular conception of the nature of reality itself, and as such it potentially affects, and is reflected in, all manner of social phenomena and their material correlates—with corresponding implications for its archaeological detection and obvious overlaps in the fields of anthropology, ethnography, sociology, and cultural theory. Shamanism's earliest and in some ways most fundamental appearance in archaeological research relates to the search for the first human spiritual expressions and patterns of consistency in ritual behaviour across large spans of time and space, ideas linked largely to its association with hunter-gatherer communities.

The material that has come under most scrutiny here is undoubtedly the parietal, and to a lesser degree the portable, 'art' of the Upper Palaeolithic in Europe—the painted caves and their analogues that date back to at least 30,000 years BP and mark a clear cognitive leap in human image-making. Early interpretations of the paintings focused heavily on sympathetic 'hunting magic', and even a rather undefined shamanism (see Bahn and Vertut 1988: 150-8 for an effective overview). This changed dramatically with the suggestion, first made in the late 1980s and elaborated ever since, that the cave walls were used by shamans to fix the visions that they had experienced while in an altered state of consciousness (ASC), combining the sensory deprivation of the deep dark with the after-effects of trance. Crucially, it was argued that this process was hard-wired into the human brain and that the types of images, or entoptic phenomena, seen in ASC could be classified in clear stages ranging from initial vortexes and geometrics to final forms that were determined by cultural context (Lewis-Williams and Dowson 1988; Clottes and Lewis-Williams 1996; Lewis-Williams 2002 with references to his very large body of work on this theme). Thus the paintings were argued to represent not just the emergence of shamanic beliefs, but also a vital moment of human cognitive evolution embodying the brain's ability to enter trance and invest it with cultural significance. According to this argument, as Piers Vitebsky has memorably put it, 'being a shaman is probably the world's oldest profession' (1995: 96). The combination of neurological constant and cultural manifestation quickly became known as the neuropsychological model. These approaches have been widely taken up in other contexts, including the European Neolithic and the western United States, both discussed below, Central Asia (e.g. Rozwadowski 2001; Rozwadowski and Kośko 2002), and Australia (e.g. Chippindale et al. 2000).

Although the model ultimately related to work on Southern African spirituality, in some ways the parallel antecedents of these ideas go back to 1978 and Anna-Leena Siikala's thesis on *The Rite Technique of the Siberian Shaman*. This book was a successor to that of Shirokogoroff (1935), in that it focused on the details of the shamanic séance, but her analysis of the neuropsychology of trance states was both new and revelatory. Consisting of a massive compendium of seance descriptions with an analysis of the different kinds of altered states of consciousness that resulted, this work set a pattern of combined neurological and cultural studies of shamanism that is still followed today.

Whitley (2005: ch. 7) provides a useful, contextualized, and well-referenced overview of the neuropsychological model, though with a tendency to smooth over the critique that was soon levelled against it. Much of the opposition to these interpretations has been unhelpfully vitriolic and unconstructive, and potentially positive academic differences have been displaced by deliberate confrontation (it seems invidious to quote examples, but they are easy to find; to give the flavour, some of those involved in these arguments have been dubbed respectively 'shamaniacs' and 'shamanophobes'). In negotiating a middle path there is little doubt that claims for evidence of shamanic signals in archaeological assemblages have occasionally—and more frequently in recent years—been overstated, but by the same token rejections of shamanic interpretations have sometimes been based on little more than Pavlovian dismissal. The case against the 'mind in the cave' has been most coherently made in a number of papers assembled in Francfort and Hamayon (2001), but while some valid points have been made about the necessity for trance states in shamanism (see below) the neuropsychologists have been wrongly accused of presenting a monolithic idea and a one-size-fits-all argument for hunter-gatherer religion, when in fact the core model proposed for the European Palaeolithic is both nuanced and cautiously defined.

It is clear that no consensus has been reached on these questions, but equally the argument for at least *some* component of visionary experience in the creation of Upper Palaeolithic 'art' remains a powerful one. The case for a neuropsychological basis for these cultural manifestations is also strong, and has potential for very broad application in the study of human spirituality and cognition. Importantly, the identification of widespread manifestations of shamanic practice—above all in the circumpolar sphere—can be independently verified, and this would support the existence of a hard-wired cognitive platform behind them. For the Palaeolithic, this material focuses *inter alia* on a variety of decorated portable art showing transformed individuals, therianthropic figures, animal sculptures, and the first evidence of burial ritual (Dowson and Porr 2001; Aldhouse-Green and Aldhouse-Green 2005: ch. 2).

A key problem in the context of Palaeolithic shamanism, however, is the role played by ecstatic experience, trance and other forms of ASC as the arguable core of shamanic practice. Their status as primary requisites for a shamanic definition derives from the text that has undoubtedly come to dominate perceptions of these belief systems in Western research, Mircea Eliade's *Shamanism: Archaic techniques of ecstasy*, first published in French in 1951 and continuously in print ever since. Almost all subsequent work has been drawn into the orbit of Eliade's book, and despite its shortcomings it is still the mostly widely used work of reference for those working in disciplines *outside* the specific study of religion. This is significant, because in practice very few comparative theologists or anthropologists rely on this work any longer, partly because of the narrow field on which it focuses, and partly because it has quite simply been superseded by a great many other publications.

Other authors have pushed Eliade's definitions of ecstatic religion into new territory, not least extending the shamanic definition to a global scale and over vast spans of time, and we find this focus in the generalizing definitions of shamanism that are still frequently employed: 'we may define the shaman as a social functionary who, with the help of guardian spirits, attains ecstasy in order to create a rapport with the supernatural world on behalf of his [*sic*] group members' (Hultkrantz 1973: 34; see also Lewis 1989). The problematic focus on ecstasy, ultimately deriving, we must remember, from a work written in the 1950s, is also the primary reason why the modern, popular definitions of shamanism are so broad, extending far beyond what many anthropologists would accept. This kind of lassitude also has other manifestations, particularly in relation to the kinds of stimulants used to enter ASC, as when scholars have ignored serious differences between narcotics, hallucinogens, the rather nebulous category of entheogens—more anthropological construct than medical classification—and indeed many other kinds of mind-altering substances (Rudgely 1999 provides a useful overview).

Importantly, it has begun to be acknowledged that alongside trance and ecstasy there are also many variants of these traditions, even in Siberia, where the shamanic communion is constructed through rituals rather than directly altered states of consciousness—this is another of the key areas that the archaeology of shamanism can illuminate, in recovering the material correlates of these performances.

4 SIBERIAN SHAMANISM AND THE POPULATING OF THE AMERICAS

One important effect of the debate on cognition and rock art has been a new focus on the geographical origins of shamanism. The supporting evidence for some kind of consistent pattern of spiritual belief, practice, and material culture across the circumpolar region is overwhelming, existing alongside a natural variation within these societies. In part this is an environmentally determinist model, which ultimately goes back to 1965 when Åke Hultkrantz first began to develop his concept of religio-ecology as a factor in the formation of the arctic belief systems. In this he followed Ohlmarks, but added that the ecological model was dynamic, 'changing with climatic fluctuations and historical developments' (1965: 286 and references therein). This remains a dominant model in shamanic studies (e.g. Pentikäinen 1996).

However, the archaeological support for the idea of a circumpolar shamanic complex is very clear. In general we can cite the very widespread use of special objects such as drums, as well as details of costume and even architecture (e.g. Gulløv and Appelt 2001). Even extended patterns of shamanic behaviour have left traces across this area, as in the prevalence of bear ceremonies and ursine burials that take strikingly similar form in many cultures over vast distances (e.g. among the Sámi: Zachrisson and Iregren 1974; and Mulk and Iregren 1995; the Finns: Pentikäinen 2007; the Scandinavians: Price 2002: ch. 5; and Näsström 2006; and the Ainu: Fitzhugh and Dubreuil 1999; for general comparisons, see Edsman 1994).

There are also more clearly quantified data. One example comes from the work of Karl Schlesier (1987: 45–9), who in studying Tsistsista (Cheyenne) religion has demonstrated an astonishing 108 direct parallels with features of Siberian shamanism. Considering the spatial distances involved, this has profound implications for cultural continuity over a very long time period indeed. The same conclusion can be reached through studies of cosmological ideas such as the 'world support', manifested as either a tree, pillar, post, or nail that holds up the cosmos. In material form it is depicted in various ways, for example on totem poles, and Hultkrantz has shown that the idea is found all across the circumpolar zone. He concludes that 'the world pillar, we may insist, genuinely represents an archaic, circumpolar world-view. Since circumpolar culture, besides being an adaptation to the Arctic and sub-Arctic environment, typifies a culture of Mesolithic-Palaeolithic origins it seems probable that the world pillar and its associated mythic-ritual complex may be traced back to this time and age' (Hultkrantz 1996: 43; see also Price 2002: ch. 5, and 2009). But where did these ideas originate?

The traditionally accepted answer, current since the eighteenth century, is that Siberia and Northern Asia may be regarded as the proverbial 'cradle of shamanism', and as we have seen above, some scholars go so far as to argue that in its 'pure' form (whatever that actually is) it is *only* found here. But to what degree does this argument depend on the historical accident that the shamanic complex was first observed and recorded here, and thereby that the artificial construct of shamanism was named after a Siberian word?

In a series of important works, the Californian archaeologist David Whitley has presented a steadily increasing body of case studies of rock art from the western United States that he has persuasively argued represent a range of shamanic traditions (overviews can be found in Whitley 2000 and 2004: 18–20, with a full list of relevant works given in Whitley 2005: 110, 202–4). In relation to this he has observed that the archaeological datings for shamanic rock art and related artefacts in the Americas are *earlier* than those from Siberia (Whitley 2009). The implications of this are profound, as it directly contradicts the received wisdom that shamanic practices, where they can be said (or claimed) to exist in the Americas, must have arrived as part of the sociocultural baggage of the first settlers moving into the New World through Beringia from what is now Siberia. If Whitley is right, then Siberian shamanism may actually have originated in the Americas, carried west as part of a long process of travel and exchange. Whichever view proves to be correct, the notion of complex interactions across Beringia seems far more sensible than a simple 'migration' in one direction. If we follow a neuropsychological model, then there is also no reason why shamanism cannot have developed independently along discrete trajectories of local cultural traditions in different places at different times (e.g. Winkelman 1992). There is as yet little consensus in this debate, but the controversy represents one of the most significant contributions that the archaeology of shamanism has made to broader prehistoric studies.

5 MESOLITHIC AND NEOLITHIC MIND-SETS

Mesolithic ritual offers no evidence as dramatic as the Palaeolithic 'art', and attempts to place shamanism in its mental toolkit have necessarily been limited to artefactual hypotheses. In this vein the antler frontlets found at the Mesolithic site of Star Carr in Britain have often been interpreted as some kind of shaman's costume on the basis of rather nebulous comparisons with earlier images like the so-called 'sorcerer' at the cave of Les Trois Frères in the Pyrenees and Celtic folk tales of the 'horned god' (Aldhouse-Green and Aldhouse-Green 2005 effectively survey these ideas). Some scholars have constructed much more comprehensive visions of Mesolithic shamanic societies, weaving together evidence from a variety of sources and heavily reliant on ethnographic analogy (e.g. Strassburg's 2000 study of Southern Scandinavia).

Shamanic manifestations have been more successfully sought in the Eurasian Neolithic, partly following neuropsychological models and the study of entopic forms, most dramatically in the rock carvings found both in the open air and in the entryways of the great Irish passage-tombs (Bradley 1989; Dronfield 1994, 1995, 1996). The stimulus for the visions thus inscribed has been sought in a variety of sources, first by Sherratt (1987, 1991) in his groundbreaking suggestion that the agriculture of the Neolithic revolution made possible the brewing of mind-altering alcohol in large quantities, with considerable implications for the changing nature of ritual practice. The potential that this afforded for increased social control of religion has been extensively debated (Lewis-Williams and Dowson 1993; Hayden 2003; a useful review of the evidence is presented by Aldhouse-Green and Aldhouse-Green 2005: ch. 3).

Building on this in combination with the neuropsychological reading of the early Stone Age, Lewis-Williams and Pearce (2005) have combined all these ideas to present a bold vision of Neolithic belief that ultimately emerged from hunter-gatherer communities to embrace the kinds of settled, complex societies found at Catalhöyük and Göbekli Tepe in modern Turkey. The presence of shamanism in state-based societies will be discussed further below.

6 ARENAS OF ACTION

Beyond these large-scale interpretations, archaeology has been used as a point of access for many aspects of shamanic behaviour and practice, even the process by which shamans become who they are. Shamanic initiations are a constant of the ethnographies (see Vitebsky 1995 for an effective review), and have been traced in rock engravings argued to replicate the paths taken by the mind on these mental journeys, for example in Australia (Sales 1992). Attempts have similarly been made to perceive shamanic cosmologies of tiered worlds in other carving traditions, such as those of the Scandinavian Bronze Age (Aldhouse-Green and Aldhouse-Green 2005: ch. 4).

It has also been possible to approach even the most intangible elements of ritual through archaeology. The role of sound and song is crucial in ethnographic accounts of shamanic performance, to the extent of forming the language of communication between the shaman and the denizens of other worlds. It has also been argued that this may be the longest-lived aspect of these ideas, and that the 'last breathing' of a dying language may be found in the sacred codes of shamanic ritual (Niemi 2001, building on Kuusi's ideas of the Stone Age origin of shaman songs; see also Siikala 1990). Though naturally harder to detect archaeologically, there have been intriguing links made between the acoustic properties of specific areas of caves and the location of Palaeolithic paintings, suggesting that sound may have played a role in their creation (Reznikoff and Dauvois 1988; Scarre 1989). Similar work has been done around Neolithic monuments including chambered tombs, showing that these places were designed with acoustic properties that actually facilitate the entering of ASC (Watson 2001).

Another important development is a tendency to shift research emphasis from process to practitioners, with a special focus now most often placed on shamanism in its social context (an approach first formally introduced by Lewis in 1981). As early as 1914, Czaplicka could perceive a chronological evolution from what she called 'family shamanism', in which the rituals were organized communally and within the household as need arose, to the later 'professional' system familiar from the early European ethnographic accounts. The broad range of personal and cultural connotations of the shamanic complex have led some researchers to seek less dogmatic terminologies, preferring to speak of 'shamanship' or 'shamanhood' (e.g. Atkinson 1989; Ripinsky-Naxon 1993; Pentikäinen 2001). These in turn link to themes of communication and reception, and the role that these practices play within, between, and outside communities.

The locus of the shaman's authority has come in for particular scrutiny in its assumption of supernatural power through a complex interplay of culture and politics, crucially expressed through the medium of personhood—the individual qualities, experience, and personality of each shaman. Particularly interesting work has been done on this in Siberia, by Vitebsky (2005) and Willerslev (2001, 2007). Here, animals are regarded not just as vessels for spirits but actually as 'persons' that are in some ways equal to—and at times even interchangeable with—humans. This has links with another key area of archaeological and anthropological research on shamanism, concerning its gender implications. The circumpolar records in particular suggest that border-crossing sexual identities were a fundamental ingredient of the shamanic experience, in terms of both behaviour and material culture, to the extent that in some societies the shaman seems equivalent to a gender category in itself (the earliest examples come from the Jesop ethnographies mentioned above, especially those of Bogoraz and Jochelson, but there are numerous other detailed case studies; Saladin d'Anglure's works from 1986–92 on Inuit shamanism provide perhaps the most in-depth analysis of this kind, but see also Lang 1998; Hollimon 2001; Price 2002: ch. 5). In becoming 'transformed' in this way, shamans gain special powers that facilitate the other processes of elision that characterize their performances.

This concept of mutability may go further still in a general fluidity of body as well as sex and its signals, including the blurring of distinctions between humans and animals (for two alternative views of these ideas as they play out in the archaeology of later Iron Age 'shamanism' in Scandinavia, see Price 2002 and Back-Danielsson 2007). The centrality of an animist world view to shamanic thought has been mentioned above, but alongside this we can trace a second strand of enquiry that explores the links between shamanism and another, equally hotly debated anthropological construct, namely totemism (discussed elsewhere in this volume, Insoll Ch. 62; see Layton 2000 for a critical review of the archaeological discussion). Though the totemic concept is now rarely employed by anthropologists, the flexible nature of animal–human identities remains a crucial part of any shamanic analysis (see Sutherland 2001 for an extended example from the high arctic).

Another aspect of this personalized level of work has been a focus on 'bodylore', deriving from Pentikäinen's definition of shamanism as 'a grammar of mind and body'. This holistic approach emphasizes the notion of shamanism as narrative performance, in which the shaman employs a deep knowledge of folklore and traditional learning within a diverse range of social roles. The key element is seen here to be the pact of responsibility entered into by the shaman with her or his community, and with the world of the spirits. This whole complex is encapsulated in the shaman's function as an embodied human repository of the knowledge required for the community to survive—culturally and spiritually as well as literally (Pentikäinen 1996, the introduction to which provides a particularly effective survey, 1998; Pentikäinen et al. 1998). It has been taken further by Price (2008) to argue that the bodylore of individual shamans represents their personal skills and techniques in physical form, akin to a ritual version of an athlete's muscle memory. Importantly, knowledge acquired, developed, and transmitted in this way need not necessarily be articulated or understood even by its possessor, taking shamanism even further away from a religious definition.

The importance of place has been noted above in relation to acoustics, but this can also apply to whole landscapes of shamanism. Peter Jordan's work with the Khanty (2001a and b, 2003) has shown how a combined network of spirits and supernatural forces encoded in the natural landscape forms a kind of sacred geography, in which the habitus of the community encodes spatial perceptions with spiritual meaning. Similar features have also been noted in the shamanic landscapes of the Nepal Himalayas (Walter 2001), and there is often a marked tendency towards liminal locations for the arenas of shamanic performance, as Bradley (2000) has noted for Sámi rituals. It is clearly in such landscape contexts that the earlier focus on animism makes most sense, as the shamans situate themselves in the midst of the 'ensouled world'. But what did shamans *do*?

The problematic legacy of Eliade's work has been mentioned above, and has also given rise to the common popular (and academic) association of shamanism almost exclusively with healing, despite the very clear evidence of specialized practices for aggressive ends. The sentiment has perhaps been expressed most succinctly by the Nivkh ethnographer Chuner Taksami, himself descended from a line of shamans, when he stated that, 'in Siberia, the drum is a weapon' (pers. comm. 2002). Added to this, we must also remember the prominence of sexual elements in the rituals. These two traits of violence and sexuality are so common among the rituals of the arctic and subarctic peoples that it is these, rather than the healing functions, which might actually be said to be typical of shamanism in the circumpolar region. Shamans were clearly people to be feared, whose glance was to be avoided and in whose presence it was difficult to be comfortable.

Shamanism has been viewed in a hunter-gatherer context as a system to cope with the need to take (animal) life in order to live oneself. In state-based societies this innate aggression takes on different overtones, as in the case of Viking Age Scandinavia where shamanism seems to have been used to provide a ritual and spiritual resource for war. Here, up to 40 different categories of shamans, bound by strict gender codes as elsewhere in the north, performed an equally broad range of tasks for their elite patrons—most commonly predicting the future and casting spells on the battlefield (Price 2002). Glosecki has argued for the same beliefs among the pagan Anglo-Saxons, visible in what he calls the 'reflexes' of shamanism. These, he contends, 'though fragmentary and widely dispersed, are too pervasive to be explained without reference to a vigorous shamanic tradition current at some point in Germanic prehistory' (Glosecki 1989: 1). For the Viking Age, this phase of shamanic 'half-life' is perhaps what was occurring in the early centuries of the High Medieval period, the time of the sagas' composition.

In Europe, there may be very long antecedents for these individuals. Classical sources mention seeresses of this kind in both Greek and Roman contexts, and also amongst what they saw as the barbarian tribes in Germania; these too have left their archaeological trace in the form of sanctuaries and offerings, together with the personal paraphernalia of these individuals. Aldhouse-Green and Aldhouse-Green (2005: chs. 5–7) have attempted to follow the roots of these traditions deep into the European Iron Age, using the evidence of sacrifices and,

FIGURE 61.3 Shamanism, syncretism, and the state: This woman lived in a firmly sedentary, agrarian, and state-based society, and was buried in the Swedish Viking town of Birka. She is marked out as a probable *völva*—the Norse equivalent of a shaman—by her exotic jewellery, clothing, and iron staff, laid here across her midriff and described in numerous Icelandic texts as the tool of a sorcerer. Alongside amulets with pagan significance, the dead woman also wears on her necklace the first crucifix known from Scandinavia—presumably as a syncretic object of power alongside the others. Birka chamber grave Bj.660, mid-tenth century AD.

amongst other finds, the bodies of humans killed and deposited in the bogs of the north-west. Beliefs in animal transformations may even be detectable in the graves, as Williams (2001) has argued in the mixture of cremated humans and domesticates in early Anglo-Saxon burials, combining their natures to make a new being for the world of the dead.

In East Asia, shamanism has even been argued to have played a fundamental role in the actual development of state-based societies. Nelson (2008) sees the roots of leadership in states such as early China, Korea, and Japan as an outgrowth of the roles played by shamans, with a very clear importance attached to female elites. The process can also work in reverse, and another key research theme is the gradual decline of shamanism under various forms of cultural stress. This was especially apparent in Siberia under the Soviet regime but occurred to a greater or lesser degree all over the world. The problem of what happened to shamanic societies when the shamanic institution itself began to fade was obvious early on, and had become apparent even by the time of the Jesup expedition. When Jochelson visited the Koryak, for example, he found only two shamans, and it was clear to him that their former power as a professional class was all but gone (1908: 49).

Caroline Humphrey's ethnographic work has made a crucial contribution here (Humphrey 1983), but several other scholars have also explored the shamanic aftermath. There have been various terms coined for such a phenomenon, equivalent to the 'post-shamanism' that Håkan Rydving studied among the Sámi (1987, 1993). Anthropologist Rane Willerslev (2001: 49), working with material culture among the Yukaghirs, writes of a 'shamanistic approach to life', in which the roles and functions of the shaman become secularized in their material representations but maintained within an approximation of the traditional world view. Sometimes foreign religious elements, such as Christianity, can be imposed upon this, but are more often merely adopted in name and adapted to local requirements (see a range of examples in Pentikäinen 1998).

7 Conclusions and Future Research Directions

Looking to the future, it seems clear from current work that the search for rigid definitions of shamanic practices is slowly being abandoned, and that such proscriptions are steadily being recognized for the follies that they are. We may expect to see lively debate around the chronological and geographical origins of shamanic concepts, reviving not only the controversies around Palaeolithic spirituality but also the emergence of human cognitive structures. Whitley's suggestion of an American core area for shamanic belief systems is also sure to stimulate much discussion, not least among Russian and Far Eastern scholars.

The study of shamanism must be freed from its straitjacketed comparison with the world's modern faith-based religions. As archaeologists we must acknowledge the dynamic nature of the shamanic concept, manifested in different ways at different times and places, and with varying degrees of social emphasis, including the operation of shamans alongside other spiritual specialists. We still need to urgently understand more about the individual artefactual repertoires of shamans within these varied traditions around the world and the materiality of bodylore mentioned above.

It can be argued that a true archaeology of shamanism needs to be all-embracing, examining not just an illusorily discrete corpus of 'ritual' material culture but in fact the total social environment as meaningfully constructed by any given community. If shamanism is nothing less than a view of the world, then it is necessarily maintained and developed by all the human and material actors that inhabit it. Archaeology's potential to access this world has few limits, embracing the material contexts of symbolic storage, portable culture, sexuality and gender, war and aggression, leadership, community and social structure, landscape, subsistence strategies, and mortuary behaviour. In pursuing these paths of evidence we will be well on the way to deeper and more nuanced perceptions of prehistoric spiritualities than anything so far seen.

Suggested Reading

Both the available and historic literature on shamanism is vast: as an example, Popov's 1932 bibliography of merely the Tsarist and early Soviet works on the subject ran to nearly 650 books, in a list that terminated more than 70 years ago. A few key texts must, however, be mentioned. The classic early overviews of shamanism as a belief system, and milestones in the development of the concept, include works such as the reports from the Jesup Expedition by Bogoras (1904–9) and Jochelson (1908, 1926), and regional studies by Czaplicka (1914) and Shirokogoroff (1935). Later syntheses of importance include those by Edsman (1967), Motzki (1971), and Furst (1974), while a selection of Hultkrantz's many publications have been cited above. Retrospective reviews of changing fashions of interpretation, and more recent responses to them, can be found in the international journal of shamanic research, *Shaman*, and in a series of influential conference publications from the last three decades (e.g. Diószegi and Hóppal 1978; Hóppal 1984; Hóppal and von Sadovszky 1989; Hóppal and Pentikäinen 1992; Siikala and Hóppal 1992; Hóppal and Howard 1993). Significant syntheses of recent years include those by Saladin d'Anglure (1996), Bowie (2000: 190–218), Larsson (2000), Price (2002: ch. 5), Harvey (2003), Stutley (2003), and Walter and Fridman (2004). While material culture is taken up in all the above works to a greater or lesser degree, strictly archaeological syntheses have been fewer in number. The primary summaries to date have been published by Price (2001), Pearson (2002), Hayden (2003), Whitley (2004) and Aldhouse-Green and Aldhouse-Green (2005), the latter including a good bibliography of key works.

References

ALDHOUSE-GREEN, M. and ALDHOUSE-GREEN, S. 2005. *The Quest for the Shaman: Shapeshifters, sorcerers and spirit-healers of ancient Europe* (London and New York: Thames and Hudson).

ATKINSON, J. M. 1989. *The Art and Politics of Wana Shamanship* (Berkeley: University of California Press).

BACK-DANIELSSON, I.-M. 2007. *Masking Moments: The transitions of bodies and beings in Late Iron Age Scandinavia* (Stockholm: University of Stockholm).

BAHN, P. G. and VERTUT, J. 1988. *Images of the Ice Age* (London: Windward).
BANZAROV, D. 1891. *Chernaja Vira ili shamanstvo u Mongolov* (St Petersburg).
BOGORAS, W. 1904-9. *The Chukchee*, Publications of the Jesup North Pacific Expedition, VII, American Museum of Natural History (Leiden: Brill).
BOWIE, F. 2000. *The Anthropology of Religion* (Oxford: Blackwell).
BRADLEY, R. 1989. 'Deaths and entrances: A contextual study of megalithic art', *Current Anthropology*, 30: 68–75.
—— 2000. *An Archaeology of Natural Places* (London and New York: Routledge).
CASTRÉN, M. A. 1853. *Vorlesungen über die finnische Mythologie*, Nordische Reisen und Forschungen, III (St Petersburg: Kaiserlichen Akademie der Wissenschaften).
CHIPPINDALE, C., SMITH, B., and TAÇON, P. S. C. 2000. 'Visions of dynamic power: Archaic rock paintings, altered states of consciousness and "Clever Men" in Western Arnhem Land', *Cambridge Archaeological Journal*, 10(1): 63–101.
CLOTTES, J. and LEWIS-WILLIAMS, J. D. 1996. *Les chamanes de la préhistoire: transe et magie dans les grottes ornées* (Paris: Éditions du Seuil).
CZAPLICKA, M. A. 1914. *Aboriginal Siberia: A study in social anthropology* (Oxford: Clarendon).
DEVLET, E. 2001. 'Rock art and the material culture of Siberian and Central Asian shamanism' in N. S. Price (ed.), *The Archaeology of Shamanism* (London: Routledge), pp. 43–55.
DIÓSZEGI, V. and HÓPPAL, M. (eds) 1978. *Shamanism in Siberia* (Budapest: Akadémiai Kiadó).
DIXON, R. B. 1908. 'Some aspects of the American shaman', *Journal of American Folkore*, 21: 1–12.
DOWSON, T. A. and PORR, M. 2001. 'Special objects—special creatures: Shamanistic imagery and the Aurignacian art of southwest Germany' in N. S. Price (ed.), *The Archaeology of Shamanism* (London: Routledge), pp. 165–77.
DRONFIELD, J. 1994. *Subjective Visual Phenomena in Irish Passage-tomb Art: Vision, cosmology and shamanism*, unpublished PhD thesis, University of Cambridge, Cambridge.
—— 1995. 'Subjective vision and the source of Irish megalithic art', *Antiquity*, 69: 539–49.
—— 1996. 'Entering alternative realities: Cognition, art and architecture in Irish passage-tombs', *Cambridge Archaeological Journal*, 6: 37–72.
EDSMAN, C.-M. (ed.) 1967. *Studies in Shamanism* (Stockholm: Almqvist and Wiksell).
—— 1994. *Jägaren och makterna: samiska och finska björnceremonier* (Uppsala: ULMA).
ELIADE, M. 1989 [1951]. *Shamanism: Archaic techniques of ecstasy* (London: Arkana).
FITZHUGH, W. W. and DUBREUIL, C. O. (eds) 1999. *Ainu: Spirit of a northern people* (Washington DC: Smithsonian Press).
FLAHERTY, G. 1992. *Shamanism and the Eighteenth Century* (Princeton: Princeton University Press).
FRANCFORT, H.-P. and HAMAYON, R. N. (eds) 2001. *The Concept of Shamanism: Uses and abuses* (Budapest: Akadémiai Kiadó).
FURST, P. 1974. 'The roots and continuities of shamanism', *ArtsCanada*, 184/7: 33–50.
GLOSECKI, S. O. 1989. *Shamanism and Old English Poetry* (New York: Garland).
GULLØV, H.-C. and APPELT, M. 2001. 'Social bonding and shamanism among Late Dorset groups in high arctic Greenland' in N. S. Price (ed.), *The Archaeology of Shamanism* (London: Routledge), pp. 146–64.
HARVEY, G. (ed.) 2003. *Shamanism: A reader* (London and New York: Routledge).
HAYDEN, B. 2003. *Shamans, Sorcerers and Saints: A prehistory of religion* (Washington, DC: Smithsonian Press).

HOLLIMON, S. E. 2001. 'The gendered peopling of North America: Addressing the antiquity of systems of multiple genders' in N. S. Price (ed.), *The Archaeology of Shamanism* (London: Routledge), pp. 123-34.

HÓPPAL, M. (ed.) 1984. *Shamanism in Eurasia* (Göttingen: Herodot).

——and HOWARD, K. (eds) 1993. *Shamans and Cultures* (Budapest: Akadémiai Kiadó).

——and PENTIKÄINEN, J. (eds) 1992. *Northern Religions and Shamanism* (Budapest: Akadémiai Kiadó).

——and VON SADOVSZKY, O. (eds) 1989. *Shamanism Past and Present*, 2 vols. (Budapest: Ethnographic Institute).

HULTKRANTZ, Å. 1965. 'Types of religion in the arctic hunting cultures: A religio-ecological approach' in H. Hvarfner (ed.), *Hunting and Fishing: Nordic symposium on life in a traditional hunting and fishing milieu in prehistoric times up to the present day* (Luleå: Norrbottens Museum), pp. 265-318.

——1973. 'A definition of shamanism', *Temenos*, 9: 25-37.

——1996. 'A new look at the world pillar in Arctic and sub-Arctic religions' in J. Pentikäinen (ed.), *Shamanism and Northern Ecology* (Berlin: Mouton de Gruyer), pp. 31-49.

——1998. 'On the history of research in shamanism' in J. Pentikäinen, T. Jaatinen, I. Lehtinen, and M.-R. Saloniemi (eds), *Shamans* (Tampere: Tampere Museum), pp. 51-70.

——1989. *Ecstatic religion: a study of shamanism and spirit possession*. 2nd edn (London: Routledge).

HUMPHREY, C. 1983. *Karl Marx Collective: Economy, society and religion in a Siberian collective farm* (Cambridge: Cambridge University Press).

HUTTON, R. 2001. *Shamans: Siberian spirituality and the Western imagination* (London: Hambledon and London).

JOCHELSON, W. 1908. *The Koryak*, Publications of the Jesup North Pacific Expedition, VI, American Museum of Natural History (Leiden: Brill).

——1926. *The Yukaghir and the Yukaghirized Tungus*, Publications of the Jesup North Pacific Expedition, IX, American Museum of Natural History (Leiden: Brill).

JORDAN, P. 2001a. 'The materiality of shamanism as a "world-view": Praxis, artefacts and landscape' in N. S. Price (ed.), *The Archaeology of Shamanism* (London: Routledge), pp. 87-104.

——2001b. 'Cultural landscapes of colonial Siberia: Khanty settlements of the sacred, the living and the dead', *Landscapes Journal*, 2(2): 83-105.

——2003. *Material Culture and Sacred Landscape: The anthropology of the Siberian Khanty* (Walnut Creek, CA: AltaMira).

KENDALL, L. and KRUPNIK, I. (eds) 2003. *Constructing Cultures Then and Now: Celebrating Franz Boas and the Jesup North Pacific Expedition* (Washington, DC: Smithsonian Arctic Studies Center).

KRUPNIK, I. and FITZHUGH, W. W. (eds) 2001. *Gateways: Exploring the legacy of the Jesup North Pacific Expedition, 1897-1902* (Washington DC: Smithsonian Arctic Studies Center).

LANG, S. 1998. *Men as Women, Women as Men: Changing gender in Native American cultures* (Austin: University of Texas Press).

LARSSON, T. P. (ed.) 2000. *Schamaner: essäer om religiösa mästare* (Falun: Nya Doxa).

LAYTON, R. 2000. 'Shamanism, totemism and rock art: "Les chamanes de la préhistoire" in the context of rock art research', *Cambridge Archaeological Journal*, 10(1): 169-86.

LEWIS, I. M. 1981. 'What is a shaman?', *Folk*, 23: 25-35.

——1989. *Ecstatic religion: a study of shamanism and spirit possession*. 2nd edn (London: Routledge).
Lewis-Williams, J. D. 2002. *The Mind in the Cave: Consciousness and the origins of art* (London and New York: Thames and Hudson).
——and Dowson, T. A. 1988. 'The signs of all times: Entoptic phenomena in Upper Palaeolithic art', *Current Anthropology*, 29: 201–45.
————1993. 'On vision and power in the Neolithic: Evidence from the decorated monuments', *Current Anthropology*, 34: 55–65.
——and Pearce, D. G. 2005. *Inside the Neolithic Mind* (London and New York: Thames and Hudson).
Motzki, H. 1971. *Schamanismus als Problem religionswissenschaftlicher Terminologia* (Köln: Brill).
Mulk, I.-M. and Iregren, E. 1995. *Björngraven i Karats. Arkeologisk undersökning* (Jokkmokk: Ájtte Svenskt Fjäll- och Samemuseum).
Näsström, B.-M. 2006. *Bärsärkarna: vikingatidens elitsoldater* (Stockholm: Norstedts).
Nelson, S. M. 2008. *Shamanism and the Origins of States: Spirit, power and gender in East Asia* (Walnut Creek, CA: Left Coast Press).
Niemi, J. 2001. 'Dream songs of the forest Nenets' in J. Pentikäinen (ed.), *Shamanhood: Symbolism and epic* (Budapest: Akadémiai Kiadó), pp. 135–54.
Nioradze, G. 1925. *Der Schamanismus bei den siberischen Völkern*. Stuttgart.
Ogden, D. 2008. *Night's Black Agents: Witches, wizards and the dead in the Ancient World* (London: Hambledon Continuum).
Ohlmarks, Å. 1939. *Studien zum Problem des Schamanismus* (Lund: University of Lund).
Pearson, J. L. 2002. *Shamanism and the Ancient Mind* (Walnut Creek, CA: AltaMira).
Pentikäinen, J. (ed.) 1996. *Shamanism and Northern Ecology* (Berlin: Mouton de Gruyer).
——1998. *Shamanism and Culture* (Helsinki: Etnika).
——(ed.) 2001. *Shamanhood: Symbolism and epic* (Budapest: Akadémiai Kiadó).
——2007. *Golden King of the Forest: Lore of the northern bear* (Helsinki: Etnika).
——et al. (eds) 1998. *Shamans* (Tampere: Tampere Museum).
Popov, A. A. 1990 [1932]. *Materialen zur Bibliographie der russischen Literatur über das Schamanentum der Völker Nordasiens* (Berlin: Schletzer).
Price, N. S. (ed.) 2001. *The Archaeology of Shamanism* (London: Routledge).
——2002. *The Viking Way: Religion and war in late Iron Age Scandinavia* (Uppsala: Uppsala University Press).
——2008. 'Bodylore and the archaeology of embedded religion: Dramatic licence in the funerals of the Vikings' in D. M. Whitley and K. Hays-Gilpin (eds), *Belief in the Past: Theoetical approaches to the archaeology of religion* (Walnut Creek, CA: Left Coast Press), pp. 143–65.
——2009. 'Beyond rock art: Archaeological interpretation and the shamanic frame' in G. Blundell and B. Smith (eds), *Seeing and Knowing: Ethnography and beyond in understanding rock-art* (Johannesburg: Witwatersrand University Press).
Reznikoff, I. and Dauvois, M. 1988. 'La dimension sonore des grottes ornées', *Bulletin de la Société Préhistorique Française*, 85(8): 238–46.
Ripinsky-Naxon, M. 1993. *The Nature of Shamanism: Substance and function of a religious metaphor* (Albany: SUNY Press).

ROZWADOWSKI, A. 2001. 'Sun gods or shamans? Interpreting the "solar-headed" petroglyphs of Central Asia' in N. S. Price (ed.), *The Archaeology of Shamanism* (London: Routledge), pp. 65–86.

—— and KOŚKO, M. M. (eds) 2002. *Spirits and Stones: Shamanism and rock art in Central Asia and Siberia* (Poznan: Instytut Wschodni UAM).

RUDGELY, R. 1999. *The Encyclopedia of Psychoactive Substances* (London: Abacus).

RYDVING, H. 1987. 'Shamanistic and postshamanistic terminologies in Saami (Lappish)' in T. Ahlbäck (ed.), *Saami Religion*, Scripta Instituti Donneriani Aboensis XII (Åbo: Donner Institute), pp. 185–207.

—— 1993. *The End of Drum-Time: Religious change among the Lule Saami, 1670s–1740s* (Uppsala: Uppsala University Press).

SALADIN D'ANGLURE, B. 1986. 'Du foetus au chamane: la construction d'un "troisième sexe" inuit', *Études Inuit Studies*, 10(1–2): 25–113.

—— 1988. 'Penser le "féminin" chamanique, ou le "tiers-sexe" des chamanes inuit', *Recherches Amérindiennes au Québec*, 18(2–3): 19–50.

—— 1989. 'La part du chamane ou le communisme sexuel inuit dans l'Arctique central Canadien', *Journal de la Société des Américanistes*, 75: 133–71.

—— 1992a. 'Le "troisième" sexe', *La Recherche*, 245(23): 836–44.

—— 1992b. 'Shamanism and transvestism among the Inuit of Canada' in A. I. Gogolev (ed.), *Shamanizm kak religiia* (Yakutsk: Yakutsk University), p. 18.

—— 1992c. 'Rethinking Inuit shamanism through the concept of "Third Gender"' in M. Hóppal and J. Pentikäinen (eds), *Northern Religions and Shamanism* (Budapest: Akadémiai Kiadó), pp. 146–50.

—— 1996. 'Shamanism' in A. Barnard and J. Spencer (eds), *Encyclopedia of Social and Cultural Anthropology* (London: Routledge), pp. 504–8.

SALES, K. 1992. 'Ascent to the sky: A shamanic initiatory engraving from the Burrup Peninsula, northwest Australia', *Archaeology in Oceania*, 27: 22–35.

SCARRE, C. 1989. 'Painting by resonance', *Nature*, 338: 382.

SCHLESIER, K. H. 1987. *The Wolves of Heaven: Cheyenne shamanism, ceremonies and prehistoric origins* (Norman and London: University of Oklahoma Press).

SHERRATT, A. 1987. 'Cups that cheered: The introduction of alcohol to prehistoric Europe' in W. Waldren and R. Kennard (eds), *Bell Beakers of the Western Mediterranean: The Oxford international conference 1986* (Oxford: BAR), pp. 81–106.

—— 1991. 'Sacred and profane substances: The ritual use of narcotics in later Neolithic Europe' in P. Garwood, D. Jennings, R. Skeates, and J. Toms (eds), *Sacred and Profane: Proceedings of a conference on archaeology, ritual and religion*, Monograph 32 (Oxford: Oxford University Committee for Archaeology), pp. 50–64.

SHIROKOGOROFF, S. M. 1935. *Psychomental Complex of the Tungus* (London: Kegan Paul, Trench and Trubner).

SIIKALA, A.-L. 1978. *The Rite Technique of the Siberian Shaman* (Helsinki: Academia Scientarum Fennica).

—— 1990. 'Singing of incantations in Nordic tradition' in T. Ahlbäck (ed.), *Old Norse and Finnish Religions and Cultic Place-names* (Åbo: Donner Institute), pp. 191–205.

—— and HÓPPAL, M. (eds) 1992. *Studies on Shamanism* (Helsinki: Finnish Anthropological Society).

STRASSBURG, J. 2000. *Shamanic Shadows: One hundred generations of undead subversion in southern Scandinavia, 7000–4000 BC* (Stockholm: University of Stockholm).

STUTLEY, M. 2003. *Shamanism: An introduction* (London and New York: Routledge).
SUTHERLAND, P. D. 2001. 'Shamanism and the iconography of Paleo-Eskimo art' in N. S. Price (ed.), *The Archaeology of Shamanism* (London: Routledge), pp. 135–45.
VITEBSKY, P. 1995. *The Shaman* (London: Macmillan).
—— 2005. *Reindeer People: Living with animals and spirits in Siberia* (London: Harper).
WALTER, D. 2001. 'The medium of the message: Shamanism as localised practice in the Nepal Himalayas' in N. S. Price (ed.), *The Archaeology of Shamanism* (London: Routledge), pp. 105–19.
WALTER, M. N. and FRIDMAN, E. J. N. (eds) 2004. *Shamanism: An encyclopedia of world beliefs, practices and culture*, 2 vols. (Santa Barbara: ABC-CLIO).
WATSON, A. 2001. 'The sounds of transformation: Acoustics, monument and ritual in the British Neolithic' in N. S. Price (ed.), *The Archaeology of Shamanism* (London: Routledge), pp. 178–92.
WHITLEY, D. S. 2000. *The Art of the Shaman: Rock art of California* (Salt Lake City: University of Utah Press).
—— 2004. 'Archaeology of shamanism' in M. N. Walter and E. J. N. Fridman (eds), *Shamanism: An encyclopedia of world beliefs, practices and culture*, 2 vols. (Santa Barbara: ABC-CLIO), pp. 16–21.
—— 2005. *Introduction to Rock Art Research* (Walnut Creek, CA: Left Coast Press).
—— 2009. *Cave Paintings and the Human Spirit: The origin of creativity and belief* (New York: Prometheus).
WILLERSLEV, R. 2001. 'The hunter as a human "kind": Hunting and shamanism among the Upper Kolyma Yukaghirs of Siberia' in T. A. Vestergaard (ed.), *North Atlantic Studies: Shamanism and traditional beliefs* (Aarhus: Centre for North Atlantic Studies, Aarhus University), pp. 44–50.
—— 2007. *Soul Hunters: Hunting, animism and personhood among the Siberian Yukaghirs* (Berkeley: University of California Press).
WILLIAMS, H. 2001. 'An ideology of transformation: Cremation rites and animal sacrifice in early Anglo-Saxon England' in N. S. Price (ed.), *The Archaeology of Shamanism* (London: Routledge), pp. 193–212.
WINKELMAN, M. 1992. *Shamans, Priests and Witches: A cross-cultural study of magico-religious practitioners* (Tempe: Arizona State University).
ZACHRISSON, I. and IREGREN, E. 1974. *Lappish Bear graves in Sweden: An archaeological and osteological study*, Early Norrland 5 (Stockholm: KVHAA).

CHAPTER 62

ANIMISM AND TOTEMISM

TIMOTHY INSOLL

1 INTRODUCTION

THE utility of the terms animism and totemism is questionable, and various anthropological observers have commented upon their problematical status and that of related terms such as 'ancestor worship' and 'shamanism'. Geertz (1966: 39), for example, has described all these terms when applied to religious traditions as denying their 'individuality' and as 'insipid categories by means of which ethnographers of religion devitalize their data'. Similarly Wendy James (1999: xv) has noted that 'such concepts as totem, taboo, animism, ancestor-worship, tribal gods, and so on... carry too much of a burden from older evolutionary thinking about religion'. Both are entirely fair criticisms. For 'totemism' and 'animism' were used to define religions themselves when in reality, if said to exist, they refer to phenomena that may or may not be present, and are usually contextualized by other religious phenomena, perhaps each other, or in relation to, for example, ancestor or earth cults in so-called 'tribal', 'primal', 'traditional', or preferably, 'indigenous' religions. They do not refer, as Ingold (2000: 112) notes, to 'coherent and explicitly articulated doctrinal systems' but are 'rather orientations that are deeply embedded in everyday practice'.

Equally, their linkage with early evolutionary approaches to religion is undeniable. E. B. Tylor (1929) and Emile Durkheim (1915), respectively, proposed that animism and totemism were the primal forms of religion. Their thinking reflected the obsessive search for origins and the impact of evolutionary theory that was current in scholarship at the end of the nineteenth and beginning of the twentieth century (Bolle 2005: 366–7). To 'animism' and 'totemism' could also be added 'fetishism' or 'preanimism' as other suggested primal religions. The concern of this entry is not with the origin and development of the terms, theories, and concepts surrounding animism and totemism in the study of religions or early anthropology. Instead their utilization and applicability within archaeological contexts will be the focus. However, it will be necessary to define what both animism and totemism mean and this is considered below.

2 ANIMISM: DEFINITION

Tylor's (1929) use of the term 'animism' refers to a theory of religion rather than a type of religion (Chidester 2005: 78). Its premise was that religion in its earliest form was characterized by ideas concerning a plurality of ghosts and spirits (Bolle 2005: 362; and see Stringer 1999 for a re-evaluation of Tylor's concept of 'animism'). Hence, the origins of religious belief were 'in the primordial mistake of attributing life, soul, or spirit to inanimate objects' (Chidester 2005: 78). Even today 'animism' is defined in the *Oxford Handy Dictionary* as 'attribution of living soul to inanimate objects and natural phenomena' (Fowler and Fowler 1986: 27). More recently animism has been reconsidered by various scholars; Bird-David (1999: S68), for instance, has contested the inadequacy of the concept of hunter-gatherer 'animism' and has argued that it has been viewed from modernist perspectives and rather should be theorized as 'animisms' and 'constitutes a relational (not a failed) epistemology'. This is not universally accepted (e.g. Morris 1999), and its validity in archaeological contexts perhaps needs further appraisal. Ingold (2000, 2006), likewise, has re-evaluated the concept of animism and argues that it is misleading to think of animism as 'a system of beliefs that imputes life or spirit to things that are truly inert' (Ingold 2006: 10). Instead he suggests it should be considered as having a transformative and dynamic potential 'within which beings of all kinds, more or less person-like or thing-like, continually and reciprocally bring one another into existence' (ibid.), i.e. constituting an 'animic ontology' (ibid.: 14). Whilst Viveiros de Castro (1998) has also considered 'animism' within the context of exploring 'perspectivism', which he defines as 'the ideas in Amazonian cosmologies concerning the way in which humans, animals and spirits see both themselves and one another' (ibid.: 469).

Using 'animism' to describe religions is untenable but it is still used by some contemporary groups, such as 'eco-pagans' to define their beliefs (Harvey 2005: 82–3). Elsewhere, using 'animism' and 'animists' now has almost pejorative connotations in setting up a simplistic juxtaposition with world religions as in West Africa where formerly it was used to describe followers of indigenous religions as opposed to those of Islam and Christianity (e.g. Trimingham 1968: 105, 1959: 21; Insoll 1996: 92). Although its application to describing religions is thus inappropriate, animism might be adapted as a term that can be utilized to describe religious phenomena but only if carefully defined and applied. This is perhaps a contentious assertion but 'animism' or rather the ascription of 'animistic' properties is perhaps a feature of, for instance, aspects of Tallensi beliefs in northern Ghana. Trees, for example, can be ascribed with elements of personification, through their potential function as the sitting place of ancestors; thus they can assume the status of an ancestral shrine (again indicating the interlocking of all these different religious elements—see Chapter 65, 'Ancestor Cults') but are not invested with personhood (Fortes 1987: 256; Insoll 2007a: 150).

Yet this raises the question as to whether this is even the ascription of 'animistic' concepts—for 'personification' is seemingly more applicable. Hence where used it may be preferable to think in terms of 'animistic' properties rather than 'animism' per se, though in truth its avoidance altogether is perhaps ultimately preferable in many contexts. Even attempting to 'question the authority of the western objectivist view of reality' rather than accepting 'a priori the nature/society dualism' (Bird-David 1999: S70) in relation to Tallensi beliefs still makes 'animism' no more comfortable to ascribe. Perhaps exploring emic/vernacular alternatives is applicable. In the Tallensi archaeological context in regard to both 'animism' and 'totemism' this is still to be explored and is beyond the confines of this chapter (but see Fortes 1945, 1987). Elsewhere more persuasive vernacular alternatives exist as with the Nigerian Yoruba concept of *Ase*, also from West Africa and parts of which seem to encompass 'animistic' type concepts as in Abiodun's (1995: 3) point that *'Ase* also pertains to the identification, activation and use of the innate energy believed to reside in all animals, plants, hills, rivers, human beings and *orisa*' (deities). However it is important to note that although *Ase* might encompass 'animism' or the ascription of animistic concepts, it also transcends them.

3 'Animism', 'Animistic' Concepts, and Archaeology

Suggesting the qualified use (if at all) of animistic concepts in certain carefully defined contexts is not synonymous with proposing the archaeology of animism. Such a concept is absurd. It is also impossible to provide clear archaeological case studies relating to either animism or animistic concepts in the same way that it might be for totemism (assuming that any archaeological interpretations are ever 'clear' in relation to ritual and religion). Marcus (2007: 51), for example, refers to the former existence of 'animatism' in Mesoamerican indigenous religion, but this appears to be more akin to 'animism', where 'the earth, hills, mountains, caves, stalactites, rocks, streams, lightning, wind, the sun, the moon, water, and many more things were all considered to be alive'. Similarly, in a dated study of prehistoric 'religions' heavily permeated with direct analogies, Lissner (1961: 263) refers to Siberian Tungus 'animism', where trees, rivers, animals, marshes, mountains, and physical objects all 'possess souls of their own', though in fairness he stresses that animism is not a religion, and does not project it onto archaeological materials. Bird-David (2006) has also explored why some hunter-gatherer groups do not depict animals in visual art. This is not written from an archaeological perspective but obviously relates to material culture and is thus of interest. She suggests that her chosen example, the so-called 'immediate-return' hunter-gatherers, omit animals as a correlate of 'an ontology which is inseparable from their animistic epistemology' (ibid.: 33).

Considering the paucity of direct examples instead it is perhaps preferable to consider, if it is at all relevant, the ascription of animistic concepts as phenomena potentially linked with all categories of materials, objects, and natural features. But this leads into determining whether there exists a danger of duplicating totemic relationships with materials, objects, and natural features. The answer to this would seem to be negative for the primary difference lies in the inherent social 'role' of totemism as described by Descola (1996: 87) in relation to their differing 'modes of identification', whereby animism endows natural beings with human social attributes and dispositions, but totemic classifications utilize observable discontinuities between natural species to bestow a conceptual order on society. Thus in archaeological contexts, the elusive nature of appropriate case studies might indicate the overall irrelevance of 'animism' as an applicable concept, or alternatively the need to further explore its relevance, allied with that of 'animistic' and perhaps 'animic' (Descola 1996: 94; Ingold 2000: 112) alternatives.

4 TOTEMISM: DEFINITION

'Animism' might have been the focus of recent debate (e.g. Bird-David 1999; Stringer 1999), but totemism has also been the subject of much discussion within the social sciences, in particular within the discipline of social anthropology both as to what it means, and if in fact it is a valid cross-culturally descriptive term for the range of phenomena it is often used to describe (Insoll 2008: 397). Hence various definitions of totemism exist but it is usually agreed that the word *totem* is derived from the Ojibwa, an Algonquin Native American ethnic group from north of the Great Lakes region in North America (Wagner 2005: 9250). Claude Lévi-Strauss (1964: 18), who has produced one of the most important works on totemism, *Totemism*, describes how the Ojibwa expression, *ototeman*, means, approximately, 'He(she) is a relative of mine'. This is significant for a useful and broad definition of totemism that could be suggested is that it refers to the use of plants or animals by social groups as guardians or emblems that are ritually celebrated (Layton 2000: 169), and in such a system different social groups are identified with different species (Insoll 2008: 397).

But it could be asked if the focus upon 'plants' and 'animals' is too restrictive. Evans-Pritchard (1956: 90) describes Nuer totems as 'an odd assortment' comprising, 'lion, waterbuck, monitor lizard, crocodile, various snakes, tortoise, ostrich, cattle egret, durra-birds, various trees, papyrus, gourd, various fish, bee, red ant, river and stream, cattle with certain markings, monorchids, hide, rafter, and rope; and, if we were to include totemistic objects, parts of beasts and some diseases'. Hence here we have a range of animals, insects, natural features, objects, and disease as totems suggesting that 'totemism' can transcend an animal/plant association. In so doing it is probably best to forgo the 'bare linking' of species with clans or other social groups, and recognize that totemic relations can also exist with parts of things and animals; tail, ears, feet, etc. as well as in homologous relation to each other (Weiner 1994: 600).

In general terms, totemism has gone through two distinct phases in how it has been considered by anthropologists (Wagner 2005: 9250). Initially, it was presented by scholars such as Émile Durkheim (1915) and Sir James Frazer (1910) within an evolutionary framework, i.e. that totemism was a unified and universal phenomenon and that it was a required state of religious belief through which all societies must proceed. The second is not so simplistic, and allows for variety in both the classificatory systems and symbolism evident in totemism in different cultural contexts. The latter is best represented, again, by the work of Claude Lévi-Strauss (1964; and see Weiner 1994; Wagner 2005 for relevant synthesis).

Today the term totemism is infrequently encountered in anthropology. Its evolutionary baggage has already been referred to, but it can be asked whether alternatives such as 'emblem' (Lienhardt 1961: 30–1) are universally preferable. Perhaps again it is a question of context for in some instances 'totem' might be better, and in others, 'emblem'. However, a potential solution, as with 'animism', is to use the emic/vernacular term, if such exists, though again in relation to most prehistoric archaeological contexts it obviously will not. Thus it would seem that recourse to qualification is required in clearly stating that material

A or B is perhaps indicative of something loosely resembling 'totemism', rather than being indicative *of* totemism. Alternatively, configuring relevant thinking in relation to archaeological materials in terms of pursuing ideas of metaphor or metonym offers another alternative, for as Weiner (1994: 597) notes, 'myth and totemism provide different avenues for the expansion of metaphor'. Tilley (1999: 23) considers how in totemic thought metaphorical transformations are culturally determined and his general approach to metaphor and material culture offers exciting possibilities for exploring relevant patterning in relation to archaeological materials. This is especially so in thinking about metaphorical understandings where metaphor serves as 'a binding element in providing an interpretative account of the world' and can 'also be conceived as a quality which links together individuals and groups' (Tilley 1999: 9). The potential for such an approach rather than admitting a strictly 'totemic' explanation is considered below in reinterpreting the ceramic figurines of Koma Land in northern Ghana.

A further alternative is to think of 'animism' and 'totemism' in the context of transformation, and how they might connect with, for example, concepts of the person, and interrelations with animals, substances, and things. Conneller (2004) ascribes neither concepts of 'animism' nor 'totemism' to the antler frontlets she discusses that were recovered from the Mesolithic site of Star Carr in Yorkshire, England, and dated to the tenth millennium BP. However, she clearly indicates how they might have had significance in peoples' thinking about animal and human identities, and how they could have been used in transforming the human body, and in making its boundaries ambiguous (ibid.: 48). To achieve this she uses and builds upon the work of, for example, Ingold (2000) and Viveiros de Castro (1998) already discussed in the context of 'animism'.

What is certain is that, as with exploring the potential of ascribing animistic concepts to archaeological contexts, thinking of totemism in the singular is flawed; where it or its cognates exist it interrelates with and is defined by other religious concepts and phenomena (Insoll 2007b: 326), be it in relation to Nuer religion (Evans-Pritchard 1956), or Tallensi religion (Fortes 1945, 1987), or Australian Aboriginal religions (Flood 1983; David 2002), all contexts in which the term 'totemism' has been employed. Evans-Pritchard (1956: 316) states this succinctly—'on one level Nuer religion may be regarded as monotheistic, at another level as polytheistic; and it can also be regarded at other levels as totemistic or fetishistic. These conceptions of spiritual activity are not incompatible. They are rather different ways of thinking of the numinous at different levels of experience.'

It might also be reasonable to suggest that totemism is sometimes subsumed within, usually erroneously, the category shamanism. Hence as a result of this, the religious beliefs and practices of hunter-gatherer communities, for instance, might be referred to almost exclusively as those of shamanism whilst totemism is largely suppressed or avoided. A good example of this is provided by Guenther's (1999) discussion of hunter-gatherer 'spirituality' that alludes to totemism in the title but then wholly ignores it in favour of shamanism. Layton (2000: 184) has referred to the shamanistic hypothesis as applied to rock art as 'a voracious beast', and this would seem an apt point to project out to the whole shamanic interpretive framework. This process might reflect the fads and fashions that scholarship like many other endeavours is subject to, and 'shamanism' is academically fashionable at present, whereas 'totemism' is not. Yet confusing the two or superimposing one upon the other is erroneous for the simple reason that totemism refers to a phenomena, even if reduced crudely to a socially symbolic relationship, whereas shamanism primarily refers to a role, that of the shaman. Hence the totem is not equivalent to the shaman.

5 TOTEMISM AND ARCHAEOLOGY

A correlate of the absence of totemism in archaeological thinking is that dedicated studies concerned with the archaeology of totemism in contrast to shamanism (Price 2001) are lacking. However, this does not mean archaeologists have neglected totemism. Burl (1981: 54, 56) for example interprets totemism in various British prehistoric contexts as in explaining the presence of the remains of an ox at the Neolithic sites of Fussell's Lodge, a long barrow, seven ox skulls at Bole's Barrow, or four heaps of jaw bones from young pigs at Hanging Grimston, the latter interpreted as a collapsed and burnt mortuary house dated to c.3540 BC. Totemism is similarly proposed to account for 24 dog skulls recorded along with 5 human skulls in the Cuween tomb at Maes Howe in the Orkney Islands, Scotland (ibid.: 115). Burl does not go for singular explanations but sees totemism functioning alongside ancestor cults or shamanism. He correctly recognizes religious complexity even if the interpretations proposed are somewhat simplistic as in the far-fetched equivalences made between the variety of faunal remains—skua, crow, cormorant, buzzard, guillemot—at Mid Howe, also in the Orkney Islands, and the existence of a naming system reminiscent of a native American one, and thus his inference that 'it is likely that they had totemistic beliefs similar to those of the Indians [sic]' (Burl 1981: 116).

Both totemism and animism have also been included within resurrected evolutionary sequences proposed to explain the development of religions. Mithen (1998: 202), for instance, has suggested that cognitive developments seemingly indicate that totemism and anthropomorphic thought developed as early as c.100,000 years ago as a result of the integration of social and natural history intelligence. Then, c.60,000–30,000 years ago, the addition of technical knowledge to this cognitive cocktail gave rise to animism, leading to Mithen's confident assertion that 'religious ideologies as complex as those of modern hunter-gatherers came into existence at the time of the Middle/Upper Palaeolithic transition and have remained with us ever since' (ibid.). The problems with cognitive processualist approaches to religion in which Mithen's model sits, have been described elsewhere (Insoll 2004: 92–7). It is an interesting argument, but the type of universalizing perspective employed, 'i.e. a defining "hey-presto" moment of religious complexity subsequent to a number of evolutionary stages' (Insoll 2004: 30), is not one supported here.

Long-standing totemic, albeit now unpopular, explanations have also existed in relation to interpreting Upper Palaeolithic rock art. Reinach (1905: 132), for example, drew parallels between French rock art and totemic cults of the Arunta of Australia. Critics of totemic interpretations of rock art have 'noted that some animals appear wounded by spears, which would be incompatible with the respect that would be due a totem' (Clottes and Lewis-Williams 1998: 66). It could be noted that this would of course depend on whether the totem was that of the spear painters! Maringer (1960: 60) has also suggested that the 'ice-age hunters' of the Upper Palaeolithic in decorating some of their tools and weapons with animal figures may have been expressing totemic beliefs. In contrast Layton (2000: 183) suggests that mobile art is more likely to have been largely 'an art of everyday hunting and gathering activities'. James (1957: 234) has also raised objections to totemic interpretations of Upper Palaeolithic material in arguing that totemism in its more developed forms 'involves a social and religious structure which is not likely to have prevailed in Palaeolithic times'. Treated as a singular 'defining' religion this is likely to be true, but more broadly construed as part of a package of beliefs it is not impossible that in some contexts totemic explanations might carry as much substance as currently popular alternatives such as shamanism.

However, Layton (2000: 182–3) also suggests that the distribution of animal motifs in Upper Palaeolithic art would tend to suggest a 'shamanic pattern' (ibid.: 182). Recent interpretations of Upper Palaeolithic rock art have certainly favoured shamanic associations rather than totemic ones (e.g. Lissner 1961; Lewis-Williams and Dowson 1988; Clottes and Lewis-Williams 1998). Layton (2000: 181) provides a pertinent discussion of these interpretations, and suggests that in shamanic rock art, the species represented will be widely depicted throughout an area as 'vehicles for spiritual encounters' or guardians available to people in many different groups; whilst he (Layton 2000: 180–1) argues that the species represented in totemic rock art are much more preferentially depicted within the group territory for which they serve as a totemic emblem. Thus it is concentrated at significant points in the territory used by a group. Elements of the later rock art of parts of Australia are often described as totemic (Layton 2000: 176), though it has to be acknowledged that, as David (2002: 21) notes, 'totemism' as a term has been 'a major stumbling block' in trying to understand Aboriginal religious organization and thought. Hence to avoid the historical implications of the latter, the concept of the 'Dreaming', i.e. creation, is often now used to replace 'totem'. Nonetheless, David (2002: 179) refers to the 'totemic landscape', whereby throughout mainland Australia the Dreaming ordered the world and those who lived in it.

This was often made manifest by rock art—of symbols and Dreaming creatures—and an example of this is provided by the rock art of Wardaman country in the Northern Territory where links with the Dreaming (David 2002: 71–88) were represented by painted Dreaming beings such as Emus, Devil Dogs, Flying-Foxes, and Nail-Tail Wallabies. Dates from the excavations in the rock shelters in which the rock art was recorded vary but suggest, for example, that the white cockatoos at Mengge-ya, appear in the late second millennium AD. Whilst the anthropomorphic Dreamtime beings at Garnawala 1 date from some time between 800 to 1,000 years ago, though the rock shelter was used much earlier at c.5200 BP (David 2002: 83, 81). Other sites linked with totemism in Australia were created in different ways and Flood (1983: 241) describes how some 'totemic increase sites', seemingly linked with maintaining natural species, were marked with arrangements of bone, as with a star-shaped pile of crocodile bones recorded on the floor of Sleisbeck rockshelter in the Northern Territory.

In the Australian examples totemism can be manifest across whole landscapes, and has been described as 'cosmological totemism' (Goody 1967: 75); in other societies it may be prominently attested in different ways, and serve a different function. Ingold (2000) has explored this in some detail in relation to the depiction of animals in art produced by peoples relating to 'animic' (ibid.: 112) and totemic ontologies. His definition of 'totemic ontology' is also derived from Australian Aboriginal examples and again is seen as linked with the land whilst the framework of 'animic ontology' is derived from the 'circumpolar North' (Ingold 2000: 113). Ingold's emphasis in considering possible meanings is less on the location of art, which is more broadly categorized than just rock art, and more upon content. The fundamental contrast, he argues, that exists between totemic and animic depictions of animals, 'is between a focus on morphology and anatomy in the former, and on posture, movement and behaviour in the latter' (Ingold 2000: 127–8).

A prominence in research focus upon 'art' exists in relation to both archaeology and material culture studies focused upon the materiality of 'totemism'. This covers a broad corpus as also manifest by the totem poles, the 'stereotypical totemic artifact', produced by various Native North American ethnic groups of the Pacific North-West Coast such as the Haida people of the Queen Charlotte Islands or the Tlingit of further north in Alaska (Malin 1986). Besides providing a further example of the variety that exists, they seem to affirm Lévi-Strauss's (1964) thesis, and the absence of a universal totemic 'template'. 'Totem poles' have also been interpreted in prehistoric European contexts. Andersson (2004: 169), for instance, provides a reconstruction drawing of the Early and Middle Neolithic settlement of Dagstorp in southern Sweden that includes an ornate totem pole.

6 THE ARCHAEOLOGY OF 'TOTEM' OR 'METAPHOR' IN NORTHERN GHANA

Totemism has been interpreted as an element of indigenous religions amongst different ethno-linguistic groups in northern Ghana by various observers, and its 'emblematic' role stressed (Goody 1967: 75). These include the Tallensi (Fortes 1945, 1987; Insoll 2007b: 326), Dagara, i.e. Goody's (1967) so-called Lo Willi, and the Bulsa (Anquandah 1998: 38). The 'emblematic' nature of the totemic species serves to indicate clan affiliation and connected with the totem is the notion of prohibition for, ideally at least, totemic observance should prohibit the consumption of certain species. Amongst the Tallensi, Fortes (1945: 142) notes that totemic avoidances have a symbolic value in relation to social organization but are not 'explicable simply as a function of the social structure'. His thinking (Fortes 1987: 123; and see Allman and Parker 2005: 39) on the role of Tallensi totemic observances was later clarified as their being 'cultural devices', thus indicating the complex role of totemism in the construction of Tallensi personhood and social relations. Initially, Fortes (1945: 145) suggested that the most widely respected Tallensi totems were 'teeth-bearers', reptiles and carnivores, but this was criticized by Levi-Strauss (1964: 75) and later admitted to be speculative (Fortes 1987: 131). Instead it is preferable to note that the totemic species can be terrestrial, arboreal, ethereal, or aquatic.

Considering its existence, totemism might then perhaps be expected to be archaeologically visible in northern Ghana. Unfortunately, in recent archaeological research completed in a main area of Tallensi settlement, the Tongo Hills, such patterning has not been evident. There has been a complete absence of, for instance, faunal remains whose patterning might have suggested 'totemic' relationships. This was because the residue of sacrifice, a primary agent in their creation (see also Chapter 11, 'Sacrifice'), is dispersed through the landscape according to strict criteria that reflect clan association and social structure (Insoll 2007b: 331). Excavation of, based on current analogy, ultimate destinations for these faunal remains such as domestic compounds has been equally negative. Presumably this is a result of processing methods, the removal and inclusion of some body parts such as skulls in shrines, and their subsequent deterioration, and the action of scavengers (Insoll, MacLean, and Kankpeyeng 2008).

Rock art is also lacking, though the use of stone arrangements as seating places by elders, chiefs, and priests recorded in one shrine, the Nyoo shrine, might have reflected totemic affiliation, but this is highly speculative and unlikely (Insoll 2007b: 332), and alternative interpretations centred upon performance can be suggested (Insoll 2009). Hence the archaeology of Tallensi 'totemism' is perhaps unsurprisingly, considering the discussion already presented, negative. More compelling is the potential for exploring metaphor based upon the patterning of the archaeological materials and this is what is being pursued (Insoll in preparation).

The work in the Tongo Hills is in progress, hence it is useful to turn to existing research to consider the potential of interpreting the archaeology of totemism in northern Ghana. Such interpretations exist, for Anquandah (1987: 180; 1998: 158–9) has suggested that some of the terracotta figurines recovered from mounds excavated in Koma Land, south-west of the towns of Sandema and Fumbisi in northern Ghana, might be indicative of totems. Anquandah's (1987: 180) interpretation is that the mounds primarily served funerary purposes (more complex interpretations less focused on a funerary role and involving thinking about fertility, witchcraft, and healing are now being explored by Kankpeyeng and Nkumbaan [2008] following renewed excavation of the Komaland mounds). Anquandah's (1987, 1998) excavation of two mounds at Yikpabongo East recorded multiple human and animal burials deposited with a range of objects such as cowrie shells, pottery discs, and copper or brass bracelets, anklets, and necklets (Anquandah 1998: 95–100, 113). Hundreds of pottery vessels, stone querns and grinders, and numerous terracotta figurines were also 'dumped' on the burials by what Anquandah (1987: 176) terms 'the clan relations of the deceased'. Two of the figurines dated by TL (thermoluminescence) led Anquandah (1987: 180) to initially suggest that the Koma complex flourished between the fifteenth to seventeenth centuries AD, but this was later revised to the period AD 1200–1800 (Anquandah 1998: 82).

The figurines representing humans (the majority), animals, camel and horse riders, and objects such as stools are of significance here. Anquandah (1987: 177–8) suggests that their producers 'were probably guided by religious and social motives to produce symbolic, naturalistic or stylized representations of clan deities, ancestral spirits, or stool and animal totems and motifs'. Local ethnography to support the interpretation of this material would seem to be lacking for according to Anquandah (1987: 177) there appears to be a rupture between the people responsible for the mounds and the contemporary population. In his later publication (Anquandah 1998) however, more explicit analogies are drawn with the Bulsa, an ethnolinguistic group now found immediately north of Koma Land. These direct links are evident in Anquandah's use of the term 'Koma-Bulsa' (1998) instead of 'Komaland' (1987). It is also evident in the more direct analogies drawn between Bulsa practices and beliefs and the Koma archaeological material. Anquandah (1987: 180) earlier refers to, in relation to the figurines, besides totems, the clan relationship with the deceased, and also '"*jadoks*" of terracotta', the latter a reference to the Bulsa concept of embodying spirits in animals (see Kroger 1982: 83). This is subsequently made much more explicit in stating that the figurines 'may be assumed to be the materialization of belief patterns which have survived in modern Bulsa *Wen-bogluta Jadoksa* and animal totemic practices' (Anquandah 1998: 159).

Whether this association is correct is unknown but it is likely that this level of analogical precision drawn from specific recent practices in relation to ancestral (*Wen-bogluk*, see Kroger 1982: 6) and totemic beliefs is insupportable. This is unfortunate as another source of evidence is available, the faunal remains described by Anquandah (1998: 92), that can be used to make interpretive suggestions about the animal figurines. What is clear is that the vast majority of identifiable bones recovered, 99.2 per cent, are from domesticated species whereas other than the dog, horse, and camel, the species represented by the figurines are wild animals—rhinoceros, hippopotamus, crocodile, lion etc. (Figure 62.1). Anquandah (1998: 91–2) notes this distinction but does not really explore its significance. Instead what might be represented, rather than necessarily 'totemism' or animal spirit beliefs based on modern Bulsa-type parallels, is the representation of symbolic or metaphorical thought; 'good to think' equals the figurine species, and 'good to eat' equals the faunal species (Insoll in preparation). Thus conceptual and metaphorical links were perhaps being formed with wild animals, hence their being rendered in clay as figurines and deposited in the mounds. The specificity of 'totemic' association is thus avoided, but the existence of complex beliefs, concepts, and metaphors is simultaneously suggested.

FIGURE 62.1 Crocodile figurine from excavations at Yikpabongo, Koma Land, January 2007. (Photograph: B. W. Kankpeyeng)

7 Conclusions

In concluding, it is best to think in terms of further archaeological implications. In relation to animism and totemism these are invariably complex and would depend, as stated, upon the context of the material examined. 'Animism' is seemingly without any value, and 'animistic' might be preferable, if at all, whilst 'totem' and 'totemism' perhaps have greater overall utility but are currently unfashionable. Nonetheless this should not preclude archaeologists from continuing to explore the efficacy of such terms even if they are materially elusive and very difficult to define adequately. It is the latter that is very much the crux of the issue and suggests that looser frameworks are preferable rather than attempting to 'fit' archaeological evidence into 'animist' or 'totemic' definitions derived from limited ethnography. Conneller (2004: 52) has stressed in relation to interpreting shamanism in Mesolithic European contexts that the level of specificity derived from present-day analogies 'is neither necessary nor often justified', and this would seemingly apply to animism and totemism as well. In summary, it will be interesting to see if in 10 or 20 years' time the status, usage, and definition of 'totemism' and 'animism' in archaeological contexts has altered, or if they remain, overall, a footnote to religious 'history'.

Suggested Reading

The entries by Bolle (2005) and Chidester (2005) in the *Encyclopedia of Religion* are useful in summarizing the history of the terms 'animism' and 'totemism'. For recent perspectives on both the reader is directed to Ingold (2000), and for animism, Bird-David (1999). For archaeological considerations and applications, see Layton (2000) and, in less detail, Insoll (2007b).

This chapter was written before the publication of Alberti and Bray's (2009) special section of the *Cambridge Archaeological Journal*, 'Animating Archaeology: Of subjects, objects and alternative ontologies', that indicates that animism is back on the archaeological agenda.

References

ABIODUN, R. 1995. *'What Follows Six is more than Seven': Understanding African art* (London: British Museum Press).
ALBERTI, B. and BRAY, T. L. 2009. 'Animating Archaeology: Of subjects, objects and alternative ontologies'. Introduction, special section, *Cambridge Archaeological Journal* 19(3): 337–43.
ALLMAN, J. and PARKER, J. 2005. *Tongnaab* (Bloomington: Indiana University Press).
ANDERSSON, M. 2004. 'Domestication and the first Neolithic concept, 4800–3000 BC' in M. Andersson, P. Karsten, B. Knarrstrom, and M. Svensson (eds), *Stone Age Scania* (Lund: National Heritage Board), pp. 143–90.
ANQUANDAH, J. 1987. 'The stone circle sites of Komaland, northern Ghana, in West African archaeology', *African Archaeological Review*, 5: 171–80.

——1998. *Koma-Bulsa: Its art and archaeology* (Rome: Istituto Italiano per l'Africa e l'Oriente).
BIRD-DAVID, N. 1999. '"Animism" revisited', *Current Anthropology*, 40 (Supplement): S67–S91.
——2006. 'Animistic epistemology: Why do some hunter-gatherers not depict animals?', *Ethnos*, 71: 33–50.
BOLLE, K. W. 2005. 'Animism and animatism' in L. Jones (ed.), *Encyclopedia of Religion*, I, 2nd edn (Detroit: Thomson Gale), pp. 362–8.
BURL, A. 1981. *Rites of the Gods* (London: Dent).
CHIDESTER, D. 2005. 'Animism' in B. R. Taylor (ed.), *The Encyclopedia of Religion and Nature*, I (London: Thoemmes Continuum), pp. 78–81.
CLOTTES, J. and LEWIS-WILLIAMS, D. 1998. *The Shamans of Prehistory: Trance and magic in the painted caves* (New York: Harry N. Abrams).
CONNELLER, C. 2004. 'Becoming Deer. Corporeal Transformations at Star Carr', *Archaeological Dialogues* 11: 37–56.
DAVID, B. 2002. *Landscapes, Rock-Art and the Dreaming* (London: Leicester University Press).
DESCOLA, P. 1996. 'Constructing natures: Symbolic ecology and social practice' in P. Descola and G. Palsson (eds), *Nature and Society: Anthropological perspectives* (London: Routledge), pp. 82–102.
DURKHEIM, E. 1915 [2001]. *The Elementary Forms of Religious Life* (Oxford: Oxford University Press).
EVANS-PRITCHARD, E. E. 1956. *Nuer Religion* (Oxford: Clarendon Press).
FLOOD, J. 1983. *Archaeology of the Dreamtime* (London: Collins).
FORTES, M. 1945 (1969). *The Dynamics of Clanship among the Tallensi* (Oosterhout: Anthropological Publications).
——1987. *Religion, Morality and the Person* (Cambridge: Cambridge University Press).
FOWLER, F. and FOWLER, H. 1986. *The Oxford Handy Dictionary* (Oxford: Oxford University Press).
FRAZER, J. G. 1910. *Totemism and Exogamy* (London: Macmillan).
GEERTZ, C. 1966 (1985). 'Religion as a Cultural System' in M. Banton (ed.), *Anthropological Approaches to the Study of Religion* (London: Tavistock), pp. 1–46.
GOODY, J. 1967. *The Social Organisation of the Lo Willi* (Oxford: Oxford University Press).
GUENTHER, M. 1999. 'From totemism to shamanism: Hunter-gatherer contributions to world mythology and spirituality' in R. B. Lee and R. Daly (eds), *The Cambridge Encyclopedia of Hunters and Gatherers* (Cambridge: Cambridge University Press), pp. 426–33.
HARVEY, G. 2005. 'Animism: A contemporary perspective' in B. R. Taylor (ed.), *The Encyclopedia of Religion and Nature*, I (London: Thoemmes Continuum), pp. 81–3.
INGOLD, T. 2000. *The Perception of the Environment: Essays in livelihood, dwelling and skill* (London: Routledge).
——2006. 'Rethinking the animate, re-animating thought', *Ethnos*, 71: 9–20.
INSOLL, T. 1996. *Islam, Archaeology and History: Gao Region (Mali) ca. AD 900–1250*, BAR S647 (Oxford: Tempus Reparatum).
——2004. *Archaeology, Ritual, Religion* (London: Routledge).
——2007a. 'Natural or human spaces? Tallensi sacred groves and shrines and their potential implications for aspects of Northern European prehistory and phenomenological interpretation', *Norwegian Archaeological Review*, 40: 138–58.
——2007b. '"Totems", "ancestors", and "animism": The archaeology of ritual, shrines and sacrifice amongst the Tallensi of northern Ghana' in D. Barrowclough and C. Malone (eds), *Cult in Context* (Oxford: Oxbow Books), pp. 326–33.

Insoll, T. 2008. 'Totemism' in W. A. Darity Jr (ed.), *International Encyclopedia of the Social Sciences* (Detroit: Macmillan Reference), pp. 397–8.
—— 2009. 'Materialising performance and ritual: Decoding the archaeology of shrines in northern Ghana', *Material Religion*, 5: 288–311.
—— in preparation. *Theoretical Explorations in African Archaeology: Contexts, materials, persons, and animals* (Oxford: Oxford University Press).
——, MacLean, R., and Kankpeyeng, B. 2008. 'Excavations and surveys in the Tongo Hills, Upper East Region, and Birifor, Upper West Region, Ghana. March–April 2008: A preliminary fieldwork report', *Nyame Akuma*, 69: 11–22.
James, E. O. 1957. *Prehistoric Religion* (London: Thames and Hudson).
James, W. 1999. 'Introduction' in D. Forde (ed.), *African Worlds* (Oxford: James Currey), pp. ix–xxx.
Kankpeyeng, B. and Nkumbaan, S. N. 2008. 'Rethinking the stone circles of Komaland: A preliminary report on the 2007/2008 fieldwork at Yikpabongo, Northern Region, Ghana' in T. Insoll (ed.), *Current Archaeological Research in Ghana*, BAR S1847 (Oxford: Archaeopress), pp. 95–102.
Kroger, F. 1982. *Ancestor Worship among the Bulsa of Northern Ghana* (Munich: Klaus Renner Verlag).
Layton, R. 2000. 'Review feature: Shamanism, totemism and rock art: *Les Chamanes de la Préhistoire* in the context of rock art research', *Cambridge Archaeological Journal*, 10: 169–86.
Lévi-Strauss, C. 1964 [1991]. *Totemism* (London: Merlin Press).
Lewis-Williams, D. and Dowson, T. 1988. 'The signs of all times: Entoptic phenomena in Upper Palaeolithic art', *Current Anthropology*, 29: 201–45.
Lienhardt, G. 1961 [1987]. *Divinity and Experience: The religion of the Dinka* (Oxford: Oxford University Press).
Lissner, I. 1961. *Man, God and Magic* (London: Jonathan Cape).
Malin, E. 1986. *Totem Poles of the Pacific Northwest Coast* (Portland, OR: Timber Press).
Marcus, J. 2007. 'Rethinking ritual' in E. Kyriakidis (ed.), *The Archaeology of Ritual* (Los Angeles: Cotsen Institute of Archaeology), pp. 43–76.
Maringer, J. 1960 [2002]. *The Gods of Prehistoric Man* (London: Phoenix Press).
Mithen, S. 1998. *The Prehistory of the Mind* (London: Phoenix).
Morris, B. 1999. 'Comment', *Current Anthropology*, 40 (Supplement): S82–S83.
Price, N. (ed.) 2001. *The Archaeology of Shamanism* (London: Routledge).
Reinach, S. 1905. *Cultes, Mythes et Religions*, I (Paris: Ernest Leroux).
Stringer, M. D. 1999. 'Rethinking animism: Thoughts from the infancy of our discipline', *Journal of the Royal Anthropological Institute*, 5: 541–55.
Tilley, C. 1999. *Metaphor and Material Culture* (Oxford: Blackwell).
Trimingham, J. S. 1959. *Islam in West Africa* (Oxford: Clarendon Press).
—— 1968. *The Influence of Islam upon Africa* (London: Longman).
Tylor, E. B. 1929. *Primitive Culture*, 2 vols (London: John Murray).
Viveiros de Castro, E. 1998. 'Cosmological deixis and Amerindian perspectivism', *Journal of the Royal Anthropological Institute*, 4: 469–88.
Wagner, R. 2005. 'Totemism' in L. Jones (ed.), *Encyclopedia of Religion*, XIII, 2nd edn (Detroit: Thomson Gale), pp. 9250–3.
Weiner, J. F. 1994. 'Myth and metaphor' in T. Ingold (ed.), *Companion Encyclopedia of Anthropology* (London: Routledge), pp. 591–612.

CHAPTER 63

NEO-SHAMANISM

Pagan and 'Neo-Shamanic' Interactions With Archaeology

JENNY BLAIN

1 INTRODUCTION: SHAMANIC PAGANISMS AND RECONSTRUCTIONIST SPIRITUALITIES

NEO-SHAMANISM, a term for today, is a problematic term. It indexes practitioners within Western 'developed' countries in the late twentieth and early twenty-first centuries who draw on 'shamanic' techniques or occasionally refer to themselves as 'shamans', but the relationship to 'traditional' shamanisms may not be clear. Equally, there is no single organization, and no single set of materials, practices, or written work which practitioners will refer to as basic to what they do. Few practitioners term themselves 'neo-shamans', preferring (for instance) 'Western Shamanic Practitioner'; some will define themselves as simply 'Pagan' or as a Heathen, Druid, Brythonic celebrant or an adherent of some other form of (broadly speaking) pagan spirituality, while pointing out that they work spiritually in ways which are shamanistic and hold a world view which may be described as either shamanic or animic (Harvey 2005), often relating to a tripartite 'upper, middle and lower world' system where all worlds are peopled with their own beings. Hence the term 'neo-shaman' has been used within academic research to refer to some varieties of pagan spiritualities within Europe and North America (e.g. Wallis 2003).

The range of variation of practitioners is large. Neo-'shamans' frequently adopt concepts and definitions of 'shamanisms' from traditional or indigenous cultures, particularly Native religious traditions of North America. They may therefore be subject to charges of appropriation of spiritualities. Not all do this, however, and of those who do, many would protest that they give what Harvey (1997: 122) terms 'extra pay' to the term 'shaman'—acknowledging that their practices are not those of 'traditional' shamans, but drawing attention to the situations of shamanic cultures in various areas of the world. Particularly in North America, these charges of appropriation may become heated. Native authors have commented on the phenomenon of 'wannabes' in articles such as 'For all who were Indian in a former life' (Smith 1993). These spokespeople object to pieces of their cultural and spiritual heritage being packaged for a 'new-age' audience and often sold for profit, and to the art and music of Native artists being used and exploited without the artists themselves being named. The anthropologist Wendy Rose has discussed the issues as they are experienced by native groups (e.g. Rose 1984, 1992). (Some of these issues are summarized for a student readership in Tepperman and Blain 2005.) Appropriation, however, is not the chief focus of this chapter; though it forms part of the relationship of neo-shamans to traditional communities, and hence shapes some interactions of neo-shamans and archaeology; not only concepts and practices but places, artefacts and monuments may be appropriated—or protected.

There are many reasons for 'Western', i.e. non-traditional or non-indigenous, practitioners to seek out 'shamanic' ways of interacting with self, gods, places, landscapes, monuments, spirit, and human communities. Mayer (2008) has discussed the attractions of 'shamanism' for a Western audience today; Hutton (2001) and Flaherty (1992) traced histories of how 'shamanism' came into the popular imagination. Practitioners vary from those who draw on shamanic cultures of past and present to develop ways of relating to 'living landscapes' of today, to those who adopt or mimic specific practices claiming 'authenticity' of transmission from spiritual teachers or books; and those working for and with a community to those who practise individually to achieve personal goals. There is therefore a tension between 'neo-shamanism' as syncretism and community service and 'neo-shamanism' as appropriation for personal development.

It can be said, of course, that all shamanic practice (or indeed most forms of spiritual expression) is appropriative: 'traditional' practices are not static, and the 'shaman' may appear as a creative forger of cultural expression, drawing on practices and concepts from many sources and using these within complex politicized contexts. Greene (1998), for instance, discussed the use of 'the shaman's needle', that is the concept of Western immunization, becoming part of a traditional practitioner's repertoire so demonstrating fluidity of shamanic practice and incorporation of ideas, and Taussig (e.g. 1987) theorizes tensions between contestation and creative uses of 'traditional' practices, by spiritual leaders, workers of magic, shamans, and/or artists within changing colonial and post-/neo-colonial contexts.

Neo-shamanism, though, involves a deliberate adoption of 'other' practices—sometimes discussed (e.g. on practitioner websites) as 'closer to nature' or indeed even as 'more primitive'—to develop ways of developing self or relating to community: a suggestion that 'premodern' sensibilities offer a way of life which is superior to the fragmentation of post-industrial society. Not all practitioners of course would take such views, but some will articulate them as a justification for appropriation of lifestyles. Blain and Wallis (2007) have discussed issues of romanticizing various 'pasts' and 'traditional cultures' within today's spiritual diversity, and implications for engagements with archaeology; since the dissemination of Western 'travellers tales' of Siberian shamans in the seventeenth and eighteenth centuries (Wallis 2003; Flaherty 1992), the attraction of the 'exotic', 'primitive' other has been manifest in various ways that involve imitation of dress, practices, and accoutrements. Hutton (1999: 90) described the attire of a Welsh 'cunning man' of the nineteenth century as apparently inspired by that reported for 'Siberian tribal shamans'. Early anthropologists living with North American peoples engaged with rituals and initiations, adopting 'native' dress and for some recreating practices and 'secret societies' in their Western lives (see Wallis 2003, 2004 for summaries). And latterly, the anthropologist Michael Harner can be seen as following this trend, publishing his account of experiences in South America and his developments, from these, of forms of Western 'shamanic' practice (Harner 1980), associated with the genesis of the Foundation for Shamanic Studies (<http://www.shamanism.org/>) and 'Core Shamanism'. Felicitas Goodman from studying body posture and 'trance' experiences became a teacher of neo-shamanic practices, through experimental work with members of non-shamanic communities (Goodman 1990, 1999). More generally, neo- or Western shamanic practitioners draw on a large range of anthropological materials (though often outdated) and on Western discussions and analyses of 'shamanism' (notably Eliade [1964]), as well as an increasing literature from various practitioners described as indigenous or traditional shamanic practitioners. There is, too, a growing literature on forms of neo-shamanism: ranging from detailed accounts of practice to the 'how-to' books familiar in other areas of alternative spirituality. Clifton (1991) has pointed to the burgeoning of a literature on 'How I became a Shaman' and indeed anthropologists are paying some attention to the phenomenon of the 'new shaman' and through this outlining some forms of practice and generation of meanings in post-industrial societies (see e.g. Greenwood 2000 and 2005; Blain 2002a; Wallis 2003).

The range of neo-shamanic practice in the UK and elsewhere today is wide: and it does not lend itself to easy classification. (For details of some practices, see e.g. Wallis 2003; Greenwood 2005; Blain 2002a; Mayer 2008.) Practitioners draw on both 'pagan' and 'new-age' concepts and contexts, and refer to practices and beliefs by a diversity of names. At one end of a continuum, 'Shamanism' is a term practitioners use for a religion (to which they see themselves subscribing), and they term themselves 'shamans'; at the other end, practitioners adopt 'shamanic' techniques and practices which are found elsewhere in cultural and spiritual contexts which could be termed 'shamanic'; they will in turn make use of these within the specific cultural and spiritual contexts of today's 'new' religions; borrowing and adapting what seems to work, but do not presume to term themselves 'shamans' though other members of pagan or spiritual communities may describe them thus. They may see themselves as guardians of place and uncoverers of tradition, and Blain and Wallis (e.g. 2007) have described practitioners as 'new-indigenes'. Somewhere in the middle lie claims for core shamanism, practices which are in some sense deemed to be culture-free. This is cross-cut by debates of what practices are 'shamanic' and which are not, of how shamanic consciousness is or should be achieved, and of the role of the 'neo-shaman' within the community. To an individual, neo-shamanism may be a means for personal development and self-empowerment, for healing or 'seeing' within a community or belief group, for personal expression or cultural change, for environmental activism and education, a means to a livelihood through teaching and 'workshops', or several of these at once. Within communities of practice, neo-shamanism, its practices, and terminology are every bit as contested as they may be in archaeological or anthropological literature. It should therefore be no surprise that neo-shamanic engagements with archaeology take a wide variety of forms. The Foundation for Shamanic Studies expresses a triple role, 'a three-fold mission to study, to teach, and to preserve shamanism' (<http://www.shamanism.org/>), and many neo-shamans who are not FSS members likewise adopt the aims of learning from and supporting traditional shamanisms—and indeed look to traditional shamanisms for justification.

2 Interactions with Archaeology: Sacred Landscapes and Monuments

For many neo-shamanic practitioners, monuments become places where ancestors, deities, or spirits of place can be accessed, communicated with, and/or where the world view of 'ancestors' who built the monument or worked the land, or in particular who visibly inscribed meanings in landscape, become more accessible. Given the extent of variation in neo-shamanic beliefs and practices it will come as no surprise that these spirits, or deities, or ancestors may be very varied; likewise the ritual practices associated with them. Attempts to understand the importance of landscape and place need to bear in mind the huge variety of practice. Again, conceptualizing a continuum is useful. At one extreme are views that all spirits are one, with 'ancient' places sought out for honouring of 'Spirit' and gaining further understanding of self—including through vision quest; at the other, animic perceptions of distinct entities of the 'other than human people' (Harvey 2005), beings of stone, birch, fox, mosquito, and others who have their own understandings and sensibilities creating a web of relationships within a place, with human people of past and present being part of this; and somewhere in the middle, understandings of 'spirit of place' or *genius loci* associated with a particular location or monument.

The term 'animic', rather than the older term 'animist', is used to distinguish today's 'new animism' as described by Bird-David (1993, 1999), Harvey (2005) and others from the nineteenth-century understandings of animist 'belief in spirits' which presented indigenous beliefs as superstitious or inferior. Harvey's understanding explores relationships between human and other-than-human people, with the 'shaman' as a mediator. This understanding allows for perceptions that other-than-human people have interests which may diverge greatly from those of the human communities with which they share space and time, and ties in with warnings of British practitioner Gordon 'The Toad' MacLellan (e.g. 1999) who cautions that the spirits met with in shamanic journeying are not necessarily 'safe'.

Together with this come understandings of the shamanic practitioner's particular 'helper' spirits and means of communication with them. Ancestors—people in the landscape, people who built monuments, or had particular associations with an area (as well as those who may have been physical ancestors of the shaman)—form part of this sense of the landscape as peopled, and of the neo-shaman acting deliberately to form relationships with these (ancestor, deity, human or other-than-human) people. Specific places, landscape, sacred sites, rock-art panels, and so forth may be seen as a doorway (in science-fiction terms 'a portal') to communication or understanding, with ritual use of place designed to further this.

Shamanic rituals generally involve some form of deliberate alteration of consciousness. Harner (1980) has popularized the concept of the shamanic state of consciousness (SSC) in which the shaman 'controls' his or her helper spirits or others met with (as opposed to, for instance, spirit possession), in line with the concept of the shaman as 'master' of spirits derived from work of Shirokogorov (1935) and recently re-presented by Jakobsen (1999). For many neo-shamans, therefore, achieving this SSC becomes the aim of ritual. There are many ways of attaining a trance or SSC: the use of percussion (drumming or rattle) is by far the most common among neo-shamans, and a group ritual may involve setting up some kind of protective circle (often based on Wiccan forms) followed by drumming until people have attained the state. They may then 'journey' in the shamanic state, and the energy or power felt by individuals within the group may eventually be directed to some end: healing the 'energies of place' or focusing on world peace in addition to increasing the well-being of practitioners through 'shamanic' healing or simply raising self-esteem. Harvey and Wallis (2007) point out that the concept of one 'shamanic state of consciousness' may over-psychologize neo-shamanic practice by focusing only on one process; and to counter it they cite Hamayon's emphasis (1993, 1996) that in Siberian shamanic communities the focus is on relationships between shaman and spirits (and, one might add, community) and in particular the 'marriage' of shaman and spirit, rather than this individualized 'ecstasy'. Blain has suggested use of 'altered consciousness' which might encompass many forms (including sleep, heightened awareness, etc.) without privileging one, and has pointed out that much of what 'traditional shamans' do is focused on the here-and-now waking deliberations and organization of everyday life (Blain 2002a; Blain and Wallis 2006b); simply put, a shaman whether traditional or 'neo-' is not only *a shaman* when in ecstasy.

Nonetheless, neo-shamans may seek out ancient monuments as places of power where spirits, deities, or ancestors are more easily met with. In addition to self-development, though, practitioners may seek knowledge of place through altering consciousness to 'know' sacred places in an attempt to understand why or how these came to be 'sacred' and to form relationships with the spiritual and physical beings there. Altered consciousness includes altered awareness of time, both the 'clock time' which the event occupies (perceived as stretched or speeding) and the awareness of change and past landscapes; paralleling some work from archaeology (e.g. Edmonds and Seabourne 2001) which attempts to reflect changing uses of landscape through poetic awareness and understanding. Protecting landscapes give another strand: Letcher (2004) indicates some derivations of 'raising the dragon', environmental protest-magic, in British folklore and in the concept not only of dragon energies of the island of Britain but of forming alliances with these energies. Some pagans, independently, speak of specific dragons in threatened landscapes, and of negotiating with these in an altered consciousness.

Altering consciousness for these ends can be attained through chant, song, dance, drumming or rattle, whistling, the use of other instruments, or the use of entheogenic (psychoactive) substances. Many neo-shamans make use of 'magic mushrooms': for some simply to attain that SSC (and a popular perception of a neo-shaman at an archaeological monument is of somebody who is 'wasted'), for others, judiciously used, to more easily enable a specific practice of healing or quest for healing or knowledge through changed consciousness. In general, these are psilocybin mushrooms. Letcher (2006) has explored the 'cultural history' of the use of these, and the generalizing of Central American indigenous practices to 'shamanism' more generally. Folklore however points to Fly Agaric (Amanita muscaria) as the 'shamanic' mushroom of North Eurasia.

Altered consciousness, though, may be attained (particularly by established practitioners) rather more simply through walking, singing, or stillness, at need or at will. Further, knowledge of place includes knowledge of the physical other-than-human people who share it. Neo-shamanic knowledge of, for instance, an upland-heath landscape (we could take the specific example of the much contested Stanton Moor in England's Peak District) could include understandings from formal ritual conducted with others; from meditative encounters with and within the stone circles; 'sacred partying' at solstice; meeting a guardian 'dragon' spirit of the moor; participating in protests against quarry threats; sleeping on the moorland; 'visiting' at all seasons over years; processing over the moor in an altered consciousness; learning the movement of birds and studying relationships between the grasses and heathers, beetles, bats, wheatears, merlins, and other heathland creatures; walking the upland paths; and exploring the history and folklores of the place, which includes industrial and post-industrial settlement as well as Bronze-Age landscape. The neo-shamanic quest for knowledge attempts to penetrate metaphysical meanings of places and pasts, constructing site as mythscape and weaving new folklores for the present day into the inscriptions of 'the past'. But patterns of movement in Britain and elsewhere in the 'West' may prevent local knowledge enabling these: a lack of local knowledge is pointed to by Nepali shaman Yarjung Tamu in dialogue with Judith Pettigrew (Pettigrew and Tamu 2002). Tamu had negotiated spirit landscapes in several parts of the world: he found it hardest, however, to practise as a shaman when living in England. Local people seeking his assistance do not have the local knowledge he needs to ascertain how he can work for them or what 'bad spirits' he has to fight (ibid.: 118). In particular, he seeks information on the source of the local water and the ancestors of/in the area.

Shamanic practitioners, though, also make pilgrimage to places which they construe as sacred—where they are not 'at home' and where they seek wisdom or understanding, again usually through altered consciousness, rituals and (often) making physical offerings. For neo-shamans, this may take the form of visiting sites associated with 'traditional' shamanic practices; amongst others, Wallis (2003) has discussed how such visitors may be regarded with examples of Pueblos where signs alert visitors to respect not only place but current practices. Sites of pilgrimage include rock-art sites and ancient monuments; spiritual tourism may be facilitated by organizations and indeed 'shamanic' pilgrimage constitutes an industry for today. Within the UK, prime neo-shamanic pilgrimage sites include Avebury and Stonehenge (see Blain and Wallis 2007 for detailed accounts of Stonehenge, 2008 for discussion of Avebury as a site of shamanic 'performance', and 2006b for a critique of 'performance' in its implications for shamanic practice; see Figure 63.1). Other visited sites include those which are managed (e.g. Sutton Hoo or Flag Fen) and those which are less known, and include places of archaeological or folkloric significance or natural beauty, or the graves or dwelling sites of historic ancestors: for some neo-shamans, the recent semi-derelict graveyard of the Glasgow Eastern Necropolis might be as much a place of pilgrimage as the 'temples' of Stonehenge, Thornborough or Kilmartin.

Finally in terms of direct engagements with archaeology, sacred places, be they ancient monuments or secluded sites, become places of initiatory journeys, lone workings by shamanic practitioners who seek first to know themselves through undergoing an event of initiation by their spirit-beings. Many practitioners have tales of their first 'sitting out', with parallels in Native American vision quests, shamanic 'death and rebirth' experiences and North European 'sitting out for wisdom' or útiseta (on which see Aðalsteinsson 1978). These may be combined with 'pilgrimage' events, with, for instance, North American 'Celtic Shamans' seeking to spend a night in a British Neolithic chambered tomb or Bronze-Age cairn (Blain 2001); a form of reverse appropriation which may not always be welcomed by local practitioners or residents.

FIGURE 63.1 Stonehenge summer solstice 2001. Partying at (and on) the stones.

3 Interactions with Archaeology: Artefacts and Reconstruction

Selected symbols of the past, through their representations by today's practitioners, become the symbols of the present informing reconstructed worldviews and materiality of religion. Practitioners of present-day animic and shamanic spiritualities draw heavily on the artefacts of past or indeed present cultures perceived as 'shamanic': musical instruments, statues, jewellery and adornments, and items of costume become part of practice. Some neo-shamanic traditions have rationalized this in terms of popular psychology: a practitioner becomes conditioned to respond to certain stimuli, these including the symbols which are otherwise connected with a shamanic world view, and which create an expectation in the community for which the neo-shaman works. Artefacts and accoutrements therefore become part of the context of neo-shamanic practice. In particular, the costumes of 'traditional' shamans give rise to the use of feathers, rattles, fringed head-dresses, beads, and crystals among practitioners drawing on 'core shamanic' resources or general 'how to be a Shaman' books (such as Harner 1980; Ingerman 2004).

Here practitioners may seek to specialize, choosing artefacts or attires that locate their practices in particular cultures or communities and potentially bringing them to examine archaeological literature or museum artefacts. Harner (1980) discusses the use of quartz crystals among indigenous groups in Australia; in some British archaeological contexts carved spheres (of chalk, etc.) are assumed to be likewise 'shamanic' and practitioners may seek to find or make copies. Blain and Wallis (2006a) give examples of the use of Scandinavian or Old English artefacts by Heathen practitioners, including amber jewellery, quartz spheres, and reproductions of Thor's hammer and other pieces. Artefacts become 'materialised ideology' (DeMarrais et al. 1996) with their selection and presentation both signifying and establishing world view and associations with (assumed) past practitioners, and so forming part of the structuring of neo-shamanic understandings of time and being.

A particular example is the reconstruction of *seidr* or North European shamanic practice, which Blain (e.g. 2002a, 2002b, 2005) has explored as both anthropologist and practitioner, noting differences in its construction which relate to relationships to deities and landscape across the Atlantic ocean. In general, she finds that North American practitioners are more focused on the deities who (in the Eddas and other North European mediaeval literature) are said to themselves practise shamanically (Freyja and Odin), while some UK practitioners have a keener focus on spirits in the land (landwights) and how the landscape shapes practice. Both groups draw inspiration from accounts in various Icelandic sagas, notably the Saga of Eric the Red which gives a more detailed account of apparently shamanic practice and costume than is found elsewhere in these works, and which has formed the basis of reconstruction of today's 'oracular seid' practice.

Briefly, a seeress comes to a Greenlandic farmstead which has fallen on hard times and is facing famine. She is asked to foresee if the luck will change (which it will). She wears a cloak decorated with stones and her gown is girdled with a belt of touchwood from which hangs a pouch containing her 'taufr'—magical objects; her shoes, gloves, and hat are described and even the knife and spoon which she carried. She bears a staff decorated with metal and with a knob at its top. A special raised platform is prepared for her and a special meal served. The next day she prepares to 'make seidr', and a circle of women chant, apparently following a lead singer (the heroine of the saga). The song calls to spirits who enable the seeress to see further and learn more than she has done previously, thanks to the excellence of the singing (summarized from Eiriks saga Rauda, ch. 5, discussed in more detail in Blain 2005 and 2002a.)

A form of practice derived initially in North America (by Diana Paxson and others) derives a highly formalized ritual structure including the seidr platform or raised chair and the song, together with drumming and other 'shamanic' performances. In Europe, Annette Høst and her colleagues have focused on the song and the staff (see e.g. her article 'The staff and the song' at <http://www.shamanism.dk/Articles.html>), in a less formalized development of shamanic techniques derived initially from 'core shamanism' but relating specifically to a North European context. Seidr practice in Sweden, as described by Lindquist (1997) and experienced by Høst, has a focus on the raised platform. Some UK practitioners combine the relative informality of the European practices with a question and answer pattern derived from the North American ritual form (Blain 2002a and b). All, though, look both to the Icelandic literature and to archaeology in exploring possibly shamanic contexts of North Europe including Scandinavia, Britain, and Iceland, and with reference to Sámi shamanisms of past and present. The work of Neil Price (e.g. 2001), exploring the phenomenon of seidr as shamanic practice referenced in Sagas and visible in contexts of

Scandinavian graves, becomes an important resource for these communities; giving materiality to concepts of the staff (wood or metal), the pouch and its possible contents (small bones, entheogenic seeds), and even the chair of the seeress.

Neo-shamans therefore have a dual relationship to archaeology in these contexts: on the one hand, consumers of archaeological materials, a readership ready to hand; on the other, creatively trialling methods and materials to discover 'what works' in the changed consciousnesses and circumstances of today. Other examples, here, include the participation of 'shamanic' Druids in the exploration of how 'burnt mounds' might indicate use of sauna or sweat-lodge techniques in Bronze Age Britain, exploring alterations in consciousness through applied archaeology, and relating material and 'alternative' knowledges. Such explorations can never be definitive but can enable imaginative or speculative reconstruction of community and world view, as well as of specific practices.

4 INTERACTIONS WITH ARCHAEOLOGY: ANCESTORS AND REBURIAL

A final dimension of this chapter, though, must relate to the question of 'ancestors'. Shamanic perceptions connect with ancestors in many ways, not all of them obvious. Included among these are ideas of ancestors within the landscape, communication with them, and (paralleling concepts articulated from many indigenous communities worldwide) the issue of respect. This is an area where neo-shamanic concepts may conflict with those of archaeologists and heritage management. If (at least some) neo-shamans consider themselves as in dialogue with other than human people and ancestors, what claims do they make and how do they relate to those who, from various needs, disturb ancestral bones and grave goods? In a notable conference at Manchester Museum in November 2006, issues of world view and perceptions of 'personhood' were debated between pagans, archaeologists, and museum personnel, with a high level of agreement on the issue of 'respect'. Yet this may not cover all aspects of the debate.

Some groups have hit headlines in the UK, as indicated by Wallis and Blain (2011). Claims have arisen from Druid and other groups in the south-west of England calling for respect and reburial of various 'ancestors', particularly high-profile and scientifically notable remains, such as at Avebury, where Druid Paul Davies has spearheaded a campaign for the reburial of 'our sister', whose remains are or were on display in the Alexander Keiller Museum there; and in Wales, a Swansea Druid group naming themselves 'Dead to Rights' have asked for the reburial of the 'Red Lady of Paviland' (these remains were discovered on the Gower peninsula by the palaeontologist and clergyman William Buckland, who incorrectly thought the red ochre indicated the skeleton was female and dated the find as Roman; it is now known to be a young man buried approximately 26,000 BP). Chris Warwick, the Druid behind 'Dead to Rights', protested at the site over a weekend in September 2006, calling for the return of the remains from Oxford University, receiving publicity from regional BBC News (see <http://news.bbc.co.uk/1/hi/wales/south_west/5372598.stm>).

Various calls for reburial or for permission to perform pagan ceremonies over human remains as they are excavated have led to the formation of HAD, an organization (though not exclusively pagan or shamanic) committed to 'Honouring the Ancient Dead' (<http://www.honour.org.uk/>). HAD aims to 'ensure respect for ancient pagan remains' with 'clear interactions between archaeologists, historians, landowners, site caretakers, museums and collectors... and the pagan community', stating:

> The purpose of this interaction is clear and positive communication that will inspire a broader and deeper understanding of the sanctity of all artefacts (notably those connected with ritual, sacrifice, burial and human remains) sourced from the Pagan eras of the British Isles. HAD will be seeking assurances that there will be communication and consultation on matters relating to such artefacts and remains. [E. Restall Orr, founder of HAD, pers. com.]

Emma Restall Orr and HAD are not calling for mandatory reburial but are more concerned with enabling dialogue between interest groups, including establishing consultation during excavations as well as the opportunity for pagans to 'make ritual in appropriate ways, honouring the spirits involved' relating both to newly found remains and to established museum exhibits. HAD has proposed a 'rite of committal of human remains' (<http://www.honour.org.uk/articles/reburial_rite.html>) to assist museum personnel or others, which takes care to specify how much is 'not known' of either the persons committed or their theology and ritual. The aims of HAD to promote dialogue and respect resulted in November 2006 in collaboration with the Manchester Museum (linked to the University of Manchester) and the Museums Association in the aforementioned conference on 'Respect for Ancient British Human Remains: Philosophy and practice'.

Some recent dialogues have concerned the display of the 'Lindow Man' remains. Originally found at Lindow Moss near Manchester, Lindow Man is on permanent display at the British Museum. On two previous occasions, Lindow Man had returned 'home' for exhibitions at the Manchester Museum. Preparation for a third exhibition between April 2008 and March 2009 involved ongoing consultation with various interest groups, including pagans. The 'Consultation Report' (Sitch 2007) of a meeting held on 10 February 2007 included a section (3.2: 4) entitled 'Spirituality':

> There was broad agreement that the approach taken to Lindow Man needed to reflect that he had been a living human being and that he was most definitely a 'he' and not an 'it', that he was an ancestor and that he must be treated with sensitivity... People felt that there is a spiritual dimension to Lindow Man and how he is treated on display, which also extends to allowing visitors to demonstrate their respect for him as an ancestor.
>
> - The Museum should explore the option to create a shrine near the Lindow Man exhibition where people could make offerings to the ancestors, of which Lindow Man is a representative but not make offerings *to* Lindow Man.
> - A Pagan perspective on Lindow Man is very important. We want to emphasize his humanity. He certainly is not a museum object.
> - Lindow Man's discovery and excavation was an intersection of then and now, of us and him, that is still on-going, evolving and certainly not over.

As a result, the exhibition has included the display of objects from local residents and other stakeholders in order to demonstrate that interest in Lindow Man since his discovery has its own history. These objects include one woman's 'Care Bear', a spade to represent his finders, and, from a pagan, some crow feathers (see the Lindow Man blog at <http://lindowmanchester.wordpress.com/> for various descriptions and comments on this process during 2007 and 2008). In a collaboration between Bryan Sitch, Head of Humanities and curator of the exhibition, with HAD and other pagans, a special event at the Manchester Museum the week after the exhibition opening involved a ceremony where several pagan and shamanic groups (including the author) came together to honour the 'ancestor' who was before us, bearing biodegradable offerings from the mosses over which we had travelled, and speaking of the winds that blew from there to where he was found and where he now lay, the people who had come, and what the concept of this ancestor did for us today in helping us to relate to environment and sacredness. Within the exhibition, an area is available for people (pagans or others), to make offerings, and these offerings are in turn the subject of study: an example of archaeology studying neo-shamanic processes. It seems, then, only right to conclude this section with a description of this pagan/neo-shamanic ritual conducted for Lindow Man, at Manchester Museum, in April 2008, as it may exemplify some points about neo-shamanic intersections with archaeology today.

Coordinated by environmental educator, performer, and artist Gordon 'The Toad' MacLellan, this ritual involved a considerably greater area than the museum exhibit space. Participants came from east, south, west, and north, representing 'four winds' which blow over the moorland and uplands around Lindow Moss. The author drove from the east, bringing biodegradable items (grasses, bog myrtle, leaf mould, and mosses) to offer to the 'ancestor' and later return to the upland landscapes. In the museum, participants processed downstairs from conference rooms into the exhibit space, bearing banners and offerings, to a chant of three runes initiated by a seid practitioner. Inside the darkened exhibit space, various participants spoke of the winds blowing over the mosses from which they had come, in verse and in prose, and said something of the history of Lindow Moss and its environment; then of the Man, his finding and what he may have to teach today's people. After spending a silent time, then giving thanks to ancestors (Lindow Man and others), the winds, and wishing health to all, participants returned in procession from the exhibit space through the museum, and eventually reassembled in the forecourt to share seedcake and mead. For those present it was a deeply moving experience. It is important to say, in this short account, that those present spoke of Lindow Man as a living presence within 'his' space, welcomed him in a return to his home territory, and yet that many of those present displayed ambivalence about whether he should be in a museum exhibit at all, considering that he should be returned to the Moss if circumstances would enable this.

In summary, the British reburial issue is coming to the fore for some pagans and neo-shamanic practitioners. Issues here are not only those of cultural continuity or direct physical ancestry—which is somewhat of a red herring where UK contexts and mobile populations are concerned.

5 CONCLUSIONS: NEO-SHAMANS AND ARCHAEOLOGY

The foregoing shows several ways in which neo-shamanisms intersect with archaeology. Neo-shamanic practitioners engage with artefacts and places; they may be critical of archaeologists as 'grave robbers' and draw inspiration from cultures elsewhere that have expressed criticism of excavation: yet many artefacts and understandings come from studies of grave goods. Concepts of communication, of discussing excavation needs *with ancestors*, and of multiple ways of showing respect inform neo-shamanic practices and interactions with archaeology. Some issues are not easily resolved. These include calls for reburial, somewhat at odds with claims of Western science, and appropriations of place and practice which are evident in 'visits' of neo-shamans to ancient monuments or 'traditional' sites, sometimes to the dismay of local residents and heritage personnel. Whose knowledge should be privileged here? The Foundation for Shamanic Studies, by its focus on study and transmission, has emphasized the importance of preserving traditional shamanic understandings and working with indigenous shamans. Within Western Europe, local 'new-indigenous' groups attempt to revive or reconstruct shamanic understandings through knowledge of place and folklore. Others may claim knowledge of 'ancient' shamanic practices through ancestral transmission. Neo-shamanism is varied and has no central spokesperson, no organizing committee, no doctrines; yet practices and world views give ways of knowing landscapes of past and present which enable concepts and speculations not otherwise evident, pointing to alternative possibilities which enrich understandings of how human people relate to those other-than-human people within many landscapes.

SUGGESTED READING

For extended discussion of interactions with prehistoric monuments, please see *Sacred Sites, Contested Rites/Rights* (Blain and Wallis 2007). For a more extended discussion of what 'neo-Shamanism' may imply see *Shamans/Neo-Shamans* (Wallis 2003) which examines some issues of British and other sites and pagan and neo-shamanic practitioners. Other key material includes Graham Harvey's work on Animism, especially his 2005 work *Animism: Respecting the living world*. For detailed discussion of one 'neo-Shamanic' set of practices see Blain's *Nine Worlds of Seid-Magic: Ecstasy and neo-shamanism in North European paganism* (2002a) which explores constructions of Northern European shamanic practice in today's world. Further recommended are works which encourage multiple or alternative views of landscape and 'site', such as Edmonds and Seabourne's work on one English region, *Prehistory in the Peak* (2001) or for more global sense of sites and interaction, see Adrian Ivikhiv's *Claiming Sacred Ground: Pilgrims and politics at Glastonbury and Sedona* (2001) and the work of Kathryn Rountree, which presents multiple views and interpretations of sites in Malta and elsewhere (e.g. 'Performing the divine: Neo-pagan pilgrimages and embodiment at sacred sites', *Body and Society*, 12(4): 95–115, 2006).

REFERENCES

AÐALSTEINSSON, J. H. 1978. *Under the Cloak*, Acta Universitatis Upsaliensis 4 (Uppsala: Almqvist and Wiksell).

BIRD-DAVID, N. 1993. 'Tribal metaphorisation of human-nature relatedness: A comparative analysis' in K. Milton (ed.), *Environmentalism: The View from Anthropology* (London: Routledge), pp. 112-25.

——1999. 'Animism revisited: Personhood, environment and relational epistemology', *Current Anthropology*, 42: 67-91.

BLAIN, J. 2001. 'Shamans, stones, authenticity and appropriations: Contestations of invention and meaning' in R. J. Wallis and K. J. Lymer (eds), *A Permeability of Boundaries: New approaches to the archaeology of art, religion and folklore*, BAR International Series 936 (Oxford: BAR), pp. 47-56.

——2002a. *Nine Worlds of Seid-Magic: Ecstasy and neo-shamanism in North European paganism* (London: Routledge).

——2002b. 'Magic, healing, or death? Issues of seidr, "balance", and morality in past and present' in P. A. Baker and G. Carr (eds), *New Approaches to Medical Archaeology and Anthropology* (London: Routledge), pp. 161-71.

——2004. 'Tracing the in/authentic seeress: From seid-magic to stone circles' in J. Blain, D. Ezzy, and G. Harvey (eds), *Researching Paganisms* (Walnut Creek, CA: AltaMira), pp. 217-40.

——2005. '"Now many of those things are shown to me which I was denied before": Seidr, shamanism, and journeying, past and present', *Studies in Religion/Sciences Religieuses*, 94(1): 81-98.

——and WALLIS, R. J. 2006a. 'Re-presenting spirit: Heathenry, new-indigenes, and the imaged past' in I. A. Russell (ed.), *Images, Representations and Heritage: Moving beyond modern approaches to archaeology* (London and New York: Springer), pp. 89-108.

—— ——2006b. 'Ritual reflections, practitioner meanings: Disputing the terminology of neo-shamanic "performance"', *Journal of Ritual Studies*, 20(1): 21-6.

—— ——2007. *Sacred Sites, Contested Rites/Rights: Pagan engagements with prehistoric monuments* (Brighton: Sussex Academic Press).

—— ——2008. 'Sacred, secular or sacrilegious? Prehistoric sites, pagans and the sacred sites project in Britain' in J. Schachter and S. Brockman (eds), *(Im)permanence: cultures in/out of time* (Pittsburgh: Centre for the Arts in Society, Carnegie Mellon University), pp. 212-23.

CLIFTON, C. 1994. 'Shamanism and neoshamanism' in C. Clifton (ed.), *Witchcraft and Shamanism: Witchcraft today, Book Three* (St Paul, Minnesota: Llewellyn), pp. 1-13.

DEMARRAIS, E., CASTILLO, L. J., and EARLE, T. 1996. 'Ideology, materialization and power strategies', *Current Anthropology*, 37(1): 15-31.

EDMONDS, M. and SEABORNE, T. 2001. *Prehistory in the Peak* (Stroud: Tempus).

ELIADE, M. 1964. 'Shamanism: Archaic techniques of ecstasy' (Harmondsworth: Penguin).

FLAHERTY, G. 1992. *Shamanism and the Eighteenth Century* (New Jersey: Princeton University Press).

GOODMAN, F. D. 1990. *Where the Spirits Ride the Wind: Trance journeys and other ecstatic experiences* (Bloomington: Indiana University Press).

——1999. 'Ritual body postures, channeling, and the ecstatic body trance', *Anthropology of Consciousness*, 10: 54-9.

GREENE, S. 1998. 'The shaman's needle: Development, shamanic agency, and intermedicality in Aguarina lands, Peru', *American Ethnologist*, 25(4): 634–58.
GREENWOOD, S. 2000. *Magic, Witchcraft and the Otherworld* (Oxford: Berg).
—— 2005. *The Nature of Magic: An anthropology of consciousness* (Oxford: Berg).
HAMAYON, R. 1993. 'Are "trance", "ecstasy"' and similar concepts appropriate in the study of shamanism?', *Shaman*, 1(2): 3–25.
—— 1996. 'Shamanism in Siberia: From partnership in supernature to counter-power in society' in N. Thomas and C. Humphrey (eds), *Shamanism, History and the State* (Ann Arbor: University of Michigan Press), 76–89.
HARNER, M. 1980. *The Way of the Shaman* (London: HarperCollins).
HARVEY, G. 1997. *Listening People, Speaking Earth: Contemporary paganism* (London: Hurst).
—— 2005. *Animism: Respecting the living world* (London: Hurst).
—— and WALLIS, R. J. 2007. *A Historical Dictionary of Shamanism* (Lanham, Maryland: Scarecrow Press).
HUTTON, R. 2011. *Shamans: Siberian Spirituality and the Western Imagination* (London: Hambledon).
—— 1999. *The Triumph of the Moon: A history of modern pagan witchcraft* (Oxford: Oxford University Press).
—— 2001. *Shamans: Siberian Spirituality and the Western Imagination* (London: Hambledon).
INGERMAN, S. 2004. *Shamanic Journeying: A beginner's guide* (Louisville, CO: Sounds True).
IVIKHIV, A. 2001. *Claiming Sacred Ground: Pilgrims and Politics at Glastonbury and Sedona* (Bloomington: Indiana University Press).
JAKOBSEN, M. D. 1999. *Shamanism: Traditional and contemporary approaches to the mastery of spirits and healing* (New York and Oxford: Berghahn Books).
LETCHER, A. 2004. 'Raising the dragon: Folklore and the development of contemporary British eco-paganism', *The Pomegranate*, 6(2): 175–89.
—— 2006. *Shroom: A cultural history of the magic mushroom* (London: Faber and Faber).
LINDQUIST, G. 1997. *Shamanic Performances on the Urban Scene: Neo-shamanism in contemporary Sweden* (Stockholm: Stockholm Studies in Social Anthropology).
MACLELLAN, G. 1999. *Shamanism* (London: Piatkus).
MAYER, G. 2008. 'The figure of the shaman as a modern myth: Some reflections on the attractiveness of shamanism in modern societies', *The Pomegranate*, 10(1): 70–103.
PETTIGREW, J and TAMU, Y. 2002. 'Healing here, there and in-between: A Tamu shaman's experience of international landscapes' in P. A. Baker and G. Carr (eds), *Practitioners, Practices and Patients: New approaches to medical archaeology and anthropology* (London: Routledge), pp. 109–24.
PRICE, N. 2001. *The Viking Way: Religion and war in Late Iron Age Scandinavia* (Uppsala: Uppsala University Press).
ROSE, W. 1984. 'Just what's all this fuss about whiteshamanism anyway?' in B. Schöler (ed.), *Coyote Was Here: Essays on contemporary Native American literary and political mobilization* (Aarhus, Denmark: Seklos), pp. 13–24.
—— 1992. 'The great pretenders: Further reflections on whiteshamanism' in M. Annette Jaimes (ed.), *The State of Native America: Genocide, colonization, and resistance* (Boston: South End Press), pp. 403–22.
ROUNTREE, K. 2006. 'Performing the divine: Neo-pagan pilgrimages and embodiment at sacred sites', *Body and Society*, 12(4): 95–115.

SHIROKOGOROV, S. M. 1935. *Psychomental Complex of the Tungus* (London: Kegan Paul, Trench, Trubner and Co.).

SITCH, B. 2007. *Lindow Man Consultation, Saturday 10th February 2007: Report*, available online: <www.museum.manchester.ac.uk/aboutus/ourpractice/lindowman/fileuploadmax10mb, 120485,en.pdf>.

SMITH, A. 1993. 'For all those who were Indian in a former life' in C. J. Adams (ed.), *Ecofeminism and the Sacred* (New York: Continuum), pp. 168–71.

TAUSSIG, M. 1987. *Shamanism, Colonialism and the Wild Man: A study in terror and healing* (Chicago: The University of Chicago Press).

TEPPERMAN, L. and BLAIN, J. 2005. *Think Twice: Sociology looks at current issues*, 2nd edn (New Jersey: Prentice-Hall).

WALLIS, R. J. 2003. *Shamans/Neo-Shamans: Ecstasy, alternative archaeologies and contemporary pagans* (London: Routledge).

——2004. 'Between the Worlds: Autoarchaeology and neo-Shamans' in J. Blain, D. Ezzy, and G. Harvey (eds), *Researching Paganisms* (Walnut Creek, CA: Altamira), pp. 191–215.

——and BLAIN, J. 2011. 'From Respect to Reburial: Negotiating pagan interest in prehistoric remains in Britain, through the Avebury Consultation', *Public Archaeology*, 10(1): 23–45.

CHAPTER 64

DRUIDISM AND NEO-PAGANISM

ALEKS PLUSKOWSKI

1 INTRODUCTION

NEO-PAGANISM, a phenomenon which started in the late eighteenth/early nineteenth century, proliferated in Western Europe and North America during the second half of the twentieth century. Today, it is represented by a diversity of religions seeking to recreate and revive extinct European pre-Christian polytheistic religions, largely based on celebrating the seasonal cycles of Nature (Adler 1986: ix). In the United States, neo-paganism can be understood, in one sense, as the search by uprooted Westerners for their own roots and origins (ibid.: 252). In Europe, this revival is, in part, focused on ceremonies conducted at prehistoric sites where neo-pagan groups have come into direct conflict with archaeologists and heritage managers. Since the 1960s, elements of neo-paganism have become interwoven with the ecology movement, the feminist movement, and libertarianism, as well as various counter-culture and alternative lifestyles. This fusion of traditions goes some way to explain the confrontations over access to sacred sites, a trend which can be traced to the earliest clashes between self-proclaimed druids and the British authorities at Stonehenge in the 1920s. But alongside the struggle for access, neo-paganism has also contributed to questioning the monopoly of orthodox archaeology over interpretations of the past. Some neo-pagans have also begun to question the excavation, removal, and display of prehistoric human remains, echoing concerns expressed by Native American and Australian Aboriginal groups. In the same way that archaeologists see themselves connecting with the past by direct contact with the material remains of extinct societies, neo-pagan engagements with the past are most significant at archaeological sites (Wallis 2001: 221).

How has academia reacted to neo-pagan interests in the past? A decade ago, Ronald Hutton (1999) published the first historical study of modern pagan witchcraft, focusing on its development in southern England from the early nineteenth century. Following on from *The Pagan Religions of the Ancient British Isles* (Hutton 1993), which distanced modern paganisms from ancient pre-Christian paradigms, *The Triumph of the Moon* systematically explored the fusion of various cultural and magical traditions within neo-pagan groups ranging from druids to Wiccans. Although Hutton reiterated the lack of continuity between modern and early paganisms, he recognized the past as a legitimate source of inspiration for contemporary neo-pagan spirituality. In a similar vein, a number of archaeologists have begun to see the reuse of prehistoric monuments by neo-pagan groups as another stage in the life cycle of these structures, perhaps even leaving new and distinct archaeological signatures. Nonetheless, alternative, neo-pagan interpretations of archaeological sites continue to be rejected by the majority of academic archaeologists and historians. Within the bewildering diversity of neo-pagan groups (e.g. see Adler 1986 and papers in Strmiska 2005) the most frequently associated with prehistoric landscapes and monuments are the druids.

2 DRUIDISM AND STONEHENGE

Many discussions of neo-paganism and the past begin and end with Stonehenge. This ruined stone circle in Wiltshire has become the quintessential European neo-pagan monument, and arguably one of the most contested archaeological sites in the world. The association between druidism and Stonehenge first appears as one of John Aubrey's speculative theories for interpreting the site at the end of the seventeenth century, reiterated by William Stukely and others in the 1740s. By this point the association with druidism had became established as national folklore (Piggott 1968: 145). When William Danby built a folly in the grounds of his home at Swinton Hall in Yorkshire, he modelled it on Stonehenge and called it a 'druid temple' (Green 1997: 145). The link with modern druidism (or neo-druidism) developed at the turn of the twentieth century, and has been thoroughly documented by Adam Stout (2008). The modern druids emerged from the Universalist movement, led by the charismatic George Watson Macgregor Reid. After a major ceremony at Stonehenge taking place during the 1905 Solstice, in which 650–700 druids participated, regular annual druidic services became the norm from 1912. Confrontations began a few years later when the local landowner enclosed the site and began charging admission.

The struggle then became one for access, but when the first major archaeological campaign was initiated at Stonehenge in the 1920s by one Colonel Hawley, representing the Society of Antiquaries, Reid described this as a form of desecration. In a letter to the head of the Society, he thundered against archaeologists, who, in his eyes, had nothing to contribute to an understanding of Stonehenge, and who could never understand or explain the site. Subsequent incidents included a petition by the druids to have two sets of ashes buried at the site, an event which provoked heavy criticism from the archaeological community and national media and culminated in the breaching of the perimeter around Stonehenge in 1925, whereupon 1,000 people incited by Reid were able to enter the site without paying. Although archaeologists such as O. G. S. Crawford attacked the validity of the association between druids and Stonehenge, the Solstice services were revived in the 1950s and are now a permanent fixture, dovetailing with the counter-culture festivals that provoked serious concerns about conserving the monument in the latter decades of the twentieth century. Today, the site both unites and divides the druid community, with divergent views regarding access and usage (Puttick 2000: 151). At one point the joint-chief of the British Druid Order clashed with heritage managers over the reburial of skeletal remains likely to be excavated at Stonehenge (Wallis 2001: 216). Although archaeologists

FIGURE 64.1 Seahenge.

have more or less accepted the right of the druids to use the site, recognizing this as another stage in the ongoing life of Stonehenge, conflicts over access and management continue.

Confrontations between archaeologists, heritage managers, and neo-pagans are not restricted to Stonehenge, but have flared up more recently around other prehistoric monuments. In 1998, a circle of 54 wooden split-oaks surrounding a single inverted post was spotted on the Norfolk coast, revealed due to the increasing erosion of the surrounding peat (Figure 64.1). In 1999, archaeologists moved in to prevent 'Seahenge' from being destroyed by the sea. On 16 June, Michael McCarthy, writing for *The Independent*, described how neo-pagan eco-warriors (including druids) occupied the circle and sought to physically stop the removal of the timbers. The druids had interpreted the central oak as an altar and accused the archaeologists of vandalizing a sacred site (Wood 2002). Excavation was delayed and the confrontation became a legal issue, with both sides trying to outmanoeuvre each other in the courtroom. The druids were initially offered the chance to build a replica of Seahenge on the spot to 'plug up the energy source', but ultimately the archaeologists won the court battle and the neo-pagans were barred from the site.

The tensions over Seahenge extended beyond the druids to the local community, and raised all manner of heritage-management issues, but the archaeologists were genuinely surprised by the reaction to what they perceived as the essential rescue of a unique site. Although no similar confrontations have reached the attention of the national media since Seahenge, neo-pagan groups maintain an active watch on prehistoric landscapes around the country. In 2003, druids gathered to protest at road building near the site of Tara in County Meath, Ireland—a complex of prehistoric monuments with links to sacral kingship. Unable to stop the development itself, they performed rituals designed to protect the Hill of Tara from damage (Butler 2005: 95). Most recently, The Dragon Network (combining neo-paganism with the ecology movement) sought to block quarrying within the vicinity of the Nine Ladies stone circle in the Peak District. The stone (or timber) circle has certainly become integrated with popular perceptions of modern druids; Douglas Cowan's (2005) recent book on the organization of paganism on the Internet is entitled *Cyberhenge*. Even modern stone circles have become the foci of neo-pagan rituals; Sam Hill built a replica of Stonehenge in Maryhill, Washington in the early twentieth century, initially as a war memorial, but which has subsequently become a site of neo-pagan worship (Kaiser 1998; Holtorf 2005: 122).

Not all see the neo-pagan reuse of prehistoric monuments in a wholly positive light. Referring to incidents such as the graffiti daubed on the Avebury stones in 1996 and the regular lighting of candles in West Kennet long barrow, Robert Wallis (2003: 168) suggested the situation was perhaps reaching 'crisis point'. Certainly visitor impact on sacred monuments—pagan or otherwise—is being increasingly monitored by organizations such as the National Trust and local heritage bodies. The balance between conservation and accessibility, rehearsed for decades at Stonehenge, is now extending to other monuments and has promoted reflection on the very purpose and extent of this conservation. Modern druids are probably the oldest group of neo-pagans who use prehistoric stone circles for religious purposes, but today these monuments attract the broadest range of groups from the neo-pagan community. Despite the variety in cosmologies, all share a broadly similar understanding of the spirituality of the landscape; a landscape organized and spiritually activated by the earliest human societies.

3 NEO-PAGAN LANDSCAPES

In the cosmologies of neo-paganism, the landscape is typically charged with varying degrees of spiritual power focused on key monuments (such as Stonehenge and Avebury). Sites across a region, and indeed across the world, are perceived as being linked by a network of spiritual energy. This network is believed to date back to a dim and distant past, linking the spirituality of modern pagans with that of their prehistoric (and sometimes historic) ancestors. The most popular and enduring expression of this spiritual power grid is the concept of ley lines. In October 1925, Alfred Watkins published *The Old Straight Track*, outlining the theory of ley lines. It became one of the most popular books on British prehistory, shortly followed by *The Ley Hunter's Manual*. Watkins initially interpreted his perceived ley lines—straight lines cutting through the landscape linking various monuments—as trade networks maintained by a community of artisans. He hinted at some esoteric knowledge associated with these alignments, and this may have prompted the development of ideas of leys as lines of spiritual energy. Watkins' ideas have been repeatedly ridiculed and criticized by archaeologists (more recently reiterated by Chippindale 2004: 243–5), but they remain popular and have, at least in part, inspired neo-pagan constructions of their sacred landscapes. Ley lines connect sites of spiritual power which modern neo-pagan groups have adopted as a link to the spirituality of their ancestors, whose organization of the landscape resulted in a national, even global, sacred geometry (Holtorf 2005: 109; Green 1997: 178). Unsurprisingly, two of the most famous ley lines in England pass through Stonehenge (see Figure 64.2; Chippindale 2004: 242). The destruction or removal of sites on ley lines threatens to disrupt their energy flows, an argument that was presented at Seahenge in an attempt to stop archaeologists tampering with the site (Wallis 2001: 222). But archaeologists and developers are not the only groups who potentially interfere with the sacred geometry of the past.

The phenomenon of 'psychic questing' was popularized by Andrew Collins in the 1990s, particularly in his *Black Alchemist* series, and painted a picture of a British landscape charged with spiritual energy that could be tapped, misused, and restored. Incorporating everything from ley lines to Gnosticism, psychic quests were partially concerned with the spiritual biographies (and 'health') of monuments in the landscape—from megaliths to monasteries. The objects of quests were a variety of spiritually and historically important

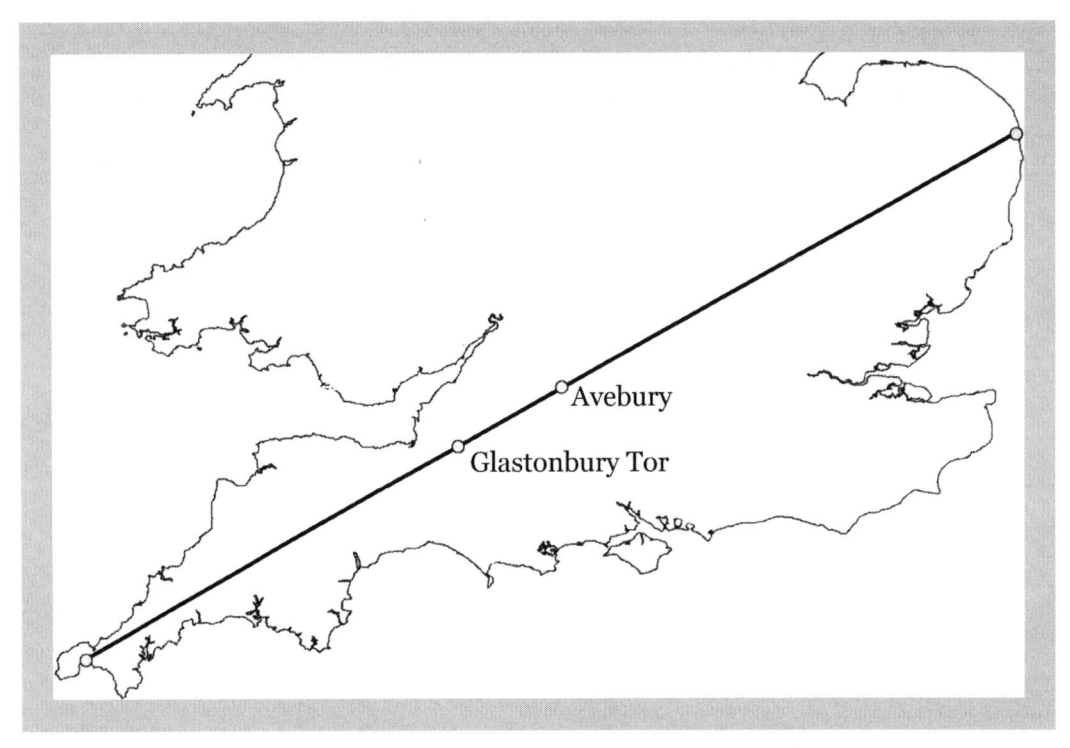

FIGURE 64.2 The St Michael ley line (cutting through Avebury and Glastonbury).

artefacts, with their own detailed spiritual biographies. The idea of a spiritually charged landscape is certainly nothing new, and societies around the world have actively organized religious space for millennia. However, his books (Collins 1988, 1991, 1994) represented a dramatic snapshot of distinct neo-pagan spiritual spaces in Britain at the end of the second millennium AD. The process of questing resulted in new 'psychic histories' of featured monuments, drawing together threads of continuity over centuries, and in some cases, millennia and culminating in the discovery of artefacts. Collins' publications documented a number of obscure occult groups and individuals visiting these sites (in addition to his own group), typically at night, to conduct magical rituals in order to tap and manipulate spiritual energy, usually for negative purposes:

> Like the Black Alchemist, the Dark Council's targets were seemingly prehistoric monuments—such as stone circles, barrows, earthworks and mounds—as well as Christian sacred places such as holy hills, wells and churchyards. At each they would conduct some form of magical rite to contain and harness the inherent energies thought to be generated at such locations. [Collins 1994: 94]

Prehistoric (pagan) and historic (Christian) sites were spiritually linked by their association with supernatural archetypes. For example, St Catherine's Hill near Winchester—an iron age hill fort with a twelfth-century chapel on its summit—was associated with the saint who was seen as embodying aspects of 'pagan dark goddesses such as Hekate', whilst the ancestral guardian of Stonehenge took the name of the Egyptian god Ptah, prompting Collins to refer to Egyptian material culture found at the site and to speculate about visits from Bronze

Age Egyptians (ibid.: 134, 221). The implications of perceiving the land as spiritually 'alive' have already been illustrated in the example of Seahenge (Blain 2005: 202), and it is clear that the archaeological landscape is not only contested between neo-pagans, archaeologists, and heritage managers, but also between neo-pagans and occult groups. In recent years Andrew Collins has moved away from psychic questing, but his popularization of a spiritually charged and contested landscape—a psychic battlefield focused on key monuments—endures. The modern neo-pagan landscape is of interest to archaeologists and historians because it is typically mapped onto a comparable spiritual landscape in the past. This past landscape is a normative one, conflating multiple prehistoric eras into a single, enduring spirituality, one which was interrupted by the introduction of Christianity. But even Christian monuments may have spiritual significance to neo-pagans; for example, Irish neo-druids believe that wells dedicated to Christian saints were previously markers of sacred springs (Butler 2005: 100). The 'conversion of the landscape' is certainly an important aspect of the Christianization of Europe, and has attracted increasing attention from scholars in recent years. But whilst the idea of spiritual landscapes is something that archaeologists and historical geographers are increasingly comfortable with, the notion of continuity and familiarity with extinct religious systems based on a shared spiritual landscape—something that certain neo-pagan groups believe—is unlikely to be recognized within mainstream scholarship.

4 ASATRU AND CONFRONTING CHRISTIANITY IN SCANDINAVIA

Described as the revival of the beliefs and practices of pre-Christian North Europeans, Asatru (after the Icelandic organization Asatruarfelagid—'the fellowship of those who follow the ancient gods') is a modern religion which developed in Iceland, Britain, and the US independently, but more or less simultaneously, in the 1970s (Adler 1986: 274–5). The differences between Icelandic and American Nordic paganism reflect the close association of the former with the country's cultural heritage. Pagan groups in Iceland are seen as quintessentially indigenous and get a lot of respect and support within the country. Asatru is largely concerned with the revival of aspects of Nordic paganism, and its members are interested in both textual and archaeological sources to inform their practices. Archaeological monuments of pre-Christian/Conversion Period Scandinavia—from Viking Age cemeteries through to the picture stones on the island of Gotland—are considered pilgrimage sites, and there is a strong awareness of scholarly debate and research developments within the Asatru community (Strmiska and Sigurvinsson 2005: 141). Archaeologists and historians, in turn, are certainly aware of neo-pagan interests in the Scandinavian pre-Christian past. A project initiated at the University of Lund in Sweden in 2000 entitled 'Vägar till Midgård' (Roads to Midgard: Norse paganism in long-term perspectives), encompassed both ancient and modern Scandinavian paganisms and sought, like Hutton (1999: 412–16), to recognize both in their broader contexts, rather than dismiss any neo-pagan use of the past as somehow incorrect. This is one example of a growing scholarly acceptance that archaeologists and historians do not have an exclusive monopoly on the past, and that multiple interpretations and recontextualizations are not only legitimate, but also inevitable and even desirable.

However, there have been occasional confrontations concerning archaeological monuments which illustrate an undercurrent of unease stretching back, at least in the imagination of contemporary groups, to the conversion period itself. The site chosen for Christian millennium celebrations in 2000—organized by the Lutheran Church—was at Thigvellir, the cherished location of the Althing parliament where Icelanders voted for Christianity at the turn of the first millennium. Members of Asatruarfelagid had celebrated the summer solstice there for a number of years, and for the millennium had intended to close a series of land and fire ceremonies, dedicated to the god Baldur, with a ritual at Thigvellir. Whilst the aim of the Christian celebrations was to present an idea of a unified, Christian Iceland, the objective of Asatruarfelagid was to revive Iceland's pagan beliefs, and by doing so heal the land. This ideological confrontation prompted the Church to push for restricted access to the newly constructed facilities at the site, on the grounds that these were intended for Christians, rather than non-Christians (Strmiska and Sigurvinsson 2005: 172–5). There was much popular sympathy and support for Asatruarfelagid, who held their ceremony in spite of the restrictions, but the whole episode illustrates a simmering tension between neo-pagan groups and Christianity which is found across contemporary Western culture.

In the early 1990s, this had evolved into an explicit confrontational ideology within certain Norwegian groups. Here, a combination of right-wing politics, Satanism, and Scandinavian neo-paganism, nurtured within the Black Metal music scene, resulted in the targeted, physical destruction of Christian monuments. The most devastating example of this anti-Christian impulse was the destruction of the twelfth-century stave church at Fantoft by arson in 1992 (Figure 64.3; see Moynihan and Søderlind 1998: 75–80). The church was subsequently rebuilt, but the incident has become an enduring element of the modern mythology of the extreme music scene. No one was convicted, although as many as 20 subsequent instances of church arsons in Norway have been linked to the Black Metal scene by the Directorate for Cultural Heritage (ibid.: 79). Varg Vikernes, the creator of Norwegian band *Burzum* and alleged founder of Norsk Hedensk Front (later Allgermanische Heidnische Front), described the fire as 'a symbol of our heathen consciousness' and suggested it was one of the main reasons for the recent growing interest in Norse mythology in Norway (ibid.: 89, 92).

There is in fact no clear link between the Black Metal scene and neo-paganism, although the physical destruction of Christian heritage is regarded by some—within the scene—as a form of revenge against what is perceived to be an oppressive, foreign religion. This opposition has come to define the extreme counter-culture of Norwegian society, but across Scandinavia today the pre-Christian past is popularly invoked to construct a sense of identity in the present. Northern Europe is not the only part of the world to have witnessed the rise of nationalist neo-paganism. Mattias Gardell (2003) documented what he described as 'racist heathenry'; a meeting between the white separatist movement and Scandinavian (or rather Germanic) neo-paganism in North America. Right-wing extremists appear to have been particularly attracted to the Odinist pagan community; more conservative in character than Asatru, emphasizing family values, courage, and warrior virtues (Adler 1986: 274). But in North America there has been little confrontation over the material culture of the past. An exceptional incident was the Asatru Folk Assembly's demand for exclusive rights to Kennewick Man—a 9,000-year-old skeleton found in Washington State in 1996—on the grounds that the bones may have been ancient European in origin (Wallis 2001: 216). Although similarities have been observed between the treatment of prehistoric sites in England and North America, with visitors occasionally leaving

FIGURE 64.3 Fantoft stave church, Norway.

votive offerings (Chippindale 2004: 257), neo-pagan groups in the United States ultimately look to Europe for their source of spirituality and inspiration.

5 CONCLUSIONS: WHAT DOES THE FUTURE HOLD FOR NEO-PAGANS AND ARCHAEOLOGISTS?

The development of tensions between neo-pagan groups and archaeologists is evident in Britain, and perhaps in other areas of the world, but at present these are limited to spectacular and relatively unique cases. Although Chippindale (2004: 255) describes modern druidism at Stonehenge as a 'mess of misunderstanding and credulity', he also admits having an 'affection and a respect for the alternative visions across the divide'. Whilst the monopoly on the past is being slowly broken by subversive theoretical elements within academic archaeology, the government and its agencies—across the world—look to archaeologists for 'the truth' about the past. Archaeologists are certainly aware of being 'truth-makers' (Stout 2008: 227), but maintain a distance from what some refer to as the 'lunatic fringe' of alternative archaeology, a category which includes neo-pagan interpretations of the past. Neo-pagan groups perceive a shared or familiar spirituality with prehistoric (and specifically pre-Christian) societies. These tend to range from the endurance of supernatural forces at prehistoric sites through to broader mythologies of pagan survivals following Christianization (e.g. on Wicca mythologies of this survival see Adler 1986: 45–6; Wallis 2001: 215; Hutton 1999). But whilst it may be easy to demonstrate the complex life histories of individual monuments on the basis of excavation and observation, it is impossible to argue against something as physically intangible as belief.

In 1993, the Insular Order of Druids was founded at Stonehenge, with an aim of recreating 'authentic' Celtic ritual (Green 1997: 170), whilst Irish neo-pagan druids strongly believe that megalithic stone circles and similar prehistoric monuments were used by the original druids, even if they did not build them (Butler 2005: 96). Unsurprisingly, many archaeologists refuse to enter into a dialogue with alternative archaeology, although there are also archaeologists who consider themselves neo-pagans. Without a detailed anthropological study canvassing both sides, it is very difficult to say whether a confrontational attitude over conflicting interpretations of the past has become ingrained. Dialogue between neo-pagans and archaeologists will occur most frequently in the sphere of heritage management of prehistoric sites. Groups which express some spiritual affiliation with a particular site have been more concerned with access to this site, rather than with engaging in academic debate. The case of Stonehenge, and more recently Seahenge, exemplifies this. Whether neo-pagan groups develop strong political lobbies that can influence the course of archaeological excavations and presentations remains to be seen, but the impulse to challenge the scholarly monopoly on the past is certainly there. Prehistory, as Stout (2008: 1) notes, is the 'place where different visions for the future are passionately fought out in the present', as neo-pagans look back to this era before the coming of Christianity. Negative attitudes to Christianity are evident to varying degrees in druidism, as well as in Scandinavian and North American neo-pagan groups. However this hostility should not be exaggerated; more popular and less confrontational uses of archaeological sites are provided by self-styled pagan weddings held at prehistoric monuments, from the stone circles at Avebury in Wiltshire to the Gollenstein menhir in Saarland, Germany (Holtorf 2005: 108), alongside the countless ceremonies which seek to tap the spiritual energies of the past.

Furthermore, despite the sensationalism of neo-pagan confrontations with archaeologists and heritage managers, alternative interpretations of the past appear to be restricted to a very small minority. Membership of individual neo-pagan groups tends to reach no more than a few thousand, and often significantly less. Moreover, John Collis (1999: 135) has observed that 'we [archaeologists] still provide the dominant, and most popular view of the past', one which is made widely accessible through school curricula as well as various forms of public media. On the other hand, Schmidt and Halle (1999: 171), considering the popular mythology surrounding the Externsteine—a rock formation in the Teutoburger Forest region of Germany, popularly perceived as a prehistoric sanctuary, attracting various neo-pagan groups—concluded that archaeologists have little if any control over public 'misinterpretations of the evidence'. In contrast, Lynn Meskell (1999: 88) has argued how in the case of neo-pagan interests in Çatalhöyük, archaeologists actually created the narratives which New Age archaeology subsequently adopted. Indeed, neo-pagans in Britain have been inspired by landscape archaeology and anthropology in recognizing the importance of place and the close relationships between people in the past, and the land they lived and worked on (Blain 2005: 201). The relationship between archaeologists working with prehistory and neo-pagans therefore appears to be more complicated than a simple confrontation between 'truth makers' and 'myth makers'.

Archaeologists working with contexts post-dating the religious conversion to Christianity rarely encounter neo-pagan interests although they are occasionally confronted with claims of indigenous religious traditions surviving the conversion. The 'green man', a popular high-medieval church decoration found across Europe, is perhaps one of the most frequently cited examples of a pagan survivor, deriving in part from assumptions that medieval Christianity perceived the natural world negatively. In fact, the notion of continuity is supported by some academics. For example, Marija Gimbutas has argued for the widespread veneration, suppression, underground survival, and then resurgence of a universal prehistoric goddess, influencing the development of neo-pagan goddess spirituality in recent decades (Hutton 1997). Gimbutas (1999: 320) refers to her homeland Lithuania as still possessing a 'sacred landscape' with holy forests and groves, miraculous springs, healing trees, and menhirs called 'goddesses' charged with 'mysterious power'. Interestingly, the Eastern Baltic is one area of Europe where there *is* good evidence for the maintenance of indigenous religious traditions alongside the acceptance of Christianity, sometimes for several centuries, but this is a far cry from druidism at Stonehenge. However, it cannot be denied that any archaeology of neo-paganism in the future will have to look to the use of prehistoric monuments and landscapes in the modern era.

Suggested Reading

For an overview of British paganism see Ronald Hutton's 1993 volume *The Pagan Religions of the Ancient British Isles: Their nature and legacy* (Oxford: Blackwell) and Adam Stout's 2008 volume, *Creating Prehistory: Druids, ley hunters and archaeologists in pre-war Britain* (Oxford: Blackwell). Hutton's 1999 volume, *The Triumph of the Moon: A history of modern pagan witchcraft* (Oxford: Oxford University Press) is recommended as a history of modern pagan witchcraft. Hutton's latest volume, *Blood and Mistletoe* (New Haven: Yale University Press) provides a definitive history of the Druids in Britain. For an introduction to paganism in other cultures see *Modern Paganism in World Cultures: Comparative perspectives* (Oxford: ABC-CLIO, 2005) edited by Michael Strmiska.

References

ADLER, M. 1986. *Drawing Down the Moon: Witches, druids, goddess-worshippers, and other pagans in America today* (Boston, MA: Beacon Press).
BLAIN, J. 2005. 'Heathenry, the past and sacred sites in today's Britain' in M. Strmiksa (ed.), *Modern Paganism in World Cultures: Comparative perspectives* (Oxford: ABC-CLIO), pp. 180–208.
BUTLER, J. 2005. 'Druidry in contemporary Ireland' in M. Strmiksa (ed.), *Modern Paganism in World Cultures: Comparative perspectives* (Oxford: ABC-CLIO), pp. 87–125.
CHIPPINDALE, C. 2004. *Stonehenge Complete* (London: Thames and Hudson).
COLLINS, A. 1988. *The Black Alchemist* (Leigh-on-Sea: ABC Books).
——1991. *The Seventh Sword* (London: Century).
——1994. *The Second Coming* (London: Arrow).
COLLIS, J. 1999. 'Of "The Green Man" and "Little Green Men"' in A. Gazin-Schwartz and C. Holtorf (eds), *Archaeology and Folklore* (London: Routledge), pp. 129–35.
COWAN, D. E. 2005. *Cyberhenge: Modern pagans on the Internet* (London: Routledge).
GARDELL, M. 2003. *Blood of the Gods: The pagan revival and white separatism* (Durham, NC: Duke University Press).

Gimbutas, M. 1999. *The Language of the Goddess* (London: Thames and Hudson).
Green, M. 1997. *Exploring the World of the Druids* (London: Thames and Hudson).
Holtorf, C. 2005. *From Stonehenge to Las Vegas: Archaeology as popular culture* (Walnut Creek, CA: AltaMira).
Hutton, R. 1993. *The Pagan Religions of the Ancient British Isles: Their nature and legacy* (Oxford: Blackwell).
——1997. 'The Neolithic great goddess: A study in modern tradition', *Antiquity*, 71: 91–9.
——1999. The *Triumph of the Moon: A history of modern pagan witchcraft* (Oxford: Oxford University Press).
——2011. *Blood and Mistletoe: The history of the Druids in Britain* (New Haven: Yale University Press).
Kaiser, D. 1998. 'Stonehenge: American style', *3rd Stone*, 32: 31–2.
Meskell, L. 1999. 'Feminism, Paganism, Pluralism' in A. Gazin-Schwartz and C. Holtorf (eds), *Archaeology and Folklore* (London: Routledge), pp. 83–9.
Moynihan, N. and Søderlind, D. 1998. *Lords of Chaos: The bloody rise of the satanic metal underground* (Los Angeles, CA: Feral House (revised 2003)).
Piggott, S. 1968. *The Druids* (London: Thames and Hudson).
Puttick, E. 2000. 'Druidry' in P. B. Clarke (ed.), *Encyclopedia of New Religious Movements* (London: Routledge), pp. 150–1.
Schmidt, M. and Halle, U. 1999. 'On the folklore of the Externsteine, or a centre for Germanomaniacs' in A. Gazin-Schwartz and C. Holtorf (eds), *Archaeology and Folklore* (London: Routledge), pp. 158–74.
Stout, A. 2008. *Creating Prehistory: Druids, ley hunters and archaeologists in pre-war Britain* (Oxford: Blackwell).
Strmiska, M. (ed.) 2005. *Modern Paganism in World Cultures: Comparative perspectives* (Oxford: ABC-CLIO).
Strmiska, M. F. and Sigurvinsson, B. F. 2005. 'Asatru: Nordic paganism in Iceland and America' in M. Strmiksa (ed.), *Modern Paganism in World Cultures: Comparative perspectives* (Oxford: ABC-CLIO), pp. 126–79.
Wallis, R. J. 2001. 'Waking ancestor spirits: Neo-shamanic engagements with archaeology' in N. S. Price (ed.), *The Archaeology of Shamanism* (London: Routledge), pp. 213–30.
——2003. *Shamans/Neo-shamans: Contested ecstasies, alternative archaeologies, and contemporary pagans* (New York: Routledge).
Watkins, A. 1925. *The Old Straight Track* (London: Methuen and Co.).
Wood, C. 2002. 'The meaning of Seahenge', *3rd Stone*, 43: 49–54.

CHAPTER 65

ANCESTOR CULTS

TIMOTHY INSOLL

1 INTRODUCTION

EXPLANATIONS involving ancestors and ancestor cults have a long tradition, 'ancestral' almost, in both archaeological interpretation (e.g. Morris 1991; Whitley 2002) and wider scholarship that falls within the remit of History of Religions (e.g. Hardacre 2005). An 'ancestor' is defined within the *Oxford Handy Dictionary* as 'any person from whom one's father or mother is descended' (Fowler and Fowler 1986: 25). This is a simple definition that belies the complexities that are denoted by a belief in the ancestors within the frameworks of religion and as the focus of ritual practices. 'Ancestor' in connection with describing the associated body of relevant practices and beliefs is often related to 'cult', as here, or to 'worship'. 'Worship' might be applicable in some contexts in indicating the level of devotion offered the ancestors, as perhaps in ancient Egypt beginning c.3100 BC, or in Mesopotamia, beginning c.2500 BC (Parker Pearson 2001: 210), but in many others 'veneration' may be preferable. This is because there are semantic differences between the two, with 'worship' meaning, among other things, 'adore as divine' (Fowler and Fowler 1986: 1046) and 'veneration', 'deep respect, warm approbation' (Fowler and Fowler 1986: 1009); whilst 'cult', though problematic if applied to describe religious practices more generally (e.g. Renfrew 1985; cf. Insoll 2004: 5), is useful in denoting a specific body of practice especially 'as expressed in ceremonies' (Fowler and Fowler 1986: 200).

As with terms such as 'animism' and 'totemism' (see Chapter 62), 'ancestor worship', and to a lesser extent 'ancestor cults' carry a lot of baggage linked with evolutionary approaches to religion (Geertz 1966: 39; James 1999: xv). In such evolutionary schema ancestor worship was seen as developing from animism and Spencer (1876), for instance, argued that at the root of every religion was ancestor worship (Parker Pearson 2001: 206). This epistemological background means that 'ancestor worship' and 'ancestor cults' can become meaningless empty categories ill-advisedly applied to archaeological contexts if caution is not exercised (see below). With ancestor cults a key difference is that these are not usually a descriptive category applied to describing religions themselves, unlike, erroneously, totemism and animism (see Chapter 62). However, exceptions exist, and Craig (1988: 61), for instance, refers to the religion of the Mountain-Ok of Central New Guinea (see below) as 'an ancestor cult'. Though in general, as Hardacre (2005: 321) notes, ancestor cults/veneration should be 'properly regarded as a religious practice, not as a religion in itself'.

2 Configuring Ancestors and Ancestor Cults in Terms of Complexity: African Analogies

Analogical frameworks for thinking about the validity of ancestors, and ancestor cult based interpretations for archaeological material are usually sought in anthropology and ethnography. But complexity in configuring ancestors also needs recognizing by archaeologists and sometimes it is not (cf. Whitley 2002: 121–2). Within the frameworks of religious beliefs of the Tallensi of northern Ghana the centrality of the ancestors is clear, and Fortes (1983: 29) notes how 'Tale (Tallensi) cosmology is wholly dominated by the ancestor cult. Even the elaborate totemic institutions, the cult of the Earth and the beliefs about the dangerous mystical qualities of evil trees, animals and other natural phenomena are subordinated to it'. Yet within this structure of ancestral primacy complexity and subtlety of ancestral beliefs, ritual actions directed toward ancestors, and the material culture denoting and linked with ancestors is evident (see below for an example). Moreover, there are what may be defined as different 'types' of ancestors, and what Fortes (1983: 11) refers to as 'a hierarchy of ancestors and ancestor shrines'. Hence although all Tallensi ancestor veneration might be structured by what Fortes (1987: 67) describes as 'geneonymy', i.e. 'the commemoration of ancestors by name', complexity exists in how these relationships and ritual congregations are configured; e.g. as in founding, lineage, and personal ancestors (cf. Fortes 1945, 1949, 1983, 1987).

Further complexity in the Tallensi context is evident in the terms used to define shrines and ancestors for Fortes also notes (1949: 325) how the term *bakologo* is applied to describe the tall conical mud shrine (Figure 65.1) and the group of ancestors that the shrine is dedicated to in the context of divination practice. Hence the word for shrine, groups of ancestor, and the associated beliefs and practices can all be applied to the *same* thing. The complexity of ancestor beliefs, again in the African context, is also well indicated by Janzen (1992: 95) who describes how 'the spirits or shades may be either direct, identifiable lineal ancestors, or more generic shades. They may include more distant nature spirits, hero spirits, or alien spirits that affect human events in many ways. They may be benign or malign; very generalised or particular; male or female; African or foreign.'

The variability in how ancestors can be conceptualized and venerated is clearly indicated by considering another classic anthropological example from Africa, that of the Ndembu of north-western Zambia. Turner (1967: 293–4) describes how among the Ndembu the ancestors do not embody or represent the moral order 'so much as continue after death to interact with their living kin, in terms of their human likes and dislikes' (ibid.: 293). Hence the remote ancestors are not involved in most ritual contexts but rather the spirits of the comparatively recently dead. A further fundamental contrast between Ndembu and Tallensi conceptions of ancestorhood would also seem to lie in Ndembu beliefs that the

FIGURE 65.1 Tallensi ancestor shrine, Tongo Hills, Northern Ghana.

moral order transcends the living and their deceased relatives, and instead, according to Turner (1967: 294), is 'in fact something axiomatic in terms of which both the living and the spirits of their ancestors must seek to become reconciled'. Thus significant differences exist between Tallensi and Ndembu ancestor concepts, materiality, and associated ritual practices and are highlighted by Turner (1957: 172–3). These include, for instance:

- constructing impermanent ancestor shrines consisting of *muyombu* saplings (in contrast to permanent Tallensi ancestor shrines)
- shrines being abandoned when a village moves to a new site (in contrast to Tallensi continuing to maintain, in most instances, ancestral shrines [see Insoll 2008])
- Ndembu beliefs relating to ancestors and the dead functioning towards the promotion of mobility (rather than emphasizing attachment to localities as amongst the Tallensi).

Within the African context, and potentially elsewhere, the often embedded nature of ancestor cults and beliefs can have psychological implications. Negotiating existential uncertainty is a recurring element of life in many parts of sub-Saharan Africa (Ferme 2001), and where, for instance, destiny or 'fate' might be contingent upon how you treat your ancestors as amongst the Tallensi (Fortes 1945: 9, 1987), the consequences of not treating them correctly—respectfully and loyally—can be profound, i.e. the descent into madness (Insoll 2008: 384). Equally, the implications for personhood, psychologically, also need acknowledging for ancestors are not only guardians but can be ultimate constituents of personhood. The profound psychological consequences that can exist have been considered by Sow (1980: 6) within the anthropological structure of madness in sub-Saharan Africa and he has stressed how 'the day-to-day psychological fate of individual human beings is modulated by a subtle dialectic of complex (often ambiguous) relations between humans and the creatures of the mesocosmos (African genies or spirits): invisible but powerful, good, or bad, gratifying or persecutory—and, as such, they can drive one mad'. Illustrative examples of madness in African societies can indicate this 'ancestral' connection. Janzen (1978: 183), for instance, refers to a young man in Lower Congo who had ordered medicine from France to make him into a French-speaking Belgian. This had driven him mad and his only cure, administered by a healer, was 'by throwing away his cherished European possessions—into the river, before the ancestors' (ibid.).

It is recognized that this complexity would be difficult, if not impossible, to reconstruct archaeologically, but this does not absolve the absence of the recognition of complexity in the first instance where hypotheses centred around ancestors and ancestor cults are considered. 'Ancestors' are not simple constructs but can be beliefs, materialized in many contexts, of recurring complexity and ontological importance.

3 ARCHAEOLOGY AND ANCESTORS

Ancestral interpretations are ubiquitous in archaeological interpretations of materials from many periods and regions of the world, as the entries in this Handbook attest. The development of theoretical approaches by archaeologists has been mobilized in considering ancestors and relationships between the living and the dead in myriad contexts (cf. Morris 1991; Parker Pearson 1993, 1999; Whitley 2002), and an example of this is provided by models developed to assess the extent to which ancestral beliefs as potentially manifest by formalized cemeteries can be modelled and interpreted as indicative of private property concerns and the development of the monopolizing of resources through inheritance by agnatic lineages. This, the so-called processual Saxe/Goldstein hypothesis was examined by Morris (1991) with reference to material both from Ancient Greece (500–100 BC) and Rome (200 BC–AD 200). And Morris (ibid.) found that there was some substance to the hypothesis but that other meanings and messages are unsurprisingly also conveyed through burial.

European prehistory seems to vary according to which religious 'form' is seen as best fit with which chronological period (Insoll 2004: 65). Hence, for instance, shamans often people the religious worlds of the Upper Palaeolithic (Lewis-Williams 2002), and the Neolithic is seen as the time when 'the cult of the ancestors was growing' (Burl 1981:

41)—an ancestral importance interpreted as linked with developing ties to the land initiated by cultivation cycles, and sedentism framed and negotiated via ancestral relationships. Thus 'ancestors' are very common in the British and European Neolithic (Edmonds 1999; Tilley 1994; Whitley 2002; cf. Cooney 2000; Parker Pearson 2000). Undeniably the archaeological record seems to attest to an intensification of what might be deemed 'ancestral' relations expanding in the Neolithic, as manifest in the British Isles by, for instance, the human remains disarticulated, sometimes sorted, and deposited in the earthen long barrows, megalithic tombs, and causewayed enclosures found (Edmonds 1999: 69–73; Parker Pearson 2000: 203; Cooney 2000: 90, 103; Tilley 1994: 169).

Evidence for the existence of the concept of collective burial has, however, been found in Early Mesolithic contexts including in southern Belgium inside caves on the Meuse River. Cauwe (2001: 151–3) describes how the skeletons, possibly all female, in one cave, the Grotte Margaux, had been deliberately selected for burial and were further distinguished by differential treatment of the remains based on cut marks present and by implication secondary burial practices involving setting apart and sorting of some of the elements. Cauwe (2001: 160–1) does not suggest a simplistic evolutionary trajectory to European Neolithic megalithic burial traditions nor deny the indisputable changes that occur in the latter, but this Mesolithic evidence is of interest in not precluding an 'ancestral' interpretation for this period. This is a theme also considered by Tilley (1994: 202) in relation to Mesolithic peoples' 'ancestral' connection with the landscape as 'embodied in the Being of the landscape and an emotional attachment to place'; and, in so doing, Tilley also recognizes a possible 'ancestral' component in Mesolithic beliefs, with, he posits, changes in ancestral relationships occurring subsequently in the Neolithic.

These exceptions aside, older sources tend to be less rigid, rightly or wrongly, in interpreting ancestor cults outside the types of schema frequently evident in European prehistory today. Maringer (1960: 60–1, 129) suggests ancestor 'worship' for both the Upper Palaeolithic and Mesolithic in Europe. Similarly, Burl (1981: 24) refers to the 'ancestor-spirits' of the Upper Palaeolithic. Perhaps the most vehement criticism of the proliferation of ancestral interpretations in European prehistory with particular reference to work on the British Neolithic has been made by James Whitley (2002). He suggests that ancestors became to 1990s archaeology (and indeed, beyond) what chiefs were to that of the 1970s. It is unnecessary to go as far as Whitley (2002: 121) to deny 'any theoretical grounds at all for holding on to ancestors in the British Neolithic'. Ancestors are a valid concept to employ in archaeological interpretation if configured according to appropriate complexity (cf. Whitley 2002: 121–2), as already discussed, and if they are 'bundled' with other religious forms, phenomena, or concepts rather than treated in the interpretive singular. Hence for example, it is often very difficult to separate a consideration of ancestor beliefs from sacrificial practices (Chapter 11), or 'totemism' and 'animism' (Chapter 62).

Ancestors can obviously also be prominent in world religious contexts, even if they are not framed in terms of ancestor 'cults', as the veneration frequently associated with cemeteries and their occupants in, for example, Islam (contrary to orthodoxy, Figure 65.2) and Christianity (Gibb and Kramers 1961; Curl 1993), or the ancestral 'worship' of Buddhism indicates (Hardacre 2005: 321). These also hold varying archaeological implications in relation to how the dead are monumentalized, materialized, and located in time and space (Simpson 1995; Insoll 1999: 166–95; Coningham 2001; Lane 2001).

FIGURE 65.2 Venerated Shi'a Saint's shrine, Shaikh Nasser shrine, Al-Helah, Bahrain. 'Ancestor' veneration in World religious contexts?

4 THE ARCHAEOLOGY OF ANCESTORS AND ANCESTOR CULTS

The ubiquity of ancestral interpretations in archaeology means selectivity has had to be employed in providing relevant examples. The underlying theme connecting these examples is a concern with materiality and substance.

4.1 The Materiality, Place, and Immateriality of Ancestors

A universally object- or iconographic-centred approach to ancestors is flawed. Iconography can depict ancestors as with the human figures rendered on Chinchawas sculptures dating from AD 500–800 described by Lau (2002: 297) from the North Highlands of Peru, but a general ancestor rendering or object association, with a type of pot perhaps, obviously does not exist for all contexts and periods. Rather, configuring ancestors in terms of substance and metaphor might be preferable in many instances. MacGaffey (2000: 20) encapsulates this well in considering various entities in the forest regions of Central Africa, including ancestors, and stating by way of summary that they are 'not primarily an object or even necessarily a definite personality, but a ritual process whose material infrastructure may include amulets, calabashes, carved figures, masks, rocks, graves, shrines, and human bodies, in any of which the divinity may be to some extent immanent, and among which enabling metaphors endlessly cycle' (Figure 65.3).

The link between substances and ancestors can be profound, positively or negatively. The Mountain-Ok peoples of New Guinea (Papua New Guinea and Irian Jaya) have an ancestor cult the maintenance of which is regarded as essential to the success of hunting, gardening, the raising of pigs, and fighting (Craig 1988). Of interest is that Craig (1988: 20) describes how 'certain substances, particularly water, are inimical to the "heat" (that is, power) of the ancestors' (see also Barth 1975: 54). In contrast the colour red is smeared on initiands' faces and ancestral bones as it is believed to impart heat to the bones (ibid.: 56) and thus has positive connotations of power in relation to the ancestors. Presumably this is obtained from the red ochre, clay, and iron deposits described by Craig (1988: 32–3), though this might be a gross oversimplification for MacKenzie (1991: 178) also refers to Baktaman initiates being painted with ceremonial paint, *bagan isak*, described as 'a potent generative mixture of red ochre from the sacred site of Safoltigin, tree sap and woman's menstrual blood'. Barth (1975), however, in his study of the Baktaman does not seem to refer to the use of the latter in mixing red paint or substances (ibid.: 74, 113), but rather provides repeated references to menstrual taboos (ibid.: 167, 205).

Notwithstanding the components of 'red', its power and symbolic importance are because it belongs, in part, 'with' the 'ancestors'. Ancestral relics, primarily human skulls and bones are kept in bilums, looped string bags, inside cult houses. MacKenzie (1991) indicates the diversity of bilum form and usage, and the complexity in belief that underpins them amongst the Telefol people of the Mountain Ok. These range from *dam laal men*, a finger-sized amulet bilum containing fragments of bone from the ancestors through to *men amen*, a 'generic term for a secret, sacred bilum containing the bones and thus the spirit of deceased ancestors' (MacKenzie 1991: 50).

In the New Guinea example, human remains constitute ancestral relics (Barth 1975: 61), and animal remains such as domestic-pig jawbones, wild-pig skulls, and cassowary leg bones function as trophies of successful pig husbandry and hunting (Craig 1988: 30), but do not seemingly constitute ancestral relics in themselves. Elsewhere ancestors can be linked more directly with animals. Politis and Saunders (2002), for example, describe how the food taboos of the Nukak, a mobile forager society of the north-west Amazon forest of Colombia, are structured by beliefs that animals can represent or contain the spirit of ancestors (see also Politis 2001: 45–6). These include jaguar, tapir, and deer, and they note (Politis and Saunders 2002: 115) how 'animals are concepts, "bundles" of meanings, whose place in local taxonomies defines the emically logical criteria for their full-, partial- or non-exploitation' (cf. Insoll 2007a: 106–10 for further discussion of animal 'classification'). These beliefs 'actively shape the archaeological record' (Politis and Saunders 2002: 125), as in, for example, the predicted absence of jaguar and deer remains other than curated, potentially ritually related items such as deer-bone flutes and necklaces of jaguar teeth.

Ancestors might also be framed in terms of place. As Lau (2002: 281) notes, ancestor cults can be reinforced by a 'genealogy of place' with little attempt made to proselytize outsiders for the cult becomes the 'specific religious domain of the descendants'. However, complexity again exists and across the board associations between ancestors and place cannot be made. For example, what are referred to as 'territorial cults' in Central Africa are considered by Schoffeleers (1979), but these have to be differentiated, essentially, from lineage

FIGURE 65.3 Ancestor-related ritual acts in the Congo. Top: The ancestor of the anaemic boy stole, his descendant is punished. For the healing, a chicken is sacrificed but must be beaten by the wings around the sick person before being killed (author's translation). Bottom: For presenting a new born to the ancestors; the village chief digs a hole at a fork in the road and pours into this palm wine and salt—wine for men and salt for women (author's translation).

cults that have recourse to the ancestors. Elsewhere such a division is not always so clear. Mathers (2003: 40), for instance, describes in detail how among the Kusasi of north-eastern Ghana, the ancestors as 'founders of the present social order are fused with the land by enshrinement'. Hence in one of the case studies he considers the tree that comprises the shrine is a product of nature, but is also a 'product of the dwelling of the ancestors' (ibid.) as they nurtured and protected the tree. Hence it becomes what Mathers refers to as a 'land god' (ibid.) but equally can be seen to have ancestral connections.

Parker Pearson and Ramilisonina (1998: 308) have explored both place and substance with reference to suggesting that the famous site of Stonehenge in south-western England could be interpreted in the Later Neolithic as 'belonging to the ancestors, a stone version for the dead of the timber circles used for ceremonials by the living'. Emphasis in developing this hypothesis was placed upon relational analogy with Madagascan beliefs that link standing stones and ancestors in various ways. This has been criticized for its 'allusion to universality' (Barrett and Fewster 1998: 849), in suggesting that ancestor cults are universal in small-scale societies where the social organization is based on kinship affiliation, and in the use of the Madagascan relational analogy. However, the suggestion of substance and ancestor links is of interest, specifically in their argument that 'stone was associated with the ancestors, as part of a process of hardening in the life–death cycle, in both cultures' (Parker Pearson 2000: 203). Whilst place is considered in relation to different 'domains' for the 'ancestors', 'living' and 'liminal' (Parker Pearson and Ramilisonina 1998: 317–18).

As with all such interpretations it remains impossible to prove (Barrett and Fewster 1998: 848), and there is a tendency to project out from the original Stonehenge case study to attempt to explain the change seen from wood to stone at other Later Neolithic sites in the British Isles under the same ancestral framework (e.g. Parker Pearson and Ramilisonina 1998: 321). Ethnography can also undermine their substance and ancestor hypothesis more generally, for counter examples, as in Barth's (1975: 139, 233) linking hardwood and the ancestors in Baktaman society, which indicate that stone, even where available, is not necessarily the substance linked with the ancestors. Equally, the ancestral hypothesis developed to account for the movement of the bluestones from their original Welsh source to Stonehenge, and the suggestion that Peterborough ware pottery be renamed 'ancestor ware' (Parker Pearson and Ramilisonina 1998: 322; and see Parker Pearson 2000: 208) can also be challenged and an alternative suggested. Namely, that the former might have occurred under a process akin to shrine 'franchising' (Insoll 2006), whilst the stone tempers of the latter might be used as they incorporate, or are associated with, powerful substances, perhaps with perceived curative properties (Insoll in preparation).

The potential immaterial element of ancestors, a contradictory position perhaps for an archaeologist, should also be remembered. In noting this, a return to points already made in the introductory chapter must be made, specifically that because of the nature of archaeological evidence the default position can become an emphasis on materiality to the exclusion of recognizing (even if they cannot be reconstructed) less tangible associations, beliefs, and immateriality. Yet, again via considering anthropological and ethnographic materials, we can see that ancestral substances, associations, shrines, etc. are often only made 'powerful' through usually immaterial acts such as speech, song, chanting, rhythm etc. Janzen (1992: 67), for example, describes how in Bantu-speaking areas of Africa the medicinal notions of *tí* (tree, stick, or medicinal plant) and *pémbà* (white river chalk or clay denotive of purity or clarity) are, 'usually not, per se, charged with overtones of power. When combined with other substances into compounds and given the "interpretation" of a spoken phrase, they become so. Such compounds, especially when spoken or sung over, become powerful medicines invoking the attributes of ancestors and spirits.' Similarly Barth (1975: 193) relates how sacrifice is '*the* means to communicate with the ancestors' and how sacrifice is invariably linked with prayer. Prayers/words/utterances serve to actualize ritual actions and activate substances linked with the ancestors. They also serve to provide the ancestors with biography and names. Hence, although the ancestors can be rendered materially, their potential immaterial aspects also need acknowledging even if archaeologically they cannot be recognized as such (and hence the anthropological emphasis taken with regard to the illustrative examples chosen here).

4.2 West African Islam and the Ancestors

For European Neolithic contexts it has been noted how interpretations have been proposed invoking the growing importance of the ancestors as a correlate of strengthening ties with the land as cultivation increased. Away from Europe it is interesting to note a reverse process where interpretations involving the shedding or loosening of ancestral ties have been suggested as a key factor amongst sedentary agricultural populations converting to Islam in West Africa. This has been tracked archaeologically in the Gao region of eastern Mali (Insoll 1996, 2000, 2003) where the variable rate of conversion was seen to be significant, occurred in three stages, and was in part based upon pre-existing religious beliefs and socio-economic lifestyle. Hence in the urban context of Gao some of the earliest evidence (c.AD 900–1250) for Islam is found such as mosques and Muslim burials. This appears to link to what has been interpreted as the appeal of Islam to urban populations, being universalistic in outlook and having the power to bring together different ethnolinguistic groups under the universal rubric of *ummah* or community (Insoll 1996: 91). The second group to convert were nomads. Outside Gao, in the Niger Bend area, the patterning of Muslim cemeteries containing inscribed tombstones clustered along trade routes and in areas currently inhabited by nomads would seem to indicate that Islam was adopted more rapidly by nomad populations at the beginning of the second millennium AD. The ease of worship that Islam enjoys has been suggested as one of the possible reasons for its appeal to nomadic groups (Lewis 1980; Insoll 1996: 92).

The third group to convert to Islam, gradually, and with varying degrees of adherence were the bulk of the population, the sedentary agriculturalists, living in the vicinity of the River Niger. The tardy, syncretic, and piecemeal nature of sedentary agriculturalist conversion can be explained by various factors, primarily that where indigenous religions formed the framework of belief centred around, though this is not certain, ancestors and the earth (Insoll 1996: 92), the appeal of Islam in loosening links with ancestors, and breaking bonds with soil, water, and bush would have been limited (Dramani-Issifou 1992: 55). Archaeological data certainly indicates that among the proto-Songhai of the Gao region Islam had little impact outside of Gao in the period c.AD 900–1250 and it was not really significant in the rural environment until the late eighteenth–nineteenth centuries AD (Insoll 1996: 14).

Through recourse to Songhai ethnography (e.g. Rouch 1954, 1989, 1997) we know that one element of indigenous religion was ancestor cults (the past tense is used here as orthodox Islamization and Wahabi influences on the Songhai have increased significantly over the past couple of decades). The ancestor cults are described by Rouch (1954: 61) as local cults addressed to the first inhabitant of an area or to a particularly powerful ancestor. The head of the family maintained the process of mediating with the ancestors, and Rouch (1989: 191) notes that ancestor cults were in principle reserved to a single family. Hence people were tied to known ancestors and places, and it is not implausible to suggest such ritual relationships and obligations formed a component of earlier proto-Songhai religiosity, in so doing helping to explain the differential archaeological patterning for Islam evident over time in the Gao region as already described.

4.3 Personhood, Personal Destiny, and the Materiality of Tallensi Ancestors

Previously, the complexity of Tallensi ancestor cults was emphasized. This also relates to materiality, and through considering *Yin* or Good Destiny (personal) shrines, an example of how they can be materialized with attendant archaeological implications is provided (Insoll 2008). Among the Tallensi, destiny is negotiated via the so-called 'good destiny' ancestors who are ritually serviced and placated through regular sacrifice, offering, and libation at shrines. The shrines are agents for unique ritual relationships between individuals whose destiny they control and unique configurations of ancestors. In this way the negotiation of destiny, and its material configuration, are distinguished from 'ritual relationships with kinsfolk and clansfolk' (Fortes 1983: 23).

Destiny is primarily negotiated via ritual action at small household shrines of generically similar types (Insoll 2008). These are usually formed of specific objects with precise associations; the material relics of events such as success in hunting for the first time, doing well in farming, or illness for instance. The elements materialized in destiny shrines—hoes, arrows, animal remains, bracelets, etc.—do not as such reflect a person's biography but play an active role in producing that biography. Of obvious significance here is the relationship between ancestors, personhood, and materiality, though it should be emphasized that personhood does not precede materiality but is produced through material practices and embodied processes (cf. Thomas 2006/2007). As this author has stated elsewhere (Insoll 2008: 387), 'notions of personhood do not exist as disembodied ideas; instead they emerge, and are reproduced and transformed, through material practices, including those related to shrines'. This is not merely of consequence to considering the materialization of ancestors but is a point applicable in other contexts elsewhere in West Africa (Ferme 2001: 4; Ogundiran 2002: 431), and in concurrence with more general archaeological readings of materiality (Hallam and Hockey 2001: 118; Tilley 2006: 61).

Exploration of the materiality of destiny shrines was achieved through recording a Tallensi compound abandoned in 1999 (Insoll 2008). This compound contained three shrines—father's, mother's, and *Yin*. Of archaeological significance is the fact that although the compound itself had deteriorated substantially, the best-preserved elements were the shrines, specifically the father's and the *Yin* shrine, being formed of more durable materials than the mud compound itself. Both shrines lacked, if indeed they had them in the first place, additional architectural features such as conical mud or clay pillars (Figure 65.1), but other elements were preserved. The primary surviving *in situ* element of the *Yin* shrine was a mud and gravel platform with a complete pot set into it. The pot contents included an iron bracelet, a potsherd, and a stone pounder/grinder, with, close by, another upturned pot with two bronze bracelets and further potsherds underneath. Scattered in front of the platform were a coin, four iron bracelets, two cowrie shells, and an iron hoe blade. These were also parts of the *Yin* shrine, though some intermixing between elements of the *Yin* and the very poorly preserved mother's shrine might also have been occurring. In contrast, the father's shrine, again a pot set in a mud platform, was well preserved and contained, for example, coins, a razor-blade holder, several bracelets, a copper bell, and a polished pebble of a type used to give a finished surface to mud plaster (Insoll 2008: 390–2).

In archaeological terms a generic 'ritual' or shrine deposit was being created through the mixing of the different shrine parts—but it was still possible to be more precise, owing to the types of material culture present, to interpret 'destiny' and 'ancestral' links. Specifically, for objects such as the razor-blade holder, polished pebble, bracelets, and hoe blade link with Fortes' description of personhood and with his comment that when an ancestor reveals themselves, 'as an agency claiming service from a particular descendant, the chosen vehicle is usually some such intimate and characteristic possession, or its replica, owned by the descendant' (1987: 267).

Ethnography facilitates such interpretations and it is seen here that precise ancestral beliefs and ritual relationships can be materialized. But although ancestors are being precisely materialized, caution must also be exercised, for a universal code for interpreting these objects does not exist. They are precise in relation to historical circumstances and questions of both structure and agency have to be considered, and considered alongside each other as operating in a dialectical relationship (Tilley 2006). Equally, the polysemic qualities of the objects present in the shrines also need recognizing and, if considered in relation to understanding ancestors in earlier periods, issues of ritual 'stability' and gender association would need due acknowledgement. Tallensi women can only nominally become custodians of ancestor shrines if they are the sole survivors of a lineage and must still contact a man to sacrifice for them. Yet we do not know if women were excluded from the direct act of sacrifice at shrines in the past (Insoll 2008: 388). Certainly female 'ancestresses' are important and Fortes (1983: 11) notes that although the lineage ancestor cult is by definition that of the patrilineal male ancestors, the role played by ancestresses and maternal ancestors is very significant in a person's life (as the mother's shrine would indicate), and 'the ancestress of a lineage or segment is almost as important as the founding ancestor' (ibid.).

Similarly, among some of the Mountain-Ok groups of Central new Guinea referred to previously, such as the Telefol, Ulapmin, and Falamin, the skulls of women who were renowned for pig husbandry can be preserved as ancestral relics and invoked, and thus, as Craig (1988: 60) notes, allowing women 'a degree of access to the cult of the ancestors'; though this ritual access and ancestral status would seem to be an arena of contested gender-relations and negotiation, with variable understandings and knowledge evident (see MacKenzie 1991: 182–5). In archaeological terms, ancestors are often 'genderless', or by implication seemingly default male. 'Ancestors' do not figure in, for example, the index to Nelson and Rosen-Ayalon's (2002) study of 'worldwide archaeological approaches to gender', but Nelson (this volume, Chapter 14) does note that religions have been neglected in archaeological studies of gender. Perhaps the utility of the New Guinea and Tallensi examples lies in indicating the precision with which ancestors can be both given and provide biographies, genders, and identities, as well as in suggesting interpretive complexity in considering 'ancestors' in the archaeological record.

5 CONCLUSIONS

Interpreting the presence of ancestors based on archaeological materials has validity in some contexts, but if 'ancestors' and 'ancestor cults' are deemed interpretively relevant for archaeology then ethnographic analogy usually tells us they should not be thought of as operating in isolation, but, as already stressed earlier, as part of a multiple 'package' of phenomena, practices, and beliefs whose configuration and importance can change over time. For instance, Barth (1975: 191) in his magnificent study of the Baktaman clearly indicates the interlinking between sacrifice and ancestor veneration in stating that 'the focal operation in every Baktaman ritual is sacrifice'. Similarly, among the Tallensi, complex configurations of ancestors exist, as described, but beliefs in these and their associated ritual practices operate alongside other frames of reference such as earth cults and 'totemic' observance (Fortes 1945; Insoll 2007b). It is when we privilege singular ancestral interpretations with supposed universal applicability that interpretive complexity and subtlety is lost.

SUGGESTED READING

Literature considering the 'ancestors' in general terms is considerable and archaeological studies invoking ancestral interpretations are common, certainly for many periods of prehistory around the world. Useful further reading that could be suggested includes Hardacre's (2005) encyclopaedia entry, Parker Pearson and Ramilisonina's (1998) interesting hypothesis about Stonehenge, Whitley's (2002) criticisms of the ubiquity of ancestral interpretations in European Neolithic archaeology, and because it is such a wonderful ethnography, Barth's (1975) study of the Baktaman. Otherwise, the African focus reflects this author's expertise and depending upon the reader's interests all the references are of potential relevance.

REFERENCES

BARRETT, J. and FESTER, K. 1998. 'Stonehenge: *Is* the medium the message?', *Antiquity*, 72: 847–52.

BARTH, F. 1975. *Ritual and Knowledge among the Baktaman of New Guinea* (Oslo: Universitetforlaget).

BURL, A. 1981. *Rites of the Gods* (London: Dent).

CAUWE, N. 2001. 'Skeletons in motion, ancestors in action: Early Mesolithic collective tombs in southern Belgium', *Cambridge Archaeological Journal*, 11: 147–63.

CONINGHAM, R. 2001. 'The archaeology of Buddhism' in T. Insoll (ed.), *Archaeology and World Religion* (London: Routledge), pp. 61–95.

COONEY, G. 2000. *Landscapes of Neolithic Ireland* (London: Routledge).

CRAIG, B. 1988. *Art and Decoration of Central New Guinea* (Aylesbury: Shire).

CURL, J. S. 1993. *A Celebration of Death* (London: Batsford).
DRAMANI-ISSIFOU, Z. 1992. 'Islam as a social system in Africa since the seventh century' in I. Hrbek (ed.), *Unesco General History of Africa*, III (London: James Currey), pp. 50–62.
EDMONDS, M. 1999. *Ancestral Geographies of the Neolithic* (London: Routledge).
FERME, M. 2001. *The Underneath of Things* (Berkeley: University of California Press).
FORTES, M. 1945 (1969). *The Dynamics of Clanship among the Tallensi* (Oosterhout: Anthropological Publications).
—— 1949 (1967). *The Web of Kingship among the Tallensi* (Oosterhout: Anthropological Publications).
—— 1983. *Oedipus and Job in West African Religion* (Cambridge: Cambridge University Press).
—— 1987. *Religion, Morality and the Person* (Cambridge: Cambridge University Press).
FOWLER, F. and FOWLER, H. 1986. *The Oxford Handy Dictionary* (Oxford: Oxford University Press).
GEERTZ, C. 1966 (1985). 'Religion as a cultural system' in M. Banton (ed.), *Anthropological Approaches to the Study of Religion* (London: Tavistock), pp. 1–46.
GIBB, H. A. R. and KRAMERS, J. H. 1961. *The Shorter Encyclopaedia of Islam* (Leiden: Brill).
HALLAM, E. and HOCKEY, J. 2001. *Death, Memory and Material Culture* (Oxford: Berg).
HARDACRE, H. 2005. 'Ancestors: Ancestor worship' in L. Jones (ed.), *Encyclopedia of Religion*, I, 2nd edn (Detroit: Thomson Gale), pp. 320–5.
HOCHEGGER, H. 1981. *Le Langage des Gestes Rituels* (Bandundu: Ceeba Publications).
INSOLL, T. 1996. *Islam, Archaeology and History: Gao Region (Mali) ca.AD 900–1250*, BAR S647 (Oxford: Tempus Reparatum).
—— 1999. *The Archaeology of Islam* (Oxford: Blackwell).
—— (with other contributions) 2000. *Urbanism, Archaeology and Trade: Further observations on the Gao Region (Mali): The 1996 Fieldseason Results*, BAR S829 (Oxford: BAR).
—— 2003. *The Archaeology of Islam in Sub-Saharan Africa* (Cambridge: Cambridge University Press).
—— 2004. *Archaeology, Ritual, Religion* (London: Routledge).
—— 2006. 'Shrine franchising and the Neolithic in the British Isles: Some observations based upon the Tallensi, northern Ghana', *Cambridge Archaeological Journal*, 16: 223–38.
—— 2007a. *Archaeology: The conceptual challenge* (London: Duckworth).
—— 2007b. '"Totems", "ancestors", and "animism": The archaeology of ritual, shrines and sacrifice amongst the Tallensi of northern Ghana' in D. Barrowclough and C. Malone (eds), *Cult in Context* (Oxford: Oxbow Books), pp. 326–33.
—— 2008. 'Negotiating the archaeology of destiny: An exploration of interpretive possibilities through Tallensi shrines', *Journal of Social Archaeology*, 8: 380–403.
—— in preparation. *Theoretical Explorations in African Archaeology: Contexts, materials, persons, and animals* (Oxford: Oxford University Press).
JAMES, W. 1999. 'Introduction' in D. Forde (ed.), *African Worlds* (Oxford: James Currey), pp. ix–xxx.
JANZEN, J. M. 1978. *The Quest for Therapy in Lower Zaire* (Berkeley: University of California Press).
—— 1992. *Ngoma: Discourses of healing in Central and Southern Africa* (Berkeley: University of California Press).
LANE, P. 2001. 'The archaeology of Christianity in global perspective' in T. Insoll (ed.), *Archaeology and World Religion* (London: Routledge), pp. 148–81.

LAU, G. F. 2002. 'Feasting and ancestor veneration at Chinchawas, North Highlands of Ancash, Peru', *Latin American Antiquity*, 13: 279–304.
LEWIS, I. M. (ed.) 1980. *Islam in Tropical Africa* (London: Hutchinson).
LEWIS-WILLIAMS, D. 2002. *The Mind in the Cave* (London: Thames and Hudson).
MACKENZIE, M. 1991. *Androgynous Objects: String bags and gender in Central New Guinea* (Reading: Harwood Academic Publishers).
MARINGER, J. 1960 [2002]. *The Gods of Prehistoric Man* (London: Phoenix Press).
MATHERS, C. 2003. 'Shrines and the domestication of landscape', *Journal of Anthropological Research*, 59: 23–45.
MORRIS, I. 1991. 'The archaeology of ancestors: The Saxe/Goldstein hypothesis revisited', *Cambridge Archaeological Journal*, 1: 147–69.
NELSON, S. M. and ROSEN-AYALON, M. (eds) 2002. *In Pursuit of Gender: World wide archaeological approaches* (Walnut Creek, CA: AltaMira).
OGUNDIRAN, A. 2002. 'Of small things remembered: Beads, cowries, and cultural translations of the Atlantic experience in Yorubaland', *The International Journal of African Historical Studies*, 35: 427–57.
PARKER PEARSON, M. 1993. 'The powerful dead: Archaeological relationships between the living and the dead', *Cambridge Archaeological Journal*, 3: 203–29.
—— 1999. *The Archaeology of Death and Burial* (Stroud: Sutton).
—— 2000. 'Ancestors, bones and stones in Neolithic and Early Bronze Age Britain and Ireland' in A. Ritchie (ed.), *Neolithic Orkney in its European Context* (Cambridge: McDonald Institute), pp. 203–14.
—— 2001. 'Death, being and time: The historical context of the world religions' in T. Insoll (ed.), *Archaeology and World Religion* (London: Routledge), pp. 203–19.
—— and RAMILISONINA. 1998. 'Stonehenge for the ancestors: The stones pass on the message', *Antiquity*, 72: 308–26.
POLITIS, G. 2001. 'Foragers of the Amazon. The last survivors or the first to succeed?' in C. McEwan, C. Barreto, and E. Neves (eds), *Unknown Amazon* (London: British Museum Press), pp. 26–49.
—— and SAUNDERS, N. 2002. 'Archaeological correlates of ideological activity: Food taboos and spirit-animals in an Amazonian hunter-gatherer society' in P. Miracle and N. Milner (eds), *Consuming Passions and Patterns of Consumption* (Cambridge: McDonald Institute), pp. 113–30.
RENFREW, C. 1985. *The Archaeology of Cult* (London: Thames and Hudson).
ROUCH, J. 1954. *Les Songhay* (Paris: Presses Universitaires de France).
—— 1989. *La Religion et La Magie Songhay* (Brussels: Editions de l'Université de Bruxelles).
—— 1997. *Les Hommes et les Dieux du Fleuve. Essai Ethnographique sur Les Populations Songhay du Moyen Niger* (Paris: Editions Artcom).
SCHOFFELEERS, J. M. 1979. 'Introduction' in J. M. Schoffeleers (ed.), *Guardians of the Land* (Gweru: Mambo Press), pp. 1–46.
SIMPSON, ST J. 1995. 'Death and burial in the late Islamic Near East: Some insights from archaeology and ethnography' in S. Campbell and A. Green (eds), *The Archaeology of Death in the Ancient Near East* (Oxford: Oxbow Books), pp. 240–51.
SOW, I. 1980. *Anthropological Structures of Madness in Black Africa* (New York: International Universities Press).
THOMAS, J. 2006/2007. 'The trouble with material culture', *Journal of Iberian Archaeology*, 9(10): 11–23.

TILLEY, C. 1994. *A Phenomenology of Landscape* (Oxford: Berg).
—— 2006. 'Objectification' in C. Tilley, W. Keane, S. Kuechler-Fogden, et al. (eds), *Handbook of Material Culture* (London: Sage), pp. 60–73.
TURNER, V. 1957 (1996). *Schism and Continuity in an African Society* (Oxford: Berg).
—— 1967. *The Forest of Symbols* (Ithaca, NY: Cornell University Press).
WHITLEY, J. 2002. 'Too many ancestors', *Antiquity*, 76: 119–26.

CHAPTER 66

DIVINE KINGS

PIERRE DE MARET

1 INTRODUCTION

THE concept of divine kingship where a ruler is seen as an agent, an incarnation or a mediator of the sacred has attracted much interest since Frazer's (1913–15) seminal work on the topic more than a century ago. It has generated an enormous amount of literature, as it should be viewed in the broader context of the sacred aspects of the exercise of power, having a close relationship to both religion and politics. It has thus also often been seen as a key component in a state-formation process, a topic that has attracted the interest of many archaeologists, in the absence of written records for the earliest stages of state formation around the world. How and why could an egalitarian society that has had no previous experience of a centralized power transform itself into a functioning state?

2 POWER AND SACRALITY

The link between 'power' and 'the sacred' is both necessary and elusive, it could be more or less explicit, but it has never become undone, even in the most secular of the modern states. The sacred is part of the essence of power. How they both mix and interplay is at the core of the various polities that have arisen in the course of time around the world. But even in modern Western states, where one insists on the separation of church and state, power, with its sacred aspect, is essential as it reintroduces a symbolic and an imaginary element in social organizations that cannot function without shared emotion (Russ 1994: 319–20).

Rites, performances, metaphors, and symbols infuse an affective dimension into power and allow it to spread into the realm of fantasy. The paradox of political rituals is that 'they constantly connect emotion and device in such a way that it is unclear how one rises from the other' (Abeles 1993: 194). As disconnected as it is from the transcendental, power in today's world always reverts to the sacred because, ultimately, as soon as it takes shape, a state-like structure is driven by the desire of permanence, by the search for transcendence, and thus closely linked with sacrality, as noted by de Heusch (1962: 15). For him, 'Metaphysically, the state challenges death, it negates what is short-lived, it bridges past and future'. It is also in some aspects, an elaborate cult of the ancestor that brings together the generations in a collective pursuit of an ideal society. No wonder thus that in this quest of sacrality, the one who has the leadership ends up incarnating both the power and the existence of the state (de Heusch 1962). Sacralization of power appears to be a significant element in the birth of a state-like structure, and sacred kingship acts to reinforce its cohesion. Power relationships make themselves felt, for a significant part, through the production and the exchange of signs. Power is, to a large extent, produced by symbols which at the same time are used to legitimize it. But, behind the symbols of power, its personification appears to be the most powerful factor solidly linking and dynamizing the community from which it emanates. As noted by Abeles (1990: 101), 'the delegation that takes place from the group to the individual is in fact at the base of collective identity'. Power is crucial in preventing confusion.

In the old days, the coronation of the king, its '*sacre*', revitalized the kingdom. Nowadays, major political events, like elections, tend to redynamize countries. In the same way, the arrival of a new leader revives the organization (Russ 1994: 319). The leader incarnates the group but the group incarnates itself in its leader. And if the sacred chief or king appears in many traditional societies to have almost absolute power, he is in fact often hostage to his people and tangled in a web of complex rituals and taboos.

3 Sacred Rulers

An extraordinary symbolic device, half way between nature and culture, benevolent and malevolent, the ruler was the guarantor of world order and fecundity, the link between the spiritual and the material. A prisoner of etiquette and of many taboos, he was often put to death after a given amount of time or because he was weakening. It is this ritual killing that prompted Frazer to wonder: 'Why put a man-god or a human representative of deity to a violent death?' And his general answer was that 'the motive for slaying a man-god is a fear, lest with the enfeeblement of his body in sickness or old age, his sacred spirit should suffer a corresponding decay, which might imperil the general course of nature and with it the existence of his worshippers, who believe the cosmic energies to be mysteriously knit up with those of their human divinity'. Hence, for Frazer, 'the practice of putting divine men, and particularly divine kings, to death, which seems to have been common at a particular stage in the evolution of society and religion, was a crude but pathetic attempt to disengage an immortal spirit from its mortal envelope, to arrest the forces of decomposition in nature by retrenching with ruthless hand the first ominous symptoms of decay' (Frazer 1913–15: v).

Aside from Frazer's evolutionist and Christian bias, he must be praised for having drawn attention in anthropology to this widely spread phenomenon where the political power of leaders is believed to be connected with the power they exert on nature. In a broader and universalist perspective, Frazer must be credited for making us aware that as Evans-Pritchard (1962: 210) put it: 'kingship everywhere and at all times has been in some degree a sacred office'.

But if, in the political realm, kingship epitomizes the conjunction of power, sacrality, and ritual, one can also find examples, such as the Mongo of DR Congo, the Dogon of Mali, and the Samo of Burkina Faso, of small-scale societies without a state-like or even a chiefdom structure where nevertheless some individuals are vested with crucial ritual functions, similar to those of sacred or divine rulers. This ritual function, not the political, may well be, argued de Heusch (1997: 231), 'at the core of the institution for it appears already in small stateless societies where a man, or even a child, is torn from the everyday kinship order to take on the heavy responsibility of guaranteeing the equilibrium of the universe'. There is thus no more clear-cut separation in degrees of 'holiness' from the more simple manifestations of the sacred dimension of power to the most elaborate kind of divine kingship than there is between kingship and presidential systems in present-day states. Nowhere has the political fully emerged as an autonomous sphere from the ritual and the sacred.

The term 'divine kingship' could also be a misnomer, as in several instances the sacred king, even destined to a ritual killing, is not a spirit or a god as, for example, the Pharaoh was in ancient Egypt (de Heusch 2005). In this instance also, the precise divine nature of a ruler, in real life or after his death, is also a matter of discussion in anthropology. To what extent is the king really assimilated to a divinity? As pointed out by de Heusch, in sub-Saharan Africa for instance, there are various examples where, thanks to a special ritual of investiture, the body of the would-be king is sacralized. The body of this royal person is quite literally the interface between the natural and the cultural order, safeguarding the order of the world (de Heusch 2005). Yet, this does not transform him into a divinity, into a living god, but rather into a sort of living fetish (de Heusch 2005). He becomes the embodiment of his kingdom. Being the nexus between sacrality, power, continuity, legitimacy, and prosperity, the concept of divine kingship is also connected with the administration of the sacred. The ruler often plays a major role in rituals or in religious performances and discourses, as agent or mediator of the sacred, the sacred ruler being often both an object and a subject in this context.

In many ways, as suggested in an illuminating study of the persistence of the Aztec concept of sacred kingship today in the Mexican republic by Dehouve (2005: 6), sacred kingship 'is not only a form of government, but a form of society wholly built in order to conquest collective prosperity thanks to rituals'. In today's Mexican villages, people are still convinced that their fate is linked to 'the person in power and in the way he performs rituals' (Dehouve 2005: 5). As in African examples then, the sacred kingship model does not necessarily entail a true king but rather a central person vested with key responsibilities in order to ascertain collective prosperity thanks to rituals (Dehouve 2005: 36). When scrutinized, the concept of 'divine kingship' encompasses an extremely complex, diverse, and elusive field closely connected to power and spirituality.

From a theoretical point of view, the notion of divine kingship has generated a large amount of literature among anthropologists and historians. From a practical point of view, kingship covers a wide range of institutions within numerous historical, political, and cultural settings. Its sacred dimension varies accordingly and, being connected with the spiritual sphere, its study presents the scholar with the kind of difficulties associated with the in-depth analysis of any religious and ritual system of thought. In addition, a variety of societies move easily back and forth from a power structure at the kin-group level to a much larger chiefdom and kingdom. This of course challenges evolutionary notions of political complexity and related symbolism (Keech McIntosh 1999). Nowadays, even with living informants, it is indeed a challenging task to give an accurate account from all different angles of how sacrality, power, and leadership interplay in a given setting.

4 Divine Kingship and Archaeology

The application of the concept of divine kingship to contemporary cultures and groups is problematic, requiring an in-depth knowledge of how it operates, as well as an awareness of looking back into the past. However, taking into account its complexity, ambiguity, and variability, the concept of divine kingship remains relevant to archaeology when assessing past evidence of political and religious practices. How can one identify the sacred dimension of power in archaeological contexts? To what extent is social life identified with the life of the king and the success of royal rituals? Can we assume some sort of divinization of a king-like figure? Inscriptions and other written records, ritual remains and monuments, layout of religious or political centres, iconographic and symbolic vestiges, all bear witness to the ways that the religious and the political spheres were and are inextricably intertwined.

When written sources describe religious beliefs and practices, as well as the political system, it is possible to grasp if there was a king-like figure and to what extent it was assimilated to a divinity, like the pharaoh in ancient Egypt. The pharaoh was the human incarnation of the sun-god, but also of the vitality of the demiurge and, as the ritualist-in-chief, in charge of maintaining social as well as cosmic order (Derchain 1962; O'Connor and Silverman 1995; Wilkinson 1999; Kemp 2006; Wengrow 2006). As early as the turn of the third millennium BC at the end of pre-dynastic Egypt, thanks to a series of finely carved objects like the famous Narmer Palette or the Cities Palette, one can observe scenes combining representations of rulers and emblems of gods. In some instances, the ruler is portrayed as a dangerous animal—lion, falcon, bull, scorpion (Wengrow 2006: 208). As those animals were also associated with major gods of the Egyptian pantheon, this could be seen as the earliest evidence of divine kingship.

Pharaoh's divine nature is well documented through the whole of ancient Egyptian history. His title is that of a god and like him the gods are addressed as 'majesty'. He was a god by his nature and by his many powers. He was the chief ritualist, always on the move, but also the object of a major revitalizing ritual for himself and his land, the Sed-festival that marks his rebirth, their rejuvenation (Derchain 1962). The royal mortuary cult also provided a ceremonial framework 'through which the abstract linkage of royal body and land was reproduced and legitimised as a concrete reality. [This] reasserted the claim already apparent on the Narmer Palette: that the spatial boundaries of land and cosmos are contiguous with the agency of the royal body' (Wengrow 2006: 231).

The continuity of kingship was equated with the life principle, and the royal person was sacralized at the highest point; he belonged to the realm of the gods. Among the earliest evidence of the phenomenon of divinized kings one has also in ancient Mesopotamia a ruler who proclaimed himself as early as the twenty-third century BC to be the god of the city of Akkad, as wished by its citizens according to his own inscription. There is other evidence from Ur of the custom of self-deification, probably as part of a strategy to reinforce the king's own powers (Brisch 2008a and b). In fact, fully fledged divine kingship seems to be closely associated with the use of religion to legitimize the sovereign's power in the ancient state. It is often closely associated with literacy and an extended use of iconography in buttressing a divine king's image, mixing attributes of kings as well as symbols and names of divinity.

For example, among the Maya and the Olmec, the trefoil crown in the shape of maize leaves, connected the king with the Maize God in numerous representations. For the Maya, 'the human life cycle paralleled that of the maize—birth, maturation, death, rebirth—and the most important ritual performed by the king re-enacted the event of creation' (Fields and Reents-Budet 2006: 24). When the king dies, he is supposed to follow the path taken by the Maize God through the underworld before resurrecting and returning to the earth's surface in the guise of the Maize God (Fields and Reents-Budet 2006).

As examples from ancient China, South America (Inca in the Andes), Mesoamerica (Maya, Olmec), Japan, India, Cambodia (Khmers), the Middle East, and the Greek and the Roman worlds illustrate, the ruler could be identified with a god, regarded as a god himself, as a son of a god, or be deified only after his death (Feeley-Harnik 1985; Quigley 2005). In a monotheist state, as in Christian Europe or in the Muslim world, kings could not be God, so they had to resort to be God's mediator or agent on earth. The variation in kingdoms and in the nature of their sacrality is considerable. A systematic classification would be pointless, even in a well-documented archaeological context. When there are no written accounts, the archaeology of divine kingship remains less specific as to what can be inferred from the material remains about the precise nature of the sacred ruler. However, it was also possible to communicate their divine nature by erecting monuments expressing their political authority and recording in sculptures or in paintings their performance of rituals in which they had the paraphernalia of a deity. Thus palaces and standardized temples as well as sacred landscapes are features that have been used as diagnostic criteria for some sort of sacred rulers.

When there are no written or monumental records, symbols of individual position and role could be detected in burials and the sacrality of the dead may be inferred from grave goods or ritual practices during interment. For example, in Central Africa, the ruler is often symbolically considered as a blacksmith, being the successor of the blacksmith who is said to have started the dynasty. Anvils thus play an important role during the enthronement ritual and may be put into the king's grave. So, the discovery in some graves of a rare ceremonial axe (a symbol of political power) and of an anvil (Figure 66.1) suggests that the deceased had both political and supernatural power (de Maret 1999). When it comes to deciphering the symbolic meaning of objects and rituals, one must rely chiefly on anthropological and historical sources.

Contrary to the long-held view that power differential had its origin in control over labour and subsistence, 'African data unambiguously support the idea... that religious modes of focusing power are often primary in overcoming the critical structural weakness of non-centralized societies' (Keech McIntosh 1999: 14). In the view of Netting (1972: 233):

> To integrate a number of [localized, autonomous] units ... The overwhelming need is not to expand existing political mechanisms ... but literally to transcend them. The new grouping must be united, not by kingship or territory alone, but by belief, by the infinite extensibility of common symbols, shared cosmology, and the overarching unity of fears and hopes made visible in ritual. A leader who can mobilize these sentiments, who can lend concrete form to an amorphous moral community, is thereby freed from complete identification with his village or age group or lineage.

In many instances, politics may thus have taken shape thanks more to ritual, social, and charismatic authority, than to the strict control and coercion. It has also allowed this type of

FIGURE 66.1 Leader with an anvil and ceremonial axe from a tenth-century AD early Kisalian burial, Kamilamba, DR Congo.

politics to extend their ritual and symbolic reach far beyond the core area where their political authority was pre-eminent. In the most extreme African cases, sacred kings reign only over a ritual centre, but do not govern (MacGaffey 1987). At the core of this centre, the palace is usually the focus of ritual life and cosmogony (Asombang 1999).

For archaeologists, the many concepts developed by anthropologists in relation to divine kingship and the sacrality of power are useful in shedding light on the highly eclectic evidence from the wide range of institutions that they may unearth, as long as this does not lead them to subsume this diversity in a single category. By its nature, at the conjunction of the political and the religious spheres, the sacrality of power has often left more material remains than each of those two spheres on their own.

5 CONCLUSION

No matter how complex, ambiguous, and changing the topic of divine kingship is, tracking its evidence in the archaeological record is useful. It allows us to unravel key elements at the heart of both religion and politics in the past and to shed some light on how power and sacrality intertwine, even if our insight into their interplay will remain forever incomplete. It makes us also realize above all that, from chiefdom to kingdom, once the primacy of kinship was overcome, religious and ritual factors played a major role in the multiple and erratic pathways to complexity.

Suggested Reading

Feeley-Harnik (1985), Cannadine and Price (1987), and Quigley (2005) provide the most recent overview of the anthropological literature on divine kingship, although with a strong emphasis on African examples. For the earliest examples of divine ruler for Egypt, O'Connor and Silverman (1995) and Wengrow (2006); and for the Near-East, Brisch (2008) are useful, as are Freidel and Schele (1988) and Fields and Reents-Budet (2006) for Mesoamerica.

References

ABELES, M. 1990. *Anthropologie de l'Etat* (Paris: Armand Colin).
——1993. 'Les archaïsmes politiques français', *La Recherche*, 251(24): 192–6.
ASOMBANG, R. 1999. 'Sacred centers and urbanization in West Central Africa' in S. Keech McIntosh (ed.), *Beyond Chiefdoms: Pathways to complexity in Africa* (Cambridge: Cambridge University Press), pp. 80–7.
BRISCH, N. (ed.) 2008a. *Religion and Power: Divine kingship in the Ancient World and beyond*, Oriental Institute Seminars, 4 (Chicago: The Oriental Institute).
——2008b. 'Touched by the gods: Visual evidence for the divine status of rulers in the ancient Near East' in N. Brisch (ed.), *Religion and Power: Divine kingship in the Ancient World and beyond*, Oriental Institute Seminars, 4 (Chicago: The Oriental Institute), pp. 73–98.
CANNADINE, D. and PRICE, S. (eds) 1987. *Rituals of Royalty: Power and ceremonial in traditional societies* (Cambridge: Cambridge University Press).
DEHOUVE, D. 2005. *Essai sur la royauté sacrée en République mexicaine* (Paris: CNRS).

DERCHAIN, P. 1962. 'Le rôle du roi d'Egypte dans le maintien de l'ordre cosmique' in L. de Heusch (ed.), *Le pouvoir et le sacré* (Brussels: Université Libre), pp. 61–73.

EARLE, T. K. 1987. 'Chiefdoms in archaeological and ethnohistorical perspectives', *Annual Review of Anthropology*, 16: 279–308.

EVANS-PRITCHARD, E. E. 1962 [1948]. 'The divine kingship of the Shilluk of the Nilotic Sudan', Frazer Lecture, repr. in *Essays in Social Anthropology* (London: Faber and Faber).

FEELEY-HARNIK, G. 1985. 'Issues in divine kingship', *Annual Review of Anthropology*, 14: 273–313.

FIELDS, V. M. and REENTS-BUDET, D. (eds) 2006. *Lords of Creation: The origins of sacred Maya kingship* (London: Scala Publications).

FOGELIN, L. 2007. 'The archaeology of religious ritual', *Annual Review of Anthropology*, 36: 5–71.

FRANKFORT, H. 1948. *Kingship and the Gods: A study of ancient Near Eastern religion as the integration of society and nature* (Chicago, IL: The University of Chicago Press).

FRAZER, J. G. 1913–15. 'Preface', *The Golden Bough*, Part III: *The Dying God*, 3rd edn (London: MacMillan).

FREIDEL, D. A. and SCHELE, L. 1988. 'Kingship in the Late Pre-classic Maya Lowlands: The instruments and places of ritual power', *American Anthropologist*, 90(3): 547–67.

GUERNSEY, J. 2006. *Ritual and Power in Stone: The performance of rulership in Mesoamerican Izapan style art* (Austin, TX: University of Texas Press).

HEUSCH, L. DE 1962. 'Pour une dialectique de la sacralité du pouvoir' in L. de Heusch (ed.), *Le pouvoir et le sacré* (Bruxelles : Université Libre), pp. 15–47.

——1987. *Ecrits sur la royauté sacrée* (Bruxelles: Editions de l'Université de Bruxelles).

——1997. 'The symbolic mechanisms of sacred kingship: Rediscovering Frazer', *Journal of the Royal Anthropological Institute*, 3(2): 213–23.

——2005. 'Forms of sacralized power in Africa' in D. Quigley (ed.), *The Character of Kingship* (Oxford: Berg), pp. 25–37.

HOCART, A. M. 1969 [1927]. *Kingship* (Oxford: Oxford University Press).

——1970 [1936]. *Kings and Councilors: An essay in the comparative anatomy of human society* (Chicago: University of Chicago Press).

KEECH MCINTOSH, S. (ed.) 1999. *Beyond Chiefdoms: Pathways to complexity in Africa* (Cambridge: Cambridge University Press).

KEMP, B. J. 2006. *Ancient Egypt: Anatomy of a civilization* (London: Routledge).

MACGAFFEY, W. 1987. 'Kingship in sub-Saharan Africa' in M. Eliade (ed.), *The Encyclopedia of religion*, VIII (New York: MacMillan), pp. 322–5.

MARET, P. DE 1999. 'The power of symbols and the symbols of power through time: Probing the Luba past' in S. Keech McIntosh (ed.), *Beyond Chiefdoms: Pathways to complexity in Africa* (Cambridge: Cambridge University Press), pp. 151–65.

MOORE, J. D. 1996. *Architecture and Power in the Ancient Andes: The archaeology of public buildings* (Cambridge: Cambridge University Press).

NETTING, R. 1972. 'Sacred power and centralization' in B. Spooner (ed.), *Population Growth: Anthropological implications* (Cambridge: MIT Press).

O'CONNOR, D. and SILVERMAN, D. P. (eds) 1995. *Ancient Egyptian Kingship* (Leiden: Brill).

PUETT, M. J. 2002. *To Become a God: Cosmology, sacrifice, and self-divinization in early China* (Cambridge, MA: Harvard University Press).

QUIGLEY, D. (ed.) 2005. *The Character of Kingship* (Oxford: Berg).

ROWLANDS, M. 1999. 'The cultural economy of sacred power' in R. Pascal (ed.), *Les princes de la préhistoire et l'émergence de l'Etat*, 252 (Rome: Ecole française de Rome), pp. 165–72.

Russ, J. 1994. *Les théories du pouvoir* (Paris: Le Livre de Poche).
Spencer, C. S. and Redmond, E. M. 2004. 'Primary state formation in Mesoamerica', *Annual Review of Anthropology*, 33: 173–99.
Wengrow, D. 2006. *The Archaeology of Early Egypt: Social transformations in North-East Africa, 10,000 to 2,650 BC* (Cambridge: Cambridge University Press).
Wilkinson, T. A. H. 1999. *Early Dynastic Egypt* (London: Routledge).

Index

Abeles, M. 1060
Abercrombie, N. 169
Abiodun, R. 1006
Aboriginal Australia 484–92, 1008
   ancestral connections in 490–1
   art, spirits and ancestors in 487–8
   cosmology 483, 486, 487–8, 490, 491
   Dreamtime/Dreaming 12, 27, 321, 485–8, 490, 1010
   funerary rites 91
   sacred places 488–9
   study of 484–5
   the ocean and 491
   totemic landscapes 489–90
   see also rock art
Abraham, biblical figure 916, 970
Acheulian 338
   Middle 334
Adam, biblical figure 108, 136
Adam of Bremen 44, 160, 846
Adams, Robert 974
Aegean
   Bronze Age 695, 699
   Early Bronze Age 685, 686–7, 691
   Late Bronze Age 683, 684, 688–91, 704
   Middle Bronze Age 691, 704
   recognising ritual in prehistoric 684–5
Aegean prehistoric religions 681, 691–2
   Indo-European replacement theories and 682–3
   matriarchy, Great Earth Mother Goddess and 682
   scholarship 682–4
   see also Cyclades, the; Minoan
Æsc (Anglo-Saxon deity) 863
Æsir
   gods 848
   religion 851
'affordances' 25, 26, 28, 252

Africa
   iron-smelting/blacksmithing in 246–7, 253–4, 255, 265, 431–2, 1063
   pottery-making in 247–8, 252, 431–2
   see also sub-Saharan Africa; and individual entries
agency
   individual 175–6
   supernatural 330–1
   see also religion
Agni (Vedic deity) 51, 53–4, 57, 59
agnicayana 53, 56, 57
Ahura Mazda (Indo-Iranian deity) 812–13, 814, 816, 817, 820
Aiello, L. C. 333
Aita (Etruscan deity) 718
Aitteon, Gov. John 667
Akerman, Kim 490–1, 498
Akhenaten, Egyptian king 728
al-Baghdadi, 'Abd al-Latif 970
Alcock, Susan 700, 703
Aldhelm, Abbot of Malmesbury 864, 865
Aldhouse-Green, M. 995
Aldhouse-Green, S. 995
Alexander Jannaeus, King 914
Alexander the Great 814, 909
Algonquian (North America)
   traditions/languages/tribes 656, 658, 666, 668, 670, 671, 1007
al-'Idrissi, Abu Jafar 970
alloforms 53, 58
Alt, K. W. 365
altered states of consciousness (ASC) 313, 320, 630–1, 835, 990
   shamans/shamanism and 308, 310–11, 312, 321, 350, 523, 984, 989–91
   three-stage model 427
   see also shamanic state of consciousness
Althusser, Louis 168–9, 172–3

1070   INDEX

Alva, Walter 587
al-Walid, Caliph 972
Amazonian–Guianan mythology 519, 524
Ambibulus, Marcus 914
ambiguity 233
America
   Native 309, 310–13, 314–16, 317, 318
   see also individual regions and peoples
American Folklore Society 63
Ammonites, the 896, 900
Amorite
   burial practices 900–2
   deities 899
   dynasties 898
   ritual and religion 896, 897, 900
   royal cult 900–1
Amorites, the 895
Anahita (Old Persian deity) 814, 817, 818
An/Anu (Mesopotamian deity) 778
Anatolia 798, 800, 802
   Çatalhöyük 826, 828–9, 993, 1040
   Çayönü 828, 836
   cranial modification and body use in 836–7
   EPPNB 826, 834
   Halaf period 826
   Hassuna period 826
   human–animal relationships in 833, 835
   Kurban Höyük 836
   LPPNB 826
   MPPNB 826, 834
   Neolithic 826, 828, 829
   Nevali Çori 826, 828
   Pınarbaşı 826
   PPNA 826, 830, 834
   PPNC 826, 830
   Pottery Neolithic 826, 833
   Pre-Pottery Neolithic 826
   Samarra period 826
   studying ritual and religion in 827–30, 837
   see also Çayönü Tepesi; Domuztepe; Göbekli Tepe
ancestor
   veneration 1043–4, 1047–8, 1055
   worship 450, 451, 473, 719, 1043, 1047
   see also South-east Asia
ancestor cults 433, 1043–4, 1047
   archaeology of ancestors and 1048–54, 1055

   Egyptian 736–7
   see also Mesoamerica; Mountain-Ok peoples, the; Ndembu, the; Tallensi, the
ancestors
   animals and 1049
   archaeology and 1046–7
   materiality/immateriality and place of 1048–52, 1053–4
   west African Islam and 1052–3
   see also Eastern Woodlands; Inca/Andean religion; neo-shamanism; Northwest Coast
Anderson, Benedict 286
Andersson, M. 1011
Andronikos, Manolis 218–20
Anglo-Saxon
   gods 863, 865–6
   religion 863
   see also Bede, the Venerable; pre-Christian Britain
Anglo-Saxon England 153, 160, 269, 867
   images and iconography in 868–9
   priests and witches in 871–2
   sanctuaries/shrines and furnished burials in 870–1
   votive offerings in 870
Angola 428, 429
aniconism 904, 908
animal sacrifice 154–61
   cremations and 153, 268–9
   Greek 216–17
   see also pre-Christian Britain
animals
   divine/sacred 731
   in Mesolithic 365–6
   see also Anatolia; ancestors; Far Northeast; Ingold, T.; Malta
animism 11, 365–6, 466, 647, 1043
   animistic concepts, archaeology and 1006–7
   defining 1005–6
   new 1020
   NWC 639
   shamanism and 994, 995
   totemism and 1004, 1006, 1008, 1009, 1014
   see also Inca/Andean religion
Annapolis project 173
Anquandah, J. 1012–13

anthropomorphism 11
　see also Inca/Andean religion
Antigonus, Mattathias 913
Antilles 520, 521, 522, 531, 532, 533
　Greater 519, 524, 531, 534
　Lesser 523, 526, 534
Antiochus III the Great, King 909
antiquarianism 64-5, 67, 72
Any, Egyptian official 729, 730
Apalachee, the (North America) 624, 625
Aphrodite (Greek deity) 814
Aplu (Etruscan deity) 715-716
Apollo (Greek deity) 393, 814
Apter, Andrew 234
Aramaeans, the 896, 900
Aranyakas 925
archaeologies of the senses 208-11
　case studies 212-20
archaeology 1-2, 90, 115, 483
　feminist 174-5, 196-7, 205
　funerary 93-6
　nature of 80-1, 209
　post-processual 174, 175, 515, 788
　processual 195, 197, 375-6, 699, 788, 975
　public 71-2
　Western/modernist 209-10
　see also individual entries
archaeology of contemporary conflict
　development/study/purpose of 285-7
　see also forensic archaeology; humanitarianism
archaeo-mythology 882
Ardashir I, Sasanian king 820
Ardashir II, Sasanian king 820
Argentina 291, 295
Argentine Forensic Anthropology Team
　(EAAF) 285, 290, 295
Arikara, the (North America) 67
Aritimi (Etruscan deity) 715
Arnold, B. 198
Arrom, J. J. 528
Artaxerxes II, Persian king 814, 818
Artemis (Greek deity) 814, 817
Artumes (Etruscan deity) 717
Arunta, the (Australia) 1009
Asad, Talal 288, 373
Asatru/Asatruarfelagid 1037-8
ascetics 143

Ash, Jeremy 492
Asherah (Canaanite deity) 903, 904
Ashur (Assyrian deity) 778
Asklepios (Greek deity) 717
Askut 732
　Meryka shrine at 732, 733, 737
Asoka, Mauryan ruler 474, 936-7, 938
Asombang, R. N. 436
Assurbanipal, Assyrian king 819
Assyria 778
Assyriology 786-7
Astarte, love-goddess 715, 716
Astarte/Anat (Amorite/Canaanite deity) 899, 903, 904
Atahualpa, Inca 575
atassas 625
Athena (Greek deity) 814, 817, 908
Atran, S. 331
Aubrey, John 1033
Augustus, Roman emperor 63, 270, 710, 745, 748
　worship of 750-1
Australia 993
　archaeology in 483, 490, 491, 496, 498
　Kimberley region 490
　Lake Mungo 345, 484
　Ngarrabullgan 483, 488-9
　Ngilipitji 490-1
　Tasmania 491
　western Arnhem Land 487-8
　see also Aboriginal Australia; Arunta, the; Torres Strait; Uluru; Wardaman, the
Australopithecine cobble 426
Australopithecus 330, 332, 333, 338, 340
　afarensis 336
Avebury 18, 33, 273-4, 1022, 1025, 1034, 1035, 1040
　Henge 33, 271, 274
　St Michael ley line 1036
Avery, D. H. 254
Avesta, the 812, 814, 821
Ay, Egyptian pharaoh 84
Aztecs, the 544, 546, 549-50
　ceramics 561-2, 564
　ceremonies 564-7
　definition 557
　deities 563-4

1072   INDEX

Aztecs, the (*cont.*)
　domestic ritual 566–7
　music and 562
　religion and ritual 556–7, 567
　stone sculpture 561, 563
　temples, shrines and offerings 557–61
　use of fire/New Fire ceremony 561, 566
　see also human sacrifice; sacrifice

Baʿal (Canaanite deity) 899, 900, 903–4
Baʿal-Hadad (Amorite deity) 899
Babel–Bibel crisis 787
Babylon 780, 818, 908
　Marduk temple in 779
　New Year Festival 780, 781, 785
　see also pan-Babylonianism
Babylonian
　Creation Epic 776, 778, 785
　Epic of Gilgamesh 776, 785–6
　Map of World 785
Bachelard, Gaston 39, 252
Bachofen, Johann Jakob 682, 683
Baghat, 'Ali 969
Baik, Chanlatte 524
Bailey, D. W. 685
Baird, R. 234
Baktaman, the (PNG) 33, 1049, 1051, 1055
Baldur (Norse deity) 1038
Balfet, Hélène 245
Balibar, E. 169
Balkans, the 295
　Neolithic 252
ball parks (*bateys*) 519, 530, 531, 533
Ballard, Chris 495, 498
Baltic region
　folklore 880, 882, 883–4
　Late Bronze Age 881
　religious sites/holy places in 884–6
　Stone Age 880, 881, 887
　studying religions of 877–84, 887–8
　Viking Age 884, 886
Bandaranayake, S. D. 941
Banzarov, D. 987
Barham, L. 426
Bari, the (Sudan) 44
Barley, N. 247

Barnes, Gina 463, 465
Barrett, John 371
Barringer, Judith 701
Barth, F. 25, 28, 33, 34, 1049, 1051, 1055
Basseri, the (Iran/Iraq) 28
Batammaliba, the (western Africa) 138
Bateson, G. 25
Batswapong, the (Botswana) 69
Battersea Shield 411–12
Battuta, Ibn 973
Beard, M. 701
Beattie, J. H. M. 155
Bede, the Venerable 863, 864–5, 866, 870
Bednarik, R. G. 426
Bedouin
　Negev 975
Beek, W. van 432
Belgium 338, 363, 846, 1047
Belize 548
Bell, C. 3, 116, 117, 123, 128
Bell, Gertrude 952, 953, 969
Beltane festival 59
Benavides, G. 234
Bendall, L. M. 691
Bender, B. 68
Bendix, R. 65
Benson, Elizabeth 591
Beowulf 847
Bérard, C.
　A City of Images 700
Berchem, Max Van 969
Berdan, F. F. 561
Berezkin, Yuri 591
Bergson, H. 211
Bernice I (wife of Ptolemy I) 909–10
Bernice II (wife of Ptolemy III Euergetes) 910
Berossus, Babylonian astronomer 818
Bes (Egyptian deity) 726, 735
Betanzos, Juan de 572
Bhadravarman, King 476
Bible, the 786–7
　New Testament 108
　Old Testament 107–8, 109
　see also Hebrew Bible
Bickler, Simon 507
Binford, L. R. 171, 375, 482
Bird-David, B. 466, 573

Bird-David, N. 1005, 1006, 1020
Bishop Museum 505
Blain, J. 1018, 1019, 1021, 1024, 1025
Blair, J. 871
Bliujienė, Audrone 884
Bloch, M. 147, 262, 267, 278, 291, 377
Boas, F. 641
bodily
  boundaries 143-4, 145
  contact between mortal and divine 145
  practice traditions 142-3
  purity 143-4
body
  and soul 134-6
  personhood and the living 140
  see also death; fire; landscape; religion
bodylore 994-5
bogs 27, 46, 389-90, 410
Boisselier, J. 475
Boivin, N. 2
Bolger, Diane 201
Bonnet, C. 152, 432
Bonogofsky, M. 804
Borden, C. E. 648
Borić, D. 364, 366
Bossio, Antonio 952
Bottéro, Jean 789, 790
Boulay, Juliet du 955
Bourdieu, P. 122, 127, 179, 181, 251
Bourdillon, M. F. C. 151
Bourget, Steve 595
Bowie, F. 116
Bowler, J. M. 484
Boyer, P. 95, 97, 121, 127
Bradley, John 491, 498
Bradley, R. 123, 153, 379, 995
Brady, Liam 493
Brahma (Hindu deity) 923
Brahmanas 925
bread 250-1
Breuil, Henri 349
Brinker, Helmut 444
Brochtorff-Xagħra Circle 759, 760, 765, 769, 770
  nature of 761-2, 766-7
Brocktorff, C. F. de 760
Brokpa, the (Tibet) 29
Brontoscopic Calendar 711, 717

Bronze Age 19, 56, 321, 389, 408, 411, 864
  Britain 1025
  China 448
  cosmology/religious beliefs in European 387, 391-3
  Early 52, 55, 145, 231
  elites 394-5, 398
  Europe 95, 153, 276
  Iran 821
  Late 56, 58, 216, 391-2, 393, 396, 398, 415, 679
  Mediterranean 758, 770-1
  metalwork/metalworking 388, 389, 392, 394, 398
  ritual activities in European 395-6, 398
  ritual and religion 387-8, 398-9
  ritual practitioners in European 393-4
  role of water in rituals/religion 41
  Scandinavia 54-5, 231, 271, 853, 855, 856, 993
  South-east Asia 470, 471-2
  special places in European 389-91
  see also Aegean; Baltic region; caves; Crete; Cyclades, the; Greece; Levant, the; megalithic tombs; Middle East; water
Brookes, S. O. 625
Brown, Wendy 297
Brück, J. 125, 266, 379-80, 415
Brumfiel, E. M. 152
Buckland, William 1025
Buddha 142, 478, 926
  Gautama 934
  Kanakamuni 937
  lifetime of the 935-7
Buddhism 135, 136, 140, 142, 372, 815, 927
  Hinduism and 922, 925-6
  in China 141, 442
  in Japan 457, 465-6
  in South-east Asia 474, 475-6, 478-9, 480
  origins and development of 934-5
Buddhist
  First Council 936
  Fourth Council 937
  landscapes/monasteries 940-4
  monuments 937-40
  Pali canon 936, 937
  scholarship 934-5
  Temporalities Ordinance 942
  Third Council 936

Buden, Stephanie 204
Bulsa, the (Ghana) 1011, 1012–13
burial 359, 1047
   Aegean 686–7
   Anatolian 830, 832–3
   Aztec 559
   British 409–10
   Caribbean 526
   Christian 951
   Etruscan 717–18
   gender, religion and 197–8
   history/development of 94–5, 338–9
   Iranian 815
   Iron Age 409–10, 433
   Japanese 460
   Jewish 912–13
   Levantine 795, 797, 798, 799, 802–3, 900–3
   Lower/Middle/Upper Palaeolithic 337–9, 344–8
   Mesoamerican 198, 544, 545, 547–8
   mirror 410, 415
   NWC 640, 647, 648, 650
   Pacific Islands 507, 508–9, 512
   Pueblo 609, 611
   Scandinavian 855
   secondary 433, 547, 832–3
   South-east Asian 470–3
   see also individual entries
Burke, H. 174
Burkert, Walter 702, 703–4
Burkina Faso 428, 431, 434, 1061
Burl, A. 1009, 1047
Busby, C. 136
Butrimas, A. 881
Byzantine churches 212–13, 949
Byzantium 949, 950

Caesar, Julius 406, 720, 750
camac concept 574–5, 576
Cambodia 473
   Angkor Kingdom 476–80
   Angkor Thom 479, 939
   Angkor Wat 478–9
   Bakong temple 477
   Chenla states in 475–6
   Prasat Thom temple 477–8
   Preah Ko temple 476

Cambridge, University of 968
Cameroon 247, 253, 254, 433, 436
Campbell, Matthew 511, 514
Canaanite
   burial practices 901, 903
   deities 899–900, 903–4
   ritual and religion 895–6, 897
Capella, Martianus 712
Capitoline Hill/Triad 748, 750, 755
Caribbean, the 519
   Golden Rock site 523, 527
   horticulturalists in 524–5
   iconography and symbolism in 527–30
   pottery in 530, 531
   settlement 520, 523, 525–7
   see also rock art; Saladoids, the; Taíno, the
Carlson, R. L. 648
Carr, G. 409
Carrasco, D. 82, 567, 589
Carrithers, M. 940
Carter, J. 152, 156
Carthage 953
Caruana, A. A. 760
Casimiroids, the (Caribbean) 520–1, 523, 524
Caskey, J. L. 689
castes 110–11
   Ethiopian 30, 32
   Hindu/Indian 30, 106, 135, 141, 925, 935
   see also Rajput caste
Castrén, M. A. 986
Catholic
   Church 96, 551, 953, 968
   fasting 187
   priests 144
   saints 141, 145
Cauvin, J. 801, 805, 828
Cauwe, N. 1047
cave art
   Upper Palaeolithic 349–51, 364
   see also hunter-gatherers
caves 27, 29, 276, 363
   Bronze Age use/views of 389–90
   Upper Palaeolithic use of 352–4
   see also France; Pyrenean caves; sanctuaries; Spain
Cavtha (Etruscan deity) 715–16
Çayönü Tepesi
   Skull Building 826, 830–3

Celts, the 405
Central African Republic 436
Cerberus (Greek monster) 718
Ceschi, C. 761, 763
Chaco Canyon 607, 608–9
Chadwick, J. 683
chaîne opératoires 245–6, 256, 266
Chakrabarti, D. 921–2
Chalcolithic 98, 805
  see also India
Chamoux, Marie-Noël 245
Chang, K. C. 448
Chapman, J. 685, 687
Charon, Greek ferryman of dead 718
Charun (Etruscan demon) 718
Chatterton, R. 367
Chichen Itza 545, 548, 550, 551
Childe, V. Gordon 170–1, 374
Childeric, king of Franks 869
Childs, S. T. 432
Chile 11
  Purén-Lumaco monuments 13, 17
China 34, 471, 997
  Anyang 442, 449, 450–1
  Banpo 443
  Dawenkou culture 445
  Dian culture 473–4
  Dong Son culture 474
  Dongshanzui 198, 444–5
  evidence for religion in 443–7
  Han dynasty 442, 447–8, 449, 453
  Hongshan culture 444–5
  interpreting archaeological finds in 447–8
  Liangzhu culture 445–6, 449
  Lijiashan 473
  Longshan culture 445, 449
  Majiayao culture 444
  Neolithic 197, 198, 201, 443–4, 445, 447, 448–9, 451
  Niuheliang 196, 197, 198–9, 200, 444–5, 448
  Qujialing culture 447
  Sanxingdui 451
  Shang dynasty 203, 205, 442, 448, 450–3
  Shijiahe culture 447
  Shizhaishan 473
  tombs in 443–4, 445, 447–8, 449, 451, 453
  Xishuipo 197, 443–4, 447–8
  Yaoshan 445
  Yuanjunmiao 197
  Zhou dynasty 448, 451
  see also Buddhism; South-east Asia
Chippindale, C. 318, 491, 1035, 1039
Chola dynasty 928–9
Chouin, G. 434
Christensen, L. B. 830
Christian
  architecture 138
  art, sculpture and portable objects 950–1
  churches/monasteries 949–50
  landscapes 955–6
Christianity 134, 136, 372, 745, 747, 811
  archaeology of 948–53, 958–9
  archaeology of communities and 954–8
  Baltic 881
  centrality of belief in 373
  Eastern Orthodox 212
  Greek Orthodox 218–19, 249
  in Judea 916–17
  Jesus Christ in 141–2
  Late Antique 950, 952, 957
  neo-paganism and 1038, 1040–1
  Nestorian 815
  personhood in 137
  power, conflict, colonialism and 957–8
  Resurrection and 138–9
  water and 46, 143
  see also Estonia; Latvia; Lithuania
Chuci, the 449
Cicero, Roman philosopher 710, 712
Cieza de León, P. de 572
Claassen, Cheryl 196
Clark, C. M. 186
Clark, J. G. D. 69, 358
classical archaeology 701, 703
  ancient history and 697–700, 702
Claudius, Roman emperor 745
Clendinnen, Inga 589
Cleopatra 722
Clifton, C. 1019
Clottes, J. 354, 364
Clovis, the (North America) 647
CNRS 245
Coast Salish 641, 646, 648

Coast Salish (*cont.*)
  region 640, 642, 643, 644–5, 648, 649, 650, 652
Cobo, B. 572
codices 556–7, 561, 562, 565, 566, 567
Coifi, pagan priest 864, 865
Collins, Andrew 1035–7
Collins, J. M. 641
Collins, S. 135, 142
Collis, John 1040
colonialism 227, 229, 230–1, 235, 237, 286
  see also Christianity
Colonna, G. 715
Colt Hoare, R. 760
Columbia River 644
Columbia-Fraser Plateau 639, 645
Columbus, Christopher 519, 520, 528, 532
commensal hospitality 182, 183
Committee for the Conservation of Arab Art 969
commodity fetishism 167
Communion 137, 144
comparative ethnography 34
Coningham, R. 110–11, 935, 941
Conkey, Margaret 175, 318
Connah, G. 162
Conneller, C. 1008, 1014
Connelly, Joan 201
Constantine I, Roman emperor 949
contextualization 126–7
Cook, Capt. James 105, 506
Cook Islands 511
Coponius, Roman procurator 914
Cordy-Collins, Alan 595
Cortés, Hernando 556
cosmogony
  consuming humans as 81–3
  cremation and 79–80, 140
  definition 76, 77
  nature of 77, 85
  see also myths; religions
cosmology 482–3, 484
  Inca/Andean 575, 576–8, 579
  see also individual entries
cosmovision 560
Cowan, Douglas 1034
Cox, Margaret 290, 293–4

Craig, B. 1043, 1049, 1054
Crawford, O. G. S. 375, 1033
Cree, the (North America) 671
Creek Indians 625, 628
cremation 57, 58, 59, 396, 870
  English 409–10
  Etruscan 718
  Mesoamerican 546
  see also animal sacrifice; cosmogony; fire sacrifice; Hindu; Scandinavia
creolization 227, 235–6
Creswell, Bob 245
Creswell, K. A. C. 969
Crete 396
  Aghia Triadha 688
  Atsipadhes Korakias sanctuary 390
  Bronze Age 394, 683
  Early Minoan 691
  Knossos 681, 683, 687, 688, 690–1
  Later Bronze Age 685
  Middle Bronze Age 684
  Middle Minoan 687–8
  Minoan 214, 681, 683, 684, 686
  Neopalatial 687
  Post-Palatial 688, 689
  Shrine of the Double Axes 688
crimes against humanity 289
critical theory 172, 175
Croatia
  Krapina 338, 339
Crosby, Andrew 514
Crouch, Joe 492
Crown, P. L. 611
Cuba 520
cultural
  change 171–2, 175
  ecologists 171–2
  mixing/pluralism 228
Cunningham, Alexander 934
Cunnington, Maud 97
Curatola Petrocchi, M. 575
Cusa (Old English name/person) 866
Cushing, Frank Hamilton 602
Cyclades, the 681, 684, 685, 686–7, 691
  Ayia Irini 689, 690, 691
  Late Bronze Age 688–91
Cycladic

Early 686
Late 689
Cyprus 201, 204, 288–9, 826
Cyrus Cylinder 908
Cyrus the Great 813, 818, 908
Czaplicka, M. A. 994
Czech Republic
    Dolní Vestoniče 94, 346, 348
    Mšecké Žehrovice 408
    Pavlov 348

Dagara, the (Ghana) 1011
Dagon (Canaanite deity) 899
Daguan, Zhou 478
Dahlberg, A. 137, 145
Daim, Falco 95
Dall, W. H. 649
Danby, William 1033
Daoism 464
Dappula V, King 943
Darius I, Persian king 812, 813, 819
Daston, Lorraine 294
Daugudis, V. 881
David, B. 483, 487, 488, 489, 491, 492, 493, 495, 1010
David, N. 247, 433, 436
Davidson, I. 320
Davies, Druid Paul 1025
Deacon, H. J. 426
Deacon, J. 70, 426
Dead Sea Scrolls 897
death 58, 96, 576
    anthropology and sociology of 90–3
    archaeology and 89–90, 92
    body and 138–40
    humans, knowledge and 97–8
    pollution 292–4
    religion and 91–2, 95
    see also Egypt; Mesoamerica; Mesolithic;
        Mesopotamia; rituals; sub-Saharan Africa
decomposition/recomposition 139
Deetz, James 171
Dehouve, D. 1061
Delitzsch, Friedrich 787
Delle, J. A. 71
Demeter (Greek deity) 719

Deminán (Taíno mythic figure) 519, 522–3,
    528, 529, 530, 531, 532
Denmark 866–7
    Ejsbøl 867
    Fårdal 394
    Fulemile 365, 366
    Gongehusvej 7, 359
    Grevensvænge 394
    Gudme 867
    Holmegård V site 360
    Hvidegård 393
    Illerup 853, 867
    Lundby 363
    Møllegabet II site 363
    Nydam 867
    Prejlerup 363
    Rørby 392
    Vedbæk Bøgebakken cemetery 359, 360,
        361–2, 363, 365
    see also Old Norse and Germanic religion;
        Trundholm chariot
Dennell, R. 335
Derks, Ton 753
D'Errico, F. 333
Derrida, Jacques 92
Derveni papyrus 698
Descola, P. 365, 1006
destiny 1053–4
Deyts, S. 408
Di (Shang deity) 450
Diamond, M. C. 121
Dias, Malini 942, 943
diasporic identity 228
Dieterlen, G. 429–30
Dievas/Dievs (Baltic deity) 848, 882
Diez Canseco, Maria Rostworowski de
    see Rostworowski, M.
diffusion 228
Ding, Wu 451
Dinka, the (Sudan) 156
Dionysus (Greek deity) 719
direct ethnographic approach 484
Direct-Historical Approach 318, 319
disciplined invariance 117
Divakarapandita, Angkor priest 478
divination 203–4

divination (*cont.*)
   oracular 574–5, 580
   see also Etruscan
divine kingship 1059, 1061
   archaeology and 1062–5
   see also power; sacred rulers
Djoser, Egyptian pharaoh 43, 83
Djungan, the (Australia) 488–9
dlugal-NIM (Iranian deity) 812
dnin-šušinak (Iranian deity) 812
Dobres, M.-A. 255
Dockall, H. D. 71–2
Dogon, the (Mali) 429–30, 1060
Domalde, Uppsala king 44
Dominican Republic 520, 522, 529
Domitian, Roman emperor 914
Domuztepe 836
   Death Pit 826, 833–4
Donald, M. 121
Donnan, Christopher 586, 587–8, 591, 592, 593
double hermeneutic 90
Douglas, M. 109, 126, 143, 262, 429
Dowson, T. A. 364
Dronfield, Jeremy 376
Droogers, A. 236
Drucker, Philip 640
Druids 66, 406, 409, 415, 752, 755
   see also Great Britain; Stonehenge
dual historical method 484, 487, 498
Dumuzi (Mesopotamian deity) 779
Dunbar, R. I. M. 332, 333, 339, 340
Dundes, Alan 77
Duodoward, Gerry 649
Durand-Forest, J. de 561, 567
Durga (Hindu deity) 923
   temple (Aihole) 927
Durkheim, Emile 91, 118, 122, 155, 372, 684, 1004, 1007
Duviols, Pierre 572, 579
Dworkin, Ronald 297
Dyas (Sanskrit name of deity) 848

Ea (Mesopotamian deity) 777
   see also Enki/Ea
Eadbald, Kentish king 865
Ealdwulf, East Angles ruler 864

'earth as sacred' concept 32
earth figures/rock alignments 315–16
Easter Island 11, 510, 515
Eastern Woodlands (North America)
   ancestor shrines 630, 631
   Archaic 623, 625, 627, 628, 629, 630
   ceremonial centres 629–30
   earthen mound-building 625, 627–630
   Historic 624, 625, 628, 630, 631–2
   history 623–4
   iconography 632–3
   Mississippian stage 623, 624, 625, 627, 628–9, 630, 631–4
   Palaeoindian stage 623, 624, 625
   researching the 633–4
   ritual use of weapons in 624–5, 626
   tobacco use in 630–2
   Woodland stage 623, 627–8, 629, 630, 632–3
Echo-Hawk, R. C. 67
Eckstorm, F. H. 668
Eddius Stephanus
   Life of St Wilfrid by 864, 865
Edomites, the 896, 900
Edwin, Deiran ruler 864
Eggan, Fred 602, 606
Egypt 107, 139, 266, 909–10, 1043, 1062
   Akhetaten 728, 730
   Amarna 728–30, 734, 736
   Asyut 731
   Avaris 902
   conception of universe in 722–3
   Coptos 724
   death, burial and afterlife in 736–7
   domestic altars in 731–32, 735
   Dynastic 42
   dynasties/periods 723
   Early Dynastic 724, 730
   Eighteenth Dynasty 730
   Elephantine 730
   Fifth Dynasty 725
   Fourth Dynasty 83
   Fustat 969, 973, 974
   Graeco-Roman 42
   Great Aten Temple 728–30
   human-divine communication in 722–3
   Late 731
   life-giving water in 42–3

Luxor 732
Middle Kingdom 734, 735
Mirgissa 734
mortuary cult in 83–5, 1062
New Kingdom 107, 725, 726, 727, 731–2, 735, 736
Nile river 41, 42–3
offerings in 728–31, 734, 736
Old Kingdom 83, 85, 730, 736
Pharaonic 42
pre-dynastic 1062
Ptolemaic 43, 724, 735
pyramids in 83–5, 90
religion and ritual of 723–7, 737–8
rites in 728–37
Saqqara 731
temple cult 728, 734, 738
Thebes 732
Third Dynasty 83
Third Intermediate 731
Thirteenth Dynasty 732
see also purification rituals
Ehecatl (Aztec deity) 558, 561, 563
Eisinger, M. 561
Ekroth, G. 158
El (Canaanite deity) 899
Elamites, the (Iran) 812, 815, 817, 819–20
Eliade, Mircea 77–8, 243, 427, 990, 995, 1019
thought/criticism of 80–1, 85
Engels, Friedrich 167, 168, 682, 973
England 846
Aylesford 414
Bath 752
Bidford-on-Avon 872
Blacklow Hill 871
Bryher 415
Coventina cult 751
Deal 414, 416
Durrington Walls 377–9, 380–3
Goodmanham 864
Harlow 408
Hayling Island 408
Itford Hill 395
King's Barrow Ridge 16
Lindow Man remains 1026–7
Loose Howe 392
medieval 956

river Avon 380–1
river Witham 411
Roos Carr 408
Seahenge 1034, 1035, 1037, 1040
Slonk Hill 871
Snettisham 412–13
South Cadbury hill fort 396
Staffordshire hoard 873
Star Carr 358, 363, 366, 992, 1008
Sutton Hoo 869, 1022
Thames river 411–12, 870
Thornborough circles 18
Trethellen Farm 396
West Kennet long barrow 33, 371–2, 435, 1035
Westhampnett 410
Winterslow 41
Yeavering 870, 871
see also Anglo-Saxon England; Avebury; cremation; Stonehenge
Enheduanna, daughter of Sargon of Akkad 780
Enki/Ea (Mesopotamian deity) 785
Enlil (Mesopotamian deity) 776, 778, 780, 785
environment
cosmology and 27–8, 29
verticality of 29–30
Eos, goddess of dawn 714
Epipalaeolithic 795
Erdosy, G. 944
Eric the Red, Saga of 1024
Eriksen, Thomas 228
Essenes, the 909
Estonia 877–8, 883–4, 887
Christianization of 879
cup-marked stones in 884–5
Paluküla 886
studying 880–1
Tõrma hill 886
see also Baltic region
Ethiopia 295
Bodo 338
Hadar 336
Omotic-speaking people of 30–2
ethnocentrism 124, 127
Etrusca disciplina 711, 718
Etruscan
death ritual/afterlife concepts 717–19
deities 713–17

Etruscan (*cont.*)
  divination 711–13
  nation 719–20
  ritual and religion 710–11, 718
  sanctuaries 711, 715–17
  underworld 718–19
  votive offerings 716
Europe
  early medieval 95, 951
  Late Neolithic 273
  medieval 139, 949, 951
  Mesolithic 269, 1047
  Middle Ages 950
  Neolithic 10, 18, 123, 200, 275, 373, 375, 376, 989, 1047, 1052
  Palaeolithic 427, 990
  Upper Palaeolithic 989, 1047
  see also Bronze Age; Iron Age
Evans, E. E. 70
Evans, Sir Arthur 681, 683
Evans-Pritchard, E. E. 229, 425, 1007, 1008, 1060
Eve, biblical figure 108
Evenki, the (Siberia) 366, 983, 985–6, 988
Ewe, the (Togo) 255
exhumation
  as distinct from excavation 292
  functions/nature of 290–1
  responses to 288–9
Extirpacíon de Idolatrías 572
Eyadéma, G. 255
Ezra, Hebrew biblical figure 908, 911

Fadlan, Ibn 846
Fafnisbani, Sigurd 850
false consciousness 168, 170–1, 173, 175
Far Northeast (North America) 656–7
  Archaic 656, 658–9, 663, 666–7, 669, 670, 672
  burial practices, feasts and gathering places in 666–8
  Ceramic (Woodland) 658, 666–7, 668
  Early Archaic 658, 659, 660, 661, 663, 670, 671
  Early Ceramic (Early Woodland) 666
  Early Maritime Archaic 659
  history 658–9

  hunting rituals and animal bone treatment in 670–1
  Late Archaic 658, 659, 660, 663, 667, 670
  Late Ceramic (Late Woodland) 668
  Maritime Archaic 658, 660, 661
  Middle Archaic 659
  Middle Ceramic (Middle Woodland) 667
  Moorehead phase/burial tradition 658, 659, 660, 661–6, 667, 668
  Palaeoindian 658
  petroglyphs 668–70, 671
  Rattlers Bight phase 660
  Susquehanna tradition 666
  see also Gulf of Maine
fasting 111, 187–8
feasting and 179, 187
feasting 185
  as commensal politics 183–4
  Bronze Age 394
  burial and 361
  gender and 186–7
  Greek 703–4
  political economy and 182–3
  study of 180–1
  see also Far Northeast; fasting; Levant, the; rites
Feeney, Denis 748
Feldman, Ricky 493
Felix, Antonius 914
feng shui 34
Festus, Porcius 914
figurines 199–201, 408
  Aegean 682, 685–8, 689, 690, 691
  African 428–9
  Anatolian 835
  Aztec 562, 563, 564, 566–7
  Caribbean 525
  Chinese 445, 447
  Egyptian 732, 734
  female 349, 375, 445, 680, 730, 797–8, 801, 903, 923
  Ghanaian 1012–13
  Greek 697, 705
  Indian 923, 925
  Iranian 818
  Japanese 459–60, 462
  Levantine 797, 798–9, 801

Maltese 766, 767
Mesoamerican 546, 547, 548
Middle Eastern 903
Moche 589, 593
Pueblo 606
Scandinavian 851
Fiji 508, 510
Finland 878, 880
Finno-Ugric people (Russia) 878, 880, 881
fire 51
  bodies and 58
  cosmos and 53–4
  -cracked stone 56–7
  in Iran 815–16, 817–19
  rock, wood and 59–60
  see also Aztecs, the
fire ritual
  Old Iranian 52, 53
  Scandinavian 52–5, 59
  Vedic 52–4, 57, 58, 59
  see also agnicayana
fire sacrifice 52–4
  archaeology of 55–8
  cremation as 54–5
Firth, R. 116
Fischer, A. 360
Fitzpatrick, A. P. 407, 409–10, 412, 413, 415
Flaherty, G. 1018
Fleming, A. 376
Fleure, Henry 66
Flood, J. 484, 487, 1010
Flood tablet 786
Fock, N. 523
Fogelin, Lars 556, 557, 935, 940, 943
folklore 63
  archaeology, myth and 64–8, 69–70, 71–2
  history and 65, 67, 68
  links between archaeology and 68–9, 70
  tradition and 64
Fondebrider, L. 289
food
  archaeology and 110–12
  symbolism and 33
  taboo 108, 110–12, 1049
  see also fasting; feasting; material culture
Forbes, Hamish 954
Ford, Richard 602–3

forensic anthropology 285–6, 288, 290, 296
  see also Argentine Forensic Anthropology Team; Guatemalan Forensic Anthropology Foundation
forensic archaeology 285–7, 289, 297, 359
  as sense-making practice 291–6
  inclusive 295–6
  nature of 288
  objectivity/independence in 294–6
Forest, J. D. 828
formalism 117
Fortes, M. 97, 133, 151–2, 425, 1011, 1044, 1054
Foucault, Michel 169–70, 173, 234
Foundation for Shamanic Studies 1019, 1028
fractal relations/thinking 137–9, 140
framing 124, 126
France
  Abri Pataud 345–6
  Cap Blanc 346, 347
  Carnac monuments 15–16, 17, 18
  Cathedral of Vezelay 250
  Chauvet cave 352, 353
  Coligny 408
  Combe-Grenal shelter 338
  Cougnac cave 351
  Crévic 396
  Cussac cave 346
  Duruthy shelter 348
  Gargas cave 350, 351
  Gournay-sur-Aronde 408
  Grotte de Perrats 363
  'Grotte des Enfants' 94
  Hoëdic cemetery 358
  La Ferrassie 338, 339
  la Quina 339
  La Roche Cotard 334–5
  Le Mas d'Azil 346
  Les Trois Frères cave 353, 354, 992
  L'Hortus 339
  Lourdes 145
  Moula Guercy cave 338
  Pergouset cave 351
  'Princess of Vix' burial 198
  Sources de la Seine 408
  Téviec cemetery 358, 361
  Villards d'Héra 408
  see also Roman religion; Romans, the
Francfort, H.-P. 990

Frank, B. 431
Frankel, David 485
Frankfurt School 167, 174
Fraser River 647–8, 649, 652
Frazer, Sir James 91, 105, 127, 152, 249, 1007, 1059, 1060
Frend, W. H. C. 948, 952
Freud, S. 106, 152
Freya/Freyja (Norse deity) 848, 851, 1024
Freyr (Norse deity) 848, 851, 854, 864
Friedman, Jonathan 172
Frigg (Germanic deity) 863, 865
Fritz, John 602
Fry, G. 70
Fufluns (Etruscan deity) 719
functionality of form 702

Gaja Bahu I, King 942
Galilee 910, 911, 913
 Nabratein 915–16
 Sepphoris 910, 911, 916
Galison, Peter 294
Gamble, C. 332, 336, 337
Garanger, José 508
Gardell, Mattias 1038
Garfinkel, Y. 805
Gautama Siddhartha
 see Siddhatta Gautama/Gautama Siddhartha
Gavampti, Buddhist missionary 475
Gazin-Schwartz, A. 70
Geertz, C. 373, 684, 1004
Gell, A. 213, 254, 574
Gellner, David 230
Gellner, Ernest 92
gender
 in Iron Age studies 415–16
 religious activities and 203–4
 see also feasting; rites of passage
gender and religion in archaeology 204–5
 study of 195–7
 types of evidence 197–202
Gennep, A. van 26, 91, 106, 127, 263–4, 288
 on rites of passage 118, 261–2, 265, 266
genocide 289, 295
Geoffrey of Monmouth 66
George, A. R. 786

Germany
 Acholshausen 392
 Bad Dürrenberg 365
 Bedburg Königshoven 366
 Berlin Biesdorf 366
 Bilzingsleben 335, 336–7
 Ezelsdorf-Buch 394
 Feldhoffer cave 339
 Gevelinghausen 394
 Gönnersdorf 348
 Gross Perschnitz cemetery 391
 Grosse Ofnet 358, 363
 Grünhof-Tesperhude 396
 Hermannshagen 392
 Hirshlenden 408
 Hohen Viecheln 366
 idols, cult sites, sacrifices and offerings in 866–8
 Kallmünz 398
 Migration period 867
 Mittelberg hill 392
 neo-paganism in 1040
 Osternienburg 394
 Roman religion in 752, 753
 Totenstein outcrop 390
 Unterglauheim 392
 see also Old Norse and Germanic religion
Gernet, A. von 631
Gero, Joan 175, 196
Gesell, G. C. 688
Ġgantija 759, 760, 763, 764–5, 766–7
 period 761–2
Ghana
 Koma Land 429, 1012, 1013
 totemism in 1011–13
 see also Kusasi, the; Tallensi, the
Gibson, J. 25, 252
Gilchrist, R. 138
Gimbutas, Marija 197, 200, 375, 882, 1041
Glassie, H. 64
Glob, P. V. 410
Glory, André 350
Glosecki, S. O. 995
Gnostics 136
Göbekli Tepe 11, 124–5, 798, 826, 828, 993
 art forms at 834–5
 Layer II/III 834
 religion and ritual at 835–6

Goddess (Devi) 930
Goddess theory 374-6
goddesses 195, 197, 199, 201, 204, 683
   mother 199, 204, 374-6, 577-8, 683, 685, 764, 768, 801, 828, 923, 925
   see also Aegean prehistoric religions; Hinduism; Nerthus
Goldhahn, J. 45
Golding, William 261
Golte, Jürgen 592
Goodison, L. 687
Goodman, Felicitas 1019
Goody, J. 127, 425, 1011
Gosaliputra of the Ajivikas 936
Gosden, C. 333
Gose, Peter 572
Gosselain, Olivier P. 252, 431
gouges 659, 663, 664, 665
Grammaticus, Saxo 846
Gramsci, Antonio 168, 169
Grand Menhir Brisé 17
Gratus, Valerius 914
grave
   boundaries/delineation 292-4
   contamination 293-4
   see also mass graves; monuments; Scandinavia
'grave of flowers' 94
Graves, Robert 374
Gravettian period 344, 349
Great Britain
   druids in modern 1025, 1034
   Later Neolithic 1051
   Neolithic 15, 33, 145, 270, 374-5, 380-3, 833, 1009, 1047
   neo-shamanism in 1021-2, 1025
   pagans in modern 1025-7, 1040
   Roman 413, 416
   see also England; Iron Age; Mesolithic; pre-Christian Britain; Roman religion; Scotland; Wales
Greece 201, 204, 214, 396, 910
   Agios Konstantinos sanctuary 214-17
   Akrotiri 689
   archaeology of 697-8, 700
   Athens 269
   Bronze Age 683
   cities of 702-3
   Classical 269, 691
   debates concerning religion in 701-5
   Delos island 910
   gods of 713-15
   Late Bronze Age 689-91
   religion in 696-8
   sacred space in 702-3
   Vergina 218-20
   votive offerings in 704-5
   see also Aegean prehistoric religions; classical archaeology; Crete; Mesolithic; Palaeolithic; sacrifice
Green, A. 776
Green, M. A. 27
Green, M. J. 415
Green, Roger 510
Greene, S. 1018
Gregory I, Pope 870
grihas 938-9, 940
Grimes, Ronald 265
Guatemalan Forensic Anthropology Foundation 295
Guenther, M. 1008
Gulf of Maine 657, 658-9
   Moorehead burial tradition 661-6
   ritual themes 666-71
Gunaratna, Herman 943
Gunawardhana, P. 941
Gundestrup cauldron 46
Guo Yu, the 449
Gurina, N. 365
Guru Granth Sahib 142
Guss, D. M. 523
Guthrie, Stewart 573-4, 577

Haaland, R. 247, 252
Habermas, Jürgen 167-8, 173
Habu, Junko 461
HAD (Honouring the Ancient Dead) 1025-6
Hadad (Aramaean/Middle Eastern deity) 812, 899, 900
Haddon, Alfred 492, 494
Hades (Greek deity) 718
Ħaġar Qim 760, 761, 763, 764-5, 769
Hägg, Robin 702

Haglund, W. D. 294, 296
Haida, the (North America) 13, 1011
Haiti 534
hajj 145, 976
Hal Saflieni 760, 764, 765, 767, 769
    nature of 761, 766
Haldi (Urartian deity) 812
Hall, Jonathan 703
Hall, Robert 625, 627
Halle, U. 1040
Hamayon, R. N. 990, 1021
Hamdi, Osman 970
Hammarstrand, L. 935
Hannerz, U. 235
Hao, Lady 451
Hardacre, H. 1044
Harner, Michael 1019, 1020, 1024
Harrison, Jane Ellen 374
Harvey, G. 1017, 1020, 1021
Hathor (Egyptian deity) 730–1, 735, 904
    Temple of 724
Haudricourt, A.-G. 243, 245
Hauptmann, H. 828
Hawaii 17, 511–12
Hawkes, Jacquetta 374–5
Hawley, Col. 1033
Hayden, B. 184, 804
Hays-Gilpin, Kelley 198
Hebrew Bible 895, 897, 900, 905
Hebrews, the 109
Hedden, Mark 668
Hegel, Georg W. F. 167, 801
    see also Marxism
Heidegger, Martin 92
Hekate (Graeco-Roman deity) 1036
Helios (Greek deity) 814, 916
Helladic
    Early 686
    Late 688, 690
Hendrix, E. A. 685
Hengest (Anglo-Saxon deity) 863
Henninger, J. 151, 154, 160, 162
henotheism 778, 900
Henry of Livonia 883
Hera (Greek deity) 715
Heracles (Greek hero) 814
Herbert, E. 431

Herder, J. G. 879
hermeneutics 232–3, 234
    see also double hermeneutic
Herod Agrippa II 914
Herod Antipas 914
Herod Archelaus 914
Herod the Great 910–11, 911, 912
    Temple of 914
Herodian lamps 913
Herodium 910, 911
Herodotus 90, 107, 813, 816–17, 818
Herskovits, Melville 229
Hertz, R. 91, 97, 118, 288, 433
Herzfeld, E. 969
Hesiod, Greek poet 692
Heusch, L. de 1059, 1061
Hill, J. D. 414
Hill, Sam 1034
Himiko, Queen 464, 465
Hindu
    cremations 79, 140
    deities 923
    practices 144, 922–7
    sacred space 922–3, 930
    temples 927–31
    thought 80
Hinduism 29–30, 135, 136, 815
    Brahmanic 923, 925, 926
    defining archaeology of 921–2
    in South-east Asia 474, 475–7
    Mother Goddess in 39
    Preclassical 926
    Puranic 921, 922–3
    Vedic 921, 926
    see also castes; India; Shiva/Siva; Vishnu/Visnu
Hitoshi, Watanabe 461
Hocart, A. M. 92, 941
Hocquenghem, Ann Marie 591
Hodder, I. 32–3, 80, 829
Hoffman, G. L. 685
Hoffmann, Herbert 700
holism 124
Holocene 506, 623, 660
    Early 656
    Late 488, 490
Holtorf, C. 68
Homer 214, 216, 692, 714, 718

Homininae 330
Homo 336, 338
   antecessor 338
   erectus 332, 333, 336, 340
   ergaster 333
   heidelbergensis 329, 332, 336, 338, 340
   neanderthalensis 332, 333, 338–9, 340
   sapiens 329, 330, 333, 338–9, 340
   sapiens sapiens 425
Honduras 541, 542, 548
Hopewell
   ceremonial centres 629–30
   culture 632, 666
Hopi, the (North America) 67, 316, 317, 601, 606, 609, 612, 613
Horemheb, Egyptian official 726
hörgr 56–7
Hornborg, A. 573
Horsa (Anglo-Saxon deity) 863
Horus (Egyptian deity) 84, 107
   Temple of 734
Høst, Annette 1024
Houel, Jean 758, 760
Hoyle, Larco 591
Huascar, Inca 575, 580
Huayna Capac, Inca 575
Hubert, H. 120, 161
Hudson, Mark 462
Huffman, T. 435
Hughes, D. D. 159–60, 161
Huitzilopochtli (Aztec deity) 558, 564
Huli, the (PNG) 495
Hultkrantz, Å. 987, 991, 992
human sacrifice
   Aztec 82, 152–3, 556, 558, 561, 564–5, 566
   Chinese 473–4
   Egyptian 734
   evidence for 152–3
   Inca 575
   Mesoamerican 44, 550
   Moche 588–9
   Swedish 44
   see also pre-Christian Britain
humanitarianism 287
   human rights, mortuary ritual and 288–91
Humphrey, C. 28, 34, 264, 997
Hungarian Revolution 288

Hungary 393
   Rinyaszentkirály 394
Hunter, John 290, 292, 293–4, 296
hunter-gatherers 154, 359, 471, 989
   Jomon 460
   monuments 10
   rock/cave art and 308, 322, 354
   world views/cosmology of 364–5, 366
Huntington, R. 433
Hutton, R. 374, 986, 1018, 1032, 1037
hybridity 228
hydrological cycle 42, 47

Ice Age 346, 349–51, 623
Iceland 864, 1037–8
   see also Old Norse and Germanic religion
ideological state apparatuses (ISA) 168–9
ideology
   archaeology and 166, 170–6
   concept of 166–70
   discourse, hegemony and 169–70
   hegemony and 168
   Marxist archaeology and 172–4
   social relations and 173–4
Ijzereef, F. G. 110
Imhotep, Egyptian official 43
Inanna (Mesopotamian deity) 779, 819
Inca Sun cult 578, 581
Inca/Andean religion 571–2, 578–80
   animism, anthropomorphism and 572–5, 577
   gods, ancestors and 575–8, 579
   huacas, oracles and 574–5, 576–7, 578–80, 582
India
   Bharhut 934, 939
   Bodhgaya 936
   Chalcolithic 925
   Early Middle 927
   Ganges river 39, 79
   Kusinagara 936
   literary traditions in 925
   Mathura 922, 926
   Middle 926, 927–31
   milk churning in 249
   'Painted Grey Ware' period 925, 926
   Rajagriha 935, 936, 937
   Rajgir 936, 939

India (cont.)
 religious communities in 136
 Sanchi 926, 934, 936, 937, 938, 940
 Sarnath 936, 937, 938
 Taj Mahal 83
 Tirupati 922
 Upper Palaeolithic 923
 Vaisali 936, 937
 Varanasi 79–80, 140, 922
 see also castes; Hindu; Hinduism; Khasi, the; Munda, the; South-east Asia
Indian Island 667–8
Indigenous Hellenism 218
Indo-European studies 52
Indo-Iranian/Old Iranian religious tradition 812
 see also Ahura Mazda
Indravarman, King Jaya 476
Indravarman I, Angkor king 476–7
Indus civilization 923–5
Ingold, T. 25, 155, 210, 365, 466, 573, 1008
 on animal art 1010–11
 on animism 1004, 1005
Ingui (Anglo-Saxon deity) 863
Innu, the (Montagnais-Naskapi) (North America) 658, 671
Insoll, T. 110, 371, 482, 573, 576, 977, 1053
Inšušinak (Susian deity) 813, 815, 820
intentionality 332, 333
International Commission on Missing Persons 288
Inti (Inca deity) 572, 575, 576, 596
 see also Viracocha
Inuit, the
 (Eastern Eskimo) (Labrador, North America) 658
 Greenland 987
Iran 826
 Achaemenid 812, 814, 816, 819–20, 821
 Bisotun 813, 814
 Choga Zanbil 815, 816
 Dahan-e Ghulaiman temple 817
 Hamadan 814
 Kuh-e Khwaja temple 817
 Nush-i Jan Central Temple 815–16
 offerings/sacrifice in 813–14, 816–817, 820
 Parthian 820, 821
 Pasargadae 813, 818, 819

Persepolis 813, 814, 817, 818
Rayy 967
representations in 819–20
rituals and religion in 811–15
Sasanian 813, 814, 817, 819–20, 821
sites and temples in 815–18
Susa 812, 814, 815, 818, 819, 974
see also Basseri, the; fire; fire ritual
Iraq 777, 786, 789, 800, 802
 Abbasid palaces 969, 972
 Abu Dulaf mosque 972
 Great Mosque 972
 Samarra 969, 972
 Shanidar 90, 94, 338, 339
 see also Basseri, the; Kurdistan; Mesopotamia
Ireland 70, 376
 medieval literature of 406–7
 Newgrange 19, 68, 377
 Ralaghan 394
Irian Jaya 249
Iron Age 691, 718, 755, 897
 archaeological evidence for religion/ritual 407–15, 416
 Britain 409–10, 869, 871, 1036
 calendars 408–9
 depositions in water 410–12
 Early 27, 56, 58
 Europe 153, 276, 995
 France 198
 Greece 683
 hoards 412–13
 iconography 408
 India 926
 Iran 812, 815, 821
 Israel 899–900, 903, 904–5
 Late 56, 408
 Levantine 900, 903
 literary evidence for religion 405–7, 415, 416
 Middle 409
 Scandinavia 855, 856, 867
 shrines/sacred spaces 407–8
 South-east Asia 470, 473–4
 see also burial; Middle East
Iroquois, the (North America) 63, 623
Iršenas, M. 881
Isaac, biblical figure 916

Ishmael, biblical figure 970
Ishtar (Mesopotamian deity) 777
Isis (Egyptian deity) 42
Islam 136, 372, 747
   Christianity and 955
   food categories in 110
   teachings/beliefs of 134–5, 138
   see also ancestors; *hajj*; Mohammed/
      Muhammad/Muhammed, Prophet;
      mosques; Qur'an, the; Ramadan
Islamic
   art/antiquities 968–9
   cities/urban life 973–4
   Indian Ocean trade 972–3
   palaces/centres of power 971–2
   practices 142, 143
Islamic archaeology 976–7
   European secular tradition in 968–9
   historiographies of 967–70
   indigenous/Muslim tradition in 969–70
   rural and environmental studies in 974–5
   sites/themes in 971–6
Išnikarab (Susian deity) 815
Israel 28, 826, 903
   Amud cave 338, 339
   Berekhat Ram 333–4
   Ein Gev I 797
   history of 895
   Kebara cave 795
   Kfar HaHoresh 798, 799, 800,
      802, 804–5
   Mallaha 797
   Masada 28
   Nahal Hemar 798, 802
   Negev, the 975
   Neve David 797
   Tabun cave 339
   see also Iron Age; Levant, the; Palestine
Israelite ritual and religion 895–7,
      900, 904–5
Italy
   Barme Grande 94
   Belvedere temple 715–16
   Castel di Guido 338
   Christian Rome 949, 952, 955–6
   Neolithic 198
   'Prince' burial 344–5

   Pyrgi 714–16
   Romito 94, 346
   Tarquinia 711, 715, 716, 720
   Toirano cave 352
Iteanu, A. 139
Iwao, Oba 458

Jaanits, L. 880
Jacobsen, Thorkild 788–9
Jacobson-Widding, A. 432
Jainism 922, 926, 927, 938
   see also Mahavira of the Jains
Jakobsen, M. D. 1020
James, E. O. 1010
James, Liz 213
James, Wendy 1004
James, William 97
Janik, L. D. 360
Janzen, J. M. 1044, 1046, 1051
Japan 997
   agriculture in 461–2, 464
   cosmology in 459, 461, 465, 466
   Jomon 199, 457, 458–61, 462, 464
   Kofun 204, 457, 464–6
   Miwa Court 465
   Mukaisamada 460
   Oshoro stone circles 459
   Oyu stone circles 458
   Takamatsuzuka 466
   tombs in 464–6
   'woman man stone' site 459–60
   Yayoi 457, 458, 461–4
Jastrow, M. 787
Jayavarman I, Chenla ruler 475
Jayavarman II, Angkor king 476
Jayavarman IV, Angkor king 477–8
Jayavarman VII, Angkor king 478–9, 480
Jeanjean, A. 255
Jensen, J. S. 228, 233
Jericho
   Herodian 910, 911
   skulls 98
   see also Palestinian Territories
Jerusalem 898, 903, 905, 949, 975
   First Temple 896, 909, 914
   pilgrimage to 904, 913

Jerusalem (*cont.*)
   Second Temple/Second Temple period 895, 904, 911, 913, 915, 916
   Temple in 908, 909, 910, 913
   Temple Mount 911, 915
   Theodotus inscription in 910, 915
Jesup North Pacific Expedition 986, 997
Jesus Christ 137, 138, 144
   mills, metaphors and 250–1
   see also Christianity
Jewish
   art 914, 916
   coins 913–14
   ritual/ritual baths 910–12
   suicides at Masada 28
Jochelson, W. 997
Jogaila, Grand Duke 879
Johanson, Donald 336
John Hyrcanus I, King 909, 913, 914
Johnson, M. 26
Jonaitis, A. 640
Jones, R. F. J. 95
Jones, Rhys 490–1
Jordan 110, 826, 971
   'Ain Ghazal 798–9, 802
   Khirbat Faris Project 974
   see also Levant, the
Jordan, P. 366, 995
Josephus, Jewish historian 909
Joyce, R. 139, 141
Joyner, C. 65
Jubayr, Ibn 970
Judah 890, 903
   Arad temple 890, 901
Judaism 134, 747, 811, 815
   early Roman period 910–15
   Hellenistic period 909–10
   late Roman period 915–17
   Persian period 908–9
   use of term 895
Judea 909, 913, 916
   Gamla 910, 911
   Modi'in 910, 911
   Qumran 909
   Shuafat 910, 911
   see also Christianity; Yehud
Juno (Roman deity) 748
Jupiter (Roman deity) 748, 848

Kalevelis (Baltic deity) 882
Kamstra, J. H. 232
Kanishka, Kushan king 937
Kankpeyeng, B. 1012
Kantner, J. 608
Kanuri, the (Niger) 254–5
Karlström, A. 2
katsinas 602, 603, 610–12, 613
Keane, W. 2, 211, 252–3, 373
Kearney, Amanda 491
Keightley, David 448, 449
Kelly, E. P. 410
Kemosh (Middle Eastern deity) 900
Kemp, B. J. 724
Kennedy, Mary 196
Kenya
   Manda 972
   see also Kikuyu, the
Kenyon, K. 802
Kertzer, D. I. 180, 560
Khafre, Egyptian pharaoh 83
Khanty, the (Siberia) 983, 995
Khasi, the (India) 32
Khufu, Egyptian pharaoh 83–4
Kidder, Edward 463, 465
Kikuyu, the (Kenya) 186
King, Capt. James 105
Kirch, Patrick 507, 510, 512
Kirdir, *magus* 815
kivas 602, 603, 604, 610, 611–12
   Basketmaker great 605, 608
   Chaco 608
   nature/development/use of 606–8
Knight, V. J. 634
knowledge 25, 33, 171, 254, 601, 604
   see also death
Knüsel, C. 409
Kojiki, the 465
Korea 997
   Silla kingdom 201–2
Koryak, the (Siberia) 983, 997
Kouremenos, T. 698
Kramer, Samuel Noah 789
Krishna (Hindu deity) 926
Kroeber, Alfred L. 307
Kuba, R. 434
Kubra, Najm al-Din 976
Küchler, S. 251

kuel 13, 17
Kuijt, I. 803, 829
Kumeyaay, the (North America) 312
Kurdistan (Iraqi) 295
Kusasi, the (Ghana) 434, 1050
Kutscher, Gerdt 591
Kwakiutl, the (North America) 151
Kwakwakawkw, the (North America) 641, 645, 646, 650
Kyriakidis, E. 116, 685, 687
Kyrieleis, Helmut 702

Laclau, E. 169–70
Ladefoged, Thegn 511
Lagamar (Susian deity) 815
Laidlaw, J. 122, 127, 264
Laima (fertility deity) 882, 884
Lakoff, G. 26
Lakshmi (Hindu deity) 923, 930
Lambert, W. G. 776
Laming-Emperaire, Annette 349–50
landscape 24
  body and 29
  painting/theory 25–6
  phenomenology 210, 211
  ritual/ritual perspectives on 25–6, 27–30, 33, 34–5
Lane, Paul 954, 959
Laos 478
Lapita (Melanesia)
  culture/pottery 496, 505, 506–7, 508
Laqueur, Thomas 287
Larco Herrera, Rafael 586, 587, 595
Larsson, L. 358, 360–1, 365, 366
Larsson, T. B. 231
Las Casas, Bartolomé de 520, 533
Latour, Bruno 573
latte stones 512
Latvia 360, 877, 883, 887
  Christianization of 879
  holy places in 885, 886
  Semigallia 885
  studying 880–1
  Zebrene Idol hill 886
  see also Baltic region
Lau, G. F. 1048, 1049
Laurence, Ray 270

Laurentian tradition 658, 665
Lavigerie, C.-M. A. 952–3, 954, 957
Laws of Manu 111
Lawson, E. T. 121
Layton, R. 319, 490, 1008, 1009–10
Leach, E. 77
Lebanon 896
Lebeuf, J.-P. 428
Lechtman, Heather 244–5, 246, 247
Lee, Georgia 515
Lemonnier, Pierre 245, 246, 249, 252, 256
Lentz, C. 434
Lenus Mars (Celtic/Roman deity) 752, 753
Leone, M. 70, 172–3
Leopold, A. M. 228, 233
Leroi-Gourhan, André 245, 333, 349–50
Letcher, A. 1021
Levant, the 826, 896
  boundaries, domestication and supernatural in 805–6
  Bronze Age/Middle Bronze Age/Late Bronze Age 897, 900
  Ebla 898–9
  feasting/dancing in 804–5
  Hazor 898–9
  Kebaran period 795
  Late (Pottery) Neolithic 795, 799–800, 802, 805, 806
  Natufian/Late Natufian period 795, 797, 802, 804
  Neolithic 795, 797, 803, 805
  Neolithic religion in 801–2
  Palaeolithic/Middle Palaeolithic/Upper Palaeolithic 795, 801
  Pre-Pottery Neolithic A (PPNA) period 795, 797–8, 801, 802
  Pre-Pottery Neolithic B (PPNB) period 795, 798–9, 800, 802–3, 804, 806
  Pre-Pottery Neolithic C (PPNC) period 798, 804
  skull cult 802–4
  studying ritual and religion in 800–1, 806
  temples in 898
  see also burial; Iron Age
Lévi-Strauss, C. 98, 429, 507, 1007, 1011
Lewis, I. M. 427, 994
Lewis-Williams, J. D. 829, 832, 835, 993
  on rock art/shamanism 27, 319–20, 364, 376

ley lines 1035–6
Lienhardt, G. 156
life crises 312
'life lines' 45
liminality
   in archaeology of ritual 263–4
   sacred domains and 275–6
   social/spatial 26, 27, 28
Lindquist, G. 1024
Linear A 687
Linear B 681, 684, 690, 691
linguistics 235
Lissner, I. 1006
lithophones 352, 430
Lithuania 877, 887, 1041
   Christianization of 879
   holy places in 885
   studying 880, 881
   see also Baltic region
Livingstone Smith, A. 431
Livy, Roman historian 710
Logan, Melissa 200
López, Rodríguez 526
Lorzing, Han 24, 35
Lõugas, V. 880
Louis XVI, King 760
Louisiana
   Crooks site 627
   Poverty Point 627, 628, 629
   Watson Brake 627, 629
Lourandos, Harry 483, 485
Luba, the (Congo) 432
Luiseño, the (North America) 312
Lukács, Georg 167, 168
Lycett, M. T. 928

maat 723
McBryde, Isabel 485
McCarthy, Michael 1034
McCauley, R. N. 121
MacCormack, S. 575, 576
MacDonald, P. 415
Macedonia, Former Yugoslav Republic of 218
McFadyen, Alistair 137
MacGaffey, W. 1048
Machias Bay 657, 668–70

MacKenzie, M. 1049
MacLellan, Gordon 1020, 1027
McNiven, Ian 482, 491, 492–4
Magar, the (Nepal) 29
Magdalenian period 344, 348
Magi 813–14, 817
magic
   fertility 349, 352
   hunting 308, 312, 319, 320, 349, 352
   sympathetic 349
   see also Mesopotamia; techniques
Maglemosian period 360
Magri, Father Emmanuel (Manuel) 760
Mahabharata epic 925, 926
Mahavira of the Jains 936
Mahias, Marie-Claude 245, 246, 249
Maimonides, Moses 108
Maize God (Mesoamerican deity) 1063
Makowski, Krzysztof 591–2
Mali
   Gao region 1052–3
   Jenne-jeno 428
   Tondidarou 436
   see also Dogon, the; Mande, the
Maliseet, the (North America) 658, 667
Mallory, J. P. 161
mallquis 576, 577, 579
Malta
   animal/human representations in 764–5, 767, 768, 770
   funerary megalithic structures in 766–7, 768
   Neolithic 199
   temples in 762–6, 769
Maltese megaliths
   historical development of 761–2
   landscape setting of 768
   Mgarr phase 761
   religion/cosmology of 768–70
   researching 758–61
Mama Quilla (Andean deity) 576, 577–8
Mamacocha, the (Andean deity) 577
Manchester Museum 1025, 1026–7
Mande, the (Mali) 431
Manetho, ancient priest 723
Mangut, J. 434
Mania, D. 337
Mania, U. 337

Manichaeism 811, 815
Maori, the (New Zealand) 514
Mapuche, the (Chile) 11
Maquinna, Nuu-chah-nulth chief 641
marae 510–11, 514
Marcus, J. 201, 1006
Marduk (Babylon deity) 778, 780, 781, 785
   see also Babylon
Maret, P. de 425, 426, 429, 432
Marianas, the 512
Marinatos, Nanno 702
Maringer, J. 1009, 1047
Marrett, R. R. 97
Marriott, M. 136
Mars (Roman deity) 753, 848, 851
Marshall, John 934, 940
Martyr, Peter (Pietro Martire d'Anghiera) 520, 534
Marx, Karl 167, 169, 170, 171, 175, 682
Marxism
   archaeologists and 170
   French structural 168–9, 172, 174, 175
   Hegelian 172
   Western 167–8
   see also ideology
Mary, biblical figure
   see Virgin Mary
masks 366
Mason, R. J. 67
mass graves
   excavations of 295
   exhumations of 285, 289
   in Yugoslavia 288, 289, 290
Masson Detourbet, A. 428
Masterman, Margaret 97
Mata, Roy 508–9
material culture 2
   food/drink as 179, 181
   gender and religion in 197
   of rites of passage 270–1, 277
Mathers, C. 434, 1050–1
Mauritius 235
Mauss, M. 120, 161, 183, 244, 245
Maya 44, 141, 546–7, 550, 557, 1063
   Classic 139, 543, 544–5, 546, 548, 549, 551
   Lacandon 547
   monuments 17–18

   Postclassic 551
Mayadevi, Queen 935
Mayer, G. 1018
Mbiti, J. S. 426–7
Mead, M. 106
Medes, the (Iran) 816
megalithic tombs 19
   as Neolithic cult temples 371, 373–4
   Bronze Age 68
   Neolithic 10, 68, 123
Melanesia 505–6, 507, 508
   see also Lapita
Mellaart, J. 682
Mellitus, Bishop of London 870
memory 3
   of missing/disappeared 291–2
Menkaure, Egyptian pharaoh 83
Menrva (Etruscan deity) 714, 715–17
Mercury (Roman deity) 749, 752, 848, 851
Merwe, N. J. van der 254
Meryra, Egyptian official 729
Meskell, L. 2, 139, 723, 1040
Mesoamerica 269, 624
   ancestor cults in 548
   Archaic 543, 548
   ball courts in 546–7, 548, 559
   Classic 543, 544, 545, 548, 549, 550–1, 565
   definition 541–2
   Early Formative 542, 544, 548, 549, 550
   Formative 201, 542, 544, 545, 546, 548, 549
   Late Formative 542
   Later Postclassic 544
   Palaeoindian 542
   Postclassic 543, 545, 548, 549, 550–1
   religion and the living person in 546–7
   ritual/ritual practices/ritualization in 542–3, 544–6, 548–9
   state and regional-scale religion in 549–51
   time/calendars in 541, 543–4, 546–7
   treatment of dead in 547–8
   see also Aztecs, the; burial; human sacrifice; Maya; sacrifice
Mesolithic 154, 992
   birth in 359–60
   Britain 363, 374, 1008
   death/burial in 360–2, 363–4, 365
   Early 1045

Mesolithic (cont.)
    Greece 683
    initiation in 360
    Neolithic transition 111
    religion and ritual 358–9, 367
    sacred places 362–4
    see also animals; Europe; rites of passage; shamanism
Mesopotamia 712, 758, 826, 898–9, 1043
    Achaemenid Persian 775
    death/burial in 784–5
    divine kingship concept in 1062
    institutions of 778–80
    Iran and 812, 819
    Neo-Babylonian 780
    Old Babylonian 782
    omens, divination and magic in 784, 785
    personal devotion and votives in 781–4
    religion and ritual in 775–7, 780–5
    studying religion of 786–9
    Ur 779, 781, 1062
Mesopotamian
    archaeology 776–7
    cosmology 785–6
    cult statues 780–1
    gods 777–8
    iconography 776, 777, 819
    kings 779–80, 785
    temples 778–9, 780
Metcalf, P. 433
Mexica, the
    see Aztecs, the
Mexico 200, 624, 1061
    Calixtlahuaca 561
    Cholula 562
    Oaxaca 201, 548
    Teopanzolco 559
    Teotihuacan 544, 545, 549, 550, 551, 563, 565
    Tlatelolco 560
    Yukatan 44
    see also Tenochtitlan
Michaels, A. 926
Michell, G. 928
Micmac, the (North America) 658, 670
Micronesia 505–6, 512–13
Middle East
    Bronze Age 898, 904
    Iron Age 896, 898, 903–4
    Late Antique 973
    Late Bronze Age 896, 898–900, 901–2, 903–4
    Late Iron Age 901
    Middle Bronze Age 898–904
    popular cult in 901–3
    state cult in 898–901
    migdôl/tower temples 898–9
Miller, D. 174
mills 250–1
Mimbres, the (North America) 611
Mímir, Norse mythological figure 868
Min (Egyptian deity) 724
Minerva (Roman deity) 748, 752
Minoan 390
    iconography 394
    Late 159, 688
    -Mycenaean religion 681, 683–4
    palaces 395
    pottery 687
    religion 687–8
    see also Crete
Mintzberg, H. 253
Miocene
    Late 330
misrepresentation 167, 170
Mitchell, J. 255
Mitchell, P. 426
Mithen, S. 121, 1009
Mithra (Zoroastrian deity) 814, 817, 820
Mitra, D. 934, 938
Mizoguchi, Koji 462, 463
Mizue, Mori 458
Mnajdra 759, 760, 761, 763, 764–5
mnemonic sensuous field 211
Moabites, the 896, 900
Moche
    art 585–7, 588–9, 595
    ceramics/pottery 585–6, 589–91, 592–3, 595
    deities 586–7, 588, 591–2, 593–4, 595
    huacas 587, 589, 591, 593
    Presentation Theme/Sacrifice Ceremony 586, 588–9, 591, 592
    public art and politics 593–6
    rituals 588–90
Moche religion 595–6
    concepts 589–95

interpreting 585–7
Thematic Approach to 586
Moctezuma, Eduardo Matos 557
Mohammed/Muhammad/Muhammed, Prophet 108, 142, 967, 970, 975
Molech (Middle Eastern deity) 900
Mongols, the 28
monuments
  future research into 19–20
  grave 32
  land and 12–13, 15–16, 32–4
  nature of 10
  people and 17–18
  sky/cosmology and 18–19
  supernatural and 10–11, 12–13, 15
Moravia 348
Morgan, Catherine 700, 702, 703
Morgan, Jacques De 974
Morgan, Lewis Henry 682
Mormons, the 187
Morocco
  Tan-Tan 334
Morphy, H. 27, 34, 491
Morris, B. 426
Morris, I. 700, 1046
Morrison, K. D. 928, 930
Moses, biblical figure 107–8
mosques 974, 975–6
  see also Iraq
Moszynska, W. 155
Motecuhzoma, Aztec emperor 562
Mouffe, C. 169–70
mounds
  boulder 659, 660
  burial 11, 19, 627–8, 629
  burnt 55, 56–8, 1025
  effigy 19
  platform 627–8, 629
Mount Meru 477, 478, 479
Mountain-Ok peoples, the (PNG/Irian Jaya) 1043
  ancestor cult of 1049, 1054
mourning 288–9, 290, 297
movement 3, 270–1, 273
mummies/mummification 731, 736
Mumtaz Mahal, Empress 83
Munda, the (India) 32
Munro, Neil Gordon 459

Murngin, the (Australia) 486
Musée de l'Homme 245
Museum of Arab Art 969
Myanmar 474, 937
Mycenae 681, 684, 688
  Temple at 689–90
Mycenaean
  burials/tombs 396, 398
  feasting 703
  palaces/shrines 681
  sanctuaries 214–17
  tablets 690–1
  tree and pillar cult 683
Mylonas, G. E. 689
myth 63, 77
  see also folklore
myths 46, 71
  cosmogenic 76, 77–8, 81, 84, 85
  creation 27, 52–3, 77–8, 487, 543, 724, 785
  origin 66, 67, 204–5

Nabonidus of Babylon 780
Nagas (Hindu serpent-beings) 923, 926, 930
Nagy, Imre 288
Nakamura, Oki 461
Namibia 321
  Apollo II cave 427
Nanna/Sin (Mesopotamian deity) 780
Naram-Sin of Akkad 779
Narmer Palette 1062
Nash-Williams, V. E. 953, 954
Natchez, the (North America) 624
Native American Graves Protection and Repatriation Act 604
Naumov, Goce 252
Navarro, J. M. de 411
Nazca lines 19, 35
Ndembu, the (southern Africa) 380
  ancestors 1044–5
Neanderthal interments 90, 94, 338–9
Nebra disc 392–3, 398
Nebwawi, Egyptian scribe 730
Needham, R. 93
Nehemiah, Hebrew biblical figure 909, 911
Nelson, S. M. 196, 997, 1054
neo-evolutionists 171–2
Neolithic 56, 145, 232, 321, 435, 682, 1046

Neolithic (*cont.*)
  Aegean 685–6, 687, 691
  archaeology of ritual 377–80
  Early 125–6, 272, 1011
  India 921
  Iran 818
  Late 273–4, 377, 382, 686, 795
  Middle 1011
  religious experience 373–7
  ritual and religion 371–3, 380–3
  Scandinavia 44, 851
  South-east Asia 470, 471, 472
  Western 374
  see also Anatolia; Balkans, the; China; Europe; Great Britain; Italy; Levant, the; Malta; megalithic tombs; Mesolithic; shamanism; Syria
neo-paganism
  archaeology and 1039–41
  landscapes and 1035–7
  monuments and 1034–5
  nationalist 1038
  nature of 1032–3
  see also Asatru/Asatruarfelagid
neo-shamanism
  ancestors, reburial and 1025–7
  archaeology and 1028
  artefacts, reconstruction and 1023–5
  nature of 1017–19
  sacred landscapes, monuments and 1020–2
Nepal 29–30
  Lumbini 936
Neptune, Clara 669
Neptune, Lt.-Gov. John 667, 669
Nerthus (fertility deity) 848, 851, 864
Nerva, Roman emperor 914
Netherlands, the 846
  Bargeroosterveld 395
  Rhenen-Remmerden 396
  Velserbroek P-63 396, 397
Netting, R. 1063
neuropsychological (N-P) model 319–20, 321, 989–90, 992, 993
New Caledonia 508, 510
New Georgia Archaeological Survey 507, 515
New Guinea
  see Papua New Guinea

New Zealand 505, 514–15
Nibelungenlied 847
Nicholls, R. V. 691
Nicolar, Joseph 669, 671
Niger 431
  see also Kanuri, the
Nigeria 434, 436
  Igbo-Ukwu site 152
  Nok culture 428
  see also Yoruba, the
Nihon Shoki, the 465
Nihongi, the 465
nilometres 42–3
Nilsson, Martin 681, 683, 690, 692
Ninhursag (Mesopotamian deity) 782
Nintoku, Japanese ruler 465
nirvana 135
Njord (Norse deity) 848, 851
Njrðr (Norse deity) 864
Nkumbaan, S. N. 1012
Noah, biblical figure 108
Nooter Roberts, M. 2
North America 600, 623, 639, 656
  Late Palaeoindian 666
  neo-paganism in 1038–9
  see also Arikara, the; Eastern Woodlands; Far Northeast; Haida, the; Iroquois, the; Kumeyaay, the; Kwakiutl, the; Luiseño, the; Northwest Coast; Nunamiut, the; Ojibwa, the; Pawnee, the; Pueblo/Pueblos, the; Tsistsista, the; Yokuts, the
Northern Ireland
  Dunaverney 394
  King's Stables 398
Northwest Coast (NWC) (North America)
  art 649–50
  early historic 639
  Early period 647
  ethnohistoric 640, 647, 650
  feeding ancestors along the 641, 644, 645, 646–7, 648, 650, 652
  historic 644, 648
  Late period 650–1
  Locarno Beach phase/site 647, 649
  Marpole phase/site 643, 646, 647, 648–9
  Middle period 640, 647–9
  proto-historic 639

religious beliefs/practices 639–47, 648, 649
secret societies 644, 645, 648, 649, 650, 651
Norway 1038–9
see also Old Norse and Germanic religion
Nowell, A. 333
Nubian fortresses 734
Nuer, the (Sudan) 1007, 1008
Nukak, the (Amazon) 112, 1049
Numic-speaking people (North America) 311
Nunamiut, the (North America) 482
Nuwa, Changing Woman 205

Obalara's Land site 156
objects
   as 'living' things 270
   Aztec cult 562–3
   in Iran 818–19
   jade 445–6, 449, 451
   sacrifice of 153
   see also Christian; portable ritual objects; ritual
Octavian, Roman triumvir 910
Odin/Óðin (Norse deity) 46, 848, 849–51, 868, 872, 1024, 1038
Ogden, Daniel 988
Ohlmarks, Å. 987, 991
Oho-mono-nushi-no-kami (Japanese deity) 465
Ojibwa, the (North America) 1007
Old Norse and Germanic religion
   archaeology of 849–55
   'central places' in 854
   mythology/cosmology 848, 849–52
   offerings in 853
   rituals and ritual sites/buildings 848–9, 853–5
   sacrifice in 849, 854
   studying 847, 856
   textual background 846–9
   world tree in 848, 851–52, 854
Oliver, Jose 141
Olmec, the (Mesoamerica) 542, 546, 548, 550, 1063
operational sequence
   see chaîne opératoires
Oppenheim, A. Leo 787–8
oracle bones

Japanese 462, 464
Shang 203, 205, 442, 449, 450
Orientalism 967, 968
orientational metaphors 26
Orme, B. 360, 362
Orokaiva, the (PNG) 139, 264
Orpheus (Greek mythic figure) 719
Orphism 698
Ortiz, Alfonso 602
Ortíz, Hernán 529
Ortoiroids, the (Caribbean) 521, 523, 524
Osborne, R. 703
O'Shea, J. 365
Osiris (Egyptian deity) 41, 42–3, 84, 726, 731
Ostionoid culture (Caribbean) 522, 524, 529, 530, 531
Oswald of Northumbria 866
otherness 275–6
Oviedo y Valdéz, Gonzalo Fernandez de 520, 528
Owoc, M. A. 277
Oxford, University of 968
Özbek, M. 832

pa 514
pacarina concept 576, 578
Pachacamac 578, 579
   temple/site 578, 596
   -Vichma cult 571, 578, 581
Pachacuti, Inca 580, 591
Pachamama, the (Andean deity) 577–8
Pacific Islands 505
   see also Melanesia; Micronesia; Polynesia; rock art
Paekche, King of 465
Pakistan
   Mohra Moradu 939
   Taxila 934, 936, 937, 940
Palaeolithic 232, 321, 329, 334, 375, 991, 992
   Greece 685
   Late 458
   Late Middle 339
   Lower 330, 334–6, 340
   Middle 330, 334, 335, 340, 353, 1007
   Middle Upper 98, 335
   Upper 94, 199, 269, 319, 320–1, 335, 337, 340, 363, 427, 989

see also burial; cave art; caves; Epipalaeolithic; Europe; India; Levant, the; portable art; rock art; shamanism
Palau 512–13
Palestine 975
   Ramla 972–3
Palestinian Territories 826
   Jericho 798, 802, 832, 908, 910
   Mt Gerizim 909, 910
   see also Levant, the
pan-Babylonianism 787
Pané, Friar Ramón 519, 520, 524, 527, 528
Papua New Guinea (PNG) 495, 507
   archaeology in 483, 495, 496, 498, 507
   cosmology 495–6, 507
   settlement 506
   see also Baktaman, the; Mountain-Ok peoples, the; Orokaiva, the
Paranavitana, S. 941
Paranthropus 330, 336
Paris School 700
Parker Pearson, M. 271, 1051
Parry, J. 291
Parsons, Elsie Clews 602
Parvati, wife of Shiva 930
Pascal, Blaise 169
passages to other worlds 270–1
Passamaquoddy, the (North America) 658, 667, 668, 670, 671
Passássoglou, G. M. 698
Pasupati (Hindu deity) 923
Patil, C. S. 930
Patočka, Jan 92
Paulinus, Bishop 865
Pawnee, the (North America) 67
Paxson, Diana 1024
Pearce, D. 829, 832, 835, 993
Peirce, Charles Sanders 253
Penda, Mercian king 866, 873
Pender Canal site 642, 644, 647, 648
Penobscot, the (North America) 657, 667–8, 670
Pentikäinen, J. 994
Pequart, M. 361
performance 117–18
Perkūnas (Baltic deity) 882, 884
Persephone (Greek deity) 718

personhood 994
   ancestors and 1046, 1053–4
   conceptualizing 133–42
   cosmology and 141, 146
   relational 137–40
   religious beliefs about 133–7
   ritual, bodily action and 142–5
   states of being and 268–70
persons
   religious/divine 141–2, 144
   transformation of 144–5
Peru
   Chavín de Huantar 20
   Cuzco 575, 578, 596
   Huaca Cao Viejo 587, 588, 594, 595–6
   Huaca de la Luna 586, 587, 588–9, 593–4, 595
   Huancaco 587
   Huaricoto site 196
   San José de Moro 587
   see also Moche religion
Petersen, Henry 849
Peterson, Nicholas 486
Pétrequin, Anne-Marie 497, 498
Pétrequin, P. 249, 497, 498
Petroski, H. 246
Pettigrew, Judith 1022
Pettitt, Paul 338
Phear, Sarah 513
Phersipnei (Etruscan deity) 718
Philip II of Macedonia 218, 220
Phillips, Caroline 514
Phoenicians, the 896, 900
Phylakopi 681, 684, 691, 699
   West Shrine at 689, 690
Piacenza bronze liver 712–13
pierres figures 333–5
pig prohibition
   explanations for 108–9
   religion and 107–8
   see also food
Piggott, Stuart 371, 374
pilgrims/pilgrimages 143, 144–5, 264
   Buddhist 936, 941
   Christian 957
   Mesoamerican 550–1
   rock art and 316

shamanic 1022
see also hajj; Jerusalem
Plato 138
Pleistocene 335, 340, 506, 623
   Late 484
   Middle 329
   post- 520
   Upper 329, 623
Pliny, Roman historian 42, 712
Pliocene 340
   Early 330
Plot, Robert 64
plummets 660, 664, 665
Pococke, Prof. Edward 968
Poetic Edda 846, 848
poetry
   Eddic 52, 56
   Skaldic 56, 849, 851, 856
Poland
   Jędrychowice 396
Polignac, François de 700, 702–3
Politis, G. G. 112, 1049
Pollock, S. 196, 927
pollution 143
   see also death
Polynesia 105–6, 514–15
   archaeology in 505–6, 510
   central and eastern 510–12
   ritual/temples in 510–12
   settlement 505, 508
Pope, R. 415
Porr, M. 365
Port au Choix 661, 665, 670
portable art
   Palaeolithic 990
   sub-Saharan 427
   Upper Palaeolithic 348–9, 989
portable ritual objects 428–31
Portonaccio sanctuary 715–16, 717
Poseidon (Greek deity) 691
Postgate, J. N. 776
post-modernism 175–6
potlatches 151
   NWC 180, 645, 647, 648
Potnia ('mistress') 691
pottery-making 247–9, 253
   see also Africa

Powell, L. C. 71–2
power
   'places of' 10
   sacrality and/of 1059–60, 1064–5
   see also spirit; syncretism
PPNB 32
   see also Anatolia; Levant, the
pre-Christian Britain 863
   human and animal sacrifice in 869–70
   names and 865–6
   pagans in 864–5
   shrines/*fana* in 864–5, 870
Prematilleke, P. L. 934
Price, N. S. 123, 995, 1024
projectile points 658–9, 665, 670
Protestantism 144
psychic questing 1035–7
Ptah (Egyptian deity) 1036
Ptolemy, Roman general 910
Ptolemy I, ruler of Egypt 909–10
Ptolemy III Euergetes, ruler of Egypt 910
Puabi/Pu-abi, Queen 90, 780
Pueblo
   Acoma 606
   Bonito 602, 608–10
   Grasshopper 611
   Jemez 601
   Revolt (1680) 600, 612–13
   San Juan 602
   Santa Clara 613
Pueblo/Pueblos, the (North America) 66, 624
   Basketmaker beginnings of 605–6
   Basketmaker III period 605, 606
   cosmos 608
   dual divisions among 610
   history 602–3
   iconographies 610–11, 613
   languages of 601
   maize and 601, 603, 606
   migration and reorganization of 609–10
   pottery of 605–6, 608, 610–12
   Pueblo I period 606
   Pueblo II period 606, 607, 608
   Pueblo III period 609, 610, 611
   Pueblo IV period 610, 611
   religion and ritual 600–2, 613
   researching 602–4

Pueblo/Pueblos, the (North America) (*cont.*)
　Spanish and 612–13
　violence and 610, 613
Puerto Rico 520–1, 523, 524
　Caguana 519, 527, 533
　Jacaná 533
　Maisabel 526, 529, 530, 531
　Mora Cavern 532
Puranas 925, 934
purification rituals
　Egypt 40–1, 735
　Ethiopia 32
　with water 39–41, 143–4
Purusa, giant 52, 53
Pye, Michael 233
Pyrenean caves
　Enlène 348
　Erberua 348
　Fontanet 352
　Labastide 348
　Le Tuc d'Audoubert 352, 353
　Montespan 353

Qaus (Middle Eastern deity) 900
Quetzalcoatl (Aztec deity) 560, 563
Quilter, Jeffrey 588
Qur'an, the 969–70, 975

Ra (Egyptian deity) 43
Radcliffe-Brown, A. R. 106
Radovanovic, Ivana 364
Rædwald of the East Angles 864
Ragana (fertility deity) 882
Rainbow Serpent 488
Rajendravarman, Angkor king 478
Rajput caste (Punjab) 134
Ramadan 187
Ramah chert 660, 664, 665
Ramayana epic 925, 926
Rameses II, Egyptian pharaoh 107
Ramilisonina 1051
Rangi, the (Tanzania) 111
Rapa Nui
　see Easter Island
Raphael, Max 349

Rapoport, Amos 560
Rappaport, R. 25, 116, 172, 320
Rawlinson, George 786
Rawlinson, Henry 786
Rawson, Jessica 451
Ray, H. P. 927
Read, K. A. 81
Reformation, the 958
regeneration 644, 648
rehuekuel 13
Reichel-Dolmatoff, G. 314
Reid, George Watson Macgregor 1033
Reinach, S. 1009
religion
　bodies in 141–2
　definitions of 329–30, 442, 684
　ecological information and 331–2
　individual agency and origins
　　of 331–5
　psychological origins of 330–1
　understanding 373
　see also individual entries
religions 211
　African indigenous 426–7, 429, 434
　cosmogenic 76, 77–8, 81, 82
　syncretism and 227–8, 230, 232, 237
　traditional 371–2, 426
　transcendental 76, 77–8, 81
　world 371–2, 425
　see also Buddhism; Christianity; Hinduism;
　　Islam; Sikhism; Taoism; Zoroastrianism
religious fusion 226, 233, 235
　see also syncretism
Renfrew, C. 116, 121, 699–700
Renshaw, Layla 290, 295
repressive state apparatus 169
Reshef (Amorite/Canaanite deity) 899
Restall Orr, Emma 1026
Rév, István 288, 291
Rhodes, Cyril 952
Richards, C. 271, 377
Richards, Francis 488
Richardson, Ruth 294
Ricoeur, P. 233
Rimbert, German historian 846
rites
　affliction 120, 732–4

aggregation/reaggregation 261–2, 263–4, 267, 271–2
ancestor 276
calendrical and commemorative 120
exchange and communion 120, 727–31
fertility 276, 314–15
funerary 90–1
increase 317
initiation 266, 271, 312–13, 315, 360
liminal 261–2, 263, 272, 275–6
of feasting, fasting, and festivals 120
separation 261–2, 263–4, 272
transition 271–3
rites of passage 118, 121, 141, 145, 187
　archaeology of 267–76, 277
　as journeys 264–5
　cosmic order, classificatory schemes and 266
　Egyptian 735–7
　funerary 268–9
　gendered 266
　Mesolithic 359–62
　potentiality in 269
　power/violence and 267
　purpose of 265, 267
　Scandinavian 856
　technology and 265–6
　tripartite structure of 261–2, 264
ritual
　anthropological approaches to 121–2, 128
　archaeology of 277–8
　attributes of 117–18
　'breaking of the red pots' 726, 736
　definitions of 116, 118, 330, 377, 379
　distinction between religious and secular 685
　killing of artefacts/objects 27, 411, 416, 526, 716, 867
　nature of 379–80, 656
　problems with 123
　recognizing and reconstructing 124–7
　religion and 124, 211–12, 339–40
　sacrificial 158–62
　space 335–7
Ritual Form model 319, 320
rituals
　atonement 143–4
　attachment 332, 337
　creation and 77–8
　death 39, 41
　detachment 333
　devotion 144–5
　feasts as 180, 183
　functions of 118
　life-cycle 26, 39, 546
　migrations and 28
　political 121
　rain-making 43–4
　religious/non-religious 118, 121–2
　shamanistic 27, 29
　types of 118–21
　see also fire ritual; purification rituals; and individual entries
Rivers, W. H. R. 91, 93, 437
Rives, James 747–8, 750
Robbins, Maurice 659
Roberts, A. F. 2, 429
Robertson Smith, William 105, 152, 155
Robinson, B. S. 665
rock art
　Aboriginal Australian 316–17, 319, 320, 321, 484–8, 489–90, 492, 1010
　archaeology of religion and 322
　biographic 318
　Caribbean 520, 530–1
　formal interpretation of 318, 319–20
　gender, religion and 198
　informed interpretation of 318–19
　nature of 307
　non-shamanic/non-shamanistic 308, 314, 316
　non-visionary 308–9, 314–18
　NWC 641, 645
　origin of religions and 320–1
　origins/functions of 308–9
　Pacific Islands 515
　Pueblo 605–6, 610, 611–12
　Saharan 354
　San 70, 311
　Scandinavian 391, 394
　shamanic/shamanistic 308–12, 314, 320–1, 992, 1010
　Siberian 984
　sub-Saharan 427–8
　Swedish engraving 44–5, 59, 392
　totemic 1009–11
　Upper Palaeolithic 319, 320–2, 354–5, 1009–10
　visionary 308–14
　see also cave art

Roe, Peter 523, 529
Rogers, R. W. 787
Roman religion 745
　emperor-worship in 750–1
　imperial 747–52, 753, 754
　imperial temples 753–4
　in Gaul and Britain 752–5
　offerings/sacrifices in 748, 749, 753, 755
　public cults in 748
Romanization 231
Romans, the
　gods of 713–15
　in Iron Age Gaul 406
　see also Great Britain; Judaism
Rose, Wendy 1018
Rosen-Ayalon, M. 1054
Rosenfeld, Andree 490
Rosmerta (Celtic deity) 752
Ross, J. 320
Rostworowski, M. 572, 575
Rouch, J. 1052
roundhouses 415
Rouse, I. 524
Rousseau, Jean-Jacques 801
Rowlands, M. 172, 247, 254, 265
Rudolf, K. 233
Rudra (Vedic deity) 922, 923
rule-governance 117
Rumu, the (PNG) 495–6, 497
runes 869, 1027
runestones 850–1, 951
Russell, Lynette 492
Russia
　'holy stone', Kanin Nos peninsula 10
　Katyn 285
　Kostenki I site 349
　Sungir 94, 344–5, 346
　see also Finno-Ugric people
Rwanda 286, 287, 295
Rydving, H. 983, 997

Saami/Sámi, the (Scandinavia) 855, 986, 991, 995, 997, 1024
sacred marriage (Sumerian ceremony) 775, 779, 785
sacred-profane distinction 91, 124, 126
sacred rulers 1060–1

sacrifice
　Anatolian 833
　archaeology of 152–63
　Aztec 81–2, 544
　blood 152, 154–5, 703, 704, 748, 813
　child 97
　concept/definitions of 151–2, 153
　Etruscan 711
　gender and 203
　Greek 158–9, 703–4
　in pre-Christian Britain 864
　in religion 81, 97
　Indo-European 161
　Mesoamerican 44, 81
　nature/purpose of 81, 120, 161
　shamanic 155
　Shang Chinese 451, 452
　times of 162
　totem and 155
　see also animal sacrifice; fire sacrifice;
　　Germany; human sacrifice; Iran; Old
　　Norse and Germanic religion; ritual;
　　Roman religion; Scandinavia; Tallensi,
　　the; water
Sagona, Antonio 491
Sahagún, Fray Bernardino de 558
Said, Edward 967
St Augustine 373
St Cuthbert 952
St Peter's Basilica 949, 955
St Wilfrid 865
　see also Eddius Stephanus
Saladoids, the (Caribbean) 520, 524, 530, 531, 532
　Cedrosan 524–7, 528, 529
　Huecan 524–7, 528
Sales, Kim 491
Salih, Prophet 970
šaman 985–6, 987, 988
Samaria 909, 910, 911, 913
Samaritans, the 909–10
Samoa 508, 510
San, the (southern Africa) 70, 349, 427
　see also rock art
Sanballat, governor of Judea 909
sanctuaries 689
　bench 688
　cave 687, 688, 691
　Greek temples 702

peak 681, 684, 685, 687, 688, 691
  see also Anglo-Saxon England; Etruscan; Mycenaean
Sanday, Peggy 204
Sando, Joe 601
Sanford, Victoria 295
Sanger, D. 670
Sangha, the 936, 937, 939–40, 942, 943
Sanjar, Sultan 974
Sanskrit 927
Sant Cassia, P. 288–9
Sao, the (Chad) 428
Sapa Inca 580
Sapo mask (Liberia) 429
Sarapis (Greco-Egyptian deity) 42–3
Saravati (Hindu deity) 923
Sargon of Akkad 780
Sarmiento de Gamboa, P. 572
Saudi Arabia
  Mecca 970, 971, 973, 975, 976
  Medina 970, 973, 975
Saunders, J. W. 627
Saunders, N. J. 112, 1049
Saxe/Goldstein hypothesis 1046
Scandinavia 872
  cremation graves in 58, 851–2
  deposits in 853–5, 866–8
  idols, cult sites, sacrifices and offerings in 866–8
  Migration period 867
  pre-Christian 56–7, 160, 846, 1037–8
  Viking Age 995, 1037
  see also Bronze Age; figurines; fire ritual; Iron Age; Neolithic; Old Norse and Germanic religion; poetry; rock art; Saami/Sámi, the; shamanism; Sweden
Schechner, R. 265
Schechter, Esther 496
Schinkel, K. 527
Schlesier, Karl 991
Schmidt, K. 836
Schmidt, M. 1040
Schmidt, R. 365
Schoffeleers, J. M. 1049
Scotland 70
  Orkney islands 18, 273, 1009
  Sculptor's Cave 389–90

Scott, J. 168
Sears, William 633
Seaxneat/Saxnot (Anglo-Saxon deity) 863
secularization 230
Segadika, P. 69
seid/*seiðr*/*seidr*/*sejdr* 849, 855, 868, 871, 872, 1024, 1027
Selene (Greek deity) 814
Seler, Eduard 556, 561
Selk'nam, the (Patagonia) 118, 119
semiotics/semiotic forms 253, 373
Senanayake, D. S. 943
Seneca, Roman writer 712, 714
sensory experience 209, 210
  synaesthetic 210
Serbia
  Dupljaja 392
  Korbovo 393
  Lepenski Vir 358, 364, 366
  Male Vrbica 393
Seth (Egyptian deity) 107, 734
Severanus (Oratorian) 952
Shad Island 668
Shah Jahan, Mughal emperor 83
shamanic
  crystals 523
  druids 1025
  landscapes 995
  origins and cognitive archaeology 989–90
  power acquisition 310–12
  rulership in Mesoamerica 549
  studies/research 986–92, 994, 997–8
  world renewal 314
shamanic state of consciousness (SSC) 1020–1
shamanism 136, 139, 197, 218, 376, 647
  Caribbean 523
  cave art and 350–1
  Chinese 448–9
  core 1019, 1023, 1024
  debate over 427–8
  defining/discovering 983–7, 988, 990–1
  Eastern Woodlands 630–1, 632, 633
  family 994
  Far Northeast 666–8
  in Australia 491
  Japanese 463
  Mesolithic 364–5, 992

shamanism (*cont.*)
   Neolithic 993
   North American 321, 991–2
   NWC 639, 641, 644–5, 649, 650
   Palaeolithic 989
   puberty, cult initiations and 312
   Scandinavian 848, 855
   Siberian/North-east Asian/Eskimo 321, 350, 644, 983, 986, 991–2, 1018, 1021
   state-based societies and 995–7
   totemism and 1008–9
   Upper Palaeolithic 1046
   see also altered states of consciousness; neo-shamanism; rituals; rock art; sacrifice; trance; water
shamans 219, 269
   gender of 203–4
   power manipulation and 312, 314
Shamash (Mesopotamian deity) 777
Shanks, M. 90
Shaw, J. 926, 940, 943
Sheppard, Peter 505, 507
Shepseskaf, Egyptian pharaoh 83
Sherratt, A. 993
Sheshbazzar, prince of Judah 908
Shintoism/State Shinto 457, 458, 466
Shirokogorov, S. M. 989, 1020
Shiva/Siva (Hindu deity) 30, 476–7, 478, 923–4, 926, 930–2
Shreeve, James 336
sí 68
Siberia 987, 988, 991, 994, 995, 997
   Ust-Polui 155
   see also Evenki, the; Khanty, the; Koryak, the; rock art; shamanism; Tungus-speaking peoples
Siddhatta Gautama/Gautama Siddhartha 142, 935–6
Sigaut, F. 243, 245
Siikala, Anna-Leena 989
Sikhism 135, 136, 142, 144
Sillar, B. 247
Silva, R. 941
Simoons, F. J. 107, 108
Simpson, Barry 292, 296
Simpson, J. 160
Sipán 587, 588, 589, 592, 595
   Lord of 586

Sitch, Bryan 1027
Siva
   see Shiva/Siva
Skinner, Mark 292
Skjærvø, P. O. 812
skulls 156
smell 213
smelting/blacksmithing 246–7, 249, 270
   Scandinavian 855
   see also Africa
Smith, George 786
Smith, Mike 489–90
Smith, S. T. 731
Smithsonian Institution 602
Sneferu, Egyptian pharaoh 83
Snodgrass, Anthony 699–700, 702
So, the
   see Sao, the
social order 34
Sockalexis, Michael 670
Socrates 253
Soctomah, Donald 670
Soler, J. 107, 109
Solomon Islands 505, 506
   Roviana chiefdom 507–8
Sona, Buddhist missionary 474
Songhai, the (Mali) 1052–3
Sorg, Marcella 294
South Africa
   Blombos Cave 425
   Cederberg region 354
   Klasies River 425
   Makapansgat 426
   Sterkfontein Stw 93, 338
South America
   Early Intermediate 585
   Late Intermediate 580
South Asia
   Early Historic 921, 922, 925, 926, 940, 943, 944
South-east Asia
   ancestor worship in 472–3
   death rituals in 470–2
   first farmers in 470–2
   Funan 475
   links to China and India 473, 474
   pottery 471
   states in 474–6
   see also Buddhism; Cambodia; Hinduism

'Southwestern Regional Cult' 611, 612
Sow, I. 1046
Spain 295
   Atapuerca 338
   Candamo 351
   La Garma cave 348, 351
   Maltravieso cave 351
   taula monuments 395
   Tito Bustillo cave 351
Speck, F. G. 671
Spencer, H. 1043
spirit
   power 641, 643, 648, 649–50
   quest 644–5
Spiro, M. E. 684
Srejović, Dragoslav 358
Sri Lanka 111, 936, 937
   Anuradhapura 937–8, 940, 941–3
   Maduru Oya 943–4
   Polonnaruva 937, 940
Srinivasan, D. M. 926
Srinivasin, S. 929
standing stones 11
   Africa 436
   ancestors and 1051
   Australia 491
   Britain 18
   Egypt 724
   France 16, 17
   Levantine 898
   Vanuatu 508–9
Stead, I. M. 408, 412
Steadman, D. W. 296
Stein, B. 929
Steiner, F. 105–6
Stephano, Mzee 253–4
Stevens, Thaddeus 71
Stevenson, Mathilda Coxe 602
Steward, Julian 171–2, 602, 606
Stirrat, R. 145
Stone Age 993
   see also Baltic region
Stonehenge 97, 273, 362, 435, 836, 1022–3, 1036
   ancestors and 1051
   druidism and 1032, 1033–4, 1039–40, 1041
   Durrington Walls and 381, 382
   ley lines 1035

   orientation/alignments 19, 34
   Riverside Project 377
   stones of 13–15, 66, 1051
Stout, Adam 1033, 1040
Strabo, Greek historian/geographer 814, 816–17
Strassburg, J. 359–60, 362, 364, 365, 366
Stringer, M. D. 573
Strong, W. D. 644
structuralism 700
Stukely, William 1033
stupas 934, 936–8, 939
Sturluson/Sturlusson, Snorre/Snorri 44, 52, 856
   Snorri's Edda by 846, 848
Stutz, Nilsson 359, 361, 362
subjection 169
sub-Saharan Africa 1061
   archaeology of 425–6, 437
   ceramics in 431
   death/burial in 432–4
   iron production in 431–2
   madness in 1046
   sacred groves, shrines and monuments 434–6
   see also portable art; portable ritual objects; rock art
Sudan, the 428
   Kerma 152–3, 432
   see also Bari, the; Dinka, the; Nuer, the
Suddhodana, king of Kapilavastu 935
Sulis Minerva (Roman/Celtic deity) 752
Sumer
   see Iran; Mesopotamia; sacred marriage
Sundstrom, L. 319
surface survey 698, 699
Suri (Etruscan deity) 715–16
Suryavarman I, Angkor king 478
Suryavarman II, Angkor king 478–9
Suttles, W. 640
Sweden
   Åamossen 363
   Bökkeberg 363
   Gotland island 392, 849–51, 856, 1037
   Hogsbyn 271
   Laxforsen 44–5
   Lund 868
   Nämforsen 44–5
   Öland island 852, 853

Sweden (cont.)
 Rönneholm 363
 Skåne region 854, 867, 868
 Skateholm 154, 155, 358–9, 360–2, 363, 365, 366
 Uppåkra 854, 868, 871
 Uppsala 160, 702, 854
 see also Old Norse and Germanic religion; rock art
Swentzell, Rina 613
Switzerland
 Hannig Pass 390
 Lake Neuchatêl 411
symbolic systems 252–3
symbolism
 sacral 117
 see also Caribbean, the; food; Turner, V.
synagogues 910, 911, 913, 914–17
syncretism 226
 anthropology of 229–30
 anti- 230
 archaeology of 230–2
 definition/concept of 227–9
 experiential-performative approaches to 232–4
 'from within'/'from without' 233
 power and 234–7
 types of 228–9
Syria 826, 972
 Jerf el Ahmar 797–8
 Mureybet 797, 798
 Neolithic 127
 Qatna 784, 900–1, 902
 Raqqa 969
 Tell Aswad 803–4
 Tell Sabi Abyad I 799
 Ugarit 896, 898–9
 see also Levant, the
Szynkiewics, S. 28

Taboo
 archaeology and 108, 111–12
 blood 108
 concept of 105–7
Tacitus, Roman historian 46, 53, 415, 519
 Germania by 752, 847, 865–6, 867, 871
 on gods 848, 851
Taçon, P. S. C. 318, 319, 486–7

Tages (Etruscan figure) 711
Tagliaferro, N. 760
Ta'Ḥaġrat 761, 763, 769
Tai, Kang 474
Taíno, the (Caribbean) 141, 519–20, 526
 art of 522–3, 525, 527, 529, 530, 531
 cosmos 531–2
 heritage 524
 huts of 527–8
 mythology 527, 528
 religion 532–4
Taksami, Chuner 995
Talalay, L. 685
Tallensi, the (Ghana) 133, 160, 1005–6, 1008
 ancestors 1044–6, 1053–4, 1055
 Nyoo shrine 431, 1012
 sacred groves/shrines 434–5, 1053–4
 sacrifice and 155, 156, 157, 158, 161, 162, 1054
 totemism and 1011–12
Tambiah, S. J. 98, 116
Tamla, T. 880
Tamu, Yarjung 1022
Taoism 135–6
 see also Daoism
Tarxien 763, 764–6, 770
 period 761–2, 770
Tas Silġ 764, 765, 770
Tate, Winifred 289
Tatsuo, Kobayashi 459, 462
tattoos 144
Taussig, M. 1018
Taweret (Egyptian deity) 735
Taylor, Gerald 572, 574
Taylor, Ross 711
technical
 practice 243–5
 systems 246, 247
techniques
 background/nature of 243–4
 culture and 245, 255
 magic and 254–5
 production 249
 rituals and 255–6
technology 243
 materiality and 431–2
 problems and cultural approaches to 251–5
 ritual and 250, 254, 265–6

Tenochtitlan 544, 560, 562, 566
  Templo Mayor of 549–50, 557, 558, 560, 563, 564, 565, 567
Terrell, John 496
Tewa, the (North America) 601, 602
Tezcatlipoca (Aztec deity) 562, 563
Thailand 473, 476
  Ban Don Tha Phet 474
  Ban Non Wat 470–2, 479
  Dvaravati state in 475
  Khok Phanom Di 471
Tharapita (Baltic deity) 884
Thero, Rev. Matara Kithalagama Sri Seelalankara 943
Thesan (Etruscan deity) 714, 716
Thietmar of Merseburg 846
Thom, Alexander 19
Thomas, J. 33, 35, 111, 271, 377
Thompson, T. 68–9, 72
Thoms, William 63
Thor (Norse deity) 44, 848, 851, 1024
three-pointers (*trigonolitos*) 528–30, 533
Thunor (Germanic deity) 863, 865, 869
Tiberius, Roman emperor 750
Tibet 29
Tilley, C. 32, 90, 174, 271, 1008, 1047
Tinia (Etruscan deity) 714–15, 716
Tiruvengalanatha (form of Vishnu) 928
Tiryns 681, 684, 689, 690
Titus, Roman emperor 911, 913, 914
Tiw (Germanic deity) 863, 865
Tlacaxipeualiztli festival 566
Tlaloc (Aztec deity) 558, 559, 560, 564
Tlingit, the (North America) 640, 641, 644, 645, 646, 649, 1011
Tolkien, J. R. R. 847
Tonga 105, 508, 510
Topa Inca 575
Torah, the 911, 913, 915–16
Torres Strait
  religion and ritual in 492–5
totem poles 1011
totemism 1043
  archaeology and 1009–11
  defining 1007–9
  see also animism; Ghana
Tracy, Destutt de 166

traditionalism 117
'Trail of Dreams' 312, 313
trance 350
  experiences 311, 376
  imagery 320, 321
  shamanic 427, 649, 989–91
  tobacco and 630
transformation
  Japanese 461, 464
  NWC 641–2, 644, 647
  technologies of 265–6
  see also persons
transformations
  boundaries, portals, thresholds and 271–5
  of identity and states of being 268–9
transition 271–3
transnationalism 228
transposition 232
Trundholm chariot 387, 388, 391, 856
truth 169
  see also water
Tsantsanoglou, K. 698
Tsistsista, the (North America) 991
Tswana, the (southern Africa) 958
Tungus-speaking peoples (Siberia) 983, 986, 988, 1006
Turan (Etruscan deity) 715
Turkey
  Maussolleion of Halikarnassos 153
  see also Anatolia
Turkmenistan 976
  Merv 974
Turner, V. 26, 118, 425, 1044–5
  communitas idea of 264
  model of 'social dramas' 263
  on rites of passage 262
  on symbols 380
Tutankhamun, Egyptian pharaoh 84, 722
Twiss, K. C. 804
Tylor, E. B. 127, 152, 466, 573
  on animism 1004, 1005
Tyr (Norse deity) 848, 851
tzitzimime (Aztec deities) 559, 564

Ubbelohde-Doering, Heinrich 591
Ucko, Peter 93, 682, 685

INDEX

Udaya I, King 942
Udaya III, King 942
Uganda
  Ngono 433
Ugaritic texts 896–7, 899
Ugolini, L. M. 760–1
Uhle, Max 586
Uku (Baltic deity) 884
Ullr (Norse deity) 848, 854
Uluru (Ayers Rock) 12, 483
Umayyad palaces 970–1
Underground Railroad 71
Uni (Etruscan deity) 714, 716
United Nations 289, 295
Upanishads 925
Urbanavicius, V. 881
Urdr (Norse deity) 848
Uruk 786
  period 779, 781
Ushas (Vedic deity) 922
Usimu, Mesopotamian attendant 777
Uta-napishti, survivor of Flood 785–6
Uttara, Buddhist missionary 474

Vaisnavism 926
Vaitkevičius, V. 880
Valk, Heiki 885
Vanir gods 848, 872
Vansina, J. 3
Vanth (Etruscan demon) 718
Vanuatu 508–9
Vedic
  culture/society 924–5
  deities 922, 923, 926
  see also fire ritual; Hinduism
Vega, Garcilaso de la 572, 578
veintena ceremonies 565–6
Velnias (Baltic deity) 882
Venezuela 524
Ventris, M. 683
Venus (Roman deity) 749, 848
Verdery, Katherine 290, 296
Verghese, A. 929
Verhoeven, Marc 124, 799, 804, 805
Vernant, Jean-Pierre 702, 703–4
Vertumnus/Vortumnus (Etruscan deity) 715

Vespasian, Roman emperor 914
Vidudabha, King 935
Viereckshanzen 407
Vietnam 471, 473, 474
  Champa states in 476
viharas 939–40, 942, 943–4
Vijayanagara 928, 930
Vikernes, Varg 1038
Viking gods 124
Vinaya, the 936, 937
Viracocha (Inca deity) 572, 576, 579
  -Inti 578–9, 581
Virgin Mary 138, 142, 143
Vishnu/Visnu (Hindu deity) 135, 140, 475, 478,
    923, 926, 928, 930
  temple (Deogarh) 927
vision quests 625, 644, 645, 668
Vitebsky, Piers 989, 994
Vitellius, Roman emperor 914
Viveiros de Castro, E. 1005, 1008
'Vogelbarke' motif 396
Völund (Wayland the Smith) 849–50
Voltaire 90
Voltumna (Etruscan deity) 715
Vroom, Hendrik 232
vulva-forms 349, 432
  cupules and 314–15

Wabanaki, the (North America) 658, 662,
    668–9, 670, 671
  see also Maliseet, the; Micmac, the; Passa-
    maquoddy, the; Penobscot, the
Wagner, Richard 847
Wagoner, P. B. 930
Wainwright, Geoffrey 377, 381
Waiwai, the (South America) 523, 533
Wales 70, 953
  Anglesey 411, 416
  Llyn Cerrig Bach 411
  medieval literature of 406–7
  Pentre Ifan 12
  Preseli 15
  Severn Sisters 413
Walker, William 603
Wallis, R. J. 1018, 1019, 1021, 1022, 1024, 1025, 1035
Walter, Richard 505, 507, 514

Wano, the (PNG) 498
war
    crimes 289, 295
    events/honours 318
Warburton, D. A. 829
Wardaman, the (Australia) 487, 1010
Ware, J. 606
Warlpiri, the (Australia) 486
Warnier, J.-P. 247, 254, 265
Warwick, Chris 1025
water 38
    as cure 46–7
    Bronze Age special places in/near 389
    burials near 363, 364, 365
    deposits in/near 853
    difference between holy/sacred 39–40, 41, 45–6
    in cosmos 46–7
    life-giving 42–4
    malevolent 39, 43–4
    ritual use of 39–42, 78
    sacrifices to 46, 817
    shamanism and sound of 44–6
    sun/fire and 41–2, 46–7
    truth and 46
    see also Christianity; Iron Age; purification rituals
Waterloo Helmet 411
Watkins, Alfred 1035
Watkins, T. 801, 805
Watson, Patty Jo 196
Webster, J. 231, 236, 407, 753–4
Wei Zhi/Zhih 462, 463
Weiner, J. F. 1008
Weinstein, R. A. 624
wells 46–7, 389
Wepwawet (Egyptian deity) 731
Werbner, R. 157
whetstones 659, 663, 664, 665
Whitcomb, Donald 977
White, Leslie 171
White, N. M. 624
White, Neville 490–1
White, Peter 506
Whitehouse, Ruth 198
Whiteley, P. M. 65, 67, 613
Whitley, D. S. 319, 990, 992, 997
Whitley, James 705, 1047

Whittaker, C. 749
Wickler, Steve 512
Wild, Robert A. 42
Willerslev, R. 994, 997
Williams, A. 144
Williams, H. 153, 997
Wilson, M. 488
Winckler, Hugo 787
Windmill Hill people 374
Winkulkueltun 17
witchcraft 144, 426
Wittgenstein, Ludwig 97, 99
Wobst, Martin 244
Woden (Germanic deity) 863, 865, 868–9, 872
Woolley, Sir Leonard 782
Wright, D. 494
Wright, Marcia 253–4

Xemxija 761
Xerxes I, Persian king 819
Xipe Totec (Aztec deity) 566
Xoc, Lady 17

Yahweh (Israel deity) 900, 904
    House of 908
Yakshas (Hindu nature spirits) 923, 926
Yakshinis (Hindu nature spirits) 923
Yama 848
    see also Purusa
Yamato, Princess
    see Himiko, Queen
Yamen, ancient Egyptian priest 726
Yanyuwa, the (Australia) 491
yarrow sticks 203–4
Yasovarman, Angkor king 477
Ye'cuana, the (South America) 523
Yehud 908–9
Yi, Zeng Hou 448
Ymir, primordial giant 52, 848
Yokuts, the (North America) 311
Yoruba, the (Nigeria) 1006
Young, R. 110–11
Yugoslavia 287, 295
    Vukovar 289
    see also mass graves

Yukaghir, the (Siberia) 983, 997
Yuman-speaking people (North America) 311, 312, 316

Zammit, T. 760
Zangato, E. 436
Zapotec, the (Mesoamerica) 546
Żebbuġ 761
 phase 761–2, 767
Žemyna (fertility deity) 882
Zeus 691, 714, 814, 848
 temple of 701
ziggurats 779, 816, 819
Zimbabwe 435
Zizek, Slavoj 170
zodiac, the 916
Zoroaster, Prophet 812–13
Zoroastrianism 134, 135, 142
 in Iran 811, 812–15, 816, 817, 818–19
 ritual washing in 143–4
Zubayr, Ibn 970
Zuckerman, Sharon 899
Zuidema, Tom 572
Zvelebil, M. 155, 364–5

The manufacturer's authorised representative in the EU for product safety is Oxford University Press España S.A. of El Parque Empresarial San Fernando de Henares, Avenida de Castilla, 2 - 28830 Madrid (www.oup.es/en or product.safety@oup.com). OUP España S.A. also acts as importer into Spain of products made by the manufacturer.

Printed and bound by CPI Group (UK) Ltd, Croydon, CR0 4YY

15/03/2025

01833748-0007